A CATALOG OF FILES AND MICROFILMS
OF THE GERMAN FOREIGN MINISTRY ARCHIVES
1920-1945

VOLUME IV

Compiled and edited by

GEORGE O. KENT

Department of History

UNIVERSITY OF MARYLAND

HOOVER INSTITUTION PRESS
STANFORD UNIVERSITY
STANFORD, CALIFORNIA

1972

Hoover Institution Publications 120
International Standard Book Number 0-8179-1201-0
Library of Congress Card Number 69-19204
© 1972 by the Board of Trustees of the
    Leland Stanford Junior University

PREFACE

The Hoover Institution on War, Revolution and Peace takes pride in publishing the fourth and final volume of *A Catalog of Files and Microfilms of the German Foreign Ministry Archives, 1920-1945* and thus completing a cooperative publication venture with the U.S. Department of State.

The availability of new materials, specifically the files from various German missions and consulates in Europe as well as from some of the overseas offices, necessitated publication of this additional volume. The documents listed here supplement and complement the files of the political archives at the German Foreign Ministry *(Politisches Archiv des Auswärtigen Amtes)* for the period 1920-1945.

Members of the scholarly community who are interested in recent German and European history again owe a great debt to Dr. George O. Kent, not only for his painstaking work in compiling this last volume but for the unflagging enthusiasm and perseverence he brought to the ten-year task of preparing all four volumes of this superb reference tool.

The work could not have been done without the constant support of the Historical Office at the U.S. Department of State. Grateful thanks are due Dr. Bernard G. Noble, former Director of that office, under whom the work was begun, and his successor, Dr. William M. Franklin, who continued to provide advice and encouragement.

August, 1972

Richard F. Staar
Associate Director
Hoover Institution

TABLE OF CONTENTS

INTRODUCTION

This, the fourth and last volume of the Catalog, lists the files of the major European missions and consulates as well as some non-European ones. The deficiency of records in the non-European area is due to loss and destruction of entire sets of files during and after the second world war. Some that were not at Whaddon Hall were later recovered and are now in the foreign ministry in Bonn. There are also gaps in some European mission files such as London, Brussels, the Hague, and others. (These can be spotted either by the absence of files for certain periods or by the omission of individual volumes from a set of files). Another problem facing the user of this volume, especially in connection with material that has not been microfilmed, arises from the reorganization of mission files currently being undertaken in the political archive of the German foreign ministry. Inquiries pertaining to these matters should be directed to the Director of the Political Archive, Foreign Ministry, Bonn, Federal Republic of Germany.

The microfilmed material is identified, as in previous volumes, by serial and frame numbers. In some cases it was impossible to determine which files or volumes were microfilmed, in others no volume numbers were noted in the original lists. In all such cases the serial and frame numbers pertain to the entire set of files.

The material listed in this volume is richer and more diversified than may appear at first glance. It pertains not only to the country in which a particular mission was located, but also includes material on German domestic and foreign affairs (sent to the mission by the foreign ministry for the information of the mission's staff) and information on other countries and regions, as well as on international problems. Material on certain subjects can be found only in the mission files; thus the files listed in this volume complement as well as duplicate those listed in previous volumes of the Catalog.

In general, pre-1920 files have not been listed. Exceptions were made in cases when a series seemed important enough and when the omission of a pre-1920 volume would have created an awkward gap;

or when documents in a volume started before 1920 but the bulk of the volume covered the subsequent period. A number of pre-1920 mission files are listed in <u>A Catalogue of Files and Microfilms of the German Foreign Ministry Archives 1867-1920</u> (Oxford 1959), pp. 1188-1217.

I want to express my thanks to all those who have supported this project for more than a decade; especially to Drs. G.Bernard Noble and Witold S. Sworakowski, who were instrumental in getting it started, and Drs. William M. Franklin and Richard F. Staar, who sustained it to the end; to Robert Wolfe, of the National Archives and Record Service who answered countless questions and provided the National Archives Supplements, and, finally, to my wife who first wished that I had never started it and later feared that I would never complete it.

Washington, D.C.   George O. Kent
June 1972

Akten-zeichen	Inhalt	Band	Datum	Serial Nr.
Pers.G 5	Botschaftsgrundstück	1	1924-29	
Pers.G 7	Botschaftsgebäude und Grundstük-ke Pera und Therapia	3	1924-38	
Pers.G 5	Botschaft Ankara, Bau, Gebäude, Grundstück	1-6	1924-33	
Pers.R	Übersiedlung der Botschaft nach Angora	1	1928-30	
Pers.G 6	Botschaftsgarten Angora	1	1924-39	
	Angora Botschaftspark	1	1924-28	
Pers.G 8[a]	Gewächshaus Therapia	1	1937-39	
	Dienstkraftwagen, Spezialakte Benzin		1931-39	
Pers.G 22	Speditionen und Transporte für die Botschaft	1-2	1940-42	
Pers.P 3	Besoldungs- und Dienstalters-verhältnisse der Beamten und Angestellten der Botschaft	3-4) 6)	1927-39	
	Botschaftsrat Fabricius, dienstlicher Schriftwechsel	1-1a 2	1928-36	K1554/K384828-36
	Schriftwechsel Botschafter v.Keller mit Botschaftsabteilung Ankara, Sommer 1936	1	1936	
	Vertrauensarzt der Botschaft	1	1926-35	K1555/K384837-43
	Personalien der Botschaftsange-hörigen Jordan, Keßler, Bischoff, Bornstein, Stockmann, Scheel, Jacob, Albrecht, Egger, Repnow, Loewe, Strehlow, Dittler, Maack, Zoelch	15 Hefte	1924-30	
	Schriftverkehr der Botschaft mit dem türkischen Aussen-ministerium	1	1940	
	Diplomatische Privilegien: Anweisungen für die Botschafts-mitglieder und Anmeldung	1	1924-30	
	Einzelne Umzüge	1	1927-38	
	Zoll und Steuerbehandlung	1	1924-37	
Pers.A 3	Deutsche Konsularbehörden in der Türkei, Konsulatsbezirke	1	1924-29	K1556/K384844-52
	Konsulate und Konsularbezirke	1	1927-28	
Sonder-akte Gen	Konsulat Beirut	1	1940	
	Deutsches Generalkonsulat Istanbul	1	1931-37	
	Deutsches Konsulat in Mossul (ehemaliges)	1	1924-30	
Pers.A 5	Deutsches Generalkonsulat Smyrna (Ismir)	1-3	1924-40	

Akten-zeichen	Inhalt	Band	Datum	Serial Nr.
Pers.A 6	Deutsches Konsulat Trapezunt	1-2	1925-40	
Prot. 2^b	Fremde diplomatische und konsularische Behörden in der Türkei	1	1925-36	
Prot. 3	Türkische Konsularbehörden in Deutschland und anderen Ländern	1	1924-38	
	Personalien der türkischen Diplomaten	1	1927-28	
	Ordensangelegenheiten, Auszeichnungen und Ehrenzeichen	1-3	1924-40	
	Spezialakte Ehrenkreuz des Weltkrieges	1	1933-35	
Pol 2^a	Deutsch-türkische Beziehungen	1	1924-39	K1557/K384853-69
	Politische Beziehungen der Türkei zu Deutschland, anderen Staaten und zwischen anderen Staaten, Verträge	2) 3) 4)	1940-42	K1558/K384870-84 K1558/K384885-922 K1558/K384923-29
	Weltpolitik	1	1925-40	K1559/K384930-52
Pol 2	Politische Übersichten	2	1936-40	7240/E531452-525
Pol 2^a	Politische Stimmungsberichte der Konsulate	1	1940	K1560/K384953-57
Pol 1^a	Sandjak Alexandrette	3	1938-39	K1561/K384958-60
Pol 2 Nr. 2^a	Politische Beziehungen der Türkei zu Deutschland: Der Deutsche Militär- Luftfahrt- und Marineattaché in der Türkei (persönlich)	1	12.1935-10.1941	2789/D547378-83
2^b	Politische Beziehungen der Türkei zu Deutschland: Deutscher Militär- und Luftfahrt-Attaché in der Türkei - Geheim- (Chiffre-Telegramme vom und an das Auswärtige Amt in geheimen Kommandosachen)	1	7.1936-8.1940	2789/D547384-519
	Der deutsche Militärattaché in der Türkei (geheim, Chiffre-Telegramme von und an das Auswärtige Amt in geheimen Kommandosachen)	1	6.40-8.43	
		2	8.41-10.41	
		3	8.41-4.42	
		4	4.42-9.42	
2^c	Marineattaché bei der Deutschen Botschaft Ankara, geheime Berichte des Marineattachés in geheimen Kommandosachen, Chiffretelegramme vom und an den Marineattaché	1	1939-40	
2^d	Der Deutsche Marineattaché in der Türkei (Geheim, Berichte des Marineattachés an die Kriegsmarine, Chiffretelegramme)	1-2	1940-42	
3^a	Russisch-finnischer Konflikt	1	1939-40	

Akten-zeichen	Inhalt	Band	Datum	Serial Nr.
Pol 2 Nr. 3	Türkei in ihren Beziehungen zur englischen Einkreisungspolitik und die damit zusammenhängenden politischen Vorgänge auf dem Balkan (auch deutsch-italienisches Militärbündnis)	2	1939	
3^b	Amerikanisch-japanische Beziehungen	1	1940	
D Pol Nr. 2^f	Der deutsche Luftattaché (Geheime Chiffretelegramme vom und an das Auswärtige Amt)	1-2	1940-42	
Pol 2 Nr. 3^a	Europakonflikt	2,3, 4	1939-40	K1562/K384961-63
D Pol Sd Akte 3	Europakonflikt	1-3	1940-42	K1563/K384964-69
	Änderung der deutschen Prisenordnung im Europakonflikt	1-3	1939-40	8490/E596892-94
	Deutsche und englische Prisenordnung, Sonderakte: Berichte des Oberkommandos der Kriegsmarine über die fremde Handelsschiffahrt	1	1942	
D Pol 2 Sd Akte 3		4-7	1940-42	
	Transportfragen, auch Charterung von Schiffen		1941-42	
	Austausch der deutschen und sowjetrussischen Mitglieder der gegenseitigen Vertretungen durch Vermittlung der türkischen Regierung	1-2	1941-42	
	Politische Strömungen im Kaukasus	1	1941-42	
	Rücktransport der Iran-Deutschen	1-2	1941-42	
Pol 2 Nr. 3^e	Syrien, geheim	1))) 2)) 3)	1940-42	4759/E234125-72 3864/E045233-57 K1564/K384970-5216 3864/E045258-315 K1564/K385217-536 K1564/K385537-890
Pol 3	Staatsoberhäupter	1	1924-28	
	Besuche führender Staatsmänner·	4	1935-39	7853/E569708-22
	Reisen	1	1941-42	
	Flaggenfragen	2	1935-39	
	Kleine Entente	1	1924-39	
	Pan-Europa	3	1931-36	
	Kongresse, politische	4	1939	
	Politische Konferenzen	1	1937-40	

Akten-zeichen	Inhalt	Band	Datum	Serial Nr.
Pol 3	Panama-Konferenz	1	1939-40	
	Spionage	1-2	1925-40	
	Afghanistan		1935-41	
	Albanien		1936-39	
	Arabien		1936-39	K1565/385891-981
	Argentinien		1925-39	
	Armenien		1925-39	
	Balkan	5	1936-40	
	Belgien		1926-39	
	Bulgarien	3	1935-40	
	Danzig		1939	
	Ägypten	3	1939	K1565/K385982-6007
	England	3)		5835/E425383-99
		)		7622/E545033-52
		)	1936-40	
		4)		3103/D626778-800
		)		4412/E083804-23
	Finnland		1924-39	
	Frankreich	5	1938-40	
	Griechenland	6	1939	
	Irak	1	1924-28	K1565/K386008-97
		12	1939	K1565/K386098-108
	Italien	6	1938-40	
	Japan	1	1924-40	
	Jugoslawien	3	1939-40	
	Kurdistan		1930-38	
	Litauen		1925-39	
	Mandschukuo		1938	
	Mexiko		1924-39	
	Niederlande		1925-39	
	Norwegen		1924-39	
	Palästina		1924-38	K1565/K386109-338
	Persien	1	1926-28	K1565/K386339-469
		5	1937-39	K1565/K386470-82
	Polen		1927-28	
	Portugal		1926-39	
	Rumänien	3	1939	

Akten-zeichen	Inhalt	Band	Datum	Serial Nr.
Pol 3	Russland	1	1924-28	
		9	1939-40	
	Schweden		1939-40	
	Schweiz		1935-39	
	Spanien	2	1938-39	
	Südamerikanische Staaten		1939	
	Syrien	5	1936-39	K1565/K386483-719
	Ungarn	2	1936-39	
	Vereinigte Staaten	2	1936-39	
	Völkerbund	13	1938-39	
Pol 3 Nr. 1	Innenpolitik der Türkei (Innere Verwaltung, jetzt Ministerien)	2	1931-42	K1566/K386721-22
	Reformen für die Europäisierung der Türkei	2	1929-37	
Pol 4	Judentum	1) 2)	1925-39	K1567/K386773-7133 K1567/K387134-219
	Bolschewismus und Kommunismus	2	1932-39	
	Minderheiten (Minoritäten)	2	1930-40	
	Militär- und Marineangelegen-heiten	1	1924-26	2789/D547335-46
	Marineangelegenheiten Allgemeines	1) 3)	1928-39	2789/D547368-74 2789/D547375-77
	Militärangelegenheiten	2	1934-40	2789/D547347-67
D Pol	Deutschlands auswärtige Politik, allgemein	5	1939	
	Reisen deutscher Staatsmänner	1	1939	
	Deutsche Kolonialpolitik	1	1937-39	
	Sammelmappe für politische Erlasse	1) 2)	1939-40	K1568/K387220-40
	Geheime Erlasse des Auswärtigen Amtes soweit nicht in Pol 2 Geheim oder andere politische Spezialakte gehörig; Berichte hierzu	1) 2) 3)	1941-43	2361/488817-37 3867/E045609-17 5169/E304597-621 9905/E693955-61 3867/E045618-713 K1568/K387241-43 3867/E045714-64 K1568/K387244-47

Akten-zeichen	Inhalt	Band	Datum	Serial Nr.
D Pol	Geheime Erlasse, Berichte, Telegramme Streng geheim (nur von Hand zu Hand)	10)	1940	2361/488061-131 3562/E023395-437 4511/E132673-77 K1568/K387248-53
		11)		2361/488132-99 3578/E024205-58 9902/E693939-41 K1568/K387254-69
		12)		2361/488200-68 3636/E028314-55 4554/E147292-94 K1568/K387270-73
		13		3614/E027042-72 2361/488269-344 K1568/K387274-84
		14		2361/488345-87 3637/E028359-401 K1568/K387285-86
		15		2361/488388-476 3613/E026978-7038 K1568/K387287-88
		16	1941	2361/488477-554 3883/E048146-209 K1568/K387289-92
		17		2361/488555-650 3883/E048210-36 1568/K387293-94
		18		2361/488651-736 3883/E048237-82
		19		2361/488737-816 3883/E048283-310 K1568/K387295-302
		20	1942	3862/E044948-93 5166/E304290-366 K1568/K387303-
		21		3862/E044914±47 5139/E302769-815 K1568/K387307-08
		22		3862/E044994-5009 5166/E304367-95
		23		3862/E045010-40 5166/E304396-437 K1568/K387309-312
		24		3862/E045041-92 5166/E304438-73 K1568/K387313-18
		25)	1942-43	3865/E045318-51 5165/E304271-87 K1568/K387319-21
		26)		3865/E045352-406 5446/E304515-56
		27		3865/E045407-90 5446/E364551-615 K1568/K387322-28

Akten- zeichen	Inhalt	Band	Datum	Serial Nr.
Pol 4 D Pol	Geheime Erlasse, Berichte, Telegramme Streng geheim (nur von Hand zu Hand)	28	1942-43	3865/E045491-536 5446/E364616-48 K1568/K387329-36
		29		3865/E045537-606 5446/E364649-729 6863/E518225-28
D Pol 3 Nr. 1	Deutschlands Innere Politik Deutsche Innenpolitik, Auslandsorganisation	6 1	1938-40 1940-42	4704/E227423-29 3890/E048780-92 K1569/K387337-45
		2	1937	3890/E048793-808 6855/E518149-54 K1569/K387346-63
	Ortsgruppe Ankara der Auslands- organisation der NSDAP	1-2	1931-40	
D Pol 3 Nr. 2	Reichsparteitage, Sonderakte	1	1939	
	Politische Attentate	1	1938-39	K1570/K387364-65
W 1	Wirtschafts- und Handelspolitik der Türkei	1	1927-29	7239/E531418-50
W 2 Nr.1	Deutsch-Türkische Wirtschaftsab- kommen	3	1936-37	7243/E531555-72
	Deutsch-Türkische Wirtschafts- verhandlungen	1)) 2)	1937-38	7242/E531542-53
	Wirtschaftsverhandlungen 1938-39 und Wirtschaftsvertrag 1938	1-2	1938-39	
	Wirtschaftsverhandlungen, wirtschaftliche Beziehungen der Türkei zu Deutschland	1))) 2) 3) 4)	1939-40	8342/E590137-87 8493/E596910-30 9792/E687359-61 8493/E596931-63 8493/E596964-7007 8493/E597008-18 9257/E654883-99 9885/E693526-30
		5 6 6a-8	1940	9886/E693532-35 9906/E693963-88
		9-12	1941	
	Wirtschaftsstruktur der Türkei, W.v.Flügge (Unterlagen zu Wirt- schaftsverhandlungen)	1	1939-40	
W 2 Nr.1a	Wirtschaftsbeziehungen der Türkei zu Deutschland	4-7	1940-41	
W 2 Nr.1c	Durchführung des Wirtschafts- abkommens vom 25.Juli 1940, Versandmeldungen	1	1941	
W 2 Nr.1d	Kompensationsgeschäfte ausser- halb des Wirtschaftsabkommens zwischen Deutschland und der Türkei	1	1941	

Akten-zeichen	Inhalt	Band	Datum	Serial Nr.
W 2 Nr.2	Wirtschaftliche Beziehungen der Türkei mit anderen Ländern	16-17	1940-41	
	Verträge: Türkei mit anderen Staaten ausser Deutschland	3	1933-39	
W 2 Nr.3	Beratungsstelle für Wirtschafts- und Transportfragen	1	1940	
W 3	Ausfallgarantie, allgemein	2	1938-39	
	Wirtschaftsbeziehungen und Bestrebungen Frankreichs auf dem Balkan	1	1938	9258/E654902-06
	Türkisch-englische und französische Wirtschaftsbeziehungen sowie Wirtschaftsbestrebungen dieser Länder zum Südosten	1-2	1937-39	
	Kriegswirtschaft der Westmächte	1	1940	
	Marktberichte	1	1940-42	
	Deutsche Aussenhandelspolitik (Runderlasse)	1	1934-39	7549/E541803-24 7875/E570488-502
W 2	Verträge Deutschlands mit anderen Staaten ausser der Türkei	1	1925-40	
	Deutschlands Finanzen	5	1939	
W 4	Deutsch-russische Wirtschafts-beziehungen	1	1939	
Geheim	Deutsch-italienischer Wirt-schaftskrieg gegen England	1-2	1940-42	
W H 1	Handelsvertrag	1-2	1925-27	
W F 1	Finanzen in der Türkei	1,9	1925-39	
W F 3	Deutsche Reichsschatzanweisungen, Reichsschatzscheine in der Türkei	1	1929	
W I 3 Nr. 10	Rüstungsindustrie	5		2361/E488838-75 8343/E590189-218
		6	1938-40	2361/E488876-905 8491/E596896-98
	Junkers Unternehmungen	1	1928-31	
	- 1,4,5,5a,5b,6,7		1924-30	
W E 1	Eisenbahnen	1	1926-28	
W P	Post- und Telegrafenwesen	1	1924-34	
W Sch	Türkische Schiffahrt, allgemein	1	1940	
W V 4	Strassenbau	1	1927	
W L u	Flugwesen (Fluggenehmigungen)	1-4	1924-38	
		5-8	1939-42	
W L-11	Das Postwesen (Türkei)	1-2	1928-41	

Akten-zeichen	Inhalt	Band	Datum	Serial Nr.
W L 11	Türkische Gesetzgebung Allgemeines	1-4	1924-39	
Spezial-Akte	Das neue türkische Berufsaus-übungsgesetz	1-2	1931-36	
	Konsularvertrag	1-2	1927-28	
	Rechtshilfevertrag	1	1927	
	Niederlassungsvertrag	1	1926-28	
	Verträge, allgemein	1	1927-28	
	Besteuerung von Ausländern	1	1925-28	
	Steuerangelegenheiten Deutschland-Türkei	1	1924-29	
D R 3 Nr. 1a	Ausbürgerungen	1	1938-40	
1b	Staatsangehörigkeitssachen, Einzelfälle	1	1925-38	
D R 3 la S 1	Sonderakte Melzig	1	1939-41	
D R 3 Nr. 3e	Nachlass Egger	1	1935-36	
	Ableben und Nachlass des Reichsangestellten Dr. O. Hülsmann	1	1936-37	
	Nachlass Ranich	1	1939	
	Nachlass Wallner	1	1938-39	
	Nachlass Jensch	1-2	1924-41	
R 3	Ermordung deutscher Reichsange-höriger in der Türkei, Fall Stoll und Bozold	1	1927-29	
R 5	Anlieferungen, Verhaftungen, Deutsch-türkischer Auslie-ferungsvertrag	1	1925-37	
	Auslieferungen, Verhaftungen Spezialakte	1-2	1924-29	
D R	Auslieferungen von Verbrechern, Verhaftungen	1	1925-28	
D R 3	Auslieferungen und Verhaftungen Spezialakten Siek	3	1930-32	
D R 5 Nr. 2a	Paßsachen, Spezialia	1-4	1927-38	
		5-7	1938-41	
D R 5 Nr. 3a	Ausweisungen	1-2	1926-40	
	Aufenthalt und Reisen in der Türkei (Schwierigkeiten der Polizeibehörden)	1	1929-39	
	Polizeiwesen	1	1924-34	
	Autounfall Sodemann	1	1933-38	

Akten-zeichen	Inhalt	Band	Datum	Serial Nr.
Pers.G.20	Briefweiterleitungen und Nach-richtenübermittlung	3-6	1941-43	
	Türkische Forderungen gegen Firmen und Privatpersonen	1	1923-36	
	Amtliche und private Forderungen gegen die türkische Regierung, Allgemeines (Requisitionsfor-derungen)	1	1924-38	
	Amtliche und private Forderungen (Requisitionen) Spezial	3	1924-33	
	Forderungen gegen die türkische Regierung: Speziell Siemenssche Familienbesitzverwaltung, Quarzehana	1	1928-30	
	Forderungen gegen die türkische Regierung: speziell Bernhard Stiel	1	1928-31	
	Forderungsangelegenheit Wermann	1	1929-35	
	Requisitionsangelegenheit Newman	1	1920-34	
	Schadenersatzansprüche, allgemein	1	1924-26	
	-Spezialakte Caravia	1	1924-25	
	-Spezialakte Wezasek	1	1924-32	
	Angelegenheit D.Zimmer, Omasia	1	1925-57	
	- Przedecki-Ottoman-bank	1	1921-28	
	Beschlagnahme deutschen Eigen-tums	1	1924-32	
	Speziell Beschlagnahme deutscher Goldbestände in der Türkei	1	1924-31	
	Erwerb und Kauf von Grundeigen-tum durch Ausländer	1-2	1925-28	
	Abtransport deutschen Flücht-lingsguts	1	1925-26	
	Pensionsangelegenheiten Allgemeines	1	1924-34	
	Pensionsangelegenheiten Spezialband, Verschiedenes	1-3	1924-38	
	Pensionsangelegenheiten Spezialakte Kalau v.Hofe, Grumbkow, Düffel, Rieder, Witwe Mahmud Feydt Bey, Frau Auguste Stupe	1-3	1924-38	
	Pensionsangelegenheiten Kamphövener-Pascha	1	1928-35	
	Pensionsangelegenheiten, Spezielles für Mitglieder der ehemaligen deutschen Militär-mission	1	1924-30	

Akten-zeichen	Inhalt	Band	Datum	Serial Nr.
R 6	Sozialpolitik	1	1924-40	
R 7	Internationale Schiedsgerichts- und Gerichtshöfe	1	1925-37	
Kult 2	Kulturpropaganda	1	1927-28	
	- a) Lesehallen	2	1939	
	Kulturfonds	8	1939	
	Kunst und Wissenschaft	1	1925-28	
Kult 3	Vereine	1	1928	
	Deutscher Verein in Konstantino-pel	1	1929-34	
	Deutsche Vereine und Anstalten in Smyrna	1	1924-28	
	Deutscher Verein Alemania	1	1929-33	
	Deutscher Verein in Angora	1	1928-35	
	Deutsche Vereinigung in Reki-Schehir	1	1927-28	
	Deutsche Kolonie	1	1928-36	
	Wohltätigkeits- und andere Vereine in der Türkei und im Ausland	1	1925-39	
	Mädchenheim	1	1925-26	
Kult 4	Evangelische Kirchengemeinde (auch Seelsorge evangelischer und katholischer Pfarrer)	1	1929-37	
Kult 4 Nr. 1	Spezial: Hilfsbund für christ-liches Liebeswerk im Orient	1-3	1924-35	
Kult 8 Nr. 1	Türkisches Schulwesen	1	1924-37	
	Türkisches Schulwesen und fremde Lehranstalten in der Türkei	1-4	1924-40	
Kult 8 Nr. 2	Deutsches Schulwesen in der Türkei	1	1925-40	
	Deutsche Schulen und Lehrer in der Türkei	1	1927-28	
	Deutsche Schulgemeinde in Konstantinopel	1	1924-26	
	Deutsche Schulgemeinde in Pera	1	1929-39	
	Verein ehemaliger Schüler der deutschen Oberrealschule in Konstantinopel	1	1929-32	
	Schulen und Vereine in Deutsch-land und in anderen Ländern	1	1926-38	
Kult 8 Nr. 2b	Deutsche Schule in Pera	1-4	1928-39	
Kult 9 Nr. 1	Pflege und Förderung der deutschen Sprache	1	1927-29	

Akten-zeichen	Inhalt	Band	Datum	Serial Nr.
Kult 9 Nr. 2	Deutsche Lehrkräfte an türki- kischen und fremden Schulen (Sprachkurse)	1	1926-39	
	Anatolische Lehrer	6	1938-39	
	Sprachlehrer Wendler	1	1939-40	
	Sprachlehrer Dr.Heinz Kristinus	1	1939	
	Sprachlehrer Engesser-Hemmerling	1	1939-40	
Kult 9 Nr. 3	Deutsche und Fremde in türki- schen Diensten	1	1925-28	
	Deutsche und ausländische Fach- leute in türkischen Diensten	1	1924-40	
D Kult 10	Studium	8-9	1938-39	
Kult 10 Nr. 3	Landwirtschaftliche Hochschule in Ankara	8-9	1938-40	
Kult 11 Nr. 1	Ausstellungen, Kongresse	3-4	1936-39	
Kult 11 Nr. 5	Gesundheits-, Medizinalwesen, Quarantäne	1-3	1924-40	
Kult 11 Nr. 6	Krankenhäuser in der Türkei, Pflegepersonal und Schwestern für dieselben	1-2	1924-37	
Kult 11 Nr. 6b	Zulassung deutscher und auslän- discher Ärzte und Apotheker in der Türkei	1	1924-36	
Kult Spezial	Viehseuchen	1	1924-39	
Kult 11 Nr. 8	Absatz deutscher Bücher	2	1927-40	
	Bücherei	3	1935-39	
	Buchgemeinschaft (früher Kaiserl.) Eski-Sehir	1	1927-32	
	Zuwendung von Büchern (Bücherprämien)	1-3	1931-40	
	Drucksachenverwertung	13	1939-40	
Kult 11 Nr. 9	Archäologisches Institut (Einrichtung)	1	1927-29	
	Archäologisches Institut Istanbul	3	1936-39	
	Altertümer - Ausgrabungen	1	1925-28	
Kult 12	Reden und Vorträge	1	1924-39	
Kult 12 Nr. 1-3	Kunst-, Musik- und Theaterwesen in der Türkei (Verpflichtung deutscher Kräfte)	1-3	1929-40	
Kult 12 Nr. 1	Konzert- und Theaterunternehmun- gen , deutsche Gastspiele	1	1929-38	

Akten-zeichen	Inhalt	Band	Datum	Serial Nr.
Kult 12 Nr. 7 Spezial	Musikalische und sonstige Veranstaltungen in der Botschaft	3	1935-39	
Nr. 4	Filmwesen	7	1938-40	
Nr. 5	Segelflugsport	2	1934-38	
	Sonderakten Frh. Max v.Oppenheim	1	1926-27	
	Verschiedenes	1	1936-39	
	Presse	1	1924-28	
P 1^a	Presse, Allgemeines	5 6	1934-40	K1571/K387366-67
P 1^b	Türkische Presse, allgemein	9 10	1938-40	K1572/K387368-70
P 2	Propaganda (Presse) in der Türkei, jetzt: Beziehungen zu Deutschland und anderen Ländern	1	1939-41	K1573/K387371-74
P 2 Nr.1^b	Erlasse des Auswärtigen Amtes in Einzelfällen über Verwertung und Verbreitung pressepropagandistischer Nachrichten, Artikel und Bildmaterial, Anfragen über türkische Presseartikel oder Artikel in sonstigen Zeitungen des Auslands	1 2	1940-42	K1574/K387375-401 K1574/K387402-5
Nr.1^b II	Wochenfunkspiegel	1	1941	K1575/K387406-13
Nr.1^e	Presse und Propagandawesen: Beziehungen der Türkei zu Deutschland, hier: Berichte des Pressereferenten der Botschaft über Schreibweise der türkischen Presse und sonstige Presseangelegenheiten	1	1940-41	K1576/K387414-20
Nr.1^e II	Pressedienst Berlin	1	1942	K1577/K387421-23
Nr.1^f	Erlass der Informationsabteilung und Berichte an diese in Propagandaangelegenheiten	1 2 3	1940-42	K1578/K387424-26 K1578/K387427-29 K1578/K387430-43
Nr. 1^g	Druckschriften der Propagandaabteilung	1 2-3	1940-42	K1579/K387444-48
Nr. 1^h I	Berichte des Berliner Türkeisenders	3	1942	
Nr.1^h III	Sonderdienst Seehaus	1	1941	
Nr.2	Beziehungen der Türkei zu anderen Staaten, ausländische Presse und sonstige (politische) Propaganda in der Türkei	1	1940-42	
P 3	Gründung einer deutschen Zeitung in Konstantinopel ("Türkische Post)	1-5	1925-29	
	Presse "Universum" früher "Türkische Post"	1-2	1928-30	

Akten-zeichen	Inhalt	Band	Datum	Serial Nr.
P 3	Briefwechsel , Türkische Post, Verlag v.Ritgen & Co., Dr. Schmidt-Dumont	1	1926-27	
P 3 Nr.2	Bücher, Zeitschriften, Druck-sachen, Bildmaterial propagan-distischer Art, deren Absatz und Verwertung, Beanstandungen derartiger Propagandamittel durch das Gastland.(Akte ent-hält nur Schriftstücke, die nicht betreffen die Informations-abteilung und D IV)	1 2	1940-42	K1580/K387449-52
P 4^a	Pressevertreter, allgemein	5	1936-40	K1581/K387453-55
P 4^b	DNB	2	1928-39	K1582/K387456-64
P 4^d	Presse, Agence d'Anatolie	1	1929-39	
P 6	Beanstandungen in Presse und Propaganda, Greuel- und Hetz-presse, Hetzfilme, Bildfälschun-gen, Beanstandungen der Türken in deutscher Presse und Propa-ganda, deutsche Beanstandungen in türkischer Presse und Propa-ganda, auch sonstige ausländi-sche Hetzpropaganda, gegen die Verwahrung eingelegt wird.	1	1940-42	
P 6^b	Beanstandungen in Presse und Propaganda, Pressefehde in Istanbul	1	1939	
P 7	Presseberichte Dr.Schmidt-Dumont	1	1939-40	
P 8	Dr.Schmidt-Dumont, Presse-attaché	2	1934-43	
P 3 Nr.1 Sonder-akte Syrien	Syrien: Pressepropaganda	1 2 3 4 5 6	1940-42	K1583/K387465-805 K1583/K387806-8227 K1583/K388228-577 K1583/K388578-675 K1583/K388676-9024 K1583/K389025-328
P geheim	Pressefonds geheim	1	1929-39	
	Geheimerlasse der Abteilung Information und D IV	1	1940-42	K1584/K389329-32
Nr. 1 geheim	Beziehungen der Türkei zu Deutschland (Schriftliche und telegrafische Berichte des Bot-schafters und des Gesandten in Presse-und Propagandaange-legenheiten, Geheimerlasse des Auswärtigen Amtes in Presse- und Propagandaangelegenheiten) auch Abkommen Presseattaché	1	1940-41	
P geheim	Presse und Propaganda geheim	1,2 3 4	1939-43	5167/E304476-513 K1584/K389333-36 5469/E381607-80
R geheim	Rundfunkpropaganda	1-2	1939-42	

Akten-zeichen	Inhalt	Band	Datum	Serial Nr.
I B 1 e (SA)	Unterschlagungen Konsulats-sekretär Moeller		1935-37	
I B 6 a	Abrechnungen	1	4.33-12.36	
		2	1.37-12.37	
	Zusammenstellungen über Etat Haushaltjahr		1937	
	Berichtigung zur Abrechnung		10.37-12.37	
	Abrechnungsbemerkungen		36- 7.39	
6 b	Geldüberweisungen		1935-37	
I B 7 Geheim	Überprüfung Fernsprechleitung der Gesandtschaft, Kopplungs-freiheit		1939	
I C 1 Geheim	Umwandlung Saloniki in General-konsulat		11.38- 1.39	
	Beschuldigung Papanaeum gegen Konsulatssekretär Paulus		6.39	
	Depeschenkastenverkehr Athen - Saloniki		1939	
I C 7	Beschuldigung Aurich- Konsul Acker		1929-30	
I D	Fremde Gesandtschaften und Konsulate	3-5	1930-35	
		1	1935-38	
I E	Sprachzwischenfall (Gesandter von Schoen)	1		
I F	Protokoll, Landesfeiern, Flaggen	2	1927-30	
	Korrespondenz des Prinzen Reuß XXXIII		1940	
Pol Nr.1	Aussenpolitik		1927-38	
Pol 2 Nr. 1 b	Griechenland, Zwischenfälle und Beschwerden über griechische Behörden		1927-39	
Nr. 3	Griechenland und andere Staaten		4.36-9.39	7854/E569724-32
Nr. 4	Griechenland, Balkanstaaten, Kleine Entente und Balkankon-ferenzen	5-7	1938-39	
Nr. 5	Balkanpakt		1934-39	
Pol 3 Nr. 1	Griechische Regierung und Parlament		1933-36	
	Griechenlands Innenpolitik Regierung und Parlament		1937-38	
Pol 3 Nr. 2	Griechisches Königshaus		1938	

Akten-zeichen	Inhalt	Band	Datum	Serial Nr.
Pol 3 Nr. 4	Griechenlands Innenpolitik		1927-38	
	Kirchenpolitik	2	1927-28	
Nr. 3	Griechenlands Heer und Flotte, Lieferungen		1936-39	
	Ankauf deutscher Flugzeuge durch die griechische Regierung		1935	
Nr. 5	Griechische Grenz- und Minderheitsfragen, Dodekanes, Cypern		1934-39	
Pol 4 Nr. 1	Völkerbund		1931-39	
II V (SA)	Völkerbund und Abrüstung		1934-38	
	Völkerbund	3	1927-29	
		4	1930-31	
Nr. 2	Kommunismus, sozialistische Bewegung, Freimaurertum	1 2	1927-39	7854/E569733-41
Nr. 5	Informationserlasse des Auswärtigen Amtes		1939-40	
II G	Griechenland, Jahresübersicht	2	1932-35	
II G J Nr. 2	Griechenland, Innenpolitik		1927-39	
Nr. 3	Griechenland: Heer und Flotte		1.34- 3.36	
	Entsendung deutscher Offiziere nach Griechenland, Major Habicht und Korvettenkapitän Mirus		1936-38	
II G A 4	Griechisch-türkische Beziehungen		1933-38	
A 2 A	Griechenland und andere Staaten	3	4.27-12.29	
		4	1.30-12.35	
II B B	Balkan, Bulgarien	3	8.27- 8.32	
		4	8.32-12.34	
II B J	Balkan, Jugoslawien	2	4.27- 3.34	
II B T	Balkan, Türkei	4	7.33- 5.36	
D Pol Nr. 1	Griechenland, deutsch-griechische Beziehungen		1933-39	
D Pol 2 Nr. 1	Politische Beziehungen Deutschlands zu anderen Staaten		1939	

Akten-zeichen	Inhalt	Band	Datum	Serial Nr.
D Pol 2 Nr. 2	Deutsch-polnische Beziehungen, Krieg mit Polen		1939	
Nr. 3	Einkreisungspolitik		1939	6521/E487389-422
Nr. 5	Informationserlasse		1939-40	
D Pol 3 Nr. 1	Deutschland		1936-39	
Nr. 2	Der Führer und Reichskanzler		1934-39	
Nr. 4	Reichsparteitag und Tagungen der NSDAP		1936	
Nr. 8	Schwarze Front: Rudolf Aurich		1934-37	
	-Otto Strasser und Frau Gertrud Strasser		1935	
	-Dr.Meyer-Henrath und Zeitung "Griechische Post"		1935-36	
	Emigranten		1935-39	
Nr.10	Wiedervereinigung Oesterreichs mit dem Deutschen Reich		1938-39	
Nr.11	Sudetendeutschtum		1937-39	6641/E504547-49
Nr.12	Liquidierung der ehemaligen tschechischen Gesandtschaft, Protektorat Böhmen-Mähren, Slowakei		1939	
II D	Deutschland		1.34- 5.36	
II D 3	Deutschland, Heer und Flotte, Ausrüstung, Waffenhandel	1-3	1927-38	
D 9	Deutschland, Versailler Vertrag		1935-37	
II D S.A.	NSDAP und antideutsche Propaganda		1933	
		2	1.34-10.34	
	Nationalsozialismus	I	7.36- 3.39	
		II	8.34- .6.38	
II M N	Mittel- und Nordeuropa	2-3	4.27- 6.39	
II O	Osteuropa	3-4	1927- 6.39	
II S	Südeuropa	2	4.27- 6.33	
		3	1934-39	
II W	Westeuropa	3	12.35- 6.39	
II S	Pan-Europa		5.30- 8.37	

Akten-zeichen	Inhalt	Band	Datum	Serial Nr.
II P	Erlass Pressegesetz vom 29.V.36 betr. Zusammensetzung des Auslandspressebüros G.m.b.H.			
	Achilles Kyros, Chourmousis, Kostas Uranie (Reise nach Berlin)		6.37	
	Frau Anamides, Saloniki		3.39- 5.39	
	Karl Pilz		11.37- 2.38	
	Wissenschaftliche Erscheinungen		1933-37	
			7.38	
	Krallis, Saloniki		4.39- 5.39	
	Ausstellungen über internationa-les Witzblatt (Geheim)		3.39- 4.39	
	Beeinflussung Presse Nordgrie-chenlands (Haesele, Dremm an Herrn Johannsen, Hamburg		10.37-12.37	
	Deutsches Informationsmaterial für griechische Zeitungen		6.39- 8.39	
II P 2	Vertrauensbruch Athener Zeitung (Eleftheron Vima)		4.39	
P 1	Einzelakten: Presse in Deutsch-land		1937-39	
P 2	Presse in Griechenland		1933-39	
III A 3	Abwanderung von Facharbeitern auf Textilindustrie		1938-39	
	Auswanderung deutscher Fach-arbeiter		1936-39	
III B	Meldepflicht deutscher Staats-angehöriger im Ausland		8.38	
	Währungen und Handelspolitik		11.36	
	Zusammenstellung über deutsche Auslandsverschuldung		1936	
	Anmeldung jüdischen Vermögens		1938	
B 1	Finanzierungspolitik des Reiches		1938-39	
III B (S.A.)	Naphtalin		1.38	
	Deutsch-griechischer Waren-verkehr		2.38	
	Zwangsgesetz über Beschränkung der Einfuhr vom 1.1.38-30.6.38		3.38	
	Relation zwischen Schilling und Währung dritter Länder Oesterreichs		4.38	

Akten- zeichen	Inhalt	Band	Datum	Serial Nr.
III B (S.A.)	Reisemöglichkeiten nach Deutsch- land, Fahrkartenbezahlung		5.38	
	(A) Otavi-Minen, Vereinigte Aluminiumwerke (Gravia, Bauxit)		1.39	
III B K 1	Fragen aus der Eingliederung Böhmen-Mährens		4.39	
III C 2	Handelsverträge Griechenlands im ersten Halbjahr 1938		7.38	
	Deutsch-griechische Wirtschafts- verhandlungen Berlin		8.37	
	Griechisch-amerikanische Handelsabkommen		11.38	
III C 2a	Einkommensteuer für deutsches Personal der Telefongesellschaft		8.31	
	Gesandter Erbach-Moraht		6.39	
	Spitta - Varvaresses - Regierungsanschlußverhandlungen		9.38	
	Flaggen-Diskriminierung RM-Kurs		10.38	
C 2 a a	Spitta			
Ca 3	Charilaos, Griechische Handels- politik		1.32	
Ca 3 c	von Rohrer - Frangopoulos Frères		1.39	
	Tarnungsmethoden jüdischer Vertreter deutscher Firmen		12.38	
4 a	Korinthun		6.34	
C 5	Bergbau und Schmirgel		1.37- 6.39	
C 6	Wirtschaftsgruppe Chemische Industrie - Handelspolitische Beziehungen zu Griechenland		7.37	
	Athanil - Chromanil - Hambros Bank Ltd.		9.38	
	Phathina AG., Camphausen, Fikus, Zeitungsartikel in "Akropolis"		2.39	
C 6a	Lage der Textilindustrie			
	Wollstoffe, Baumwollstoffe, Bevorzugungsprozentsatz		5.38	
C 10	Feuerwehrgeschäft (Wolf-Köln)		5.39	
C 14	Erbach-Moraht		6.39	
	Umbau der deutsch-griechischen Wirtschaftsvereinigung (Dukas-Heinrich)		10.38- 2.39	

Akten-zeichen	Inhalt	Band	Datum	Serial Nr.
III C 14	Deutsch-griechische Handels-kammer in Athen		2.35	
	Unterstützungsgesuch deutsch-griechischer Handelskammer		7.35	
	Zuschuss aus Reichsmitteln deutsch-griechischer Handel		8.36	
	Bildung eines "Ständigen Ausschusses"		8.36	
	Dukas - Patentanwaltskammer		10.36	
	Dukas - Mitteleuropäischer Wirtschaftstag		12.36	
	Kordt - Hahn		12.36	
	Dukas - RfA		10.37	
	Deutsch-griechische Wirtschafts-vereinigung			
	Eiswaldt - von Horvay		8.38	
	Siegert - Dukas		9.38	
	Dukas		9.38	
	Gesandter Mohrat		12.38	
	Dukas - Telegramme		12.38	
	Dukas - Schlagdenhaufen - Dieck-mann		12.38	
	Wirtschaftsvereinigung Patentanwaltskammer		1.39	
	Schroetter - Wingen - Dukas		1.39	
III D 1	Verkehrspolitik der griechischen Regierung		4.37	
D 3	Errichtung Radiosendestation in Athen (Telefunken)		1934-36	
	Geheim, angeblicher Radiosender bei deutschem Konsulat Saloniki		10.36	
	Rundfunkkonzession (Valpietis, Tasedakis)		1938	
W 2	Schwarze Liste		1939-40	
W 2 Nr.2	Deutsch-amerikanische Handels-beziehungen		7.38	
	Sowjetunion-Bulgarien Handelsabkommen (auf dem Balkan)		1.39	
	Englisch-griechische Wirt-schaftsverhandlungen		1.40	3102/D626758-75
	Französisch-griechisches Handels-abkommen		1.40	
W 4	AFAG-Tsaconas-Luftfahrt-ministerium - Flieger-Hand-kameras		12.39	

Akten-zeichen	Inhalt	Band	Datum	Serial Nr.
W A 2	Saloniker Messe		9.39	
D W A 2	Votsis (Akropolis) Wiener Messe		2.40	
	Griechische Journalisten Wiener Messe		8.39	
	Verzollung von Werbematerial, Wiener Messe		7.39	
D W F	Pfundguthaben-Gefährdung in neutralen Ländern		9.39	
	Deutsche Aussenhandelsbilanz			
	Halbjahresbericht der Reichs-kredit-Gesellschaft		7.39	
	Verschuldung des Deutschen Reiches		7.39	
	Durchführungsverordnung zum neuen Finanzplan		5.39	
	Finanzlage und finanzielle Kriegsmaßnahmen		10.39	
W F 2 S 1	Neue englische Gesellschaft für den Handel mit den Neutralen		11.39	
W F 3	Banque d'Athènes		11.39- 1.40	
D W P 3	Verwendung von Registerguthaben im Generalgouvernement		1.40	
	Schülke R.Mayr (Merchantbank) (Nemere)		2.40	
W F 4 S 1	Krupp-Erstlieferungen - Makris		2.40	
D W F 4	Zahlungswertgrenzen		9.39	
	Sauerbrey-Köttinghoff (gr.Kurserhöhung)		10.39	
	Wertgrenzen für Devisenbeschei-nigungen		3.40	
W H 2 Nr. 2	Treibstoffaufspeicherung in Saloniki für englische Flotte		11.39	
Nr. 2 S 1	Braunstein-Teintze		10.39	
	Bauxit de Parnasse-Teintze		11.39-1.40	
	Konsulat Patras - Exportge-schäft mit Deutschland		9.39	
	Erleichterung der Reichsbank für die deutsche Ausfuhr		5.39	
	Gesetz über Aus- und Einfuhrver-bote		4.39	
W H 2 Nr. 6	Einfuhrquotenerhöhung für französische Zeitschriften		10.39	
	Krupp, Erschliessung von Erz-vorkommen		10.39	

Akten-zeichen	Inhalt	Band	Datum	Serial Nr.
W H 2 Nr. 7	Automobilexport nach Griechen-land		9.39	
	Sonderkontingent für Kraftfahr-zeuge		8.39	
Nr. 2	Wirtschaftsgruppe Elektro-industrie, Einfuhr Großdeutsch-lands 1.Halbjahr 1937		2.40	
	Campbell-Varoudakis, Kandia-Rosinen		1.40	
	Konsulat Canes, Rosinen-Export-Gesellschaft		11.39	
W H 6	Mittel zur Ausgestaltung wirtschaftlicher Berichterstat-tung und Aussenhandelsförderung		9.39	
W H 7 S 1	Zuschussüberweisung der deutsch-griechischen wirtschaftlichen Vereinigung		4.40	
W H 9	Midland Corporation of Athens. Rohöl		3.40	
W H 15	X. Kongress der Internationalen Handelskammern in Kopenhagen		7.39	
W H S 2	Polen: Einziehung polnischer Rückstände des polnischen Generalkonsulats in Amsterdam		10.39	
W H S 3	Arische Vertreter		7.39- 5.40	
W H S 4	Kreditunwürdige und zweifelhafte Firmen		1.33- 4.40	
W H S 7	Kündigung der Auslandsvertreter deutscher Firmen		10.39	
	Beitreibung von Forderungen in Arisierung begriffener deut-scher Firmen von jüdischen Inhabern		7.39	
W J 3 S 1	Triebwagen, Eisenbahn- und Strassenbahnmaterial für den griechischen Staat		1933-39	
W J 3 Nr. 1	Deutsche Beteiligung an schwedischer Ausbeutung griechi-scher Chromerzvorkommen		2.40	
	Molybdänerzvorkommen Arioupolis-Krupp		3.40	
	Teintze, deutsch-griechische Wirtschaftsvereinigung		2.40	
	Lazar, Einstellung von Gruben-arbeiten		3.40	
W J 3 Nr. 5	Deutschlands Eigenversorgung mit Textilrohstoffen		10.39	

Akten-zeichen	Inhalt	Band	Datum	Serial Nr.
W J 3 Nr. 6	Sicherung des deutschen Eisen- und Stahlbedarfs im Kriege		10.39	
	Tsalikis, Aluminiumsyndikat - Siemensgruppe		11.39	
	Commerciale et Miniere, Societé Anonyme Winkelmann-Hartblei		4.40	
	Melchers & Co. Papasotiriou		2.40	
W J 3	Erfindung von Schaumgranaten		10.39	
W L	Ewert - Auswärtiges Amt - Baumwollsamen		1.40	
W L 7	Statistik verschiffter Sulta- ninen und Korinthen, Konsulat Patras		12.39	
	Rosinenmarkt - Les Fils de N. Constantinides		11.39	
	Korinthen-Sultaninenpreise - Ausfuhr Konsulat Patras		9.39	
	Einkauf von griechischen Korinthen der englischen Regierung		9.39	
	Export frischer Weintrauben nach Deutschland Konsulat Patras		9.39	
W V Polen	Zahlungs- und Kreditverkehr im besetzten Polen		10.39	
	Polnisches Verrechnungsinstitut in Belgrad gegründet		1.40	
W P 2 S 1	Telefon		1929-40	
W S 3 Nr. 9	(alt) Waffenlieferungen an griechische Regierung		1936-37	
W Sch S	Angelegenheit der Donauländer, Donaukommission		7.32- 8.39	
W Z S 2	Schmuggel		1928-38	
IV A 3	Schulbeihilfen für Athen und Saloniki		1935-39	
IV A 5	Saloniki - Schule		1937-39	
IV A 4 a	Verschwinden Pfarrer Kindermann		2.36- 9.36	
	Beurteilung Pfarrer Schäfers durch Professor Louvaris		12.37	
IV A 4 b	Vortrag Dr. Paulsen, Verlassen des Saales (Aufführung gegen Christentum)		1935	
IV C	Reise des früheren griechischen Finanzministers Posmazoglu nach Berlin		11.-12.38	

Akten-zeichen	Inhalt	Band	Datum	Serial Nr.
IV C	Dr.med. Tsoumerkistis		1938	
IV D	Griechisch-französische und griechisch-deutsche Kultur-abkommen		12.38- 4.39	
	Aufwendung des Auslandes für kulturpolitische Zwecke		2.39- 3.39	
	Kultur- und pressepolitische Tätigkeit der britischen Aus-landsvertretungen		3.39- 4.39	
	Universität Grégoire in Brüssel Einfluss jüdischer Byzantine-logen		12.38	
IV D 2	Besichtigung von Hochschulen durch Ausländer und Beschäfti-gung dort (streng vertraulich)		. 3.38	
IV G	Deutsche Kriegergräber und Ehrenmal bei Saloniki (Tumba)		1934-39	
	Geheimakten	1	1937	3880/E046888-7025
	Geheimakten	1	1938	3880/E047026-31

Akten-zeichen	Inhalt	Band	Datum	Serial Nr.
Pers.	Banic	1	1943	
	Bartick	1	1944	
	Bauer	1	1943-44	
	Bauer, Evelyn	1	1944	
	Rednarzik	1	1943-44	
	Begovic	1	1924-44	
	Benzler, Gesandter	1-2	1941-44	
	Dr. Berge	1	1939-44	
	Bernik	1	1944	
	Biegler	1	1944	
	Boucheaux	1	1940-44	
	Brink	1	1940-43	
	Brude	1	1944	
	Buchta	1	1939-44	
	Burgemeister	1	1941	
	Bürg	1	1942-44	
	Deutsch	1	1943	
	Dobsay	1	1941-44	
	Donner	1	1944	
	Dr. Feine	1-2	1938-44	
	Feninger	1	1941-44	
	Dr. Fischer-Wellenborn	1	1942-44	
	Frenzel	1	1944	
	Galle	1	1941-44	
	Galler	1	1928-44	
	Dr. Gärtner	1	1941-44	
	Frau Gärtner	1	1943-44	
	Dr. Gredler	1	1943-44	
	Gstöttenbauer	1	1944	
	Hämmerle	1	1944	
	von Heeren	1-2	1937-42	
	Hoffmann	1	1941-44	
	Jaksch	1	1941-44	
	Husseini	1	1943-44	
	Janda	1	1943-44	
	Jandali	1	1944	
	Jarzembowski	1	1931-42	
	Jenko	1	1942-44	
	Junker	1	1944	
	Juric	1	1928-43	
	Dr. Kaernbach	1	1939-44	
	Kahr	1	1938-44	
	Frau Kahr	1	1943-44	
	Kamphoevener	1	1944	
	Keller	1	1940-44	
	Koepke	1	1937-41	
	Kölcer	1	1940-44	
	Dr. Klaiber	1	1942-44	
	Klethi	1-2	1928-42	
	Knappik	1	1944	
	Kucan	1	1941-43	
	Lange	1	1944	
	Langer	1	1940-44	
	Lechner	1	1940-44	
	Neubacher	1	1943-44	
	Reinelt	1	1940-42	
	Schatton	1	1939-42	
	Schiller	1	1937-43	
	von Schmidt	1	1944	
	Schönberg	1	1944	
	Schulte	1	1944	
	Schulz	1	1941-44	

Akten-zeichen	Inhalt	Band	Datum	Serial Nr.
Pers	Seifert-Riesche	1	1941-43	
	Simic	1	1941-44	
	Spiegel	1	1943-44	
	Stemner	1	1941-44	
	Thiele	1	1942-43	
	Veselitsch	1	1943	
	Vice	1	1943-44	
	Wagner	1	1928-44	
	v.Wallfeld	1	1941-44	
	Walter	1	1938-44	
	Frau Walter	1	1943-44	
	Wawretzko	1	1944	
	Dr. Wege	1	1942	
	Wiesing	1	1944	
	Wolschendorf	1	1944	
	Ziemendorf	1	1943-44	
	Personalien, verschiedene Namen	1-2	1941-44	
Pers R 5	Kassenabrechnung	1-6	1933-34	
		7-14	1935-36	
		15-22	1937-38	
	Abrechnung	1-3	1941	
		4-7	1942	
		8-12	1943-44	
Pers Si 1	Sicherung der Gebäude gegen Anschläge, Einbruch, Feuer	1	1939-40	
Pers Si 5	Chiffrierdienst	1	1939-40	
	Sicherheitsdienst	1	1940	
Po 1	Allgemeine auswärtige Politik	1	1937-38	
Po 2	Politische Beziehungen Jugosla-wiens zu Deutschland	1-2	1920-29	
		1	1938-39	8419/E592831-35 9538/E672312-13
Po 2 Nr.1	Politische Beziehungen Deutsch-lands zu fremden Staaten	1	1921-26	
	(Tschechische Krise, auch Polen-Krise)	1-2	1938-39	
	Übernahme der ehemaligen tschechoslowakischen Gesandt-schaft	1	1939	3122/D641632-79
Nr.2	Frage des Anschlusses Deutsch-Oesterreichs an Deutschland	1	1920-34	K1172/K301437-777
Nr.3	Politische Beziehungen Jugosla-wiens zu Deutschland, Film-propaganda	1	1921-32	
Po 2 K A	Kulturabkommen	1	1937-38	

Akten-zeichen	Inhalt	Band	Datum	Serial Nr.
Po 2 S	Sympathiekundgebungen	1	1938-39	
Po 2 B	Besuche Deutschland-Jugoslawien	1 2	1935-39	7861/E569912-50
Po 3	Politische Beziehungen zwischen Jugoslawien und Albanien	1	1921-27	
	- Bulgarien	1-4	1920-33	
	- England	1	1926-39	
	- Frankreich	1-2	1920-29	
	- Griechenland	1-2	1922-28	
	- Sonderband: Salonikikonvention	1	1921-33	
	Politische Beziehungen zwischen Jugoslawien und Italien	1-7	1920-39	
			1929-39	
	Albanienkonflikt	1	1927	
	Politik, Kleine Entente	1 2	1924-33	9708/E683094-101
	Politische Beziehungen zwischen Jugoslawien und Rumänien	1	1920-39	
	- Ungarn	1	1921-29	
	- fremden Staaten	1-6	1920-32	
		1	1938-39	
	Politische Beziehungen zwischen fremden Staaten	1-3	1920-29	
	Europäischer Zollverein, Zollfrieden, Agrarblock	1-7	1929-34	
	Europäischer Zollverein, Deutschland-Oesterreich	1-2	1931-33	
Po 4 Nr.1	Politik, Völkerbund	1-6	1921-38	
Po 4 O	Zwischenstaatliche aussenpolitische Probleme, Ostpakt	1	1933-38	
Po 5	Innere Politik Jugoslawiens, Parlament, Parteiwesen	1-11	1922-33	
		1	1938-39	
		2		7889/E570901-04
	- Fall Dr. Kraft	1	1925-28	

Akten-zeichen	Inhalt	Band	Datum	Serial Nr.
Po 5	Innere Politik Deutschlands	1-3 4 5	1922-39	K1594/K390536-634
Po 6	Minderheiten	1-6	1921-39	
	Wenden	1	1921-29	
	Ungarn	1	1930-32	
Po 6 Nr.1	Deutschtum in Jugoslawien	1-5	1922-27	
	- (Minderheiten)	6-10	1928-33	
	Deutsche Minderheit in Jugosla-wien	1-3	1936-39	
	- Beiakte	1-4	1938-39	
	- Kulturbund	1	1927-33	
	Deutsch-evangelisches Kirchen- und Schulwesen	1	1926-30	
	Katholisches Kirchen- und Schulwesen	1	1926-32	
	Deutsche Minderheiten, Schulgesetze	1	1932-39	
Nr.2	Deutschtum in Jugoslawien (Deutsche Kolonie)	1-2	1923-39	
Po 6 V L	Wochenberichte der Völkerbunds-liga der Deutschen in Jugosla-wien	1	1929-30	
Po 8	Politik, diplomatische und konsularische Vertretungen	1	1920-26	
Po 12 I	Jugoslawische Presse	1-4	1920-34	
12 II	Deutsche Presse	1	1920-28	
12 III	Deutsche Korrespondenzen	1	1920-32	
12 V	Pressemeldungen, Falschmeldun-gen	1-2	1921-34	
12 VI	Telegraphenagenturen, Aufklä-rungsdienst	1-2	1922-34	
Po 13	Politik, Militärangelegenheiten	1	1921-29	
Po 14	- Marineangelegenheiten	1	1927-31	
Po 16	Religions- und Kirchenwesen	1-2	1920-30	
		1	1936-39	
Po 18	Politik, Anleihen	1-3	1924-32	
	Ansprüche deutscher Gläubiger aus Vorkriegsanleihen	1	1927-30	
Po 19	Bolschewismus, Kommunismus	1-2	1920-36	

Akten-zeichen	Inhalt	Band	Datum	Serial Nr.
	Politik, Verschiedenes	1	1920-23	
		1	1932-39	
I	Berichte der Botschaft Ankara	1	1924-35	
II	Berichte der Gesandtschaft Athen	1	1923-33	
III	Berichte der Gesandtschaft Bukarest	1	1923-31	
IV	Berichte der Botschaft London	1	1923-36	5844/E425956-6526
V	Berichte der Botschaft Paris	1	1923-34	
VI	Berichte der Gesandtschaft Prag	1	1923-34	
VII	Berichte der Botschaft Rom	1-3	1923-35	
VIII	Berichte der Gesandtschaft Sofia	1-2	1922-35	
IX	Berichte der Vertretung Tirana	1	1923-34	
X	Berichte der Gesandtschaft Wien	1	1923-34	
XI	Berichte des Konsulats Genf	1	1923-35	
	Politische Wochenberichte	1	1927-30	
G 1	Politisches, Geheim	1-4	1920-27	
		5-6		
		7		3647/E032888-97 7861/E569951-56 K1595/K390635-41
			1928-39	
		8		3647/E032898-915 K1595/K390642-51
G 1 Nr.1	Ruhr-Einbruch	1	1923	
Nr.1 a	Geheime Ausgaben	1	1927-30	
G 2	Wirtschaftliches, Geheim	1		9340/E662281-310
		2		3717/E036906-27 9340/E662311-17
			1920-39	
		3		3717/E036928-46
		4		3717/E036947-7043
G 4	Chiffrierwesen, Geheim	1	1920-32	
G 5	Presse und Presseausgaben	1-2	1921-35	
G 6	Kulturprogramm	1-7	1927-37	
	- Kassensachen	1	1930-34	
G 6 G	- Einzelfragen - Gesandtschaft	1	1928-33	
G 6 S	- - Konsulat Sarajewo	1	1928-36	
G 6 Z	- - Konsulat Zagreb	1	1927-36	

Akten- zeichen	Inhalt	Band	Datum	Serial Nr.
G 6 a	Abrechnungen über den Wi.Fonds	1	1931-33	
Po 13 g	Militärangelegenheiten, geheim	1-2	1929-32	
I g	Italienisch-jugoslawische Verhandlungen	1	1926	
II g	Deutsches Haus Novisad	1	1929-31	
III g	Wegerer-Artikel über Kriegs- schuldfrage in Deutsche Allgemeine Zeitung	1	1926-27	
IV g	Aufzeichnungen der Unterredun- gen mit dem König Jugoslawiens	1	1931-33	
Pol geheim	Jugoslawiens Haltung zu Deutschland nach dem 1.9.1939 und gegenseitige Lieferung	1	1939	8283/E588298-303
W Sch	Handelsschiffahrt im Kriege	1	1939-40	
Kult 3 g	Deutsche Volksgruppen und ihre Organisationen	1	1939-40	
Pol 1 Nr. 1a	Aussenpolitische Reden und Erklärungen des Gastlandes	1	1940	
Nr. 1b	Tagesbefehle, Stabsbefehle	1	1944	
Pol 2 Nr. 1	Politische Beziehungen des Gast- landes zu Deutschland	1 2	1939-43	4673/E221661-87
Nr. 1a	Politische Verträge mit Deutsch- land	1	1939-40	
Nr. 2f	Deutscher Handelsattaché und sonstige Stellen wirtschaft- licher Art	1	1940	
Nr. 3	Politische Beziehungen und Verträge des Gastlandes und Deutschlands zu Bulgarien	1	1940	
	- England	1	1939-40	
	- Frankreich	1	1939	
	- Italien	1	1939-40	
	- Polen	1	1939-40	3122/641776-800
	- Rumänien	1	1940	
	- Russland	1	1939-40	
	- Serbien	5	1944	6185/E464532-56
	- Slowakei	1	1939-40	3122/641680-89
	- Protektorat	1	1939-40	3122/641690-775
	- Ungarn	1	1940	

	- Vereinigte
	    Staaten von
	    Amerika
		1	1940	

Akten-zeichen	Inhalt	Band	Datum	Serial Nr.
Pol 3 Nr. 1	Ministerium (Neu-, Umbildungen) und die innere Lage Jugoslawiens	1 3	1939-40 1942-44	
Nr. 1a	Königshaus, Flaggen, Wappen	1	1941-42	
Nr. 1b	Militärbefehlshaber in Serbien	1	1942	
Nr. 2	Personalien des Staatsoberhauptes und prominenter Persönlichkeiten	1-2	1940-44	
Nr. 2a	Interventionen für Kriegsgefangene	1	1942-43	
Nr. 2b	Verhaftungen, Internierte, Serbien-Kroatien	1	1942	K1596/K390652-71
Nr. 3	Militärangelegenheiten und sonstige Kriegsvorbereitungen	1-2	1939-43	
Nr. 3a	Arbeitsdienstangelegenheiten in Jugoslawien	1	1941-44	
Nr. 4	Staatsschutzbestimmungen	1	1942-43	
Nr. 4a	Spione, Agenten, Tito-Partisanen	3	1942-44	6184/E464525-30
Nr. 4b	Kommunismus und seine Bekämpfung	1 2	1939-44	6183/E464514-23
Nr. 4c	Judenangelegenheiten	1 2	1939-44	K1597/K390672-83 5799/E422514-32 K1597/K390684-811
Nr. 4f	Kirchenwesen	2-3	1942-44	
Nr. 5	Gedenk- und Feiertage, Flaggen	1-2	1939-43	
Nr. 6	Wahlen im Gastland	1	1939-40	
Nr. 7	Parteiwesen - Politische Verbände und Organisationen	1	1939-40	
Nr. 9	Reichs- und Protektoratsangehörige im Gastland	1	1939	K1598/K390812-21
Nr. 9a	NSDAP und ihre Nebenorganisationen	1	1939-40	
Nr. 9c	Aussiedlung Volksdeutscher	1	1939-40	
Nr. 9d	Kroatische Frage	1	1939-40	
Nr. 9e	Minderheiten in Jugoslawien (ausser Deutschen, Kroaten und Slowenen)	1	1939-40	
Nr. 10	Politische Verhältnisse in Slowenien und Grenzberichte	1-2	1939-40	
Nr. 11	Hetze und Protestkundgebungen	1	1939-40	
Nr. 11a	Verunglimpfungen des Führers (auch Attentate)	1	1938-40	
Pol 4 Nr. 3	Internationales Freimaurertum	1	1940	

Akten- zeichen	Inhalt	Band	Datum	Serial Nr.
Pol 5	Politische Auskünfte und Nachforschungen	1	1938-40	
		4	1943-44	
D Pol 1 Nr. 1a	Aussenpolitische Reden und Erklärungen	1	1939-40	
D Pol 3 Nr. 3	Militärangelegenheiten in Deutschland	1	1939	
Nr. 3a	Luftfahrtangelegenheiten	1	1939	
Nr. 4a	Agenten und Spionagewesen	1	1939-40	
Nr. 5a	Gedenk- und Feiertage	1	1939-40	
Nr. 8	Kolonialfragen in Deutschland	1	1939	
Nr. 9	Jugoslawische Staatsangehörige in Deutschland	1	1940	
	Veesenmayer	1	1941-42	
	Stab	1	1944	
	Austausch	1	1944	
	Bombardierung Belgrads	1	1944	
	Standesamtliche Register	11 Bü- cher	1907-44	

Akten-zeichen	Inhalt	Band	Datum	Serial Nr.
	Nicht registrierte Akten von			
	etwa 1916 - 1928			
	Kanzleiakten und Geschäfts-betrieb	1	1916-19	
		1	1918	
	Personenlisten	1	1918-20	
	Internierten- und Personal-angelegenheiten	1	1917-19	
		2	1918-19	
	Verschiedene Personalsachen	1	1918-22	
		1	1919	
	Personenliste Abteilung B., Original	1	1917-19	
	Personalakten der Presseabtei-lung und Verschiedenes	1-2	1918-20	
	Kanzleiverfügungen	1	1922-24	
	Vereidigungen	1-2	1919	
	Bewerbungen zum Eintritt in die konsularische Laufbahn	1	1918	
	Gesandtschaftspässe	1	1922-23	
	Steuern der Konsulatsbeamten	1	1920-23	
	Gesandtschaftsorganisation	1	1918-19	
	Einschränkung der Gesandtschaft, Abbau der Konsulate, Auflösung Abteilung J.	1	1919-22	
	Gesandtschaftshaus, Reparaturen	1-2	1919-24	
	Aufhebung der Passtellen Kreuzlingen-Schaffhausen	1	1920-21	
	Kanton Thurgau - Konsulat St.Gallen	1	1921	
	Errichtung einer Konsularagen-tur in Luzern	1	1919-20	
	Handakten des Gesandten, 4 Umschläge		1916-18	
	Handakten, Verschiedenes	1-3	1915-20	
	Pressefeldzug gegen Deutsche Gesandtschaft	1	1918-19	
	Badisch-schweizerische Grenze, Gemeinde Büsingen und Verenahof	1	1928	
	Sozialpolitik, Allgemeines	1	1918-21	
	Internationaler Frauenkongress	1	1918-19	

Akten-zeichen	Inhalt	Band	Datum	Serial Nr.
	Internationaler christlicher sozialer Arbeiterkongress	1	1919	
	Auslandssammlungen	1	1923-24	
	Spende für das deutsche Schrifttum	1	1922-23	
	Schweiz, Ernährungshilfsaktion für Deutschland	1	1923	
	Literatur, Kunst und Wissenschaft, Allgemeines	4	1922-24	
	Hochschulfragen, Allgemeines	1	1920-24	
	Studentenfragen	1-2	1920-23	
	Deutsche Kunst- und Literaturpropaganda	1	1917-20	
	A.N. Pressekonferenz	1	1919-20	
	Choulat "Agentur Republica"	1	1919-21	
	"Die Arbeit", Halbmonatsschrift für Kulturgemeinschaft deutscher Sprache	1	1919-20	
	Politische Akten 1920 - 1938			
Schweiz a	Schweiz, Allgemeines	1-3		
		4	1923-37	3835/E044086-92
		5		3835/E044093-96
b	Innere Verwaltung	1-5	1923-30	
		6-7		
		8	1931-38	6099/E451886-92
		9		6099/E451893-918
		10		
	Material über die Wahlen zur schweizerischen Bundesversammlung	1	1925	
		1	1928	
	Sessionsberichte	1-3	1923-35	
c	Kirchen- und Schulangelegenheiten	1-2	1924-38	
d	Zonenfrage	1-3	1923-36	
e	Tessin	1-4	1923-38	
f	Schiedsgerichte und Vergleichsverträge	1-3	1920-37	
g	Die Nuntiatur in der Schweiz	1	1920-35	
h	Neutralität der Schweiz	1-2	1919-37	
		3		6101/E451997-2034
				M62/M001728-64

Akten-zeichen	Inhalt	Band	Datum	Serial Nr.
Schweiz i	Frauenstimmrecht	1	1926-37	
k	Ordensfrage	1	1927-37	
l	Schweizer Nationalsozialismus und Frontenbewegung	1		
		2	1932-38	6102/E452036-57
		3		6859/E518176-79 9912/E694095-99
m	Flaggenzwischenfälle	1-2	1933-38	
m 1	Zwischenfälle	1	1938	
n	Maßnahmen gegen schweizerische Staatsangehörige in Deutschland	1	1933-38	K1585/K389337-48
		2		K1585/K389349-64
	- Einzelfälle	1	1933-38	
n geheim	Verfahren gegen Schweizer	1	1936-37	K1586/K389365-67
o	Spitzel- und Spionagewesen	1-3	1935-38	
q	Beziehungen zu Deutschland	1	1937-38	3842/E044219-38
r	Beziehungen zu anderen Ländern	1	1937-38	
s	Politische Parteien	1	1937-38	
t	Wahlen	1	1937-38	
u	**Maßnahme** gegen den Kommunismus in der Schweiz	1	1938	3856/E044516-21
Deutschld a	Deutschland, Allgemeines	1-7	1922-38	
a 1	Nationale Erhebung	1-4	1933-37	
a 2	N.S.D.A.P.	1	1931-37	
a 3	Angriffe und Verunglimpfung des Reichskanzlers und von Regierungsmitgliedern	1-2	1933-38	
b	Bayrische Sonderbestrebungen	1	1923-37	
c	Abtrennungsbestrebungen, Büsingen	1	1923-36	
d	Danzig	1-3	1923-38	
e	Memelgebiet	1-2	1923-37	
f	Oberschlesien	1-2	1923-38	
h	Eupen-Malmedy	1	1923-37	
i	Mit fremden Regierungen abgeschlossene Verträge	1	1923-35	
k	Minderheiten in Deutschland	1	1929-38	
l	Rechtsverhältnisse des Tägermoos bei Konstanz	1	1933-37	
m	Reise der deutschen Delegationen nach Genf unter Bewachung	1	1926-37	

Akten-zeichen	Inhalt	Band	Datum	Serial Nr.
Deutschld n	Deutscher Nationalsozialismus in der Schweiz	1 2-4	1931-35	8544/E598032-38
		5 6	1935-38	6100/E451920-83
		7 8		6100/E451984-95
n 1	Fall Dr. Kittelmann	1	1935-36	
n 2	Ermordung Gustloffs	1		3857/E044526-64 6108/E452355-75
		2	1936	3857/E044565-77 6108/E452376-407
	- Prozess Frankfurter	3	1936-37	6108/E452408-18
		4		6108/E452419-24
n 3	Deutsche Professoren in der Schweiz	1-2	1933-38	
o	Grenzzwischenfälle, Grenzver-letzungen	1-2	1933-38	
p	Reichstagsbrandprozess	1	1933-37	
q	Kirchliche Angelegenheiten	1-2	1933-38	
r	Deutsch-russische Beziehungen (Rapallo-Vertrag)	1	1933-37	
s	Musterung und ärztliche Unter-suchung (Schriftwechsel)	1	1935-38	
Afrika	Afrika, abessinisch-italieni-scher Konflikt	1-3	1923-37	
Amerika	Vereinigte Staaten	1	1923-38	
	Lateinamerika	1	1923-38	
Arabien		1	1923-37	
Balkan	Albanien, Montenegro, Serbien	1	1923-36	
Belgien	Belgien	1-2	1923-38	
Bulgarien	Bulgarien	1	1923-37	
China	China, allgemein	1-2	1923-37	
Dänemark	Dänemark, allgemein	1	1923-37	5954/E438037-50
England	England, allgemein	1-2	1923-38	
	England-Tschechoslowakei 1938, Informationserlasse und poli-tische Übersichten	1	1938	
Estland	Estland, allgemein	1	1923-32	
Finnland	Finnland, allgemein	1	1923-32	
Frank-reich	Frankreich, allgemein	1-7	1923-38	

Akten-zeichen	Inhalt	Band	Datum	Serial Nr.
Frank-reich b	Elsass-Lothringen	1	1923-37	
c	Französische Fremdenlegion	1	1928-37	
Griechen-land	Griechenland, allgemein	1	1923-38	
Irland	Irland, allgemein	1	1937-38	
Italien a	Italien, allgemein	1-3	1923-38	7217/E530135-37
		4		
b	Faschismus	1-2	1923-36	
	– Zwischenfall Cesare Rossi	1	1928-37	
	– – Bassanesi	1	1930	
c	Südtirol	1	1923-35	
Japan	Japan	1	1923-38	
Jugosla-wien	Jugoslawien	1-2	1923-38	
Lettland	Lettland	1	1923-36	
Liechten-stein	Liechtenstein	1	1923-38	
Litauen	Litauen	1	1923-37	
Nieder-lande	Niederlande	1	1923-38	
Norwegen	Norwegen	1	1923-38	
Oester-reich a	Oesterreich, allgemein	1-4	1923-37	
c	Vorarlberg	1	1923-31	
d	Anschlussbestrebungen	1	1923-36	
e	Deutsch-oesterreichische Wirtschaftsvereinbarung	1-2	1931	
f	Donaukonföderation	1	1932-36	K1171/K301170-435
		2-3		
g	Neutralisierung Oesterreichs	1	1933-36	
h	Sprengstoffschmuggel Bodensee	1	1934-35	
i	Deutsch-oesterreichisches Abkommen vom 11.7.1936	1	1936	
Palästina	Palästina	1	1922-37	K1587/K389368-422
Persien	Persien	1	1923-36	
Polen a	Polen, allgemein	1		K1588/K389423-29
		2	1923-27	K1588/K389430-34
		3		
		4-7	1927-38	
b	Polnischer Korridor	1-2	1925-36	

Akten-zeichen	Inhalt	Band	Datum	Serial Nr.
Polen c	Deutsche Minderheiten in Polen	1	1926-34	
Portugal	Portugal	1	1924-36	
Rumänien	Rumänien	1-2	1923-38	
Russland a	Russland, allgemein	1-7	1923-38	
b	Russische Flüchtlinge	1	1925-30	
c	Monarchistische Bewegung	1	1923-26	
d	Ukraine	1	1931	
e	Beziehungen zur Schweiz	1	1923-36	
f	Georgien	1	1924-34	
Schweden	Schweden	1	1923-38	
Spanien	Spanien	1-2	1923-37	
Tschecho-slowakei	Tschechoslowakei	1-2	1923-38	
Türkei	Türkei	1	1923-38	
b	Lausanner Friedenskonferenz	1-3	1922-24	
Ungarn		1	1923-38	
Vatikan		1	1923-37	
II 1	Friedensvertrag	1-2	1920-22	
		2	1931-36	
II 2	Reparationsverhandlungen	1,2 2a,3	1920-22	
		4-7	1922	
II 2 a	Reparationen, allgemein	1-3	1923-37	
	- Steuer- und Zollstatis-tiken	1-2	1923-32	
II 2 b	- Informationserlasse des Auswärtigen Amtes	1-7	1923-37	
II 2 c	- besetztes linkes Rhein-ufer	1-4	1923-28	
	- Sonderbände	1-2	1923-28	
II 2 d	- Holz- und Kohlenlieferun-gen	1-3	1923-28	
II 2 e	- Besatzungskosten	1	1923-26	
II 2 f	- Saargebiet	1-3	1920-22	
		1-14	1923-36	

Akten-zeichen	Inhalt	Band	Datum	Serial Nr.
II 2 f	Reparationen, Saargebiet 1.Beiheft: Saarabstimmung	1-4	1934-36	
	- 2.Beiheft: Abstimmungsberech-tigte	1	1934	
	- 3.Beiheft: Handakten für Gesandten, ein Saaratlas	1	1934	
II 2 g	- Ruhr	1-7	1923-24	
	-- 1.Beiheft: Besatzungstruppen	1-2	1923-24	
	-- 2.Beiheft: Schweizerische Einfuhrschwierigkeiten seit Ruhraffaire	1	1923-24	
II 2 h	- schwarze Besatzungstruppen	1	1923-25	
II 2 i	- Wiesbadener Abkommen	1	1923	
II 2 k	- Moratorium	1	1923	
II 2 l	- vollzogene Reparations-leistungen	1-2	1923-32	
II 2 m	- Sachverständigengutachten	1-4	1924-25	
	- Dawes-Plan	5-17	1925-29	
	- Young-Plan	18-22	1929-34	
II 2 m a	- -Internationale Zahlungsbank, Basel	1	1930-31	
	- 1.Beiheft: Presseregie bei der B.J.Z. (Bank für inter-nationalen Zahlungsausgleich)	1	1930-37	
II 2 m b	-- Young-Plan, Lausanner Konferenz	1	1932-33	
II 2 m 2	- Behandlungen des feindlichen Privateigentums	1-3	1924-37	
II 2 n	- Pariser Finanzministerkon-ferenz	1-2	1925-35	
II 2 o	- Sicherheitsfrage, Investiga-tionen, Locarnopakt	1 2 3	1925-37	6396/E474537-647
II 2 p	- Mandatsfrage der Kolonien	1	1925-35	
II 2 r	- Kriegsächtungspakt (Kellogpakt)	1	1928-35	
II 3	Völkerbund, allgemein	1	1919-22	
II 3 a		4	1929-38	6397-/E474649-57
II 3 a 1	Radiostation des Völkerbundes	1	1930-35	
II 3 b	Völkerbund, Zusammensetzung, Personalien, Delegationen	3	1931-38	

Akten-zeichen	Inhalt	Band	Datum	Serial Nr.
II 3 c	Völkerbund, Berichte über Völkerbundstagungen	4-6	1927-38	
II 3 c 1	- Abrüstung	1-7	1925-32	
		14	1934-38	
II 3 c 3 b	- Ostpakt	2	1935-36	
II 3 c 3 c	- Westpakt	1	1936-37	
II 3 c 4	- Minderheitenschutz	2	1936-37	
II 3 c 7	- Ausschüsse, Konferenzen und Kongresse	1	1929-37	
II 3 d	- Völkerbundsdrucksachen	12	1933-34	
II 3 e	- Schweiz und der Völkerbund	2	1929-38	
II 3 e 1	- Schweizerische Vereinigung für den Völkerbund	1	1923-32	
II 3 f	- Deutschland und der Völker-bund	4	1926-38	3841/E044214-16
II 3 g	• - Verschiedenes	1	1924-35	
II 3 h	- Völkerbundsvereinigungen	1	1924-37	
II 3 k	- Mädchen- und Kinderhandel	1	1923-36	
II 3 m	- Weltwirtschaftskonferenz	2-3	1930-37	
II 3 o	- Bekämpfung des Handels mit unzüchtigen Veröffentlichun-gen	1	1923	
II 3 p	- Welthilfsverein	1	1927-37	
	Völkerbund-Protokoll Nr.17-19		1935-38	
II 4	Schuldfrage	1-5	1923-37	
II 4 1	- Aktenpublikation des Auswärtigen Amtes	1	1922-29	
II 4 2	- Filmpropaganda	1	1924-25	
II 4 3	-, Veröffentlichungen von Dr. Heiders "Ceinturon"	1	1926-28	
II 5	Friedensbestrebungen	1-2	1923-38	
II 6	Interparlamentarische Union	1	1924-33	
II 7	Internationales Friedensbüro, Genf	1	1923-34	
III 1	Haager Schiedsgericht	1	1923-37	
III 2	Internationaler Gerichtshof	1	1923-36	
III 3	Schiedsgerichtsverträge, Allgemeines	1	1923-35	
III 3,1	- Deutschland-Belgien	1	1923-25	
III 3,2	- -England	1	1923-26	

Akten-zeichen	Inhalt	Band	Datum	Serial Nr.
	Schiedsgerichtsverträge			
III 3,3	Deutschland-Finnland	1	1923-29	
III 3,4	-Frankreich	1	1923-26	
III 3,5	-Elsaß-Lothringen Versorgung	1	1923-24	
III 3,6	-Griechenland	1	1923-24	
III 3,7	-Italien	1	1923-24	
III 3,8	-Jugoslawien	1	1923-33	
III 3,9	-Niederlande	1	1923-28	
III 3,10	-Polen	1	1923-37	
III 3,11	-Portugal	1-2	1923-30	
III 3,12	-Rumänien	1	1923-35	
III 3,13	-Schweden	1	1923-26	
III 3,14	-Schweiz	1	1923-24	
III 3,15	-Tschechoslowakei	1	1923-25	
III 3,16	Schiedsgerichtsvertrag deutsch-französisch	1	1923-35	
III 3,17	-schweizerisch	1	1923-36	
III 3,18	-italienisch	1	1923-30	
III 3,19	-polnisch	1	1923-35	
III 3,20	-belgisch	1	1923-34	
III 3,21	-tschechoslowakisch	1	1923-37	
III 3,22	-dänisch	1	1923-32	
III 3,23	-amerikanisch	1	1928	
III 3,25	-türkisch	1	1931-38	
III 3,26	-luxemburgisch	1	1931-37	
III 4	Rechtsstreitfälle	1	1923-27	
III 5	Haager Friedenskonferenz	1	1923-26	
III 6	Haager Privatrechtskonferenz	1	1923-27	
III 7	Haager Staatsangehörigkeits-abkommen	1	1930-32	
IV 1	Internationales Arbeitsamt	1-3	1923-34	
	Veröffentlichungen	1	1923-30	
IV 1 a	Internationale Arbeitskonferen-zen	1	1930-37	
IV 2	Sozialismus	1-2	1923-38	
IV 3	Bolschewismus, Kommunismus	1-7	1923-38	

Akten-zeichen	Inhalt	Band	Datum	Serial Nr.
IV 4	Internationale Vereinigung gegen die III. Internationale	1-3	1925-36	
IV 5	Gottlosenbewegung	1	1933-34	
IV 6	Freimaurertum	1	1937	
V	Kolonialfragen	1	1923-38	
V 1	- Kolonialdrucksachen	1	1923-38	
VI	Presse, allgemein	1-5	1919-22	
VI 1	- Propaganda, allgemein	2	1933-38	
VI 2 d 1 a	Schweizer Presse, allgemein (vergleiche 13)	2-3	1926-36	
VI 2 d 2	- Spezielles (vergleiche 13a)	1-7	1923-37	
VI 2 d 2 a	- Presseberichte	1	1923-24	
VI 2 d	Presseberichte russischer Blätter	1	1923-24	
VI 2 g	Skandinavische Presse	1	1923	
VI 2 h	Der Reichsdeutsche	1	1933-37	
VI 2	Auslandspropaganda gegen Deutschland	3	1937-38	
VI 3	Reichsministerium für Volksaufklärung und Propaganda	1	1933-38	
VI 4	Pressebeirat	2	1938	
VI 5	Presse und Buchdruck	1	1923-38	
	Sportpropaganda	1	1933-35	
VI 6	Deutsches Nachrichtenbüro	1	1923-38	
VI 7	Deutsche Presse und Propaganda	4	1937-38	
VI 8	Vertreter reichsdeutscher Blätter in der Schweiz	2	1936-38	
VI 9	Deutsches Institut für Zeitungskunde	1	1930-33	
VI 10	Depeschenbureau "Europapress"	1	1934-35	
VI 11	Auslands-Pressebüro	1	1934-38	
VI 12	Französische Presse und Propaganda	1	1938	
VI 13	Schweizer Presse, allgemein (vergleiche 2 d 1 a)	4	1936-38	6860/E518181-90
VI 13 a	- Spezielles (vergleiche 2 d 2)	8	1937-38	
VI 13 b	Hetzkampagne und Zeitungsverbote	7-8	1937-38	
VI 13 c	Hetzkampagne "Kämpfer"	1	1933-36	
VI 13 d	- "Vaterland"	1	1934-38	

Akten-zeichen	Inhalt	Band	Datum	Serial Nr.
VI 13 e	Hetzkampagne "Volksstimme"	1	1933-38	
VI 13 f	- "Neue Züricher Zeitung"	1	1933-38	
VI 13 g	- "Berner Tageblatt"	1	1935-38	
VI 13 h	- "Neue Basler Zeitung"	1	1937	
VI 13 i	- "Nationalzeitung"	1	1938	
VI 13 k	- "Die Weltwoche"	1	1938	
VI 14	Schweizer Pressetelegraf und Depeschenagentur	1	1923-38	
VI 15	Schweizer Pressevertreter	1-3	1933-38	
VI 16	Presse und Propaganda verschiedener Länder	1	1923-38	
VI 17	Deutsche Wochenzeitung	1-2	1926-38	
VI 18	Deutsche Informationen	1	1938	
VI 19	Filmwesen	1-5	1923-38	
VI 19 a	Vermittlung von Tonfilmen	1-3	1934-38	
VI 19 b	Schweizer Filmproduktion	1	1938	
VI 20	Kultur- und Kunstpropaganda	1-2	1923-37	
VI 21	Vortrags- und Rundfunkpropaganda	1-3	1923-37	
VI 22	Deutschenhetze, Greuelpropaganda	1		
		2	1923-38	6861/E518192-205
		3		6862/E518207-23
VI 23	Hetzliteratur	1	1937-38	
VI 24	Deutsche Zeitung in der Schweiz	1	1938	
VII 1	Heer, Allgemeines	1-2	1926-37	
VII 1 1	Heereswesen, allg.Militärattaché	1	1933-37	
VII 1 2	- Bericht des Militärattachés	1	1933-37	
VII 1 a	Schweizer Heereswesen	1-4	1923-38	
VII 1 b	Schweizerische Militärmissionen und schweizer Offiziere im Auslande	1	1926-35	
VII 1 a	Teilnahme von schweizer Offizieren an deutschen Manövern	1-2	1923-35	
VII 1 d	Erfindungen	1	1923-38	
VII 1 f	Austausch militärischer Drucksachen	1	1925-36	
VII 1 g	Teilnahme deutscher Offiziere an schweizerischen Manövern und Besichtigungsreisen	1-2	1927-37	
VII 2	Kriegsmarine	1	1923-35	

Akten-zeichen	Inhalt	Band	Datum	Serial Nr.
VII 3	Luftfahrtwesen	1-2	1923-38	
	Sonderband: Flugzeugunglück Ilfingen	1	1936-37	
VII 3 a	Ziviler Luftschutz	1	1925-36	
VII 4	Kriegslieferungen, Rüstungs-industrie	1	1923-38	
VII 5	Waffenhandel	1-2	1927-38	
VII 6	Gaskrieg und Abwehr	1-2	1928-36	
VII 7	Kriegswesen und Rüstungen Verschiedenes	1	1930-38	
VII 8	Anti-Militarismus	1	1932-37	
	Informationsmaterial über das Heereswesen fremder Staaten	1	1920-23	
VIII	Jüdische Angelegenheiten	1		K1589/K389435-39
		2	1923-25	K1589/K389440-44
		3-4		
		5		
		6		K1589/K389445-50
		7	1926-29	
		8		K1589/K389451-53
		9		K1589/K389454-58
		10	1930-33	
		11		K1589/K389459-525
		12	1934-38	K1589/K389526-786
		13		K1589/K389787-90011
VIII a	Prozess, "Protokolle der Weisen von Zion"	1	1933-38	K1590/K390012-223
VIII b	Presseausschnitte Zionistenkongress	1	1937	
IX 1	Kriegsgefangenenabkommen	1-2	1928-35	
IX 2	Seeabrüstungskonferenz	1	1930-37	
IX 3	Konferenzen der Kleinen Entente	1	1923-37	
IX 4	Europäischer Nationalitäten-kongress	1	1931-34	
IX 5	Politische Kongresse und Konferenzen	1	1923-34	
X 1	Diplomatisches Korps in der Schweiz, allgemein	1-2	1921-37	
X 1 a	— Spezielles	1-4	1923-38	

Akten-zeichen	Inhalt	Band	Datum	Serial Nr.
X 1 b	Fremde Konsulate in der Schweiz	1	1923-38	
X 3	Schweizer Vertretungen im Auslande	1-2	1923-38	
X 4 a	Verschiedene politische Persön-lichkeiten, Deutsche	1	1923-33	
X 4 b	- Schweizer	1	1923-33	
X 4 c	- Fremde	1	1923-33	
XI 1	Politische Vereine: Deutsche Vereine und Deutschtum im Auslande	1	1923-38	
XI 2	Schweizer Vereine und Schweizer im Auslande	1	1923-38	
XI 3	Sonstige politische Vereine und Allgemeines über politische Vereine	1	1923-38	
XII 1	Verschiedene Einzelpersonen	1-7	1923-38	
XII 2	- Spionage	1-3	1923-38	
XII 2 a	- - Duffort	1	1923-27	
XII 2 b	- - d'Armont	1	1923-30	
XII 2 c	- - Andon Bey	1	1923-33	
XII 3	Verschiedenes über Einzelper-sonen: M.Färber, Zürich	1	1923-26	
XII 4	- Prinz Friedrich Leopold von Preussen	1	1923-32	
XII 5	- John de Kay	1	1923-30	
XII 6	- Isidor Kreil	1	1923-26	
XII 7	- Ad.Müller-Hippele	1	1923-34	
XII 8	- Eduard Pfeffer, Genf	1	1923-25	
XII 9	- Fritz Platten	1	1923	
XII 10	- R.Hellweger, Genf	1	1923-27	
XII 11	- Hans Unger	1	1923-34	
XII 12	- Robert von Schenk	1	1923-25	
XII 13	- C.Mertens	1	1923-32	
XII 14	- Dr.Alexander Klein	1	1923-31	
XII 15	- Dr. Johann Wilhelm Muehlon	1	1923-35	
XII 16	- Dr. Hellmuth Sticherling	1	1923-38	
XII 17	- von Siebert	1	1923-28	
XII 18	- Angehörige des Hauses Hohenzollern	1	1923-35	
XII 19	- von Sonnenburg	1	1923-31	
XII 19 a	- Martin	1	1923-27	

Akten- zeichen	Inhalt	Band	Datum	Serial Nr.
XII 20	Deutsche Emigranten	1-3	1923-38	
XII 21	Jacob Salomon und Wesemann	1-2	1923-37	
XIII	Verschiedenes, politischer Natur	1	1923-29	
XIV	Stinnes	1	1923-25	
	Rathenau-Mord	1	1922	
	Mord Erzberger	1	1922-27	
XV	Wochenberichte der Abteilung II des Auswärtigen Amtes	1-2	1923-29	
XVI	Bücher- und Zeitschriftenbestellung, politisch	1	1923-35	
XVII	Politische Zeitschriften, Broschüren	1-3	1925-37	
	Nichtpolitische Akten 1920-1939			
I 1 1 a	Allgemeine Dienstvorschriften	1	1924-38	
I 1 1 b		1	1925-38	
I 1 2 b	Ernennungen im Auswärtigen Amt und bei den Schweizer Behörden	1	1924-38	
I 1 3 a	Dienstbetrieb der Gesandtschaft: Geschäftsordnung	1	1925-38	
I 1 3 b	- Abbau und Einschränkung	1-2	1925-38	
I 1a 2	Ernennungen im Auswärtigen Amt und bei den Schweizer Behörden	1	1931-38	
I 1a 4	Verkehr mit deutschen Länder- regierungen	1	1933-38	
I 2 1 a	Gesandtschaftspersonal (Rang, Urlaub)	1-2	1924-38	
1 b		1	1924-38	
I 2 2 a	Umzugskosten, Umzugsgut, Zollangelegenheiten der Beamten	1	1924-38	
2 b		1	1924-38	
I 2 3 a	Reisekostenpauschalen	1	1932-35	
I 2 3 b	Liquidierung von Reisekosten	1	1924-38	
I 2 4 a	Steuern der Beamten und Ange- stellten der Gesandtschaft	1	1924-38	
4 b		1	1924-38	
I 2 5 a	Pass- und Sichtvermerksangelegen- heiten	1	1924-38	
5 b		1	1924-38	
I 2 6 a	Diensteinkommen, Teuerungszulage	2-3	1932-38	
6 b		1	1924-36	
	Gehaltszahlungen, Sonderbände	1-4	1931-36	
I 2 7 b	Mitteilungen an den Schweizer Bundesrat über Personalverän- derungen	1	1924-38	

Akten- zeichen	Inhalt	Band	Datum	Serial Nr.
I 2 8 b	Personalveränderungen im AA	1	1924-38	
I 2 9 a	Beamtenfragen, Allgemeines	1	1924-38	
I 2 9 b		1	1926-38	
I 2 10 a	Exterritorialität	1	1923-38	
I 2 10 b		1	1926-38	
I 2 11 a	Anmeldung der Beamten der deutschen Konsulate in der Schweiz	1	1926-38	
I 2 13 a	Angestelltenversicherung der Gesandtschaftsangestellten	1	1925-38	
I 2 13 b		1	1931-38	
I 2 17 b	Dienstpersonal des Herrn Gesandten (An-und Abmeldungen)	1-2	1926-38	
I 2a 1	Beitritt der Beamten und Ange-stellten zur NSDAP, NSV	1-2	1932-38	
I 3 1 a	Rechnungswesen, Kassenführung, allgemein	1-2	1925-38	
I 3 1 b	Kassensachen, Verschiedenes	1-2	1925-38	
	Ausgabenmeldung der Gesandt-schaft, Sonderband	1-2	1929-38	
I 3 2 a	Spezialfonds	1	1923-33	
I 3 2 b		1	1925-38	
I 3a 2	Kulturfonds, Beiheft	1-9	1928-38	
I 3 3 a	Gebührengesetz- und Tarif	1	1924-36	
I 3 3 b	Vierteljahresabrechnungen der Gesandtschaft	1	1924-38	
I 3 5 b	Gelderhebung bei den schweizeri-schen Banken	1-2	1924-38	
I 3 6 a	Gegenseitigkeitsgebühren (Sichtvermerke)	1	1924-38	
I 3 7 b	Zahlungen an Konsulate und von Konsulaten	1-2	1924-38	
I 3 8 b	Berichte über Kassenbestände	1	1924-38	
I 3 9 b	Gebührenwesen (Verschiedenes)	1	1924-38	
I 3 10 b	Gebührenlisten	1-2	1922-38	
I 3 11 b	Hinterlegungen	1	1925-38	
I 3 12 b	Gegenseitigkeitsgebühren (Sichtvermerke)	1	1924-38	
I 3 13 b	Weihnachtsgeschenke und Neujahrs-trinkgelder der Gesandtschaft	1	1923-38	
I 4 1 a	Gesandtschaftsgebäude, Repara-turen, Möbelausstattung, Garten	1-3	1924-38	

Akten-zeichen	Inhalt	Band	Datum	Serial Nr.
I 4 1 a	Ausbesserungsarbeiten im Gesandt-schaftshaus	1	1933	
I 4 1 a	Elektrischer Aufzug, elektrische Warmwasseranlage	1	1922-26	
I 4 1 a	Kaufvertrag für eine Gartenpar-zelle zum Gesandtschaftsgrund-stück	1	1928-37	
	Unterhaltung der reichseigenen Gebäuder und Gärten	1	1924-28	
	Anschaffung und Reparaturen von Ausstattungsgegenständen	1	1925-27	
I 4 1 b	Reparaturen, Ausstattung, Garten, Unterhalt	1-2	1924-38	
I 4 4 a	Garagenwohnung, Garage	1	1922-37	
I 4 6 a	Brandversicherung, Gas- und Wassergelder	1	1927-35	
I 4 6 b		1	1927-38	
I 4 8 b	Allgemeine Hausordnung, Reinigungspersonal	1	1927-38	
I 4 9 a	Kraftwagen, Reparaturen, Werkzeuge	1	1926-37	
I 4 9 b	Kraftwagen der Gesandtschaft, Reparaturen	1-2	1924-38	
	Der neue Kraftwagen für die Ge-sandtschaft	1	1933-38	
I 4 11 a	Inventar der Gesandtschaft	1	1925-38	
I 4 11 b	- Verschiedenes	1-2	1924-38	
I 4 13 a	Bibliothek der Gesandtschaft	1	1925-38	
I 4 13 b		1-3	1924-38	
I 4 14 a	Materialbeschaffung	1	1931-38	
I 4 14 b		1-2	1924-38	
I 4 15 a	Kanzlei-Neubau	1-4	1922-38	
I 4 15 b		4	1936-39	
I 4 22 b	Kohlenbelieferung der Gesandt-schaft	1-2	1924-38	
I 6 1 a	Kurierverkehr, Kuriergepäck, Depeschenkasten	1	1924-38	
I 6 1 b	Mitteilung der Kuriergelegenhei-ten, Beförderung verschiedener Sendungen durch Kurier, Kurier-reisen	1→2	1924-38	

Akten-zeichen	Inhalt	Band	Datum	Serial Nr.
II 1 a	Errichtung von deutschen Konsulaten in der Schweiz	1	1926-38	
	Konsulat Lausanne, Beiheft	1	1936-38	
II 2 a	Konsularschutz	1	1926-38	
II 2 b	Angelegenheiten des General-konsulats Zürich	1-2	1924-38	
II 3 a	Konsulatswesen und Auslands-vertretungen, Verschiedenes	1	1924-38	
II 3 b	Angelegenheiten des Konsulats Basel	1-2	1924-38	
II 4 b	- Genf	1-2	1924-38	
II 5 b	- St.Gallen	1	1924-38	
II 6 b	- Lugano	1-2	1924-38	
II 7 b	- Davos	1	1924-38	
II 8 b	Fremde Gesandtschaften und Konsulate	1-2	1920-38	
II 4 a	Übernahme österreichischer Vertretungen (Generell)	1-2	1938-39	
II 9 b	- Spezielles	1	1938	
III 1 a	Ermächtigung zur Ausübung konsularischer Befugnisse	1	1925-38	
III 1 b	Aufnahme von Notariatsakten und Beglaubigung von Unterschriften in notarieller Form	1	1924-38	
III 2 a	Beglaubigungen und Legalisatio-nen	1	1924-38	
III 2 b	Beglaubigungen in nicht nota-rieller Form, Legalisationen und Lebensbescheinigungen auf Renten- und Pensionsquittungen	1-4	1924-38	
III 3 b	Bescheinigung über die Matrikel-eintragung	1	1927-38	
III 4 b	Verschiedenes	1	1925-38	
III 5 a	Pensions- und Rentenwesen (Allgemeines)	1	1931-38	
III 6 b	- Verschiedenes	1	1924-38	
III 7 b	Bescheinigungen verschiedener Art	1-2	1924-39	
IV 1 b	Zeremoniell	1	1922-24	
		1-2	1924-38	
IV 1 a		1	1925-38	
	Trauerfeier und Trauerkundgebun-gen anlässlich des Hinscheidens des Reichspräsidenten von Hindenburg, Sonderband	2	1935	

Akten-zeichen	Inhalt	Band	Datum	Serial Nr.
IV 1 a	Trauerfeier für den Reichs-präsidenten Friedrich Ebert	1	1925	
IV 2 a	Nationalfeiertage, Festtage, Flaggen	1-3	1924-38	
	30.Januar und Heldengedenktag, Sonderband	1	1936-38	
	1. Mai, Nationalfeiertag, Sonderband	2	1936-38	
	Erntedankfest, Sonderband	3	1935-38	
	Redneranmeldungen	4	1936-38	
IV 2 b	Nationalfeiertage, Festtage, Flaggen	1-2	1925-38	
IV 3 a	Orden, Titel, Adelsprädikate	1	1928-38	
IV 3 b	- Rettungsmedaillen	1-2	1923-38	
IV 4 a	Ehrenzeichen des Deutschen Roten Kreuzes	1-2	1924-38	
	Verleihung des Ehrenkreuzes des Weltkrieges, Sonderband	1	1934	
IV 4 b	Glückwunsch- und Beileids-schreiben	1-3	1925-37	
IV 6 b	Trauerkundgebungen anlässlich des Ablebens Dr.Stresemanns	1	1929-31	
	Anträge für Ehrenkreuz	1	1934-35	
V 1	Überfremdungsfrage	1	1919-20	
V 1 a	Erneuerung des Deutsch-schweizerischen Niederlassungs-vertrages	1	1923-34	
V 2 a	Niederlassungsverträge der Schweiz mit anderen Staaten	1	1928-38	
V 4	Niederlassungsfragen in der Schweiz	1	1920-23	
V 4 a	- Münchener Verhandlungen	1-2	1926-27	
	Schweizer Niederlassungsfragen Verschiedenes	1-7	1924-38	
V 4 b		1-8	1924-38	

Akten-zeichen	Inhalt	Band	Datum	Serial Nr.
V 4 b	Schweizer Niederlassungsfragen	1	1932-36	
V 5 a	Deutsche Niederlassungsfragen, Verschiedenes	1	1926-38	
	Verordnung über ausländische Arbeitnehmer in Deutschland vom 23.1.1933 Verhandlungen mit der Schweiz, Beiheft	1	1933	
V 5 b	Deutsche Niederlassungsfragen, Verschiedenes	1-2	1925-39	
V 8 a	Ausweisungen, Aufenthaltsverweigerungen, unerlaubte Grenzüberstellungen und Abschiebungen, Verweigerung der Ausübung eines Gewerbes durch die Schweiz	1	1925-38	
V 8 b		1-2	1924 -38	
V 9 a	– durch Deutschland	1	1926-38	
V 9 b		1	1924-38	
V 10 a	Staatsangehörigkeitsfragen, allgemein	1	1926-39	
V 10 b	– Verschiedenes	1-3	1924-39	
V 11 a	Wiedereinbürgerungen in Deutschland, Ausbürgerungen	1-2	1924-38	
V 11 b	Wiedereinbürgerungen in Deutschland, Entlassungen aus dem deutschen Staatsverband	1-2	1924-38	
V 12 a	Erwerbung des Schweizer Bürgerrechts und Beibehaltung der deutschen Reichsangehörigkeit	1	1925-38	
V 12 b		1	1924-38	
V 13 a	Heimatscheine	1	1924-38	
V 14 a	Schweizerische Fremdenpolitik	1	1924-38	
V 14 b		1	1924-38	
V 15 a	Deutsche Fremdenpolitik	1	1930-38	
V 15 b		1	1925-38	
V 16 a	Verletzung des deutsch-schweizerischen Niederlassungsvertrages durch die Schweiz	1	1925-38	
V 17 a	Kleiner Grenzverkehr, Verschiedenes (auch Warenaustausch)	1	1933-38	
V 17 b		1	1928-38	
V 18 b	Erledigte Heimatpapiere	1	1926-38	
V 19 b	Passwesen, allgemein	1	1924-38	

Akten-zeichen	Inhalt	Band	Datum	Serial Nr.
V 20 b	Fremdenpolitik, italienische amerikanische	1	1926-38	
VI 1 a	Deutsche Pass- und Sichtvermerks-bestimmungen	1-3	1924-38	
VI 1 b	Paßkorrespondenz	1-4	1924-38	
VI 2 a	Deutsche Einreise-, Ausreise- und Durchreisebestimmungen	1	1924-38	
VI 2 b	Einreise nach Deutschland	1-2	1924-38	
VI 3 a	Vergünstigungen bei Pass- und Sichtvermerkserteilung	1	1924-38	
VI 3 b		1	1924-38	
VI 4 a	Diplomatische Pässe und Sicht-vermerke	1	1924-38	
VI 4 b		1-2	1924-38	
VI 5 b	Umgehung der deutschen Einreise- und Ausreisevorschriften	1	1924-38	
VI 6 a	Schweizer Reisebestimmungen	1	1924-38	
VI 6 b	Einreise in die Schweiz	1	1927-38	
VI 7 a	Schweiz, Vereinbarungen und Abkommen mit anderen Staaten über den Reiseverkehr	1	1924-38	
VI 7 b	Schwarze Liste, Einreiseverwei-gerungen	1	1924-36	
		1	1936-38	
VI 9 a	Reisebestimmungen für den kleinen Grenzverkehr	1	1924-38	
VI 9 b		1	1924-38	
VI 10 a	Reiseverkehr mit Kraftfahrzeu-gen	1	1924-38	
VI 10 b		1	1924-38	
VI 11 a	Förderung des Fremdenverkehrs nach Deutschland	1	1924-38	
VI 11 b	Förderung und Schädigung des Fremdenverkehrs nach Deutsch-land und Ausland	1-2	1924-38	
VI 12 a	Grenzempfehlungen, Laissez-passer	1	1924-38	
VI 12 b		1-3	1924-38	
VI 13 a	Leichenpässe	1	1924-38	
VI 13 b		1	1924-38	

Akten-zeichen	Inhalt	Band	Datum	Serial Nr.
VI 14 a	Schweizer Fremdenverkehr	1	1924-38	
VI 14 b		1	1924-38	
VI 15 a	Reiseausweise für Staatenlose, Russen	1	1924-38	
VI·15 b	Unbedenklichkeitsvermerk der Finanzämter	1	1924-38	
VI 16 b	Reiseausweise für Staatenlose, Russen	1	1925-38	
VI 17 b	Internationale Passregelung	1	1925-38	
	Ein- und Ausreise von Schweizern	1	1918-20	
	Ein- und Ausreise von Ausländern	1-3	1918-20	
VII 1 a	Standesamtliche Fragen Allgemeines	1	1925-38	
VII 1 b	Auskunftserteilung über Ehe-schliessung	1	1924-38	
VII 2 a	Ehescheidungen	1	1927-38	
VII 2 b	Ehesachen, Ehescheidungen, Vermittlung in Ehestreitigkei-ten	1-2	1924-38	
VII 3 a	Ehe- und Güterrecht	1	1926-38	
VII 3 b	Ehefähigkeitszeugnisse	1	1924-38	
VII 4 a	Austausch von Personenstands-urkunden	1	1924-38	
VII 4 b		1-6	1924-38	
VII 5 a	Nachlass- und Erbschaftssachen (Verschiedenes)	1	1924-38	
VII 5 b		1-5	1924-38	
VII 6 a	Vormundschaftssachen (Alimente)	1	1925-33	
VII 6 b		1-2	1924-38	
VII 7 b	Beschaffung von Zivilstands-urkunden	1-5	1924-38	
VII 8 b	Verschiedenes (Namensänderungen)		1925-38	

Akten-zeichen	Inhalt	Band	Datum	Serial Nr.
VIII 1 a	Rechtswesen, generell, Gesetze und Verordnungen	1-2	1924-38	
VIII 1 b	Rechtsfragen, Verschiedenes	1	1924-38	
VIII 2 a	Rechtswesen (Direkter Verkehr der deutschen und schweizerischen Gerichtsbehörden)	1	1927-38	
VIII 2 b		1	1931-38	
VIII 3 a	Rechtseinheit	1	1937-38	
VIII 4 a	Rechtshilfe	1	1925-38	
VIII 4 b	Rechtshilfesachen	1-3	1925-38	
VIII 5 a	Gegenseitigkeit in der Vollstreckung deutscher und schweizerischer Urteile	1-2	1922-38	
VIII 5 b		1	1924-38	
VIII 6 a	Entwurf eines neuen schweizerischen Strafgesetzbuches	1	1927-38	
VIII 6 b		1	1930-38	
VIII 7 a	Zustellungen	1	1924-38	
VIII 7 b		1	1924-38	
VIII 8 a	Entscheidungen des Schweizer Bundesgerichts in Lausanne	1	1927-38	
VIII 9 b	Verhandlungen und Berichte des Schweizer Jugendgerichtstages	1	1930-31	
VIII 10a	Deutsches Strafgesetzbuch	1	1924-25	
VIII 10b	Reklamationen, Forderungssachen	1-10	1924-38	
VIII 11a	Vertrauensanwälte der Gesandtschaft	1	1925-38	
VIII 11b	Beschwerden gegen Schweizer Behörden	1-2	1925-38	
VIII 12a	Arrest- und Zwangsvollstreckungsmaßnahmen der Schweiz gegenüber Vermögen fremder Staaten	1	1926-38	
IX 1 1 a	Deutsche Gesetzgebung	1	1925-38	
IX 1 2 a	Eidgenössische Gesetzgebung	1	1924-38	
IX 1 2 b		1	1924-38	
IX 1 3 b	Gesetzgebung, Kantonale	1	1931-38	
IX 1 4 a	Internationale Gesetzgebung	1	1924-38	
IX 1 4 b		1	1927-38	
IX 1 9 a	Gesetzgebung Basel-Stadt	1	1931-38	

Akten-zeichen	Inhalt	Band	Datum	Serial Nr.
IX 1 11 a	Gesetzgebung Kanton Bern	1	1925-38	
IX 1 12 a	Kanton Freiburg	1	1926-38	
IX 1 14 a	Kanton Genf	1	1928-38	
IX 1 18 a	Kanton Neuenburg	1	1930-38	
IX 1 23 a	Kanton Thurgau	1	1935-38	
IX 1 27 a	Kanton Waadt	1	1928-38	
IX 1 29 a	Kanton Zürich	1	1925-38	
IX 2 1 a	Deutsche Reichsverfassung	1	1919	
IX 2 2 a	Schweizerische Bundesverfassung	1	1938	
IX 2 3 a	Ausübung des Wahlrechts der Deutschen in der Schweiz	1-2	1933-38	
IX 2 3 b		1	1930-38	
IX 3 1 a	Deutsche Statistiken (ausser Handel)	1	1933-38	
IX 3 2 a	Schweizerische Statistiken (ausser Handel)	1	1927-38	
IX 3 3 a	Bevölkerungsstatistiken der Schweiz	1	1928-38	
IX 4 1 a	Geschäftsberichte der Schweizer Bundesbehörden	1	1924-38	
IX 4 4 a	Austausch von Gesetzessammlungen	1	1925-38	
X 1 a	Auslieferungsverträge	1	1923-38	
X 1 b		1	1925-38	
X 2 a	Auslieferungen	1	1930-38	
X 2 b		1-2	1924-38	
X 3 a	Durchlieferungen, Verschiedenes	1	1926-38	
X 3 b		1-2	1924-38	
X 4 a	Strafverfolgungen, allgemein	1	1927-38	
X 4 b	Strafsachen, Verschiedenes	1-2	1924-39	
X 5 b	Strafverfolgungen in der Schweiz für Vergehen in Deutschland	1	1924-38	
X 6 a	Strafregisterauszüge und Strafnachrichten	1	1925-38	
X 6 b	Strafregisterauszüge	1-3	1924-38	
	Gebührenerhebung für die Beschaffung von Strafregisterauszügen, Sonderband	1	1926-36	

Akten-zeichen	Inhalt	Band	Datum	Serial Nr.
XI 1 a	Internationales Gesundheitswesen	1	1928-38	
XI 2 a	Krankheiten, Seuchen, Epidemien der Menschen	1	1924-39	
XI 2 b		1	1924-38	
XI 3 a	Krankheiten der Tiere, Seuchen, Veterinärvorschriften	1	1930-38	
XI 3 b		1	1924-38	
XI 4 a	Gesundheitswesen, Verschiedenes	1	1926-38	
XI 4 b		1	1932-38	
XI 5 a	Zulassung deutscher Ärzte, Zahnärzte und Apotheker in der Schweiz und schweizerischer in Deutschland	1	1924-38	
XI 5 b		1	1927-38	
XI 6 a	Deutsche Heilstätte in Davos	1-2	1924-38	
XI 6 b		1	1924-38	
XI 7 a	Deutsche Heilstätte in Agra	1-2	1925-38	
XI 7 b		1	1924-38	
XI 8 a	Deutsches Kriegerkurhaus in Davos	1-2	1924-38	
XI 8 b		1-2	1924-38	
XI 9 a	Tierschutz, Vogelschutz	1	1924-38	
XI 10 a	Reblaus	1	1924-38	
XI 11 a	Deutsches Studentenheim in Arosa	1	1926-38	
XI 11 b		1	1926-38	
XII 1 a	Ausstellungen und Messen (nicht in Handelssachen)	1	1925-38	
XII 1 b		1-3	1924-38	
XIII 1 a	Kultur, Kunst, Wissenschaft und Literatur	1-3	1925-38	
	Das deutsche Buch in der Schweiz Beiheft	1	1926-38	
XIII 1 b	Literatur, Kunst und Wissenschaft	1-2	1924-38	
XIII 2 a	Geschichte, Geographie und Meteorologie	1	1925-38	
XIII 2 b		1	1924-38	

Akten-zeichen	Inhalt	Band	Datum	Serial Nr.
XIII 3 a	Erdkunde, Naturwissenschaft, Welt-Naturschutz	1	1927-38	
XIII 3 b		1	1924-38	
XIII 4 a	Kongresse, Konferenzen, Veranstaltungen und Vorträge	1	1924-38	
	Goethe-Gedächtnisfeiern, Sonderband	1	1932-38	
	Tomarkin-Stiftung, Beiheft	1	1931-38	
XIII 4 b	Kongresse, Konferenzen, Vorträge und Veranstaltungen über Kunst und Wissenschaft	1-9	1924-39	
	Schweizerische Kunstausstellung in Karlsruhe und Berlin	1	1924-25	
XIII 5 a	Broschüren über Kultur, Kunst, Wissenschaft und Unterricht	1	1924-38	
XIII 5 b	Deutsches Schulwesen, Studium und Unterricht (vergleiche auch 7 a)	1-4	1924-39	
	Alexander von Humboldt-Stiftung, Beiheft	1	1932-38	
XIII 6 a	Museen und Kunsthistorisches Institut in Florenz	1	1933-38	
XIII 6 b	Schweizerisches Schulwesen, Studium und Unterricht (vergleiche 8a)	1-3	1924-38	
	Unterstützung von Universitäten	1	1927-38	
XIII 7 a	Deutsches Schulwesen, Unterricht und Studium (Vergleiche 5b)	1-3	1924-38	
XIII 7 b	Deutsche und Schweizer Fach- und Privatschulen, Mädchen-pensionat (vergleiche 9a)	1-3	1924-30	
		5-6	1936-38	
XIII 8 a	Schweizerisches Schulwesen, Unterreicht und Studium (vergleiche 6b)	1-4	1924-38	
	Beiheft: Deutsche Professoren an Schweizer Hochschulen	1-2	1929-38	
XIII 8 b	Schulwesen, Unterricht und Studium (Verschiedenes) Schülerzeitung "Hilf mit"	3	1937-38	
XIII 9 a	Deutsche und schweizerische Fach- und Privatschulen (vergleiche 7b)	1	1927-38	
XIII 9 b	Studentenfragen, Organisationen, Kongresse (Verschiedenes)	1-3	1924-39	

Akten-zeichen	Inhalt	Band	Datum	Serial Nr.
XIII 9 b	Deutsche Studentenverbindung Teutonia	1	1925-35	
	Germania	2	1925-37	
XIII 10a	Schulwesen, Unterricht, Studium (Verschiedenes)	1	1925-38	
XIII 10b	Anerkennung von Reifezeugnissen (vergleiche 13 a)	1	1924-38	
XIII 11a	Studentenfragen, Organisationen und Kongresse	1	1924-38	
XIII 11b	Verleihungen von Ehren-Doktor-Titeln	1	1924-38	
XIII 12a		1	1925-38	
XIII 12b	Gleichstellung ausländischer Studierender in Deutschland und deutscher in der Schweiz (vergleiche 15 a)	1	1925-38	
XIII 13a	Anerkennung von Reifezeugnissen (vergleiche 10 b)	1	1925-38	
XIII 13b	Internationales Weltsprachenamt (vergleiche 16 a)	1	1925-38	
XIII 14a	Einführung einer neuen deutschen Rechtschreibung	1	1933-34	
XIII 14b	Fridericianum Davos (vergleiche 17 a)	1	1919-24	
		1-3	1924-38	
XIII 15a	Gleichstellung ausländischer Studierender in Deutschland und deutscher in der Schweiz (vergleiche 12 b)	1	1924-38	
XIII 15b	Institut für Hochgebirgsphysiologie und Tuberkuloseforschung in Davos (vergleiche 18 a)	1	1924-38	
XIII 16a	Internationales Weltsprachenamt (vergleiche 13 b)	1	1933	
XIII 16b	Kirchliche Angelegenheiten (vergleiche 19 a)	1-2	1924-38	
XIII 17a	Fridericianum Davos (vergleiche 14 b)	1-2	1924-38	
	Lyceum Alpinum, Zuoz	1-2	1926-38	
	Institut Dr.Schmidt in St.Gallen	1	1932-38	
	Schulunterstützungsgesuche	1-2	1931-38	
XIII 17b	Sportliche Veranstaltungen (vergleiche 20 a)	2-4	1929-38	

Akten-zeichen	Inhalt	Band	Datum	Serial Nr.
XIII 17b	Olympiade, Beiheft	1-2	1935-38	
XIII 18a	Institut für Hochgebirgsphysio-logie und Tuberkuloseforschung in Davos (vergleiche 15 b)	1	1924-38	
XIII 18b	Beschaffung von Material und Auskünfte für Doktordisserta-tionen	1	1924-38	
XIII 19a	Kirchliche Angelegenheiten (vergleiche 16 b)	1-2	1926-38	
XIII 19b	Ausländische Bestrebungen gegen deutsche Kunst und Wissenschaft (vergleiche 21 a)	1	1925-38	
XIII 20a	Sport, Verschiedenes (vergleiche 17 b)	1	1925-38	
XIII 20b	Förderung und Unterstützung von wissenschaftlichen und kulturel-len Bestrebungen	1-5	1924-38	
	Theaterdirektor Edmund, Sonderband	1	1920-25	
	Verbreitung des wissenschaft-lichen deutschen Buches im Auslande	1	1928-30	
XIII 21a	Ausländische Bestrebungen gegen deutsche Kunst und Wissenschaft (vergleiche 19 b)	1	1925-38	
XIII 21b	Deutsche Einheitskurzschrift (vergleiche 23 a)	1	1925-38	
XIII 22a	Förderung und Unterstützung von wissenschaftlichen Bestrebungen	1	1925-38	
XIII 22b	Internationales Hochgebirgs-sanatorium und Universität	1	1926-38	
	Davoser Hochschulkurse, Sonderband	1	1928-31	
XIII 23a	Deutsche Einheitskurzschrift (vergleiche 21 b)	1	1924-38	
XIII 23b	Mitteleuropäisches Forschungs-institut in Genf	1	1931-38	
XIII 24b	Ausländische Volkshochschulen und Kurse	1	1931-38	
XIII 25b	Vermittlung deutscher Tonfilme und Filmgeräte	1	1938-39	
XIV 1 a	Auswanderung, Abwanderung (auch Abwanderung von Facharbei-tern)	1-2	1924-38	
XIV 1 b		1-5	1924-38	

Akten-zeichen	Inhalt	Band	Datum	Serial Nr.
XV 1 a	Pflege des Deutschtums im Aus-lande (Verschiedenes)	1-2	1925-38	
XV 1 b		2	1936-39	
XV 2 a	Deutsche Vereine in der Schweiz (ausser Hilfsvereine)	1	1925-38	
XV 2 b		1	1924-38	
XV 3 a	Deutsche Institute und Anstalten im Auslande	1	1930-38	
XV 3 b		1	1925-38	
XV 4 a	Die deutschen Kolonien in der Schweiz	1	1931-38	
XV 4 b		1	1928-38	
	Zuzugslisten und Wegzugslisten von Deutschen in Bern	1-2	1927-38	
XV 5 a	Die deutsche Kolonie in Bern	1	1925-38	
XV 5 b		1-2	1924-37	
XV 6 a	Zusammenschluss aller deutschen Vereine in der Schweiz	1	1924-38	
XV 6 b		1	1924-38	
XV 7 a	Vorträge und Veranstaltungen	1	1927-38	
XV 7 b		2	1938	
XVI 1 a	Soziale Fragen (Verschiedenes)	1	1924-38	
	Sozialpolitische Berichte, Sonderband	1	1930-31	
XVI 2 a	Sozialversicherungen, Verschiedenes	1	1925-38	
XVI 3 a	Kranken- und Unfallversicherung	1	1924-38	
XVI 5 a	Deutsch-schweizerisches Unfall-versicherungsabkommen	1	1929-38	
XVI 6 a	Alters-, Invaliditäts- und Hinterbliebenenversicherung	1	1925-38	
XVI 8 a	Arbeiterfragen und Arbeiter-gesetzgebung	1-2	1924-38	
XVI 9 a	Arbeits- und Erwerbslosenfür-sorge, Arbeitslosenversicherung	1-2	1922-38	
XVI 12a	Arbeitsdienstpflicht	2	1937-38	
XVI 12b		2	1935-38	
XVI 13a	Internationale Kongresse und Konferenzen für Arbeiterschutz	1	1924-38	
XVI 13b		1	1925-38	
XVI 14a	Mieterschutz und Wohnungswesen	1	1925-38	
XVI 14b		1	1925-38	
XVI 17b	Lotteriewesen	1	1925-38	

Akten-zeichen	Inhalt	Band	Datum	Serial Nr.
XVI 18b	Ortsverein Basel zur Ruhe gesetzter deutscher Beamten und Hinterbliebenen	1	1925	
XVII 1a	Fürsorgeangelegenheiten	1	1927-28	
XVII 1b	Fürsorgeangelegenheiten, Unterstützungsgesuche	2-3	1929-38	
XVII 2a	Schweizer Hilfe für deutsche Not	1	1924-38	
XVII 2b		1	1924-38	
XVII 3b	Schweizerisch-deutsche Hilfskommission, Studentenhilfe	1-3	1930-38	
XVII 4b	Auslandssammlungen	1	1924-38	
	Deutsches Winterhilfswerk, Beiheft	1-3	1933-38	
	Reichsdeutschenhilfe, Sonderband	1	1937-39	
	Schlußfeier der schweizerischen Hilfsaktion für Deutschland	1	1927-31	
XVII 5b	Liebesgabensendungen	1	1924-38	
XVII 6a	Jugendfürsorge, Ferienkinder	1	1924-38	
XVII 6b	Jugendfürsorge, Schweizerbund, Kinderverschickung	1-2	1924-38	
XVII 7a	Übernahme von Armensachen und Geisteskranken	1	1925-38	
XVII 7b		1-2	1924-38	
XVII 8a	Heimschaffung von mittellosen Deutschen	1	1924-38	
XVII 8b		2-4	1927-38	
XVII 9b	Wohltätigkeitsveranstaltungen	1	1926-38	
XVII 10b	Stiftungen	1	1925-38	
XVII 11a	Ehrung von Personen, die sich um die Wohltätigkeit verdient gemacht haben	1	1925	
XVII 11b		1	1925	
XVII 12a	Verteilung von Wohltätigkeitsschriften	1	1924-38	
XVII 13a	Deutsche Hilfsvereine in der Schweiz	1-2	1924-38	
	Reichsbeihilfe an die deutschen Hilfsvereine in der Schweiz, Sonderband	1-2	1927-38	
XVII 13b	Deutsche Hilfsvereine in der Schweiz	1	1924-38	

Akten-zeichen	Inhalt	Band	Datum	Serial Nr.
XVII 14a	Sonstige gemeinnützige Anstalten und Vereine	1	1925-38	
XVII 14b		1	1925-38	
XVII 15b	Internationales Rotes Kreuz und andere Rote Kreuz Organisationen (ausser Deutsche)	1	1925-38	
XVII 16a	Deutsches Rotes Kreuz	1	1925-38	
XVII 16b		1	1917-38	
XVII 17a	Unterstützungen an Kriegsteilnehmer und Hinterbliebene und Veteranbeihilfen	1	1924-38	
XVII 17b		1-3	1924-38	
		1	1926-32	
	Spenden des Herrn Gesandten	1	1930-37	
	Kassenbelege der Arbeitsgemeinschaft der Organisation der deutschen Kriegsbeschädigten, Hinterbliebenen und Kriegsteilnehmer in der Schweiz	1	1926	
XVII 18a	Kriegergräberfürsorge	1	1924-38	
XVII 18b		1	1918-38	
XVII 19a	Deutsche Darlehnsgenossenschaft in der Schweiz	1	1925-38	
XVII 19b		1	1922-34	
XVII 20a	Unterstützung bedürftiger deutscher Sozial- und Kleinrentner	1	1924-38	
XVII 21a	Verein Deutscher Heimstätten in der Schweiz (Altersheim Pieterlen)	1	1924-38	
XVII 22b		1	1925-38	
XVII 22a	Altersfürsorge für bedürftige deutsche Reichsangehörige	1	1925-38	
XVII 23b		1	1926-38	
XVIII 2a	Internationaler Postvertrag, Weltpostverein	1	1924-38	
XVIII 4a	Internationale Telegrafen-Union	1	1925-38	
XVIII 5a	Radiowesen, Verschiedenes	1	1924-38	
XVIII 7a	Funkstationen, Funkkonferenz	1	1926-38	
XIX 1a	Deutsche Reichseisenbahnen	1	1924-38	
XIX 1b		1	1931-38	
	Reichsbahnbüro Zürich	1	1935-37	

Akten- zeichen	Inhalt	Band	Datum	Serial Nr.
XIX 2 a	Schweizer Bundesbahnen	1	1924-38	
XIX 3 a	Internationales Eisenbahnbüro	1	1928-38	
XIX 3 b	Internationales Eisenbahnwesen	1	1925-38	
XIX 4 a	Eisenbahn- und Verkehrswesen, Verschiedenes	1	1924-38	
XIX 4 b		1	1925-38	
XIX 5 a	Fracht- und Personenverkehr	1	1925-38	
XIX 6 a	Gotthardbahn und Vertrag	1	1925-38	
XIX 7 a	Verkehrskonferenzen	1	1924-38	
XIX 7 b		1	1924-38	
XIX 7 a	Zusatzakte zum Internationalen Übereinkommen vom 23.Oktober 1924 betr. die Beförderung von Waren durch die Eisenbahn, Sonderband	1	1926-38	
XIX 8 a	Verkehrsabkommen	1	1924-38	
XIX 10 a	Luftschiffahrt	1-2	1924-38	
XIX 11 a	Verkehrstarifpolitik	1	1924-38	
XIX 12 a	Verkehrsfragen, Automobilverkehr	1	1931-38	
XIX 13 b	Luftschiffahrt	1-3	1924-38	
XX 1 a	Schiffahrtswesen(Verschiedenes)	1	1924-38	
XX 1 b		1	1925-38	
XX 2 a	Rheinfragen	1-7	1924-38	
XX 2 b		1	1924-38	
XX 2 a	Rheinfragen betr. Rheinregulie- rung, Sonderband	1-2	1927-38	
	Rheinschiffahrtsverband Konstanz	1	1933	
	Zentral-Kommission für die Rheinschiffahrt	1	1922-30	
XX 3 a	Rhone-Rhein-Schiffahrt	1	1926-38	
XX 3 b		1	1924-38	
XX 4 a	Wasserwesen, Wasserkräfte und ihre Ausnützung	1	1924-38	
XX 4 b		1	1924-38	
XX 5 a	Schweizerische Handelsschiffahrt	1	1925-38	
XX 5 b		1	1925-38	
	Basler Rheinschiffahrt,	1-2	1927-38	

Akten-zeichen	Inhalt	Band	Datum	Serial Nr.
XX 6 a	Schweizerisch-italienische Wasser- und Schiffahrtsfragen	1	1925-27	
XX 7 a	Schweizerisch-französischer Wasserweg; Genfersee-Rhone-Mittelmeer	1	1924-38	
XX 7 b		1	1926-38	
XX 8 a	Internationale Wasserfragen	1	1925-38	
XX 9 a	Wasserweg Venedig-Lago Maggiore-Gotthard	1	1925-38	
XXI 1 a	Militär- und Heeressachen (auch fremdes Heerwesen)	1	1925-38	
XXI 1 b	Verschiedenes	1	1924-39	
XXI 2 b	Amnestierung der Fahnenflüchtigen	1	1927-38	
XXI 3 a	Schweizer Polizeiwesen	1	1927-38	
XXI 3 b		1	1928-38	
XXI 4 b	Erfindungen für das Heerwesen	1	1924	
XXII 1a	Fischereiwesen, Verschiedenes	1	1924-38	
XXII 2a	Jagdwesen, Verschiedenes (Landwirtschaft siehe XXIV)	1	1925-38	
XXIII 1a	Deutsches Bank- und Finanzwesen, Verschiedenes	1-5	1924-38	
	Deutsches Transfermoratorium Sonderband	1-3	1933-38	
	Deutsch-schweizerisches Verrechnungsabkommen (Reiseverkehrsabkommen) Sonderband	1-4	1934-38	
	Vorschriften über die Verwendung von Registerguthaben	1	1936-38	
XXIII 1b	Deutsches Bank- und Finanzwesen, Verschiedenes	1-2	1924-38	
		1-2	1924-38	
XXIII 2a	Schweizerisches Bank-und Finanzwesen, Verschiedenes	1-4	1924-38	
	Clearingabkommen der Schweiz mit anderen Staaten, Sonderband	1-3	1931-38	
	Schweizerische Verrechnungsstelle, Sonderband	2	1936-38	
XXIII 2b	Schweizerisches Bank- und Finanzwesen, Verschiedenes	1-3	1924-38	

Akten-zeichen	Inhalt	Band	Datum	Serial Nr.
XXIII 3a	Bank- und Finanzwesen anderer Länder	1	1925-38	
XXIII 3b		1	1924-38	
XXIII 4a	Staatshaushalt der Schweiz (Voranschlag)	1	1924-38	
XXIII 4b		1	1924-38	
XXIII 5a	- (endgültig)	1	1924-38	
XXIII 5b		1	1926-38	
XXIII 6a	Staatshaushalt Deutschlands und seiner Länder	1	1926	
XXIII 7a	Deutsches Kapital im Ausland	1	1931-38	
XXIII 7b		1-2	1924-38	
XXIII 8a	Kreditaufnahme in der Schweiz	1	1925-38	
XXIII 8b		1	1924-38	
XXIII 9a	Goldhypotheken-Abkommen	1	1924-38	
XXIII 9b		1	1926-38	
XXIII 10a	Vertrauensstelle für Gold-hypotheken	1	1925-38	
XXIII 10b		1	1924-38	
XXIII 11a	Valutaschulden	1	1924-38	
XXIII 12a	Subventionen des Bundesrates	1	1926-38	
XXIII 13a	Einschmelzung fremder Goldmün-zen	1	1927-38	
XXIII 14a	Schweizer Steuerfragen	1-2	1924-38	
XXIII 15a	Deutsche Steuerfragen	1	1924-38	
XXIII 16a	Doppelbesteuerung	1	1924-38	
	Verhandlungen zwischen Deutschland und der Schweiz betreffend Abschluss eines Ab-kommens zur Vermeidung der Doppelbesteuerung, Sonderband	1	1927-38	
XXIII 17a	Steuerfragen, Verschiedenes	1	1921-38	
XXIII 17b		1	1925-38	
XXIII 18a	Monopole	1	1932-38	
XXIII 19a	Deutsche Aufwertungsfragen	1-3	1924-38	
XXIII 19b		1-2	1924-38	
XXIII 20b	Abwicklungsstelle für Hypotheken, Liegenschaften	1	1925-38	
XXIV 1 a	Wirtschaft, Handel, Industrie und Gewerbe	1-2	1925-38	

Akten-zeichen	Inhalt	Band	Datum	Serial Nr.
XXIV 2a	Deutsch-schweizerischer Handels-vertrag	1-3	1925-38	
XXIV 3a	Schweizerisch-italienischer Handelsvertrag	1	1925-38	
XXIV 4a	Schweizerisch-französischer Handlesvertrag	1	1925-37	
XXIV 5a	Schweizerische Handelsverträge mit verschiedenen Ländern	1	1925-38	
XXIV 6a	Handelsverträge Deutschlands mit anderen Staaten	1	1925-38	
XXIV 7a	Handelsverträge anderer Länder	1	1925-38	
XXIV 8a	Zulassung zum Handels- und Gewerbebetrieb	1	1925-38	
XXIV 9a	Vorbereitung eines neuen deutsch-schweizerischen Handels-vertrages	1-2	1924-28	
XXIV 10a	Handelsbeziehungen Schweiz - Deutschland	1	1925-38	6109/E452426-29
XXIV 11a	- Italien	1	1925-38	
XXIV 12a	- Frankreich	1	1925-38	
XXIV 13a	- Russland	1	1925-38	
XXIV 14a	- Schweden	1	1932-38	
XXIV 15a	- Holland	1	1930-38	
XXIV 16a	- Ungarn	1	1938	
XXIV 18a	- Nordamerika	1	1925-38	
XXIV 19a	- Südamerika	1	1933-38	
XXIV 20a	- Rumänien	1	1925-38	
XXIV 21a	- Tschechoslowakei	1	1925-38	
XXIV 22a	- mit anderen Ländern	1	1925-38	
XXIV 23a	- Deutschland - Frankreich	1	1927-38	
XXIV 24a	- - Italien	1	1928-38	
XXIV 26a	- - mit anderen Ländern	1	1926-38	
XXIV 27a	- verschiedener anderer Länder mit anderen Staaten	1	1925-38	
XXIV 28a	Deutschland, Wirtschaft, Handel und Industrie, allgemein	1-3	1926-38	
	- Beiheft	1	1929-33	
XXIV 29a	Schweiz, Wirtschaft, Handel und Industrie, allgemein	1-5	1925-38	
XXIV 31a	Frankreich, Wirtschaft, Handel und Industrie, allgemein	1	1925	

Akten-zeichen	Inhalt	Band	Datum	Serial Nr.
XXIV 32a	Wirtschaft, Handel, Industrie anderer Staaten	1	1925-38	
XXIV 33a	Internationale Wirtschafts-fragen	1	1925-38	
XXIV 34a	Deutsche Handelsstatistik	1-2	1925-38	
XXIV 35a	Schweizer Handelsstatistik	1-3	1925-38	
XXIV 36a	Deutsche Einfuhr-, Ausfuhr- und Durchfuhrbestimmungen	1	1925-38	
	Zusammenstellung in Deutschland bestehender Einfuhr-, Ausfuhr-verbote, sowie Beschränkungen	1	1936-38	
XXIV 37a	Schweizerische Einfuhr-, Ausfuhr- und Durchfuhrbestim-mungen	1	1925-38	
	Deutsch-schweizerisches Wirt-schaftsabkommen, Zusatzabkommen, Sonderband	1-4	1933-38	
	Einfuhrbeschränkungen, Kontingentierung, Einfuhrdros-selung durch Zollerhöhung der Schweizer Regierung	1-11	1932-38	
XXIV 38a	Deutsche Handelskammern in der Schweiz	1-4	1925-38	
XXIV 39a	Deutsche Handelskammern in Deutschland und in anderen Ländern	1-2	1926-38	
XXIV 40a	Schweizer und andere Handels- und Gewerbekammern	1	1928-38	
XXIV 41a	Handelsverbände und Organisa-tionen in Deutschland	1	1925-38	
XXIV 42a	- in der Schweiz	1	1925-38	
XXIV 43a	Vorschriften über Handels-auskunftserteilung, allgemein	1	1925-31	
XXIV 44a	Normierungsbestrebungen	1	1925-38	
XXIV 45a	Schmuggel und Schiebungen	1	1925-38	
XXIV 46a	Handels- und Wirtschaftsspionage	1	1925-38	
XXIV 47a	Unlauteres Geschäftsgebahren deutscher Firmen	1	1933-38	
XXIV 48a	Schweizerische Hotelindustrie	1-2	1931-38	
XXIV 49a	Freiland, Freigeld, Freiwirtschaftsbewegung	1	1932-38	

Akten-zeichen	Inhalt	Band	Datum	Serial Nr.
XXIV 51a	Errichtung von Filialen in der Schweiz	1	1931-38	
XXIV 52a	Veredelungsverkehr	1	1925-38	
XXIV 53a	Deutsche Landwirtschaft	1	1929-38	
XXIV 54a	Schweizerische Landwirtschaft	1-2	1925-38	
XXIV 55a	Wirtschaftliche Jahresberichte	1-3	1924-38	
	Wirtschaftlicher Enquête-Bericht	1	1926-28	
XXIV 56a	Geschäftsberichte Schweizer Handelsgesellschaften	1	1925-38	
XXIV 57a	Rechtsfragen in Handelssachen	1	1925-38	
XXIV 59a	Lebenshaltung und Lohnverhält-nisse in der Schweiz und in anderen Staaten	1	1926-38	
XXIV 60a	Ausstellungen und Messen des Handels und der Industrie in Deutschland	1	1925-38	
XXIV 61a	Leipziger Mustermesse	1	1925-38	
XXIV 62a	Frankfurter Mustermesse	1	1925-38	
XXIV 63a	Kölner Mustermesse	1	1938	
XXIV 64a	Ausstellungen und Messen in der Schweiz	1	1925-38	
XXIV 64b		1+4	1926-38	
XXIV 65a	- in anderen Ländern	1	1936-38	
XXIV 66a	Wirtschaftskongresse und -konferenzen	1	1926-38	
XXIV 67a	Internationaler Mittelstands-kongress	1	1924-38	
XXIV 68a	Submissionen	1	1926-38	
XXIV 69a	Patent-, Muster- und Marken-schutz	1	1926-38	
XXIV 70a	Deutsch-schweizerisches Abkom-men über Einfuhrbeschränkungen	1	1924-38	
XXIV 71a	Schweizer Getreidemonopol	1-2	1925-38	
XXIV 72a	Monatsberichte der Gesandt-schaft von Equador	1	1925	
XXIV 73a	Automobilmarkt, Schweizer	1	1925-38	
	Schweizerische Automobil-statistik	1-2	1926-38	

Akten-zeichen	Inhalt	Band	Datum	Serial Nr.
XXIV 74a	Holzmarkt	1	1925-38	
XXIV 75a	Elektrizitätswirtschaft	1	1925-38	
XXIV 76a	Wirtschaftliche Überfremdung der Schweiz	1	1925-38	
XXIV 77a	Ausländische Wirtschaftspropaganda	1	1925-30	
XXIV 78a	Kinomatographie, Gesetze und Verordnungen	1-4	1925-38	
XXIV 79a	Schweizer Uhrenindustrie	1	1925-38	
XXIV 10b	Auskünfte über Firmen und Personen	6	1938	
XXIV 18b	Kreditunwürdige Firmen	1	1925-32	
XXIV 23b	Handelsauskünfte über Kreditunwürdigkeit, Werbemethoden, Exportschädigungen	1	1925-38	
XXIV 25b	Wirtschaftliche Neugründungen und Umsiedlungen nach der Schweiz	1	1925-38	
XXV 1 a	Schweizer Zollwesen, allgemein	1-6	1925-38	
	Kartoffeleinfuhr in die Schweiz, Kartoffelzölle, Beiheft	1	1926-38	
XXV 2 a	Schweizer Zolltarif	1-2	1925-38	
XXV 3 a	Deutsches Zollwesen, allgemein	1-3	1925-38	
XXV 4 a	Zollwesen anderer Länder	1	1925-38	
XXV 5 a	Deutsch-schweizerischer Zolltarif, Verhandlungen	1	1924-38	
XXVI 1 a	Internationale Verträge, Konventionen und Konferenzen (Verschiedenes)	1-2	1924-38	
XXVI 2 a	Internationale Organisationen, Büros	1	1929-38	
XXVI 5 a	Internationale Fachkongresse verschiedener Art	1-3	1924-38	
XXVI 6 a	Weltwirtschaftskonferenz	1	1932-38	
	Weltkongress für Freizeit und Erholung, Beiheft	1-2	1935-38	
XXVII 1 a	Gefangenen- und Interniertenfragen	1	1925-38	
XXVII 1 b		1-4	1925-38	
XXVII 2 a	Sequester, Schadensanmeldungen für im Ausland erlittene Kriegsschäden	1	1924-38	
XXVII 2 b		1	1924-38	

Akten- zeichen	Inhalt	Band	Datum	Serial Nr.
XXVII 2 b	Wiedergutmachung der Kriegs- schäden von Schweizern, Sonderband	1-2	1928-38	
XXVII 3 a	Vertretung deutscher Interessen durch neutrale Staaten	1	1924-38	
XXVII 4 a	Kassensachen (Verschiedenes) Forderungen und Erstattungen	1	1928-38	
XXVII 5 a	Weltkrieg 1914-1918, Verschie- denes	1	1925	
XXVIII 2a	Option in den abgetretenen Landesteilen	1	1924-25	
XXIX 4 b	Nachforschungen (ausser in Vormundschafts- und Nachlaß- sachen)	1-4	1924-38	
XXIX 8 b	Schwarze Liste (ausser in Paß- und Handelssachen)	1	1924-38	
XXIX 9 b	Zweifelhafte Personen (ausser in Paß- und Handelssachen)	1	1924-38	
XXIX 10 b	Auskunftserteilung	1-3, 5	1924-37 1939	
	Verschiedenes A - Z	1	1939	

Akten von 1939 - 1943

Akten- zeichen	Inhalt	Band	Datum	Serial Nr.
Pers.A.4	Rückkehr der in Belgien tätig gewesenen Beamten und Angestell- ten des Auswärtigen Amtes und Abtransport des Umzugsgutes aus dem Feindesland	1	1940	
Pers.P	Angestellte, Anmeldung bei Behörden	1	1939-40	
Pers.P.3	Bewerbungen um Beschäftigung bei der Gesandtschaft	1-2	1939-42	
Pers.G.2	Dienstbetrieb, Anordnungen des Behördenleiters, Organisation der Gesandtschaft, Geschäftsver- teilung	1	1939-41	
Pers.G.4 Nr.1	Grundstücksverwaltung Dienstwohnungen	1	1939-41	
Pers.G.5 Nr.3	Büromaterial	1	1939-42	
Pers.G.5 Nr.4	Bibliothek der Gesandtschaft	1	1939-40	
Pers.G.5 Nr.5	Beschaffung von Druckschriften und Materialien für innerdeut- sche Stellen	1-2	1939-42	
Pers.G.8a	Bezug von Zeitungen und Zeit- schriften für das Auswärtige Amt	1	1939-41	

Akten-zeichen	Inhalt	Band	Datum	Serial Nr.
Pers.G.9.	Konsulat Basel	1	1939-42	
	Genf	1	1939-42	
	St.Gallen	1	1939-42	
	Lausanne	1	1939-42	
	Generalkonsulat Zürich	1-2	1939-43	
Pers.G 10	Studienreisen und Informations-reisen deutscher Beamten, Kommissionen und Delegationen nach dem Ausland	1-2	1939-42	
Pers.G 13	Weiterleitung von Briefen	1-8	1939-42	
Pers.G 14	Glückwünsche und Beileids-schreiben	1	1939-42	
Pers.G 15	Empfehlung beziehungsweise Einführung deutscher Kommissio-nen, Delegationen und Einzel-personen	1	1939-42	
	Empfangsbestätigungen und Dank-schreiben für Übersendungen von deutschen Aufklärungsschriften	1	1940-41	
Pers.G 17	Übernahme der Tschechischen Behörden	1	1939-43	
	Tschechische Mappe, Einzelfälle	1	1939-40	3122/D641801-16
Pers.R.2. Nr.1	Kassensachen, Spezielles	1-5	1939-42	
Pers.R.2. Nr.2	Kassenbestandsverstärkungen	1	1941-42	
Pers.R.2. Nr.4	Bestandsverstärkungen für die Konsulate	1	1941-42	
Pers.R.4. Nr.2 a	Beantragung, Zuteilung und Ver-teilung der Kulturfonds	1	1939	
Pers.R.8.	Besoldung der Beamten	1	1939-41	
Pers.R.17	Kassenangelegenheiten der ehe-maligen Tschechischen Vertre-tungen	1	1939-40	
Pers.Si.5	Chiffrierdienst und Fernschrei-ber	1	1939-42	
Pers.Si.6	Kurierangelegenheiten, Speziel-les	1-3	1939-42	
	Kurierangelegenheiten, Generelles	1	1939-43	
Pol. 1	Allgemeine Aussenpolitik der Schweiz	1	1939-42	4825/E240946-1008
Pol. 1 Nr. 1	Die Neutralität der Schweiz	1 2	1938-40	3286/E588318-23

Akten-zeichen	Inhalt	Band	Datum	Serial Nr.
Pol.1 Nr.2	Kriegsmaßnahmen der Schweiz	1	1939-42	5319/E337937-40 9877/E693135-37
Pol.1 Nr.3	Belästigung von Deutschen und Angriffe auf Deutsche	1	1939	9913/E694100-13 K1591/K390224-31
Pol.2 Nr.1	Politische Beziehungen der Schweiz zu Deutschland	1	1939-42	3918/E051017-62
		2		3918/E051063-115 5320/E337942-58
Pol.2 Nr.1a	- Grenzzwischenfälle	1	1939	
Pol.2 Nr.1b	- Sonstige Zwischenfälle	1	1939-40	
Pol.2 Nr.6	Politische Reden und Vorträge	1	1941-43	5321/E337960-71 6003/E443135-40
Pol.2	Anonyme Schmähschriften und andere Zuschriften	1	1939	
Pol.3	Innenpolitik der Schweiz im Allgemeinen	1	1939-41	
Pol.3 Nr.1	Bundesrat, Politische Departements	1	1939-42	
Pol.3 Nr.2	Personalien des Bundespräsiden-ten, der Bundesräte, prominenter Staatsmänner	1	1939-41	
Pol.3 Nr.2a	Alt-Bundesrat Musy	1	1939-42	4835/E244249-338
Pol.3 Nr.2b	Oberst Däniker	1	1940-42	
Pol.3 Nr.3a	Militärische Angelegenheiten der Schweiz	1	1939-41	3911/E050249-66
Pol.3 Nr.4c	Kommunistische Partei der Schweiz, Bekämpfung kommunisti-scher Agitation	1	1939-42	3920/E051194-206
		2		3920/E051207-20 5323/E337983-88
Pol.3 Nr.6	Wahlen in der Schweiz	1	1939-42	
Pol.3 Nr.7	Politische Parteien und Verbände	1-2	1939-42	
Pol.3 Nr.7a	Die nationalen Erneuerungsbewe-gungen in der Schweiz	1		3938/E053154-96
		2	1939-41	3938/E053197-242
		3		3938/E053243-316
		4		3938/E053317-57
		5	1941-42	3938/E053358-84
		6		3938/E053385-437
		7		3938/E053438-465
		8		3938/E053466-507
Esap.Geh.	Eidgenössische Sozialistische Arbeiter Partei	1	1939-40	

Akten-zeichen	Inhalt	Band	Datum	Serial Nr.
Esap. Nr.7d	Bund Nationalistischer Schweizer Studenten	1	1941-42	
Esap. Nr.7f	Verhaftung beziehungsweise Verurteilung der Schweizer Wilhelm Schärer und Paul Gfeller	1	1941-42	
Esap. Nr.12	Judenfrage in der Schweiz	1	1939-43	K1592/K390232-509
Pol.4 Nr.1	Völkerbund	1	1939-41	
Nr.3	Freimaurer-Logen	1	1939-42	5322/E337973-81
Nr.6	Danziger Frage	1	1939-40	
Nr.7	Memel-Frage	1	1939	
Nr.8a	Fürstentum Liechtenstein, Politisches	1	1926-41	
Nr.8b	- Innere Angelegenheiten	1	1926-41	
Nr.12	Übernahme des Protektorats über die Tschechei und die damit zusammenhängenden politischen Aktionen	1	1939-41	3122/D641817-45
Nr.17	Politische Fragen über das ehemalige Oesterreich	1	1940	
Nr.18	Der ehemalige Staat Polen, seine Scheinregierung, Sammlungen	1-2	1939-43	
Nr.18a	Polnische Greuelpropaganda und Bekämpfung derselben	1 / 2	1940-42	K1593/K390510-23 / K1593/K390524-34
Nr.19	Finnisch-russischer Konflikt	1	1940	
Nr.22	Carol von Rumänien	1	1940	3900/E049611-21
Nr.23	Die internationalen Büros in der Schweiz	1	1940-42	
Schweiz 2	Grenzverletzungen durch Deutschland, Fliegerzwischenfälle	1	1939-42	
Schweiz 3	Neutralitätsverletzungen durch die Alliierten	1	1940-42	
Schweiz 6	Rückkehr der in der Schweiz internierten belgischen Soldaten und Arbeitern	1	1940-41	
	Rücktransport von Kriegsmaterial aus der Schweiz	1	1940-42	
	Preispolitik und Preisbewegung in der Schweiz	1	3.1940	
	Anlage: Übersicht der Preisvorschriften des Eidgenössischen Volkswirtschafts Departments		9.39- 2.40	
Deutschld 2	Kriegsmaßnahmen für die Schiffahrt	1	1939-40	
4	Deutsches Weißbuch und Kriegsschuldfrage	1-2	1939-42	

Akten-zeichen	Inhalt	Band	Datum	Serial Nr.
Deutschld 5	Vertrauensmänner, Agenten	1	1939-43	
9a	Spenden für das Deutsche Rote Kreuz	1	1939-40	
13	Kirchliche Hilfsaktionen, Seelsorge für die Kriegsgefangenen in Deutschland und im Feindesland	1	1940	
14	Kriegsgefangene in Deutschland	1	1940-41	
14a	Flucht des französischen Generals Giraud aus deutscher Kriegsgefangenschaft	1	1942	3898/E049560-90
Belgien 1	Belgien im Krieg	1	1940-43	
2	Belgien, Angelegenheiten von Privaten	1	1940-42	
Elsass 1	Elsass-Lothringen, Politisches	1	1940-42	3907/E050006-20
2	Internierte Elsass-Lothringer und Flüchtlinge in der Schweiz	1	1940-41	
Frank-reich 1	Krieg mit Frankreich, Allgemeines	1	1939-42	3901/E049624-27
2	Angelegenheiten von Privatpersonen	1	1940-43	
4	Berichtesammlung des Konsulats in Genf über Frankreich	1	1940	3901/E049628-65
Niederl.1	Niederlande im Krieg	1	1940-43	
Rußland 1	Der Kampf gegen Sowjet-Rußland, Allgemeines, Politisches	1	1941-43	
2	Russische Emigranten und Faschisten, Nationalkomitee der Weissrussen	1	1941-42	
3	Reisen an die Front und die besetzten Ostgebiete im propagandistischen Interesse	1	1941-42	
4g	Einstellung beziehungsweise Annahme von Schweizern zum Kampf gegen die Bolschewisten	1	1941-43	4830/E242735-77
5	Schweizer Ärztemissionen für die Ostfront	1	1941-43	5324/E337990-97
7	Ukrainer in der Schweiz	1	1940-42	
9	Russischer Massenmord an polnischen Offizieren in Katyn, Massenmorde in Winniza	1	1943	5827/E424229-399 7225/E530368-70
Gen. 4	Stimmungsberichte	1	1939-40	3879/E046860-84
Gen. 5	Presseberichte über Lage und Stimmung in Frankreich	1	1939-42	
Gen. 6	Abwehr, Spionage	1 2	1939-43	3919/E051119-88 3919/E051189-91

Akten-zeichen	Inhalt	Band	Datum	Serial Nr.
Gen. 7	Berichte über Verhältnisse in den Feindstaaten, Kriegsziele, Friedensfühler	1	1939-43	3921/E051224-302
		2		3921/E051303-86
		3		3921/E051387-505 5436/E364413-19
		4		3921/E051508-84 5437/E364421-23 6597/E494844-49
Gen. 8	Berichtssammlung Prof.Grimm	1	1939	
Gen. 9	Berichte und Aufzeichnungen des Frh.Schenk zu Schweinsburg	1	1939-40	
Gen.13	Maßnahmen der Feindstaaten nichtmilitärischen Charakters wie Post, Zensur, Störung der Sender	1	1939-40	
Gen.15	Informationserlasse des Auswärtigen Amtes in politi-scher und wirtschaftlicher Hin-sicht zum Krieg	1	1940	
Gen.17	Verwendung von Giftgasen in der Kriegführung	1	1939-43	
Gen.20	Englische und französische Kriegspropaganda, Englisches Blaubuch, Französisches Gelb-buch	1	1939-42	
D.Pol.1	Die deutsche Aussenpolitik	1	1939-43	5189/E307430-34 3874/E046748-82
		2		3874/E046783-89
D.Pol.2	Politische Beziehungen Deutschland-Ägypten	1	1941-42	4799/E236717-61
	-Baltische Staaten	1	1939-41	4969/E276989-7015
	-Frankreich	1	1940-42	3837/E044104-26
	-Großbritannien	1	1939-41	
	-Italien	1	1939-43	5898/E433421-29
	-Jugoslawien	1	1940-41	
	-Portugal	1	1942	3905/E049928-36
	-Russland	1	1939-41	
	-Spanien	1	1940-42	
	-Türkei	1	1941-42	1965/437718-27
	-Ungarn	1	1940-43	
	-Vereinigte Staaten	1	1940-42	1965/437728-51
D.Pol.2 Nr.1 geheim	Rumänisch-ungarische Gegensätze Friedensfühler beider Länder	1	1940-42	5429/E363747-4016
D.Pol.3 Nr.1	Der Führer und Reichskanzler	1 ·2	1939-42	3899/E049592-608
D.Pol.3 Nr.1a	Attentat auf den Führer in München	1	1939-42	4027/E059586-616

Akten-zeichen	Inhalt	Band	Datum	Serial Nr.
D.Pol.3 Nr.3	NSDAP und ihre Gliederungen	1	1939-42	3904/E049917-25
Nr.3c	Zentralamt für internationale Sozialgestaltung	1	1941-42	
Nr.3d	NS-Frauenschaft	1	1939-42	
Nr.6	Reichsparteitage	1	1939	
D.Pol.5	Angliederung Oesterreichs an Deutschland	1	1938-42	
D.Pol.6d	Deserteure	1	1939-43	
R.2 Nr.1	Austausch von Standesamtsurkunden und Strafregisterauszügen	1	1939-42	
R.3 Nr.5a	Professor Lüdke,Verschiedenes	1	1940	
Nr.6c	Austausch von Häftlingen	1	1942	
R.5 Nr.5	Polizeisachen, Einzelfälle	1	1939-40	
Nr.6	Durchlassscheine für Protektorat Böhmen und Mähren	1	1939	
R.6 Nr.8	Verschickung von Kindern zur Erholung nach der Schweiz und von der Schweiz nach Deutschland	1	1939-42	
Nr.9	Schweizerische Arbeitskräfte für Deutschland und Rückführung reichsdeutscher Facharbeiter	1	1937-41	
Nr.10	Sammlungen und Spenden	1	1940-42	
R.7 Nr.3	Internationales Rotes Kreuz	1-2	1939-43	
Kult 2 Nr. 1	Kulturpolitische Beziehungen zwischen Deutschland und der Schweiz	1	1939-41	
Nr. 2b	Ausländische Kulturpropaganda in der Schweiz	1	1939-41	
Kult 3 Nr. 6b	Koloniefilme, Einzelfilme	1-2	1939-41	
Nr. 6d	- Wochenschauen	1-7	1939-42	
Kult 8 Nr. 1b	Deutsche Schulen in der Schweiz, Fridericianum Davos	1	1937-40	
Kult 10 Nr. 1	Professoren, speziell	1	1939-41	
Nr. 2	Studentenwesen	1	1938-40	
Nr. 6	Bücherspenden an Schulen in der Schweiz	1-2	1939-41	
Kult 11 Nr. 6a	Deutsche Heilstätte Davos	1-2	1938-40	
Kult 12 Nr. 2	Theaterwesen	1	1939-41	
Nr. 3	Musikwesen in der Schweiz	1	1939-41	

Akten-zeichen	Inhalt	Band	Datum	Serial Nr.
Kult 12 Nr. 4	Schweizerisches Filmwesen	1-2	1939-41	
Nr. 4b	Filmzensur, Lage des deutschen Films in der Schweiz	1-2	1939-42	
Nr. 4c	Filmwesen, Spezielles, Einzelfilme	1-2	1939-41	
Nr. 5	Sportwesen	1-2	1939-41	
P 1	Presse- und Propagandawesen, Allgemeines	1	1939-42	
P 2 Nr.1	Pressebeziehungen Schweiz zu Deutschland	1-2	1939-42	
P 2 Nr.2	Pressebeziehungen Schweiz zu anderen Staaten	1	1939-42	
P 2 Nr.3	Berichterstattung über Haltung der Schweizer Presse	1-2	1939-42	
P 2 Nr.3a	Meldungen in der Schweizer Presse über Errichtung einer zweiten Front	1	1942-43	
P 2 Nr.4	Deutsche Presspropaganda	2-3	1940-43	
P 2 Nr.4a	Bild-Pressedienst	1	1939-42	
P 2 Nr.4b	Propaganda der Reichsbahnzentrale	1	1940-42	
P 2 Nr.5	Studienfahrten Schweizer Journalisten nach Deutschland und deutscher nach der Schweiz	1	1941-43	
P 2 Nr.6	Verwertung der Pressetelegramme, Gegenpropaganda, Herausgabe der "Mitteilungen der Deutschen Gesandtschaft"	1	1939-42	
P 3	Verlagsanstalten, Zeitungen, allgemein	1	1939-41	
P 3 Nr.1	Nachrichtenbüros und Telegrafenagenturen in der Schweiz	1	1939-41	
P 3 Nr.1a	Schweizerische Depeschenagentur, Sonderheft	1	1938-42	
P 3 Nr.1b	Geopress (Atlas-Permanent) Sonderheft	1	1936-40	
P 3 Nr.2	Die deutschen Zeitungen in der Schweiz	1-2	1939-42	
P 3 Nr.2a	Bodensee-Rundschau	1	1939-40	
P 3 Nr.9	Gazette de Lausanne	1	1939-42	
P 3 Nr.40	Nationale Hefte	1	1939-42	
P 3 Nr.78	"La jeune Suisse"	1	1941-43	
P 4 Nr.1b	Berichterstatter und ihre Organisationen	1-2	1939-41	
P 4 Nr.2a	Dr.Reibstein, Vertreter des Deutschen Nachrichtenbüros	1	1939-41	

Akten-zeichen	Inhalt	Band	Datum	Serial Nr.
P 6 Nr.1	Greuel- und Hetzpresse, Einzelfälle	1	1939	
P 6 Nr.4	Beanstandungen in Presse und Propaganda, Deutsche Beanstandungen	1-4	1939-42	
P 7	Dichter und Schriftsteller Jacob Schaffner	1	1940-42	
P 7a	Schriftsteller René Sonderegger	1	1940-41	
P 8	Verbot deutscher Zeitungen und Zeitschriften, sowie Beschlagnahme von deutschem Propagandamaterial	1-2	1939-41	
P 9	Neutralitätswidriges Verhalten der Schweizer Presse	1	1939-42	9914/E694114-25
P 10	Schweizer Presseamt (Armeestab, Zensur)	1-2	1939-42	
P 11	Anfragen wegen deutscher Veröffentlichungen, Führerreden	1	1939-42	
P 12	Feindliche Propaganda	1-3	1939-43	
P 12a	Feindhetze, betreffend die besetzten und angegliederten Gebiete	1-2	1939-42	
P 15	Bolschewistische und antibolschewistische Propaganda in der Schweiz	1-4	1939-43	
P 20	Nachrichtendienst über England, Auslandsdienst	1-2	1941-42	
	V.-Aktion (Victory")	1	1941	
D P 1	Presse und Propagandawesen in Deutschland	1	1939-43	
D P 1c	Angelegenheiten des Pressebeirats Oberregierungsrat von Chamier	1	1940-42	
D P 3 Nr.2	Zeitschrift Berlin-Rom-Tokio	1	1939-43	
Nr.5	Ausländische Korrespondenten in Deutschland	1-2	1939-43	
D P 4	Verbote von Zeitungen, Druckschriften und Büchern in Deutschland	1	1939-42	
D P 8	Europa Sonderdienst (Kaufmann)	1-2	1939-42	
D P 12	Predigten des Bischofs von Galen in Münster	1	1941-42	
D P 16	Berichte der Verbindungsoffiziere des Auswärtigen Amtes bei den Armee-Oberkommandos	1	1941-42	3997/E057902-8166
S	Mitteilungen der Deutschen Gesandtschaft seit Kriegsausbruch	1	1939-40	

Akten-zeichen	Inhalt	Band	Datum	Serial Nr.
S geheim	Radio-Mondial (Rundfunk-Nachrichten-Agenten)	1	1941-43	
S	Aufzeichnungen über Kanzler Wagner	1	1942-43	
	Dr.Thoenen, Zweisimmen, (Obersimmental)	1	1940-43	
	Friedensburg, Ferdinand	1	1942-43	
	Kiefer, Wilhelm (Deutscher Reichsangehöriger)	1	1940-43	
	Verschiedenes A - G, Ordner	1	1940	
	H - N, Ordner	2	1940	
	O - S, Ordner	3	1940	
	Sch - Z, Ordner	4	1940	
	Verschiedene Briefe und Aufzeichnungen von Jacob Sulzer	1 Bün-del	1940	
		1 Bün-del	1940	

Akten-zeichen	Inhalt	Band	Datum	Serial Nr.
	Personalakten von Gesandtschafts-Angehörigen			
	Achelis Ursula			
	Achilles			
	Alt Anton			
	Alt Elsbeth			
	Altendorf Elisabeth			
	Aschmann			
	Ashton			
	Assmann Max			
	Baehr			
	Bäumler Dora			
	Barth Hermann			
	Bartlome Flora			
	Baumann Karl			
	Becker, Dr.			
	Beer, Dr. Max			
	Belke Margarethe			
	Bendler Walter			
	Bensing Rudolf			
	Benzler			
	von Berchem,Graf			
	von Berg Walter			
	Bern			
	Berthold Rudolf			
	v.Bethmann-Hollweg			
	v.Bibra,Freiherr			
	Biengräber Hans			
	v.Bismarck, Major			
	Bissants Rudolf			
	Bitzer Jakob			
	v.Blankenburg			
	Blankenhorn Herbert			
	Blasen Liselotte			
	Blochwitz Walter			
	Blume Charlotte			
	Bodenstedt			
	Bodo Friedrich			
	Börger Karl			
	Böhme Georg			
	Bolwin, Dr.			
	Bolwin			
	Bonacker Frieda			
	Borchard Käthe			
	Borchers, Dr.			
	v.Bose, Major			
	v.Brauchitsch, Hauptmann			
	Brauer Wilhelm			
	v.Brentano di Tremezzo			
	Brielmaier Charlotte			
	Brielmaier Josef			
	Bring Paul			
	Budde, Dr.			
	v.Bülow			
	Burghardt			
	Busse Dorothea			
	Calender Lorenz			
	Capitaim Edmund			
	v.Chamier			
	Christlein			
	Claas			
	v.Courten			
	Cramer			
	Cunitz Charlotte			

Akten-zeichen	Inhalt	Band	Datum	Serial Nr.
	Dammann Erich			
	Dankwort, Dr.			
	Dannenberg Elsa			
	Delling Elisabeth			
	Diel			
	Dietrich Erwin			
	Dopp Hubert			
	v.Dorrer Susanne			
	Dr.Dreihann-Holema			
	Dressler			
	Eberth Oskar			
	Eggers Anna			
	Eggers			
	Eichel Charlotte			
	Eichholtz Edith			
	v.Einsiedel-Wolkenburg			
	Eisenhuth Ruth			
	Encke Ursula			
	Engel Adolf			
	Dr.Engerth Wilhelm			
	Epler			
	v.Ernst			
	Falk Max			
	Fass,Dr. Friedrich			
	Feihl			
	Fickler			
	Figge Eduard			
	Fischer			
	Flamm			
	Flügel Martha			
	Franke			
	Frei			
	Freitag Ottmar			
	Freund Charlotte			
	Friedensburg, Dr.			
	Fritsch			
	Fuehr, Dr.			
	Gamper Theodora			
	Gastl Friedrich			
	Geffken, Dr.			
	Geiger Fritz			
	Geyger Elisabeth			
	Gierling Adolf			
	Glasemann Erich			
	Glinz			
	Goetzke Carla			
	v.d.Goltz, Freiherr			
	Grabenstein Franz			
	Gradenwitz Willy			
	Gräbner Hermann			
	Gramatte Karl			
	Grimm, Dr.			
	Groh			
	Grosse Fritz			
	Grosse			
	Grossmann Irma			
	Haack			
	Haasemann, Dr. Hans			
	Hack Wilhelm			
	Häckl Heinrich			
	Hänsel Gertrud			
	Häussler			
	Hager Ferdinand			
	Haid Eugen			
	Hamel Carl Curt			
	Hanesse			

Akten-zeichen	Inhalt		Band	Datum	Serial Nr.
	Harazim	Elfriede			
	v.Hardt				
	v.Hartung				
	Hartmann	Eva			
	Hartung, Dr.	Erich			
	Hartung	Friedrich			
	Hasenbach	G.W.			
	Hasslacher, Dr.	Fritz			
	Hauck	Karl			
	Heidling	Otto			
	Heinecke, Dr.				
	Heiner				
	Heinrich	Max			
	Hemmen, Dr.	Hans			
	Henning				
	Henschel	Reinhard			
	Hensel	Lotte			
	Herbrand	Margarete			
	v.Herff				
	Hermoneit				
	Herrmann				
	Hessler	Anna			
	Hetzel				
	Heymann				
	v.Hindenburg				
	Hintze	Hertha			
	Hitzler	Georg			
	Höcker	Kurt			
	Hoffmann				
	Hoffmeister	Friedrich			
	Hohlfeld				
	v.Holbein	Charlotte			
	v.Holbein	Elsa			
	v.Holten, Dr.				
	Horazek	Barbara			
	Hermes	Anny			
	Hüffer,Dr.	Hermann			
	Humpert	Ottilie			
	Immelen				
	Isler	Mina			
	Janssen				
	v.Jecklin				
	Jessen	Hellmuth			
	Jolles	Bernhard			
	Jünke	Arnold			
	Junecke				
	Kann	Edith			
	v.Kardorff				
	Kasting	Wilhelm			
	Kempa	Heinrich			
	v.Kessel, Dr.				
	v.Ketelhodt	Ulrike			
	v.Keudell				
	Kietzmann				
	Kiliani				
	Kirmis				
	Kling	Mina			
	Knabbe	Erik			
	Knipping				
	Knoerle	Eugen			
	Koch	Erno			
	Körner				
	Kordt, Dr.	Erich			
	Kratzsch				
	Krebs,Dr.				
	Kropp	Brunhild			

Akten-zeichen	Inhalt	Band	Datum	Serial Nr.
	Kudajewski Marie			
	Kühn			
	Kuhlmann Lieselotte			
	Kuhn Lotte			
	Kummer			
	Kurlbaum			
	Kuske			
	Langen Paula			
	Langen, Dr.v.			
	Lasswitz, Dr.			
	Lauterbach			
	Leisewitz, Dr.			
	Lenz			
	Lerch			
	Linnekogel Elisabeth			
	v.d.Lippe			
	Litten Wilhelm			
	Loeff Wolfgang			
	Loewengard Eduard			
	London Nelly			
	Lüders Sophie			
	v.Lüttichau			
	Lutzeyer			
	Maier Marie-Luise			
	Majer,Dr. Otto Eberhard			
	Mankowski Franz			
	Mantey Ellen			
	Marti Emmi			
	Martin Barbara			
	Marum			
	Matulat Erika			
	Mayer Viktor			
	Mechlenburg, Dr.			
	Meintzinger Konrad			
	Melchers			
	Mey			
	Meyer, Hedwig			
	Meyer Carl Hermann			
	Meyer Robert			
	Meyer Wilhelm			
	Möbius Ernst			
	Möhlmann Friedrich			
	v.Montgelas, Graf			
	Mühl Walter			
	Müller, Dr. Adolf			
	Müller Anna			
	Müller August			
	Müller Friedrich			
	Müller Ilse			
	Müller Justus			
	Müller Mina			
	Müller-Palm Charlotte			
	Muff			
	Mulert Walter			
	Näher Hans			
	Nasse, Dr.			
	Natus Hugo			
	Neef			
	Nölting			
	Obst			
	Oertel,v. Kurt			
	v.Oswald Kurt			
	Paniowski Margarethe			
	v.Passavant Hermann			

Akten-zeichen	Inhalt	Band	Datum	Serial Nr.
	Peinert Max			
	Peter, Dr. Ernst			
	Peter Maria			
	Petschat			
	Pfennig-Kinder			
	Pickert Margarethe			
	v.Plessen			
	v.Podewils-Duernitz			
	v.Podewils-Duernitz,Gräfin			
	Poensgen, Dr.			
	Polak Georg			
	Posselt Ernst			
	Prevot, Dr.			
	Probst Werner			
	Radbruch			
	v.Radowitz			
	Raedecke			
	von Rath			
	v. Rechberg			
	v. Reden-Pattensen			
	v.Reibnitz Ursula			
	Reinhards Johanne			
	Reinhold Friedrich,			
	Richard			
	Reiser Albert			
	v.Renthe-Fink			
	Renz, Dr. Willi			
	Rettig Fritz			
	Rieger Ilse			
	Rigg Hans			
	Rinneberg			
	Ritter			
	Robé Kurt			
	Rodi Hermann			
	Rössler Gertrud			
	Rohrbach Alice			
	v.Romberg			
	v.Rosenberg			
	Rosenberg Eduard			
	Rottmoser Anton			
	Rudeloff Karl			
	Rück Christian			
	Rummel			
	Sailer Christian			
	Salin, Dr. Edgar			
	Sander			
	Salzer Trudel			
	Sannecke Theodor			
	Saxe Irmgard			
	Schaffert Reinhold			
	Scharffenberg			
	Scheffler Bernard			
	Schellberg			
	v.Scheller			
	Schenk			
	Scheps Paul			
	Scherer			
	Scheuerl Anni			
	Schick			
	Schinzel Heinrich			
	Schmid Josef			
	Schmid-Büchler			
	Schmidts			
	Schmitt Adelheid			
	Schneider			
	Schnorbus			
	Schön Nora			
	Schönenberg			
	Scholl			

Akten-zeichen	Inhalt	Band	Datum	Serial Nr.
	Schroeder Gerda			
	v.Schröder,Freiherr			
	Schrott Eberhard			
	v.Schubert, Dr.			
	Schütt			
	Schuflitowski			
	v.d.Schulenburg,Dr.			
	Schwaynoch			
	Schweinsburg,Freiherr Schenk zu			
	Schweinsburg			
	v.Schwerin			
	Schwiebus Elisabeth			
	Seidel Gerda			
	Seidl Eduard			
	Selner			
	v.Selzam, Dr. Edwart			
	Sichel Josefa			
	Smend, Dr.			
	Smiers			
	Solinski			
	v.Specht			
	Sprenger Annemarie			
	Sprenger Rudolf			
	Staehle Walter			
	Stefanski Hedwig			
	Stehr, Dr.			
	Stein, Dr.			
	Steinecke August			
	Steuer Theo			
	Stobbe			
	Strittmatter Anni			
	v.Sydow Amelia			
	Tafel Marianne			
	v.Tattenbach, Graf Eberhard			
	v.Tattenbach, Graf Franz			
	Tepper Hans			
	Tettenborn, Dr.			
	Teuber Hedwig			
	Thiele			
	Thielert			
	Thiess Karl			
	Thomas Helene			
	Tilse			
	Treu Werner			
	Trost Heinrich			
	Ulrich, Dr.			
	Velhagen, Dr. Adolf			
	v.Vietsch			
	Virgien Helene			
	Vogel Elisabeth			
	Voigt Ursula			
	Waag			
	Waibel Johanna			
	Walbaum Therese			
	Wallerstein Ernst			
	Walser Karl			
	Warnecke			
	Waskowitz			
	Wehrkamp Emmy			
	Wehrmann Gisela			
	Weström Barbara			
	Weissenborn			
	Weiz, Dr.			
	v.Weizsäcker			

Akten-zeichen	Inhalt		Band	Datum	Serial Nr.
	Werner	Ursula			
	Werz				
	Wetteran	Käthe			
	Wiesner				
	Wille	Liselotte			
	Winden	Hans			
	Winkel				
	Witt				
	Wolff, Dr.	Ernst			
	Wolters	Jack			
	Wunder	Franz			
	Zacharias				
	Zander	Marie			
	Zimmermann				

Akten-zeichen	Inhalt	Band	Datum	Serial Nr.
A 1 –90g	Geheimakten	1	2.39– 5.39	1338/353016–90
91 –180g		2	5.39– 9.39	1345/353733–893 8367/E590634–44 8369/E590646–64
181 –250g		3	8.39–12.39	1348/354357–93
251 –313g		4	9.39– 7.40	1349/354396–477
1 –150		1	1.40–10.40	4692/E226335–58
151 –320		2	3.40– 9.40	672/258220–38 4692/E226359–80 659/257016–40
321 –502		3	10.40–12.40	4692/E226381–408
1 –300		1	1.41– 5.41	1192/330674–1152
301 –480		2	5.41– 9.41	1315/350503–773 4850/E247550–73
481 –636		3	9.41– 3.42	1330/352401–570 4850/E247574–604
1 –150		1	1.42– 4.42	1156/326045–187
151 –250		2	6.42	1157/326191–285
251 –350		3	5.42– 9.42	1175/328860–994
351 –450		4	7.42– 9.42	1177/329091–211
451 –628		5	9.42– 3.43	1186/330012–206
	Auslandsdienst der Deutschen Gesandtschaft Bern (England-Nachrichten)		1.44– 7.44	
			8.44–11.44	

Akten-zeichen	Inhalt	Band	Datum	Serial Nr.
Pol 1	Aussenpolitik Belgiens	1	1939-40	4021/E059230-93 2856/D551422-23 1601/385180-284 8346/E590231-34
Pol 2 Nr.1	Politische Beziehungen Belgiens zu Deutschland, Verträge, Allgemeines	1	1939	1602/385288-301
Pol 2 Nr.3 c	Politische Beziehungen Belgien - Niederlande	1	1939-40	1747/403616-23
Pol 3	Innenpolitik Belgiens, allgemein	1	1939	3949/E054342-52
Pol 3 Nr.1	- Ministerien	1	1939-40	1734/401888-914
Pol 3 Nr.3	Militär-, Marine- und Luftange-legenheiten	1	1939-40	1740/402496-532
Pol 3 Nr.4	Staatsschutzbestimmungen, Agenten und Spionage und Kommunismus	1	1939-40	1748/403627-31
Pol 3 Nr.7	Parteiwesen, politische Verbände	1	1939-40	2847/D551247-55 3948/E054324-38
Pol 3 Nr'.9	Eupen-Malmedy	1	1939	3947/E054310-20
Pol 4 Nr.1	Völkerbund	1	1939-40	
D Pol 1	Deutsche Aussenpolitik, allgemein	1	1939-40	4001/E58554-59 2144/468484-91 1559/377956-8016
D Pol 2 Nr. 2 b	Politische Beziehungen Deutsch-lands zu Frankreich Berichte Dr.Sieburg	1 2	 1931-40	4020/E059113-215 1636/389998-90061 4020/E059217-25 1679/395481-677
D Pol 3 Nr. 8	Deutsche Innenpolitik, Militär-, Marine-, Luftfahrtangelegen-heiten, Arbeitsdienstpflicht	1	1939-40	1694/397974-8019
W 1	Oslo-Konvention	1	1937-38	1089/317622-804
W H 2 Nr. 1	Beziehungen Belgiens zu Deutsch-land, Handelsvertragsverhältnis	1	1939-40	
W V 9	Speditionswesen	1	1939-40	
	Akten der Presseabteilung der Deutschen Botschaft, Brüssel	1 2 3	 1939-40	1091/317919-8094 3950/E054356-78 2841/D549456-57
	- Aufzeichnungen	1	1939	
	- Beschwerden	1	1939-40	1090/317808-915
	Propaganda	1 2	 1939-40	4052/E065395-403 1587/383257-68 4052/E065404-31 1600/385145-76

Akten-zeichen	Inhalt	Band	Datum	Serial Nr.
W V 9	Getarnte bolschewistische Propaganda (Drucksachen, Zeit-schriften)	1	1937	
	Berichtverzeichnisse	1-3	1937-39	
	Secreta	1		1307/346519-63
		2		1333/352680-90
		3		3944/E054005-90 1333/352692-704
		4	1931-37	3944/E054092-114 1425/362705-844 7597/E543731-47
		5		3944/E054116-57 1444/364615-80
	(6 fehlt)	6		
		7		3944/E054159-200 2845/D551180-204 1456/366239-418
		8		3944/E054202-27 1496/370167-301
		9	1939-40	3944/E054229-73 2845/D551206-35 1524/373425-68
		10		3944/E054275-95 4243/E074738-42 1544/375879-904
	- Informationsdienst	1	1939-40	1290/344763-875
	Legationsrat Werkmeister	1	6.40- 9.40	P 6a/P00312a-77a

Akten-zeichen	Inhalt	Band	Datum	Serial Nr.
I	Geschäftsübergaben	1	1935-1936	
I 1	Personalien, Allgemeines	1	1926-1939	
I 1	– Hilfskräfte	1	1923-1936	
I 1	– Sonderrechte der Beamten	1	1922-1936	
	Aktenverzeichnisse	1	1925-1928	
I 2	Personalien, Einzelnes	1	1936-1938	
I 2	Pers.-Namen:			
	Arlt, Ella	1	1938-1942	
	Bauer	1	1924-1938	
	Baur	1	1935-1938	
	Benzler, Felix	1	1926-1931	
	Benzler, Gesandter	1	1944	
	Bertram, Marianne	1	1934-1939	
	Blümel, Johanna	1	1939-1940	
	Broich-Oppert	1	1927-1934	
	Brude, Eugen	1	1941-1944	
	Brükler, Arthur	1	1932-1939	
	Bunde, geb.Hage	1	1941-1944	
	von der Damerau	1	1943-1944	
	Dembinsky	1	1940-1942	
	Dietzler	1	1928-1929	
	Dittmar	1	1941-1943	
	Dumke	1	1910-1933	
	Ebner	1	1940	
	Eitler	1	1944	
	Emde	1	1942	
	Ender	1	1940-1941	
	v.Erdmannsdorff	1	1937-1943	
	Finger	1	1939-1943	
	Fischer	1	1938-1943	
	Fritzer	1	1941	
	Graeb	1	1936-1938	
	Gregory	1	1943	
	Gechwind	1	1939-1942	
	Hassler	1	1940-1941	
	Hedelt	1	1941-1944	
	Hellwig	1	1940-1943	
	Henning	1	1944	
	Henschel	1	1938-1943	
	Hermandinger	1	1938	
	Hezinger	1	1944	
	Hoffmann, Günther	1-2	1940-1944	
	Hofer	1	1940-1944	

Akten-zeichen	Inhalt	Band	Datum	Serial Nr.
I 2	Pers.-Namen:			
	Hofmann, Hamilkar	1	1944	
	Hofmann, Josefine	1	1939-1943	
	Holzer	1	1940-1941	
	v.Jagow	1	1941-1944	
	Kaldor	1	1911-1934	
	Kienast	1	1940-1942	
	Kiewnick	1	1927-1928	
	Klarner	1	1902-1940	
	Kornhauser	1	1913-1936	
	Koepke	1	1932-1941	
	Kraft	1	1939-1940	
	Krappe	1	1939-1941	
	Kühnemann	1	1925-1940	
	Kuszmits	1	1923-1936	
	Leise	1	1940-1941	
	Lenz	1	1936-1940	
	Luft, Attaché	1	1935-1938	
	Mittelstädt	1	1937	
	Möller	1	1937-1943	
	Mutscheller	1	1938-1944	
	Nentwig	1	1941-1942	
	Nikolowsky	1	1940-1944	
	Overbeck	1	1937-1943	
	Pfeiffer	1	1939	
	Plischke	1	1941-1942	
	Prachar	1	1940-1941	
	Prettenhofer	1	1940	
	v.Richthofen	1	1940-1944	
	Rothen-Schaub	1	1944	
	Schnurre, Dr.	1	1930-1936	
	Scholz	1	1941-1944	
	Schulz, Eva	1	1938-1943	
	Schulz, Louis	1	1941-1944	
	Simon	1	1943	
	Solms	1	1939-1941	
	Strachwitz	1	1939-1943	
	Struve, Dr.	1	1940-1943	
	Szabadka	1	1941-1943	
	Thiede	1	1940	
	Vaubel	1	1942-1943	
	Wagner, Dr.	1	1942	
	Welck	1	1939-1942	
	Werkmeister, Dr.	1	1936-1939	
	Weisse, Dr.	1	1937-1944	

Akten-zeichen	Inhalt	Band	Datum	Serial Nr.
I 2	Abgelegte Personalakten:			
	A–D		bis 1938	
	E–J		bis 1938	
	K–L		bis 1938	
	M		bis 1938	
	N–P		bis 1938	
	R–Sz		bis 1938	
	T–Z		bis 1938	
	Namenverzeichnis der Angehörigen der Gesandtschaft	1–2	1944–1945	
II 1	Gebäude	1	1921–1937	
II 2	Dienstwohnung	1	1921–1936	
III 1	Ausbau der Handelsabteilung	1	1936	
III 1	Wirtschafts-Fonds	1	1927–1936	
III 1	Institut für Wirtschaftsfor-schung	1	1928–1935	
III 1	Salzeinfuhr nach Ungarn	1	1929–1935	
III 1	Bücher, Absatzförderung des deutschen Buches	1	1926–1930	
III 1	Staatliche Vergünstigungen und industrielle Entwicklung	1	1931–1932	
III 1	Agrar-Kontingentierung in Deutschland	1	1932–1935	
III 2	Kompensationsgeschäfte	1	1933	
III 2	Entwicklung des deutsch-ungarischen Warenverkehrs	3	1936–1937	9784/E687214-18
III 2	Ungarische Kohleneinfuhr	1	1931–1936	
III 2	Deutsch-ungarisches Weizen-geschäft	1	1932–1937	
III 2	I.G.-Farbenindustrie	1	1927–1936	
III 2	Schweinegeschäft	1	1935–1938	
III 2	Ölsaatenanbau	1–2	1933–1936	
III 2	Schweineschmalzfrage	1	1934–1935	
III 3	Regierungsausschuss für die deutsch-ungarischen Wirtschafts-beziehungen	1–4	1934–1936	
	dazu eine Anlage		1934	
III 3	Regierungsausschuss für Jugoslawien	1	1934	
III 3	– Frühjahrsverhandlungen in München	1	1936	
III 3	Regierungsausschussverhandlungen in Budapest und in Berlin	1–3	1936–1937	

Akten-zeichen	Inhalt	Band	Datum	Serial Nr.
III 4	Deutsch-ungarischer Handelsver-trag	1-5	1924-1938	
III 5	Ungarns Handelsverträge und Abkommen mit anderen Ländern	1	1924-1925	
III 5	Handelsvertrag Ungarn-Tschechoslowakei	1-2	1926-1938	
	- Italien	1-2	1926-1938	
	- Frankreich	1-2	1925-1937	
	- Oesterreich	1-2	1926-1934	
	- Rumänien	1	1930-1938	
	- Türkei	1	1926-1937	
	- Polen	1	1928-1938	
	- Jugoslawien	1	1926-1937	
III 5	Deutsch-ungarische Handelskammer	1-2	1920-1937	
III 6	Staatliche Ausfuhrförderung in Ungarn	1-2	1928-1936	
III 6	Transdanubia	1	1935-1936	
III 6	Triester Frage	1	1933-1938	
III 6	Osthandel A.G.	1	1929-1930	
III 6	Pakt von Rom	1	1934-1935	
III 7	Präferenzfrage	1-2	1933-1934	
III 7	Verhandlungsprotokolle	1-2	1933-1934	
III 7	Deutsch-ungarisches Weizen-geschäft	1	1932	
III 7	Hühnerweizen-Ausfuhr nach Deutschland	1	1932	
III 7	Clearing-Abkommen	1	1934-1935	
III 7	Vortragsreise des Geheimrats Benzler bei verschiedenen Aussenhandelsstellen	1	1931	
III 7	Wirtschaftsverhandlungen im Juli 1933	1	1933	
III 7	Vertragstexte	2	1935-1938	
III 9	Adressbuch - Schwindelfirmen	1	1929-1932	
VI 3	Fluggenehmigungen	1	1931-1937	
VI 7	Reiseverkehrsabkommen	1	1934-1937	
VII 1	Kulturelles und Soziales: Kunst und Wissenschaft	1-4	1925-1936	
VII 1	- Generelles, Einzelfälle	1	1925-1936	
VII 1	- Goethe Gedenkjahr	1-2	1932	

Akten-zeichen	Inhalt	Band	Datum	Serial Nr.
VII 1	Dreihundertjahrfeier der Universität Budapest	1	1935	
VII 1	Besuch Homans in Berlin Kulturabkommen	1	1935-1936	
VII 1	Professoren- und Studenten-austausch	1	1934-1938	
VII 2	Reichsdeutsche Schule	2-4	1910-1918	
VII 2		5-7	1919-1924	
VII 2		1-5	1925-1931	
VII 2		5-8	1931-1935	
VII 2		9-11	1935-1938	
VII 2	Lehrkräfte der Reichsdeutschen Schule	1-3	1925-1935	
VII 2		4-5	1935-1937	
VII 2	Bücher, Broschüren und Lehr-mittel	1-2	1932-1938	
VII 3	Reichsdeutscher Kindergarten	1	1926-1938	
VII 4	Deutsche Akademie München	1-2	1934-1936	
VII 4	Deutscher akademischer Aus-tauschdienst	1	1936-1938	
VII 5	Reichsdeutsche Lektoren in Budapest	1-5	1924-1935	
VII 5		6-7	1934-1937	
VII 6	Sprach- und Handelskurse	1	1931-1935	
VII 6	Bibliothek der deutschen Sprach- und Handelskurse	1	1926-1937	
VII 6	Deutsche Sprach- und Handels-kurse	1	1926-1938	
VII 6	Humboldtstiftung	1-2	1925-1933	
VII 6	Stipendien an deutschstämmige Studierende aus Ungarn	1	1925-1934	
VII 7	Kirchenwesen, Allgemeines	1	1925-1938	
VII 8	Waisenhaus-Bethanien	1	1925-1938	
VII 9	Deutsche Heime	1-4	1934-1936	
VII 12	Reichsdeutscher Verein	1-2	1920-1938	
VII 13	Sportklub Wacker	1	1925-1936	
VII 15	Olympiade in Berlin	1-3	1933-1937	
VII 15	Weltjamboree in Gödöllö	1	1933-1937	
VII 15	Studentenweltmeisterschaft in Budapest	1	1935	
VII 15	Kulturelle Tagung und Kongresse	1	1925-1932	

Akten-zeichen	Inhalt	Band	Datum	Serial Nr.
VII 16	Filmwesen und Filmindustrie	1-2	1926-1938	
VII 17	Kriegergräber	1	1916-1924	
VII 17		1-2	1925-1938	
VII 19	Arbeiterfragen und Gewerkschaft	1	1919-1929	
VII 19	Ungarische Saison- und Landar-beiter	1	1926-1931	
VII 20	Ein- und Auswanderung	1-2	1914-1935	
VII 21	Rotes Kreuz, generell	1	1925-1935	
VII 21	Rotes Kreuz, Ehrenzeichen	1-2	1923-1938	
VII 21	Olympia-Ehrenzeichen	1	1936-1938	
VII 22	Orden, Festliche Veranstaltungen	1-2	1930-1936	
IX 1	Volksabstimmung im Saargebiet	1	1934-1935	
IX 3	Novembermagyaren	1	1919-1920	
IX 12	Deutsches Heim	1-5	1911-1923	
IX 7	Stiftungen	1	1915-1924	
VIII	Rechtsangelegenheiten, Allgemeines	1	1928-1933	
VIII a	Staatsangehörigkeit, Matrikel	1	1913-1929	
VIII b	Staatsverträge und Abkommen	1-2	1909-1933	
VIII c	Staatsangehörigkeitszeugnisse	1	1925-1929	
VIII c	Ungarische Staatsangehörigkeits-fragen	1	1924-1931	
VIII d	Nachlassangelegenheiten	1	1927-1934	
VIII 1	Einbürgerungsanträge	1-2	1925-1928	
VIII 1		3-5	1929-1934	
VIII 1		6-7	1935-1936	
VIII 2	Heimatscheine	1-2	1925-1928	
VIII 2		3-4	1931-1936	
VIII 3	Matrikulierungen und Auskünfte über in Ungarn ansässige Perso-nen	1	1930-1935	
VIII 3	Oesterreichische Flüchtlinge	1	1933-1936	
VIII 3	Vormundschafts- und Alimenten-sachen	1	1926-1929	
VIII 3		2-3	1930	
VIII 3		4-5	1931-1932	
VIII 3		6-7	1933-1934	
VIII 3		8-9	1935-1936	
VIII 4	Nachlässe	1-12	1915-1936	

Akten-zeichen	Inhalt	Band	Datum	Serial Nr.
VIII 6	Handhabung der Fremdengesetz-gebung gegen Deutsche	1-2	1924-29	
		4	1931-36	
VIII 7	Strafsachen, Steckbriefe, Auslieferungen	1	1932-36	
VIII 8	Übernahmen, Ausweisungen	1	1928-36	
VIII 10	Legalisationen und Beurkundungen, generell	1	1933	
X a	Militaria, Deutsches Heer und Marine	1	1925-36	
X c	- Versorgung	1	1925-34	
X c	Militärrenten	1	1926-29	
X c	Militaria, Versorgung ausser-ehelicher Kinder von Angehörigen der früheren K.K.Wehrmacht	1	1921-33	
P 1	Politische Lage in Deutschland	1-18	1920-38	
P 1	Ableben des Reichspräsidenten	1	1934	
P 1 spez	Politik in Deutschland	1	1933-37	
P 1 bes	Kraft durch Freude-Weltkongresse	1	1935-38	
P 2	Deutschlands auswärtige poli-tische Beziehungen	1-9 10 10-12	1920-38	7681/E547655-61
P 3	Deutsch-ungarische Beziehungen	1-10 11 12-13	1920-30 1931-38	7864/E569975-79
P 3 a	Studentenaustausch und dergleichen	1-5	1921-35	
P 4	Gehässige Presseartikel gegen Deutschland	1-11	1920-38	
P 10	Deutsche Presse	1-11	1920-38	
P 11	Pressefonds	1-2	1921-28	
P 12	Völkerbund	1-3	1923-26	
P 13	Deutsche Propaganda	1-6	1923-38	
P 13 a	Französische Propaganda	1-5	1923-35	
P 14	Ungarns innere politische Lage	1-11 12 13-14	1920-38	7864/E569980-82
P 15	Ungarische Regierung, Kabinett, Ministerien	1-11	1920-38	
P 16	Horthy	1	1923-24	

Akten-zeichen	Inhalt	Band	Datum	Serial Nr.
P 16	Besuch in Berlin, Horthy Sonderband	1	1938	
P 17	Ungarische Armee	1-7	1920-38	
P 17 a	Luftschiffahrt	1-7	1922-36	
P 17 a	Luftschutz	1	1935-36	
P 18	Monarchistische Bewegung in Ungarn	1-7	1920-38	
P 19	Ungarischer Friedensvertrag	1-13	1920-38	
P 20	Ausländische Missionen in Budapest	1-10	1920-38	
P 21	Ungarische Grenzregulierungen	1	1922-23	
P 22	Donau-Konföderation	1-7	1925-35	
P 22	Internationale Donaukommission	1	1936	
P 22	Deutsche Stromfreiheit	1	1937	
P 23	Pan-Europa	1-4	1928-36	
P 24	Nationalitäten in Ungarn, deutsche Minderheiten	1	1920-24	
P 24		1-12	1923-31	
		13	1932	M76/M002910-17
		14	1933-35	9722/E683406-29
		15		9722/E683430-81 9722/E683482-505
		16		9722/E683506-92
		17		9722/E683593-659 M240/M008061-81
		18		9722/E683660-711
		19	1936-37	
		20		7864/E569983-97
		21		
	Deutsch-ungarische Besprechun-gen zur Minderheitenfrage	1	1936-37	7368/E539234-334
	Deutsche Volksgruppen in Ungarn	1	1938	
P 24 a	Deutsche Sprachkurse	1-3	1922-27	
P 24 b	Minderheiten allgemein und ungarische Minderheiten	1-13	1923-38	
P 24 c	Genossenschaften unter der deutschstämmigen Bevölkerung Ungarns	1	1924-33	
P 25	Soziale und kulturelle Verhält-nisse, Kirchen, Schulen	1-9	1920-38	
P 26	Ungarische Presse	1-12	1920-38	
P 27	Revue de Hongrie	1	1915-34	
		1	1938	

Akten-zeichen	Inhalt	Band	Datum	Serial Nr.
P 28	Hamburg-Amerika-Linie	1	1920-24	
	Norddeutscher Lloyd	1	1921-25	
	Arbeiterbewegung, Streiks	1	1921-23	
P 31	Ungarns auswärtige politische Beziehungen	1-14	1920-34	
		15		7864/E569998-70032
		16-17	1934-38	
P 32	Beziehungen zu den Entente-Staaten	1-7	1920-38	
P 33	- Randstaaten	1-2	1920-22	
P 34	Deutsch-Österreich	1 2-7	1923-33	K1170/K303138-271
		8-13	1934-38	
P 35	Tschechoslowakei	1-9	1920-35	
	- Kleine Entente	1-3	1936-37	
		4	1938-39	2004/442441-507
		5		2004/442707-38
P 35 a	Tschechoslowakischer Konflikt ausgehende Telegramme	1	1938	
	- eingehende Telegramme	1	1938	2004/442508-90
	- Erlasse	1	1938	2004/442591-696
	- Berichte	1	1938	2004/442697-706
	- Karpathorussland nebst Kartenmaterial	1	1938	2004/442739-42
P 36	Rumänien	1-11	1920-38	
P 37	Jugoslawien	1-12	1920-38	
P 38	Ukraine	1	1920	
P 39	Republik Fünfkirchen, Baranya	1	1920-21	
P 40	Polen	1-10	1920-38	
P 41	Türkei	1-9	1921-38	
P 42	Bulgarien	1-9	1921-38	
P 45	Kommunismus	1-10	1920-38	
P 46	Geheimsachen	1-3	1920-30	
		4	1930-36	7864/E570033-70 9586/E675620-69 K1599/K390822-60
		5	1937	3626/E027943-8068 K1599/K390861-907
		6	1938	3626/E028069-122 K1599/K390908-41

Akten-zeichen	Inhalt	Band	Datum	Serial Nr.
P 46	Geheimsachen	7	1939	3626/E028123-52 6642/E504551-54 K1599/K390942-97
	Geheim, Mackensengüter	1	1920-25	
	Pol. Fonds, geheim	1	1924-28	
	Anforderungen für kulturpoliti-sche Zwecke	1-2	1927-35	
	Kuriere	1	1921-24	
	Hugo Stinnes	1	1922-24	
	Deutsch-österreichisch-ungari-scher Wirtschaftsverband	1	1923-24	
	Verfolgung der Erzbergermörder	1-4	1920-25	
	Kapitän Erhardt	1	1923-25	
	Hakenkreuzler, Putschisten	1	1924-33	
	Kapp-Putsch, Bauer-Heim, Lincoln-Trebitsch	1	1920-26	
	Fonds und Belege	1	1920-36	
P 47	Turanische Frage	1	1916-22	
	Russland	1-9	1924-38	
P 48	Jahresberichte	1-2	1929-38	
P 49	Agrarverhandlungen in Osteuropa	1-4	1930-33	
P 50	Deutsch-österreichische Zoll-union	1-2	1931	
P 51	Französisch-italienische Ver-handlungen, Donaupakt	1-2	1935	
	Donaupaktfragen	1	1936	9600/E676766-81 M241/M008082-91
P 52	Deutsch-schweizerisches Schieds-gericht in der Angelegenheit Jacob	1	1935	
P 53	Italien, italienisch-abessini-scher Konflikt	1-3	1935	
		1-3	1936	
		1	1937-38	
P 54	Dardanellenfrage, Konferenz von Montreux	1	1936	
P 55	Bürgerkrieg in Spanien	1	1936	
	Spanische Revolution	1	1937	
	Spanien	1	1938	
	Memelfrage	1	1934-35	
	Varia	1	1920-25	

Akten-zeichen	Inhalt	Band	Datum	Serial Nr.
Pers R 2	Amtliches Konto bei Pester Ungarischer Commercialbank	1	1939-43	
	Sammlung der Zusammenstellungen über Einzahlungen zu Gunsten Dritter	1	1937-43	
	Kassenbestandsverstärkung und Ablieferung an die Konsulate in Grosswardein, Kaschau, Klausenburg und Szeged	1	1939-44	
Pers R 5	Abrechnungen	1	1936-38	
		1-4	1941	
		1-4	1942	
		1-4	1943	
	Vorschusszahlungen	1	1942	
Pers R 8	Zahlungslisten	1	1943	
	Hauptbuch, Einzahlungen		1941	
	- Auszahlungen		1941	
	Sachbuch		1943	
Pers R 13	Unterstützungen im Auslande	1	1929-39	
Pers R 14	Heimschaffungen	1	1939-41	
Prot 2	Diplomatisches und konsularisches Korps	1	1939-41	
Prot 5	Staatsbesuche Deutschland-Ungarn	1	1935-40	
Prot 6	Staatsbesuche zwischen Ungarn und anderen Staaten	1	1939-41	
D Pol 3 Nr. 1	Der Führer und Reichskanzler, Verschiedenes	1	1939-41	
		1	1939-41	
		1	1939-41	
		1	1939-41	
D Pol 3 Nr. 5	NSDAP	1-4	1935-41	
	- Veranstaltungen	1	1941	
	Deutsche Arbeitsfront	1	1936-41	
D Pol 3 Nr. 7	A.O.-Tagungen in Stuttgart	1	1939-40	
D Pol 3 Nr. 8 b	Wehrpflicht, Arbeitsdienstpflicht	1	1939-40	
D Pol 3 Nr. 11	Freimaurertum und Judenfragen	1	1939	K1600/K390998-1023
D Pol 3 Nr. 12	Kolonialfragen	1	1939-41	K1601/K391024-30
	Einkreisungsbestrebungen Sonderband	1-2	1939	

Akten- zeichen	Inhalt	Band	Datum	Serial Nr.
D Pol 3 Nr. 12	Danziger Frage	1	1939	
	Ukrainer in Polen	1	1938-39	
	Deutsch-polnische Zwischenfälle	1	1939	
	Dankschreiben anlässlich Rück- gliederung Siebenbürgens	1	1940	
	Eingehende Telegramme	1-4	1938-40	
	Eingehende Multex-Telegramme	1	1940	9919/E694612-13
	Eingehende Presse-Telegramme	1	1940	
	Ausgehende Telegramme	1 2 3 4 5 6	1938-40	8376/E591184-88 9506/E670023-28 9506/E670029-32
	Politische Berichte Sammelakten Nr.1 - 4039	1-8	1940	
W 1 Nr.1	Ungarische Wirtschaftspolitik	1	1939-41	K1602/K391031-280
W 2 Nr.1	Wirtschaftliche Beziehungen Ungarns zu Deutschland	1	1939-41	
W 2	– anderen Staaten	1	1939-41	
W 2 Nr.5	– Polen	1	1939-41	
W E 1 Nr.1	Eisenbahn, allgemein	1	1939-41	
W E 2 Nr.1	– Ungarn-Deutschland	1	1939-41	
W F 1	Finanzwesen, allgemein	1	1939-41	
W F 2 Nr.1	Finanzen Ungarn/Deutschland	1	1939-41	
W F 2 Nr.2	– - zu anderen Staaten	1	1939-41	
W F 3	Devisengesetzgebung in Ungarn	1	1939-41	
W F 4	Banken, Sparkassen	1	1939-41	
W H 1	Handel, allgemein	1	1939-41	
W H 2 Nr.1	Deutsch-ungarischer Handelsver- trag	1-2	1939-40	
	– Einzelakte	1	1939-41	
	Aufgeldbefreiungsfonds	1-2	1938-41	
W H 2 Nr.2	Deutschland-Ungarn, Ein- und Ausfuhr	1	1939-41	
W H 5 Nr.5	Deutsch-ungarische Handelskammer	1	1938-40	
W H 3	Beziehungen Ungarns zu anderen Staaten	1	1939-41	

Akten-zeichen	Inhalt	Band	Datum	Serial Nr.
W J 1	Staatliche Vergünstigungen und industrielle Entwicklung	1	1933-1939	
W J 1	Industrie, Technik, Gewerbe, allgemein	1	1939-1941	
W J 2 Nr.1	Industrie-Beziehungen zu Deutschland	1	1939-1941	
W J 2 Nr.1a	Erfindungsangebote an Deutschland	1	1939-1941	
W L 1 Nr.1	Landwirtschaft, allgemein	1	1939-1941	
W L 2 Nr.1	Landwirtschaft Ungarn - Deutschland	1	1939-1941	
W L 3	Ackerbau und Plantagenwirtschaft	1	1939-1941	
W L 5	Viehzucht in Ungarn	1	1939-1941	
W L 8	Forstwirtschaft	1	1939-1941	
W L 9	Jagd in Ungarn	1	1939-1941	
W Lu 1	Luftfahrt (zivile) allgemein	1	1939-1941	
W Lu 2 Nr.1	- Ungarn-Deutschland	1	1939-1941	
W P 1 Nr.1	Post, Telegraf, Radio, allgemein	1	1939-1941	
W P 2 Nr.1	Post, Telegraf, Radio zu Deutschland	1	1939-1941	
W P 2 Nr.2	Post, Telegraf, Radio zu anderen Ländern	1	1939-1941	
W R 1	Rohstoffe und Rohwaren, allgemein	1	1939-1941	
W Sch 2 Nr. 1	Seeschiffahrt Ungarn-Deutschland	1	1939-1941	
W Sch 2 Nr. 2	Binnenschiffahrt Ungarn-Deutschland	1	1939-1941	
W Sch 2 Nr. 2	Donaukommission	1	1938-1940	
W Sch 3 Nr.1+2	See- und Binnenschiffahrt Ungarns mit anderen Ländern	1	1939-1941	
W Sch 4	Schiffbau und Hafenangelegenheiten	1	1939-1941	
W Sch 5 Nr.1+2	See- und Binnenschiffahrtsunternehmungen	1	1939-1941	
W V 2 Nr.1	Verkehr Ungarn-Deutschland	1	1939-1941	
W V 3	Reiseverkehrswerbung	1	1939-1941	
W V 4	Verkehr, Strassenwesen, Strassenbau	1	1939-1941	

Akten-zeichen	Inhalt	Band	Datum	Serial Nr.
D W 1	Deutsche Wirtschaftslage	1	1939-1941	
D W 1	Englisch-französische Blockade-maßnahmen	1-2	1939-1941	
D W 2	Wirtschaftliche Beziehungen Deutschlands zu anderen Staaten	1	1939-1941	
D W A	Ausstellungen	1	1939-1941	
D W E	Eisenbahnen	1	1939-1941	
D W F	Deutsche Finanzen, allgemein	1	1939-1941	
D W F	Deutsche Devisengesetzgebung	1	1939-1941	
D W H	Handel	1	1939-1941	
D W J	Industrie, Technik, Gewerbe	1	1939-1941	
D W Kr.	Kraftfahrwesen	1	1939-1941	
D W L	Landwirtschaft, Ernährung und Forstwirtschaft	1	1939-1941	
D W Lu	Luftfahrt	1	1939-1941	
D W P	Post, Telegraf	1	1939-1941	
D W R	Rohstoffe und Rohwaren	1	1939-1941	
D W Sch	Schiffahrt	1	1939-1941	
D W St	Steuern, Monopole	1	1939	
D W V	Verkehr	1	1939-1941	
D W Z	Zollwesen	1	1939-1941	
R 2 Nr.1	Rechtliche Beziehungen Ungarns zu Deutschland	1	1939-1941	
R 2 Nr.1a	Grenzfragen	1	1939-1941	
R 3 Nr.1	Staatsrecht, Strafrecht	1	1939-1941	
R 3 Nr.3	Zivilrecht und Bodenreform	1	1939-1941	
R 3 Nr.5	Handelsrecht und Prozessrecht	1	1939-1941	
R 3 Nr.6	Strafrecht, Rechtshilfe	1	1939-1941	
R 4 Nr.1	Lohnfragen, Streiks	1	1940-1941	
R 5 Nr.1	Aufenthaltsbestimmungen	1	1940-1941	
R 5 Nr.2	Sonstige Polizeisachen	1	1940-1941	
R.6 Nr.1	Sozialpolitik und Gesetzgebung	1	1940-1941	
R 6 Nr.2	Sozialversicherung	1	1940-1941	
R 6 Nr.3	Wohnungs-und Siedlungswesen	1	1940-1941	
R 6 Nr.4	Übernahme und soziale Fürsorge	1	1940-1941	
R 6 Nr.5	Freizeitgestaltung	1	1940-1941	
R 7	Internationales Rechtswesen	1	1940-1941	

Akten-zeichen	Inhalt	Band	Datum	Serial Nr.
D R 1 Nr.1	Rechtswesen in Deutschland	1	1939-1941	
D R 3 Nr.7	Deutsche Wahlen und Volksab-stimmungen	1	1939-1941	
D R 5 Nr.4	Grenzempfehlungen	1	1939-1941	
D R 5 Nr.7	Polizeisachen, Geheime Staats-polizei	1	1939-1941	
D R 6 Nr.1	Sozialpolitik	1	1939-1941	
D R 6 Nr.3	Freizeitgestaltung	1	1939-1941	
Kult 1	Allgemeine Kulturpolitik in Ungarn	1	1939-1941	
Kult 2 Nr. 1	Kulturpolitische Beziehungen Ungarns zu Deutschland	1	1939-1941	
Kult 2 Nr. 1	Wissenschaftliche Fachbespre-chungen	1	1939-1941	
Kult 2 Nr. 1a	Handwerker, Kaufleute, Kinder-austausch	1	1939-1941	
Kult 2 Nr. 1a	Kindererholungsaktion Sommer	1	1940-1941	
Kult 2 Nr. 1c	Gastvorlesungen- Ungarische Wissenschaftler nach Deutsch-land	1	1939-1941	
Kult 2 Nr. 1d	Gastvorlesungen in Ungarn	1	1939-1941	
Kult 2 Nr. 2	Kulturbeziehungen Ungarn – Deutschland	1	1939-1941	
Kult 3 Nr. 1	Reichsdeutsche Kolonie	1	1939-1941	
Kult 3 Nr. 2	Volksdeutsche in Batschka, Siebenbürgen, Westungarn	1	1939-1941	
Kult 3 Nr. 2	Volksgruppenabkommen	1	1939-1941	
Kult 3 Nr. 3	Zustellung an Kulturverband "Kultura"	1	1939-1941	
Kult 3 Nr. 4	Volksdeutsche Bücherei	1	1939-1941	
Kult 3 Nr. 6	Deutsche Minderheiten	1	1939-1941	
Kult 5	Ein-, Aus- und Rückwanderung	1	1939-1941	
Kult 7	Jugendbewegungen in Ungarn	1	1939-1941	
Kult 8 1-9	Schulwesen in Ungarn	1	1939-1941	

Akten-zeichen	Inhalt	Band	Datum	Serial Nr.
Kult 8 Nr. 3	Reichsdeutsche Schule	12	1939-1941	
Kult 8 Nr. 3b	Lehrmittel der Reichsdeutschen Schule	1	1939-1941	
Kult 9 Nr. 2	Lehrer der deutschen Sprach-schule	1	1939-1941	
Kult 9 Nr. 3	Sprachkurse und Sprachunter-richt	1	1939-1941	
Kult 9 Nr. 4	Leihbücherei der deutschen Sprachschule	1	1938-1941	
Kult 10 Nr. 1	Hochschulen in Ungarn	1	1939-1941	
Kult 10 Nr. 2	Professoren und Lehrer	1	1939-1941	
Kult 10 Nr. 3	Reichsdeutsche Lektoren	1	1939-1941	
Kult 10 Nr. 4	Studentenwesen	1	1939-1941	
Kult 11 Nr. 1	Kongresse und Ausstellunger	1	1939	
Kult 11 Nr. 2	Museen	1	1939-1941	
Kult 11 Nr. 3	Forschungswesen	1	1939-1941	
Kult 11 Nr. 4	Wissenschaftliche Institute	1	1939-1941	
Kult 11 Nr. 5	Gesundheitswesen und Sanitäts-abkommen	1	1939-1941	
Kult 11 Nr. 6	Deutsche Krankenhäuser und medizinisches Personal	1	1939-1941	
Kult 11 Nr. 7	Veterinärwesen	1	1939-1941	
Kult 11 Nr. 8	Buchwerbung und Ausstellungen	1	1939-1941	
Kult 12 Nr. 1	Kunst	1	1939-1941	
Kult 12 Nr. 1a	Literatur	1-2	1939-1941	
Kult 12 Nr. 2	Theater	1	1939-1941	
Kult 12 Nr. 2b	Gastspiele deutscher Künstler	1	1939-1941	
Kult 12 Nr. 3	Musikwesen	1-2	1939-1941	
Kult 12 Nr. 4a	Filmwesen, ungarisches	1	1939-1941	
Kult 12 Nr. 4b	Filmwesen, ungarisches-deutsches	1	1939-1941	

Akten-zeichen	Inhalt	Band	Datum	Serial Nr.
Kult 12 Nr. 4c	Deutsche Filmaufführungen	1	1939-1941	
Kult 12 Nr. 5	Sport	1	1939-1941	
D Kult 1 Nr. 1	Kultur (Abkommen und Verträge)	1	1939-1941	
D Kult 1 Nr. 2	Deutsche Kulturwerbung im Ausland	1	1939-1941	
D Kult 2	Kulturpolitische Beziehungen zu anderen Staaten	1	1939-1941	
D Kult 4	Kirchenwesen in Deutschland	1	1939-1941	
D Kult 5	Ein-, Aus- und Rückwanderung	1	1939-1941	
D Kult 5	Umsiedlung Volksdeutscher	1-2	1939-1941	
D Kult 7 Nr. 1	Hitlerjugend	1	1939-1941	
D Kult 7 Nr. 2	Jugendtreffen und Kongresse	1	1939-1941	
D Kult 7 Nr. 3	Wanderungswesen	1	1939-1941	
D Kult 6	Nachforschungen im Inland	1	1939-1941	
D Kult 8 Nr. 1	Versorgung der Auslandsschulen mit Büchern, Zeitschriften und Lehrmitteln	1	1939-1941	
D Kult 8 Nr. 3	Auswahl, Vermittlung und Betreuung der Lehrkräfte	1	1939-1941	
D Kult 8 Nr. 3	Deutscher Schüleraustausch	1	1939-1941	
D Kult 8 Nr. 4	Reichssportführer	1	1939-1941	
D Kult 9	Sprachlehrer	1	1939	
D Kult 10 Nr. 1	Hochschulwesen	1	1939-1941	
D Kult 10	Professoren, nichtarische	1	1939	K 1603/K391281 -504
D Kult 10 Nr. 2	Stipendien für Studien in Deutschland	1	1939-1941	
D Kult 10 Nr. 2	Stipendien des Mitteleuropäischen Wirtschaftstages	1	1936-1938	
D Kult 10 Nr. 2	Humboldtstiftung	1	1933-1939	
D Kult 10 Nr. 3	Deutscher akademischer Austauschdienst	1	1936-1942	
D Kult 10 Nr. 3	Studienreisen und Tagungen	1	1939-1941	
D Kult 11 Nr. 1	Archive und Bibliotheken	1	1939-1941	

Akten-zeichen	Inhalt	Band	Datum	Serial Nr.
D Kult 11 Nr. 2	Gesundheitswesen, Veterinärwesen	1	1939-1941	
D Kult 11 Nr. 3	Deutsche Wissenschaftler	1-2	1939-1941	
D Kult 11 Nr. 4	Wissenschaftliche Institute und Vereinigungen	1	1939-1941	
D Kult 12 Nr. 1	Kunst	1	1938-1941	
D Kult 12 Nr. 2	Theaterwesen	1	1939-1940	
D Kult 12 Nr. 3	Musikwesen	1	1939-1941	
D Kult 12 Nr. 4	Filmwesen	1	1939-1941	
D Kult 12 Nr. 5	Sportwesen	1	1939-1941	
P 2 Nr.1b	Presse und Propagandawesen	1	1939-1941	
P 2 Nr.1b	Artikel für ungarische Presse	1-2	1940-1942	
P 2 Nr.1b	Feindhetze betreffend die besetzten und angegliederten Gebiete	1	1941	
P 2 Nr.1b	Propagandistische Verwertung von Informationen	1	1939-1940	
P 2 Nr.1b	Europa-Sonderdienst	1	1939-1941	
P 2 Nr.1d	Presse, Einsichtsberichte anderer deutscher Missionen	1	1939-1941	
P 2 Nr.2	Presse- und Propagandawesen zu anderen Staaten	1	1939-1941	
P 2 Nr.2a	Englische und französische Presse und Propaganda	1	1939-1941	
P 4 Nr.1a	Bildberichterstatter	1	1939-1941	
P 4 Nr.2	Vertreter deutscher Zeitungen in Ungarn	1	1939-1941	
P 4 Nr.2a	Reisen deutscher Schriftleiter nach Ungarn	1	1939-1941	
P 6 Nr.1a	Greuel- und Hetzpresse	1	1939-1941	
P 6 Nr.1b	Hetzfilme	1	1939-1941	
P 6 Nr.1c	Hetzsender	1	1939-1941	
P 6 Nr.1d	Flugblätter	1	1940	
P 6 Nr.2	Deutsche Beanstandungen in der ungarischen Presse	1	1939-1941	
P 6 Nr.3	Ungarische Beanstandungen in der deutschen Presse	1	1939-1941	
D P 1	Presse und Propagandawesen in Deutschland, allgemein	1	1939-1941	

Akten-zeichen	Inhalt	Band	Datum	Serial Nr.
D P 3 a	Verlagsanstalten	1	1939-1941	
D P 3 b	Zeitungen und Zeitschriften	1	1939-1941	
	Deutsch-italienische Offiziers-kommission in Siebenbürgen	1	1940-1944	
		2	1940-1944	

Akten-zeichen	Inhalt	Band	Datum	Serial Nr.
I A	Politische Berichte	1	1938-39	
I A 1	Deutschland aussenpolitisch, auch Ost- und Westpakt	4 5 6	1936-40	3709/E036604-20 3764/E040668-85
I A 1a	Wiedervereinigung Österreichs mit dem Reich	1-2		
I A 2	Deutschland innenpolitisch	2-10	1933-37	
	- Einzelmappe	1	1936-39	
I A 2a	Saargebiet, Einzelmappe	2	1935-36	
I A 2a	Reichstagswahl	1-2	1936-38	
I A 3	Politische Beziehungen Deutschland-Rumänien	1-2 3 4	1932-39	3715/E036789-800 3715/E036802-47 6643/E504556-60 7486/E540440-45
Po IV Nr. 1	Auswärtige Politik, Allgemeines	1	1926-31	
Po IV Nr. 2	Politische Beziehungen Rumänien - Deutschland	1	1925-31	
	- Bulgarien	1	1926-31	
	- Frankreich	1	1926-31	
	- Italien	1	1926-31	
	- Jugoslawien	1	1931	
	- Lettland	1	1929-32	
	- Polen	1-2	1926-32	
	- Russland	1	1925-30	
	- Ungarn	1-2	1926-32	
I A 4	Rumänien aussenpolitisch	1 2 3 4-5 6	1932-36	7860/E569889-91 6520/E487337-87 7999/E575644-49 8357/E590539-43 8377/E591190-93
Po IV 8	Rumäniens Innenpolitik, Allgemeines	1-4	1926-31	
Po IV 11	Bessarabien	1-2	1924-29	
I A 5	Rumänien innenpolitisch	5-9	1936-40	
I A 5 a	- Einzelmappe-Jahresberichte	1	1935-39	7860/E569892-910
I A 5 b	- Prozess Codreanus	1	1938	7887/E570891-95
I A 6	Räterussland politisch	1-3 4 5	1932-40	7998/E575637-42
I A 7	Politische Beziehungen Räterussland - Rumänien	1-2	1932-39	

Akten-zeichen	Inhalt	Band	Datum	Serial Nr.
I A 8	Polen politisch	1-4	1932-39	
		6-7	1939-40	
I A 9	Politische Beziehungen Polen - Rumänien	1-2	1932-39	
I A 10	Ungarn politisch	1-2	1932-40	
I A 11	Politische Beziehungen Ungarn - Rumänien	1	1932-39	7063/E524156-60 8378/E591195-202
I A 12	Tschechoslowakei politisch	2-3	1936-39	
I A 12a	Deutsch-tschechoslowakische Optionsbestimmungen	1	1939	
I A 13	Politische Beziehungen Tschechoslowakei - Rumänien	1	1936-39	
I A 14	Jugoslawien politisch	2	1935-39	
I A 15	Politische Beziehungen Jugoslawien - Rumänien	1	1932-39	
I A 17	- Bulgarien- Rumänien	1	1931-39	
I A 18	Österreich politisch	2	1935-37	
I A 22	Politische Beziehungen Frankreich - Rumänien	1	1934-39	
I A 23	England politisch	1	1932-38	
I A 25	Vatikan politisch	1	1934-39	
I A 27	Türkei politisch	1	1932-36	
I A 28	Balkan politisch	1-3	1932-40	
I A 29	Italienisch-abessinischer Konflikt	4-5	1936	
I A 30	Albanien politisch	1	1935-39	
I A 31	Spanien politisch	1-2	1936-39	
I A 32	Römisches Protokoll, Italien-Österreich-Ungarn	1	1936-37	
I A 33	Sonstige europäische Staaten	1-2	1932-39	
I A 34	Kleine Entente politisch	1 2-3	1932-39	9827/E691839-41
Po IX 1	Politische Beziehungen zwischen anderen Staaten	1-2	1926-31	
Po IX 2		1	1926-30	
I A 35	Donauförderation	1 2 3	1932-39	9848/E692475-90
I A 36	Meerengenfrage politisch	1	1934-39	

Akten-zeichen	Inhalt	Band	Datum	Serial Nr.
P IV 10	Sozialismus, Kommunismus, Faschismus	1	1925-26	
P IV 4	Judenfrage	1	1926-31	K1604/K391505-65
I A 37	Kommunismus	1-2	1932-39	
I A 38	Nationalsozialismus	1-6	1932-40	
I A 38 a	Verbot nationalsozialistischer Zeitungen	1-2	1934-40	
I A 38 b	Reichsparteitag	1	1934-39	
I A 39	Rumäniens Politik gegen Fremde	1-2	1934-38	
I A 40	Internationale Vereinigungen und Kongresse politischer Natur	1-2	1932-40	
I A 42	Deutsche Kolonialforderung	1	1937-38	
I A 44	USA - Politisches	1	1932-40	
I A 45	Sonstige amerikanische Staaten - Politisches	1	1932-39	
I A 46	Afrikanische Staaten Politisch	1	1933-39	
I A 47	Ostasien politisch	1	1932-40	
I A 48	Sonstige asiatische Staaten politisch	1	1932-39	
I B 1	Völkerbund, Allgemeines	2	1934-39	6398/E474659-700
I B 2	- Besonderes	1	1932-38	
I B 3	Abrüstung	3	1934-38	
I B 4	Reparationen	2	1933-36	
Po IV 18	Internationales Recht	1	1928-31	
I B 5	Internationales Schiedsgerichtswesen	1	1930-39	
I B 5 speziell	- Fall Göppert-Paleologu	2	1935-39	
I B 5 speziell	Rückgabe Donaukähne	1	1934-36	
I B 6	Reparationssachleistungen	2	1936-38	
Po IV 2	Deutsch-rumänischer Handelsvertrag	1	1929-30	
		1-2	1930-32	
	Deutsch-rumänische Handelsvertragsverhandlungen	1	1930	
I C 4	Handelsvertrag Deutschland mit Rumänien	1-8	1932-38	
I C 5	Politische Verträge Rumäniens	1	1932-36	
H 4	Handelsverträge Rumäniens und anderer Staaten	1-4	1926-32	
Po III	Deutsch-österreichische Zollunion	1-2	1930-31	

Akten-zeichen	Inhalt	Band	Datum	Serial Nr.
Po IV 6	Rumänisches Königshaus - Karlfrage	1	1926-31	
Po IV 6 a	Tod des Königs Ferdinand	1	1922-27	
I D 1	Personalia des rumänischen Königshauses	1-2	1932-40	
I D 3	Der deutsche Reichspräsident	1	1932-34	
I D 6	Ordensangelegenheiten, Allgemeines	1	1933-39	
I D 7	- Besonderes	1-2 3 4	1932-40	8920/E623211-25
I D 7	Ehrenkreuz des Weltkrieges	1	1934-38	
	Verwundetenabzeichen	1	1936-39	
	Liste der mit dem Roten Kreuz ausgezeichneten Personen	1	1936-39	
E 2	Rumänische National- und Feiertage, Rumänische Orden, Protokoll-sachen, Ernennung von fremden Missionschefs zu Botschaftern aus Anlass des Todes Königs Ferdinand	1	1926-31	
E 4	Fremde Missionen, diplomatisches Korps, Konsularkorps	2	1931	
Po IV 3	Diplomatische und konsularische Vertretungen Rumäniens	1	1927-32	
PO 10	Deutsche diplomatische und konsularische Vertretungen in Rumänien	1	1921-23	
I E 1	Personalien des diplomatischen und Konsular-Korps in Rumänien	1-6	1929-40	
I E 2	Der Doyen des diplomatischen Korps	1	1933-39	
I E 3	Rechte und Privilegien des diplomatischen Korps	1-2	1930-40	
I F 1	Deutsches Heerwesen	1-2	1932-39	
Po IV 14	Flottenbesuche	1	1926-30	
Po V 2	Landheer und Marine Rumäniens	1	1926-32	
Po V 4	Einziehung Deutscher zum rumänischen Heeresdienst	1	1922-30	
I F 2	Rumänisches Landheer	1-2	1932-39	
I F 3	Rumänische Kriegsflotte	1	1932-39	
I F 4	Militär-Luftflotte Rumäniens	1	1932-39	
I F 5	Heereswesen anderer Staaten	1	1932-39	
I F 7	Rumänische Aufrüstung	1	1936-39	7997/E575632-35
I G 1	Rumänische Verwaltungsorganisation	1	1932-34	

Akten-zeichen	Inhalt	Band	Datum	Serial Nr.
I G 2	Personalien des rumänischen Hof-, Aussen-, Innen- und Militärdienstes	1	1932-38	
I G 3	Personalien des rumänischen Parlaments	1	1932-35	
I G 4	Rumänische Staatsjugend	1	1936-40	
I H 3	Agenten- und Spionagewesen	1	1926-31	
I H 3	Spionageabwehr	1	1932-1939	
I H 5	Kulturelle Bewilligungen	1-2	1931-33	
	- Allgemeines	1	1939	
	- Kult	1	1939	
	- Spenden	1	1938-39	
	- Schulfonds	1	1939	
	- Amtsbezirk Galatz	1	1939	
	- - Kronstadt	1	1939	
	- - Temesvar	1	1939	
	Deutschtumsarbeit Österreichs	1	1938	
I H 7	P. Fonds	2	1937-40	
Po VIII 1	Deutsche politische Propaganda	1	1926-30	
Po VIII 3	Korrespondenten und Mitarbeiter deutscher Zeitungen	1-2	1926-31	
Po VIII 4	Die rumänische Presse	1-2	1926-31	
Po VIII 4 a	Bukarester Tageblatt	1-2	1926-31	
Po VIII 5	Filmwesen	1	1926-30	
Po VIII 6	Bücher, Zeitschriften und Zeitungen	1-6	1926-31	
I J 1	Deutsche Presse, allgemein	4	1938-40	
I J 2	Rumänische Presse	2	1935	
		8	1938	
		10	1939-40	
I J 2 a	Bildfoto-Material	1	1936-40	
I J 3	Deutsche Pressevertreter in Rumänien	2	1935-36	
		4	1938-40	6644/E504562-65
I J 3 b	Presseattaché	1	1936-39	
I J 4	Politische Theaterstücke und Filme	2	1936-39	
I J 5	Nachrichtendienst, Presseattaché	1	1939-40	
I J 6	- Allgemeines	1	1936	
Gg 3	Gesandtschaftsgebäude	1-3	1926-28	
	Personalien der Gesandtschaft	1	1920-26	

Akten-zeichen	Inhalt	Band	Datum	Serial Mr.
Gg 4	Personalien der Gesandtschaft:			
	Bahr	1	1921-25	
	Busch, Dr.	1	1921-25	
	Deppe	1	1924-26	
	Dittmar	1	1921	
	Freytag	1-3	1921-27	
	v.Grundherr	1	1921-24	
	Hollmann	1	1921-23	
	Heinburg, Dr.	1	1921-24	
	Kiewitz	1	1925-29	
	Kirchholtes, Dr.	1	1928-32	
	Mohrmann, Dr.	1	1927	
	v.Mutius	1-3	1923-31	
	Neumann, Dr.	1	1925-26	
	Schwarz, Dr.	1	1925-27	
	Springer	1	1921-25	
	Schmidt-Tube, Dr.	1	1929	
	v.Stein, Freiherr	1-2	1929-33	
	v.Stetten	1	1926-28	
	Sucker	1	1926	
	Toepke	1	1924-30	
	v.Tucher, Freiherr	1	1929	
	Zorn	1	1921-27	
II A 1	Personalien der Beamten, Allgemeines	1-3	1932-40	
II A 1 b	Mitgliedschaft der Beamten und Angestellten bei der NSDAP	1	1934	
II A C	Angestellten- und Invaliden-versicherung	1	1921-31	
II A 2	Personalien:			
	v.Adelmann, Graf	1	1936-38	
	v.Bargen, Dr.	1	1934	
	Bährens, Dr.	1	1934	
	Bauer	1	1939	
	Blücher	1	1925-39	
	v.Dehn-Schmidt	1	1934-35	
	v.Doernberg	1	1930-36	
	v.Gerstenberg, General	1	1938-39	
	Giffels	1	1939	
	Fabricius	1-5	1936-39	
	Fabian	1	1937-41	
	v.Haeften	1	1937-39	
	Haschke	1	1938-39	
	Haushofer	1	1938	
	Heinburg, Dr.	1	1935	
	Hollmann, Professor	1	1932-33	
	Kirchholtes,Dr.	1	1927-35	
	Klugkist	1	1936-39	
	Konradi	1	1936-40	

Akten-zeichen	Inhalt	Band	Datum	Serial Nr.
II A 2	Personalien:			
	Korter	1	1935-38	
	Krause-Wichmann, Dr.	1	1932-36	
	Krüger	1	1926-36	
	Martin	1	1925-39	
	v.d.Marwitz	1	1939	
	Niedermayer, Dr.	1	1936-37	
	Ortmann	1	1926-39	
	v.Pochhammer	1	1934-39	
	Pusch, Dr.	1	1934-40	
	v.Rantzau	1	1933-36	
	Ostermann v.Roth	1	1935-36	
	Schmidt, Dr.	1	1938-39	
	v.d.Schulenburg	1	1931-36	
	Sochor	1	1938-39	
	Stelzer, Dr.	1	1938-39	
	v.Stohrer	1	1935-36	
	Voss	1	1939-40	
	Wahle	1	1938-39	
	Weisse, Dr.	1	1936	
II A 3	Personalien der Angestellten, Allgemeines	1	1932-37	
II A 4	Personalien der einzelnen Angestellten	1-3	1932-40	
II A 6	Gehaltsfragen und Teuerungs-berichte	1	1932-39	
II A 11	Beschwerden über die Gesandt-schaft	1-2	1927-33	
II B 4	Bewirtschaftung der sonstigen Fonds	1	1932-39	
II B 6	Kriegsrentenwesen	1	1932-36	
II B 7	Sozialrentenwesen	1	1931-37	
	Monatliche Überweisungen des Versicherungsamtes München-Land	1-3	1929-40	
II C 1	Allgemeine Runderlasse, Geschäftsgang	1	1927-40	
II C 2	Sommeraufenthalt in Sinaia	1	1921-40	
II D 1	Unterstellte Konsulate, Allgemeines	2	1931-39	
II D 2	Konsulat Braila	2	1932-39	
	Vizewahlkonsulat Campina	1	1936-39	
	Konsulat Czernowitz	1-3	1923-39	
	– Craiowa	1	1930-40	
	– Galatz	1-3	1923-40	
	– Grosswardein	2	1932-38	

Akten-zeichen	Inhalt	Band	Datum	Serial Nr.
II D 2	Vizekonsulat Kischineff	1-2	1932-1938	
II D 2	Konsulat Klausenburg	2	1931-1939	
II D 2	- Konstantza	2	1932-1940	
II D 2	- Kronstadt	1-3	1923-1940	
	Konsulat Kronstadt an Gesandt-schaft Bukarest abgegebene Akten	1	1932-1942	
II D 2	Vizekonsulat Lugosch	2	1933-1934	
II D 2	Konsulat Orsova	1	1934-1940	
II D 2	- Ploesti	1-2	1926-1932	
II D 2	- Temesvar	1-3	1923-1939	
III A 2	Deutsche Einzelpersonen A,B,C,D,E,G	1-6	1932-1936	
III A 2	H, T,U,V,W,Y,Z	1-6	1932-1936	
III A 9	Heimschaffungen	1	1931-1932	
III A 9		1-2	1932-1933	
III A 9		3-7	1933-1935	
III A 9		8-11	1935-1937	
D 8	Unterstützungen	2	1931-1932	
III A 11		1-5	1932-1934	
III A 11		6-9	1935-1937	
III A 11	Fürsorgeverbände	1	1932-1936	
III A 11	Unterstützungsquittungen (lose)	1 Bd1	1932-1940	
III A 13	Nachforschungen	5-6	1934-1935	
R 8	Staatsangehörigkeitsfragen	2	1930-1932	
III B 1	- allgemein	1	1932-1936	
III B 2	- Einzelfälle	2-3	1935-1936	
R 20	Ausweisungen, Übergriffe gegen Deutsche	1-2	1926-1932	
III B 3	Ausweisungen von Rumänen aus Deutschland und Übernahme	1	1932-1936	
IV 3	Rumänisches Staatsrecht	1	1932-1936	
IV 3 a	Rumänische Staatsangehörigkeit	1	1932-1936	
IV 3 a	Stinnes ./. Wildermann (Einzelmappe)	1	1932-1936	
IV 6	Rumänisches Familienrecht	1	1932-1936	
R 15	Vormundschafts-und Unterhalts-sachen	2	1930-1932	

Akten-zeichen	Inhalt	Band	Datum	Serial Nr.
IV 8	Unterhaltssachen	1-3	1932-1936	
IV 8	Sonderakte Wilhelms ./. Bürger	1	1928-1933	
R 10	Nachlaßsachen, Testamente	2	1930-1932	
IV 8 a	Nachlaßsachen (Einzelfälle)	1-2	1932-1936	
IV 8 a	Nachlaßangelegenheit Riesen-berger	1	1921-1932	
R 9	Standesamtliche Urkunden	2	1930-1932	
IV 9	Standesamtssachen	1-2	1932-1934	
IV 9		3-6	1934-1937	
IV 15	Rumänische Zivilprozesse Allgemeines	1	1932-1936	
IV 20	Notariatssachen und Beglaubigun-gen, allgemein	1	1932-1936	
IV 24	Rechtsanwaltsbenennung	1	1932-1934	
IV 30	Rumänisches Strafrecht	1	1932-1936	
IV 31	Anträge auf Strafverfolgungen	1	1932-1936	
IV 31	Strafsache gegen Hirschmann	1	1932-1935	
IV 32	Strafprozess Roselius und andere	1	1936-1940	
IV 33	Aus- und Durchlieferungen (Einzelfälle)	1	1932-1936	
IV 33	Auslieferung Anton Weisskopf	1	1934-1935	
H 19	Handelsrechtsfragen, Patent-sachen	1-6	1930-1932	
IV 25	Rumänisches Handelsrecht	1	1932-1936	
IV 42	Entschädigungsansprüche gegen die rumänische Regierung	1	1932-1936	
IV 42	- drei Sonderhefte		1932-1936	
R 19 Nr. 1	Sequestriertes Vermögen von Reichsdeutschen	1	1921-1923	
R 19 Nr. 1	Beschlagnahme deutschen Eigen-tums in Rumänien	1	1922-1925	
IV 44	Liquidationsangelegenheiten	1	1933-1936	
IV 44	Fall Heinrich Voigt	1	1929-1934	
IV 44	Freigabe der beschlagnahmten Schiffe des Bayrischen Lloyds	1	1929-1934	
	Handelsberichte	1	1882-1888	
H 16	Wirtschaftliche Berichte der Konsulate	1-2	1930-1932	
V 3	Wirtschaftliche Lage Rumäniens und Bericht darüber	2	1933-1936	

Akten-zeichen	Inhalt	Band	Datum	Serial Nr.
Wi 6	Wirtschaftliche Verhältnisse der deutschen Volksgruppe	1	1936-39	
Wi 2	Staatliche wirtschaftliche Maßnahmen,Devisenordnungen, Moratorien, neue Gesetze	1-5	1930-32	
Wi 4	Wirtschaftliche Projekte, Neu-gründungen in Handel und In-dustrie, Verbesserungen auf wirtschaftlichem Gebiet	1-3	1930-31	
H 3	Handelsstatistik, Handelszeit-schriften, Handelsmuster, Export-musterlager	1-2	1930-31	
V 4	Rumänien-Deutschland, wirtschaftlich	1-7	1932-38	
V 7	— Tschechoslowakei	1	1932-39	
V 5	— Österreich	1	1932-37	
V 11	— Übrige	1	1932-36	
V 16	Rumänische Kompensationsbestre-bungen	1-2	1932-34	
H 6	Handelskammern, Handelsverbände	1	1930-31	
V 17 a	Rumänisch-deutsche Handelskammer	1	1932-37	
V 18	Ausschreibungen	1	1933-35	
	— Hirsch-Kupfer	1	1931-33	
H 7	Ausstellungen, Messen, Märkte	1-2	1930-32	
V 19	Messen und Ausstellungen	1-3	1932-37	
V 22	Kreditunwürdige Firmen und schwarze Listen	1-3	1931-40	
V 26	Handelsreklamationen gegen die rumänische Eisenbahn	1-6	1932-33	
		1-5	1933-35	
	J.A.Maffei A.G. ./. Rumänische Eisenbahn	1	1929-32	
V 27	Handelsreklamationen gegen sonstige rumänische staatliche Stellen	1-6	1934-38	
V 39	Julius Berger, Tiefbau	1	1932-36	
VI 3	Rumänische Industrie und Bericht darüber	1	1932-37	
J 5	Petroleumindustrie, Naphta-produkte	1-2	1926-31	
J 7	Erdöl	1	1921-25	

Akten-zeichen	Inhalt	Band	Datum	Serial Nr.
VI 4	Erdöle	1	1932-1938	
V 1	Eisenbahnwesen, Allgemeines	1	1926-1931	
VIII 4	Deutsch-rumänische Eisenbahnbe-ziehungen	1	1935-1938	
VIII 9	Deutsche Flugzeuge und Flug-schiffe in Rumänien	1-2	1932-1937	
VIII 9 a	Luftverkehrsabkommen	1	1936-1939	
VIII 18	Beschwerden der deutschen See-schiffahrt	1	1932-1937	
VIII 19	Europäische und Internationale Donaukommission	1-2 3 4-5	1932-1940	7308/E534515-32
Fi 1	Rumänisches Geld-, Bank- und Börsenwesen	1	1925-1932	
Fi 2	Staatshaushalt	1	1927-1932	
Fi 3	Französisch-rumänische Kriegs-schuldenfrage	2	1928-1932	
Fi 3 Nr.1	Rumänische Wertpapiere	1	1926-1930	
Fi 3 Nr.2	Deutsch-rumänische Anleihe			
	Konflikt wegen Banca-Generala-Noten	1	1921-1929	
	Rumänische finanzielle Ansprüche aus dem Versailler Friedensver-trag	1	1926-1928	
VIII 18	Beschwerden der deutschen See-schiffahrt	1	1932-1937	
VIII 19	Europäische und Internationale Donaukommission	1-5	1932-1940	
Fi 1	Rumänisches Geld-, Bank- und Börsenwesen	1	1925-1932	
Fi 2	Staatshaushalt	1	1927-1932	
Fi 3	Französisch-rumänische Kriegs-schuldenfrage	2	1928-1932	
Fi 3 Nr.1	Rumänische Wertpapiere	1	1926-1930	
Fi 3 Nr.2	Deutsch-rumänische Anleihe	1-6	1926-1929	
Fi 6	Banca-Generala, Notenfrage	1-2	1926-1927	
F 6 a	Rumänische Forderung wegen Banca-Generala-Noten	1	1925-1926	
IX A 2	Rumänische Staatsfinanzen	1-3	1932-1938	

Akten- zeichen	Inhalt	Band	Datum	Serial Nr.
IX A 4	Rumänische Währungsfragen	1	1932	
IX A 4 a	— Allgemeines	1-2	1932-36	
IX A 4 b	— Einzelfälle	1-6	1932-34	
		12	1935	
		17 - 19	1936	
IX A 6	Rumänische Finanzfragen und Konvertierung	1	1932-34	
IX A 7	Rumänisches Steuerwesen	1-2	1932-37	
IX B 4	Rumänische Nationalbank	1	1932-36	
Z 2	Zollpolitik, Zollgesetze, Zoll- organisation in Rumänien	1	1930-31	
Z 3	Rumänischer Einfuhrzolltarif	1-9	1930-32	
IX C 4	Rumänisches Zollwesen	1	1932-36	
IX C 5	Rumänischer Zolltarif	1-3	1929-38	
IX C 7	Rumänische Einfuhrverbote und Beschränkungen	1-3	1932-35	
IX C 7 a	- Kontingentierungen, Einzelfälle	1	1932-33	
IX C 7	Rumänische Einfuhr, Verbote und Beschränkungen	2	1937-38	
IX C 7 a	Kontingentierungsmaßnahmen	2	1936-37	
		1	1937-38	
Po VII 1	Allgemeine Kirchenfragen in Rumänien, Kirchengesetze	1	1926-30	
Po VII 2	Römisch-katholische Kirche, Konkordatsfrage	1-3	1924-30	
Po VII 3	Evangelische Kirche, englische und amerikanische protestanti- sche	1	1926-31	
X A 1	Kirchliches, allgemeine Kirchen- und Schulgesetze	1	1933-39	
X A 2	Orthodoxe Kirche	1	1932-38	
X A 3	Römisch-katholische Kirche	1	1932-37	
X A 4	Deutsch-katholische Seelsorge	1	1931-39	
X A 5	Evangelische Landeskirche	1-2	1932-39	
X A 6	Andere protestantische Kirchen	1	1932-40	
Po VII 4	Schulwesen in Rumänien	1	1926-31	
Po VII 5	Deutsches Schulwesen in Rumänien	1	1926-32	
Kw 1	Rumänisches Hochschulwesen	1	1926-32	
Kw 4	Deutsches Hochschulwesen	1-2	1926-31	

Akten-zeichen	Inhalt	Band	Datum	Serial Nr.
X B 3	Rumänisches Schulwesen	1-4	1932-40	
	- Sonderband	1	1938-40	
X B 4	Deutsche Lehrkräfte in Rumänien	1-3	1932-40	
X B 5	Rumänische Schüler und Studenten in Deutschland	1-5	1932-40	
X B 5 a	Gegenseitige Anerkennungsrechte für Diplome	1	1938-39	
X B 6	Alexander von Humboldt Stiftung	1-4	1932-39	
X B 7	Schulreform	1	1938-40	
X B 8	Zweigstelle des Deutschen Akademischen Austauschdienstes in Bukarest	1	1938-40	
Kw 6	Kunst und Wissenschaft, Allgemeines	2	1930-32	
X C 3	Rumänische Kunst und Wissenschaft Allgemeines	1	1932-39	
X C 4	Kunstausstellungen	1	1932-40	
X C 5	Deutsche Künstler in Rumänien	1	1932-40	
X C 6	Archäologie	1	1932-39	
X C 7	Erdbeben- und Vulkanologie	1	1929-38	
X C 8	Rumänisch-deutsche wissenschaft-liche und künstlerische Beziehun-gen	1-12	1932-39	
X C 8 a	Goethejahr	1-2	1932-38	
X C 8 b	Wagnerfeier (50jähriger Todestag)	1	1933-39	
X C 9	Deutsche Wissenschaft und Wissenschaftler in Rumänien	1	1932-39	
X C 11	Wissenschaftliche Kongresse	1-3	1930-40	
X C 14	Rumänisches Filmwesen	1	1933-40	
X D 2	Rumänisches Gesundheitswesen	1	1932-39	
X D 3	Seuchen	1-2	1932-39	
X D 4	Deutsche Krankenhäuser, Ärzte in Rumänien	1-2	1932-40	
	- Einzelmappe	1	1932-33	
X D 4 a	- Revision der ärzt-lichen Approbatio-nen	1	1938-39	
X D 5	Zulassung zur Registrierung von pharmazeutischen und sonstigen chemischen Erzeugnissen	1	1932-36	
Po VI 1	Minderheiten, allgemein	1-2	1926-32	
Po VI 2	Deutschstämmige Minderheiten in Rumänien	1-2	1926-32	
Po VI 3	Ungarische Minderheiten und an-dere Minderheiten	1-2	1926-32	

Akten-zeichen	Inhalt	Band	Datum	Serial Nr.
X E 1	Minderheiten, Allgemeines	1	1932-39	
X E 2	- ausser Rumänien	1	1932-35	
X E 3	Deutsche Minderheiten in Rumänien	1-11	1932-40	
X E 3 a	- Einzelmappe	1	1937-39	
X E 3 b	- Volksdeutsche Jugender-ziehung	1	1938-39	
	- Wirtschaftsprogramm	1	1938-39	
X E 5	Deutschstämmige Minderheiten, Altreich-Dobrudscha	1	1932-39	
X E 6	- im Banat	1-3	1932-39	
X E 7	- in Bessarabien	1	1932-39	
X E 8	- in der Bukowina	1-3	1932-39	
X E 9	Deutschtumsbewegung in Satmar	1-3	1931-37	
X E 10	Deutschstämmige Minderheiten in Siebenbürgen	1-2	1932-39	
X E 11	Ungarische Minderheiten in Rumänien	1	1932-39	
X E 12	Sonstige Minderheiten in Rumänien	1	1932-39	
	- Stoyanoff und Gospodinoff, Völkerbundsbeschwerde Einzelmappe	1	1930-33	
X E 13	Judenfrage	1	1932-39	
X E 14	Russenflüchtlinge	1-3	1930-39	
	Volksgemeinschaft der Deutschen in Rumänien	1-2	1935-37	
	Mittelstelle, Akten Rittmeister Fabricius Rosch aus der Bukowina, Verschiedenes	1	1935-37	
Kw 7	Sportwesen	1	1926-31	
X F 2	- Verschiedenes	2	1937-39	
Kw 2 a	Auslandsfahrten von Jugendbünden	1	1931-32	
X F 3		1-7	1932-39	
X F 4	Sportolympiade 1936 Berlin	1-2	1933-39	
Kw 3	Kulturpropaganda	2-3	1929-32	
X G 2	Deutsche Kulturpropaganda in Rumänien	1-9	1931-40	
	Kulturbericht des Gesandten Kirchholtes betreffs Rumänien	1		
X G 2 a	Deutsche Kulturpropaganda in Rumänien, Einzelmappe, Bücher-prämien	1-2	1932-39	
X G 2 b	- Einzelmappe, Bücher-sendungen	1-2	1935-38	

Akten-zeichen	Inhalt	Band	Datum	Serial Nr.
X G 3	Französische Kulturpropaganda in Rumänien	1	1931-40	
X G 4	Sonstige Kulturpropaganda in Rumänien	1	1933-39	
S 1	Soziale Verhältnisse, Sozial-politik im allgemeinen	1	1925-31	
S 2	Sozialversicherung	1	1925-27	
S 4	Streiks, Aussperrungen	1	1925-26	
S 5	Arbeiterfragen, Zeitschriften, Statistiken darüber	1	1926-32	
XI 2	Rumänische Sozialversicherung	1	1932-33	
XI 3	Mädchenhandel	1	1932-34	
		1	1937	
XI 5	Wohlfahrtseinrichtungen deutschen Charakters in Rumänien	1	1932-38	
XI 8	Kriegsgräberfürsorge, Allgemeines	1	1932-35	
XI 9	- Spezial	1-4	1932-39	
XI 9 a	- Ehrenstätte Petrisoru-Racoviteni Einzelmappe	1	1937-39	
Kg 2	Kriegsgräberabrechnungen	1	1928-32	
XI 10	-	1	1932-39	
XI 11	Beauftragter für die deutschen Kriegergräber in Rumänien	1-2	1931-38	
XI 12	Auswanderungswesen	1	1933-36	
XII A 2	Rumänisches Postwesen	1	1932-39	
XII C 2	Rumänisches Telefonwesen	1	1935-40	
XII C 3	Rundfunk	1	1932-40	
XIII	Curiosa	1-2	1932-40	
	Akten für Friedensverhandlungen Verschiedenes	1	1921-24	
G 3	Äussere Rumänienpolitik	1	1922-28	
Geh. Ukraine	Die ukrainische Lage	1	1925-31	
G 5	Königlicher Hof	1	1921-28	
Geh. 7	Sathmarer Schwaben (einschließ-lich Kirchen- und Schulwesen)	1-2	1923-29	
Geh. 8	Presse- und Nachrichtenwesen	2	1925-29	
Geh. 9	Deutscher Pressedienst während des Krieges in Rumänien	1	1918-19	
	Fremder Nachrichtendienst	1	1927-29	
M 1 gen.	Militärangelegenheiten	1	1924-26	
M 3 gen.		2	1928-29	

Akten-zeichen	Inhalt	Band	Datum	Serial Nr.
Geh. 19	Kirchen- und Schulwesen	1-7	1921-31	
Geh. 20	Minderheiten	2-3	1926-32	
Geh. 21	Stipendien und andere Schulange-legenheiten	1-2	1925-31	
Geh. 23	Gründung eines Mitteleuropa-Institutes	1	1928-31	
Geh. 22	Kulturpolitik Banat	1	1927-29	
	- Siebenbürgen	1	1928-29	
	- Bukowina, Nordbessarabien	1	1928-29	
	- Südbessarabien, Dobrudscha, Altreich	1	1928-29	
Pol.Arch. 250g/43	Geheimakten			
	Verwaltungsorganisation		4.36- 3.43	3712/E036714-38
	Geheimpersonalien		3.38- 1.43	902/292759-919
	Politisch		4.39- 9.42	895/291517-663
	Minderheiten		1.36-12.40	3711/E036662-711
	Wirtschaftlich		3.36- 8.42	903/292922-3050
	Verschiedenes		12.37- 5.42	889/290779-97
	Krisenmaßnahmen		6.38- 8.39	
	Militärisches		8.38-12.42	3710/E036623-59
	NSDAP Parteiangelegenheiten, Korrespondenz mit Parteigenossen Konradi, Landesgruppenleiter		10.37-10.40	
	Handelsattaché Konradi		5.38-10.39	
	Telegramme aus Berlin an Bukarest		1941	4685/E225264-304
			1942	5430/E364018-31

Akten-zeichen	Inhalt	Band	Datum	Serial Nr.
Pers A 1	Organisation, Geschäftverteilung im Auswärtigen Amt		1922-44	
Pers A 2	Die Deutschen Auslandsvertretungen in China und Ostasien, Allgemein		1937-41	
Pers A 2-1	Konsularbezirk Canton		1920-43	
2-2	Konsularbezirk Chungking		1920-41	
2-6	Amtsbezirk Japan		1938-44	
2-10	Konsularbezirk Shanghai		1920-39	
2-12	Konsularbezirk Tientsin		1921-41	
2-13	Amtsbezirk Tsingtau, Tsinanfu		1943	
2-16	Hsinking, Harbin, Manchouli		1941-42	
2-20	Amtsbezirk Chefoo		1943-44	
Pers A 3	Personalveränderungen im Auswärtigen Amt			
Pers P 1	Allgemeine Beamtenfragen		1929-44	
1-2	Zollfreiheit für deutsche Beamte allgemein		1937-41	
	- Einzelfälle,Bescheinigungen		1942-44	
Pers P 2	Heimaturlaub der Beamten, Generalia		1922-42	
2-1	Sommerurlaub der Beamten der Botschaft		1921-45	
2-2	Erholungsurlaub, Specilia Konsulatsbehörden		1935-42	
2-4	Stenotypistinnen der Botschaft, allgemein		1932-35	
2-6	Personalien der Hilfsangestellten		1936-45	
3-1	Nachweisungen über das Personal der Behörde		1936-43	
3-4	Betriebsgemeinschaften		1942-45	
3-5	Lettres, Chinesische Angestellte		1936-45	
3-6	Chinesisches Unterpersonal		1944-45	
3-7	Bewerbungen für den Konsulatsdienst		1940-44	
Pers G 1	Aktenplan der Botschaft		1940-44	
G 1 a	Aktenabgabe, Versendung		1940-45	

Akten-zeichen	Inhalt	Band	Datum	Serial Nr.
Pers G 2	Dienstbetrieb, Anordnungen des Behördenleiters, Organisation, wichtige Beschwerden, Geschäfts-verteilung		1941-45	
2 - 1	Dienstanweisungen des Auswärtigen Amtes über Berichterstattung		1938-44	
2 - 1 b	- über telegrafische Bericht-erstattung		1944-45	
2 - 2	- der Botschaft an die Dienststellen		1941-45	
Pers G 3	Grundlegende und von Zeit zu Zeit in Umlauf zu setzende Erlasse		1938-45	
Pers G 4 - 1 a	Dienstwohnungen der Beamten in Nanking		1941-42	
4 - 1c,d	Angemietete Diensträume in Nanking		1941-43	
4 - 2	Grundbesitz in Nanking		1945	
	Grundbesitz der Botschaft Generalia		1920-44	
4 - 2 b	Hospitalgelände in Peking		1922-27	
4 - 2 c	Ostgelände (Offiziersgelände) in Peking			
4 - 2 d	Enklave Gombojeff		1905-37	
4 - 2 e	Lichtbilder der reichseigenen Gebäude in Peiping und Peitaiho		1933	
4 - 2 f	Reichseigene Wohnungen in Peking		1933-45	
4 - 2 g	Dienstwohnungen, Wohnungsblätter Peiping		1929-44	
4 - 2 h	Garagen Stallungen		1932-44	
4 - 3	Verpachtungen, Vermietungen allgemein, Mietgesuche		1922-45	
4 - 3 a	Pachtvertrag F.W.Basle		1925-45	
4 - 3 b	- F.W. D.A.B.		1921-42	
4 - 3 c	- F.W. Max Hartung		1925-45	
4 - 3 d	- F.W. Peking Club		1910-31	
4 - 3 e	- F.W. Petric Electric Co.		1925-44	
4 - 3 f	- F.W. Portugiesische Gesandtschaft		1921-45	
4 - 3 g	- F.W. Reitzig		1939-45	
4 - 4 a	Mietvertrag D.N.B. (Dr.Müller)		1937-44	
4 - 4 b	- Deutsche Gemeinde Peking,(Lehrerhaus)		1939-44	
4 - 4 c	- Deutsches Hospital		1941-42	

Akten-zeichen	Inhalt	Band	Datum	Serial Nr.
Pers G 4 - 4d	Mietvertrag Deutsche Schule		1933-42	
4 - 4e	– Hübner		1937-45	
4 - 4f	– Huwer		1934-42	
4 - 4g	– Kirchengemeinde		1935-42	
4 - 4h	– Marschall		1929-45	
4 - 4k	– Secker früher Stolz		1934-42	
4 - 4L	– Transocean		1937-45	
4 - 4m	– Illies		1940-45	
4 - 4n	– Dr.Eckert		1936-42	
4 - 4o	– Füllkrug		1943	
4 - 4p	– K.Beister		1945	
4 - 5	Oesterreich-ungarische Gesandt-schaft		1941-44	
4 - 6	Unterhaltung der Gebäude Generalia		1921-44	
4 - 6b	Gärten in Peking und Peitaiho		1922-44	
4 - 6c	Bausachen, Voranschläge, Baube-darfsnachweisungen Peking		1936-41	
Pers G 5	Ausstattungsgegenstände und Geräte in den Diensträumen und Dienstwohnungen, allgemein		1936-41	
5 - 2	Inventarverzeichnis B , Bücher Karton		1936-45	
5 - 3	Schreibmaschinen		1925-42	
5 - 4	Materialbestellungen		1939-45	
5 - 5	Reichsgesetzblatt		1936-43	
5 - 6	Telefonanlage		1934-45	
5 - 7	Dienstauto, allgemein		1941-44	
5 - 8	– spezialia		1937-44	
Pers G 6	Beflaggung der Behörde an Feier-tagen und aus besonderen Anläs-sen		1944	
6 - 1	Dienstbetrieb an Feiertagen		1941-45	
Pers G 7	Zeitungsbezug, allgemein		1941	
7 - 1	Zeitungsbezug, speziell		1938-45	
7 - 2	Übersichten über den Bezug von Zeitungen und Zeitschriften		1938-41	
Pers G 8	Geschäftsübergabe, Protokolle		1921-39	
8 - 8a	Verlegung der Botschaft		1940-41	
8 - 1	Mitteilung von der Übergabe oder Übernahme der Geschäfte		1931-41	

Akten-zeichen	Inhalt	Band	Datum	Serial Nr.
Pers G 8 - 2	Jährliche Berichte der Dienst-stellen über wichtige Daten im Amtsbezirk		1941	
Pers G 9	Verkehr mit den Behörden des Gastlandes (nach Bedarf auszu-bauen)		1941	
Pers G 4 - 6a	Bausachen, spezialia		1944-45	
4 - 7d	Reichseigenes Grundstück in Chinwangtao		1912-42	
4 - 7n	Grundbesitz in Peitaiho, spezial		1922-44	
4 - 7q	Konsulatsgrundstück Tsinanfu		1941	
Pers R 1	Haushaltswesen und Kassensachen, allgemein		1929-42	
1 - 1	Sparerlasse		1921-40	
1 - 2	Kassensachen, specialia, auch Sparmaßnahmen		1939-40	
1 - 2			1945	
1 - 3	Voranschläge für Mittel zur eigenen Bewirtschaftung		1938-45	
1 - 3a	Haushaltsanträge der Dienst-stellen		1941-44	
1 - 4	Voranschläge zur Förderung des Aussenhandels		1937-43	
1 - 5	Bankvollmachten, Zeichnungs-befugnisse		1935-45	
Pers R 2	Kassenordnung		1941-45	
2 - 1	Kassenprüfungen		1941	
Pers R 4 4 - 1	Pressefonds		1941	
4 - 2	Pressefonds, Abrechnung Shanghai		1941	
4 - 3a	Abrechnung Promi		1941	
4 - 4	Fonds für kulturelle Zwecke		1942-45	
Pers R 5 5 - 1	Amtliche Vierteljahrsabrechnun-gen Nanking, Peiping, Chungking		1936-39	
5 - 1a	Abrechnung Grundstück		1938-45	
5 - 2	Abrechnung Nanking über politi-sche Ausgaben. Peitaiho Generalia		1922-41	
5 - 3	Beiträge zu den Dekanatsausgaben		1938-44	
Pers R 6	Prüfungsbemerkungen des Auswärtigen Amts und des Rech-nungshofes		1940-41	
Pers R 7	Konsulatsgebührengesetz		1944-45	

Akten- zeichen	Inhalt	Band	Datum	Serial Nr.
Pers R 8	Besoldung, Löhne, Unterstützun- gen der Beamten und Angestellten Allgemeines		1933-45	
R 8			1945	
8 - 1	Teuerungsberichte		1942-44	
8 - 2	Kinderzuschläge. Jährliche Meldungen betreffs Teuerungs- berichte jeden 25.Februar		1928-45	
8 - 4	Neujahrsgratifikation		1936-45	
8 - 5	Zahlungslisten für Angestellte		1943-45	
8 - 6	Erhebung von Gehältern		1940	
Pers R 9	Umzugskosten, allgemein		1927-44	
9 - 1	Anforderungen von Reisekosten- mitteln		1936-42	
9 - 2	Dienstreisen des Botschafters		1942-44	
9 - 3	- der Beamten der Botschaft		1936-44	
9 - 4	- der Beamten der Dienststellen		1936-42	
9 - 5	- des Handelssach- verständigen		1936-40	
Pers R 10	Steuern der Beamten und Lohn- steuern der Angestellten		1929-42	
10 - 1	Angestellten-und Invalidenver- sicherung		1932-43	
Pers R 11	Devisenangelegenheiten des Auswärtigen Amts und der Vertretungen		1935-40	
Pers R 13	Unterstützungen im Ausland, allgemein		1934-45	
13 - 1	- Einzelfälle		1943-45	
Pers R 14	Heimschaffungen, allgemein		1934-41	
14 - 1	- Einzelfälle		1931-43	
Pers R 15 15 - 1	Pensionen und Versorgungsge- bühren der Beamten, Einzelfälle		1939-45	
15 - 3	Pensions- und Rentensachen, allgemein		1941-45	
15 - 4	Militärische Versorgungsgebüh- ren		1944-45	
Pers R 16	Sammlungen im Ausland, allge- mein		1944	
16 - 1	- Einzelfälle		1936-40	
16 - 2	Hindenburgspende		1937-40	
16 - 3	Winterhilfswerk		1934-45	
16 - 4	NS-Volkswohlfahrt		1935-41	

Akten-zeichen	Inhalt	Band	Datum	Serial Nr.
Pers R 16 16 - 5	Zahlungen an das Deutsche Rote Kreuz		1940-45	
Pers Si 3	Telegrammerlass und Berichtkontrolle		1944-45	
Pers Si 5 5 - 4	Chiffriermaterial in Peiping, Meldungen über Bestände		1940	
Pers Si 6	Kurierangelegenheiten, allgemein		1944-45	
6 - 1	Kuriere, Kurierausweise		1944-45	
6 - 1			1945	
6 - 2a	Kuriersendungen fremder Staaten		1941	
6 - 3	Kurierreisekosten		1940-45	
Pers Si 7 7 - 2	Geheimsachen, Wirtschaft			
Prot 1	Einführung beim Staatsoberhaupt, Überreichung der Beglaubigungs- und Abberufungsschreiben		1938-40	
1 - 1	Zeremonielles		1938-45	
1 - 2	Empfänge		1937-44	
1 - 3	Todesfälle von Staatsoberhäuptern		1941-45	
1 - 4	Glückwunsch- und Beileidsschreiben		1922-45	
1 - 5	Exequatur für deutsche Konsuln in China		1929-40	
1 - 7	An- und Abmeldung der Botschafts- und Konsulatsbeamten beim Waichiaopu		1935-41	
Prot 2 A	Diplomatisches Korps		1941-45	
A - 1	Personalien der ausländischen Botschafter, Gesandten		1940-45	
A - 2	Materialsammlung über diplomatische Beamte aller Staaten		1940-45	
A - 3	Mitteilungen über Dienstantritt, Urlaub, Versetzungen der ausländischen Botschafter, Gesandten		1940-44	
A - 3a	Diplomatisches Korps, Nationalfeiertage		1931-43	
A - 3 a	Fremde Nationalfeiertage		1944-45	
A - 5	Dekanat		1938-41	
A - 6	Chinesische Botschaft in Berlin		1939-41	
Prot 2 B	Konsularkorps		1940-44	
B - 1	Seniorrat		1915-40·	
B - 2	Konsularkorps, Personalien		1939-41	
B - 2a	— Mitteilungen über Geschäftsübergaben		1941	

Akten- zeichen	Inhalt	Band	Datum	Serial Nr.
Prot 3	Orden und Ehrenzeichen, allgemein		1938-44	
Prot 3-1	Ehrenkreuz des Weltkrieges		1938-41	
3-1a	Kriegsverdienstkreuz		1941-45	
3-2	Ehrenkreuz für deutsche Mütter		1939-41	
3-3	Sonstige Ordensangelegenheiten		1938-45	
Pol 3-1	Chinesische Regierung, Ministerium, Personalien		1936-44	
3-1a	Chinesische Gesandtschaften und Konsulate		1940-41	
3-3b	Marineangelegenheiten in China		1944	
3-5	Chinesische Wappen, Hoheitszei- chen, Flaggen, Nationalhymne		1943	
3-6	Chinesische Feiertage		1940-43	
3-9	Kommunale Angelegenheiten, Volkszählungen		1922-44	
4-1	Völkerbund, allgemein		1933-40	
4-5a	Juden deutscher Staatsangehörig- keit, Emigration in China, Einzelfälle		1940-42	
5-1	Persien, Afghanistan		1925-35	
5-4	Balkanstaaten		1944	
5-6	China - Deutschland		1932-41	
5-8	England, politisch		1925-42	
5-9	Englische Kolonien politisch Dominions, Indien		1922-44	
5-10	England - Ostasien		1937-41	
5-11	Frankreich - Europa		1920-44	
5-12	Indochina, Frankreich, Ostasien		1920-45	
5-13	Italien		1943-44	
5-15	Japan - Russland, politisch		1945	
5-16	Japan - Ostasien, politisch		1945	
5-17	Mandschurei - Osthopei		1944-45	
5-20	Niederlande und Kolonien poli- tisch		1941	
5-21	Iran politisch		1935	
5-22	Randstaaten		1929-40	
5-24	Philippinen, politisch		1943	
5-25	Russland, politisch		1936-41	

Akten-zeichen	Inhalt	Band	Datum	Serial Nr.
Pol 5-26	Russland - China politisch		1937-42	
5-27	Siam (Thailand)		1935-43	
5-28	Südamerika		1929-40	
5-30	Spanien		1927-43	
W 1	Wirtschaftspolitik, allgemein		1940-44	
W 1a	Wirtschaftliche Lage in China		1941-45	
W 1-1	Wirtschaftsberichte der Botschaft und deren Dienststellen		1944-45	
W 1-2	Wirtschaftsberichte anderer Dienststellen		1940-41	
1-3	Berichte der Handelssachverständigen		1937-41	
1-4	Zivilberater		1939-40	
1-5	Ernährungslage und Preiskontrollmaßnahmen in Nordchina		1942-44	
2-2	Japanische Wirtschaftspläne in Mittel- und Südchina		1940	
2-2b	Statistische Erhebungen über fremde Betätigung in China		1944	
2-2d	Central Trust of China		1937-41	
2-3	Wirtschaftsverträge China - England		1925-41	
2-3	Wirtschaftliche Beziehungen Chinas zu anderen und zwischen anderen Ländern		1941-44	
3-1	Anmeldungen von Projekten deutscher Firmen, allgemein		1937-43	
3-1a	- Einzelfälle		1937-41	
3-2	Lokomotiven		1941	
WA 1	Ausstellungen und Messen, allgemein		1941-42	
WE 1	Eisenbahnen in China, allgemein		1944-45	
WA 1-2	Eisenbahnen speziell, auch Projekte		1937-44	
1-3	Nordchina Verkehrsgesellschaft North China Communication Co.		1942-44	
WE 2-2a	Abkommen, Frachtenverkehr, Transitverkehr, FRAKO		1940-44	
WF 1	Chinesisches Finanz-, Bank- und Geldwesen, allgemein		1936-44	
1-1	Chinesische Staatsfinanzen, allgemein		1941-45	
1-2a	- Anleihen, Einzelfälle		1934-43	

Akten-zeichen	Inhalt	Band	Datum	Serial Nr.
WF 1-2	Chinesische Anleihen, allgemein		1934-41	
1-4	Berichte über das chinesische Finanzwesen		1941	
1-5	Berichte über Provinzialfinanzen		1931-40	
2-2	Finanzielle Beziehungen Chinas zu und zwischen anderen Ländern		1941	
2-2a	Salzgabelle		1938-41	
3	Chinesisches Währungswesen Münzen, Banknoten		1936-44	
3			1945	
3-1	Devisenbeschränkungen		1939-42	
4-1	Chinesische Banken, allgemein		1937-44	
5	Lotterien, Spielbanken		1942	
6	Fremde Banken in China		1935-41	
6-1	Internationales Bankenkonsortium		1941	
6-2a	Deutsch-Asiatische Bank, Anleihen		1936-42	
WH 1	Handel in China		1940-42	
1-1	Handelsberichte der Botschaft		1941	
1-1a	— der Konsulate		1938-45	
1-1b	— des H.S.		1941	
1-2	Gesetzgebung, Ein-, Aus- und Durchfuhrverbote		1936-45	
1-2a	Transitpässe		1937-40	
1-2a			1938-42	
1-2b	Küstenhandel		1941-42	
1-4	Kriegsmateriallieferungen Einzelfälle		1936-41	
1-4a	— allgemein		1940	
2-1	Handel China - Deutschland, Verträge		1942	
2-1b	Handelsvertragsverhandlungen		1941	
2-2	Beziehungen Chinas zu Deutschland, Ein-, Aus- und Durchfuhrverbote, allgemein		1937-43	
2-3	— Austauschgeschäfte		1940	
2-3b	Nordchina Verrechnungsabkommen (Woidt)		1939-41	
2-3c	Otto Wolff - Project		1936	

Akten-zeichen	Inhalt	Band	Datum	Serial Nr.
WH 2-4a	Absatzmöglichkeiten für deutsche Waren		1937-40	
2-4b	Handelsvertreter, Handelsagenten		1941	
2-7	Berichte der Handelskammern		1944	
2-8	Geschäftsberichte deutscher Chinafirmen		1924-41	
2-10	Verbände, Kumiais und sonstige Wirtschaftsorganisationen		1942-44	
3	Monopole		1926-40	
6-1	Berichte der chinesischen und fremden Handelskammern		1937-41	
7-1	Eintragungen von Firmen in das chinesische Handelsregister		1937-43	
11	Kreditunwürdige und unzuverläs-sige Firmen in China		1941	
11-1	Kreditauskünfte über Firmen in China		1935-40	
15-1	Normungsbestrebungen		1936-40	
17	Handelsadressbücher und Adress-bücher			
WJ 1	Chinesische Industriepolitik		1930-43	
1a	Industrieberichte		1937-41	
1b	Berichte der Dienststellen		1939	
2-1	Industrie, Technik, Gewerbebe-ziehungen Chinas zu Deutschland, Verträge		1942	
2-2	Industrie, Technik, Gewerbebe-ziehungen Chinas zu und zwischen anderen Ländern, allgemein		1941	
3	Industrie, Kartelle, Trusts allgemein, Genossenschaften		1941	
3a	North China Development Company		1943-45	
3-1	Bergbau, Hüttenwesen, Gesetz-gebung		1942-43	
3-1a	Kohlenbergbau		1938-44	
3-1b	Eisen- und Stahlindustrie		1942-44	
3-1c	Eisenerz, Eisen- und Stahlin-dustrie in Mengchiang		1944	
3-2	Metallindustrie		1940-41	
3-3	Textilindustrie		1943-44	
3-3a	Teppiche		1939	
3-4	Chemische Industrie		1942-44	
3-5	Elektro-Industrie		1942-45	
3-5a	Elektrizitätswerke, Kraftwerke		1936-41	

Akten-zeichen		Inhalt	Band	Datum	Serial Nr.
WJ	3-11	Maschinenbauindustrie		1941	
	5-2	Handelsmarkengesetz, Warenzeichen und Musterschutz, allgemein		1942-44	
	5-3	Warenzeichen und Musterfälschungen, Einzelfälle		1944	
WL	1	Landwirtschaft auch Gesetzgebung allgemein		1941-45	
	3-2	Landwirtschaftliche Verbände		1942-43	
	5	Forstwirtschaft, Gesetzgebung		1941-42	
WLu	1	Zivile Luftfahrt, allgemein		1935-43	
	1-1	Pläne für den Bau von Flugzeugen		1943	
	2-1	Luftfahrt, Beziehungen Chinas zu Deutschland		1943	
	2-1a	Eurasia Aviation Corporation		1944-45	
	3	Flugpläne, Fluglinien, Flugtarife		1941-44	
WP	1	Post, Telegraf, Fernsprecher, Kabel Radio, allgemein		1942-45	
	1-1	Post Generalia		1937-44	
	1-2	Telegrafen, auch drahtlose Telegrafie		1936-45	
	1-3	Radio auch Rundfunk		1944	
	1-3a	Radio, Rundfunk, Entzug von Kurzwellen, Deutsches Programm		1943-44	
	2-1	Post, Telegrafen, Rundfunk Beziehungen Chinas zu Deutschland		1937-41	
	2-1a	Postwesen, Zensur, Brieföffnung, Briefspionage		1940-41	
	2-2	Beziehungen Chinas zu und zwischen anderen Ländern		1942-43	
	3	Postgebühren		1943-45	
	5	Postpaketverkehr über Sibirien		1926-41	
WR	1	Baumwolle		1938-44	
	2	Bohnen, Bohnenprodukte		1938-40	
	3	Borsten, Haare		1939	
	4	Eier und Eierprodukte		1939-42	
	5	Erdöl			
	6	Federn		1939-40	
	7	Felle, Pelze, Häute, Leder, Därme		1938-44	
	8	Getreide, Mehl		1939	

Akten-zeichen	Inhalt	Band	Datum	Serial Nr.
WR 9	Gummi		1941	
10	Hanf, Jute, Ramie, Chinagras		1938–41	
11	Holzöl und andere vegetablische Öle		1938–41	
12	Ingwer, Kampfer, Cassia		1938	
15	Erdnüsse, Walnüsse, Galläpfel		1938	
16	Reis		1938–41	
18	Salz, Soda		1938–44	
19	Seide		1939–41	
21	Tabak		1938–41	
23	Tee		1941	
24	Wolle		1939–40	
25	Rohrzucker, Zucker		1938–43	
WSch 1-1	See- und Binnenschiffahrt allgemein		1941–42	
1-1a	Schiffahrtsberichte der Botschaft und Konsulate		1937–41	
4-1	Seeschiffahrt, Schiffbau		1938	
5-1	Seeschiffahrt, Schiffahrtsunter-nehmungen		1936–42	
6-1	Seeschiffahrt, Fracht- und Personentarife		1941	
7-1	Hypotheken, Verkäufe		1941	
8	Chinesische Häfen, Flußregu-lierungen		1940–43	
8-2	Haiho Conservancy District		1937–40	
8-3	Drucksachensammlung der Whangpo-Conservancy Board		1941	
8-7	Lotsenwesen-Hafenvorschriften		1939–40	
9-1	Seezeichen, Leuchtfeuer, Leucht-schiffe, Bojen in Shanghai		1941	
9-3	Notices to Mariners		1941	
WSt 1	Steuern, Monopole, allgemein		1944–45	
1a	Staatliche Erhebungen zum Zwecke der Besteuerung		1937–44	
1-2	Gewerbesteuergesetz		1942	
1-3	Einkommensteuergesetz		1941–42	
1-4	Verbrauchersteuer-Warensteuern		1941	
1-9	Salzsteuer (Salztabelle siehe unter WF 2 Nr.2a)		1941	

Akten- zeichen	Inhalt	Band	Datum	Serial Nr.
WV 1	Verkehr, allgemein		1938-44	
2-2	Verkehr, Beziehungen Chinas zu und zwischen anderen Ländern		1941	
4	Strassenwesen, Strassenbau, Autostrassen		1938-43	
5	Wasserwesen, Wasserbau, Kanäle		1941-45	
6	Reiseverkehr über Sibirien		1939-41	
7	Fremdenverkehr		1921-41	
9	Speditionswesen		1937-41	
10	Verkehrsgesellschaften		1941	
11	Reiseberichte von Privatleuten		1938-40	
WZ 1	Chinesische Seezollverwaltung, allgemein		1930-43	
2-1a	Zollbehandlung deutscher Waren		1920-40	
2-2	Zollwesen, Beziehungen Chinas zu und zwischen anderen Ländern		1944	
3	Statistiken des Seezollamtes		1936-45	
4	Ein- und Ausfuhrzoll, Goldzölle		1943-44	
4-1	Zolltarif		1934-40	
7	Inlandpässe (Huchaos)		1941-42	
WJ 3-1b	Eisen- und Stahlindustrie in Nordchina		1944-45	
R 1	Chinesisches Rechtswesen, allgemein		1941-44	
1-1	Chinesische Gesetze, Verordnungen, Zusammenstellungen		1942-44	
3	Staatsrecht, Zivil- und Strafrecht, Gerichtswesen, Verfassung, Verwaltung allgemein		1943	
3-1	Staatsangehörigkeitsfragen allgemein		1939-43	
3-2a	Chinesisches Bürgerliches Gesetzbuch, einzelne Rechtsfragen		1942	
3-3	Grundbuchsachen, Landgesetz Erwerb von Grundeigentum, allgemein		1944	
3-3a	Eintragungen von Grundeigentum und Hypotheken, Grundbriefe		1942-44	
3-4d	Eheschliessung Deutscher mit anderen Ausländern, Einzelfälle		1944	
3-5a	Zivilprpzessrecht		1944-45	
3-5c	Rechtsanwaltsordnung, Zulassung von Rechtsanwälten		1943	

Akten-zeichen	Inhalt	Band	Datum	Serial Nr.
R 3-5d	Deutsche Rechtsanwälte		1941-42	
3-5e	Schutz deutscher Interessen in China		1944-45	
3-5f	Forderungen gegen chinesische Behörden		1942-44	
3-5h	- Chinesen		1939-43	
3-5j	- Deutscher gegen Ausländer		1940-44	
3-5k	Gehaltsforderungen gegen chinesische Behörden		1944-45	
3-5L	Buchhändlerforderungen		1939-40	
3-5p	Forderungen aus dem japanisch-chinesischen Konflikt, allgemein		1937-43	
3-5q	- Mission in Nanking		1938-43	
	- Hackmack, Tiensin		1936-41	
	- Beamte, Hempel		1938-42	
	- Sammelband		1938-40	
	- Gebr. Roese		1939-41	
	- Sammelband		1941-43	
	- Tiyuanfu		1937-42	
	- Rückgabe von Fabriken		1941-43	
	- Siemens		1938-40	
	- - D.A.B. Chung Hsing Coal Mg		1937-40	
	- - Chia-Chia-Wang-Mine		1938-40	
3-6a	Strafsache gegen Lassota-Herbold		1938-42	
3-7a	Genossenschaftswesen in China		1941	
3-7d	Wechselproteste		1921-37	
4	Arbeits- und Gewerberecht, Lohnfragen, Streiks, Aussperrungen, Arbeitsmarkt und Arbeitslosigkeit		1936-45	
5	Passrecht und Fremdenpolizei im Ausland, allgemein		1940	
5-1	Chinesische Pass- und Sichtvermerksbestimmungen		1942-45	
5-2	Reiseverbote, Reisebeschränkungen in China, allgemein		1942-45	
5-2a	Inlandreisescheine, Torpässe, Bescheinigungen		1941-44	
5-3	Pass- und Reisevorschriften		1936-45	

Akten-zeichen	Inhalt	Band	Datum	Serial Nr.
R 5-6	Einlasskarten, Besichtigung chinesischer Sehenswürdigkeiten		1922-44	
5-7	Chinesisches Polizeiwesen, allgemein		1943-44	
6-1	Sozial- und Fürsorgewesen in China		1941	
7	Internationales Rechtswesen		1942	
7-5	Fremde Niederlassungen in China		1942-44	
7-6	Rotes Kreuz		1942	
7-12	Exterritorialität		1943-45	
7-13	Diplomatisches Quartier in Peking		1940-44	
7-15	Urheberrecht, Schutz geistigen Eigentums		1941-43	
Kult 1	Allgemeine Kulturpolitik Chinas		1941-45	
1a	Kulturpolitik in Mengchiang		1942-44	
1-1	Kulturelle Organisationen und Vereinigungen		1941-44	
2-1	Kulturpolitische Beziehungen Chinas zu Deutschland, allgemein		1939-41	
2-1c	Anträge auf Bewilligung von Mitteln für kulturelle Zwecke		1944-45	
2-1d	Deutsch-chinesische Freund-schaftsvereine		1941	
2-1f	Chinesisch-deutscher Kultur-verband (DOES Club)		1937-41	
2-1h	China Institut, Frankfurt am Main		1925-41	
2-1j	Übersetzung deutscher und chine-sischer Literatur		1943-44	
2-2	Kulturpoltische Beziehungen Chinas zu und zwischen anderen Ländern, allgemein		1932-45	
2-3	Japanische Kulturpolitik		1943-44	
3-1	Reichsdeutsche Kolonie		1940-45	
3-2	Deutsche Vereine		1938-41	
3-3	Deutsche Gemeinde Peking		1940-45	
3-3a	Deutsche Selbstversorgergenos-senschaft		1944-45	
3-3b	Deutsche Hilfswerke		1945	
3-4	Deutsche Auslandsbüchereien		1936-41	
3-7	Deutsche Mitgliedschaften in fremden Klubs und Vereinen		1936-44	
4	Kirchenwesen in China		1941-44	

Akten- zeichen	Inhalt	Band	Datum	Serial Nr.
Kult 4-1	Missionswesen, allgemein		1939-43	
4-2	Missionen, Missionare, Missions- kongresse		1939-44	
4-3	Landerwerb der Missionen		1941	
4-4	Missionarspässe, Schutzpässe		1939-41	
4-5	Gewaltakte gegen Missionen und Missionare		1938-42	
4-7	Vatikan		1929-40	
4-8	Deutsche Kirchengemeinde in China		1938-44	
4-9	Deutsche Friedhöfe, allgemein		1936-38	
4-10	Friedhöfe, Geldmittel		1925-45	
4-11	Deutsche Friedhöfe in den Amts- bezirken		1941-45	
5	Wanderungswesen, allgemein		1942	
5-4	Stellenvermittlung, Einzelfälle		1937-45	
5-4a	Stellengesuche von Chinesen		1938	
5-6	Aufenthalts- und Niederlassungs- fragen		1943	
6-1	Nachforschungen nach Personen, Anschriftenvermittlungen		1938-45	
7	Jugendbewegung in China		1941	
7-1	Chinesische Jugendorganisationen		1932-42	
8-1	Schulwesen in China, allgemein		1940-44	
8-3	Lehrmittel und Lehrmittelzusen- dungen für deutsche und chinesi- sche Schulen		1940-44	
8-4	Buchprämien		1940-42	
8-5	Deutsch-chinesische Mittelschu- len, allgemein (nach Orten ge- trennt)		1940-41	
8-5a	Deutsch-chinesische Mittelschule Canton		1940	
8-5e	- Tsingtau		1924-41	
8-6	Deutsche Schulen in China, all- gemein (nach Orten getrennt)		1937-43	
8-6b	Deutsche Schule in Kunming, all- gemein auch Abschlussprüfungen und Jahresberichte		1940-41	
8-6c	Deutsche Schule Peking		1945	
	- Personalien der Lehrer		1941-45	
8-6d	Deutsche Schule Shanghai		1935-40	

Akten-zeichen	Inhalt	Band	Datum	Serial Nr.
Kult 8-6e	Deutsche Schule Tientsin,allge-mein, auch Abschlussprüfungen und Jahresberichte		1939-44	
8-6f	Deutsche Schule in Tsingtau, Jahresberichte		1940-45	
8-6h	– Nanking		1937-45	
8-6j	Deutsche Schulen in China und Ostasien allgemein, Personalien der Lehrer		1940-44	
8-7	Schulbeihilfen, Anträge, Bewilli-gungen und Nachweisungen der Mittel		1938-45	
8-7a	Lehrer, Gehälter, Bezüge		1941-45	
8-8	Qualifikationsberichte über Lehrer		1938-40	
8-9	Fremde auch Missionsschulen in China		1941-42	
9-1	Deutsche Sprachwerbung		1940-45	
9-2	Deutsche Akademie in München		1941-45	
10-1	Universitäten in China (nach Namen getrennt)		1942-44	
10-1a	Technische Schulen in China, allgemein		1940	
10-1b	Studien an chinesischen Hoch-schulen		1943	
10-2	Dozentenberufssicherung		1935-42	
10-3	Chinesisches Studentenwesen		1942	
10-3a	Chinesen in Deutschland		1925-41	
10-8	Katholische Universität in Peking		1942	
10-12	Tungchi Technische Hochschule, allgemein		1941	
10-12a	Anträge, Bewilligungen und Abrechnungen der Beihilfen		1940-41	
10-12c	Personalien der Lehrer		1942	
	Tungchi Technische Hochschule Personalien Hefter		1941	
10-12f	Mittelschule der Tungchi-Hoch-schule		1941	
10-12g	Deutsche Medizinische Akademie, Shanghai		1942-44	
11-3	Forschungsreisen und Expeditio-nen, allgemein		1942	
11-3a	Expedition Filchner		1937-40	

Akten-zeichen	Inhalt	Band	Datum	Serial Nr.
Kult 11-3a	Expeditionen Sven Hedin		1938-40	
11-4	Wissenschaftliche Institute und Vereinigungen, allgemein		1942-44	
11-4a	Durchreise und Vorträge deutscher Wissenschaftler und Gelehrter		1940-45	
11-4b	Wissenschaftliche Veröffentlichungen		1938-45	
11-4d	Medizin und Kultur		1942	
11-5	Gesundheitswesen, Sanitätsabkommen		1941	
11-5a	Ärztekongresse in Ostasien		1938-43	
11-5b	Chinesische Quarantäneverordnungen und Einrichtungen, Seuchen und ihre Bekämpfung		1941-45	
11-5e	Deutsche praktische Ärzte, Zahnärzte, Apotheken		1940-44	
11-5f	Zulassung von deutschen Ärzten und Apothekern		1944-45	
11-5h	Deutsche Krankenhäuser und Apotheken in China, allgemein		1940-44	
11-5k	Fremde Krankenhäuser in China		1941-42	
11-5L	Billroth-Stiftung		1940-41	
11-5m	Paulus Hospital in Shanghai		1940-42	
11-7	Veterinärwesen, allgemein		1937-40	
11-8	Klimatische Verhältnisse		1942	
11-10b	Deutsche Buchhandlungen		1940-41	
11-10c	Bücherangebote		1942-45	
12-1a	Kunstausstellungen		1938-44	
12-3	Musikwesen		1942	
12-4	Chinesisches Filwesen, allgemein		1940-43	
12-4d	Fremde Filme und Filmgesellschaften, auch in Deutschland unerwünschte Filme			
12-4e	Hetzfilme, allgemein		1941	
12-4f	Hetzfilme, Verhinderungen der Aufführung		1940-44	
12-6	Sportwesen in China		1941-42	
12-6b	Olympiade		1936-37	
P 1	Presse und Propagandawesen in China, allgemein		1937-45	
1a	Chinesische Propagandaschriften		1944-45	
1-1	Chinesisches Pressegesetz, Zensur		1944-45	

Akten-zeichen	Inhalt	Band	Datum	Serial Nr.
P 1-2	Chinesische Presse		1941-45	
1-3	Presseberichte der Botschaft		1938-44	
1-3a	Presseberichte der Dienststellen		1938-39	
1-4	Übersichten der in den Amtsbezirken erscheinenden Zeitungen		1938-43	
1-5	Fremde Presse in den Amtsbezirken (nach Orten geordnet)		1937-45	
2-1	Presse- und Propagandawesen, Beziehungen Chinas zu Deutschland, allgemein		1943-44	
2-1a	Abkommen über Presseattachés		1941	
2-2	Presse- und Propagandawesen, Beziehungen Chinas zu und zwischen anderen Staaten		1941	
2-3	Pressetelegramme Cordt Shanghai		1941	
3-1	Nachrichtenbüros Chinas		1940-41	
3-1a	Chung Hua News Agency		1941-44	
3-2a	Reuter News Agency		1941-42	
3-2b	Havas		1944-45	
3-2c	Domei News		1941	
3-2f	Radio Roma		1940-42	
3-3	Deutsche Zeitung und Zeitschriften in China, allgemein		1940-44	
3-3a	Ostasiatischer Lloyd		1940-44	
3-3b	Deutsche Zeitung für Nordchina		1938-44	
3-3c	International News und Far Eastern Illustrated News		1940-44	
3-4	Jüdische Presse		1940	
4-1	Pressevertreter, Schriftleiter		1937-44	
4-2	Vertreter deutscher Zeitungen in China		1941-45	
4-3	Vertreter fremder Zeitungs- und Nachrichtenbüros in China		1940-43	
DPol 1a	Protektorat Böhmen und Mähren		1938-42	
1a-2	Umsiedlung deutscher Volksgenossen		1940-42	
2-2a	Deutsch-russische Verträge		1938-41	
2-2a	Verträge Deutschlands mit anderen Staaten		1940-44	
3-1	Der Führer und Reichskanzler		1934-45	

Akten-zeichen	Inhalt	Band	Datum	Serial Nr.
DPol 3-1a	Reichsregierung und Reichstag		1937-41	
3-2	Hervorragende Staatsmänner und Parteiführer		1938-41	
3-3d	Wehrdienst, Arbeitsdienst		1940	
3-3j	Erfassung von Offizieren A.D.		1942	
3-5	Hoheitszeichen, Flaggen in Deutschland		1938-41	
3-6	Nationalfeiertage, Erlasse		1934-44	
3-6a	Berichte über nationale Feiertage		1936-41	
3-6a2			1942-45	
3-7	NSDAP , Gliederungen und angeschlossene Verbände		1941-43	
3-7c	Auslandsorganisation			
3-8	Deutsche Kolonien		1937-41	
DW 1-1	Deutsche Wirtschaftslage		1936-41	
2	Deutsch-russische Verträge		1921-40	
DWF 1	Finanzwesen in Deutschland, allgemein		1935-41	
1-1	Anleihen für Deutschland		1941	
1-2	Devisengesetzgebung, allgemein		1941	
1-3	Devisenangelegenheiten		1940-45	
1-4	Handelsbilanz		1940	
3	Deutsche Währung		1942	
3-2	Ausserkurssetzung Münzen		1938-40	
DWH 1-1	Gesetzgebung: Aus-, Ein- und Durchfuhrverbote		1936-41	
1-2	Handelsstatistiken		1941	
2-1	Handelsbeziehungen Deutschlands zu anderen Staaten als China, allgemein		1941	
2-2b	Handelsbeziehungen zu Manchoukuo		1941-42	
3	Anfragen wegen Geschäftsverbindungen in Deutschland		1937-41	
4	Handelsanfragen deutscher Firmen, Benennung von Vertretern		1941	
6-1	Reichsstelle für Aussenhandel		1931-36	
6-10	Ostasiatischer Verein Hamburg		1940	

Akten-zeichen	Inhalt	Band	Datum	Serial Nr.
DWLu 1-1	Deutsche Lufthansa		1941	
DWP 1	Post, Telegraf, Kabel, Radio, allgemein		1942	
DWSch 1-1	Schiffahrt, allgemeine Erlasse		1940	
1-9	Erwerb und Verkauf von Schiffen im Kriegsfalle		1940	
1-10	Beschlagnahme deutscher Schiffe im Kriege		1940	
6	Seemannsamt, Seemannsordnung		1941-42	
DWZ 1-1	Der deutsche Zolltarif			
3	Zollbehandlung von Liebesgaben		1940-41	
4	Zollbehandlung von Umzugs-, Heirats- und Erbschaftsgut, allgemein		1937-38	
DR 1	Deutsches Rechtswesen, allgemein		1936-39	
3-2	Staatsangehörigkeitsfragen, allgemein		1942-43	
3-2a	Einbürgerung, Wiedereinbürgerung		1944-45	
3-2g	Meldepflichtgesetz, allgemein		1937-40	
3-3b	Freiwillige Gerichtsbarkeit, allgemein		1922-23	
3-3b1	Beglaubigungen von Unterschrif-ten, Abschriften, Übersetzungen, Gegenzeichnungen		1924-43	
3-3b2	Lebensbescheinigungen, Renten-quittungen		1922-45	
	Legalisationen			
3-3b3	Bescheinigungen aller Art (Umzugsbescheinigungen siehe DWZ 4 Nr.1)		1941-45	
3-3b4	Notariatsakte*		1923-45	
3-3b5a	Testamente, Hinterlassungen, Erbverträge, Einzelfälle		1933-45	
3-3b6	Nachlasssachen, allgemein		1934-45	
3-3b6a	Schiedsansprüche, Einzelfälle		1938-45	
	Nachlasssachen allgemein Wilhelm Michels		1943	
	- Sauer		1939-41	
	- Benck		1942-43	
	- Lassotta		1945	
	- Jean Renaud		1938-40	
	- Arthur u.Anne Ferchel		1943-44	
	- Dr.Ernest Schierlitz		1941-44	

Akten- zeichen	Inhalt	Band	Datum	Serial Nr.
DR 3-3b6a	Nachlasssachen:			
	- B. Rüdorff		1944-45	
	- A. Marschall		1944	
	- M.Karius		1944	
	- K.Heinze		1945	
	- Adolf Wittig		1941-42	
	- Jansen		1943	
	- F.W.Basel		1944	
3-3b7	Vormundschaften, Pflegschaften, Alimentensachen, Entmündigungen		1933-45	
3-3b9	Firmenregister, allgemein		1938-42	
3-3b9a	Eintragungen in das Firmenregister Bescheinigungen Einzelfälle		1936-45	
3-3g	Reichsarbeitsdienst		1936-41	
3-4	Familienrecht, Ehe- und Personenstandsangelegenheiten, allgemein		1932-45	
3-4a	Anfragen, Auskünfte über Personenstandsangelegenheiten		1938-45	
3-4b	Eherecht		1941-44	
3-4c	Eheschliessungen, Aufgebote		1937-45	
3-4d	Geburtsurkunden, Einzelfälle		1937-45	
3-4e	Sterbefälle, Leichenpässe, Einzelfälle		1937-45	
3-4f	Ehelichkeitserklärungen, Annahme an Kindesstatt		1942	
3-4g	Namensänderungen, auch zusätzliche Vornamen bei Juden		1938-39	
3-4h	Standesamtliche Jahresberichte		1937-44	
3-5	Zivilprozessrecht, Handelsrecht Schiedsgerichtswesen		1940-45	
3-5b	Zustellungen, Einzelfälle		1921-41	
3-6	Strafrecht, Strafprozessrecht, Auslieferungen, Gefangenenaustausch		1941	
5-1	Deutsche Passvorschriften, allgemein		1938-45	
5-1a	Passvorschriften für Emigranten		1943	
5-1b	Deutsche Pass- und Sichtvermerksgebühren,		1936-39	
5-2	Einreisevorschriften für Chinesen		1921-39	

Akten-zeichen	Inhalt	Band	Datum	Serial Nr.
DR 5-4	Ausstellung deutscher Pässe und Kinderausweise		1942-45	
5-5	Verlust von Reisepässen		1938-45	
5-6	Sichtvermerke für Diplomaten		1929-41	
5-6b	Sichtvermerke Einzelfälle		1939-41	
5-7	Sichtvermerke für Diplomaten		1935-41	
5-8	Grenzempfehlungen		1936-41	
6	Sozial- und Fürsorgewesen		1942-43	
DKult 1	Kulturpolitik Deutschlands		1940-41	
5	Ein-, Aus- und Rückwanderung, allgemein		1934-39	
5-1	Umsiedlung deutscher Volksge-nossen, Rückwanderung nach Deutschland		1940-41	
8-2	Aktenregister			
12-4	Filmwesen		1944-45	
S 1	Weitergabe von Briefen, Paketen		1944-45	
2	Empfehlungen des Auswärtigen Amtes		1938-41	
2a	Empfehlungen der Botschaft und anderer Dienststellen		1941-44	
4	Verschiedenes		1944-45	
10-5	Pressepropaganda		1941	
10-5d	(Inhalt unbekannt)		1941	
10-7	Deutsche Zahlungsverbote		1940-41	
10-8	Betreuung von Heimkehrern, Flüchtlingen		1941-42	
10-8c	Abrechnungen der N.S.V. über Rückwandererbeihilfen			
10-9	Anmeldungen deutscher Verluste im feindlichen Ausland		1942-45	
	Liquidation deutschen Eigentums, allgemein		1940-42	
10-12	Wehrwirtschaftsreferat (Woidt)		1945	
10-12/2			1945	
10-10	- in Hongkong		1940-41	
10-11	(Inhalt unbekannt)		1940	
10-12a	Geldbeschaffungen		1941	
10-13	Deutsche wirtschaftliche Mass-nahmen aus Anlass des Krieges		1939-41	

Akten-zeichen	Inhalt	Band	Datum	Serial Nr.
S 10-22	Deutsche Kriegsgesetze über Wirtschaft und Handel		1939	
10-23	Wirtschaftlicher Verkehr		1940-41	
29	Kriegsschuld			
3300	Denkschrift des Dr.Gerhard Rose		1933-37	
3500	Deutsches Hospital Generalia		1921-36	
6603	Kassensachen		1938-39	
6621	Abrechnung		1939-40	
6646	(Inhalt unbekannt)		1938-39	
	Akten enthalten Kopien von Briefen und Meldungen mit Kurier nach Berlin gesandt			
	Meldungen, Listen			
	Rechnungen (Autoreparaturen)		1939	
			1939-41	
			7.41- 9.41	
			9.41-12.41	
			12.41	
	Verschiedenes, ungeordnet		1941	
			1941	
			1.42- 3.42	
			3.42- 6.42	
			7.42- 1.43	
			2.43- 8.43	
			9.43- 1.44	
			2.44- 6.44	
			6.44-11.44	
			12.44- 3.45	
			4.45- 8.45	
	Botschaft, Pressesachen		1943-45	
	Tagesberichte der Botschaft Peking		1941-43	
	Berichte		1941-43	
	Deutsche Schule Peking, chinesische Veröffentlichungen		1935-41	
	Personalakten		1938-45	
	Protokollbuch	2	1927-35	
	Weltkrieg I, Botschaftsmaterial		1913-17	

Akten-zeichen	Inhalt	Band	Datum	Serial Nr.
	Deutscher Schulverein, Peking		1936-45	
			1930-45	
	Botschaft, Geschäftsakten			
	Northe persönliche Briefe und Briefe vom I.Weltkrieg			
Pers R 13-1	(Akten)			
13-1	(Akten)			
DKult 4	Kirchenwesen in Deutschland			
D 3-3b6a	Nachlass Ziegler			

Akten-zeichen	Inhalt	Band	Datum	Serial Nr.
	Nach dem Kriegsausbruch, 11.Dezember 1941, entstandene Akten.			
	An das Auswärtige Amt gerichtete Telegramme ab 11.Dezember 1941	9		
	Generalakten (Schriftverkehr, Aufzeichnungen, Telegrammver-kehr) nach dem Kriegseintritt der Dominikanischen Republik, 11.Dezember 1941	10		
	Schriftwechsel mit dem spani-schen Gesandten seit Kriegsaus-bruch zwischen Dominikanischer Republik und Deutschland	11		

Akten-zeichen	Inhalt	Band	Datum	Serial Nr.
Nie 5	Aussenpolitik	2	1.38- 4.39	2852/D551342-69
Nie 15	Jahresbericht, Lageberichte über Holland		1.35- 4.39	6810/E517686-94
Pers. P.1a	Der Vertreter des Auswärtigen Amtes im Stabe des Reichskommissars für das besetzte niederländische Gebiet. Allgemeines			7778/E556045-63
Pers. P.2	Urlaubsbestimmungen Urlaubspläne		4.41- 3.44	7779/E556065-146
Pers. P.3	UK - Stellung	3	1944	7780/E556148-283
Pers. G.2	Sonderheft. Gen.v.Unruh Aktion		1943	7781/E556148-324
Pers. P.3	W.Janke		8.40- 3.43	7782/E556326-407
	Gesandter Bene		9.40- 7.44	7783/E556409-615
	Personalia, Presse Referat		3.42- 7.44	7784/E556617-87
	Legationssekretär Betz		1941-43	7785/E556689-768
	Abteilung Rundfunk		1941-44	7786/E556770-921
	Protektorat Böhmen und Mähren, Slowakei	2	3.39- 4.39	3122/D641846-920
	Belgien		1.37- 5.38	7599/E543754-60
	Niederlande - Nationalsozialistische Bewegung in den Niederlanden		6.38- 4.39	2854/D551376-413
Deut. 8	Deutschland. Kolonialpolitik		1.35- 4.39	2885/D565348-75
	Vertreter des Auswärtigen Amtes (Pressereferent)		9.41- 6.42	7777/E555970-6043

Akten-zeichen	Inhalt	Band	Datum	Serial Nr.
	Erlasse Nr. 201-600		1941	5085/E292971-86 6434/H059185-282
	Nr. 1-499		1940	6434/H059283-665
	Nr. 1-500		1940	5085/E292987- 992/2 6434/H059666- 60104
	Nr. 501-813		1940	6434/H060105-574
	Nr. 601-1100		1941	5085/E292993- 3004 6434/H060575-955
	Nr.1101-1349		1941	5085/E293005-10 6435/H060957- 1101
	Nr.1350-1535		1941	5085/E293011-26 6435/H061102-420
	Nr.1536-1712		1941	6435/H061421-724
	Drahterlasse und Drahtberichte		12.39- 3.40	6436/H061726-44
	Berichte Nr. 902-1299			6436/H061745- 2121
	Drahtberichte Nr. 2-399		1943	5683/E412567-573 6436/H062122-626
	Nr. 400-900		1943	5683/E412574-85 6436/H062627- 3256
	Drahtberichte Geheim		1944	5683/E412586-89 6436/H063257-559
	Drahterlasse Nr. 501-761		1940	6437/H063561-860
	Nr. 1-219		1943	6437/H063861- 4121
	Nr. 220-500		1943	5683/E412525-27 6437/H063122- 4411
	Nr. 501-599		1943	6437/H064412-529
	Nr. 600-749		1943	6437/H064530-682
	Nr. 750-860		1943	5683/E412528-35 6437/H064683-798
	Nr. 861-999		1943	6437/H064799-939
	Nr.1000-1120		1943	6438/H064941- 5075
	Nr.1121-1200		1943	6438/H065076-181
	Nr.1201-1300		1943	6438/H065182-292
	Nr.1301-1494		1943	6438/H065293-553
	Nr.1303-1800		1943	5683/E412536-57 6438/H065554-891
	Nr.1804-2230		1943	6438/H065892- 6246

Akten-zeichen	Inhalt	Band	Datum	Serial Nr.
	Drahterlasse Nr. 2231-2587		1943	5683/E412558-61 6438/H066247-558
	Berichte Nr. 1-250		1941	4963/E276573-74 6440/H066560- 7063
	Nr. 251-550		1941	4963/E276575-77 6440/H067064-522
	Nr. 551-1000		1941	4963/E276578-80 6440/H067523- 8125
	Nr.1,001-1400		1941	4963/E276581-99 6440/H068126-671
	Drahtberichte Nr. 1-2225		1942	5223/E308349-91 6441/H068673- 9322
	Nr.261-1728		1942	5223/E308392-401 6441/H069323-69
			1939- 3.40	6441/H069370-623
			1939- 3.40	6441/H069624-886
	Nr. 1-200		1941	4963/E276600-14 6441/H069887- 70020
	Multex-Telegramme Nr. 1-900		1941	5160/E303745-51 6506/H070022-294
	Nr.901-1142		1941	5171/E305761-959 6506/H070295-550
	Nr. 1-301		1942	
	Nr.302-947		1942	5171/E305960- 6239 6506/H070551-858
	Nr. 1-512		3.40- 1.41	6507/H070860- 1044
	Nr.354-790		1943	6507/H071045-169
	Nr. 7-487		1943	6507/H071170-358
	Nr.803-1004		1943	6507/H071359-448
	Nr.1005-1361		1943	6507/H071449-670
	Persönliche Reklamationen		1944	6508/H071672-733
	Wehrpflichtigenliste, Stand		1. 9.1939	6509/H071735-68
	Buch X für Schiffs- und See-mannsangelegenheiten		5.29-12.31	6509/H071769- 2059
	Telegramme Nr. 155-211 Nr. 482-485		22. 6.1941	6509/H072060-100 6509/H072101-07
	Freiwilligenfrage Telegramme Nr. 208-428		3.41- 6.41	6509/H072108-80

Akten-zeichen	Inhalt	Band	Datum	Serial Nr.
	Schriftwechsel des Schiffahrts-sachverständigen beim deutschen Konsulat in Petsamo		9.40- 7.41	6509/H072181-847
	Petsamo Telegramme Nr. 1-803		1940	6509/H072848-992
	Nr. 1-808		1941	4964/E276617-47 6509/H072993-3144
	Schiffe		1918-20	6510/H073146-356
			1921	6510/H073357-484
	Freigabe der Schiffe "Irma"		11.19- 7.20	6510/H073485-582
	Freigabe deutscher Schiffe speziell Ravensberg		6.18-12.23	6510/H073583-651
	Freigabe deutscher Schiffe		3.18-11.23	6510/H073652-80
	Freigabe deutscher und finni-scher Schiffe: "Worms"		3.18- 1.21	6510/H073681-875
	- "Aallotar""Helmi"		9.19- 7.23	6510/H073876-4070
	Nachforschungen bei Geldhinter-legungen		5.20- 4.23	6510/H074071-188
	Nachforschungen		6.20-11.21	6510/H074189-203
	Nachlass Becker		7.21- 6.22	6510/H074204-572 6510/H074573-706
23 VI	Pass-Sachen Buch IV - f.6		3.22- 6.22	6511/H074708-5298
23 VII	Buch IV - 7		6.22- 9.22	6511/H075299-699
23 VIII	Buch IV - 8		9.23- 2.23	6511/H075700-6263
23 X	Buch IV - 10		7.23- 9.24	6511/H076264-839
	Nachlass		6.18-11.21	6512/H076841-7030
			1922-23	6512/H077031-332
			1920-27	6512/H077333-74
	Notenwechsel über Waffenhilfe, Prisenschiffe, Schiffsabgaben	1	12.21- 4.22	6512/H077375-654
		2	4.22- 2.23	6512/H077655-789
	Nordische Woche		3.21- 8.24	6512/H077790-861
	Deutsche Schule in Helsingfors		4.89- 7.14	6512/H077862-8029
	Deutsche Vereine		10.18-12.22	6512/H078030-102
	Jahresbericht über das Geschäftsjahr		10.36- 9.37	
	Juden		4.18-11.18	6512/H078103-32
	Oberschlesien		7.20-12.21	6513/H078134-285

Akten-zeichen	Inhalt	Band	Datum	Serial Nr.
	Sache Transoceanic o/a Schichau		1.25- 5.26	6513/H078286-382
	Notariatsakte		8.20- 8.21	6513/H078383-94
	Hauptgräberlisten			6513/H078395-629
	Politik		1912-32	6514/H078631-80081
			1919-32	6515/H080083-1095
			1926-32	6516/H081097-2890
	Hilfsamtdiener Hartig		1921-27	6517/H082892-939
	Overbeck, Karl Kuno Attaché Gg.5 Overbeck		1935-37	6517/H082940-3015
	Kanzler Schaller		1927-37	6517/H083016-96
	Pache		1922-23	6517/H083097-177
	Fräulein Schreiber, Frau Haaser		1918-24	6517/H083178-210
	Crull, Hoffmann Legationsrat		1919-20	6517/H083211-95
	H.Toivonen Siilinjärvi (Finnland)		1921	6517/H083296-342
	Dr.Friedmann		1924	6517/H083343-45
	Militärattaché Marine Vertreter		1918-22	6517/H083346-440
	Graf du Moulin		1921-23	6517/H083441-87
	Brück		1920-24	6517/H083488-507
	Meynen		1922-26	6517/H083508-650
	Hintze		1918-23	6517/H083651-70
	Fogelholm		1900-22	6518/H083672-764
	Kanzler Wucherpfennig		1923-29	6518/H083765-876
	Hahn		1921	6518/H083877-79
	Lampe		1919-24	6518/H083880-900
	v.Küchler		1918-22	6518/H083901-79
	Gesandtschaftsrat Dr.v.Grundherr		1925-35	6518/H083980-4300
	Preusker		1920-34	6518/H084301-500
	Teiskonen Marta, geborene Liebe		1918-31	6518/H084501-62
	Personalien S (S)		1918-21	6518/H084563-634
	Milewski		1920-24	6518/H084635-67
	Hollberg		1922-23	6518/H084668-85
	Handelsabteilung Personalien H.1.		1920	6518/H084686-866
	Ausgeschiedene Personen Höhere Beamte		1918-20	6518/H084867-947
	Ausgeschiedene mittlere Beamte Personalien		1918-20	6518/H084948-5216

Akten-zeichen	Inhalt	Band	Datum	Serial Nr.
88 R 10	Deutsche Bestimmungen betreffend Entschädigung von Kriegsschäden		1918-30	6671/H085218-6036
	Deutsche Zivilschäden in Finn-land, ihre Rechts- und Verhand-lungslage		1918-30	6671/H086037-79
	Material für deutsche Zivil-schadenanmeldungen		1918-30	6671/H086080-213
	Schriftwechsel mit Geschädigten speziell A-O		1918-30	6671/H086214-562
89 R 9 d	Aufruhrschäden, Schriftwechsel mit Geschädigten A-Z			6672/H086564-7963
	Protokolle des deutschen Aus-schusses. Abrechnungen des Kulturbeitrages		1927-35	6672/H087964-9155
91 Ww 9	Walther			6672/H089156-537
Ws 10	Frau Irene Schmidt geborene Fliegenring			6672/H089538-702
	Berichtverzeichnisse	1	1942	6673/H089704-990
		2	1943	6673/H089991-90284
		3	1944	6673/H090285-459
	Schriftwechsel geheim	1	1941-42	5112/E295447-60 6674/H090461-866
		2	1941-42	5112/E295461-94 6674/H090867-1280
		3	1941-42	6674/H091281-596
		4	1941-42	6674/H091597-952
	Schriftwechsel verschiedene		1940-43	6674/H091953-2217
	Schriftwechsel geheim	5	1942-43	6675/H092219-591
		6	1942-43	5223/E308402-09 6675/H092592-842
		7	1942-43	5683/E412562-66 6675/H092843-3198
		8	1943-44	6676/H093200-498
		9	1943-44	6676/H093499-874
		10	1943-44	6676/H093875-4196
		11	1943-44	6676/H094197-481
	Depots bei Gesandtschaft Helsinki		1943-44	6676/H094482-589
	Verfügungen des Auswärtigen Amtes (Verschiedenes) Tagebücher 1 2 3 4 5		1941-43	6676/H094590-890

Akten-zeichen	Inhalt	Band	Datum	Serial Nr.
	Konsulatsgebührengesetz		10.3.1936	
	Schnetzer Privata		1943	6677/H094892-96
	Schnapp Privata		1943	6677/H094897-912
	Goldbeck Privata		1943	6677/H094913-5221
	Berichte vom VAA beim AHQ über sowjet-russisches Heer		10.1941	6677/H095222-315
	Varia der Gesandtschaft Helsinki		8.1943	6677/H095316-403

Akten-zeichen	Inhalt	Band	Datum	Serial Nr.
VIII/36	Kulturelle Angelegenheiten Sport	1	1928-36	4745/E233293-322
		2	1936	4745/E233323-25
		3	1934-38	4745/E233326-44
VIIIa/35	Vorträge, Musik, Theater	1	1935	4755/E233689-98
VIIIa/36		2	1936-37	4755/E233699-724
VIIIa/37		3	1936-37	4755/E233725-31
VIIIa/37		4	1937	4755/E233732-39
VIIIa/38		5	1938	4755/E233740-96
VIIIa		6	1938-39	4755/E233797-829
XV/1928	Oelsner & Co.		1928-39	
	Deutsche Kolonie, deutsche Kirchen, Schulen, Vereine		1926-31	
			1931-32	
			1933	
			1934	
			1935	
			1936	
			1937	
			1938	
XVI	Rotes Kreuz, Kinderaustausch		1929-35	
	Kinderfürsorge, Liebesgabensendungen, Sammlungen		1937	
XVII	Verschiedenes		1928-31	
			1931	
			1932	
			1933	
			1934	
			1935	
			1936	
			1937	

Akten-zeichen	Inhalt	Band	Datum	Serial Nr.
XVII	Verschiedenes		1938	
	Plakate und Prospekte		1932	
	Fachschulen, Prospekte		1932	
r.588 Ia/21	Zusammenlegung des Generalkonsulates und der Gesandtschaft		1920–21	4754/E233679–86
Ia/1929	Dienstbetrieb	1	1929	
Ia/1930		2	1930	
		3	1931–33	
		4	1934	4753/E233675–76
		5	1934	
		6	1935	
		7	1936	
		8	1937	
		9	1938	4752/E233658–72
		10	1939	
Ib	Diplomaten	1	1924–27	
		2	1926–38	4751/E233644–55
Ib/37			1931–36	
			1934–38	
Ib/38			1935–38	
	Generalia	1	1925–34	4750/E233614–22
		2	1935–39	4750/E233623–41
IV/1933	Schiffahrt und Fischerei	1	1929–34	4749/E233529–76
IV/1934		2	1933–35	4749/E233578–611
IV/1935		3	1933–35	
IV/1936		4	1935–36	
IV/1937		5	1937	
IV/1938		6	1936–38	
V	Eisenbahn, Post, Telegrafie, Zollwesen	1	1929–32	4761/E234203–09
		2	1934	
		3	1936–37	4761/E234210–11
		4	1938	

Akten-zeichen	Inhalt	Band	Datum	Serial Nr.
VI	Luftverkehr, Kraftfahrzeuge	1	1932-35	4762/E234214-19
VI/37		2	1936-37	4762/E234220-29
VI/38		3	1938	4762/E234230-37
IX/33/35	Passangelegenheiten		1926-35	
IX/36			1936	
IX/37			1936-37	
X/30/32	Internationale Abkommen und Institute, Ausstellungen, Konferenzen	1	1930-32	
X/33/34		2	1933-34	4763/E234240-51
X/35		3	1935	
X/36		4	1936	4763/E234252-55
X/37		5	1937	4763/E234256-62
X/1-285/ 38		6	1938	
X/286/38		7	1938	4763/E234263-67
Ic/28	Kanzlei		1928-38	
Id	Pressebeirat Dietrich		1927-37	4771/E234512-76
Id/37	Hauswart, Reinigung der Büroräume		1921-38	
Ie/20-22	Berufskonsulate, Konsulatsabteilung		1919-25	
Ie/38	Berufskonsulat Apenrade		1921-38	4770/E234489-509
If/37	Konsulat Reykjavik		1925-38	
If	Wahlkonsulate, Verschiedenes, Bewerbungen für nicht errichtete Wahlkonsulate und Konsularagenturen. Allgemeine Vorgänge		1922-39	4772/E234579-90
If/28	Wahlkonsulate A - Z		1923-38	
II	Rechtshilfe, Auslieferungen, Heimschaffungen, Fürsorge, Auslandsdeutschtum, Kirchen, Schulen, Religion	1	1927-39	4773/E234593-96
		2	1930-32	4773/E234597-611
		3	1933-35	
		4	1936-37	
	Rechtssachen		1938	4764/E234270-87
III	Handel, Industrie, Landwirtschaft	1	1929-32	4765/E234290-98
		2	1933-35	
		3	1936-37	
		4	1938	
	Veterinärpolizeiliche Angelegenheiten		1927-30	

Akten-zeichen	Inhalt	Band	Datum	Serial Nr.
XII	Nichtpolitische Militär- und Marineangelegenheiten		1929-38	
VIII	Kulturelle Angelegenheiten		1930-38	
XIII	Vermittlungen von Sendungen		1933-35	
XI	Ordenssachen, Ernennungen		1930-38	
Nr.214 P 21	Journalist Ernst Harthern		1919-22	4766/E234301-402
P/8/263	Presse, Telegramme und Presseberichterstattung		1939	4767/E234405-19
P/6/267	Presse		1939-40	
P 250-299			1939	4768/E234422-55
D Pol 3/318 3/330	Reichsparteitag		1939	4769/E234458-86
303	Drucklegung des deutschen Weissbuches in dänischer Sprache		1939	4774/E234614-15
2/303	Der Ausbruch des Krieges und Haltung der dänischen Regierung gegenüber Polen			4775/E234618-65
3/357	Konterbande (Prisenordnung)		1939	2695/D529755-863
	Wirtschaftspolitische Front der Neutralen gegen England		1939	4776/E234668-88
	Zeitungsartikel		1939	
3/323	Deutsche Flaggen, Generelles		1933-38	4777/E234691-96
D.R.350-399	Rechtswesen		1939	
27.0/32	Dänischer Kapitän Lembourn	1	1928-33	4788/E235404-663
		2	1932-33	4788/E235664-75
	Nordschleswig		1923-24	
	Verschiedene Zeitungsausschnitte		1929-30	
	Politische Wochenberichte		1925-30	
	Rechtsanwalt Heinrich A.Möller	1-2	1900-28	
	Wichtige Akten allgemein politischen Inhalts		1917-20	4792/E235849-6181
	Zusammenstellung der politischen Verträge Europas, der Verträge und Vereinbarungen Dänemarks seit Abschluss des Weltkrieges		1935-36	
	Politische Übersicht		1935-36	
95 X 36	Politische Verträge Europas seit Abschluss des Weltkrieges		1927-37	
34 B 35	Pensionen in Nordschleswig		1925-37	
57 A/32	Fremde Diplomaten	1	1926-34	
399 E/34	Das Ostseeproblem		1924-34	4814/E238898-9115

Akten-zeichen	Inhalt	Band	Datum	Serial Nr.
209/25.IV	Dänische Lotsenordnung		1920-26	4815/E239118-52
305/IV.26	Aufbringung und Beschiessung deutscher Fischdampfer in isländischen Gewässern	1-4	1926-29	
6.IV.30		5	1929-30	
9.IV.31		6	1930-32	
8.IV.31		6a	1930-32	
1.IV.35		7	1932-36	
13 C.1/29	Schleswig-holsteinischer Universitätstag Dr.Schifferer, Professor Scheel	1	1927-28	4779/E234725-934
	Zeitungsausschnitte zur Sache, Schleswig-Holsteinischer Universitätstag		1927-29	
107 C.1/31	Deutsch-nordische Woche in Kiel		1928-31	4780/E234936-98
48 C.1/26	Deutsch-dänischer Schiedsvertrag	1	1922-25	4781/E235001-29
172 C.1/37		1	1926-37	4781/E235030-64
196 C.1/35	Dänische Schiedsverträge mit fremden Staaten		1928-37	
85 C.1/30	Die deutsch-dänische Passfrage		1925-31	4782/E235066-161
9 M/32	Die dänische Grenzwehr und militärische Mitteilungen betreffend Nordschleswig		1925-32	4783/E235164-254
70 M/26	Gestellung und Einziehung Deutscher zur dänischen Wehrpflicht		1920-26	4784/E235257-65
26 M/35	Grundsätzliche Bestimmungen für den Besuch dänischer Häfen durch deutsche Kriegsfahrzeuge		1912-32	
27 M/35	Anlaufen von Bornholm und Christiania, Durchfahrt bei Samso durch deutsche Kriegsfahrzeuge, jährliche Anmeldung der Dienstsegelboote		1932-38	4785/E235268-74
5 M/35	Die dänische Abrüstungsfrage, dänisches Heer und Flotte		1929-36	4889/E253426-54
25 M/35	Fischereischutzdienst		1921-38	
272 B/38	Fischerei in der Flensburger Föhrde		1920-38	4786/E235276-355
	Professor Aage Fries		1922-34	4891/E253510-660
18 B/30	Das Kreditinstitut Vogelgesang		1927-30	2697/D530036-291
135 B/32	Kranken- und Angestelltenversicherung, Invaliditäts- und Altersversicherung Nordschleswig	1	1922-30	4892/E253663-71
2 B/33	Kranken- und Altersversicherung Invaliden- und Altersversicherung, Kriegsverletzte und Hinterbliebene		1931-33	4892/E253672-748
2 B/35			1933-36	4892/E253749-836

Akten-zeichen	Inhalt	Band	Datum	Serial Nr.
29 B/27	Pastor Schmidt-Wodder und Cornelius Petersens Bendestyre Bergung		1926-27	2698/D530294-302 4843/E245470-96
2 B/32	Ausstückung in Nordschleswig		1926-32	4844/E245499-576
43 B/29	Die deutschen Zeitungen in Nord-schleswig, deutsche Einheits-zeitung		1926-29	2748/D534531-615
78 B/26	Kraftlastwagenverkehr an der deutsch-dänischen Grenze in Nordschleswig		1922-26	
66 B/26	Der Durchgangsverkehr nach Sylt		1922-26	
202 V/34	Verbindung Kopenhagen-Berlin		1928-32	
99 IV/31	Kiel Korsar		1925-31	
43/VIII/37	Internationale Meeresforschung		1922-37	
/ P 1925	Presse		1925	
P 1929			1929	4901/E255003-55
P 1930			1930	4901/E255056-85
P 1931			1931-32	4902/E255088-134
P 1932			1932	4902/E255135-40
P 1933			1933	4903/E255143-93
P 1934		1	1934	4898/E254848-56
		2	1934-35	4898/E254857-68
P 1935			1935	4898/E254869-83
P 1936	- Propaganda	1	1936	4917/E255938-99
P 1937	- Nr. 1 - 252	2	1937	4917/E256000-31
	- Nr. 253	3	1937	4917/E256032-164
P 1938	- Nr. 1 - 180	4	1938	4917/E256165-301
	- Nr. 183	5	1938	4917/E256302-22
P 39	-	6	1939	4917/E256323-34
W.1929/31	Arbeiterbewegung, Sozialpolitik		1929-31	
W.1932			1932	
W.1933			1933	4916/E255874-88
W.1934			1934	4916/E255889-915
W.1935			1935	4916/E255916-35
W.1936	- - Kommunisten, Emigranten		1936	4918/E256337-75
W. /37			1937	4918/E256376-461
W. /38	- Nr. 1 - 293		1938	4918/E256462-98
	- Nr. 294		1938	4918/E256499-537
W. /39	-		1939	4918/E256538-71

Akten-zeichen	Inhalt	Band	Datum	Serial Nr.
6 B/36	Minderheiten und Schulfragen S.N.Sch. /504	5	1934-39	2699/D530305-518
	- 500-549		1939	8276/E588229-33 2700/D530521-636 4845/E245579-618
	- Spezialakten 550		1939	4915/E255869-71
L.1929	Völkerbund		1926-29	4941/E273084-103
L.1930			1930	2941/E273104-21
L.1931			1931	
L.1932			1932	4941/E273122-39
L.1933			1933	4941/E273140-46
L.1935			1935	4941/E273147-83
L.1936			1936	4941/E273184-91 4941/E273192-207
L.1937/ 38			1937	4941/E273208-48
M	Militär- und Marinesachen		1920-25	4942/E273251-319
	Heer und Marine		1930	4943/E273322-40
M.1931			1930-31	4943/E273341-45
M.1932			1932	
M.1933			1933	4943/E273346-61
M.1934			1934	4943/E273362-75
M.1935			1935	4943/E273376-436
M.1936			1936	4943/E273437-80 5951/E437775-901
M.1937			1937	4943/E273481-522
M.1938	Militär und Marine Nr. 1 - 242		1938	4943/E273523-68
M/38	- Nr. 24		1938	4943/E273569-80
0/38	Politische Agenten, vertrauliche Auskünfte über Personen		1920-38	2701/D530638-751
	Wirtschaftspolitisches		1932-34	
Kult 12/ 223 43P 49 P/33 29 P/34	Dänisches Filmwesen generell			
D.Kult spez.420			1939	
D.Kult 1 - 400			1939	
Kult 200- 249			1939	5010/E286548-84
D.Kult 400-449			1939	

Akten-zeichen	Inhalt	Band	Datum	Serial Nr.
R.150–199			1939	
D.Pol.300 –311	Politische Angelegenheiten		1939	8284/E588303–11 5019/E286868–960
312–349			1939	5019/E286961– 7021
450–499	Presseangelegenheiten		1939	5019/E287022–24
100–149	Politische Angelegenheiten		1939	5019/E287025–109
	Simmermann		1934–35	
Pers.	Pers. Si und Bibl		1939	
	Namen		1939	
	Protokollangelegenheiten		1939	5018/E286850–65
	Pers. A–P–G–R		1939	
A.1933	Deutsche Politik		1933	5020/E287112–16
A.1935			1935	5020/E287117–22
A/36			1936	5020/E287123–63
A/37			1937	5020/E287164–70
A/38			1938	5020/E287171–99
B/35	Nordschleswig B. 1 – 200	1	1935	4833/E243356–411
	201 – 390	2	1935	4833/E243412–506
B/36		3	1936	4833/E243507–643
B/37	1 – 160	4	1937	4833/E243644–758
	182	5	1937	4833/E243759–891
B/38	1 – 126		1938	4833/E243892– 4008 2702/D530753– 1048
	127		1938	4833/E244009–217 2703/D531050–157
D	Skandinavien		1920–28	4991/E281471–606
			1929–30	4991/E281607–16
			1931–33	4991/E281617–35
			1933–36	4991/E281634–76 6020/E444402–45
D/37			1937	7550/E541826–41 4991/E281677–94 6020/E444446–99
D/38			1938	7028/E522475–84 4991/E281695–715
D/39			1939	4991/E281716–18

Akten-zeichen	Inhalt	Band	Datum	Serial Nr.
C.1/27	Dänische Politik Deutsch-dänische Beziehungen		1937	7551/E541843-47 4996/E282663-765
C.1/38			1938	4996/E282766-838
E.	England		1929-33	4997/E282841-47
			1934-38	4997/E282848-51 5840/E425556-62
E.39			1939	4997/E282852-57
F 34-36	Frankreich		1934-36	4997/E282858-67
F/1937-38	Frankreich, Belgien, Niederlande, Spanien, Portugal, Italien, Schweiz, Luxemburg		1937-38	4997/E282868-82
F/39	Frankreich		1939	
H	Österreich, Ungarn, Türkei, Balkanstaaten		1932-37	
H/38			1938	
J	Afrika, Amerika, Asien		1932-38	
L.34/Saar	Saar		1934	
A	Deutsche Politik		1920-24	4999/E282990-3037
A/1931			1931	
A/1932			1932	
A/1934			1934	
	Nordschleswig	1	1920	4838/E244630-728
		2	1920	4838/E244729-831
		3	1920	4838/E244832-969
B/1920/22	Deutsch-dänische Verhandlungen		1920-22	2704/D531160-91 4823/E239615-739
	Tischler Verhandlungsprotokolle		1921	4842/E245151-467
B.1/2/1920	Nordschleswig Nr.400 - Schluss (670 B 2)		1920	4867/E249892-50000
B.1921	— Nr. 1 - 50		1921	4867/E250001-159
	— Nr. 51 - 200		1921	4867/E250160-491
	— 201 - 461		1921	4867/E250492-858
B.1922	— 1 - 100		1922	4868/E250861-985
	— 100 - 335		1922	4868/E250986-1159
B.1923	— 1 - 214		1923	4868/E251160-282
B.1924	— 1 - 300		1924	4868/E251283-586
B.1925/27			1925-27	4869/E251589-2065
B.1928			1928	4869/E252066-219

Akten-zeichen	Inhalt	Band	Datum	Serial Nr.
B/1929	Nordschleswig		1929	4869/E252220-349
B/1930			1930	4869/E252350-503
B/1931			1931	4871/E252651-96
B/1932			1932	4871/E252697-917
B/1933			1933	4871/E252918-3039
B/1934	- 1 - 350		1934	4870/E252506-623
	- 351 - 486		1934	4870/E252624-48
	Anlage zu 328 B 1935 Erl.W spec. 807 vom 18.10.1935 Karte über Bodenverteilung in den nordschleswigschen Grenz-zonen			
C. 1	Dänische Politik		1920-21	5000/E283041-122
	- Vertrag zwischen Deutschland und Dänemark		1922	5000/E283123-281
	- Deutsch-dänische Beziehungen		1925-27	5007/E286002-176
			1928-29	5007/E286177-252
			1930	5007/E286253-71
			1931	5007/E286272-305
			1932	5007/E286306-43
			1933-34	5007/E286344-70
			1935-36	5007/E286371-421
C. 2	Dänische Gesetzgebung		1920-27	
	Dänische Politik, deutsch-dänische Gesetzgebung		1928-38	
C. 3	Dänische Politik Island		1920	
	Dänische Nebenländer Grönland, Island, Färöer		1923-30	
			1931-33	5008/E286424-47
			1934-37	5008/E286448-50
			1938	5008/E286451-82
			1939	
G. 1	Russland		1930-39	
G. 2	Randstaaten		1929-32	
			1933	5009/E286485-511
			1934	5009/E286512-20
			1935-36	5009/E286521-34
			1937	5009/E286535-41
			1938	5009/E286542-45

Akten-zeichen	Inhalt	Band	Datum	Serial Nr.
G. 2	Randstaaten Memel		1939	
G. 3			1939	
H. 38			1936	
J.	Übersee		1929-33	
37.I.f.	Konsulat Reykjavik		1939	
47.XI.	Ehrenzeichen des deutschen Roten Kreuzes		1938-39	
46.XI.	Verdienstorden vom deutschen Adler		1937-39	5012/E286670-84
II	Verschiedenes. Legate, Dienstreisen		1938-39	
III			1939	
IV			1939	
V			1939	
VI			1939	
VII			1939	
VIII			1939	
VIII a			1939	5014/E286752-70
IX			1939	
X			1939	
XI			1939	
XII			1938-39	
XV			1939	
XVII			1939	
I b			1939	
I d			1937-38	
I c	Kraftwagenführer Olsen		1933-37	
I e	Apenrade		1939	
10 b C.3	Julius Schepka		1939	
C. 1	Verschiedenes		1939	5015/E286773-805
C. 2	Dänisches Pressegesetz 114		1939	
J. 39	Afrika, Amerika, Asien		1939	5016/E286806-12
L. 39	Verschiedenes		1939	
35.S/39			1939	
A/39			1939	5017/E286815-47
B/39			1939	5011/E286587-667
216 A	Protektorat Böhmen und Mähren		1939	
8/A Nap.	Nichtangriffspakt mit den Nord-staaten		1939	

Akten-zeichen	Inhalt	Band	Datum	Serial Nr.
R/39	Pontoppidan Affaire, Vorgänge siehe 176 R/39			4944/E273583-608
DD	Anlagen zu 215 X/39			
	– zu Erlass 83-21 17/2 Ang.II vom 14.3.39 37 P/39			
	– zu 201 B/39			
	– zu Ber.vom 30.10.39 siehe Verschiedenes 554		1939	
	– zu Prot.A.1609/39 V 63 vom 23.2.39 – 45 XVII/39			
	– zu Bibl./57 Erl 16.10.39 R.24466/39 Ang.II		1939	
	Musiklehrer Modis der St.Petri-Schule	1	1929-34	4953/E274800-71
	Studienrat Heidrich, Deutsche Petri-Schule	2	1934	4953/E274872-94
	Dekorierung von Mitarbeitern des dänischen Roten Kreuzes	6	1918-25	
	Politische Register		1920-35	
33 L/32	Dr.Heerfordt		12.25- 2.32	
	Besuche von dänischen Häfen durch deutsche Flotteneinheiten		1939	
	Schriftwechsel zwischen Gesandt-schaft und Firmen, insbesondere mit Waldemar Oelsner & Co., Kopenhagen		1933-39	
	Besatzungskosten			
	Nr. 151 - 300		1944	
	Nr. 601 - 800		1944	
	Nr. 801 - 919		1944	2504/D519198-202
	Winterschule für Nordschleswig		8.37- 4.38	2505/D519205-07
	Politisches Journal I und II		1936-39	
	Nichtpolitisches Register I u.II		1914-39	

Akten- zeichen	Inhalt	Band	Datum	Serial Nr.
Pers.A 1	Das Auswärtige Amt Organisation, Geschäftsübersich- ten		12.37-10.40	
Pers.A 2 Nr.1a	Die deutschen Auslandsvertretun- gen, Allgemeines, Berichterstat- tung, Schriftwechsel		2.38- 2.41	
Nr.1b	Die deutschen Auslandsvertretun- gen, Schriftwechsel (Schliessung der deutschen Gesandtschaft Kowno)		7.40- 3.41	
Nr.2	Geschäftsverkehr mit der Reichs- stelle für den Aussenhandel		5.33- 1.40	
Nr.3	Allgemeine Angelegenheiten der Beamten und Angestellten des Auswärtigen Dienstes		1938-40	
Nr.4	Veränderungsanzeigen		1.38- 8.40	
Pers.P 1	Allgemeines			
Pers.G 1	Aktenplan der Gesandtschaft		5.37- 3.41	
Pers.G 2	Dienstbetrieb, Anordnungen des Behördenleiters, Organisation, wichtige Beschwerden, Geschäfts- verteilungsplan		4.33- 7.40	
Pers.G 3	Grundlegende und periodisch in Umlauf zu setzende Erlasse		4.38- 1.39	
Pers.G 4 Nr. 1a	Dienstgebäude der Gesandtschaft		3.37- 1.39	
Nr. 1b	Gesandtschaft Schriftwechsel		1.39-12.40	
Nr. 1c	Diensträume, Militärattaché		3.40- 7.40	
Nr. 2	Gesandtenwohnhaus (Villa)		4.38- 2.41	
Nr. 3a	Dienstwohnungen, Dienstwohnungs- vorschriften, Allgemeines		7.37-12.38	
Nr. 3b	Dienstwohnungen, Diensträume (Schriftwechsel)		3.38- 1.41	
Nr. 4a	Fernsprecher		3.37-11.39	
Nr. 4b	Fernsprecher (Schriftwechsel)		6.36- 1.41	
Nr. 5a	Dienstkraftwagen, Allgemeines		3.30- 2.35	
Nr. 5b			3.38- 3.41	
Nr. 6	Versicherung Dienstkraftwagen		9.35- 3.41	
Nr. 7	Bezug und Verbrauch von Benzin	1	6.37- 8.40	
		2	9.40- 1.41	
Pers. G 5 Nr. 1	Inventar, allgemeines Inventar- verzeichnis A. und B.		2.38	
Nr. 2	Ausstattungsgegenstände und Geräte in Diensträumen und Dienstwohnungen, Beschaffung von Inventar		6.37-10.40	

Akten-zeichen	Inhalt	Band	Datum	Serial Nr.
Pers.G 5 Nr. 3	Büromaterialien		1937-41	
Pers.G 8 Nr. 1	Generalkonsulat Memel	1	1.37- 3.39	
Nr. 1a	– Wilna		5.40- 9.40	
Nr. 4	Anträge an die litauische Valuta-kommission Verschiedenes		2.40- 8.40	
Pers.R 1a	Haushaltswesen, Voranschläge, Bedarfsnachweise, Allgemeines		1.36- 8.40	
Pers.R 1b	Haushaltswesen, Voranschläge, Schriftwechsel		12.37-10.40	
Pers.R 2d	Verzeichnisse von abgesandten Wertdepeschen nebst Empfangsbe-stätigungen (Quittungen)		2.40- 3.41	
Pers.R 2b	Kassen- und Rechnungswesen, Schriftwechsel	1	2.38- 3.41	
		2	10.40- 3.41	
Pers.R 2c	Einzahlungen Dritter	1	1.38-11.40	
		2	11.40- 3.41	
Pers.R 2d	Versendung von Wertsachen		2.41- 3.41	
Pers.R 7b	Gebührenlisten, Schriftwechsel		1.38- 2.41	
Pers.R 8a	Besoldung und Abgaben der Beam-ten und Angestellten des Auswär-tigen Dienstes		1927-40	
Pers.R 9a	Umzugskosten, Reisekosten Allgemeines		1.34- 1.41	
Pers.R 9b	– Schriftwechsel		1.38- 2.41	
	Verzeichnis der erteilten Eisen-bahnstundungsbescheinigungen		11.40- 3.41	
Pers.R 10a	Steuern, Angestellten- und Inva-lidenversicherung, Allgemeines		8.23- 1.41	
Pers.R 10b	– Schriftwechsel		2.38- 2.41	
Pers.R 11a	Devisenangelegenheiten des Auswärtigen Amtes und dessen Vertretungen, Allgemeines, Bestimmungen		7.34- 4.37	
Pers.R 11b	– Schriftwechsel		12.37-11.39	
Pers.R 14	Heimschaffungen		9.40	
Pers.R 16	Litauische Kommerzbank		1.35- 1.41	
Pers.R 17a	Abrechnung mit Militär- und Marineattaché, Allgemeines		11.38- 1.39	
Pers.G 17b	– Schriftwechsel		9.38- 8.40	
Pers.R 18	Portoangelegenheiten		3.38-12.40	

Akten-zeichen	Inhalt	Band	Datum	Serial Nr.
Pers.Si 1	Sicherung der Gebäude gegen Anschläge, Einbruch, Feuer		3.38-10.39	
Pers.Si 2	Mob-Fragen		4.37- 1.41	
Pers.Si 3	Telegramm, Erlass- und Bericht-kontrolle		12.37- 2.41	
Pers.Si 4	Aktenvernichtung		1.40	
Pers.Si 5 b	Chriffrierdienst, Schrift-wechsel		1.41- 2.41	
	Nachrichtenwesen, Fernschreiber (Schriftwechsel)		3.39- 2.41	
Pers.Si 6a	Kurierangelegenheiten,Depeschen-listen, Allgemeines	1	3.22- 2.41	
Pers.Si 6 b		2	10.40- 2.41	
Bibl. 1	Bibliothek, Schriftwechsel		12.38- 1.41	
Prot. 1	Allgemeines (Einführung beim Staatsoberhaupt in Litauen, Zeremonielles, Empfänge)		6.38- 2.40	
Prot.1 Nr. 1	Litauische Staatsmänner		1.20- 3.20	
Prot.2 Nr. 1	Diplomatisches und Konsulari-sches Korps in Kowno und Memel		1.30-11.40	
	Schriftverkehr mit der russi-schen Gesandtschaft, Kowno	2	9.40	
Nr. 2	Ausländische diplomatische und konsularische Vertretungen im Ausland		12.37- 2.41	
Nr. 3			9.33- 9.40	
Nr. 4	- in Deutschland		7.38- 8.40	
Prot.3 Nr. 1	Verleihung von Orden und Ehren-zeichen durch den Führer und Reichskanzler		1.38- 3.41	
Nr. 2	Verleihung von Orden und Ehren-zeichen durch die litauische Regierung und durch Regierungen anderer Staaten		2.38-12.40	
Prot.6	Uniformfrage in Litauen		7.39- 8.39	
Pol.1 Nr. 1	Litauische Aussenpolitik (aussenpolitische Reden, Kurs, Orientierung)		10.38- 6.40	
Nr. 2	Litauische allgemeine Politik, Regierungserklärungen	1	1.38-12.40	
		2	6.40-11.40	
Nr. 3	Jahresberichte über Litauen		1.38- 3.40	
Pol.2 Nr. 1	Politische Beziehungen Litauens zu Deutschland		3.38- 9.40	3645/E032854-65
Nr. 2	Deutscher Militär-, Marine- und Luftattaché in Litauen		11.37-10.39	

Akten-zeichen	Inhalt	Band	Datum	Serial Nr.
Pol 2 Nr. 3	Politische Beziehungen Litauen- Lettland		1.38- 2.40	
Nr. 4	- Polen		4.39-12.40	8439/E594070-103
	- Polen (pol- nisch-litauischer Zwischenfall)		1.38- 3.39	
Nr. 5	- UdSSR	1	1.38- 5.40	
		2	5.40- 8.40	
Nr. 6	- Frankreich		3.38- 2.39	
Nr. 7	- Italien		1.38- 7.40	
Nr. 8	- Tschechoslowa- kei		2.39- 6.39	
Nr. 9	- U. S. A.		2.38- 7.40	
Nr. 10	- Estland		2.39- 6.39	
Nr. 11	- Spanien		3.39	
Nr. 12	- England		7.39- 4.40	
Nr. 13	- Finnland		11.39- 3.40	
Nr. 16	Litauische Mobilmachung gegen Polen. Polnische Internierte in Litauen		9.39- 3.41	
Nr. 20	Baltische Entente-Länder		2.38- 7.40	
Nr. 21	Baltische Aussenministerkonfe- renzen		12.37- 3.40	
Nr. 22	Lettland	1	12.37- 6.40	
		2	6.40-12.40	
Nr. 23	Estland	1	1.38- 5.40	
		2	11.39- 6.40	
Nr. 24	Finnland	2	1.40- 8.40	
Nr. 29	UdSSR	2	7.40- 9.40	
Pol. 3 Nr. 1a	Litauen. Ministerien, Minister- kabinett, Regierungsbildung		6.40- 9.40	
Nr. 1b	Memelstatut		3.38-11.38	
Nr. 1c	Memelgebiet. Gouverneur		4.38- 1.39	
Nr. 1d	- Vetierung von Ge- setzen durch den Gouverneur		3.38- 8.38	
Nr. 1e	- Direktorium		12.38- 1.39	
Nr. 3a	Grosslitauen. Militär-, Marine- und Luftfahrtangelegenheiten		5.38-10.40	
Nr. 3b	Memelgebiet Militär-Marine und Luftfahrtangelegenheiten		4.38-11.38	
Nr. 4b	- Staatsschutz		12.38- 3.39	

Akten-zeichen	Inhalt	Band	Datum	Serial Nr.
Pol. 3 Nr. 4c	Verhaftungen und Prozesse deut-scher Reichsangehöriger und Volksdeutscher wegen Spionage und staatsgefährlicher Betäti-gung gegen Litauen		3.38- 1.41	
Nr. 4e	Neumann-Sass-Prozess		1.38- 3.39	
Nr. 4g	Beamtenspionageprozess		1.38	
Nr. 4h	Prozess gegen Wilhelm Starost-Vydunas		3.38- 2.40	
Nr. 5b	Hoheitszeichen, Flaggen, Feier-tage im Memelgebiet		5.38- 2.39	
Nr. 6c	Landtagswahlen im Memelgebiet		3.38- 3.39	
Nr. 6d			1.38- 2.39	
Nr. 7a	Parteiwesen, Politische Verbände in Grosslitauen		10.37- 6.40	
Nr. 7b	- Politische Verbände im Memelgebiet		5.38- 3.39	
Nr. 8a	Innere Angelegenheiten in Gross-litauen	1	12.38- 6.40	
	Innere Angelegenheiten in Sowjetlitauen		10.40- 2.41	
Nr. 8b	Allgemeine politische Lage im Memelgebiet	1	10.37-12.38	
			1.39- 3.39	
Nr. 8c	Bodenenteignungen in Memel und im Kreise Memel durch Gesetz der litauischen Regierung	1	9.37-11.37	
		2	11.37- 1.39	
	Bodenreform, Landenteignung in Litauen	3	1939-40	
Nr. 8d	Litauischer Kauf von Grundstük-ken im Memelgebiet		8.38- 4.40	
Nr. 9b	Memelgebiet. Judenfragen	1	12.38	
Nr. 10	Polentum in Wilna		11.39- 3.41	
Nr. 11	Weissrussische Bestrebungen in Wilna		12.39- 3.40	
Pol. 4 Nr. 1	Völkerbund		2.38- 6.40	
Nr. 2	Bolschewismus, Kommunismus		5.30-10.39	
Nr. 5	Judenfrage, Minderheiten in Europa		8.38- 6.39	
Nr. 3	Freimaurer		8.40- 9.40	
W.1 Nr.1	Wirtschaftspolitik, Wirtschafts-lage, Moratorien, Zahlungsver-bote in Grosslitauen	1	1.38- 4.40	
		2	6.40- 1.41	

Akten-zeichen	Inhalt	Band	Datum	Serial Nr.
W 1 Nr.2	Memelgebiet, Wirtschaftspolitik	1	11.38-12.38	
	Litauen - Lettland		1.39- 2.39	
Nr.3	Allgemeine Wirtschaftsberichte		3.38- 1.40	
W 2 Nr.3	Wirtschaftliche Beziehungen			
	Litauen - Finnland		8.38	
Nr.4	- Polen		3.38- 2.40	
Nr.5	- UdSSR		1.38- 2.40	
Nr.6	- England		9.39- 5.40	
Nr.7	- Spanien		1.38- 2.38	
Nr.8	- Ungarn		1.38	
Nr.9	- Amerika		12.38- 3.39	
Nr.10	- Schweiz		3.38- 9.38	
Nr.11	- Türkei		7.39	
Nr.12	- Schweden		1.40- 8.40	
Nr.13	- Dänemark		6.40	
Nr.16	Handelskrieg. (Prisenordnung, Banngut, schwarze Firmenlisten) allgemein		9.39- 5.40	
Nr.19	Finnland		8.39- 3.40	
Nr.20	Baltische Entente		2.38- 5.40	
Nr.21	Lettland		12.37- 7.40	
Nr.22	Estland		1.38- 3.39	
Nr.23	Polen		2.38- 1.40	
Nr.24	UdSSR		2.38- 3.39	
Nr.25	Dänemark		7.39-12.39	
Nr.26	Schweden		1.40- 8.40	
Nr.27	U.S.A.		11.38- 4.40	
Nr.28	Norwegen		3.40- 4.40	
Nr.29	England		4.40- 5.40	
W 3	Internationale Wirtschaft Weltwirtschaft·		7.38- 8.38	
W.A.1 Nr.1	Ausstellungen, allgemein in Grosslitauen		1.40- 2.40	
Nr.2	Ausstellungen allgemein, Beziehungen zu Deutschland		5.40- 7.40	
W.E.1 Nr.1	Eisenbahnen-Grosslitauen		11.38- 1.40	
Nr.2	Eisenbahnen allgemein, im Memelgebiet		4.38-11.38	

Akten-zeichen	Inhalt	Band	Datum	Serial Nr.
W.E.2 Nr. 1	Eisenbahnen. Beziehungen Litauen zu Deutschland (Konferenzen, Grenzfragen)		6.39- 8.40	
Nr. 2	Eisenbahnbeziehungen Litauens zu anderen und zwischen anderen Ländern (Konferenzen, Mitropa, Wagons Lits)		2.39- 3.40	
W.F.1 Nr. 1	Staatsfinanzen allgemein Staatshaushalt, Anleihen, Wert-papiere in Grosslitauen, Staats-bank		1.38- 3.40	
Nr. 2	Finanzen allgemein, Haushalt, Anleihen, Wertpapiere im Memel-gebiet		4.38- 3.39	
W.F.2 Nr. 1	Finanzielle Beziehungen Litauens zu Deutschland		7.39- 3.41	
Nr. 2	Finanzielle Beziehungen Litauens zu anderen und zwi-schen anderen Ländern		4.39- 6.39	
W.F.3	Devisengesetzgebung in Litauen		4.38- 8.40	
W.F.4 Nr. 1	Banken, Sparkassen, Kredit-institute in Grosslitauen		2.38-12.40	
Nr. 2	im Memelgebiet		12.37- 2.39	
Nr. 4	Deutsche Genossenschaftsbank in Kowno		2.38- 2.41	
W.Fs.2	Deutsch-litauisches Fischerei-abkommen		10.37- 8.38	
W.H.1 Nr. 2	Handel allgemein, allgemeine Berichte im Memelgebiet		9.38-10.38	
W.H.2 Nr. 1a	Beziehungen Litauens zu Deutsch-land. Handelsvertragsverhältnis, deutsch-litauische Abkommen über den gegenseitigen Warenver-kehr		6.39- 6.40	
	Beziehungen Litauens zu Deutsch-land (Protektorat Böhmen und Mähren) Handelsvertragsverhält-nis.	1	8.39- 9.40	
		3	6.40- 2.41	
Nr. 1b	Devisenbescheinigungen für die Ausfuhr von Litauen nach Deutschland		1.38- 6.39	
Nr. 2a	Beziehungen Litauens zu Deutschland. Ein-, Aus- und Durchfuhr, allgemeines litaui-sches Vertretergesetz		2.38- 2.41	
Nr. 2b	Ein-, Aus- und Durchfuhr Memel-gebiet	1	2.39	
Nr. 4	Beziehungen zu Deutschland Angebote, Nachfragen, Preisbil-dung, Absatzmöglichkeiten		9.39- 1.40	

Akten-zeichen	Inhalt	Band	Datum	Serial Nr.
W.H.3	Beziehungen Litauens zu anderen Ländern, Verträge		10.39-12.40	
W.H.4 Nr. 1	Innenhandel in Grosslitauen Absatz, Ausschreibungen		9.38- 3.39	
Nr. 2	Inländische Marktberichte (Dr.Lee)		1.38- 8.40	
Nr. 2b	- (Jehnke)		3.40- 9.40	
Nr. 3	Innenhandel im Memelgebiet		1.38-11.38	
W.H.5	Aussenhandel Litauens		2.38- 8.40	
W.H.6	Halbstaatliche Organisationen des Aussenhandels in Litauen		6.40	
W.H.7	Handelskammer, auch ausländische Handelskammern in Litauen		1.38- 8.39	
W.J.1 Nr. 1	Industrie, Technik, Gewerbe, Allgemeines in Grosslitauen		5.38-10.38	
W.J.2 Nr. 1	Industrie, Technik, Gewerbe, Beziehungen Litauens zu Deutschland		7.40- 1.41	
Nr. 2	Industrie, Technik, Gewerbe, Beziehungen Litauens zu und zwischen anderen Ländern		3.39- 6.39	
W.J.5	Gewerbe und Handwerk in Litauen (auch Schutz des gewerblichen Eigentums, Markenschutz, Musterschutz)		7.39- 8.39	
W.Kr.1	Kraftfahrwesen in Litauen		10.37- 1.41	
W.L.1 Nr. 1	Landwirtschaft allgemein in Grosslitauen		3.38- 3.39	
Nr. 2	- im Memelgebiet		12.37- 2.39	
W.L.2 Nr. 1a	Landwirtschaftliche Beziehungen Litauens zu Deutschland		11.39- 5.40	
Nr. 1b	Deutsch-Litauischer Forst- und Holzwirtschaftlicher Ausschuss		2.38- 3.41	
W.L.4	Landwirtschaftliche Genossenschaft in Litauen		1.38- 2.39	
W.L.5	Viehzucht in Litauen		5.38- 8.38	
W.L.6	Forstwirtschaft in Litauen		9.37-10.40	
W.L.7	Tierschutz in Litauen		1.39	
W.Lu.1	Litauen Luftfahrt (zivile)		2.39- 3.39	
W.Lu.2 Nr. 1a	Luftfahrt (zivile) Beziehungen Litauens zu Deutschland Luftverkehrsabkommen		3.37- 3.40	
Nr. 1b	Überflug- und Landungsgenehmigungen deutscher Flugzeuge über litauischem Gebiet		4.38- 9.40	

Akten-zeichen	Inhalt	Band	Datum	Serial Nr.
W.Lu.2 Nr. 1c	Grenzverletzungen durch deutsche und litauische Flugzeuge			
W.P.1 Nr. 1	Post, Telegraf, Fernsprecher (Kabel) Radio allgemein in Grosslitauen		5.38- 5.40	
Nr. 2	- - im Memelgebiet		3.38- 2.39	
W.P.2 Nr. 1	Post, Telegraf, Fernsprecher, (Kabel) Radio, Beziehungen Litauens zu Deutschland (auch deutsche Postämter in Litauen)		2.38- 3.40	
W.Sch.1 Nr. 1	Seeschiffahrt allgemein in Litauen, allgemeine Berichte		5.39- 8.40	
W.Sch.2 Nr. 1	Seeschiffahrt, Beziehungen Litauens zu Deutschland		7.39- 7.40	
	Binnenschiffahrt, Beziehungen Litauens zu Deutschland, Verträge		5.38- 2.41	
W.Sch.3 Nr. 1	Seeschiffahrt Litauens, Beziehungen zu und zwischen anderen Ländern, Verträge		1.38-12.40	
Nr. 2	Binnenschiffahrt		2.39- 3.39	
W.Sch.4 Nr. 1a	Seeschiffahrt, Hafenangelegen-heiten, Schiffbau in Litauen		12.37-10.39	
Nr. 1b	Memeler Freihafen		6.39- 8.40	
	Memeler Hafen		7.38- 2.39	
W.St.1 Nr. 1	Steuern, Monopole, allgemein in Grosslitauen		1.38	
Nr. 2	Memelgebiet, Steuern		1.39- 2.39	
W.St.2 Nr. 1	Steuern, Monopole, Beziehungen Litauens zu Deutschland		2.39- 6.40	
W.V.1 Nr. 1	Verkehr, Grenzangelegenheiten allgemein in Grosslitauen		5.40- 8.40	
Nr. 2	- - im Memelgebiet		5.38- 1.39	
W.V.2 Nr. 1a	Verkehr, Beziehungen Litauens zu Deutschland		3.39- 1.40	
Nr. 1b	Deutsch-litauischer kleiner Grenzverkehr		8.36-10.40	
Nr. 1c	Grenzzwischenfälle (Verletzungen) auf deutscher und litauischer Seite, Übergriffe		7.38- 7.40	
Nr. 1d	Regulierung des deutsch-litaui-schen Grenzflusses Schwirwindt		11.37- 5.40	
Nr. 2	Verkehr, Beziehungen Litauens zu und zwischen anderen Staaten		3.39- 4.39	
W.V.3 Nr. 1	Reiseverkehr, Verkehrswerbung, Reisebüros, Reiseberichte in Grosslitauen		3.39- 4.40	
Nr. 2	- - im Memelgebiet		1.38- 8.39	

Akten-zeichen	Inhalt	Band	Datum	Serial Nr.
W.V.4 Nr. 2	Verkehr, Strassenwesen, Strassen-bau im Memelgebiet		7.38- 2.39	
W.V.5	Wasserwesen, Wasserbau in Litauen		4.38- 2.39	
W.Z.1 Nr. 1	Tarife, Zollorganisationen (Zollämter, Grossbahnhöfe) in Grosslitauen		1.38-11.40	
W.Z.2 Nr. 1	Zollwesen, Beziehungen Litauens zu Deutschland (auch Beschwerden allgemein)		5.39- 8.39	
R.1 Nr.1	Rechtswesen allgemein, Grosslitauen		2.39- 11.40	
R.2 Nr.1a	Rechtliche Beziehungen Deutschland - Litauen		9.38-11.40	
R.2 Nr.1b	Deutsch-litauischer Konsular-vertrag		8.38- 9.39	
R.2 Nr.1c	Deutsch-litauisches Abkommen über Urheberrecht (Schutz des gewerblichen Eigentums)		2.37-12.38	
R.2 Nr.1d	Deutsch-litauisches Schiedsge-richt über Staatsangehörigkeits-fragen		3.38- 8.39	
R.2 Nr.1e	Deutsche Kriegsgräberfürsorge in Litauen. Allgemeine Bestimmun-gen		10.36- 8.38	
	- Schriftwechsel		1.38- 1.41	
R.2 Nr.2	Rechtliche Beziehungen Litauens zu anderen Staaten und zwischen fremden Staaten		3.39	
R.3 Nr.1a	Staatsrecht, Zivil- und Straf-recht, Gerichtswesen, auch Ver-fassung, Verwaltung in Gross-litauen		1.38-12.39	
R.3 Nr.1b	Memelgebiet. Staats-, Zivil- und Strafrecht, Gerichtswesen, Ver-waltung		12.38- 2.39	
R.3 Nr.2	Staatsangehörigkeitsfragen in Litauen		11.37- 2.41	
R.3 Nr.3a	Zivilrecht, auch Bodenreform, Pfandrecht, Grundeigentum, Nachlassrecht, Justizverwaltung in Grosslitauen		3.38- 7.40	
R.3 Nr.3b	- Beziehungen zu Deutschland		3.38- 7.40	
R.3 Nr.4	Familienrecht, Ehe- und Personen-standsangelegenheiten in Litauen		12.37- 8.40	
R.3 Nr.6a	Strafrecht, Rechtshilfe in Straf-sachen, Auslieferung, Strafvoll-zug, Gefangenenaustausch in Grosslitauen		2.38-11.40	
R.3 Nr.6b	- im Memelgebiet		1.38- 2.39	

Akten-zeichen	Inhalt	Band	Datum	Serial Nr.
R.4 Nr.1	Lohnfragen, Streiks und Aussper-rungen, Arbeitsmarkt und Arbeits-losigkeit in Grosslitauen		2.38- 9.40	
R.4 Nr.2	– im Memelgebiet		6.38- 3.39	
R.5 Nr.1	Aufenthaltsbestimmungen, Grenz-empfehlungen, Pässe und Sicht-vermerke in Grosslitauen		12.37-12.40	
R.5 Nr.2	Sonstige Polizeisachen in Gross-litauen		10.39	
R.5 Nr.3	Memelgebiet, Aufenthalt, Pässe, Sichtvermerke		4.37- 2.39	
R.5 Nr.4	Sonstige Polizeisachen im Memel-gebiet		1.38- 2.39	
R.6 Nr.1a	Sozialpolitik und Gesetzgebung in Grosslitauen		11.39- 8.40	
R.6 Nr.1b	– im Memelgebiet		8.38	
R.6 Nr.2a	Sozialversicherung in Gross-litauen		10.38-12.39	
R.6 Nr.2b	Memelgebiet, Versicherungswesen Sozialversicherung		4.38- 3.39	
R.6 Nr.4b	Übernahme und soziale Fürsorge im Memelgebiet. Pensionen		11.37-11.40	
R.6 Nr.6	Soziale Frauenarbeit		2.40- 2.41	
Kult 1 Nr. 1	Allgemeine Kulturpolitik in Grosslitauen		10.37- 4.38	
Nr. 2	– im Memelgebiet		9.37- 2.39	
Nr. 3	Kulturelle Betätigung Litauens in Wilna		12.39- 4.40	
Kult 2 Nr. 1a	Kulturpolitische Beziehungen Litauens zu Deutschland, Verträ-ge, Litauische Minderheiten in Deutschland		10.38- 6.40	
Nr. 1b	Kulturpolitische Beziehungen Litauens zu Deutschland, Propaganda, allgemein		12.39-10.40	
Nr. 2	Kulturpolitische Beziehungen Litauens zu anderen Ländern und zwischen anderen Staaten, Welt-verband der Auslandslitauer, ausländische Kulturpropaganda		1.38- 5.40	
Nr. 3	Ukrainer in Litauen			
Kult 3 Nr. 1	Reichsdeutsche Kolonie in Kowno		5.28- 3.41	
Nr. 2a	Deutsche Volksgruppen und ihre Organisationen (Kulturverband)	1	2.38- 6.40	
			7.40- 2.41	
Nr. 2b	Umsiedlung der deutschen Volksgruppen aus Litauen		10.39- 8.40	

Akten-zeichen	Inhalt	Band	Datum	Serial Nr.
Kult 3 Nr. 2c	Deutsche Vorumsiedler aus Litauen		9.40- 1.41	
Nr. 2d	Vermögenswerte Tillmanns		12.39- 1.41	
Nr. 2e	Beschaffung des Lebensmittel-bedarfs für die deutsche Volks-gruppe		12.40	
Nr. 2f	Wohnungs- und Inventarbeschlag-nahme durch die russischen Behörden		1940	
Nr. 3	Zustellung von Briefen und Paketen an den Kulturverband	1	1.38- 6.39	
		2	6.39- 1.41	
Nr. 4	Volksdeutsches Büchereiwesen		5.38-12.40	
Nr. 6	Memelländischer Kulturverband		8.38-10.39	
Nr. 7	Deutsche Minderheiten im Aus-land (Auslandsdeutschtum,VDA, Auslandsinstitut Stuttgart) Saisonarbeiter		5.37- 8.39	
Nr. 8	Bund Deutscher Osten, Berlin		11.37- 3.39	
Nr. 9	Institut für Osteuropäische Wirtschaft		11.37- 4.38	
Kult 4 Nr. 1	Kirchenpolitik, Glaubensbewegun-gen, Sekten und Religionsgesell-schaften, Verhältnis zum Heiligen Stuhl, Kirchenkongresse und Tagungen in Grosslitauen		2.38-11.40	
Nr. 2	- im Memelgebiet		12.37- 3.38	
Nr. 3	Deutsche Kirche in Litauen		1.38- 1.41	
Kult 5 Nr. 2	Ein-, Aus- und Rückwanderung im Memelgebiet		1.38- 7.38	
Kult 8 Nr. 1	Schulwesen in Grosslitauen allgemein		6.38- 4.40	
Nr. 2	- im Memelgebiet		1.38- 9.39	
Nr. 3	Deutsches Schulwesen in Litauen allgemein		2.38- 2.41	
Nr. 4	Anforderungen an den Kultur- und Schulfonds	1	11.37- 2.41	
		2	2.40- 2.41	
Nr. 5	Deutsches Gymnasium in Kowno		1.38- 3.41	
Nr. 6	Litauisches Schulwesen in Deutschland		7.39-10.39	
Kult 9 Nr. 1	Deutsche Sprachwerbung in Litauen		2.39- 9.40	
Kult 10 Nr. 1	Hochschulwesen in Grosslitauen		7.38- 4.40	
Nr. 2	- Beziehungen zu Deutschland		5.40- 6.40	

Akten-zeichen	Inhalt	Band	Datum	Serial Nr.
Kult 10 Nr. 3	Deutsche Dozenten an der Universität in Kowno (Professor Jungfer) Lektoren		12.37- 3.41	
Nr. 4	Volksdeutsche Studentenverbindung in Kowno		12.37- 4.38	
Nr. 5	Stipendien		3.38- 1.40	
Kult 10 Nr. 6	Litauische Studenten in Deutschland. Stipendien		2.40- 8.40	
Kult 11 Nr. 4	Wissenschaftliche Institute und Vereinigungen (auch Drucksachenaustausch) in Litauen		4.39-12.40	
Nr. 5	Gesundheitswesen und Sanitätsabkommen in Litauen		1.39- 5.39	
Nr. 6	Deutsche Krankenhäuser und deutsches medizinisches Personal (auch Apotheker) Epidemien in Litauen		10.40- 2.41	
Nr. 7	Veterinärwesen, Abkommen mit Deutschland, Viehseuchen (Maul- und Klauenseuche) Quarantäne Konferenzen in Litauen		9.37-12.39	
Nr. 8a	Buchwerbung und Buchausstellungen in Grosslitauen, Literatur		1.38-12.40	
Nr. 8b	- im Memelgebiet		3.38- 2.39	
Nr. 9	Archäologie in Litauen		9.39-10.39	
Kult 12 Nr. 1	Kunst in Litauen		10.39- 6.40	
Nr. 2a	Theaterwesen in Grosslitauen		10.39- 4.40	
Nr. 2b	- im Memelgebiet		2.38- 2.39	
Nr. 3	Musikwesen		12.38- 5.40 12.40	
Nr. 4a	Filmwesen in Grosslitauen		10.37- 3.41	
Nr. 4b	- im Memelgebiet		2.39	
Nr. 5a	Sportwesen in Litauen, deutsch-litauische Sportbeziehungen, deutsche Ruderriege		4.38- 2.41	
Nr. 5b	- im Memelgebiet		5.38- 2.39	
Kult 13	Internationale kulturelle Angelegenheiten		1.38- 7.40	
P.1.Nr.1	Presse und Propagandawesen in Grosslitauen		5.38-10.39	
P.1.Nr.2	- im Memelgebiet		12.38- 1.39	
P.1.Nr.3	Übersichten über die litauische Presse (Einsendung von Belegexemplaren)		7.39- 9.40	
	Presseberichte, Rundfunknachricht		8.39- 9.39	

Akten- zeichen	Inhalt	Band	Datum	Serial Nr.
P.1.Nr.4	Laufend telefonische Berichter- stattung. Akten über die litau- ische Presse		4.40- 7.40	
P.2.Nr.1	Presse und Propagandawesen Beziehungen zu Deutschland, Ab- kommen Presseattachés allgemein		5.39- 8.40	
P.2.Nr.2	Presse und Propagandabeziehungen zu anderen Staaten und zwischen anderen Staaten, Abkommen, Presseattachés		2.39- 6.40	
P.2.Nr.3	Vom Auswärtigen Amt übersandtes Pressematerial (Presserundtele- gramme, Presseaufzeichnungen) zur Unterbringung in der litau- ischen Presse oder Sprachrege- lung		7.39-10.39	
			10.39- 6.40	
P.2.Nr.4	Auswertung von Pressematerial der Informationsabteilung im Auswärtigen Amt, Presse, Bulle- tins	1	10.39-12.39	
		2	12.39- 1.40	
	An die litauische Presse zur Veröffentlichung versandte Presseberichte (Pressebulletins)			
P.2.Nr.5	Deutsche Bildpropaganda in Litauen		9.39- 7.40	
P.2.Nr.5a	Sammlung von deutschen Bildsen- dungen		12.39- 1.40	
P.3.Nr.1a	Nachrichtenbüros, Telegrafen- agenturen "Elta" Tageszeitungen in Grosslitauen		5.39- 6.40	
P.3.Nr.1b	— im Memelgebiet		3.38- 2.39	
P.3.Nr.2a	Deutsche Zeitungen und Zeit- schriften in Grosslitauen		12.37- 3.40	
P.3.Nr.2b	Deutschland-Litauen "Deutsche Nachrichten"		1.38- 2.41	
P.3.Nr.3	Polnische Minderheitenpresse		11.39- 6.40	
P.3.Nr.3a	Polnische Presseübersichten		2.40- 8.40	
P.4.Nr.1a	Pressevertreter, Redakteure, Berichterstatter und ihre Orga- nisation in Grosslitauen		6.39- 1.40	
P.4.Nr.2a	Vertreter deutscher Zeitungen in Grosslitauen		9.39- 8.40	
P.4.Nr.2b	Litauische Pressevertretung in Deutschland		5.38- 8.40	
P.5.Nr.1a	Zeitungsaustausch		4.39- 1.40	
P.5.Nr.2	Verbreitung von deutschen Druck- schriften in Litauen	1	6.39- 4.40	
		2	4.40- 2.41	

Akten-zeichen	Inhalt	Band	Datum	Serial Nr.
P.5.Nr.2a	Sammlung der in Litauen verbrei-teten deutschen Druckschriften		10.39- 2.40	
P.6.Nr.1a	Greuel- und Hetzpresse, Greuel-propaganda		2.38- 7.40	
P.6.Nr.1b	Hetzfilme		12.37- 3.40	
P.6.Nr.2	Deutsche Beanstandungen über litauische Presse, Bücher		2.38- 4.40	
P.6.Nr.3	Litauische Beanstandungen über deutsche Presse, Bücher		1.38- 8.40	
P.6.Nr.4	Jüdische Presseübersichten (Dr.Leo)		8.39- 4.40	
D.Pol.1 Nr. 1	Deutsche Aussenpolitik	1	1.39- 5.40	
Nr. 2	Deutsche allgemeine Politik		2.38-10.39	
D.Pol.2 Nr. 1	Politische Beziehungen Deutschland - Lettland		2.38- 7.40	
Nr. 2	- Estland		5.38- 8.40	
Nr. 3	- Finnland		6.38- 8.40	
Nr. 4	- Polen		1.38- 7.39	
Nr. 5	- UdSSR		12.37-11.40	
Nr. 16b	Deutsche Warngebiete während der Kriegsdauer		9.39- 1.41	
Nr. 18	Politische Beziehungen Deutschland - Slowakei		6.40	
Nr. 19	- Norwegen		9.39- 5.40	
Nr. 20	- Balkanstaaten		1.40- 2.40	
Nr. 21	- Japan		10.39-11.39	
Nr. 22	- U.S.A.		9.39- 2.41	
Nr. 23	- Südamerika		9.39-11.39	
Nr. 24	- Mittelamerika		10.39-11.39	
Nr. 25	- Türkei		11.39- 1.40	
Nr. 26	- Skandinavien		3.40- 4.40	
Nr. 27	Kriegsführung gegen die West-mächte		5.40- 6.40	
Nr. 28	Politische Beziehungen Deutschland - Schweiz		4.40	
D.Pol.3 Nr. 1	Führer und Reichskanzler		3.39- 2.40	
Nr. 2	Die Reichsregierung, Reichstag, Reichstagswahlen		3.36-12.38	
Nr. 3	Ministerien		4.39- 5.39	

Akten- zeichen	Inhalt	Band	Datum	Serial Nr.
D.Pol. 3 Nr. 5	NSDAP, Gliederungen und ange- schlossene Verbände		12.35- 4.40	
Nr. 5b	- Schriftwechsel		9.39- 8.40	
Nr. 6	Deutschland, Reichsparteitage in Nürnberg		9.37- 8.39	
Nr. 8b	Wehrpflicht	1	7.39-11.40	
		2	6.35- 6.39	
Nr. 8c	Wehrstammrolle, Anmeldeblätter		9.39- 3.41	
Nr. 8d	Arbeitsdienstpflicht		1.38- 2.41	
Nr. 9	Staatsschutzbestimmungen (auch Antikomintern)		6.37- 6.39	
Nr. 10	Hoheitszeichen, Flaggen, Feiertage		6.39- 8.40	
Nr. 11	Freimaurertum, Judenfrage		7.37-12.40	
Nr. 12	Kolonialfragen		10.37-10.39	
Nr. 14	Generalgouvernement Polen		1.40- 5.40	
D.W.2	Wirtschaftliche Beziehungen Deutschlands zu anderen Staaten als Litauen		3.38- 9.40	
D.W.3	Wirtschaftliche Beziehungen zwischen Deutschland und Sowjet- russland		8.39- 5.40	
D.W.A.	Ausstellung in Deutschland		3.39- 8.40	
D.W.E.	Deutsche Eisenbahnen		3.39- 3.40	
D.W.F.1	Deutsche Finanzen allgemein		4.38- 7.40	
D.W.F.2	Deutsche Devisengesetzgebung		2.38-12.40	
D.W.F.3	Deutsche Devisenerlasse (Druck)	1	1.38- 8.39	
		2	3.40- 7.40	
D.W.F.4	Deutsche Registermarkbestimmun- gen		2.38- 3.41	
D.W.H.2	Deutscher Aussenhandel		3.38- 8.39	
D.W.H.3	Deutsche Ausfuhr allgemein (Vertreter im Ausland)		7.36-10.39	
D.W.H.4	Deutsche Ein- und Ausfuhrbestim- mungen		11.37- 2.41	
D.W.H.5	Deutsche Ein- und Ausfuhr von Kriegsgerät		8.37- 1.39	
D.W.H.6	Binnenhandel in Deutschland, Marktverhältnisse		6.38- 39	
D.W.H.7	Wirtschaftsorganisationen in Deutschland		4.38-12.40	
D.W.J.	Deutsche Industrie, Technik, deutsches Gewerbe		1.39	

Akten-zeichen	Inhalt	Band	Datum	Serial Nr.
D.W.Kr.	Deutsches Kraftfahrwesen		3.39- 4.40	
D.W.L.	Deutsche Landwirtschaft		1.39	
D.W.Lu.	Deutsche Luftfahrt (zivile)		3.38- 5.40	
D.W.P.	Deutsche Post, Telegrafen, Fernsprecher, Radio, Kabel		10.38-10.40	
D.W.R.	Deutsche Rohstoffe und Waren		1.38-10.39	
D.W.Sch.1	Deutsche Schiffahrt		5.38- 7.40	
D.W.Sch.2	Deutsches Seemannsrecht		12.37- 5.38	
D.W.St.	Deutsche Steuern, Monopole		8.38	
D.R.1	Rechtswesen in Deutschland allgemein		5.38- 5.40	
D.R.2	Rechtliche Beziehungen Deutsch-lands zu anderen Ländern als Litauen		2.39- 2.40	
D.R.3 Nr. 2a	Staatsangehörigkeitsfragen		7.38-12.40	
Nr. 2b	Ausbürgerungen		1.38- 6.39	
			5.39-11.39	
Nr. 3	Bürgerliches Recht, auch Boden-reform, Pfandrecht, Grundeigen-tum, Nachlassrecht, Beglaubi-gungen		4.38-11.39	
Nr. 4	Familienrecht, Ehe- und Per-sonenstandsangelegenheiten		9.38- 7.40	
Nr. 6	Strafrecht, Rechtshilfe in Strafsachen, Auslieferung, Strafvollzug, Gefangenenaus-tausch, Kriminalität		9.38- 9.40	
D.R.4 Nr. 1	Lohnfragen, Arbeitsmarkt, Beschäftigung ausländischer Wanderarbeiter		7.38- 5.40	
Nr. 2	Deutsches Gewerberecht		1.39- 2.39	
D.R.5 Nr. 1	Aufenthaltsbestimmungen		10.30-11.39	
Nr. 2	Passangelegenheiten		10.37- 7.40	
Nr. 21	Passvordrucke (Nummernkontrolle)		12.39- 2.41	
Nr. 3a	Sichtvermerksangelegenheiten Allgemeine Bestimmungen		3.34- 2.41	
Nr. 3b			1.40-11.40	
Nr. 4	Grenzempfehlungen		3.36- 2.41	
Nr. 5	Autopassierscheine		4.38- 2.41	
Nr. 6	Meldepflicht der Reichsdeut-schen im Ausland		4.38- 1.40	
Nr. 7	Polizeisachen, geheime Staats-polizei, Grenzpolizei		2.34-12.39	

Akten-zeichen	Inhalt	Band	Datum	Serial Nr.
D.R.6 Nr. 1	Sozialpolitik und Gesetzgebung Sozialversicherung		2.38- 2.41	
Nr. 2	Übernahme und soziale Fürsorge, Unterstützungen, Pensionen, Winterhilfswerk		2.38- 1.41	
D.Kult 1 Nr. 2	Deutsche Kulturwerbung im Ausland		4.39- 7.40	
D.Kult 2	Kulturpolitische Beziehungen Deutschlands zu anderen Staaten als Litauen		6.39-11.39	
D.Kult 4	Kirchenwesen in Deutschland		10.37- 6.40	
D.Kult 5	Ein-, Aus- und Rückwanderung Abwanderung		4.38- 3.40	
D.Kult 6	Nachforschungen im Inland		2.40- 5.40	
D.Kult 7 Nr. 1	Hitlerjugend		2.39-10.40	
D.Kult 8 Nr. 1	Allgemeine Versorgung der Auslandsschulen mit Büchern, Zeitschriften und Lehrmitteln		3.38- 3.40	
Nr. 3	Deutscher Lehrer- und Schüleraustausch		1.38	
Nr. 4	Reichssportführer und Reichsakademie für Leibesübung		3.38- 3.40	
D.Kult 10 Nr. 1	Hochschulwesen		2.38- 1.40	
Nr. 2	Stipendien für Studium und Weiterbildung von Ausländern in Deutschland, Ferienkurse		5.39- 5.40	
Nr. 3	Studentenreisen, Tagungen und Lager		6.39- 8.39	
D.Kult 11 Nr. 1	Allgemeine Archive, Bibliotheken, Literatur		11.37-12.39	
Nr. 2	Gesundheitswesen, Veterinärwesen		3.38-12.40	
Nr. 3	Forschungsreisen und Expeditionen sowie Reisen von deutschen Professoren ins Ausland		1.39-12.40	
Nr. 4	Wissenschaftliche Institute und Vereinigungen, Preussisches geheimes Staatsarchiv (Publikationsstelle)		1.38- 5.39	
D.Kult 12 Nr. 1	Kunst		6.39- 7.39	
Nr. 2	Theaterwesen		1.38- 7.38	
Nr. 3	Musikwesen		4.38- 4.40	
Nr. 4	Filmwesen		3.39- 3.40	

Akten-zeichen	Inhalt	Band	Datum	Serial Nr.
D.P.1	Presse und Propagandawesen in Deutschland, allgemein		8.37- 7.40	
D.P.2	Beziehungen Deutschlands zu anderen Staaten als Litauen		10.39-10.40	
D.P.3	Nachrichtenbüro, Verlagsanstalten, Telegrafenagenturen, Zeitungen		7.39- 9.39	
D.P.4	Telegramme		9.39	
D.P.5	Militärische Massnahmen gegen Polen und Rückwirkungen auf die internationale Lage		9.39	
S.1	Geheim, Memelpolitik		10.36- 2.39	
S.2	Wirtschaftspolitik, Memelgebiet Geheim		10.37- 6.38	
S.3 Pol	Geheime politische Angelegenheiten. Verschiedenes		12.36-11.40	
S.3 W	Geheime wirtschaftliche Angelegenheiten (Verschiedenes)		1.37-12.40	
S.3 Kult	Geheime kulturelle Angelegenheiten (Verschiedenes)		5.37- 9.40	
S.5	Gesetz über die Wiedervereinigung Oesterreichs mit dem Deutschen Reich vom 13.März 38 Überleitung und technische Abwicklung		3.38-10.39	
S.6	Rückgliederung der sudetendeutschen Gebiete an das Deutsche Reich, Abkommen von München		9.39- 5.39	
S.7	Angliederung Böhmen-Mähren an Grossdeutschland	2	8.39- 7.40	
S.8	Rückgliederung des Memellandes an das Deutsche Reich		3.39- 5.39	
			6.39-10.39	
S.9	Einkreisungspolitik England, Frankreich, Russland, USA, gegen die Achse		3.39- 5.39	
S.14	Telegramme, Militärattaché (Berichterstattung an Oberkommando)		8.39- 8.40	
S.3	Litauen-Russland Verschiedenes Strengst geheim		6.40- 9.40	
S.3 Pol.	Geheime politische Angelegenheiten, Verschiedenes		6.35- 6.36	
S.3 Pers.	Personalien, Geschäftsgang Haushalts-, Protokollsachen. Litauische Bank		2.40-11.40	
S.3 R.	Geheime rechtliche Angelegenheiten. Verschiedenes		4.37-10.40	
S.3 P.	Geheime Presseangelegenheiten Verschiedenes		6.38- 6.40	

Akten-zeichen	Inhalt	Band	Datum	Serial Nr.
S.4	Kartei - Einzelfälle, geheim		11.36- 1.41	
			8.40- 2.41	
B.1 Ges.a	Gesandtschaft, Geschäftsgang I Vorschriften		1.35-12.37	
B.1 Ges.b	Geschäftsgang II, allgemein		1.35-12.37	
B.1 Ges.c	Kurierangelegenheiten und Postangelegenheiten		1.35-12.37	
B.1 Ges.d	Zeremonien, Etikette		1.35-12.37	
B.1 Ges.e	Diplomatisches und konsularisches Korps in Kowno		1.35-12.37	
B.1 Ges.f	Zoll-, Gebühren- und Steuerfreiheit für Gesandtschaftsgut, ausser Kraftwagen für Generalkonsulat Memel		1.35-12.37	
B.1 Ges.g	Privatkraftwagen der Beamten, Zoll- und Gebührenfreiheit		1.35-12.37	
B.1 Ges.h	Personalangelegenheiten allgemein, Urlaubsplan		1.35-12.37	
B.1 Ges.m	Inventar, allgemein		1.35-12.37	
B.1 Ges.n	Dienstgebäude		1.35-12.37	
B.1 Ges.o	Gesandtenvilla		1.35-12.37	
B.1 Ges.p	Dienstauto	1	1.30-12.35	
		2	1.36-12.37	
B.1 Ges.p	Dienstfahrrad, Dienstrundfunk		1.35-12.37	
B.1 Ges.qu	Brennmaterial		1.35-12.37	
B.1 Ges.r	Büromaterialbestellungen		1.35-12.37	
B.1 Ges.s	Zeitungsbestellungen	1	1.35-12.36	
			1.37-12.37	
B.1 Ges.t	Bibliothek		1.35-12.37	
B.1 Ges.u	Drucksachen m.Angel. Brockhaus-Lexikon 1932-1933			
B.1 Ges.v	Orden-Deutschland		1.35-12.37	
B.1 Ges.v Li	Orden-Litauen		1.35-12.37	
B.1 Ka.a	Kassensachen I (Vorschriften)		1.31-12.33	
B.1 Ka.b	Kassensachen II, allgemein		1.23-12.37	
B.1 Ka.c	Zahlstelle der Legationskasse		4.33-12.37	
B.1 Ka.d	Bedarfsanmeldungen		10.33- 6.34	
B.1 Ka.cl	Überweisungen, Einzahlungen		11.35-12.37	
B.1 Ka.e	Devisenanforderungen		10.37-12.37	
B.1 Ka.g	Kassenrevisionen		3.21-12.37	

Akten- zeichen	Inhalt	Band	Datum	Serial Nr.
B.1 Ka.h	Amtliche Abrechnungen		1.35-12.35	
			7.34-12.34	
			1.35- 6.35	
			7.36-12.36	
			1.37- 6.37	
			7.37-12.37	
B.1 Ka.k	Kassensachen, Gebührenkonto des Auswärtigen Amtes		1.35-12.37	
B.1 Ka l	Gehälter der Beamten und Ange-stellten		3.27- 6.38	
B.1 Ka.m	Gehalts- und Zahlungslisten		1.35-12.37	
B.1 Ka.n	Landesversicherung		1935-1937	
B.1 Ka.o	Reichsversicherung für Ange-stellte		1.24-12.37	
B.1 Ka.p	Litauische Einkommensteuer		1.35-12.37	
B.1 Ka.q u	Litauische Wohnungssteuer		5.28-12.37	
B.1 Ka.r	Wohnungs- und Möbelmieten der Beamten und Angestellten Heizmaterial und Wassergeld		1.35-12.37	
B.1 Ka.u	Dienstreisen		1.35-12.37	
B.1 Ka.v	Dienstreisen nach Eydtkuhnen		1.35-12.37	
B.1 Ke.w	Kriegsgräberfürsorge		1.35-12.37	
B.1 Ka.a	Kassensachen		1940	
B.2.b.	Rechtswesen allgemein Gerichtswesen Litauen		1.35-12.37	
B.2.c.	Rechtsstellung der Ausländer in Litauen: Gesetze, Bestimmungen		1.35-12.37	
B.2.d.	Aufenthalts- und Arbeitsangele-genheiten für Reichsdeutsche in Litauen. Sammelintervention der Gesandtschaft		1935-1936	
B.2.c.	Aufenthalts- und Arbeitsangele-genheiten für Litauer in Deutschland		1935-1937	
B.2.f.	Rechtshilfe: Zeugenvernehmungen Zustellungen		1935-1937	
B.2.g.	Rechtsauskünfte		1.35-12.37	
B.2.h.	Rechtsschutz (Urheberrecht, Patentwesen, Warenzeichen- und Musterschutz)		1.35-12.37	
B.2.i.	Fahndungs-, Haft- und Strafsa-chen.		1935-1937	
B.2.k.	Nachlasssachen		1935-1937	

Akten-zeichen	Inhalt	Band	Datum	Serial Nr.
B.2.m.1	Übernahmesachen		1935-37	
B.2.m.	Beurkundungen, allgemein		1935-37	
B.2.o.	Grenz- und andere Zwischenfälle		1935-37	
B.2.qu.	Entschädigungsansprüche		1935-37	
B.2.r.	Konsulats- und Rechtssachen Notarielle Urkunden		1935-37	
B.2.s.	- Kriegsgräberfür-sorge		1935-37-43	
B.3.a.	Staatsangehörigkeit I Gesetzliche Bestimmungen		1935-37	
B.3.d.	Staatsangehörigkeit, Ausbür-gerungen		1935-37	
B.4.b.	Finanz- und Bankwesen Deutschland Devisen		1935-37	
B.4.a.	Finanz- und Bankwesen Litauen allgemein, spezielle Auskünfte in Valutaangelegenheiten	1	10.35-12.36	
			1.37-12.37	
B.4.c.	Finanz- und Bankwesen Deutschlands Registermark		1935-37	
B.4.a.	Finanz- und Bankwesen Litauen allgemeine Staatsfinanzen, Budget, Gesetzgebung		1.35-12.36	
			1.37-12.37	
B.4.b.	- Staatsbank, Anlei-hen, Zinsendienst		1935-37	
B.4.c.	- Privatbanken		1936-37	
B.4.d.	- Steuern		1929-37	
B.5.a.	Verkehrswesen, Post, Telegr. Funkwesen		1935-37	
B.5.b.	Eisenbahn		1935-37	
B.5.c.	Kraftfahrt, Strassenbau		1935-37	
B.5.d.	Schiffahrt	1	1.35- 9.36	
		2	10.36-12.37	
B.5.e.	Luftfahrt und Flugwesen Deutschland		1935-37	
	- Litauen		1935-37	
	- Baltikum		1935-37	
B.5.f.	Reisewesen, Fremdenverkehr		1935-37	
B.6.a.	Landwirtschaft Litauen. Gesetz-gebung und Kreditwesen		1935-37	
B.6.b.	Litauen. Landwirtschaft allgemein Ackerbau		1935-37	

Akten-zeichen	Inhalt	Band	Datum	Serial Nr.
B.6.d.	Landwirtschaft, Viehzucht, Viehmarkt und Ausfuhr, Schlacht-industrie "Maistas"		1935-37	
B.6.e.	Litauen. Landwirtschaftliche Genossenschaften "Pinocentras" "Lietukis"		1935-37	
B.6.f.	Litauen. Landwirtschaftl. Veteri-närwesen und Schädlingsbe-kämpfung. Berichte über Tier-seuchen		1935-37	
B.7.b.	Soziale Angelegenheiten, soziale Fürsorge, Allgemeines, Winterhilfe		1924-37	
B.7.c.	- Sammlung St.Organia		1935-37	
B.7.e.	- Arbeiterlohnfragen		1935-37	
B.7.f.	- Arbeitsdienst		1935-37	
B.7.g.	- Aus-, Ein- und Rückwanderung Beratung von Rückwanderern		1935-37	
B.7.h.	- Gesundheitliche Verhältnisse Ärzte, Krankenhaus- Apothekerwe-sen. Berichte über Epidemien.		1935-37	
115.g.	Liste Vermögensbeschlagnahme			
	Vorumsiedler (Doppel)		1940-41	
	Umsiedlung Litauen K-Liste und U-Liste			
W.H.2.	Deutschland Aussenhandelsrege-lung, Liste der Einfuhr- und Ausfuhrverbote und Beschränkun-gen.		1935-37	
W.H.2a.	Deutschland. Aussenhandelsrege-lung. Regelung der Einfuhr von Milchprodukten		1.35- 5.35	
W.H.3.	Deutsch-litauischer Grenzverkehr (auch Kleiner Grenzverkehr)		1935-37	
W.H.4.	Zollsachen allgemein (auch Schmuggel)		1935-37	
W.H.4a.	Zollsachen, Einzelfälle		1935-37	
W.H.5a.	Deutschland, Aussenhandel Kohlenstatistik		1935-36	
W.H.6	- Reichsstelle für den Aussen- handel		1.35- 6.36	
			7.36-12.36	
			1.37- 6.37	
			7.37-12.37	
Wi.1.	Wirtschaft Litauen, allgemein		1933-37	
Wi.3.	- Wirtschafts- und Handelsgesetz-gebung und Recht		1935-37	

Akten-zeichen	Inhalt	Band	Datum	Serial Nr.
Wi.4.	Wirtschaft Litauen, Industrie einschliesslich Gewerbe, Handwerk, allgemein. Einzelne Industrien		1935-37	
Ia.1.	Litauen, Aussenhandel		1935-37	
Ia.2.	Litauischer Zolltarif		1935-37	
Ia.3.	Litauen. Aussenhandelsregelung Ausfuhr, Durchfuhr- und Einfuhrbestimmungen		1935-37	
Ia.3a.	- Einfuhrlizenzen allgemein		1935-37	
Ia.3b.	- Einzelfälle alphabetisch		1935-37	
Ia.3c.	- Kompensations- und Verrechnungsgeschäfte		1935-37	
Ia.4.	Wirtschaft Litauen. Ausschreibungen litauischer Behörden		1935-37	
Ia.6.	Heeresgerät		5.36- 4.37	
2.	Memel. Politik	13	10.26- 2.27	
3.		14	3.27- 6.27	
4.		15	6.27- 8.27	
5.		16	8.27-10.27	
6.		17	11.27- 4.28	
7.		18	1.28- 4.28	
99.		19	4.28- 6.28	
100.		20	6.28-10.28	
101.		21	11.28- 2.29	
102.		22	3.29- 4.29	
103.		23	5.29- 6.29	
104.		24	5.29- 6.29	
105.		25	7.29- 8.29	
106.		26	9.29-10.29	
107.		27	10.29-11.29	
108.		28	12.29	
109.		29	1.30- 2.30	
110.		30	3.30- 4.30	
111.		31	5.30	
112.		32	6.30	
113.		33	7.30	
114.		34	8.30	
115.		35	9.30	

Akten-zeichen	Inhalt	Band	Datum	Serial Nr.
116.	Memel. Politik	36	10.30	
117.		37	11.30	
118.		38	12.30	
119.		39	1.31- 2.31	
120.		40	3.31	
121.		41	4.31- 5.31	
122.		42	6.31- 7.31	
123.		43	8.31- 9.31	
124.		44	10.31-12.31	
125.		45	1.32- 5.32	
126.		46	6.32- 9.32	
127.		47	9.32- 1.33	
128.		48	2.33-11.33	
129.		49	12.33- 3.34	
130.P.81		50	4.34- 5.34	
131.P.81		51	6.34- 7.34	
132.P.81		52	8.34- 9.34	
133.P.81		53	10.34-11.34	
134.P.81		54	12.34	
135.P.81b	- Sonderband bei Entlassung reichsdeutscher Beamter und Verweigerung von Arbeitsgenehmi- gungen für reichsdeutsche Arbeitnehmer im Memelgebiet	1	12.33-12.34	9798/E687577-631
136.P.81c	Memelgebiet. Neumann Prozess. Hierzu ein Band mit Zeitungs- ausschnitten		1.34-12.34	
	Politik. Memelgebiet	5	10.23-12.23	
		6	1.24- 3.24	
		7	3.24- 7.24	
		8	10.23- 4.24	
		9	7.24-11.24	
		10	11.24- 2.25	
		11	3.25-10.25	
		12	10.25- 9.26	
M.1.	Memelgebiet. Autonomie	1	1.35- 4.35	
			1.35-12.37	
		2	5.35- 6.35	
		3	7.35-10.35	

Akten-zeichen	Inhalt	Band	Datum	Serial Nr.
M.1.	Memelgebiet. Autonomie	4	11.35- 5.37	
		5	5.37-12.37	
M.2.	– Direktorium		1.35-12.37	
M.3.	– Gouvernement		1.35-12.37	
M.4.	– Landtag	1	1.35- 8.35	
		2	8.35- 9.35	
		3	10.35- 9.36	
		4	10.35-12.37	
M.5.	– Generalkonsulat		1.35- 9.37	
			10.37-12.37	
M.6.	– Kulturelle Angele-genheiten		1.35-12.37	
M.7.	– Schulwesen		1.35-12.37	
M.8.	– Kirchliche Angele-genheiten		1.35-12.37	
M.9.	– Parteiwesen		1.35-12.37	
M.10.	– Presse. Drucker-zeugnisse		1.35-12.37	
M.12.	– Aufenthalts-Arbeitsgenehmigun-gen, Ausweisungen, Einreisen		1.35- 5.37	
			6.37-12.37	
M.13.	– Beamtenangelegen-heiten		1.35-12.37	
M.14.	– Pensionen		1.37- 4.37	
			5.37-12.37	
M.15.	– Finanzwesen		1.35-12.37	
M.15a.	– Bankwesen		8.37-12.37	
M.16.	– Versicherungswesen		1.35-12.37	
M.17.	– Gerichtswesen		1.35-12.37	
M.18.	– Haftsachen		1.35-12.37	
M.19.	– Neumann-Sass-Prozess		12.34- 8.35	
	– Neumann-Sass-Prozess, Zeitungs-ausschnitte		1.35- 2.35	
			3.35-12.37	
			9.35- 8.37	
			8.37-12.37	
M.20.	– Memel-Abt. bei Ober-tribunal		1.35-12.37	

Akten-zeichen	Inhalt	Band	Datum	Serial Nr.
M.21.	Memelgebiet. Staatsangehörig-keitsangelegenhei-ten, Bürgerrecht, Passsachen	1	1.35- 9.36	
		2	10.36-4. 37	
		3.	4.37-12.37	
M.22b.	– Verkehrswesen, Eisenbahn		1.35-12.37	
M.22a.	– Postverkehr (auch Rundfunk)		1.35-12.37	
M.22c.	– Schiffahrt		1.35-12.37	
M.22d.	– Kleiner Grenz-verkehr		3.30-12.37	
M.23.	– Memelhafen		1.35-12.37	
M.25.	– Wirtschaft, Land-wirtschaft, Ein- und Ausfuhr, Handel		1.35- 2.37	
			3.37-12.37	
M.26.	– Verschiedenes		1.35-12.37	
M.28.	– Kriegsgräberfür-sorge		12.35-12.37	
M.29.			5.37-12.37	
P.1.	Politik. Allgemeine Angelegen-heiten	1	1.35- 8.35	
		2	8.35-12.37	
P.1a.	– Jahresübersichten der Gesandtschaften und anderen deutschen Aus-landsbehörden		1.35-12.37	9814/E691094-126 5921/E435326-441
P.3.	– Deutschland, Äusseres		1.35-12.37	
P.4.	– Litauen, Inneres	1	1.35- 3.36	
		2	4.36- 5.37	
P.4a.	– Weltverband der Litauer		5.36- 2.38	
P.5.	– Litauen, Äusseres		1.35-12.37	
P.6.	– Deutsch-litauische Be-ziehungen		1.35-12.37	9812/E691066-70
P.7.	– Kommunismus-Russland		6.35-12.37	
P.8a.	– Deutsch-litauische Wirtschaftsverhandlun-gen	1	1.36- 9.36	9800/E687669-726
			1.38- 9.38	9007/E631621-24
		2	9.36-12.37	
P.9.	– Litauische Wirtschafts-politik		1.35-12.37	
P.8.	– Deutschlands Wirtschafts politik		1.35-12.37	

Akten-zeichen	Inhalt	Band	Datum	Serial Nr.
P.10.	Politik. Baltikum	1	1.35-11.35	
		2	12.35- 4.36	
		3	5.36- 6.37	
		4	6.37-12.37	
P.11.	– Baltenpakt		12.34-12.37	
P.12.	– Ostpakt		1.35-12.37	
P.13.	– Litauisch-polnische Beziehungen		1.35-12.37	
P.13a.	– Polen		12.35-12.37	
P.13b.	– Litauisch-russische Beziehungen		1.37-12.37	
P.14.	– Kommunistische Agita-tion in Litauen und ihre Bekämpfung		5.37-12.37	
P.14a.	– Anforderungen an den Kultur- und Schul-fonds	1	1.35- 3.36	
		2	4.36-12.37	
P.14b.	– Deutsche Nachrichten		1.35-12.37	
P.14c.	– V.D.A.		1.35-12.37	
P.14d.	– Allgemeine deutsche kulturelle Angelegen-heiten		2.35-12.37	
P.14e.	– Evangelische Kirche in Litauen und im Ausland		1.35-12.37	
P.14f.	– Kirchenwesen in Deutschland und Be-ziehungen zum Ausland	1	5.37-12.37	
P.14f.1.	Schulwesen allgemein		1.35-12.37	
P.14f.3.	Arminia		1.35-12.37	
P.14f.4.	Stipendien		6.35-12.37	
P.14f.6.	Kulturverband		1.35-12.37	
P.14f.7.	Deutsches Hochschulwesen		1.35-12.37	
	Briefe an den Kulturverband		9.36-12.37	
P.14g.1.	Deutsche Kolonie, Veranstaltung		1.35-12.37	
P.14g.3.	Ruderriege		1.35-12.37	
P.14g.4.	Allgemeine Sportangelegenheiten		1.35-12.37	
P.14g.5.	Deutsche kulturelle Angelegen-heiten, Olympiade 36		2.35-12.37	
P.14g.7.	Büchereien		1.35-12.37	
P.14g.6.	Deutscher Buchhandel		7.35-12.37	

Akten-zeichen	Inhalt	Band	Datum	Serial Nr.
P.14g.8.	Wissenschaftliche, künstlerische Angelegenheiten	1	1.35- 4.37	
		2	5.37-12.37	
P.14h.1	Litauische kulturelle Angelegenheiten, Schulerziehungswesen, Frauenfragen		1.35-12.37	
P.14h.2.	Universität Kowno		1.35-12.37	
P.14h.3.	Lehrstuhl für deutsches Recht		1.35-12.37	
P.14h.4	Deutsche Dozenten an der Universität Kowno		1.35-12.37	
P.14h.5	Studentenangelegenheiten		1.35-12.37	
P.14h.6.	Katholische Kirche in Litauen		1.35-12.37	
P.14h.7.	Vereinswesen		2.36-12.37	
P.14h.8.	Litauische künstlerische Angelegenheiten		5.35-12.37	
P.14h.9.	Allgemeine kulturelle Beziehungen zum Ausland		1.35-12.37	
P.14i.	Polnische kulturelle Angelegenheiten		1.35-12.37	
P.14k.	Kulturelle Angelegenheiten der Minderheiten in Deutschland		1.35-12.37	
P.15.	Propaganda (deutsch)		1.35-12.37	
P.16.	Greuelpropaganda, Boykott	1	1.35-11.35	
		2	12.35-12.37	
P.16a.	Hetzfilme gegen Deutschland		5.37-12.37	
P.17.	Antideutsche Kundgebungen Zwischenfälle		1.35-12.37	
P.18.	Minderheiten		1.35-12.37	
P.19.	Militärische Angelegenheiten		1.35- 5.37	
			5.37-12.37	
P.20.	Spionage		1.35-12.37	
P.21.	Saargebiet		1.34- 5.36	
P.22.	Danzig		4.35-12.37	
P.23.	Österreich		10.35-12.37	
P.24.	Völkerbund	1	1.35- 7.36	
		2	8.36-12.37	6399/E471460-77
P.25.	Abrüstung		1.35-12.37	
P.27.	Deutsche Presse		1.35-12.37	
P.27a.	Deutsches Pressematerial		12.35-12.37	

Akten-zeichen	Inhalt	Band	Datum	Serial Nr.
P.28.	Deutsche Presse in Litauen		1.35-12.37	
P.29.	Litauische Presse. Bücherei-gesetz		1.35- 4.37	
P.30.	Polnische Presse		1.35-12.37	
P.31.	Russische Presse		1.35-12.37	
P.32.	Presseübersichten der deutschen Gesandtschaft Reval		1.37-12.37	
P.34.	Diplomatisches und konsulari-sches Korps, Auswärt. Dienst		1.35-12.37	8212/E583331-33
P.35.	Geheim. Verschiedenes		1.35-12.37	
P.36.	Spanien		4.37-12.37	
Abt.VI	Personalangelegenheiten. Entlas-sungen, Urlaub		1.19-11.19	
	Gesuche und Anfragen		3.19-11.19	
	Abtransport der deutschen Trup-pen aus Litauen		12.18-12.19	
	Bericht der "Geheimen Feldpoli-zei"		3.19-10.19	
	Schriftwechsel mit dem litaui-schen Ministerium des Innern in Kowno		6.19- 8.19	
	Schriftwechsel mit dem litaui-schen Ministerpräsidenten in Kowno		3.19- 6.19	
7a.	Telegramme an Auswärtiges Amt	1	12.18- 8.19	
8.		2	8.19-11.19	
9.	Vorfall Metropol		3.19- 6.19	
10.	Lage im Baltikum		8.19-10.19	
14.b.	Rechtssachen, Minderheitenschutz	2	11.25-12.29	
		3	1.30-12.34	
14.c.	Rechtssachen, Schadenersatz	2	1.22- 6.26	
14.d.	Forderungen gegen Lützendorf		5.27-12.30	
14.e.	Rechtssachen specialia	3	1.31-12.34	
	Rechtsstellung von Ausländern in Litauen	1	6.30- 6.31	
14.g.	Rechtssachen, Sonderband Rechts-hilfe		10.31- 4.34	
15.	Zustellungen	6	8.26- 7.27	
		7	8.27- 5.29	
		8	6.29-12.30	
		9	1.31-12.34	
16a.	Forderung Walter Hinnenthal an das litauische Kriegsministerium		1.29- 9.29	

Akten-zeichen	Inhalt	Band	Datum	Serial Nr.
16a.	Forderung C.Charles Carol an litauische Regierung		5.25-12.32	
	Steinhof Pecht Königsberg c/a. Litauische Staatsbank		5.28- 6.31	
	Schadenersatzanspruch des deutschen Deckereibesitzers Seedat			
	Nachnahmeschwindeleien im Verkehr zwischen Tilsit und Memel		3.27-10.31	
	Fall Hellwege (Warschuck alias Karschuck)		12.26- 3.28	
	Ersatzansprüche des Majors a.D. Ludwig Baehr an den litauischen Fiskus		4.20- 8.33	
	Reklamation der Firma Robert Neyhöfer in Königsberg		10.27- 8.33	
16b.	Arbeitsgenehmigungen für Reichsdeutsche in Litauen. Grundsätzliche Verhandlungen Einzelfälle siehe Akten 14e spec		10.30-12.33	
16b.gen.	Rechtsstellung von Reichsdeutschen in Litauen. Arbeitsgenehmigungen für Reichsdeutsche in Litauen. Grundsätzliche Verhandlungen	2	1.34-12.34	
16b.	Unterbringung von 18 Reichsdeutschen im städtischen Betriebswerk Memel		4.33-11.33	
16b.spec.	Rechtsstellung von Ausländern (speziell Reichsdeutschen) in Litauen, Arbeitsgenehmigungen, Aufenthaltsgenehmigung		7.31-12.32	
	Aufenthalt Pastor Eckart in Kibarti		11.27-10.31	
	Rechtsanwalt Baumgärtel (Staatsangehörigkeit, Aufenthaltsgenehmigungen)		9.21- 7.34	
16c.	Rechtssachen, Fahndungs- und Haftsachen, unerlaubter Grenzübertritt	3	1.32- 9.34	
	Haftsache David Spugies		9.25-11.30	
	Haft der reichsdeutschen Kommunisten Pöhle, Sakantzky und Schwindt (Bemühungen der "Roten Hilfe")		10.27-11.29	
	Sonderakten Bergles		12.26- 2.28	
	Sonderband Strafsache Karl Gerlach		7.26- 2.28	
	Sonderband Rutkowski (unerlaubter Grenzübertritt.)		9.31- 3.32	
	Sonderakten Wilhelm Bolz		12.27- 6.29	

Akten-zeichen	Inhalt	Band	Datum	Serial Nr.
15c.	Verhaftung und Verurteilung des Reichsdeutschen Martin Sakuth wegen Desertieren		6.32-11.33	
	Haftsachen Richard Himkus		4.34- 6.36	
16d.	Rechtssachen- Ausweisungen	1	4.24- 7.31	
16a.	Rechtssachen, spec. (Zeugenvernehmung)	1	1.26-12.26	
		1a	1.27-12.28	
		2	1.29-12.30	
16b.	Aufenthaltssachen		1.26- 4.33	
16c.	Rechtssachen, Fahndungs- und Haftsachen, unerlaubter Grenz-übertritt	1	5.24-12.29	
		2	1.30-12.32	
16d.	Rechtssachen, Ausweisungen	2	8.31-12.34	
	Grundsätzliche Verhandlungen über Entschädigung der fünf aus dem Memelgebiet ausgewiesenen Reichsdeutschen: Daniel, Schneider, Knoblich, Bukowski und Ellnitz		7.31-11.33	
16d.Sbd	Ausweisung Bruno Schneider		10.30- 9.31	
16d.	- der Eheleute Pommere-ning		5.28- 6.32	
16d.Sbd	- Ida Schewitz		12.25- 1.28	
	- Henele Hoffmann		4.27- 3.28	
16e.	Ausländer (Litauer) in Deutsch-land. Arbeitsgenehmigung und sonstige Behandlung		6.31-12.34	
18a.	Spec. Passsachen		1.27-12.34	
18b.	Student Sang.		10.23- 2.25	
18c.	Jacob Bielogurski		4.22- 6.28	
18d.	J.Kopelovicius-Josefsonas		6.22-10.24	
18e.	Pass- und Sichtvermerksstatistik		6.25- 8.28	
18f.	Litauische Pass- und Sichtver-merksbestimmungen		6.31-11.34	
20.	Nachforschungen		7.22- 4.24	
21.	Nachlasssachen	1	5.20-12.30	
		2	1.31-12.34	
24b.	Staatsangehörigkeit Memel-Optanten	3	1.30- 7.33	
22.	Hinterlegungssachen, generalia		7.34- 8.34	
25.	Grenzverkehr, gen.	1	4.26- 3.27	

Akten-zeichen	Inhalt	Band	Datum	Serial Nr.
25.	Grenzverkehr, gen.	2	3.27-12.29	
24.	Staatsangehörigkeit gen.	2	1.30-12.34	
24b.	- Memel-Optanten	1	7.25-12.27	
25.	Grenzverkehr, gen.	4	1.33-12.34	
25a.	- allgemein		1920-22	
	Sonderband. Grenzverkehrsange-legenheit des Pastors Metz, Kybarti mit grundsätzlichen Ausführungen zu Artikel 2 des Grenzverkehrsabkommens		2.32- 8.33	
	Grenzverkehr spec.	2	1921-24	
25b.	Schirwindt-Brücke		3.20- 7.22	
	-(Vertrag und Repa-ratur)		5.23- 1.30	
25c.	Grenzverletzung bei Kummetschen Frl. Lengnick		2.24-12.29	
25d.	Grenzempfehlungen		4.20-11.34	
25e.	Autopassierscheine		1925-34	
26.	Litauische Krankenversicherung und litauisches Krankenkassen-gesetz		5.28- 3.34	
27.	Vereinswesen		1.20-12.27	
	- , Verbände und Genossenschaften	2	1.28-12.30	
		3	1.31-12.34	
27a.	Verein der Reichsdeutschen in Litauen		2.27- 7.33	
27b.	Veranstaltungen (Festlichkeiten)	1	1.34-12.34	
	Verzichtscheine auf gezeichnete Anleihe		4.29- 5.29	
	Mitarbeiter des Kulturverbandes		11.40-12.40	
28.	Schulwesen (auch Minderheiten-schulen)	4	1.31-12.34	
28a.	Oberrealschule Kowno	1	1920-22	
		2	1923-29	
		3	1.30-34	
28b.	Schulwesen, Oberrealschule Kowno.(Deutsches Gymnasium) Lehrerangelegenheiten		1923-34	
28.	Schulwesen	1	1.20- 3.22	
		2	1.23-12.28	
		3	1.25-12.30	

Akten-zeichen	Inhalt	Band	Datum	Serial Nr.
29.	Kirchliche Angelegenheiten		1.25-12.34	
30.	Litauische Presse (Übersetzungen)		1.19- 1.25	
	Polnische Presse		7.20- 9.27	
30a.	Presse spec.		1.23-12.31	
30b.	Presseübersichten	4	1.31- 5.31	
30a.	Polnische Presse Sonderband "Slowo"	1	1.27- 4.28	
30b.	Presseberichte		7.20- 1.28	
	Presseübersichten	1	1.30- 4.30	
		2	5.30- 8.30	
		3	9.30-12.30	
		5	6.31- 9.31	
		6	10.31- 2.32	
		7	3.32- 6.32	
		8	7.32-12.32	
		9	1.33- 6.33	
30a.	Presse spec.		8.32-12.34	
30b.	Presseübersichten	10	7.33-10.33	
		11	11.33- 2.34	
		12	3.34- 6.34	
30c.	Sonderakte Einstellung der "Königsberger Allgemeinen Zeitung" gegenüber Litauen		7.27- 2.28	
30d.	Litauische Presse. Berichte an das Auswärtige Amt Übersetzungen		1.20-12.34	
30e.	Polnische Presse (u.a.Dementi)		1920-34	
30f.	Russische Presse	1	1924-34	
30g.	Wilnaer Presse ("Slowo" "Kurier Wilenski"	2	5.28-12.34	
30h.	Sonderband. Weissrussische (Weissruthenische) Angelegenheiten		8.22-11.23	
31.	Propaganda	1	1.23-12.23	
		2	1.24- 6.25	
		3	7.25-12.26	
		4	1.27-12.29	
		5	1.30-12.31	
		6	1.32-12.34	

Akten-zeichen	Inhalt	Band	Datum	Serial Nr.
31a.	Film, Theater und Vorträge, Kunst und Kunstgewerbe	1	5.25-12.29	
		2	1.30-12.31	
		3	1.32- 5.34	
		4	6.34-12.34	
31b.	Deutsche Buchhandlung in Kowno. Beziehungen zum deutschen Buchhandel		5.30-12.34	
31c.	Sonderband. Goethe-Zentenarfeier 1932. Goethe-Spende		4.31- 6.32	
31d.	Sonderband. Genehmigung der Einreise deutscher Sport- und Gesangvereine sowie Schauspielertruppen in das Memelgebiet, Gewährleistung der Gegenseitigkeit		10.31-12.34	
31e.	Sport		1.31-12.34	
31f.	Propaganda. Sonderband: Ilgner		5.33- 4.34	
32.	Ausübung der ärztlichen Praxis in Litauen durch reichsdeutsche Ärzte		1.23- 8.32	
33a.	Gesundheitsverhältnisse. spec.		12.20-12.34	
32.	Ausübung der ärztlichen Praxis in Litauen durch reichsdeutsche Ärzte		5.20-12.22	
34.	Diplomatisches und konsularisches Korps	1	4.22-12.24	
		2	1.25- 4.28	
		3	5.28- 6.30	
		4	7.30-12.34	
34a.	Sonderband Zoll- und Steuererlass für Gesandtschafts- und Konsulargut		8.24-12.33	
			1.34-12.34	
34b.	Zollfreiheit für Privatkraftwagen der deutschen diplomatischen und konsularischen Beamten in Litauen und dem Memelgebiet		5.29-12.34	
35.	Hiesige Behörden	1	2.21- 6.25	
35a.	Ausschreibungen, Projekte und Unternehmungen	1	6.26- 4.28	
	- Wettbewerbe	2	5.28-12.30	
		3	1.31-12.34	
35.	Hiesige Behörden	2	7.25-12.34	
35b.	Ausschreibungen betr. Bahnbau Telschi-Krottingen		11.27- 1.30	

Akten-zeichen	Inhalt	Band	Datum	Serial Nr.
36.	Deutsch-litauische Finanz- und Wirtschaftsverhandlungen 1922	1	2.21- 5.22	
		2	1.21- 8.22	
		3	9.22- 6.23	
		4	6.24- 9.26	
36a.			10.21- 6.33	
39.	a) Finanzwesen Baltikum b) - Litauen			
	Litauisches Staatsbudget Litauische Staatsverschuldung	1	12.22- 1.31	
		2	8.31-12.34	
39a.	Baltikum, Verkehrswesen		11.23-10.34	
39b.	- Verträge	1	5.22- 5.25	
		2	7.25-12.34	
39c.	- Wirtschaftsverhältnis-se	1	12.22- 4.26	
		2	4.26-12.29	
		3	1.30-12.34	
39d.	Litauisch-lettländischer Handelsvertrag		1.29-11.34	
40.	Memel, allgemein	1	5.24-12.29	
		2	1.30-12.34	
40e.	Holzflösserei		1923-30	
40f.	Memel. Beamtenverhältnisse	1	1927-28	
		2	1928-34	
40g.	- Aufwertungsfrage		5.28- 1.33	
40h.	Memelländisches Beamtengesetz und Beamtensprachgesetz		1928-31	
40a.	Pensionszahlungen im Memelgebiet Memelländisches Versorgungs-gesetz	1	7.23-12.30	
		2	1.31-12.33	
		3	1.34-12.34	
40b.	Memelakten. Fall Heidemann		1924-32	
40i.	Memelländisches Umzugsdrittel		1925-31	
40k.	Ansprüche der aus dem litaui-schen Postdienst entlassenen memelländischen Postbeamten		1929-32	
40l.	Ausweisung des reichsdeutschen Robert Daniel und seiner Ehefrau aus dem Memelgebiet		1929-33	
40m.	Presseberichte über die Zeitun-gen des Memelgebietes	1	10.31-10.34	

Akten-zeichen	Inhalt	Band	Datum	Serial Nr.
40m.	Generalkonsulat Memel	2	6.34-12.34	
40n.	Sonderband. Die im Memelgebiet tätigen deutschen Privatversi-cherungsunternehmungen		3.32-10.34	
40o.	Sonderband. Kündigung von reichs-deutschen Lehrern im Memelgebiet		3.32- 9.33	
40p.	Verlegung der memelländischen Abteilung des litauischen Ober-tribunals nach Kowno		3.32-12.34	
40qu.	Abgeltung der memelländischen Beamten (Differenzzahlungen)		12.29-12.33	
40r.	Schiffsbesuche in Memel		6.32-12.34	
40s.	Memel, Presse	1	7.33-12.34	
40t.	Memeler Hafen	1	8.33-12.34	
40u.	Benennung der Post- und Telegra-fenanstalten des Memelgebietes. Adressierung der vom General-konsulat aufzugebenden Postan-weisungen		7.32-12.34	
	Landreform, Einzelaufzeichnungen des Gesandtschaftsrates Freundt		1.19-10.31	
	Landreform. Gesetzgeberisches Material.			
	Aufzeichnung über Agrarreklama-tionen 2.Auflage			
	- 3.Auflage			
37a.	Sonderband. Verkehr zwischen Deutschland und Litauen		7.29-10.32	
37b.	Litauische Einfuhrlizenzen	1	1.33- 6.34	
		2	7.34-12.34	
38.	Zwischenfälle	1	1926-28	
		2	1.29-11.34	
38a.	Emil Rodloff		4.24- 5.24	
38c.	Motorsegler "Malaga" Kapitän v.Stosch		5.25-11.27	
38d.	Motorboot "Bärbchen" Pol.26 Gebr.Koske		6.25-11.33	
38e.	Sache Schurz		6.23- 9.23	
38f.	Sonderakte. Zwischenfall Motorkutter "Käthe" (Kapitän Handel und Genossen)		3.27-11.29	
40c.	Memeler Putschisten. Korrespon-denz sowie Pakete	1	12.24- 2.26	
	Memeler Putschisten		8.24- 5.25	
		3	3.25- 5.28	
		2a	2.20- 7.20	

Akten-zeichen	Inhalt	Band	Datum	Serial Nr.
40 d	Memel. Aufenthaltssachen	1-3	7.25-12.34	
	Sonderband. Aufenthalt der Reichsdeutschen a) Eheleute Laaser b) Bruno Kaspereit im Memelgebiet		5.32-10.32	
	Sonderakte. Einreise des Lepra-kranken Stammler in das Memel-gebiet		10.31- 4.32	
41	Agrarreform und unsere Reklama-tionen dagegen	2-7	1922-34	
41 a	- Sonderakten: Agailo (Gräfin von Medem)	1	1.24-12.27	
	- Administrator Richard Henkel	2	2.28- 9.29	
	- Birschtany, Arnold		1.24- 2.32	
	- Gut Gugrary (Bräutigam)		5.24- 3.34	
41 d	- Henke's Erben (Gut Ros-helen)		7.24- 6.32	
41 e	- Keyserlingk (Gut Staning		4.24- 9.33	
41 f	- v.Hahn (Güter Weiss-Plonian, Gedutschy)		1.24- 5.34	
41 g	Restgut Skordupiany		3.27-10.28	
	Agrarreform. v.Poschinger v.Frauenau Gut Pobolwiany		12.25-10.32	
	- Zellstoff-Fabrik Waldhof-Tilsit, Gut Gawri		6.22-12.28	
41 h	Waldakten. Gut Stanieung Graf Erich Keyserlingk			
42	Grenz- und Binnenschiffahrts-fragen	1	5.23-12.27	
		2	1.28-12.34	
43	Ruhrspende. Sammlung für die Notleidenden in Deutschland		12.25- 1.26	
44	Kili		1922-28	
45	Wissenschaftliche Angelegen-heiten		1.27-12.34	
45 a	Lehrstuhl für deutsches Recht an der Universität Kowno		7.31-12.34	
46	Ostpreussen und seine Beziehun-gen zu Litauen	3	1.32-12.34	
		1	12.26-12.28	
		2	1.29-12.31	

Akten-zeichen	Inhalt	Band	Datum	Serial Nr.
P.51.	Ausweisungsfälle. Eckart, Südoff, Brieskorn, Leubner, Warm,Esch-mann	1	9.22- 9.27	
P.52.	Specialakten: Radzevicius - Jakuzaitis		10.26-11.26	
P.53	Wirtschaftspolitische Verhält-nisse in Litauen und deutsch-litauische Wirtschaftsbeziehun-gen		6.26-10.27	
	- Deutsch-litauischer Handels-vertrag	2	11.27- 2.29	
		3	3.29- 6.30	
		4	7.30- 2.33	
		5	3.33- 9.34	9801/E687728-31
		6	10.34-12.34	
P.53a.	Deutsch-russisch-litauisches Schweinekontingent		4.33- 5.33	
	Litauen, Veterinärfragen		1928-33	
P.54.	Auslegung des Artikels 6 des deutsch-litauischen Handelsver-trages. Rechtsstellung und Zu-lassung von Aktiengesellschaften und Handelsgesellschaften		4.30- 3.31	
P.55.	Völkerbund	3	1.31-12.31	
		4	1.32-12.34	
P.56.	Deutsch-litauische Verträge	1	4.28- 3.29	
		2	7.28- 9.29	
		3	10.29- 6.30	
	Deutsch-lit. Vertragswerk	4	7.30- 7.33	
P.57.	Geheim. Sonderakten betr."Eiser-nen Wolf"		7.28-10.29	
	Deutsch-österreichische Zollunion und Deutsch-Österreich allgemein		3.31-11.34	
P.58.	Sonderband. Kellog-Pakt (Kriegsächtungspakt)		1.28- 3.30	
P.59.	Deutsch-litauisches Abkommen über den Rechtsverkehr		6.29-12.34	
P.60.	Deutsch-litauische Vergleichs-verhandlungen	1	7.31- 4.33	
		2	4.33-11.34	
P.60a.	Sonderband. Deutsch-litauische Vergleichsverhandlungen. Beson-dere Wünsche deutscher Firmen und Organisationen		3.33-10.33	
P.61.	Sonderakten: Finanzausgleichs-verhandlungen der litauischen Regierung mit dem Memelgebiet		10.29- 7.33	

Akten-zeichen	Inhalt	Band	Datum	Serial Nr.
P.62.	Annulierung der Wahlen zum Kreistag des Landkreises Memel		1.32- 2.32	
P.63.	Entsendung memelländischer Vertreter zur Völkerbundstagung		2.32	
P.64.	Sonderband Böttcher (Zwischenfall Baltromejus)	1	12.31- 2.32	
		2	2.32	
		3	2.32	
		4	2.32	
		5	3.32	
II.b.R. Gen.II.43	Akten der Zivilverwaltung Litauen, Rechtsabteilung. Kriegs-schadensansprüche		1918-19	
P.65.	Abrüstungsfrage, Abrüstungskonferenzen und Propaganda	2	8.33-12.34	
P.66.	Verhaftung des Reichsdeutschen Beckers und des Schulrats Meyer in Memel		3.32- 5.33	
P.67.	Antideutsche Demonstrationen in Litauen		8.32-12.35	
P.68.	Litauisch-polnische Beziehungen		3.32-11.34	
11.	Abt.VI. Schriftwechsel Generalbevollmächtigte für Litauen mit den Abwicklungsstellen		1.19- 8.19	
12.	Berichte aus Rückwanderlager		5.19- 7.19	
13.	Telegramme vom Auswärtigen Amt		1919	
14.	Flugblätter		2.19- 3.19	
15.	Ausfuhrverbot von Lebensmitteln		3.19	
16.	Differenzen mit militärischen Stellen		2.19- 7.19	
18.	Telegramme		7.19	
19.	Vorschläge zur Regelung der Passfrage bei Einreise deutscher Staatsangehöriger nach Litauen		5.19- 7.19	
20.	Vorfall Tensnie		5.19- 7.19	
26.	Grenzpolizei Tätigkeitsberichte		3.19-10.19	
30.	Telegramme des Auswärtigen Amtes		10.18- 5.19	
31.	Berichte und Tagesbefehle Freikorps Diebitsch, VI.Res. Korps		10.19	
37.	Auflösung der Dienststelle Kibarty		9.19-11.19	
41.	Telegramme des Auswärtigen Amtes und Material über die Anerkennung des selbständigen Litauischen Staates		5.18- 6.18	

Akten-zeichen	Inhalt	Band	Datum	Serial Nr.
42.	Politik Litauen		1918	
46.	– Verschiedenes		2.19– 6.19	
51.	Preussisch Litauen		2.19– 7.19	
52.	Telegramme an das Auswärtige Amt Politik, Verschiedenes		1.19– 5.19	
54.	Flugblätter Grodno-Suwalki			
58.	Meldungen V.V. Hauptmann Tschunke		9.19–10.19	
59.	Kompetenzfragen		3.19– 9.19	
60.	Jüdische Angelegenheiten		1.20– 8.20	
6a.	Sonderband Personalien Dr. Jungfer		12.23– 5.34	
8a.	Inventar spec.	1	1920,21,22	
		2	1923–24	
		3	1.25–12.27	
		4	1.28–12.34	
8d.	Hausbau	1	1.23–12.25	
	Gesandtenwohnhaus		2.24–12.24	
			1.25–12.27	
	Inventarverzeichnis der Deutschen Gesandtschaft in Litauen		4.25–10.27	
	– B.Bücher, alt			
8b.	Inventar, Wagen, Auto	1	1920–29	
8d.	Gesandtenwohnhaus	4	2.28–12.29	
		5	1.30–12.34	
8e.	Inventar. Zeitungsbestellungen	1	1.20–12.30	
8f.	Dienstgebäude der Gesandtschaft		1.26– 9.33	
		2	9.33–12.34	
8g.	Inventar. Materialbestellung	1	1.34–12.34	
9a.	Kassensachen allgemein	2	8.20–12.22	
9b.	Kassensachen spec. Litauische Kommerzbank		12.22– 6.28	
			7.28–12.34	
9c.	Gebührenwesen	1	1920–24	
		2	1.25–12.34	
9d.	Gebührenkonto des Auswärtigen Amtes		6.22– 4.28	
			4.28– 3.31	
			4.31–12.34	

Akten-zeichen	Inhalt	Band	Datum	Serial Nr.
9e.	Kassensachen. Gehälter der Beamten und Angestellten	1	12.20- 7.27	
	Gehalts- und Zahlungslisten	2	4.27-12.29	
		3	1.30-12.33	
9f.	Z.A.K. Kriegsgräberfürsorge. Gen.	2	1.25- 3.28	
10.	Steuerabzug	1	2.24- 8.28	
		2	8.28-12.34	
10a.	Beihilfen, Dienstreisebestimmungen, Reisekosten, Umzugskosten		6.24- 1.34	
	spec. Reisekostenrechnungen		9.29-12.34	
10b.	Heimschaffung	2	11.22-12.29	
		3	1.30-12.34	
	Johann Kallweit (Heimschaffung)		2.28- 5.32	
	Heimschaffung (Übernahme) Eugen Burba		8.29- 3.32	
	Heimschaffung Ludwig Motzkat		10.30-12.31	
	Deutsche Kolonistentransporte aus Sowjetrussland		11.29-12.29	
	Sonderband Iwanow		4.29-1934	
10c.	Amtliche Abrechnungen	7	1.32- 6.33	
	Amtliche Abrechnungen Rechnungsjahre	2	1922-23	
		3	1924	
		4	1926,27,28	
		5	1928-29	
		6	1930-31	
			7.33- 6.34	
10f.	Kassensachen. Reichsversicherung für Angestellte	1	9.20-12.23	
10h.	Dienstreisen nach Eydtkuhnen		1.30-12.34	
11.	Finanzwesen. Aufwertung (Deutschland)	1	9.23- 2.26	
		2	3.26-12.33	
12.	Notarielle Beglaubigungen	1	12.25- 7.34	
13.	Steuerbeschwerde der Vereinigten Stahlwerke A.G. in Berlin		10.28- 7.33	
13a.	Steuerbeschwerde der Firma Kohlen-Import und Poseidon-Schiffahrt		2.29-11.30	
13b.	Konzession der Hamburg- Südamerikanischen Dampfschiffahrtsgesellschaft		5.31- 1.32	

Akten-zeichen	Inhalt	Band	Datum	Serial Nr.
13c.	Steuersache Hermann Gerlach, Eydtkuhnen		5.29-10.32	
14.	Rechtssachen generalia	4	1.34-12.34	
14a.	Rechtsschutz	1	12.22- 4.28	
	- Patent- und Waren- zeichenschutz	2	5.28-12.34	
14b.	Rechtssachen (Minderheitsschutz)	1	7.21-10.25	
P.64.	Böttcher Zwischenfall Baltro- mejus	6	3.32- 4.32	
		7	3.32- 5.32	
		8	5.32- 6.32	
		9	6.32	
		10	6.32- 7.32	
		11	7.32- 8.32	
P.67.	Zwischenfall vor der deutschen Buchhandlung und Fall Essen		1.32-11.32	
P.70a.	Pol. Baltikum, Baltenpakt (Litauen, Lettland, Estland)		2.33-12.34	
P.70b.	Pol.Baltikum, Ostpakt	1	7.33- 7.34	
	Pol.Baltikum (Randstaaten) Ostpakt	2	8.34-12.34	
P.71.	Greuelhetze gegen Deutschland und Boykott	1	3.33- 4.34	
		2	5.34-12.34	
P.82.	Memelgebiet. Kirche und Schule		5.24-12.34	
P.84.	Geheim. Sonderband: Kulturelle Angelegenheiten	1	12.25-12.28	
		2	1.29-12.30	
		3	1.31-12.31	
		4	1.32-12.33	
		5	1.34-12.34	
	Specialfonds		1927-32	
P.87.	Geheim. Militärisches	2	1.30-12.34	9974/E697351-61
P.85.	Politik. Geheim. Generalia	1	6.22-10.22	
		2	11.22- 6.23	
		21	1933	
		22	8.33- 2.34	
		23	1934	
P.86.	Geheim. Verschiedenes		3.19- 1.22	

Akten-zeichen	Inhalt	Band	Datum	Serial Nr.
P.86.	Geheim. Verschiedenes	1	12.24-11.25	
		2	11.25-12.27	
		3	1.28-12.34	
P.86a.	Sonderband. Litauische Unabhän-gigkeitsfeier im Mai 1928		4.28- 1.29	
P.86c.	Sonderband, Woldemaras, Prozesse		1931-34	
P.87.	Militärisches, Geheimsachen		11.21-12.29	
	Militaria		10.24-11.27	
P.88.	Geheim. Kirchliche Angelegen-heiten	2	9.27-12.33	
		3	1.34-11.34	
	Sonderband 1. (zu den Akten Memelpolitik) Kompetenzkonflikt zwischen der litauischen Mili-tärbehörde und der memelländi-schen Justizbehörde		6.28- 8.28	
	Sonderband. Kirchliche Angelegen-heiten	1	1.26- 8.27	
P.90.	Deutschland, äussere Politik		2.27-11.34	
P.90a.	Freie Stadt Danzig	1	11.26- 1.34	
P.90b.	Deutschland. Politik. Äusseres Korridorfrage	1	7.33- 9.34	
P.92.	Politik, Deutschland, Inneres		3.22-12.23	
	Deutschland, innere Politik	4	6.34-12.34	
81c.	Memel. Pol. Neumann-Sass-Prozess Zeitungsausschnitte		12.34	
P.93.	Deutsche Wirtschaftspolitik	1	12.33-12.34	
P.94.	Geheim. Deutsch-litauische Beziehungen	2	1.27-12.34	
P.95.	Litauen, Innere Politik	4	1.29- 9.34	M 117/M004588-92
		5	10.34-12.34	
P.96.	Litauen, Politik, Äusseres	9	8.26- 8.27	
		11	1.29-12.34	
	Politik, Geheim, Generalia	11	6.26- 2.27	
	Politik Generalia	12	3.27- 8.27	
		13	8.27- 2.28	
		14	3.28-12.29	
		15	1.29- 6.29	
		16	7.29- 1.30	
		17	2.30- 9.30	
		18	10.30- 4.31	

Akten-zeichen	Inhalt	Band	Datum	Serial Nr.
	Politik Generalia	19	5.31-12.31	
		20	1.32- 2.33	
30b.	Presseberichte	13	7.34- 9.34	
	Presseübersichten	14	10.34-12.34	
	Deutsche Presse	1	7.20- 5.34	
30c.		2	6.34-12.34	
	Steuern		1.32-12.34	
	Finanz- und Banksachen, Finanz-wirtschaft		1.33- 6.34	
	Deutsche Finanzwirtschaft		7.34-12.34	
	Handel, Einfuhr, Ausfuhr, Statistik		1.30-12.32	
	Handel, Einfuhr, Durchfuhr, Statistik	2	1.33-12.34	
	Sonderheft. Gesamtausfuhr deutscher Brennstoffe. Monat-liche Statistiken des Reichs-kohlenkommissars, Berlin		1930-34	
C.9d.	Verkehr. Luftfahrt		2.33- 9.34	
C.12. gen.	Deutsche Zoll- und Handelspoli-tik		1.30-12.32	
			1.33-12.34	
	Politik L-A.	2	1.23- 5.23	
		3	6.23- 5.24	
		4	5.24- 9.24	
		5	10.24- 3.25	
		6	4.25- 8.25	
		7	8.25-12.25	
		8	1.26- 7.26	
	Litauen, Politik, Äusseres		9.27-12.28	
	Innerpolitische Angelegenheiten Litauens	2	4.20-12.21	
	Politik L-J.	1	8.22- 9.24	
		2	10.24- 9.26	
P.95.	Litauen. Politik. Inneres	3	10.26-12.28	
P.95b.	- Gerichtswesen	1	4.33-12.34	
P.92.	Deutschland. Innere Politik		1.24-11.29	
		3	10.29- 5.34	
	Politik Litauen und Randstaaten		6.22-12.22	

Akten- zeichen	Inhalt	Band	Datum	Serial Nr.
1.	Politische Angelegenheiten	1	1.20-10.20	
2.		2	10.20-12.20	
3.		3	1.21- 4.21	
4.		4	5.21- 9.21	
5.		5	9.21-12.21	
6.		6	1.22- 2.22	
7.		7	3.22- 5.22	
8.		8	5.22- 6.22	
	Passsachen, Grenzempfehlungen		1935-37	
	- Autopassierscheine		1935-37	
	- Noten betr.Passvisa		1937-41	
	Legationssekretär Dr.Karl Geffcken		10.36-10.38	
	Militärattaché		9.34-12.37	
	Passsachen Ib. Litauer Pass- und Sichtvermerksbestim- mungen mit Gebührenverzeichnis R.5.Nr.1.		1.35-12.37	
	Passsachen Ia. Ausländer Fremdenpässe, Sichtvermerke (Bestimmungen) mit Gebührenver- zeichnis D.R.5 Nr.2.		1.35-12.37	
	Gehalts- und Zahlungslisten		1.34-12.34	
	Kriegsgräberfürsorge	3	4.28-12.30	
		4	1.31-12.34	
	Akten betr. die Tätigkeit des Beauftragten des Zentralnach- weisamtes für Kriegerverluste und Kriegergräber in Litauen	1	6.21-10.24	
	Berichtverzeichnisse an das Auswärtige Amt	1	12.36- 3.39	
		2	3.39-12.39	
		3	1.40- 3.41	
	Fremde Vertretungen	1	3.20-11.21	
	Rechtssachen. Schadensersatz- anmeldung	1	4.19-10.21	
	Rechtssachen. Haftsachen	2	3.20-10.21	
	Rechtssachen allgemein	1	12.19- 9.20	
	Polnische Flüchtlinge		2.40- 9.40	
	Volksdeutsche Internierte		1939-40	
	Litauische Listen			
	Einr. Kr.Gefangener		11.39-12.40	

Akten-zeichen	Inhalt	Band	Datum	Serial Nr.
	Beschwerde Kriegerhilfe Ost vom 4.4.19 an das Auswärtige Amt			
	Internierte		10.39-10.40	
Pol.3. Nr.40.	Geheim. Verhaftungen und Prozesse deutscher Reichsangehöriger und Volksdeutscher wegen Spionage gegen Litauen. Betr.König, Hoffmann, Huff, Lukat		1.37- 9.40	
	Polnische Angelegenheiten. Vertrag Buehlmann-Kolankowski. Grodno-Suwalki	1	1.19-10.19	
		2	1.20- 7.20	
	Innerpolitische litauische Angelegenheiten	1	10.19- 5.20	
	Bolschewismus		3.19- 1.22	
	Geheim. Deutsch-litauische Beziehungen	1	11.25-12.26	
	Weissrussische politische Angelegenheiten		1.21- 3.22	
	Herstellung der Personalunion Litauens mit Preussen		4.18	
	Persönliches Verhalten der Konsuln		3.75- 3.14	
	Austausch Radek		7.19-10.19	
	Politik Litauen auch Kirchliches		1.18- 4.18	
	Litauische Miliz		1.19- 6.19	
	Gerichtssachen, allgemein	1	12.18-11.19	
	Verkehrseinrichtungen		4.19-12.19	
	Schiedsgericht		12.18- 1.20	
	Deutsche Interessenvertretung		7.19- 8.20	
	Militärabkommen mit litauischer Regierung 14.II.19		4.18- 2.19	
1.	Geschäftsgang generalia	3	7.32-12.32	
		2	1.23- 6.28	
			8.19-12.22	
	Geheim. Sonderakten betr. Schiedsgericht im Streit Baumgärtel/Rogall		8.31-10.31	
G.G.	Geheimakten		8.19- 9.20	
	Generalakten der Deutschen Gesandtschaft Kowno		1.38	
	Politische Akten betr. Marineangelegenheiten		1909-11 1912-13	
	Betreuungen		6.40- 7.40	

Akten-zeichen	Inhalt	Band	Datum	Serial Nr.
A.II.3d.	Gesandtschaft, Heizungsanlagen, Brennmaterialien		1.38-12.38	
	Rückzahlungen von Unterstützungen durch Bemate und Angestellte der Verwaltung		12.36- 3.37	
W.F.4. Nr.3.	Memelgebiet. Agraria und Kredit-verbände, Bankfusion		4.37- 5.39	
	Einrichtung des Deutschen Generalkonsulats in Wilna		6.40	
	Kassensachen, Armenpflege	2	9.21-11.23	
J.Nr.123.	Akten		1928-29	
	Dampfer Remholz. Schiffahrt		9.19-10.19	
R.Einr.	Landrat Ebenrode		6.39- 8.40	
I.c. 10715/15	Die für verdächtig gehaltenen Schriftstücke und Karten		8.97- 5.99	
	Memeler Hafen		11.38- 4.39	
26.	Sonderband. 2.Kompetenzkonflikt zwischen litauischer Militärbe-hörde und memelländischer Justiz-behörde		8.28-10.29	
B.1.v.4b.	Ehrenkreuz für Frontkämpfer, Kriegsteilnehmer, Witwen und Eltern		8.34- 3.37	
536.	Ostjudenliste			
	Nachweis über ausländische Ver-sicherungsbeiträge für die Büro-angestellten. Reichskostenrech-nungen		7.38- 9.38	
1.	Loge Memphis		2.25- 7.27	
2.	Memelländischer Verein gegen den Alkoholismus		2.29- 6.29	
3.	Memelländische Rundschau		11.26- 2.32	
4.	Memelländische Volkszeitung		2.27- 1.31	
5.	Verein der Kolonialwarenhändler		11.30	
6.	Memeler Dampfboot		4.27- 2.32	
29.	Holzindustrie A.G., Wischwill		12.25- 5.32	
30.	Handwerker Verein, Nattkischken		6.28- 7.28	
31.	Textilwerke Memel A.G.		12.26- 4.33	
32.	"Lietuvos Eksportas" Schlachthaus		9.30- 2.32	
33.	Zellulosefabrik Memel		11.26-10.31	
36.	Geschäftsbetrieb. Geheim		6.25- 2.33	
1.	Personalien. Gesandtschaftsrat Dr. Freundt		7.25- 8.28	
2.	- Kurt Edelmann		2.20- 4.22	

Akten-zeichen	Inhalt	Band	Datum	Serial Nr.
3.	Personalien. Gesandter und Minister Schroetter		5.24- 3.27	
4.	– Oberinspektor L.Schöne		3.33- 8.33	
5.	– Dr.Schmidtlein		8.27- 9.27	
6.	– Dr.Schoenberg		2.20- 8.23	
7.	– Oberinspektor Windhausen		1.27- 6.32	
8.	– Konsulatssekretär Arnold Pfeiffer		4.37- 6.39	
9.	– Konsulatssekretär Heinrich Clausen		10.36- 3.39	
10.	– Gesandtschaftsrat Sayur		5.28- 1.35	
11.	– Kurier Lange		7.23- 7.26	
12.	– Legationssekretär Hencke		1.30- 8.30	
13.	– Dr.Hahn		7.20- 9.21	
14.	– Attaché Dr. Pawelke		4.31- 6.34	
15.	– Attaché Werner Picot		3.36- 8.37	
16.	– Oberstleutnant a.D. Hans Klein		12.24- 2.39	
17.	– Legationssekretär Dr.Mohrmann		8.33- 2.37	
18.	– Konsulatssekretär Otto Scholz		9.20- 6.37	
20.	– W.L.R. Dr.Olshausen		5.22- 7.24	
21.	– Legationssekretär Fricke		10.21- 1.26	
22.	– Legationssekretär Jung		12.27-10.29	
23.	– Legationssekretär Hess		4.28- 1.29	
24.	– Dr.Leopold Krafft von Delmensingen		4.35-10.37	
25.	– Dr. A.Tichy		3.34- 3.35	
26.	– Legationssekretär Unversehrt		9.28-12.35	
27.	– Verwaltungsassistent Vogel		12.22- 6.26	
28.	– Legationssekretär Dr.Weber		2.35- 8.36	
29.	– Legationssekretär Dr.Werkmeister		5.31-11.34	

Akten-zeichen	Inhalt	Band	Datum	Serial Nr.
30.	Personalien. Legationssekretär Windecker		8.23-11.26	
31.	— Bruno Thomas		1.32- 3.32	
32.	— v.Stolzmann		12.25-10.29	
33.	— Gesandtschaftsrat Seiler		4.20- 1.34	
34.	— Barbara Oldenburg		3.36- 3.37	
35.	— Charlotte von Freysleben		7.22- 9.23	
36.	— Frl.Käte Gonzen		2.24-10.26	
37.	— Frl.Demant		11.20-11.23	
38.	— Straube		8.20-12.24	
39.	— Skwirbliss		3.21- 4.21	
40.	— Seifart, Wilhel-mina		1.21-10.21	
41.	— Hedwig Dobrindt		1.21- 1.22	
42.	— Margot Kaiser		7.29- 2.37	
43.	— **Frl.** Gutjahr		11.20- 8.27	
44.	— Frl. Klenzmann und Schiemann		6.23- 2.29	
45.	— Elly Maursch		3.21-12.33	
46.	— Helene Mathien		10.35- 3.36	
47.	— Gnädig		12.26-10.37	
48.	— Frl.Martha Johannson		7.21-12.23	
49.	— Dorothea Witthöft		12.36- 4.39	
50.	— Kutscher		4.25-11.25	
51.	— Chauffeur Schweyer		10.25- 2.37	
52.	— Wächter der Ge-sandtenvilla		8.24-10.35	
53.	— Legationssekretär Blanck		11.28- 6.34	
54.	— Gesandter und be-vollmächtigter Minister Moraht	2	1.29-10.38	
55.	—	1	1926-28	
56.	— Dr.Wellberg		10.21- 3.39	
57.	— Legationssekretär Ried		9.24-10.27	
58.	— Podczus		6.20- 2.22	
59.	— Konsulatssekretär Pallat		2.20-12.20	

Akten-zeichen	Inhalt	Band	Datum	Serial Nr.
61.	Personalien Kanzler Forner		5.20- 2.39	
62.	- v.Riesen		3.21- 5.23	
63.	- Konsulatssekretär Bethge		12.25-11.35	
64.	- Dipl.Ing.Schult		5.24-12.37	
65.	- Pförtner Emil Klein		9.28- 4.39	
66.	- Frau Schult		7.23- 8.37	
67.	- Liselotte Kneip		1.37- 2.38	
68.	- Margarita Gerhard		1.34- 9.34	
69.	- Elfriede Kummert		6.32- 1.38	
106.	- Raoul Löffler		8.24-12.40	
	- Laurintschik		7.40- 2.41	
	- Kanzler Waldemar Kurschat		8.38- 3.41	
	- Assistent Johann Lunkeit		5.39-12.40	
	- Marineattaché		3.40- 6.40	
	- Rechtsanwalt Ernst Lichtenstein		10.36- 3.41	
	- Helene Hamm		12.37- 4.40	
	- Helbig		1.40-10.40	
	- Konsulatspraktikant Georg Fabian		2.39- 3.41	
	- Dorothea Faden		3.31- 1.41	
	- Cramer		10.39-11.40	
	- Hartwich		1.41	
	- Heinrich Brockbals		4.22- 3.41	
	- Irmgard Behrens		5.38-12.40	
	- Graf Adelmann		9.39- 3.41	
	- Dr. Haasemann		3.40- 9.40	
	- Günther		6.40-10.40	
	- Domela, Meta Dolmetscherin		4.21- 2.41	
	- Gesandter Dr.Erich Zechlin		10.32-10.37	
	- Zöllner		1.41- 3.41	
	- Oberinspektor Bruno Rentz		8.33- 3.38	
	- Elisabeth Reh/Müller		3.39- 2.41	

Akten-zeichen	Inhalt	Band	Datum	Serial Nr.
106.	Personalien Attaché Hermann Schall		5.38- 1.41	
	– Gustav Kiele		7.36- 1.40	
	– Oberst Just, Militär-attaché		3.39- 1.41	
	– Hildebrandt		7.40- 3.41	
	– Hoffmann		7.40- 3.41	
	– Adele Scholdonat		7.40- 9.40	
	– Lothar Schulz-Schwieder, Paul Stockinger		12.38-12.40	
	– Dr.Heinz Trützschler von Falkenstein		9.39	
	– Legationssekretär von Ungern-Sternberg		7.37-10.40	
	– Hans Werrlich		1.35- 6.40	
	– Reinert-Agafanow		6.39-10.40	
	– Reinert		2.40- 2.41	
	– Graf v.Hardenberg		3.36-12.39	
	– Erich Wollert		9.36- 3.41	
	– Dagobert Wiese		2.40- 2.41	
	– Wenk		1.39-11.40	
	– Gesandter Dr. Erich Zechlin	2	1.37- 3.41	
	– Plamsch		3.40- 3.41	
	– Dr.Pusch		1.40-11.40	
	– Elisabeth Balzer		4.40- 3.41	
	– Dorothee Lutz		4.40-11.40	
01.	– Postschaffner Jakeit		12.25- 4.27	
92.	– Postbeamter Ilhauds		4.26-12.30	
93.	– Martin Joneleit		7.25- 4.27	
94.	– Martin Josatitis		1.25-10.26	
95.	– Postsekretär Junker		4.24- 5.24	
96.	– Postbote Jakumeit		3.27- 6.27	
97.	– Max Juckat		4.27- 7.27	
98.	– Otto Jurgeleit		5.27- 9.28	
99.	– Telegr.Arb.Jagomast		10.27-12.27	
100.	– Otto Jagomast		10.27-12.27	
213.	– Ella Reimer		10.25- 4.26	

Akten-zeichen	Inhalt		Band	Datum	Serial Nr.
214.	Personalien	Postagentin Else Reinecker		3.26- 6.27	
215.	–	Postangest.Riemann		8.25-11.30	
216.	–	Wilhelm Riess		7.26- 3.30	
217.	–	Adam Rupkalwies		5.26- 5.33	
218.	–	Oberpostschaffner Richter		5.24	
220.	–	Postangestellte Gertrud Ruhnke		12.27- 5.28	
221.	–	Walter Romeikat und Richard Danner		3.28- 1.30	
266.	–	Postschaffner a.D. Tischner		1.27- 1.28	
267.	–	Tel.Ass.Gertrud Till		3.25- 9.26	
269.	–	Elise Trauschies		3.26-10.30	
270.	–	Hedwig Trauschies		12.24- 4.26	
271.	–	William Tydecks		8.25- 3.30	
272.	–	Postangest. Teichert		8.26- 3.30	
273.	–	Postangest.de Terra		4.27- 4.30	
274.	–	Postbeamter August Torkel		12.28	
275.	–	Tarwitz		6.29- 7.29	
277.	–	Martin Tarwitz		3.30	
278.	–	Martin Tydecks			
279.	–	Anna Tendies			
283.	–	Ewald Walter		2.26- 3.26	
279a.	–	Karl Thiel		3.30	
280.	–	Usch und Gen.Post-schaffner Uschtrin, Gutweth, Kruschat		5.25-10.31	
282.	–	Waiczys, Brandt, Ponell		1.25- 2.32	
284.	–	Postangest. Wapsa		10.25-12.25	
285.	–	Felix Wroblewski		8.22- 5.25	
286.	–	Artur Wiegratz		1.26- 6.26	
288.	–	Postsekretär Winter		9.24	
289.	–	Fr.Wohlgemuth		4.21- 4.26	
290.	–	Anna Wottrich		8.24	
292.	–	Adam Willums		5.28-10.28	
293.	–	Albert Willomatz		10.28- 1.29	

Akten- zeichen	Inhalt	Band	Datum	Serial Nr.
294.	Personalien Carl Wiese		1.29- 3.30	
295.	- Kurt Wisbar		4.29- 7.30	
296.	- Theodor Weichert		3.30- 4.30	
297.	- Frau Margarete Wilck		11.30	
298.	- Albert Waitschies		11.30- 6.31	
299.	- Hildegard Witten- born		2.30	
304.	- Herta Zander		10.27- 6.28	
B.2.	Rechts- und Konsulatssachen Dienstpflicht		1.35-12.37	
B.3.	Staatsangehörigkeit c) Einzelfälle alph. A - K		1.35-12.39	
	Renten, Alimente, Einzelfälle alph. A - K		1.35-12.37	
	Staatsangehörigkeit c) Einzelfälle L - Z		1.35-12.37	
	Renten, Alimente Einzelfälle alph. L - Z		1926-34	
B.4.	Beurkundungen A - F			
	- G - K		bis Ende 34	
	- L - R		bis Ende 34	
	- S - Z		bis Ende 34	
	Finanzen De. b)spec. Anträge auf Devisenfreigabe		1.35-12.37	
	Beurkundungen A - K	8a	1927-31	
B.6.	Einzelfälle alph. A - Z		1927-34	
	Regierungsanzeiger		1935-37	
	Betr. Besuche der Leipziger Messe. Jo - Jz.		3.40	
	Regierungsanzeiger Nr.571-640		3.37- 4.39	
	Amtsblatt des Memelgebiets		1937-38	
B.2.m.	Beurkundungen A - B		1.35-12.37	
	Regierungsanzeiger Nr.641-730		1939-40	
	Beurkundungen G - H		1.35-12.37	
B.2.	Rechtswesen m)Beurkundungen, Einzelfälle C - F		1.35-12.37	
B.2.m.	Beurkundungen L - M		1.35-12.37	
	- Einzelfälle J - K			
	- N - R		1.35-12.37	
	- S - Sch		1.35-12.37	

Akten-zeichen	Inhalt	Band	Datum	Serial Nr.
B.2.	Rechtswesen. d)Aufenthalts- und Arbeitsangelegenheit für Reichs-deutsche A - K		1.35-12.37	
	Rechtswesen. m) Beurkundungen Einzelfälle St - Z		1.35-12.37	
	Rechtswesen. d)Aufenthalts- und Arbeitsangelegenheit für Reichs-deutsche L - Z		1.35-12.37	
	Kleine Anfragen, Ermittlungen A - K		1.35-12.37	
	- L - Z		1.35-12.37	
	Rechtswesen. e)Aufenthalts- und Arbeitsangelegenheit für Litauer		1.35-12.37	
	Finanzwesen, Anleihen, Bankwesen. Steuern, Versicherungen	3	1.27-12.30	
	Finanzwesen, Anleihen, Bankwesen	2	1.24-12.26	
C.2.	- Versicherungswesen	4	1931-33	
	Finanzwesen, spec. Bankwesen	5	1931-34	
C.	Handel, generalia,	7	6.26-12.32	
	Einfuhr von Schnellwaagen		1.30-12.32	
C.6.	Handwerk, Industrie, Technik		1928-32	
C.7.	Landwirtschaft und Erzeugnisse nach Ernteberichten			
C.8.	Soziale Frage. Generalia, Specialia, Arbeitsfrage, Auswan-derung, polnische Wanderarbeiter Soziale Fürsorge, litauische Arbeiter, Arbeitsdienst		1.33-12.24	
			1.21-12.32	
C.9.	Verkehrswesen. Schiffahrt, Telegrafie, Eisenbahnen, Frem-denverkehr		1.30-12.34	
	Verkehr. Allgemein, Funkwesen, Kraftfahrwesen, Luftfahrt		1.31-12.34	
C.10.	Verträge, Abkommen, Konventionen		1.23- 9.29	
			10.29-12.31	
			1.32-12.34	
C.13.	Litauisches Gesetz und Verord-nungen		8.20-12.31	
C.15/3.	Hochschulwesen		1920-29	
	Stipendien		1925-34	
B.9.	Memelschiffer Kai - Kap.		1939-40	
	Matrikel		4.30- 6.34	
	Sichtvermerke A - Z			

Akten-zeichen	Inhalt	Band	Datum	Serial Nr.
B.9.	Fremdländische Sichtvermerke	1	1.32- 5.32	
	Forderungen VI Fo.	1	1.32- 5.32	
	- II	4	1909	
		2	5.32- 7.32	
		3	8.32-11.32	
		1	1.33-10.33	
		4	1.31-12.32	
B.6.	Landwirtschaft. c)Einzelne Land- und forstwirtschaftliche Erzeugnisse. Alph.		1.35-12.37	
B.7.	Soziale Angelegenheiten d) Renten, Unterstützungen. Alph.		1.35-12.37	
455.B.7.	- L - Z			
456.	Handelsbestimmungen. Steuer-Zollbestimmung			
457.B.8.	Staatsangehörigkeit H - J		bis 12.34	
458.B.8.	- M - S		bis 12.34	
459.B.8.	- Q - Sch		bis 12.34	
460.B.8.	- St.- Z		bis 12.34	
461.B.11.	Ermittlungen, Nachforschungen		1.30-12.34	
462 Ha.5.	Auskünfte		1.35-12.37	
463 Ha.5.			1.35-12.37	
464 Ha.5.			1.35-12.37	
465 Ha.5.			1.35-12.37	
466 Ha.5.			1937	
467 Ha.5.	alte Auskünfte über Personen und Firmen		1.29-12.34	
468 Ha.5.			1.29-12.34	
469 Ha.5.			1.29-12.34	
470 Ha.5.			1.29-12.34	
471 Ha.5.			1.29-12.34	
472/475 Ha.6.	Absatz deutscher Waren A - Z		1.35-12.37	
476 Ha.j.	Vertreter A - Z		1.32-12.37	
477/480 Ha.6.	Handelsauskünfte nach Branchen A - Z		1.31-12.34	
481 Ha.8.	Beschwerden A - Z		1.35-12.37	
482 Ha.9.	Handelsempfehlungen A - Z		1935-37	

Akten-zeichen	Inhalt	Band	Datum	Serial Nr.
483.W.B.	Wirtschaft Baltikum und umlie-gende Länder		1935-37	
484.Wi.2.	Wirtschaft Litauen. Wirtschaft-liche und Handelsbeziehungen zu anderen Ländern (alph.)		1.35-12.37	
485.	Verzeichnis der nach Moskau abgegebenen Vorgänge. 1941		1940-41	
Pers.R. 2b.	Versendung von Wertsachen (Name)	2	1940-41	
Pol.2. Nr. 42.	U.S.A.		9.37- 1.40	
Nr. 43.	Japan		1.38- 1.40	
Nr. 44.	Amerika		12.38- 1.40	
Nr. 45.	Italien		4.38-10.39	
Nr. 46.	Spanien		1.39- 2.40	
Nr. 47.	Portugal		11.39- 1.40	
Nr. 48.	Ukraine		4.39- 7.39	
Nr. 49.	Belgien		6.39- 9.39	
Nr. 50.	Bulgarien		10.39	
Nr. 51.	China		12.39- 1.40	
Nr. 22.	Hinterlegungssachen allgemein		11.13-10.29	
Nr. 24.	Staatsangehörigkeit Generalia	1	1920-29	
Nr. 24b.	Memel-Optanten/Kowno. Staatsangehörigkeit		3.25- 6.29	
	Staatsangehörigkeit Polen-Optan-ten		6.22- 9.26	
	Sonderband Gertrud Blode Staatsangehörigkeit		8.27-12.27	
Nr. 25.	Grenzverkehr generalia	3	1.30-12.32	9973/E697343-49
Pol.3. Nr. 1a.	Grosslitauen, Ministerien, Ministerkabinett, Regierungs-bildung		7.37- 3.41	
Nr. 2.	Litauisches Staatsoberhaupt prominente Staatsmänner		5.38- 2.41	
Nr. 4a.	Staatsschutzbestimmungen, Agenten- und Spionagewesen, Bekämpfung kommunistischer Agitation in Grosslitauen			
Nr. 4d.	Verhaftungen, Verurteilungen, Prozesse litauischer Staatsange-höriger wegen Spionage und staatsgefährlicher Betätigung gegen Deutschland		7.38- 9.39	
Nr. 4f.	Spionageprozess König, Geld-überweisungen		3.37-11.40	

Akten-zeichen	Inhalt	Band	Datum	Serial Nr.
Pol. 3. Nr. 5a.	Hoheitszeichen, Flaggen, Feier-tage in Grosslitauen		1.38- 1.41	
Nr. 6a.	Wahlen in Grosslitauen. Seimwahlen		6.40- 7.40	
Nr. 6b.	Grosslitauen, Seimsitzungen		1.39	
Nr. 9a.	Judenangelegenheiten in Gross-litauen		4.37- 2.41	
Pers. Si. 6b.	Kurierangelegenheiten, Depeschen-listen, Schriftwechsel		1.38- 3.41	
D.Pol.2. Nr.4.	Politische Beziehungen Deutschland - Polen		8.39- 5.40	
Nr.6.	- Dänemark		4.38- 4.40	
Nr.7.	- England		11.37- 9.40	
Nr.8.	- Frankreich		8.37- 7.40	
Nr.9.	- Italien		5.38-12.40	
Nr.10.	- Jugoslawien		1.38- 6.39	
Nr.11.	- Rumänien		8.38-12.39	
Nr.12.	- Tschechoslowakei		5.38- 8.38	
Nr.13.	- Ungarn		8.38- 1.39	
Nr.14.	- Schweden		1.39- 8.40	
Nr.15.	- Baltische Staaten		1.39- 9.39	
Nr.16.	Deutsche Militärmassnahmen gegen .Polen und deren Rückwirkungen auf die internationale Lage	1	8.39- 9.39	
		2	9.39-10.39	
D.Pol.3. Nr.7.	A.O. Tagungen in Stuttgart		10.37- 9.40	
Nr.8a.	Militär-, Marine- und Luftfahrt-angelegenheiten		1.38-12.40	
9.	Zahlungen an Beamte		1935-36	
	Einnahmen		1914	
	Politische Berichte		1886-97	
			1898-1907	
			1901-1906	
557.	VI. Urkunden			
537.	Litauische Anschriften aus allen Gebieten des öffentlichen Lebens		6.40	
538.	Zusammenstellung der von den Antragstellern nicht erhobenen Beiträge			

Akten-zeichen	Inhalt	Band	Datum	Serial Nr.
542.	Abkommen über den gegenseitigen Warenverkehr zwischen dem Deutschen Reich und der Republik Litauen		5.39	
547.	Verzeichnis der von der Deutschen Gesandtschaft für Litauen benannten Vertreter. Ein offener Brief.		6.40	
544.	Verzeichnis der deutsch-litauischen Vereinbarungen		4.40	
P.III.1a.	Traduktion Discours prononcé par le Führer Chancelier au Reichstag		1.39	
	Translation Speech of the Führer and Chancellor of the German Reich before the Reichstag		1.39	
Nr. 24b.	Staatsangehörigkeit Memel-Optanten	2	1.28-12.29	
	Reisepass Frau Voss			
	Abrechnung von 1891 bis 1.4.09 über die den Erben des verstorbenen Generalleutnants Baron Karl Karlowitsch Stackelberg gehörigen Bilette der inneren Anleihe mit Gewinnbeteiligung			
P.27.	Sonderheft. Ressortbesprechung		3.23- 6.23	
	Asservatenliste			
	Abschlüsse der Konsulatskasse		1.13- 7.14	
	Nebenkasse		1914	
	Ausgaben		1914	
	Tageskassenbuch		10.13- 7.16	
	Aktenstück in russischer Sprache			
	Schriftwechsel wegen Geburtsurkunden		1937-38	
	Anträge von Privaten an die Gesandtschaft		1938-40	
	Schriftwechsel wegen Urkunden.			
	Anträge von Privaten an die Gesandtschaft		1937-38	
	Schriftwechsel wegen Urkunden		1938	
			1938-39	
	Kasse des Verwaltungsstabes des deutschen Generalbevollmächtigten für Litauen. Abrechnung mit der Darlehnskasse Ost, Königsberg			
	Schriftwechsel betr. Reichsdeutsches Eigentum		1937-41	

Akten-zeichen	Inhalt	Band	Datum	Serial Nr.
P.27.	Schriftwechsel betr. Einbürger-ungsanträge		1938-41	
	Schriftwechsel betr. Genehmigung zu Einreisen ins Reich		1938-39	
	Anträge von nicht deutschen Privaten an das Generalkonsulat der Gesandtschaft in Kowno		1939-40	
	Schriftwechsel wegen Einreise-genehmigungen		1940-41	
			1940	
			1939-40	
	Schriftwechsel in Staatsangehö-rigkeitsangelegenheiten		1937-39	
			1940	
58.	Schriftwechsel betr. Regelung der Staatsangehörigkeit		1940-41	
59.	Schriftwechsel betr. Übernahmen		1939-40	
8.	Schriftwechsel wegen Urkunden		1939	
9.			1939-40	
10.	Schriftwechsel in Urkunden und Devisenmangel		1939-40	
17.	Warnungen vor Erteilung von Einreisegenehmigungen		1938-41	
18.	Schriftwechsel wegen Zeitungs-bestellungen		1937-40	
19.	Zustellungen		1939-40	
20.	Czerweny v.Arland Boisa		9.39-12.40	
21.	Zustellungen		1940	
22.			1940-41	
23.	Schriftwechsel betr. Kongresse		1938-40	
24.	Schriftwechsel betr. Sport		1938-39	
25.	Schriftwechsel betr. Konzerte		1937-39	
26.	Anträge auf Einbürgerungen und Einreisen nach Deutschland		1939-41	
27.	Schriftwechsel wegen Umsiedlung		1940	
	Eine Urkundenregistermappe dazu		1940-41	
28.	Schriftwechsel betr. Auskünfte		1938-40	
29.			1937-40	
30.	Schriftwechsel betr. Aufwertun-gen		1939-40	
	Schriftwechsel betr. Arbeits-genehmigungen		1937-39	

Akten-zeichen	Inhalt	Band	Datum	Serial Nr.
31.	Schriftwechsel betr. Ausweisungen		1937-40	
32.	Schriftwechsel betr. Reisebescheinigungen		1937-41	
	Schriftwechsel wegen Übersiedlung von Volksdeutschen nach Deutschland		1940-41	
	Anträge auf Einreisegenehmigungen nach Deutschland und Generalgouvernement		1940-41	
41.	Abgelehnte Anträge auf Einreisen ins Generalgouvernement		1940	
42.	Abgelehnte Anträge auf Einreisen		1939-40	
44.	Anträge auf Einreiseerlaubnis			
45.	Anträge von nichtdeutschen Privaten an die Gesandtschaft in Kowno			
46.	Schadenersatzanträge von Deutschen		1937-40	
44.	Anträge auf Einreiseerlaubnis			
47.	Erbschaftsangelegenheiten		1937-41	
49.	Anträge auf Einreisegenehmigungen nach Deutschland. Meldeblätter		1938	
50.	Schriftwechsel betr. Meldungen über Aufenthaltsänderungen		1937-39	
51.	Schriftwechsel betr. Nachforschungen		1938-39	
52.	Schriftwechsel der Gesandtschaft mit geheimer Staatspolizei		1940	
	Kulturverband der Deutschen Litauens			
	Deutsche Botschaft in Moskau und Auswärtiges Amt wegen Nachforschung nach Polen, Litauern, Reichs- und Volksdeutschen		1940	
	Schriftwechsel wegen Nachforschungen		1939-40	
53.	Schriftwechsel wegen Personen		1938-39	
54.	Schriftwechsel betr. Beglaubigungen		1939-40	
55.	Schriftwechsel betr. Rentenangelegenheiten		1935-40	
60.	Unterstützungsangelegenheiten		1935-39	
61.			1937-41	
39.	Anträge auf Einreisegenehmigungen nach Deutschland und Generalgouvernement		1940-41	

Akten-zeichen	Inhalt	Band	Datum	Serial Nr.
62.	Vormundschaftsangelegenheiten		1938-40	
63.				
64.	Schriftwechsel in Wehrangelegen-heiten		1938-40	
65.	Reiseverkehr nach dem Ausland			
66.	Messeangelegenheiten		1938-40	
67.	Verschiedenes		1938-41	
68.	Schriftwechsel betr. Wettbewerb für den Bau eines Staatspalais in Kowno		2.39- 2.41	
	Schriftwechsel mit Firmen		1939	
	Schriftwechsel mit Reichsstelle für Aussenhandel und anderen Aussenhandelsstellen und Firmen		1938-39	
69.			1939-40	
70.			1939-40	
71.	Schriftwechsel in Devisenange-legenheiten		1937-39	
72.	Schriftwechsel mit Firmen		1939-40	
73.	Schriftwechsel mit Aussenhan-delsstellen und Firmen (Einfuhr-lizenzen)		1938-39	
74.	Schriftwechsel betr. Warenein- und -ausfuhr		1938-40	
75.	Schriftwechsel mit Ministerien, Aussenhandelsstellen und Firmen		1940-41	
76.	Schriftwechsel mit Aussenhandels-stellen und Firmen		1937-40	
77.			1929-39	
78.			1938-39	
79-80.	Forderungen von Firmen und Privaten an Litauen		1934-39	
80a.	Schriftwechsel mit Firmen		1939-41	
81.			1939-40	
82.	Schriftwechsel mit Aussenhandels-stellen und Firmen wegen aus-stehender Forderungen		1940-41	
83.	Schriftwechsel betr. Forderungen deutscher Firmen		1940	
84.	Schriftwechsel mit Aussenhandels-stellen und Firmen		1940-41	
85.			1938-40	
86.			1938	
87.			1938	

Akten-zeichen	Inhalt	Band	Datum	Serial Nr.
88.	Schriftwechsel mit Aussenhandels-stellen und Firmen		1939	
89.			1939-40	
90.	Schriftwechsel betr. Wirtschafts-kredite		1940	
91.	Schriftwechsel betr. Kreditwür-digkeit von Firmen		1940	
92.	Schriftwechsel wegen wirtschaft-licher Reklamationen		1937-40	
93.			1940	
94.	Schriftwechsel betr. wirtschaft-licher Vertretungen		1937-38	
95.	Schriftwechsel betr. wirtschaft-licher Vertreter		1938	
96.	Schriftwechsel mit Aussenhandels-stellen und Firmen		1938	
97.			1938-39	
98.			1939-41	
99.	Schriftwechsel betr. wirtschaft-licher Vertretungen		1939	
100.			1939-40	
101.			1940	
102.			1940	
103.			1940	
104.	Schriftwechsel in Zonentarifan-gelegenheiten		1938-40	
105.	Schriftwechsel in Steuerangele-genheiten		1938-40	

Akten-zeichen	Inhalt	Band	Datum	Serial Nr.
B.I.	Personalveränderung im Auswärtigen Amt	1-2	4.21- 8.38	
B.II.	Wiedereinrichtung der Gesandt-schaft und Konsulate	1-2	6.20-12.28	
	Einrichtung Gesandtschaft und Konsulate. Exequatur für Konsuln	1	4.29- 4.38	
B.1.	Halbamtlicher Schriftwechsel der Gesandtschaft		1933-34	
	Allgemeine Personalien	1	6.20- 4.24	
B.2.	Bewerbungsschreiben um Stellun-gen		6.20- 7.38	
B.3.	Geschäftsträger Wirkl.Leg.Rat Haug.		6.20- 1921	
	Personalien des Gesandten Freytag		9.32-12.34	
	- betr. Gesandten Voretzsch		11.22-11.33	
B.3a.	- Gesandten Horstmann	2	2.31-10.34	
	Geschäftsübergabe, Urlaubsvertr.		1.35- 9.38	
	Halbamtlicher Schriftwechsel des Gesandten Freytag		1.33-12.33	
B.3b.	- betr. Gesandten Horstmann		4.31-10.35	
B.3c.	Eintreffen des Gesandten Horst-mann		4.31- 1.34	
B.3.	Geschäftsübergabe	Sbd.	4.26-12.34	
B.4.	Personalien der Ges.Räte und Legationssekretäre	1-3	6.20- 9.34	
		4		
	- Graf Du Moulin	1-2	8.32-11.38	
	- Ges.Rates Rahn	1-2	2.38- 8.42	
B.4a.	- Ges. Rat Dr. Völckers		12.26- 7.29	
B.5.	Personalien Daehnhardt		6.20-12.35	
B.6.	- des Kanzlers		6.20-12.39	
B.7.	- Kanzleipersonal		6.21- 4.36	
	Personalverstärkung	Sbd.	4.38- 8.38	
B.9.	Konsulate in Portugal	1-2	6.20- 1.39	
B.9a.	- in Coimbra		2.24- 4.29	
	Personalien Götz		1.39- 6.41	
	- Trosch		1.39- 5.41	
B.10.	Konsulat Funchal Madeira	1-2	6.20- 9.38	
	Konsul Gesche	2		

Akten-zeichen	Inhalt	Band	Datum	Serial Nr.
B.11.	Konsulat Azoren	1-4	6.20-12.39	
B.11a.	- in Horta		10.27- 7.38	
B.12.	- in Sao Vincente	1-2	6.20- 5.38	
B.13.	- in Guinea	1-2	6.20-11.39	
adh.	Erbschaft Schacht			
B.14.	Konsulat St.Thomé und Prinicipe		6.20- 7.29	
B.15.	- Benguela-Lobito		6.20-11.38	
B.15a.	- Luanda	1-2	1.21-12.29	
B.16.	- Lourenco Marques	1-2	6.20-12.38	
B.16a.	- Beira		11.20- 9.34	
B.16b.	- Mozambique		10.26-12.37	
B.17.	Personalien der Konsulate in Portug.Indien		4.30-10.38	
B.18.	Militär-, Marine- und Luft-attaché	1-2	1.33-12.38	
B.20.	Dienstkleidung des Hilfspersonals		4.33- 4.38	
B.21.	Invalidenversicherung		2.32- 2.39	
B.22.	Umzugs- und Reisekosten		1.34- 7.38	
B.23.	Urlaub		5.30- 7.38	
B.25.	Attentat Baligand		6.30- 6.35	
B.25a.	Kondolenz Baligand		6.30	
B.26.	Personalien Ponto		6.20-12.41	
B.28.	- Scheibel		8.22- 6.40	
B.30.	Hilfskräfte bei Gesandtschaft und Konsulatsabteilung	1-2	6.20- 2.39	
B.31.	Personalien Attaché Schmidt		7.37-12.38	
B.32.	- Handelsattaché Clausen		10.37-12.38	
C.I.	Runderlasse des Auswärtigen Amtes	1-3	6.20-12.29	
C.Ia.	Erlasse für neueintreffende Beamte		6.28- 1.31	
C.II.	Allgemeine Dienstanweisung des Auswärtigen Amtes		6.20- 7.33	
C.IIa.	Erlasse für neueingerichtete Konsulate		1.31	
C.III.	Beflaggen der Gebäude		1.38-11.38	
C.VIII.	Kassenwesen	1-2	6.20- 7.38	
C.XIII.	Bestimmungen über Kurier-, Briefbeutel- und Depeschenverkehr		3.30- 1.39	

Akten-zeichen	Inhalt	Band	Datum	Serial Nr.
C.2.	Propagandaministerium		8.33-12.37	
C.3.	Geschäftsgang und Geschäftsver-teilung		6.20-10.38	
C.5a.	Telefonanlage		8.28- 6.37	
C.5b.	Kanzleigebäude		6.26-12.34	
C.5c.	Einbruch auf der Gesandtschaft		7.27- 5.28	
C.5d.	Hausverwaltung		5.29- 8.31	
C.6.	Inventarverzeichnis	1-7	6.20-12.38	
C.6a.	Eisschrank		7.24- 5.36	
C.7.	Inventarverzeichnis B.	1-9	6.20-10.31	
	Bibliothek der Gesandtschaft	10-12	10.31-11.38	
C.9.	Abrechnung	1-7	6.20- 7.37	
C.10.	Geldbeschaffung	1-3	6.20-10.38	
	Escudenfonds	Bei-heft	7.31- 1.32	
C.11.	Gehaltslisten	1-2	6.20-10.36	
C.12.	Verschiedene Kassensachen	1-5	6.20- 1.39	
	Überweisung der Bezüge		12.22- 4.27	
C.13.	Kurierverkehr	1-5	6.20- 9.39	
		6-9	10.32-12.38	
C.13a.	Berichteverzeichnisse	3-4	1.33-11.35	
C.14a.	Automobilverkehr		9.26-12.35	
C.15.	Steuernachweise	1-2	12.24- 7.32	
C.16.	Gehaltsüberweisungen	1-4	6.27-12.38	
C.17.	Scheckübersendungen		10.28- 1.38	
C.18.	Rundfunk	1-2	12.28-12.38	
C.19.	Selbstbewirtschaftungsfonds	1-3	1.30-12.38	
C.20.	Post-, Telegrafen- und Fern-sprechbetrieb		9.33-12.38	
C.21.	Zeitungen	1-2	12.35- 1.39	
D.I.	Paßsachen	1-3	6.20- 2.38	
D.II.	Staatsangehörigkeit		6.20- 2.38	
D.III.	Personenstandsachen		6.20-11.38	
D.IV.	Militär-und Marinesachen	1-2	6.20- 6.35	
D.IVa.	Flaggenordnung		11.20-10.37	
D.IVb.	Ausbildungsreisen der Marine	1-3	6.26-12.31	
D.IVb.	- der Deutschen Flotte	4	1.32- 1.34	
		5	1.34- 7.35	

Akten-zeichen	Inhalt	Band	Datum	Serial Nr.
D.IVe.	Deutsche Flottenbesuche in Lissabon		6.27	
	Flottenbesuche in den Kolonien			
D.V.	Juden und Emigranten	1-3	5.33-10.39	
	Aufenthalts- und Einreise-erschwerung für Deutsche	Sbd.	2.38-10.39	
D.VI.	Rassebestimmungen		11.35- 9.37	
D.VIII.	Unterstützungen, Renten		6.20- 2.38	
D.IX.	Mädchenschutz		6.20- 5.30	
D.XII.	Fremde Flottenbesuche in Portugal		10.24- 7.34	
D.1.	Paßwesen, Anfragen und dergl.		6.20- 8.27	
	Passangelegenheiten	1-2	1.30- 5.38	
D.1a.	Anträge - Grenzempfehlungen und Sichtvermerke		12.32-10.40	
D.2.	Anträge über Staatsangehörig-keitssachen		6.20- 2.38	
D.3.	Personenstandssachen, Geburten, Eheschliessung und Todesfälle		6.20- 9.38	
D.4.	Angelegenheiten deutscher Wehrmacht	1-2	6.35- 2.38	
D.5.	Personen-Adressenermittlung	1-4	6.20-10.38	
D.6.	Geld-, Brief- und Drucksachen	1-9	6.20-10.39	
D.6a.	Deutsche Drucksachen für portu-giesische Behörden	2	8.28-12.34	
D.6b.	Austausch von Drucksachen von der portugiesischen Regierung für das Auswärtige Amt	Sbd.	6.20- 6.31	
D.6a.	Austausch von Drucksachen vom Auswärtigen Amt für die portu-giesische Regierung	Sbd.	6.20- 7.38	
D.6b.	Austausch von Drucksachen an deutsche Behörden	2 Sbd.	7.31- 6.35	
D.6a.	Zeitschriften- und Bücherweiter-gabe an Lesehallen, National-Bibliothek, Deutsche Institute und Schulen	1	2.30- 8.34	
D.7.	Beschaffung von Urkunden, Geburts- und Totenscheinen, Verehelichungspapiere		6.20-12.37	
D.8.	Gesetzliche Unterstützung, Renten, Pensionen, Hinterblie-benenfürsorge, Armenpflege, Wohltätigkeit, Heimschaffung	1-5	6.20-12.38	
D.9.	Portugiesisches Vereinswesen	1	1.37- 6.37	
D.10.adh	Empfehlungen an spanische Burgos Regierung		9.36-10.38	

Akten-zeichen	Inhalt	Band	Datum	Serial Nr.
D.10.	Empfohlene und verdächtige Personen	1-6	6.20-12.38	
D.14	Deutsche Flottenbesuche in Portugal und portugiesischen Besitzungen	1-5	2.35-12.37	
D.11.	Portugiesische Paßsachen		5.26-12.38	
D.12.	Fremde Flottenbesuche in Portugal und in portugiesischen Besitzungen	1-2	8.34-12.38	
D.13.	Deutsche Marine (allgemein)	1	6.22- 6.36	
D.14.		1-3	12.35- 9.38	
	Besuch des Vermessungsschiffes "Meteor 2" in Lissabon		4.37- 5.37	
	- des Panzerschiffes "Deutschland" in Lissabon		2.38- 3.38	
	- des Segelschulschiffes "Horst-Wessel" in Lissabon		10.38-12.39	
	- des Kreuzers "Köln" in Lissabon		9.37-10.37	
	- des Linienschiffes "Schleswig-Holstein" in Horta		3.37- 4.37	
	- des Panzerschiffes "Admiral Scheer" in Lissabon		9.37	
	Bergung eines deutschen Torpedos durch Fischdampfer "Cabo Sta. Maria"		9.37-11.37	
D.15.	Portugiesische Flottenbesuche		6.35- 2.38	
D.16.	Weitergabe deutscher Druckschriften an portugiesische Stellen		1.35- 1.39	
D.17.	Austausch von Druckschriften von portugiesischen an deutsche Stellen		6.35-12.38	
D.18.	Weitergabe von Druckschriften an Lesehallen, Nationalbücherei, deutsche Institute, Schulen	1-2	1.35- 1.39	
D.19.	Heimschaffungen	1-2	10.34- 2.39	
D.20.	Weitergabe von Büchern an deutsche Schulen und sonstige Organisationen	1-2	12.35- 2.39	
E.I.	Rechtswesen (Generell)	1-3	6.20- 3.39	
E.Ia.	Deutsch-portugiesisches Abkommen über Wiederinkraftsetzung des Hager Zivilprozessabkommens		7.23- 7.27	
E.2.	Zustellen und Zeugenvernehmungen	1-8	6.20- 5.38	
E.3.	Auslieferungen	1-2	6.20- 1.35	

Akten- zeichen	Inhalt	Band	Datum	Serial Nr.
E.3.	Otto Schmidt, Entschädigungs- sache	Sbd.	6.33- 9.38	
E.4.	Nachlasssachen, Testamentssachen	1-2	6.20-12.38	
E.5.	Vormundschaft		6.20-11.31	
E.6.	Allgemeine Rechtshilfe und Aus- künfte, Benennung von Rechtsan- wälten, Beschwerden gegen deut- sche und portugiesische Behörden	1-6	6.20- 5.38	
	Theodor Lehrfeld	Sbd.		
E.7.	Schuldforderungen und sonstige Reklamationen gegen Private und dergleichen	1-3	6.20- 8.38	
	Angelegenheit Schöss		10.32- 8.40	
E.7a.	Deutsche Vorkriegsforderungen, Sonderheft	1-2	6.20- 5.34	
E.7b.	Entschädigungsansprüche Deutscher	1-2	6.20-12.35	
E.8.	Notariatssachen, Beglaubigungen, Lebensatteste, Bescheinigungen, Zertifikate, Atteste		6.20- 2.38	
F.I.	Schiffs- und Seemannsamtssachen, auch Schiffsunfälle	1-4	6.20-11.38	
	Schiffsverkehr mit Portugal		12.35- 8.38	
F.II.	Schiffsuntergang des Dampfers "Deister"		2.29- 8.29	
G.I.	Unterrichtswesen, Religions- Missionswesen	1-2	6.20- 1.39	
G.II.	Schulunterstützungen		2.35-10.38	
G.III.	Ibero-Amerikanisches Institut Museum		10.35- 1.39	
G.IV.	Kunst und Wissenschaft	1-5	6.20-12.29	
	Allgemeine Kulturpropaganda, Kulturbestrebungen, allgemeiner Art. Kulturpolitische Erlasse und Berichterstattungen, Fonds, Maßnahmen allgemeiner Art.	6	4.29-11.38	
	Deutsches Institut in Coimbra	1-2 Sbd.	9.25- 4.31	
G.IVa.	Vortragsreisen deutscher Wissen- schaftler nach Portugal	1-2	10.25-12.34	
	Vortrag Prof.Askanapp, Genf, betreffend und Graf Keyserling Beiheft.		11.29- 4.30	
G.IVb.	Ereignisse und Veranstaltungen auf künstlerischem und wissen- schaftlichem Gebiet, mit Zutun der Gesandtschaft	1-3	4.29- 6.34	
	Lessingfeier, Beiheft		8.28-12.29	

Akten-zeichen	Inhalt	Band	Datum	Serial Nr.
G.IVd.	Unterstützung und Vermittlung der Gesandtschaft in speziellen und kulturellen Studienfahrten	1-4	6.29- 7.35	
G.IVf.	Kulturfonds 1929	1	1929	
	- 1930	2	4.30- 5.33	
G.V.	Deutsche Reichsangehörige in Portugal und Kolonien, deutsche Vereine	1-2	6.20-11.38	
G.VI.	Allgemeine Schulangelegenheiten der deutschen Schulen in Portugal	1-2	1.35-12.38	
G.VII.	Sport und Olympische Spiele	1-3	3.26- 7.38	
G.VIII.	Deutsche Lesehalle in Lissabon	1-4	1.29-11.38	
G.IX.	Naturereignisse, Erdbeben	1-2	2.23- 7.38	
G.X.	Errichtung eines deutschen Lese-sales im Institute Superior de Ciencias Economicas e Finan-cieras	1-3	11.33-12.38	
G.XI.	Academia da Historia zur Geschichte		7.27-12.38	
G.1.	Bücher, allgemeine Verbilligung des deutschen Buches, Angebot		9.35-10.38	
G.2.	Deutsche Schulen in Lissabon	2-4	1.35-12.38	
	Akten der Deutschen Gesandt-schaft in Portugal		8.27	
	Deutsche Schulen in Lissabon und Porto, Schulunterstützungen	1-8	8.20- 9.33	
G.2a.	Deutsche Schule Lissabon und generelle Erlasse des Auswärtigen Amtes	1	10.33-12.35	
G.2b.	Deutsche Schule Porto	1-2	10.33- 1.39	
G.2c.	- Funchal	1-2	10.33-12.38	
G.2d.	- Horta auf Fajal-Azoren		5.37-11.38	
G.3.	Deutsche Kirche, Friedhof, Bartholomäus-Brüderschaft, Deutsches Krankenheim	1-2 Sbd.	11.20- 2.39	
G.3a.	Deutsche katholische Kirche		11.26-12.38	
G.3b.	Deutsches katholisches Heim		6.28- 5.32	
G.3c.	Deutsches Krankenhaus Lissabon und Hilfsverein		1.30- 1.38	
G.4.	Gliederungen der NSDAP., HJ., BDM., NSV., Arbeitsfront	1-2	11.35-12.38	
G.4.adh.	NSDAP.		9.36-12.38	
G.4.	Reichsredner Prinz Schaumburg-Lippe		1.38-12.38	

Akten-zeichen	Inhalt	Band	Datum	Serial Nr.
G.4.	Reichs-Parteitag 1938 und Aus-landstagung in Stuttgart 1938	Sbd.	3.38- 9.38	
	Besuch des Stabsführers der HJ., Hartmann Lauterbacher in Lissa-bon 1938	Sbd.	1.38- 3.38	
G.4a.	Portugiesische Jugendbewegung Novidade Portuguesa		7.36-12.38	
G.5.	NSDAP., Ortsgruppe Portugal		8.33-10.38	
G.6.	Sammlungen für Wohlfahrtszwecke	1-5	6.20-12.38	
G.7.	Olympiade 1936 in Berlin	1-4	1.34- 9.38	
	Film über Olympiade 1936 in Berlin		9.36- 2.39	
G.7.Adh.	Winter-Olympiade		1.36- 3.36	
	Eintrittskarten Olympiade		12.35- 3.36	
G.8.	Vortragsreisen deutscher Wissen-schaftler nach Portugal	1-2	1.35- 1.39	
	Prof. Georgii			
	Vortragsreise Prof.Dr.H.Cramer, Berlin-Zehlendorf, nach Lissabon 1938		7.38-11.38	
	Prof.Dr.Werner Mulert nach Lissabon, Studienreise 38		6.38	
	Prof.Dr.Harri Meier, Studien-reise		6.38- 7.38	
	Vortrag Prof.Leutensach in Lissabon		3.38- 1.39	
	Prof. Müller-Hehs		11.35-12.37	
	Studienreise Prof.Dr. Daue		9.38	
G.9.	Ereignisse und Veranstaltungen auf künstlerischem und wissen-schaftlichem Gebiet mit Zutun der Gesandtschaft		7.34- 2.38	
G.10a.			4.29-10.38	
G.11.	Unterstützungen und Vermitt-lungstätigkeit in speziell kulturellen Belangen		7.37- 2.39	
G.12.	Kulturbestrebungen fremder Staaten, Auftreten fremder Künstler und Wissenschaftler kulturelle Veranstaltungen fremder Staaten	1-2	4.29-12.38	
	Spez. Camoes Literaturpreis			
G.13.	Kulturfonds Beantragungen, Zahlungen	1-3	6.33- 1.39	
G.15.	Studienreise von Portugiesen nach Deutschland mit deutschen Verkehrsmitteln	1-3	7.35-12.38	

Akten-zeichen	Inhalt	Band	Datum	Serial Nr.
G.15.	Vortrag Prof.Dr.Cabral de Moncada, Nat.-Soz.-Rechtswahrer-Bund		12.37-11.38	
G.16.	Deutsches Institut in Coimbra		5.31-10.38	
G.16.adh	400-Jahrfeier der Universität Coimbra. Überreichung eines Festgeschenkes		10.36- 3.38	
G.17.	Fest des Deutschen Buches, der Deutschen Schule		5.34-12.38	
G.18.	Vortragsreisen deutscher Künstler		8.32- 6.38	
	Reisen deutscher Künstler nach Portugal und portugiesi-scher Künstler nach Deutschland	2	6.38-12.38	
	Konzert Prof.Wilhelm Backhaus in der Gesandtschaft		6.38	
	Dirigentenbesuch Schulz-Dornburg, Austausch-Konzert, Empora Nacional		12.38	
G.19.	Deutsche wissenschaftliche Institute		10.35-11.35	
	Fall Leutensach	Sbd.	4.38- 4.39	
G.20.	Humboldt-Stiftung, Akademischer Austauschdienst	1-2	5.35-11.38	
G.21.	Schwimmwettkämpfe zwischen Portugal und Deutschland	Sbd.	6.37-11.38	
	Ruderwettkämpfe Deutschland-Portugal	Sbd.	6.37- 3.39	
	Jugendsegelregatta in Estoril	Sbd.	1.38- 8.38	
	Fussballspiele, Internationale Spiele	Sbd.	1.35- 3.39	
G.22.	Lehrstühle für deutsche Professoren in Portugal		1.35-11.38	
G.23.	Portugiesisch-brasilianisches Institut, Universität Köln, Prof.Lejeune - Prof.Dané		1.36-12.38	
G.24.	Portugiesische Lektorate in Deutschland		10.37-12.38	
G.25.	Schallplatten		2.38-12.38	
H.1.	Deutsche Schiffahrt		6.20-11.38	
H.2.	Portugiesische Schiffahrt Hafenangelegenheiten	1-4	6.20- 5.28	
		5-9	5.28-12.38	
H.2a.	Kai-Abgabe auf den Azoren Dekret 11190		10.25-12.34	
H.3.	Fremde Schiffahrt		6.20- 9.38	
H.4.	Post-, Telefon-, Telegrafen-, Kabel-,Telefunkenwesen	1-4	6.20- 5.36	

Akten- zeichen	Inhalt	Band	Datum	Serial Nr.
H.5.	Eisenbahnen und Verkehrswege	1-2	6.20-12.38	
H.6.[1]	Luftschiffahrt-Flugwesen Beiheft	1-3	9.21- 2.31	
		1-4	6.20- 9.30	
		5-9	10.30- 7.38	
H.7.	Speditionswesen		6.20- 6.32	
H.8.	Kohlen- und Oelstationen		6.20- 4.26	
H.9.	Diskriminierung der fremden Flagge	1-4	4.29-11.35	
H.10.	Portugiesisches und fremdes Flugwesen	1-2	11.35-11.38	
H.11.	Segelflug		11.34-12.38	
H.12.	Reiseverkehr, Fremdenverkehr, Verkehrswerbung, Verkehrsvereine, Reisebüros		6.36- 2.39	
H.13.	Reiseabkommen mit Portugal		2.37-10.37	
J.I.	Deutsche Maßnahmen und Bestim- mungen zur Regelung der Ein- und Auswanderung		6.20-10.38	
J.II.	Portugiesische Maßnahmen zur Regelung der Ein- und Auswan- derungen, Siedlung, Bestimmungen über Fremdenkontrolle		6.20- 1.36	
J.1.	Ein- und Rückwanderung nach Deutschland		10.37- 3.38	
J.3.	Arbeits-, Wohnungs- und Stellen- vermittlung, Einreisegesuche, Lebensbedingungen in Portugal und Madeira	1-2	6.20-11.38	
J.4.	Arbeitsstellenvermittlung , Einreisegesuche, Lebens-Ansied- lungsbedingungen in Angola	1-5	6.20- 5.38	
J.5.	- in Mozambique	1-3	6.20- 1.38	
J.6.	- Azoren,Cap Verd Inseln,Guinea, Insel St.Thomé und Principe (Golf v.Guinea) Macao(China) Timor(Ostindien) Coa und Damao (Vorderindien) und alle Anfra- gen ohne nähere Bezeichnung der Kolonie		6.20- 7.37	
J.7.	Zulassung von deutschen Ärzten, Apotheken und freien Berufen		6.20- 1.38	
K.I.	Versicherungswesen		6.20- 6.38	
K.II.	Patentwesen, Markenschutz, Urheberrecht		6.20-11.38	

Akten-zeichen	Inhalt	Band	Datum	Serial Nr.
K.III.	Gesundheitswesen		1.20- 9.33	
K.VIII.	Sozialisierung		6.20- 6.34	
K.IX.	Staatsfinanzen, Finanzwirtschaft	1-3	6.20-11.28	
Pol.3	Portugal: Finanzen	1	1912-16	
K.IX.	Portugiesische Staatsfinanzen,	1-7	3.39-12.39	
K.IXa.	Aufnahme des Zinsendienstes der Portugiesischen Vorkriegs-anleihen	1-2	4.28- 4.37	
K.X.	Allgemeine wirtschaftliche Lage in Portugal, Madeira und Kolonien	1-2	6.20-11.38	
K.XI.	Allgemeine Wirtschaftslage Deutschlands	1-8	6.20- 5.38	
K.XII.	Wirtschafts- und Finanzlage fremder Staaten	1	1920-36	
K.XIII.	Internationale Konferenzen und Kongresse	1-4	11.24- 7.38	
	Zweiter Internationaler Kongress für Brückenbau und Hochbau. Dritter Internationaler Kongress für das ärztliche Fortbildungs-wesen. Tuberkulose-Kongress, Früchteverwertung. Erster Kon-gress der Geschichte der Portu-giesischen Expansionen. Welt-milchkongress. Siebter Interna-tionaler Kongress für Entomologie Berlin		1937-38	
	Kongress über Freizeit- und Feierabendgestaltung, Deutscher Forstkongress		10.35- 7.36	
	Internationaler Kongress für gerichtliche und soziale Medizin		8.38	
	Internationaler Gartenbaukongress		8.38	
	- Forstkongress		5.38- 6.39	
	Tagung der Taubstummenlehrer International		10.38	
	Internationaler Bäderkongress		8.38-11.38	
	-Kongress Städterei-nigung		5.38- 8.38	
	-Touristenkongress, Lissabon		5.38	
	-Kinderschutzkongress		4.38- 7.38	
	-Kongress Unfall-Medizin und Berufs-krankheiten		3.38-11.38	
	-Kongress für Singen und Sprechen		4.38- 5.38	
	-Weinbaukongress		3.38- 1.39	

Akten-zeichen	Inhalt	Band	Datum	Serial Nr.
K.XIII.	Internationaler Kongress für Archäologie, Berlin		10.38-10.39	
	Internationaler Landwirtschafts-kongress, Dresden		9.38- 6.39	
	Anti-kommunistischer Weltkongress		11.37-11.38	
	Internationaler Prüfungs- und Treuhandkongress			
K.4.	Deutsches Ausstellungswesen und Reklame	1-4	6.20- 7.38	
K.5.	Fremdes Ausstellungswesen	1-2	6.20-11.38	
K.6.	Landwirtschaft, Forstwesen, Fischzucht, Weinbau, Pflanzen und Tiere		6.20- 9.38	
K.7.	Bankwesen, Münzen, Maasse, Gewichte, Genossenschaftswesen	1-3	6.20-11.38	
	Errichtung einer deutschen Bank-Filiale in Lissabon		1.37- 1.39	
K.8.	Devisenbestimmungen, auch Anträge auf Freigabe von Devisen	1-2	7.34-11.38	
K.9.	Deutsche Kongress-Zentrale		12.35	
L.I.	Deutsche Zollgesetzgebung		6.20- 1.39	
L.II.	Portugiesische Zollgesetzgebung		6.20- 9.38	
L.III.	Portugiesische Gesetzgebung über pharmazeutische Artikel		1.32- 2.39	
L.IV.	Beantragung zollfreier Einfuhr		5.36- 7.36	
L.V.	Zollvergünstigung diplomatischer Vertretungen		1.29- 5.38	
L.XV.	Deutsche Steuergesetzgebung und Monopole		6.20- 2.38	
L.XVI.	Portugiesische Steuergesetzgebung und Monopole		6.20- 8.36	
L.XVII.	Fremde Steuergesetzgebung und Monopole		6.20- 7.21	
L.XVIII.	Portugiesische Gesetzgebung über pharmazeutische Artikel		2.28-12.31	
L.1.	Deutsche Zölle und Zolltarif (Anfragen)		6.20- 3.38	
L.2.	Portugiesischer Zolltarif und Zölle	1-2	6.20-11.38	
L.3.	Fremde Zollgesetzgebung		6.20- 9.37	
L.4.	Zollbehandlung von Umzugs-, Heirats- und Erbschaftsgut		6.20- 4.36	
L.5.	Zollbefreiung, Zollvergünstigung für die Gesandtschaft		6.20-12.38	
L.6.	Zollbeschwerden	1-2	6.20-12.38	

Akten-zeichen	Inhalt	Band	Datum	Serial Nr.
L.7.	Ursprungserzeugnisse, Konsulats-fakturen, Reinheitszeugnisse	1-3	6.20- 8.38	
L.8.	Portugiesische Konsulatsgebühren	1	10.21- 9.38	
L.9.	Untersuchungszeugnisse und Ursprungszeugnisse, Port- und Madeira-Weine	1-2	4.26- 5.36	
M.I.	Industrie in Deutschland		6.20- 9.38	
M.II.	Industrielle Entwicklung Portugals		6.20-10.38	
M.1.	Gewerbe und Handwerk in Deutschland		2.37-11.38	
M.2.	Gewerbe und Handwerk in Portugal		1.37-11.38	
M.3.	Elektro-Industrie, Wasserkraft		6.20- 5.38	
M.4.	Portugiesische Bergwerksindu-strie Kohlen		6.20- 8.38	
M.5.	Kriegslieferungen		11.35- 4.38	
	Protokoll über die Regelung der Zahlungen für die Lieferung deutscher Kriegsgeräte in Portugal, Waffenlieferung	2-3	1.37-12.38	
	Deutsche Waffenlieferungen an die portugiesische Regierung Protokoll über die Zahlungs-regelung	Sbd	1.38- 6.40 6.38	
N.1.	Handelsbeziehungen Portugals zu Deutschland	1-2	3.38- 2.39	
	Deutsch-portugiesische Wirt-schaftsverhandlungen einschließ-lich Abkommen anlässlich der Rückgliederung Oesterreichs und des Sudetenlandes	1-2 Sbd.	3.38- 2.39	
N.2.	Handelsbeziehungen zwischen Deutschland und anderen Staaten		6.20- 7.38	
N.3.	Handelsbeziehungen zwischen Portugal und anderen Staaten	1-2	6.20-12.38	
N.4.	Handelsbeziehungen zwischen fremden Staaten		6.20-12.38	
N.5.	Handelskongress		6.20- 8.27	
N.6.	Deutscher Innenhandel (auch Statistik)		6.20- 4.36	
N.7.	Portugiesischer Innenhandel (auch Statistik)		6.20- 6.34	
N.8.	Deutscher Aussenhandel und Maßnahmen zu seiner Förderung (Statistik)	1-4	6.20-12.38	
N.9.	Portugiesischer Aussenhandel, Maßnahmen zu seiner Förderung (Statistik)	1-2	6.20-12.38	
N.10.	Sonstige Handelsstatistik soweit nicht in 6-9		6.20- 7.32	

Akten-zeichen	Inhalt	Band	Datum	Serial Nr.
N.11.	Handelssachen fremder Länder mit Ausschluss von Deutschland und Portugal		6.20- 4.34	
N.12.	Deutsche Aus- und Einfuhrbestim-mungen (amtliche Verzeichnisse der Waren, deren Ausfuhr aus Deutschland gestattet ist)	1-2	6.20- 9.38	
N.13.	Portugiesische Aus-und Einfuhr-bestimmungen (Verbote)	1-4	6.20-11.38	
N.15.	Ausschreibungen von Werklieferun-gen	1-2	6.20- 3.39	
N.16.	Klagen über deutsche wirtschaft-liche Maßnahmen und Geschäfts-praktiken und Gegenvorschläge		6.20-12.38	
N.17.	Firmen und Kreditauskünfte Schwindelfirmen	1-2	6.20-10.38	
N.18.	Benennung und Angebote von Vertreterfirmen		6.20-12.38	
N.19.	Handelsauskünfte	1-2	6.20- 6.38	
N.20.	Handlungsreisende und Waren-musteraustausch junger Kaufleute		6.20-10.38	
N.21.	Handelsadressbücher, Handelszei-tungen und Zeitschriften, Berich-te von Banken, Handelskammer	1-3	6.20- 5.37	
N.22.	Berichte deutscher Grossbanken über die wirtschaftliche Lage Deutschlands	1-2	1.26- 6.26	
N.23.	Bearbeitung des Fragebogens des Enquete-Ausschusses		11.26- 6.29	
N.24.	Berichterstattung an die Zentral-stelle für Aussenhandel, soweit Berichte nicht zu einer Materie gehören		10.29-11.35	
N.25.	Beschwerden über Erledigung von Handelsangelegenheiten		1.32- 1.39	
N.26.	Ananas-Ausfuhr		10.35-10.37	
N.27.	Vertretung: Bildienst für Aussenhandel und Auslandswirt-schaft		3.36- 7.38	
N.28.	Deutsche Handelskammer Lissabon		8.35- 6.37	
N.29.	Kompensationsgeschäfte		1.37- 2.39	
O.1	Empfänge	1-2	6.20- 5.35	
O.2a.	Portugiesische Ingenieurerzeug-nisse		12.26- 8.38	
O.3.	Einladungen zu Festlichkeiten, feierlichen Begebenheiten	1-3	6.20- 1.39	
O.3a.	- Audienzen		4.26-12.38	
O.4.	Zeremonielles		6.20- 7.38	
O.5.	Portugiesische Nationalfeiertage		11.27-10.38	

Akten-zeichen	Inhalt	Band	Datum	Serial Nr.
O.6.	Ordensauszeichnungen fremder Staaten		3.29- 1.39	
O.5.	Portugiesische Ordensverleihung an deutsche Reichsangehörige	1	1.39	
O.7.	Verschiedenes	1-2	1.32- 3.39	
O.8.	Ehrenkreuz für Frontkämpfer des Weltkrieges, Verwundeten-abzeichen	1-2	8.34- 9.38	
	Verzeichnis und Anträge auf Weltkriegs-Ehrenkreuze	Sbd.	1.35- 7.38	
O.9.	Bestellungen (Christbäume)		11.35- 3.39	
O.10.	N.S. Gemeinschaft Kraft durch Freude	1-3	12.35-11.38	
	Reichstagung der NSG.-Kraft durch Freude 1937 Weltkongress Arbeit und Freude, Rom		6.38- 7.38	
	Besuch der K.d.F.-Flotten	Sbd.	4.38	
O.11.	Nationalsozialistische deutsche Kriegsopferversorgung N.S.K.O.V.		7.35- 1939	
O.12.	Darbietungen, Wünsche an Führer und Reichsregierung		1936-38	
P.1. Nr.1	Presse und Propagandawesen in Portugal (Allgemeines)	1-5	1.39- 1.43	
Nr.2	- in anderen Ländern		11.39- 6.41	
P.2.	Propagandamappe Verteilung von Propagandamaterial	1-4	1.39- 1.41	
P.2. Nr.1	Deutsche Propaganda und Aufklä-rung und Pressebeziehungen Deutschland - Portugal	1 2 3	1.39- 4.40	7231/E530542-48
		4-7	1.40- 9.40	
		8-15	8.40- 1.43	
	Presserundtelegramme	1-2 Sbd.	9.39- 6.40	
	Pressestimmen (Anlage)	2	9.39	
	Rheinpresse	Sbd.	2.41- 2.42	
P.2. Nr.1a.	Übersetzer für Presse		3.40- 9.40	
Nr.1b.	Europa-Sonderdienst		3.40-12.41	
Nr.1c.	Technischer Aparat für Propa-ganda-Abteilung		9.40-12.40	
P.2. Nr.2.	Presse und Propagandabeziehun-gen zwischen Portugal und ande-ren Staaten, fremde Presseatta-chés, feindliche Propaganda (soweit nicht Hetze)	1-3	1.39- 9.42	
Nr.3.	Pressepolitische Berichte der Gesandtschaft und Berichte des Pressebeirates	1-2	1.39- 1.42	

Akten-zeichen	Inhalt	Band	Datum	Serial Nr.
P.2. Nr.4	Telefonisch durchgegebene Meldungen der D.N.B. nach Berlin	1-3	1.40- 2.42	
P.3. Nr.1	Portugiesische und sonstige Journalisten, Schriftleiter, einschliesslich Auslandsreisen	1	1.39-12.41	
Nr.2	Deutsche Journalisten und Schriftleiter einschliesslich Reisen ins Ausland	1-3	1.39- 4.42	
P.4.	Zeitungsaustausch		1.39- 3.39	
P.5.	Deutschfeindliche Presse, Theater- und Rundfunkhetze in Portugal und sonstigen Ländern	1-5	1.39- 7.42	
Po.1.	Politische Beziehungen zwischen Portugal und Deutschland, auch Handelsverträge		1.20-10.38	
	Material zum Abschluss des Handelsvertrages	1	3.22- 2.27	
Po.2.	Politische Beziehungen zwischen Portugal und anderen Staaten, auch Handelsverträge	1-5	6.20- 1.39	
	Englische Militärmission in Portugal	Sbd.	10.37	
Po.3.	Politische Beziehungen zwischen Deutschland und anderen Staaten, auch Handelsverträge	1-4	6.20-10.38	
Po.4.	Zwischenstaatliche politische Beziehungen, auch Handelsverträge		6.20-10.38	
Po.5.	Politik fremder Staaten mit Ausnahme Portugals und Deutschlands	1-4	6.20-12.38	
Po.6.	Allgemeine auswärtige Politik Portugals	1-2	6.20-11.38	
	Allgemeine Angelegenheiten und Kolonien		1.39- 6.39	
Po.7.	Portugals innere Polotik, Parlaments- und Parteiwesen	Sbd.	6.20- 9.25	
	Zeitungsausschnitte über portugiesische innere Lage	1	6.20-12.21	
	Portugals innere Politik, Parlaments- und Parteiwesen	1-4	1.22-12.32	
		5-9	1.33- 2.39	
	Ausrüstung der portugiesischen Legion	Sbd.	5.37- 3.38	
	Feier der 12.Wiederkehr des Tages der Nationalrevolution Portugals	Sbd.	5.38	
	Übersetzung der Reden von Dr. Oliveira Salazar	Sbd.	3.37-11.38	

Akten-zeichen	Inhalt	Band	Datum	Serial Nr.
Po.7.	Verleih der Filme vom 28.Mai 37 "Legiao Portuguesa"	Sbd.		
	"Mocidade Portuguesa" an die "Tobias" in Deutschland		5.37	
Po.8.	Portug. Ministerien		6.20- 9.38	
	Angelegenheiten des Presserefe-renten bei der Gesandtschaft Madrid		2.40- 8.41	
Po.9.	Portugiesische diplomatische und konsularische Vertretungen im Auslande (auch Deutschland)	1-3	6.20-10.38	
Po.10.	Fremde diplomatische und konsu-larische Vertretungen in Portu-gal und anderen Ländern	1-4	6.20-12.38	
Po.11	Personalien und Reisen bedeuten-der Persönlichkeiten: Staats-oberhäupter, Militärs, Journa-listen, geistliche Würdenträger	1-3	6.20- 9.38	
Po.12.	Portugiesische Militär-und Marine angelegenheiten	1-2	6.20-12.38	
Po.13.	Portug. Missions-, Religions- und Kirchenwesen		6.20-10.38	
Po.14.	Portug. Unterrichtswesen und Bildungswesen	1-2	10.28- 7.38	
Po.14a	Portug. innere Verwaltung		1.29- 1.38	
Po.15.	Deutschlands innere Lage, Verfassung, Nationalfeiertage	1-5	6.20- 4.34	
		6-8	5.34-12.38	
Po.15a.	Verfassung, Flaggenfrage		4.29- 6.38	
Po.15b.	Deutsche Nationalfeiertage	1	4.29-10.38	
Po.16.	Deutschlands äussere Lage und Politik		6.20- 2.39	
Po.17.	Soziale Verhältnisse	1-2	6.20-12.38	
Po.19.	Bolschewismus, Kommunismus	1-2	6.20-12.38	
Po.19a.	Politische Übersichten		1.30- 2.31	
	Bolschewismus in Portugal		5.27-12.37	
Po.20.	Liquidation des deutschen Eigen-tums	1	6.20-11.20	
		2	11.20- 7.21	
		3-4	9.21-11.33	
		4	10.21-10.24	
		5	11.24-10.26	
Po.20a.	Liquidation des Eigentums der deutschen Wahlkonsuln		6.20- 1929	
Po.21.	Herausgabe der Privateffekten, die von Portugal auf deutschen Dampfern beschlagnahmt worden sind	1-2	6.20-11.26	

Akten-zeichen	Inhalt	Band	Datum	Serial Nr.
Po.22.	Herausgabe des Seemannsgepäcks		6.20- 6.22	
Po.23.	Ladungen der beschlagnahmten deutschen Schiffe	1-2	6.20- 9.32	
Po.24.	Beschlagnahme der deutschen Schiffe		9.19- 1.27	
Po.24a.	- der kaufmännischen Archive		8.20- 2.21	
Po.25.	Beschlagnahmtes deutsches Eigentum in den portugiesischen Kolonien	1-2	5.19-10.27	
Po.25. III.			11.27- 1932	
Po.26.	Assyrische Altertümer	1-2	6.20- 5.29	
Po.27.	Private Wirtschaftsverhandlungen	1-2	7.23- 5.24	
	Verhandlungsakten über beschlagnahmtes Eigentum	1-6	9.20-12.36	
	Handelsvertragsverhandlungen mit Portugal	Sbd. 1-7	9.21-10.31	
	- Zeitungsausschnitte zu den Verhandlungen		7.21- 8.21	
	- Verhandlungen	Sbd.		
Po.28.	Verhandlungen über eine deutsch-portugiesische Literaturkonvention		7.23- 1.27	
Po.29.	Verhandlungen über einen deutsch-portugiesischen Konsularvertrag		9.26- 7.27	
Po.30.	Zahlungsabkommen Deutschland-Portugal	1-4	9.33- 1.39	
Po.31.	Beglaubigungsschreiben der Missionschefs		1.35-11.38	
Po.32.	Deutsche Journalisten		12.35-10.38	
	Journalist Dr.Schulz	Sbd.	12.37-10.38	
Po.33.	Kirche und Nationalsozialismus		10.35-10.38	
Po.34.	Jahresberichte, frühere Jahresberichte		1.38	
Po.35.	Rückgliederung Oesterreichs		3.38-11.38	
Po.39.	Deutscher Nachrichtendienst, Transocean-Ges., Radio		6.20- 5.38	
Po.40.	Deutsche Presse	1-3	6.20-12.38	
Po.41.	Bonaventura	Sbd.	1.35-10.38	
	Portugiesische Presse, deutscher Nachrichtendienst für portugiesische Presse	1-4	6.20- 4.35	
		5-8	4.35-12.38	

Akten-zeichen	Inhalt	Band	Datum	Serial Nr.
Po.42.	Fremde, nichtdeutsche und nicht-portugiesische Presse		6.20- 4.36	
Po.43.	Deutsche Propaganda, Aufklärungs-dienst	1-6	6.20- 4.23	
		7-15	8.23- 3.30	
		16-20	4.30- 5.35	
	Nachrichten für Herrn Mielitz. Propagandamaterial über Anfänge des Hitlerregimes	1	3.33- 9.33	
	Deutsche Propaganda und Aufklä-rungsdienst	21-25	6.35- 2.39	
	Salazar, Einrichtung von Lese-sälen an den portugiesischen Universitäten betr. Faschismus und Nationalsozialismus	Sbd.	4.37-10.38	
Po.43a.	Deutsche Pressebeiträge	1-5	12.28-12.30	
		6-10	1.31- 5.37	
Po.43b. gen.	Zeitungsaustausch zum Zwecke von Propaganda über das Neue Deutsch-land	1	2.37-11.38	
Po.43b. spec.	Zeitungsaustausch	1	9.37-11.38	
Po.43b.	"Eine Handvoll Statistik"		11.30- 4.31	
Po.44.	Fremde (feindliche) Propaganda	1-2	6.20-11.38	
Po.45.	Filme	1-5	6.20-12.38	
Po.46.	Fremde Propaganda in Portugal		11.35-12.36	
Po.47.	Übersendung von Filmen	1-2	8.35-12.38	
Po.48.	Portugiesische Kolonien (allge-mein) Portugiesisch-koloniale Reichskonferenz		7.36-12.38	
Po.49.	Wirtschaftsabkommen für portu-giesische Kolonien		11.35- 3.38	
Po.50.	Azoren und Madeira	1-2	6.20-11.38	
Po.51.	Cap Verdische Inseln		6.20- 2.37	
Po.52.	Portugiesisch Guinea, Westafrika	1-2	6.20-11.38	
Po.53.	Die Inseln St.Thomé und Principe (Golf v. Guinea)		6.20-10.34	
Po.54.	Angola (Westafrika)	1-4	7.20-10.27	
	Politik in Angola	5-9	10.27- 1.39	
Po.54. adh.	Stauerei in Lobito		9.37- 3.39	
	Fall Paul Losch		10.35- 9.36	
	Bericht über eine Dienstreise durch den belgischen Kongo	Sbd	11.36- 6.37	

Akten-zeichen	Inhalt	Band	Datum	Serial Nr.
Po.55.	Mozambique (Ostafrika)	1-4	6.20- 5.29	
		5-9	5.29-12.38	
Po.56.	Macao (China), Timor (Ostindien)		6.20-12.38	
Po.57.	Portugiesische Presse, neue Kolonien für Deutschland	1 2 3 4 5	10.29-11.38	M276/M011448-81
	Angeblich Angola-Verhandlungen (Eintritt) Katzenstein und Vor-gänge Compannia Cabinda	Sbd	4.36- 6.37	
Po.58.	Locarno und Deutschlands Eintritt in den Völkerbund	1-4	12.25-12.30	
	- und Völkerbunds-fragen	5 6 7	1.31- 5.37	6428/E479963-75
	Völkerbundsfragen	1	3.36-12.38	6428/E479976-80
Po.58a.	Internationales Arbeitsamt beim Völkerbund	1-2	3.27- 7.32	
Po.59.	Rüstungs- und Abrüstungsfragen	1-3	10.28-11.36	
Po.60.	Young-Plan Konferenzen	1 2 3 4	1929-30 1930-31 1931-32 1932-34	
	Liquidierung der Vergangenheit	5-6	1.35-11.36	
	Young-Plan-Gesetzgebung Beiheft		6.29- 1930	
	Vorkriegsforderungen, Beiheft		1920-31	
Po.70.	Friedensvertrag von Versailles und seine Folgen	1-3	1920-38	
Po.71.	Sanktionen in Portugal und ande-ren Ländern		1921	
Po.72.	Reparationsfrage in Deutschland	1-6	6.20- 1.23	
		7-10	1.23- 6.23	
		11-15	6.23- 3.24	
		16-20	3.24- 3.28	
		21-25	4.28- 4.29	
		26-30	4.29- 3.33	
Po.73.	Oberschlesien	1-2	6.20- 3.27	
Po.74.	Polnische Fragen		6.20- 8.33	
Po.75.	Die Schuldfrage	1-2	6.20- 4.27	
Po.76.	Deutsch-portugiesisch gemischte Schiedsgerichtshöfe und portu-giesische Forderungen auf Repara-tionskonto	1-3	6.20- 3.35	
	- mit Zeitungsausschnitten		6.20- 6.36	

Akten-zeichen	Inhalt	Band	Datum	Serial Nr.
Po.76a.	Überführung eines Greifbaggers nach Lissabon		9.22- 7.27	
Po.76b.	Überführung von drei Einbaggern nach Lissabon		6.23	
Po.77.	Schulden der Alliierten	1-2	9.25- 1.37	
Po.78.	Kriegsschulden Portugals an England		6.25-11.30	
Po.79.	Interviews		12.27-11.34	
Po.80.	Internationale Vorträge, Pan-Europa-Bestrebung	1-2	4.29- 7.38	
Po.81.	Lausanner Abkommen		7.32-10.32	
Po.82.	Saarfrage	1-2	1.34- 3.35	
Po.83.	Memel		3.35- 5.38	
Po.84.	Spanien - Italien	1-3	9.35-12.38	
Po.84. adh.1.	Deutsche Flüchtlinge aus Spanien		12.36- 3.38	
adh.2.	Napierala		9.36-11.38	
adh.3.	Kriegsschiffe in Spanien	1	7.36-12.37	
adh.4.	Waffenlieferung an Spanien	1	7.36-11.36	3371/E010612-29
adh.5.	Spanien: Nichteinmischungspakt Waffenembargo, Freiwilligenfrage	1 2 3 4	11.36-12.38	3369/E010560-77 3369/E010578-82 3369/E010583-600 3467/E017875-77
Po.84b.	Deutsche Botschaft und Konsulate in Spanien		7.37-12.38	
Po.84.	Spanien, Privatbriefe mit Personal	Sbd. 6	7.37-12.38	
Po.85.	Politik der Westmächte, England, Belgien, Holland, Frankreich, Schweiz		1.34- 5.38	
Po.86.	Sowjet-Union, Verhältnis zu Deutschland		11.36- 1938	
Po.90.	Wehrpolitik, Auf- und Abrüstung (allgemein)		9.36-11.36	
Pol.1.	Portug.Aussenpolitik, allgemein		1.39- 2.43	2949/D576498-513
Pol.2. Nr. 1	Politische Beziehungen Deutschlands zu Portugal		1.39- 9.42	2942/D569960-64
	Neutralität Portugals im deutsch-englischen Kriege		1.39- 7.40	
	Schutzmachtangelegenheiten Belgisch-Kongo	Sbd. 1-2	10.40- 2.43	
Nr.2.	Besuche deutscher Kriegsschiffe in portugiesischen Häfen, Hoheitsgewässern, Besitzungen und sonstigen fremden Ländern		1.39- 7.39	

Akten-zeichen	Inhalt	Band	Datum	Serial Nr.
Pol.2. Nr.2.	Besuch deutscher Kriegsschiffe in Portugal	Sbd.	4.39- 5.39	
Nr.3.	Angelegenheit der deutschen Militärattachés		1.39- 5.42	
Nr.3a.	Militärattaché v.Horn		11.38-12.40	
Nr.4.	Insel Timor	1-2 Sbd.	11.41- 1.43	
Nr.5.	Besuche fremder Kriegsschiffe in portugiesischen Häfen, Hoheitsgewässern und Besitzungen		1.39-11.41	
Nr.6.	Politik fremder Staaten, Innen- Aussen-Kolonialpolitik und politische Beziehungen zu son- stigen fremden Staaten	1 2 3	1.39- 1.43	2936/D569609-37
Nr.7.	Wehrmachtsangelegenheiten und Sonstiges fremder Staaten		4.39	
Nr.8.	Spanien und spanischer Bürger- krieg einschliesslich Nicht- einmischung, Aufbau	1	1.39- 2.43	2937/D569640-89
Pol.3.	Innenpolitik Portugal		1.39- 2.43	
Pol.3. Nr.1.	Ministerien		1.39- 1.43	
Nr.2.	Portug. Militärangelegenheiten		1.39- 1.43	
Nr.3.	Portug.Heeresbesuche in Deutsch- land und fremden Staaten		1.39-11.42	
Nr.4.	Portug.Marinebesuche in Deutsch- land und anderen Staaten		1.39-12.42	
Nr.5.	Portug.Luftwaffenbesuche in Deutschland und anderen Staaten		1.39- 5.40	
Nr.5a.	Portug.Polizeibesuche in Deutschland und anderen Staaten		1.39- 1.42	
Nr.6.	Portug.Frontkämpferverbände und Legion		1.39-12.42	
Nr.7.	Kommunismus in Portugal		1.39- 2.43	
Nr.9.	Juden in Portugal, auch Einwan- derung		1.39-12.42	
Nr.10.	Portug. Kolonialpolitik	1 2	1.39- 2.43	1095/318227-29
Nr.11.	Portug.Kolonien, Azoren, Madeira und Cap Verdische Inseln		1.39- 4.40	
Nr.13.	Angola (Westafrika)		1.39-10.40	
Nr.14.	Mozambique (Ostafrika)		1.39- 5.40	
Nr.15.	Insel Timor		1.39-12.39	
Nr.16.	Kolonie Macao		1.39	
Pol.4. Nr.1.	Völkerbund		1.39- 1.41	
Nr.2.	Bolschewismus-Kommunismus- Sozialismus-Freimaurertum		1.39- 2.43	

Akten-zeichen	Inhalt	Band	Datum	Serial Nr.
Pol.4. Nr.3.	Abrüstung, Rüstung allgemein		1.39- 7.39	
Nr.4.	Judenfrage, Rassenfrage, ausser in Deutschland und Portugal		1.39- 7.39	
Nr.6.	Flaggenführung und Salutordnung einschliesslich Kriegs- und Handelsschiffe (Flaggenvergehen)		1.39- 2.39	
D.Pol.1.	Deutsche Aussenpolitik	1-2	1.39- 2.43	
	Hess	Sbd.	5.41	
D.Pol.2.	Deutsch-polnischer Krieg 1939 und dessen Auswirkung bezüglich England und Frankreich	1 2 3 4 5 6 7 8	1.39- 4.40 4.40- 7.40 6.40-10.40 lo.40- 8.41 9.41- 5.42 3.42-10.42	1116/320849-50 9920/E694615-45 4852/E247719-24 5392/E362135-45
	Navicerts	Sbd. b.	7.40- 1.42	
	Politische Beziehungen zu anderen Staaten ausser Portugal, auch Verträge und Abkommen	1 2 3	1.39-12.41	5130/E295947-48
	Deutsch-englischer Konsulataustausch	Sbd. c. 1-3	8.40- 4.42	
	König Carol von Rumänien	Sbd. d.	7.40- 7.42	
	Deutsch-amerikanischer Konsulat-austausch	Sdb. f. 1-4	7.41- 5.42	
		5-9	5.42-10.42	
D.Pol.3.	Deutsche Innenpolitik, allgemein (Staat, Kirche und Partei, Wehr-politik, Bevölkerungs- und Pressepolitik, Deutsche Polizei)		1.39- 1.43	
Nr.2.	Deutsche Wehrmacht allgemein Wehr- und Arbeitsdienstpflicht, Pflichtjahr für Mädchen		1.39-12.42	
Nr.3.	Deutsches Heer		1.39- 3.42	
Nr.4.	Deutsche Kriegsmarine		1.39- 2.41	
Nr.5.	Deutsche Luftwaffe		1.39- 8.42	
Nr.6.	NSDAP und Nationalsozialismus		1.39- 5.41	
Nr.7.	NSDAP Landesleitung Portugal und Ortsgruppen Lissabon, Porto, Funchal	1-2	1.39- 2.43	
Nr.8.	Reichsparteitag	Sbd.	1.39- 7.39	
Nr.9.	Reisen von Parteiführern und Führern der Parteigliederungen (SA) nach Portugal und sonstigen Ländern		1.39- 8.41	
Nr.10.	Hitlerjugend auf Reisen nach Portugal und anderen Staaten		1.39- 1.43	

Akten-zeichen	Inhalt	Band	Datum	Serial Nr.
D.Pol.3 Nr.10.	Reise General Carmona nach Mozambique	Sbd	1.39- 9.39	
Nr.11.	Frontkämpferverbände, NS-Kriegs-opferversorgung		1.39- 6.39	
Nr.13.	Reisen prominenter deutscher politischer Persönlichkeiten nach Portugal		1.39-12.42	
Nr.14.	Protektorat Böhmen und Mähren		1.39- 4.42	
Nr.15.	Abgetretene Gebiete (Danzig, Korridor, Schleswig auch frühe-res Memelland)			
Nr.17.	Lösung der Judenfrage		1.39-12.42	5798/E422508-12 K1605/K3911566-695
	Portugiesische Gesellschaft		3.22- 5.28	
	Streitfrage Josef Henn (Commercial)		10.26- 8.27	
	Zahlungslisten		12.22- 3.27	
			1927- 3.30	
			4.31- 3.33	
	Wochenberichte		4.27-10.30	
	Sympathie- und Antipathiekundge-bungen einzelner Portugiesen		1.39-10.41	
	Pressestimmen die Gesandschaft und deren Tätigkeit betreffend		1.29- 3.31	
	Portugiesische Pressestimmen über Deutschland		12.27- 3.30	
			4.30- 8.30	
			9.29-11.29	
			9.30-12.30	
			1.31-12.33	
			1.34	
	Deutsche Zeitungsausschnitte	1-3	11.28-12.29	
	Briefwechsel Deutschland - Spanien A.		10.36-11.36	
	B.		10.36-11.36	
	C.		8.36- 3.37	
	D.		10.36-11.36	
	E.		9.36- 8.37	
	F.		8.36- 1.37	
	G.		9.36-11.36	
	H.		9.36-10.37	
	I.J.		9.36- 3.37	
	K.		9.36- 8.38	

Akten-zeichen	Inhalt	Band	Datum	Serial Nr.
	Briefwechsel, Deutschland – Spanien L.		8.36– 2.41	
	M.		8.36– 3.37	
	N.		9.36–10.36	
	O.P.		9.36–10.36	
	Q.R.		9.36–10.36	
	S.		9.36– 8.38	
	T.U.		9.36–12.38	
	V.W.		9.36–11.36	
	X.Y.Z.		9.36–11.36	
	Warnungen vor Personen		11.35– 1.36	
	Costa/Weiss gegen Stadt Berlin		1.35– 2.38	
	Personalien		7.35– 6.38	
	Presse, Auslands-Presse-Büro G.m.b.H., Pressebeirat	1-2	1.36–12.38	
	Kommunismus	1	7.36– 7.38	
	Spanien-Vertraulich-Geheim	1	9.38– 4.39	
	Politische Übersichten	1	8.38–10.38	
	Wehrpflicht, Arbeitsdienst-pflicht, Reichswehr	1	8.35–12.38	
	Vertrauliche Erlasse des Auswärtigen Amtes	1 2 3 4	2.34– 3.39	6984/E522071-232
	Anfragen über Inkunabeln von Martin Kurz	1	3.25– 5.32	
Pers.G.15	Schriftwechsel der Gesandt-schaft mit der Botschaft in Spanien und Deutschen Konsula-ten in Spanien und spanischen Besitzungen	1-6	1.39– 7.42	
Pers.G.16	Schriftwechsel mit der Gesandt-schaft, mit sonstigen deutschen ausländischen Vertretungen	1	1.36–12.41	
Pers.G.17	Arbeits- und Stellenvermittlung (auch für Portugiesen) Auskünfte über Einzelpersonen		1.39–12.40	
Pers.G.18	Abgehende Minero-Telegramme	1-2	9.41– 6.42	
	Weiterleitung von Briefen nach Funchal und Azoren und portu-giesische Kolonien	Sbd.	3.41– 1.43	
	Weiterleitung von Briefen, Paketen, Geld und sonstige Vermittlungen	1-5	1.39– 3.41	
		6-10	3.41– 3.42	

Akten-zeichen	Inhalt	Band	Datum	Serial Nr.
Pers.G.18	Weiterleitung von Briefen, Paketen, Geld sowie sonstige Vermittlungen	11-15	3.42-10.42	
			5.41-12.42	
Pers.G.22	Bezüge und Weiterleitung von deutschen Zeitungen, Zeitschriften und sonstigen Drucksachen (ausgenommen Bücher für deutsche Institute in Portugal, Schulen, Gremio, Lesesaal, Parteidienststellen)	1	1.39- 6.41	
Pers.G.23	Bezüge von portugiesischen und anderen ausländischen Gesetz- und Verordnungsblättern, Zeitungen und Zeitschriften für das Auswärtige Amt und deutsche Behörden, Institute	1-5	1.39- 3.42	
Pers.G.30	Konsulat Lourenco Marques und Mozambique	1 2	1.39-12.41	1096/318233-43
Pers.G.31	- Luanda	1	1.39-11.41	1094/318215-24
Pers.G.32	- Porto	1-3	1.39- 5.41	
Pers.G.33	- Funchal-Madeira	1-4	8.39- 2.42	
		Sbd.	1.39-12.39	
Pers.G.35	- Sao Vicente (Cap Verde)		9.39- 6.41	
Pers.Si 2	Kurierwesen, Briefbeutel, Depeschenverkehr, auch Telegrammverkehr mit Auswärtigem Amt	1-5	1.39-11.42	
Pers.G.36	Konsulat Ponta Delgada, Azoren	1-4	1.39- 5.42	
	Beleidigungsklage Kons. Gesche-Sandberger	Sbd	1939-41	
	Personalien über Maria Tomala		1.41-11.42	
	- Vicekonsul Krumbholtz		9.40- 3.41	
	Kons.Sekr. Gerstberger		1.31- 6.42	
	Handelsattaché Claussen		1.31- 6.41	
	Kanzler Burgemeister		12.41-12.42	
	Kons.Sekr. Pfeiffer		9.41-12.42	
	Botschaftsrat Friedr.Sieburg		2.39- 4.41	
	Attaché Dr.Schmidt		1.39- 6.42	
	Presseattaché Schmitt		9.42-12.42	
	Leg.Sekr.Raven u.Karstlof		1.39-11.40	
	wissenschaftl.Mitarbeiter von Fetter		2.42-12.42	
	Hilfsamtsgehilfe W.Kunert		4.41-11.43	
	wissenschaftlicher Hilfsarbeiter Fritz Cramer		10.40-12.40	
	Stenotypistin Frl.Block		10.41-10.42	
	- Frl.Hirschmann		3.41- 7.42	
	- Frl.Maria von Poser-Schmidtmann		9.42- 1.43	
	- Frl.von Wetter,		1.39-10.40	
	- Frl.Elisabeth Sahrbach			
	- Frl.Frieda Meinhardt			
	Hilfsamtsgehilfe Edgar Scharf		11.41- 1.43	
	Druckfachmann Redepenning		7.42- 8.42	

Akten-zeichen	Inhalt	Band	Datum	Serial Nr.
	Personalien über:			
	Regierungsinspektor W.Nebe		3.41- 3.42	
	Stenotypistin Brandenburg		6.39- 1.42	
	Frau Ruth Lorentz		11.41-12.42	
	Frau Ingeborg Evert		4.40- 3.41	
	wissenschaftl.Hilfsarb.Alexander		9.41- 8.42	
D W I	Wirtschaftspolitik allgemein wirtschaftliche Lage und wirtschaftlicher Aufbau Deutschlands		1.31- 2.43	
D W II	Wirtschaftliche Beziehungen Deutschlands zu anderen Staaten ausser Portugal		1.39-10.42	
D W A	Deutsches Ausstellungs-, Markt- und Messewesen		1.39- 1.43	
D W A I	Internationale Verkehrsausstellung 1940 in Köln		11.38- 8.39	
D W E	Deutsches Eisenbahnwesen und Beziehungen zu anderen Ländern		1.39- 2.43	
D W F I	Staatsfinanzen und Finanzwirtschaft in Deutschland		1.39- 7.41	
D W F II	Deutsches Bank- und Geldwesen, Maaße und Gewichte		1.39- 8.41	
D W F III	Devisenbestimmungen		1.39-11.42	
D W F IV	Registermark		1.39- 2.41	
D W H I	Deutscher Innen- und Aussenhandel, (allgemein) Verfügungen und Maßnahmen zur Förderung, Exportpropaganda, Boykottbekämpfung		1.39- 2.43	
D W H II	Handelsbeziehungen zwischen Deutschland und anderen Ländern, ausgenommen Portugal		1.39- 2.41	
D W H III	Reichsstelle für den Aussenhandel		1.39- 1.40	
D W J I	Industrie, Technik, Gewerbe, Handwerk in Deutschland		1.39- 3.40	
D W Kr.	Deutsches Kraftfahr- und Strassenwesen einschliesslich Reichsautobahn		1.39- 7.41	
D W Lu	Deutsche Luftfahrt und Beziehungen zu anderen Ländern einschl. Abkommen		1.31- 6.42	
D W P	Deutsches Post-, Kabel-, Telegrafen- Radio- und Fernsprechwesen einschliesslich Beziehungen zu anderen Ländern		1.39- 1.43	
D W Sch	Deutsche Schiffahrt einschliesslich Seeleute, Seemannsämter, See-und Binnenwasserordnung, auch Beziehungen zu anderen Ländern (Verträge)		1.39-10.42	
D W Z V I	Deutsches Verkehrswesen allgemein(Beziehungen zu anderen Ländern)		1.31- 8.40	

Akten-zeichen	Inhalt	Band	Datum	Serial Nr.
D W Z I	Deutsche Zollorganisation und Zollgesetzgebung und Beziehungen zu anderen Ländern		1.39-12.42	
D W Z II	Zollvergünstigungen für diplomatische und konsularische Vertretungen in Deutschland		1.39- 8.42	
Prot.1.	Allgemeines Zeremoniell, Einführung beim Staatsoberhaupt, Empfänge, Besuche, Besuchsordnung, Audienzen		1.39- 8.42	
Prot.2.	Diplomatisches und Konsularisches Korps Lissabon, allgemeine Erleichterungen ausser Zollvergünstigungen, Exterritorialität der Auslandsvertretung		1.39- 4.42	
Prot.3	Einladungen, Veranstaltungen, Feiern der Gesandtschaft		1.39- 4.42	
Prot.4.	Einladungen, Veranstaltungen, Feiern portugiesischer und sonstiger fremder Behörden, anderer Missionen, Personen		1.39-12.42	
Prot.5.	Glückwünsche, Beileidsbezeugungen, Kartenabgabe, Geschenke und Wünsche an Führer, Reichsminister, Gesandten und sonstige prominente Personen und sonstige Zuschriften		1.39- 1.42	
Prot.7.	Diplomatische und Konsularische Vertretungen Deutschlands und Portugals		1.39- 6.42	
Prot.8.	Diplomatische und Konsularische Vertretungen in sonstigen Ländern		1.39- 4.42	
Prot.9.	Diplomatische und Konsularische Vertretungen Portugals in Deutschland		6.39- 1.43	
Prot.10.	Diplomatische und Konsularische Vertretungen Portugals und sonstiger Länder		1.39- 1.43	
Prot.11.	Fremde diplomatische und konsularische Vertretungen in Portugal und sonstigen Ländern, auch Militär- und Marineattachés	1 2 3	1.39- 1.43	1115/320844-46
Prot.13.	Deutsche Ordensverleihungen Einzelverleihungen	1	1.39- 2.41	
	Ordensvorschläge, Buchausstellung Berlin	Sbd.	3.38- 7.41	
	Ordensvorschläge	Sbd.	2.39- 7.41	
Prot.14.	Deutsche Einzelauszeichnungen, Titel und Ehrungen		1.39-11.42	
	Providencia und Moneade		9.40- 3.41	
	Forderungen der Firma Richard Zeeck betreffend	Sbd. 6	3.34-12.34	

Akten-zeichen	Inhalt	Band	Datum	Serial Nr.
Prot.15.	Portugiesische Ordensverleihungen an deutsche Staatsangehörige		1.39-10.42	
Prot.16.	Portugiesische Ordensverleihungen an fremde Staatsangehörige		1.39-10.42	
Prot.17.	Portugiesische Einzelauszeichnungen, Titel, Ehrungen		1.39- 9.41	
Prot.18.	Auszeichnungen, Titel, Ehrungen und Ordensverleihungen sonstiger Staaten		1.39-12.42	
R.1.	Portugiesisches und sonstiges Rechts- und Gerichtswesen		1.39- 9.42	
R.2.Nr.1.	Rechtliche Beziehungen Portugals zu Deutschland, einschliesslich Rechtsverträge und Abkommen		1.39- 7.42	
R.3.Nr.1.	Portugiesische und sonstige Staatsangehörigkeitsfragen		1.39- 7.40	
Nr.3.	Nachlass, Erbschaft, Testamente speziell		3.39- 3.40	
Nr.4.	Familienrecht, Ehe, Personenstandsangelegenheiten		1.39- 4.40	
Nr.6.	Amnestie und Begnadigungen, Fahnenflucht, Gefangenenaustausch und Beförderung, Steckbriefe. Desertion von Seeleuten auf Handelsschiffen, Strafregister		1.39- 7.40	
Nr.7.	Verhaftung, Ausweisung, Aufenthaltserschwerung, Auslieferung deutscher Staatsangehöriger durch fremde Staaten, auch Portugal	1-2	1.39- 1.43	
Nr.8.	Notariatssachen, Legalisationen, Beglaubigungen, Vollmachten, Notariatsregister		1.39- 9.41	
Nr.9.	Erfindungen, Erfinder und Urheberrecht, Patentwesen		1.39- 2.42	
Nr.11	Kriegsschädenforderung an portugiesischen Staat, auch Handelsentschädigungen		1.39-11.41	
R.4.Nr.1	Arbeits- und Gewerberecht, Lohnfragen, Streiks		1.39- 1.40	
Nr.3	Wahrnehmung der Interessen deutscher Staatsangehöriger im Ausland durch Asylgewährung an fremde Auslandsvertretungen		1.39-12.40	
Nr.4			1.39-10.41	
	Gefangennahme von Deutschen auf portugiesischen Schiffen	Sbd.	11.39- 3.40	
Nr.5	Arbeitszulassung in Portugal, Dentist Wasser, Porto	Sbd.	7.38- 3.40	
R.5.Nr.1	Portugiesisches und sonstiges Passwesen	1-3	1.39-12.42	
	Visen für Kraftfahrer Spanien		12.40- 5.42	

Akten- zeichen	Inhalt	Band	Datum	Serial Nr.
R.5.Nr.2.	Empfohlene Personen und Firmen		1.39- 4.42	
Nr.3.	Verdächtige und unsichere Personen und Firmen, Warnungen		1.39-12.42	
R.6.	Sozial- und Fürsorgewesen, Sozialpolitik und Gesetzgebung		1.39- 5.41	
R.6.Nr.2.	Sozialversicherung und Freizeitgestaltung		1.39- 4.40	
Nr.4.	Kriegsgräberfürsorge		1.39- 1.40	
Nr.5.	Sammlungen für nationale und wohltätige Zwecke in Portugal und fremden Staaten		1.39- 4.41	
R.7.	Kinderhilfsaktion	Sbd. a	2.41- 9.41	
	Begleitschreiben an portugiesisches Rotes Kreuz zur Briefpost an deutsche Gefangene in Canada		11.40- 6.42	
	Internationales Rechtswesen	1-2	1.39- 4.42	
D R 1.	Deutsches Rechts- und Gerichtswesen, allgemein. N.S.-Rechtswahrerbund, Staatsrecht		1.39- 4.42	
D R 2.	Rechtliche Beziehungen Deutschlands zu anderen Ländern ausser Portugal		1.39- 6.42	
D R 3. Nr.1	Reichs-Staatsangehörigkeit, Einbürgerung, Heimatschein, Matrikel, Meldewesen		1.39- 5.41	
Nr.2.	Doppelte Staatsangehörigkeit		1.39- 3.41	
	Frage der doppelten Staatsangehörigkeit von Reichsdeutschen in Portugal	Sbd.	3.36-10.42	
Nr.3.	Ausbürgerungen, Aberkennung und Ausscheiden aus der deutschen Staatsangehörigkeit		1.39-11.41	
Nr.4.	Ausbürgerungslisten		1.39- 2.40	
Nr.5.	Verhaftung, Ausweisung und Auslieferung fremder Staatsangehöriger durch deutsche Behörden		1.39- 7.42	
Nr.6.	Beteiligung Auslandsdeutscher an deutschen Wahlen		1.39- 4.40	
D R 4.	Arbeits- und Gewerberecht, Lohnfragen, Arbeitsmarkt		1.39- 4.40	
D R 5.	Deutsches Pass- und Sichtvermerkswesen		1.39-10.42	
D R 5. Nr.1.	Sonderakte Frau von Jessenszhy	Sbd.	2.41- 8.41	
Nr.2.	Ausstellung von deutschen amtlichen Bescheinigungen, Attesten, Grenzempfehlungen, ausser für Spanien		1.39- 2.43	

Akten-zeichen	Inhalt	Band	Datum	Serial Nr.
D R 5. Nr.3.	Empfehlungsschreiben zur Ein-reise nach Spanien, allgemein		1.39- 3.39	
Nr.4.	- Einzelpersonen		1.38- 6.42	
D R 6. Nr.1.	Sozial- und Fürsorgewesen, Gesetzgebung Vers.		1.39- 2.41	
Nr.2.	Freizeitgestaltung "Kraft durch Freude"		1.39- 4.41	
	Besuch des KdF-Schiffes "Robert Ley"		4.39	
Nr.3.	Sammlungen für nationale und wohltätige Zwecke in Deutschland W.H.W.	1-2	1.39-10.42	
D Kult.1. Nr.1.	Deutsche Kulturpolitik und all-gemeine deutsche Kulturpropa-ganda (auch Kulturabkommen mit anderen Staaten ausser Portugal)		1.39- 1.43	
Nr.2.	Zwischenstaatliche Gesellschaf-ten		1.39- 2.41	
D Kult.2.	Kulturpolitische Beziehungen Deutschlands zu anderen Staaten (ausser Portugal)		1.39-11.39	
D Kult.3.	Fremde Volksgruppen in Deutsch-land		1.39- 3.39	
D Kult.4.	Kirchenwesen in Deutschland und deutsches Missionswesen (auch Nationalsozialismus und Kirche)		1.39-12.39	
D Kult.5. Nr.1.	Deutsche Maßnahmen und Vor-schriften zur Regelung der Ein-, Aus- und Rückwanderung, allgem.		1.39- 3.40	
D Kult.7.	Schulwesen in Deutschland		1.39- 4.40	
D Kult.8. Nr.1.	Deutsches Hochschulwesen, NS-Studentenschaft		1.39- 5.42	
Nr.2.	Deutsch-akademischer Austausch-dienst		1.39- 4.41	
D Kult.9. Nr.1.	Deutsche Wissenschaft, Expedi-tion		1.39- 4.42	
Nr.3.	Portugiesisch-brasilianisches Institut, Universität Köln		1.39- 3.41	
Nr.4.	Sonstige portugiesische Insti-tute in Deutschland		1.39- 8.41	
Nr.5.	Sonstige deutsche wissenschaft-liche Institute		1.39- 6.41	
Nr.6.	Gesundheitswesen in Deutschland		1.39- 4.39	
Nr.7.	Veterinärwesen, Tier- und Pflanzenschutz, Tier- und Bota-nische Gärten in Deutschland		4.39- 6.39	
Nr.8.	Deutsches Buchwesen und deutsche Literatur, allgemein		1.39- 2.43	
D Kult 10 Nr.1.	Deutsche Kunst		1.39- 6.42	

Akten-zeichen	Inhalt	Band	Datum	Serial Nr.
D Kult 10 Nr.2.	Deutsches Rundfunkwesen	1-3	1.39- 1.43	
Nr.2a.	Amtsstube		2.41- 6.42	
Nr.3.	Deutsches Filmwesen allgemein		1.39- 1.43	
Nr.4.	Deutscher Sport allgemein		1.39-12.41	
Nr.5.	Reichsakademie für Leibes-übungen, auch Ausländerkurse		1.39	
D P 1.	Deutsche Presse, allgemein		1.39- 8.41	
D P 2.	Pressebeziehungen Deutschlands zu anderen Ländern		1.39-11.40	
Kult 1.	Allgemeine Kulturpolitik Portugals (kulturelle Organisa-tionen und Vereinigungen, soweit nicht Sonderband)		1.39- 9.42	
	Jahrhundertfeier Portugals	1-4	6.38- 9.40	
Kult 2. Nr.1.	Deutsch-portugiesische Kultur-beziehungen, auch Kulturreferent und Kulturpropaganda in Portugal	1-3	1.39-10.42	
Nr.2.	Kulturabkommen Deutschland-Portugal		1.39- 2.39	
Nr.3.	Kulturpolitische Beziehungen Portugals zu anderen Ländern und zwischen anderen Ländern, auch Abkommen, ausländische Kulturpropaganda		1.39- 2.43	
Kult 3. Nr.1.	Deutsche Reichsangehörige in Portugal und portugiesischen Besitzungen		1.39- 1.43	
Nr.2.	Reichsangehörige in Lissabon, auch Deutscher Verein		1.39- 5.42	
Nr.3.	Deutsche Reichsangehörige in Porto, auch Deutscher Verein		1.39- 7.41	
Kult 4. Nr.1.	Kirchenwesen, Glaubensbewegungen, Sekten, Missionswesen, Verhält-nis zum Heiligen Stuhl,Kirchen-kongresse und Tagungen		1.39- 9.42	
Nr.2.	Deutsches Kirchenwesen in Portugal (deutsche evangelische und katholische Kirche, auch deutsches Haus, Pfarrer Wurzer, deutsche Friedhöfe)		1.39-12.42	
Nr.3.	Stellung des Auslandes zum Kirchenwesen in Deutschland, auch Hetze		1.39-12.42	
Kult 5.	Ein-, Aus- und Rückwanderung (Portugal und sonstige Staaten)		1.39- 4.39	
Kult 6.	Nachforschungswesen		1.39- 8.41	
Kult 8. Nr.2.	Deutsches Unterrichtswesen, deutsche Auslandsschulen, allgemein	1-2	1.39- 6.42	

Akten-zeichen	Inhalt	Band	Datum	Serial Nr.
Kult 8. Nr.3.	Deutsche Schule Lissabon	1-4	1.39- 6.42	
Nr.4.	- Porto	1-3	1.39- 9.42	
Nr.9.	Kultur- und Schulbeihilfen	1-6	1.39- 6.42	
Kult 9. Nr.1.	Deutsche Lektorate, Sprachlehrer in Portugal	1-2	1.39- 4.42	
Nr.2.	Portugiesische Lektorate, Sprachlehrer, Sprachkurse in Deutschland und anderen Ländern		1.39-10.42	
Kult 10. Nr.1.	Portugiesisches Hochschulwesen		1.39- 6.42	
Nr.2.	Universität Coimbra (auch deutsch-portugiesische Veranstaltungen)	1	1.39- 6.40	
Nr.3.	Universität Lissabon und Porto		1.39- 3.42	
Kult 11. Nr.1.	Portugiesische und sonstige Wissenschaft		1.39- 7.42	
Nr.2.	Studien- und Vortragsreisen deutscher Wissenschaftler nach Portugal und sonstigen Ländern	1	1.39- 7.41	
Nr.3.	Studien- und Vortragsreisen portugiesischer Wissenschaftler nach Deutschland und sonstigen Ländern	1-2	7.39- 3.42	
Nr.5.	Deutsch-portugiesische Gesellschaft (Roth, Dr.Polster)	1	1.31- 3.41	
Nr.6.	Deutscher Lesesaal am Instituto Superior de Ciencias Economias e Financiales und Institut selbst		1.39- 8.42	
Nr.9.	Portugiesisches und sonstiges Gesundheitswesen und Sanitäts-abkommen		1.39-10.42	
Nr.12.	Portugiesische Buchausstellung Berlin 1938-1939	1-2	11.37- 2.40	
	Portugiesisches und sonstiges Buchwesen, Literatur, portugiesische Buchausstellung		1.39- 2.43	
Nr.13.	Deutsche Buchwoche und Ausstellung Deutschland und Ausland		1.39- 4.39	
Nr.14.	Deutsche Buchspenden und Bücherprämien und Weitergabe an deutsche Schulen in Portugal	1	1.39- 9.40	
Nr.15.	Deutsche Bücherspenden und Buchspenden und Weitergabe an deutsche Institute in Portugal		1.39-12.41	
Nr.16.	Deutsche Bücherspenden und Buchprämien für portugiesische Behörden und Institute sowie Schulen		1.39- 3.43	
Nr.17.	Bücherspenden und Übermittlung von portugiesischen Büchern an deutsche Behörden, Institute	1-4	1.39- 1.43	

Akten-zeichen	Inhalt	Band	Datum	Serial Nr.
Kult 12. Nr.1.	Portugiesische und sonstige Kunst und Künstler, Theater, Film, Architektur, Malerei, Musik, sonstige Kunst		1.39- 1.43	
Nr.2.	Studien- und Vortragsreisen deutscher Künstler nach Portugal und sonstigen Ländern	1-3	1.39-11.42	
	Konzert Wilhelm Kempff am 26.4.39 in Lissabon	Sbd.	1.39- 8.40	
Nr.3.	Studien- und Vortragsreisen portugiesischer Künstler nach Deutschland und anderen Ländern	1	9.38- 7.41	
Nr.4.	Studien- und Vortragsreisen sonstiger ausländischer Künstler		1.39-12.42	
Nr.5.	Portugiesisches Rundfunkwesen			
Nr.7.	Portugiesisches und sonstiges Filmwesen		1.39- 2.43	
Nr.8.	Deutscher Filmabsatz in Portugal und sonstigem Ausland	1-2	1.39- 2.42	
Nr.9.	Vermittlung und Weitergabe deutscher Filme und Vorführung bei Partei, Schulen, deutscher Kolonie, Firmen in Portugal (Filmapparate)	1	1.39- 4.41	
Nr.10.	Vermittlung deutscher Filme für portugiesische Behörden, Institute, Armee, politische Verbände		1.39-11.41	
Kult 13. Nr.1.	Portugiesischer und sonstiger fremder Sport allgemein		1.39- 1.43	
Nr.2.	Beteiligung deutscher Sportler an sportlichen Veranstaltungen in Portugal		1.39-10.42	
Nr.3.	Beteiligung portugiesischer Sportler an sportlichen Veranstaltungen in Deutschland		1.39- 7.42	
Nr.4.	Portugiesisches und sonstiges fremdes Segelflugwesen (auch deutsche Segelfluglehrer in Portugal und sonstigem Ausland)	1	1.39-12.41	
Nr.5.	Deutsche Sportlehrer für Portugal und sonstige Länder und Ausbildung portugiesischer Sportlehrer in Deutschland, auch Studienreise Prof.Magalhaes		1.39-10.42	
Nr.7.	Olympiade 1940		1.39- 5.42	
Kult 14.	Unterstützungen und Vermittlungstätigkeit der Gesellschaft in kulturellen Angelegenheiten		1.39- 9.40	
Kult 15.	Internationaler Kongress für 1. Verwaltungswissenschaft 2. Tuberkulosebekämpfung 3. Weinbau 39 4. Kriminalpolizei, Kommiss. 39 5. Ärztekongress 1939	Sbd.	1.39-12.42	

Akten-zeichen	Inhalt	Band	Datum	Serial Nr.
Kult 15.	Notgemeinschaft deutscher Wissen-schaftler im Ausland	Sbd.	1.38- 3.40	
	Werkstoffausstellung	Sbd. 1-2	10.41- 1.43	
	Architekten-Ausstellung in Lissabon 1941	Sbd. 1-2	8.40- 8.42	
W.1.	Wirtschaftspolitik und allge-meine Wirtschaftslage sowie wirtschaftlicher Aufbau (Korporationen) in Portugal	1	1.39-11.41	
W.2. Nr.1.	Wirtschaftliche Beziehungen Portugals zu Deutschland, auch Studien- und Vortragsreisen deutscher Wirtschaftler nach Portugal	1	1.39-12.41	
Nr.2.	Studien- und Vortragsreisen portugiesischer und sonstiger Wirtschaftler nach Deutschland		1.39- 7.41	
Nr.3a.	Sardinen (Weissblech)	1-2	7.40-10.41	
Nr.3.	Wirtschafts- und Handelsverhand-lungen und Verträge sowie son-stige Wirtschaftsabkommen zwischen Deutschland und Portu-gal	1-2	1.39-12.41	
Nr.3b.	Bericht Dr.Georg Fischer über Wolfram	1-2	1942	
Nr.4.	Wirtschaftliche Beziehungen Portugals sowie Verhandlungen und Verträge Portugals mit anderen Ländern	1	1.39-12.41	
Nr.5.	Wirtschaftliche Beziehungen, Verhandlungen und Verträge zwischen anderen Ländern		1.39-12.41	
Nr.6.	Wirtschaftspolitik, allgemein Wirtschaftslage und wirtschaft-licher Aufbau in sonstigen Staaten		1.39- 2.39	
Nr.9.	Ausschreibungen und Angebote in Portugal und sonstigen Län-dern		1.39- 1.40	
W.A.2.	Einzelausstellungen		1.39- 2.42	
W.E.2. Nr.1.	Eisenbahnbeziehungen Portugals zu Deutschland		1.39-10.39	
W.F.1.	Staatsfinanzen und Finanzwirt-schaft in Portugal, auch An-leihen, Wertpapiere	1-2	1.39-11.40	
W.F.2. Nr.1.	Finanzielle Beziehungen Portu-gals zu Deutschland, auch Abkommen	1-2	1.39-12.41	
Nr.3.	Finanzielle Beziehungen Portu-gals zu anderen Ländern und zwischen anderen Ländern (auch Finanzen in anderen Ländern)		1.39-11.41	

Akten-zeichen	Inhalt	Band	Datum	Serial Nr.
W.F.3.	Portugiesisches und sonstiges Bank- und Geldwesen		1.39- 4.39	
W.H.1.	Portugiesischer Innen- und Aussenhandel, allgemein, Verfügungen und Dekrete zur Förderung, Ein- und Ausfuhrbestimmungen	1	1.39-12.41	
W.H.2.	Handelsbeziehungen zwischen Portugal und Deutschland	1-3	1.39- 1.42	
W.H.2. Nr.1a.	Halbamtlicher Schriftwechsel einzelner Firmen mit Dr.Weber	Sbd.	12.40-12.41	
Nr.4.	Auskünfte über Firmen und Handelspersonen in Deutschland		1.39-12.41	
W.H.3.	Handelsbeziehungen zwischen Portugal und anderen Ländern		1.39-10.41	
W.H.4.	Handelsbeziehungen fremder Staaten		1.39- 3.41	
W.J.1.	Industrie, Technik, Gewerbe und Handwerk in Portugal, allgemein		1.39- 5.40	
W.J.2. Nr.1.	- Beziehungen Portugals zu Deutschland		1.39- 3.42	
			12.40- 1.42	
W.H.2. Nr.7.	Klagen und Beschwerden über portugiesische und fremde Firmen und Handelsvertreter		1.39- 4.40	
W.Kr.	Portugiesische und sonstige Kraftfahrer und Strassenwesen sowie Beziehungen zwischen sämtlichen Staaten		1.39- 1.40	
W.L.II. Nr.1 u. W.H.1.	Landwirtschaftliche Beziehungen zu Deutschland		1.39- 3.41	
W.Lu.1.	Portugiesische und sonstige fremde Luftfahrt		1.39- 4.41	
W.Lu.2. Nr.1.	Luftfahrtbeziehungen Portugals zu Deutschland, einschliesslich Abkommen		1.31-10.41	
Nr.2.	Luftfahrtbeziehungen Portugals zu anderen Ländern und zwischen anderen Ländern, einschliesslich Abkommen		1.31-12.41	
W.P.1	Portugiesisches Post-, Kabel-, Telegrafen, Radio- und Fernsprechwesen		1.39- 3.42	
W.P.2. Nr.1.	Portugiesisches Postwesen, Beziehungen zu Deutschland		1.39-12.41	
Nr.2.	- zu und zwischen anderen Ländern		1.39- 1.42	
W.Sch.1.	Portugiesische und sonstige Schiffahrt	1	1.39- 3.42	

Akten-zeichen	Inhalt	Band	Datum	Serial Nr.
W.Sch.2. Nr.1.	Portugiesische Schiffahrt, Beziehungen zu Deutschland, Verträge	1	1.39-11.41	
Nr.2.	Schiffahrtsbeziehungen Portugals zu anderen und zwischen anderen Ländern, auch Verträge		1.39-11.41	
W.V.1.	Portugiesisches und sonstiges Verkehrswesen, allgemein		1.39-12.41	
W.V.2. Nr.1.	Verkehrsbeziehungen Portugals zu Deutschland, auch Verträge		1.39-12.41	
V.W.3.	Portugiesischer und sonstiger fremder Reise- und Fremdenverkehr Verkehrswerbung, Reisebüros		1.39-12.42	
W.Vers.	Portugiesisches und sonstiges Versicherungswesen		1.39- 9.39	
W.Z.1.	Portugiesische Zollorganisationen und Zollgesetzgebung		1.39- 7.40	
W.Z.2. Nr.2.	Zollwesen- Beziehungen Portugals zu Deutschland (auch Beschwerden)		1.39- 6.42	
W.Z.4.	Zollgesetzgebung sonstiger Länder		1.39-12.41	
Geheim	Harz	4	1.39- 9.41	
	Kork	6	9.41- 4.42	
	Ausfuhr von Leder	7	8.41- 1.42	

Akten-zeichen	Inhalt	Band	Datum	Serial Nr.
	Geheimakten			
D Pol 2 Sbd a	Lage in England	1 2 3 4 5 Sbd a	7.40- 9.43	3084/D613459-706 4362/E080809-62 4362/E080863-909 5434/E364385-90 4362/E080910-47 5435/E364392-411 4362/E080948-98 6093/E451765-801
Sbd g	Lage in Amerika	1 Sbd g	1.42- 8.43	4375/E082766-822
	Britische I.S.Tätigkeit. Kommunistische und liberale Machenschaften (Umsturzversuche)	1	1942	
	Dr.Schwonder, Reisebericht an das Auswärtige Amt über Erkundungsreise in Angola (Portug. Westafrika)	1	1928	
	Mob.-Sachen	1	4.37-11.38	
	Abrüstungsmemorandum	1 Um-schl	1934	
	Kongoakte	1 Um-schl	1943	
	Flaggendiskriminierung	1 Um-schl	1943	
	Photokopiertes Heft mit einer Anlage: Bases pour l'étude de l'établissement de l'industrie sidérurgique au Portugal	1 Um-schl		
Vertr.Pol	Geheimakte	1	1942	
		1	1943	
		1	1943	
		1	1943	
Vertr. Pers.		1	1942	
		1	1943	
		1	1943	
		1	1943	
	Hollmüller	1	1943	
W V 4	Bruno Lesser	1	1942-43	
	Sonimi-Lobar (Waldthausen)	1	1942-43	
W H 1 a	Kurt Porst	1	1942-43	
	Knigge	1	1942-43	

Akten-zeichen	Inhalt	Band	Datum	Serial Nr.
Geheim				
W H 1 c	Wimmer	1	1943	
W V 4	Strafsache Cotter	1	1943	
	Roubaud und Holz "Cotmarsum" (Dampfer)	1	1942-43	
W H 1 d	"Cofor" und "Sapem"	1	1942-43	
	Geheimakte	1	1942-43	9925/E694707-14
		1	1941-43	
		1	1942-43	
W A		1	1942-43	
	Flugzeuge	1	1942-43	
	Schiffe	1	1943	
	Lettischer Dampfer "Klints"	1	1941-43	
	Verkauf portugiesischer Motor-wachboote und Fischdampfer an England Bau Fischdampfer für England	1 Sbd.	1941-43	
	W-Bezüge Feindmächte (auch Ver-träge Feindmächte)	1	1942-43	4376/E082825-37
	Gummi	1		
	Kohlen	1		4377/E082840-63 6528/E487622-29
W H 1	Schafdärme	1	1943	
	Öl	1	1943	
	Kaffee	1		
	Sisal	1		
W 2 Nr.3 f	Beryll	1		
W 2 Nr.3b	Wolfram-Abkommen	1	1941-42	516/236083-256
	Wolfram-Gesellschaften Organisation, Ausbau der Minen, Förderung, Wolframbeauftragter, Bergbaubeauftragter	1	1942-43	
	Wolfram-Weber	1	1942-43	
	Zinn- und Wolframbezüge der Italiener und Sonstiges betr. Italien	1	1942-43	
W 2 Nr.3c	Angelegenheiten Wolfram, Grube Borralha	1 2	1941-43	4360/E080491-671 4360/E080672-783
	Vertrauliche Akten Pol, Kult, Pers, Presse, Recht,	1	1940-43	515/235988-6081

Akten-zeichen	Inhalt	Band	Datum	Serial Nr.
I.Deutsch-land 9	Deutschland. Armee und Kriegs-flugwesen	5	6.34-11.36	5759/E419198-327
I.Deutsch-land 10	Marine	4	9.29- 9.37	7364/E538986-9005 7631/E545353-56
I.Frank-reich	Frankreich	4	1.30- 5.31	
I.Frankr. adh.		4	11.24- 2.32	
I.Groß-britan-nien 7	Auswärtige Angelegenheiten	9	11.27- 6.29	
		10	6.29- 9.34	7568/E542394-404
9	Großbritanniens Armee	4	11.29-10.30	
		5	10.30-12.33	
		6	2.34- 8.36	5758/E419164-96
10	Marine	7	4.28- 5.31	
		8	6.31- 4.35	
		9	4.35- 4.37	
III.Spio-nage 8	Spionage	2	4.20-12.30	
		3	12.30- 4.38	
9a	Bekämpfung des Bolschewismus und Kommunismus	1	10.20-12.31	
		2	11.21- 3.30	
V.adh. 1	Major E.W.Pelson-Newman		9.28- 1.32	
	Lt.-Col. G.S.Hutchison		5.32-12.33	
	The Polish Corridor and the Consequences Buch von Sir Robert Donald		12.26- 1.30	
V. 1a	Informationsbüro über Danzig	1	1.26- 7.28	
1b	Informationsdienst Deutschland – England	1	4.26- 2.29	
V. 1	Presse	2	12.20- 9.22	1572/380420-716
		3	1.23- 1.29	1572/380717-926
VII.	Personalia. Geheim	1	1872-90	
		2	1899-1912	
		3	11.22-11.28	1572/380927-52
F.IX.6a	Die deutsche Wiederbesetzung des Rheinlandes	1	5.-12.3.36	
		2	13.-20.3.36	
		3	20.-24.3.36	
		4	24.3.-6.4.36	
		5	7.-21.4.36	

Akten-zeichen	Inhalt	Band	Datum	Serial Nr.
F.IX.6a.	Die Deutsche Wiederbesetzung des Rheinlandes	6	22.4.- 5.36	
		7	6.5.- 7.36	
F.XV.1.	Gespräch zwischen Führer und Sir John Simon am 25.3.1935			1572/380347-419
A.		1	3.20- 2.22	K2090/K566034-317
		2	3.22- 5.24	K2090/K566318-749
		3	5.24- 9.25	K2090/K566750-7179
		4	10.25- 7.26	K2090/K567180-624
		5	8.26-11.27	K2090/K567625-804
		6	5.28-12.31	K2090/K567805-8237
	Friedensvertrag	1	2.20- 1.21	K2091/K568238-472
		2	2.21- 7.22	K2091/K568473-611
	Rudolf Said Ruste		7.20- 5.31	
	Rostin über Unterredung mit Russen, Bogolomov, Lindenberg und Rosengolz		1926	K2092/K568612-646
	Die zu den Botschaftsakten genommenen Handakten des früher bei der Botschaft tätig gewesenen Gesandtschaftsrats Dr.E. Kordt:			
	Flottenverhandlungen		1937	K2093/K568647-732
	Notenwechsel seit dem Austritt Deutschlands aus dem Völkerbund bis Ende April 1934			
	Ostpakt			
	Österreich			
	Waffen-Embargo-Ausschuss betr. Spanien	1 2		
	Europäische Paktverhandlungen ab 1.Januar 1935			
I.2.	Ministerien	3	1920-28	
I.3.	Parlament	3-4	11.20- 4.29	
I.4.	Finanzen	3	4.20-11.29	
I.6.	Innere Angelegenheiten	6-7	2.20-1928	
I.6. adh.III.	Streiks	1	10.20- 3.24	
I.7.	Auswärtige Angelegenheiten	6-8	2.20-11.27	
I.7. adh.I.	Beziehungen zu Deutschland	8	2.20-10.29	
adh.V.	- - Amerika	1	9.20- 2.28	
adh.VI.	- - Frankreich	1	3.27-12.28	

Akten-zeichen	Inhalt	Band	Datum	Serial Nr.
I. 8.	Koloniales	2	12.20- 8.29	L981/L277346-413
I. 8. adh.I.	Beziehungen zu den Besitzungen	3	6.20- 5.28	L981/L277414-735
adh.II.	Koloniale Konferenzen	2	11.20-10.26	L981/L277736-957
I. 9.	Armee	3	2.20-11.29	
I. 10.	Marine	6	2.20- 3.28	
I.	Sonstige britische Besitzungen	3	2.20- 1.30	
	Abessinien	2	2.22-11.26	
I. adh.		2	8.21- 9.26	
I.	Afghanistan	2	9.20-12.28	
I. adh.		2	9.21- 8.29	
I.	Albanien	2	6.20- 6.27	
	Armenien	1	5.20- 8.20	
	Argentinien	2	12.20-12.29	
	Australien	3	4.20-12.29	L944/L271534-645
	Belgien	2	10.20- 2.29	
I. adh.		2	3.20- 9.26	
I.	Bulgarien	2	2.20- 8.28	
	Chile	2	11.20- 4.32	
I. adh.		2	7.26- 6.29	
I.	China	3-5	5.20- 5.29	
I. adh.		4-6	5.26- 1.29	
I.	Ägypten	3	4.20-12.27	
I. adh.		3-4	12.21- 2.28	
I.	Estland	1	5.20-11.29	
	Dänemark	2	2.20- 1.30	
	Finnland	1	5.20-10.29	
	Frankreich	2-3	3.20-12.29	
	Französische Besitzungen	2	1.24- 1.31	
I. adh.	Frankreich	3	1.21-10.24	
I.	Georgien	1	9.20- 8.26	
I. adh.		1	7.20-10.24	
I.	Griechenland	1	10.20- 1.29	
I. adh.		2	6.21-10.28	
I.	Indien	3	2.20- 1.28	
I. adh.		3	2.22- 3.29	
I.	Italien	2	3.20- 1.27	

Akten-zeichen	Inhalt	Band	Datum	Serial Nr.
I.adh.	Italien	1	6.21- 4.26	
I.adh.I.		1	8.23-10.23	
I.	Japan	2	6.20-12.29	
I.adh.		2	1.22- 5.29	
I.	Jugoslavien	1	5.21- 7.28	
I.adh.	Kanada	2	5.21- 3.26	
I.	Korea	2	6.21	
	Liberia	2	2.20-12.28	
	Litauen	1-2	2.20- 3.28	
	Marokko	7	12.20- 8.27	
	Mexiko	3	7.20-12.29	
	Niederlande	2	10.20- 5.30	
	Niederländische Besitzungen	2	12.24-12.29	
	Norwegen	1	7.22- 2.30	
	Oesterreich	1	11.20-11.29	Kl181/K303489-705
I.adh.		1	11.21-10.28	Kl180/K303427-88
I.	Persien	7	4.20- 6.28	
I.adh.		4	8.20-11.26	
	Peru	2	6.25- 9.28	
I.	Polen	1-5	2.20- 5.27	
I.adh.		1-2	8.21- 4.27	
	Portugal	3	6.22- 7.29	
I.	Portugiesische Besitzungen	4	11.20-12.29	
I.adh.		3	2.23- 7.29	
	Rhodesien	1	1.21-10.27	
I.	Rumänien	1	6.20- 2.28	
I.adh.		2-3	2.21- 6.28	
I.	Russland	3-6	2.20- 5.27	
I.adh.		3-6+8	8.21- 6.27	
I.	Schweden	1	11.20- 7.29	7437/E540132-49
I.adh.		2	4.20-11.32	
I.	Südafrikanische Union	3	5.20- 9.29	
I.adh.		2-3	3.21-10.28	
I.	Tibet	2	7.22- 2.25	
I.adh.		2	7.24- 6.27	
I.	Tschechoslowakei	1	6.20-11.25	
I. adh.		1	5.20- 7.29	

Akten-zeichen	Inhalt	Band	Datum	Serial Nr.
I.	Türkei	6-7	2.20-12.25	
I.adh.		4-6	8.20-12.27	
I.6.	Palästina	1	2.20- 2.28	
I.7.	Irak	1	8.23-12.28	
I.9.	Hedschas Yemen	1	5.23- 3.29	
I.	Ungarn	1	5.20- 6.28	
I.adh.		1	6.21- 4.28	
I.	Vereinigte Staaten von Amerika	2	9.20- 3.28	
I.adh.		2	1.21- 4.28	
	Besitzungen Vereinigte Staaten	2	12.23- 9.26	
II.1.	Handelsbeziehungen zu Deutsch-land	2	7.21-10.26	K2094/K568733-9089
		3		K2094/K569090-471
II.2a.	Deutsch-englische Zusammenarbeit zur Erschliessung Russlands	1	7.21- 1.24	K2095/K569472-505
II.5.	Handelsbeziehungen zum Ausland	2	2.20- 4.23	
II.6.	- und auswärtigen Besitzungen	2	5.21- 9.27	
III.3.	Schiedsgerichtsverträge	2	11.20- 7.28	
III.9.	Bolschewismus	1	9.20-12.26	
III.11.	Kriegsschuldfrage	1-2	1.21- 1.28	
adh.	- Material	1-2	1.20-11.28	
III.14.	Giftige Gase	1	10.20- 4.29	
adh.		1	10.21- 1.22	
III.15.	Allgemeine Abrüstung	1-3	10.21-12.28	
III.17.	Minderheitsfrage	1	5.25- 9.29	
adh.		1	7.26	
F.III.1.	Militärkontrolle in Deutschland	1-4	2.20-10.29	
F.IV. 1.	Deutsche Kolonien	1-2	2.20-12.26	
	Kriegsgefangene und Zivilinter-nierte	1	4.20- 3.23	
F.VII.1.	Auslieferungsfrage	1-3	2.20-12.26	
F.VII.2.	Kaiser Wilhelm II. und das Kaiserliche Haus	1	6.20- 9.27	
F.IX.6.	Sicherheitsfrage	1 2	1.23-11.25	K2096/K569506-845 K2096/K569846-70119
		3 4		K2096/K570120-425 K2096/K570426-724
F.IX.7.	Micumverträge	1-2	10.23- 9.24	
F.IX.10.	Kriegsschulden der Alliierten	1-2	11.21-11.27	
F.X. 1. adh. 2	Zwangsmaßnahmen Wiedergutmachung	1-2	3.21- 9.28	

Akten-zeichen	Inhalt	Band	Datum	Serial Nr.
F.XII.2.	Auswandererkonzessionen	1	11.20- 6.21	
F.XIV.3.	Räumung der besetzten Gebiete	1-2	2.23- 9.28	
Nachtrag	Privatbriefe des Botschafters und Geh.Rat Dufour.		1921-24	
Marine-attaché	Flottenkonferenz		1934-35	M335/M014221-34
Botsch. Dirksen	Privatbriefe		1933-34	M336/M014235-987

Akten-zeichen	Inhalt	Band	Datum	Serial Nr.
A.I.	Luxemburg-Aufwertung		1.32-12.33	
A.I.a.1.	Vorschriften über die Ehe von Diplomaten		5.95- 9.33	
	Reichsbund der Deutschen Beamten		12.33- 9.36	
	Allgemeine Personal- und Besoldungsangelegenheiten	1-2	12.26- 7.37	
A.I.b.1.	Graf v.Podewils		3.34-12.37	
	Frh.v.Ow-Wachendorf		7.33- 9.35	
	Der Gesandte		10.31-12.38	
A.I.b.2.	Militärattaché in Brüssel		7.38-11.38	
	Presseattaché		9.34- 5.39	
	Handelsattaché		8.35- 6.40	
	Gesandtschaftspersonal	1-6		
A.I.b.3.	Personal der Gesandtschaft	1-11		
A.I.b.4.	Kanzler, Putzfrau Behelfe für den Dienstbetrieb	1-2 3 Hef- te		
A.I.d.1.	Gesandtschaftsgebäude	1-2	10.33- 1.37	
	Neubau des Kanzleihauses	Sbd.		
	Gesandtschaftsgrundstück und Neues Kanzleigebäude	1-4	1.27- 9.33	
A.I.d.2.	Gesandtschaft, Hauseinrichtung, Büromaterial	1-2	1.37-12.37	
A.I.e.1.	Kassensachen	1-2	6.33- 6.36	
	Abwicklung des deutschen Generalkonsulats Luxemburg	Sbd.		
A.I.f.4.	Reichstagswahl		9.3.36	
	Deutsche und andere National-feiertage		1931-10.33	
	National-Hoheitszeichen, Nationalhymne, Nationalfeiertage Staatsoberhaupt, Flaggenvor-schrift	1-2	1.34-12.35	
A.II.	Zweifelhafte Personen		4.28-12.33	
A.II.a.1.	Deutsch-luxemburgisch-belgi-sches Verrechnungsabkommen		9.34	
	Einzelfälle	1-2	1935-37	
	Deutsch-luxemburgisch-belgi-sches Verrechnungsabkommen		9.34-12.35	
A.II.a.7.	Luxemburgische Kammer: Verhand-lungen über Eisenbahnverträge und Beiheft zu Akten Eisenbahnen	1-3	12.24- 1.25	
	Verhandlungen mit Luxemburg über Kriegsschaden und Eisen-bahnforderungen		1925-12.36	

Akten-zeichen	Inhalt	Band	Datum	Serial Nr.
A.II.a.7.	Kriegsschäden, Entschädigungs-protokoll		1922	
A.II.a.8.	Grenzsachen und Abkommen	1-2	1.31-12.33	
A.II.b.1.	Grenzzwischenfälle, allgemein	1-2	1938-40	
A.II.b.2.	Einzelne Grenzzwischenfälle	1-2	1926-39	
A.II.c.4.	Luftfahrt, Einzelfälle		1935-37	
A.II.d. 1.d.	Luxemburgische Studenten an deutschen Hochschulen. Alexander v.Humboldt-Stiftung, Einzelfälle	1-2	1935-37	
1.b.	Deutsches Theater		1934-35	
1.d.	Luxemburgische Studenten an deutschen Hochschulen		10.22-12.33	
1.e.	Alexander v.Humboldt-Stiftung	1-3	1925-32	
1.f.	Kunst und Wissenschaft	11	1.33- 1.34	
A.II.d.2.	Drucksachenaustausch		1.32-12.33	
	Zeitungsaustausch	Sbd.	10.36- 6.38	
A.III. 1.c.	Luxemburgs Eintritt in den Völkerbund, Neutralitätsfragen	1 2 3	10.20- 9.25 1926-36	2863/D563264-69 2864/D563278-340 2863/D563271-74
	Luftschutz in Luxemburg		1936-39	2865/D563344-58
A.III. 2.a.	Besteuerung des Nassauischen Hausfideikommissvermögens, sowie die Fideikommisserhaltung und dergleichen	1-2	12.20-10.33	
2.b.	Die Luxemburgische Regierung, (Neu- und Umbildung, Personalien Innenpolitik) (Maulkorbgesetz)		6.37- 7.37	
	Beamte der Grossherzoglichen Regierung	1	3.10- 8.32	
A.III. 2.g.1.	Volkszählung	2	1922-33	
2.g.2.	Hundertjahrfeier der Unabhän-gigkeit Luxemburgs		1939	
A.III. 3.a.	Presse: Escher Tageblatt Presseprozess gegen das Escher Tageblatt	Sbd.	10.38-12.38	
A.IV.1.	Personalien des Missionschefs		1920-32	
	− Gesandter von Gülich		5.25- 3.27	
	− Gesandter Mertens		4.27- 6.29	
	Kanzler Fenselau		3.12-12.24	
	Äussere Politik Deutschlands		1928-32	
A.IV. 1.a.2.	Abrüstung		12.33-11.36	

Akten-zeichen	Inhalt	Band	Datum	Serial Nr.
A.IV. 1.c.3.	Saargebiet, Geheimakten	1	8.34- 6.35	
	Saar, Einzelfälle		1934	
	Saarländer, allgemein		12.34	
	Saarabstimmung	1-11	1934-35	
A.IV. 1.c.5.	Französisch-sowjet-russischer Beistandspakt und Militarisierung der Rheinlandzone		5.35- 7.37	2866/D563362-68
1.d.	Schiedsgerichts- und Vergleichsangelegenheiten	3	11.35- 6.37	
A.IV.2.	Sekretär Fibelkorn		7.21- 2.22	
A.IV.2.i.	Nationale Erhebung Einzelfälle A - Z			
A.IV.6.	Personalien des Gesandtschaftspersonals		4.10- 5.27	
A.IV.7.	Personalakten Stenotypistin Doempke		9.27-11.27	
	- Stenotypistin Güssow		3.26- 5.27	
	- E.Richter		12.27-11.29	
	Gehaltsangelegenheiten, Spezialakten		1.24-12.28	
	Diensteinkommen der Gesandtschaft		9.15-10.23	
A.V.	Internationale Konferenzen, Kongresse, Zusammenkünfte		12.38	
A.VI.1.	Diplomatisches Korps	5	1.36-12.36	
B.I.1. gen.	Nationalität: Erwerb, Verlust; Feststellung der Staatsangehörigkeit		1928-32	
B.I.1a.	Gesetz betr.Luxemburgische Staatsangehörigkeit und Identitätskartenfrage ab 1.Januar 1937	2	1.34- 4.38	
B.I.7.	Allgemeine Lage und gesetzliche Bestimmungen über den Arbeitsmarkt in Luxemburg			
B.I.8a.	Arbeitsbeschaffung		1939-40	
B.II.3.	Luxemburgische Gesetze		8.34- 3.39	
B.III.1.	Haftsachen, Strafauszüge, Führungszeugnisse, Auslieferungen Einzelfälle	1-3		
B.III.1a.	Zeugenvernehmungen	1	3.14-12.33	
	Beschwerden über Rechtsanwälte A - Z		1933-37	
B.III.8.	Wohlfahrtsakten	1-5	1933-35	
B.III.10.	Ermittlungen, Auskünfte (Einzelfälle)	1 2	4.33-12.35 1935-36	

Akten-zeichen	Inhalt	Band	Datum	Serial Nr.
B.III.11.	Zivilstandsangelegenheiten	2	1925- 9.30	
		3	10.30-12.33	
	Aufgebote in Luxemburg, Ehesachen Legitimation von Kindern, Namens-erteilung	1-3	1908-33	
	Austausch von Heiratsurkunden		1920-31	
	Erledigte Einzelfälle: Beschaffung von Urkunden in Personenstandssachen, Ehefähig-keitszeugnisse und andere Ehe-sachen	1-2		
		1-9		
	Erledigte Sachen	19 Hefte		
B.III.14.	Beglaubigungen, Bescheinigungen, Übersetzungen, Übermittlungen, Legitimationen	1-4		
B.III.15.	Erledigte Nachlassachen	1		
B.IV.10.	Sport, Tourismus	1		
B.IV.10a.		1		
B.IV.11.	Fürsorge allgemein, mit Ausnahme von Irrenwesen	1	10.27-11.33	
	Irrenwesen, allgemein	1	1.33	
B.IV.14.	Auszahlungen von Pensionen und Renten, Veteranenbeihilfen, Für-sorgemaßnahmen für deutsche Kriegsrentenempfänger in Luxem-burg (Rentenakten generell)	1	1925-33	
	Rentenakten	1-28	2.20- 2.27	
B.V.1a.	Deutsche Vereine in Luxemburg		1934-37	
	Bernh.Gesellgen		1929-38	
B.V.1b.	NSDAP-Landesgruppe Luxemburg		1933-34	
B.V.2.	Ehrenkomitée			
B.VI.5.	Immobilien, Einzelfälle			
B.VII.1.	Arzneitaxe		4.07-1933	
B.VIII.3.	Kriegsgräber in Luxemburg, Gedenktafeln	1-11	1920-36	
B.X.9.	Unfreundlichkeit von Luxemburger Beamten und Behörden, Einzelfälle			
C.XI.2.	Berichte der Landesgruppe über Rückwanderer, Geschäftsanfragen			
E.1.	Eisenbahnen	1-4	7.24- 4.29	
E.5.	Ourtalsperre		1925-29	
G.13.	Weingesetz		1922-29	

Akten-zeichen	Inhalt	Band	Datum	Serial Nr.
G.1.B.1.	Grenzzwischenfall Schengen		3.32- 5.36	
K.1.	Konzerte, Vorträge		10.32-12.32	
K.3.	Luxemburger Studenten an deutschen Hochschulen		9.30- 3.31	
K.4.	Protestantische Kirche in Luxemburg		1891-1933	
M.4.	Kriegsgräber in Luxemburg		1.29-11.29	
N.3.	Nachlass- und Erbschaftsangelegenheiten	1-3	1908-33	
S.2.	Saargebiet	2-9	3.27- 6.36	
S.1.	Sanitäts- und Veterinärwesen	3-4	1.25- 3.30	
S.3.	Sozialpolitik	2-5	2.22- 4.33	
V.2.	Das staatliche Versicherungswesen Unfallversicherung, Alters-und Invalidenversicherung	7	1.33- 3.34	
P.1.	Presse- und Propagandawesen		5.39- 3.40	
P.1.g.	Pressesachen	Sbd. 3	2.37- 8.38	
P.3.Nr.1.	Nachrichtenbüros und Telegrafenagenturen Luxemburg und Belgien		12.39	
P.3.Nr.2.	Deutsche Zeitungen und Zeitschriften in Luxemburg		11.38- 4.40	
			5.40	
P.6.Nr.1a	Beanstandungen in Presse und Propaganda. Krise 1938	Sbd.		
P.6.Nr.2	Hetzfilme	8		
Nr.4	Antideutsche Propaganda		4.38- 4.40	
Nr.4a	Deutsche Beanstandungen		5.39- 7.39	
P.12.	Deutsche Propaganda		1.40- 2.40	
D.P.1.	Presse- und Propagandawesen in Deutschland		5.39- 7.39	
P.1. u. D.P.1.	Pressesachen, Einzelfälle		1939-40	
Pol.3. Nr.2.	Das Grossherzogliche Haus		1939-40	
Pol.2. Nr.1g.	Luxemburgische Sicherheitsfragen		9.38- 8.39	8505/E597271-73
Nr.3g.	"Moderne Garantien", Luxemburg		3.37- 7.39	2870/D563399-485
Nr.3a.g.	Politische Beziehungen Luxemburgs zu Belgien und Frankreich		1.35- 4.37	2879/D565210-23
Nr.4g.	Konferenz der Neutralen	Sbd.	6.38- 2.39	2867/D563372-76
Pol.3. Nr.1a.	Darlehn, Aufwertung, Evangelische Kirchengemeinde, Wiesbaden-Biebrich,Rh.Langgries, Vermögensverwaltung der Grossherzogin von Luxemburg		2.36- 2.40	

Akten-zeichen	Inhalt	Band	Datum	Serial Nr.
Pol. 3. Nr. 1g.	Luxemburgische Regierung: Neu- und Umbildung, Personalien, Innenpolitik		8.37-12.37	2868/D563380-86
Nr. 4g.	Spionagesachen		2.25- 1.38	
Pol. 4. Nr. 1g.	Völkerbundangelegenheiten		10.34- 3.39	
Nr. 2g.	Antifaschismus, Marxismus, Kommunismus, Antikomintern		1.38- 7.39	
	Kommunisten, Marxisten, Emigran-ten		2.35- 3.37	
Nr. 3g.	Rotary-Club und Internationales Freimaurertum		2.36- 3.38	
Nr. 4g.	Luxembg. faschistische Bewegung		5.33- 3.40	4427/E084209-15
D.Pol.2. Nr. 1g.	Wiedervereinigung Deutschland-Oesterreich	*	10.31- 4.39	
Nr. 1ag.	Habsburger Frage und sonstige österreichische Geheimsachen		8.30- 3.37	
Nr. 2g.	Deutschland-Russland	Sbd.	2.37- 3.37	
Nr. 2.			8.35- 3.39	
Nr. 3.	Politik Deutschland-Amerika		1.29- 7.38	
Nr. 4.	Deutschland - Asien		1.35- 3.36	
Nr. 5g.	Oberschlesien und Polen, Danzig und die Minderheitenfrage		1.34- 7.39	
Nr. 6.	Vatikan	2	10.1934	
Nr. 10ag.	Deutsch-französische Annäherung, deutsch-französisches Studien-komité		1.37- 2.37	
Nr. 10g.	Deutschland-Frankreich		2.31- 8.39	
Nr. 12.	Politische Beziehungen Deutsch-lands zu Belgien		1.35-10.39	
Nr. 12g.	Belgien geheim		3.27- 6.39	
Nr. 13.	Politische Beziehungen Deutsch-lands zur Schweiz		3.35- 8.39	
Nr. 14g.	Deutschland-England		2.35- 6.39	
Nr. 15g.	Italien		5.36- 4.38	
Nr. 15.	Italien und italienisch-abessi-nischer Konflikt		5.35- 9.38	
Nr. 16.	Norwegen, Schweden, Dänemark		2.37- 8.39	
Nr. 17.	Die Randstaaten		6.36- 1.40	
Nr. 18.	Deutschland-Spanien		3.36- 5.39	
Nr. 19.	Politische Beziehungen Deutsch-lands zum Balkan		8.36-11.37	
Nr. 20.	Deutschland-Holland		9.36- 7.39	

Akten-zeichen	Inhalt	Band	Datum	Serial Nr.
D.Pol.2 Nr. 21.	Orient und Südafrika		1.37-12.37	
Nr. 23.	Japan		1.38-12.39	
Nr. 24a.	Sudetenland-Option		11.38- 3.39	
Nr. 24g.	Tschechoslowakei		8.38-12.38	
Nr. 25.	China		1938	
Nr. 27.	Ukraine		1939	
Nr. 28.	Memel		12.38- 4.39	
Nr. 29.	Slowakei			
Nr. 30.	Rumänien		1939	
D.Pol.2E	Gestellungsbefehle an Volksdeutsche polnischer Staatsangehörigkeit in Luxemburg		10.39- 1.40	
	Nachrichtenmaterial		1939-40	
	Brüssel		10.39- 4.40	4423/E084084-94
	Krise Sommer 1939: Einkreisung und Abwehr, Polen-Danzig, Garantie Englands für Polen, Verhandlungen England-Frankreich-Russland		3.39-12.39	
D.Pol.3g	Deutschland, Geheimakten		9.29- 7.39	
D.Pol.3. Nr. 9.	Feiertage: 1.Mai	1-2	1939-40	
Nr.11g.	Konzentrationslager		12.35-10.38	
Nr. 1.	Der Führer und Reichskanzler		1939-40	
Nr. 12.	Deutschland und die Kolonien		1939	
R.II.	Unterhaltsforderungen, Vormundschaftssachen	19-20	7.31- 8.38	
R.III.	Rechtshilfe	1-3	1906-09-13	
R.2.Nr.1.	Rechtshilfeverkehr zwischen Luxemburg und Deutschland	1	1.29- 4.30 1939-40	
Nr.3.	Kriegergräber, allgemein		1.34- 6.40	
R.3. Nr. 2g.	Gesetz betr. Luxemburgische Staatsangehörigkeit, Einbürgerungsbereitschaft		3.37- 9.37	
R.5. Nr. 3.	Ausweisungen und sonstige luxemburgische Polizeisachen, Einzelfälle			
Nr. 3a.	Bekämpfung des Mädchenhandels		8.37- 2.38	
R.6. Nr. 1.	Sozialpolitik und Sozialgesetzgebung		1.37- 2.40	
	Einzelfälle an Arbeiterfragen			
Nr. 1a.	Material zur Lohnfrage		1935	
Nr. 2a.	Doppelversicherung auf dem Gebiete der Krankenversicherung		4.37	

Akten-zeichen	Inhalt	Band	Datum	Serial Nr.
R.6. Nr. 5.	Freizeit und Erholung in Luxemburg			
R.7. Nr. 1.	Friedensvertrag von Versailles, seine Anwendung, Auslegung betr. Deutscher Wasserstrassen		1936	
Nr. 1a.	Verhandlungen mit Luxemburg über die Kriegsschäden und Eisenbahn-forderungen (Goldklauselprozess)		1939-40	
Nr. 2.	Kriegsschädenersatzansprüche, allgemein und Einzelfälle		1.40- 5.40	
Nr. 3.	Rotes Kreuz		9.39- 5.40	
Nr. 4.	Humanisierung des Krieges, Militärärztekongress in Luxem-burg		6.38- 3.40	
Nr. 5.	Internierte, Deserteure		2.39- 6.40	2869/563390-95
D.R.1.	Rechtswesen, Rechtshilfeverkehr		12.33	
	Einzelfälle			
D.R.3. Nr. 2.	Reichsbund der Deutschen Beamten, Rechtswahrerbund			
	Geyer, Wilh. Rost für Dampf-lokomotiven		11.37-11.38	
	Fragebogen betr. Erwerb der Deutschen Staatsangehörigkeit in den eingegliederten Ostge-bieten Einzelfälle			
Nr. 2g.	Allgemeine deutsche Staatsange-hörigkeitsfragen		2.36- 2.39	
Nr. 3.	Allgemeine Beglaubigung, Bescheinigungen, Übersetzungen		2.34-10.39	
	Einzelfälle		1936-39	
Nr. 3a.	Zustellungen, Übermittlungen		2.35- 5.40	
	Einzelfälle			
Nr. 3b.	Nachlasssachen allgemein	1	1.34- 2.39	
Nr. 4g.	Blutschutzgesetzgebung		10.36	
Nr. 3b.	Nachlasssachen Einzelfälle			
Nr. 4.	Allgemeines, Beschaffung von Urkunden in Personenstandssachen Standesamtssachen, Ehefähig-keitszeugnisse	13 Hefte	4.37- 2.40	
Nr. 6.	Gnadengesuche, Einzelfälle			
Nr. 7.	Wahlen		10.4.38	
D.R.4.	Beschaffung von Urkunden in Personenstandssachen, Ehefähig-keitszeugnisse und andere Ehe-sachen, Einzelfälle			

Akten-zeichen	Inhalt	Band	Datum	Serial Nr.
D.R.4.	Lage und gesetzliche Bestimmungen über den deutschen Arbeits-markt	2	11.34- 3.40	
	Herr Mosel		1.35- 6.40	
D.R.5.	Aufenthaltsbestimmungen, Einzelfälle			
D.R.6. Nr. 5.	K.d.F.	1-2	10.36- 8.39	
Nr. 6.	Renten- und Versorgungsbezüge von Deutschen im Ausland		1.39- 4.39	
Kult.2. Nr. 3.	Intellektuelle Beziehungen Luxemburgs zu Frankreich und Belgien	2	1936	
Kult.3. Nr. 1a.	Filme für Landesgruppe der NSDAP		11.35-12.39	
		2	12.39- 4.40	
Nr. 1g.	NSDAP.		1.36- 2.40	
	NSDAP Landesgruppe Luxemburg (allgemein)	2	4.34-12.35	2878/D565172-206
Kult.4. Nr. 2g.	Katholische Kirche in Luxemburg (Bischof)		1.35- 3.36	
Kult.12. Nr. 2a.	Casino und sonst.Varieté		12.37- 3.38	
Nr. 3a.	Rundfunk in Luxemburg		6.39- 7.40	
Nr. 3b.	Pensis-Radio-Orchester		4.35- 2.40	
Nr. 3c.	Deutsche Konzerte und Konzerte von prominenten Ausländern Einzelfälle	1-3		
Nr. 4.	Filmwesen in Luxemburg		1.38- 6.40	
D.Kult.1.	Deutsche Kulturpolitik		1.39- 3.40	
D.Kult.1. Nr. 2.	Deutsche Kulturwerbung im Ausland Propagandamaterial, Verteilung von Druckschriften		10.38- 5.40	
	Deutsche Kulturpropaganda, Einzelfälle, ärztliches Fortbil-dungswesen		1936-39	
	- Lackas, Kratzenberg, Büchereiwesen			
	Deutsche Kulturpropaganda	3	1936-40	
Nr. 2a.	Archiv für politische Plakate, Propagandamaterial		1935-39	
Nr. 2g.	Kulturpropaganda		1937-38	
Nr. 3.	Buchprämien an luxemburgischen Lehranstalten und Pfarreien		1939-40	
D.Kult.4.	Auseinandersetzungen zwischen Kirche und Staat		11.37- 4.39	
D.Kult.4. Nr. 2.	Deutsche katholische Kirche		3.34- 6.40	

Akten-zeichen	Inhalt	Band	Datum	Serial Nr.
D.Kult.4. Nr. 3	Deutsche protestantische Kirche		2.34- 4.40	
D.Kult.8.	Schulwesen, Einzelfälle			
D.Kult.8. Nr. 3.	Luxemburger Studenten an deut- schen Hochschulen		1.34- 3.38	
			4.38- 6.40	
Nr. 3a.	Schüleraustausch mit dem Ausland		3.38- 2.39	
D.Kult.10 Nr. 2.	Alexander v.Humboldt-Stiftung		1.33- 7.38	
			8.38- 4.40	
Nr. 3.	Studentenreisen-Tagungen und Lager		7.39	
D.Kult.11. Nr. 1.	Einzelfälle (Kongresse, Fort- bildungskursus)			
Nr. 5.	Vorschriften über ärztliche Prüfungen, Zulassung von Auslän- dern zu den Prüfungen und zur Ausübung der Praxis		1.34- 6.40	
D.Kult.12. Nr. 1.	Kunst und Wissenschaft		7.38-12.39	
Nr. 1a.	Deutsches Schrifttum		1.37- 3.40	
Nr. 3ag.	Rundfunk		8.36- 7.37	
Nr. 5.	Sportwesen, Einzelfälle		1939	
Nr. 5a.	Nürburgring		1.37- 6.39	
Pers.R.1. Nr. 1.	Gesandtschaftsgebäude	3	2.37-12.39	
		4	1.40- 6.40	
Nr. 2.	Haus- und Büroeinrichtungs- gegenstände		1.38-12.39	
			1.40- 6.40	
Pers.R.2.	Kassensachen	4	1.38-12.39	
	Abrechnungen: Prüfungsbemerkun- gen des Auswärtigen Amtes und des Rechnungshofes		1.39- 9.39	
Pers.R.4. Nr. 2	Kriegergräber, Rechnungen		5.31- 1935	
	Baukonto der Gesandtschaft		10.27- 7.30	
Pers.G.2.	Diensteinteilung und Dienstauf- sicht		11.33- 4.40	
Pers.G.4.	Dienstwohnungen		6.30-12.38	
Pers.G.5. Nr. 1	Telef. Einrichtung		1.39- 8.40	
Pers.P.1. Nr. 1.	Personal- und Besoldungsfragen, allgemein	3	7.39- 7.40	
Pers.P.2.	Urlaubsbestimmungen und Pläne		4.21- 7.40	

Akten-zeichen	Inhalt	Band	Datum	Serial Nr.
Pers.P.2.	Meldungen über Urlaubsantritt und Rückkehr		11.32- 4.40	
Pers.	Nachtwächter		1.37- 8.40	
	Kurtze, Bostedt, Thum		4.37- 6.40	
	Beihilfen, Zeugnisse		1940	
	Der Gesandte		1.39- 5.40	
W.2.Nr.2.	Luxemburg-Belgische Zoll-Union		12.33- 4.40	
W.2.Nr.3.	Handelsbeziehungen der Luxemburg-Belgischen Wirtschaftsunion mit fremden Staaten		1.34- 5.40	
W.H.Nr.13	Einzelfälle			
W.J.6.	Patentsachen, Urheberrechtsschutz, Einzelfragen			
D.W.Fs.g.	Fischereischeine		3.35- 3.39	
Prot.3. Nr. 1.	Luxemburgische und ausländische Ordenssachen		1934-40	
Nr. 2.	Ehrenzeichen des Deutschen Roten Kreuzes, jetzt "Ehrenzeichen für Deutsche Volkspflege"		4.34- 1940	
Nr. 3.	Ehrenkreuz des Weltkrieges		8.34- 1940	
	Briefwechsel betr.Ehrenkreuz für Frontkämpfer, Anhang A	1 Heft	1934-36	
	Anhang B	1 Heft	1934-38	
	Erstes Heft: Alphabetisches Verzeichnis der Ehrenkreuz-Anträge			
	Zweites Heft: Nummernliste der Ehrenkreuze für Frontkämpfer			
Nr. 4.	Deutsches Olympia-Ehrenzeichen		1936-37	
Nr. 5.	Verdienstorden vom Deutschen Adler		1937-40	
Nr. 6.	Ehrenkreuz der Deutschen Mutter		3.39	
Prot.	Orden und Ehrenzeichen, Einzelfälle		1937-39	
	Personenverzeichnisse,Einzelfälle Lordt, Robert Lucks Lucks, Lyon M - Z A - Z	1-4 1-12		
	S., Sch.- T			
	Berichtverzeichnisse der Gesandtschaft an das Auswärtige Amt		1922-24	
			1927-28 1929 1930 1931 1932+1933	

Akten-zeichen	Inhalt	Band	Datum	Serial Nr.
	Berichtsammlung		8.34-12.34 1.35- 4.35 5.35- 8.35 9.35-12.35 1.36- 6.36 7.36-12.36	
			1.37- 9.37 10.37- 6.38 7.38-12.38 1.39-10.39 11.39- 3.40	6809/E517681-84 8285/E588313-16
	Deutscher Hilfsverein Luxemburg Ausgaben-Belege			
	1.) ab Gründung bis 12.30 2.) 1930 3.) 1.Vierteljahr 1931 4.) April bis Dezember 1931 5.) April bis Dezember 1931 6.) April bis Dezember 1931			
W.gen.	Vereinbarungen bezüglich Arbeitslosenfürsorge für Deut- sche in Luxemburg:	1 2 3	8.20-12.31 1.32- 8.32 11.32- 8.34	
U.l.	Unterstützungskasse, Belege	1-2	1928-33	
	Fürsorge, allgemein		10.33- 3.37	
	Wohlfahrt, allgemein		1.38- 3.39	
	Abrechnungen mit Landes-Fürsorge- verbänden und Wohlfahrtsämtern	21 Hefte	1.37- 6.40	
	Landesgruppe Luxemburg der NSDAP.(Angelegenheit Geh.Hildebrand)		8.33-12.34	
		Heft 2	10.35- 7.39	
	Beiträge von Gesandtschaftsmit- gliedern zur NS-Volkswohlfahrt		1.36-12.39	
	Rote Kreuz-Spenden der Beamten und Angestellten der Gesandt- schaft		1939-40	
	Reichsdeutsche in Luxemburg A-Z	1-2		
P.l.	Deutschtum in Luxemburg und üb.Ausland	2	1929-33	
	Pazifistische Bestrebungen (Kriegsächtungspakt)	1	1927-28	
	Auslieferungen, Durchlieferungen und andere Strafsachen	3	1.28- 7.29	
	Verschiedenes: Behandlung von Geheimakten, Kurierdienst, Radio	1 Heft	11.34- 4.40	
	Wehrwirtschaftsvorbereitungen Bescheinigungen, Ablieferungen, Auftragszahlungen	1 Heft	10.39	
	Telegrammkosten	1 Heft	12.39	

Akten-zeichen	Inhalt	Band	Datum	Serial Nr.
	Unterstützungszahlungen	1 Heft	10.39-12.39	
	Baukonto	1 Heft		
	Rechnungen	1 Heft		
	Ein Erlass	1 Heft		
	Aktenpläne der Gesandtschaft	3 Hefte		
	Gräberliste Grossherzogtum Luxemburg			
	Abwicklung	1		
	Geheime Eingänge und Ausgaben seit 10.Mai 1940	1 Heft		4424/E084098-145
	Einladungen	1 Heft		
	Teuerungsverhältnisse	1	1.30- 8.33	
	Dienstanweisungen für Auslands-vertretungen, Telegramme	1	1938-39	2876/D565152-55
M.W.	Erzlieferungen	1 Heft	9.39- 2.40	2872/D565043-66
	Geh.Tagebuch des Gesandten		8.39-12.39	8302/E589630-97
	Telegramme	1	1939	4428/E084218-47
	Villa: Inventarverzeichnis			
	Versetzung Luxemburg	1 Heft	7.36- 1.37	
	Gehaltsangelegenheiten			
	Geheime Einzelfälle		1939-40	
	Rohstoffe		1938	
	Einstellung in den Wehrdienst		1939	
	Fragebogen und interne Dienst-anweisung		8.39	
	Wirtschaftspolitische Telegramme und Berichte		9.39- 2.40	
	Ein- und Ausgänge bei der Abwicklungsstelle		5.40- 7.40	
	Akte "Abwicklung"		7.40- 9.40	
	Ablieferungen, Auftragszahlungen		11.39- 3.40	
	Verzeichnis der Ferngespräche		11.39	
	Wasser- und Koksverbrauch, Rechnung		12.39	
	Verfügung		5.40	
	Eine Beihilfs-Jahresquittung			

Akten-zeichen	Inhalt	Band	Datum	Serial Nr.
	Telegramme		5.40- 8.40	
	Gratulationen, Abschiedsschrei-ben anlässlich Ernennung zum Gesandten 1936	1 Heft		
	Ein Postscheck-Konto-Gegenbuch			
	Landesfürsorgeverband Düsseldorf	1	1.38- 1940	
	Landesfürsorgeverband Berlin	1	1938-39	
	Ausgabe - Fürsorge-Belege	1	1939-40	
	Verrechnung: Wohlfahrtskasse mit Zahlstelle. Kriegsnothilfe, Winterhilfe	1 Sbd.		
	2 Kassenbücher (III.und XI.)für Fürsorgesachen und Wohlfahrtsunterstützungen		1937-40 1936-39	
	Ein Registerkasten mit Kartei			
	Ein Registerkasten			
	Briefe betr.Kriegsehrenkreuz-anträge	4 Bdl.		
	Paßjournal		5.21- 9.21	
	Paßregister		9.32	
			11.27- 5.30	
	Beglaubigungsjournal		1922-26	
	Beglaubigungsregister		1.27-12.31	
		4	1.32- 7.40	
	Notariatsregister		1922-39	

Akten-zeichen	Inhalt	Band	Datum	Serial Nr.
M^1:	Militaria		1916-28	
M.1. Nr.5.	Aus feindlicher Kriegsgefangen-schaft nach Spanien entkommene deutsche Heeresangehörige	4-6	1918-22	
M.1.	Militaria		bis 1928	
M.II	Marineattaché und Marine		1928	
Pol. Nr.1a.	Argentinien		1875-1928	
Nr.1b.	Bolivien		1871-1928	
Nr.1c.	Brasilien		1890-1926	
Nr.1cc	Canada			
Nr.1d.	Chile		1865-1928	
Nr.1e.	Columbien		1881-1928	
Nr.1ee.	Costa Rica		1910-1928	
Nr.1f.	San Domingo auf Haiti		1865-1923	
Nr.1ff.	Cuba		1920-28	
Nr.1g.	Ecuador		1871-1928	
Nr.1h.	Guatemala		1874-1928	
Nr.1hh.	Honduras		1907-21	
Nr.1i.	Mexiko		1901-28	
Nr.1k.	Nikaragua		1876-1928	
Nr.1 l.	Paraguay und Uruguay		1874-1928	
Nr.1m.	Peru		1804-1923	
Nr.1n.	San Salvador		1921-26	
Nr.1o.	Venezuela		1869-1926	
Nr.1p.	U.S.A.		1871-1928	
Nr.1q.	Panama		1904-25	
Nr.2.	Belgien		1914-28	
Nr.2a.	Abessinien		1916-26	
Nr.3.	Bulgarien		1872-1918	
Nr.4a.	China		1879-1928	
Nr.4c.	Japan		1883-1925	
Nr.6.	Curie	1-2	1866-1927	
Nr.7.	Dänemark		1883-1925	
Nr.8a.	Deutsches Reich, Varia I		1874-1921	
	- Varia II		1922-25	
	Deutschland		1922-28	
	Flaggen des Deutschen Reiches		1921-28	

Akten-zeichen	Inhalt	Band	Datum	Serial Nr.
Pol. Nr.8f.	Deutsche Kolonialangelegenheiten		1884–1928	
Nr.8h.	Presse	6-9	1917–28	
	Spezial-Pressebüro der Bot-schaft. Dr.Zechlin-Motschmann	1	1918–21	
	La Nacion und Neutralität Propaganda Mp.3.	1		
	– Kl Dia, Mel-garejo, Villar	2-3	1916–27	
	Pressetelegramme	6-9	1925–26	
	Presseberichte	1-4	1922–28	
	Pressetelegramme nach Santa Cruz de Tenerife und Las Palmas	6-8	1926–28	
	Pressetelegrammkosten nach Santa Cruz de Tenerife und Las Palmas Mp.1.		1924–28	
Pol.8i. Nr.18.	Der Frieden: 3 Mappen		1920–22	
	Die Schuldfrage	1-3	1921–35	
	Das Saargebiet Mp.2.			
Nr.19.	Die Konferenz in Brüssel			
	Die Konferenz in Spa Mp.2.			
	Die Konferenzen in Genf, Paris und London Mp.3.		1.21– 3.21	
	Mp.4.		4.21–12.21	
	Mp.5.		1.22– 3.22	
	Mp.6.		4.22–12.23	
Nr.20.	Oberschlesien Mp.1.	1	bis 3.21	
	Mp.2.		4.21– 6.21	
	Mp.3.		7.21– 9.21	
	Mp.4.		10.21–12.28	
	Entscheidungen durch den Völker-bund	1		
Nr.21.	Reklamationen		1918–28	
Nr.22.	Die Kriegsgefangenen Mp.1.			
Nr.23.	Liebesgaben	1		
Nr.23a.	Übergabe deutscher Schiffe an die Spanische Regierung Mp.51.			
Nr.24.	Besetzte Gebiete (Rheinland u.a.)	1-2	11.22–12.28	
Nr.25.	Rheinlandkommission	1		
Nr.26.	Die Reparationsfrage	1-3	1920–28	

Akten-zeichen	Inhalt	Band	Datum	Serial Nr.
Pol.8i. Nr. 26.	Die Reparationsfrage	4-7	1920-28	
		8-10	bis1928	
	Deutsches Angebot zur Regelung der Reparationsfrage vom 2.5.23 und die sich daran anschliessenden Verhandlungen. Beiakten	1		
Nr. 27.	Der Ruhreinbruch	1-3	1.23- 7.24	
	Sammlungen für die Ruhrbevölkerung	3	1923	
Nr.28.	Die separatistische Bewegung in Westdeutschland. Beiakten	1	1923-25	
Pol.8 k.	Freistaat Danzig (ab 1.1.29 "Danzig")			
8 n.	Die Finanzen Deutschlands	1-3	1922-28	
Pol.9.	Ägypten			
Pol.11.	Frankreich		1902-28	
Pol.11a.	Finnland			
Pol.12.	Griechenland			
Pol.13.	Holland			
Pol.13a.	Luxemburg			
Pol.13b.	Liberia			
Pol.15.	Mannesmann		1926-28	
	Marokko Erlasse und Berichte Mp.38-41		1920-24	
		42-46	8.25-12.28	
Pol.16.	Oesterreich-Ungarn Mp.1.		1908-28	
Pol.17.	Portugal Mp.2.		1918-28	
Pol.17a.	Polen Mp.1.		1918-28	
Pol.17.	Deutschland: Krieg mit Portugal	9-11	1918-28	
Pol.18.	Rumänien		1880-1925	
Pol.19.	Rußland		1891-1928	
Pol.19a.	Lettland Mp.1.		1921	
Pol.19b.	Litauen Mp.1.		1887-1928	
Pol.20.	Schweden Mp.1.		1917-28	
Pol.20a.	Norwegen Mp.1.		1905-25	
Pol.21.	Schweiz Mp.1.		1871-1924	
Pol.22.	Serbien-Jugoslavien Mp.1.		1875-1927	
Pol.23a.	Spanien Erlasse und Berichte Mp.50		1920-22	

Akten-zeichen	Inhalt	Band	Datum	Serial Nr.
Pol 23a	Spanien Erlasse und Berichte Mp 50		1920-22	
Nr. 1	Ministerkrisen und innere Lage I.und II.Teil	1-2		
Nr. 2	- Äussere Politik	1		
Nr. 3	- Diplomaten und Konsuln	1		
Nr. 4	- König, Kgl.Familie und Reisen	1		
Pol 23t	Spanien: Fernando-Po Mp 1		1884-1928	
Fasc. 1	Gründung einer deutschen Marine-station auf Fernando-Po			
Fasc. 2	Varia betr. Fernando-Po			
Fasc. 3	Verpachtung von Fernando-Po an ein ausländisches Syndikat Spanien, Deutschland, Belgien			
Pol 23	Spanische Kolonialangelegenhei-ten Ost-und Westafrika Mp 1-2		1909-27	
Pol 23 Nr. 7 a	Spanische Fremdenlegion Mp 1 Mp 2 Mp 3		1923-25 1925-26 1926-28	
Pol 24	Türkei Mp 1-2		1916-25	
Pol 25	Erlasse und Berichte Mp 6		1907-28	
25 a	Kommunismus Mp 1		1924-28	
26	Tschechoslowakei Mp 1		1919-26	
27	Ungarn Mp 1		1922-27	
P 1	Geh.Kzl.Sekr.Reetz Ges.Graf Solms Leg.Rat Graf Tattenbach Leg.Rat Graf Wallwitz Mil.Att.Rittm.von Bülow Leg.Sekr.Prinz Hohenlohe Attaché Leutn. von Eck Attaché von Below Leg.Rat Prinz Taxis Diäter H.Zander Attaché Graf Lynar Leg.Rat Graf Henckel Attaché von Quast Attaché von Eckardstein Leg.Sekr.von Waldthausen Leg.Kzl.Bieler Leg.Sekr.Graf Pückler Botschafter von Stumm Leg.Rat von Gaertner Leg.Sekr.Graf Linden Leg.Sekr.Frhr.von Wangenheim Kanzleidiener Lersch			

Akten-zeichen	Inhalt	Band	Datum	Serial Nr.
P 1	Kanzleisekr. Simroß			
	Attaché Prem.Ltn.von Reinhardt			
	Leg.Kzl.Dr. Grade			
	Leg.Sekr. von Portatius			
	Attaché Ltn.von Schmeling			
	Leg.Rat Frhr.von Montzingen			
	Mil.Att. Major von Funcke			
	Leg.Rat Graf Arco			
	Leg.Rat Erbgraf zu Castell			
	Attaché Ltn.Eggers			
	Diäter H.Hell			
	Leg.Sekr.Graf Wedel			
	Attaché Ltn. Krosta			
	Korv.Kap.von Krosigk			
	Hptm.von Weise			
	Leg.Sekr.von Below-Saleske			
	Leg.Rat von Bülow			
	Leg.Rat Frhr.von Seefried auf Buttenheim			
	Attaché von Radowitz			
	Leg.Rat Graf von der Groeben			
	Leg.Sekr.von Brüning			
	Mil.Att.Major von Etzel			
	Leutnant von Riepenhausen			
	Attaché Frhr.von Nagel			
	Kzl.Rat Supply			
	Leg.Rat Graf von Eberndorff			
	B.R.Renner	1 R	1923-28	
	Ges.R. Prinz Erbach			
	Leg.S. von Heinz			
	Leg.S.Dr. Kissling			
	Leg.S.v.Tucher			
	Kons.S. Kienle			
	O.Insp.Mieschel			
	Hilfsschrb. Frömke			
	Hilfsschrb. Ludwig			
	Stenotyp. Frl. Meene			
	Stenotyp. Frl.Eberhardt			
P 1 a	Botschafter v. Radowitz			
	Botschafter Graf Tattenbach	2	1909-20	
	Prinz Ratibor	1-2		
	Prinz Ratibor, Abberufung	1		
	Botschafter Frhr.v.Langwerth-Simmern	1-2	1922-28	
P 1 b	Personalien der Leg.Sekr. und Attachés		1903-22	
	Attaché v.Kamphövener Kons.Frhr.v.Stengel			
P 1 c	Personalien der Militär-und Marineattachés	1-8	1902-28	

Akten-zeichen	Inhalt	Band	Datum	Serial Nr.
P 1 d	Personalien der Attachés und kommandierenden Offiziere	1-15	1903-28	
P 1 e	- der Kanzleivorsteher	1-4	1879-1929	
P 1 f	- der Legationskanz-listen und Diätare		1895-1922	
P 1 g	- der Kanzleidiener und Scheuerfrauen Kzl.Diener Gottwald	1		
P 1 h	- der Hausmaschinisten			
P 1 i	- der Portiers, Hilfs-amtsgehilfen, Chauf-feure Kübler	1	1895-1928	
	Damaso Rodriguez Cobian	1		
	Angulo Gareia	1		
P 1 k	- der Gärtner	1		
P 1 l	Sommeraufenthalt der Botschaft in San Sebastian	1-7	1895-1922	
		8	1923-27	
		9	1928	
P 1 m	Beurlaubung der Beamten und Angestellten	1	1921-28	
P 2	Personalien der Botschafts Advokaten		1869-1928	
	- Advokat M.Feronda u.Rodriguez			
H 1	Handel und Industrie Mp. R		1919-21	
	Nr.101 Güterabfertigung und Warenstockung in spanischen Häfen und Grenzstationen	1		
	Handel und Industrie		1922-24	
			1925-25	
			1927-28	
	Nr.2 Goldaufschlag		1922	
	Warenaustausch mit Deutschland	1		
	Olivenausfuhr	1		
	Handel und Industrie Patent- und Markenschutz	1-7	1888-1928	
		8-9	1894-1928	
		10-14	1875-1928	
			1922-28	
			1928	
	Verkehrswesen (Auto)	1		

Akten-zeichen	Inhalt	Band	Datum	Serial Nr.
H 1	Verkehr mit den Aussenhandels-stellen Nr.1-58 Nr.1-5		1920-27 1928	
	AH Enquete-Ausschuss	1	1926-27	
	AH 29 Berichte über Wirtschafts-lage		1929	
	AH 16 Kohlenversorgung in Deutschland		1920	
H 1 a	Handel, Industrie, Banken und Handelsgesellschaften		1920-24	
			1925-26	
H 1 a 21	Nr.18 Bankberichte		1921-26	
H 1 b	Einzelne Handelsfirmen		1919-28	
H 1 e	Messen (namentlich)		1919-28	

	Fasc. Frankfurt/Main
	          Leipzig
	          Barcelona			

H 1 d	Handelskammer Barcelona	1	1922-28	
H II	Allgemeines		1923-28	
H II Nr.1	Vertragsverhältnis Spaniens zu Anam			
Nr.2	Argentinien			
Nr.3	Belgien			
Nr.3a	Bulgarien			
Nr.4	Bolivien			
Nr.4a	Brasilien			
Nr.5	Canada			
Nr.6	Chile			
Nr.7	China			
Nr.8	Columbien			
Nr.9	Costa Rica			
Nr.9a	Cuba			
Nr.10	Dänemark			
Nr.20	Deutsch-spanische Handelsbezie-hungen		2.09-1925	
	Deutsch-spanische Handelsver-tragsverhandlungen	1-4		
	Der provisorische Zolltarif	3		
Nr.21	Deutsch-spanische Handelsver-tragsverhandlungen			
Nr.11		1-11	8.21- 8.26	

Akten-zeichen	Inhalt	Band	Datum	Serial Nr.
H II	Deutsch-spanische Handelsver-tragsverhandlungen Beiakten: Protokoll 1922			
	Delegation			
H II Nr.11 21 adh	1.) Verzollung deutscher Waren in Span.-Neu-Guinea	1-3	1926- 7.27	
H II Nr.12	Vertragsverhältnis Spaniens zu Santo Domingo			
Nr.13	Ecuador			
Nr.14	Ägypten			
Nr.14a	Estland			
Nr.15	England			
Nr.15a	Finnland			
Nr.16	Frankreich			
Nr.17	Griechenland			
Nr.18	Guatemala			
Nr.19	Hawai			
Nr.20	Holland			
Nr.21	Honduras			
Nr.22	Italien			
Nr.22a	Island			
Nr.22b	Island			
Nr.23	Japan			
Nr.23a	Luxemburg			
Nr.24	Marokko			
Nr.25	Mexiko			
Nr.26	Nicaragua			
Nr.27	Oesterreich-Ungarn			
Nr.28	Paraguay			
Nr.29	Persien			
Nr.30	Peru			
Nr.30a	Polen			
Nr.31	Portugal			
Nr.31a	Rumänien			
Nr.32	Rußland			
Nr.33	Salvador			
Nr.34	Schweden-Norwegen			
Nr.35	Schweiz			
Nr.35a	Serbien			
Nr.36	Siam			
Nr.36a	Tschechoslowakei			
Nr.37	Türkei			
Nr.38	Tunis			
Nr.39	Uruguay			
Nr.40	Venezuela			
Nr.41	Vereinigte Staaten von Amerika	1-3		

Akten-zeichen	Inhalt	Band	Datum	Serial Nr.
H 2	Heimatwesen, Passangelegenheiten, Matrikel und Schutzscheine			
	Cedulas de vecindad		1900-23	
H III Nr.1-8	Handelsverträge mit anderen Ländern Mp 1		1861-1928	
H IV Nr.1a	Vorschriften betr. Erteilung von Pässen und Visa a) Deutsch	1-4	1871-1928	
	b) Spanisch		1895-1928	
H IV Nr.2	Erwerb und Verlust Mp 1 a) der spanischen Staatsangehörigkeit		1851-1928	
	b) der deutschen Reichsangehörigkeit			
Nr.3	Cedulas de vecindad (Personalscheine) konsularische Matrikel und Matrikelscheine			
Nr.4	- in Cuba und den Philippinen			
Nr.5	Varia lt Rotulus Nr.1			
Nr.6	Passangelegenheiten auf Cuba			
H IV	Spanische Fremdenkontrolle (Dekret vom 12.März 1917-1928)	1		
P I Nr.1	Postverträge Mp 1		1900-28	
Nr.2	Internationaler Telegrafenvertrag			
Nr.3	Einführung des Postpaketdienstes in Spanien. Rückerstattung der Zollbeträge und Nebenkosten bei Rück- und Nachsendung von Postpaketen	1		
Nr.3a	Postanweisungs-, Giro- und Scheckverkehr	1		
Nr.3b	Postverkehr nach Spanien und Portugal	1		
Nr.4	Post-, Eisenbahn- und Telegrafenverhältnisse von Cuba			
Nr.5	Varia lt.Rotulus Nr.1-73			
P I E	Eisenbahnangelegenheiten lt. Rot.		1918-28	
	Nr.29 Beschaffung von Eisenbahnmaterial durch spanische Regierung. Bildung einer technischen Kommission	1		
P I K Nr.3	Kabelverbindung zwischen Kamerun und Fernando Po	1-2		
	Kabel lt.Rot.Nr.1-11			

Akten-zeichen	Inhalt	Band	Datum	Serial Nr.
P I K Nr.7	Kabelverbindung zwischen Emden - Vigo	1-2		
Nr.8	Kabelverbindung zwischen Deutschland - Südamerika und Westafrika			
P I T 1	Telegrafen und Telefone Mp 1		1890-1928	
2	Konferenzen betr.Funkentelegrafie Mp 1	1-2		
3	Listen über Funkstationen der Erde	1		
4	Drahtlose Telegrafie in Spanien und Kolonien Mp 1	1-2		
5	Drahtlose Telegrafie Varia Mp 1		1879-1928	
	Nr.1. Erfindung des Telegrafenbeamten Balsera	1		
	Nr.2. Spanische Vorschriften betr. Ausrüstung der Handelsschiffe mit Funkgeräten	1		
	Nr.3. Einrichtung spanischer Kriegsschiffe mit drahtloser Telegrafie	1		
	Nr.4. Dahtlose Telegrafie. Verschiedenes	1		
	Nr.6. Radioverkehr Deutschland-Spanien	1-2		
	Nr.6a.Pressefunkdienst Barcelona (Vanguardie)	1		
C 1 Nr.1-9	Civilstandsangelegenheiten Mp 1		1900-28	
	- (Nr.128-193) Mp 5		1918-28	
C II	Konsulatswesen Mp 1-3		1874-1928	
	Mp 2		1874-1928	
E 1	Erbschafts- und Nachlasssachen Z I		1900-28	
Z I Nr.16	Ursprungszeugnisse Mp 4	1-7	1868-1928	
Nr.17	Zölle, Zolltarif, Steuern, Abgaben lt.Rot.Nr.1-58 Mp 5,1		1870-1928	
	Nr.23 Pulver- und Explosivstoffmonopol	1		
	Nr.26 Zahlung der Zölle in Gold	1		
	Nr.29 Behandlung der Warenmuster deutscher Handlungsreisender in Spanien	1		
	Nr.31 Getreidezölle in Spanien	1		
	Nr.43 Die Einkommensteuer in Spanien	1		
	Nr.45 Bergwerkssteuer	1		

Akten- zeichen	Inhalt	Band	Datum	Serial Nr.
Z I Nr.17	Nr.51 Industrie- und Handels- steuer	1		
	Zölle, Zolltarif, Steuern, Abgaben Mp 5,2			
	Nr.1 Konsum- und Mietsteuer	2		
	Nr.2 Transportsteuer	2-3		
	Nr.4 Grundsteuer	2		
	Nr.14 Stempelsteuergesetz	2		
	Nr.15 Grenzempfehlungen	2		
	Nr.26 Schmuggel der deutschen Schiffsbesatzung	1		
	Nr.27 Besteuerung deutscher und fremder Banken und Handels- gesellschaften in Spanien	1		
	Zoll- und Steuervergünstigungen der diplomatischen und konsulari- schen Beamten (Gesandtschaftsgut)	1		
Z I Nr.17/1a	- Varia Mp 5,3		1912-23	
	Mietsteuer	1		
	Kraftwagen der Diplomaten in Spanien	1		
Z I Nr.18	Zolltarife lt.Rot.1-9 Mp 6		1876-1928	
	Nr.2 Zolltarif für die spanische Halbinsel und Balearen	1		
	Nr.3 Deutscher Zolltarif	1		
	Nr.5 Zolltarif für Cuba und Puerto Rico	1		
	Nr.8 Zolltarif für die spanischen Besitzungen am Golf von Guinea	1		
Z I Nr.19	Klassifikation und zollamtliche Befugnisse von Häfen und Küsten- plätzen.Errichtung neuer Zoll- ämter Mp 7		1877-1928	
Nr.20	Zollentscheidungen Varia bis 1925 lt.Rot.Nr.1-220			
	Nr.155 Zollfreie Einfuhr von Büchern und Katalogen	1		
	Nr.162 Einfuhrverbot bestimmter Messerarten	1		
	Nr.171 Grenzkarten für Radfahrer und Motorfahrer	1		
	Nr.180 Verzollung von Doublé- waren	1		
	Nr.188 Verzollung von Thioxin	1		
	Nr.191 Verzollung von Treiböl für Dieselmotoren	1		

Akten-zeichen	Inhalt	Band	Datum	Serial Nr.
Z I Nr.20	Zollentscheidungen Varia, 1925-1928 lt.Rot.Nr.1-29 Mp 8			
	Einfuhrverbot für Weizen und Mehl nach den Kanarischen Inseln	1		
	Verzollung von Jutesäcken	1		
Nr.21	Die Juntas arbitrales in Spanien Mp 9	1	1906-28	
Nr.22	Freihafen-Gesetzgebung für die Kanarischen Inseln	1		
Nr.23	Allgemeine Jahresberichte betr. Gesetze aus dem Gebiete der Zölle und indirekten Steuern	1		
Nr.24	Ungenauigkeit der spanischen Handelsstatistik			
Z I	Zollfreie Einfuhr von Sendungen für Gesandtschaftsmitglieder		1880-1928	
Z 2	Zoll- und Steuerreklamationen Mp 2		1916-28	
	Sicherheits- und Zolldienst		1920	
V 1	Verträge (Rotulus) Mp 1-2		1877-1928	
	Deutsche Vereine		1896-1928	
O 1	Verschiedene unvollständige Akten betr.Orden, Titel, Geschenke von Fürstlichkeiten u.a. aus Anlass der Thronbesteigung Alfons XIII.		1914-21	
	Ordensverleihungen: aus Anlass des Krieges		1900-28	
	Ehrenzeichen des Deutschen Roten Kreuzes		1924-28	
	Ordensverleihungen an Kolonialbeamte		1914-21	
	Verdienstkreuz für Kriegshilfe		1917-21	
U 1 1.	Unterstützungen, Heimschaffungen	1,1a 2-3	1920-28	
U 1a 2.	Sammlungen für deutsche Nothilfe		1923-25	
U 1b	- für die Intellektuellen Deutschlands		1923-24	
U 1c	Hilfsaktion des Spanischen Roten Kreuzes		1923-28	
L 1	Literatur, Kunst und Wissenschaft lt.Rotulus Nr.1-62 Mp R Nr.3 Deutsche wissenschaftliche Bücherverbreitung in Spanien		1920-21	
	Nr.7 Reise spanischer Universitätsprofessoren nach Deutschland			
	Nr.37 Deutsches Auslands-Institut in Stuttgart			

Akten-zeichen	Inhalt	Band	Datum	Serial Nr.
L 1	Nr.17 Wagneraufführungen in Madrid			
	Nr.48 Organ.student.Selbsthilfe			
	Nr.36 Boykott der deutschen Wissenschaft			
	Nr.39 Vortragsreisen deutscher Gelehrter in Spanien			
	Literatur,Kunst und Wissenschaft Mp R lt.Rotulus Nr.1-87		1922	
	Nr.14 Lehreraustausch			
	Nr.17 Ausländernachweis an deutschen Universitäten			
	Nr.18 Centro Ibero americano in Hamburg			
	Nr.19 Stud.-Reisen deutscher Akademiker nach Spanien			
	Nr.31 Deutsche Professoren in Spanien			
	Nr.54 Einladung spanischer Gelehrter nach Deutschland			
	Nr.68 Görres-Gesellschaft			
	Nr.70 Ausländer-Reifezeugnis			
	Nr.72 Stud.-Reise spanischer Studenten nach Deutschland			
	Nr.86 Wirtschaftshilfe der Deutschen Studentenschaft			
	Literatur,Kunst und Wissenschaft Mp 1 R lt.Rotulus 1-92		1923	
	Nr.1 Notgemeinschaft der deutschen Wissenschaft			
	Nr.25 Wiegendrucke			
	Nr.41 Ferienkurse			
	Literatur,Kunst und Wissenschaft lt.Rotulus Nr.1-146 Mp 1 R		1924-25	
	Nr.39 Span.Stipendien für Deutschland			
	Nr.74 Deutsche Kurse für Spanisch in Madrid			
	Nr.76 Deutsche Akademie			
	Nr.105 Besprechung deutscher Bücher im Auslande			
	Nr.127 Deutsch-spanische Wissenschaftsbeziehungen			
	Nr.131 Ausländische akademische Titel in Spanien			
	Nr.133 Stipendien von ausländ. Studenten in Spanien			

Akten-zeichen	Inhalt	Band	Datum	Serial Nr.
L 1	Nr.134 Görres-Gesellschaft			
	Nr.135 Prof.Finke und Schreiber			
	Nr.137 Forschung und Fortschritte			
	Nr.144 Deutsche Stipendien (Humboldt-Stiftung)			
	Literatur,Kunst und Wissenschaft Mp 1 R		1926-27	
	Nr.9 Deutscher Sprachunter-richt in Spanien			
	Nr.19 Wagner-Mozart-Festspiele			
	Nr.42 Prof.Finke und Heuss			
	Nr.59 Dr.H. Petriconi			
	Nr.75 Prof.Dr.Weise			
	Nr.76 Prof.Dr.Meyer-Lübke			
	Nr.77 Prof.Dr.Rauchhaupt und Obermaier			
	Nr.85 Reform der Real Academia			
	Nr.91 Arbeitsgemeinschaft für ausw.Kulturbeziehungen in Spanien			
	Nr.3 Übersicht betr.Ausländer an deutschen Hochschulen			
	Nr.5 Ferienkurse für Deutsche im Ausland			
	Nr.8 Deutsches Opernensemble in Madrid			
	Nr.13 Verleihung span.akadem. Titel an Ausländer			
	Nr.23 Dr.Hans Fahrenberg			
	Nr.26 Dtsch.-span.Komitee (Dtsch-südam.Kom.)			
	Nr.38 Kulturpolitische Bedürf-nisse			
	Nr.41 Einladung spanischer Pro-fessoren an deutsche Uni-versitäten			
	Nr.60 Span.Stipendien für aus-ländische Studierende			
	Nr.72 Lehrstühle für ausländi-sche Sprachen und Litera-tur in Madrid			
	Nr.73 Giudad Universitaria			
	Nr.74 Prof.Dr.Weise und Elias Termo y Monzo			
	Nr.86 Kulturpropaganda für deutsche Hochschulen			

Akten-zeichen	Inhalt	Band	Datum	Serial Nr.
L 1	Nr.88 Ges. für Erdkunde			
	Nr.90 Katholizismus in Spanien			
	Nr.91 Buchstiftungen im Ausland			
	Nr.1 Blner Südam. Institut		1928	
	Nr.2 Spanisch-amerikanische Kulturbeziehungen			
	Nr.7 Kulturpolitische Bedürf-nisse			
	Nr.8 Prof.Obermaier			
	Nr.11 Prof.Schaefer			
	Nr.20 Lehrstuhl für deutsche Sprache in Madrid			
	Nr.22 Notgemeinschaft der Deutschen Wissenschaft			
	Nr.46 Austausch-Professuren zwischen Deutschland und Spanien			
	Nr.60 Kaiser Wilhelm Gesell-schaft zur Förderung der Wissenschaften			
	Nr.73 Wagner-Mozart-Festspiele			
	Nr.77 Reise spanischer Profes-soren ins Ausland			
	Nr.89 Wiegendrucke			
	Nr.93 Prof.Gamillscheg und Prof.Castillejo			
	Nr.99 Bedingungen für Studium in Deutschland			
	Nr.100 Handbuch der Kaiser-Wilhelm-Gesellschaft			
	Verträge		1898-1928	
	Die Arbeitsstelle für deutsch-spanische Wissenschaftsbeziehun-gen in Madrid	1-4	1921-28	
	Dtsch.-wiss. Vermittlungsstelle in Barcelona	1	1922-28	
	Kunst und Wissenschaft Arbeitsstelle für deutsch-spanische Wissenschaftsbeziehun-gen		1929	
L 2	Bildungsanstalten		1904-28	
L II	Landwirtschaft		1890-1928	
L 3	Luftschiffahrt		1914-28	
	Nr.12 Span-Luft-Einheits-Gesellschaft	1	1927-28	
	Nr.28 Junkers-Flugzeuge	1	1923-28	

Akten-zeichen	Inhalt	Band	Datum	Serial Nr.
L 3	Nr.41 Luftdienst Spanien-Südamerika	1	1921-28	
	Nr.48 Deutsche Lufthansa (Ceridor Syndikat)	1	1926-28	
S 1	Schiffs- und Hafenangelegenheiten Mp 5 R		1921-28	
	Nr.54 Untersuchung dtsch. Dampfer D.Ruhr	1		
	Schiffs- und Hafenangelegenheiten Besetzung und Beschlagnahme deutscher Schiffe in spanischen Häfen	1-5		
	Geldangelegenheiten	6		
	Reisen deutscher Kriegsschiffe		1926-28	
	Dampfer Lützow		1927-28	
	Besuch der Kriegsschiffe: span.Häfen		1929	
	Auslandsreise der deutschen Flotte	1	1927	
	"Kreuzer Berlin"		1928	
	"Kreuzer Emden"		1926-28	
	"Kreuzer Hamburg"		1927	
	"Linienschiff Hannover"		1927	
	"Vermessungsschiff Meteor"			
	Nr.10 Anmeldung der Schiffs-kapitäne bei deutschen Konsuln, der Kommandanten bei Missionen im Ausland		1879-1925	
	Nr.13 Besuchsordnung (fremde Kriegsschiffe)		1885-1928	
	Nr.1-10 Schiffahrt und Seewesen		1871-1928	
	Nr.11-13		1875-1928	
	Nr.14	1-3	1908-28	
	Nr.15-17 - Kaiser Wilhelm-Kanal		1890-1928	
	Nr.18 Kohlendepots		1905-09	
	Nr.18a-21 Prisenmeldung		1915-28	
S 2	Schiffsvermessungen (Verträge)		1906-28	
	Nr.3 Statistik		1900-28	
K 1	Krankheiten von Menschen, Tieren und Pflanzen		1917-28	

Akten-zeichen	Inhalt	Band	Datum	Serial Nr.
K la	Das deutsche Krankenheim in Madrid	1-2	1922-28	
K 2	Protestantische und katholische Kapellen, Schulen und Gemeinden, Friedhöfe		bis 1928	
	Nr.3 Deutsch-evangel.Gemeinde in Madrid	1 la 2 3	1900-28	2046/446946-53 2046/446954-63 2046/446964-7010
	Deutsche katholische Gemein-de in Madrid		1925-28	
K 3	Deutsche Schulen in Spanien, Allgemeines	1-2	1923-28	
	Deutsche Schulen in Madrid	5a-8		
	- in Barcelona	1-3	1894-1929	
	- in Bilbao		1928	
	- in Gijón		1921-28	
	- in Malaga	1-2	1898-1928	
	- in Las Palmas		1920-25	
	- in Santa Cruz de Tenerife		1926-28	
	- in San Sebastian		1920-28	
	- in Santandor		1924-28	
	- in Sevilla		1916-28	
	- in Tanger		1920-28	
	- in Valencia	1-2	1920-28	
	- in Vigo	1-2	1916-28	
	- in Saragossa		1926-28	
K 4	Kongresse und Konferenzen Mp 1		1907-21	
	Mp 2		1921-28	
F 1	Filmwesen	1-2	1920-28	
	Das Vizekonsulat in Las Palmas	1-4	1876-1920	
	Das Konsulat in Vigo	1-2	1868-1922	
	- in Saragossa	1	1891-1921	
	- in Sevilla	1-4	1868-1922	
	Das Vizekonsulat in Granada	1-2	1874-1923	
	- in Larasch	1	1914-26	
	Das Konsulat in Tetuan	1-2	1913-22	
	- in Santa Cruz de Tenerife	1-4	1896-1922	
	- in Santa Isabel	1	1899-1922	

Akten-zeichen	Inhalt	Band	Datum	Serial Nr.
	Das Generalkonsulat in Barcelona	5-8	1918-29	
	Das Konsulat in San Sebastian		1875-1922	
	- in Bilbao	1-2	1856-1922	
	Das Vizekonsulat in Alicante		1868-1922	
	Das Konsulat in Madrid	7-9	1904-21	
A I	Allgemeine Dienstangelegenheiten	1-16	1863-1928	
A II	Auslieferungsverträge, Generalia betr.Strafsachen			
A 1	Inventar, Kraftwagen		1923-28	
A 2	Auslieferungen und Ausweisungen		1913-28	
A 5	Ausstellungen		1908-28	
A 6	Botschaftsgebäude	1-22	1876-1928	
B I	Beglaubigungen		1900-25	
G I	Spanisches und deutsches Rechts-wesen. Gesetzgebung	1-16	1879-1928	
G II		12-16		
N 1	Notifikationen		1806-1928	
R 1	Requisitionen und Insinuationen		1891-1928	
01 - 3	Geschäftsverfügungen der Bot-schaft		6.87-12.31	
3a	Geschäftsverteilung (auch mit Kons.Abt.)		11.99-12.31	
5	Das Archiv		1.29-12.35	
8	Depeschenbeförderung, Verschie-denes	1-2	1.29-12.32	
Ø1 - 10	Zeitungsabonnements		1.29-12.32	
11a	Horchwagen des Herrn Botschaf-ters Graf von Welczek		5.30- 4.36	
12	Büromaterialien (u.a.Flaggen, Dienstsiegel)		1.29- 6.33	
14	Bibliothek		1.29-12.33	
02 - 1	Das Dienstgebäude	1-3	1.29-12.31	
5	Das Inventar, Verschiedenes		1.29- 6.33	
03 - 3	Personalien der Beamten und Angestellten der Botschaft A-W			
03 - 6	Beiakten 29-34: Dienstbezüge Einzelkassenanweisungen		1.29-12.34	
	Beiakten: Gehaltsaufbesserungs-material		1.31- 5.34	
10b	Legitimation (auch Honorarkon-suln)		1.29-12.32	
04 - 2	Kassensachen, Verschiedenes		1.29-12.31	

Akten-zeichen	Inhalt	Band	Datum	Serial Nr.
04 - 3	Amtliche Abrechnungen	2-4	1.31-12.34	
4	Gehaltslisten	1-2	1.29-12.35	
4a	Zahlungslisten der Angestellten	1-2	1.29-12.34	
5	Steuerabzugslisten		1.29- 7.32	
6	Vorschüsse aus der Legations-kasse (Kassenbestandsverstärkung) Bereitstellung von Devisen	1-2	1.29-12.34	
10	Erinnerungen des Rechnungshofes des Deutschen Reiches		1.30- 2.32	
13	Nachweisungen über ständige Einnahmen- und Auszahlungsan-ordnungen		5.34-10.34	
06 - 1	Heimats- und Staatsangehörig-keitssachen, Pass- und Unter-stützungswesen, Generalia		1.29- 9.30	
08 - 1	Handel und Industrie Deutsch-lands, Allgemeines	1-4	1.29-12.39	
1/1	Übersicht über die deutsche Handelsbilanz	1-2	1.32-12.39	
2a	Handel und Industrie Spaniens, Allgemeines	1-2	1.29-12.39	
2b	Wiederaufbaupläne und Bauvor-haben im Nat.Spanien	1-2	8.37-11.39	
2	Handel und Industrie Spaniens, Verschiedenes	1-2	1.29-12.39	
2/1	Spanische Rüstungsindustrie		1.29- 9.35	
2/2	- Automobilindustrie		1.29- 7.35	
2/3	Spanisches Petroleummonopol		1.29- 1.36	
2/4	Spanische Minenkonzessionen		1.29-11.34	
2/5	Kontingentierungsmaßnahmen Spaniens	1-2	12.31-12.38	
2/6	Preisüberwachung		1.38-12.39	
3	Deutsch-spanische Wirtschafts-beziehungen	1-2	6.36- 1.40	
	Deutsch-spanisches Handelsabkom-men und Handelsbeziehungen	1-3	1.29- 5.36	
3/1	Deutsch-kanarische Kompensa-tionen		5.37- 9.39	
4	Handelsabkommen, Allgemeines		1.29-11.35	
5	- Deutschlands mit anderen Ländern		1.29- 9.34	
6	- und Beziehungen Spaniens mit anderen Ländern		1.29- 5.36	
	Ägypten		1.29- 8.30	
	Argentinien	1-2	1.29- 5.39	
	Ecuador		1.29- 8.33	

Akten-zeichen	Inhalt	Band	Datum	Serial Nr.
08 - 6	Handelsabkommen und Beziehungen Spaniens mit anderen Ländern:			
	El Salvador		1.29- 7.35	
	Uruguay		1.29- 7.35	
	U.S.A.	1-2	1.29- 9.39	
	China		1.29- 5.30	
	Japan		1.29- 2.35	
	Türkei		1.29- 9.38	
	Belgien	1-2	1.29- 6.39	
	Bulgarien		1.29- 2.30	
	Dänemark		1.29-10.35	
	England	1-2	1.32- 7.39	
	Estland		1.29- 5.35	
	Frankreich	1-2	1.29- 1.40	
	Holland	1-2	1.29-12.38	
	Irland		1.29- 4.35	
	Italien	1-2	1.29- 9.39	
	Jugoslavien		1.29- 5.36	
	Norwegen	1-2	1.29-10.39	
	Polen	1-2	1.29- 4.38	
	Portugal		1.29- 6.31	
	Rumänien		1.29- 5.35	
	Rußland		1.29-12.34	
	Schweiz		1.29- 8.39	
	Ungarn		1.29- 3.29	
	Oesterreich		12.38- 3.39	
7	Handel und Industrie, Verschiedenes		1.29-10.35	
9	Patent-, Marken- und Musterschutz in Spanien	1-2	1.29-10.39	
10	Patent-, Marken- und Musterschutz, Allgemeines		1.29- 2.35	
	- Verschiedenes	1-2	1.29- 8.39	
12	Banken, Industrie- und Handelsunternehmungen in Spanien	1-2	1.29- 9.39	
13	Deutsche Handelskammern in Spanien (und fremde)		1.29-12.35	
14	Messen		1.29- 5.35	
15	Ursprungszeugnisse		1.29- 6.36	
16	Aussenhandelsstellen des Auswärtigen Amtes		1.29- 6.39	
17	Bankberichte		1929-32	
18	Abkommen über Warenverkehr		1934	
19	Reichsstelle für den Aussenhandel		11.38-12.39	

Akten-zeichen	Inhalt	Band	Datum	Serial Nr.
09 - 1	Zoll- und Steuerangelegenheiten Allgemeines		1.32-10.33	
2	Deutscher Zolltarif		1.29- 1.34	
3	Spanischer Zolltarif	1-2	1.29- 6.36	
3/1	Zollrückvergütungen (u.a.Auto- mobile) Spaniens		5.33- 2.35	
4	Steuern und Abgaben in Deutsch- land		1.29- 6.32	
5	- in Spanien		1.29- 1.34	
5/1	Besteuerung von Schulen und Kirchen		1.29- 3.33	
9	Zollreklamationen Zollabfertigung		7.37- 1.40	
10 - 1	Deutsch-spanische Kulturbe- ziehungen, Allgemeines		1.29- 3.39	
1/1	Deutsch-spanischer Professoren-, Studenten- und Schüleraustausch	1-3	1.29-12.39	
1a	Kulturpolitik, Allgemeines und Jahresbericht der Botschaft	1-2	11.37- 9.39	
	Kulturpolitische Beziehungen Spanien-Deutschland, Verträge		1937-39	
	Subventionen für Schulen	1-7 + 11	1.29-11.39	
1b	- (Kassentechnische Behand- lung)	1-2	12.33- 5.35	
2	Kunst und Wissenschaft, Verschiedenes		1.29-12.39	
2/1	Lehrerin Frl.Vietmeyer		1.29- 2.36	
2/2	Lieferung von wissenschaftlichen Lehrmitteln		1.29-11.39	
2/3	Entleihung von Handschriften		1.29- 4.39	
3	Literatur		1.29- 9.39	
3/1	Deutsch-spanischer Bücher- und Zeitschriftenaustausch		1.29-12.39	
3/2	Versorgung des Auslandes mit deutschen Büchern und Zeit- schriften		1.29-11.40	
3/3	Deutsche Bücher, Broschüren und Zeitschriften, Einzelfälle		1.29-10.39	
3/4	Spanische Bücher, Broschüren und Zeitschriften, Einzelfälle		1.29- 3.39	
3/5	Sondernummer der deutschen Illustrierten Rundschau		1.29-12.29	
3/6	Revista médica germano-ibero- americana		1.29- 3.39	
3/7	Revista Alemana		1.29- 5.37	
3/8	Graf Keyserling		1.29- 1.36	

Akten-zeichen	Inhalt	Band	Datum	Serial Nr.
10 - 3/9	Übersetzungsrechte deutscher Bücher		9.37-1939	
10 - 4	Malerei		1.29-12.38	
5	Baukunst (Architektenwesen)		1.29-10.39	
5a	Bildhauerei		1.29-1934	
6a	Musikerberufsausübung, Allgem.		1.29-1936	
6	Musik	1-3	1.29-10.39	
6/1	Studium der Musikwissenschaft (u.a.Kurse)		1.29- 8.39	
7	Theater		1.29-12.39	
7a	Tanzkunst		1.29-12.34	
8a	Filmwesen und Filmindustrie	1-2	1.29-11.39	
8	Filme, Verschiedenes	1-3	1.29-12.39	
8a	Entleihung von Filmen und deren Vorführung		2.34-10.39	
9a	Studienreisen und Vorträge, Allgemeines		1.29- 2.38	
9	- Einzelfälle (ausser Presse)	1-6	1.29-12.39	
9U	- Unterteilung		12.35- 9.39	
10	Stipendien (Alex.v.Humboldt-Stiftung)		1.29-11.39	
11	Besichtigung von Schulen, Museen		1.29- 8.35	
12	Besichtigung des Real Palacio, Eintritt in das Parlament		1.29- 3.36	
13	Eintritt in das Casa de Campo, El Pardo		1.29-12.33	
14	Die Arbeitsstelle für deutsch-spanische Wissenschaftsbeziehun-gen in Madrid (ab 20.2.34 Zweig-stelle des deutschen akademi-schen Austauschdienstes, Zweig-stelle Madrid)	2-3	1.30-12.39	
15	- Zweigstelle Barcelona		1.29- 3.39	
16	Die Goerresgesellschaft		1.29-11.34	
17	Die Kaiser-Wilhelm-Gesellschaft		1.29- 4.39	
18	Das deutsch-spanische Komitee	1-2	1.29-11.34	
19	Die Union Intelectual Espanola		3.30- 4.30	
20	Ibero-amerikanische Institute		9.29- 7.39	
21	Die Universitätsstadt Madrid und das deutsche Studentenhaus		4.30- 6.39	
22	Welt-Goethe-Ehrung	1-2	11.29- 7.34	
23	Vogelwarte Rossitten und Helgoland	1	1.29-12.41	

Akten-zeichen	Inhalt	Band	Datum	Serial Nr.
10 - 24	Naturschutz	1	1.29- 5.34	
25	Deutsche Lektoren und Dozenten in Spanien	1	1.29-1940	
25a	Spanische Lektoren und Lektorate in Deutschland	1	1937-39	
25/1	Prof.Dr.Schaefer	1	1.29-12.39	
25/2	Dr.Wilh.Bierhenke	1	2.33- 4.36	
26	Deutsche Vereinigungen Kulturelle und sonstige Ein-richtungen in Spanien	1	1929-40	
27	Hochschulstudium in Deutschland, Allgemeines		1.29- 7.39	
27/1	Besuch von deutschen Schulen und Hochschulen im Inland, Einzelfälle	1	1.29-10.39	
28	Wissenschaftliche und andere kulturelle Institute und Verei-nigungen in Deutschland		1.29- 2.40	
29	Das Archäologische Institut des Deutschen Reiches		1.29-10.39	
31	Schul- und Hochschulwesen in Spanien, Allgemeines		1.29-1940	
31/1	Gesuche von Deutschen betr. span.Schulen und Hochschulen, Einzelfälle		1.29-12.39	
32	Wissenschaftliche und andere kulturelle Institute in Spanien		1.29- 5.39	
33	Private und halbamtliche wissen-schaftliche und kulturelle In-stitute und Vereinigungen in Spanien		1.29-1940	
34	Besondere spanische Gelehrte und Künstler		1.29-11.39	
35	Spanische Kulturpropaganda im Auslande		1.29-1940	
36	Kulturpolitik ausserdeutscher Länder in Spanien (u.Portugal)		1.29- 2.39	
37	Die Sommer-Universität in Santander		1.29- 8.39	
38	Achúcarro-Preis		1.29- 6.33	
39	Ausfuhr von Kunstgegenständen aus Spanien (Kunstbesitz)		1.29- 6.39	
40	Ferien-und Fortbildungskurse in Deutschland		1.29- 4.32	
41	Studienkurse in Spanien und anderem Ausland		1.29- 4.35	
42	Akademische Titel		1.29-10.39	
43	Schutz des literarischen, künstlerischen und wissenschaft-lichen Eigentums		1.29-11.35	

Akten-zeichen	Inhalt	Band	Datum	Serial Nr.
10 - 44	Deutsche Sprachpropaganda in Spanien		3.38-12.39	
45	Buchausstellung, Woche des deutschen Buches		1.37-10.40	
46	Zeitungsausschnitte		1938	
10 - 50	Kultur, Verschiedenes		1940-41	
11 - 1	Ausstellungen, Allgemeines		1.29- 8.39	
2	- in Deutschland und anderen Ländern	1-2	1.29- 7.39	
3	- in Spanien	1-2	1.21- 7.39	
4	Die Internationale Ausstellung in Barcelona 1929	1-3	1.27- 3.31	
5	Die Ibero-amerikanische Ausstellung in Sevilla 1929	1-2	1929- 5.36	
6	Deutsche Buchausstellung in Madrid		1928	
12 - 1	Kongresse und Konferenzen Verschiedenes	1-2	1.29-10.39	
2	Internationale Arbeiter- und Sozialkonferenzen	1-2	1.29- 5.39	
3	Panamerikanische Kongresse		1.29- 9.39	
4	Haager Friedenskonferenzen		1.29	
5	Minoritätenkongresse	1-2	1.29- 8.35	
6	Verkehrskonferenzen		1.29- 8.35	
7	Wirtschaftskonferenzen	1-3	1.29-12.39	
8	Interparlamentarische Konferenzen		1.29- 3.35	
9	Wissenschaftliche Kongresse	1-6	1.29-10.39	
9/1	Kongresse für Bibliotheken- und Bücherkunde		5.34- 6.38	
9/2	Amerikanisten-Kongress		7.34-11.35	
10	Reichstagungen, Gemeinschaft KdF		1938-39	
13 - 1	Land- und Forstwirtschaft in Spanien, Allgemeines		1.29-12.39	
2	- Verschiedenes		1.29-12.39	
3	Spanische Agrarreform		1.29-12.35	
4	Spanische Aufforstung		1.29-12.38	
5	Spanischer Weinbau und Handel		1.29-12.34	
6	Veräusserungsbeschränkungen für ländl. Grundstücke in Spanien		8.31-12.32	
14 - 1	Rechtssachen, Allgemeines		1.29- 2.40	
1a	Internationales Abkommen zur Vereinheitlichung des Wechsel-rechts		5.32- 9.33	

Akten-zeichen	Inhalt	Band	Datum	Serial Nr.
14 - 2	Deutsche Gesetze und Verordnungen		1.29- 1.40	
4	Auslieferungsverträge und Strafrechtshilfe, Allgemeines		1.29- 3.39	
5	Deutsch-spanischer Auslieferungsvertrag und Verfügung betr. Verfahren bei Auslieferung und Übermittlung von Strafurteilen, Generalia		1.29-12.32	
6	Auslieferungen und Strafrecht, Einzelfälle	1-5	1.29- 3.36	
8	Zivilrechtshilfeabkommen und Verkehr, Allgemeines		1.29- 6.36	
8a	Vollstreckung deutscher Urteile in Spanien und umgekehrt, Allgemeines		1.29-11.38	
9	Deutsch-spanische Zivilrechtshilfe, Einzelfälle		1.29- 4.39	
9/1	Erbschaftsangelegenheit Manuel de la Torre		1.29-12.35	
9/2	Francisco Batalla Monleón		1.29-1934	
10	Requisitionen und Insinuationen, Einzelfälle		1.29- 8.40	
11	Reklamationen, Einzelfälle	1-2	1.29- 6.40	
11/1	- Renschhausen		1.29-12.38	
11/2	- Langenheim	1-2	1.29-12.37	
11/3	- Dr.Cassel		1.29- 5.35	
11/4	- Sager und Woerner		1.29- 6.36	
11/5	Spitzsche Erben		1.29- 3.31	
11/6	Reklamationen bei spanischer Regierung, Allgemeines (u.a. deutsche Schutzgenossen in Marokko)		1.29- 9.32	
11/7	- deutsche Schutzgenossen in Marokko, Einzelfälle		1.29- 7.34	
11/8	Prinz Ludwig Ferdinand von Bayern		4.33- 1.34	
12	50-jähriges Jubiläum des Deutschen Reichsgerichts		1.29-11.29	
15 - 1	Sozialangelegenheiten, Allgemeines		1.29-12.38	
2	- Verschiedenes		1.29- 1.40	
3	Versicherungswesen in Deutschland (priv.)		1.29- 5.35	
4	- in Spanien (priv.)		1.29- 8.39	

Akten-zeichen	Inhalt	Band	Datum	Serial Nr.
15 - 5	Arbeitsmarkt, Arbeiterfragen, Gewerkschaftswesen, Streiks u.a. in Spanien, Allgemeines	1-2	1.29-10.39	
5a	Streikbewegungen in Spanien	1-2	1.29- 6.36	
6	Deutsch-spanische Vereinbarung betr. Arbeitnehmer	1-2	1.29- 6.39	
16 - 1	Kirchen, Allgemeines		1.29- 8.39	2045/446820-47
2	Deutsch-evangelische Gemeinden in Spanien		1.29-11.39	2045/446848-924
2a	Die deutsche evangelische Gemeinde in Madrid		1.29- 5.39	2045/446925-42
3	Deutsch-katholische Gemeinden in Spanien		1.29-12.38	
3a	Die deutsche katholische Gemeinde in Madrid		1.29-11.39	
4	Friedhöfe		1.29- 6.39	
17 - 2	Deutsche Schulen in Spanien Cartagena		7.31- 2.34	
	Madrid	2	1.30- 3.33	1331/352574-615
		3		1331/352616-56
	Sta.Cruz de Tenerife		1.29- 7.34	
3	Bücher und Druckschriften für Schulen	1-3	1.29- 3.34	
3a	Schulprämienbücher	1-2	1.29- 6.39	
18 - 1	Deutsche Vereine in Spanien, Verschiedenes	1-2	1.28- 6.36	
2	Deutscher Verein Germania, Madrid		1.29-10.33	
3	Deutscher Turnverein in Madrid	1-2	1.25- 6.36	
4	Deutscher Handlungsgehilfen-Verband, Ortsgruppe Madrid		1.29-1933	
5	Deutscher Hilfsverein in Madrid		1.29- 6.36	
6	Verein für Bewegungsspiele in Madrid		1.29- 2.33	
7	Bund der Auslandsdeutschen (Sitz in Berlin) und Verband reichsdeutscher Vereine im Ausland	1-2	1.28- 6.36	
8	Deutsche Pfadfindergruppen in Madrid		1.29- 6.29	
9	Gewerkschaftsbund der Angestellten (CdA), Ortsgruppe Madrid		1.29- 2.32	
10/1	Parteiabzeichen der NSDAP (Einfuhr nach Spanien) (Stahldrahtknüppel)		6.33- 2.34	
11	Deutsche Angestelltenschaft Deutsche Arbeitsfront (DAF)		3.34-12.38	

Akten-zeichen	Inhalt	Band	Datum	Serial Nr.
18 - 12	Vereine, Verbände und Organisationen in Deutschland		1.29-12.35	
13	Vereine in Spanien und anderen Ländern (ausser Deutschland)		1.29- 9.39	
19 - 1	Gemeinnützige Anstalten, Verschiedenes	1-3	1.29- 2.38	
1a	Arbeitsspende und Winterhilfswerk		7.33- 3.36	
2	Das deutsche Krankenheim in Madrid	2	4.35-12.39	
3	Das deutsche Marienheim in Madrid		1.29-1933	
4	Gemeinnützige deutsche Anstalten in Spanien, Verschiedenes		1.29- 1.39	
20 - 1	Verkehrs- und Nachrichtenwesen, Allgemeines		1.29- 3.39	
1/1	Der Welttelegraphen- und Funkkongress in Madrid 1932 und der Weltnachrichtenvertrag		5.34- 5.36	
2	Verkehrs- und Nachrichtenwesen, Verschiedenes		1.29- 9.39	
3	Postwesen	1-2	1.29- 6.40	
3/1	Internationale Postkongresse und Abkommen		1.29- 5.39	
4	Eisenbahnen		1.29-10.39	
5	Kraftwagenverkehr		1.29-11.39	
6	Telegraphie		1.29- 7.33	
7	Fernsprechwesen		1.29-1931	
8	Funkwesen		1.29- 3.39	
9	Kabelangelegenheiten		1.29- 3.36	
10	Fremdenverkehrswerbung	1-2	1.29- 5.39	
10/1	Presseberichte der deutschen Reichsbahnzentrale Madrid		11.35- 5.36	
21 - 1	Luftverkehr, Allgemeines		1.29-12.38	
2	- Verschiedenes	1-2	1.29- 5.36	
3	Flugwesen in Deutschland		1.29- 9.39	
3/1	Deutsche Luftfahrt-Industrie		1.29-12.39	
3/2	Private Auslandsflüge von Deutschen		1.29- 3.39	
4a	Flugwesen in Spanien, Allgemein. (Militär und Zivil)		1.29- 9.39	
4	- Verschiedenes		1.29- 9.38	
5	Luftschiffe und Luftschiffahrten	1-2	1.29- 2.36	
6	Luftverbindung Spanien-Südamerika		1.29-10.35	

Akten-zeichen	Inhalt	Band	Datum	Serial Nr.
21 - 7	Spanisches Luftverkehrsmonopol (Classa & Lapo)	1-2	1.29- 9.39	
8	Junkers Flugzeuge		1.29- 8.39	
9	Die Lufthansa		1.29-11.39	
10	Deutsch-spanisches Luftverkehrs-abkommen (Berlin-Madrid)	1-2	1.27- 6.34	
11	Deutsch-spanische Sonderverein-barung betr.Luftschifflinien	1-2	1.29- 4.39	
12	Deutscher Transozeanluftverkehr und Zusatzabkommen zum deutsch-spanischen Luftverkehrsabkommen (Flugzeuge)	1-2	1.29-10.35	
13	Internationaler Europa-Rundflug		1.29- 9.34	
14	Luftverkehr Spaniens mit anderen Ländern (ausser Deutschland)		1.29- 6.39	
15	Segelflugwesen		1.29- 7.36	
22 - 1	Schiffahrt, Allgemeines		1.30- 3.39	
1a	Internationales Abkommen betr. Schiffahrt		7.32-10.38	
2	Deutsche Schiffahrt, Allgemeines		1.29- 5.39	
3	Spanische Schiffahrt,Allgemeines	1-2	1.29-11.39	
4	Schiffahrt, Verschiedenes	1-4	1.29-10.39	
4a	Norddeutscher Lloyd	1-2	12.30- 8.38	
4b	Germanischer Lloyd		1.29- 8.33	
4c	Hamburg-Amerika-Linie	1-2	12.31- 1.39	
4d	Hamburg-Südamerikanische Dampf-schiffahrtsgesellschaft		11.33- 6.35	
4e	Rückgabe spanischer Dampfer		6.37- 5.35	
4f	Beschlagnahme von Dampferladun-gen, an denen deutsches Interes-se besteht		8.38-11.38	
5	Besuch deutscher Handelsschiffe in Spanien (Flaggenzwischen-fälle)	1-2	1.29- 2.38	
5/1	KdF-Schiffe (Besuch in Spanien)		1939	
6	Besuch deutscher Kriegsschiffe in spanischen Häfen	2,3, + 5	1.30- 2.39	
6a	Deutscher Kreuzer "Berlin"		1.29- 3.29	
6b	Deutscher Kreuzer "Emden"		1.29- 1.39	
6c	Deutsches Linienschiff "Schlesien"		9.35- 4.36	
7	Besuch ausländischer Kriegs-schiffe in spanischen Häfen und benachbarten Gewässern (Einzel-fälle)		7.32- 7.39	

Akten-zeichen	Inhalt	Band	Datum	Serial Nr.
22 - 8	Kaiser-Wilhelm-Kanal (Betriebsordnung)		1.29- 2.39	
9	Deutsche amtliche Schiffahrts-liste		1.29-10.39	
10	Spanische amtliche Schiffahrts-liste		1.29- 8.35	
11	Internationales Signalbuch		1.29- 9.38	
12	Nautisches Jahrbuch und Ver-zeichnis der Zeitsignalstationen		1.29- 7.39	
13	Befeuerung der spanischen Küste und Handelsschiffahrt (Telegr.-, Funkstationen, Funkfeuer, Lotsen-zwang)		1.29- 3.36	
14	Spanische Flaggen- und Salut-vorschriften (Handels- und Kriegsmarine)		1.29- 7.39	
15	Flaggen und Hoheitszeichen der deutschen Kriegsschiffe. Bei Auslandsbesuchen zu beach-tende Zeremonalien. Kreuzerhand-buch		1.29- 8.35	
16	Einteilung der Kriegsschiffs-besuche in offizielle und inof-fizielle		1.29-11.32	
17	Auslandsreisen der Kriegsschiffe und Besuchsabstattung bei kirch-lichen Würdenträgern		1.29- 4.34	
18	Desinfektion der Handelsschiffe		1.29-10.39	
19	Spanisches Auswanderungsgesetz und Bestimmungen für Schiffe		1.29- 5.30	
20	Schiffsabgänge		1934-35	
21	Schiffsmeldungen		1939-40	
22	Einschiffungslisten		1936	
23	Begegnungen neutraler und feindlicher Schiffe		1939-40	
24	Festliegende deutsche Dampfer	1-2	9.39- 3.40	
23 - 1	Sport	1-2	1.23- 7.39	
1a	- (Reit-und Fahrsport) (Pferde)	1-2	1.29- 5.39	
1b	Olympische Spiele	1-2	1.29- 6.39	
1c	Deutsche Automobilklubs und Auslandfahrten (auch Rennfahrer)		1.29- 7.39	
24 - 1	Statistik		1.29- 4.36	
1/1	Übersicht der Einnahmen des Reiches an Steuern, Zöllen und Abgaben		1.29-1932	
1/2	Deutsche Hochschulstatistik		1.29- 5.35	

Akten-zeichen	Inhalt	Band	Datum	Serial Nr.
24 - 2	Berichterstattung über den Schiffsverkehr in den nat.span. Häfen		6.37- 1.39	
25 - 0	Verschiedenes	1-2	1.29- 3.40	
1	Dr.v.Weickhmann		1.29-12.34	
2	Baronin v.Loen		1.29- 7.34	
3	Dr.Ernst Kocherthaler (und Kono Kocherthaler)		1.32- 5.39	
4	van Vollenhoven		1.29- 5.34	
5	Lewin		12.37- 3.38	
27 - 3	Schieds- und Vergleichsabkommen (ausser deutsch-spanisch)	1-2	1.29- 4.35	
28 - 1	Jugendbewegungen		1936-39	
2	Jugend in Deutschland		1936-39	
3	Jugend in Spanien		1937-39	
99 - 3	Deutsche Konsulate in Spanien Einzelakten: Kons.Agt.Aguilas	1	1871-1934	
	Kons.Agt.Alicante	1-10	1936	
	Vizekonsul Almeria	2	3.24- 5.30	
	Kons.Agt. Arrecife de Lanzarote	1	1914-20	
	Kons.Bilbao	3	1923-32	
	Kons.Cadiz	2	1923-36	
	Kons.Cartagena	1-2	1875-1929	
	Kons.Agt.Castellon de la Plana	1	1904-22	
	Kons.Agt. Ceuta & Malilla	1	1908-32	
	Vizekonsul Corcubion	1	1903-34	
	Kons.Agt. Córdoba	1	1910-21	
	Kons. La Coruna	2	1912-31	
	Kons.Agt.Denia	1	1871-1934	
	Kons.Agt. Ferrol	1	1862-1924	
	Kons.Agt. Candia	1	1904-33	
	Kons.Agt. Gibraltar	1	1914-25	
	Kons. Gijon	1-2	1868-1925	
	Vizekons.Granada	3	1932-34	
	Kons. Huelta	2	1925-35	
	Kons.Agt. Huesca	1	1922-29	
	Kons.Agt. Irun	2	1902-30	
	Kons.Agt.Jerez de la Frontera	1	1871-1935	
	Kons. Larache			
	Kons.Agt.León	1	1932-35	
	Kons.Agt.Lérida	1	1922-32	
	Kons.Madrid	10	1922-34	
	- Sekretäre und Dolmetscher	1	1900-22	
	Kons. Mahòn	2	1929-36	
	Kons. Malaga	3	1919-33	

Akten-zeichen	Inhalt	Band	Datum	Serial Nr.
99 - 3	Deutsche Konsulate in Spanien, Einzelakten:			
	Vizekons. Monforto de Lemon (siehe Vivero)	1-2	1907-35	
	Kons. Las Palmas	5-6	1922-35	
	Kons. Palma de Mallorca	1-2	1868-1936	
	Kons.Agt. Port Bou	1	1902-32	
	Kons. Santa Isabel	2	1923-36	
	Vizekons.Salamansa	1	1927-35	
	Vizekons.San Feliu de Guixols	2-3	1908-31	
	Kons. San Sebastian			
	Vizekons. Sta.Cruz de la Palma	1	1931-35	
	Kons.Sta.Cruz de Tenerife	5-6	1923-36	
	Kons. Santandor	2	1901-34	
	Kons. Sevilla	5-6	1923-32	
	Kons./1 Ehem.Wahlkonsul Otto Engelhardt	1	1929-35	
	Kons. Tarragona	1-2	1868-1935	
	Kons. Tetuan	3-4	1923-33	
	Kons.Agt. Torrevieja	2	1903-33	
	Kons. Valencia	2-3	1895-1936	
	Vizekons. Valladolid	1	1905-35	
	Kons. Vigo	3	1923-36	
	Kons.Agt. Villagarcia	1	1904-32	
	Kons. Zaragoza	2	1923-33	
200 - 0	Politik, Allgemeines	1	1.29- 7.32	
201 - 0	Abrüstung und Sicherheitsfrage (Luftpakt)	1+9	12.34- 2.37	
1	Locarno-Pakt - Rheinlandmilitarisierung	1	3.36- 7.36	
202 - 0	Sozialismus (intern.Arbeiterfrage)	1	1.29- 7.36	
203 - 0	Kommunismus (Anarchismus) Allgemeines (intern)		8.38- 7.39	
	Kommunismus, Stand und Fortschritte in Spanien		5.36	
204 - 0	Minoritäten	1-2	1.29-11.35	
205 - 0	Freimaurer und intern.Judenfrage		6.37- 2.40	
210 - 0	Völkerbund	3-6	1.32- 6.40	
1	- Ratstagung Madrid		1929	
2	Gaskrieg und Luftkriegverbot		1899-1934	
230 - 0	Politische Paktprojekte (Ostpakt, Donaupakt)	1	7.34-12.39	
250 - 0	Italien-Abessinischer Konflikt	4-5	1.36- 6.36	
300 - 0	Afrika, Allgemeines	1	4.39- 6.39	
2	Ägypten	1	1.39- 4.39	

Akten-zeichen	Inhalt	Band	Datum	Serial Nr.
310 - 1	Marokko, Allgemeines	4	10.34-11.41	
		5		4096/E069603-45
				4937/E264135-85
1a	– Feindpropaganda	1	1.41-10.41	
2	– Kapitulationen	1-2	1.29-12.32	
3	Die Tangerzone	2		
		3	1.32-11.41	4090/E069282-330
4	Mannesmann-Interessen	1-2	1.29- 4.36	
5	Ifni-Gebiet	1	3.34- 8.41	
6	Angeblicher Waffenschmuggel deutscher Schiffe nach Marokko		3.34-12.36	
7	Einreise Deutscher nach Marokko und Tangerzone, Einzelfälle	1	1.29- 5.36	
8	Marokko, Wirtschaftsangelegen-heiten	1	1.37- 9.39	
10	Französisch Marokko	1	1.40-11.41	
400 - 1	Argentinien	1	1.39- 5.40	1937/434093-129
2	Bolivien	1	1.39- 4.40	1937/434130-40
3	Brasilien	1	1.39- 7.40	1937/434141-55
4	Chile	1	1.39- 3.40	1937/434156-89
5	Canada	1	1.39- 9.39	
6	Columbien	1	1.39- 2.40	1937/434214-22
7	Costa Rica			
8	Cuba (Dominik.Republik)		1.39- 7.40	1937/434190-213
9	Ecuador		1.39- 5.40	1937/434223-28
10	Guatemala		1.39- 4.40	1937/434229-47
11	Honduras		1.39- 5.39	
12	Mexiko		1.39- 5.40	1937/434248-62
13	Nicaragua		1.39- 6.39	
14	Panama		1.39- 7.40	1937/434263-69
15	Paraguay		1.39- 9.39	1937/434270-75
16	Peru		1.39- 5.40	1937/434276-86
17	El Salvador		1.39- 9.39	
18	Uruguay		1.39-10.39	
19	Venezuela		1.39- 3.39	
20	Vereinigte Staaten von Amerika		1.39- 8.40	
500 - 1	Afghanistan	1-2	1.29- 8.39	
2	China	1	1.39- 6.40	
3	Japan		1.39- 7.40	
5	Iran (Persien)	1-2	1.29- 9.39	
7	Türkei		1.39- 1.40	
8	Mandschukuo		1.39- 5.40	
600 - 0	Australien, Allgemeines		1.39-12.39	
700 - 1	Albanien		1.39- 7.39	
2	Belgien		7.38-1940	
3	Bulgarien		1.39-1940	

Akten-zeichen	Inhalt	Band	Datum	Serial Nr.
700 – 4	Röm.Curie (Vatikan)		3.37– 5.40	
5	Dänemark		10.37– 4.40	
7	England (auch Dominions)		12.36– 5.40	2772/D536938-53 3050/D601048-125
7a	Irland		1.39– 1.40	
8	Estland		1.39–10.39	
9	Frankreich		5.37– 7.40	2806/D548444-540 2667/D528000-010 2960/D577787-807
10	Finnland		12.38– 4.40	
11	Griechenland		1.39– 4.40	
12	Holland		10.38–12.39	
13	Italien		12.36– 5.40	
14	Jugoslavien		12.36– 5.40	
15	Lettland		6.39–10.39	
16	Litauen		3.39–11.39	
17	Luxemburg		1.38– 7.39	
18	Norwegen		10.38– 4.40	
19/1	Oesterreich, Allgemeines		1.29– 4.36	
20	Polen		12.36– 4.40	
20a	Deutschenhetze in Polen		5.39– 9.39	
21	Portugal		1.38– 5.40	
22	Rumänien		12.36–1939	
23	Rußland		11.38– 5.40	
24	Schweden		1.39– 4.40	
25	Schweiz		7.38– 4.40	
26	Tschechoslowakei		11.38– 4.39	
27	Ukraine		1.39	
28	Ungarn		12.36–12.39	
710 – 1	Deutschland – Allgemeines		12.38	
2/1	Reichsparteitage		6.37– 8.39	
2	Innere Angelegenheiten	4-5	1.35– 7.40	
2a	NSDAP (Parteisachen)	2	9.38–1939	
2b	Arbeiterfragen und Sozialange-legenheiten	1-3	1.29– 4.40	
2c	Oesterreichische Fragen		3.38– 6.38	
2e	Deutscher Arbeitsdienst		7.39–12.39	
3	Auswärt.Angelegenheiten		12.36– 6.40	
3a	M.d.R.Schreiber	1	3.30–1937	
4	Verfassung und Reichstag (Staatsrecht)	1	1.39– 2.36	
4a	Wahlen und Abstimmung		10.38–12.38	
5	Reichspräsident (Führer)	1-2	1.29–11.39	
6	Ministerien, Minister und Staatsmänner (ausser Auswärtiges Amt)		1.29–11.35	

Akten-zeichen	Inhalt	Band	Datum	Serial Nr.
710 - 7	Das Auswärtige Amt	1-3	1.29- 6.40	
	Beiakten: Etatsverhandlungen (D.R.Anz.)		1.31	
8	Finanzen	1-5	1.29- 3.36	
	Deutsche Finanzen (Registermark)		1938	
8a	Auswirkungen der deutschen Finanz- und Wirtschaftskrise in Bezug auf den deutsch-spanischen Handel (u.a.Devisenzahlungsab-kommen)	1-4	11.31-12.38	
8/1	Finanzangelegenheiten, Einzelfälle	1-2	1.29-12.39	
8/2	Alte Markbesitzer		1.29- 2.35	
8/3	Reichsbanknoten und Reichsmünzen		1.39- 7.39	
8/4	Rückwanderer (Registermark)		8.38-1939	
9	Heer und Flotte	1-2	1.29- 2.40	
9e	Deutsche Militär-, Marine- und Luftattachés		2.33- 5.36	
9/1	Heer und Flotte, Einzelfälle		1.29- 6.40	
10	Presse	2-3	1.34- 7.39	
10a	Handbuch der Weltpresse und bibliothekarische Behandlung der Zeitungen		1.29- 9.35	
10b	Verbreitung innerdeutscher Zeitungen und Zeitschriften im Auslande und Belieferung der Botschaft und anderer wichtiger Stellen mit solchen Zeitungen und Zeitschriften	1-2	1.29- 5.39	
10b/1	Zeitschrift "Völkerbund und Völkerrecht"	1-2	5.34-1940	
10c	Verzeichnis der ständigen Ver-treter innerdeutscher Zeitungen in Spanien		1.29-1936	
10d	Vertreter innerdeutscher Zeitun-gen in Spanien und deren Bericht-erstattung	1-2	1.34- 3.39	
	Handakten: Zeitungsausschnitte deutscher Pressevertreter		1.29- 3.30	
10e	Die hauptsächlichen Zeitungen deutscher Sprache im Auslande (Spanien)		1.29-12.35	
10f	Deutschsprachige Zeitungen und Zeitschriften in Spanien, Verschiedenes	2	10.33- 1.35	
10g	Zeitungsausschnitte		5.29-12.33	
10h	- (San Sebastian)		1937-39	
11	Pressetelegrammdienst		1.29- 2.35	

Akten-zeichen	Inhalt	Band	Datum	Serial Nr.
710 - 11a	Pressetelegramme	1-3	1.29- 3.35	
11b	Ein- und abgehende Fernschreiben	1-5	1928-39	
12	Weltkrieg (Vertrag von Versailles)	1-5	1.29-10.38	
12a	Kriegergräber		1.29- 1.35	
13	Auslandsdeutschtum (deutsche Minoritäten, Anschlussfrage) Allgemeines	1-2	1.39-12.39	
14	Kolonialangelegenheiten	1-2	1.29- 5.40	
14/1	- laufende Veröffentlichung		7.37- 3.39	
15a	Deutsche Propaganda im Auslande, Allgemeines		1.39- 6.40	
15	- (Bücher, Broschüren, Zeitschriften)	1-3	1.29- 5.39	
15/1	Segeljacht "Deutschland"		1.34- 7.34	
15/2	Deutscher Fichtebund		1.33-10.36	4401/E083345-96
15/3	Propagandareisen spanischer Politiker nach Deutschland	1-2	5.34-11.41	
16	Deutschfeindliche Propaganda (ausser Presse) Allgemeines	2-3	8.33- 7.41	
15/4	Reisen deutscher Persönlichkeiten in Spanien		9.38-11.41	
16a	Spanische Kundgebungen gegen Deutsche Regierung Hitler	1 2 3 4	2.33-11.39	4403/E083456-65
16b	Manifestationen gegen deutsche Vertretungen in Spanien	1 2 3	2.35- 5.36	4394/E083269-72
16c	Überwachung deutscher Emigranten und verdächtiger Personen, Allgemeines		4.39-11.39	
16d	Deutschfeindliche Propaganda in Marokko	2	1.34- 2.36	4399/E083336-38
18	Abgetrennte und besetzte Gebiete (Grenzproblem)	1-2	1.29- 4.39	
18a	Das Saargebiet	1-4	1.29-12.35	
	Beiakten: 1. Das Ausland über die Saar (Informationsblatt)	1-2	3.34- 2.35	
	Beiakten: 2. Saarabstimmungs-berechtigte deutsche Reichsange-hörige in Spanien.		3.34- 9.35	
19	Reden deutscher Politiker Interviews	1-3	1.39- 2.40	
20	Führer-Reden		11.37-39	
770 - 1	Spanien, Allgemeines	1-2	1.29- 9.39	

Akten-zeichen	Inhalt	Band	Datum	Serial Nr.
770 - 2	Das spanische Königshaus	1-2	1.29-11.39	
2a	Der Präsident der spanischen Republik	1-2	12.31- 1.40	
3	Nationale Erhebung	1		3207/D697818-53 4687/E225358-583
		2		3207/D697854-81 4687/E225584-604 5076/E292415-17
			1936	
		3		3207/D697882-95 4687/E225605-08
		4		3207/D697896-98 4687/E225609-11
	Innere Angelegenheiten	1-2 3	1.37- 1.42	5145/E302965-3504
3a	Katalonien	1-3	4.31- 5.40	
3/1	Falange Espanola	1	6.37-11.41	1899/427778-802
		2		1899/427803-30 4411/E083745-801
4	Auswärtige Angelegenheiten	2		1899/427717-58
		3	1.32- 6.40	1899/427759-63 4391/E083249-56
		4		1899/427764-77 4091/E069333-47
4a	Spanisch-französische Beziehungen	1	1.29- 6.40	1912/430233-64
		2		1912/430265-94
4b	Spaniens und Frankreichs Bestrebungen zur Sicherung der Verbindung mit den afrikanischen Kolonien		1.29-12.36	
4c	Spanisch-russische Beziehungen		1.29-12.36	1912/430295-330 4395/E083275-80
4d	Spanischer Volkssturm im Ausland		2.39- 7.40	1912/430331-32
4e	Spanisch-italienische Beziehungen		7.39- 9.41	
5	Ministerien, Minister und Staatsmänner	2 3	1.32- 9.41	4406/E083611-68
	Beiakten: Diverse spanische Persönlichkeiten (Bildersammlung)		4.31-10.38	
5a	Schriftverkehr mit den spanischen Staaten		1.29-12.39	
5/1	Verschiedene spanische und ausserdeutsche Personen		11.38- 3.40	
5/3	Mitglieder internationaler Schiedsgerichtskommissionen		1.34- 8.40	
6A	Span.auswärt.Dienst (auch Kons. und Kons.-Agt.)		1.29- 7.40	
6	Span.Diplom. und Konsular-Korps	3 4	1.32- 5.41	4392/E083259-60
6a	Die spanische Botschaft in Berlin		1.29- 6.40	

Akten-zeichen	Inhalt	Band	Datum	Serial Nr.
770 – 6b	Spanische Militär-, Marine- und Luftattachés		1.29-10.41	4393/E083263-66 8402/E592333-63
6c	Spanisches Konsularkorps in Deutschland		1.29- 1.40	
7	Diplom. und Konsularkorps in Spanien	3-4 5	1.33-12.41	4409/E083689-716
7a	Diplomatenliste und Liste der Konsuln, Vizekonsuln und Kons. Agt. in Spanien		1.31-11.41	
8	Finanzen	1-5	1.29-12.39	
8/1	Finanzangelegenheiten, Einzel-fälle	1-2	1.29-12.39	
8/2	Verrechnungsabkommen Handel mit Devisen		9.38-12.39	
9	Militär und Polizei	2	7.32-12.41	4893/E253839-48
9/1	– Einzelfälle		1.29- 7.39	
10	Die spanische Fremdenlegion, Allgemeines		1.29- 2.36	
11	– Verschiedenes	1-5	1.29- 1.36	
11a	Französische Fremdenlegionäre		1.29- 3.39	
11/1	Die spanische Fremdenlegion Sonderfälle:Heinicke und Genossen	1-2	6.32- 5.36	
11/2	– Dietrich Sieverling-Frehse		6.31- 1.34	
11/3	– Jacob Wisemann alias Jaques del Norte		3.31- 3.36	
12	Marine	2	1.32- 5.40	
13A	Presse, Allgemeines (deutscher Einfluss auf spanische Presse)	2	1.34- 9.39	4400/E083341-42
13Md	Madrider Presse, Verschiedenes	1-2	1.29- 9.39	
13MdU	– Unterteilung	1-2	1.29- 5.35	
13Prv	Provinzpresse, Verschiedenes	1-6	1.29-10.39	
Prv.U 13	– Unterteilung		5.35- 7.39	
13/1	Madrider Presse, Eizelakten (bes.Liste)		1.29- 5.35	
	Unterteilung der Einzelakten "Madrider Presse"			
	A B C		1.29- 5.35	
2	Blanco y Negro		1.29- 2.36	
3	El Debate		1.29- 5.36	
4	El Sol		1.29- 1.36	
5	Informaciones		1.29- 5.36	
6	Ahora		12.30-12.35	
7	La Voz		1.29- 9.35	
8	Luz		3.33- 7.33	

Akten-zeichen	Inhalt	Band	Datum	Serial Nr.
770 - 9	Diario de Madrid		10.34- 2.36	
10	Ya		1.35- 9.35	
11	Heraldo de Madrid		1.29-12.35	
12	La Libertad		1.29-10.35	
13	El Liberal		1.24- 9.35	
14	El Socialiata		3.33- 4.36	
15	La Tierra		3.31-12.34	
16	La Lucha		3.34- 4.34	
17	El Pueblo		12.34- 6.39	
18	La Nacion		1.29- 6.35	
19	El Imparcial		1.29- 5.33	
20	La Epoca		1.29- 3.36	
21	Domingo		10.39-11.39	
13B	Spanischer Presseverkehr		12.38- 8.39	
13a	Pressesammel-Artikel (Büro Hansa, Johannsen, Transocean)	1-2	1.29- 7.36	
13b	Monatliche Presseberichte	1-2	11.33- 5.39	
13c	Verzeichnis der für das Reichs-gebiet verbotenen ausländischen Druckschriften		1.34-11.38	
13d	Ausländische Telegrafenbüros und Presseagenturen. Vertreter aus-ländischer Zeitungen sowie deren Berichterstattung (Pressekon-ferenzen, Pressevereinigungen) (ausser deutsche)		1.29- 9.39	
13e	Presseartikel deutscher und ehemaliger deutscher Reichsange-höriger in spanischer Presse		1.29- 9.39	
13f	Deutsche Pressepropaganda in Spanien (Org.)		12.34-11.38	
13g	Berichte der Presseabteilung		12.38- 9.39	
14	Pressetelegrammdienst WTB - FABRA und DNB-Dienst		1.29- 7.39	
15	Kirchen, Allgemeines	1-2	1.29-11.41	
15/1	- Verschiedenes		1.29-12.39	
16	Kolonien		1.30- 5.41	
16a	Spanisch-Guinea		1.29- 7.39	
17	Spanische Verfassung		1.29- 4.39	
19	Reden spanischer Politiker		4.38- 1.40	
20	Deutsch-spanische Polizeikommis-sion		11.37- 6.39	
Sa.2e	Beiakte Einladungen	1	1936-38	
	Weiterleitungen von Briefen	1-4	12,36-12.39	
2f	Brief- und Telegrammweiterlei-tungen	1-5	1940-42	

Akten-zeichen	Inhalt	Band	Datum	Serial Nr.
Sa. 3I	Spanischer Krieg	1 2 3	11.36- 6.39	4305/E077958-8003
3Ia	Nichtinterventionspolitik	1 2 3 4	11.36- 6.39	3372/E010633-57 3372/E010658-74 3372/E010759-73 3372/E010675-758 3468/E017880-81
		5-8	11.37- 6.39	
3Ib	Verstösse gegen Nichteinmi-schungsabkommen	1-4	5.36- 3.39	
3IbA	Angebliche deutsche Waffen-lieferungen	1	1937-38	
3Ic	Diplomatische Vertretungen der National-spanischen Regierung	1	12.36-10.38	
3Id	Diplomatische Vertretungen bei der Spanischen Nationalregierung		1.37-10.38	
3Ie	Ausländische Beobachter der spanischen Vorgänge		12.36- 2.39	
3Ig	Fremde Konsulate in Spanien (mit Ausnahme der deutschen und italienischen)	1	3.37- 7.38	
3Ih	Beziehungen Nationalspaniens zu fremden Staaten		12.36-11.38	
3Ii	Personalien spanischer Behörden (Beiakte)		1.37-10.38	
3Ik	Marokko	1 2	12.36- 9.38	3376/E011149-63
3Im	Gesundheitswesen	1	3.38	
3In	Spanische Aussenpolitik	1	4.38	
3II	Diplomatische Vertretung in Rotspanien, Asylfrage (Beiakte)	1	11.36-1938	5174/E306997-99
	Politische und wirtschaftliche Lage in Rotspanien		11.36- 5.39	
3IIa	Illegaler Goldexport, Wertsachen-Raub (Beiakte)	1	11.36- 7.38	
	Rotspanische Beziehungen zu fremden Ländern	1	11.36- 4.39	
3IIb	Zwischenfälle zur See	1	12.36- 6.38	
3IIc	Rote Propaganda und Machen-schaften	1	12.36- 2.39	
3IId	Anti-Komintern und sonstige Gegenarbeit in Spanien		12.36-10.38	
3 IIIb	Europa (ausser Rußland)		11.36- 9.38	
3 IIId	Ibero-Amerika	1	11.36- 7.38	
3 IIIe	Andere Staaten	1	12.36-10.38	
3 IIIf	Bolschewistische und kommunisti-sche Tätigkeit und Machenschaf-ten, Angelegenheiten UdSSR.	1		

Akten-zeichen	Inhalt	Band	Datum	Serial Nr.
3 III g	Logen und logenähnliche Organisationen		1937	
Sa. 4	Zensur	1	12.36-10.38	
	Verkehrsakten	1	12.36- 8.38	
	Heeres-, Marine- Luftsachen (Beiakte)	1	12.36- 1.37	
4 b	Luftverkehr	1	5.37- 7.38	
4 c	Schiffahrt	1	11.36-10.38	
4 d	Kriegsschiffsbesuche und Besuche von Hilfsfahrzeugen in spanischen Häfen	1	6.36- 9.38	
4 e	Herunterholen von Passagieren von spanischem Dampfer "Marques de Comillas"	Sbd.	4.41- 5.42	
Sa. 5	Fürsorge allgemein, Heimkehr Spanier aus Deutschland	1	12.36- 8.38	
	Spanische verwundete Offiziere und deren Betreuung durch den Kyffhäuserbund	1	1937-38	
5 b	Austausch gefangener Flieger	1-3	12.37- 1.39	
	Gefangene in Rotspanien (Beiakte)	1-3	1937	
	Fliegeraustausch bes.Komsomol und Smidovich	1	5.37- 1.38	
	Austausch Antonio Gabriel Rodriguez	1	2.38- 4.39	
	Austausch Zivilgefangener in Rotspanien	4-6	6.37- 5.38	
5 c	Sowjet.-rotspan. Gefangenenaustausch	1	3.40- 7.41	
	Geflüchtete Rotspanier in Frankreich und anderen Ländern	1	2.40- 9.41	
6	Rückwandererlisten deutscher Staatsangehöriger aus Spanien		1936	
7	Schadenanmeldungen Kaltwinkel	1		
8	Wissenschaft	1-2	11.37- 3.38	
8 a	Literatur	1	1936-38	
8 b	Kunst und Kult	1	1.37- 5.38	
	Evangelische Kirche (Beiakte)		11.36-1938	
8 d	Sport	1	3.37- 8.38	
8 e	Deutsch-akademischer Austausch-dienst	1	4.37- 6.38	
8 f	Deutsch-akademisches Recht	1	1.37- 5.38	
8 g	Vorträge		1.37-12.37	
Sa.10	Beiakte. Wirtschaft. Bananen auf den Kanarischen Inseln	1-2	8.37- 6.39	

Akten-zeichen	Inhalt	Band	Datum	Serial Nr.
Sa – 10 A	Wirtschaftssachen	1	5.37– 8.38	
10 a	– Einzelfälle	1-6	10.36– 2.40	
10 b	Handelssachen (Vertreter)	1-2	1.37–12.39	
10 c	Zahlungsverkehr, allgemein	1	9.37– 7.38	
		1-3	11.36– 1.40	
10 g	Spanische Wirtschaft	1-2	12.36–11.39	
10 h	Deutsche Wirtschaft	1	11.36– 8.38	
10 i	Spanische Finanzen	1	12.36–11.39	
	– Notenabstempelung	1	12.36– 7.39	
10 k	Deutsche Finanzen	1	1936-39	
10 l	Monopole (Tabak, Benzin)		1939	
10 m	Deutsche Industrien in Spanien	1	3.37– 8.39	
10 n	Versicherungen	1	2.37– 9.39	
Sa 10 a 1	Handelssachen, Einfuhrschwie-rigkeiten	1-3	8.37– 2.40	
Sa 10 a 2	– Forderungsange-legenheiten	1-4	2.37–12.39	
	Schadensersatzforderungen	1	10.37– 2.40	
10 a 2/1	Bescheinigungen für Firmen	1	12.37– 8.39	
10 a 3	Handelssachen: Zollsätze	1	10.37–11.39	
10 a 4	Auskünfte über Firmen	1-3	8.37– 1.40	
10 a 5	Reklamebezeichnungen, Waren-marken	1	9.37–11.37	
10 a 6	Unsichere Firmen	1-3	7.34– 6.38	
10 a 7	Deutsche Handelskammer in Spanien	1-2	2.40– 9.42	
	Steuern	1	10.37–12.39	
10 a 8	Beschlagnahmte deutsche Ware in Marseille	1	6.40– 3.42	
10 a 9	Transporttaxen	1	3.39–12.41	
10 a 10	Spanischer Schiffsverkehr nach Übersee	1	12.41– 3.42	
10 a 11	Schiffsverladungen von spani-schen Häfen über Marseille nach Deutschland	1	6.41–12.42	
10 a 12	Apfelsinenexport nach Deutsch-land	1	10.40– 9.41	
10 a 13	Schwefelkies- und Eisenerzver-schiffungen nach England	1	12.39–12.42	4247/E074789-816
10 a 14	Häute- und Schuhgeschäft H.v.Holloufer	1	7.40–11.41	
10 a 15	Preispolitik	1	12.40– 3.42	1961/437596-613

Akten-zeichen	Inhalt	Band	Datum	Serial Nr.
Sa.10a 16	Banknotenaustausch	1	2.37- 2.41	
10 a 17	Olivenöl	1	4.42	1961/437591-95
10 a 18	Emilio Kiechle	1	10.42	1961/437585-90
10 a 19	Berichte Ehlert	1	11.41	
10 a 20	Roubaud	1	1.41-11.41	1961/437571-84
10 a 21	Kriegsgewinnsteuer	1	1.39- 6.41	1961/437515-70
10 a 22	Deutsche Waren im spanischen Zoll	1	3.39-10.42	
10 a 23	Geleitscheinwesen, Verbleibskon-trolle	1	1.41- 8.42	2010/443157-71
10 a 24	Carbonell y Cia de Cordoba, SA.Cordoba, H.Bade & Co., Hamburg	1	2.38- 4.41	2010/443172-75
10 a 25	Warenbezug aus den besetzten Gebieten	1	8.40-12.41	
10 a 26	Barcelona	1	12.41- 4.43	
10 a 27	Spanische und deutsche Bezugs-wünsche innerhalb des normalen Warenverkehrs	1	9.40-11.41	2010/443176-93 4244/E074745-56
10 a 28	Wirtschaftskrieg, deutsch-italienische Zusammenarbeit	1	8.40- 7.41	2010/443194-201
10 a 29	Dampfer "Usaramo"		9.39- 3.42	
10 a 30	Maßnahmen geflüchteter Regierun-gen. Norw. Handels- und Schif-fahrtsdelegation in London	1	6.40- 4.41	
10 a 31	Frachten verschiedener Dampfer	1	1939-40	
10 a 32	Sonstige Industrien	1	12.34- 5.36	
10 a 33	Neutralitätsverletzungen		11.39- 7.40	
10 a 34	Nachlassakten, Einzelfälle	1	4.35- 5.36	
10 a 35	Vertreter Thissen	1	1940	
10 a 36	Wirtschaftsabteilung, Allgemeines Nr. 1 -400	1-2	1940	
10 a 37	Nr. 401 -800	3-4	1940	
10 a 38	Nr. 801 -2000	5-7	1940	
10 a 39	Nr.2001 -2629	8-10	1940	
		1 Bündl	1939-41	
12 a	Deutsch sprechende Spanier	1	4.37-12.39	
12	Verkehr mit Staatsministerien, sonstigen und spanischen Behör-den	1	12.36-10.37	
15	Sympathiekundgebungen für Deutschland	1-3	12.36-11.38	
15 a	Glückwünsche für spanische und nichtdeutsche Persönlichkeiten	1	6.37-11.38	

Akten-zeichen	Inhalt	Band	Datum	Serial Nr.
Sa 15 b	Beileidsbezeugungen Kreuzer "Deutschland"	1	1937	
16	Presse, allgemein	1	1.37-10.38	
16a I	Deutsche Presse	1	4.37- 7.38	
16a II	Deutsche Pressevertreter	1	12.36-11.38	
16b I	Spanische Presse	1	12.36-10.38	
16b II	Spanische Pressevertreter	1	12.36-10.38	
16c I	Fremde Presse	1	12.36- 8.38	
16c II	Fremde Pressevertreter	1	1.37- 9.38	
16d	Presselenkung	1-3	1.39-12.41	
Sa 17	Filme, allgemein	1	12.36- 5.39	
17a	- Weiterleitung	1	12.36-11.38	
17b	Hetzfilme	1	11.36- 3.39	
18	Sozialpolitik	1	11.36- 3.38	
18a	Besuche, Kindergärtnerin	1	11.37	
18b	Rückgliederung der Dolmetscher, allgemein	1	1.37- 1.39	
20	Angelegenheiten der NSDAP Landesgruppe Spanien	1	12.36-11.38	
	Deutsche Arbeitsfront in Spanien	1	1.36- 8.38	
20b	Nationalsozialismus, Organisa-tion, Besuche	1	12.36- 8.38	
20c	Einladungen von Spaniern und spanischen Gruppen nach Deutsch-land	1	1.37- 7.38	
20e	Anfragen von Spanien und deut-schen Einrichtungen	1	12.36- 9.38	
21	Falange Espanola	1	12.36- 7.37	
22	Requeté	1	12.36- 1.37	
23	Lieferscheine und Briefsendun-gen des Auswärtigen Amtes	2-3	1935-39	
24	Kuriersendungen	1-3	1929-34	
25	Briefbeutelsendungen	1-2	1923-36	
26	Schreiben für das französische Konsulat	1	1936	
27	Angekommene Depeschen	1-4	1937	
28	Bestellungen bei verschiedenen Firmen	1-7	1930-35	
29	Eingegangene Verbalnoten	1	1.40- 5.41	
30	Abgegangene Verbalnoten	1 2	1.35- 7.36	4410/E083719-42

Akten-zeichen	Inhalt	Band	Datum	Serial Nr.
Sa 31	Verbalnotenliste	1	1931	
32	Berichtverzeichnisse Nr.1 - 12	1-12	1925-36	
33	Sammlung der Berichte	1 2	8.41- 6.42	4980/E278695-736
34	Berichte	1	7.41- 9.41	
35	Reg. Pol. Allg.	1 2		4897/E254687-715 4897/E254716-40
36		3 4		4897/E254741-54 4897/E254755-96
37		5 6		4897/E254797-828 4897/E254829-32
38		7 8		4897/E254833-45
39		9 10	1940-41	4895/E253941-85
40		11 12		
41		13 14		4894/E253851-938
42		15 16 17		4306/E078008-341
Kr. 1a	Ursachen des Krieges, Vorgeschichte, Schuldfrage		11.39	3027/D599476-82
	- Weissbücher	Sbd.	9.39-10.39	3027/D599483-504
1b	Kriegserklärung, Kriegseintritt		10.39	3027/D599505-12
1c	Stand des Kampfes, Aussichten		1939	3027/D599513-15
2a	Deutschland im Kriege, innerpolitische Kriegsmaßnahmen, Stimmung im Volk		1939	
2b	Polen im Krieg, Aufteilung, "Neue Regierung"		11.39- 6.40	
2c+d	Wirtschaft, Kriegswirtschaft	1	10.39-11.39	3027/D599519-43
2e	England und Frankreich, Beistandspflicht gegen Polen		1939	3027/D599516-18
2g	Kriegsakten ausgezeichnet		1939	3027/D599544-54
3a	Ziele, Maßnahmen, Methoden der deutschen Kriegsführung		1939	
	- Schiffsmeldungen	Sbd.	1939	
3b	Deutsche Kriegshandlungen, Kriegserfolge		1939	
3c	Beeinflussung der spanischen Presse	Sbd.	1939	
4a	Ziele, Maßnahmen, Methoden der feindlichen Kriegsführung (Blockade)		1939-40	3027/D599555-61

Akten-zeichen	Inhalt	Band	Datum	Serial Nr.
Kr.4b	Kriegshandlungen der Feindstaaten, Neutralitätsbrüche		1939	3027/D599562-63
4c	Feindliche Kriegspropaganda, Pressehetze		1939	3027/D599564-70
5a	Die Neutralen, allgemein		1939	
	Haltung Spaniens		1939	4103/E070535-65
	- Freundschaftsbeweise	Sbd.	1939	
	- Die spanische Presse zum Krieg	Sbd.	1939	
	- Spanische Zensur	Sbd.	1939	
5b	Haltung der U.S.A. Waffenembargo		1939	
5c	Haltung Sowjet-Rußland		1939	
	Haltung der Neutralen (ausser Spanien, U.S.A., Rußland, Italien)			3027/D599571-85 4218/E073914-28
6c	Panama-Konferenz			
6b	Konferenz der Oslo-Staaten		11.39	3027/D599586-97
7a	Der türkisch-englisch-französische Pakt		11.39	
8a	Deutschland-Friedensbemühungen, Hitlers Vorschläge und ihre Beurteilung		1939	
8b	Vermittlungsversuche, Friedensappelle		1939	
9a	Heimschaffung Reichsdeutscher aus französisch Marokko	Sbd.	6.40- 3.41	
	Kriegsakte		1939	
9b	Reisehilfe, Unterstützungen		10.39	
9c	Deutsche Schiffe und Schiffsbesatzungen		10.39-12.39	
9d	Ladungen der in Spanien zurückgebliebenen deutschen Schiffe		2.39-1940	
9e	Internierungen von Reichsdeutschen. Ausschiffung in feindliche Häfen	1-2	9.39- 4.40	
9f	Angebote Deutscher für Kriegszwecke		1939	
10a	Prisenwesen-Konterbande, Banngut Schwarze Liste		10.39- 5.40	4245/E074759-71
	Kriegsauswirkungen auf Handel und Wirtschaft		1940	
10b	Versicherungen gegen Kriegsrisiko und sonstige Maßnahmen im Schiffsverkehr		10.39- 1.40	
10c	Deutscher Handel über neutrale Länder		1939-40	

Akten-zeichen	Inhalt	Band	Datum	Serial Nr.
Kr. 11	Kriegsorganisation der Botschaft Hilfspersonal		9.39	
12	Verschiedenes		9.39- 7.40	
H. 1	Wein, Öl, Südfrüchte	1	9.37-12.39	
2	Gemüse, andere Früchte und sonstige Produkte	1	8.37-11.39	
3	Getreide	1	9.37- 1.40	
4	Holz, Kork, Harze, Terpentin	1	8.37-12.39	
5	Leder, Lederwaren und Felle	1	9.37- 8.39	
6	Erze, Metalle und sonstige Rohstoffe	1	11.36-11.39	
7	Kohle	1	10.37- 8.39	
8	Farben, Lacke und verwandte Artikel		10.37- 1.40	
9	Medizinische Produkte aller Art	1	8.37-12.39	
10	Lebensmittel und Getränke	1	8.37- 7.39	
11	Handelsstatistiken	1	7.38- 1.39	
12	Maschinen für Industrien aller Art	1	8.37-12.39	
12a	Landwirtschaftliche Maschinen	1	1.38- 8.39	
13	Kleineisenwaren	1	9.37-10.39	
14	Büro- und Haushaltungsmaschinen	1	1937-38	
15	Papier und Büromaterialien	1	8.37-10.39	
16	Textilindustrie und Waren	1	9.37-12.39	
17	Hausgeräte und Baumaterialien	1	8.37-12.39	
18	Bijouterie, Edelmetalle und Geschenkartikel	1	10.37-12.39	
19	Chemische Waren	1	8.37-10.39	
20	Medizinische und chirurgische Instrumente und Präzisions-instrumente, Orthopädische Apparate	1	8.37-11.39	
21	Spielzeuge, Sportartikel, Musik-instrumente	1	8.37-11.39	
22	Fahrzeuge und Automobile	1	8.37-12.39	
23	Optik und Kinoapparate, Rundfunkapparate	1	8.37-12.39	
24	Elektro-Motoren, Maschinen und Kleinwaren	1	7.37- 9.39	
25	Anfragen allgemeiner Art in Handels- und Wirtschaftssachen	1	8.37- 2.40	
26	Speditionsfirmen	1	9.37- 5.39	
27	Motoren und Zubehör	1	9.37-10.37	

Akten-zeichen	Inhalt	Band	Datum	Serial Nr.
H. 28	Waffen, Munition, Kriegsmaterial	1	10.37- 5.39	
29	Glas, Porzellan, Steingut	1	6.37- 8.39	
30	Sonstiges nicht Erwähntes	1	8.37-12.39	
31	Kosmetische Artikel	1	11.37-11.39	
32	Vieh	1	1937	
33	Fachzeitschriften für Handel und Industrie	1	1.38-12.39	
34	Sanitäre Einrichtungen	1	4.38- 9.39	
	Musik, Theater, Kunst		7.39- 8.40	
	Film		5.39- 8.39	
	Propaganda	1-2	1937-38	
		3-4	11.38-12.39	
			12.34- 8.39	
			8.39	
	Presse und Schrifttum		4.39- 8.39	
	Feindpropaganda		3.38- 6.39	
	Presseberichte		3.38- 8.39	
	Nachrichtendienst im Spanischen Bürgerkrieg für Presse und Rundfunk in spanischer und deutscher Sprache	1	1937	
	Rote Berichte		3.38- 8.39	
	Nachrichtendienst		5.37- 6.37	
	Verschiedenes mit Promi		1939	
	Spanier in Deutschland		7.39- 8.39	
	Deutsche in Spanien		6.39- 8.39	
	Besorgung spanischer Passmuster		1945	
	Statistik, Material, Hisma und Arbeitsfirmen		1937-38	
	Material und Unterlagen		1937-38	
	Belege für die kleine Kasse		3.38- 7.38	
	Belege für Portokasse		6.38-12.38	
	Postquittungen für Telegramme		6.38	
	- für Einschreiben		6.38	
	Nummarbriefe		1937	
	Aussenhandel		1924	
	Devisenerlasse	1-2	1938-41	
	Benachrichtigungen allgemein	1-2	1936	
	Auxilio - Social		1938-39	

Akten-zeichen	Inhalt	Band	Datum	Serial Nr.
	Falange - Exterior			
	Falange Organisation Tradicionalista			
	51 Journale		1875-1928	
	3 Journale Nr. 1 - 5661		1938-39	
	1 - 3499			
	9 Journale - Telegramme		1907-28	
	4 Tagebücher		1935-37	
	1 Paßregister		1937-40	
	1 Buch Kassenschrank			

Akten-zeichen	Inhalt	Band	Datum	Serial Nr.
770-9/2.	Lieferungen deutschen Kriegs-geräts	1	6.38- 7.38	3202/D697565-79
710-13/1	Sudetendeutsche Frage und mitteleuropäische Krise	1	5.38- 1.39	2685/D528845-908 5194/E307465-69
	Handakten Kanzler Schiffsmeldungen Einzelfälle	1	8.39- 1.40	3852/E044440-42
	Handakten Kanzler Pressepolitik und Propaganda	1	3.39- 9.39	2947/D576418-69
100 - 9	Legion Condor	1	6.39- 1.40	2948/D576473-96
	Getarnte Warensendung aus Übersee "Get.Sdgn."	1	3.41-10.42	3871/E046506-48
	"Gr.Plan" Grosser Plan 1942	1	1.42-12.42	5185/E307398-408
	Carol Geheim: Exkönig von Rumänien Carol	1	9.40- 1.42	3908/E050023-82
	Montana	1	10.37- 6.38	2946/D576031-230 4445/E086244-59 5149/E303623-45
		2	6.38- 8.39	2946/D576231-414 5156/E303703-09
II/1	Verschiedenes		1939-40	1308/347770-8034 3850/E044425-33
II/2	Quecksilber		1940	1308/348035-122
II/3	Sofindus		1940	1308/348123-302
II/4	Störungskäufe		1940	1308/348303-38
II/5	a Projekt Lieferungen für Luft-fahrtindustrie b Luftfrachtsonderdienst Wolfram		1939-40	1308/348339-463
II/6	Handelsvertragsverhandlungen Deutschland-Spanien u.a. Länder		1939-40	1308/348464-638
II/7	Wehrwirtschaftliche Beurteilung Englands und Frankreichs		1939-40	1308/348639-85 3851/E044436-37
II/8	Getreidelieferungen		1939-40	1308/348686-749
II/9	Transitverkehr		1941	1308/348750-821
II/10	Deutsche Beteiligungen in Spanien		1940	1308/348822-64
II/12	P.P.P./Campsa		1941	1308/348865-943
II/13	Verrechnungspartner mit Spanien		1940-41	1308/348944-78
II/14	Eigentumsübertragungen und "Orconera"		1940-41	1308/348979-9278
II/17	Ausländische Kapitalbeteiligun-gen in Spanien		1942	1308/347200-769
II/18	Störungskäufe der Feindmächte, feindliche Firmen		1942	
II/19	Verschiedenes		1941-42	
II/20	a Besprechungen mit span.Handels-minister Carceller b Bernhardt (Sofindus)		1941-42	1308/346843-7199

Akten-zeichen	Inhalt	Band	Datum	Serial Nr.
II/21	Geschenke an Beamte des spanischen Handelsministeriums		1941-42	
II/22	Zollpolitik		1941	1308/346571-842
II/23	Wolfram		1942	
II/24	Schiffsangelegenheiten		1942	
Kur.	Kurierverkehr Depeschenbeförderung	1	8.40-12.42	479/230373-603
Fern.	Fernsprech- und Fernschreibbetrieb der Botschaft	1	7.40-12.42	480/230606-944
Arb.	Deutsch-spanische Beziehungen auf dem Gebiet des Arbeitsrechts. Einsatz spanischer Arbeiter in Deutschland	1	10.40-12.41	481/230947-1251
I/1 38/40	Handels- und Wirtschaftsangelegenheiten		1938-40	5206/E307776-832
I/2 39			1939	5206/E307833-78
I/3 38/39			1938-39	5178/E307022-26
I/4 38/39			1938-39	5206/E307879-914
I/5 39			1939	5206/E307915-17
I/6 39			1938-39	5206/E307918-28
I/7	Material für Handelsvertrag		1939	4365/E081980-2297
I/8	Handels- und Wirtschaftsangelegenheiten		1939	4366/E082300-70
I/9	Deutschlands Zahlungen an Spanien, Finanzplan, Ein- und Ausfuhrstation Spanien		1942	4367/E082373-437
I/10	Telegrammwechsel Wirtschaftsverhandlungen		1942	4368/E082440-515
I/11	Oliven für Amerika		1941-42	4369/E082518-57
I/12	Wolfram		1942	4370/E082560-82
I/13	Chinin und Lebertran		1942	4371/E082585-649
I/14	Angaben über spanische Kolonien		1941	4372/E082652-58
I/15	Kohle		1941-42	4373/E082661-84
I/16	Handels- und Wirtschaftsangelegenheiten		1942	4374/E082687-763
	Innere Lage in Spanien	1	7.39- 9.41	492/232742-3075
		2	10.41- 7.42	498/233877-4187
	Übergabe Mercedes-Wagens an Franco als Geburtstagsgeschenk des Führers	1	9.42-12.42	3848/E044410-16 5187/E307421-22
	Deutschlandreise des spanischen Parteiministers Arrese, Januar 1943	1	10.42- 2.43	3869/E046475-95 5188/E307425-27

Akten-zeichen	Inhalt	Band	Datum	Serial Nr.
Mon.	Restaurationsfrage in Spanien: Wiedereinführung der Monarchie	1	1.39–12.42	497/233585–874
Sp.Ber.	Berichterstattung der spanischen Auslandsvertretungen über Zustände im neutralen und feindlichen Ausland	1	10.39– 7.43	499/234190–257
Bl.Div.	Spanische Freiwillige in Rußland "Blaue Division" (Division Azul)	1	7.41– 8.42	502/234667–899
Scheinr.	Diplomatische und konsularische Vertretungen der Scheinregierungen in Spanien	2	1.42–12.42	446/222009–297
Engl.Vertr.adh.2 Engl. Botsch.	Periodische Meldungen des Polizeiattachés über die Besucher in der Englischen Botschaft	1	11.42– 3.43	445/221965/1–2006
Scheinr.	Diplomatische und konsularische Vertretungen der Scheinregierungen in Spanien	1	10.39–12.41	448/222372–619
	Deutsches Konsulat San Sebastian	1	1940–43	3902/E049668–702 5190/E307437–38
Vertr.Fr.	Fremde Vertretungen in Spanien, ausser von England, Frankreich, Italien, USA und Scheinregierung	1	10.39–12.42	454/223473–565
Ital.	Italien und italienische Beziehungen zu Spanien	1	12.39–12.42	454/223567–624
Frankr.	Frankreich und Beziehungen zu Spanien	1	2.39–12.42	454/223627–775
	Antikominternpakt, auch Verlängerung und Reise Serrano Suner nach Berlin	1	11.36–11.41	462/225457–782 3203/D697582–85
	Berlin, Verschiedenes	1	1940–41	457/224292–507
	Entwicklung der allgemeinen Kriegslage	1	9.39–12.42	1631/389691–780 3025/D599382–410 3891/E048811–35
	Illegaler Grenzverkehr (Durchschleusung wehrfähiger der Feindländer) (1624a g – 4405 g)	1	9.40– 8.42	1653/392246–334 2342/487371–72
		2	9.42–12.42	1654/392340–439 2343/487376–406 3849/E044419–22
	Meldungen über Landungsabsichten der Alliierten (Schaffung einer zweiten Front) Landung der Alliierten in West- und Nordafrika	1	9.40–12.42	1630/389516–686 3895/E049056–64 6462/E482680–85
	"Seekrieg" und seine Auswirkungen auf Spanien (1043g – 2778g)	1	9.39–12.41	1672/394797–904 3893/E048934–72
	– (2835g – 5733g)	2	1.42–12.42	1673/394907–08 3893/E048973–9002 5391/E362129–32
Seekr. adh.2.	"Bandalona"		1941–43	1674/394911–39

Akten-zeichen	Inhalt	Band	Datum	Serial Nr.
Seekr. adh.4.	San Diego, Ladung des französischen Dampfers San Diego, Bilbao		11.40- 5.42	3847/E044403-07
Seekr. adh.5.	U-Boot 573 in Cartagena beschädigt eingelaufen	1	5.42- 2.43	3855/E044496-513
Seekr. adh.7.	U-Boot 167 Las Palmas, Besatzung des deutschen versenkten U-Bootes		4.43- 4.43	3853/E044445-54

Akten-zeichen	Inhalt	Band	Datum	Serial Nr.
A I	Allgemeine auswärtige Politik Russlands	1 2 3 4	1921- 4.38	1536/374514-794 1537/374798-5126 1538/375130-333 1539/375336-76
A II	Politische Beziehungen Russlands zu Deutschland	1 2 3 4	1921-25	1563/378125-464 1564/378467-727 1565/378730-9155 1566/379158-439
	– geheim	5	1924	1567/379442-71
	Innerpolitische Verhältnisse in der UdSSR	2,3,5 7-9 10	1929-32 1934-36	7223/E530351-54
A 2	Neue Sowjetverfassung in der UdSSR	11 12 13 14	1937-38	7222/E530331-49
	Innere Politik der UdSSR, Beiakten zu Beschränkung des Konsularnetzes	1-2	1937-38	
	Mitteilungen wirtschaftlichen und sonstigen Inhaltes Charkow		1931-39	
	Kiew		1933-35	
	Leningrad		1931-34	
	Nowosibirsk		1932-34	
	Odessa		1930-34	
	Tiflis		1930-34	
	Wladiwostok		1930-34	
A 2 a	Innere Politik Rußlands, Parteiwesen	1-4	1926-38	
A 2 b	Fall Peters	1	1934	
	Innere Politik der Sowjetunion, Kongresse, Konferenzen	1 Sbd.	1932	
		2	1934-38	
A 2 c	Berliner Zwischenfall		1924	
	Innere Politik der UdSSR, Verwaltung GPU	1-3	1927-38	
A 2 d	Kommunistische Partei und Internationale		1927-31	
A 2 e	Kommunistenprozesse in Deutschland		1925-26	
	Innere Politik Rußlands, Finanzwesen		1926-31	
A 2 f	Prozess gegen Bund zur Befreiung der Ukraine		1929-30	
A 2 g	Bessedowski		1929-31	
A 2 h	Prozesse gegen Industriepartei		1930-31	
A 2 i	Sträflingsarbeit		1931	
A 2 k	Prozesse gegen Menschewisten-organisation		1931	

Akten-zeichen	Inhalt	Band	Datum	Serial Nr.
A 2 l	Trotzkistenprozess Pjatzkow-Radek		1937	5944/E437562-610
A 2 m	– Jagoda,Bucharin und Genossen		1938	
	Politische Beziehungen der UdSSR zu anderen Staaten	3	1931-36	
A 3	Sonderband: Allgemeine Fragen			
	Politische Beziehungen der Sowjetunion zu Afghanistan		1925-38	
	– Amerika	1-3	1925-38	
	– Belgien		1932-36	
	– Bulgarien		1933-38	7859/E569884-87
	– China und Japan		1926-27	
	– China	2 3	1927-38	9113/E645537-43
	– China, Japan, Mongolei		1925	
	– England	1-4	1926-38	
	– Finnland		1933-38	7552/E541849-52 L288/L087621-77
	– Frankreich (Nichtangriffs-pakt)	1 2 3 4 5	1926-38	9446/E666674-79
A 3 A	– Sonderband: Nicht-angriffspakt und Schlichtungsabkom-men		1932-33	
A 3 B	– Sonderband: Reise Pierre Oot's nach der UdSSR		1933	
A 3 C	– Reise Herriot's nach der UdSSR		1933	
A 3	– Iran	1-2	1926-38	
	– Italien	1 2	1925-37	7221/E530325-29 9462/E667452-54
	– Japan	1 2 3		8984/E630025-29 M144/M005067-72
	– Japan, Grenzzwi-schenfälle, mong.-mandsch.Grenze	Sbd.	1936-38	
	– Japan, China, Mongolei, Sonder-akten	1-2	1922-25	
	– Jugoslavien		1932-37	
	– Kleine Entente		1932-37	
	– Mandschukuo		1932-37	
	– Mongolei		1926-36	
	– Oesterreich		1932-37	
	– Polen	1-3	1922-38	
	– Polen, geheim		1931-33	

Akten-zeichen	Inhalt	Band	Datum	Serial Nr.
A 3	Politische Beziehungen der Sowjetunion zu den Randstaaten Sonderband, Nichtangriffspakt der Sowjetunion mit den Baltischen Staaten und Finnland	1-2	1926-35	
	– zu den Randstaaten Estland, Lettland, Litauen, Finnland	2-5	1927-37	
			1933-38	7601/E543776-85 7601/E543786-88
	– Rumänien, Bessarabische Frage	1	1926-36	
	– – Sowjet-rumänischer Nichtangriffspakt		1937-38	
	– Schweiz		1932-38	
	– Skandinavien und Dänemark		1931-38	
	– Spanien	1		1810/414240-538
			1931-37	
		2		1811/414541-84
	– Südamerika		1931-37	1814/414958-5020
	– Tschechoslowakei	1 2	1936-38	1812/414588-876 1813/414879-955
	– Türkei	1 2	1926-38	1589/383475-880 1590/383884-4042
	– Ungarn		1931-38	
	– Vatikan		1926-36	
A 3 I	Sowjetisch-rumänische Nichtangriffspaktverhandlungen		1931-32	
A 3 a	Sowjetisch-polnische Nichtangriffspaktverhandlungen	1 2	1925-34	K1904/K482305-317
A 3 Ia	Nichtangriffspakt Sowjetunion-Baltische Staaten		1926-33	
A 3 Ib	Osteuropa-Pakt		1933-36	
A 3 Ic	Italienisch-sowjetischer Freundschafts-, Nichtangriffs- und Neutralitätsvertrag		1933	
A 3 Id	Französisch-sowjetischer Beistandspakt	1 2	1933-37	M150/M005185-193
A 3 Ie	Sowjetisch-polnischer Garantiepakt über Unabhängigkeit der Randstaaten			
A 3 If	Litwinow-Vorschlag über Unabhängigkeit der Baltischen Staaten			M268/M011338-42
A 3 Ig	Litwinow-Barthou-Ostpakt	1 2 3 4	1934-35	8758/E610871-73 8812/E613720-22
A 4	Militär- und Marineangelegenheiten	1-5	1926-36	
		6-7	1937-38	
A 5	Religions-, Kirchen- und Schulwesen		1926-34	

Akten-zeichen	Inhalt	Band	Datum	Serial Nr.
A 4 b	Kirchenprozesse		1923	
A 6	Verkehrswesen		1926–34	
A 7	Verbindung der Komintern mit den kommunistischen Parteien aller Länder, Arbeiterbewegung	1	1925–26	
		6–7	1932–37	
A 7 b	Kommunistische Propaganda und KPD in Deutschland		1934–38	
A 7 d	Kommunistische Propaganda unter deutschen Arbeitern in der UdSSR, Resolution deutscher Arbeiter in Nadeschdinsk			
A 8	Deutsche Vertretungen, Konsulate und Delegationen in Rußland	1		
	Russische Emigranten und ihre Organisation	1–2	1926–38	
A 8 a	Alexander-Hospital in Petersburg		1921–23	
	Solonewitsch		1934–38	
A 9	Politische Beziehungen zwischen Deutschland und der UdSSR	1 2 3 4	1926–31	1841/419277–486 1842/419490–916 1843/419920–20258 1844/420263–725
A 9 Gen.		5 6 7 8 9 10 11	1931–36	1882/424692–5076 1883/425079–330 1884/425333–415 1885/425418–540 1904/428506–825 1905/428828–996 1906/428999–9284
		12	1937–38	1907/429289–386
A 9 Geh.		1 2	1933–38	1908/429390–761 1909/429766–30028
A 9 a	– Unfreundlichkeiten			
A 9 b	– russische Dokumenten-fälscher in Berlin, Orloff und Genossen		1929–32	
A 9 c	– Zwischenfälle am 1.Mai		1929	
A 9 d	– Pol. Beschwerden und Bereinigung		1930	
A 9 d I	Bereinigungsaktion	1–2	1930	
	– sowjetische und deut-sche Pressestimmen		1930	
	– Generalia, Berliner Vorgänge		1930	
	– deutsche Pressestimmen		1930	
A 9 e	Sonderakte: Attentat auf Bot-schaftsrat von Twardowski		1932	

Akten-zeichen	Inhalt	Band	Datum	Serial Nr.
A 9 f	Sonderakte Abberufung der Sowjetkorrespondenten aus Deutschland, Ausweisung der deutschen Korrespondenten aus der UdSSR, ausländische Zeitungsvertreter im Reichstagsbrandprozess Leipzig		1933	
A 9 g	Sonderband: Angriffe gegen Dr.Schiller			
A 9 h	Pol.Beziehungen Geheim, sowjetische Verdächtigung eines deutschen Konsulatsmitgliedes in Wladiwostok		1932	
A 9 i	- Sonderband: Hugenberg-Memorandum mit Weltwirtschaftskonferenz London		1933	
A 9 K	- Vergehen gegen "Derop"		1933	9459/E667355-425
A 9 l	- Zeitungsverbote	1-3	1933-37	
A 9 m	- russisch-nationalsozialistische Organisationen (Rond.)		1933	
A 9	Sonderband Spec. Russische Beschwerden über Verhaftungen, Verhaftungen, Haussuchungen bei Sowjet-Staatsangehörigen in Deutschland	1 2	1933	9525/E671706-16
A 9	- Verhaftungen	3-5	1933-36	
	- Fall Kulenskaja		1936	
	- Fall Tönsow Knapp		1936	
A 10	Wirtschaftliche Beziehungen Rußlands zu Deutschland		1926-32	L354/L107498-534
A 10 a	- Handelsvertrag		1928-31	L355/L107535-56
A 10 b	- Beitritt deutscher Banken der internationalen Vereinigung der Rußlandgläubiger		1928	
A 10 c	- Deutsch-französische wirtschaftliche Zusammenarbeit in der UdSSR			L356/L107557-80
A 11	Geschäftsgang der deutschen Vertretung in Rußland	1-2	1924-37	
A 11 a	Militär- und Marineangelegenheiten, allgemein		1922-24	
A 12	Innerpolitische Verhältnisse in Deutschland	3-6	1931-37	
	- Sonderakten zum Tode Stresemanns		1929-32	
A 12 a	Stahlhelm		1927-30	
A 14	Bolschewistische Propaganda im Ausland	1-3	1922-25	
	November-Verhaftungen Reichsdeutscher		1936	

Akten-zeichen	Inhalt	Band	Datum	Serial Nr.
A 14	Verhaftungen Reichsdeutscher Juli 1937		1937	
A 14 I	Politische Haftsachen	1-2	1925-33	
A 14 b	Tscherwonetz -Notenfälscherprozess in Berlin		1928-32	
A 14 d	Sonderband: Verhaftungen bei Controll-Co., Beschuldigungen gegen Bahn in Odessa - (Hahn, Karl und Wehrmann)			
A 14 e	Haftsache Vasel			
A 15 b	Presse, speciell deutsche	1-2	1933-37	
A 15 B I	- DNB, Pressebeirat Baum, Stein, Dr.Schüle, Hellschreiberanlage			7538/E541711-21
A 15 bII	- Köln, Zeitungsvertreter A.Zust		1933-37	
A 15 b III	- Moskau-Aufenthalt des Korrespondenten Görbing(jun tim Görbing-Hoffmann, Görbing-Klimow, Prawda)		1936	
A 15 d	Presseberichte aus Peking Deutsche Militärinstrukteure in China		1928-29	
A 15 e	Russische Presseübersichten (in Harbin)		1930-31	
A 15 f	Moskauer Politische Presse	10 -12	1936-38	
	Presseberichte aus Charkow		1929-33	
	- Kiew		1929-33	
	- Leningrad		1929-34	
	- Nowosibirsk		1930-35	
	- Odessa		1929-33	
	- Tiflis		1934	
	- Wladiwostok		1930	
A 15 h I	Deutschfeindliche Karikaturen	3	1936	
A 15 h	Deutschfeindliche Sowjetpresse	5-6	1935-38	
	Russische Emigranten und ihre Organisationen			
A 16	Russische Monarchisten	1	1922-25	
	Beziehungen Deutschlands zu anderen Ländern (ausser Rußland) mit Aktenliste	7	1933-38	

Akten-zeichen	Inhalt	Band	Datum	Serial Nr.
A 16 a	Beziehungen Deutschlands zu Oesterreich und Wiedervereinigung mit Deutschland	2	1934-38	
A 16 b	- zu Polen	1 2 3	1932-38	9222/E648203-13
A 16 c	- Litauen und Memelgebiet	2+4	1935-38	
A 16 d	- Frankreich		1933-38	
A 16 e	- Italien		1934-38	
A 16 f	- England		1935-36	7630/E545301-51
	Ministerbesuch in Berlin		1935	
	Blaubuch		1936	
A 16 g	Beziehungen Deutschlands zu Estland		1933-38	
A 16 h	- Lettland		1933-38	
A 16 i	- Tschechoslowakei		1933-38	
A 16 j	- Japan		1934-38	
A 17	Sonderband: China, ostchinesische Eisenbahn	2	1929-35	
A 18 b	Nordpaktfragen, Locarno-Vertrag		1926-28	
A 18 c	Mossul-Frage		1925-34	
	Polnisch-litauische Beziehungen (auch Wilna-Frage)	2-3	1931-38	
A 18 k a	Pakt der Uferstaaten des Schwarzen Meeres	1-2	1934-37	
b	Meerengenfrage			
c	Meerengenkonferenz von Montreux	1-2		
A 18 m	Beziehungen der baltischen Staaten untereinander, Litauisches Memorandum, Baltenblock	1-2	1933-38	
A 18 o	Lage im fernen Osten	1 2	1932-37	9148/E643544-61
A 19 a	Deutsch-russischer Vertrag	1-2	1926	
A 19 b	Kellogpakt, Litwinoff-Protokoll	1-2	1928-36	
A 19 c	Berliner Vertrag, Erneuerung		1930-33	
A 19 d	Viermächtepakt, geheim		1932-34	
A 20 i	Beziehungen der Sowjet-Union zum Völkerbund (Eintritt Rußlands in den Völkerbund)		1934-36	
A 23	Haftsachen		1922-25	
	Berichte des Kons. in Nowosibirsk		1929	
A 24	Verschiedenes (Telegramme)	6-8	1928-38	

Akten-zeichen	Inhalt	Band	Datum	Serial Nr.
A 24 b	Paßsachen, Empfehlungen		1925-38	
A 24 c	Zweifelhafte Persönlichkeiten, anonyme Eingänge, Denunziationen, Drohbriefe	1-2	1930-38	
A 24 e I	Politischer Emigrant Prof. Schaxel	Sbd.	1934	
A 24 e II	Personalien Jurik		1935	
A 24e III	- Rudi Pfeiffer		1936-37	
A 24 f	Nachforschungen und Auskünfte über Personen		1932-38	
A 24 g	Geschäftsgang, Dienstbetrieb		1932-38	
A 24 g I	Beschaffung sowjetischer Zeitschriften und Bücher für deutsche Interessenten (nur geheime Sachen)		1938	
A 24 h	Spionage, Werkspionage, Wirtschaftsspionage		1931-37	
A 25 b	Deutschfeindliche und Gegenpropaganda	1 2 3	1933-37	9535/E672204-14
A 26	Lausanner Konferenz	1-2	1922-28	
A 29	Informatorische Übersichten für Petersburg und Charkow		1923	
A 30	Memel		1923-25	
A 33 d+f	Personalien des Herrn Botschafters Nadolny	1-2	1933-34	
	Konsulntreffen und -besprechungen		1934-37	9456/E667176-253
A 35 N 2	Blattsammlung, geheim		1926-33	
A 36	Diplomatisches und konsularisches Korps in Moskau	1-2	1929-32	
A 38	Jahresübersichten der Botschaft auf politischem, wirtschaftlichem und kulturellem Gebiet		1928-32	
A 39 a	Jahres- und Halbjahresberichte des Deutschen Generalkonsulates in Leningrad		1930-36	
A 39 b	- in Charkow		1930-37	
A 39 c	- Odessa		1930-34	
A 39 d	- des Deutschen Konsulates Tiflis		1930-36	
A 39 e	- des Konsulates Kiew		1930-34	
A 39 f	- des Konsulates Nowosibirsk			

Akten-zeichen	Inhalt	Band	Datum	Serial Nr.
A 39 g	Jahres- und Halbjahresberichte des Deutschen Konsulats Wladiwostok			
A 40	Politische Jahresberichte der Botschaft an das Auswärtige Amt (geheim)		1930-33	1931/433150-216
	Politische Berichte	1 2 3	1922-26	K1905/K482318-594 K1905/K482595-953 K1905/K482954-3060
	Rundtelegramm betr. Schliessung der Konsulate Odessa und Wladiwostok		1937	
	Politische Lage im Ausland		1926-28	
	Besprechungen mit Volkskommis-saren			
	Auskünfte über fremde Diplomaten		1927-28	
	Anti-Sowjet-Campagne		1930	M318/M013295-98
	Lenin		1923-24	
	Kindermann Ehrenfrage		1925	
	Vasel in Sinkiang		1934-35	
	Mukden und Pekingvertrag		1924	
	Garantievertrag mit der Sowjet-regierung		1926	
	Zwischenfall Berliner Handels-vertretung		1924	K1906/K483061-156
	Versöhnungsprotokoll (deutsch-russischer Entwurf)			
	Abteil.D.H.6.Junkerswerke	1 2	1922-32	9444/H273079-346 9444/H273347-54
	Entwicklung der Beziehungen zu Junkers und dem Reich bezgl. Zusammenarbeit in Rußland		1922	9472/H273735-843
	Abt.D.Geh.Akten aller Art, Inhaltsverzeichnis	1 2	1924-37	7498/E540776-81
	Abt.E.Geheim-Akten kulturellen Inhalts	1-2	1929-35	
	Schriftwechsel mit Herrn Reichsminister des Auswärtigen von Rosenberg		1923	L336/L100403-30
	"Kupferberg-Gold" Aufzeichnungen	1 2	1923-28	L337/L100431-543 L337/L100544-712
	"Kupferberg-Gold" Briefwechsel mit dem Reichskanzler und Mini-ster des Auswärtigen	3	1923-28	L337/L100713-958
	v.Koerner, dienstliche Korres-pondenz		1925	L338/L100959-1001
	Völkerbund Locarno		1924-25	L339/L101002-46
	Mission Heller-Morsbach Aufzeichnungen für Berlin		1923-28	L340/L101047-233

Akten-zeichen	Inhalt	Band	Datum	Serial Nr.
	Geheime Erlasse des Auswärtigen Amtes		1936-38	
C allg.	A - U (Einzelnamen, siehe alte Moskauer Liste)		1939-41	
C I a 1	A - L (Einzelnamen, siehe alte Moskauer Liste)		1926-41	
C I a 1 gen.	Auslegung des deutschen Staats-angehörigkeitsgesetzes, Einbür-gerungen und Wiedereinbürgerun-gen		1931-39	
C I a 2 gen.	Auslegung des sowjetischen Staatsangehörigkeitsgesetzes		1931-39	
C I a 2 II	Russ.Teil: Sowjetisches Staats-angehörigkeitsgesetz, Anerken-nung deutscher Staatsangehörig-keit	2	1931-33	
C I a 3 gen.	Aberkennung der deutschen Staatsangehörigkeit und Widerruf der Einbürgerung (auch Ausbür-gerungslisten)		1933-38	
C I a 3	Namenliste F - Sch			
C I a 4 gen.	Annahme der Sowjetischen Staats-angehörigkeit durch Reichs-deutsche, Namen von B - St			
C II a 2	B - J		1926-40	
C II a 3	B - R			
C IIIa 2	E - V			
C III e	Hildebrand		1936-40	
C III d	Lukasch, Ludwig			
C IV a	Namen A - R		1936-40	9444/H273079-346
C IV a gen.	Verhaftungen in Tiflis und Batum		1936	9444/H273347-54
C IV a	Haftliste Charkow			
	- Moskau H - L	1		
	November-Verhaftungen	1 2 3	1936	7220/E530250-323
		4-5		
C IV a adh.	Verhaftungen, Haftlisten	6		
	Haftsache Berndt			
	Namen E - St			
C V f	Kessal und Sachert		1936-37	
C VII a	Namen A - W			
C VIII a	Friedhofsort Korenowo			

Akten-zeichen	Inhalt	Band	Datum	Serial Nr.
R 2 Nr.1	Kriegsgräberfürsorge (Ehrenstät-ten in von Rumänien an Rußland abgetretenen Gebieten) D - P			
R 2 Nr.1 gen.	Ansprachen des Botschafters zum Heldengedenktag in Moskau		1940-41	
R 3	Handelskammer Puchalski			
R 3 Nr.2	Namen B - s			
R 3	H - S			
R 3 Nr.2 gen.	Staatsangehörigkeitsverhältnis der Bewohner der an Sowjetrußland abgetretenen Gebiete des ehema-ligen Polens			
R 3 Nr.2	Friedhöfe der Volksdeutschen in Bessarabien, Namen A - Z			
R 3 Nr.3	A - Z			
R 3 Nr.4	Personenstandsurkunden Moskau Namen K - Z			
	Urkundenbescheide, Moskau B - Z , positiv - B - V, negativ			
R 3 Nr.4 Spec.	- B - V			
R 3 Nr.5	- B - T			
R 3 Nr.5 Gen.	Rechtshilfe, Ersuche, Namen A - Z			
R 3 Nr.6	A - Z			
	L - W Haftliste Moskau, Auswei-sungen Reichsdeutscher und Protektoratsangehöriger			
R 6	Namen A - W			
R 6 Nr.1	H - W			
R 6 Nr.3	Betriebsschutzgesetz			
DR3Nr.2	Namen A - Z			
DR3Nr.2 Prot	Namen A - W			
DR3Nr.3	- B - U			
DR3Nr.4 Gen.	Schriftwechsel			
DR 3 Nr.4	Urkundengesuche, Ariernachweise F - Z			
DR 3 Nr.8	Urkundengesuche			
DR 5	Bleckmann, Brand, Klambeck			
DR 5 L	Passangelegenheiten, Einzelfälle A - V			

Akten-zeichen	Inhalt	Band	Datum	Serial Nr.
DR 6	Paßangelegenheiten Einzelfälle A - Z			
	12 Fälle Rentenakten			
Kult	Kriegsgefangene. (36 Deutsche, 67 Polen)			
	Umbettung von gefallenen deutschen Heeresangehörigen in Polen			
Kult 5	Generalakten			
Kult 5 Nr.1 So	Heimschaffung reichsdeutscher Kinder			
Kult 6 a	Namen von A - Z			
Kult 6 b So	Namen von A - Z			
	Lettland, Namen A - Z			
	Estland, - A - P und zwei Verhaftete: Dunkel und Siwitzki			
Kult 6 b	Litauen, Namen L - S			
Kult 6 b So	Nachforschung nach vermissten Heeresangehörigen			
	Liste über die im Gebiet des ehemaligen Polens vermissten deutschen Heeresangehörigen sowie Reichsdeutschen			
Kult 6 b	Deutsche Heeresangehörige in der UdSSR			
Kult 6 b So	Balzer und Balzer Katharina			
	Namen Haa - T			
Kult 6 b So gen.	Rückholung von Flüchtlingen nach dem Generalgouvernement			
Kult 6 b	Umsiedlungsangelegenheiten Namen A - Z			
D Kult 6 a	- B - W			
	Litauische und polnische Kinder im Generalgouvernement bezw. Deutschland			
D Kult 6 b So	Namen B - Z			
	Weiterleitung von Briefen für Kriegsgefangene in Polen			
Pol. 2	Umsiedlung aus den Balkanstaaten, Sonderakte			
Pol. 3	Prozesse: König, Hoffmann, Huff, Lukat (Lokys)			
	Sondermappe: Einreiseanträge der Volksdeutschen aus den Balkanstaaten			

Akten- zeichen	Inhalt	Band	Datum	Serial Nr.
D Pol 3	Anträge Wehrpflichtiger, Namen B - Z			
	Auslandspost			
D Pol 3 Nr. 1	Juden und ehemalige Ostpolen (mit alphabetischem Namensver- zeichnis, Flüchtlinge) Namen L - Sch			
	- F			
St 1 gen.	Staatsangehörigkeit, Einbürgerungen	2		
St a	Namen D - V			
WZ	- B - P			
DWZ	- B - Sp			
WZ 2 Nr.1	- B - Z			
WV Nr.1	- B - S			
DWH S Pol 2 Wi IV	Schadenersatzforderungen im bessarabischen Gebiet und Nord- bukowina. Verschiedene Firmen- forderungen			
DWH	Forderungen Namen A - W		1941	
WF 2Nr.1	- D - W			
DWF	- B - S			
W Sch 1 Nr.1 gen.	Schriftwechsel			
W E 1	Ungarische Gesandtschaft		1940	
W 22	Listen der deutschen Fachleute in Sowjetdiensten		1930-31	
I A 8	Tiflis, von Nymann (Haftfall)			
I D 1	Deutscher Wehrdienst und Gesetze über Meldepflicht	1+2	1935-39	
I e 2	Verdrängung deutscher Reichsan- gehöriger		1929-38	
I e 3	Lage der deutschen Reichsange- hörigen in der UdSSR		1930-34	
I f	Konsularrecht			
II a 1	Finanzrecht, sowjetisches Steuerrecht		1930-33	
II a 2	- sowjetische Zollvor- schriften		1928-39	
II a 3	Bank- und Versicherungswesen in der UdSSR	1+2	1927-38	
II a 4	Finanzrecht, deutsches Finanz- recht	1	1931-40	
II b	Verwaltungsrecht		1930-34	

Akten-zeichen	Inhalt	Band	Datum	Serial Nr.
II c	Handelsrecht		1928-30	
II d	Arbeitsrecht, Arbeitsmarkt in Deutschland		1929-39	
II d 1	Arbeitsrecht, Arbeitsverhältnisse in der UdSSR			
II e	Vereins-, Versammlungs- und Pressewesen			
III a 1	Forderungen, Zessionen		1929-38	
III a 2	Sachenrecht		1929-39	
III b	Vertragsrecht		1929-37	
III c 1	Familien- und Erbrecht, Urkunden- und Eherecht, Arbeitsgesetzgebung	1-3	1928-31	
III c 2	Erbrecht		1929-39	
III c 3	Unterhaltungspflicht		1929-36	
III d	Rechtshilfe, Zustellungen, Zeugenvernehmungen		1929-39	
III e	Urheber- und Erfinderrecht		1929-41	
III f	Legalisierungen, Notariatswesen		1930-39	
III g	Gerichtsverfassung, Prozessrecht		1928-39	
IV a Gen	Straf- und Prozessrecht	1	1928-34	
IV a 2	Mainzer, Wilhelm		1937	
V a	Deutsches Sozialrecht, Renten	1	1935-39	
V b	Sowjetisches Sozialrecht		1929-39	
V c	Übernahme hilfsbedürftiger Sowjet-Staatsangehöriger		1930-33	
V d	Rückwanderer, Heimschaffung der Reichsangehörigen		1929-39	
V e	Unterstützungen notleidender Reichsangehöriger		1933-39	
V f	Hilfskasse		1923-40	
VI b	Verkehr und Schiffahrt	3	1935-39	
VI d	— Flugwesen		1932	
VI e	— Kraftwagen und Strassen		1931	
VII a	Fremdenpolizei, Meldewesen		1931-39	
Pers.	Protektorat Namen B - Z			
	Mappe Wyschinski		1941	
	Restumsiedlungen			
	Persönliches Schreiben des Botschafters in Sachen Sapieha			
Prot.2 D K	Protokoll Diplomatisches Korps	3	1941	

Akten-zeichen	Inhalt	Band	Datum	Serial Nr.
VI E 1 adh.	Ausweisungen	2	1937-38	
	Drucksachen zu den Vertrags- und Schlichtungsverhandlungen	2	1930	
Nr. 1	Namensverzeichnis A – W von Schreiben der deutschen Botschaft			
Nr. 2	Namensverzeichnis A – Z			
Nr. 4	– A – W von Schreiben der deutschen Botschaft	1-5	1940-41	
	Sichtvermerke und Grenzüberschreitungsscheine A – Z		1941	
	Nachforschungen, Auskünfte, Geld- und Effektenbetreuung, Vormundschaftsangelegenheiten		1926-41	
	Namensverzeichnis, Wiedervorlagen, Grenzempfehlungen, Paßbegleitscheine, Verschiedenes, Aktenverzeichnis Pa, Aktenverzeichnis Generalakten, Kirchliche Eheschliessungsstatistik nach Ort und Zeit			
	Umbettung gefallener deutscher Soldaten aus ehemaligem polnischen Gebiet der UdSSR		1940	
	Umsiedlung, Rückwanderer		1941	
	Rückwanderer A – Z		1940	
	Sichtvermerksanträge E – T Hilfskasse		1940-41	
Pers G 17 gen.	Anschriftenverzeichnis der Ministerien		1940	
	Erlasse Moskau Konsulatsabteilung	1+2	1936-41	
	Namen-Indexe: Moskau Konsulatsabteilung	1-3	1937-39	
Kult.	Namensverzeichnis A – Z			
	Moskau Konsulatsabteilung		1940	
Abt.A-D 4	Deutsche Schulen, Deutschtum in Georgien	1+2	1923-26	
Abt.D L 1	Landwirtschaft in Rußland	4	1929-31	
Abt.D L 1 a	Vieh- und Geflügelzucht (auch deutsche Lieferungsanträge)	1	1923-37	
Abt.D L 3	Fischerei, Jagd (auch deutsche Lieferanträge)	2	1922-27	
	Namensverzeichnis von B			
	Paul, Liefke, Stauff, Stump, Bach, Bier, Gutmann,Völker, Awrutin, Hennig, Höhne, Andrasek, Steinadler			

Akten-zeichen	Inhalt	Band	Datum	Serial Nr.
	Schuldanerkenntnisse und Gepäck-angelegenheiten		1940-41	
	Reichsstelle für Sippenforschung "Genkin"			
	Unerledigte Eingänge		1941	
	– Rentensache "Steiner"		1941	
	Akten und Karten der Umsiedlungs-kommission			8433/E593906-59
	Generalkonsulat: R.v.Saucken			
	Namensverzeichnis Nr.9 A – Z			
	Deutsch-russisches Abkommen über Grenzwasserläufe		1939-40	
	Inventar- und Materialbeschaf-fung			
	Angebote und Offerten			
	Besuche und Empfänge			
	Fremde Missionen			
	Verschiedenes	1-3		
	Wirtschaftliche Berichte			
	Russischer Warenverkehr mit ausserdeutschen Ländern			
	Finanzen, Währung, Banken			
	Schriftverkehr mit den Bevoll-mächtigten des Kriegsministeriums			
	Sitzungsberichte des Berliner Ständigen Ausschusses			
	Warenaustausch			
	Schriftwechsel mit der Russi-schen Regierung über Warenaus-tausch			
	Eisenbahnen			
	Wirtschaftliche Berichte des Generalkonsulats Petersburg			
	Schriftwechsel mit der Russi-schen Regierung (allgemein)			
	Auswärtige Handelskammern			
	Organisation Personalien			
	Handakten Dr. List	1-2		
	Deutsche Reichangehörige Buchstabe K		1926-40	
	Einreisegesuche		1937-39	
	Staatenlose A – M		1940	

Akten-zeichen	Inhalt	Band	Datum	Serial Nr.
Pol 2 Nr.1	Politische Beziehungen der Sowjet-Union zu Deutschland	1	1.39- 8.39	127/69455-5582 644/254831-49 695/260260-467 8515/E597403-07
		2	9.39-12.39	127/69585-864 644/254851-72 4139/E071559-62
		3	1.40-12.40	127/69866-968 1379/357600-926 3590/E025873-82 4138/E071550-56
Pol 2 Nr.3 Balk.	zu den Balkan-Pakt- Staaten (Bulgarien, Griechenland, Jugo- slawien, Rumänien, Türkei) Balkan-Pakt Mittelmeerfragen, Schwarzmeerpakt, Bessarabien	1	12.38-12.39	370/207703-964
		2	1.40- 6.40	372/208185-408 4184/E072300-03
		3	6.40- 1.41	380/210212-503 4183/E072296-97
	zu den Baltischen Staaten	1	1.39- 5.40	466/226781-7025
		2	5.40- 9.40	432/219311-530
Pol 2 Nr.3 England	zu England(engli- sche Einkreisungs- politik, Garantien, Paktverhandlungen mit der SU, der Türkei)	1	1.39- 6.39	258/169024-473
		2	7.39-12.39	361/204313-668
Pol 2 Nr.3 Italien	zu Italien	1	5.39- 4.41	366/206700-824
Pol 2 Nr. 3 Polen	zu Polen (Ukraine Frage-Russisch- Polen)	1	12.38- 4.41	500/234260-318 2494/D517975-92
Pol 2 Nr.3 Sp.Gef.	zu Spanien: Gefan- genenaustausch	1	9.38- 1.41	2801/D548233-68 7992/E575527-34 8422/E592918-31
Pol 2 Nr.3 Nord	zu den Nordischen Staaten (Finnland, Schweden,Norwegen, Dänemark) Aalandfra- ge-Finnische Inseln	1	12.38-12.39	429/218483-723 2492/D517960-62 3426/E015976-96 4448/E086701-03 L286/L087492-552
		2	1.40- 3.40	171/134070-579 4447/E086695-98
		3	3.40- 6.40	171/134582-5014
		4	7.40- 5.41	171/135017-305
Pol 2 Nr.3 Japan	zu Japan. Mandjukuo, Chin.-jap.Krieg, Zwischenfälle an mongol.- mandschur. Grenze	1	1.39- 3.40	166/131710-902 7992/E575535-39 7995/E575620-22
Pol 2 Nr.3	zu anderen Staaten (sofern sie nicht in die Einzelakten gehören) und polit. Beziehungen zwi- schen anderen Staa- ten(Aussenpoliti- sche Informationser- lasse)	1	1.39- 3.39	167/132667-976

Akten-zeichen	Inhalt	Band	Datum	Serial Nr.
Pol 2 Nr.3	Politische Beziehungen der SU zu anderen Staaten (sofern sie nicht in die Einzelakten gehören) und polit.Beziehungen zwischen anderen Staaten (Aussenpolitische Informationserlasse)	2	3.39-12.39	167/132979-3525
		3	1.40-12.40	167/133529-4066
Pol 2 Nr.3 I	Politische Verhältnisse in anderen Ländern (innerpolit.Informationserlasse)	1	1.39-12.39	433/219533-20072
Pol 3 Nr.1	Innenpolitik der SU	1	2.39- 5.41	493/233078-272
		2	1.39- 5.41	494/233275-310 7992/E575540-42
Pol 4 Nr.2	Zwischenstaatliche aussenpolitische Probleme: Bolschewismus, Sozialismus.	1	1.39-10.40	215/146984-7403
		2	11.40- 5.41	215/147404-538
Pol 4 Nr.6	Russische Emigranten	1	2.39- 2.41	215/146966-983
Pol 3 Nr.3	Innenpolitik der SU Militär, Marine, Luftfahrt	1	4.39- 5.41	215/146207-415
D Pol 2 Balt.	Politische Beziehungen Deutschlands zu den Baltischen Staaten (auch Memel)	1	12.38- 2.41	215/146495-820
D Pol 2 Balk.	zu den Balkanstaaten	1	3.39- 4.41	215/146821-965
D Pol 2 Engl.	zu England (Einkreisungspolitik).	1	2.39-10.39	215/146416-94
D Pol 2 It.	zu Italien	1	4.39- 4.40	363/205175-221 4185/E072306-10
D Pol 2 Nord	zu den Nordischen Staaten	1	1.39- 5.41	441/221241-360 L287/L087553-620
D Pol 2 Sp.	zu Spanien	1	6.39- 9.39	487/232001-22
D Pol 2 Ung./Sl.	zu Ungarn und der Slowakei	1	1.39-11.40	2533/D520418-24 4435/E084987-98
D Pol 2 Pol.	zu Polen, auch Danzig	1	1.39- 8.39	461/225036-454
		2	9.39-12.39	477/229661-30247 7992/E575543-49
	zu Polen,Scheinregierung	3	1.40- 8.40	488/232025-134
D Pol 3 Antik.	Deutsche Innenpolitik, Staatsschutzbestimmungen, Antikommitern.	1	11.37-11.39	418/216205-43
D Pol 3 Mil.	Militär-, Marine-, Luftfahrtangelegenheiten, Wehr- und Arbeitsdienstpflicht.	1	6.39- 5.40	4191/E072468-509 7992/E575550-53
D Pol 3 Prot.	Protektorat Böhmen und Mähren(Angelegenheiten, die sich auf die ehemalige Tschechoslowakei beziehen)	1	3.39- 8.40	414/215900-6028 2922/D566751-54

Akten-zeichen	Inhalt	Band	Datum	Serial Nr.
SD Pol 2 Krieg Sonder-akte	Politische Beziehungen Deutschlands zu anderen Staaten Krieg (Krieg mit Polen besonders: DPol 2 Pol)	1	10.39-12.39	352/202607-940 3066/D611868-91 7775/E555879-90
		2	1.40- 4.40	354/203098-304 3066/D611892-945 8836/E614877-87
		3	4.40-10.40	357/203854-4048 2763/D535574-78 3066/D611946-60 4190/E072438-64 7775/E555891-97 8836/E614888-90
		4	11.40- 5.41	359/204171-265 4189/E072431-35
P 2	Presse- und Propagandawesen: Beziehungen zu Deutschland, Presseattachés.	1	10.38-12.40	7992/E575554-57
P 4	Pressevertreter, Redakteure, Berichterstatter und ihre Orga-nisationen. Vertreter des DNB und deutscher Zeitungen.	1	1.39- 5.41	410/215170/2-202
D P 1	Presse- und Propagandawesen in Deutschland, Allgemeines	1	1.39-10.40	2830/D549099-102 7992/E575558-59
Pol g	Geheime politische Akten	1	4.40- 8.40	270/175301-712
		2	8.40-10.40	285/181595-873
		3	11.40- 3.41	165/131656-86 1447/364920-5250
		4	4.41	165/131688-707 597/246385-86 1448/365254-433
Pol Mil g	Militärische Angelegenheiten	1	4.40- 5.41	426/217942-8181
S Pol g Sonder-akte	Politik geheim	1	11.40- 3.41	292/183844-905
S Pol g Lit.Son-derakte	Litauischer Gebietsstreifen	1	12.40- 1.41	359/204114-69 644/254739-41 4100/E070506-07
Pers.Si	Sicherheitsfragen	1	11.37- 5.41	7992/E575560-62
Pers.Si g	MOB und Nach-richtenwesen	1	4.40- 5.41	4087/E069228-239
B g	Geheime Sachen der Abteilung B.	1	4.40- 5.41	4086/E069223-25
C g	Abteilung C.	1	4.40- 4.41	4082/E069189-205
P A g	Abteilung P A	1	4.40- 3.41	4137/E071539-47
S P a Sonder-	Paßabteilung	1	12.39- 8.40	4085/E069218-20
	Akten betr.:Tschechoslowakei	1	2.38-12.38	397/212695-909
SD	Sonderakten Abteilung D.	1	1.39- 5.40	2801/D548269-91
	G-Sachen (Verschiedenes)		1.39- 3.40	425/217725/1-938

Akten-zeichen	Inhalt	Band	Datum	Serial Nr.
SD	Lose G-Vorgänge		1938	315/191139-940
	Personalia	1	10.38- 5.41	349/201866-2015
	Politisches Schulenburg	1	10.38- 8.40	276/178362-703
		2	9.40- 5.41	277/178707-828
	Personalia	3	10.38- 5.41	273/177530-621
	Handakten Schulenburgs aus ver-schiedenen Sachgebieten (D Pol 1, D Pol 2, Pol 4,Wi) überwiegend Mai-Juni 1941/ 19.VII.39-16.VI.41			2119/461750-856

Akten-zeichen	Inhalt	Band	Datum	Serial Nr.
1 c 1	Beiakte 1: Grundabtretung zur Strassenerweiterung		1925–26	
	Beiakte 6. Verlängerung des Abflussrohres		1926–35	
1 d 4	Baufonds-Abrechnungen	1	1.26–32	
1 d 5	Beiakte 1: Gebäudeunterhaltung		1929	
	Gesandtschaftsgebäude: Unterhaltung in Instandsetzung		1928–30	
4	Gesandtschaftskanzlei, Geschäfts-verkehr, Bürobedürfnisse, Inventarien, Zeitungsabonnement	3–4	1912–22	
4 a	Gesandtschaftsgrundstück in Kristiana	1	1907–24	
	Garten		1936–40	
	Rechnungen über Reparaturen	1 Heft	1939–40	
	Hauskauf		1925–26	
	Hausangelegenheiten		1925–26	
	Kosten für Hauserwerb		1925–26	
	Hauskauf		1924–25	
	Baukosten		1925	
17 a	Dampfer Valeria		1918–21	
27 a	Strassenbaumaschinen		1927–28	
27 o	Büromaterialien		1927–29	
29 a	Hilfskreuzer Berlin		1918–25	
34 m	Nobel-Institut, Nobel-Vortrag und Aufenthalt des Reichsaussen-ministers Stresemann in Oslo		1926–27	
42	Kunst und Wissenschaft, deutsche Kulturpropaganda		1923–25	
	Passangelegenheiten	1	1926	
A II h	Prof. Wieth-Knudsen, Drontheim		1934	
	Humboldt-Medaille der Deutschen Akademie		1935	
	Weihnachtskrippenausstellung Oslo 1933		1933	
A II h 1	Forderung der norwegisch-schwedi-schen Importvereinigung an die Reichsregierung (U-Boot-Affäre)		1926–30	
A III C.13b	Deutsche Kriegsschiffbesuche in Norwegen		1926–29	
A A	Audienzen bei den norwegischen Majestäten		1911–20	
A Aa	Aaland-Inseln		1917–21	

Akten-zeichen	Inhalt	Band	Datum	Serial Nr.
A B	Beisetzungen		1925-26	
A C	Die internationalen Konferenzen und Verträge, Schiedsgerichte, Abschluss von Verträgen zwischen verschiedenen Ländern	1	1907-24	
		2-3	1908-25	
A D	Diverses	1-3	1913-25	
	Norwegens diplomatische Vertretungen, Budget für die auswärtige Vertretung Personalien norwegischer Diplomaten		1905-21	
A D I	Norwegisches Pressewesen, norwegische Handels-, Sozialpresse, Militärattachés		1917-23	
A E I	Fischerei im nördlichen Eismeer		1910-22	
A E II a	Spitzbergen		1920-25	
A E II b	- Bäreninsel		1918-25	
A E III	De Norske Kulfelter Spitzbergen		1921	
A F	Fremde Kriegsschiffe in norwegischen Gewässern		1906-25	
A F I	Deutsche Flottenbesuche in Norwegen		1905-22	
	Finnland		1914-25	
A G I	Feier nationaler Gedenktage in Norwegen		1906-25	
A H	Der Königliche Hof von Norwegen, Reisen der norwegischen Majestäten, sonstige Hofnachrichten		1906-25	
A I	Norwegens Novembertraktat von 1855 und der Neutralitätsvertrag 1907. Integritätsvertrag		1906-23	
A K	Das deutsche Kaiserhaus, deutsche Bundesfürsten, Geburtstagsfeier des Kaisers		1906-25	
A K i	Kirchenbewegung in Norwegen		1920-25	
A P I	Deutschlands innere und äussere Politik		1907-21	
A P II	Deutsch-norwegische Beziehungen		1906-24	
A P II a	Deutsche Propaganda, Generalia (auch Mundpropaganda)	3	1920-25	
A P II b	Deutsche Propaganda, spez.	1-2	1914-24	
A P II d	Deutschfeindliche norwegische Propaganda, Spezialia		1914-25	
A P III	Norwegisch-schwedische Beziehungen (Defensionsbündnis)	1	1907-25	
A P IIIa	Norwegens politische Beziehungen zu anderen Ländern		1906-22	

Akten-zeichen	Inhalt	Band	Datum	Serial Nr.
A P IV	Internationale Politik		1908-24	
A P V	Norwegische Arbeiterfragen		1919-25	
A P VI	Personalien fremder Diplomaten	1-2	1905-25	
A P VII	Presseangelegenheiten, Verkehr mit Pressevertretern, interna-tionale Telegrafenagenturen	1-2	1906-20	
A P VIIb	Radio - Verkehr		1920-25	
A Pol gen.	Politisches, generell		1908-25	
A R i	Reisen fürstlicher Persönlich-keiten und anderer Staatsober-häupter	1	1914-25	
A R u	Rußland	2-3	1919-25	
A S I	Ostsee- und Nordseeangelegen-heiten		1907-24	
A S II	Skandinavische Gelehrte, Dichter, Presseäusserungen		1906-25	
A S III	Die Sprachenfrage in Norwegen		1907-24	
A S k	Skandinavismus, skandinavische Zusammenarbeit		1903-22	
A S z.	Die Sozialdemokratie in Norwegen	1+3	1906-25	
A V	Norwegische Verfassung		1913-20	
	Deutsche Verfassung		1919-22	
A V I	Militärangelegenheiten		1912-25	
A V I a	Marineangelegenheiten		1907-24	
A V II	Kommandierung deutscher und anderer Offiziere nach Norwegen		1909-22	
A W	Die wirtschaftliche Lage Nor-wegens, Staatsfinanzen, Handels-politik, das jährliche Budget, Alkoholverbot	1-2	1915-20	
	Abkommen Alexander		1919-22	
	- Nosta II + III		1919-24	
	- allgemein		1920-25	
	Industrie-Tran-Abkommen		1919-22	
	Abkommen fremder Staaten		1918-20	
	Politische Wochenberichte		1925	
	Geheimakten		1917-22	
	Betr.: Frieden		1919-20	
	Kriegsgefangene		1918-20	
	Befreiung Kriegsgefangener		1916-21	
	Kindertransporte		1917-21	

Akten-zeichen	Inhalt	Band	Datum	Serial Nr.
	Norwegische Presseübersichten		1920-21	
	Norwegische Presse		1918-23	
			1922	
	Presse, Verschiedenes		1919-25	
	Presse und Propaganda (Gen.)		1914-24	
	Presse, spez.	1	1920	
		2	1920	
	Feindliche Propaganda, besonders Frankreich		1922-25	
	Deutsche Propaganda		1920	
			1921	
	Reichsversicherung für Angestellte bei der Gesandtschaft Kristiania		1912-22	
	Ruhrbesetzung		1923	
	Reparationen		1924	
	Keynes zur Reparationsfrage		1921	
	See-Unfälle, Unterstützung, Heimschaffung von Seeleuten		1925	
	Schleswig		1919-25	
	Saargebiet, Verschiedenes		1919-23	
	U-Boot-Krieg		1920-25	
	Verwertung, Verschiedenes		1920	
			1921-22	
	Zustellungen, Verordnungen		1920	
	Handelsbeziehungen mit Rußland		1920	
	Auslandskredite		1920	
	Björnson & Co.		1920	
	Centrosojus		1920	
	Frischheringsabkommen		1920	
	Neue Salzheringe		1920-21	
H I 2 a 1	Gehärtete Trane, Walöl, Tiertalg, Öle und Fette		1934	
7 b	Vertreter		1926-29	
I 13	Kraftübertragungsprojekt Norwegen-Deutschland		1929-31	
I 14	Kornmonopol		1926-33	
I 15 a	Wirtschaft, allgemein, Norwegen, Wirtschaftsberichte, vierteljährlich		1926-29	
I 15 c	Ermittlungen für den Wirtschafts-ausschuss		1926-29	

Akten-zeichen	Inhalt	Band	Datum	Serial Nr.
H II 5	Fischerei	1	1926-27	
H II 6	Walfang	1-2	1930-35	
		3-5	1936-38	
H IV 6 a 1	Norwegischer Zoll		1929-32	
H IV 1 e	Handels- und Schiffahrtsver-träge		1926-39	
II 4	Dienstbetrieb, Verschiedenes		1918-24	
III Gen.	Kassensachen		1919-25	
III 3	- Postscheckkonto		1919-22	
III 4	- verschiedener Konsulate	1-10	1918-22	
III 5	- Depositen		1918-22	
IV 4	Rechts- und Polizeisachen, Todesfälle, Leichenpässe, Nachlässe		1918-25	
IV 5	- Alimente verschiedener Personen	1-8	1915-25	
IV 6	- Beglaubigungen, Nota-riatssachen	1-2	1919-20	
IV 8	Entschädigungen der Auslands-deutschen		1919-23	
V 1	Matrikel des Generalkonsulates in Kristiania		1895-1922	
V 4	Staatsangehörigkeit, Abstim-mungsangelegenheiten		1920-21	
VII 12	Schwarze Liste, Warnung vor unwürdigen Personen und Firmen		1916-25	
IX 1-2	Land- und Forstwirtschaft, Viehzucht 1. Landwirtschaft 2. Viehzucht, Seuchen, Aus- und Einfuhrbestimmungen	1-2	1920-23	
X 1	Schiffahrt und Fischerei: Schiffsmeldungen, Berichte über deutschen Schiffsverkehr		1920-21	
X 2	- An- und Abmusterungen Desertionen		1919-25	
X 3	- Heimschaffung von Seeleuten		1919-25	
X 4	- Strafsachen		1919-25	
X 5	- Seeunfälle		1919-25	
X 6	- Lotsen		1919-25	
X 7	Schiffahrt			
X 8	Schiffahrt und Fischerei: Fischerei Norwegens		1919-25	
X 10	- Seemanns- und Schiffs-nachlässe		1919-25	

Akten-zeichen	Inhalt	Band	Datum	Serial Nr.
X 13	Schiffahrt und Fischerei: Konsulatsfragebogen der Seewarte		1919-25	
X b	- Generalia b Norwegen		1919-25	
XI 3	Ceremonial, Orden		1919-21	
XII 1	Gesundheitswesen, epidemische Krankheiten		1919-25	
XII 2	- Ärzte und Apotheker		1919-25	
XIII 3	Verschiedenes		1918-20	
XIV 3	Begräbnisstätten	1-2	1916-21	
K I 5 a	Auslieferungen, Fahndungser-suchen, Einzelfälle		1927-37	
K I 6	Strafverfolgungen, Sonderheft Heinrich Mohr		1927-35	
K I 9	Alimente	1-3	1926-37	
K I 10	Eheschliessung, Allgemeines und Einzelfälle	1-2	1927-37	
K I 11		1-2	1927-39	
K I 12	Strafnachrichten, Allgemeines und Einzelfälle	1-2	1928-39	
K I 15	Vormundschaftssachen		1922-28	
K I 16	Forderungen: Sonderheft Annette Hirschbühl		1928-33	
	Sonderheft 2: Reichsfiskus gegen Norcanners		1925-33	
	Forderungssachen	4	1931-33	
K I 17	Nachlass Gesandtschaftsamts-diener Adolf Seybold		1934	
K I 17a	Nachlässe, Todesfälle, Einzel-fälle	1-3	1926-38	
	Beiakte: Berndt, Oberländer, Rauhut, Rentiera		1929-38	
K I 18	Beschaffung von Urkunden, Personenstandssachen, Ehefähig-keitszeugnisse	1-3	1926-38	
K I 19	Beglaubigungen, Bescheinigungen, Übersetzungen	1-2	1930-39	
K II 3	Pässe und Visa, Einzelfälle		1930-33	
K II 4	Russenvisa		1934-38	
K III 2	Staatsangehörigkeitsnachweise, Heimatscheine, Einzelfälle	1-2	1929-38	
K III 3	Einbürgerungen in Deutschland		1922-38	
K III 4	Entlassungen aus der Reichsange-hörigkeit		1928-36	
K IV 4	Streitigkeiten mit Arbeitgebern		1928-38	

Akten-zeichen	Inhalt	Band	Datum	Serial Nr.
K V 2	Übernahme, Heimschaffung durch Vermittlung der Gesandtschaft, Einzelfälle		1926-35	
K V 4	Ausweisungen, Einzelfälle	1-2	1926-37	
K V 5	Arbeitslosen-Unfall-Versicherung		1925-38	
K V 6	Renten, Allgemeines und Einzel-fälle		1928-38	
K V 7	Wohnungswesen		1928-38	
K V 9	Unterstützungen		1926-38	
K V 11 So	Unterstützung Frau Palmyra Schuster		1926-32	
K V 11	Geisteskranke		1926-38	
K V 12	Sammlungen und Spenden		1926-28	
K VI 3	Ärzte, Apotheker, Hospitäler		1926-38	
K VI 4	Gesundheitsstatistik	1-2	1926-38	
K VI 5	Deutsches Hygiene-Museum, Dresden		1933-37	
K VII 2	Schiffsverkehr		1926-38	
K VII 4	Schiffahrtsbestimmungen		1926-38	
K VII 7	Betriebsunfälle und Krankheiten	1-2	1925-38	
K VII 8	Darlehn auf Schiffe		1926-38	
K VII 9	Flaschenzettel und Strandgut		1926-38	
K VII 10	Heimschaffungen und Entweichun-gen		1926-38	
K VII 11	Lotsensachen		1926-38	
K VII 14	Seemannsnachlässe		1926-38	
K VII 16	Seeunfälle und Verklarungen	1-3	1926-38	
K VII 17	Seewarte		1922-28	
K VII 18	Fischdampfer "Preussen"		1934-35	
K VII 19	Unterstützungen von Seeleuten	1-2	1926-38	
K VIII 1	Nachforschungen nach Personen	2-3	1932-37	
K VIII 4	Auskünfte und Vermittlungen	1-3	1931-38	
1	City of Flint		1939-40	3007/D587775-803
2	Internierte		1939-40	
3	Friedensbestrebungen		1939-40	3073/D612899-903 3677/E034671-86
4	Spionage		1939-40	
5	Luftverkehr, Sperrballons, deutsche Flugzeuge		1939-40	3660/E034108-15
6	Lotsenwesen		1939-40	

Akten-zeichen	Inhalt	Band	Datum	Serial Nr.
7	Vercharterung norwegischen Schiffraums		1939-40	3074/D612906-21 3663/E034143-67 9868/E693031-40
8	Schiffahrtssachverständige in Norwegen		1940	3661/E034118-21
9	Norwegische Neutralitätspolitik		1939-40	3706/E036526-57 3075/D612925-44
10	Verletzung norwegischer Neutralität durch Flugzeuge		1939-40	3662/E034124-40
11	Seekriegsführung		1939-40	3676/E034657-68
12	Englische Neutralitätsverletzungen in den norwegischen Hoheitsgewässern		1940	3668/E034360-88 3078/D613000-17
13	Respektierung norwegischer Hoheitsgewässer		1939-40	3686/E035523-33 3077/D612986-96
14	Überfall des M/S "Altmark"	1	1940	3687/E035536-66 3076/D612948-76 8389/E591799-801
15		2	1940	3687/E035567-92 3076/D612977-82
16	— Presse	1	1940	
17	"U 21"		1940	3079/D613020-47
18	Besetzung Norwegens- Geheim		1940	2953/D576581-657
19	— Okkupationspolitik		1940	2969/D578454-667 3664/E034170-260
20	— Okkupation, militär.		1940	3081/D613176-319 3766/E040706-09
21	— Okkupationsverwaltung		1940	3080/D613051-172 4452/E086789-90 3746/E040414-23
22	Geheime Reichssachen, Einzelfälle		1939-40	2972/D579467-78
23	Geheime Verschlusssachen		1940	3741/E040261-64
24	Rückführung der Nachrichtengeräte		1940	
25	Gehaltszahlungen an Landeskreisleiter der NSDAP Pg Spanaus		1938-40	3740/E040257-58
26	Überweisung der Daimler-Benz-Werke		1930-39	
27	Sicherung des Gesandtschaftsgebäudes		1937-40	
28	Propagandafonds		1940	3705/E036511-23
29	Geheimer Pressefonds		1937-40	2970/D578670-703 3704/E036489-508
30	Gesandtschaftsgrundstück		1912-37	
	Island		1925-38	

Akten-zeichen	Inhalt	Band	Datum	Serial Nr.
	Osa-Kraftanlage		1930	
	Allgemeines		1940-41	
	Gesandtschaft Oslo, Vertreter des Auswärtigen Amtes beim Reichskommissar		1940	3735/E037472-75
	Besprechungen mit den Konsuln		1939	3742/E040267-323
	Erlasse und Reden des Führers		10.33	
	Rest, Konzepte		1941	
	Streitsache Hildisch-Firma Up-meyer, Margarineherstellung		1936-40	
	Instandsetzungen		1934-36	
	Abrechnungen: Januar - März		1939	
	Juli - Dezember		1939	
	Inventarverzeichnis A. (Amtsgebäude)		1940	
	Stücknummerliste zum Inventar-verzeichnis A.(Amtsgebäude)		1937-39	
	Verhandlungen betr. Übergabe der Gebäude und der Einrich-tungsgegenstände		1940-41	
	Abwicklung der Geschäfte		1940-41	3743/E040326-45
	Personalangelegenheiten		1940-41	
	Konto des ehemaligen Konsulats in Drontheim		1940	
I.5.Pers.	Vizekonsulat Grimstad		1907-25	
Pers.	Friedr. Gelderblom, Bürohilfs-arbeiter		1940	
Nr.3/1. Pers.	Oltn.Gädeke, zur Gesandtschaft kommandiert		1911-13	
	Günther Kern		1937-38	
	Stenotypistin Gerda Metje		1925-41	
	Dr. Marhefka		1930-32	
	Pastor Günther		1933-39	
	Dr. U. Noack		1936-40	2973/D579481-587
I/5.Pers.	Carl P.C.Albretsen (Tod)		1922-25	
	Vizekonsulat Bodö		1919-24	
I/1 Pers.	Generalkonsul		1919-22	
I/3 Pers.	Hilfspersonal		1919-22	
Pers.	Stenotypistin Sophie Bollhagen		1939-40	
	H.W.Biswanger, Hilfsarbeiter		1939-40	

Akten-zeichen	Inhalt	Band	Datum	Serial Nr.
A.I.f.1. Pers.	Bergenser Konsuln: Heldal, Küchler, Strahl		1927-36	
I.5. Pers.	Konsulat Bergen		1918-25	
	Berthold Benecke, 2.Handels-attaché		1939-40	
	Leg.Sekr. Gerhard Graf		1939-40	
	Stenotyp. Maria Donhäuser		1939-40	
	Schiffssachverständiger John Alfred Edye		1939-40	
	Erich Engel, Amtsgehilfe		1939-40	
	Ilse Rittershausen, Stenotyp.		1933-40	
	Attaché Dr.Wilhelm Lehmann		1938-40	
	Alfred Liegl, Gärtner		1933-40	
	Werner Rudolf, Bürohilfsarbeiter		1939-40	
	Hofrat Ferdinand Carow, Kanzler a.D.		1924-38	
	Hofrat Ferdinand Carow, Kanzler I.Kl.		1940	
	Hugo Fischer, Prof.		1939	
I.5.a Pers.	Vizekonsulat Aalesund		1914-22	
I.5.b Pers.	Konsulat Arendal		1917-25	
	Erich Alexander, Amtsgehilfe		1940	
	Frau Inga Behrens		1939-40	
	Gesandtschaftsrat Baron von Behr		1932-39	
	Wilhelm Beck, Bürohilfsarbeiter		1940	
	Kons.Sekr.I.Kl. Fritz Bauer		1940	
	Karl Bartels, Amtsgehilfe		1935-40	
A.I.b.6. Pers.	Pressebeirat Behrens		1919-38	
I.5.d. Pers.	Konsulat Drontheim		1918-25	
I.5.6a. Pers.	Konsulat Drammen		1917-21	
3.F.1. Pers.	Hofrat Fröhlich		1912-24	
I.7. Pers.	Fremde Konsuln in Norwegen		1918-21	
I.5. Pers.	Vizekonsulat Fredriksstad		1918-25	
	Vizekonsulat Fredrikshald		1919-21	
	Frau Gertrud Fischer,Stenotyp.		1939-40	
	Konsul Fischer, Mukden		1920-26	
	Günther Fiedler, Amtsgehilfe		1940	
	Prinz Erbach-Schönberg		1921-23	

Akten-zeichen	Inhalt	Band	Datum	Serial Nr.
I.5. Pers.	Karl Engelbert, Nachtwächter		1940	
	Gesandter Dr. Rhomberg		1920-26	
	Eugen Schick, Pianostimmer		1920-22	
	Ges.Freiherr v.Weizsäcker		1931-33	
	Stenotyp.Charlotte Wiemann		1940	
III.6. Pers.	Versorgungsgebührnisse W.Wiencke		1924-25	
	Gustav Frank Züchner, Journ.		1937-40	
	Margot Winter, Senotyp.		1940	
	Dr. Frank Weiland, Hilfsarbeiter		1939-40	
	Ges.Rat Dr.Walter Weber		1939-40	
5 b Pers.	Missionschef Ges.Dr.Wallroth		1928-32	
7 Pers.	Generalkonsul Dr. Voretzsch	2	1917-20	
	Fritz Volberg, Presseattaché		1938-40	
	Johannes Viefhaus, Kons.Sekr.		1939-40	
	Verschiedenes		1939-40	2974/D579590-93
	Vereidigung der Beamten und Angestellten der Gesandtschaft		1918-25	
I 5 Pers.	Vizekonsulat Vardö		1917-25	
	General von Uthmann, Militär-attaché		1938-40	
	Konsulat Tromsö		1918-24	
	Konsulat Tönsberg		1918-25	
	Leg.Sekr. Henning Thomsen		1936-39	
	Hans Steinhaus, Amtsgehilfe		1926-40	
	Konsulat Stavanger		1913-23	
	Albert Stark, Hilfsamtsgehilfe		1939-40	
	Friedrich Spörl, Bürohilfsarb.		1939-40	
	Hauptm.Eberhard Spiller, Luftattaché		1939-40	
	Karl Spanaus, Hilfsarbeiter		1939-40	
3 S I Pers.	Willi Skerra, Bürohilfsarbeiter		1940	
I 5 Pers.	Vizekonsulat Skien		1922	
	Marie Simonet, Stenotyp.		1939-40	
I 2 Pers.	Sekretäre		1918-26	
	Hermann Schnabel, Nachtwächter		1940	
	Hans Schütt, Kons.Sekr.		1940	
	Korvettenkapitän Schreiber, Marineattaché		1939-40	

Akten-zeichen	Inhalt	Band	Datum	Serial Nr.
I 2 Pers.	Fritz Schmidt, Kons.Sekr.I.Kl.		1938-40	
I 5 Pers.	Vizekonsulat Sandefjord		1916-24	
	Vizekonsulat Sarpsborg		1923-33	
4 C Pers.	Geheim		1918-28	2975/D579596-604
	Friedrich Perkunder, Kanzler		1938-40	
	Erich Opitz, Bürohilfsarbeiter		1939	
	Ges.Rat I.Kl.Hans Joachim von Neuhaus		1935-40	
I 5 Pers.	Narvik		1918-25	
	Namsos		1915-24	
Pers.	Generalia		1918-25	
A Ib 6 Pers.	Männliche Angestellte		1926-30	
I 5 Pers.	Konsulat Mandal		1919-23	
	Dr. Mangelsdorf, Handelsattaché		1938-40	
3 I Pers	Leg.Sekr.Freiherr von Maltzan		1909-10	
	Militärattaché bei den Skandina-vischen Reichen		1911-20	
3 Pers.	von Mutius(amtl.Akten)		1918-20	
	Christian Müsch, Assistent		1940	
	Gesandter Rohland		1934-36	
	Polit. Personalaffären, verdäch-tige Personen		1914-20	
	Kons.Sekr. I.Kl. Jos.Müller		1914-39	
I 5 Pers.	Vizekonsulat Moss		1919-25	
	Vizekonsulat Molde		1921-25	
5 b Pers.	Missionschef		1926-29	
	Joachim Meyer, Kons.-Sekr.		1939-40	
I 5 Pers.	Vizekonsulat Melbo		1921-24	
	Vizekonsulat Larvik		1916-25	
	Else Krüger, Stenotypistin		1940	
	Vizekonsulat Kragerö		1920-22	
	Vizekonsulat Kristiansund N.		1917-25	
	Vizekonsulat Kristiansund S.		1917-26	
	Sonderbeauftragter für kultur-politische Fragen Reg.Rat Dr.Werner Knab		1940	
	Kapitän Kempf, Gehilfe des Schiffahrtssachverständigen		1940	
	Marie-Luise Keilwagen, Angestellte		1940	

Akten-zeichen	Inhalt	Band	Datum	Serial Nr.
I 5 Pers.	Ingo Kaul, Hilfsarbeiter		1940	
	Helene Kanaschöfsky, Angestellte		1940	
5 c Pers.	Gesandtschaftsräte		1925-30	
	Hans Jamber, Bürohilfsarbeiter		1939-40	
	Anneliese Imhoff, Stenotypistin		1933-40	
3 Pers.	Gesandtschaftsrat Horstmann		1920-29	
	Wilhelm Hoppe, Kons.Sekr.		1939-40	
	Gertrud Holzhäuser, Stenotyp.		1937-40	
	Leg.Sekr. Dr.Holm, Freiherr von Berchem, Dr.v.Putlitz, Dr. Pfeiffer, Freiherr v.Schwarzenberg, Dr.Schumburg, Attaché Velhagen		1925-35	
	Joh.Wilh.Hohnsbein, Hilfsamtsgeh.		1939-40	
	Kanzler Hoffmann		1924-25	
3 II Pers.	Hilfsbeamte		1916-26	
	Frau Henriksen, Hausverwalt.		1939-40	
	Hausangestellte		1939-40	
I 5 Pers.	Harstad		1920-21	
	Vizekonsulat Hammerfest		1918-23	
	Haugesund		1918-25	
	Studienrat Dr. Haintz		1937-40	
	Helmut von dem Hagen, Presse-beirat		1938-40	
	Mitteilungsblätter des Presse-beirats in norwegischer Sprache über die aktuellen politischen und wirtschaftlichen Vorgänge Januar bis April 1940		1940	
	Norwegische Ausgabe des Deut-schen Weißbuches "Polnische Dokumente zur Vorgeschichtes des Krieges" Erste Folge Auswärtiges Amt 1940 Nr.3		1935-39	
Kult 1	Allgemeine norwegische Kultur-politik 1939			
D Kult 1	Nordische Gesellschaft		1936-39	3747/E040427-64
D Kult 1-3	Deutsche Kulturpolitik, zwischen-staatliche Gesellschaften, Nordische Gesellschaft, Nordi-sche Verbindungsstelle		1938-39	
Kult 2 Nr.1	Kulturpolitische Beziehungen zu Deutschland		1937-40	
Nr.2	Norsk-Tysk Forening		1939-40	

Akten-zeichen	Inhalt	Band	Datum	Serial Nr.
Kult 2 Nr. 2	Norwegischer Verein für kulturelle Verbindung mit Deutschland - Oesterreich		1928-38	
Nr. 3	Norsk-Tysk Selskab und andere norwegisch-deutsche Gesellschaften		1934-39	
			1939-40	
Nr. 4	Kulturpolitische Beziehungen des Gastlandes zu anderen Ländern und zwischen anderen Staaten		1938-40	
Nr.2-6	Kulturpolitische Beziehungen Deutschlands zu anderen Staaten, fremde Volksgruppen in Deutschland, Kirchenwesen in Deutschland, Ein-, Aus- und Rückwanderung, Nachforschungen im Inland		1939-40	
Kult 3 Nr. 1	Deutsche Kolonie, deutsche Vereine		1939	
	Deutsche Vereine in Oslo und Vereine ausserhalb Norwegens		1927-38	
	Deutsche Vereine (deutsch-norwegische) in Norwegen		1926-34	
Nr. 2	Deutsche Heime		1938-40	
Kult 4 Nr. 1-4	Kirchenpolitische Religionsgesellschaften, deutsche Kirche, katholische Kirche, Kirchenkongresse und Tagungen		1939-40	
Nr. 2	Evangelische Gemeinde		1926-38	
Nr. 3	Katholizismus		1925-38	
Kult 7 + D Kult 7	Jugendbewegungen und Jugendverbände		1926-38	
Kult 8	Schul- und Unterrichtswesen		1926-33	
	E.G.Kern		1926-38	
Kult 8 Nr. 8a	Schulwesen, Kernsche Schule		1939-40	
Kult 9 Nr.1-2	Deutsche Sprachwerbung, Buchprämien		1939-40	
Kult 10 Nr. 1	Professoren, Lektoren, deutsch-akademischer Austauschdienst		1939-40	
Nr. 2-3	Studentenwesen, Hochschulfeiern und Hochschulkongresse		1939-40	
Kult 11	Wissenschaft, Verschiedenes		1926-38	
			1939	
Kult 11 Nr. 1	Wissenschaftliche internationale Kongresse und Ausstellungen		1939	
Nr. 2	Museen		1939-40	
Nr. 3	Forschungsreisen, Expeditionen		1939-40	
	Polarforschung		1925-30	

Akten-zeichen	Inhalt	Band	Datum	Serial Nr.
Kult' 11 Nr. 3	Forschungen		1925-38	
Nr. 4	Wissenschaftliche Institute und Vereinigungen (Drucksachenaus-tausch		1939	
Nr. 8	Buchwerbung, Buchausstellungen		1939-40	
			1936-40	
Nr. 9	Archäologie		1939-40	
Nr. 10	Nobelinstitut		1939-40	
			1927-36	
Kult 12	Kunst		1939-40	
Kult 12 Nr.1-2	Theaterwesen, Musikwesen		1939-40	
Nr.3,3a	Filmwesen, Filvermittlung		1939-40	3745/E040405-11 2976/D579607-12
Nr. 4	Filme		1931-38	
	Sportwesen		1938-39	
Nr. 5	Architektur		1939	
Nr. 6	Vorträge		1939-40	
Nr. 7	Literatur, Bibliotheken		1939-40	
Nr.7-9	Jugendbewegung, Schulwesen in Deutschland, Auswahl und Ver-mittlung von Sprachlehrern		1939-40	
Nr. 8	Bibliotheken. Literatur		1925-32	
	Kriegsliteratur		1926-38	
Nr.10	Hochscnulwesen in Deutschland, Humboldt-Stipendium, Ferienkurse, Studentenreisen		1939-40	
Nr.11-12	Wissenschaft, Kunst		1939-40	
P 1	Presse- und Propagandawesen in Norwegen, allgemein		1939-40	
P 2 Nr. 1	Pressewesen, Beziehungen zu Deutschland, Abkommen Presseab-teilung		1939-40	
	Norwegische Presse		1937-38	
Nr. 2	Pressewesen, Beziehungen zu anderen Staaten		1939-40	
P 3 Nr. 1	Nachrichtenbüros, Telegrafen-agenturen		1939	
Nr. 2	Deutsche Zeitungen und Zeit-schriften in Norwegen		1938-40	
P 4 Nr. 1	Pressevertreter, Redakteure, Berichterstatter		1939-40	
	Presseagenten		1927-35	

Akten-zeichen	Inhalt	Band	Datum	Serial Nr.
P 4 Nr. 1 a	Freifahrten für norwegische Pressevertreter		1927-38	
Nr. 2	Freifahrten norwegischer Journa-listen in Deutschland		1939	
Nr. 3	Vertreter deutscher Zeitungen in Norwegen		1939	
P 6	Greuelpresse, Hetzfilme, Beanstandungen		1933-39	
	Interventionen		1938-40	
D P 1	Presse- und Propagandawesen in Deutschland		1939	
Prot.1	Reisen, Festlichkeiten und Antrittsbesuche, Audienzen		1926-36	
Prot.1a	Björnson-Jubiläum		1932-33	
	Nationaltag 1.Mai		1926-38	
	Goethe-Jubiläum		1931-32	
	Nationaltage, Königliche Geburts-tage, Tag des deutschen Buches, Erntedanktag, Heldengedenktag		1927-38	
	Reichsgründungstag		1930-36	
	Attachés		1933-39	2977/D579615-16
Prot.2	Doyenat un Personalien der diplomatischen russischen Sowjetvertretung		1927-39	
Prot.3	Orden und Titel		1933-38	
	Orden und Ehrenzeichen, Auszeichnungen		1939-40	
	Ordensrückgabe, Belege über Zuwendungen		1928-38	
Prot.3a	Norwegische Orden und Ehrenzei-chen		1935-36	
Prot.3b	Ehrenkreuz der deutschen Mutter		1939-40	
So 1	Verschiedenes		1939-40	
So 2 Nr. 3	Kriegsgräber, Denkmäler		1930-40	
So 4 Nr. 5	Empfehlungen für Norweger, für Deutsche		1939-40	
So 6	Auskünfte über Norweger		1939-40	
So	Dänemark, Finnland, Schweden	2	1930-40	
	Hilfsamtsgehilfen		1931-39	
	Konflikt Finnland-Rußland und damit zusammenhängende Fragen	1	8.39- 2.40	
	Der finnisch-russische Konflikt	2	3.40	
	Konsulatsangelegenheiten		1940	

Akten-zeichen	Inhalt	Band	Datum	Serial Nr.
Kri-Pre	Allgemeines		1939-40	
	Wochenberichte		1939-40	2982/D584317-504
Kri-Pro	Propaganda	2	1939-40	
		3	1939-40	2983/D584506-08
Kri-Prop	- Fichtebund, Weissbuch		1939-40	
Kri-Schiff	Schiffahrt, Frachten, Schiffs-meldungen	1	1939-40	
	Schiffahrt 1940	2	1939-40	
	Allgemeines	3	1939-40	
	Deutsche Schiffe, Einzelfälle		1939-40	
Kri-Wi	Deutsch-norwegische Wirtschafts-verhandlungen, England-Norwegen		1939-40	
		2	1939-40	
Kri-Blo	Blockade, Bannware, Schwarze Liste, deutsche Prisenordnung	5	1939-40	
Kri-Verl	Norwegische Schiffsverluste, Beschlagnahme, u.a.Einzelfälle		1939-40	
Kri-Versch	Verschiedenes, Stimmung in anderen Ländern		1939-40	
Kri-Rundfunk	Rundfunk		1939-40	
WV 2a,2b	Reisen von Deutschen, Reisen von Norwegern		1939-40	
	Personalakten		1939-40	
	Akten betr. Jaspis		1939-40	
	Verbände vom 1.10.28 - 30.6.33		1927-33	
	Verkehr mit Reichskommissionen		1940	
	Verkehr mit norwegischen Behör-den		1940	
	Verkehr mit Militärdienststellen		1940	
	Ehrenkreuz des Weltkrieges, Einzelfälle		1935	
	- Allgemeines, Verwundetenabzei-chen, allgemein, verschiedene Einzelfälle		1934-40	
F	Firmen A - Z		1930-33	
Pol 1	Aussenpolitik Norwegens		1939-40	
Pol 2 Nr. 1	Verschiedene Abkommen zwischen Deutschland und Norwegen		1926-38	
	Politische Beziehungen Norwegens zu Deutschland		1939-40	
Nr. 1a	Norwegen, Deutschland und die Antarktis	1	1938-39	
2	Waffenattachés		1939-40	

Akten-zeichen	Inhalt	Band	Datum	Serial Nr.
Pol 2 3	Politische Beziehungen Norwegens zu anderen Staaten		1939	
			1926-38	6021/E444501-21
	Politische Beziehungen Norwegens zu Frankreich, Oesterreich, Polen, Ungarn		1926-36	
	Schiedsverträge, Verträge Norwegens mit anderen Ländern		1928-38	
Pol 2 3a	Skandinavismus	1	1926-38	
		2	1939	
3b	Politische Beziehungen zwischen anderen Staaten		1939	
	Grönland	1	1935-38	
		2	1939	
4b	Deutsche Kriegsschiffsbesuche in Norwegen	1	1926-39	
		2	1930-38	
		3	1938-39	
	Deutsche Flottenbesuche in Oslo		1932+34	
Pol 3	Norwegische Innenpolitik		1939-40	
Pol 3 1	Königliche Familie und Hof		1922-39	
Pol 3 2	Ministerien, Minister, prominente Persönlichkeiten		1926-29	6021/E444522-46
Pol 3 3a	Die Armee		1924-38	6021/E444547-65
	Armee, Marine		1939-40	
3b	Norwegische Marine		1927-39	
4	Staatsschutzbestimmungen, Agenten und Spionagewesen		1939-40	
5	Hoheitszeichen, Feiertage		1927-37	
6	Thronreden und Stortingwahlen		1927-38	7553/E541854-58
	Storting und Regierung		1926-38	
	Wahlen, Regierung und Storting		1939-40	
7	Politische Parteien Norwegens		1937-39	
8	Nordnorwegen		1931-39	
8b	Spitzbergen: Allgemeines, Verwaltung, Ansprüche, Ausbeute		1926-39	
8c	Südpolargebiet, Nordpolargebiet, Spitzbergen, Jan Mayen, Franz-Josefsland		1922-39	
9	Jahresübersichten		1930-38	
4 1	Völkerbund		1939	

Akten-zeichen	Inhalt	Band	Datum	Serial Nr.
Pol 4 2	Kommunistische Bewegung		1927-38	
	Kommunismus, Bolschewismus		1937-40	
Pol 4 3	Freimaurerei und andere Bünde		1939	
Pol 4 5	Indienfrage		1939	
Pol 4 6	Flüchtlingsfragen		1933-39	
D Pol 1	Deutsche Aussenpolitik		1938	
D Pol 1 1-2 3	Auflösung Tschechei, Rückkehr Memel Danzig		1939	8153/E582580-82
D Pol 2	Amerika		1939-40	
	Balkan, Türkei, Ungarn		1939-40	
	Baltische Staaten: Estland, Lettland, Litauen		1939-40	
	Belgien, Holland, Luxemburg		1939-40	4250/E075395-473
	England, Frankreich	1	1939-40	3091/D626006-091
		2	1940	3091/D626092-125
	Italien, Irland, Portugal, Schweiz, Spanien		1939-40	3091/D626126-28
	Rußland, Polen, Afrika, Asien	1	1939-40	
	Skandinavien, Dänemark, Finnland, Schweden	1	1939-40	4299/E077812-49
D Pol 3	Deutsche Innenpolitik		1940	
D Pol 3 Nr. 1	Führer und Reichskanzler	1	1939	
Nr. 2+3	Reichsregierung, Reichstag, Ministerien, Minister und andere prominente Persönlichkeiten			
Nr. 4	Reden		1939	
Nr. 5	NSDAP		1934-36	
Nr. 5-6	NSDAP, Gliederungen, angeschlossene Verbände, Reichsparteitage		1939-40	
Nr. 7-8	Auslandsorganisation, Tagungen in Stuttgart		1939	
Nr. 9-10	Militär-, Marine- und Luftfahrtangelegenheiten, Arbeitsdienst	1	1939	
Nr.11-13	Staatsschutzbestimmungen (auch Antikomintern), Hoheitszeichen, Flaggen, Feiertage, Kolonialfragen		1939	
Pers A 1	Auswärtiges Amt, Organisation, Geschäftsübersichten		1939	
Pers A 2	Die deutschen Auslandsvertretungen, auch monatliche Veränderungen		1939-40	
Pers G 1	Aktenplan, Registratur		1930-40	

Akten-zeichen	Inhalt	Band	Datum	Serial Nr.
Pers G 2	Dienstbetrieb		1939-40	
Pers G 2a	Weiterleitung von Briefen, Sendungen		1939-40	
Pers G 4	Dienstkraftwagen, Garage		1928-34	
	Rangieren vor der Gesandtschaft, Besteuerung des Gesandtschafts-grundstückes		1926-38	
	Gebäudeunterhaltung		1926-37	
	Gesandtschaftsgebäude (Haupt-akten), Dienstwohnungen		1924-38	
	Drammenson		1939-40	
	Sonderakte: Klingenberg		1939-40	
Pers G 4a	Versicherung von Chauffeur und Kraftwagen		1924-38	
	Gärtnerunterhaltung		1928-40	
Pers G 4b	Dienstkraftwagen, -führer, Ver-sicherung		1940	
Pers G 5	Ausstattungsgegenstände, Wohn-haus und Bürohaus	1	1925-38	
			1930-38	
		2	1939-40	
Pers G 5a	Büromaterialien		1931-40	
Pers G 5b	Hausfernsprecher		1939-40	
Pers G 6	Gedenktage, Feste, Flaggen, Allgemeines		1926-38	
	Beflaggung der Behörde			
	Kurierangelegenheiten		1939-40	
Pers G 7a	Drucksachenaustausch, norwegische		1931-37	
Pers G 7b	- deutsch		1924-39	
Pers G 8a	Vom Auswärtigen Amt gelieferte Zeitungen, Zeitschriften		1926-38	
	Drucksachen, Zeitungen für die Gesandtschaft		1926-38	
	Zeitungen, Zeitschriften		1939-40	
Pers G 8b	Drucksachenbeschaffung für andere Stellen		1939-40	
Pers G 9	Allgemeine Vorschriften für die Konsuln und den Konsulatsdienst, Einteilung des Amtsbezirkes		1926-39	
	Kriegskonsulate, Kirkenes, Kristiansand , Narvik, Stavanger		1939-40	
	Kriegskonsulate, Allgemeines Haugesund		1939-40	
Pers G 9a	Konsulat Bergen	1	1928-38	

Akten-zeichen	Inhalt	Band	Datum	Serial Nr.
Pers G 9a	Konsulat Bergen	2	1939-40	
Pers G 9b	Trontheim	1	1926-39	
		2	1939-40	
	Wahlkonsulate: Aalesund und Bodö		1926-39	
	- Haugesund und Harstad			
	- Honningsvaag, Kirkenes, Kristiansand, Melbo, Narvik, Stavanger, Namsos			
	- Egersund, Florö und Hammerfest		1926-40	
	- Salvaer, Tromsö, Vardö		1926-40	
Pers G 9c	- Risör, Tönsberg, Sandefjord, Sarpsborg		1924-37	
	- Halden, Kragerö, Kristiansand, Larvik, Mandal, Moss,Porsgrund			
	- Arendal, Drammen, Fredriksstad, Grimstad, Holmestrad, Faresund, Flekkefjord		1924-39	
Pers P	Vertragsangestellte (männliche)		1926-38	
	Gesandtschaftsgärtner		1926-28	
	Gesandter Dr.Sahm		1936-39	
	Gesandter		1939-40	3779/E041135-45
Pers P 1	Allgemeines, Gesetz zur Wiederherstellung des Berufsbeamtentums, Verzeichnis des beschäftigten Personals	1	1935-39	
		2	1940	
Pers P 1a	Rechtsstellung der Gesandtschafts mitglieder (Amtsbefugnisse, Vorrechte, Meldepflicht, Ausweise)		1926-38	
Pers P 1b	Steuer- und Zollfreiheit		1939	
Pers P 1c			1926-38	
	Kraftwagensteuer		1939	
Pers P 1d			1926-38	
Pers P 2	Urlaubsbestimmungen, - pläne		1929-4C	
Pers P 5b	Oberinspektor Schmidt und Konsulpraktikant K.Skinbach		1926-38	
Pers P 6a	Vertragsangestellte (weiblich)		1918-34	
Pers R 1	Haushaltswesen, Voranschläge, Bedarfsnachweisungen		1938-40	
Pers R 2	Kassenordnung, Kassenprüfung		1939-40	

Akten-zeichen	Inhalt	Band	Datum	Serial Nr.
Pers R 3	Beschaffung von Betriebsmitteln		1928-39	
Pers R 4a	Kulturpolitischer Fonds	1	1927-37	
		2	1938-40	
Pers R 5	Abrechnungen		1930-39	
Pers R 6	Prüfungsbemerkungen des Auswärtigen Amtes und des Rechnungshofes		1929-39	
Pers R 7	Gebühren, Tarife		1939	
Pers R 8	Besoldungsfragen, Löhne		1927-40	
Pers R 9	Reise- und Umzugskosten		1925-40	
Pers R 10	Steuern, Angestellten- und Invalidenversicherung		1926-37	
Pers R 11	Devisenangelegenheiten		1940	
Pers R 17	Abrechnung der Konsulate		1925-31	
Pers R 16		2	1939-41	
Si 3	Telegramme, Erlasse, Berichtkontrolle		1939-40	
Si 6	Kurierangelegenheiten			
R 5	Grenzempfehlungen, Allgemeines, Einzelfälle		1939-40	
R 6 5	Freizeitgestaltungen		1939-40	
R 7 1	Friedensbestrebungen		1939	
R 7 2	Neutralität Norwegen		1938-40	8568/E600180-85
A I	Gräber		1919-34	
	Denkmäler		1933-39	
	Handbücher, Jahresberichte		1925-38	
A II	Musik	1	1926-36	
		2	1936-39	
	Theater, Tanz, Zirkus	1	1925-35	
		2	1936-38	
	Kunst, Kunstausstellung, Museen		1925-38	
	Deutsche Kunstausstellung in Norwegen		1929-32	
	Filmvermittlungen		1930-37	
	Cavell-Film (Im Westen nichts Neues)		1928-36	
	Sonderteil: Olympia-Ehrenzeichen		1935-40	
	Propaganda		1926-38	
			1933-38	

Akten-zeichen	Inhalt	Band	Datum	Serial Nr.
A II	Deutsche Presse		1926-37	
	Gesuche Deutscher Zeitschriften, Anschriften		1924-38	
	Verschiedene Reisen Deutscher, Reisen von Norwegern		1933-38	
	Reisen von Norwegern		1935-38	
	Deutschlandfahrt norwegischer Journalisten		1933	
	Austausch und Reisen von Studie-renden, deutsch-norwegischer Schüleraustausch und Schüler-reisen		1927-38	
	Empfehlungen für Norweger und andere Ausländer		1926-38	
	Empfehlungen für Deutsche		1926-32	
	Überfliegen norwegischen Staats-gebietes durch deutsche Flugzeuge Flugrouten der Lufthansa durch Norwegen		1928-33	
	Flugwesen		1926-38	
	Vereinbarung betr. Kriegsschaden aus dem U-Boot-Krieg		1927-37	
	Schadenersatzforderung der Norweger	1-2	1928-38	
	Flaggen-Inzidente		1933-38	
	Vorträge	1	1931-35	
		2	1936-38	
	Korrespondenz		1933-38	
	Verschiedenes	1	1926-36	
		2	1926-38	
	Erfindungen, Patente		1926-37	
	Deutsch-norwegische Handelspoli-tik -		1927-37	
	Eisenbahn, Strassenbahn, Autobahn		1926-31	
	Kraftwagen		1926-40	
	Post, Telegraf, Telefon und Radio		1925-38	
	Förderung des Auslandsdeutschtums		1927-38	
	Grenzempfehlung, Allgemeines, Einzelfälle		1920-37	
	Auskünfte über Schulen und Hoch-schulen	1	1926-37	
		2	1927-39	
	Kraftübertragungen von Norwegen nach Deutschland		1929-31	

Akten-zeichen	Inhalt	Band	Datum	Serial Nr.
A III	Alkoholverbot- und handel		1926-37	
	Oslo-Konventionen, Osloer Zoll-frieden		1930-38	
	Auskünfte über Schriftsteller		1937-38	
	Arbeiterfragen (Streiks)		1926-33	
	Lektorat Norwegen	1	1933	
	Gesetzgebung und Verwaltung		1927-35	
	Nobelpreis		1934-38	7554/E541860-62
	Trotzky		1935-38	
A IV	Deutsche Reichswehr		1926-38	
	Internationales Rotes Kreuz, deutsch-norwegische Wochen		1928-36	
	Kirchliche Angelegenheiten		1933-36	
	Kreditabkommen, Transfermora-torium		1933-34	
	Deutsches Transferabkommen		1931-38	
	Kriegsächtung (Kellog-Pakt)		1928-33	
	Kriegsschuldfrage		1918-20	
	Kommunistische Proteste gegen die Entwicklung in Deutschland		1933-36	
	Minderheiten Kolonien		1927-38	
	Minister und andere Beamte, Regierungswechsel ehemaliger deutscher Fürsten		1926-36	
	Übernahme früherer österreichi-scher Vertretungen		1938	
A V	Dänemark, Island, Farör		1927-38	5952/E437903-94
	Dänemark		1938-39	
	Finnland		1936-39	5808/E423631-85
	Schweden		1937-38	5911/E433786-832
	Handelsangelegenheiten		1920	
	Handel, Eisen-Kohle, Generalia		1919-22	
	Rechtssachen (Ehe)		1923-24	
	Ausgehende Korrespondenzen		1915-20	
	Rechtssachen (Verschiedenes)		1924-25	

Akten-zeichen	Inhalt	Band	Datum	Serial Nr.
	Abessinien	1-4	8.06- 7.35	
		5-7	7.35-10.35	
		8		
		9	10.35- 5.38	
		10		9911/E694091-94
		11		
I adh.1		1-4	10.35- 8.36	
	Afghanistan	1-2	6.28- 8.39	
	Albanien	1-2	8.21-10.38	
	Andorra	1	9.21-11.36	
	Armenien	1	7.21-10.32	
	Australien	1	10.38- 8.39	L945/L271646-77
	Baltenpakt	1	1.34- 2.39	
	Belgien	1-4	4.20- 2.27	
		5-8	2.27- 6.29	
		9-12	6.29-12.33	
		13-16	1.34- 8.39	
	Bulgarien	1-4	10.20- 7.39	
	Chile	1	7.20- 8.39	
	China	1-4	4.20- 1.30	
		5-8	3.30- 4.32	
		9-12	4.32- 7.39	
	Dänemark	1-3	3.20- 8.39	
	Donauproblem	1		3550/E022508-694
		2	7.33-12.37	3550/E022695-804
I adh.1.		1	1.34- 8.35	3550/E022466-507
	Agypten	1		K1006/K391697-739
		2	8.20- 8.39	K1006/K391740-2088
		3		K1006/K392089-387
		4		K1006/K392388-702
	England	1-5	2.20-11.31	
		6		7633/E545362-80
		7	11.31- 8.39	5836/E425401-38
		8		5836/E425439-77
		9		
		10		
	Kleine Entente	1	9.33- 5.38	3114/D632924-35
	Estland	1	1.21- 8.39	
		2		5923/E435486-564
	Finnland	1-3	12.20- 9.38	
	Griechenland	1-3	8.20- 4.30	
		4-5	4.30- 8.39	
adh.1.		1	8.23-12.23	
	Haiti	1-2	9.20-11.36	
	Japan	1-4	9.20- 7.39	
	Indien	1	1.22- 2.39	K1607/K392703-3130
	Irak	1	7.26- 8.39	
	Iran	1	3.30- 3.39	
	Irland	1	8.38- 7.39	
	Italien	1-5	11.20-11.31	

Akten-zeichen	Inhalt	Band	Datum	Serial Nr.
	Italien	6 7 8 9	11.31- 8.39	2039/445977-6005 7207/E529827-40 2039/446006-32
	Italien-Rußland	1	8.33- 9.34	
	Jugoslavien	1-4	2.21- 7.32	
		5-6	8.32- 8.39	
	Kanada	1	9.21- 8.39	
	Korea	1	6.20- 6.21	
	Lettland	1-2	11.20- 6.39	
	Liberia	1	9.21- 6.39	
	Litauen	1-4	10.20- 4.28	
		5-9	4.28- 7.39	
	Luxemburg	1-2	4.20- 8.39	
	Mandschukuo	1	3.34- 2.38	
	Marokko	1-5	1.20- 6.30	
		6-8	8.30-11.34	
		9 10	12.34- 4.38	5501/E383486-99
adh.1		1	4.29- 7.33	
adh.		1	3.33- 1.39	5218/E308289-304
	Mesopotamien	1 2 3 4	6.24- 3.37	K1608/K393131-435 K1608/K393436-742 K1608/K393743-873 K1608/K393874-4059
	Mexiko	1-2	5.20-12.38	
	Mittelmeer	1	8.20- 2.38	K1609/K394060-149
	Monaco	1-2	1.20- 3.37	
	Mongolei	1	10.22- 6.23	
	Montenegro	1	8.20- 9.20	
	Niederlande	1-3	4.20- 7.39	
	Norwegen	1-2	5.20- 6.39	
	Oesterreich	1 2 3 4 5	4.20- 3.32	K1167/K298071-173 K1167/K298174-470 K1167/K298471-852 K1167/K298853-9081 K1167/K299082-351
		6 7 8 9 10	3.32- 1.34	K1167/K299352-589 K1167/K299590-822
		11 -13	1.34- 3.38	
adh.2.		1	5.33- 6.34	
adh.1.	Oesterreich-Wiedervereinigung	1 2	2.38- 7.38	1716/399042-183 1716/399184-206
adh.2.		1-2	3.38-12.38	
adh.3.		1	3.38- 5.38	
	Ostpakt	1 2	7.34- 6.37	8760/E610897-941 M 37/M001042-53 8760/E610942-59
adh.1.		1 2	5.34- 9.35	8759/E610875-95

Akten-zeichen	Inhalt	Band	Datum	Serial Nr.
	Palästina	1	3.20- 8.39	K1610/K394150-209
		2		K1610/K394210-517
adh.		1-2	3.20- 3.21	
		3-6	4.21- 9.23	
adh.		7-10	9.23-12.27	
		11-14	12.27- 3.33	
	Persien	1-2	12.21- 3.30	
	Polen	1-2	9.20- .7.22	
		3-6	9.22-10.26	
		7-10	10.26-10.29	
		11-14	12.29- 5.33	
		15 16 17 18	5.33- 8.39	1948/435851-6161 1948/436162-291 1948/436292-404
	Portugal	1-2	5.21- 6.39	
	Rumänien	1-3	12.20- 2.29	
		4-7	3.29- 6.39	
	Rußland	1-5	6.20- 1.25	
		6-10	1.25- 7.27	
		11-15	7.27-12.30	
		16-20	12.30- 4.37	
		21	4.37- 8.39	1791/408276-96 4864/E248622-36
		22		1791/408297-358
		23		1791/408359-63
	Schweden	1-2	4.20- 8.39	
	Schweiz	1-4	9.20- 8.39	
	Siam	1-4	4.20- 5.37	
	Slowakei	1	7.38- 8.39	3114/D632936-37
	Spanien	1-4	7.20-10.35	
		5	11.35-11.36	1819/415881-942 3206/D697677-78 4444/E086234-41 4405/E083588-607
		6		1819/415943-58
		7		1819/415959-84 3206/D696679-83
		8		1819/415985-6038 4798/E236711-14
		9	10.36- 3.37	1819/416039-140 3206/D697684-93 5072/E292326-29
		10		
		11		1819/416141-43 3206/D697694-701
		12		1819/416144-171 3206/D697702-03
		13	3.37- 7.37	1819/416172-216 3206/D697704-08

Akten-zeichen	Inhalt	Band	Datum	Serial Nr.
	Spanien	14	3.37- 7.37	1819/416217-290 3206/D697709-12
		15		1819/416291-326 3206/D697713-44
		16	7.37- 6.38	1819/416327-97 3206/D697745-64
		17		1819/416398-407 3206/D697765-85
		18	6.38- 7.39	1819/416408-23 3206/D697786-807
		19		1819/416424-63 2654/D527365-71 3206/D697808-14 5154/E303689-91
		20		1819/416464-86 2655/D527375-434 2941/D569910-57
adh 1		1	8.36- 7.38	1819/416487-91
	Südafrika	1	8.29-10.37	M173/M005490-93
	Südamerika	1-5	3.20- 7.39	
	Syrien	1		K1611/K394518-874
		2		K1611/K394875-5149
		3	8.28- 8.39	K1611/K395150-547
		4		K1611/K395548-6304
		5		K1611/K396305-563
	Tschechoslowakei	1-4	8.20- 6.32	
		5-8	5.32- 2.39	
	Türkei	1		K1612/K396564-629
		2		K1612/K396630-7141
		3	3.20-10.30	K1612/K397142-500
		4		K1612/K397501-870
		5		K1612/K397871-8250
		6		K1612/K398251-686
		7	10.30- 7.36	K1612/K398687-9037
		8		K1612/K399038-374
		9		K1612/K399375-893
		10.		K1612/K399894-40050̸3
			7.36- 8.39	7453/E540380-84
		11		K1612/K400504-28
	Ukraine	1	3.31- 7.39	K1613/K400529-31
		2		
	Ungarn	1-5	10.20- 7.39	
	Vatikan	1-4	7.21- 3.29	
		5-6	4.29- 7.39	
	U.S.A.	1-5	1.21- 8.39	
	Deutschland Präsident und Minister	1-3	1.20- 3.35	
		4		7700/E548612-17 M127/M004682-84
		5	3.35- 3.39	
		6		
I D 1 a	Mein Kampf franz.	1		
I D 1 b	Veröffentlichungen "Journal Magazin" über Führer		4.39- 5.39	
I D 1 adh	Führerreden	1	2.36- 5.36	

Akten-zeichen	Inhalt	Band	Datum	Serial Nr.
I D 2	Innere Angelegenheiten	1-15	3.20- 6.39	
I D 2 adh 1.	Zwischenfälle mit Mitgliedern der Ententekommission	1-3	3.20- 7.27	
I D a adh 2.	Militärputsch 1920, Ruhrunruhen	1-2	3.20- 7.21	
I D 2 adh 3.	Besetzungen im Westen	1-85	6.20- 7.37	
	Spezialband Klump	1	7.31- 2.35	
I D 2 adh 3a.	Verhandlungen Hirsch-Seydoux in Koblenz	1	7.21-12.22	
I D 2 adh 3b.1	Verhandlungen der Saardelegation	1-2	11.29- 7.30	
adh 3b.2	Association Francaise de la Sarre	1	5.28- 1.35	
adh 3b.3	Französische Presse zur Saar-frage	1-2	5.34-11.34	
adh 3b.4	Union Franco-Sarroise	1	9.34- 2.35	
adh 3b.3	Französische Presse zur Saar-frage	3-4	12.34- 1.35	
adh 3b.5	Dreierkomité	1	9.34-12.34	
adh 3b.6	Wirtschaftsfragen	1	9.34-12.35	
adh 3b.7	Rundfunkpropaganda über Saar-frage	1	11.34- 3.36	
adh 3b.8	Ausweisung Röchling	1	11.34-12.34	
adh 3b.9	Entmilitarisierung des Saar-gebietes	1	1.35- 3.35	
adh 3b.10	Handakten Botschafter Köster	1	10.34-12.34	M31/M000958-70
I D 2 adh 4.	Wirtschaftsangelegenheiten	1-3	4.20-12.22	
		4-5 6	12.22- 1.37	9399/E665551-60
adh 5.	Kindernot in Deutschland	1	6.21-10.21	
adh 5a.	Schriftwechsel mit Dr. Pierre Thomas über Kinderhilfe	1	11.20- 9.22	
adh 7.	Reichstagsbrand	1-2	6.33-10.36	
I D 3.	Auswärtige Angelegenheiten	1-3	8.20- 5.39	
		4-6	8.20- 5.39	
I D 3 adh 1.	Deutschland und der russisch-polnische Krieg	1	7.20-10.20	
adh 2.	Beziehungen zu den Staaten der ehemaligen österreich-ungari-schen Monarchie	1	9.20- 4.38	
adh 3.	Beziehungen zu Rußland	1-3	12.21- 4.39	
	Spezialband Rußland	1	4.26- 8.26	
adh 4.	Beziehungen zu Polen	1-2	2.33- 6.39	

Akten-zeichen	Inhalt	Band	Datum	Serial Nr.
I D 4.	Militärangelegenheiten	1-5	3.20- 4.39	
I D 5.	Kolonien	1 2 3	9.20- 5.37	L982/L277958-88 L982/L277989-8106 L982/L278107-469
		4 5 6		L982/L278470-617 L982/L278618-886 L982/L278887-9004 2484/D517785-826
I D 6.	Schiffahrt	1	12.20- 5.25	
I D 6a.	Deutsch-französische Differenzen	1	2.22- 2.23	
I D 6b.	Schiffsverkehr mit den ehemaligen deutschen Kolonien	1	7.21- 1.23	
I D 7.	Luftschiffahrt	1	1.21- 4.28	
I D 8.	Deutsch-französische intellektuelle Beziehungen	1	1.26- 2.39	
I D 10	Protektorat Böhmen und Mähren	1	3.39- 5.39	2819/D548708-41 3114/D632938-3016
I Fr.1	Präsident und Minister (Frankreich)	1-4	1.20- 3.39	
I Fr.1a	Attentat in Marseille	1	10.34-12.34	
I Fr.2	Innere Angelegenheiten	1-33	1.20- 7.38	
		34		2536/D520502-35 2594/D525142-45 5207/E307930-34
		35 36	7.38- 6.39	2536/D520536-92 2536/D520593-634
I Fr.2 adh 1.	Kirchen- und Schulangelegenheiten	1-2	7.20- 8.37	
adh 2.	Politische Vereinigung	1-2	3.20- 6.39	
adh 3.	Kommunistische Umtriebe und Propaganda	1-4	2.21- 4.39	
adh 4.	Antinationalsozialistische Ausstellung in Paris		1.38- 3.38	K1614/K400532-641
Pol.Spec. 37	Innere Angelegenheiten	1	5.39- 6.39	2808/D548549-59 8203/E583088-91 K1615/K400642-43
I Fr.3	Auswärtige Angelegenheiten	1-4	6.20-12.27	
		5-7	2.28- 7.36	
		8-9 10 11	7.36- 6.39	2469/D517463-83 7805/E566362-67
I Fr.3 adh 1.	Beziehungen zu Deutschland	1-29	3.20- 8.36	
		30	8.36- 6.39	5500/E383476-84 7603/E543802-15 7728/E553256-63 5522/E383963-4096
		31 32		
adh.1a.	Grenzzwischenfälle und andere Einzelzwischenfälle	1-4	3.33- 1.39	

Akten-zeichen	Inhalt	Band	Datum	Serial Nr.
I Fr.3. spezial	Vorg. Gersdorf, Springer und Distelbarth	1	1932-34	
I Fr.3.	Parlamentariergruppe zum Studium deutsch-französischer Fragen	1 Sbd.	6.28-12.33	
I Fr.3. adh.spez 1. 2. 3. 4. 5.	Denkmalfragen, Basilika St.Quentin Kaiserstandbilder in Straßburg Armeemuseum Inschrift Nizza	1	1929-39	
I Fr.3. adh.1 aa	Deutsch-französische Verständigung (Briand)	1	9.21-11.22	
adh.1b.	Austausch von politischen Gefangenen Deutschland-Frankreich	1-2	2.24- 7.37	
adh.1 d	Fahne des 3.Garderegiments	1	9.29- 2.34	
adh.2	Beziehungen zu England	1-7	4.20- 1.39	
adh.3	- Italien	1-4	12.20- 2.32	
		5-6 7	2.32- 6.39	2537/D520638-71
adh.4	- Ungarn	1	8.20-12.22	
adh.5	- U.S.A.	1-4	7.21- 9.38	
adh.5 a	Besuch der American Legion in Paris 1927	1	6.27- 3.28	
adh.6	Beziehungen zu Rußland	1-7	8.20- 1.32	
		8-10	1.32- 5.34	
		11 12 13	5.34- 1.39	197M/M006137-57 8747/E610528-33
adh.6 a	Frankreich - Rußland (Handakten Botschaft Köster)	1	11.32-12.35	198M/M006158-75 8748/E610535-78
adh. 7	Beziehungen zu Polen	1-4	7.20-10.38	
I Fr. 4.	Militärangelegenheiten	1-14	3.20- 4.39	
I Fr. 5.	Kolonien, Mandate und Protektorate	1-11	9.20- 5.39	
I Fr. 6.	Elsaß-Lothringen	1-5	3.20-12.27	
adh. 1	Rechtswidrige Behandlung Deutscher in Elsaß-Lothringen	1	9.20- 5.34	
	Elsaß-Lothringen	6-12	12.27- 6.34	
adh. 1		13 14	8.34- 4.39	7831/E568729-50
	Rechtswidrige Behandlung Deutscher in Elsaß-Lothringen	1	9.20- 5.34	
II. 1	Weltwirtschaft	1-2	3.20- 1.36	
II. 2	Reparationsfrage	1-50	4.20- 1.29	
		51 52	1.29- 5.29	M287/M012036-38 M208/M006630-32 M208/M006633-34

Akten-zeichen	Inhalt	Band	Datum	Serial Nr.
II. 2	Reparationsfrage	53 -80	1.29-12.36	
II. 2 adh.1	Garantiekomité	1	5.21- 9.21	
adh.2	Vorschlag Hoover	1-6	6.31- 3.33	
II. 6	Debetsaldenübertrag im Ausgleichsverfahren	1	10.20- 1.21	
II. 7	Vorschläge Henri Bazin	1	8.20- 9.20	
II. 8	Genfer Konferenz und Vorkonferenz in Brüssel	1	7.20- 2.21	
II. 9	Deutsch-französische Sachverständigen Vorbesprechungen	1	9.20-10.20	
II. 10	Verhandlungen in Boulogne, Hythe, Spa und San Remo	1-4	5.20- 3.23	
II. 11	Brüsseler Finanzkonferenz	1	9.20- 2.21	
II. 12	Pariser Konferenz des Obersten Rates	1	1.21- 2.21	
II. 13	Londoner Konferenz	1	2.21- 3.21	
II. 14	Konferenz in Genua	1	1.22- 3.23	
II. 15	— im Haag	1	6.22- 7.22	
II. 16 adh.1 a	Zeppelinfahrten	1-2	2.29- 5.32	
	Wochenberichte zu Abt.II		9.26-11.30	
III. 1	Versailler Diktat, allgemein	1-8	11.19- 4.37	
III. 1 adh. 1	Kriegsschuldfrage	1-18	12.19- 1.39	
adh. 1 a	Leipziger Kriegsbeschuldigungsprozesse	1-2	1.21-10.22	
adh. 1 b	Fall Nathusius	1-2	11.24- 1.26	
adh. 1 c	Strafsache Ludw. Falk	1-2	3.25- 1.28	
adh. 1 d	Kriegsbeschuldigte	1	8.25-12.35	
III. 1 a	Revision der Verträge	1-2	11.29- 2.37	
III. 1 adh. 2	Entwaffnung Deutschlands	1	2.20	731/L222826-38
		2-25	2.20- 2.31	
		26	12.29- 2.31	732/L222839-83
		27 -30	2.31-11.35	
adh. 2 a	Deutsche Werke	1	11.21- 2.22	
adh. 2 c	Deutsche Rüstungsgleichberechtigung	1-2	8.32- 2.33	
adh. 2 b	Entmilitarisierung der Rheinbahnen	1-4	5.22- 7.31	
adh. 3	An Polen abgetretene Gebiete, Danzig, Oberschlesien	1-27	2.20- 5.38	

Akten-zeichen	Inhalt	Band	Datum	Serial Nr.
III.1 adh.3 spezial	Abrechnung	1	10.22- 9.29	
III.1 adh.4	Herausgabe von Kriegstrophäen	1-2	10.20- 2.23	
III.1 adh.5	Memel	1-18	3.22- 4.39	
III.1 adh.6	Weichselfrage	1-4	6.21- 7.25	
III.1 adh.7	Danzig	1-4	3.22- 3.33	
	Danzig	5 6 7	3.33- 7.39	2371/D495541-724 2371/D495725-6264 2371/D496265-305
adh.7 a	Danzig und Ostfragen, Handakten Botsch. Köster	1	1933-34	9214/E647949-993
adh.8	Posen und Westpreussen	1	2.22- 8.30	
adh.9	Ostpreussen	1	3.22- 1.38	
adh.10	Leistungen aus dem Waffenstill-standsvertrag	1	1.22- 1.38	
adh.11	Grenzkommissionen, allgemein	1-2	1.23-12.30	
III.2	Völkerbund	1-18	2.20- 3.33	
		19 20 21	4.33- 4.39	6399/E474702-15
III.2 adh.1	Mitteilungen der Völkerbunds-sekretariate	1	2.20	
adh.2	Ratskommissionen	1-3	4.26- 9.26	
adh.3	Sonstige Völkerbundsinstitute	1	1.27-12.33	
adh.4	8.Völkerbundsvollversammlung	1	9.27	
adh.5	Arbeitsberichte der Ratstagungen	1	1931-34	
III.3	Verträge	1-7	7.20- 8.38	
III.4	Ein- und Ausreisen	1	3.20-12.34	
III.8	Deutsches Garantieangebot, Sicherheitspakt Locarno	1-11	1.25- 1.26	
		12		7965/E574932-37
		13	1.26- 3.36	6403/E474915-62 7965/E574938-39 M208/M006624-29 M287/M012027-35
		14		6403/E474963-5055 M208/M006630-32
		15	3.36- 1.37	7965/E574940-90 M208/M006633-34
		16		
III.9	Rückwirkungen der Locarno-Verträ-ge	1-3	9.26- 8.28	

Akten-zeichen	Inhalt	Band	Datum	Serial Nr.
III.10	Allgemeine Abrüstung und Rüstung	1 2 3 4	10.26-12.29	K1785/K445441-42
		5-12	1.30- 2.33	
		13 -16 17	2.33- 7.37	6400/E474717-55
III.10 adh.	Havas-Meldungen hierzu	1-3	12.29- 5.30	
III.10a	Abrüstung, Handakten Köster	1 2 3 4	5.33- 5.35	8681/E607300-43 8681/E607344-49 M38/M001054-61
III.10 adh.1	Genfer Abrüstungskonferenz	1-3a	1.32-10.32	
		4-8	11.32- 9.35	
adh.2	Viermächtepakt	1	3.33- 1.34	
adh.2a	- Handakten Köster	1	3.33- 8.33	8906/E621718-20
adh.3	Französisch-englische Abmachungen in London	1	1.35- 2.36	
spez.	Handakten Köster (Londoner Communiqué)	1	1.35- 5.35	M11/M000329-36
adh.4	Stresa-Konferenz	1	4.35- 5.35	
III.11	Kriegsächtungspakt	1-4	1.28- 3.35	
III.12	Minderheiten	1-4	1.29- 5.36	
adh.1	Polnischer Wahlterror	1-2	11.30- 8.31	
III.13	Allgemeine Schiedsverträge	1-2	10.28-11.37	
III.13a	Havas-Meldungen hierzu	1-2	8.29- 1.30	
III.14	Haager Regierungskonferenz	1-6	6.29- 5.30	
III.14a	Young-Komité	1-2	9.29- 1.30	
adh.	Telegramm der Delegation Dorn	1	9.29- 5.30	
III.15	Luftpakt (Handakten Botschafter Köster)	1	2.35- 6.36	7845/E569261-64
ohne Signatur	Beratungen der Kommission für die Zusammensetzung des Völkerbundrates (Erlasse und Berichte)	1-6	1926	
IV.1	Deutsche Missionen und Konsularvertretungen in Frankreich	1	6.20-10.37	
adh.1	Übernahme der Geschäfte durch den Geschäftsträger	1	1.20- 2.20	
IV.2	Deutsche Missionen und Konsularvertretungen im sonstigen Ausland	1	3.20- 5.38	
IV.3	Französische Missionen und Konsularvertretungen in Deutschland	1 2	2.20- 5.39	8213/E583335-43

Akten-zeichen	Inhalt	Band	Datum	Serial Nr.
IV.3 adh.1	Französische Gesandtschaft in München	1	7.22- 9.34	
adh.2	Francois Poncet, Handakten Köster	1	7.34- 7.34	8211/E583304-29 M48/M001212-22
IV.4	Französische Missionen und Konsularvertretungen im sonstigen Ausland	1-5	4.20- 3.39	
IV.5	Sonstige fremde Missionen und Konsularvertretungen in Deutschland	1	10.21-12.38	
IV.5a	Sonstige fremde Vertretungen im Ausland (ausser Deutschland und Frankreich)	1	10.21-12.38	
IV.6	Sonstige fremde Missionen und Konsularvertretungen in Frankreich	1-3	5.20-11.38	
IV.7	Sozialattachés	1	1.20- 2.20	
IV.8	Militärattachés	1	7.27- 7.36	
IV.8 adh.1	Deutsche Militär- und Marineattachés in Paris, allgemein (Anlage Personalien Hauptmann Janensch)	1	1.33- 7.37	
adh.4	Personalien Generalmajor Kuhlenthal und Hauptmann Speidel	1	3.33- 4.35	
adh.5	- Korvettenkapitäne Wever und Lietzmann	1	3.33- 3.36	
adh.6	Berichterstattung Militärattachés	1 2	4.33- 6.36	K2101/K571528-853 K2101/K571854-72
adh.7	- Marineattachés	1-2	4.33- 3.35	
IV.9 adh.1	Presseattachés Allgemeine Regelung der Tätigkeit	1	10.33-12.36	
adh.2	Berichterstattung (Anlage 1: Berichte von Dincklage 2: Ilgner Berichte)	1	12.33- 9.34	
V.1	Allgemeines	1-3	2.20- 7.33	
		4-6	7.33- 6.39	
V.1a	Presse Geheim	1	2.21- 5.35	3547/E022169-375
V.2	Deutsche Journalisten in Frankreich	1-5	2.20- 6.39	
V.2 adh.1	Ausweisung Koerber	1	9.32-11.34	
adh.2	Akten Heimburg	1	1.34- 3.34	
adh.3	- Dr.Ihlefeld	1	12.33- 6.37	
V.2a	Fremde Journalisten in Frankreich	1	1.21- 5.38	
V.3	- in Deutschland	1-4	5.20- 7.39	
V.3 adh.1	Journalist Loudre	1	3.33- 3.33	

Akten-zeichen	Inhalt	Band	Datum	Serial Nr.
V.4	Beschaffung und Einreichung von Drucksachen	1-4	1.20- 8.38	
V.4 adh.1	Beschaffung von Drucksachen für Deutsche Allgemeine Zeitung	1	10.20- 3.21	
V.5	Französische Presse	1-11	1.20- 3.38	
		12 13 14 15 16	3.38- 6.39	2493/D517965-67 2493/D517968-72
V.5 adh.	"Matin"	1	1.33	
	"Echo de Paris"	1	2.?	
	"Vendêmiaire"	1	12.33- 1.35	
	Deutsche Artikel in "Revue de Paris" Thibaut	1	3.35- 1.36	
V.5a	Auszüge aus französischen Zeitungen	1-2	12.20- 9.22	
V.5b	Zeitungsberichte von Bordeaux	1-2	1.31-10.37	
V.5c	— von Tunis	1	11.30- 9.33	
V.5d	Verbot französischer Zeitungen und Bücher in Deutschland	1	2.33- 6.39	
V.6	Französische Pressepropaganda im Ausland	1	4.20- 4.30	
V.7	Deutsche Presse	1-2	5.21- 6.39	
V.7 adh.1	Provinzpresse, Wochenberichte	1	10.20- 4.21	
V.8	Deutsche Presse in Frankreich, Verbote, Grüne Post	1-2	9.26- 3.34	
V.8 adh.	Pariser Tageblatt, Pariser Zeitungen und verschiedene	1	10.34- 1.39	
V.9	Presseberichte und Telegramme Dr.Feihl	1-3	11.34- 2.39	
V.10	Tribune-International	1	11.34- 6.35	
V.11	Aufklärungsausschuss Hamburg-Bremen Dr.C.K.Johannsen	1	7.34-10.37	
V.12	Sammlung der Berichte der Presseattachés (Promi)	1	4.37-10.37	
VI.1	Allgemeines	1-3	8.20- 4.39	
VI.2	Chiffrierwesen	1-2	11.20- 1.36	
VI.3	Dienst- und andere Angebote	1-3	5.21- 5.39	
VI.4	Allgemeine Friedensbestrebungen	1-5	7.25-10.30	
		6-9	7.30-12.38	
VI.4 adh.1	Deutsch-französisches Studienkomité (Mayrisch-Komité)	1 2 3	1.26-12.38	K2097/K570726-964 K2097/K570965-1250

Akten-zeichen	Inhalt	Band	Datum	Serial Nr.
VI.4 adh.2	Plan de Vignaud, Schaff.v. deutsch-französischen Arbeitsl.	1	4.33-12.33	K2097/K571251-383
VI.5	Propaganda und Gegenpropaganda	1-5	1.26- 8.38	
VI.5 adh.1	Angeblich deutsches Propaganda-dokument (Pt.Parisien)	1	11.33- 5.34	M181/M005737-872
adh.2	Greuelpropaganda	1-4	3.33- 7.39	
VI.6	Vereinigte Staaten von Europa	1 2 3 4	7.29- 5.31	K2102/K571873-2073 K2102/K572074-172 K2102/K572173-430 K2102/K572431-533
VI.6a	Juden und Freimaurer	1 2	1.37- 5.39	K1616/K400644-854 K1616/K400855-97
VI.6 adh.1	Deutsch-österreichisches Zoll-abkommen	1 2 3 4	3.31-12.31	M189/M005985-87 K1168/K299823-80 K1168/K299881-966 K1168/K299967- K300168 K1168/K300169-254
VI.7	Comité des Forges	1	1932-33	7834/E568900-26
VI.8	Kriegsteilnehmer und Kriegs-beschädigte	1 2-5	2.30- 5.39	M49/M001223-25
VI.8 spez.	Angebliche Spionage Rathke-Frischmann	1	11.34-11.35	
VI.9a	Ausländische Orden und Ehren-zeichen	1	5.36- 6.39	
VI.9b	Deutsche Orden und Ehrenzeichen	1	1937-38	
VI.9b adh.1	Ehrenzeichen des Deutschen Roten Kreuzes	1	1934-39	
adh.2	Verdienstorden vom Deutschen Adler	1	5.37- 4.39	
	Material zur Oberschlesienfrage	1		
I D 2 adh.3 b	Saargebiet	1-37	10.20- 6.38	
I D 2 adh.3 c	Besetzung des Ruhrgebietes	1-22	10.20-12.32	
1 adh.II	Norris-Vorgänge	1	9.34-1935	
2	Frankreichs Finanz- u.Geldwesen	1-25	2.20- 8.39	
2 a	Banque Industrie de Chine	1	5.21-11.28	
2 b	Frankenkurs	1	1.23- 7.26	
2 adh.I	Französische Finanzen	1-3	12.34- 7.39	
4	Internationales Abkommen, Kongresse, Institut	1-19	5.21- 8.39	
4 a	Internationale Handelskammer	1-7	7.21- 7.39	
4 b	Schiedsklausel im Handelsverkehr	1	10.24-11.34	
4 c	Weltwirtschaftskonferenz	1-3	12.25- 8.31	

Akten-zeichen	Inhalt	Band	Datum	Serial Nr.
4 d	Internationales Weinamt	1-11	12.27- 7.39	
6 a	Doppelbesteuerung	2-6	11.30- 7.39	
8	Französischer Aussenhandelsver-kehr (Statistik)	1-7	4.20- 8.39	
9	Ein- und Ausfuhr, deutsch-französische Verhandlungen	1	1.20- 9.26	
10	Elsass-Lothringen	1-4	2.20- 8.39	
11	Französische Ein- und Ausfuhr-vorschriften	1-14	2.20- 8.39	
11 b	Einfuhrverbot für deutsche Kohle	1	8.25-11.26	
11 adh.I	Einfuhr von Fieberthermometern nach Frankreich	1	5.25-10.36	
adh.II	Ursprungsbezeichnungszwang (Handexemplar)		1934-37	
	Markierungszwang	1-3	1.32- 4.34	
	Ursprungsbezeichnungszwang (Handexemplar)	4-8	3.34- 8.39	
15 b	Stickstoff	1-4	9.24- 5.39	
16	Konferenz von Spa	1	5.20- 7.20	
17 a	Deutsche Handelskammer Paris allgemein	1-9	9.22- 6.39	
17 b	Organisationsformen für den deutschen Wirtschaftsverkehr in Frankreich	1-4	6.26- 2.32	
18	Ausführung des Versailler Diktats, Sequester	1-3	1.20- 3.38	
19	Deutsche und französische Aussen-handelsförderung	1-4	5.20-12.32	
		5-9	2.33- 8.39	
20	Messen und Märkte,Ausstellungen	1-24	2.20- 7.39	
20 adh.	Internationales Ausstellungsbüro	1-4	1.34- 7.39	
20 adh. I	Deutsche Ausstellungen	1-3	1.30- 7.39	
	Hygiene-Ausstellung Dresden	1 Sbd.	12.29- 3.31	
	I P A.(Internationale Pelzaus-stellung in Leipzig)	1 Sbd.	2.30- 7.31	
	Kolonialausstellung	1-2 Sbd.	3.31- 9.32	
	Weltausstellung Chicago	1 Sbd.	3.30- 4.34	
20 adh. V	Internationale Ausstellung Paris 1937	1-2 3 4-5	4.34-12.36	7701/E548619-21
		6-9	12.36- 3.39	
	Nebenbände	1-2	10.35-11.37	

Akten-zeichen	Inhalt	Band	Datum	Serial Nr.
20 adh. V	Besuch Dr.Schacht	1 2	8.36- 6.37	3545/E022117-21
	Sonderakte: Grundsteinlegung des Deutschen Pavillons		1.37	
	Handakte zur Internationalen Ausstellung Paris		1937	
	Internationale Tagungen und Kongresse auf der Pariser Welt-ausstellung 1937	1-3	12.35- 2.39	
20 adh. VI	Internationale Ausstellung New York 1939	1	7.37- 7.39	
21	Vorkriegsverträge	1	4.20- 1.23	
21 a	Deutsch-französische Staatsver-träge	1	8.24- 9.24	
22	Deutsche Wirtschaftslage, Lebensverhältnisse, Lebensmit-telversorgung	1-13	5.20- 8.39	
22 a	Deutsche Wirtschaftskurven	1-2		
23	Wiederaufbau, Wiedergutmachung	1-5	1.20- 7.28	
23 a	Nebenband hierzu	1	3.21- 2.25	
23 b	Deutsche Sachleistungen	1-13	12.21- 9.35	
23 b I	— Listen			
24	Auskünfte über Firmen und Personen	1-17	5.20- 8.39	
24 a	Unzuverlässige Firmen	1-9	10.30- 6.39	
25	Personalia führender fanzösi-scher Persönlichkeiten	1	6.28- 7.39	
25 adh.	Personalien Elbel	1	11.38- 1.39	
26 adh. V.	Deutsche und französische Merk-blätter für den Aussenhandel	1	4.37- 8.39	
27	Deutsch-französische Handels-beziehungen, Anbahnung	1-12	2.20- 7.39	
27 a	Kompensationsgeschäfte	1-4	10.35- 8.39	
27 b	Lizenzvergebung	1	5.38- 1.39	
27 adh.	La Vie Technique Industrielle	1	4.25- 2.27	
27 adh. II	Boykott deutscher Waren	1-3	3.33- 3.39	
27 adh. b.1.	Illustration Economique et Financière	1	1.26- 1.27	
28	Landwirtschaft	1-31	6.20- 8.39	
29	Löhne, Preise und Kosten der Lebenshaltung, Preispolitik	1-8	2.20- 7.39	
30	Europäische Wirtschaftsfragen, Weltwirtschaft	1-8	1.20- 7.39	
adh. 1	Zollfrieden	1-2	9.29-10.33	

Akten-zeichen	Inhalt	Band	Datum	Serial Nr.
30.adh. II.	Automobilindustrie	1-2	9.29-10.35	
adh.III.	Wiederaufbau von Mittel- und Osteuropa- Stresa	1	5.32-12.33	
adh.IV	Weltwirtschaftskonferenz und Weltweizenkonferenz der Goldblockländer	1-3	8.32- 3.35	
31.	Rheinlande	1	2.20-12.25	
31 a	– Währungsfragen	1	1.23-11.23	
32	Saargebiet	1-2	1.23- 9.34	
34	Deutsch-französische Zeitungs-gründung, Zeitungspropaganda	1-6	6.20- 2.39	
	Comité National d'Expansion Economique	1 Sbd.	8.21- 5.27	
36	Arbeiter-, Beamten- und sonstige Fragen	1-16	9.20- 8.39	
36 a	Unterrichts- und Lehrlingsfragen Gewerbekammer	1-3	3.23- 1.38	
36 b	Arbeitslosigkeit, Arbeitslosen-fürsorge, Arbeitsbeschaffungs-maßnahmen	1-4	11.30- 5.39	
36 c	Arbeitszeit und -dauer	1-3	1.22- 5.39	
38	Exchanges generaux, Paris		4.20- 7.20	
39	Schiffahrt, Hafenbauten, Fischerei, Meeresforschungen	1-21	8.20- 8.39	
39 a	Binnenschiffahrt, Kanäle	1-4	3.24- 7.39	
39 b	Behandlung deutscher Schiffe in französischen Häfen	1-3	8.22-11.35	
39 adh.I.	Hochseeschiffsfunk	1	3.24- 2.30	
adh. II	Suezkanal, Anstellung von Deutschen	1-4	11.29- 8.39	
41	Arbeitsverträge Frankreichs mit anderen Staaten	1	1.20- 7.31	
42	Seuchenwesen, Gesundheitswesen	1-6	8.20- 7.39	
42 adh.	Sanitätsabkommen	1	9.26- 7.39	
42	Gesundheitswesen, (Verschiedenes)	1	12.27- 1.36	
45	Eisenbahnen, Verkehr	1-11	10.20- 8.39	
50	Französische Industrie, allg.	1-16	11.20- 7.39	
50 adh. II.	Film, Deutschland und Frankreich	1-6	2.28- 8.39	
50-a	Französischer Handel, Handels-recht, Allgemeines	1-11	1.21- 7.39	
50 b	Französische Wirtschaftsorgani-sation	1	3.25- 6.34	
51	Kolonien	1-14	11.20- 8.39	

Akten-zeichen	Inhalt	Band	Datum	Serial Nr.
51	Koloniale Wirtschaftskonferenz	1 Sbd.	2.33- 4.35	
	Deutsche Kolonial- und Rohstoff-fragen	1-2 Sbd.	4.36- 4.39	
51 a	Marokko, Rechtsverhältnis zu Deutschland	1-3	8.26- 9.38	
51 adh. I.	Marokko, Wirtschaftsverhältnisse	1-4	8.27- 8.39	
adh.II.	Algerien und Tunis	1-8	7.29- 8.39	
adh.III	Französisch Westafrika und Französisch Äquatorialafrika	1-2	10.29- 7.39	
adh.IV.	Indochina	1-3	9.29- 8.39	
51 b	Französische Kolonialprojekte	1	7.20- 6.39	
51	Ruete	1-2	12.26- 4.33	
54 adh. I	Kolonialzollwesen, Ursprungsbe-zeichnungszwang in den Kolonien	1-10	4.24- 8.39	
54 adh.	Wertverzollung	1	5.29-11.38	
55	Allgemeines, Sammelberichte über französische Handelsvertrags-politik	1-2	12.20- 7.39	
	Wirtschaftliche Beziehungen Frankreichs zu Belgien-Luxemburg	1-7	12.20- 7.39	
	- China	1	2.23- 7.39	
	- Ägypten,Abessinien	1	7.28- 3.38	K1617/K400898-949
	- England, Irland engl.Dominiens	1-3	3.21-11.33	
	- England, Irland engl.Dominiens	4-6	12.33- 8.39	
	- Finnland	1	7.21- 7.39	
	- Griechenland	1-3	5.22- 7.39	
	- Holland	1-2	11.22- 6.39	
	- Japan	1-2	1.22- 8.39	
	- Jugoslavien Albanien	1-3	5.21- 7.39	
	- Italien	1-5	7.20- 8.39	
	- Mittel- und Süd-amerika einschl. Haiti	1-6	12.21- 7.39	
	- Monaco	1	11.32- 8.39	
	- Oesterreich, Ungarn	1-4	7.21- 6.39	
	- Polen	1-5	8.21- 8.39	
	- Portugal	1	5.21- 4.37	
	- Rumänien, Bulgarien	1-3	12.20- 7.39	
	- Baltenstaaten	1-3	1.21- 5.39	
	- Russland	1-5	11.20- 4.39	
	- Schweiz	1-3	12.21- 7.39	
	- Siam	1	6.25- 4.39	

Akten-zeichen	Inhalt	Band	Datum	Serial Nr.
55	Wirtschaftliche Beziehungen Frankreichs zu Skandinavien	1-2	7.20- 4.39	
	– Spanien	1-4	12.20- 8.39	
	– Slowakei	1		
	– Tschechoslowakei	1-2	4.21- 6.39	
	– Böhmen u. Mähren	3-4		
	– Türkei, Syrien, Irak, Libanon, Persien und Afghanistan	1-3	10.22- 8.39	
	– U.S.A., Kanada	1-4	2.21-12.31	
	–	5-6		
		7	11.31- 7.39	6339/E473189-210
		8		6339/E473211-23
56	Französische allgemeine Wirt-schaftsfragen	1-17	12.20- 7.39	
56 adh.I	Französisch Nationaler Wirt-schaftsrat	1-3	2.24- 8.39	
adh. II	Französische Planwirtschaft Industrievereinbarung	1	10.35- 6.39	
adh. IV	Kriegs- und Wehrwirtschaft	1-2	9.38- 8.39	
56 spez.	Enquête	1-3	11.26- 1.38	
56		1	1927	
63	Luftfahrt	1-6	1.21-10.28	
64	Ruhrbesetzung	1-2	1.23- 9.26	
64 a	Rückwirkung derselben auf französische Wirtschaft	1-2	1.23- 2.28	
65	Wochenbericht der französischen Wirtschaft	1-3	1.22- 2.23	
70	Deutsch-französische Wirtschafts-kommission	1-2	12.31- 3.33	
71	Deutsch-französische privat-wirtschaftliche Abmachungen	3-8	2.32- 3.39	
75	Deutsch-französische Wirtschafts-politik, Handelsvertragsverhand-lungen	1-2	7.32- 2.33	
		11 -13	9.34- 3.35	
		14 -18	3.35- 3.36	
		19		7604/E543817-44 7829/E568715-23
		20	3.36-11.38	7640/E545731-42
		21		
		22		
		23		
		24		2485/D517829-63
		25	4.38- 8.39	2485/D517864-71
		26		
75 adh.I		1-10	11.32- 9.34	

Akten-zeichen	Inhalt	Band	Datum	Serial Nr.
75 adh. II	Deutsche zollrechtliche Stellung in Syrien nach Austritt aus SDN	1-3	6.35- 6.39	
adh.III	Vereinbarung über Pariser Internationale Ausstellung	1	4.37-10.37	
adh. I	Wertfestsetzung	1-3	4.36- 8.39	
	Telegramme	1-2	2.32- 6.39	
	- Weymann	1	7.35	
76	Saarakten	1-9	3.25-12.32	
I 9 a	Geldüberweisungen an Avignon-gefangene	1	10.20-10.21	
I 9 adh.	v. Mutius	1	2.32- 8.32	
I 10	Französische Beamte, In- und Auslandsdienst	1-2	1.20- 7.36	
I 25	Hauptausschuss für Kriegsgefan-gene	1	3.20-10.22	
I 25 adh.	Unterschlagung Lepper	1	9.20-12.22	
I 28	Friedensdelegation	1	11.19- 5.27	
I 28 a	Kriegslastenkommission	1-2	6.20-10.33	
I 28 b	Vertreter der Ruhrkohlenkommis-sion	1	11.22	
I 28 c	Delegationsverhandlungen Grünau, Ritter	1	2.29-11.35	
I 30 k	Reichspräsident	1-4	3.25- 1.37	
	Französische Statistiken	1	4.21- 6.26	
II 2	Eisenbahnen	1-2	4.20-10.35	
II 3	Schiffahrt, allgemein	1	6.20-10.35	
II 3 a	Lotsenwesen	1	12.20- 1.21	
II 3 b	Kieler Kanal, Kaiser Wilhelm-Kanal	1	6.20- 4.29	
II 3 c	Prisenurteile	1	3.20- 3.27	
II 3 d	Vermessungen	1	7.14- 9.20	
II 3 e	Suez-Kanal	1	7.20- 1.27	
II 3 f	Schiffsunfälle	1	4.20- 4.29	
II 3 g	Binnenschiffahrt, Rheinlandkom-mission, Oderakte, Oderkommission Donauschiffahrt, Donaukommission und Konferenz	1-14	9.20- 7.39	
	1 Beiheft: Bemannung der Rhein-schiffe		1.24-11.27	
II 3 g adh.	Eichung der Binnenschiffe	1-2	11.25-11.35	
II 3 h	Nautisches Jahrbuch, Signal-stationen	1	6.21- 4.36	

Akten-zeichen	Inhalt	Band	Datum	Serial Nr.
II 3 i	Deutsche Vertreter bei den Internationalen Stromkommissionen	1-3	5.22-10.36	
II 4	Luftwesen	1-9	2.20- 5.30	
II 4 a	Handelsluftfahrt	1	12.28- 3.29	
II 5	Post, Telegrafen, Funk	1-3	4.20- 4.36	
II 5 a	Postdienstgebühren Mühlhausen	1	2.20- 4.21	
II 6	Internationales Büro für Maße und Gewichte	1-3	5.20- 1.34	
II 9	Ein- und Auswanderung	1	12.20- 5.34	
II 10	Wirtschaftssachen, Verschiedenes	1	8.20-11.35	
II 10 a	Handelsanfragen	1	1.20- 3.26	
II 11	Kongresse, Konferenzen, Verschiedenes	1-11	1.21-12.38	
II 11 a	Sonderband: Weltkongress für Freizeit und Erholung in Hamburg		10.35- 7.36	
II 11 adh.	Deutsch-französische Katholische Konferenz 1929 in Berlin	1	8.28- 4.30	
II 11 adh.1.	Belgisch-deutsche katholische Besprechungen	1	5.30- 7.30	
II 11 a	Internationale Donaukonferenz	1-2	9.20-11.30	
II 11 c	Interparlamentarische Konferenz 1927	1	6.27- 7.30	
II 11 d	Europäische Donaukommission	1	5.27-10.30	
II 12	Patente, Erfindungen, Lizenzen	1	8.20-10.35	
II 13 d	Sanitätsübereinkunft 1912 und 1926	1	7.20- 7.26	
II 14	Kolonialwesen	1	1.20- 9.31	
II 16	Kleiner Grenzverkehr und Saarangelegenheiten	1-4	3.28-12.38	
II 18	Ausstellungen	1-7	3.20- 1.37	
II 18 adh.1	Goethefeier 1932	1-2	7.31-12.33	
adh.2	Internationale Ausstellung 1937	1	4.35- 8.35	
II 19				
	Internationaler Landwirtschaftsverband	1	9.20- 5.22	
II 22	Internationales Kraftfahrzeugabkommen		3.21- 7.33	
III 4	Erfüllung Versailler Diktate	1-2	2.20- 6.36	
III 4 a	Ablieferungen	1	2.24- 4.24	
III 4 b	Verlängerung der Fristen Versailler Diktat Art.300 und 301	1	10.20-10.22	

Akten- zeichen	Inhalt	Band	Datum	Serial Nr.
III 5	Strafgefangene und Kriegsgefan- gene. Kriegsvermisste A - Z			
	- Allgemeines	1-3	1.20- 6.39	
III 5 adh.1	Zivil- und politische Gefangene in Frankreich	1-2	12.26-12.36	
III 5 a	Holtz und Carmelich 1 Beiband	1-3	4.20- 7.23	
III 5 b	Haase, Düring, Theissen	1	8.21- 9.21	
III 5 c	Saargefangene generell	1	8.21- 2.22	
III 5 d	Ruhrgefangene generell	1-4	7.23-12.24	
	Saargefangene und Ruhrgefangene gen. spezial	1-3	9.23-11.32	
III 5 e	Ruhrfonds und Sonderhefte	1	1923-25	
III 5 f	Daubmann	1	5.32- 9.32	
III 5 g	Paoli Schwartz	1-4	7.20- 1.33	
III 5 g adh.2	Guyanagefangene	1-2	7.25- 9.35	
adh.2 spez.	Gefangener Schrempf	1	8.28- 6.30	
	Gef.Kreuzer Salamis	1-2	11.26- 4.32	
III 6	Kriegerfriedhöfe, Denkmäler, Kriegergräbergrunde	1	6.37-12.38	
III 6 adh.5	Kriegerfriedhöfe in Frankreich	1	1.37- 5.39	
adh.2/3	Kriegerdenkmäler in Frankreich		2.37- 1.39	
adh.4	Kriegergräber in Frankreich nebst Kolonien		3.37-12.38	
adh.7	Besuch der Schlachtfelder	1	6.38- 3.39	
	Der Delegierte für die amtliche deutsche Kriegsgräberfürsorge. Zentralnachweisamt für Krieger- gräber und Kriegerverluste	1	7.37- 2.39	
III 8	Fremdenlegion, einzelne nament- liche Vorgänge A - Z		1920-28	
	- A.Berger		1920-28	
	- Bernhard-Bütz		1920-28	
	- Carly-Dussmann		1920-28	
	- Eberhardt Fütter		1920-28	
	- Gaebel-Gutmidl		1920-28	
	- Haag-Heinzmann		1920-28	
	- Hebl-Hüttner		1920-28	
	- Ihrig-Kessler		1920-28	
	- Kiby-Kriessel		1920-28	
	- Kuberzig-Loewen- hardt		1920-28	
	- Linkenhausen- Muth		1920-28	
	- Naab-Pullmann		1920-28	

Akten-zeichen	Inhalt	Band	Datum	Serial Nr.
III 8	Fremdenlegion, einzelne nament-liche Vorgänge P		1920-28	
	- P		1920-28	
	- Quedt-Rux		1920-28	
	- R - Z		1920-28	
	Fremdenlegion-Anwärter und Eisenbahnunfall in Algier betr: 100 Fremdenlegionäre		1920-28	
III 9	Kohlenabkommen von Spa	1	8.20- 6.21	
III 12	Sequester (Namen) A - Z		1920-28	
III 12 a	Sequester, Allgemeines, Ver-schiedenes	1-5	1920-28	
III 12 b	Monaco Fall Glimmann, Sequester	1-2	6.20- 5.26	
III 12 c	Sequester Boulogne	1	9.20- 8.20	
III 12 d	- Marokko	1	6.20- 1.32	
III 12 e	- Staatenlose	1	6.20-12.20	
III 12 f	- Lyoner Messe	1-3	6.20- 2.31	
III 12 g	- Ostafrikadeutsche	1	3.20- 7.20	
III 12 h	- Religiöse Anstalten	1-2	2.14- 7.32	
III 12 i	Schule in Rustschuk	1	9.21-12.21	
III 12 k	Schule und Kirche in Konstanti-nopel	1	1.22- 8.30	
III 12 l	Johanniter-Hospital in Beirut	1-2	1.25- 6.31	
III 12 m	Beschlagnahmte Goldbestände der Deutschen Orientbank in Kospoli	1	5.24- 7.31	
III 12 n	Evangelisch-lutherische Kirche Paris,Rue Blanche	1		
III 12 o	Borromäerinnen, Beirut	1	7.26-10.30	
III 12 q	Katholische Kirche, allgemein	1-2	6.30- 9.39	
III 12 r	Evangelisch-lutherische Kirche, allgemein	1-2	7.31- 3.39	
III 12 t	Kirchliche und religiöse Ange-legenheiten	1	1.37- 6.39	
III 12	D."Goeben"	1	9.21- 3.31	
	"Viktoria" Versicherungsgesell-schaft	1	1.28- 2.32	
	Gesellschaft Südkamerun		4.32- 8.37	
III 17	Elsass-Lothringen Angelegenheiten	1-8	1.20-12.36	
III 21	Schiedsgericht Marokko	1	2.20- 3.22	
III 22	Militaria, allgemein	1	9.20-11.33	
	Einreise deutscher Offiziere nach Frankreich	1	6.26- 5.39	
	Tragen von Uniform, Waffen, Parteiabzeichen,Zeigen fremder Flaggen	1	12.29- 7.37	

Akten-zeichen	Inhalt	Band	Datum	Serial Nr.
III 22	Rechtssachen, grundsätzlich	1	7.36- 6.39	
	- Einzelnes	1	9.38- 7.39	
	Ansprüche und Beschwerden gegen den französischen Staat	1	2.37- 8.39	
	Ansprüche und Beschwerden gegen den deutschen Staat	1	6.38	8372/E590680-82
	Schiedsgerichtsverträge	1	3.24-12.29	
V 1	Kunst und Wissenschaft, allgemein	1-23	6.20-12.36	
V 1 adh.	Messages	1	4.31- 8.33	
V 1 a	Grab und Denkmal Heinrich Heine	1	3.23-12.35	
V 1 b	Theater, Konzerte, Vorträge	1-14	10.26- 1.37	
V 1 c	Kulturfonds	1-5	2.29- 8.39	
V 1 d	Deutsche Kunstgesellschaft, Kunstaustausch	1	4.28- 3.35	
	Kulturpolitik, internationale Kulturbeziehungen	1-2	12.36- 8.39	
V 1 e	Jenner Welttheater	1	12.27	
V 2	Empfehlung für Nationalbibliothek	1-2	1920-27	
V 3	Handschriftenbeschaffung	1-13	1920-37	
	Handschriften Archivbenutzung	1-3	1.37- 8.39	
V 4	Schulwesen, Hochschule, Schüler, Lehrlings- und Gesellenaustausch	1-18	6.20- 2.37	
	Bildungswesen, Erziehung und Unterricht	1	2.38- 5.39	
	Schulen, Universitäten, Studium, Unterricht	1	1.37- 8.39	
	Austausch von Schülern, Besuche, Reisen und Briefwechsel	1	12.36- 7.39	
	Lektoren, wissenschaftliche Assistenten, Sprachklubs	1	12.36- 8.39	
	Deutsch-französische Gesellschaft	1-2	11.33- 5.39	
	Lifa	1 Sbd.	1.30- 4.34	
adh.1	Academie Diplomatique Internationale	1	1.38- 6.39	
V 4 a	Solbergkreis	1	6.31- 7.35	
	Professoren, Lehrer und Studentenaustausch, Besuche, Reisen		10.37- 8.39	
	Studentenangelegenheiten	1-5	9.26- 1.37	
V 4 b	Deutsche Studentenvereinigungen in Frankreich	1	1.27- 5.36	

Akten-zeichen	Inhalt	Band	Datum	Serial Nr.
V 4 c	Cité Universitaire	1	1.28-12.36	
V 4 e	Französische Kulturbeziehungen zum Ausland	1-2	6.30-12.36	
V 4 g	Deutsch akademischer Austausch-dienst	1-4	1.30- 8.39	
V 5	Wohltätigkeit	1	1.37- 8.39	
V 10	Vereine, Gesellschaften, Stiftungen	1	7.25- 6.39	
V 11	Filme und Filverleih	1	12.36- 8.39	
V 12	Wissenschaft	1-4	12.36- 8.39	
	Rassenfrage, Vererbungslehre, Forschungs- und Studienreisen	1-3	12.36- 8.39	
V 13	Internationaler Jagdrat	1-2	5.32- 4.38	
	Literatur, Kunst	1	12.36- 6.37	
	Museen	1	1.37- 8.39	
V 14	Theater, Musik, Tanz	1-2	12.36- 6.39	
V 15	Vorträge und sonstige Darbietun-gen	1	1.37- 8.39	
V 16	Ausstellungen	1-2	11.37-10.39	
V 17	Pariser internationale Ausstel-lung für moderne Kunst und Technik 1937	1-2	1.37- 5.38	
V 18	Tagungen, Sitzungen, Zusammen-künfte, Kongresse	1-5	3.37-1939	
V 19	- anlässlich Pariser Ausstellung für moderne Kunst und Technik	1	2.37- 9.37	
V 20	Jugendbewegung, deutsche und französische		6.37- 3.39	
	Hitlerjugend		3.37- 8.39	
	Nationalsozialismus, NSDAP und Gliederungen	1-3	6.33- 7.39	
	Parteitag, Tagungen, Zusammen-künfte	1	4.37- 8.39	8371/E590671-78
	R.D.B. Reichsbund deutscher Beamter	1	4.38- 8.39	
	Arbeitsfront, Arbeitsdienst, KdF., NSV., AO. und Auslands-deutschtum	1	7.33- 7.39	
	Propaganda	1	2.37- 5.39	
	Depeschenkasten	1	1939	
	Presseausschnitte aus französi-schen Zeitungen A - Z		1940-44	
	Ausschnitte aus Tageszeitungen A - U		1940-44	

Akten-zeichen	Inhalt	Band	Datum	Serial Nr.
	Presseausschnitte von folgenden französischen Persönlichkeiten:		1942-43	
	De Gaulle			
	Doriot			
	Chatel			
	Peyroutou			
	Deàt			
	Paul Marion			
	Ferdinand de Brion			
	Légion Combattant			
	Abel Bonnard			
	L.V.P.			
	Admiral Robert			
	Jacques Benoist-Mechin			
	Pucheu			
	Barthelemy			
	Laval			
	Bucard			
	Catroux			
	Bichelonne			
	Giraud			
	Jean Lagarigue			
	Georges Suarez			
	Henry Lebre			
	Guy Crouzet			
	Marcel Dèat			
	Wochenzeitschriften (Ausschnitte)		5.43- 8.43	
	Ausschnitte aus "La France Socialiste"			
	Presseberichte der Deutschen Botschaft Paris an das Auswärtige Amt		1942-44	
	Zeitungen, Zeitschriften		1943-44	
	Akten der Presseabteilung		1943-44	
	Essen und Empfänge		1940-43	
Pers.G 5	80 rue de Lille 15 Av.Charles Floquet 205, Bd.St.Germain			
Pers.P 3	Personal, allgemein			K1618/K400950-99
Inf.1	Propagandamaterial			
Inf.1 a	Broschürenanforderung und -verteilung			
Inf.1 A K	Propaganda und Auslagen			
Inf.1 b	Hellschreiberempfang, Infa - Fernschreiberdienst			
Inf.I St	Stoßaktion			

Akten-zeichen	Inhalt	Band	Datum	Serial Nr.
Inf.II	Militärische Nachrichten und Propagandadienst/Funk			
Inf.IIa	Verbindungsoffiziere des Aus-wärtigen Amtes bei den Heeres-gruppen			
Inf.IIb	Material über feindliche Kriegs-greuel, Bekämpfung der Kriegs-greuel, Material aus den besetz-ten Gebieten			
Inf.III	Artikel-Bilderdienst			
Inf.IIIa	Schriftverkehr mit den Partei-stellen und anderen deutschen Stellen - nicht Militär			K1619/K401000-002
Pol.3 Nr. 3a	Freiwilligenlegion			
Nr. 7	Parteiwesen - Politische Verbän-de			
Nr. 7a	Groupe Collaboration			
Nr. 9	Comité Ouvrier de Secours Immédiat			
R 4	Arbeiterfragen, allgemein			K1620/K401003-008
R 5	Aufenthaltsbestimmungen Grenzempfehlungen, Sichtvermerke			
S 1	Sammlung von ein- und ausgehen-den Telegrammen			
S 9	Wirtschaftsnachrichten			
S 14	Judenfragen, allgemein			
P 1	Presse und Propagandawesen in Frankreich	1 2 3	1942-43	K1621/K401009-011
		4 5-7	1943-44	K1622/K401012-017
P 1 a	Französische Regierung Verordnungen			
P 2 Nr.1	Presse- und Propagandabeziehun-gen zu Deutschland			
Nr.1a	Aufbaumeldungen			
Nr.1b	Pressestimmen - Wochenzeitungen			
P 3 Nr.1	Französische Zeitungen Französische Nachrichtenbüros Telegrafenagenturen (Havas-Agence - Hachette-Konzern in den besonderen Aktenstücken)			
Nr.1b	France au Travail France Socialiste			
Nr.1d	L'Illustration			
Nr.1f	Zeitungsgründungen und Vorschlä-ge			

Akten-zeichen	Inhalt	Band	Datum	Serial Nr.
P 3 Nr. 1g	Papierfragen der französischen Zeitungen			
Nr. 1j	Paris-Soir			
Nr. 1k	Semaine			
Nr. 1 l	Inter-France			
Nr. 1m	Petit Parisien			
Nr. 2	Deutsche Zeitungen und Zeit-schriften			
P 4 Nr. 1d	Reisen ausländischer Journali-sten nach und durch Deutschland			
Nr. 1a	- Amerika			
Nr. 1e	- Europa			3713/E036742-63 3714/E036766-85
Nr. 1j	- Italien			
Nr.1frz	- Frankreich			
Nr. 1f	- Ferner Osten			
Nr. 1Sp	- Spanien			
Nr. 2	Vertreter deutscher Zeitungen			
P 5 a	Ein- und Ausfuhr von Zeitungen			
P 5	Zeitungstausch			
P 7	Hachette-Konzern			
	Jüdische Zeitungen, Judentum im Kampf gegen Hitler-Deutschland	1 2	1934	K1623/K401018-104
Kult 1	Allgemeine Kulturpolitik des Gastlandes (Frankreich)			
	Kulturelle Organisationen und Vereinigungen			
Kult 2 Nr. 1	Französisch-deutsche Kultur-beziehungen, Vorträge			
Nr. 2	Französische Kulturbeziehungen zu anderen Ländern und zwischen anderen Staaten. Ausländische Kulturpropaganda			
Kult 3	Reichs- und Volksdeutsche in Frankreich Deutsche Vereine, Deutsche Volks-gruppen und ihre Organisation Deutsche Heime, Volksdeutsches Büchereiwesen			
Kult 3a	Rückführung (Elsass-Lothringen)			
Kult 4	Kirchenwesen			
Kult 7	Jugendbewegung - Jugendtreffen und Jugendkongresse			
Kult 8	Schulwesen - Deutsche Schulen Paris Beihilfen			
Kult 9 und 9 Nr. 1	Sprachwerbung			

Akten-zeichen	Inhalt	Band	Datum	Serial Nr.
Kult 10	Hochschulwesen - Professoren - Lektoren			
Kult 10 Nr.1	Deutsch-akademischer Austausch-dienst			
Nr.2	Stipendien			
Kult 11	Wissenschaft			
Kult 11 Nr.1	Wissenschaftliche Kongresse Ausstellungen			
Nr.1 a	Internationale Kongresse			
Nr.1 b	Deutsche Akademie und Lektorate in Frankreich			
Nr.1 c	B I E - Bureau International Expositions			
Nr.4	Deutsches Institut und andere Institute			
Nr.4 a	Personal des Deutschen Instituts			
Nr.4 b	Deutsche Akademie und Lektorate in Frankreich			
Nr.4 c	Personal - Deutsche Akademie und Lektorate			
Nr.4 d	Gesundheitswesen und **S**anitäts-abkommen			
Nr.7	Veterinärwesen			
Nr.8	Buchwesen - Werbung und Aus-stellungen			
Nr.8 a	Verlage			
Kult 12 Nr.1	Kunst			
Nr.2	Theaterwesen			
Nr.3	Musikwesen			
Nr.4	Filmwesen			
Nr.3 a	Schallplattenarchiv Paris			
Nr.4 g	Berichte über deutsche Filme			
Nr.4 f	Verbot ausländischer Filme für Deutschland			
Nr.4 d	Monaco-Film			
Nr.4 e	Propagandistischer Filmeinsatz			
Nr.5	Sport			
Nr.6	Architektur			
D Kult 1	Deutsche Kulturpolitik			
D Kult 1 Nr.1	Deutsche Kulturwerbung im Aus-land, Vorträge			

Akten-zeichen	Inhalt	Band	Datum	Serial Nr.
D Kult 2	Kulturbeziehungen zu anderen Staaten als Frankreich			
D Kult 9	Auswahl und Vermittlung von Sprachlehrern			
D Kult 10	Hochschulwesen			
D Kult 12	Kunst-Theater-Musik-Film-Sport-Architektur			
Kult R	Rundfunkreferat			3105/D626869-87
Kult Ra	Ru - Propaganda Nordafrika			
Kult Rl	Abhörstelle - Aussenstelle West			
Kult R Ru	Verhandlungen mit der französischen Regierung			3105/D626165-868
	Radio - Mondial			
Ru Nr.2	Radio-Diffusion National			3105/D626862-64
Nr.3	Radio-Monaco			
Nr.4	-Paris			3105/D626853-61
Nr.5	-Lille			
Nr.7	Maghrebinische Sendungen			
Nr.8	Funkspiegel			3105/D626888-89
Nr.9	Sonderaufträge - Durchreisen			
Nr.9a	Ru - Mitarbeiter			3105/D626890-7043
Nr.11	Radio-Stuttgart			
Nr.11a	Sendung "Voix du Reich"			
Nr.12	Interradio			
Nr.13	Radio-Toulouse			
Nr.14	Brazzaville			
Nr.15	Radio-Vichy			
Nr.16	- Metropol			
Pers.R 1	Kassensachen - allgemein Voranschläge			2455/D515419-23
R 2	Kassenordnung - Kassenführung			2455/D515424-63
R 3	Beschaffung von Betriebsmitteln (Fonds)			2455/D515464-68
R 5	Abrechnungen Kult R - Rundfunk und Presse			2455/D515469-500
R 8	Presse, Löhne, Gehälter, Zahlungslisten			2455/D515501-73
R 8 Kult	Kult-Rundfunk, Löhne, Gehälter, Zahlungslisten			
Pers.R 8	Nouvelles Continentales Löhne, Gehälter, Zahlungslisten			
R 9	Reisekosten			

Akten-zeichen	Inhalt	Band	Datum	Serial Nr.
Pers.R 10	Steuern, Angestellten- und Invalidenversicherung			
Pers.R 15	Presse, Presseauftragszahlungen			
Pers.R 13 Kult	Kult-Rundfunk, Auftragszahlungen			
R 15 N.C.	Nouvelles Continentales			
R 21	Ausgabebelege			
Pers. 3 Nr.1 NVG	Nordische Verlagsgesellschaft			
Pers. G 1	Geschäftsgang			
D IV Mundus	Mundus-Angelegenheiten		1943	
Pers. P 3	Personal - allgemein		1943	
Pers. P A	Sonderbeauftragte		1943	
Inf.Pol.3	Französische Kriegsgefangene		1943	
Inf.I	Propagandamaterial		1943	
Inf.I a	Broschüren		1943	
Inf.I b	Hellschreiberempfang		1943	
Inf.II	Militärische Nachrichten und Propagandadienst		1943	
Inf.II a	Verbindungsoffizier des Auswärtigen Amtes bei den Heeresgruppen		1943	
Inf.III	Artikelbilderdienst		1943	
Inf.III a	Schriftverkehr mit den Parteistellen und anderen deutschen Stellen		1943	
D Pol 2	Danzig		1939	7991/E575458-62 K1624/K401105-10
	Politische Beziehungen zu Deutschland		1943	3521/E021333-36
Pol 2 Nr. 1	Politische Beziehungen Deutschland - Frankreich		1939-43	2318/E485154-83 2807/D548543-46 2318/E485184-203 3546/E022125-64
Nr. 2	Deutsche Kontrollkommission im unbesetzten Frankreich und in den französischen Kolonien		1942-43	K1625/K401111-130
Nr. 5	Politische Beziehungen Frankreich - England		1943	3522/E021339-43
Pol 3	Innenpolitik Frankreich, allgemein		1943	2318/485242-327 3551/E022808-33 K1626/K401131-36
Pol 3 adh.1	Riom Prozesse		1943	5634/E407339-43
Pol 2 Nr. 1 a	Internierte Minister Reynaud, Mandel, Blum		1943	2318/485204-06

Akten- zeichen	Inhalt	Band	Datum	Serial Nr.
Pol 3 Nr. 2b	Verhältnis Pétain - Laval		1943	2318/485207-41 3523/E021346-51
Pol 3 Nr. 3	Militär-, Marine- und Luftfahrt- angelegenheiten		1943	2335/E486930-69 3797/E042713-25
Nr. 3a	Freiwilligenlegion		1943	
Nr. 4a	Groupe Collaboration		1943	2335/486970-89 3814/E043096-132 2335/486990-7006
Nr. 4b	Anwerbung französischer Arbeits- kräfte für Deutschland		1942-43	3813/043077-92
Nr. 7	Parteiwesen - Politische Ver- bände		1943	2346/487456-65
Nr. 7a	Groupe Collaboration		1943	
Nr. 9	Comité Ouvrier de Secoure Immediat		1943	2346/487466-76
Pol 4 Nr. 2	Bolschewismus, Kommunismus, Sozialismus		1943	
Nr. 3	Freimaurer		1943	6453/E482157-59
R. 4	Arbeiterfragen, allgemein		1943	3789/E042292
R. 5	Aufenthaltsbestimmungen, Sicht- vermerke		1943	2456/D515577-81
S 1	Sammlung von ein- und ausgehen- den Telegrammen,(Depeschenkasten)		1943	3789/E042289-91
S 2	Umläufe		1943	
S 3	Berichtsammlung Auswärtiges Amt Berlin		1943	2456/D515582-602
S 7	Bescheinigungen allgemein		1943	
S 12	Sammlung Schwendemann		1943	2456/D515603-28 3789/E042293-94
S 10	Monatsberichte		1943	2543/D520739-96
S 9	Wirtschaftsnachrichten		1943	
S 13	Englische Sendungen		1943	
S 14	Judenfrage		1943	3796/E042687-709 K1627/K401137-385
S 15	Rahn		1943	2623/D525898-931 K1628/K401386-441
Zu Kult 12 Nr. 4	Cinepress		1943	2623/D525803-97
P 1	Presse- und Propagandawesen in Frankreich	1-3	1943	
P 1a	Französische Regierung Verordnung		1943	
P 2 Nr. 1	Presse- und Propagandabeziehun- gen zu Deutschland		1943	
Nr. 1b	Pressestimmen, Wochenzeitungen		1943	

Akten-zeichen	Inhalt	Band	Datum	Serial Nr.
P 2 Nr.2	Beziehungen zu anderen Ländern		1943	
Nr.2 a	Presseberichte		1943	
Nr.2 b	Presseabendberichte		1943	
P 3 Nr.1 f	Zeitungsgründungen und Vorschläge		1943	
Nr.1	France Continentale		1943	
Nr.1 g	Papierfragen der französischen Zeitungen		1943	
P 4 Nr.1	Journalisten Spanien		1943	
	– Italien		1943	
	Gaillard Bourrageas		1943	
Nr.2	Vertreter deutscher Zeitungen		1943	
P 5	Zeitungstausch		1943	
P 5 a	Ein- und Ausfuhr von Zeitungen		1943	
P 6	Beanstandungen in Presse und Propaganda		1943	
P 7	Hachette-Konzern		1943	
P 8	Garde Francaise		1943	
D P 1	Presse und Propaganda in Deutschland	1	1942-43	
		2	1943	
D P 2	Presse und Propagandabeziehungen Deutschlands zu anderen Staaten in Frankreich		1943	
D P 3	Verlagsanstalten		1943	
P 3 Nr.1 a	Havas – Ofi – Afip		1940-44	
S 8	Geheim		1940-44	3844/E044279-331 3112/D632215-379
P 3 Nr.1	Französische Zeitungen		1943	
Nr.1 b	France au Travail France Socialiste		1943	
A	Abri		1943	
Kult 1	Allgemeine Kulturpolitik		1943	
Kult 1a	Übernahme Prop.Abt. auf Botschaft		1943	
Kult 2 Nr.1	Französisch-deutsche Kulturbeziehungen		1943	
Nr.2	Französische Kulturbeziehungen zu anderen Ländern - ausländische Kulturpropaganda		1943	
Kult 3a	Rückführung Elsass-Lothringen		1940-43	

Akten-zeichen	Inhalt	Band	Datum	Serial Nr.
Kult 11 Nr.1	Wissenschaftliche Kongresse, Ausstellungen		1943	
Kult 10	Hochschulwesen	1-2	1943	
Kult 12 Nr.1	Kunst			
Kult 11 Nr.8	Buchwesen	1-2	1943	
Nr.4 a	Personal der deutschen Institute	1-2	1943	
Nr.4	Deutsches Institut,u.a.Institute		1943	
Nr.8 a	Verlage		1943	
Nr.8 b	Einzelverlag		1943	
Kult 12 Nr.1	Kunst		1943	
Nr.2	Theaterwesen		1943	
Nr.3	Musikwesen			
Nr.4	Filmwesen	1-2	1943	
Nr.4 b	Deutsch-französische Wochen-schau		1943	
Nr.4 a	Deutsch-italienisches Film-abkommen		1943	
Nr.4 c	Französische Zensurgesetzgebung		1943	
D Kult 1 Nr.1	Deutsche Kulturwerbung im Ausland	1-2	1943	
D Kult 2	Kulturbeziehungen zu anderen Staaten als Frankreich		1943	
Kult R	Rundfunkreferat		1943	
Kult R a	Rundfunkpropaganda Nordafrika		1943	
Kult R Ru	Verhandlungen mit französischer Regierung		1943	
Ru 2	Radio Diffusion Nationale		1943	
Ru 3	Radio Monaco		1943	
Ru 4	– Paris		1943	
Ru 6	Bose-Sendungen		1943	
Ru 9	Sonderaufträge		1943	
Ru 11	Radio Stuttgart		1943	
Ru 13	– Toulouse		1943	
Ru 14	Brazzaville		1943	
Ru 15	– Vichy		1943	
Pers R 15 Presse	Auftragszahlungen		1943	
Pers R 8 Presse	Löhne,Gehälter, Zahlungslisten		1943	

Akten-zeichen	Inhalt	Band	Datum	Serial Nr.
Pers R 15 Heim	Auftragszahlungen		1943	
Pers R 19	Fonds		1943	
DR	Doppelrechnungen		1943	
Pers R 21	Ausgabebelege		1943	
Pers R 8 NC	Nouvelles Continentales		1943	
Pers R 9	Reisekosten		1943	
Pers R 15 Ru	Auftragszahlungen		1943	
Pers R 20	Einnahmebelege		1943	
Pers R 16	Gestetner Doppel		1943	
Pers R 8 Ru	Nouvelles Continentales	1-2	1943	
Pers R 6	Prüfungsbemerkungen des Auswärtigen Amtes für KIPD		1943	
Pers R 17	Zentralwerkstätte		1943	
Pers R 15 D IV	Auftragszahlungen		1943	
Pers R 3	Beschaffung von Betriebsmitteln		1943	
Pers R 2	Kassenordnung - Kassenführung		1943	
Pers R 15	Mundus		1943	
	Nouvelles Continentales		1943	
	Inf.		1943	
NC	Belege	1-6	1943	
Pers R 5	Abrechnungen Kult., Inf., Presse	1-2	1943	
Pers R 1	Kassensachen allgemein		1943	
Pers R 8	Mundus		1943	
Pers R 5	Abrechnungen Kult., Inf., Presse	3	1943	
B	Sonderband I Belege		1940-43	
	- II Belege			
	- III H-Belege			
	- IV Belege			
	2 Kontobücher			
Pers R 5 Kult R	Belege		1941	
D IV K	Kartenmaterial		1943	
Pers G 3 a	Eingaben		1943	

Akten-zeichen	Inhalt	Band	Datum	Serial Nr.
Pers G 8	Weiterleitungen		1943	
Pers G 8 a	Weiterleitung Artikeldienst Deambrosis Martins		1943	
Pers G 8 b	Artikeldienst Camille Mauclair		1943	
Pers P 2	Urlaub		1943	
Inf.Pol 3 a	Kriegsgefangene (Rahn)		1943	
Pers G 5	Ausstattungsgegenstände in den Dienstgebäuden		1943	
Pers R 5 a	Mitarbeiter Ru		1943	
P 2 Nr. 2 a	Presseberichte		1943	
Nr. 2 N	Pressebeziehungen anderer Länder zu Nordafrika		1943	
S 6	Telegrammsammlung Auswärtiges Amt, Berlin		1943	
	Telegramme und Berichte	1-3	1943	
	Telegrammausgänge		1943	
	Informationstelegramme		1939	7991/E575463-525 8132/E582067-89 9887/E693537-73 9968/E696719-21
Ref. 1	Staatsangehörigkeit, Einbürgerungen		1942-44	
Ref. 2	Zivilrechtsfragen, Schadenersatz		1944	
Ref. 3	Urkundenbeschaffung, Standesamt, Eheschliessungen		1944	
	Aufgebote,Abwicklung		1944	
	Rückführungen		1944	
	Familienunterhalt		1942-44	
	Kassenbelege		1943	
	Abrechnungen		1942-43	
	Barbelege		1940-42	
	Verschiedenes		1943	
	Durchschläge		1941-42	
	Verladeanzeigen		1939	
WH 12 Nr. 1	Afrika		1942-43	4648/E209541-84
Nr. 4	Marokko		1941-43	5638/E407720-92
Nr. 2	Algerien		1942	K1629/K401442-45
Nr. 3	Tunis		1942	

Akten-zeichen	Inhalt	Band	Datum	Serial Nr.
WH 12 Nr. 5	Westafrika		1942	5616/E402763-73
Nr. 6	Syrien		1942	K1630/K401446-66
Nr. 7	Neukaledonien		1941	K1631/K401467-85
W 1979	La route de l'Huile Marokko - Senegal		1941	
W	Kommerzienrat Lehrer Siemens	1-2	1924-41	
	Passangelegenheiten		1940-44	
			1942-43	
D I	Broschürenpropaganda, allgemein 133 Vorgänge Teil I		1940-42	
D II	- 70 Vorgänge Teil II		1942-43	
D I	Broschüreneingang von Berlin, 112 Vorgänge Teil I		1942	
	- 105 Vorgänge Teil II		1943	
D II	Broschürenherstellung in Paris 107 Vorgänge		10.41-12.43	
D III	Broschürenvertrieb durch Hachette 7 Vorgänge			
D IV	Broschürenversand nach Berlin 40 Vorgänge Teil I		2.41- 7.42	
	- 51 Vorgänge Teil II		5.42-11.43	
D V	Broschürenversand innerhalb Frankreichs und Belgiens 42 Vorgänge		1.42-12.43	
D VI	Schriftverkehr mit Verlegern, 28 Vorgänge		7.42- 3.43	
D VII	- mit den Militärstellen 100 Vorgänge			
D VIII	- mit den Botschaftsdienst-stellen, 178 Vorgänge, Teil I			
	23 Vorgänge, Teil II			
D XI	Lastwagentransporte 15 Vorgänge			
D XIV	Verteilungsplan 8 Vorgänge			
D XV	Schriftwechsel D IV - Le Pont 16 Vorgänge			
D 16	Material für Technischen Apparat 24 Vorgänge			
D 17	Schriftverkehr mit Schrift-stellern 4 Vorgänge			
D 18	Betreuungs- und Karteiberichte 9 Vorgänge			

Akten-zeichen	Inhalt	Band	Datum	Serial Nr.
R 5	Passierscheine 25 Vorgänge			
Pers R	Kassensachen 137 Vorgänge			
Pers G	Geschäftsgang 108 Vorgänge Teil I		1942	
	– 151 Vorgänge Teil II		1943–44	
Pers C 3 a	Eingaben, Bewerbungen 7 Vorgänge			
Pers C4	Grundstückverwaltung 21 Vorgänge		1941–42	
Pers C5	Büromaterial, Inventar 31 Vorgänge		1941–43	
Kult 11 Nr. 2	Fotos, Plakate, Flugblätter 136 Vorgänge			
	Allgemeines 185 Vorgänge		1941–43	

	Rednereinsatz
	    allgemein 21 Vorgänge
	    Schürmann 2 Vorgänge
	    Dr.Jessen 36 Vorgänge
	    Zapp 50 Vorgänge			

	Judenfragen 23 Vorgänge		1942–44	
	Schaufenster in Paris und Bann- meile 19 Vorgänge			
	Notizen Teil I 405 Vorgänge			
	Notizen Teil II 257 Vorgänge			
	Berichtsammlung 668 Vorgänge		1941–42	
	– 463 Vorgänge			
	Sammlung ausgehender Telegramme Teil I und II 107 Vorgänge			
	Veranstaltung, Verschiedenes		1942	
Kult I	Allgemeine Kulturpolitik des Gastlandes (Frankreich) Kulturelle Organisationen und Vereinigungen		7.42–12.42	
Kult 2 Nr. 1	Französisch-deutsche Kulturbe- ziehungen. Vorträge		7.42–12.42	
Nr. 2	Französische Kulturbeziehungen zu anderen Ländern und zwischen anderen Staaten, ausländische Kulturpropaganda		7.42–12.42	
Kult 3	Reichs- und Volksdeutsche in Frankreich - Deutsche Vereine Deutsche Heime. Volksdeutsches Büchereiwesen		7.42–12.42	
Kult 4	Kirchenwesen		7.42–12.42	
Kult 10	Hochschulwesen - Professoren - Lektoren		7.42–12.42	
Kult 11 Nr. 1	Wissenschaftliche Kongresse, Ausstellungen		7.42–12.42	

Akten-zeichen	Inhalt	Band	Datum	Serial Nr.
Kult 11 Nr. 1	Wissenschaftliche Kongresse, Ausstellungen		7.42-12.42	
(Breker)	Breker-Ausstellung in Paris		1942	
Kult 11 Nr. 1 A	Internationale Kongresse		7.42-12.42	
Nr. 4	Deutsches Institut Paris und andere Institute		7.42-12.42	
Nr. 8	Buchwesen - Werbung und Ausstellung		7.42-12.42	
Nr. 8 A	Verlage		7.42-12.42	
(Sorlot)	Verlag Sorlot		1942	
Kult 12 Nr. 1	Kunst		7.42-12.42	
Nr. 2	Theaterwesen		7.42-12.42	
Nr. 3	Musikwesen		7.42-12.42	
Nr. 4 I	Filmwesen		1.42- 6.42	
Nr. 4 II			7.42-12.42	
D Kult I	Deutsche Kulturpolitik		7.42-12.42	5639/E407794-811
D Kult I Nr. 1	Deutsche Kulturwerbung im Ausland Vorträge		7.42-12.42	
P 1 (I u.II)	Presse- und Propagandawesen in Frankreich		1.42-12.42	
P 1 A	Französische Regierung Verordnungen		1.42-12.42	
P 2 Nr.1	Presse- und Propagandabeziehun-gen zu Deutschland		1.42-12.42	
P 2 Nr. 1 A	Aufbaumeldungen		1.42-12.42	
P 2 Nr.2	Beziehungen zu anderen Ländern		1.42- 6.42	
			7.42-12.42	
Nr. 2 A	Presseberichte		1.42- 8.42	
I u. II			8.42-12.42	
P 2 Nr. 2 N	Beziehungen zu anderen Ländern (Nordafrika)		10.42-12.42	
Nr. 2 B	Presse-Abendberichte		1.42-12.42	
P 3 Nr.1	Französische Zeitungen, Französisches Nachrichtenbüro, Telegrafenagenturen		1.42-12.42	
P 3 Nr. 1 B	- France au Travail		8.40- 9.42	
Nr. 1 C	- Nouvelles Continen-tales		1.42-12.42	
Nr. 1 D	- L'Illustration		8.40- 9.42	
Nr. 1 E	- La Terre Francaise		4.41-12.42	

Akten-zeichen	Inhalt	Band	Datum	Serial Nr.
P 3 Nr. 1 F	Französische Zeitungsgründungen und Vorschläge		7.41- 9.42	
Nr. 1 G	Papierfragen der französischen Zeitungen		1941-42	
Nr. 2	Deutsche Zeitungen und Zeit-schriften		6.40-12.42	
P 4 Nr. 1 D	Reisen ausländischer Journali-sten nach und durch Deutschland		9.41- 9.42	
P 4 Nr.1 Frank-reich	Französische Jornalisten		7.42-12.42	
Europa	Journalisten allgemein		1942	
Italien	Italienische Journalisten		1942	
Spanien	Spanische Journalisten		1942	
P 4 Nr.2	Vertreter deutscher Zeitungen		1942	
P 5	Zeitungstausch		1942	
P 5 A	Ein- und Ausfuhr von Zeitungen		1942	
P 6	Beanstandungen in Presse und Propaganda		1942	
P 7	Hachette-Konzern		1941-42	
D P 1	Presse und Propaganda in Deutschland		1942	
D P 2	Presse- und Propagandabeziehun-gen Deutschlands zu anderen Staaten als Frankreich		1942	
D P 3	Verlagsanstalten, Zeitungen, Nachrichtenbüros, Telegrafen-agenturen		1940-42	
Kult R	Rundfunkreferat		1.42-12.42	
Kult R-Ru	Verhandlungen mit der Französi-schen Regierung		1.42-12.42	
Kult R Nr. 1	Abhörstelle Aussenstelle West		1.42-12.42	
Ru Nr. 2	Radio-Diffusion National		1.42-12.42	
Ru Nr. 4	Radio-Paris		1.42-12.42	
Ru Nr. 7	Maghrebinische Sendungen		1.42-12.42	
Ru Nr. 9	Sonderaufträge Durchreisen		1.42-12.42	
Ru Nr.10	Radio Travail		1.42-12.42	

Akten-zeichen	Inhalt	Band	Datum	Serial Nr.
Pol 2 Nr. 1	Beziehungen Frankreichs zu Deutschland	1	6.40-11.40	3485/E019424-63 2624/D525934-47
		2	12.40- 6.41	3485/E019464-68 2670/D528133-289
		3	6.41-12.42	3485/E019469-505 2724/D532744-81
		4	1.43- 7.44	
Pol 2 Nr. 1 a	Beziehungen Frankreichs zu Deutschland, Gesuche	1	6.40-12.40	3649/E032992-3020 2932/D567032-50
		2	1.41- 5.41	2940/D569859-907 K2098/K571384-414
		3	5.41-12.41	
		4	1942-44	2939/D569841-56
Pol 2 Nr. 1 b	Gesuche, Schadenersatzansprüche, Erlaubnisscheine	1	6.40-12.40	K1632/K401487-498
		2	11.40- 2.41	K1632/K401500-03
		3	3.41- 6.42	K1632/K401504-33
		4	7.42-44	K1632/K401546-86
		5	1944	K1632/K401534-45
Pol 2 Nr. 1 c	Häftlinge	1	6.40- 8.41	2985/D584525-59 K2099/K571415-63
		2	9.41- 7.44	2985/D584560-662 K2099/K571464-519
Pol 2 Nr. 1.d	Flüchtlinge, Betreuung durch NSV	1	6.40-12.42	
Pol 2 Nr. 1 e	Waffenstillstandskommission (Wako)	1	6.40- 9.40	3697/E035908-54
		2	9.40-10.40	3697/E035955-6046
		3	11.40- 5.41	3697/E036047-146 4635/E208787-842
		4	5.41-12.42	4635/E208843-936
Pol 2 Nr. 1 f	Vertreter des Auswärtigen Amtes beim AOK(VAA)	1	6.40-12.42	4659/E211076-091
Pol 2 Nr. 1 g	Friedensvorbereitungen	1	6.40-12.42	4646/E209480-93
Pol 2 Nr. 3	Politische Beziehungen Frankreichs zu anderen Staaten	1	6.40-12.42	3698/E036149-54 3038/D600476-82
Pol 2 Nr. 6	Diplomatische und konsularische Vertretungen Frankreichs und anderer Staaten	1	6.40-12.42	3106/D627049-68
Pol 2 Nr. 7	Comité France-Allemagne	1	6.40-12.42	

Akten-zeichen	Inhalt	Band	Datum	Serial Nr.
Pol 3 Nr. 1	Französische Regierung, Zusammensetzung der Kabinette, Übersiedlung nach Versailles	1	6.40-12.42	3699/E036159-219 4651/E209786-811 3120/D641618-19 4430/E084276-77
		2	1.43- 7.44	
Pol 3 Nr. 2	Französische Persönlichkeiten (Politiker, Wissenschaftler)	1	6.40- 6.41	3121/D641622-27
		2	7.41- 2.42	4652/E209814-29
		3	3.42-12.42	
		4	1.43- 7.44	
Pol 3 Nr. 3	Französische Militärangelegen-heiten (Kriegsschäden, Fremden-legion, Exhumierung von Soldaten)	1	6.40-12.42	
Pol 3 Nr. 4	Französische Vereine, Versamm-lungen, Veranstaltungen, Genehmigungen	1	6.40- 2.41	
		2	3.41- 5.41	
		3	6.41- 7.41	
		4	8.41-12.41	
		5	1.42- 7.44	3248/E000157-168
Pol 3 Nr. 4 RNP.	Rassemblement National Populaire	1	5.41-11.41	
		2	11.41- 7.44	
Pol 3 Nr. 4 a	Kampf gegen Kommunisten	1	6.40- 7.41	3780/E041149-61 4647/E209496-538 K2100/K571520-27
		2	8.41- 1.44	3780/E041162-64 4653/E209832-61
Pol 3 Nr. 4 b	Arbeitseinsatz, Unterstützungen	1	6.40- 3.41	4645/E209379-477
		2	1.42- 4.43	6442/E481012-57
		3	5.43-10.43	
Pol 3 Nr. 5	Juden und Freimaurer in Frank-reich	1	6.40- 4.41	3748/E040473-85 K1636/K401587-914
	- Teil I	2	5.41-12.42	3748/E040486-95 4636/E208939-76 K1633/K401915-2136
	- Teil II	3	1.43- 6.44	3748/E040496-516 6442/E481058-062 K1633/K402137-804
Pol 3 Nr. 6	Deutsch-französisches Liquida-tionsabkommen	1	6.40-12.42	4650/E209678-783
		2	1.43- 9.43	
Pol 3 Nr. 7	Französische Kolonien, Mandate, Protektorate, Kolonialministerium	1	6.40- 7.41	4649/E209587-675
		2	7.41- 3.42	4654/E209864-920
		3	4.42-12.42	5633/E407309-37
		4	1.43- 6.44	6442/E481063-94

Akten-zeichen	Inhalt	Band	Datum	Serial Nr.
Pol 3 Nr. 8	Berichte über innere Verhältnisse in Frankreich	1	6.40- 4.41	3790/E042299-336 K1634/K402805-938
		2	5.41-12.42	3790/E042337-78 4637/E208979-9039 5800/E422534-40 K1634/K402939-3066
		3	1.43- 7.44	3790/E042380-90 6442/E481095-331 K1634/K403067-73
D Pol 2 England	Beziehungen Deutschlands zu England	1	6.40-12.42	
D Pol 2 Italien	- zu Italien	1	6.40-12.42	
D Pol 2 USA	- USA	1	6.40-12.42	3548/E022379-98
D Pol 2 UdSSR	- UdSSR	1	6.40-12.42	3702/E036380-90
D Pol 3 Nr.4 b	Familienunterhalt, Unterstützungen (Generalia)	1	8.40- 1.43	
		2	9.42- 6.43	
		3	6.42- 2.44	
		4	1.42-12.44	
		5	4.41- 7.44	
	N SV Winterhilfswerk, Deutscher Hilfsverein	6	1.40- 7.44	
D Pol 3 Nr. 9	Protektorat Böhmen und Mähren	1	6.40-12.42	4713/E227965-66 K1635/K403074-80
	Freimaurerausstellung, Berichte	1	9.38- 1.42	
		2	6.41- 9.42	
Pers G 8	Verkehr mit der Deutschen Botschaft Paris und Generalkonsulat Marseille, Algier, Casablanca	1	1941-42	
Pers G 9	Auftragszahlungen	1	6.40-12.41	
		2	1.42- 7.44	
Prot 1 Nr. 2	Glückwünsche, Weiterleitung von Briefen	1	7.40	
		2	4.43- 7.44	
R 6	Fremdenlegionäre, Rentenansprüche und Unterstützungen	1-11	1942-44	
	Termine, Renten, Pensionen, Fremdenlegionäre	11a	1941-44	
	Generalerlasse	12	1942-44	
S	Ägypten und Palästina	1	6.40-12.42	K1636/K403081-102
S	Arabien	1	6.40-12.42	K1637/K403103-22
S	Argentinien	1	6.40-12.42	
S	Belgien	1	6.40-12.42	4807/E237704-83 5896/E433397-414 K1638/K403123-26

Akten-zeichen	Inhalt	Band	Datum	Serial Nr.
S	Bolivien	1	6.40-12.42	
S	Bulgarien	1	6.40-12.42	
S	China	1	6.40-12.42	4683/E225041-51
S	Costarica	1	6.40-12.42	
S	Ecuador	1	6.40-12.42	
S	England	1	6.40-12.42	3089/D625913-51
S	Finnland	1	6.40-12.42	
S	Griechenland	1	6.40-12.42	
S	Holland	1	6.40-12.42	4803/E237268-324
S	Indien	1	6.40-12.42	
S	Irak	1	6.40-12.42	4743/E233254-55 K1639/K403127-36
S	Iran	1	6.40-12.42	
S	Irland	1	6.40-12.42	3089/D625952-58
S	Italien	1	6.40-12.42	
S	Japan	1	6.40-12.42	
S	Jugoslavien	1	6.40-12.42	K1640/K403137-42
S	Mexico	1	6.40-12.42	
S	Panama	1	6.40-12.42	
S	Peru	1	6.40-12.42	
S	Portugal	1	6.40-12.42	4840/E245095-129
S	Rumänien	1	6.40-12.42	
S	Schweiz	1	6.40-12.42	4826/E241011-072
S	Skandinavien	1	6.40-12.42	
S	Slowakei	1	6.40-12.42	
S	Spanien	1	6.40-12.42	4246/E074774-86 5184/E307317-95
S	Südamerika	1	6.40-12.42	4810/E238071-195
S	Syrien	1	6.40-12.42	4760/E234175-200
S	Thailand	1	6.40-12.42	4682/E225013-038
S	Türkei	1	6.40-12.42	K1641/K403143-66
S	Ungarn	1	6.40-12.42	
S	UdSSR	1	6.40-12.42	K1642/K403167-71
S	Uruguay	1	6.40-12.42	
S	USA	1	6.40- 7.41	
		2	8.41-12.42	
S	Vatikan	1	6.40-12.42	
Kult 1	Kulturelle Organisationen und Vereinigungen	1	6.40-12.42	
Kult 2 Nr. 1	Kulturpolitische Beziehungen Frankreich-Deutschland	1	6.40-12.42	
Nr. 1 a	Deutsches Institut	1	6.40-10.41	
	Goethehaus	2	11.41-12.42	
Nr. 1 b	Vorträge im Rahmen des Deutschen Institutes	1	6.40- 6.41	
		2	7.41-12.42	

Akten-zeichen	Inhalt	Band	Datum	Serial Nr.
Kult 2 Nr. 2	Kulturpolitische Beziehungen Frankreichs zu anderen Staaten, ausländische Kulturpropaganda	1	6.40-12.42	
Kult 3	Reichs- und Volksdeutsche in Frankreich	1	6.40-12.42	
Kult 3 Nr. 1	Fremde Volksgruppen in Frank-reich	1	6.40-12.42	4638/E209042-044
Kult 4	Kirchenwesen in Frankreich	1	6.40-12.42	
Kult 5	Ein-, Aus- und Rückwanderung	1	6.40-12.42	
Kult 6	Nachforschungswesen, Warnungen	1	6.40-12.42	
Kult 7	Jugendbewegung	1	6.40-12.42	
Kult 8	Schulwesen	1	6.40-12.42	
Kult 9 Nr. 1	Deutsche Sprachwerbung	1	6.40-12.42	
Kult 10	Hochschulwesen	1	6.40-12.42	
Kult 10 Nr. 1	Deutsch akademischer Austausch-dienst	1	6.40-12.42	
Kult 11	Wissenschaft	1	6.40-12.42	
Kult 11 Nr. 1	Wissenschaftliche Kongresse und diesbezügliche Ausstellungen	1	6.40-12.42	
Nr. 2	Museen, technische und andere Ausstellungen	1	6.40-12.42	
Nr. 3	Forschungsreisen und Expedi-tionen	1	6.40-12.42	
Nr. 4	Wissenschaftliche Institute und Vereinigungen	1	6.40-12.42	
Nr. 5	Gesundheitswesen	1	6.40-12.42	
Nr. 6	Deutsche Krankenhäuser, deutsches medizinisches Personal, deutsche Kriegergräber	1	6.40-12.42	
Nr. 7	Veterinärwesen	1	6.40-12.42	
Nr. 8	Buchwerbung und Buchausstellung, Übersetzungen	1	6.40- 6.41	
	Austausch, Buchhandel, Verlage	2	7.41-12.42	
Nr. 9	Archäologie, Archivwesen	1	6.40-12.42	
Kult 12	Kunst	1	6.40-12.42	
Kult 12 Nr. 1	Malerei, Bildhauerei	1	6.40-12.42	
Nr. 2	Theaterwesen	1	6.40-12.42	
Nr. 3	Musikwesen	1	6.40- 6.41	
		2	7.41-12.42	
Nr. 4	Filmwesen	1	6.40-12.42	
Nr. 5	Sportwesen	1	6.40-12.42	
Nr. 6	Architektur	1	6.40-12.42	

Akten-zeichen	Inhalt	Band	Datum	Serial Nr.
D Kult 1	Deutsche Kulturpolitik	1	6.40-12.42	
D Kult 2	Kulturpolitische Beziehungen Deutschlands zu anderen Staaten als Frankreich	1	6.40-12.42	
Spanien	Spanisch-Deutsche Gesellschaft (Asociacion Hispano-Germano)	1	6.40-12.42	
D Kult 4	Kirchenwesen in Deutschland	1	6.40-12.42	
D Kult 6	Nachforschungswesen	1	6.40-12.42	
D Kult 7	Jugendbewegung	1	6.40-12.42	
D Kult 7 Nr. 1	Hitlerjugend	1	6.40-12.42	
D Kult 7 Nr. 2	Jugendtreffen und Jugendkongresse	1	6.40-12.42	
D Kult 8 Nr. 2	Auswahl, Vermittlung und Betreuung der Lehrkräfte	1	6.40-12.42	
D Kult 10	Hochschulwesen in Deutschland	1	6.40-12.42	
D Kult 11	Wissenschaft	1	6.40-12.42	
D Kult 12 Nr. 2	Theaterwesen	1	6.40-12.42	
D Kult 12 Nr. 3	Musikwesen	1	6.40-12.42	
D Kult 12 Nr. 5	Sportwesen	1	6.40-12.42	
D Kult 12 Nr. 6	Architektur	1	6.40-12.42	
	Telegramme Botschaft Paris an Auswärtiges Amt über die Vorkriegsereignisse August 1939			2273/479636-44
Pol 3 Nr. 4 b	Französisches Gewerkschaftswesen, Sozialpolitik, Einsatz französischer und anderer ausländischer Arbeiter in Deutschland	1	2.41- 8.42	4660/E211094-334 5635/E407345-55
		2	9.42-11.42	5637/E407370-718
Pol III 4	Gardes Territoriaux		1941-42	4661/E211337-85
Pol 3 Nr. 4 b	Französisches Gewerkschaftswesen, Sozialpolitik, Einsatz französischer Arbeiter in Deutschland	2	11.41-11.42	3821/E043500-64 4655/E209923-10062 5636/E407357-68
		3	12.42- 4.43	3821/E043565-680 6443/E481333-78
Pol II 1 a	Besetzung Frankreichs und sich daraus ergebende Fragen		11.42- 4.43	3652/E033043-60 6443/E481379-87
Pol II 1 d	Verhaftungen, Interventionen für Verhaftete, Auslieferungen allgemein und nach Namen: A - K		1.43- 9.43	279/179129-579
	L - Z			279/179581-891

Akten-zeichen	Inhalt	Band	Datum	Serial Nr.
Pol III 2	Persönlichkeiten		1943	3681/E035164-93
Pol III 7	Algerien und Marokko		1.43- 6.43	3599/E026312-34
	Antillen	3	4.43- 8.43	3616/E027109-94
Pol III 8 c	Lageberichte über Nordafrika und Besetzung Frankreichs durch Achsentruppen		2.42- 5.43	3597/E026245-308 6028/E444609-67 M74/M002624-905
Pol II 3	Italien, Politische Beziehungen Frankreichs zu Italien		1.43- 9.43	3633/E028225-75
Pol III 7	Französisch Nordafrika	1	5.43-10.43	3624/E027674-764 6443/E481388-403
W	Französische Wirtschaft, Handel, Industrie, Verkehr	1	1943	6551/E489393-439
Pol I (g)	Aussenpolitik Frankreichs		1.43- 3.43	3833/E044079-83 6443/E481404-10
Pol II 1 a II	Nebenakte Demarkations- und Rhonelinie		12.42- 5.44	3843/E044243-74 6443/E481411-71
Pol II 1 a II	Der Militärbefehlshaber in Frankreich	1	3.41- 4.44	3758/E040521-47 6027/E444589-607
Pol II 1 a III	Der Höhere SS- und Polizeiführer im Bereich des Militärbefehls-habers in Frankreich	1	4.42-10.43	3760/E040562-70 4644/E209340-76
Pol II 1 a IV	Der Befehlshaber der Sicher-heitspolizei und des SD im Bereich des Militärbefehlshabers in Frankreich	1	6.42- 6.44	3761/E040574-89
Pol II 1 c	Kriegsgefangenenwesen		5.42- 4.44	450/223133-235
Pol II 1 e	Deutsche Waffenstillstands-kommission in Wiesbaden, deut-sche Waffenstillstands-Delega-tion für Wirtschaft		11.42- 5.44	3839/E044138-85
Pol II 1 g	Friedensvorbereitungen, - Fühler-Angebote		5.43- 4.44	450/223237-58
Pol II 1 h	Illegaler Grenzverkehr		12.42- 5.44	6443/E481472-764
Pol II 1 i	Berichterstattung Botschafter Abetz an RAM und andere Persön-lichkeiten des Auswärtigen Amtes Berlin und des Führerhauptquar-tiers und Schriftwechsel Gesandter Schleier an Abetz in Berlin		11.42-11.43	455/223777/1-826
Pol II 1 L	Abwehrsachen, spionagepolizei-liche Auskunft und Ermittlungen	2	12.42- 4.44	478/230250-369
Pol III 7	Französisch Nordafrika	2	10.43-12.43	6559/E489636-93
	Tunis		12.42- 9.43	6443/E481765-94
Pol III 8	Frankreich		11.42- 6.44	5857/E428814-22

Akten-zeichen	Inhalt	Band	Datum	Serial Nr.
Kult	Nebenakte, Katholische Kirche		11.4.- 6.44	6443/E481795-886
Prot 2	Italien: Italienische diploma-tische und konsularische Vertre-tungen in Frankreich		12.43- 6.44	282/180463-681
D Pol 3	Deutsche Innenpolitik (Führer, Reichsregierung, Reichs-tag, Ministerien, Personalien prominenter Staatsmänner und Parteiführer, NSDAP, Ostgebiete)		3.40- 3.44	6443/E481854-86
Pol.Arch. 1272/38	Ein Briefumschlag enthaltend privaten Schriftwechsel zwischen Botschafter von Hoesch und Staatssekretär von Schubert			4642/E209279-92

Akten-zeichen	Inhalt	Band	Datum	Serial Nr.
A	Berichtsverzeichnisse	10	1920-29	
		7	1930-36	
A I a 1	Allgemeine Personal- und Besoldungsangelegenheiten	8-11	1931-39	
A I a 2	Rechtliche Stellung der Gesandt-schaftsmitglieder und der Mit-glieder der nachgeordneten Dienststellen(Exterritoriale Vorrechte, Meldepflicht)	1-5	1925-38	
A I a 2 spez.	Spezialband betr. zollfreier Einfuhr von Kraftfahrzeugen		1936-38	
Ergän-zungs-band	Zollfragen (Umzugsgut, Auto)		1928-38	
A I a 3	Rückgliederung Österreichs in das Reich. Übernahme der öster-reichischen Vertretungen und damit zusammenhängende Maßnahmen	1-2	1938-39	
A I b 1	Gesandter Dr. E. Eisenlohr	3	1935-39	
A I b 2	Leg.Sekr.G.A.v.Halem	1	8.36- 4.39	
	Handelsattaché Dr.Richter	1	6.37-12.38	
	Attaché Eugen Betz	1	3.37- 1.39	
	Attaché Dr.Hofmann	1	7.37- 5.39	
	Kanzler Carl Menne	1	5.36- 1.39	
	Kons.Sekr.Josef Stechele	1	10.37- 1.38	
	Kons.Sekr. Fritz Niepel	1	11.37- 5.38	
	Kons.Prakt.G.Haubold (später Sekretär)	1	7.35-12.38	
	Generalvertretung der Deutschen Reichsbahn für die Tschechoslo-wakei (Reg.Rat Freytag, Reichs-bahnrat Müller)	1	1.21- 5.38	
	Vorübergehend zugeteilte Beamte	1	1.24- 5.39	
	Personalien:			
	Leg.Sekr. Dr. v. Trützschler	1	3.39- 5.39	
	Kons.Sekr. Roeseler	1	4.38- 5.39	
	Militär- und Luftattaché Oberst Toussaint	1	10.36- 4.39	
	Luftattaché Major Friedrich Möricke		5.37- 4.39	
	Presseattaché Dr.Karl Frhr. von Gregory		3.38- 4.39	
	Ges.Rat Frhr.von Winter		11.38- 4.39	
	Leg.Sekr.Dr.Krafft von Dellmensingen		11.38- 4.39	
	Kanzler Fischer, Joosten, Wegener		11.38- 4.39	
	Ob.Insp. Karl Ahlbrecht		11.37- 4.39	
	Kons.Sekr. Fritz Geuther		11.38- 4.39	
	Kons.Prakt. Johannes Teumer		4.34- 4.39	
	Gesandtschaftsbaurat		12.34- 4.38	

Akten-zeichen	Inhalt	Band	Datum	Serial Nr.
A I b 2	Der Leiter der Wohlfahrtsstelle des Deutschen Reiches für die Tschechoslowakische Republik		8.33- 8.35	
C III spec.	Akten des Kons.Reichenberg betr. Heinrich Gesellensetter, Über-setzer		12.32- 8.39	
A I b 3	Stenotypistin Charlotte Intrau		5.15- 8.39	
	- Margarethe Vetters		4.21- 8.39	
	- Irene Friedrich		4.38- 8.39	
	- Hildegard Hähne		10.36- 8.39	
	Amtsgehilfe Erich Rinkert		10.36- 2.39	
	Putzfrauen: Marie Kraitl, Anna Lang, Emilie Schuh Heizer Anton Wollein		8.38- 5.39	
	Übersetzer(in) Irmgard Jung, Albert Illgen, E.Schubert	1	4.34- 5.39	
	Johann Oxenbauer, Hilfsamtsgeh.	1	7.23- 2.39	
	Oskar Gilbert, Hilfsamtsgehilfe	1	2.38-12.38	
	Wilhelm Trampler, Hilfsamtsgeh.	1	1.37- 4.39	
	Personalien vorübergehend be-schäftigter Angestellter	1	10.33- 5.39	
A I b 5	Angebote von Beamten und Hilfs-kräften	2	1.35-12.38	
		3	1.39- 5.39	
A I b 6	Urlaub	1-2	1925-39	
A I c 1	Nachgeordnete Dienststellen Allgemeines mit 1 Faszikel: Nachgeordnete Dienststellen in der Tschechoslowakei 1925-28	1	1921-37	
A I c 2	Konsulat Pressburg	1-3	5.23-39	
	- Reichenberg	1-2 3	1925-38	3108/D628968-71
	- Kaschau	1-2	1926-38	
	- Brünn	1-3	1922-38	
	- Chust	1	1939	
	- Mährisch-Ostrau	1	1938-39	
	- Eger	3 4 5	1932-39	3108/D628972-73 3108/D628974-76
A I d 2	Anlageband betr.Schreibmaschinen	1	10.19- 2.35	
A I f 1	Dienstbetrieb a) Weisungen zur Regelung	1	10.22-10.38	
		1	1.25-12.37	
		2	4.31- 5.39	
A I f 2	Kurierverkehr		9.38- 4.39	
A I f 3	Benutzung der Verkehrsmittel		3.26-10.38	

Akten-zeichen	Inhalt	Band	Datum	Serial Nr.
A I g 2	Verkehr mit den Behörden und Organisationen im Reich		12.22- 5.39	
A I g 4	Verkehr mit den reichsdeutschen Kolonien	2	1.31-10.38	
	Hilfsverein Deutscher Reichsan-gehöriger, Prag, Vereinshaus		11.27- 2.36	
			9.28-10.28	
A I g 3	Verkehr mit den tschechoslowa-kischen Behörden		12.21- 3.39	
A I g 6	Konsulate anderer Staaten in der Tschechoslowakei		1.24-12.38	
A I g 5	Beziehungen zu inländischen Organisationen, Vereinen, Klubs	3	1933-39	
A allgem.	Sonstiges	1	1938-39	3108/D628977-9005
A II geheim	Geheime Zahlungen	2	1936-38	3108/D629006-438
A I f 4	Flaggen, nationale Feiertage	2-7	1930-39	
A II A 1	Rechtshilfsvertrag	1-5 +7	1919-34	
A II A 2	Nachlassakten	1	1923-32	
A II A 3	Pflegschaftsabkommen	1	1923-25	
A II A 6	Unmittelbarer Schriftverkehr Abkommen	1	1924-34	
A II A 7	Weitergeltung alter Verträge	1	1920-27	
A II b Ia	Grenzregulierung Schwarze-Pockau	1-2 Sbd	1920-28	
	- Egerland	1 Sbd	1921-22	
	- Georgswalde-Ebersbach	1 Sbd	1920-23	
A II b Ib	Grenzverletzungen	4-5	1935-37	
A II c Ib	Eisenbahnen im Grenzgebiet	2	1927-32	
A II c 3	Oder-Elbe-Donau	3-4	1929-38	
A II c 3a	Abkommen mit Deutschland betr. Elbschiffer	1	1924-31	
A II c 4	Luftverkehr	1-3	1921-38	
A II c 5	Post-Telegraf-Funkspruch	1	1923-34	
A II d	Förderung kulureller Beziehungen	3	1936-37	
A II d allg.		1	1938-39	
A II d I	Kultur. Sudetendeutschtum, Unterstützungen	1-2	1923-25	
		12 -21	1933-39	

Akten-zeichen	Inhalt	Band	Datum	Serial Nr.
A II d 1 a	Deutsch-evangelische Schule	1	1921-37	
	Kultur. Finanz, Unterstützungen	3	1930-38	
	Laufende Beihilfen für Kultur und Schulzwecke	1-2	1935-39	
	1 Sonderheft: Anforderungen an Kultur- und Schulfonds		1939	
A II d 1 a Nr.5	Evangelische Gemeindeschule Eger	1	1926-31	
Nr.7	Volksbund deutscher Katholiken in Reichenberg	1	1927-30	
Nr.8	Reichsbund katholischer Deutscher Jugend	1	1927-30	
Nr.17	Deutsche Akademie für Musik	1	1926-37	
Nr.32	Unterstützungen Professor Otto	1	1925-32	
Nr.38	Hilfsbund der katholischen Deutschen, Privatschulen	1	1925-35	
Nr.41	Deutsches Theater in Prag	1	1928-36	
Nr.42	Stipendium für Deutschstämmige	1	1925-36	
A II d 8	Deutsches Theater in Mährisch-Ostrau		1939	
A II d 1 a Nr.44	Deutsches Theater in Brünn	1-2	1932-39	
Nr.63	- in Eger		1928-38	
A II d 2	Hilfsvereine deutscher Reichsan-gehöriger in der Tschechoslo-wakei	1	1938-39	
A II d 5	Verein deutsche Akademie für Musik und darstellende Kunst in Prag	1	1938-39	
A II d 6	Studienreisen, Einladung zu Sportveranstaltungen, Buchaus-tausch	1-2	1938-39	
A II d 7	Verein für Kammermusik in Prag		1939	
A II d 8	Sport. Jugendertüchtigung		1937	
A II d 1 a 60	"Rixi" Böhmerwald Hotel G.m.b.H.	1	1937-38	
69	Buch von Schürer		1929-35	
71	Lesehalle der Deutschen Studen-ten in Prag	1	1929-37	
72	Deutsche und tschechische Staatsstipendiaten	1-3	1929-38	
77	Tatrapresse	1	1929-30	
A II e allg.	Schutz deutscher Reichsangehö-riger	1-4	1938-39	

Akten-zeichen	Inhalt	Band	Datum	Serial Nr.
A II e gen.	Schutz deutscher Reichsangehöri-ger	3 4	1936–37	3108/D629439–46 3108/D629447–67
A II e Versch.		2		
A II e Asch		1	1933–38	
A II e	Verzeichnis der Sonderakten	1		
22 a	Schutz Heinrich Hoffe		1921–37	
25	— Heinemann	1	1929–33	
26	— Gröschel	1	1929–31	
A II e	Haftfälle A — Du		1934–36	
	— E — Grü		1934–36	
	— Gru — Hur		1934–36	
	— H — Klar		1934–36	
	— Kl — Lang		1934–36	
	— Lang — Mordan		1934–36	
	— Mor — Ra		1934–36	
	— Ra — Su		1934–36	
	— Sp — Z		1934–38	
	— H — U		1935–38	
	— T — Z		1935–38	
A II f allg.	Reichsdeutsche Presse und ihre Beziehungen zur CSR(Allgemeines)	1	2.39– 5.39	
A II f 1	Vertreter reichsdeutscher Zeitungen in der CSR.	1	11.38– 5.39	
A II f 2	Pressepropaganda, Warnung vor und Empfehlung von Zeitungen und Zeitschriften	1	11.38– 5.39	
A II f 3	Presseausgaben	1	1919–23	
	Vertrieb und Verteilung von Zeit., Büchern und Briefen	1+16	1937–39	
A III 1 Allg.	Aussenpolitik	2–4 5	1933–39	3108/D629468–87 5201/E307690–700
A III 1a 1	Aussendienst	2	1929–33	3108/D629488–514
A III 1b 6	Politische Beziehungen Tschechoslowakei zum Britischen Imperium		1938–39	
8	Politische Beziehungen zu Deutschland	1–8	1921–34	
		9	1934	M75/M002907–09
		10 –12		
		13	1934–35	1976/438436–55
		14		1976/438456–99
		15	1935–39	1976/438500–59

Akten-zeichen	Inhalt	Band	Datum	Serial Nr.
A III 1b 8	Politische Beziehungen zu Deutschland	16		1976/438560-615
		17		1976/438616-36
		18	1935-39	1976/438637-60
		19		3108/D629515-26 1976/438661-79
	Schwarze Front		1933-37	9706/E683067-73
	Schauspiel "Rassen"	1 Sbd.	1934	
	Dr.Frank, Reichsjustizkommissar	1	1934	
	Vorfall auf dem Reichenberger Bahnhof		1937	
	Emigranten	1-6 Sbd.	1933-37	
A III 1b 10	Beziehungen zu Frankreich	1	1922-24	
21	– zu Österreich	1 2	1922-36	K1173/K301778-2049 K1173/K302050-334
23	– Polen	1-3	1923-39	
27	– Rußland	1-2 3	1921-39	3701/E036370-77
33	– Ungarn	1-3	1921-39	
34	– zum Vatikan	1	1920-28	
29	– zu Spanien und Portugal	1	1938-39	
30	Teschener Plebiszit		1920-22	
32	Unabhängige Balkanblockade	1	1923-25	
A III 1c 1	Minderheitenschutz	1	1938-39	
A III 2	Innenpolitik	1-2 3 4	1924-39	3109/D629530-46 3109/D629547-83
A III 2a	Aktenmaterial Brünn über Ent-stehung der Republik	1	1918-19	
	Entstehung, Verfassung des Staates	1-2	1919-39	
A III 2 allg.	Abtretung des sudetendeutschen Gebietes	1 2 3	1938-39	3109/D629584-92 3109/D629593-606
	Sonderheft. Auszahlung von Gehältern an sudetendeutsche Beamte, Offiziere		1938-39	
A III 2c	Aussenminister Benes	1-2	1923-26	
A III 2b 2	Präsident der Republik		1938-39	3109/D629607-66
A III 2d	Kabinett		1938-39	3109/D629667-86
A III 2b	Präsident Masaryk		1930-37	3109/D629687-88

Akten-zeichen	Inhalt	Band	Datum	Serial Nr.
A III 2 g 4	Innenpolitik, Verwaltung, Gesetz-gebung	2 3	1930-39	3109/D629689-756 3109/D629757-58
A III 2 g 2	Beamte	1	1938-39	
	Maßnahmen gegen deutschstämmige Beamte	Sbd.	1938-39	
A III 2 f	Parteien allgemein	4-6	1933-39	
A III 2 f 1	NSDAP	2 3	1933-39	9542/E672354-71
A III 2 f 2	Sudetendeutsche Heimatfront (Henlein)	1 2 3	1933-37	3109/D629759-838 3109/D629839-948 3109/D629949-30105
	Auseinandersetzungen in der SDP	1	1936-38	3109/D630106-210
A III 2 f 9	Parteien, Kommunisten und schwarze Liste		1919-24	
A III 2 h	Minderheiten	5-7	1930-35	
		1 2 3	1938-39	5200/E307685-87
	Prozess Patschneider u.Gen. Sonderband III	1	1934-36	
A III 2 h 1	Innenpolitik	1 Sbd.	1919-36	
	Nationalitätenfragen allgemein	1	1938-39	3109/D630276-89
A III 2 h II	Lage des Sudetendeutschtums in CSR Deutsches Landestheater	Sbd.	1920-22	3109/D630211-75
A III 2 h 3	Innenpolitik, Minderheiten	1 4-5	1920-39	
A III 2 h 4	Polen	1	1938-39	
A III 2 h 5	Karpatho-Ukraine	1	1938-39	
A III 2 i	Hultschin	1-3	1919-34	
A III 2 k allgem.	Konfessionsfragen in der CSR, Allgemeines	1	2.39- 4.39	
A III 2 k 1	Tschechische Nationalkirche	1	12.38- 4.39	
A III 2 k 2	Katholische Kirche in der CSR.	1	10.38- 4.39	
A III 2 k 3	Protestantische Kirche in der CSR.	1	10.38- 4.39	
A III 2 k 5	Orthodoxe in der CSR.	1	3.39- 4.39	
A III 21	Bodenreform: Ansprüche der Herzogin von Schleswig-Holstein	1	12.38- 4.39	
A III 21 1	Bodenreform Fürstbistum Breslau	6 1-2	1919-30	
A III 21	Allgemeine Bodenreform		1938-39	

Akten-zeichen	Inhalt	Band	Datum	Serial Nr.
A III 2m	Tschechoslowakische Armee	1-3	1919-24	
	Armeespionage	7 8	1932-39	3109/D630311-38 3109/D630290-310
A III 2m 1	Armee, Militärvorbereitungen	1-3 4	1921-39	3110/D630343-45
A III 2m 3	Armeelegionäre	2-3	1930-39	
A III 2n	Sprachengesetz, Sprachenfrage		1919-25	
A III 3a	Presse - Rundfunk	3 4	1929-39	3110/D630351-62
	Sudetendeutsche Presse	1 Sbd.	1929-35	
A III 3 allg.	Presse allgemein	1 2	1920-39	3110/D630346-50
A III 3a 1	Politischer Nachrichtendienst allgemein		1919-24	
	Deutsche Presse in der Tschecho-slowakei		1938-39	
A III 3a 2	Pressezensur	1	1921-33	
	Deutsches Nachrichtenbüro	1	1938	
A III 3a 3	Presse-Aventinsky Magazin	1	1930	
A III 3a 4	Pressegesetzgebung, Zensur, Postdebit		1938-39	
A III 3b	Kulturelle Einrichtungen, Wissenschaft, Lehranstalten	1-5	1926-37	
	Lehranstalten, deutsche Hoch-schulen und Universitäten	1-5	9.38- 4.39	
	Schwestern an den deutschen Universitätskliniken		12.38- 3.39	
A III 3b 2	Deutsches Schulwesen in der CSR.	1	11.38- 5.39	
A III 3b	Schulsteuern Oberulersdorf		1928-36	
	Unterstützungszahlungen für Universität Prag	Sbd.	1938-39	
	Zuschüsse des Reiches für Extern-ärzte	Sbd.	1939	
A III 3c	Kunst, Film, Sport	1	11.38- 5.39	3110/D630363-75
A III 3c	Sokol	1	1938-39	
A III 5	Auskünfte über Personen	2-4 5	1933-35	3110/D630376-83
		6 7 8 9	1935-39	3110/D630384-409 3110/D630410-30 3110/D630431-66 3110/D630467-576
	Auskünfte Einzelfälle	1	1933-34	

Akten-zeichen	Inhalt	Band	Datum	Serial Nr.
A III 5	Fälschung von Bezugsscheinen über Margarine (Geheim)	1	1937-38	3110/D630624-73
A III 5 A	Auskünfte über Personen, Agenten		1938-39	3110/D630674-705
A III 5 k	Kommunisten		1938-39	3110/D630577-623
A III 6	Propaganda für Wenden in Deutschland	1	1926-32	
	Wendisches Seminar		1921-33	
A III 7	Wirtschaftl. pol. Verhältnisse	1	1921-30	
A III 8	Tschechisierungsbestrebungen	1-2	1924-35	
A III 10	Tschechische Schulen in Deutschland, allgemein		1938-39	3110/D630706-14
A III 11	Deutschfeindliche Propaganda	2-4	1929-39	
A III 12	Protektorat Böhmen-Mähren (Militär. Besetzungs-, Flücht-lingsfragen, Verhaftungen)		1939	3110/D630715-838
A IV 1 allg.	Deutschlands Aussenpolitik	1	1938-39	
	Politische Beziehungen Deutschlands zu anderen Staaten	1	1938	
A IV 1 a	Deutschland und der Völkerbund	1-3	1920-39	
A IV 1 b 2	Politische Beziehungen Deutschlands zu Amerika	1	10.38- 1.39	
A IV 1 b 9	- Danzig	1	12.38- 4.39	
A IV 1 b 12	- Italien	1	11.38-11.38	
A IV 1 b 13	- Jugoslawien	1	10.38-11.38	
A IV 1 b 17	- Niederlanden	1	2.39- 2.39	
A IV 1 b 18	- Nordstaaten	1	10.38-10.38	
A IV 1 b 20	- Polen	1-2	1923- 3.39	
A IV 1 b 22	- Randstaaten	1	11.38-11.38	
A IV 1 b 23	- Rumänien	1	10.38-10.38	
A IV 1 b 24	- Rußland	1	12.38	
A IV 1a 1	Minderheitenschutz	1-3	1924-38	
A IV 1 b 27	Deutschland - Tschechoslowakei	1-4 5 6 7-8	1923-36 1936-39	3110/D630839-46
A IV 2	Innenpolitik	1-3	1926-39	
A IV 2 a l	Wenden	1-4 Sbd.	1919-28	
A IV 1 c allg.	Friedensvertrag und Revisions-bestrebungen	1	1938-39	
A IV 1 c l	Informatorisches Material über Lage und Politik Deutschlands, Reparationen	1	1921-25	

Akten-zeichen	Inhalt	Band	Datum	Serial Nr.
A IV 1c 2	Informatorisches Material über Lage und Politik Deutschlands, Schuldfrage	1	1921-25	
A IV 1c 4	– Garantiepakt und Genfer Konferenz	1	1925	
A IV 2 b	Innenpolitik Deutschlands, Verfassung	1	1919	
A IV 2 c	Reichspräsident	1	1924-26	
	Führer und Reichskanzler	1	1938-39	
A IV 2 d	Innenpolitik Deutschlands, Kabinett	1	1920	
A IV 2 e	– Reichstag und Reichsrat	1	1920	
A IV 2 a	Minderheiten in Deutschland	1	3.39- 3.39	
A IV 2 a 2	Tschechische Minderheit in Deutschland	1	1.39- 3.39	
A IV 2 d	Reichsregierung	1	4.39- 4.39	3110/D630847-51
A IV 2 f	Wehrmacht, Gendarmerie, Polizei	1	11.38- 5.39	
A IV 2 g	Kulturelle Einrichtungen in Deutschland, Alexander von Humboldt-Stiftung	1	12.38- 3.39	3110/D630852-60
A IV 2 h	Presse, Rundfunk und Film in Deutschland	1	12.38- 1.39	
A IV 3	Auslandsdeutschtum, Institut Stuttgart		1938-39	
A IV 4 a	NSDAP	1	10.38- 5.39	
A V 2	Informatorisches Material über Amerika	1	10.38- 4.39	
A V 4	– Albanien	1	10.38- 4.39	
A V 5	– Balkan (allgemein)	1	2.39- 4.39	
A V 6	– Belgien	1	2.39- 4.39	
A V 7	– Britische Imperium	1	10.38- 4.39	
A V 8	– Bulgarien	1	11.38- 4.39	
A V 9	– Danzig	1	10.38- 4.39	
A V 11	– Frankreich	1	10.38- 4.39	
A V 12	– Griechenland	1	10.38- 4.39	
A V 13	– Italien	1	11.38- 4.39	
A V 14	– Jugoslawien	1-2	1924- 4.39	
A V 15	– Kleine Entente	1	11.38- 4.39	
A V 16	– Luxemburg	1	10.38- 4.39	
A V 17	– Memel	1	12.38- 4.39	
A V 18	– Nordstaaten	1	10.38- 4.39	
A V 19	– Niederlande	1	10.38- 4.39	
A V 21	– Polen	1-2	1923-39	
A V 22	– Portugal	1	10.38- 4.39	
A V 23	– Randstaaten	1	10.38- 4.39	
A V 24	– Rumänien	1	11.38- 4.39	

Akten-zeichen	Inhalt	Band	Datum	Serial Nr.
A V 25	Informatorisches Material über Rußland	1-3	1921-39	
A V 26	— über die Schweiz	1	10.38- 4.39	
A V 27	— Spanien	1	10.38- 4.39	
A V 29	— Ungarn	1	11.38- 4.39	
A V 30	— den Vatikan	1	3.39- 4.39	
A V 31	— den Völkerbund	1	1938-39	
A V 32	Judenfragen, Freimaurertum	1	11.38- 4.39	
A V 33	Informatorisches Material über die Ukraine	1	12.38- 4.39	
A V allg.	Kongresse, Tagungen	1	10.38- 4.39	3110/D630861-63
A VI 1	Biographien der Diplomaten mit Ausnahme der tschechoslowakischen	1	11.38- 5.39	
A VI 3	Diplomatisches Korps (Etikette)	1	10.38- 5.39	
A VI 4 Anlage-akten	Bescheinigungen und Bestätigungen	1-2	11.38- 5.39	
A VI 5	Deutsche Orden und Ehrenzeichen	1	11.38- 5.39	
B allgem.	Kleine Anfragen, Interventionen und Einladungen	1-4	1924-38	
	Festabzeichen	1	1934-36	
	Meldungen, Jugendliche	1	1937	
B I 1	Staatsangehörigkeit (allgemein)	5-6	1930-35	
B I 2	— Ausstellung von Heimat-scheinen F - R		1935-37	
B I 4	Aufnahme in den tschechoslowakischen Staatsverband	1	1920-24	
B I 5	Option Hultschin gen.	1-2	1920-38	
B I 5a	Optionen, diverse Angelegenheiten der Optanten	2	1923-27	
B I 7a	Aufenthaltsbestimmungen für Ausländer in Deutschland	2	1925-32	
B I 7d	Befreiungsschein	1	1937	
B I 8a	Arbeitsgesuche A - Z	1	1937	
B II 1d	Eheschliessungen und Scheidungen	1	1937	
B III 1b	Rechtspflege in Deutschland Verschiedenes	1	1923-32	
B III 7	Fahndungsersuchen und Auslieferungen	1-3	1920-37	
B III 8	Vormundschaftssachen, Alimentationsangelegenheiten	1-2	1924-37	
B III 9	Mahnungen und Schadenersatzforderungen	1	1937	
B III 11	Personenstands- und Standesamtssachen	1-2	1920-33	

Akten-zeichen	Inhalt	Band	Datum	Serial Nr.
B III 13b	Grenzverkehr, Preussen, Sachsen	1-2	1928-33	
B III 13c	Rechtsstellung der Bediensteten der beiderseitigen exponierten Zoll- und Eisenbahnamtsstellen		1921-27	
B III 14	Beglaubigungen, Bescheinigungen	1	1920-32	
	- A - Z	5	1937	
B III 15	Nachlasssachen, allgemein	1	1922-29	
B III 20	Erbschaftsangelegenheiten	1	1937	
	Rechtsfragen, die durch Abtretung des Hultschiner Gebietes entstehen	3	1927-30	
B III 21	Gnadengesuche	1	1922-29	
B IV 1 a	Versicherungen, Rentensachen	1	1935-37	
B IV 1 b	Unfallversicherung	1	1921-33	
B IV 1 f	Sozialversicherung, Soziale Gesetze	3-4	1926-34	
B IV 1 g	Selbständige Versicherung	1	1925-27	
B IV 1 i	Bruderladen	1	1925-36	
B IV 6 a	Heimarbeiter	1	1919-32	
B IV 6 b	Deutsche Betriebsräte	1	1922-28	
	Tschechoslowakische Betriebsausschüsse und Räte	1	1921-27	
B IV 6 c	Arbeits- und Gewerbeinspektion	1	1921-26	
B IV 6 d	Erwerbslosenfürsorge	7	1930-34	
B IV 6 I	Arbeiterurlaub	1	1922-34	
B IV 6 f	Masaryk-Akademie der Arbeit	1	1921-26	
B IV 7 a	Bau- und Wohnungswesen in Deutschland	1	1924-33	
B IV 8	Mieterschutz in der Tschechoslowakei	2	1929-36	
B IV 8 b	Mieterschutz in Deutschland	1	1922-28	
B IV 9	Rückwanderer	1	1937	
B IV 11	Übernahme	1-3	1935-37	
B IV 11 a	Übernahme gen.	1	1921-35	
B IV 11	Fürsorgewesen, Armen- und Jugendfürsorge, allgemein	2	1926-28	
B IV 11/12 gen.	Allgemeine Fürsorge	2+4	1932-33	
		5-7	1933-36	
B IV 12	Wohlfahrt-Unterstützung	1-4	1935-37	
B IV 13 a	Rentenabkommen gen.	1	1921-28	
B IV 13 b	Deutsche Kriegsbeschädigtenfürsorge	2	1924-34	

Akten- zeichen	Inhalt	Band	Datum	Serial Nr.
B VI 8	Listen des reichsdeutschen Gross- grundbesitzes in der Tschecho- slowakei	1	1921-29	
B VI 8 b	Bodenreform in anderen Staaten	1	1921-30	
B VI 8 g	– reichsdeutschen Grossgrundbesitzes, allgemein	2 3+5	1926-29	
B VI 7	Städtischer Grundbesitz von Ausländern in Deutschland	1	1922-33	
B VI 8 d/1	Bodenreform Gräfin Althann	1	1921-28	
B VI 8 d/2	– Bayer. Königin (Erben)	1	1921-25	
B VI 8 d/4	– von Ehrenthal	1	1921-23	
B VI 8 d/5	– Mitglieder ehemaliger Herrscherhäuser	1	1921-23	
B VI 8 d/6	– Baron Gemming'sche Erben	1	1920-26	
B VI 8 d/7	– Prinz Alexander Hohenlohe-Waldenburg	1	1922-30	
B VI 8 d/8	– Hohenzollern	1	1919-22	
B VI 8 d/9	– Lichnowsky	1	1922-28	
B VI 8 d/10	– Fürst Löwenstein	1	1921-29	
B VI 8 d/11	– Pinkus	1	1920-27	
B VI 8 d/12	– Herzog von Ratibor	1-2	1922-33	
B VI 8 d/13	– Röders, August	1	1920-21	
B VI 8 d/14	– Schaumburg-Lippe	1	1922-27	
B VI 8 d/15	– Graf Tiele-Winckler	1	1921-25	
B VI 8 d/15	– v. Bettschart	2	1937-39	
B VI 8 d/16	– Thurn-Taxis	1	1919-32	
B VI 8 d/17	– Böhmerwald-Waldhaus	1	1920-32	
B VI 8 d/22	– Fürst Hohenlohe	1	1921-34	
B VI 8 f	Die reichsdeutschen Güterbeamten und Angestellten des beschlag- nahmten Grossgrundbesitzes	2	1926-28	

Akten-zeichen	Inhalt	Band	Datum	Serial Nr.
B VII 1	Deutsch-tschechisches Akommen über den Nachrichtenaustausch beim Auftreten übertragbarer Krankheiten	1	1932	
B VII 2	Gesundheitswesen: Geschlechts-krankheiten	1	1921-33	
B VII 3a	- Ärzte	1	1920-37	
B VII 3d	- Bäder	2	1928-33	
B VIII 1	Entschädigung der Auslands-deutschen	1	1921-34	
B VIII 4 b	Kriegerdenkmäler Königgrätz	1	1920-34	
B VIII 4 c	Schwerin Denkmal in Sterbehol	1	1908-25	
B VIII 4 d	Kriegergrab in Lundenburg	1	1925-26	
B VIII 4 f	Kriegerdenkmal in Oderberg	1	1936	
B VIII 8	Schiedsgerichtshof	1	1927	
B IV 14	Militärakten, Verschiedenes		1920-32	
	- A - Z		1933-39	
I 1 a	Wirtschaftslage der Tschechoslo-wakei, Sudetenländer	8	1936-39	
I 1 a Einlage	Tschechoslowakische Exportgesell-schaften	1	1936-39	
	Exportförderung der tschechi-schen Industrie	1	1927-38	
	Tschechoslowakische Produktions-statistik	1	1927-36	
I 1 b	Wirtschaftslage der Industrie der Slowakei und Karpathoruß-lands	1	1923-38	
I 1 c	Sudetendeutscher Anteil an der tschechoslowakischen Industrie-wirtschaft	1	1924-39	
I 2	Tschechoslowakischer Aussenhandel Statistik, Handelsbilanz	2+4	1932-39	
I 3 a	Zahlungsbilanz der Tschechoslo-wakei	1	1928-36	
I 3 b	Reichsdeutsche Kapitalsbeteili-gung an tschechoslowakischen Industrieunternehmungen	1	1938-39	
I 3 c	Drittländische Kapitalsbeteili-gung an tschechoslowakischen Industrieunternehmungen	1	1924-35	
I 3 d	Tschechoslowakische Kapitals-beteiligung an ausländischen Industrieunternehmungen	1	1927-39	

Akten-zeichen	Inhalt	Band	Datum	Serial Nr.
I 4 a	Übersichtsberichte zur Wirt-schafts- und Finanzlage der Tschechoslowakei	2	1931-38	
I 4 b	Rückwirkung des Ruhreinbruchs auf die tschechoslowakische Volkswirtschaft	1	1923-26	
I 5 b	Tschechoslowakische Kartelle und Konzerne	1	1931-32	
I 6 b	Wärmewirtschaftsorganisationen	1	1922-39	
I 7 c	Freie Verbände der Industrie und Handel	1	1922-39	
I 7 e	Austausch kaufmännischer Jugend	1	1937-39	
II 1 a	Automobilindustrie und Handel	2	1929-34	
II 4	Buchhandel	1-2	1931-39	
II 5	Chemische Industrie	1	1924-39	
II 6	Eisen und Stahl	3-4	1927-39	
II 7 a	Tschechoslowakische elektrotech-nische Industrie, Einfuhr elek-trischer Artikel in die Tsche-choslowakei	1	1922-39	
II 7 b	Elektrifizierung der Tschecho-slowakei	1	1922-39	
II 7 c	Radiomaterial	1	1923-33	
II 10	Filmmarkt in der Tschechoslo-wakei	4-5	1932-39	
II 11	Ein- und Ausfuhr von Blumen und Pflanzen aus Deutschland	1	1920-37	
II 12 a	Tschechoslowakische Glasindustrie	1	1931-38	
II 12 b	Gablonzer Industrie	1	1920-39	
II 13	Gerste und Malz	1	1920-35	
II 14	Graphisches Abkommen	1	1919-37	
II 15	Einfuhr von Gummiwaren	1	1920-39	
II 16	Hopfen	2-3	1925-38	
II 17	Holzausfuhr aus der Tschecho-slowakei	4-5	1928-39	
II 18	Kalk	1	1921-34	
II 19 a	Kohlenlage in der Tschechoslo-wakei	3	1925-38	
II 19 b	Einfuhr deutscher Eisenbahn-dienstkohlen	1	1924-38	
II 20	Leder und Häute	2	1926-38	
II 21 a	Tschechoslowakische Maschinen-industrie	2	1928-38	
II 21 b	Landwirtschaftliche Maschinen	1	1922-38	

Akten-zeichen	Inhalt		Band	Datum	Serial Nr.
II 21 c	Skoda-Werke		1	1938-39	
II 22	Tschechoslowakische Papier-industrie		2	1931-39	
II 23 a	Pharmazeutische Präparate		2	1927-39	
II 23 b	Rauschgifte		1	1929-36	
II 24	Fotografische Bedarfsartikel		1	1922-34	
II 25 a	Tschechoslowakische Porzellan-industrie		1	1921-38	
II 25 b	Kaolin		1	1923-32	
II 26	Schuhe		2	1929-35	
II 28	Spiritus		2	1927-39	
II 27	Spielwaren		1	1924-35	
II 29	Stickstoffindustrie		1	1925-35	
II 30 a	Tschechoslowakische Textil-industrie, allgemein		1	1925-39	
II 30 b	Tschechoslowakische Woll- und Tuchindustrie		2	1927-38	
II 30 c	Flachsbau und Leinenindustrie		1	1921-37	
II 30 d	Seiden- und Kunstseidenindustrie		1	1921-39	
II 31 a	Vieh und andere Haustiere		1	1928-39	
II 31 b	Tschechoslowakische Veterinär-abkommen mit dritten Ländern		1	1925-28	
II 31 c	Wild (Ein-, Aus- und Durchfuhr), Edelpelztierzucht		1	1925-35	
II 32	Waffen		1	1922-39	
II 33	Wein		1	1921-39	
II 34	Zementausfuhr aus der Tschecho-slowakei		1	1919-39	
II 35 a	Zucker		3	1928-39	
II 35 b	Zuckerrübensamen		1	1921-33	
II 36 b	Landwirtschaftliche Erzeugnisse		2-3	1929-39	
II 36 a	Wirtschaftslage einzelner tschechoslowakischer Industrien	A - D	1-12	1927-39	
		E - J	1-19	1927-39	
		K - M	1-20	1927-39	
		N - Z	1-17	1927-39	
III 1	Kreditauskünfte		1-2	1932-36	
III 2 a	Forderungen	A - Z	1	1934	
	-	A - Z	1-2	1935-36	
	-	A - Z	1	1937	
	-	A - Z	1	1938	

Akten-zeichen	Inhalt	Band	Datum	Serial Nr.
III 2 b	Forderungen generell	1	1924-39	
III 2 c	Nichterfüllte Lieferungsver-pflichtungen	1	1924-39	
III 2 d	Schwarze Liste	1	1923-32	
	Marsik (Firma)	1	1928-34	
III 3 a	Vertreter deutscher Firmen in der Tschechoslowakei	2-3	1929-39	
III 3 b	Gewerbelegitimationskarten für Handlungsreisende	1	1926-39	
III 4	Handelsspionage	1	1929-35	
IV 1 a	Handelspolitik der Tschechoslo-wakei	1	1937-38	
IV 2 c	Internationale Wirtschaftskon-ferenzen	2	1930-36	
IV 3	Zollunion der Nachfolgestaaten	1-3	1923-33	
IV 4 a	Deutsch-tschechoslowakischer Handelsvertrag	4-6	1924-33	
		7 10 -11	1934-39	
	Deutsch-tschechoslowakisches Wirtschaftsabkommen	1-3	1920-37	
	Regelung des Wirtschaftsverkehrs zwischen dem Protektorat und dem Ausland	1	1939	
	Wirtschaftsverkehr zwischen Deutschland und der Slowakei	1	1939	
	Anschluss Sudeten - Deutschland	1	1938-39	
Einlage	- Oesterreichs	Sbd. 1	1938	
	Ausdehnung des deutsch-tschecho-slowakischen Vertrages auf Oesterreich	1-2	1936-38	
	Autokontingent	1	1935-38	
	Hamburger Verhandlungen Oktober 1937	1	1937	
IV 4 c	Deutsch-tschechoslowakisches Liquidationsabkommen	1	1919-27	
IV 5	Tschechoslowakisch-belgischer Handelsvertrag	1	1921-39	
IV 7	Tschechoslowakisch-bulgarischer Handelsvertrag	1	1920-38	
	Tschechoslowakisch-dänischer Handelsvertrag	1	1922-38	
IV 8	Handelsvertrag Tschechoslowakei mit Großbritannien	1	1921-39	
IV 9	- mit Estland	1	1923-38	
IV 10	- Finnland	1	1923-38	

Akten-zeichen	Inhalt	Band	Datum	Serial Nr.
IV 11	Tschechoslowakisch-französischer Handelsvertrag	1	1925-39	
IV 12	Handelsvertrag mit Griechenland	1	1921-38	
IV 13	– Holland	1	1921-39	
IV 14	– Italien (Triester Hafen)	3-4	1925-39	
IV 15	– Japan	1	1922-35	
IV 16	– Jugoslawien	2	1931-39	
IV 17	– Lettland	1	1922-36	
IV 18	– Litauen	1	1922-34	
IV 19 a	– Oesterreich	3-4	1927-38	
IV 19 b	Tschechoslowakisch-österreich-ischer Doppelbesteuerungsvertrag	1	1922-36	
IV 20	Handelsvertrag mit Polen	3-4	1928-39	
IV 21	– Rumänien	1	1921-38	
IV 22	– Rußland	3-4	1927-39	
IV 23	– mit der Schweiz	1	1923-36	
IV 24	– mit Spanien	1	1923-37	
IV 25	– mit der Türkei	1	1923-38	
IV 26	– mit Ungarn	2-3	1927-38	
IV 27	Handelsbeziehungen mit Schweden	1	1925-37	
	– USA	1	1921-39	
	– sonstigen Staaten	1	1921-39	
V 1a	Entwicklung der tschechoslowa-kischen Krone	1	1925-39	
V 1 b	Tschechoslowakische Nationalbank	1	1925-38	
V 1 d	Devisenverkehr speziell A – Z	5	1934-36	
	– –	1	1939	
	Devisenordnung, Valuta bei Ein- und Ausfuhr	7	1936-39	
V 1 e	Geldwesen, technische Fragen	1	1921-38	
V 1 d	Erholungsreisen auf deutschen Schiffen	1	1932-33	
V 2 a	Tschechoslowakisches Bankwesen	2-3	1925-34	
V 2 b	Bankwesen in der Tschechoslo-wakei	1	1921-38	
V 2 c	Tschechoslowakische Sparkassen		1933-36	
V 3 c	Konto W.	1	1921-27	
V 3 e	Tschechoslowakisch-Oesterreich. Clearing (alte Kronen-Forderun-gen)	1	1921-34	

Akten-zeichen	Inhalt	Band	Datum	Serial Nr.
V 3 f	Forderungen an die ehemalige österreich-ungarische Heeresver-waltung	1	1924-34	
V 4	Börsenwesen	1	1921-32	
VI 1 a	Tschechoslowakisches Versiche-rungswesen, allgemein	1-2	1921-37	
VI 1 b	Deutsche Versicherungsgesell-schaft in der Tschechoslowakei	3	1921-31	
VI 1 c	Versicherungen speciell	1	1934-39	
VI 2	Tschechoslowakische Versicherungs-abkommen mit Oesterreich, Italien und Ungarn	1	1924-30	
VII 1	Tschechoslowakische Staats-finanzen	3-5	1921-39	
VII 4 b	Tschechoslowakische Steuern, alphabetisch	1	1928-37	
VII 4 a	- -	4	1931-37	
VII 4 c	Tschechoslowakische Umsatz- und Luxussteuern	6	1932-38	
VII 4 d	Doppelbesteuerung und Vermögens-abgabe	2-3	1923-39	
VII 4 e	- speziell	1-2	1926-38	
VII 5 a	Tschechoslowakisches Zollwesen, allgemein	1-2	1926-37	
VII 5 b	Tschechoslowakischer Zolltarif	3-4	1928-38	
VII 5 c	Tschechoslowakische Zolltarif-entscheidungen	1	1925-37	
VII 5 d	Veredlungsverkehr	1	1925-37	
VII 5 e	Ursprungserzeugnisse	1-3	1927-38	
VII 5 f	Zollfreilager	1	1923-30	
VII 5 g	Zoll speciell	1	1931-34	
		2-3	1935-37	
VII 5 h	Zollrückerstattung speciell	1	1932-33	
VII 5 i	Gefällsstrafverfahren	1-2	1928-38	
VII 6	Tschechoslowakisches Antidumping-gesetz	1	1924-27	
VII 7	Tschechoslowakische Ein- und Ausfuhrgebühren	1	1923-32	
VII 7 a	Tschechoslowakische Aussenhan-delskontrolle	3-4	1929-38	
VII 7 b	Ausfuhr von Wolle aus der Tschechoslowakei	1	1934-35	
	Tschechoslowakische Aussenhan-delskontrolle speciell	1-3	1929-39	
VII 8 a	Staatsmonopole: Radium-Monopol	1	1923-39	

Akten-zeichen	Inhalt	Band	Datum	Serial Nr.
VII 8 b	Staatsmonopole: Salz	1	1921-36	
VII 8 c	- Tabak	1	1926-39	
VII 8 d	- Süssstoff	1	1937-38	
VII 9	Kommerzialisierung der Staats-betriebe	1	1923-30	
VII 10	Tschechoslowakische Lieferungs-ausschreibungen	1	1920-38	
VII 11 a	Tschechoslowakische Staats-finanzen, ausländische Verschul-dung	1	1920-39	
VII 11 b	- Innere Anleihen	1	1920-39	
VII 12 a	Oesterreichische Vorkriegsrenten	1	1920-39	
VII 12 b	Ungarische Vorkriegsrenten	1	1920-32	
VII 12 c	Oesterreichische und ungarische Vorkriegsrenten, Gemeinsames	2	1927-31	
VII 12 d	Vorkriegsrenten speciell	1	1928-39	
VII 13 a	Eisenbahn-Prioritäten	2-3	1926-39	
VII 13 b	Interventionen der Gesandtschaft betr. Eisenbahn-Prioritäten	2	1928	
VII 14	Sonstige Wertpapiere speciell	1	1926-39	
VIII 1 a	Personenkraftwagenverkehr	3-4	1927-39	
VIII 1 d	Kraftwagenlinien im Grenzgebiet	1	1921-38	
VIII 2	Radfahrer-Grenzverkehr	1	1921-38	
VIII 3 a	Tschechoslowakische Eisenbahnen	3-4	1928-39	
VIII 3 b	Verkehr Kaschau-Oderberger Bahn	1	1920-27	
VIII 3 c	Tschechoslowakisch-deutscher Verkehrsverband	1	1924-30	
VIII 4	Tschechoslowakisches Flugwesen	6	1936-38	
VIII 5 a	Tschechoslowakische Post, Flugpost	2	1934-38	
VIII 5 b	Verkehr, Telefon	1	1921-32	
VIII 5 c	Telegrafie	1	1921-34	
VIII 6	Verkehr, Diverses	1	1921-39	
VIII 7 a	Tschechoslowakische Binnen-schiffahrt	1-2	1921-39	
VIII 7 b	Elbe	3+5	1924-39	
VIII 7 c	Donau	4	1934-39	
VIII 7 d	Oder	2-3	1922-39	
VIII 7 e	Tschechoslowakische Wasserstras-sen-Bauprojekte	1	1921-39	
VIII 8 a	Tschechoslowakische Seeschiffahrt	1	1921-38	

Akten-zeichen	Inhalt	Band	Datum	Serial Nr.
VIII 8 b	Hamburg - Triest	1	1921-36	
VIII 8 c	Tschechoslowakische Freihafen-zonen in Hamburg und Stettin	1	1922-35	
IX 1 b	Prager Messe	1	1928-39	
IX 1 c	Reichenberger Messe	3	1925-32	
IX 2 a	Automobilausstellung in Prag	1	1920-39	
IX 2 c	Landwirtschaftliche Ausstellung in Prag	1	1921-38	
IX 2 d	Verkaufsausstellung in Brünn	1	1922-30	
IX 2 e	Ausstellungen in der Tschecho-slowakei Verschiedenes	2	1922-38	
IX 3	Ausländische Ausstellungen und Messen	1	1925-38	
X 1 a	Gründungswesen (grundsätzliches Material)	2	1932-39	
X 1 b	- (statistisches Ma-terial)	1	1923-38	
X 1 c	Gründungswesen speciell	1-3	1931-39	
	Bromografia - Emil Pinkau, Leipzig	1	1935-37	
X 2 a	Tschechoslowakischer Patent-, Marken- und Musterschutz	2	1931-38	
X 2 b	Patent- und Markenschutz, spec.	1-2	1937-39	
X 2 c	Urheberrechtsschutz	1	1921-38	
X 3 a	Handelsgebräuche in der Tschecho-slowakei	1	1922-38	
X 3 d	Tschechoslowakische Konkurs- und Ausgleichsordnung	1	1931	
X 4	Kaufmännische Buchführung	1	1927-34	
X 5	Deutsch-tschechoslowakisches Handelsschiedsgericht	1	1921-35	
XI 1 a	Deutscher Aussenhandel (Handels-politik)	1-2	1922-39	
XI 1 b	Deutsche Aussenhandelskontrolle	4-6	1925-39	
XI 1 c	Deutsche Handelspolitik, Verträge Gesamtübersicht	1 2	1921-39	7555/E541864-86
XI 1 d	Handelsverträge Deutschlands mit dritten Ländern	1	1932-35	
XI 1 e	Handelsvertrag Deutschlands mit Frankreich	1	1921-39	
XI 1 f	- mit Italien	1	1925-39	
XI 1 g	- Jugoslawien	1	1928-39	
XI 1 h	- Oesterreich	1	1925-37	
XI 1 i	- Polen	1	1925-38	
XI 1 k	- Rumänien	1	1931-39	

Akten-zeichen	Inhalt	Band	Datum	Serial Nr.
XI 2 a	Zweig- und Reichsnachrichten-stellen, Vorschriften betr. wirtschaftliche Berichterstat-tung der Gesandtschaft	1-2	1919-33	
XI 2 c	Handbuch für den Aussenhandel	1	1922-37	
XI 2 d	Gebührentarif	1	1923-37	
XI 2 e	Deutsche Auslandshandelskammern	1	1928-38	
XI 3 a	Deutschlands Wirtschaftslage	6-7	1930-39	
XI 3 a	Tschechoslowakische Presse-stimmen über die deutsche Wirtschaft	1	1926-37	
XI 3 b	Boykott ausländischer Waren in Deutschland. Einlage: Boykott deutscher Waren in der Tschecho-slowakei	1	1930-39	
XI 3 c	Wirtschaftslage der deutschen Industrien	1	1921-33	
XI 3 d	Deutschlands Kohlenlage	3	1924-32	
XI 3 e	Deutsche Industriekonzerne, Trust	2	1925-26	
XI 3 f	Internationale Kartelle mit deutscher Beteiligung	1	1926-36	
XI 4 a	Deutsche Finanzfragen, allgemein	1	1931-38	
XI 4 b	Deutsche Steuern	3	1926-36	
XI 4 c	Deutsche Umsatz- und Luxus-steuern	1	1920-32	
XI 4 d	Deutsches Zollwesen	1-2	1920-39	
XI 5 a	Deutsche Währungsfragen	1	1921-38	
XI 5 b	Deutsche Devisenordnung	1 2 3	1931-36	7851/E569680-90 9443/E666627-71
		4-5	1936-39	
XI 5 c	Stillhalteabmachungen mit Deutschland	1	1931-37	
XI 5 d	Deutsche Reichsbank	1	1922-33	
XI 5 e	Deutsches Bank- und Börsenwesen	1	1921-39	
XI 5 f	Entschuldung der deutschen Landwirtschaft	1	1931-37	
XI 6 a	Deutsches Verkehrswesen	1	1922-	
XI 6 b	Deutsche Handelsflotte, Hamburg	2	1925-36	
XI 6 c	Deutsche Binnenschiffahrt	1	1926-38	
XI 7 a	Deutsches Gründungswesen und handelsrechtliche Sonderfragen	1	1922-39	
XI 7 b	Patent- und Musterschutz in Deutschland	1	1921-36	

Akten-zeichen	Inhalt	Band	Datum	Serial Nr.
XI 7 c	Deutsche Urheberrechtsfragen	1	1927	
XI 8 b	Leipziger Messe	2	1925-32	
	Handelsauskünfte A - Z	1-9	1934-39	
	Kompensationsanträge 1 - 5592		1935-38	
	Tschechoslowakische Einfuhr und deutsche Ausfuhrstatistik			
	Reichsstelle für den Aussenhandel	1-2	1937-39	
	Einfuhrbewilligung für Hafer	1-3	1935-37	
		1-2	1937-38	
	Personalbogen für Vertreter		1938	
	Vertreter		1938	
	Kontingente	1-13	1938	
	Verordnungen und Berichte		1938	
	Berichte Regierungsrat Freyberg		1931-36	
	Reichs- und Länderanleihen (Ablösung)		1920-28	
			1920-28	
	Irrenverpflegungskosten, Heim-beförderung (Einzelfälle)		1936-38	
	Meldepflicht Deutscher Staats-angehöriger im Ausland A - Z		1936-38	
	Passfragebogen, Einzelfälle		1935-38	
	Durchlassscheine		1938	
	Meldeblätter, Einzelfälle Dittmann, Horawetz, Hornek, Kaser, Nickerl, Sach Scha-Schl, Schm-Scho, Schr-Schw, St, T, U, V, Wa-We, Wi-Wy, Zy		1936-38	
	Durchlassscheine, Liste fehlen-der Pässe, Liste ausgestellter Grenzübertrittsscheine		1938	
	Passliste 1 - 8, Aufzeichnungen der deutschen Zivilverwaltung Empfangsbestätigung der Gestapo		1939	
	Spendenliste Verschiedenes		1938	
	Berichte an das Auswärtige Amt Unterstützungsakten		1924-29	
	Telegrammabschriften, Aufzeich-nungen	1-4 5-8	1938-39	
I 5 a	Tschechoslowakisches Kartell-gesetz	1	1922-38	
I 5 b	Tschechoslowakische Kartelle und Konzerne	2	1933-39	

Akten-zeichen	Inhalt	Band	Datum	Serial Nr.
I 6 a	Normung in der Industrie	1	1920-35	
I 7 a	Tschechoslowakische Handels- und Gewerbekammern	1	1921-38	
I 7 b	Tschechoslowakischer Wirtschafts-beirat	1	1920-36	
II 1 a	Automobilindustrie und Handel	3	1935-39	
II 1 b	Tschechoslowakische Automobil-zölle	2	1927-38	
II 2	Bier	2	1928-39	
II 3	Bleistiftindustrie	1	1923-39	
II 7 c	Radiomaterial	2	1934-39	
II 8	Edelmetallindustrie, Pforzheimer Waren	1	1923-39	
II 9 a	Farben	2	1925-38	
II 9 b	Lacke	1	1925-32	
IV 1 a	Handelspolitik der Tschechoslo-wakei	2	1939	
IV 1 b	Handelsverträge der Tschechoslo-wakei	1	1924-39	
IV 2 a	Interparlamentarische Handels-konferenz	1	1922-36	
IV 2 b	Internationale Handelskammer	1	1920-37	
IV 2 c	- Wirtschaftskonferenzen	3	1937-38	
IV 2 d	Internationaler landwirtschaft-licher Kongress in Prag	1	1931-33	
IV 2 e	Internationale Wirtschaftslehr-kurse	1	1938-39	
	Internationaler Kongress für kaufmännisches Unterrichtswesen	1	1935	
IV 2 f	Tagung des internationalen Statistischen Instituts Prag 1938	1	1937	
IV 3	Zollunion der Nachfolgestaaten	4	1933-39	
IV 4 a	Deutsch-tschechoslowakische Vereinbarungen vom 15.12.1938	1	1938-39	
Einlage	Kontingentbescheinigungen	1	1934-37	
IV 4 a	Deutsch-tschechoslowakischer Handelsvertrag	8+9	1935-36	
IV 4 b	Deutsch-tschechoslowakisches Kohlenabkommen	1	1920-38	
IV 4 c	- Liquidationsabkommen	2	1928-38	
V 1 c	Bankausweise	6	1935-38	
V 1 d	Tschechoslowakische Devisenord-nung, Valuta bei Ein- und Ausfuhr	5+6	1932-36	
VII 2	Tschechoslowakische Staatsfinan-zen, Allgemeines	1	1920-37	

Akten-zeichen	Inhalt	Band	Datum	Serial Nr.
VII 3 a	Landes- und Kommunalfinanzen	1	1921-37	
VII 3 b	Finanzen der Stadt Prag	1	1921-33	
VII 4 a	Tschechoslowakische Steuern	5	1938-39	
VIII 1 c	Autoverkehr, speziell	1	1932-38	
VIII 1 b	Lastkraftwagen-Grenzverkehr	1	1923-39	
VIII 5 a	Tschechoslowakische Post Flugpost	1	1920-33	
VIII 7 c	Donau	3	1927-33	
IX 1 a	Messe- und Ausstellungswesen, allgemein	1	1922-38	
IX 1 c	Reichenberger Messe	4	1933-38	
IX 1 d	Internationale Donaumesse Pressburg	1	1921-38	
IX 2 b	Tschechoslowakische Flugzeug-ausstellungen	1	1921-37	
X 1 a	Gründungswesen (grundsätzliches Material)	1	1921-31	
X 2 a	Patent- und Musterschutz in der Tschechoslowakei	1	1919-30	
X 2 d	Warenherkunftsbezeichnung	1	1921-38	
X 2 e	Bekämpfung unlauteren Wett-bewerbs	1	1921-38	
X 3 b	Wechselordnung und Scheckrecht	1	1926-39	
X 3 c	Tschechoslowakische Eichordnung	1	1930-38	
XI 1 c	Material zu den deutsch-schweize-rischen Handelsvertragsverhand-lungen Stand vom 1.5.26	1	1926	
XI 1 m	Handelsvertrag Deutschland mit Russland	1	1921-39	
XI 1 n	— — Schweiz	1	1926-38	
XI 1 o	— — Ungarn	1	1931-39	
XI 1 p	— — USA	1	1921-38	
XI 2 a	Reichsstelle für den Aussenhan-del, Vorschriften betr. wirt-schaftlicher Berichterstattung der Gesandtschaft	3	1927-39	
XI 2 b	Deutscher Überseedienst, Eildienst	1	1921-30	
XI 8 a	Deutsches Messewesen, allgemein	1	1920-38	
XI 8 b	Leipziger Messe	3	1933-39	
XI 8 c	Frankfurter Messe	1	1921-28	
XI 8 d	Deutsche Messen und Ausstellungen	1	1934-38	
XI 8 e	Kongresse	1	1932-38	

Akten-zeichen	Inhalt	Band	Datum	Serial Nr.
	Kompensationsanträge, Wiedervorlagen	1	1935-38	
	Kompensationsgeschäfte, erledigte Anfragen	1-2	1935-38	
	Kompensationsanträge 1101 - 5350		1936-38	
	Geheimakten.			
1/1	Telegrammabschriften, Aufzeichnungen		5.39- 5.39	37/26116-252
1/2	Telegramme vom Auswärtigen Amt und anderen Behörden		1.38-10.38	28/18860-9289
1/3	Telegramme an das Auswärtige Amt und andere Behörden		9.38-10.38	28/17752-8071
1/4			1.38- 9.38	28/18362-859
2/5	Telegramme vom Auswärtigen Amt und von anderen Behörden		10.38-12.38	28/19290-434
2/6	Telegramme an das Auswärtige Amt und andere Behörden		10.38-12.38	28/18072-361
2/7	Telegramme vom Auswärtigen Amt und anderen Behörden		1.39-10.39	28/19435-636
2/8	Telegramme an das Auswärtige Amt und andere Behörden		1.39- 5.39	28/17506-751

Akten-zeichen	Inhalt	Band	Datum	Serial Nr.
Pers.	Personalakten der Gesandtschaft Pressburg A - Z		bis 1944	
Pers.A	Frau Irma Richter	1	1941	
Pers.A 1	Landkarte der Slowakei für geographischen Dienst	1	1941-43	
Pers.A 2	Die deutschen Auslandsvertretungen	1	1932-44	
Pers.A 3	Deutsches Konsulat Preschau	1	1940-44	
Pers.A 3 (K)	Konsulat Preschau	1	1940-44	
Pers.A 4	Deutsch-slowakischer Konsular-vertrag	1	1941-42	
Pers. Berater	Beraterberichte	1	1941	
	Berater A - Z	1-3	1941-44	
	Dr. Werner Brocke	1	1941-44	
	Krim.Rat Franz Goltz	1	1941-44	
	Dr. Hamsche, Johann	1	1940-44	
	Albert Smagon	1	1940-44	
	Dieter Wisbiceny	1	1940-44	
Pers. Bibl.	Bibliothek des Konsulats, Buchbestellung	1-3	1939-44	
Pers.G (K)	Geschäftsgang bei der Konsulats-abteilung	1	1939-42	
Pers.G 1	Aktenplan der Behörde	1	1938-41	
Pers.G 2	Dienstbetrieb Anordnung des Behördenleiters	1	1920-44	
Pers.G 2a	Verfügungen und Umläufe	1-3	1939-43	
Pers.G 3a	Heizung des Konsulatsgebäudes	1	1940-43	
Pers.G 4	Grundstücksverwaltung, Dienst-wohnung, Mietvertrag	1	1939-43	
Pers.G 4a	Dienstwohnungen	1	1931-43	
Pers.G 4b	Dienstkraftwagen	1	1937-42	
	Fernsprecheinrichtung	1-3	1939-43	
Pers.G 4i	Dienstgebäude Schillerstrasse, Gundulicgasse	1-2	1941-42	
Pers.G 5 (K)	Beschaffung von Einrichtungsge-genständen, Materialbestellungen	1	1942-43	
Pers.G 5a	Bürobedarf	1-2	1931-44	
Pers.G 5b	Einrichtungsgegenstände	1	1929-43	
Pers.G 5c		1-2	1939-43	

Akten-zeichen	Inhalt	Band	Datum	Serial Nr.
Pers.G 5d	Einrichtungsgegenstände für Sonderbeauftragte	1	1940	
Pers.G 6	Beflaggung der Behörde, Feiertage, Hoheitszeichen	1	1931-40	
Pers.G 7	Bezug von Zeitungen und Zeitschriften	1-2	1932-43	
Pers.G 8	Verkehr mit den Behörden des Gastlandes.	1-2	1939-44	
Pers.G 9	Verkehr mit innerdeutschen Behörden	1-2	1933-44	
Pers.G 10	Schriftverkehr des Militärattachés	1	1939	
Pers.G 11	Weiterleitung von Briefen	1-3	1941-44	
Pers.P	Ärzte (auch Vertrauensärzte der Gesandtschaft)	1	1940-44	
Pers.P 1	Personalien der Beamten und Angestellten der Behörde, Allgemeines	1-3	1938-44	
	Anlagen, Abbaukommission	1	1942	
	- Personalausweise	1	1933-44	
	- Arbeitseinsatz der Frauen	1	1943	
Pers.P 1a	Bewerbungen	1	1940-43	
Pers.P 1c	- A - Z	1-6	1940-43	
		1-4	1939-44	
Pers.P 1e	Wirtschaftsstelle Lebensmittelverteilung	1-2	1940-43	
	Anlagen, Bezugsscheine für Schuhe und Sohlen	1	1942-43	
Pers.P 2	Urlaub und Bestimmungen	1-2	1924-44	
Pers.P 3	Angestellte, Allgemeines	1	1923-43	
Pers.R	Gebührenwesen	1	1937-43	
Pers.R 3	Beschaffung von Betriebsmitteln, Kassenbestandsverstärkungen	1	1939-44	
Pers.R 4	Fonds, Geschäftsbedürfnisse, Kult, Presse	1	1939-41	
Pers.R 5	Abrechnungen	2-5	1941-42	
	- Verschiedenes		1941-43	
Pers.R 6	Prüfungsbemerkungen des Auswärtigen Amtes und des Rechnungshofes	1	1935-36	
Pers.R 7	Gebühren (Tarife)	1	1929-40	
Pers.R 8	Besoldungen, Löhne und Unterstützungen der Beamten und Angestellten, Vorschüsse	1-3	1922-43	

Akten-zeichen	Inhalt	Band	Datum	Serial Nr.
Pers.R 8	Teuerungen in der Slowakei	1-3	1940-43	
Pers.R 8a	Zahlungslisten für Beamte	1	1943	
Pers.R 9a	Umzugskosten, Reisekosten, Dienstreisen	1	1941	
Pers.R 10	Steuern, Angestellten- und Invalidenversicherung	1	1921-41	
Pers.R 11	Devisenangelegenheiten des Auswärtigen Amtes und der Vertretung	1	1939-43	
Pers.R 12	Verwahrgüter, Vorschüsse und Kosten	1	1939-43	
Pers.R 13	Unterstützungen im Ausland	1	1927-44	
Pers.R 14	Pensionen und Versorgungsge-bühren	1	1926-43	
Pers.Si 1	Sicherung des Gebäudes	1	1935-43	
Pers.Si 2	Telegramme, Erlasse und Berichts-kontrolle, Luftschutzanordnungen	1-2	1921-44	
Pers.Si 5	Lebensmittelsendungen	1	1941-42	
	Kurierausweise, Benutzung des Postfachs, in Engerau und Ku-rierverbindungen	1-3	1941-44	
	Kurierangelegenheiten	1-2	1931-43	
Pers.	Versorgung	1	1941-44	
B I 1	Generalia Verzeichnis der Beamten und Angestellten		1923-37	
B I 1a	Wiederherstellung des Berufs-beamtentums		1933-39	
B I 2	Personalien des Kons.Leg.Rat Dr.Schellert		1927-33	
B I 6	Personalveränderungen im Auswärtigen Amt		1926-39	
B I 7	Personalien, Allgemeines (Offerten, Stellengesuche)		1930-39	
B I 8	Kanzler Sebald		1938-40	
B I 9	Anna und Josef Kulacs, Rein-machefrau, Hausmeister und Gärtner		1938-40	
B I a 1	Generalia	1-2	1923-29	
B I a 2	Inventar und Anschaffungen	1	1924-35	
B I a 3	Bibliothek	1	1929-39	
B I a 4	Amtslokal	2-3	1928-39	
B I a 5	Wohnungsangelegenheiten	1	1924-31	

Akten-zeichen	Inhalt	Band	Datum	Serial Nr.
B I a 6	Kontrollberichte	2-4	1934-39	
B I a 7	Kurierangelegenheiten	2	1933-39	
B I a 8	Gesandtschaft Prag und andere deutsche Vertretungen in der Tschechoslowakei	1	1926-38	
B I a 9	Geschäftsverkehr mit den tschechoslowakischen Behörden		1922-38	
B I a 10	Flagge, Hoheitszeichen		1921-38	
B I a 11	Zeremonielles		1929-33	
B I b 1	Generalia	1-2	1922-29	
B I b 2	Bankverkehr und Geldbeschaffung	2	1936-39	
B I b 4	Kassensachen, Verschiedenes		1930-39	
B I b 5	Kassenabschlüsse		1928-39	
B I b 6	Kassenrevisionen		1922-33	
B II 1	Staatsangehörigkeit, Gen.	1	1925-38	
B III 1	Rechtssachen, Gen.	1	1932-38	
B III 1a	Arbeit und Aufenthaltsbewilligung		1931-38	
B IV 1	Generalia	1	1919-37	
B IV 2	Unfallsachen, Renten, Unterstützungen, Balosak, Sahl		1937-38	
B IV 5	Wohlfahrtsstelle des Deutschen Reiches, Prag		1933-39	
B VI 1	Kriegsfolgen, Kriegsgräber, Gen.		1926-36	
	Ehrenkreuz	2	1934-38	
B VI 3	Kriegsgräber, allgemein Schriftverkehr		1929-38	
B VI 4	Heldengedenktag		1929-38	
B VI 4a	Fotografische Aufnahmen		1937	
B VII 1	Generalia		1932	
B VII 2	Land- und Forstwirtschaft, Viehzucht, Seuchen	1	1929-38	
B VII 3	Jagd und Fischerei	1	1934-36	
B VII 4	Bodenreform	1	1928-38	
B VIII 1	Wirtschaft, Handel Gen.		1924-38	
B VIII 1b	Wirtschaftliche Lage der deutschen Minderheiten in der Tschechoslowakei		1930-38	
B VIII 3	Internationale Donaumesse	2	1934-38	
B VIII 7	Handel, Industrie und Gewerbe, allgemein		1931-38	
B VIII 7a	Deutscher Wirtschaftsdienst		1931-35	

Akten-zeichen	Inhalt	Band	Datum	Serial Nr.
B VIII 12	Finanzen, Banken, Geldwesen		1932-39	
B VIII 14	Holzindustrie		1935-39	
B VIII a 1	Generalia		1929-39	
B VIII a 3	Zollsachen, Ausfuhr aus der Tschechoslowakei nach Deutschland		1929-38	
B VIII a 4a	Verkehrsnachrichten		1936-39	
B VIII a 4b	Verkehrswerbung		1930-39	
B VIII a 5	Schiffahrt, Donauhäfen	3	1936-38	
B VIII a 5a	Russische Warentransporte auf der Donau		1927-39	
B VIII a 6	Kraftfahrzeuge		1922-35	
B VIII a 6a	Auto des Konsuls		1938-39	
B IX 1	Grenzverkehr		1927-39	
B IX 3	– und Grenzzwischenfälle		1934-39	
B IX 5	Russenvorschriften		1922-38	
B IX 6	Russenfragebogen		1925-28	
B X 1	Prisota Gen.	1	1934-39	
B XI 1	Zeitungen Gen.	1	1923-27	
B XI 3	Verschiedene Zeitungen, Zeitschriften	3	1935-39	
B XII 3	Pressburg	1	1924-38	
B XIII 1	Wehrerziehung und Luftschutz in der Tschechoslowakei		1938	
Kult 1	Allgemeine Kulturpolitik des Gastlandes und zu anderen Staaten	1	1941-43	
Kult 1 Nr. 1	Kulturpolitische Beziehungen der Slowakei zu anderen Ländern	1	1939-44	
Kult 2	Kulturpolitische Beziehungen des Gastlandes zu Deutschland	1	1939-44	
Kult 2 D.W.I.	Deutsches wissenschaftliches Institut	1	1943-44	
Kult 2 a	Kulturpolitische Arbeitsbe-sprechung	1	1942	
Kult 2 Nr. 1	Auslandsreisen von Persönlich-keiten aus der Slowakei, Studienreisen, Einladungen	1	1939-43	
Kult 2 Nr. 2	Deutsch-slowakische Gesellschaft	1-6	1939-43	

Akten-zeichen	Inhalt	Band	Datum	Serial Nr.
Kult 3	Reichs- und Volksdeutsche im Gastlande		1939-43	
	Reiseverkehr nach der Slowakei	1	1939-43	
Kult 3 Nr. 1	Reichsdeutsche und ihre Organisationen	1	1939-43	
Kult 3 a	Maler Kurth	1	1939-42	
Kult 3 b	Juden und Emigranten	1	1930-44	
Kult 3 Nr. 2	Volksdeutsche in der Slowakei	1-4	1939-44	
	Anlagen. Schallplattenarchiv, wissenschaftliche Arbeiten, Nationalitätenkataster und Verschiedenes		1939-44	
Kult 3 Nr. 3	Ausbildung von Volksdeutschen im Reich, Einzelfälle	1-2	1936-40	
Kult 3 Nr. 4	Deutsche Schulen in der Slowakei und Verschiedenes	1	1938-43	
Kult 3 Nr. 5	Wochen- und Tätigkeitsberichte für Landwirtschaft, Presse und Propaganda, Hauptamt für Kultur		1940-44	
Kult 3 Nr. 7	Gegner der Volksgruppe	1	1940	
Kult 4	Kirchenwesen	1 2	1939-43	3115/D633106-17
Kult 5	Ein-, Aus- und Rückwanderung, auch Amerika-Slowaken, slowakische Minderheiten im Ausland	1	1939-42	
Kult 5 a	Minderheiten in der Slowakei (ausser deutsche Volksgruppen)	1	1941-43	•
Kult 6	Nachforschungswesen	1	1940-44	
Kult 8	Kinderlandverschickung in die Slowakei, Meldeblätter und Listen A - Z	1-3	1940-44	
	K.L.V. Erweiterte Kinderlandverschickung	1-4	1940-43	
		1-3	1941-44	
	- Monatliche Abrechnung	1	1941-42	
	Schulwesen	1-2	1939-43	
	- Verschiedenes	1	1940-44	
Kult 9	Sprachwerbung	1-3	1939-42	
		4-6	1942-43	
	- Verträge, Ferienlager, Verschiedenes		1940-43	
Kult 10	Hochschulwesen	1-3	1939-42	
	- Gastvorlesungen	1	1940-42	
	- Studentenaustausch	1	1940	

Akten-zeichen	Inhalt	Band	Datum	Serial Nr.
Kult 10	Hochschulwesen: Verschiedenes		1941-43	
	- Professoren und Studenten		1940-44	
	- Professoren und Studentenaustausch		1940-44	
Kult 10 Nr. 2	- Akademischer Austauschdienst	1-3	1940-43	
Kult 11	Vortragsdienst verschiedener Professoren		1940-43	
	- und Verschiedenes		1940-43	
	Buchausstellung, Buchaustausch		1939-42	
	Gesundheitswesen	1	1939-42	
	Wissenschaft, Verschiedenes		1939-43	
	Veranstaltungsplan und Künstler		1939-43	
	Musik, Quartette, Dichterlesung		1939-43	
Kult 12	Kunst, Theaterwesen, Musikwesen	1-4	1939-43	
	Deutscher Theaterverein	1-2	1939-43	
	Kulturelle Veranstaltungen	1-3	1939-43	
	Musikkorps, Philharmonisches Orchester, Gesangvereine und Zirkus		1939-43	
Kult 12 Nr. 1	Slowakische Wochenschaulieferungen	1-3	1940-44	
	Filmwesen in der Slowakei	1-5	1939-43	
	Schmalfilmgesellschaft	1-2	1939-42	
	Filmwesen in der Slowakei, Einzelfälle		1939-43	
	Film und Rundfunk	1	1932-39	
Kult 12 Nr. 2	Sport	1-2	1930-43	
Kult 13	Auskünfte aller Art	1-2	1938-44	
Kult 14	Ferienveranstaltungen in der Slowakei	1	1943-44	
D.Kult 1	Deutsche Kulturpolitik (Allgemeines)	1	1937-42	
D.Kult 2	Kulturpolitische Beziehungen Deutschlands zu anderen Staaten als zum Gastland	1	1937-42	
D.Kult 2 Nr. 1	Geschäftsreisen nach der Slowakei	1	1937-42	
	Auslandsreisen von Persönlichlichkeiten aus dem Reich, Einzelfälle		1937-42	
	-	8-12	1941-44	

Akten-zeichen	Inhalt	Band	Datum	Serial Nr.
D.Kult 3	Minderheiten in Deutschland, Einzelfälle		1934-44	
D.Kult 4	Kirchenwesen in Deutschland	1	1934-43	
D.Kult 5	Ein-, Aus- und Rückwanderung deutscher Flüchtlinge	1	1935-44	
D.Kult 6	Nachforschungswesen	1	1939-43	
D.Kult 6a	Urkundenbeschaffung, Allgemeines	1	1927-43	
D.Kult 7	Jugendbewegung K.L.V.	1	1934-44	
D.Kult 8	Schulwesen in Deutschland	1	1939-44	
D.Kult 10	Deutsches Hochschulwesen	1-2	1939-44	
D.Kult 11	Wissenschaft, verschiedene Einzelfälle		1939-44	
D.Kult 12	Kunst	1-3	1939-44	
	– Einzelfälle		1939-44	
R 1	Rechtswesen, Allgemeines	1	1939-44	
R 2 Nr.1	Rechtliche Beziehungen der Slowakei zu Deutschland, Nacheilevertrag, Beglaubigungs-abkommen	1-3	1939-43	
R 2 Nr.2	Rechtliche Beziehungen des Gast-landes zu anderen Staaten	1	1939-42	
R 3 Nr.1	Staatsrecht, Zivilrecht, Straf-recht, Gerichtswesen auch Ver-waltung, Einzelfälle	1	1939-43	
R 3 Nr.2	Staatsangehörigkeitsfragen, Verträge, Einzelfälle		1939-44	
R 3 Nr.3	Zivilrecht, auch Bodenreform, Pfandrecht, Grundeigentum, Nachlassrecht, Einzelfälle	1-2	1939-42	
R 3 Nr.4	Handelsrecht und Prozessrecht, Rechtshilfe in Zivilsachen, Justizverwaltung, Einzelfälle		1939-42	
R 3 Nr.5	Handelsrecht und Prozessrecht, Einzelfälle		1939-42	
	Patentrecht und Markenschutz-gesetz	1	1939-42	
	Genossenschaftswesen	1	1939-42	
R 3 Nr.6	Strafakten und Gnadengesuche, Einzelfälle		1939-42	
R 4 Nr.1	Lohnfragen und Streiks	1	1942-43	
R 4 Nr.2	Arbeitskräfte aus der Slowakei	1-3	1939-44	
	– Einzelfälle		1939-44	
R 5 Nr.2	Grenzempfehlungen, Pässe und Sichtvermerke, Einzelfälle		1939-44	
R 5 Nr.3	Grenzverkehr	1	1939-44	

Akten-zeichen	Inhalt	Band	Datum	Serial Nr.
R 5 Nr.4	Sonstige Polizeisachen, Grenz-verletzungen	1	1940-42	
R 6 Nr.2	Sozialversicherung	1	1939-42	
R 6 Nr.3	Wohnungs- und Siedlungswesen	1	1940	
R 6 Nr.4	Übernahme und soziale Fürsorge	1	1939-42	
R 6 Nr.6	Unfälle, ärztliche Gutachten	1	1941-44	
R 7	Internationales Rechtswesen	1	1940-44	
R 8	Gesundheitswesen	1	1940-43	
R poln.	Staatsangehörigkeit und Passangelegenheiten A - Z Einzelfälle		1940-44	
R poln. gen.	Angelegenheiten polnischer Staatsangehöriger	1	1939-41	
D R 3	Staatsrecht, Zivil- und Straf-recht	1	1933-41	
D R 1	Rechtswesen in Deutschland, allgemein	1	1939-43	
D R 3 Nr. 1	Allgemeiner Reiseverkehr	1	1941-42	
	Staatsangehörigkeitsfragen, Ein- und Ausbürgerungen	1	1939-44	
D R 3 Nr. 1 Gen.K	Staatsangehörigkeitsfragen all-gemein, auch Einbürgerungen, Entlassungen	1-2	1936-44	
D R 3 Nr. 1 a	Staatsangehörigkeitsfragen, Einzelfälle	1-5	1940-44	
D R 3 Nr. 1 b Gen.K	Ausbürgerungen, allgemein (auch Ausbürgerungslisten)	1-4	1940-44	
D R 3 Nr. 1 b	Listen der Ausbürgerungen	1	1938-39	
	Staatsangehörigkeit: Einbür-gerungen,Einzelfälle		1939-44	
D R 3 Nr. 1 c	Staatsangehörigkeit, Ein- und Ausbürgerungen, Einzelfälle		1939-44	
D R 3 Nr. 1 d	- Einzelfälle A - Z		1940-44	
D R 3 Nr. 1 a	- A - Z		1940-44	
D R 3 Nr. 2	Bürgerliches Recht, Bodenreform, Grundeigentum, Pfand, Nachlass-recht, Einzelfälle	1	1940-42	
D R 3 Nr. 2a	- A - Z		1940-44	
D R 3 Nr. 2 b	Beglaubigungen A - Z Einzelfälle		1940-44	
D R 3 Nr. 2 c	Rechtshilfeersuchen, Einzelfälle A - Z		1940-44	

Akten-zeichen	Inhalt	Band	Datum	Serial Nr.
D R 3 Nr. 2 d	Aktenübergabe: Urkunden, Straf-sachen, Kriegsbeschädigtenfür-sorge, Wehrstammblätter, Einzelfälle A - Z		1940-44	
D R 3 Nr. 2 e	Urkunden, Sichtvermerke Einzelfälle A - Z		1940-44	
D R 3 Nr.3 Gen.	Zwischenstaatlicher Austausch von Personenstandsurkunden	1	1936-42	
D R 3 Nr. 3	Familienrecht, Ehe, Personen-standsangelegenheiten	1	1933-44	
	- Einzelfälle A - Z		1940-44	
D R 3 Nr. 3 a	- A - Z		1940-44	
D R 3 Nr. 3 b Gen.	Verpflegungskosten	1-3	1939-44	
D R 3 Nr. 3 b	- Einzelfälle A - Z		1940-44	
D R 3 Nr. 4 Gen.	Zivilrecht	1	1939-43	
D R 3 Nr. 4	Handels- und Prozessrecht, Rechtshilfe in Zivilsachen	1-2	1940-42	
	- Einzelfälle A - Z		1940-44	
D R 3 Nr. 4 a	Rechtshilfe in Zivilsachen, Justizverwaltung, Einzelfälle	1	1941-43	
	- Einzelfälle A - Z		1940-44	
D R 3 Nr. 4 b	Rechtshilfe in Zivilsachen, Forderungen, Einzelfälle A - Z	1	1940-44	
D R 3 Nr. 4 d	Aussenhandelsstelle für das Sudetenland, Benennung von Rechtsanwälten, Einzelfälle		1940-44	
D R 3 Nr. 4 e Gen.	Kriegssachschäden slowakischer Staatsangehöriger	1	1942-44	
D R 3 Nr. 5 Gen.	Orts- und Gerichtsverzeichnis	1	1940	
D R 3 Nr. 5	Strafrecht, Rechtshilfe in Strafsachen	1	1937-43	
D R 3 Nr. 5 a Gen.	Strafprozessrecht (Generalia)	1	1939-41	
D R 3 Nr. 5 a	Strafrecht, Einzelfälle	1	1941-44	
	- - A - Z		1940-44	
D R 3 Nr. 5 b	Strafrecht, Auslieferung, Aus-weisung, Einzelfälle B - Z		1940-44	

Akten-zeichen	Inhalt	Band	Datum	Serial Nr.
D R 3 Nr. 6	Beglaubigungen, Bescheinigungen, Zeugenvernehmung, Allgemeines und Einzelfälle	1-2	1921-44	
D R 3 Nr. 7	Zustellungsersuchen (Reichsprot.)	1-5	1941-44	
D R 4	Arbeits- und Gewerberecht	1	1941	
D R 4 Nr. 1 Gen.	Arbeits- und Stellenvermittlung, auch Ein- und Rückwanderung, allgemein	1	1935-43	
D R 4 Nr. 3 Gen.	Kleiner Grenzverkehr	1	1940-44	
D R 4 Nr. 3	- Einzelfälle A - Z		1940-44	
D R 5 Nr. 1	Aufenthaltsbestimmungen in Deutschland, Einzelfälle	1	1939-44	
	Fremdenpolizeiliche Bestimmungen in Deutschland	1	1939-43	
	Dr. Sarsun Ausweisung	1	1942-43	
D R 5 Nr. 2	Deutsche Grenzempfehlungen	1	1936-44	
D R 5 Nr. 3 Gen.	Behandlung polnischer Reisepässe	1	1939-40	
D R 5 Nr. 3	Deutsche Pässe, Heimatscheine, allgemein	1	1932-42	
	Donauschiffer-passtechnische Behandlung	1	1942-44	
	Pässe und Sichtvermerke, Erlasse	1	1939-43	
	Sichtvermerksgebühren	1	1941-44	
	Sichtvermerke und Passbestim-mungen	1	1940-42	
	Sichtvermerke, Durchlass-Scheine, Einzelfälle	1-3	1939-44	
	Schwierigkeiten beim Grenzüber-tritt	1	1942	
	Sichtvermerke Margarete Spiller	1	1940-41	
	- Johann Lichy	1	1942-43	
	Sichtvermerks- und Passbestim-mungen	1-3	1920-39	
D R 5 Nr. 3 a	Durchlass-Scheine und Sichtver-merke	1	1926-44	
D R 5 Nr. 3 b	Norwegen: Passausstellung (Allgemeines)	1	1943	
D R 5 Nr. 3 c	Ungarn: Passierscheine	1	1944	
	- Durchlass-Scheine nach Ungarn	1	1944	
	Personenverkehr nach Ungarn	1	1944	

Akten-zeichen	Inhalt	Band	Datum	Serial Nr.
D R 5 Nr. 3 c Gen.	Leichenpässe (Allgemeines)	1-2	1931-44	
D R 5 Nr. 3 c	- Einzelfälle A - Z		1940-43	
D R 5 Nr. 3 d Gen.	Rückkehr von Protektoratsange-hörigen aus der Slowakei	1	1939-40	
D R 5 Nr. 3 e Gen.	Umsiedlung deutscher Volksange-höriger	1	1939-43	
D R 5 Nr. 3 f Gen.	Evakuierungen ins Reich und Protektorat	1	1944	
D R 5 Nr. 4 Gen.	Meldepflicht der Reichsange-hörigen	1	1938-44	
	- in Dubnica (Skoda-Werke) A - Sch	1	1940-44	
D R 5 Nr. 4 a	Meldepflicht der Reichsdeutschen (Einzelakte)	1	1938-44	
D R 5 Nr. 5	Juden, Emigranten, Pass-Sachen, allgemein, Einzelfälle A - Z	1	1934-44	K1643/K403173-297
D R 6	Sozial- und Fürsorgewesen, Pensionssachen	1-2	1933-43	
D R 6 a	- Einzelfälle	1	1941-43	
	Sozial- und Fürsorgewesen, Funk, Emil	1	1941-42	
D R 6 Nr. 1	Pensions- und Rentenangelegen-heiten (Allgemeines)	1	1940-42	
	Sozial- und Fürsorgefälle, auch pol. und Protektorat, Einzel-fälle	1	1941-44	
	Wollsachensammlung für die Front	1	1941-42	
	Metall-Sammlung	1	1940-43	
	Erholung von Angehörigen der Waffen-SS in der Slowakei	1	1940-42	3115/D633118-24
	Renten, Versorgungsangelegen-heiten, Einzelfälle A - Z		1940-44	
D R 6 Nr. 2	Wohlfahrtsunterstützung und Heimschaffung von Hausgehilfin-nen, Einzelfälle A - Z		1940-44	
D R 6 Nr. 2 a	Heimschaffung deutscher Haus-angestellter ins Reich	1	1941-42	
D R 6 Nr. 2 c	Gewährung und Rückzahlung eines Darlehens, Einzelfälle A - Z		1940-44	
D R 6 Nr. 4 Gen.	Vertretung slowakischer Interes-sen durch das Reich im Auslande	1	1940-42	

Akten- zeichen	Inhalt	Band	Datum	Serial Nr.
D R 6 Nr. 4	Vertretung slowakischer Interes- sen durch das Reich im Auslande Einzelfälle A - Z		1940-44	
D R 6 Nr. 5	- B - Z		1940-42	
D R 7	Sammlungen des Auslands-Winter- hilfswerkes, allgemein und Einzelfälle	1	1933-44	
Rp Gen.	Angelegenheiten von Protektorats- angehörigen	1	1939-44	
Rp	Schriftwechsel mit Protektorats- angehörigen im Auslande, Einzelfälle A - Z		1940-44	
Rp Spez.	Ausweisungen aus der Slowakei Einzelfälle A - Z		1940-44	
S.Urk. Gen.	Urkundenbeschaffung	1	1940-44	
S.Urk.	- Einzelfälle A - Z		1940-44	
	- Reichsdeutsche,erledigte Einzelfälle		1940-44	
	- Protektoratsangehörige, erledigte Einzelfälle		1940-44	
Pol 1	Aussenpolitik der Slowakei, Allgemeines	1	1944	3115/D633165-93
Pol 2	Politische Beziehungen der Slowakei zu anderen Staaten	1 2	1939-44	3115/D633125-64 3115/D633194-314
	- Romreise Dr.Tukas	1	1940-42	3115/D633315-44
	- Kleine Entente	1	1941-43	3115/D633345-78
	- Balkankonferenz	1	1940	3115/D633379-403
	- Kroatien	1	1940-43	3115/D633404-35
	- Rumänien	1	1942-43	3115/D633436-45
	- Vatikan	1	1940-43	3115/D633446-91
Pol 2 Nr. 1	- Deutschland	1	1940-43	3115/D633492-96
Pol 2 Nr. 1 a	Propaganda und Hetze gegen Deutschland in der Slowakei, deutschfeindliche Tätigkeit	1	1939-42	3115/D633497-617
Pol 2 Nr. 1 b	Grenzzwischenfälle	1-2	1939-42	
Pol 2 Nr. 2	Politische Beziehungen der Slowakei zu Ungarn	1 2 3 4	1938-42	3115/D633618-823 3115/D633824- 4100 3115/D634101-239 3115/D634240-390
	-	5	1942-43	
	Dr. J.O.Petreas, Das neue Europa und die Slowakei	1	1942-43	

Akten-zeichen	Inhalt	Band	Datum	Serial Nr.
Pol 2 Nr. 2 a	Politische Beziehungen der deutschen Volksgruppe in der Slowakei zu Ungarn	1	1939	
Pol 2 Nr. 2 b	Beschwerden der deutschen Volksgruppe und Interventionen des deutschen Staatssekretariats	1	1939–43	
Pol 2 Nr. 3	Politische Beziehungen der Slowakei zu Polen	1	1938–39	
	Kommunistische und deutsch-feindliche Propaganda	1	1941–44	
Pol 3	Innenpolitik des Gastlandes, allgemein	1	1939–43	3115/D634391–591
Pol 3 Nr. 1	Ministerien, Staatsrat, Bücher für Propagandachef Murgas	1	1941	3115/D634592–613
Pol 3 Nr. 2 a	Sidor	1	1939–41	3115/D634614–44
Pol 3 Nr. 2 b	Dr. Klinovsky	1	1939	3115/D634645–61 4431/E084280–82
Pol 3 Nr. 2 c	Staatspräsidentenwahl	1	1939	3115/D634662–69
Pol 3 Nr. 3	Marine, Luftfahrt, Militär, Arbeitsdienst in der Slowakei	1 2	1939–44	3115/D634670–88 3115/D634689–858
Pol 3 Nr. 4	Staatsschutzbestimmungen des Gastlandes, auch Agenten- und Spionagewesen	1	1941–42	
Pol 3 Nr. 5	Hoheitszeichen, Flaggen, Feier-tage, Ferien	1	1938–42	3115/D634859–902
Pol 3 Nr. 6	Wahlen im Gastlande, Volksab-stimmungen	1	1944	3115/D634903–05
Pol 3 Nr. 7	Parteien, Politische Verbände (allgemein)	1 2	1939–40	3115/D634906–50 3115/D635150–54
Pol 3 Nr. 7 a	– (slowakische)	1 2	1939–44	3115/D6634958–5149 3115/D634951–57
Pol 3 Nr. 7 b	– (volksdeutsche)	1	1939–42	
Pol 3 Nr. 7 c		1	1941	
Pol 3 Nr. 7 d		1	1941–42	
Pol 3 Nr. 8	Warnungen, Empfehlungen	1–2	1939–44	
Pol 4	Zwischenstaatliche aussenpoliti-sche Probleme	1 2 3	1940–44	6791/E514090–114 6792/E514116–46
Pol 4 Nr. 1	Völkerbund	1	1940	

Akten-zeichen	Inhalt	Band	Datum	Serial Nr.
Pol 4 Nr. 2	Judentum, Frage, Freimaurertum, Gesetze und Vorträge, Reden		1939-43	K1644/K403298-584 K1644/K403585-695
Pol 4 Nr. 4	Tschechoslowakische Restaurationsbestrebungen, Expräsident Benesch, Masaryk	1 2 3	1939-43	3115/D635155-384 3115/D635386-496 3115/D635497-509
Pol 4 Nr. 5	Informationserlasse	1	1937	
	Liquidierung des Vermögens der ehemaligen tschechoslowakischen Republik	1	1939-41	3115/D635510-55
Pol 4 Nr. 5 a	Schriftgutaushändigung	1	1939-43	
D Pol 1	Deutsche Aussenpolitik, allgem.	1	1931-43	3115/D635556-61
	Konsul v.Druffel(Pol.Handakten)	1	1932-37	
D Pol 1a	Umsiedlung der deutschen Volksgruppen in die südost-europäischen Staaten	1 2	1924-41	3115/D635562-74
D Pol 2	Politische Beziehungen Deutschlands zu anderen Staaten als dem Gastland	1	1938-43	3115/D635575-730
D Pol 2 Nr. 1	Politische Beziehungen Deutschlands zu Polen	1	1939-43	
D Pol 2 Nr. 2	Protektorat (allgemein)	1	1938-42	
D Pol 2 Nr. 3	Slowakei	1	1940-44	
D Pol 2 Nr. 4	Estland, Lettland, Litauen und Finnland	1	1939-40	
D Pol 3 Nr. 1	Führer und Reichskanzler, die Reichsregierung, Reichstag, Ministerien	1	1941-44	
D Pol 3 Nr. 2	Personalien prominenter deutscher Staatsmänner und Parteiführer	1	1933-41	
D Pol 3 Nr. 3	Internationale Frauentagung NSDAP		1933-44	
D Pol 3 Nr. 4	Militär- und Arbeitsdienstangelegenheiten	1-3	1935-44	
	Militär-Marine-Luftfahrtangelegenheiten	1	1941-44	
	Unruh-Kommissionen			
D Pol 3 Nr. 4 a	Militaria, Erfassung, Musterungen, Einberufungen, Familienunterstützungen	1	1920-43	
D Pol 3	Ausreise Wehrpflichtiger nach der Slowakei	1	1944	
	Liste der Drückeberger	1	1944	

Akten- zeichen	Inhalt	Band	Datum	Serial Nr.
D Pol 3 Nr. 4 a	Militaria pers.	1	1939-41	
	— spec. Einzelfälle		1939-43	
	Reichsarbeitsdienstangelegen- heiten, Einzelfälle		1939-43	
D Pol 3 Nr. 4 b	Arbeitsdienstpflicht, Allgemei- nes und Einzelfälle	1	1939-43	
	Wehrpflichtige Reichsangehörige, die ohne Einschaltung der Gesandtschaft die slowakische Staatsangehörigkeit erworben haben, Verschiedenes	1	1940-44	
D Pol 3 Nr. 4 c	Familienunterhalt für Angehörige slowakischer Soldaten	1	1939-42	
D Pol 3 Nr. 4 d	Familienunterhalt SS	1	1941-44	
D Pol 3 Nr. 4 b	Wehrpflichtige, Einzelfälle A - Z		1940-44	
D Pol 3 Nr. 4 c	Familienunterhalt, Kriegsbesol- dung, Einzelfälle A - Z		1940-44	
D Pol 3 Nr. 4 d	Kriegsgefangene A - Z		1940-44	
D Pol 3 Nr. 5	Staatsschutzbestimmungen, Kommunismus, Freimaurertum, Judenfrage in Deutschland	1	1933-42	K1645/K403696- 721
D Pol 4 Nr. 2	Judenfrage Generell, Einzelfälle	1	1939-41	K1646/K403722-49
D Pol 5 Nr. 1	Gen.Sammlungen im Ausland, WHW	1	1940-41	
	Sammlungen in der Konsulats- abteilung	1	1944	
D Pol 3 Nr. 7	Deutsche Kriegergräber	1-2	1940-44	
D Pol 6 Nr. 1	Kriegsgräberfürsorge und Gräber- listen	1-2	1940-44	
P 1	Presse- und Propagandawesen im Gastland (Allgemeines)	1-3	1939-43	
	— (Verschiedenes)	1-5	1940-43	
P 2	Beziehungen zu Deutschland und anderen Ländern, Presse	1	1939-44	
P 3	Verlagsanstalten, Zeitungen, Buchhandlungen	1-6	1940-43	
P 3 Nr. 1	Nachrichtenbüro, Telegrafen- agenturen	1	1940-43	
P 3 Nr. 2	Zeitungsbetriebe slowakische	1	1940-43	
P 3 Nr. 3	Firma Karl Ruszioska	1	1942-43	
P 3 Nr. 5	Rudolf Kremayer	1	1941-44	

Akten-zeichen	Inhalt	Band	Datum	Serial Nr.
P 4	Pressevertreter, Redakteur Berichterstatter und ihre Organisationen	1	1941-43	
P 4 Nr. 3	Deutsche Informationsstelle	1	1941-43	
P 5	Zeitungsaustausch	1	1940-43	
	Pressebericht-Süd	1	1943	
P 6	Beanstandungen in Presse und Propaganda	1-3	1939-43	
D P 1	Presse und Propagandawesen in Deutschland (Allgemeines)	1-16	1939-43	
	Anti-bolschewistische und anti-kommunistische Propaganda	1-4	1941-44	
	Anti-englisch-amerikanische Propaganda	1-4	1941-44	
	Propagandamaterialversendung	1-2	1940-43	
	Propagandamaterial,Verschiedenes	1-18	1940-44	
	Propagandawesen: Broschüren, Bücher	1-24	1940-44	
D P 1 a	Pressetelegramme	4	1940	
D P 1 b	Belegexemplare für Presse-telegramme	1	1940	
D P 1 c	Propaganda in der slowakischen Presse, Presse-Echo	1-6	1940-44	
	- Schriftenreihe, Pressedienst,	1-3	1934-42	
	Berichte	1-7	1940-44	
D P 1 d	Pressedienst	1	1940-43	
D P 3	Verlagsanstalten, Zeitungen	1	1936-43	
D P 4	Pressevertreter, Redakteure, Berichterstatter	1	1935-36	
D P 5	Arbeitsberichte der Presseab-teilung	1	1942	
W 1	Wirtschaftspolitik des Gast-landes, allgemein	1	1939-41	4434/E084896-918
		2		4737/E232609-862 4434/E084919-84
	Wirtschaftsberichte	1	1940-43	4433/E084335-893
		2		
	Bäderbewirtschaftung	1	1940-43	
	Raumordnungsfragen, Pauschal-kuren, Auskunftserteilung	1-4	1940-44	
	Agrarpolitische Berichte der deutschen Partei	1	1940-41	
W 1 Nr. 1	Gründung einer slowakischen Ein- und Ausfuhr-Gesellschaft (Dovus)	1	1939-43	

Akten-zeichen	Inhalt	Band	Datum	Serial Nr.
W 2	Wirtschaftliche Beziehungen zu den einzelnen Staaten und zwischen den einzelnen Staaten	1-3	1939-42	
	Russland	1	1939-41	
	Pferdelieferungen	1	1940-42	
	Zelluloselieferungen	1	1940-41	
W 2 Nr. 1	Wirtschaftliche Beziehungen der Slowakei zu Deutschland	1-13	1939-43	
	Wirtschaft, Handel, Industrie Generalia	1	1930-42	
	Wirtschaftliche Beziehungen der Slowakei zu Deutschland. Lieferung von Obst, Gemüse, auch Hülsenfrüchte	1	1940-43	
	Öl, Schmieröl, Mineralöl	1	1940-43	
	Krautlieferungen	1	1940-42	
	Kartoffellieferungen	1	1941	
	Heu und Stroh	1	1940-43	
	Kraftwagen und Pneulieferungen	1	1940-43	
	Vieheinkäufe	1	1940-43	
	Kunstdüngereinfuhr	1	1940-43	
	Umsatzsteuerfragen, sudetendeutsche Lieferungen	1	1940-43	
	Ein- und Ausfuhr verschiedener Firmen,		1940-43	
W 2 Nr. 1 a	Slowakisch-deutsche Wirtschaftsverhandlungen	1-7	1939-43	
	- Arbeitskräfte für Deutschland	1-2	1940-44	
	Deutsch-slowakisches Clearing und 1 Anlage	1-2	1940-43	
W 2 Nr. 1 a Gen.	Firmen und Vertreterbenennungen	1	1939-44	
	Handelsauskünfte, Forderungen und Vertretungen	1	1941-42	
	Verzeichnisse von Firmen und Personen	1	1941	
	Vereinbarung über Beamte und sonstige Bedienstete	1	1942-44	
	Deutsch-slowakische Vereinbarungen und Berichte und eine Anlage	1	1940-43	
W 2 Nr. 1 c	Forderungen, Auskünfte,		1940-44	
	Einzelfälle, Auskünfte	1	1940-42	

Akten-zeichen	Inhalt	Band	Datum	Serial Nr.
W 2 Nr. 2	Wirtschaftliche Beziehungen zu Polen	1	1939	
W 2 Nr. 3	Filialbetriebe ausländischer Unternehmungen in der Slowakei	1	1941	
W 2 Nr. 4	Geschäftsverkehr mit dem General-gouvernement	1	1940-42	
W 2 Nr. 5	Schulungen	1	1940-41	
W 2 Nr. 6	Wirtschaftsberatungsstelle	1	1940	
W 2 Nr. 7	Tagungen der Handelsattachés im Südostraum	1	1943	
W A	Ausstellungen, Museen, Kongresse Verschiedenes	1-17	1940-43	
W E	Eisenbahnen	1-2	1939	
	- Kaschau-Oderberg	1	1940-44	
	Elektrifizierung der Staats-bahnen	1	1941-43	
W F	Finanzwesen der Slowakei	1	1939-41	
	Finanzen	1-3	1940-43	
	Staatsschuld und Eigentum, Verschiedenes	1-9	1939-43	
W F a	Slowakische Nationalbank	1	1939-43	
W F a Nr. 1	Bankenzusammenlegung	1-4	1939-43	
	Spiritus und Hefefebrik	1	1940-41	
	Pressburger Börse	1	1940-41	
W F a Nr. 2	Bau- und Sparkassen	1	1941	
W F s	Fischerei	1-2	1940-43	
W H	Handel der Slowakei	1	1939-43	
	Preispolitik - Preiserhöhungen	1-2	1939-43	
	Handel, Handelskammern	1	1940-41	
W H Nr. 1	Versicherungswesen	1-2	1940-43	
W H Nr. 2	Revisions- und Treuhandgesell-schaft	1	1940-41	
W J	Industrie, Technik und Gewerbe		1939-44	
W J 1	Arisierungsmaßnahmen in der Slowakei	1-2	1939-42	
	- verschiedener Firmen	1-15	1939-42	
W Kr.	Kraftfahrwesen	1-2	1938-43	
	Autoklub	1	1941-43	
W L	Landwirtschaft, Ernährung, Forstwirtschaft und Jagd	1-2	1939-44	

Akten-zeichen	Inhalt	Band	Datum	Serial Nr.
W L	Landwirtschaft, Ernährung, Verschiedenes	1-11	1939-44	
W L Ho.	Holzindustrie in der Slowakei	1-2	1939-43	
	- Verschiedenes			
W P	Post, Telegrafen, Fernsprecher, Kabel	1	1939-43	
	Feldpostsendungen und Brief-markensammler	1-2	1939-44	
W P 1	Radio und Rundfunkbesprechungen	1-3	1941-43	
	Radiojournal, slowakische Betei-ligung	1	1941-43	
	Rundfunkorchester	1	1942	
	Feindsendungen und Störaktion	1	1939-43	
	Ukrainische und russische Sen-dungen	1-2	1941-43	
	Radio	1-8	1939-44	
W R	Rohstoffe und Waren	1-2	1936-44	
	Erdölvorkommen und Vertrag	1	1939-43	
	F.W.Schmidt, Kaufmann	1	1939-42	
W.Schif-fahrt	Gen.Schiffahrt	1	1939-40	
W.Sch.		1-2	1939-43	
W.St.	Steuern - Monopole	1	1939-43	
W.V.	Verkehr	1-2	1939-43	
	- Strassen, Postkraftwa-gen, Güterverkehr, Holz-gasgeneratoren-Einsatz	1-11	1939-43	
W Z Gen.	Zollwesen, allgemein	1	1939-43	
W Z	-	1-2	1940-42	
	- Verschiedenes	1-18	1940-44	
W Z Nr. 1	Zollgrenzschutz	1	1940	
W Z Nr. 3	Liebesgabensendungen	1	1940-42	
D W A	Ausstellungen und Tagungen in Deutschland	1-2	1939-44	
D W A allg.	Ausstellungen und grössere Kon-gresse in anderen Staaten	1	1939-42	
D W E	Deutsche Eisenbahnen	1	1939-44	
	Fahrkarten der Abordnung der Hlinka-Jugend	1	1942-43	
D W F	Finanzwesen des Reiches	1	1939-44	
	Deutsche Finanzen, auch Devisenbestimmungen	1-3	1931-44	

Akten-zeichen	Inhalt	Band	Datum	Serial Nr.
D W F	Deutsche Finanzen und Devisen-bestimmungen, Verschiedenes	1-8	1940-44	
	Slowakisch-deutsche Handels-kanzlei	1	1942-43	
	Reichsverbürgte Kredite	1	1939-42	
D W F Nr. 1	Generelle Devisenbestimmungen	1	1939-44	
	Staatszuschüsse der Tschecho-slowakei für den Wohnungsbau	1	1940	
D W F Nr. 2	Deutsches Vermögen im feindli-chen Ausland	1	1940	
D W H	Deutscher Handel	1	1934-44	
D W J	Deutsche Industrie, Technik, Gewerbe	1-2	1936-44	
D W Kr.	Kraftfahrwesen	1	1937-43	
D W L	Landwirtschaft und Ernährung, Forstwirtschaft und Jagd	1	1939-44	
D W Lu	Deutsche Luftfahrt (Zivile)	1	1940-43	
D W P	Deutsche Post, Fernsprecher, Telegrafen	1	1939-43	
	Tatra-Sender	1	1941-42	
	Sonderdienst Seehaus	1	1941	
D W R	Deutsche Rohstoffe und Waren	1	1939-42	
D W Sch	Deutsche Schiffahrt Oder-Donau-Kanal	1-2	1933-43	
D W St	Deutsche Steuern	1	1936-37	
D W V	Deutscher Verkehr	1	1939-43	
D W Z	Deutsches Zollwesen	1-2	1933-43	
D W 1	Deutsche Wirtschaftspolitik allgemein	1-2	1939-44	
	-	1	1932-41	
D W 2	Wirtschaftspolitische Beziehun-gen Deutschlands zu anderen Staaten als dem Gastland	1	1939-43	
	Erlasse 1941, 2 Anlagen		1941-42	
	Donau-Kommission	1-8	1921-27	
	- Verschiedenes	1-5	1921-27	
Prot. E	Einladungen, Glückwünsche	1-2	1939-41	
Prot. 1	Konsularisches Korps im Gastland	1	1943	
Prot. 4	Staatsbesuche zwischen dem Gast-land und Deutschland	1-2	1938-42	
Prot. 5	Orden und Ehrenzeichen	1	1922-44	
Prot. 5 a	Mutterkreuze	1	1939-43	

Akten-zeichen	Inhalt	Band	Datum	Serial Nr.
Prot. 5b	Frontkämpfer Ehrenkreuze, Verwundetenabzeichen	1	1934-44	
Prot. 6	Empfänge, Diners, Einladungen, Glückwünsche, Kondolenzen, Kränze	1-2	1940-44	
Prot. 7	Besuch offizieller Persönlichkeiten im Amtsbezirk	1	1940-42	
	Staatshaushalt	1	1940-44	
	Amtsblatt	1	1943-44	
	Erlasse des Auswärtigen Amtes ohne besondere Bedeutung für Behörde	1	1918-39	
	Verzeichnis über abgesandte Berichte an die Deutsche Gesandtschaft	1	1940-43	
	- an das Auswärtige Amt	1	1940-43	
	Statistische Berichte	1	1941-44	
	Slowakische Gesetze 1943	1	1943	
	Sonstiges	1	1939-43	
	Meldeblätter allgemein A - Z		1938-44	
	Sammelpässe		1940-42	
	Sichtvermerkserteilung		1940-44	
	Melderegister abgereister Deutscher A - Z		1938-44	
	15 Tagebücher		1939-43	
	1 Sichtvermerk		1941-44	
	1 Buch Berichte an das Auswärtige Amt		1939-41	

Akten-zeichen	Inhalt	Band	Datum	Serial Nr.
	A n h a n g			
Pa.	Pass-Angelegenheiten A - Z			
	- Protokoll-Angelegenheiten			
	Buchstabe Pa-Pr			
	Pa-Pr Juden			
	Pa-Pr Dubnica			
	Pa-Pr Podbrezora			
	Pa-Pr Bystrica			
W 2 1 a	Anfragen ob Juden oder Arier			
W 2 1 b				
W 2 1 d				
W 2 1 i				
D W F 1	A - Z			
	Fragebogen für Reichsdeutsche und Protektoratsangehörige			
	Staatsangehörigkeit Ungarn			
	Sichtvermerke			
	Rd Reichsdeutsche			
	Slowaken			
	Juden			
	KLV (Kinderlandverschickung)			
	Dubnica			
	Diverse			
	Diverse Karteien			

Akten-zeichen	Inhalt	Band	Datum	Serial Nr.
1	Wahlkonsulat Reval		1924-39	
1a	Gesandtschaftsakten Haus	1-7	1920-40	
	Bauabrechnung		1938	
3a	Geschäftsbetrieb	2	1938	
		4	1938	
4	Zeremonielle Angelegenheiten		1930-40	
5	Verhandlungen über den deutsch-estnischen Konsularvertrag		1924-25	
6	Konsularvertrag			
7a	Persönliche Berichte		1919	
7b	Persönliche,politische Angele-genheiten mit estnischem Aussen-ministerium		1919	
7c,7d	Persönliche Berichte		1919	
8a	Personalien allgemein	2	1924-29	
8b		4	1934-36	
8c		5	1936-39	
9	- Geheimsachen		1924	
10	Specialia Dienstreisen, Umzugs-kosten		1930-38	
11a	Personalia Einzelhefte: Badendieck		1935-41	
11b	Dr.Breer		1935-41	
11c	Edel Herda		1935-41	
11d	Erdmann		1935-41	
11e	A.Friedmann jun.		1935-41	
11f 1+2	Minister Dr.Frohwein		1935-41	
11g	Hansen			
11h	Höntsch			
11i	Kiele			
11k	Knüpfer			
11L	Nill			
11m	Otto			
11n	Prawitz			
11o	G.Reinhardt			
11p	L.Reinhardt			
11q	Frhrr.v.Schleinitz-Prokesch			
11r	Schmidt			
11s	Schulmann			
11t	Seipel			
11u	Spelsberg			
11v	Tommark			
11w	Thomas			
11x	Vockrodt			
11y	Dr.Weiss			

Akten- zeichen	Inhalt	Band	Datum	Serial Nr.
	Personalia Einzelhefte: Westereten			
	Zimmer			
	Zobel			
	Umlauf			
	Jahresberichte		1936-40	
Prot.1	Zeremonielles		1939-40	
Prot.2	Diplomatisches und Konsulari- sches Korps		1939-40	
Prot.3	Orden und Ehrenzeichen		1939-41	
Prot.5	Staatsbesuche		1939	
Pers.G. 4a	Dienstkraftwagen		1939-41	
Pers.G.8	Drucksachenaustausch		1939-41	
Pers.R.6	Prüfungsbemerkungen		1939	
Pers.R.11	Devisenangelegenheiten		1939-40	
Pers.Si.6	Kurierangelegenheiten gen.		1939-40	
Pers.Si. 6a	- spec.		1939-40	
	Vizekonsular Dorpat	1	1919-31	
		2	1931-40	
	Wahlkonsulat Arensburg		1928-40	
	Konsulat Narva			
	Abrechnung Oktober bis Dezember		1939	
	- 1939		1939	
	- ab 1.Oktober 1940		1940	
	Zahlungslisten (Beamte)		1940	
	- (Angestellte)		1940	
	Einzahlungen zu Gunsten Dritter		1935-41	
	Nebenkassenbuch Belege		1935-40	
	Kassensachen		1939-41	
	Fürsorgezahlungen		1939-40	
	Angestelltenversicherung		1919-39	
	Dienstreisen und Umzugskosten, allgemein		1924-41	
	Abgabe von Akten der Gesandt- schaft an das Auswärtige Amt			
	Kistenverzeichnis der mit Abzug der Gesandtschaft abgefertigten Kisten mit Akten und Büromaterial			
	Abzug der Gesandtschaft		1940-41	

Akten- zeichen	Inhalt	Band	Datum	Serial Nr.
Pers.R 4. 2	Auftragszahlungen, Fonds, Kult		1939-41	
Pers.R 11	Devisenangelegenheiten des Auswärtigen Amtes und der Gesandtschaft		1940	
	Übersiedlung		1939-41	
	Kiviöli (Merits)		1939-41	
	Abwicklung der Gesandtschaft Reval, Kassenangelegenheiten		1941	
	Wertsendungen aus Anlass der Umsiedlung	2	1940-41	
	Umsiedlungswertsendungen		1940-41	
	Wertverzeichnisse			
	1 Mappe Umsiedlung		1940	
	1 Mappe Einbürgerungen		1940	
	Treuhandstellen		1940	
	Konsulatsgebühren		1924-41	
	Sonderdienst Kulturaustausch gen.		1939-41	
	Reichsversicherungsanstalt, Landesversicherungsanstalt		1938-41	
	Passbestimmungen		1940	
	Bestimmungen über Verschluss- sachen		1938-40	
	Kassensachen	1-4	1937-41	
	Verschiedenes		1941	
	Abrechnung für Waffenattachés		1939-40	
	Konsulat Dorpat		1940	
	- Pernau		1939-40	
	Verkehr mit vorgesetzten Dienst- behörden	2	1919-20	
	Berichtverzeichnisse		1939-41	
	Kriegswinterhilfswerk 1940/41		1940-41	
	Inhaltsverzeichnis der Geheim- akten		1924	
	Dienstliche Briefe in privater Form		1924	
Pers.R 12	Verwahrgüter		1939-40	
Pers.R 13	Beschaffung von Betriebsmitteln		1939-40	
	Inventarverzeichnis		1924	

Akten-zeichen	Inhalt	Band	Datum	Serial Nr.
Pers.	Korvettenkapitän Cellarius		1939-40	
	Pförtner Friedmann		1923-39	
	Dr.Hartisch		1939	
	Kapitänleutnant Junghans		1939-40	
	Kube		1935	
	H.Kubitz		1940	
	W.Nickel		1939-40	
	K.S. Karl Stark		1939	
	Wiese		1939-40	
	Beihilfen		1935-39	
	Zahlungsanordnungen		1940	
	Handakten, Verschiedenes		1926-41	
	Personalia:			
	G.R.Dittmar		1924-26	
	L.S.Duckwitz		1928-31	
	M.Drost		1919-24	
	Frl. M.Ernst		1921-22	
	Frl. M.Bielib		1922-25	
	Minister Frank		1925-26	
	Kanzler Gehrmann		1920-21	
	Minister Frank		1924-28	
	L.S.Henkel		1920-23	
	R.R.von Hentig		1921-26	
	Attaché Graf Hohenthal		1928	
	Leg.Sekr. Jung		1922-24	
	Frl. A.Kaselitz		1927-30	
	L.S.Dr.H.Koester		1922-23	
	L.S.Dr.Kreutzwald		1925-28	
	Diätar R.Lüneburg		1922-23	
	Kanzler Limberts		1922-33	
	Chauffeur Markin		1920-21	
	L.S. Mey		1929	
	Minister Moraht		1924-25	
	L.S.v.Neuhaus und G.B.Noeldecke		1923-24	
	Kanzler Max Pache		1921-23	
	Amtsdiener Poller		1920-21	
	v.Pressentin		1920-21	
	Frl. Seiler		1920-22	
	Bürohilfsarbeiter Siegfried		1922-35	
	Stelzer		1929	
	Amtsdiener Stübing		1921-24	
	Diätar Fritz Schmidt		1921-32	
	Minister Schroetter		1928-33	
	Minister Reinebeck		1932-38	
	Karl Telschow		1919-20	
	Oskar Thomas		1919-23	
	Hilde Thomas		1920-31	

Akten-zeichen	Inhalt	Band	Datum	Serial Nr.
Pers.	Personalia:			
	Amtsdiener R.Rohde		1920-23	
	Max Vogl		1919-25	
	Warrlich		1929-35	
	Minister Wedding		1923-25	
	Frhrr.v.Welck		1930-32	
	Wezels		1923-27	
	G.R.Weirauch		1925-28	
	Hilfsarbeiter G.Wüstefeld		1922-26	
	L.S.Dr.Zwade		1921-22	
	L.S.A.v.Stockhammer		1936-37	
	Bürohilfsarbeiter Schiller		1934-37	
	HAG.König		1924-35	
	L.S.v.Rosen			
	Frl.E.Erbrecht		1933-37	
	S.Conrad		1938	
	Frl.J.Gründemann		1937-38	
	Kanzler W.Pierau		1933-39	
	L.S.Frhrr.v.Doernberg		1933-37	
C 1	Estland politisch		1939	
C 3 a	Estland-Russland		1938-39	
Pol 1	Aussenpolitik Estlands		1939-40	
Pol 2/1	Politische Beziehungen Estlands zu Deutschland		1939-41	
Pol 2/1a	Enteignung und andere Maßnahmen gegen Reichs- und Volksdeutsche		1941	
Pol 2/3	Politische Beziehungen Estlands zu Lettland und Litauen		1939-40	
Pol 2/4	－ Finnland und Skandi-navien		1939-40	
	－ Räterussland		1939-40	8511/E597371-74
Pol 2/8	－ England und Frankreich		1939-40	
Pol 2/11	－ anderen Staaten		1939-41	
Pol 3/2/1	Innerpolitische Lage		1939-41	
Pol 3/4	Staatsschutzmaßnahmen		1939-40	
Pol 3/6	Wahlen, Politische Verbände, Parlament		1940-41	
Pol 4/1	Völkerbund		1939-40	
Pol 4/2/3	Bolschewismus, Kommunismus, Sozialismus, Freimaurerei		1940-41	
	Kommunismus, Maßnahmen gegen Staatsfeinde		1935-40	
Pol 4/5	Judenfrage		1939-40	
	Juden und Freimaurerei		1936-38	
D Pol L3	Krieg	1-3	1939-40	

Akten-zeichen	Inhalt	Band	Datum	Serial Nr.
D Pol 2/3	Freiwillige, Sonderheft		1939-40	
D Pol 3/2	NSDAP		1938-40	
D Pol	Buchliteratur über NSDAP in Deutschland		1937-40	
	Verhaftung des Konsuls Allik		1940-41	
	Auslieferungsvertrag		1926-34	
C 1	Deutsch-estnischer Konflikt		1928	
Geh.2 b	Estland wirtschaftlich politisch		1919-22	
	Estland wirtschaftlich speziell Narowa Wasserfälle		1924-31	
	Rigaer Abrüstungskonferenz		1925	
	Estland wirtschaftlich	1-9	1924-37	
	Politik der Randstaaten unter-einander	1-17	1922-38	
C 1 I	Estlands Beziehungen zu Deutsch-land	1-4	1932-40	
		5		5922/E435443-46
		6-8	1932-40	
		9		7795/E566005-07
		10		9623/E678919-22
	Deutschlands politische Bezie-hungen zu den Randstaaten	1-2	1922-32	
C 1	Estland innerpolitisch und seine Beziehungen zu Deutschland	1-10	1923-34	
		11		
		12	1934-38	
		13		5922/E435447-50
		14		
	Minderheiten	1-7	1921-39	
	Memelfrage	1-4	1923-39	
	Ostpaktverhandlungen	1-3	1934-37	
	Paktverhandlungen England-Frankreich-Russland		1939	
C 2 a	Estlands politische Beziehungen zu Lettland	1-4	1922-39	
C 2 b	- Litauen		1922-39	
C 2 d	- Polen	1-2	1923-40	
C 1 b	Politisch wichtige Persönlich-keiten	1	1920-26	
	Wichtige Persönlichkeiten Est-lands		1923-25	
	Beihilfen für die deutschen Schulen	1-3	1922-36	
C 3 a	Estlands politische Beziehungen zu Russland	1-3	1925-37	

Akten-zeichen	Inhalt	Band	Datum	Serial Nr.
C 3 b	Estlands politische Beziehungen zu Frankreich	1-2	1922-35	
C 3 c	- Skandinavien	1-2	1922-39	
C 3 d	- England	1-2	1923-39	
C 3 e	- anderen Staaten	1-3	1923-39	
D 1	Politik der Randstaaten unter-einander	18	1918-39	
D 2	Politik der Randstaaten gegen-über anderen Staaten	10	1938-39	
D 1	Deutschlands politische Bezie-hungen zu den Randstaaten	1-2	1932-39	
	Marineattaché		1937-39	
Pol 3-5b			1940	
	Militärattaché		1934-37	5922/E435451-84
			1937-39	
Pol 3-5a	Allg.persönl. Militärattaché		1939-40	
	Berichte Militärattaché	1+3	1939-40	
	Flottenbesuche gen.	1-2	1924-37	
	Besuch des Kreuzers "Thetis"		1924-25	
	Hilfsaktion für im finnischen Meerbusen im Eise eingeschlos-sene deutsche Schiffe		1926-27	
	Flottenbesuche 1927, 1929, 1931, 1932			
	Kreuzer "Hessen"		1933	
	Flottenbesuch "Königsberg"		1934	
	- 2.Torpedobootflotille		1936	
	- Kreuzer "Leipzig"		1937	
	- "Rolshoven"		1938	
	Ostseefahrt S/S "Tannenberg"			
	Flottenbesuch "Admiral Hipper"		1939-40	
	Flugzeugbau in Estland		1933-39	
	Militärakten, Bescheinigungen, Meldeblätter		1936-38	
Pol 3-3	Militär-, Marine- und Luftfahrt-angelegenheiten			
	Ehrenkreuz	1	1934-40	
	Ehrenkreuzverzeichnis der EK-Inhaber	2		
	Abwicklung aus der Okkupations-zeit		1919-20	
	Militärdienst Spezielles A-Z		1935-40	

Akten-zeichen	Inhalt	Band	Datum	Serial Nr.
	Militärisches, Abrüstung	2-3	1935-39	
	Häfen und Kanäle in Estland		1932-39	
W Sch 8			1939-40	
W Sch 1	Schiffahrt Estlands		1939-41	
W Sch 2	- Estland-Deutschland		1940	
D W Sch	Deutsche Schiffahrt		1941	
	Geleitscheinstelle		1940	
	Seemannsheim		1937-39	
	Wirtschaftsverhandlungen		1937-39	
	- Eisenbahnmateriallieferungen		1938	
	Abkommen zwischen Deutschland und den Sozialistischen Sowjet-republiken über gegenseitige Vermögensansprüche betr. Litauen, Lettland, Estland			
	Ratifikation von Urkunden: Deutsch-estnisches Abkommen über Warenverkehr		1938-39	
	- über Handel mit Betäubungs-mitteln		1925-30	
	Deutsch-estnischer Handelsvertrag	1+2	1928-32	
	Deutsch-estnisches Wirtschafts-abkommen	2	1923-27	
		3	1933-37	
	Deutsch-estnische Ausgleichsver-handlungen		1920-24	
	Handakten des Herrn Gesandten Schroetter zum deutsch-estni-schen Wirtschaftsvertrag		1928	
W 1	Wirtschaftspolitische Lage		1938-40	
W A	Wirtschaftliche Ausstellungen in Estland		1939-41	
W E	Eisenbahnen in Estland		1940-41	
W F	Estland-Finanzen		1939-41	
W 2/1	Finanzielle Beziehungen Estland-Deutschland		1939-41	
W 2/1a	Devisenangelegenheiten Estland		1939-40	
W 2/2a	- Einzelfälle		1939-40	
W H	Handel Estlands (Verordnungen)		1939-41	
W 2/1	Handelsbeziehungen Estland-Deutschland		1939-41	

Akten-zeichen	Inhalt	Band	Datum	Serial Nr.
W H 2/3	Handelseinzelgeschäfte Deutschland-Estland	1	1939-40	
		2	1940-41	
W H 3	Handelsbeziehungen Estlands zu anderen Staaten		1939-40	
W J	Industrie, Technik und Gewerbe		1939-40	
W L	Landwirtschaft, Ernährung, Forstwirtschaft,Jagd in Estland		1939-40	
	1 Mappe Kreditbeschaffung für die Landwirtschaft		1926	
	Landkauf der Reichsdeutschen		1938-39	
	Agrarabkommen		1926-34/35	
	Darlehnsbescheinigungen für Estländer, Landwirtschaftsverein für zinsfreie Darlehn		1933-34	
W Lu 1	Luftfahrt allgemein (zivile)		1939-41	
W Lu 2/1	- Beziehungen Estland-Deutschland		1937-40	
	Estnisch-deutscher Wirtschafts-verband		1923-26	
W K	Kraftfahrwesen		1939-41	
W P	Post, Telegraf, Kabel, Radio allgemein		1939-41	
W V	Verkehr, allgemein		1938-40	
W Z	Zollwesen		1939-40	
W St	Steuer		1940	
W R	Rohstoffausbeutung		1939-40	
m 3	Steuerwesen		1924-37	
m 4	Öffentliche Unternehmungen		1923	
n 12-13	Bergbau allgemein Industrie und Technik	1-2	1920-33	
n 14	Handwerk und Gewerbe		1922	
n 15	Soziale Verhältnisse		1920-33	
n 17	Wohnungs- und Bauwesen		1921-31	
n 18	Handel allgemein		1920-24	
n 18 b	Aussenhandel allgemein		1921-27	
n 18 c	Ausfuhr allgemein		1921-24	
n 18 e	Durchfuhr allgemein		1921-24	
n 18 f	Ein- und Ausfuhrregelung		1921-38	
	Handelskrieg, Durchfuhrverbote, Geleitscheine		1939-40	
n 18 h	Staatliche Handelsorganisationen		1920-21	

Akten-zeichen	Inhalt	Band	Datum	Serial Nr.
n 21	Maße und Gewichte		1921-26	
n 23	Geldwesen		1921-36	
	Valutafragen		1922-23	
n 25	Auskunftswesen im allgemeinen		1921-23	
n 26	Wirtschaftliche Interessenver-tretung		1921-26	
n 27	Genossenschaftswesen		1920-28	
n 28	Verkehrswesen im allgemeinen		1921-35	
n 29	Landstrassen, Wege, Brücken		1921-29	
n 30	Eisenbahnen, Strassenbahnen, Kraft- und sonstiges Verkehrs-wesen		1920-34	
n 31	Hafen und Kanäle	1	1921-31	
n 32	Seeschiffahrt und Schiffbau		1921-26	
n 33	Binnenschiffahrt		1921	
n 35	Luftschiffahrt und Flugwesen		1921-23	
n 36	Pressewesen		1921-22	
n 40	Speditions- und Lagerwesen		1923	
n 41	Fremdenindustrie		1921	
n 43	Reklamewesen		1921-23	
n 37	Versicherungswesen		1920-35	
0	Aufenthaltsbedingungen für Aus-länder		1921-32	
	Schiffahrtswesen	5-7	1926-35	
	Angelegenheit "Oostzee"		1919-25	
	Wracks		1920-28	
	Reparatur der Dampfer "Heidel-berg", "Petersburg" S/S"Kronos"			
	Totalverlust S/S "Wagrien"		1936	
	- Dampfer "Möwe"		1927	
	Kabelwerk Vogel Köpenick		1926	
	Geldmarkt und Börsenberichte (Devisen, Effekten, Kurse und Notierungen)	1-3	1921-36	
	Beschaffung von Büchern und Lehrmitteln für deutsche Schulen	1-3	1920-39	
	Liste reichsdeutscher Firmen in Estland			
	Klaus Scheel, G.Scheel & Co.			
	Unerledigtes		1940	
	Kartei und Runderlasse des Referats "H" HFA-Angelegenheiten		1925-27	

Akten-zeichen	Inhalt	Band	Datum	Serial Nr.
	Waldhof-Pernau		1920-38	
	Ausweisung Renter		1933-35	
	Firmensachen A - Z		1940	
	Holzexport Nord-Lettland		1936-37	
	Schiffssachen		1938-40	
	Universität Dorpat	1-8	1920-39	
Kult 1	Allgemeine Kulturpolitik in Estland		1939-40	
Kult 2	Kulturpolitische Beziehungen, Verträge		1939-40	
Kult 3	Reichsdeutsche Kolonie		1939-40	
Kult 4	Kirchenwesen		1940	
Kult 8	Schulwesen		1939-40	
Kult 10	Hochschulwesen		1939-40	
Kult 11 3	Studien- und Vortragswesen		1940	
Kult 11 3a	Dienstreisen verschiedener Persönlichkeiten		1939-40	
Kult 12 1	Kunstausstellungen, Kunst		1940	
Kult 12 2	Theaterwesen		1939	
Kult 12 3	Musikwesen		1940-41	
Kult 12 4	Filmwesen		1939-41	
Kult 12 4a	Kolonie und Propagandafilme		1939-41	
Kult 12 4b	Hetzfilme		1940	
Kult 12 5	Sportwesen			
Kult 12 5a	Olympische Spiele		1939	
	Rundfunk, Radio		1934-39	
	Deutsches Theater in Reval, Konzertreisen	5-6	1936-39	
	Wagner-Konz.Prof.Mikorey		1923-24	
	Kirche	1-3	1923-39	
	Schulsachen allgemein	1-3	1921	
	Goetheschule in Jekaterinburg		1922	
	Ordensangelegenheiten und Aus-zeichnungen	1-2	1921-39	
	Verleihung von Ehrenkreuzen des Roten Kreuzes, Ehrenkreuze für Mütter		1927-40	

Akten-zeichen	Inhalt	Band	Datum	Serial Nr.
	Film allgemein		1936-39	
	Film (Hetze, Kolonie, Filme)	1-2	1929-39	
	Medizinalwesen	2	1935-39	
	Vortragsreise Prof.Schreiber		1926-27	
	Sonderdienst		1939	
	Telegramme und Berichtkontrolle		1920-37	
	Estnische Journalisten über ihre Deutschlandreise		1936-37	
	Reichstagswahl und Volksabstimmung		1933	
	Abstimmung		19.8.34	
	Reichstagswahl 1936 und Abrechnung			
	- und Abstimmung		1938	
	Wohlfahrtsunterstützung, Krankenhäuser Seevald		1922-35	
	Nationale Vereinigung (Bewegung)		1934-38	
	Vereinswesen in Deutschland	1-2	1920-32	
	Deutscher Wohltätigkeitsverein, Bund der Reichsdeutschen, Verband der Reichsdeutschen in Estland		1920-39	
	V.D.A.		1933-38	
	Kongresse	1-4	1935-39	
	Kulturfond	1-3	1933-38	
	Anfragen und Auskünfte	1-4	1920-41	
	Auskünfte und Kartenmaterial		1922-30	
	Kriegsgräberpflege		1938-40	
			1932	
	Alphabetisches Ortsverzeichnis Hauptgräberlisten			
	Gräberlisten der Inseln			
	- Oesel,Arensburg			
	- Nachtrag			
	Kriegsgräber		1931-37	
	Deutsche Kriegergräber auf dem Johannisfriedhof bei Narwa		1926-37	
	Umsiedlunsverhandlungen allg.	1-9	1939-41	
	Umsiedlung Geisteskranker		1939-40	
	- Strafgefangener		1939-40	
	- der Banken		1939-40	

Akten-zeichen	Inhalt	Band	Datum	Serial Nr.
	Umsiedlung Transport allgemein und speziell	1-2	1939-41	
	- Heimschaffung von Polen		1939-41	
	- Rückkehr der Protektorats-angehörigen		1940-41	
	- Zusatzband		1941	
	- Dorpat		1939	
	- Anfragen		1939-40	
	- Leichentransport Kapitän Meislahn		1941	
	Transporte		1939-40	
	Liste der aus estnischer Staats-angehörigkeit ausgeschiedenen und umgesiedelten Personen			
	Liste der Reichsdeutschen in Estland			
	Verzeichnis der Reichsdeutschen im Bezirk der Tallinn-Harrien-schen Präfektur		1932	
	Verzeichnis der aus Estland nach Deutschland Umgesiedelten		1939	
	Umsiedlung		1940	
	Übertritt Reichsdeutscher in den estnischen Untertanenschafts-verband		1934-40	
	Listen Deutscher Reichsangehöri-ger und Erklärungen		1937-39	
	Kirchliche und Standesamtsakten		1933-40	
	Optionen			
	Meldewesen		1938-40	
	Kartei der Konsulatsmeldepflicht			
DR 5/4	Deutsche Pässe und Sichtvermerke	1-2	1939-41	
	Als Volksdeutsche Anerkannte, die ohne Rückfrage Sichtvermerke in Berlin erhalten		1941	
	Zugelassene Volksdeutsche mit Sichtvermerk mit ausländischen Pässen		1941	
	Estnische Gesetze und Verordnun-gen	4	1937-39	
	Deutsche Gesetze und Verordnun-gen		1919-39	
	Schutz des Urheberrechts		1920-40	
	Deutsch-estnischer Schiedsge-richts- und Vergleichsvertrag		1925-33	
	Deutsch-estnischer Übernahme- und Niederlassungsvertrag		1924-29	

Akten-zeichen	Inhalt	Band	Datum	Serial Nr.
	Deutsch-estnisches Vormund-schaftsabkommen		1925	
	Notariatsregister		1939	
R 2/1	Rechtliche Beziehungen Estlands zu Deutschland		1939-40	
R 5	Passrecht, Fremdenpolizei und sonstige Polizeisachen		1939-40	
R 6	Sozial- und Fürsorgewesen in Estland		1939-40	
DR 6	Deutsches Sozial- und Fürsorge-wesen in Estland		1939-41	
	Übernahmen		1924-39	
	Bescheinigungen und Beglaubi-gungen	8-9	1937-40	
	- Heimatscheine, Einbür-gerungsurkunden		1936-39	
	Staatsangehörigkeit, Einbürgerung		1925-29	
	- Steuersachen		1939-40	
	Urkunden und Bescheinigungen		1934-40	
	Offene Schulden auf Urkunden-beschaffung		1935-40	
	Verschiedene juristische Ange-legenheiten, Stackelberg-Pellin		1940	
	Strafsache Kienast-Leucht S/S Taube		1929-34	
	Sichtvermerksfragebogen von Polen		1940-41	
	- A - Z		1940-41	
	Passakten der in Estland verblie-benen Reichsdeutschen		1940-41	
	Meldeblätter		1939-40	
	Kartothek Meldegesetz		1939-40	
	Passanträge mit Fragebogen A - Z		1939-40	
	Gütersachen allgemein	1-14	1920-39	
	Güterentschädigungen: Gut Massau-Scott von Pistohl-ckors		1921-31	
	Narwa Flachsmanufaktur und Narwa Tuchmanufaktur			
	Gut Saarahof-Johann Baron Ungern Sternberg		1921-27	
	Gut Wandorfer-Buxhoevden			
	Gut Kesküll-Persen		1919-20	
	Gut Stahlberg v.Ekkespaerre		1922-31	
	Gut Patsal - von der Becke		1920-30	

Akten- zeichen	Inhalt	Band	Datum	Serial Nr.
	Güterentschädigungen:			
	Gut Alexandrowsk		1922-23	
	Gut Paddenorm-Uexküll		1920-23	
	Gut Ulzen und Freienhof-Samson Himmelstjerna		1923	
	Gut Loper - Dr.Bolz		1922-27	
	Gut Willust - G.v.Roth			
	Gut Hattoküll - v.Rosen		1922-27	
	Gut Neu Löwen - v.Dittmar		1919	
	Gut Wacküll - v.Lueder		1933	
	Güter Uhla und Surra - Gräfin Hännin		1920-34	
	Gut Hukkas-Rausch v. Trauberg		1927-32	
	Gut - d.Ilse Catani		1937-38	
	Gut Waggenküll - Hugo v.Stryck		1934	
	Gut Mohrenhof- Heinrich Stackel- berg		1920-35	
	Gut Baronin Baggo of Bao		1934	
	Gut Poll - Wilhelm Wockenfuss		1930-34	
	Gut Kergel - v.Sievers		1929-34	
	Gut Tammik-Rathleff		1933-35	
	Gut Saggad-v.Günderrode		1921-25	
	Gut Neu Werpal - Baumsteiger		1921-22	
	Gut Kuckers - v.Toll		1920-22	
	Gut Zintenhof-Stael Holstein		1921-24	
	Gut Fetenhof - v.Rosen		1922-28	
	Gut Kosch - Bruno Stein		1920-21	
	Gut Kertelhof - Moenting		1919-20	
	Gut Warrol - Toepffer		1921-23	
	Gut Piersal - Ebba Rein		1919-35	
	Gut Allo - v.Verschuer		1920-21	
	Gut Matsal - v.Hoyningen-Huene		1921-28	
	Gut Koiküll - Boehmer		1919-30	
	Gut Allenküll - Alexander Baron Engelhardt		1921-32	
	Gut Kolossowka - v.Derjugin		1922-23	
	Gut Ledes - Pommeranz		1922	
	Gut Schwarzen - von Pollar		1920-22	
	Gut Menzen - Wulff		1933-36	

Akten-zeichen	Inhalt	Band	Datum	Serial Nr.
	Güterentschädigungen:			
	Gut Kock & Asserin - Wetter - Rosenthal		1923-24	
	Gut Karnus - v.Dalwigk-Lichten-fels		1920-38	
	Gut Georg Lilienfeldt		1938	
	Gut Friedrich v.Moeller		1938	
	Gut Seydell - Hans Baron von Schilling		1924-37	
	Gut Lelle - Hoyningen Huene u.a.		1926-34	
	Feudehof		1934-39	
	Eichhorn		1936-39	
	Einbürgerung Frau Nora v.z. Müh-len		1935-40	
	Gut Serrist - Helene Jäger		1929-31	
	Gut Avakar - Prof.v. Rohland		1923-36	
	Gut Aja - v.Brasch		1931-34	
	Gut - W.Hammerbeck		1929-34	
	Alt und Neu Piigant-Ungern Sternberg		1933-35	
	Gut Palme - v.Devis		1920-36	
	Gut Lesle - Hoyningen Huene			
	Gut Rapkoy - v.Grotthue		1935-37	
	Maidla - E.v.Sievers			
	Gut Kollo - Baron Engelhardt - Freifrau von Hahn		1930-34	
	Gut Laimjall - de Russe		1922	
	Gut Kuiwast - v.Devitz		1919-29	
	Gut Lilienbach - v.Lerchenfeld		1920-34	
	Gut Oskar von Stryck		1938-40	
	Gut Heinrich v.Stryck-Liegnitz		1934-40	
	Gut Ingeborg von Hubatius		1922-39	
	Gut Waiwara v.Korff		1934-35	
	Gut Piep & Sellie - von Baehr		1935	
	Gut Pajack, Markgraf		1922-35	
	Gut Ayakar - Prof.W.Rohland	1	1919-23	
	Gut Alt Fennern - Baronin Lilien-feldt		1922	
	Gut Polenhof - Wold v.Roth		1919-31	
	Gut Lechts - Hoyningen Huene		1922-26	

Akten-zeichen	Inhalt	Band	Datum	Serial Nr.
	Güterentschädigungen:			
	Gut Teilitz - Preetzmann		1921-23	
	Gut Uxnorm - Schottländer Amtro-poff		1923	
	Gut Muddis - L.Greifeld		1924	
	Gut Wissust - Oettingen		1922-24	
	Gut Grewenhagen - Selma Becker		1922-26	
	Gut Kleskowo Saweljewo - Kraus		1922-23	
	Gut Kabbel - Olewa.Lemmatri - v.Nolken		1931-35	
	Unterstützungsrenten:		1936-40	
	Abdank, Arndt Pauline, Arndt Wilhelm,Bartels, Bartsch, Bauer, Behrens, Berger, Daubert Werner und Wilhelmine,Desenick, Dieck, Doege, Doerwaldt,Dreger, Ebert, Ebhardt, Eggers, Eichfuss, Esser, Fick, Pundt, Redin, Reichmann, Ross, Schmidt, Schroeder, Schwartze, Schwarz, Seifert, Spicker, Taubeles, Traeyer, Viertel, Wangerin, Westren-Doll, Wiener, Wittke, Giese, Griese, Helbrich, Hoppe, Jacobi, Jaedicke, Jann Bernhardine, Jann Jenny, Justus, Kahlan, Kaiser, Kalff, Kamm, Kanngiesser, Kauffeldt, Kessler, Kickhöfer, Kirschner, Köckert, Köhler Ada Hermine, Köhler Georg Roman, Köhler Wilhelm, König, Kreutz-berger, Kracht, Lange, Laufenberg Andreas, Laufenberg Anna, Lemke Berta, Lemke Emma, Lutz, Martignoni, Mikur, Müller, Neels, Nicolai, Pfennigwerth, Pomronig, Pressentin			
	Unterstützungen: Einzelfälle			
	Arndt Johann August		1935-36	
	Daubert Wilhelmine		1934-35	
	Bielib Wilhelmine		1930-34	
	Eichelberg Ewald Hermann		1932-33	
	Erdreich Gustav, Dietrich, Karl		1935-37	
	Erdmann Bernhard, Rappin		1928-36	
	Fohlmeister Gretchen und Tochter Gerty		1927-33	
	Füllgraf Amalie geb.Lins		1929-34	
	Gebert Egon		1937-38	
	Heiseler Heinz		1924-29	
	Hohmann Ewald Richard Herrmann		1934-38	
	Ketturek Friedrich		1927-32	
	Läckschewitz Adele		1931-34	
	Laufenberg Theodor		1934-38	
	Lemke Ernst		1935-38	

Akten-zeichen	Inhalt	Band	Datum	Serial Nr.
	Unterstützungen: Einzelfälle			
	Letz		1936-37	
	Laess Ida		1927-38	
	Michaelis Edgar		1933-35	
	Neumann Emil Gustav		1928-31	
	Nietz Friederike, Auguste, Susanne		1930-33	
	Reinhardt Gustav Otto		1937	
	Reinke Karl Albert Robert		1932-35	
	Rohde Emma geb. Grass		1929-33	
	Schütz Caroline		1928-37	
	Seifert Oskar		1933-37	
	Seifert Paul		1935-36	
	Schütz Wilhelmine geb.Schultz		1929-37	
	Thiem Karl Robert		1934	
	Waag Tekla		1935	
	Wuttke Erich Emil Georg		1935	
	Maßnahmen zum Schutze des deutschen Blutes		1934-40	
	Lutherakademie		1936-39	
	Siedlungswesen Beihilfen	1-2	1934-39	
	Güterentschädigung Gut Wacküll		1921-31	
	Einlösung von Hypotheken		1930-32	
	Bescheinigungen in Güterangele-genheiten		1925-28	
	Rechtsstreit Rosenkranz gegen Reichsfiskus		1922-26	
	Doppel in Güterentschädigungs-angelegenheiten			
	Bescheinigungen, Beglaubigungen	1-5	1924-32	
	Doyenat	1-2	1931-37	
	Geheim Politisches		1924-25	
	Wochenberichte des Referats IV Rd		1927-32	
	Schwarze Liste		1922-34	
	A.Heide, Pressebüro, Deutsches Nachrichtenbüro		1933-40	
	Passbestimmungen, Emigranten-wesen		1935-40	
	Blattsammlung, Politische Per-sönlichkeiten		1936-40	
	Hetze gegen Deutschland, Lügen-meldungen		1937-39	
Ordner 1 - 5	Passakten A - Z		1934-39	
6	-		1940	

Akten- zeichen	Inhalt	Band	Datum	Serial Nr.
Ordner 7	Passangelegenheiten		1940-41	
8 - 10	Passsachen		1929-32	
11	Durchlassscheine		1941	
12	Zugelassene Volksdeutsche ohne Sichtvermerk mit Auslandspass		1940-41	
13 - 15	Umsiedlung A - Z		1939-40	
16 - 17	Urkundennachforschungen		1930-36	
18	-		1938-40	
19	Bescheinigungen		1924-40	
20	Bescheinigungen, Umsiedlungs- fragen		1939-40	
21	Ein- und Ausbürgerungen		1940-41	
22 - 23	Reichsangehörige mit ständiger Wohnung, Meldeblätter		1938-40	
24	Einbürgerung und Entlassungen		bis 1933	
25	- -		1933-35	
26 - 29	- - A - Z		1936-39	
30	- aus der deutschen Reichs- angehörigkeit A - L		1922	
31 - 36	Notariatssachen A - Z		1924-38	
37	Todesfälle und Nachlasssachen		bis 1928	
38 - 39	Notariatssachen A - Z		1939-40	
40 - 41	Todesfälle, Nachlasssachen A - Z		1929-40	
42	Eintragungen in die Matrikel		1924-31	
43	Erblegitimationen und Nachlass- sachen		1921-38	
44	Kriegsschädenforderungen		1921-30	
45	Auskünfte, Beschwerden über Firmen		1940	
46 - 47	Zustellungen, Strafsachen A - R		1933-40	
48	Arbeits- und Aufenthaltsgenehmi- gungen		1940	
49 - 50	Ablagen E - Z		1940-41	
51 - 52	Rohstoffe A - Z		1931-39	
53	Gerichtsforderungen		1940-41	
54	Forderungen		1940	
55	Unterstützungen		1924-26	
56	- L - Z		1927-40	
57 - 58	-		1930-41	

Akten-zeichen	Inhalt	Band	Datum	Serial Nr.
Ordner				
59	Auskünfte		1934-41	
60	Canaris-Cellarius	1	1938-41	
61	-	2	1941	
62	D-Fonds		1924-40	
63	Erfindungen		1937-41	
64	NSDAP		1934-39	
65	Kultur		1938-40	
66	Landesverteidigung		1936-38	
67	Mob.	1	1936-38	
68	-	2	1938-40	
69	P-Fonds		1929-41	
70	Politische Fragen	1	1936-38	7802/E566163-65
71	-	2	1938-39	
72	-	3	1939-41	
73	Propaganda		1940	
74	Revalsche Zeitung		1940	
75	Sicherung		1935-40	
76	Spionage		1934-40	
77	Verschiedenes		1938-41	
78	Vorträge, Filme		1936-40	
79	Matrikel A			
80	- Ba - Z			
	Staatsangehörigkeitssachen			
	Beglaubigungsregister Reval		1938-40	
	- Tallinn		1940	
	Schiffsregister		1936-38	
	-		1940	
	Passregister		1921	
	- (Fragebogen)		1931-36	
	Passjournal		1926-39	
	Sichtvermerke		1922	
	Notariatsregister Pernau		1910-40	
	- Dorpat		1920-37	
	Alte Matrikelscheine Dorpat		1932	
	Matrikelregister Dorpat		1919-38	
	Matrikelprotokolle			
	Tagebücher A		1938-41	

Akten-zeichen	Inhalt	Band	Datum	Serial Nr.
	Tagebücher B		1938-40	
	Beglaubigungsregister (3 Stück)		1924-38	
	Unterstützungskartei (Anleihe-gläubiger)		1926-27	
	Namensverzeichnisse, Auslands-gebühren, Erlasse des Auswär-tigen Amtes und der Deutschen Gesandtschaft in Estland		1928-35	
	Sichtvermerkbuch		1923-27	

Akten-zeichen	Inhalt	Band	Datum	Serial Nr.
Gg 1	Dienstbetrieb, Neuorganisation im Auswärtigen Amt und seinen Auslandsvertretungen, Personalveränderungen	3	1940-41	
Gg 2	Dienstbetrieb in der Gesandtschaft, generelle Verfügungen und Erlasse, Hauserlasse, Geschäftsverteilung	2	1937-40	
Gg 2 b	Anträge an die Valutakommission		1939-41	
Gg 2-1	Dienstbetrieb in der Gesandtschaft (Kassenführung)	1-4	1921-41	
adh.	Kassenrevisionen, Kassenabschlüsse		1933-38	
Gg 2-1 A	Amtliche Vorschüsse	1-2	1929-40	
Gg 2-1 A C	Devisenbeschaffung für die Gesandtschaft, Amtliche Vorschüsse		1935-39	
Gg 2-1 B	Abrechnungen 1936		1936-37	
Gg 2-2	Schriftverkehr mit Behörden und diplomatischen Missionen, Verkehr der Mitglieder der Gesandtschaft mit Mitgliedern fremder Vertretungen, Protokollsachen, Etikette	4	1937-41	
Gg 2-3	Depots, Überweisungen	1-3	1930-41	
	Portogebühren		1920-41	
Gg 2-4	Telefon, Lichtanlagen		1922-40	
	Generelles des Auswärtigen Amtes für die Zahlstelle		1931-38	
Gg 2-5	Richtlinien für die Berichterstattung		1920-41	
Gg 2-6	Archivalien, Registraturordnung		1924-40	
Gg 2-9	Vorschriften über den Verkehr mit Privaten		1934-38	
Gg 3	Etatsangelegenheiten einschliesslich Konsulat Libau		1922-28	
Gg 4	Urlaub, Urlaubsbezüge	1-2	1921-41	
Gg 5	Materialien	3	1937-41	
Gg 6	Bücherbeschaffung (Bibliothek)	1-6	1922-40	
Gg 6-1	- für die lettland-deutsche Schulverwaltung		1920-40	
Gg 7	Inventar	1-4	1923-41	
	Inventarverzeichnis A			
	- - B			
Gg 7 a	Radio		1934-39	
Gg 7 c A	Wasch- und Wringmaschine		1938-40	
Gg 7	Einrichtungsgegenstände		1920-23	

Akten-zeichen	Inhalt	Band	Datum	Serial Nr.
Gg 7	Registratur			
	Alte Inhaltsverzeichnisse			
Gg 8	Kuriere, Kurierdienst	5	1938-41	
Gg 8 a	Kurierbescheinigungen aus Berlin	5	1940-41	
Gg 8 b	Verzeichnisse der Wertbriefe	1-2	1923-41	
Gg 8 c	Kurierbescheinigungen nach Berlin	3+4	1936-41	
Gg 8 c spez.	Kurierausweise für Gelegenheits-kuriere		1939-41	
Gg 8 d	Kurierpaketverzeichnisse	5	1937-41	
Gg 8 e	Berichtverzeichnisse	5	1938-41	
Gg 8 f	Verzeichnisse der abgegangenen Geheimsachen		1940-41	
Gg 9	Kraftwagen, Fahrräder	1-3	1920-41	
	Dienstkraftwagen (Mercedes Benz)		1939-41	
Gg 9 spez.	Autoversicherung für Opel Nr.64		1937-38	
	Versicherung des Kraftwagens "Adler"		1935-39	
Gg 11	Dienstreisen		1923-41	
Gg 12	Besoldungen, (Vermögens- und Einkommensteuer der Beamten)	1-3	1920-39	
	Besoldungen	4	1939-41	
Gg 12-1	Teuerung, Teuerungsberichte		1921-41	
Gg 13	Hauskauf, Hausverwaltung, Unterhaltung einschliesslich	1-6	1920-40	
Gg 13-1	Dienstwohnungen, Mieten	1-2	1921-40	
Gg 13 a	Garteninstandhaltung		1937-39	
Gg 13 b	Strandgrundstück "Bulduri"		1939-42	
Gg 13 c	Büroräume: Raina Buly II		1940-41	
	Umbauten im Gesandtschafts-gebäude		1936-37	
Gg 13-4	Baubedarfsnachweisung	1-2	1935-40	
Gg 13	Unterhaltung des reichseigenen Dienstgebäudes		1921-22	
	Belege zum Hausreparationskonto		1921-22	
Gg 16	Reichsdeutsche Kolonie		1920-41	
Gg 16-1	Reichsdeutscher Verein Riga	1-3	1924-41	
Gg 16-1 A	Eigenheim des reichsdeutschen Vereins		1935-39	
B	"Mitteilungsblatt" des Reichsdeutschen Vereins		1936-40	

Akten-zeichen	Inhalt	Band	Datum	Serial Nr.
Gg 16-1 spez.	Streitsache Lüth-Molls		1933-34	
Gg 16-1c	Verlettisierung deutscher Namen		1934-39	
Gg 16-2	Verein reichsdeutscher Republi-kaner	1	1926-33	
Gg 16-4	Deutsches Altersheim	1-2	1922-39	
Gg 16-5	Unterstützung und Heimschaffung hilfsbedürftiger Reichsdeutscher		1924-40	
Gg 16-6	Reichsdeutsche Schule	1-2	1932-41	
	Ein Kassenbuch der Schule des Reichsdeutschen Vereins in Riga mit zwei Heften Belege		1940-41	
Gg 18	Personalien des Gesandten Dr.Stieve	1-2	1928-33	
	- des Gesandten Dr. Martius		1932-34	
	- des Ges.Rat Dr.Weyrauch		1931-36	
	- Lütkene	1	1927-29	
	- Leg.Sekr.Dr.Schaller		1936	
	- v.Bargen		1927-32	
	- Kons.Sekr.Otto	1	1926-37	
	- Kons.Sekr.Zobel		1921-40	
	- Kanzler Ephan		1924-36	
	- Kons.Sekr.Neugebauer		1932-38	
	- Leg.Sekr.Frhr.Marschall v.Bieberstein		1934-37	
	- Attaché Dr.G.Federer		1936-38	
	- Gesandter Dr.v.Schack	1-2	1934-41	
	- Hoffmann		1925-41	
	- der Übersetzer der Ge-sandtschaft		1923-41	
	- v.Stolzmann		1940-41	
	- Bawart		1939-41	
	- Gesandter v.Kotze		1938-41	
	- Dr.Hartisch		1939-41	
	- Kleu		1938-41	
	- Ahlbrecht		1939-41	
	- Dr.Kutscher		1936-41	
	- Erdtmann		1936-41	
	- Vietz		1939-41	
	- Kröger		1938-41	
	- Nowak	1	1928-40	

Akten-zeichen	Inhalt		Band	Datum	Serial Nr.
Gg 18	Personalien	Dr.Lecksyck		1936-40	
	–	Sthamer		1938-41	
	–	v.Stockhammern		1936-39	
	–	Betz		1939-40	
	–	Weber		1937-40	
	–	Wendt		1924-38	
	–	Dr.v.Schilling		1920-38	
	–	Bildt		1940	
	–	Pleinert		1939-40	
	–	Stresow		1923-40	
	–	Forstattaché		1940	
	–	Welkisch		1940	
	–	Bode		1938-39	
	–	Rössing		1935-36	
	–	Würfel		1939-41	
	–	Schmidt		1937-41	
	–	Schenkenberger		1935-41	
	–	Gerndt		1938-40	
	–	Chauffeur		1922-41	
	–	Dr.Brosch		1922-28	
	–	Pubantz		1922-23	
	–	Lüneburg		1923-25	
	–	Schneemann		1920-30	
	–	Reinhardt		1926-28	
	–	Landwirtschaftlicher Beirat Mönke und später Darré		1923-29	
	–	Dr.Weber		1921-23	
	–	v.Tippelkirch		1928-31	
	–	Comick		1930-32	
	–	v.Neuhaus		1922-24	
	–	Hagemeier	1	1928-30	
	–	Dornbusch, Willi		1923-27	
	–	Schaller		1921-24	
	–	Riesser		1923-26	
	–	G.K.Riesser		1926-27	
	–	Schau		1925-28	
	–	Wucherpfennig		1922-23	
	–	Dr.Köster	1-3	1922-31	
	–	allgemein	1-4	1920-41	
	–	weibliche Angestellte	1-2	1921-41	
	–	männliche Angestellte	1-2	1920-41	
Gg 18-1	Bewerbungen		2	1921-41	
Gg 18-2	Steuern und Versicherungen			1923-39	
Gg 18-3	Allgemeine Beamtenfragen		1-2	1919-41	
Gg 18-4	Geschenke an Gesandtschaftsange-hörige			1939-41	

Akten-zeichen	Inhalt	Band	Datum	Serial Nr.
Gg 18-5	Zahlungslisten der Angestellten		1935-37	
Pers. Kons.	Personalien Sekr.Schulze		1925-26	
16 Sond.	– Konsul Seelig		1921-24	
Spez.	Leg.Rat Weber (Umzugsgut)		1922-24	
Gg 19	Umzüge, Umzugskosten, Einrichtungsgelder		1921-41	
Gg 20	Beschaffung von Gesetzesmaterial, Gefälligkeiten, durchlaufende Briefe, Telegramme		1938-41	
Gg 21	Beschwerde über den Geschäftsbetrieb sowie über Mitglieder der Gesandtschaft, Bestechungsversuche		1923-40	
Gg 21-1	Zollschwierigkeiten, Beschwerden der Gesandtschaft gegen lettische Behörden und Einrichtungen		1921-40	
Gg 22	Sonderabmachung und Vergünstigungen für die Gesandtschaft (Zollangelegenheit)		1921-41	
Gg 22-1	Zollangelegenheit der Gesandtschaft und des Personals	1-2	1921-34	
Gg 23	Zeitungs- und Zeitschriftenabonnements, Freiabonnements	3-6	1930-41	
Gg 24	Deutsches Krankenhaus, Krankenhausverein		1921-26	
Gg 25	Holzkauf für die Gesandtschaft		1920-41	
Gg 26	Theaterverein: Deutsches Theater in Riga		1921-25	
Gg 27	Durchreisende Persönlichkeiten	2	1927-41	
Gg 28	Haushaltsmittel, Fondsverwaltung, Etat	1-3	1931-40	
A II Gg	Dienstbetrieb in der Gesandtschaft		1920-23	
IV 29	Gesandtschaftsgebäude (Miete)		1920	
	Das Deutsche Haus in Riga (Grundrisszeichnungen)			
A II	Personalien Leg.Sekr. Rudolph		1921-23	
	– Kons.Sekr.Gaebler		1921	
	– Grabowsky		1923	
	– Eckardt		1921-23	
	– Göring		1920-21	
	– Min.Dr.Wewer		1920-21	
	– Dr.Wallroth		1921-23	
	– v.Radowitz		1920-22	
	Amtsantritt des neuen Gesandten Minister Dr.Köster		1922-23	

Akten-zeichen	Inhalt	Band	Datum	Serial Nr.
Kons.Sta. A - Z	Staatsangehörigkeit Einzelfälle		1920-40	
Kons.Sta.	Professor Dr.Sokolowski		1925-28	
Sta.	Staatsangehörigkeit, Einzelfälle A - Z		1939	
	Angaben zum Einbürgerungsantrag A - Z		1939-40	
St.gen. Nr.1	Staatsangehörigkeitssachen, Heimatscheine, deutsche Pässe, Generalia		1920-26	
Kons.Sta. gen.	Aberkennung der deutschen Reichs-angehörigkeit (Sonderakte)		1933-38	
Sta.gen.	Staatsangehörigkeit, Gen.	2-3	1927-39	
Kons.Sta 2.gen.			1934-40	
St.2	Stadtmüller (Staatsangehörigkeit)		1940	
	Seuberlich -		1940	
	Baltisches Familienarchiv		1940	
	Anfragen über Landessippenstelle Posen		1940-41	
Kons.St.2	Urkundenbeschaffung, Einzelfälle A - Z		1938-40	
	Urkunden, Staatsangehörigkeit A - Z		1940-41	
St.3 Nr.6	Staatsangehörigkeit, Einzelfälle		1926-27	
St.6 Nr.4			1923	
Nr.7-9			1925-27	
R 1	Allgemeine Rechtssachen, Gesetzgebung		1922-36	
R 1 gen.	Internationales Recht, interna-tionale Rechtsfragen, Internatio-nales Privatrecht		1929-40	
R 1-1	Internationales Rechtsabkommen auch Arbeitsrecht		1930-40	
R 1a gen.	Eherecht		1921-38	
R 1b gen.	Anerkennung von Urteilen und Schiedssprüchen		1921-33	
R 1c gen.	Haager Abkommen		1926-39	
R 1f gen.	Erbrecht		1923-39	
R 1g gen.	Legitimierung, Adoption		1939	
R 1h gen.	Wechselrecht		1932	
R 2	Rechte von Exterritorialitäten, Privilegien, Reziprozitätsfragen	1-2	1922-41	
R 2 gen.	Spezialgesetz		1923-40	

Akten-zeichen	Inhalt	Band	Datum	Serial Nr.
R 3	Agrargesetz, Schädigung des reichsdeutschen Grundbesitzes	2	1926-37	
R 3 Beiheft	Evangelisches Brüderinstitut		1923-26	
R 3 spez.	Agrar (Einzelfälle)		1920-41	
R-Agr.	v.Hohendorf		1920-37	
R 4	Beschlagnahmen		1923-24	
R 7 gen.	Alimentationsrecht		1935-36	
Kons.R 7	Brecht		1936-40	
	Martin Vecars Karl Heinz Pade		1932-39	
	Rudolf Schalcher Ruth Fischer		1928-39	
	Krause August		1936-39	
	Höfer Albert		1928-39	
	Hartwig Wilhelm und Charlotte		1924-38	
	Geiger		1926-40	
	Irene Friedmann Johanna Gerson		1932-40	
	Grepp Harry		1939-40	
	Brozek Ottilie		1925-27	
	Martha Dannehl		1922-38	
Kons.R 12	Nachlass Elbo		1933-38	
Kons.R 12 Rieck.	Nachlasssache Falk		1939-41	
Kons.R 12	Englert-Schubert		1936-40	
	Nachlass Kerkovius		1938-39	
	– Ehling		1935-38	
	– Pusch, Ella		1938-40	
	– U.v.Lochow		1936-39	
	– Treffkorn		1933-37	
R 12	Nachlässe, Einzelfälle		1920-36	
R 13 Z.R.H.O.	Rechtshilfeordnung in Zivil-sachen		1922-38	
Kons.R 13	Moskau-Windau-Rybinsker Eisen-bahn		1934-38	
	Angelegenheit Sirek		1938-39	
	Wilhelm Renner		1934-37	
	Sonderakte A.E.G.		1929-34	
	v.Bergmann		1935-40	
	Gutachten von Herrn v.Bergmann		1934-37	
Kons.R 19 St.R.H.O.	Rechtshilfeordnung in Strafsachen		1925-39	
	Rechtssachen, Einzelfälle		1920-40	

Akten- zeichen	Inhalt	Band	Datum	Serial Nr.
R 19-1 gen.	Strafrecht		1925-39	
	Riga'ische Zeitschrift für Rechtswissenschaft		1925-39	
R 19-4 gen.	Strafverfolgungen wegen Wehr- pflicht- und Spionagevergehen		1934	
R 19-4	v.Schilling, Wolfgang		1929-33	
R.20^{I}	Entlassung aus der Staatsange- hörigkeit, Einzelfälle		1921-25	
R.20^{II}	Einbürgerungen, Einzelfälle		1920-26	
R.20^{III}	Staatsangehörigkeitsnachfor- schungen, Einzelfälle		1920-26	
R 21	Casselmann		1935-37	
	v.Rentnern		1935-37	
	Minuth		1935-38	
	Müller (Eugen und Konstantin) Guthof		1935-37	
	v.Schwürk		1936-39	
R 22 a	Heimschaffungen		1939-41	
R 24	Pensionen und Renten		1930-31	
	Geburtsurkunden, Einzelfälle		1939-40	
	Sterbeurkunden, Einzelfälle		1935-39	
	Urkunden von Reichsdeutschen, Einzelfälle		1921-22	
	Belege zu den Gebührenüberwei- sungslisten (bare Auslagen) der Konsulatsabteilung	1	1937-40	
	Französisch-deutsche Wortzusam- menstellung für amtlichen Schriftverkehr	1		
	Aktenverzeichnis, Konsulatsab- teilung	1		
	Wer ist's in Lettland?	1		
	Pensionen		1917-39	
Kons.R 28 gen.	Übersetzungsrecht an deutschen Werken der Literatur und Kunst		1930-40	
Kons.R 29 gen.	Steuersachen		1934-38	
R 32 gen.	Rechtsabkommen Lettlands mit anderen Staaten ohne Deutschland		1929-38	
R 35 gen.	Drucksachen		1927-35	
R 7	Alimentensachen, Einzelfälle A - Z		1920-40	
R 10	Deutsche Entschädigungen, Ein- zelfälle A - Z		1920-40	
R 12	Nachlässe, Einzelfälle A - Z		1920-40	
R 13	Rechtshilfe, Einzelfälle A - Z		1920-40	

Akten-zeichen	Inhalt	Band	Datum	Serial Nr.
R 14	Rechtsauskünfte, Einzelfälle A - Z		1920-40	
R 21	Vermittlungen aller Art, Einzelfälle A - Z		1920-40	
	Verschiedenes, Einzelfälle	2	1920-40	
R 24	Pensionen und Renten Einzelfälle A - Z		1920-40	
	Notariatsakten		1921-35	
	Beurkundungen und Beglaubigungen		1936-37	
Kons. gen.	Entschädigungen		1920-37	
	- Einzelfälle		1929-30	
Kons.	- Keyso		1925-34	
	Schadenersatzkommission		1922	
	Entschädigungen verschiedener Einzelfälle		1920-41	
Pa gen.	Passangelegenheiten		1930-33	
	Sichtvermerksangelegenheiten		1934-35	
	Ersatzakte		1939-41	
	Messen		1940	
Kons. Pa 2	Ausreisen der Missionen und Kolonien aus Lettland und Estland		1940	
Pa 9 gen.	Leichenpässe		1909-38	
Pa	Warnungen		1920-21	
Kons. Übern.	Jacobsohn, Jacob		1932-36	
	Haeckel, Gert		1931-38	
	Marcuse		1930-32	
	Kaschube, v.Antonius, Lasers, Schultz Harb.		1935-40	
gen.	Rückführung Juli 1940	1-3	1940-41	
Kons.	Umsiedlung, Generalia N.1 (Optionsvertrag, Optionsverhandlung, deutsche Verhandlungsdelegation, Staatsangehörigkeit)		1939-40	
	Umsiedlung, Generalia Nr.1	2	1940	
	- - Nr.2(Kulturgüter)	1-2	1939-41	
	-, Gen.2a Protokolle, Aufzeichnungen, Sitzungsberichte des Paritätischen Ausschusses		1939-40	
	-, Gen.Nr.3 (Transport)		1939-40	
	-, Gen.Nr.3 (Empfehlungsschreiben für Umsiedler, die mit der Bahn reisen)		1940	

Akten-zeichen	Inhalt	Band	Datum	Serial Nr.
Umsiedlg. Gen.Nr.4	Libauer Bank, speziell Deutsche Gesellschaft, Rücktransport (Kassengeschäfte, Devisensachen, Transfer)		1939-40	
Nr.5	Utag	1	1939-40	L388/L112597-614
		2	1940	L388/L112615-35
Nr.6	Generelle Sammelfälle		1939-40	
Nr.7	Straf- und Untersuchungsgefangene		1939-40	
Nr.8	Baltendeutsche Legate und Sterbekassen		1940-41	
	Fortbestand deutscher Handels- und Industrieunternehmungen nach dem Umsiedlungsvertrag		1939-40	
	Deutsch-lettischer Umsiedlungsvertrag und zusätzlicher Schriftwechsel		1939-40	
	Umsiedlungsverträge 1. Südbukowina, Dobrutscha 2. Bessarabien 3. Litauen		1940	
	Handakte des Herrn Gesandten über Rückführung		1940-41	
	Fortsetzung des Umsiedlungsverfahrens Nr.1 II		1940	
	Handakten Korrespondenz Berlin (Umsiedlung)		1940	
	Abwanderung, Handakte des Herrn Gesandten		1939	
	Durchführung der Umsiedlung		1939-40	
	Kulturgüter bei Umsiedlung		1939	
	Umsiedlung, Eigentums- und Vermögensreklamationen (Einzelfälle)		1939-40	
	Immobilien (Einzelfälle)		1939-40	
	Vermögensbescheinigungen		1939-40	
	Geisteskrankentransport		1939	
	Rückwandererlisten		1939-40	
	Umsiedlerlisten		1939-41	
	Umsiedlerkartei, Einzelfälle A - Z		1939-41	
	Kons-Umsiedlung Einzelfälle A - Z		1939-41	
	Nachträgliche Gesuche, Umsiedlung spez. A - Z		1940-41	
	Umsiedlung Utag, Einzelfälle A - Z		1939-41	
	Entschädigungsansprüche der Umsiedler aus Estland und Lettland auf Grund der Agrarreform		1940	

Akten-zeichen	Inhalt	Band	Datum	Serial Nr.
	Entschädigungsansprüche der Um-siedler aus Estland und Lettland auf Grund der Agrarreform Einzelfälle A - Z		1940	
	Umsiedlungen, speziell, Beschei-nigungen Einzelfälle A - Z		1939-41	
	- Legate, Sterbekassen, Vereine, Auslösung Einzelfälle		1939-41	
	Forderungen von Reichsdeutschen		1920	
	Unterstützungs- und Heimschaf-fungskosten, Einzelfälle A - Z		1920-41	
Kons.V 2	v.Hertzberg Clemence		1935-39	
K 1	Kunst und Wissenschaft, allgem.	1-10	1923-41	
K 1-1 A	Kulturpropaganda, Studentenaus-tausch, Sportvereine	6 7 8 9 10 11	1930-40	K1649/K403821-25 K1649/K403826-31 K1649/K403832-37 K1649/K403838-39 K1649/K403840-42
K 1 spez.	Hygieneausstellung "Gesunde Frau-gesundes Volk"		1934-38	
K 1-1 B	Vorträge, Gastspiele, Konzert-reisen		1937-40	
K 1-2	Filmwesen	1-5 +7	1923-40	
Wi 27	- Wirtschaftsabteilung	1-2	1926-37	
K 1-3	Kulturpropaganda, Geschenkwerte, Propagandamaterial	1-3	1923-29	
		4	1936-41	K1650/K403843-47
A 1 16	Evangelische Kirche in Lettland	1	1921-23	
	Katholische Kirche in Lettland	2	1921-23	
A 1 16-c	Kirche und Schulwesen, Mittel-schulen		1920-22	
d	- Fachschulen		1921	
K 2 a	Handakte zum Kirchenwesen (Verfassung der evangelisch-luth. Kirche)			
K 2	Kirchenwesen	1-2	1923-33	
		3	1933-35	K1651/K403848-63
		4	1935-41	K1651/K403864-66
K 3	Akten der deutschen Gesandtschaft in Riga			
	Unterrichtswesen, Ausländerstu-dium in Deutschland	1-5	1923-31	
	Unterrichtswesen, Kurse, Auslän-derstudium in Deutschland (auch St.Josefs-Verein)	10	1939-41	
K 3-1	Humboldtstiftung	1-2	1925-39	

Akten-zeichen	Inhalt	Band	Datum	Serial Nr.
K 3 a	Befreiung reichsdeutscher Kinder vom lettischen Sprachunterricht		1936-38	
K 3-2	Stipendienfürsorge	1-2	1925-39	
K 5	Herder-Institut	1-8	1921-40	
	- - Geheim		1937-41	
K 5 a	Rektor Prof.Dr.W.Klumberg		1936-37	
K 5 b	Leihgaben für das Herder-Institut		1936-39	
K 5-1	Pädagogisches Institut		1928-30	
K 6	Lettländische Hochschule	1-3	1920-40	
K 6 Sonder-aktenst.	Angeblicher Bruno Hartmann		2.24- 3.24	
K 6-1	Akademische Arbeitsgemeinschaft für Ostfragen in Königsberg		1928-35	
K 7	Kulturpolitik		1937-40	
K 8	Studien- und Gesellschaftsreisen	1 2	1938-40	K1652/K403867-71
S 2	Arbeiterfragen, Arbeiterräte		1922-37	
S 5	Siedlungs- und Wohnungswesen		1921-34	
S 6	Rotes Kreuz, Rettungswesen		1923-40	
S 6 Beiheft	Liste der mit dem Ehrenkreuz des deutschen Roten Kreuzes ausgezeichneten Personen		1924-39	
	Schulverhältnisse in Lettland		1919-21	
R 11	Vergünstigungen auf der Eisen-bahn	1	1925-30	
	Protektorat Böhmen und Mähren		1939-41	
	Österreich		1938-39	
	Grenzempfehlungen, Generalia		1929-40	
	Briefmarkenschwindel Julius Popp alias Bergmann		1923-25	
E 1	Eisenbahnwesen, allgemein	1	5.23- 3.27	
E 2	- in Lettland	1	4.23-11.23	
E 6	Eisenbahnstatistiken	1	7.22- 9.27	
E 13	Eisenbahnkonferenzen	1	4.25-10.27	
Aw.1	Reichswanderamt	1	2.23- 2.28	
G. 1	Gesundheits- und Medizinalwesen, allgemein	1	11.26- 9.28	
G. 2	Seuchen Quarantänemaßnahmen (Konventionen)	1	6.23- 5.27	
G. 3	Gesundheitswesen, Konventionen, Konferenzen	1	4.23- 2.28	

Akten-zeichen	Inhalt	Band	Datum	Serial Nr.
Fi 1	Finanzwesen Deutschland einschl. Banken	1	11.22- 8.27	
Fi 2	Lettland	1	4.23- 4.28	
Fi 3	Finanzwesen fremder Staaten	1	9.23- 1.28	
Fi 4	Finanzielle Beziehungen zwischen fremden Staaten	1	7.26	
Fi 15	Notenwesen	1	9.26- 9.29	
K gen.	Kassen- und Geldsachen		1920-26	
K 1 spez.	Auszahlungen		1921	
K 1-1 spez.			1921-25	
K 1-2 spez.	- Einzelfälle		1926-28	
K 2 spez.	Darlehen Stockholm		1921-25	
K 3 spez.	Nachforschungen nach Sachen-depots bei den ehemalig deut-schen Vertretungen in Russland		1920-24	
K 4 Nr.1 spez.	Rückgabe von Gelddepots der ehemaligen Vertretungen in Russ-land		1920-21	
K 4 spez.	- der ehemalig deutschen Vertretungen in Russland (Einzelfälle)		1921-27	
K 4 Nr.2 spez.			1921	
K 4 Nr.3			1920-22	
K 5 spez.	Vorschüsse		1921	
K 6 spez.	Reichsversicherung für Angestell-te der Gesandtschaft		1921	
K 7 spez.	Konsulatsgebühren		1920-23	
K 8 spez.	Aushändigung von Wertpapieren		1920-21	
K 9 spez.	Rechnungs- und Kassenwesen		1921-23	
K 10/2	Bankguthaben und Umwechselungen		1920-23	
Sekt.IV Nr.26	Überweisungsverkehr der deut-schen Fürsorgeabteilungen in Riga und Libau während des Kriegs-zustandes mit Lettland		1919-20	
Sekt IV Nr.27	Schwarzer Fonds der Fürsorge		1920	
Sekt.IV Nr.28	Nachforschungen nach den beiden früheren deutschen Vertretungen in Russland hinterlegten Depots		1920	

Akten-zeichen	Inhalt	Band	Datum	Serial Nr.
F 1 Nr.1 spez.	Forderungen		1920	
F 1 Nr.2 spez.			1921-26	
	Bankguthaben Darlehnskasse Ost		1922-23	
	Staatsbank Lettlands		1921-24	
	Abrechnungen		1930-39	
	Fond des Auslandspressebüros Geh.Rat Heide		1939-41	
S 1	Soziale Verhältnisse allgemein		1923-41	
S 4 spez.	Winterhilfswerk		1935-40	
S 4	Wohltätigkeit, Veranstaltungen von Sammlungen, Auslandshilfe, Spenden	5	1939-41	
S 7	"Kraft durch Freude"		1938-39	
Kons.Z I	Zoll Einzelfälle A - Z		1940	
Z 2	Zollvergünstigungen Behandlung Diplomatengepäck durch Zollbeamte		1923-41	
Z 2 a	Zollbefreiung von Diplomatengut	3	1940	
Z 3	Zollschmuggel, Zollstrafgesetzgebung, Zollbeschwerden		1923-27	
Post 1	Post-, Telegrafen- und Fernsprechwesen, Flugpost		1921-41	
Ps. 3	Post-, Telegrafen-und Fernsprechbeziehungen zwischen Deutschland und Lettland		1920-40	
Post 4	- zwischen fremden Staaten		1927-28	
H 1	Handel, Verkehr und Industrie allgemein, Konkurrenz		1922-36	
H 2	Handelsbeziehungen Deutschland-Lettland		1920-26	
H 3	- Litauen-Polen		1926	
	- Lettland-Schweiz		1923	
	- - Frankreich		1923	
	- - Russland		1923	
	- - Litauen		1923	
	- - Finnland		1923	
	- - England		1923	
	- - Estland		1923	
H 5	Handelsverträge		1923-27	
H 6	- Polen	1	1927	
	Handelsbeziehungen zwischen fremden Staaten		1923-27	
Wi 1 H eft 3	Wirtschaftsabteilung Lettlands, Wirtschafts- und Handelspolitik allgemein		1931-35	

Akten-zeichen	Inhalt	Band	Datum	Serial Nr.
Wi. 1	Lettlands Wirtschafts- und Handelspolitik, allgemein	1 2 3 4 5	1925-40	K1680/K405536-60 K1680/K405561-83 K1680/K405586-605
Wi.1ᵃ Sd.Akte zu Wi.1	Niederlassungsrecht in Lettland	1	1934-35	
Wi.1ᵇ	Wöchentliche Wirtschaftsberichte	1-4	1928-36	
Wi.1ᶜ	Wirtschaftskrise und Krisenbe-stimmungen	1-4	1931-39	
Wi.1-2	Einfuhr von Salz in Lettland	1	1933-40	
Wi.2	Lettlands Handelsbeziehungen zu anderen Ländern	1	1923-27	
	- zu Belgien	1	1936-39	
	- Bulgarien	1	1928-39	
	- China und Dänemark	1	1929-39	
	- England	1	1929-40	
	- Estland	2	1937-40	
	- Finnland	1	1936-40	
	- Frankreich	1	1930-39	
	- Griechenland	1	1931-38	
	- Holland	1	1935-39	
	- Italien	1	1937-39	
	- Litauen	1	1928-40	
	- Polen	1	1927-39	
	- Rumänien	1	1929-40	
	- Russland	1	1930-40	
	- Schweden u. Norwegen	1	1929-40	
	- Schweiz	1	1933-38	
	- Tschechoslowakei	1	1937-40	
	- Türkei	1	1929-39	
	- Ungarn	1	1929-38	
	- U.S.A.	1	1939-40	
Wi.3	Lettlands Handelsverträge	1-2	1921-27	
Wi.4	Lettlands Finanzwirtschaft	1-3	1921-40	
Wi.4ᵃ	Konjunkturberichte	2-3	1933-40	
Wi.4ᶜ	Finanzwesen, Abwertung des Lat	1	1936-38	
Wi.4ᶜ ¹	Auswirkungen der Latabwertung auf deutsche Firmen in Lettland	1	1936-37	
Wi.4ᵉ	Deutsche Kapitalinteressen in Lettland	1	1938	
Wi.5	Lettlands Industrie	1-6	1921-41	
Wi.5ᵃ	Besichtigung deutscher Betriebe	1	1939	
Wi.6	Lettlands Rohstoffe (landwirt-schaftliche Produkte)	1-2	1922-40	
Wi.7	- Flachs	1-3	1921-40	

Akten-zeichen	Inhalt	Band	Datum	Serial Nr.
Wi.8	Lettlands Rohstoffe, Holz	1+3	1921-41	
Wi.8^a	Lettlands Forst- und holzwirt-schaftlicher Ausschuss	1	1939	
Wi.9	Landwirtschaft Allgemeines	1-2	1925-26	
	Viehausfuhr nach Lettland	1	1923-26	
Wi 10	Lettlands Land- und Forstwirt-schaft	2-6	1926-38	
Wi 10-2	Pferdezucht und Handel	1	1934-35	
Wi 10 B	Saatgutkäufe in Ostpreussen durch die lettländische Regie-rung	2	1929-31	
Wi.10^1	Getreide- und Kleesaatenexport nach Deutschland	1	1933-40	
Wi.10^3	Wöchentliche Exportverschiffun-gen	1	1939	
Wi.10^4	Lieferung von Landmaschinen	1	1938-40	
Wi.11	Öffentliche Ausschreibungen, Allgemeines	1	1926-28	
Wi.12	Regierungslieferungen	1-6 11-13	1922-40	
	- Sonderakte: Lieferung einer Torfbrikettierungsanlage	1	1938-40	
Wi.12/1	- Dünakraftwerk Keggum	1	1930-41	
Wi.12/2	- Lanz	1	1939-40	
Wi.12^a	Anleihen und Monopole	1	1930-36	
Wi.13	Behörden in Deutschland (Anfra-gen über Absatzmöglichkeiten)	1	1927-37	
Wi.20	Transit- und Grenzhandel	1	1921-40	
Wi.21	Lettlands Handel (Schmuggel-wesen)	1	1924-38	
Wi.22	Preise in Lettland	1-8	1920-40	
Wi.23	Lettlands Handelsstatistik	1-4	1923-40	
Wi.23^a	Statistik der Stadt Riga	1	1932-35	
Wi.24	Messewesen, Allgemeines	1-5	1922-41	
Wi.24^a	Konferenz von London 1924	1	1924	
	Konferenzen	2-4	1931-39	
Wi.24^b	Wirtschaftsdelegationen	1	1934-39	
Wi.25	Rigaer Ausstellungen	1-2	1923-39	
	Internationale Ausstellung in Riga	1	1922	
	Messen	1	1921-22	
Wi.25^b	Wirtschaftsabteilung, Lettische Studienreisen	1	1937	
Wi.28	Luftverkehr (Heft)	1	1927-28	

Akten-zeichen	Inhalt	Band	Datum	Serial Nr.
Wi.28	Luftverkehr	1-5	1922-40	
Wi.28[a]	– deutsche Bestimmungen	1	1931-36	
Wi.28[b]	Luftfahrtkonventionen	1	1923-39	
Wi.29	Verkehrswesen: Eisenbahnverkehr	1-3	1924-40	
Wi.30	– Schiffahrt	1-4	1926-39	
Wi.30 S.	Sonderakte: Schiffahrt (Kreuzer-handbuch)	1	1931-39	
Wi.30 Sonder-akte	A/S.Thalheim – A.M.Schmidt betr. Bunkerkohle für Dampfer "Brandenburg"		1939-40	
Wi.31	Kraftfahrwesen	1	1927-34	
Wi.31 S.	Sonderakte: Autobusse für die Rigaer Stadtverwaltung	1	1938-39	
Wi.33	Bankwesen	1-2	1924-31	
	Lettland: Banken (Heft 3)		1931-37	
	Bankwesen		1937-41	
Wi.33-a	Libauer Bank		1934-40	
Wi.36	Lettlands Staatsbudget	1	1921-26	
Wi.39	Lettlands Zolltarifverhandlungen	1	1923-30	
Wi.41	Patent- und Musterschutzangele-genheiten	1	1928-40	
Wi.41[a]	"Continental", Hannover gegen Kontinente, Riga	1	1935-37	
Wi.41[b]	Warenzeichen-Prozess J.G.Farben/ "Medfro" Riga	1	1937-40	
Wi.43	Lettland Arbeiter- und Angestell-tenfragen, (allgemein)		1921-40	
Wi.43 a	Berufsausbildung deutscher Jungen aus Lettland		1937	
Wi.45	Viehseuchen	1	1925-27	
Wi.46	Ausländische Konzessionen	1	1922-39	
Wi.47	Liquidationskommissionen	1	1925-32	
Wi.48	Zeitungen, Zeitschriften, Bücher	1-17	1920-40	
Wi.48 Sonder-akte	Einfuhr deutscher Bücher und Zeitschriften in Lettland	1	1937-39	
Wi.49	Unzuverlässige Firmen	1-8	1923-40	
Wi.49[a] Sonder-akte	Verzeichnis der Boykott und anderer Vertreter	1	1933-40	
Wi.49[b]	Liste kreditunwürdiger Firmen	1	1926-33	
Wi.50	Wirtschaftsabteilung Libau	1-4	1923-31	

Akten-zeichen	Inhalt	Band	Datum	Serial Nr.
Wi.50 a	Sonderakte Bolkerwerke, Libau		1932-34	
Wi.51	Wirtschaftsabteilung Russland	1-9	1921-31	
	-	1-4	1931-37	
	Deutsch-russische Verträge vom 10.I.41	1	1940-41	
Wi.52	Deutsch-russische Randstaaten	1-4	1923-36	
Wi.53	Lettländische Stellen- und Handelsorganisationen	1	1920-28	
Wi.55 a	Forderungsangelegenheit der Firma Springer & Möller,Leipzig		1939-40	
Wi.56	Handelsrechtliche Fragen	1-3	1926-34	
Wi.57	Verschiedenes	1-3	1926-29	
Wi.59	Empfehlungsschreiben (verschiedene Einzelfälle)	1	1927-41	
Wi.59^a	Militär-und Marineattaché	1	1937	
Wi.61	Wirtschaftsabteilung, Nachrichrichten aus Deutschland	1-4	1926-33	
		1-2	1933-35	
Sonder-mappe	Interessengemeinschaft der Kohlenimporteure		1940	
Wi.62^a	Veröffentlichungen der Zentralstelle für den wirtschaftlichen Nachrichtendienst	1-2	1929-31	
Wi.62	Erlasse über wirtschaftliche Berichterstattung	1	1920-25	
Wi.65	Deutsche Zoll- und Einfuhrbestimmungen	1-3	1923-39	
Wi.65^a	Deutsch-lettische Wirtschaftsbeziehungen	1-2	1935-40	
	Deutsch-lettische Verhandlungen und Wirtschaftsbeziehungen		1930-35	
Wi.65a-1	Deutsch-lettische Wirtschaftsbeziehungen	1-2	1934-36	
Wi.65a-3	Abkommen zwischen der Deutschen Reichsbank und der Latwigas Banka		1932-37	
Wi.65 b	Butterausfuhr Lettlands nach Deutschland		1932-35	
Wi.494/22	Gutachten über die Eignung des ehemaligen Kriegshafen von Libau zur Umwandlung in einen Freihafen			
Sonder-akte	Wirtschaftsabteilung: Libauer Bank		1922-24	
Wi.65^c	Lettlands Butterausfuhr nach Deutschland	2-3	1935-40	
Wi.65^d	Zollsätze für Geschenksendungen	1	1939-41	

Akten-zeichen	Inhalt	Band	Datum	Serial Nr.
Wi.65^a 1	Deutsch-lettische Wirtschafts-verhandlungen	1-2	1935-40	
Wi.65^a 2	Deutsch-lettische Handelskammern	1	1933-39	
Wi.66	Lettländische Vertreter deut-scher Firmen	1-3	1927-40	
Wi.66a	Vertreter deutscher Firmen in Lettland	1	1928-40	
Wi.66^b	Registrierung von Vertretern in Lettland	1	1936-40	
Wi.66^1	Vertretergesetz vom 15.12.37 und seine Auswirkungen	1	1937-38	
Wi.66^2	Umsiedlung volksdeutscher Vertreter	1-3	1939-41	
	Umsiedlerbescheinigungen	1	1940	
	Umsiedler-Namenssachen	1-4	1939-40	
Wi.66^3	Deutsche Wirtschaftsinteressen in Sowjet-Lettland	1-2	1940	
	Sonderakte: Schenker & Co. Deutsche Wirtschaftsinteressen in Sowjet-Lettland	1	1940-41	K1681/K405606-09
	Sonderakte: Wertpapiere	1	1940-41	K1682/K405610-12
Wi.67	Antideutsche Wirtschaftspropa-ganda	1	1922-40	K1683/K405613-17
Wi.67^a	Förderung deutschen Handels in Lettland	1	1931-40	K1684/K405618-23
Wi.67^a 1	Winzerfest in der Gesandtschaft	1	1937-38	
Wi.68	Ersuchen deutscher Auslandsver-tretungen	1	1920-30	
Wi.69	Sicherung deutschen Eigentums in Lettland	1	1923-40	
Wi.70	Aufwertung von Altbesitzanleihen	1-2	1926-28	
Wi.70^a	Kriegsschadensachen	1	1927-29	
Wi.70^{II}	Aufwertung des Neubesitzes	1	1927-37	
Wi.71	Liquidations- und Abreiseanträge deutscher Kaufleute	1	1940-41	
Wi.72	Während der Liquidation die Ver-tretung bearbeitet bezw. re-gistriert	1	1940	
Wi.N.	Lettische Nationalisierungs-gesetze	1	1940	
Wi.V.1	Vereinbarungen betr.Fortbestand und Liquidation deutscher Firmen	1	1940	
Wi.V.2	Verhandlungen über den Verbleib von Industrie- und Handelsunter-nehmen	1	1940	
Wi.V.3	Anträge und Fragebogen von Firmen zum Weiterverbleib	1	1940	

Akten-zeichen	Inhalt	Band	Datum	Serial Nr.
Wi.V.4	Anträge und Fragebogen von Einzelpersonen	1	1939	
Wi.V.5	Anträge und Fragebogen von Industriefirmen	1	1939-40	
Wi.V 6+7	Anträge, Befürwortungen von Vertreterfirmen	1-2	1939	
Wi.V.8	Listen reichsdeutscher Personen in Lettland	1	1940	
	Verbleibende Firmen, Fragebogen	1	1938-40	
	Genfer Handelsabkommen, Über-setzung	1	1930	
	Deutsche Devisenbestimmungen	1-2	1935-37	
	Abrechnungen Oktober bis Dezember 1940	1	1940	
Sonder-akte	Darlehnskasse Ost		1921-23	
	Wirtschaftsabteilung Finanz-minister Kalning		1922	
Wi.F. Sd.Akte	Übergabe der Bearbeitung von Forderungssachen an die Libauer Bank	1	1936	
Wi.F.	Forderungen A - Z Einzelfälle	1-2	1940	
	Forderung gegen den Direktor des Deutschen Schauspiels Friedrich Beng, Riga		1932-35	
	Albert Höfer, Limbach/Sa. Dora Levitan, Riga		1931-37	
	Handel. Wirtschaftspolitik A I Politisches		1920-22	
	Baltische Wirtschaftskunde		1920-23	
	Angelegenheit Gutzmann, Nordländische Film-Union		1920-21	
	Landwirtschaftskammer Königsberg-Pr. betr.: Belieferung Lettlands mit ostpreussischem Saatgetreide		1928-29	
	Ostpreussische Saatgutlieferung nach Lettland		1929-33	
	Polnische Landarbeiter gen.		1939-41	
	Polen. Soldaten und Flüchtlinge		1939-40	
	Polnische Internierte, unerledig-te Einzelfälle A - Z		1940	
	Polen und Danzig		1939-40	
	Polen verschiedene Einzelfälle		1940	
S gen.	Schiffsangelegenheiten	6-8	1933-40	
	Dampfer "Imanta" ("Laboe") Reederei Dr.Fischer, Rostock		1922-38	
S 3	Seeamtliche Strafverhandlungen		1926-38	

Akten-zeichen	Inhalt	Band	Datum	Serial Nr.
S 3	Schiffsangelegenheiten Einzelfälle		1939-40	
Kons.S 4	Thielsen Walter (Schiffsunfälle S-4)		1935-36	
	Warnungen in See- und Luft-schiffahrt		1939-40	
	Eisberichte		1941	
	Schiffseinzelfälle A - Z		1926-36	
	Wirtschaft Geheim			
We-Wi 1 geh.	Wehrwirtschaft allgemein	1	8.39- 6.40	
We-Wi 2 geh.	- Warenverkauf	1	9.39- 9.40	
We-Wi 3 geh.	- Schiffswesen	1	9.39- 9.40	
We-Wi 3-a geh.	- Schiffahrtswesen (Sondermappe)	1	9.39-10.40	
We-Wi 4 geh.	- Finanzierung (Spenden)	1	9.39- 9.40	
We-Wi 5 geh.	- besondere Geschäfte	1	9.36- 5.40	
We-Wi 6 geh.	- Sondermaßnahmen der lettischen Regierung	1	6.36- 3.40	
We-Wi 7 geh.	- Prisenrecht	1	9.39- 5.40	
We-Wi 8 geh.	- für Polen bestimmte in Riga gelöschte Schiffssendungen	1	9.39-12.40	
We-Wi 9 geh.	Transite durch Lettland	1	1.40- 7.40	
We-Wi 10 geh.	Neutrale Durchfuhr durch Deutsch-land	1	6.40- 7.40	
We-Wi 11 geh.	Geheimabkommen	1	12.39- 6.40	
We-Wi 12 geh.	Deutsche Aussenhandelsstatistik	1	9.40-12.40	
Hand-akten	Deutsch-lettische Wirtschaftsver-einbarungen	1	6.26- 6.40	
	Allgemeine Geheimakten	1-2	1.34-12.40	
Wi 1	Geheim		10.31- 9.39	
Wi 61	Allgemeine Wirtschaftsfragen der Volksdeutschen		6.39- 9.39	
Allg.18	Politisches, Lettland und andere Staaten, Lettland-Russland	1	9.20- 4.23	
	- - Frankreich	1	2.21- 4.23	
	- Randstaatenbund	1	4.20- 4.23	

Akten-zeichen	Inhalt	Band	Datum	Serial Nr.
Allg.18 Sonder-akte	Politisches, Lettland und andere Staaten, Lettland-Polen	1	9.20- 3.23	
Allg.18		1	6.21- 4.23	
	– England	1	8.20- 3.23	
	– Schweden	1	7.22- 3.23	
	– Estland	1	1.22- 3.23	
	– Balkan	1	10.22- 4.23	
	– Verträge	1	10.20- 4.23	
Allg. 1 19	Politisches, Nationale Angele-genheiten	1	8.21- 2.23	
20	– Entente und Rand-staaten	1	6.22- 3.23	
21	– Kulturpolitik	1	4.22- 3.23	
23	Kulturpropaganda fremder Staaten und Lettland	1	5.21- 2.23	
25	Antideutsche Fälschungen, Greuelhetze	1	3.21-11.22	
28	Konferenz Genua	1	2.22- 5.22	
29	Abrüstungskonferenz (Sonderakte)	1	6.22- 1.23	
30	Warschauer-Konferenz	1	3.22-12.22	
A I 9	Militärisches		1920-23	
A I 12	Russland		1920-23	
A I 13	Bermondt		1920-21	
A I 14	Bolschewismus, Kommunismus		1920-22	
A I 16	Kirche und Schulwesen, Politi-sches		1920-23	
A I 33	Zwischenfall Frau Klara Zetkin		1923	
A I	Politische Beziehungen Lettlands zu Deutschland		1920-23	
A I-1	Zusammenkunft der Vertretungen der drei Baltischen Randstaaten		1922	
Po gen.	Politisches	2-4	1928-40	
Po 1	Bundschuh Josef		1938-40	
Kons.Po 1 a	Ussleber		1938-39	
Po 1	Allgemeine auswärtige Politik Deutschlands	1-2	1923-40	
Po 1-1	Konferenzen der deutschen Gesandt-schaften in den Randstaaten	1	12.27- 2.38	
Po 2	Äussere Politik Lettlands	1-2	1923-40	
Po 2 Nr.1	De jure-Anerkennung Lettlands		1920-23	
Po 2-1	Lettland allgemein		1920-26	

Akten-zeichen	Inhalt	Band	Datum	Serial Nr.
Po 3	Politische Beziehungen zwischen Deutschland und Lettland	1-7	1923-39	
		8	12.39- 1.41	7636/E545392-98
Po 3-3	Deutsche Flottenbesuche in Lettland und umgekehrt	1-3	1924-37	
spez.	Flottenbesuch 1938 Panzerschiff "Admiral Graf Spee" Kreuzer "Köln 1939" Artillerieschul-schiff "Brummer" Torpedoschul-flotille		4.38- 8.39	
Sonder-heft	Besuch des Dampfers "Tannenberg" in Riga		5.38- 6.39	
Po 3-5	Flugwesen, Flugbesuch, Überflie-gen Lettlands		4.38- 8.39	
Po 3-6	Luftverkehrsabkommen Deutschland-Lettland		5.38- 8.39	
Po 3-4	Fremde Flottenbesuche in Deutsch-land und umgekehrt Flottenbe-suche zwischen fremden Staaten	1	1927-31	
Po 3 Nr.1 spez.	Handelsvertragsverhandlungen		1925-26	
Po 3 Nr.1	Deutsch-lettische Abrechnungsver-handlungen	1-4	1921-26	
"Sammlg"	Schadenersatzansprüche an die Lettländische Regierung		1920	
Po 3 Nr.2	Politische Beziehungen zwischen Deutschland und Lettland Sonderheft Kommissionen		1920-23	
Po 4 gen.	Aussenpolitik Deutschlands		1924-29	
Po 4	Deutschland-Amerika: Beziehungen zwischen Deutschland und Amerika	1	9.24- 6.39	
Po 4	Politische Beziehungen zwischen Deutschland - Balkan	1	3.39- 6.39	
	- Belgien	1	12.27-11.37	
Po 4 spez.	Protektorate Böhmen-Mähren	1	3.38-11.40	3122/D641961-74
Po 4 adh.	- Liquidierung der ehemaligen tsche-choslowakischen Gesandtschaft			
Po 4	Politische Beziehungen zwischen Deutschland und England	1	1.27- 6.39	
	- Estland	1-2	1923-40	
	- Finnland	1	4.22- 6.40	
	- Frankreich	1	9.35- 6.39	
	- Italien	1	4.26-12.40	
	Mussolini-Besuch	1	6.37-10.37	

Akten-zeichen	Inhalt	Band	Datum	Serial Nr.
Po 4	Politische Beziehungen zwischen Deutschland und Japan	1	11.30-10.39	
	– Jugoslawien	1	6.37- 5.39	
	– Österreich	1	10.20- 2.38	K1653/K403872-73
	– Litauen	1 2	1923-40	K1654/K403874-76
Po 4 spez.	Anschluss Österreichs an Deutschland		3.38-11.38	
Po 4	Politische Beziehungen zwischen Deutschland und Polen	1 2 3	1923-39	K1654/K403877-95 K1654/K403896-927
		4	6.39- 9.39	K1654/K403928-34
	– Russland	1 2	1923-41	K1655/K403935-42
	– Skandinavien	1	1.33- 9.39	K1656/K403943-47
	– Schweiz	1	1.34	
	– Tschechoslowakei (Sudetenfrage)	1	5.38- 5.39	
	– Türkei			
	– Ungarn	1	11.37- 1.39	
Po 5	Politische Beziehungen zwischen Lettland und Amerika	1	6.23- 9.30	
	– Asien	1	6.23- 2.37	
	– England	1-2	1923-40	
	– Estland	1-3	1923-40	
	Europa- Politische Beziehungen Lettlands zu fremden Staaten, ausser: Amerika, Asien, England, Estland, Finnland, Frankreich, Litauen, Polen, Russland, Skandinavien	1	5.23- 6.40	
	Politische Beziehungen zwischen Lettland und Finnland	1-2	1923-38	
	– Frankreich	1-2	1923-38	
	– Italien	1	1938	
	– Litauen	1-2	1923-40	
	– Polen	1-3	1923-39	
	– Russland	1-3 4	1923-39	3923/E051599-604 7600/E543762-74
	– Skandinavien	1-2	1924-38	
Po 6	Innere und äussere Politik der Staaten Nord-,Mittel- und Südamerika	1	1.33-11.40	
	– Asien	1	1.27- 4.40	K1657/K403949-55

Akten-zeichen	Inhalt	Band	Datum	Serial Nr.
Po 6	Innere und äussere Politik der Donau und Balkanländer, Klein-Asien, sowie Afghanistan und Persiens	1	4.28- 3.40	
	– Danzig	1	6.29- 5.40	
	– England	1	8.34-10.40	K1658/K403956-62
	– Estland	1 2 3 4	1925-39	K1658/K403963-65 K1658/K403966-71 K1658/K403972-94
		5	9.39- 3.40	K1658/K403995-4005
	Innere und äussere Politik Balkan, Skandinavien, Danzig und Osteuropa	1 2	1926-40	K1659/K404006-13 K1659/K404014-70
	– Finnland	1-2 3	1923-40	K1659/K404071-78
	– Frankreich	1	4.39- 6.40	
	– Litauen	1 2 3	1923-41	K1660/K404079-84 K1660/K404085-115 K1660/K404116-71
	– Polen	1 2	1925-40	K1661/K404172-80 K1661/K404181-208
	– Russland	1-2 3	1923-39	K1661/K404209-51
	– –	4	11.39- 9.40	K1661/K404252-58
	– Skandinavien (Schweden, Norwegen, Dänemark)	1 2	1923-39	K1662/K404259-62
	– –	3	10.39- 8.40	K1662/K404263-72
	– Spanien	1	8.36- 1.41	K1663/K404273-77
	– Schweiz	1	6.38-10.39	
	– Tschechoslowakei	1	4.38-11.38	
	– Ukraine	1	12.38	
	Beziehungen fremder Staaten zueinander	1	1923-34	
Po 6/2	Politische Beziehungen Danzigs zu anderen Staaten	1	3.29-12.38	
	– Estland und Finnland	1	4.27- 1.40	
	– - Polen	1-2	1924-39	
	– - Litauen	1	4.27- 2.40	
	– Finnlands zu anderen Staaten	1	9.23- 6.38	
	– - zu Schweden	1	10.23- 2.40	
	– Frankreich-Polen	1	5.23- 6.39	
	– - Vereinigte Staaten	1	1.28- 5.28	

Akten-zeichen	Inhalt	Band	Datum	Serial Nr.
Po 6/2	Politische Beziehungen Italien - Abessinien	1	10.35- 6.36	
	- - England	1	4.38- 5.40	
	Japan - China	1	12.37- 1.38	
	Litauen - andere Staaten	1	12.28- 3.37	
	- - Polen	1-4	1921-40	
	Polen - andere Staaten	1	1.27- 5.36	
	- - Japan	1	12.36	
	- - Rumänien	1	4.24-10.38	
	Russland- andere Staaten	1	1.24- 3.37	
	Estland - Russland	1-2	1.36- 7.40	
	Finnland- Russland	1-2	1924-40	
	- -	3	8.40	
	Frankreich-Russland	1-2	1923-40	
	Litauen -Russland	1	7.24- 8.40	
	Polen -Russland	1	7.23- 8.39	
	Rumänien -Russland	1	4.24- 6.40	
	Russland -Tschechoslowakei	1	4.35- 6.38	
	England -Russland	1	8.23- 1.40	
Po 7	Zwischenstaatliche aussenpolitische Probleme	1	1928-35	
	Nachforschungen nach russischen und lettischen Gefangenen in Deutschland		1920-21	
Po 8 spez.	Strafmitteilungen		1920-23	
	Reichsparteitag		1934-39	
	Teilnahme des Herrn Gesandten Dr.v.Schack am Reichsparteitag		1935-39	
	Deutschlands innere Politik, Parlament und Parteiwesen, Kabinette		1934-40	K1664/K404278-331
Po 8 a	Wahlberechtigung Auslandsdeutscher	1	1933-39	K1665/K404332-36
Po 8 b	Nationalsozialistische Emigranten in Deutschland		1933-39	K1666/K404337-40
Po 9	Lettlands innere Politik	1	1923-27	K1667/K404342-80
		2	1928-29	K1667/K404381-401
		3	1929-33	K1667/K404402-08
		4		K1667/K404409-14
		5		K1667/K404415-23
		6	1933-34	K1667/K404424-29
		7	5.34- 3.36	K1667/K404430-64

Akten-zeichen	Inhalt	Band	Datum	Serial Nr.
Po 9	Lettlands innere Politik	8	3.36- 3.39	K1667/K404465-76
		9	4.39-1941	4544/E146168-72 K1667/K404477-96
	Viehseuchen		1921	
Po 9 a	Enteignung, Gilden, Gewerbe-verein	1	1.36- 2.36	
	- Schwarzhäupterhaus	2	2.36- 8.40	
Po 9 a Beiheft	Donmuseum, Frau Dr.H.v.Ramm-Helmsing		1.36- 7.39	
	- , Familienarchiv des Freiherrn von Rosen		1936	
Po 9 b	Nationalsozialismus in Lettland	1	5.33- 1.36	K1668/K404497-515
		2	3.36- 3.37	
Po 9 c geh.	NSDAP-Stützpunkt in Lettland und Auslandsorganisation der NSDAP	1	6.33- 6.37	
		2	8.37-11.40	K1669/K404516-20
Po 9 e	Kulturkammergesetz und seine Auswirkungen	1	5.38- 1.39	
Po 10	Nationalitätenfrage, Minoritäten, Fremdvölker, Judenfrage	1	1922-31	K1670/K404521-60
		2	1926-29	K1670/K404561-609
		3	1929-33	K1670/K404610-704
		4	2.34- 1.35	K1670/K404705-947
		5	2.35- 5.40	K1670/K404948-5078
Po 10 A	Jüdisch-politische Nachrichten	1-14	1920-33	
Po 10 b	Minderheiten in Lettland	1 2	1923-32	K1671/K405079-92
Po 10 c	Deutsche Minderheiten in Lettland	1-3	7.32- 5.36	
	Deutsches Volkstum in Lettland	4-5	5.36- 5.40	
Po 10 c spez.	Konflikt Volksgemeinschaft		7.37-10.37	
	Briefe für Mitglieder der Deutsch-Baltischen Volksgemein-schaft		10.36- 6.39	
	Beschwerden von Deutschbalten		2.39- 3.39	
Po 10 d	Minderheiten Schulpolitik	1-2	3.32- 4.39	
Po 10 e	Landamt der Deutschbalten	1	1935-40	
Kons.Po 10	Sonderakte Trautmann, Jaacks, Bahl, Juchnewitz		1934-39	
	Sonderakte Grossheim-Krysko, Krupp-Druckenmüller		1934-39	
Po 11	Diplomatische und konsularische Vertretungen fremder Staaten in Lettland	1-4	1922-41	

Akten- zeichen	Inhalt	Band	Datum	Serial Nr.
Po 11 Beiheft	Ausflug des Diplomatischen Corps nach Oesel		1923–27	
Po 11/1	Diplomatische und konsularische Vertretungen Lettlands bei fremden Staaten	1–2	4.23– 9.40	
Po 11/2	Militär-Marine-Attachés	1	6.23–12.40	
Po 11/3	.– in Lettland	1–2	10.34– 1.41	
Po 11/3a	Offiziersbeurlaubungen	1	6.36– 7.39	
Po 11/4	Deutscher Marineattaché in Lettland	1	2.37– 1.41	
Po 12	Staatsoberhäupter	1–2	8.23– 3.40	
Po 12 Beiheft	Tod des Reichspräsidenten Ebert		2.25– 3.25	
Po 12 spez.	Tod des Reichspräsidenten von Hindenburg		8.34	
Po 12/1	Persönlichkeiten Lettlands	1–2	9.22–12.40	
Po 12/2	Andere Persönlichkeiten	2–3	1.27– 2.41	
Po 12/3	Personalien: Militärs	1	5.25–10.39	
Po 14	Militärangelegenheiten, Marine- Luftstreitkräfte Lettlands	2	3.30– 3.41	
Po 14/1	Militär- und Marineangelegen- heiten fremder Staaten	1	3.28– 8.40	
Po 14/2	Militärangelegenheiten. Marine- und Luftstreitkräfte Deutsch- lands	1	6.28– 1.40	
IV Po 13	Militärdienst		1936–38	
	Militärakten gen.		1938–40	
	Deutsche Reichsangehörige im lettländischen Heeresdienst spez.		1920–21	
	– generell		1920	
Mil.	Militär, Einzelfälle A – Z Militaria Pers.		1920–41	
	Luftfahrt, generell			
	Arbeitsdienst		1933–40	
Kons.	– Einzelfälle A – Z		1935	
	Richtlinien für die Beurteilung der Dienstfähigkeit und Arbeits- fähigkeit der weiblichen Jugend im RAD			
Po 13–3	Politische Wochenübersichten		1925–28	
Po 23	Politische Propaganda, Übersen- dung von Bild- und Zeitungs- material	5–7	1940–41	
Po 17	Bolschewismus, Kommunismus, Faschismus	2	11.22– 5.37	K1672/K405096–112

Akten-zeichen	Inhalt	Band	Datum	Serial Nr.
Po 17	Bolschewismus, Kommunismus, Faschismus	3	2.37- 6.40	K1672/K405113-75
Po 19	Krieg, Kriegsmaterial	1	4.23- 8.37	K1673/K405176-85
		2	5.39-12.40	K1673/K405186-88
Po 19 spez.	Internierte Flieger		9.39- 9.41	
Po 19 a	Kriegsschuldfrage 1939	1	9.39- 6.40	
Po 20	Randstaaten, Politik	4	2.30- 6.40	
Po 20/1	Randstaatenbund, Baltischer Staatenverband, Konferenzen der baltischen Aussenminister	4-5	1.26- 7.40	
Po 20/2	Politische Beziehungen Deutschlands zu den Randstaaten	1	11.23- 6.40	
zu Po 30	Karl Beschnitt, Politische Emigranten		1933-35	
F V 1	Versailler Friedensvertrag, Völkerbund, Locarno, Abrüstung	9-11	1933-40	
F V 1-4	Versailler Friedensvertrag, Deutsches Recht und Interessen ausserhalb Deutschlands (Art.118-158) Kolonien, Mandate		1927-39	
F V 1-5	Versailler Friedensvertrag, Bestimmungen über Landheer, Seemacht und Luftfahrt (Art.159-213) Wiedereinführung der allgemeinen Wehrpflicht, Stresskonferenz, Reisen Simons nach Berlin und Edens nach Moskau und Warschau		1927-28	
F V 2	Kriegsschuldfrage		1922-37	
F V 3	Besetzte Gebiete, einschliesslich Saargebiet	1,3	1923-24 1934-38	
F V 4	Reparationen	1	8.23-12.23	
	Ruhreinbruch	2	1.23- 8.24	
F V 5	Memelgebiete, Danziger Frage, Festsetzung der Grenzen Polens und Litauens	1-8	1923-39	
Extrabd.	Memelgebiet		5.37- 7.39	
F V 6	Reparationen	1-6	1.23- 1.33	
F V 1 Nr.1	Internationale Fragen, Neutralisierung	1-4	1921-40	
	Optionen, verschiedene Einzelfälle		1921-39	
	Optanten (Liste)		1939	
	- Einzelfälle, Noten u.Listen		1940	
	Vermögensanmeldungen		1940	
Po 9 d	Zusammenarbeit von Partei und Staat		10.37- 6.40	

Akten-zeichen	Inhalt	Band	Datum	Serial Nr.
Po 9 c spez.	Ortsgruppenleiter Prof.Mackensen		7.40- 8.40	
Geheim 2	Randstaatenpolitik, Warschau-Rigaer Konferenz, östliche Garantieverträge	5	4.35-10.38	7251/E532100-109
Po 11 geheim	Geheime Blattsammlung des Protokolls		1.38- 6.39	
Po 11/1 geh.	Lettische Gesandtschaft in Berlin		12.37- 1.38	
Po 12 geh.	Deutsch-lettische Abrechnungs-verhandlungen, Staatsvertrag, Agrarentschädigung		7.26- 2.39	
Po 12	Staatsverträge		5.33	
Po 12/4	Journalisten	2-4	6.30- 3.41	
Po 12/4a	V.B.Vertreter in Lettland	1	5.36- 7.38	
Po 12/5	Unzuverlässige Personen	1	8.32-10.37	
Po 13	Pressewesen, Presseangriffe, Dementi	4-11	11.32- 2.41	
	Unterstützung der lettischen Presse	2	1.34- 6.37	K1674/K405189-200
	Unterstützung der hiesigen Presse	3	4.37-11.40	
	Deutscher Bote	1	1.36- 7.39	
Po 13/1	Lettische Presse	1 2 3	4.23- 6.40	K1675/K405201-09 K1675/405210-62 K1675/K405263-78
Po 13/1 spez.	Jüdische Presse (Hajnt)		2.36- 1.38	K1676/K405279-416
Po 13/2	Nachrichtenübermittlung an Wolffs Telegrafenbüro Berlin	1	1.23- 8.33	
Po 13/4	Gesellschaftsreise lettischer Journalisten nach Deutschland und umgekehrt	1-2	7.26- 6.39	
I 4 c	Politische Angelegenheiten	1-2	9.20- 3.23	
Po 18	Konferenzen	2-3	7.30- 6.40	
Po 18 spez.	Weltkongress für Freizeit und Erholung		10.35- 6.37	
Po 20/3	Beziehungen fremder Staaten zu den Randstaaten	1	2.24- 1.34	
	- auch russisch-polnischer Paktvorschlag	2	1.34- 7.40	
Po 20/4	Neutralitätsfragen der balti-schen Staaten	1	8.38- 2.40	
Po 21	Deutschtum im Ausland	2	1.21- 3.40	
Po 22	Nationale Angelegenheiten, Ordenssachen, Hoheitsabzeichen, Flaggen, Nationalfeiertag	1-6	10.20- 1.41	

Akten-zeichen	Inhalt	Band	Datum	Serial Nr.
Po 22 a spez.	Festliche Begehung nationaler Feiertage		1.36- 4.40	
Po 22 spez.	Ehrenkreuz (Generalia)		7.34- 8.38	
A P 22 E.K.	Unerledigte Anträge auf Ver-leihung von Ehrenkreuzen		3.35- 4.36	
Po 22 spez.	Verwundetenabzeichen		1.36- 4.40	
	Ehrenzeichen für Deutsche Volkspflege		1.40- 9.40	
	Ehrenkreuz der deutschen Mutter		3.39-11.40	
	Treudienst-Ehrenzeichen		3.38- 2.41	
	Ordensverleihung		5.37- 2.41	
Po 23	Politische Propaganda, Übersen-dung von Bild- und Zeitungsma-terial	2	3.34- 5.37	K1677/K405418-30
		3	4.37- 2.40	K1677/K405431-54
		4	1.40- 9.40	K1677/K405455-57
Po 25	Einreise, Ausreise, Durchreise, Aufenthalt. Studienreise und Grenzabfertigung	1	4.33- 8.35	
Po 28	Flottenbesuche in Lettland	1	4.25- 8.35	
Po 29	Zusammenstellung der Parlamente und der einzelnen Staaten			
Po 30	Politische Emigranten, Matteotti-Komitee		3.33- 8.40	K1678/K405458-529
14 Geheim	Spionage und Agentenwesen	1-2	12.25- 4.41	
F V 5	Zu A.2215/34 Anklageschrift gegen Dr.Neumann, v.Sass		1934-35	
15 Geheim	Pressefonds	1-2	1922-40	
16 Geheim	Kulturfonds für die Rechnungs-jahre 1930-40	5-15	1930-40	
16/1 geh.	Dispositionsfonds	1-2	10.27- 3.41	
16/2 geh.	Schulhilfen für reichsdeutsche Kinder		3.27- 7.39	
16/3	Seemannsheim	1-2	3.26-12.39	
16/4 geh.	Goethe-Gesellschaft	1	8.36-11.39	
16/4 spez.	Konflikt Prof.v.Petersen - Rektor Klumburg		1.39- 7.39	
17 geh.	Theaterfonds, Deutsches Theater	1-4	1925-32	
18 Geheim	Landesverrat u.a. im Nachlass des früheren Geheimrats Weber vorgefundenes		1919-22	
20	Verschiedene reichsdeutsche Persönlichkeiten in Riga		1921-22	
21	Angelegenheit Neuhaus		1923	

Akten-zeichen	Inhalt	Band	Datum	Serial Nr.
22	Angelegenheit Indran sowie sonstige Vorgänge betr. deutsche Beamte und Angestellte in Lettland		1921-23	
23	Zifferntelegramme		1920	
24	Aufzeichnungen über Gespräche	1	1933	
25	Vertrauensmann B.		1933-34	
Geheim-akten	Akten des Beauftragten Mitau (Geheimakten der Deutschen Gesandtschaft)		1919-22	
26	Ganz geheim	1-2	8.39- 3.41	
27 Geheim	Geleitscheinstelle	1	3.40- 3.41	
28 Geheim	Liebesgabensendungen der Gesandtschaftsangehörigen	1	2.40- 7.40	
Gg 7 b geheim	Hellschreiber	1	7.39- 2.41	
Gg 2/8 geheim	Sicherung und Geheimhaltung des Aktenmaterials	1	5.23-10.39	
Geheim	Streng-Geheime-Erlasse	1	4.37- 1.40	
	Geheime Erlasse	1	3.36- 6.38	
	W.-Nachrichten	1	5.35-10.39	
Ordner A.P.22 EK.	Ehrenkreuz des Weltkrieges A - Z			
	Abgelegte Anträge A - Z			
	Geheimakten der Konsulats-Abteilung			
	Sonderakte	1-2	12.34- 2.41	
	Einbürgerung von Volksdeutschen aus Lettland von 1939-40	1		
Kons. Sonder	Sta.Kühnsdorf	1	6.34-11.40	
	Votum der NSDAP	1	10.37- 7.38	
	Runderlasse	1-4	1918-41	
	dazu ein Heft: Anlage zum Schreiben v.Z.Kastrorsky vom 27.11.1939			
	Verschiedenes			
Sond.2 a	Zuschuss für Konsul Fossé		1936-40	
Sond.2 spez.	Breuer - Fossé		1935	
	Beschwerde Kühn - Seligmann		1934	
Sonder-akten-stück Nr.3	Interviews		1923-26	

Akten- zeichen	Inhalt	Band	Datum	Serial Nr.
Sonder- akten- stück Nr.6	Sammlung von Vertragsduplikaten	1-2	1920-35	
Nr.11	Dr.Frost		1924-26	
Nr.13	Bezug von Wein, Bier, Tabak	6	1938-41	
I Nr.2	Politische Presse Lettland	5-6	1920	
Abt.IV Nr.19	Auflösung der Gesandtschaft		1920	
7.Son- derakte	Konsularagentur in Dünaburg		1923-39	
Sonder- akte 10	Bezirk Goldingen		1933-37	
Sonder- akte 8	Konsulatagent Windau		1924-38	
Po 3 a	Liquidierung der Gesandtschaft Riga	1	1940-41	
	Rigaer Presseübersichten	1	1934	
Po 5, 8 u.10	Einzelfälle A - Z	Ord- ner	1920-41	
Po 10 spez.	Militärdienst und Rentenbeschei- nigungen A - Z (nur dtsch.)		1920-41	
Po 11	Briefzustellungen A - Z		1920-41	
	Beglaubigungen		1919-30	
	Notariatsregister		1919-33	
	Kassabuch		1920-21	
	Forderungen. Konsulat Libau	1-15	1926-40	

Akten-zeichen	Inhalt	Band	Datum	Serial Nr.
	Dienstbetrieb, allgemeine Anweisungen des Auswärtigen Amtes	1-2	1920-30	
	– Verschiedenes	1-3	1920-39	
	– Depositen	1	1920-25	
	Geschäftsverteilung im Auswärtigen Amt	1	1920-32	
	Dienstbefugnisse	1	1920-39	
	Dienstbetrieb: Verfügungen des Herrn Botschafters	1-3	1920-39	
	Botschaftssitz	1	1920-22	
	Mittel für den Unterhalt der Botschaft	1-4	1928-39	
	Inventar, auch Silberinventar der ehemaligen Österreichischen Gesandtschaft (Qu.)	1	1938-39	
	– Schreibmaschinenkontrolle	1	1921-39	
	– Ausleihung von Gemälden	1	1920-39	
	– Inventarisàtionsbescheinigungen	1	1920-39	
	Bücherinventarisierung der Botschaftsbibliothek	1	1920	
	Rundfunkempfänger der Botschaft	1	1934-39	
	Dienstbetrieb: Archiv	1	1933-39	
	Abonnement von Zeitungen	1	12.35-1939	
	Beschaffung von Büchern, Zeitschriften und Büromaterial	1	6.36-1939	
	Zeitungsabonnements	1-6	1921-36	
	Bürobedarf	1-3	1921-35	
	Kurierverzeichnisse	1	1926	
	Geschäftsgang – Aussenhandelsstelle	1	1920	
	Reichsgesetzblatt	1	1920	
	Deutsche Mission – Büromaterial	1	1920	
	Akten-Geschäftsgang	1	1919-20	
	Postverkehr mit Tiflis Vertretungen	1	1920-22	
	Dienstkraftwagen der Botschaft	1-5	1920-39	
	Beantragung von Autonummern	1-3	1920-36	
	Kraftfahrzeuge (Dipl.Priv.)	1-2	1923-36	
	Wohnungsangelegenheiten Gen.	1	1922-39	
	Dienstwohnungen im Botschaftsgelände	1	1923-37	

Akten-zeichen	Inhalt	Band	Datum	Serial Nr.
	Beamtenwohnungen Celimontana und Via Zuchelli	1	1919-23	
	Gemeindehaus	1	1924-32	
	Umzugsangelegenheiten	1	1920-27	
	Personalangelegenheiten, Generalia, Etats, Bes.Gesandtschaft (Drucksachen)	1-4	1914-39	
	Personal Rom - Fasano		1944	
	Personalfragen im allgemeinen	1	1920-27	
	Personalangelegenheiten, Angestellte der Botschaft, für die keine besonderen Akten bestehen	1	1928-39	
	Gehaltsfragen: Generelles	1	1919-20	
	- Allgemeine Berichterstattung	1	1921-23	
	- - über Teuerung	1-3	1924-39	
	- Verschiedenes	1	1921-39	
	Besoldung der italienischen Staatsbeamten	1	1920-39	
	Gehaltsfragen: Material für Gehaltsberichte	1	1922-39	
	Hauspersonal, Eisenbahnabteil für Missionschef	1	1922-33	
	Missionschef	1 / 2	1922-39	K553/K155569-75
	Urlaubsfragen	1	1920-39	
	Urlaub des Missionschefs	1-2	1921-39	
	Militärattaché, allgemein	1	1927-39	K1048 /K268952-9035
	Luftattaché	1	1935-39	
	Marineattaché	1	1935-39	
	Botschaftsanwalt und Botschaftsarzt, Handelsbeirat	1	1920-39	
	Personalangelegenheiten, Stellenbewerbungen	1-3	1920-39	
	Diplomatischer- und Konsulardienst, Italien, Diplomatische Privilegien, Steuer, Miete	1 / 2	1920-36	9932/E694871-77
	- Hauszinssteuer	1	1925-33	
	- Zoll	1-2	1922-39	
	- zollfrei Gummireifen	1	1937-39	
	- Zollschwierigkeiten	1	1920-26	

Akten-zeichen	Inhalt	Band	Datum	Serial Nr.
	Vorrechte und Vergünstigungen des Diplomatischen Corps, Anforderung von Zollfreischeinen	1-2	1927-39	
	Steuerfragen	1	1922-39	
	Dienstreisen und Tagegelder für Beamte und Angestellte	1-2	1924-39	
	Versicherung der Hausangestellten der Beamten	1	1922-39	
	Meldungen und Ausweise des Esteri für mittlere Beamte	1	1921-28	
	Zeremonien-Angelegenheiten:			
	Rangordnung	1	1921-30	
	− allgemein	1	1.31- 3.36	
	− Karten für den Missionschef	1-2	1920-39	
	Anmeldung der deutschen Beamten in Italien beim Aussenministerium	1-3	1920-39	
	Verschiedener Schriftwechsel des Herrn Botschafters von Neurath	1 2 3 4-5	1922-31	K554/K155576-86 K554/K155587-90
	Personalia Missionschef v.Schubert	2	1930-33	
	Personalien und verschiedener Schriftwechsel des Botschafters H.v.Berenberg-Gossler	1	1921-22	
	Handakten für Botschaftsrat von Prittwitz	1	1921-27	K555/K155591-66
	Schriftwechsel Botschaftsrat von Prittwitz	1	1921-27	K556/K155663-77
	Privatbriefwechsel Botschaftsrat von Prittwitz	1	1927	
	Privater Schriftwechsel des Botschafters v.Hassell	1	1.34- 6.34	
		1	3.35- 1.36	8065/E579218-21
	Privatbriefwechsel des Botschafts-rates Smend	1	1928-35	
	Privater Schriftwechsel des Herrn Botschafters v.Mackensen	1-3	1938-39	
	Personalakten:			
	Dr.Altenburg	1	1922-25	
	Biasion	1	1924-28	
	Frl.Bischoff	1	1922-24	
	Attaché v.Bülow	1	1925-27	
	Legationssekretär Busch	1	1927-28	
	Geheimrat Dr.Busse	1	1935	
	v.Borosini	1	1920-31	
	v.Berenberg-Gossler	1	1920-23	

Akten-zeichen	Inhalt	Band	Datum	Serial Nr.
	Personalakten:			
	Dr.Braun	1	1923-26	
	Frl.Böttger	1	1920-22	
	Konsul Bütow	1	1920-22	
	Laurenz Caba	1	1923-27	
	Legationssekretär Dr.v.Campe	1	1924-26	
	Cecchini	1	1923	
	Legationssekretär Diel	1	1920-22	
	Frl.Eitner	1	1926-29	
	Dr.Engelberg	1	1933-35	
	Kons.Diäta Erlewein	1	1928-32	
	Frl. Faden	1	1924-27	
	Legationssekretär Dr.Freudenberg	1	1926-29	
	Dr.Frohwein	1	1921-22	
	Frau Frosch	1	1920-23	
	Professor Gagliardi	1	1920-22	
	Tito Guglielmotti	1	1921-28	
	Exp.Sekretär Gotthardt	1	1908-22	
	Gärtner Gherardi	1	1922-33	
	Frl. Gornitzka	1	1922-23	
	Frl. Gamper	1	1920-21	
	Att.Freih.v.d.Heyden-Rynsch	1	1927-30	
	Konsulatssekretär Hoffmann	1	1926-27	
	Geh.ORR.Heinke	1	1920-22	
	Generalkonsul v.Herff	1	1920-21	K557/K155678-80
	Frl. Jaia	1	1920	
	Gärtner Huber	1	1924-25	
	Frl. Lambertenghi	1	1920-21	
	Legationssekretär Dr.Kreutzwald	1	1927-32	
	Frl. Kohlmann	1	1920-27	
	Otto Kunisch	1	1926-29	
	Geheimrat Kehr	1	1921-22	
	Konsul Herm.Klee	1	1920-23	
	Frau Else Klee	1	1920	
	Charlotte Lüher	1	1921-26	
	Ilse Haumann	1	1928-31	
	Lilli Lorenz	1	1920-21	
	Geheimrat Dr.Lorenz	1	1922-28	
	Heinrich Losch	1	1924-26	
	Hermann Lacher	1	1926-28	
	Legationssekretär Freih.v.Lentz	1	1921-22	
	Frieda Kramer	1	1920-28	
	Alberto Massoni, Pförtner	1	1921-22	
	Vicekonsul Moggirath	1	1920-21	
	Geheimrat Dr. Möldike	1	1926-28	
	Anneliese Maegler	1	1929-33	
	Helene Mannheimer	1	1928-33	
	Legationssekretär Dr.May	1	1926-28	

Akten-zeichen	Inhalt	Band	Datum	Serial Nr.
	Personalakten:			
	Botschafter Freih.v.Neurath	1	1926-31	
	Konsul Fritz Nauer	1	1922-24	
	Geheimrat von Mackensen	1	1923-33	
	Otto Overhof	1	1929-33	
	Dr.Oster	1	1920-23	
	Botschaftsrat von Prittwitz	1-2	1921-32	
	Maria v.Röden	1	1920-21	
	Oscar Rind	1	1932-34	
	Legationsrat Dr. Rieth	1	1922-25	
	Gertrud Rendelmann	1	1930-32	
	Gerhard Rissmann	1	1929-35	
	Franz Simon	1	1927-28	
	Gärtner Jos.Schürger	1	1926	
	Hilfsgärtner Wilhelm Schneider	1	1923-25	
	Alma Schönemann	1	1921-30	
	Konsul Schwager	1	1921-24	
	Stadtrat Sassenbach	1	1920-21	K579/K157217-66
	Legationssekretär Dr.v.Schmieden	1	1921-24	
	Legationsrat v.Schön	1	1921-23	
	Handelsrat Hch.Strohecker	1	1920-33	
	Gertrud Schulze	1	1932-34	
	Legationssekretär Stiller	1	1920-22	
	Emil Stocker	1	1920-23	
	Legationssekretär Dr.Ulrich	1	1920-22	K580/K157267-79
	Geheimrat Dr.Thomas	1	1919-21	
	Legationssekretär Dr.Toepke	1	1920	
	Dr.Felix Tripeloury	1	1933	
	Legationssekretär v.Tucher	1	1920-23	
	Konsul Venth	1	1920-23	
	Nenny Fittstein	1	1920	
	Hofrat Wätsold	1	1903-35	
	Diätar Winkel	1	1920-25	
	Luftfahrtattaché v.Waldau	1	1935-36	
	Verschiedenes	1	1919-25	
	Gärtner Trautwein	1	1923	
	Pauli	1	1927-28	
	Kons.Diätar Roether	1	1925-28	
	Legationssekretär Dr.Richter	1	1929-32	
	Konsulatspraktikant Stark	1	1932-33	
	Konsulatssekretär Ernst	1	1920-24	
	Mühlbach Erich und Willi Kurt	1	1926-29	
	Gärtner Schweizer	1	1925-27	
	Gärtner Weber	1	1923-24	
	Gärtner v.Roth	1	1925-28	
	Bennewitz	1	1920-39	
	Bienotsch		1920-39	
	Blau		1920-39	

Akten-zeichen	Inhalt	Band	Datum	Serial Nr.
	Personalakten:			
	Böhm		1920-39	
	Bortfeldt		1920-39	
	von Bülow		1920-39	
	Duball		1920-39	
	Dr.v.Etzdorf		1920-39	
	Ettel		1920-39	
	Glatzel		1920-39	
	von Graevenitz		1920-39	
	Haussmann		1920-39	
	von Hassell		1920-39	M126/M004676-81
	Dr.Helmerking		1920-39	
	Graf von Hohenthal		1920-39	
	Holm		1920-39	
	Hausmann		1920-39	
	Schuffenhauer		1920-39	
	Immelen		1920-39	
	Kessel		1920-39	
	Kohlmann		1920-39	
	Krebs		1920-39	
	Dr.Kreutzwald		1920-39	
	Lange		1920-39	
	von Marschall		1920-39	
	Mayr		1920-39	
	Neuswirth		1920-39	
	Constantin von Neurath		1920-39	
	Dr.Gans Edler Herr zu Putlitz		1920-39	
	von Pfaler		1920-39	
	Paulus		1920-39	
	Picot		1920-39	
	Prüfer		1920-39	
	Satzke		1920-39	
	Prinz zu Schaumburg-Lippe		1920-39	
	Dr.Schmid-Krutina		1920-39	
	Schnerbus		1920-39	
	Professor Schoener		1920-39	
	Dr.Smend		1920-39	
	Vogel		1920-39	
	Diplomaten-Privilegien und Immunitäten, Allgemeines, Korrespondenten des Internationalen Arbeitsamtes in Genf, deutsche Staatsvertreter beim deutsch-italienischen Gem.Schiedsgericht	1	1922-23	
	Kredit an der Botschaft Beschwerden	1	1921-39	
	Verschiedene Angelegenheiten der deutschen Vertretungen des deutsch-italienischen Schiedsge-richtshofes und des Reichsaus-gleichsamtes	1	1922-32	

Akten-zeichen	Inhalt	Band	Datum	Serial Nr.
	Verschiedene Angelegenheiten der landwirtschaftlichen Sachver-ständigen der Botschaft	1-2	1927-39	
	Angelegenheiten betr. Vertretun-gen der deutschen Interessen durch fremde Regierungen	1	1921-33	
	Wachhund Rolf	1	1923-33	
	Deutsche Botschaft beim Päpst-lichen Stuhl	1	1924	
	Verschiedenes	1-2	1920-28	
	Mitteilungen des königlichen Hofes	1	1920-34	
	Verschiedene Erlasse und Korres-pondenz des Auswärtigen Amtes bezw. gemischten Gerichtshofes	1	1920-25	
	Erlasse des Auswärtigen Amtes betr. Handelsberichterstattung	1-2	1920-39	
	Gebührengesetz für die Auslands-behörden vom 1.7.21 nebst Tarif und Ausführungsbestimmungen			
	Gebührenwesen - Änderungen	1	1921-24	
	-	1	1919-26	
	Gebührenliste (1 Umschlag)		1928-32	
	Abrechnungen I.-IV.Vierteljahr	1-8	1920	
	Abrechnung	1	11.19- 3.20	
	Amtliche Abrechnungen	1-32	1921-33	
	Abrechnungen	1-7	1933-34	
	Alte Kassenakten des Kaiserli-chen Konsulats Rom		1900-21	
	Alte Kassenakten		1934- 7.41	
	Ausrangierte Kassenakten A - Z		1921-26	
	Kassenführung - Bestimmungen	1	1923-32	
	- Abschlüsse	1	1926-29	
	Verschiedene Korrespondenzen	1	1926-29	
	Kassenkorrespondenzen A - Z	1-2	1934	
	Erledigte Korrespondenzen A - Z	1	1932-35	
	Zahlungslisten	1	1925-27	
	Alte Zahlungslisten, Quittungen ausgesondert	1	1.27	
	Gehaltslisten, Zahlungslisten "M" Zusammenstellung	1	1936	
	Gehaltszahlungen	1	4.27- 3.28	
	Gehaltsabhebungen	1-5	1928-33	

Akten-zeichen	Inhalt	Band	Datum	Serial Nr.
	Gehaltserhebungen	1	12.33-12.34	
	Korrespondenz mit dem Konsulat betr. Gehaltserhebung	1	1931	
	Gehaltsauszahlungsanordnungen	1	1931-32	
	Gehalts- und Vergütungszahlungen, Unterstützungen	1	1935	
	Privatkassa des Botschafters v.Hassell Beleg-Nr.2-112, 800-1000, 1030-1100, 1178-1519	1-4	1935-37	
	– Beleg-Nr. 113-201, 203-271, 272-467, 601-800, 1101-1177	1-5	1934-38	
	Kassenbelege des Botschafters v.Hassell Nr.1-200, 201-400, 401-600	1-3	1932-33	
	Rechnungen v.Prittwitz	1	1927-28	
	Dr.Siebert, Kassensachen	1	1931	
	Privatakten Dr. Smend			
	Rechnungsbelege: Botschafter von Neurath, Gesandtschaftsrat von Mackensen, Attaché v.Bülow	1	1925-27	
	Belege und geschäftliche Korrespondenzen des Botschafters von Neurath	1	1921-26	
	Botschafter v.Neurath, Kassensachen	1	1930-31	
	v.Schubert, Kassensachen	1	1930-33	
	Gherardi, Gärtner - Bankkonto	1	1928-33	
	Kontokorrent Banco di Roma Gehalts-Akkreditiv, Nebenkassenbuch	1	1927-28	
	Witwe Elisabeth Franksen - Achille Raulli und verschiedene Kassensachen	1	1927-28	
	Zahlungen Odo Leypold	1	1922-32	
	Kriegerwitwe Romhilde Menken	1	1921-34	
	Reichsversicherung für Angestellte	1	1919-26	
	Invalidenversicherung	1	1923-28	
	Zigarettenbestellungen	1	1929-31	
	– Palatino	1	1931-34	
	– Wien	1	1931-34	
	–Konstantinopel	1	1931-34	
	Steuern	1	1920-34	

Akten-zeichen	Inhalt	Band	Datum	Serial Nr.
	Spezialband Lire-Depot (Devisen-bedarf der Botschaft und der Konsulate)	1	1935	
	Reichsmark-Bewilligungen	1	1930-32	
	Steuerpflicht. Nachweisungen	1-5	1924-29	
	Kontrolle des Benzinverbrauchs und der Fahrtleistungen des Dienstkraftwagens	1-2	1922-31	
	Ausgabebelege für Autobetriebs-kasse	1	1928-30	
	Benzin- und Veedolverbrauch	1	1934-35	
	Benzinverbrauch der Benzinpumpe der Botschaft	1	1931-32	
	Prämienzahlungen d.S.I.A.P.für das bei ihr gekaufte Benzin	1	4.31- 1.35	
	Benzin- und Oelverbrauch	1	11.32-12.37	
	Belegsammlung für die Benzinkasse	1	1935-36	
	Ausgabebelege zum Kassenbuch betr Kraftwagen-Betriebspauschale	1	11.32-12.34	
		1-2	1935-39	
	Belege und Schriftwechsel betr. Buchungen im H. u. V-Buch	1	1934-36	
	Beleg-Nr. 301-600 zum Erlass I,5, IV/32 ab	1	1.34- 8.34	
	Ausgabebelege	1-2	1929-33	
	Notizen betr.erledigter Kassen-aufträge	1	10.33- 6.34	
	Reichspressekammergelder	1	1935-36	
	Quittungen zu den Listen I-X betr.Geldüberweisungen seitens der Reichspressekammer	1	1935	
	Heizungskosten	1	1935	
	Gärtnerwohnung, Garagenbau	1	1935	
	Fondsbewilligungen	1-3	1929-31	
	Ausgabenmeldungen	1	7.30- 9.32	
	Erlasse und Berechnungen zu den monatlichen Wohnungszuschüssen	1	1926-29	
	Zahlungen Rechnungsjahr 1932 gem.Akten Pol.19a	1	1932-33	
	Kulturpolitische Ausgaben	1	4.33- 3.34	
	Ausgabenkontroll-Liste	1	1933-34	
	Nebenkassenbuch (Kontoauszüge, Briefwechsel)	1	1931-33	
	Kontenmässige Darstellung des Sachbuches über Hinterlegungen und Vorschüsse	1	1933	

Akten-zeichen	Inhalt	Band	Datum	Serial Nr.
	Geh.pol.Fonds	1	4.29- 3.33	
	Fernsprecher	1	1929-35	
	Vereinigung der Auslandsbeamten	1	1923-33	
	Reichsverband für höhere Verwal-tungsbeamte	1	1922-33	
	Kassenprüfungsverhandlungen	1	8.33-12.35	
	Liste über elektr.Licht-und Gas-verbrauch in den Beamtenwohnun-gen	1	1930-35	
	Verschiedene Notizen, Bankzettel	1	1934-36	
	Depeschenkästen	1	1921-22	
	Dienstbetrieb - Depeschenkasten-verkehr	1	1921-31	
	Depeschenkastenverkehr Berlin-Rom (Allgemeines)	1	1923	
	- (Spezielles)	1	1923-26	
	- nach und von Athen	1	1923	
	- Rom-Berlin, Rom-Neapel Rom-Triest	1	7.23-12.26	
	Kuriere - Allgemein	1	11.21- 6.33	
	- Schriftverkehr der Kurierstelle wegen Weiterleitung von Privatpaketen	1	12.25- 9.33	
	Kurierakten	1-3	1920-24	
	- allgemein	1-3	1921-33	
	Kuriere	1-3	1921	
	Abgefertigte Kuriere	1	1925	
	Kuriere	1-3	1926-28	
	Abgefertigte Kuriere	1	1929	
	Kuriere	1	1933-35	
	Kurierreisen	1	1920-22	
	Kurierfrachtposten	1	1928-29	
	Kurierfrachtrechnungen	1	1928-31	
	Kurierlisten	1-2	1931-36	
	Einkassierungslisten betr. Kurier-Portoanteile	1	1933-35	
	Kassenbücher	1	1922-37	
	Portobuch	1-6	1921-26	
	Kassabush (Ausg.lt.Erlass 4.6.21 I DJ 74)	1	1921-33	
	Telegramme	1-2	1920-28	

Akten-zeichen	Inhalt	Band	Datum	Serial Nr.
	Kassabuch	1	4.21-12.22	
	Einnahmebuch A	1-2	1920-22	
	Vorschuss Geheimrat Heinke	1	1921	
	Konsulate	1	1920-34	
	Nummerkontrolle der Berichte an das Auswärtige Amt	1	1928	
	Verzeichnis der einzureichenden Drucksachen			
	Deutsche Konsulate in Italien, allgemein	1-2	1920-39	
	Verteilung der Berichterstattung und diesbezügliche Weisung	1	1921-35	
	Konsulbesprechung	1	1921-39	
	Weisungen an die Konsulate und Verschiedenes	1	1920-27	
	Hafenkonsulate, Seemannsämter	1-2	1922-39	
	- Sonderband Kreuzerhand-buch	1	1931-32	
	Einteilung der Bezirke der deutschen Konsulate	1	1921-29	
	Unfallverhütungsvorschriften der Seegenossenschaft	1	1929-34	
	Deutsches Konsulat Adis Abeba	1	1936-39	
	- Ankona	1	1920-33	
	- Bari	1	1920-39	
	- Bologna	1	1921-35	
	- Brindisi	1	1921-37	
	- Bozen	1	1920-39	
	- Carrara	1	1920-27	
	- Catania	1	1920-39	
	- Fiume	1	1920-39	
	- Florenz	1-4	1920-39	
	- - (Konsul Hellwig)	1	1935-37	
	- Genua	1-3	1920-39	
	- Palermo	1-3	1919-39	
	- Livorno		1920-39	
	- Mailand	1-4	1920-39	
	- Messina		1920-39	
	- Neapel	1-3	1920-39	
	Deutsches Generalkonsulat Neapel:			
	- Presse und Propaganda	1	6.39- 7.43	
	- Gesuchte Personen und geheime Auskünfte über Personen	1	4.40- 4.43	
	- Aussenpolitisches	1	3.39- 5.43	
	- Innenpolitisches	1	5.33- 8.41	

Akten-zeichen	Inhalt	Band	Datum	Serial Nr.
	Deutsches Generalkonsulat Neapel:			
	– NSDAP	1	3.32- 2.41	
	– Handelssachen und wirtschaftspolitische Angelegenheiten	1	9.39- 6.43	
	– Geheime Weiterlei-tungssachen	1	9.38- 6.43	
	– Gehaltsfragen, Teuerungsberichte	1	10.41- 3.43	
	– Flugwesen	1	1.40	
	– Kassensachen und finanzpolitische Sachen	1	12.40- 3.41	
	– Kulturpolitisches und Sammlung "Blahut"	1	2.40-10.42	
	– Geheime Pass-Sachen und Sichtvermerk-sachen	1	9.37- 7.43	
	– Deutsches Militär in Italien	1	10.40- 9.41	
	– Mobilmachungsmaßnah-men	1	8.38- 9.39	
	– Steuerung deutscher Schiffe, Berichte (nur Schiffsmeldungen)	1	8.39- 6.41	
	– – Erlasse und Berichte (ausser Schiffsmel-dungen) u.a.Wetter-nachrichten, Sonder-anweisung für deut-sche Seeschiffe	1	5.35-10.40	
	– Restladungen aus deutschen Schiffen	1	9.39-12.40	
	– Statistische Unter-lagen für Schiffsver-kehr im Hafen von Neapel	1	8.39- 5.40	
	– Notizen für Bericht-erstattung (Geh. Schrank) Zeitungs-ausschnitte über Schiffsbewegungen	1	10.39- 2.40	
	Deutsches Konsulat: Rhodos	1	1928-33	
	– San Remo	1	1920-39	
	– Savona	1	1939	
	– La Spezia	1	1934-35	
	– Syrakus	1	1930-34	
	– Trapani	1	1924-28	
	– Terra Nova	1	1925-36	
	– Tirana	1	1939	
	– Triest	1-3	1919-39	
	– Tripolis	1-2	1920-39	
	– Turin	1-3	1920-39	
	– Venedig	1-2	1920-39	
	– Verschiedene Bewer-bungen	1	1920-33	
	– Konsulatsatteste, Einzelfälle	1	1932	

Akten-zeichen	Inhalt	Band	Datum	Serial Nr.
	IIIer Akten A Konsulatsangelegenheiten Namenssachen A - Z		1926-39	
	IIIer Akten A - Z 1 - 3930		1936-41	
	Sonderakten:			
	Attems, Olga		1941-42	
	Battistig-Burgegg, Oskar		1939-41	
	Berliner, Bertha		1939-41	
	Biro, Ludwig,Israel		1942-43	
	Bonomi, Petronella		1939-42	
	Deckarm,Josefa Maria		1941-42	
	Eisenbahnunglück 1938		1938-42	
	Falkenhayn, Marie		1941-42	
	Göschl & Verient, Firma		1941-42	
	Gregoriades, Vencaslao		1940-42	
	Heine, Friedrich		1940-41	
	Kollmar, Beatrice		1938-41	
	Mallaier, Crescenzia		1935-41	
	May, Petronella		1936-42	
	Medritzer, Othmar		1938-42	
	Orterer, Emma		1936-42	
	Röhl, Heinz		1942	
	Bottier, Joseph		1940-41	
	Pucci, Decime		1926-42	
	Schiff-Drost, Max		1941-42	
	Schmich, Isidor		1936-42	
	Schwepe, Heinrich		1937-41	
	Teodori, Ugo		1936-42	
	Topp, Wilhelm		1936-42	
	Vogelsang, Leni		1937-42	
	Werse, Gustav		1939-42	
	Winsemann, Hilde		1934-39	
	Zühlke, Kurt		1937-41	
	Leipziger Messe (allgemein) Erlasse des Auswärtigen Amtes		1940-42	
	- (Drucksachenver- sendung)		1941-42	
	- (Sichtvermerks- erteilung)		1940-42	
	Mailänder Frühjahrsmesse Sonder- schau "Kohle-Gas-Wasser" (Sichtvermerkserteilung)		1942	
	Prager Messe (Sichtvermerkser- teilung)		1942	
	Wiener -(Sichtvermerkserteilung)		1939-42	
	Wiener Modewoche		1940-42	
	Passakten A - Z	1-26	1924-27	
	- Monteure	1-3	1924-27	
	- Eisenbahner	1	1925-28	

Akten-zeichen	Inhalt	Band	Datum	Serial Nr.
	Passakten A – Z	1-42	1920-37	
	Juden-Passangelegenheiten A – Z			
	Pass – Allgemein	1	1928	
	– (Ermächtigung der Wahl-konsulate zur Passaus-stellung und Erteilung von Sichtvermerken)	1	1921-25	
	– (Bl. 1-309) mit Sonder-heft 1926 betr.S-V.D. Konsulat Genua	1	1924-26	
	– (Bl. 1-221)	1	1927-29	
	–	1	1929-32	
	– (Bl. 1-179)	1	1932-34	
	Reiseverkehr mit ausländischen Kraftfahrzeugen über die deut-sche Grenze (nur Ausstellung·von Triptyques besonders)	1	1922-38	
	Pass-Sachen, Generalia	1	1919-20	
	Kommunisten	1	1923	
	Meldungen an das Auswärtige Amt betr.Chinesen und Japaner	1	1920-23	
	Passangelegenheiten – Gebühren	1-2	1920-24	
	– allgemein	1-3	1921-23	
	–	1	1923-24	
	Pass-Sachen	1	1924-27	
	Passfragen	1-4	1922-31	
	Sammelband Verschiedenes	1-10	1926-31	
	Pass-und Sichtvermerkangelegen-heiten (Konferenzen, Abkommen)	1	1921-22	
	– Diplomaten, Kuriere	1	1922-23	
	Einreise- und Niederlassungs-verhältnisse allgemein	1-2	1921-24	
	Visum und andere kleine Geschäfts-sachen	1	1925-27	
	Passübersendungsschreiben	1	1932-35	
	Fahndungsberichte der Pass-Stelle	1	1929	
	Vermittlung von Spanien-Passagen Einzelfälle	1	1940	
	2 Beibände zu 110/39 (geh.)	1-2	1939	
	Verschiedene Korrespondenzen der Konsulatsabteilung	1	1920-24	
	Sichtvermerkstatistik	1	1926-28	
	Index der Pass-Stelle			
	Passangelegenheiten spez.Gebühren	1	1925-27	

Akten-zeichen	Inhalt	Band	Datum	Serial Nr.
	Passverordnung vom 4.6.24 nebst Ergänzungs- und Ausführungsbe-stimmungen sowie die neue Ver-ordnung über Gebühren für Aus-fertigung von Pässen	1	1924-27	
	Verschiedene Korrespondenz des Konsulats und Fragebogen	1	1918-31	
	Passakten A - G, M - R	1	1932-35	
	III C Anfragen und Auskünfte	1-4	1932-35	
Pol 1a	Politische Beziehungen Deutschlands zu Abessinien	1	1929-39	
	- Ägypten	1	1924-39	
	- Afghanistan	1	1929-39	7623/E545054-60
	- Albanien	1	1938-39	
	- Arabien	1	1929-39	
	- Argentinien	1	1937-39	
	- Belgien	1	1922-39	
	- Brasilien	1	1938-39	
	- Bulgarien	1	1924-39	
	- Chile	1	1938-39	
	- China	1	1921-39	
	- Dänemark	1	1920-39	
	- England	1	1923-39	
	- Estland	1	1928-39	
	- Frankreich	1-2	1920-39	
	- Georgien	1	1920-39	
	- Griechenland	1	1929-39	
	- Hedschas	1	1932-39	
	- Japan	1	1921-39	
	- Jugoslawien	1	1922-39	
	- Kanada	1	1933-39	
	- Lettland	1	1920-39	
	- Litauen	1	1928-39	
	- Niederlande	1	1933-39	
	- Oesterreich	1-4	1920-38	
	- Peru	1	1938-39	
	- Polen	1-7	1920-39	
	- Portugal	1	1921-39	
	- Randstaaten	1	1921-39	
	- Rumänien	1	1921-39	
	- Russland	1-3	1921-39	
	- Schweden	1	1924-39	
	- Schweiz	1	1928-39	
	- Spanien	1	1926-39	
	- Tschechoslowakei	1	1924-39	
	- Türkei	1	1921-39	
	- Ukraine	1	1922-39	
	- Ungarn	1	1928-39	
	- Uruguay	1	1937-39	

Akten-zeichen	Inhalt	Band	Datum	Serial Nr.
Pol 1a	Politische Beziehungen Deutschlands zu Vereinigte Staaten von Amerika	1	1920-39	
	– Yemen	1	1930-39	
	– übrige Länder	1	1935-39	
	Deutschland: Innen- und Aussen-politik, Allgemein	1 2	1922-29	L1701/L501072-84
Pol 1b		1		L1702/L501015-225
		2		L1702/L501226-80
		3	1920-28	L1702/L501281-322
		4		L1702/L501323-42
		1		L1702/L501343-350
		2	1928-35	L1702/L501351-418
		3		8066/E579223-39
		1	1935-39	8066/E579240-47 8762/E610989-1001
		2		
Pol 1b 1	– Verschiedenes betr.inner-pol.Angelegenheiten	1	1921-30	
	– Nationalsozialismus	1		L1703/L501419-804
		2	1923-35	8067/E579249-53
		3		
		1-3	1935-39	
	• – – Sonderband	1	1934	8949/E627784-87
	– Reichsparteitag, Sonderb.	1	1939	8279/E588251-56 8583/E602147-58
	– Hitlerjugend,Sonderbände	1-3	1933-39	
	– Stahlhelm, Sonderband	1	1927-33	
	– Deutsche Wahlen Sonderband	1	1924-36	
	– Wahlen,	1	1938-39	
	– Verhalten deutscher Mäd-chen im Ausland	1	1938-39	
	– Emigranten	1	1937	
	– Juden. Aufnahme der deut-schen Judenpolitik in Italien	1	1933-39	K1695/K405879-6173
	– Juden: Fall Ziffer	1	1935-36	K1695/K406174-99
Pol 1b 2	– Reichsverfassung, Flagge Nationalfeiertage	1-2	1920-35	
	– Verfassungsfeier	1	1926-29	
Pol 1b 3	– Berichte des Auswärtigen Amtes über innerpoliti-sche Lage	1	1920-39	
Pol 1b 4	– Notlage in Deutschland, Hilfsaktionen	1	1923-26	

Akten-zeichen	Inhalt	Band	Datum	Serial Nr.
Pol 1b 5	Wochenberichte der Abt.II des Auswärtigen Amtes	1-2	1923-39	
Pol 1c	Grenz- und Auslandsdeutschtum	1	1927-39	
Pol 2a	Italien: Aussenpolitik, Allgem.	1-3		
		4	1920-35	8073/E579387-90 8680/E607293-98
		5		9043/E633687-90 9910/E694085-90 M95/M003262-67
		1		7208/E529842-923 M299/M012736-40
		2	1935-39	7208/E529924-30
		3		7208/E529931-36
		4		
	Politische Beziehungen Italiens zu Abessinien	1	1928-36	
	– Aegypten	1	1920-39	
	– Albanien	1-3	1924-39	
	– Argentinien	1	1922-39	
	– Australien	1	1930-39	L947/L272067-72
	– Belgien	1	1921-39	
	– Brasilien	1	1925-39	
	– Bulgarien	1	1922-39	
	– China	1	1930-39	
	– Dänemark	1	1920-39	
	– England	1-3		
		4	1920-39	5837/E425479-87
		5		5837/E425488-542 7450/E540357-62
	– Estland	1	1924-39	
	– Frankreich	1-5	1920-31	
	– –	1-3	1931-39	
		4		5217/E308270-87 8916/E622205-09
	– Finnland	1	1922-39	
	– Griechenland	1-2	1920-39	
	– – Janina-Zwischen-fall	1	1923	
	– Irak	1	1938-39	
	– Irland	1	1938-39	
	– Japan	1	1921-39	7209/E529938-47 7680/E547634-42
	– Jugoslawien	1-3	1920-27	
	– –(Vertrag von Rapallo)	1	1920-22	
	– Jugoslawien	1-3	1927-39	
		4		5211/E308201-03 7852/E569692-706 9349/E662372-78
	– Litauen	1	1927-39	
	– Mandschukuo	1	1938-39	
	– Orient	1	1921-39	

Akten-zeichen	Inhalt	Band	Datum	Serial Nr.
Pol 2 a	Politische Beziehungen Italiens zu Oesterreich	1		9971/E697293-327
		2		9971/E697328-38
		3	1920-39	7210/E529949-90
				9958/E696271-75
		4		
	— Persien	1	1926-39	
	— Polen	1-2		
		3	1921-39	6381/E474483-87
	— Portugal	1	1920-39	
	— Protektorat	1	1939	
	— Rumänien	1-2	1922-39	
	— Russland	1-2		
		3	1920-39	7211/E529992-97
	— Schweden	1	1937-39	
	— Schweiz	1-2	1921-39	
	— Siam	1	1928-39	
	— Spanien	1	1921-39	
	— Südamerika	1	1921-39	
	— Syrien	1	1937-39	
	— Tschechoslowakei	1-2	1920-38	
	— Türkei	1-2		
		3	1920-39	7241/E531527-40
	— Ungarn	1-4	1920-39	
	— Vereinigte Staaten von Amerika	1	1921-39	
	— Yemen	1	1926-39	
	— Verschiedene Länder	1	1920-39	
Pol 2a 1	Deutsch-italienische Beziehungen allgemein	1-5	1920-28	
		1-4		
		5	1928-33	8054/E578937-50
		1		9807/E621723-26
		2	1933-35	8054/E578951-61
		3		8054/E578962-70
		4		8054/E578971-77
		1		3793/E042430-541
		2		3793/E042542-73
		3	1936-39	3793/E042574-99
		4		3793/E042600-01
				8002/E575666-69
	Vorbereitung, Führerbesuch, Organisation, Sonderband	1	1938	
	Ehrenkarten für Besuch des Führers	1	1938	
	Anträge auf Karten	1	1938	
	Besuch A.Hitler	1-4	1937-38	
	Zusammenkunft Mussolini-Hitler in Venedig, Sonderband	1	1934	3117/E041395-551

Akten-zeichen	Inhalt	Band	Datum	Serial Nr.
Pol 2 a 1	Deutsch-italienische Beziehungen Besuch Mussolini in Deutschland	1	1937–	7212/E529999-30007
		2		7212/E530008-14
	– Ciano	1	1936	7213/E530016-37 M297/M012686-705
	– RAM v.Neurath	1	1937	7214/E530039-42
	– Goering	1	1937	8420/E592837-92
	– Dr.Goebbels	1	1937	L1704/L501805-10
	– von Blomberg	1	1937	L1806/L521790-801
	– R.Hess	1	1937	L1705/L501811-30
	– Himmler	1	1936	L1807/L521802-52
	– Dr.Ley	1	1937	L1706/L501831-66
	– Dr.Darré	1	1937	
	– v.Tschammer u.Osten	1	1937-38	
	– Biagi	1	1938	
	– H.Neef	1	1938	
	– Milch	1	1938	
	– Lantini	1	1938	
	– Stabschef Lutze	1	1938	
	– Hueber	1	1938	
	– Funk	1	1938	
	– Dr.Frank	1	1938	
	– RM Rust	1	1937-39	
	– Speer	1	1939	
	– Scholz-Klink	1	1939	
	– Dr. Scheel	1	1939	
	– RAM v.Ribbentrop	1	1937-39	5852/E428728-47
	– NSLB	1	1939	
	– Kerrl	1	1939	
	– Benni	1	1939	7990/E575450-54
	– Schirach u.Rüdiger	1	1939	
	– Hierl	1	1939	
	– Dr.Gürtner	1	1939	
	– Esser	1	1939	
	– v.Brauchitsch	1	1939	
	– Fürst Colonna	1	1939	
	– Seldte	1	1939	
	– Sammelband	1	1939	8501/E597142-53

Akten-zeichen	Inhalt	Band	Datum	Serial Nr.
Pol 2 a 1	Deutsch-italienische Beziehungen Sammelband	2	1939	8341/E590132-35 8356/E590535-37
	– Pass-Schwierigkeiten Sbd.	1	1935-39	
	– Ausweisung Becker	1	1935	
	– Überwachung der Reichs-angehörigen	1	1934-39	
Pol 2 a 2	– Verschiedenes	1-2	1922-27	
	– Verhaftungen, Ausweisun-gen, Aufenthaltsbewilli-gungen	1	1935-39	
	– Verhaftungen von Italie-nern in Deutschland	1	1935-39	
	– Verhaftungen Deutscher in Italien, Einzelfälle	1	1920-28	
	–	1	1936	
	– – A - Z	1-2	1936-38	
Pol 2 a 3	Verhandlungen über einen deutsch-italienischen Schieds-vertrag	1 2	1926-39	K706/K157280-316
Pol 2 b	Innere Politik Italiens, allgem.	1-13	1920-39	
	– Rassen- u.Judenfrage	1-2	1938-39	
	Erdbebenkatastrophe Juli	Sbd	1930	
Pol 2b 1	Verschiedene innerpolitische Angelegenheiten	1-3	1920-39	
	Zeitungsartikel innerpol.Ange-legenheiten	1	1924	
Pol 2b 2	Italien. Neue Provinzen, allgem. auch Venezia Giulia	1-2	1921-39	
Pol 2b 4	Abgeordnetenkammer und Senat	1	1923-39	
	Verfassungsreform	1	1924-25	
Pol 2 c	Italienische Kolonien	1-5	1920-39	
Pol 3	Abessinien	1-5	1920-35	
	–	1 2	1935	8055/E578979-82 M272/M011391-95
		3		8055/E578983-95
		4		M254/M010943-54
	–	1		M272/M011396-406
		2	1935-36	M272/M011407-18
		3		7215/E530044-50
		4		7215/E530051-97
	–	1		7215/E530098-118
		2	1936-39	7215/E530119-23
		3-4		

Akten-zeichen	Inhalt	Band	Datum	Serial Nr.
Pol 3	Abessinien , Sonderband Sanktionen	1 2 3 4	1935-36	8057/E578142-46 M285/M011821-30 7216/E530125-33
	— Bank of Ethiopia	1	1937-39	
	— v.Waldheim	1	1937-39	
	— Requisitions-schäden	1	1936-39	
	— - österreichische	1	1938-39	
	— - Einzelfälle	1	1936-38	
	Ägypten	1-3	1920-39	
	Afghanistan	1-2	1921-39	
	Albanien	1-6	1920-39	
	Algier	1	1927-39	
	Anatolien	1	1920-39	
	Andorra	1	1934-39	
	Arabien	1	1920-39	
	Argentinien	1	1920-39	
	Armenien	1	1925-39	
	Australien	1	1934-39	L947/L272073-96
	Balkanstaaten	1 2-3	1921-39	**K1049** /K269036-47
	Belgien	1-2 3	1921-39	6811/E517696-706
	Bessarabien	1	1923-39	
	Bolivien	1	1939	
	Brasilien	1	1921-39	
	Bulgarien	1-3 4	1921-39	8275/E588223-27
	Chile	1	1921-39	6906/E518274-81
	China	1-6	1921-39	
	— (Mandschurei)	1-2	1932-39	
	Cuba	1	1938-39	
	Danzig	1-3	1921-32	
		4-6	1932-39	
	Dänemark	1	1920-39	
	Dodekanes	1	1924-39	

Akten-zeichen	Inhalt	Band	Datum	Serial Nr.
Pol 3	Donaustaaten	1		L1805/L521714-50
		2		L1805/L521751-68
		3	1931-32	9685/E681772-847 L1805/L521769-79
		4		L1805/L521780-89
		5		
		6		7680/E547643-49 8036/E577905-57
		7		8036/E577958- 8037
		8	1932-39	8036/E578038-64 M242/M008092-96 M298/M012706-35
		9		8932/E626179-84
	Ecuador	1	1938-39	
	Elsass-Lothringen	1	1922-39	
	England	1		
		2		7629/E545216-50
		3		7629/E545251-99
		4	1920-39	
		5		3104/E626803-49
	England-Amerika	1	1921-39	
	- Frankreich	1	1920-39	
		2		4413/E083826-32 7625/E545135-44
	- Irland	1	1938-39	
	- Japan	1	1931-39	7625/E545145-56
	- Jugoslawien	1	1924-39	
	- Portugal	1	1937-39	
	- Polen	1	1939	
	- Rumänien	1	1938-39	
	- Russland	1	1923-39	
		2		7625/E545157-58
	- Türkei	1	1921-39	
	- mit anderen Staaten	1	1922-39	
	- Grosse Entente	1	1924	
	- Kleine Entente	1-3	1920-39	
	- Estland	1	1924-39	
	Finnland	1	1921-39	
	Fiume	1-2	1921-31	
	Frankreich	1-8	1920-39	
	- Iran	1	1939	
	- Jugoslawien	1	1921-39	

Akten-zeichen	Inhalt		Band	Datum	Serial Nr.
Pol 3	Frankreich –	Litauen	1	1938–39	
	–	Polen	1	1936–39	
	–	Rumänien	1	1924–39	
	–	Russland Ostpakt	1–4	1920–39	
	–	Spanien	1	1939	
	–	Syrien	1	1936–39	
	–	Tschechoslowakei	1	1923–38	
	–	Türkei	1	1921–39	
	–	andere Staaten	1	1921–39	
	Galizien		1	1922–39	
	Georgien		1	1920–39	
	Griechenland		1–5	1920–39	
	Guatemala		1	1938–39	
	Haiti		1	1922–39	
	Indien		1	1920–39	
	Irak		1–2	1926–39	
	Iran		1	1920–39	
	Irland		1	1924–39	
	Japan		1–3	1921–39	
	Jugoslawien		1–8	1921–39	
	Kanada		1	1937–39	
	Kaukasien		1	1920–39	
	Kolumbien		1	1939	
	Korsika		1	1925–39	
	Kuba		1	1920–39	
	Lettland		1	1920–39	
	Litauen		1–6	1920–39	
	Luxemburg		1	1935–39	
	Malta		1	1923–39	
	Mandschukuo		1	1939	
	Marocco		1	1921–39	
	Memelgebiet		1–16	1923–39	
	Mesopotamien		1	1920–39	
	Mexiko		1	1921–39	
	Mittelamerika		1	1922–39	
	Mittelmeer		1	1922–39	
	Mitteleuropa		1	1920–39	

Akten-zeichen	Inhalt		Band	Datum	Serial Nr.
Pol 3	Montenegro		1	1920-39	
	Nicaragua		1	1939	
	Niederlande		1	1924-39	
	Nordstaaten		1	1935-39	
	Norwegen		1	1922-39	
	Oesterreich		1-4 5 6	1921-38	8983/E630004-22
	–	Nachfolgestaaten	1-2	1920-39	
	Orient		1-2	1920-39	
	Ostasien		1-2	1933-39	
	Palestina		1	1920-39	
	Panama		1	1938-39	
	Paraguay		1	1939	
	Peru		1	1924-39	
	Polen		1-7 8 9	1920-39	7990/E575455-56
	–	Riunione Adriatica Sicurta	Sbd	1939	
	–	Mitteilungen der Volksdeutschen Mittelstelle	1	1939	
	–	Polnische Staats-angehörige	1	1939	
	Portugal		1	1924-39	4363/E081001-51
	Rumänien		1-2 3 4	1920-39	6645/E504567-77
	Russland		1-7	1920-39	
	–	Kleine Entente	1	1937-39	
	–	Estland	1	1932-39	
	–	Finnland	1	1931-39	
	–	Japan	1	1924-39	
	–	Lettland	1	1932-39	
	–	Litauen	1	1926-39	
	–	Polen	1	1923-39	
	–	Randstaaten	1-2	1922-39	
	–	Rumänien	1	1924-39	
	–	Schweden	1	1924-36	
	–	Türkei	1	1924-39	
	–	Ungarn	1	1924-39	

Akten-zeichen	Inhalt	Band	Datum	Serial Nr.
Pol 3	Russland - Vereinigte Staaten von Amerika	1	1924-39	
	- andere Länder	1	1920-39	
	San Marino	1	1924-39	
	San Salvadore	1	1939	
	Saudi-Arabien	1	1932-39	
	Schweden	1	1928-39	
	Schweiz	1 2	1921 39	4414/E08385-41
	Siam	1	1926-39	
	Spanien	1-6 7 8-9 10 11 12 13	1924-39	7664/E547427-30 5148/E303617-20 5177/E307017-19 4219/E073931-43
	Sonderband zu Spanien, Telegramme Telefonate, wichtige Situations-berichte	1-3	1937-39	
	Südamerika	1	1923-39	
	Syrien	1-2	1920-39	
	Tanger	1-3	1923-39	
	Tirol	1	1920-39	
	Tschechoslowakei	1-4	1921-38	
	Tunis	1-3	1921-39	
	Türkei	1-3 4 5 6	1920-39	7238/E531320-79 8624/E604541-51 7238/E531380-410 8624/E604552-59 7238/E531411-16
	Ukraine	1	1921-39	
	Ungarn	1-4	1921-39	
	Uruguay	1	1939	
	Vereinigte Staaten v. Amerika	1-5	1920-39	
	Yemen	1	1938-39	
	Sonstige Länder	1-2	1920-39	
Pol 4	Internationale wirtschaftspoli-tische Fragen	1-4	1920-34	
Pol 5	Deutsche Kolonialpolitik	1-2 3 4	1920-39	7508/E540889-901
	Zeitungskopien		1925-27	

Akten-zeichen	Inhalt	Band	Datum	Serial Nr.
Pol 6	Verträge, allgemein und Verzeichnisse	1-2	1922-38	
Pol 6^a	Politische Verträge und Abkommen (soweit nicht in einzelnen Länderakten)	1	1923-33	
Pol 6^b	Internationale Verträge, Opium-Abkommen	1	1921-38	
	Kodifikation des Fremdenrechts	1	1929-32	
	Internationale Pflanzenschutz-abkommen	1	1932	
	Internationales Abkommen über Kraftfahrzeugverkehr	1	1926-27	
	Vollstreckung ausländischer Schiedssprüche	1	1929-30	
	Londoner Konvention: Sicherheit des menschlichen Lebens auf See	1	1921-34	
	Sammlung von internationalen Verträgen und Abkommen	1	1920-39	
Pol 7	Kongresse, Konferenzen	1-10	1921-36	
	− A − Z	1-3	1936-39	
	− Allgemeines		1927-39	
	Internationales Privatrecht	1-3	1924-39	
	Konferenz zur Kodifikation des Völkerrechts	1	1930	
	Weltkongress für Freizeit und Arbeit, Rom	1	1938	
	Kontinentaler Reklamekongress		1936	
	Genua-Konferenz Mai 1922	1-2	1922	
Pol 7^a	Internationaler ständiger Gerichtshof in Haag	1	1924-39	
Pol 7^a	Internationale Konferenzen	1	1921	
Pol 7^b	Internationale Wanderungskonferenz	1	1924-28	
	Internationale Konferenz für Aus- und Einwanderung	1	1924	
	Internationaler Handelskammer-Kongress, Rom	1	1923	
	Kongress für Internationale Finanzierung in Italien	1	1924	
Pol 7^c	Urheberrechtskonferenz, Rom	1-3	1922-39	
Pol 7^d	Weltnotverein (Ciradohilfswerk)	1	1923-32	
Pol 7^e	Internationale Weltwirtschafts-Konferenz	1	1926-29	
	Duplikate von Drucksachen der Urheberrechtskonferenz, Rom	1-5	1928	

Akten-zeichen	Inhalt	Band	Datum	Serial Nr.
Pol 8	Volksstämmige Minderheiten unter fremder Herrschaft (Südtirol)	1	1924–28	
Pol 8^a	Minoritätenfragen, allgemein	1		L1803/L521479–93
		2	1922–39	
		3		L1803/L521494–514
Pol 8^b	Deutsche Volksstämme unter fremder Herrschaft	1	1921–39	
Pol 8^c	Minderheitenfragen, Südtirol	1		L1514/L448644–47
		2		
		3	1920–26	L1804/L521515–27
		4		
		5		L1804/L521528–65
		6	1926–28	L1804/L521566–78
		7–10		
		11		L1804/L521579–642
		12		L1804/L521643–52
		13	1928–34	L1804/L521653–77
		14		
		15		L1804/L521678–713
		16		8058/E579148–50
		17		
		18		9045/E633697–98
		19	1935–39	
		20		
		21		7885/E570874–79
	Umsiedlung aus Südtirol, Einzel-fälle	1	1939	
	Südtirol: Umsiedlung	1	1939	
	– – Berichte aus Mailand	1	1939	
	– Geistliche	1	1935–39	
Pol 8^c 1	Vorgehen der Italiener gegen Deutsche in Südtirol	1–5	1923–39	
Pol 8^c	Zeitungsausschnitte über Südtirol	1–2	1928–33	
Pol 9^a	Völkerbund, Verschiedenes	1–10	1920–39	
	– Präferenzabmachung im deutsch-rumäni-schen und deutsch-ungarischen Handels-vertrag	1	1931	
	– Genfer Generalakte Beitritt Italiens	1–7	1931	
	– Europäische Union Sonderband	1–3	1930–32	
Pol 9^b 1	Deutschland und der Völkerbund	1–2	1920–26	
Pol 9^b 2	Völkerbund	1	1923–25	

Akten-zeichen	Inhalt	Band	Datum	Serial Nr.
Pol 9^{b} 2	Völkerbund: Italienische Vertreter	1	1920-37	
Pol 9^{b} 5	– Mandate	1-2	1924-39	
Pol 9^{b} 6	– Tagung in Rom 1924	1	1924-30	
Pol 9^{c}	– Ligen, auch Weltverband der Völkerbundligen	1	1926-31	
Pol 10^{a}	Politische Parteien in Italien, Verschiedenes	1	1920-39	
Pol 10^{b}	– Faschismus und Antifaschismus	1-8	1921-39	
Pol 10^{c}	Kommunismus in Italien	1-2	1922-39	
Pol 10^{d}	Freimaurer in Italien	1	1923-39	
Pol 10^{e}	Partito Popolare	1	1921-39	
Pol 10^{f}	Sozialisten	1	1920-39	
Pol 11	Personalien	1	1925-26	
	Italienisches Königshaus	1-2	1921-39	
Pol 11^{a}	v.Bethmann-Hollweg	1	1920-21	
	Dr. Wirth	1	1921	
	Erzberger	1	1921	
	Dr.Curtius	1	1921	
	Dr.Brüning,Reichskanzler	1	1921	
	Dr.Rathenau	1	1921-22	
	Reichspräsident Ebert	1	1925	
	Fürst u.Fürstin v.Bülow	1	1929-31	
	Stresemann	1	1929-33	
	Politische Persönlichkeiten, deutsche Sammlung	1	1930-39	
	Adolf Hitler	1-3	1933-39	
		4 5	1939	8417/E592801-07
	– Parade zum 50.Geburtstage	1	1939	
	Politische Persönlichkeiten, italienische Sammlung	1	1920-39	
	Mussolini	1-2	1922-39	
Pol 12^{a} 1	Deutscher Auswärtiger Dienst Allgemeines	1-2	1920-39	
Pol 12^{a2}	– Vertretungen	1	1920-39	
Pol 12^{a3}	– Personalveränderungen	1	1926-39	
Pol 12^{a} 4	– Konsularakademie Wien	1	1939	
Pol 12^{b1}	Italienischer Auswärtiger Dienst Allgemeines	1-4	1920-39	
Pol 12^{b2}	– Veränderungen	1-9	1920-39	

Akten-zeichen	Inhalt	Band	Datum	Serial Nr.
Pol 12^c	Auswärtiger Dienst anderer Länder ausser Deutschland und Italien	1-3	1920-39	
	– Sammlung	1	1928-39	
Pol 13^a	Diplomatisches Corps, Allgemein	1	1920-39	
Pol 13^b	Vorstellungsschreiben der akkreditierten Diplomaten	1-3	1921-39	
	Italienische Presse	1	1921	
Pol 13^c	Diplomatisches Corps, Verschied.	1	1920-39	
Pol 14	Politik, Film	1-6	1920-39	
Pol 14^a	Internationales Lehrfilm-Institut	1-2	1928-35	
Pol 14^b	Filmaustausch	1-2	1933-39	
Pol 15	Film, Verschiedenes, allgemein	1	1921-27	
	– Verschiedenes	1	1938-39	
Pol 16	Italienische Ministerien	1-2 / 3	1927-30	8059/E579152-67
	– Feuilles d'Informations Corporatives	1	1929-39	
	– Haushalt-Voranschläge	1 / 2	1925-32 / 1933-34	
	Sonderband Italienische Etats	1-4	1929-31	
Pol 17^a	Politik Vatikan	1-3	1921-29	
		4 / 5	1929-39	5222/E308345-47
	Sonderband: Material (Gesetze, Verordnungen) betr. Lateran-Verträge	1	1929	
Pol 19^{a1}	Deutschland, Propaganda, allgem.	1-6	1921-39	
	Beihilfen für kulturpolitische Aufgaben	1-6	1933-39	
	Propaganda, Buchausstellung, Sbd	1	1938-39	
Pol 19^{a2}	– Verbreitung politischer, wirtschaftlicher und wissenschaftlicher Literatur	1 / 2	1921-33 / 1934-39	
Pol 19^{a3}	– Verbreitung der deutschen Sprache	1-2	1933-39	
	Deutsche Sprachwerbung Dr.Junker	1	1938-39	
	Beiband		1938-39	
Pol 19^{b1}	Italienische Propaganda im Ausland	1-3	1921-39	
	– italienische Buchausstellung in Berlin	1	1939	
Pol 19^{b2}	– ital.Soc.Naz.Dante Alighieri	1	1921-39	

Akten-zeichen	Inhalt	Band	Datum	Serial Nr.
Pol 19^b 3	Italienische Propaganda im Ausland Lega Ital.per la tutela degli interessi italiani	1	1921-39	
Pol 19^c	Propaganda anderer Länder	1	1924-39	
	– Polen	1	1929-39	
	– Frankreich	1	1921-39	
Pol 19^d	Politischer Nachrichtendienst Spionage, Hetzpropaganda	1	1923-39	
Pol 19^d 2	Deutschfeindliche Filmpropaganda	2 3	1925-36 1936-39	
Pol 20^a	Heimschaffung deutscher Flüchtlinge	Heft	1939	
Pol 20^b	Gesuch deutscher Freiwilliger bei Kriegsausbruch	Heft	1939	
Pol 20^c	Gesuch italienischer Freiwilliger bei Kriegsausbruch	Heft	1939	
Fr. 1	Friedensvertrag, Allgemeines	1	1921-39	
	– Kriegsschuld	1	1925-26	
Fr. 1^a	– Schriftwechsel Schuldfrage	1	1920-24	
	– Schuldfrage	1	1922-39	
Fr. 1^a 2	– Schriftwechsel mit Baron Lumbroso in der Schuldfrage	1-2	1922-39	
Fr. 1^a 3	Kriegsschuldfrage. Deutsche Aktenpublikation	1	1921-24	
	– deutsche und österreichische Aktenpublikationen	1	1936-39	
Fr. 1^a 4	Italienische Aktenpublikation	1	1926- 39	
Fr. 1^a 5	Englische, französische und russische Aktenplubikationen	1	1926-39	
Fr. 1^a 6	Kriegsschuldfrage	1	1924-39	
Fr. 1^b	Revision des Versailler Vertrages	1	1922-39	
Fr. 2	Ausführungen zum Friedensvertrag Allgemeines	1	1920-26	
Fr. 3	Abstimmungs- und besetzte Gebiete, Allgemeines	1	1925-27	
Fr. 3^a	Friedensvertrag, Abstimmungsgebiete Oberschlesien	1-14	1920-25	
	Oberschlesische Frage	1	1921	
	Friedensvertrag: Werbung für die Abstimmung Oberschlesien	1-3	1920-21	
	Oberschlesien, Informatorische Erlasse und Berichte	3-4	1921-22	

Akten-zeichen	Inhalt	Band	Datum	Serial Nr.
Fr. 3^a	Akte betr.Kundgebungen aller deutschen Parteien und Stände gegen den polnischen Aufstand in Oberschlesien	1	1921	
	Friedensvertrag: Oberschlesien	1	1930-39	
	Abstimmungsgebiete: Osten	1-3	1921-39	
	- Saargebiet	1-5	1920-23	
		6-8 9	1923-34	M167./M005379-403
		10 11 12	1934	8970/E629676-77
		13		M32/M000971-76
		14 15	1934-35	
		16-18	1935-39	
	Saargebiet, Erfassung der Abstimmungsberechtigten		1934-35	
	- Reisebeihilfen		1935	
	Abstimmungsgebiete:Eupen-Malmedy	1-2	1920-39	
Fr. 3^b	Besetzte Gebiete: Rheinland und Pfalzfrage	1-9	1920-39	
	- - (Besatzungstruppen-Ausschreitungen)	1	1921-24	
Fr. 3^c	Einbruchsgebiete: Ruhr	1-6	1920-25	
Fr. 3^c Spez.	- Zeitungsausschnitte	1	1923	
Fr. 4^a	Kohlenlieferungen, Allgemeines	1		L361/L107707-62
		2		L361/L107763-802
		3 4	1920-21	L361/L107803-07
		5		L361/L107808-11
		6		L361/L107812-26
		7 8 9	1921-23	L361/L107827-63 L361/L107864-77
		10 13	1923-33	L361/L107878-932 L361/L107833-8047
Fr. 5^a	Abrüstung Landheer Seemacht, Luftfahrt	1-3	1920-22	
	-		1922-30	
Fr. 5	Beiakten: Abrüstung Dieselmotoren	1	1920-22	
	- Frage der Eisenbahnanlagen im linksrheinischen Gebiet	1-2	1922	

Akten-zeichen	Inhalt	Band	Datum	Serial Nr.
Fr. 5	Beiakten: Abrüstung Deutsche Werke	1-3	1921-22	
Fr. 5^a	Allgemeine Abrüstungsfragen	1-4	1925-30	
	Sonderband 1-3 zu Band 4 (Londoner Seeabrüstungskonferenz)		1930	
	Allgemeine Abrüstungsfragen	5-14	1931-33	
	Sonderband Mussolini _ Pakt - Vorschlag Sonderband zu	14	1933	8840/E615092-169 9931/E694866-69
	Allgemeine Abrüstungsfragen	15		
		16		8684/E607422-29
		17	1933-34	8684/E607430-39 9653/E680942-46 M149/M005178-83
		18		
		19	1934-39	8684/E607440-52
		20		
		21		
Fr. 5^b	Militärkontrollfragen	1-3	1923-26	
Fr. 6^a	Friedensvertrag: Kriegsgefangene	1	1920-39	
Fr. 6^b	Kriegsverluste und Kriegergräber	1-4	1921-39	
	Sammelgrab für die Besatzung U.C.12 in Tarent	1	1921-39	
	Campana dei Caduti in Rovereto	1-3	1924-39	
Fr. 6^c	Nachforschungen nach Kriegsge-fangenen und Kriegergräbern	1	1920-39	
Fr. 6^b	Ein Druckband (Elenco dei Militari Roma 1925)			
Fr. 7	Strafbestimmungen, Auslieferun-gen der Kriegsverbrecher	1-2	1920-39	
	Weissbuch Druckmaterial			
Fr. 8^a	Notenwechsel Allgemeines in der Reparations-frage	1-11	1922-27	
	Wiedergutmachung, Allgemeines	1-7	1920-21	
	Sonderband: Sonderabkommen mit Italien über Repara-tionen		1921-22	M355/M017812-41
	– Interalliierte Finanzministerkon-ferenz Paris		1925	
	Sonderakte: Frage der Rückliefe-rung Dezember 1922			
	Wiedergutmachung 1. Konferenz London 1921			
Fr.8$^{a\ 1}$	Informations Erlasse des Aus-wärtigen Amtes.Allgemeine Be-sprechung der Reparationsfragen	1-2	1922	

Akten-zeichen	Inhalt	Band	Datum	Serial Nr.
Fr.8^a 1	Veröffentlichungen	3-9	1922-27	
Fr.8^a 2	Material über die deutsche Wirt-schaftslage und über Reg. Maßnahmen in Bezug auf die Repa-rationsfragen	1-4	1922-27	
Fr.8^a 3	Deutsche Sachlieferungen auf Reparationskonto	1-2	1922-39	
Fr.8^a 5	Vorschläge zur Reparationsfrage (Zahlung - Pläne)	1	12.22- 5.24	
	Wiedergutmachung	2	5.22- 7.24	
Fr.8^a VI	Reparationsfrage - Sachverstän-digen-Gutachten - Dawes-Plan - Ausführung des Londoner Abkom -mens	1-25	1924-31	
Fr.8^a 6 Sbd.B	Ratifizierung Haager Abkommen		1930	
	Junkers - Siemens		1930	K1050 /K269048-67
	Bank für Internationale Zahlun-gen		1930	
	Besuch des Herrn und der Frau Grandi in Berlin vom 25.-27.10.		10.31	
	Sonderband: Besuch des Reichs-kanzlers Brüning und des RAM. Curtius in Rom am 7. u.8.8.31		8.31	L363/L108126-54
	Reparationsfrage, Kriegsschulden, internationale Verhandlungen, Ministerbesuche	1		L364/L108155-246
		2		L364/L108247-313
		3		L364/L108314-52
		4	1930-31	L364/L108353-58
		5		L364/L108359-70
		6		L364/L108371-408
		7		L364/L108409-54
		8	1931	L364/L108455-525
		9		L364/L108526-46
		10		L364/L108547-628
		11	1931-32	L364/L108629-88
		12		L364/L108690-748
		13		L364/L108749-814
		14		L364/L108815-31
		15		L364/L108832-905
		16	1932	L364/L108906-71
		17		L364/L108972-76
		18		L364/L108977-9106
		19	1932-33	L364/L109107-213
		20		L364/L109214-413
		21		L364/L109414-95

Akten-zeichen	Inhalt	Band	Datum	Serial Nr.
r.8[b]	Wiedergutmachung, Konferenzen	1	7.20- 8.21	
	Flottenkonferenzen	Heft	1936	
d.Fr.8[c]	Staatsvertrag mit Italien	1	IX.21	
d.Fr.8[d]	Noch nicht endgültige Fassung eines Vertrages zwischen Deutschland und Italien im Jahre 1922	1	1922	
r.8[c]	Wiedergutmachung, Verst.Best.Art. 231-47 Teil V 3		10.21-12.22	
	Friedensvertrag § 18 Anlage 2 zu Teil VIII	1	1924-26	
r.10	Wirtschaftliche Bestimmungen Verschiedenes	1-2	1921-28	
r.10[f] 1	- Schiedsgericht	1	1920-22	
	Deutsch-Italienischer Schiedsgerichtshof, Allgemeines	2-5	1923-30	
r.10 [f2]	Gemischter Schiedsgerichtshof, Kassensachen	1-2	1922-30	
r.10[f] 3	Deutsch-italienischer gemischter Schiedsgerichtshof, Personalfragen, verwaltungs-technische Fragen, Verschiedenes	1	1.22-11.27	
	Gemischter Schiedsgerichtshof	1	1930	
r.11	Friedensvertrag, Luftfahrt	1	1923-26	
		Heft	1936	
r.12	Sicherheitsfragen, Zeitungsausschnitte	1	1925-26	
r.12[a]	Häfen, Wasserstrassen, Eisenbahnen	1	1921-23	
r.12[b]	Donaubestimmungen	1	1920-22	
r.13[a]	Kosten der Besatzungstruppen	1	1921-26	
r.13[b]	Interalliierte Schulden	1-5	1921-36	
r.13[c]	Locarnopakt, französisch-russischer Pakt, Westpakt	1		M281/M011517-62
		2		M286/M011831-936
		3	1935-37	M286/M011937-2019
		4		M286/M012020-26
r.14	Veröffentlichungen über den Friedensvertrag und seine Folgen	1-6	1920-35	
r.15	Frontkämpfer-Konferenzen	1-2	1923-26 1936-39	
r.20	Friedensvertrag St.Germain, Folgen des Vertrages für Reichsdeutsche	1	1920-22	
		Heft	1933	

Akten-zeichen	Inhalt	Band	Datum	Serial Nr.
Fr.21	Friedensvertrag von Sèvres und Folgen des Vertrages für Reichsdeutsche	1	1921-25	
Fr.23	- v.Trianon	1	1922-23	
Mil. 1	Militärwesen: Deutschland, Reichswehr und Marine	1-5	1920-39	
	Sonderband: Deutsche Flottenbesuche	1	1930	
Mil. 2	Deutschland: Arbeitsdienstpflicht	1	1933-39	
Mil. 3	Militärpolitik allgemein (aller Staaten)	1	1939	
Mil. 5$^{a\ 1}$	Allgemeines über Organisation der italienischen Armee	1-9	1921-38	
	Material zu den Berichten über "Italienische Armee"	1	1929	
	Italienische Mobilmachungsmaßnahmen	1	1939	
Mil. 5$^{a\ 2}$	Italien. Polizeitruppen (Carabinieri)	1	1921-39	
Mil. 5$^{a\ 3}$	- Milizia Nazionale	1-2	1923-31	
Mil. 5$^{a\ 4}$	- Kolonialtruppen	1	1923-26	
Mil. 5$^{a\ 5}$	- Truppenübungen, Manöver	1	1922-27	
Mil. 5$^{a\ 6}$	- Marineangelegenheiten	1-5	1921-39	
Mil. 5$^{a\ 7}$	- Militär - Flugwesen	1-3	1922-36	
	Zeitungsausschnitte und Transozeanflug Balbos	1	1930-31	
Mil. 5$^{a\ 8}$ geh.	Italienische Rüstungsindustrie Bauten, Anlagen von militärischer Bedeutung	1	1931-39	
Mil. 5^{b}	Militär- und Heereswesen andere Länder A - Z	1-2	1923-39	
	- Frankreich	1	1922-35	
Mil. 5^{c}	Fremdenlegionen		1920-39	
Mil. 6	Austausch von Publikationen des italienischen Kriegsministeriums mit dem Reichswehrministerium		1920-39	
Mil. 10	Streichung Reichsdeutscher aus der italienischen Aushebungsliste u.a. verschiedene militärische Angelegenheiten	1 1a-5	1919-33	
	Dienstpflicht und Staatsangehörigkeitsfragen, allgemein		1939	
Mil. 15	Nachforschung nach verstorbenen Kriegsgefangenen	1	1920-22	
Mil. 16	Nachforschung nach Kriegsgefangenen	1	1920-22	
Mil. 17	Korrespondenzen mit den Versorgungsämtern	1	1920-23	

Akten-zeichen	Inhalt	Band	Datum	Serial Nr.
O 2	Anerkennungen, Auszeichnungen, Ordenssachen Verschiedenes	1	1920-27	
W.1ᵃ	Deutsche Wirtschaftspolitik, allgemein	1		L760/L224857-66
		2	1920-36	
		3		9400/E665563-77 M87/M003110-13
		4	1936-39	7814/E570460-86
		5-6		
	Wirtschaftsenquête 1927	1-3	1925-27	
W.1ᵃ Sdbd.	Beschäftigung italienischer Arbeiter in Deutschland: Land- und Bauarbeiter	1-2	1938-39	
W.1ᵇ	Deutschland mit den Staaten ausser Italien	1	1920-39	
	Wirtschaftspolitik Deutschland-Frankreich	1	1921-39	8951/E627796-804
	— Russland	1-2	1920-39	
.2ᵃ	Italienische Wirtschaftspolitik allgemein	1		L759/L224753-84
		2	1920-31	L759/L224785-95
		3	1932-35	L759/L224796-825
		4		L759/L224826-56
		5		
.2ᵃ bd.	L'Istituto per la Ricostruzione Industriale	1	1932-35	
.2ᵃ	Italienische Wirtschaftspolitik, allgemein	6-8	1935-39	
.2ᵇ	Wirtschaftsbeziehungen Italien — Ägypten		1920-39	
	— Albanien	1-2	1922-39	
	— Argentinien	1	1937-39	
	— Australien		1922-39	L947/L272097-100
	— Belgien		1922-39	
	— Bolivien		1939	
	— Brasilien		1924-39	
	— Bulgarien		1925-39	
	— Chile		1930-39	
	— China		1928-39	
.2ᵇ	— Dänemark		1929-39	
	— England		1920-39	
	— Estland		1925-39	
	— Ferner Osten		1930-39	
	— Finnland		1923-39	
	— Frankreich	1-4	1921-39	
.2ᵇ	— Griechenland	1	1924-39	
	— Japan	1	1924-39	
	— Jugoslavien	1-2	1920-39	
	— Kolumbien		1934-39	
	— Lettland		1929-39	

Akten-zeichen	Inhalt	Band	Datum	Serial Nr.
W. 2^b	Wirtschaftsbeziehungen			
	Italien - Luxemburg		1936-39	
	- Mandschukuo		1937-39	
	- Mittelamerika und Westindien		1925-39	
	- Niederlande		1934-39	
	- Norwegen		1931-39	
	- Oesterreich	1		
		2		8075/E579457-68
		3	1921-39	8973/E629731-35 K1051/K269068-84
		4		
	- Polen	1-2	1921-39	
	- Portugal	1	1929-39	
	- Rumänien	1-2	1927-39	
	- Russland	1-5	1920-39	
	- Schweden	1	1929-39	
	- Schweiz	1-2	1920-39	
	- Spanien	1	1922-39	
	- Südamerika	1	1930-39	
	- Tschechoslowakei	1	1920-38	
		2		7689/E548018-24
	- Türkei	1	1921-38	
	- Ungarn	1	1920-32	
	- -	2	1933-39	7680/E547650-53 8076/E579470-82
	- Venezuela		1921-39	
	- USA.		1929-39	
	- Yemen		1937-39	
	- Versch.Länder A - Z	1-2	1921-39	
W. 2^c	- Kolonien		1921-34	
W. 3	Albanien		1929-39	
	Abessinien		8.36-12.36	
	Italien - Ostafrika	1-4	1937-39	
	- Afrika, Libyen	1	1939	
	Belgien	1	1921-39	
	Bolivien	1	1939	
	England		1929-39	
	Frankreich		1921-31	
	Frankreich - Amerika		1937	
	Finnland		1937	
	Niederlande		1932-39	
	Norwegen		1930-39	
	Oesterreich		1923-38	K1191/K305548-9?
	Polen		1923-39	
	Russland		1920-36	

Akten-zeichen	Inhalt	Band	Datum	Serial Nr.
W 3	Schweden		1932-37	
	Spanien		1923-39	
	Türkei		1926-33	
	Ungarn		1922-38	
	Vatikansstaat		1929-31	
	USA.		1927-37	
	Verschiedene Länder		1921-39	
W 4	Deutsch-italienische Wirtschafts-beziehungen, allgemein	1 2	1931-36	8077/E579484-88
	Deutsch-italienische Wirtschafts-verhandlungen, Sonderband (Oberschlesien)		1921-23	
W 4ᵃ	Deutsch-italienische Wirtschafts-beziehungen, allgemein	1	1921-23	
W 4ᵃ	Angebl. Penetrazione Tedesca	1	1921-25	
W 4ᵇ 1	Vorbereitungen für deutsch-italienischen Handelsvertrag, allgemein	3 4	1924-25	L761/L224867-955 L761/L224956-5132
		5		L761/L225138-328
		6	1925	L810/L235788-800
		7		L810/L235801-77
	Alte Handelsverträge und Ver-handlungen	1	1920-22	L809/L235757-87 L811/L235878-911
	Deutsch-italienische Wirtschafts-verhandlungen und Vertrag	1		L812/L235912-97
		2	1920-32	L812/L235998-6098
		3		L812/L236099-167
		4		L812/L236168-278
		5		L731/L225329-34
		6	1932	L812/L236279-335
		7		L812/L236336-446
		8		L812/L236447-582
		9		L812/L236583-725
		10	1932-35	8078/E579490-95 L812/L236726-31
		11		
		12		
		13 14	1935-36	
		15		9053/E634116-17
		16		7219/E530145-69
		17	1935-37	7219/E530170-82 8078/E579496-98
		18		7219/E530183-210
		19		7219/E530211-28
		20		7219/E530229-48
		21		

Akten-zeichen	Inhalt	Band	Datum	Serial Nr.
W 4^b 1	Deutsch-italienische Wirtschafts-verhandlungen und Vertrag	22 -26	1937-38	
		28 -32	1938-39	5210/E308189-99
	Deutsche Delegation, Unterkunft	1	1924-27	
	Ergänzungsverhandlungen zum deutsch-italienischen Handels-vertrag	1	1926-28	
	Battaglia economica Italia Einfuhrverbote und Beschrän-kungen	1 2 3-4	1926-35	L813/L236732-808 L813/L236809-26
	Transitwaren Forderungen	1-2	1935-38	
	Einfuhr medizinischer Speziali-täten	1-2	1926-39	
	Vereinbarungen zwischen deut-schen und italienischen Eisen-bahnverwaltungen über Tariffra-gen	1	1926-28	
W. 4^b 1 Sbd.	Deutsch-italienisches Verrech-nungsabkommen	1	1934-35	
	Deutsch-italienischer Handels-vertrag	1 2	1935-37	7218/E530139-43
	Freistellung von Arbeitern, die in der italienischen Industrie tätig sind	3	1939-40	
	Verpflanzung italienischer Bergarbeiter aus Nordfrankreich ins Ruhrgebiet, Sonderband	1	1939	
	Deutsche Bergarbeiter in Carbonia, Sonderband	1	1939	
W. 4^b 2	Deutsch-italienisches Wirt-schaftsabkommen vom 28.8.21 und Notenwechsel über Verlängerung	1	1921-25	
W. 4^b 3	Material für deutsch-italieni-sche Wirtschaftsverhandlungen	1	1921-25	
W. 4^b 4	Petroleum, Benzin, Öl	1-4	1922-38	
W. 4^b 5	Berichtsfälschung Idea Nazionale Rom, Bericht des Handelsrats Stroheker	1	1921	
W. 5	Internationale Wirtschaftsfragen	1-4 5 6	1924-37	8079/E579500-22 9411/E665580-652
W. 6^b	Monatsberichte des Auswärtigen Amtes über die Wirtschaftslage in Deutschland	1	1920-26	
W. 6^c	Wirtschaftliche Lage in Deutsch-land	1-3	1920-39	
W. 7	− in Italien	1-4	1921-39	

Akten-zeichen	Inhalt	Band	Datum	Serial Nr.
W. 7^c	Berichte des Generalkonsulats Mailand über die wirtschaftliche Lage in Italien	1	1921-23	
W. 8^a	Gross- und Schwer-Industrie	1	1920-39	L816/L237034-41
		2		L817/L237042-65
W.9	Industrie und Technik	1	1921-28	
W.10	Verschiedene Industrien Italiens A - Z	1-2	1920-39	
	Deutsche und italienische Industrie Automobile	1-4	1922-39	
	- Aluminium	1	1925-39	
	- Brennstoffe		1921-39	
	- Elektrizität		1926-39	
	- Seide u.Kunstseide		1924-39	
	- Zusatzprotokoll betr. Kunstseide		1933-34	
W.11	- Bergbau		1920-37	L818/L237066-134
W.12	- Wasserwirtschaftliche Fragen		1920-39	
W.13	Italienische Landwirtschaft	1-9	1920-39	
W.13^a	Internationales Landwirtschafts-Institut	1-6	1920-39	
W.13^b	Landwirtschaftliche Sachverständige	1	1927-30	
W.13^d	Wein und Internationales Weinamt	1	1924-39	
W.14	Forstwirtschaft, Jagd	1-2	1923-39	
W.15	Viehwirtschaft, Veterinärwesen	1-3	1920-39	
W.15^a	Deutsch-italienische Zusammenarbeit zum Studium von landwirtschaftlichen Fragen	1	1938-39	
W.15^b	Pflanzenschutz		1939	
W.16	Fischereiwesen		1923-39	
W.17	Patente und Erfindungen	1-2	1920-39	
W.18	Handwerk, Gewerbe	1	1924-39	
W.20	Wirtschaftskongresse	1-3	1926-35	
W.30	Handel Deutschland	1-2	1920-39	
W.31	Handel Italien, Innen- und Aussenhandel	1-3	1922-39	
W.31^a	Italienisches Ausfuhrinstitut	1	1926-33	
W.32^a	Deutsch-italienische Handelsbeziehungen	1-6	1920-39	
	- Sonderband			
	Besuch deutscher Industrieller in Rom und Italien		1936	

Akten-zeichen	Inhalt	Band	Datum	Serial Nr.
W.32$^{a\ 1}$	Ursprungszeugnisse und Analysen-zertifikate für Bier und Wein	1-2	1921-37	
W.32$^{a\ 2}$	Verhandlungen mit Italien und Kohlenlieferungen		1926-27	L814/L236827-7030
W.32^{c}	Ursprungszeugnisse für den deutsch-italienischen Warenver-kehr (Bayrische Handelsgremien)	1	1925-26	
	Deutsch-italienische Handelsbe-ziehungen (Verschiedenes)		1921-24	
W.33^{a}	Deutsche Bestimmungen für den Warenverkehr aus Deutschland	1	1920-35	
W.33^{b}	Italienische Bestimmungen für den Warenverkehr aus Italien	1	1921-26	
W.33^{c}	Statistik, Handbuch für den Aussenhandel	1-2	1921-32	
W.40^{a}	Deutsche Handelskammern	1	1921-39	
W.40^{b}	Italienische Handelskammern	1	1921-33	
W.40^{c}	Deutsch-italienische Handels-kammern	1	1920-30	
	- Mailand	1	1920-39	
W.40^{d}	Internationale Handelskammern	1	1925-30	
W.41	Handelskammern anderer Länder in Italien	1	1920-24	
W.42	Sonstige kaufmännische Verbände kommerzielle Institute	1-3	1920-36	
W.43	Handelsverträge	1	1922-31	
W.44^{a}	Handelseinigungsstellen	1	1920-24	
	Handelsrechtliche Fragen ver-schiedener Art	1	1921-24	
W.45	Unlauterer Wettbewerb, Handels-spionage	1	1920-36	
W.46	Speditionswesen	1	1922-32	
W.47	Versicherungswesen	1-2	1921-38	
W.M.	Wehrwirtschaft	1-2	1936-39	
H. 1	Allgemeine Erlasse	1-3	1920-39	
	Gesetze	1-2	1938-39	
	Anschriften deutscher Firmen	1-4	1936-39	
	- Italien	1-2	1938-39	
	Italien- Ostafrika	1-3	1937-39	
	- Sbd.Berghaus	1	1936-38	
	- Sbd.Prächtel	1-2	1936-39	
	Stellengesuche	1-6	1924-39	
	Vortragsreise Dr.Graeff	1	1935	

Akten-zeichen	Inhalt	Band	Datum	Serial Nr.
H. 1	Persönliche Briefe Dr.Graeff	1-6	1934-39	
	Ausstellungen und Messen	1-9	1924-39	
	Banksachen	1-8	1923-39	
	Steuersachen	1-7	1924-39	
	Versicherungen	1-2	1924-35	
	Verschiedenes	1-4	1919-35	
	– Ein Heft Privatbriefe Dr.Holm 1933-34	1-4	1923-37	
	–	1-6	1937-38	
H. 1 W	Allgemeines	1-7	1920-37	
	Italien	1-2	1932-38	
	Deutschland	1	1926-35	
H. 1	Spezialfälle für die Kommission	1	1924	
	Eildienst	1-2	1934-38	
	Ausschreibungen	1-2	1926-34	
	Normalisierung	1	1932-35	
	Aluminium	1	1923-35	
	Ansichtskarten	1	1922-35	
	Armaturen	1	1922-35	
	Asbest	1	1922-35	
	Asphalt und Pech	1	1922-35	
	Automaten	1	1926-35	
	Automobile	1-6	1920-35	
	Baugewerbe	1-4	1923-35	
	Baumwolle	1	1923-35	
	Beleuchtungsindustrie	1-2	1923-35	
	Bergbauprodukte	1-2	1923-35	
	Bijouterien	1-2	1923-35	
	Bleistiftindustrie	1	1927-33	
	Blumen	1	1923-35	
	Brauerei	1-2	1923-35	
	Buchbinderei	1	1923-34	
	Buchdruckereibedarf	1-2	1923-35	
	Büroartikel	1-2	1923-35	
	Bürsten und Pinsel	1	1923-32	
	Celluloid	1	1926-35	
	Chemie	1-6	1923-35	
	Dachpappen	1	1924-35	
	Dampfschiffe	1	1923-33	

Akten-zeichen	Inhalt	Band	Datum	Serial Nr.
H. 1	Devotionalien	1	1923-35	
	Drogen	1	1923-35	
	Düngemittel	1	1926-28	
	Eisen	1	1922-35	
	Eisenbahnbau	1-4	1922-35	
	Eisenwaren	1-2	1922-35	
	Elektrische Apparate	1-3	1922-35	
	Elektrizität	1	1923-30	
	Emballagen	1	1922-33	
	Essenzen	1	1923-34	
	Fahrräder	1-2	1923-35	
	Farben	1-2	1923-35	
	Fässer	1	1923-33	
	Feuerfestes Material	1-2	1924-35	
	Feuerlöschapparate	1	1925-35	
	Film	1-3	1922-37	
	Fischerei	1-3	1923-38	
	Flaschenverschlüsse	1	1923-32	
	Fleisch und Geflügel	1	1923-35	
	Früchte, getrocknete	1	1923-35	
	Fussböden	1	1923-33	
	Futtermittel	1	1923-34	
	Galanteriewaren	1-2	1923-34	
	Garne und Nähseide	1	1923-35	
	Geldschränke	1	1924-33	
	Gemälde	1	1923-33	
	Gerbereien	1	1923-35	
	Getreide	1	1923-35	
	Glaswaren	1-2	1923-35	
	Gummiwaren	1-2	1923-35	
	Hanf	1	1924-35	
	Haushaltungsartikel	1-2	1923-35	
	Häuser	1-2	1923-35	
	Häute und Leder	1	1923-33	
	Heizungsanlagen	1-2	1923-35	
	Holz und Holzwaren	1-2	1922-35	
	Holzbaracken und Holzhäuser	1	1923-35	

Akten-zeichen	Inhalt	Band	Datum	Serial Nr.
H. 1	Hülsenfrüchte	1	1924-31	
	Hüte	1	1923-35	
	Installationen	1-2	1923-35	
	Kartoffeln	1-2	1923-35	
	Keramik	1	1923-31	
	Kerzen	1	1925-30	
	Klaviere	1-2	1923-35	
	Kleider	1	1923-35	
	Knöpfe	1-2	1923-35	
	Koffer	1	1923-35	
	Kohle und Brennstoffe	1-2	1923-35	
	Konserven	1-2	1923-35	
	Korbwaren	1	1923-35	
	Korkwaren	1	1923-31	
	Krankenhausbedarf	1-2	1923-35	
	Kunstblätter und Kupferdrucke	1-2	1922-35	
	Kunstgewerbe und Kunstgegenstände	1-2	1922-35	
	Kurzwaren	1-2	1923-35	
	Kühlanlagen	1	1929-35	
	Lampen	1	1922-33	
	Landkarten	1	1924-35	
	Landwirtschaft	1	1923	
	Lebensmittel, Allgemeines	1-2	1921-35	
	– Eier	1	1923-32	
	– Obst und Gemüse	1-2	1923-35	
	– Oele und Fette	1-2	1923-35	
	– Reis	1	1925-35	
	– Salz	1	1924-35	
	– Schokolade	1-2	1923-35	
	– Süßstoff u. Zucker	1	1925-33	
	– Tee u.Kaffee	1	1924-34	
	– Teigwaren	1	1923-35	
	– Wurstwaren	1	1923-35	
	– Zucker	1	1923-35	
	Erzeugnisse landwirtschaftlicher Verarbeitungsgewerbe:	1	1921-24	
	Mehl, Getreide, Futtermit-tel, Öle, Zucker, Weine, Bier	1	1921-24	
	Lederwaren und Leder	1-2	1923-35	
	Lehrmittel und Bücher	1-2	1923-35	

Akten-zeichen	Inhalt	Band	Datum	Serial Nr.
H. 1	Luftschiffahrt	1-2	1923-35	
	Maschinen-Industrielle	1-11	1920-36	
	Maschinenbau und Abbildungen	1-4	1924-35	
	Bäckerei-Maschinen	1	1931-34	
	Bergwerks-Maschinen	1	1923-34	
	Dampfmaschinen und -Walzen	1	1920	
	Druckerei-Maschinen	1	1923-35	
	Elektrische Maschinen	1-2	1923-34	
	Nähmaschinen	1	1924-35	
	Schiffsmaschinen	1	1924-33	
	Schuhmacherei-Maschinen	1	1923-34	
	Strassenbau-Maschinen	1-2	1924-34	
	Wäscherei-Maschinen	1	1923-34	
	Landwirtschaftliche Maschinen	1-5	1920-35	
	Marmor	1	1920	
	Medizinische Instrumente	1-2	1922-35	
	Metalle	1-2	1923-35	
	Milchwirtschaft	1-2	1923-35	
	Mineralwasser	1	1923-35	
	Möbel	1-2	1923-35	
	Musikinstrumente	1-2	1921-33	
	Musikalien	1	1923-35	
	Optik	1-2	1924-35	
	Papier und Pappe	1-4	1920-35	
	Papier	1	1923-35	
	Parfumerien	1-2	1923-35	
	Pelzwaren	1	1925-35	
	Petroleum	1	1923-33	
	Pharmazeutik	1-4	1923-35	
	Photografische Artikel	1-2	1923-35	
	Porzellan	1	1923-35	
	Pumpen	1	1923-34	
	Putzmittel	1	1922-35	
	Pyrotechnische Artikel	1	1923-35	
	Radio	1-2	1923-35	
	Rahmen	1	1928-32	
	Reklameschilder	1	1923-37	

Akten-zeichen	Inhalt	Band	Datum	Serial Nr.
H. 1	Rohrfabrikation	1	1923-35	
	Rohprodukte	1	1923-31	
	Sanitäre Einrichtungen	1-2	1922-33	
	Sämereien	1	1924-35	
	Schiffbau und Schiffahrt	1-6	1920-38	
	Schmuckwaren	1	1921	
	Schreibmaschinen	1-2	1923-35	
	Schuhe	1-2	1923-35	
	Schwefel	1	1924-35	
	Seide	1-2	1923-35	
	Seilerwaren und Bindfaden	1	1923-35	
	Sumach	1	1923-35	
	Spielwaren	1-2	1921-35	
	Spirituosen	1-2	1923-35	
	Sportartikel	1-2	1923-35	
	Stahlwaren	1-2	1923-35	
	Stoffe	1-2	1923-35	
	Tabak	1	1922-32	
	Tapeten und Tapeziermaterial	1	1923-35	
	Technische Artikel	1-2	1923-35	
	Teerprodukte	1	1923-35	
	Teppiche	1	1922-35	
	Textilwaren	1-4	1922-35	
	Toiletteartikel	1-2	1923-35	
	Töpferwaren	1	1923-34	
	Transportanlagen	1-2	1923-35	
	Uhren	1	1923-35	
	Weine	1-2	1923-35	
	Werkzeuge	1-2	1920-35	
	Wolle	1-3	1920-35	
	Waagen und Gewichte	1-2	1923-35	
	Wachs	1	1923-32	
	Waffen	1-2	1923-35	
	Wasserleitungen	1-2	1921-35	
	Wäsche	1-2	1923-35	
	Zahnärztliche Artikel	1	1923-34	
	Zeichen- und Malutensilien	1	1923-35	

Akten-zeichen	Inhalt	Band	Datum	Serial Nr.
H. 1	Zement	1	1923-34	
	Zigaretten	1-2	1923-35	
	Zündapparate	1	1930-35	
	Heereslieferungen	1	1935-37	
	Kohlenmarktberichte	1-3	1936-38	
H. 1 I	Obst und Gemüse	1-2	1937-38	
	Tiere, Lebensmittel, Tabak	1	1936-37	
H. 1 II	Ölsaaten, tierische und pflanz-liche Öle und Fette	1-3	1936-38	
H. 1 III	Textilien	1-3	1935-38	
H. 1 IVa	Metalle	1-3	1936-38	
H. 1 IVb	Maschinen und Apparate	1-3	1936-38	
H. 1 IVc	Geräte, Instrumente, Waffen	1-3	1936-38	
H. 1 IVd	Bau und Verkehr, Kraftwagen	1-3	1936-38	
H. 1 V	Mineralien	1-3	1936-38	
H. 1 VI	Holz	1-3	1936-38	
H. 1 VII	Chemische Erzeugnisse	1-3	1936-38	
H.1 VIII	Verschiedene Waren	1-3	1936-38	
H. 2[a]	Deutschland: Aussenhandel, allg. spez.Aussenhandels-kontrolle und Abga-ben	1	1920-21	
	– Aussenhandelsför-derung, allgemein	1	1920	
	Italien: Aussenhandelskontrolle	1	1920-21	
	– Aussenhandelsförderung, allgemein	1	1920-21	
	Kapitalbildung und Kapitalbe-schaffung	1	1920	
	Geldverkehr, allgemein	1-13	1935-40	
	Banco Carpi.Gieffers & Co.	1	1935-37	
	Istituto Fiduciario Italien	1	1924-33	
H. 2[b]	Clearingüberweisungen	1-9	1936-40	
H. 2[c]	Überweisungen ausser Clearing	1-5	1935-39	
H. 2[d]	Devisenbestimmungen Italien – Deutschland	1-2	1936-39	
	Devisenbestimmungen Deutschland	1	1939	
	Devisen – Schillinge	1	1938-39	
H. 2[e]	Deutsche Verrechnungskasse	1-2	1937-39	
	Lire – Abwertung	1	1936-37	
H.	Verschiedene Zeitungsausschnitte	1-4	1938-40	

Akten-zeichen	Inhalt	Band	Datum	Serial Nr.
H.	Durchdrucke der in Registratur abgelegten Akten	1	1939	
H. 3	Kompensationsgeschäfte	1-5	1935-39	
	Sonderband "Miag"	1	1938-39	
	Lizenzen	1-9	1938-39	
H. 3^a	Italien - Ein- und Ausfuhr	1-4	1920-36	
	- Aussenhandel-Statistik	1-4	1937-40	
	Deutschland - Aussenhandel - Statistik	1-3	1927-40	
H. 3^b	- Einfuhr	1-2	1920-35	
	- Ausfuhr	1	1920-36	
	- Allgemeines	1-3	1920-39	
	Italien: Allgemeines	1	1920	
	- Einfuhr	1-22	1920-40	
	- Ausfuhr	1-2	1920-36	
H. 3^c	- Durchfuhr	1	1922-33	
	- Ausfuhr	1-2	1924-36	
	- - Einzelfälle	1-4	1937-39	
	- -	1-2	1937-38	
	Deutschland: Durchfuhr	1	1923	
	- Ausfuhr	1	1923-36	
	- - Einzelfälle	1-2	1937-39	
	- Einfuhr	1-2	1923-37	
	- - Einzelfälle	1-2	1937-39	
	Italien : Einfuhr	1-47	1920-39	
	- - Sonderband Lizenz-system	1	1936	
H. 3^d	- Einfuhr	1-47	1921-36	
	- Zollwesen	1-9	1937-39	
	- Sonderband zu Zoll-tarif	1-3	1937-39	
H. 3^d spez.	- Verzollung von Doublé-Waren	1	1927-33	
	- Verzollung von Auto-mobilzubehör-teilen	1	1930-33	
	- - Bilderbüchern	1	1927-35	
	- Eduard Hueck, Lüden-scheid	1	1932-34	
	- Zollsache Wieland-Werke, Ulm	1	1933-34	

Akten- zeichen	Inhalt	Band	Datum	Serial Nr.
H. 3^d	Deutschland: Zollwesen	1	1937-38	
	– Beiband Zolltarif	1	1937-38	
H. 3^e	Erschwerung der Einfuhr deut- scher Waren, Bevorzugung ita- lienischer Waren	1-3	1923-39	
H. 3^h	Ein- und Ausfuhrbolletten	1-4	1938-39	
H. 3^i	Ein- und Ausfuhr - Zusatzkontin- gente	1	1938	
H. 3^k	– – Kolonien	1-2	1938-39	
H. 4	Treuhandwesen	1-2	1937-39	
	L.Starke, Bolzano, verschiedene Korrespondenz	1	1934-36	
	Deutsche Handelskammer in Mailand	1-3	1936-39	
H. 4^a	Handelskammern	1	1923-30	
		1-2	1937-39	
	Internationale Handelskammern spezialia	1	1920-25	
H. 4^b	Sonstige Organisationen	1-5	1923-38	
H. 5^a	Bücher-Lehrmaterial	1	1936	
	Nachrichtenwesen, Bücher, Publikationen	1-2	1937-38	
	Veröffentlichungen, Deutschland	1-3	1939	
	– Italien	1-3	1939	
H. 5^b	Zeitschriften, Deutschland	1-4	1923-38	
	– Italien	1-3	1923-38	
H. 5^c	Adressbücher, Deutschland	1-4	1923-39	
	– Italien	1-3	1923-39	
H. 5^d	Eildienst des Auswärtigen Amtes	1	1920	
H. 5^e	Italien	1	1923-29	
H. 5^f		1-4	1923-38	
	Deutschland	1	1924-36	
H. 6^a	Vertreter allgemein	1-12	1920-39	
H. 6^b	Vertreter bieten sich an	1-3	1936-39	
H. 7^a	Fakturen, Versand und Ursprungs- zeugnisse	1	1923-34	
H. 7^c	Mustersendungen, Preislisten, Kataloge	1	1924-35	
H. 7	Lieferungen, Muster	1-2	1938-39	
H. 8^{a+b}	Handelsgepflogenheiten (Gebräu- che, Missbräuche, allgemeine Winke für den Handel)	1-2	1923-36	

Akten-zeichen	Inhalt	Band	Datum	Serial Nr.
H. 8^c	Unlauterer Wettbewerb	1-4	1923-38	
H. 8^d	Unsichere Firmen "Kartei"	1-2	1936-38	
H. 9	Reklamationen und Forderungen Deutschland	1-76	1920-39	
H. 9	— spez. Hermann Dick - Zittignani, Colombo	1	1931-37	
	Reklamationen und Forderungen Italien	1-10	1920-39	
H.10	Handelsspionage	1	1924-34	
	Transit-Sondergeschäfte	1-2	1940	
H.11	Speditions- und Lagerwesen	1-5	1920-40	
	Sonderband Reichsbahn Mailand	1-3	1937-40	
	— Verkehr	1	1937-38	
	— Rundschreiben der Reichsbahn Mailand	1	1940	
H.12	Reklamewesen	1-4	1923-41	
H.13	Handelsrecht	1-10	1923-40	
H.14	Einzelauskünfte, spez.	1-29	1920-39	
	Auskunftswesen, allgemein	1-5	1923-40	
H.15^a	Patentrecht, Einzelfälle	1-6	1922-40	
H.15^b	Erfindungen und Patente Einzelfälle	1-5	1923-39	
H.15^c	—	1-5	1923-40	
H.16	Zuständigkeit deutscher Konsulate			
	Addis-Abeba	1	1937-40	
	— Barcelona	1	1940	
	— Bari	1	1936-40	
	— Bozen	1	1939-40	
	— Carrara	1	1937	
	— Catania	1	1936-38	
	— Fiume	1	1940	
	— Florenz	1	1936-40	
	— Genua	1-4	1936-40	
	— Livorno	1	1937-40	
	— Mailand	1-5	1936-40	
	— Messina	1	1938-40	
	— Neapel	1	1936-40	
	— Palermo	1	1938-40	
	— San Remo	1	1936-37	
	— Tirana	1	1939-40	
	— Triest	1	1936-40	
	— Tripolis	1	1936-40	
	— Turin	1	1936-40	
	— Venedig	1	1937-41	

Akten-zeichen	Inhalt	Band	Datum	Serial Nr.
H.17	Preisentwicklung in Italien	1-2	1940	
Spez. Akte	Korrespondenz Dr.Daffina-Hinderer	1	1928-30	
	- Clemens Claus Thalheim	1	1933-34	
	- Stahlhaus G.m.b.H., Düsseldorf	1	1927-30	
	- Cresta-Mario	1	1920-25	
	- Bogen Giovanni	1	1921-37	
	- Barbaners Davis	1	1920-27	
	- Scheidemantel, Karl	1	1922-27	
	- Paul Holländer Söhne	1	1920	
	- R.Wolf A.-G.,Magdeburg	1	1920	
	- Graf Henckel v.Donnersmarck - Beuthen	1	1920	
	Mitteleuropäisches Reisebüro Italien, Reiseverkehrs-Gesellschaft	1	1930	
	Internationale Valutakonferenz und Valuta-Fragen	1-2	1920	
	Internationale Konferenz über Normalisierung in der Metallindustrie	1	1920	
	Internationale Verkaufsbedingungen in Italien	1	1929	
	Documenti Scarico Campioni	1	1931-32	
	Verzeichnis deutscher Vertreter in Italien	1	1930-31	
Hi. 1	Italien, spez.Ansaldo	1	1920	
	Maschinen, spez.Siegfeld & Co.	1	1920	
Hi. 2	Erze und Bergwerke	1	1923-35	
	Kohle	1-2	1922-35	
Hi. 3	Verschiedenes	1	1920-22	
Hi.	Verschiedene Korrespondenzen von Handel und Industrie, lose Akten	1-7	1920-22	
W V Nr. 6	General-Konsulat Mailand: Schwarze Listen, engl. u. franz.	1	1939	
	Wirtschaftliche Spionage	1	1940	
	Handelsauskünfte: Compagnia Italo-Jugoslava	1	1939-40	
	Englische Handelskammer in Mailand	1	1940	
	Ursprungszeugnisse, Bescheinigungen	1	1940	
W.J. Nr. 7	Handelsbedingungen für pharmazeutische Spezialitäten	1	1937-41	
n 24[a]	Auskunft über Auslandsbank	1	1920	
H	Korrespondenzen des Exportförderungs-Instituts der österreichischen Handelskammer in Wien			

Akten-zeichen	Inhalt	Band	Datum	Serial Nr.
H	Österreichische Ministerien und Behörden	1	1938	
	Inkasso	1	1937-38	
	Österreichisches Export Förde-rungs-Institut	1	1938	
	Österreichische Firmen A - Z Deutsche (österr.) Firmen Osterr. Fachverbände	1-4	1938 1938 1938	
	Österreichisches Bezugsquellen-verzeichnis		1938	
	Italienische Behörden und öster-reichische Gesandtschaft	1	1938	
	Italienische Firmen	1	1938	
	- A - Z	1-4	1938	
H + W	Material für die Wochenberichte	1-2	1920-25	
A. 1	Ausstellungen, Allgemeines	1	1921-39	
A. 2 Sdbd.	Weltausstellung Rom 1942 Bewerbungen um Vergebung von Arbeiten	1	1939	
A. 3	Ausstellungen in Deutschland	1-3	1921-39	
A. 4^a	- Italien	1-4	1920-39	
Sdbd.	Weltausstellung Rom 1941	1	1937	
A. 4^b	Kunstausstellung in Mailand (Monza)	1-2	1923-36	
A. 5	Ausstellungen verschiedener Länder (ausser Deutschland und Italien)	1	1921-39	
A.10	Messen, Allgemeines	1	1920-39	
A.11	- in Deutschland	1-2	1920-39	
A.11^b	Leipziger Messe	2-3	1927-39	
A.11^c	Messen in verschiedenen Ländern	1	1920-39	
A.12	- Italien	1-2	1920-39	
	Mailänder Messe	1-4	1920-39	
A.12^b	Messen: Pieri del Lavanti Bari	1-2	1927-39	
	Neapolitaner Messe		1920-40	
	Internationale Mustermessen Padua		1921-35	
	Triester Messe		1920-22	
	Mustermesse in Tripolis		1920-39	
A.13	Ausstellungen über Wesen und Bedeutung des Nationalsozialis-mus	1	1939	
A.14	Wiener Messe	1	1939	
A.15	Prager Messe	1	1939	

Akten-zeichen	Inhalt	Band	Datum	Serial Nr.
V. 1	Verkehrswesen, Allgemeines	1	1920-39	
V. 2	Verkehr, Touristik, Reiseverkehr	1-5	1920-39	
V. 3	Deutsch-italienischer Reiseverkehr	1-3	1920-39	
V. 4	- Reklamationen, Beschwerden	1	1920-27	
V. 4^a	Autoreiseverkehr,Führerscheine	1	1922-24	
V. 5	Verkehrspropaganda aller Art	1-4	1921-39	
V. 6	Verkehrskonferenzen	1	1923-39	
V.E. 1	Deutsches Eisenbahnwesen	1	1921-39	
V.E. 2	Italienisches Eisenbahnwesen	1-2	1920-39	
V.E. 3	Internationaler Eisenbahnverkehr	1	1921-39	
V.E. 4	Alpenbahnen	1	1921-39	
V.E. 5	Deutsch-italienischer Eisenbahnverkehr	1	1921-39	
V.E. 6	Verschiedenes im deutsch-italienischen Eisenbahnverkehr	1	1922-27	
V.E. 7	Eisenbahnkongresse	1	1921-39	
V.Fl.1	Deutsches Flugwesen, allgemein	1-3	1920-39	
V.Fl.2	Italienisches Verkehrsflugwesen	1	1928-30	
V.Fl.2^a	- Flugwesen, allgemein	1	1923-25	
	- - gesetzliche Bestimmungen	1-2	1921-38	
	- - allgemein	1-2	1920-28	
V.Fl.2^b	- -	1-4	1921-29	
	Flugverkehr Italiens und anderer Länder (ausser Deutschland)	2-3	1926-39	
V.Fl.2^c	Italienisch-deutscher Flugverkehr	1-2	1929-39	
V.Fl.3	Internationaler Flugverkehr	1-3	1920-39	
V.Fl.4	Flugwesen anderer Länder (ausser Deutschland und Italien)	1	1933-39	
V.Fl.5	Flugwesen, Verschiedenes (auch Sport)	1-8	1921-39	
V.Fl.6	Konferenzen und Ausstellungen betr. Flugwesen	1-2	1920-37	
V.P. 1^a	Post u.Telegraph, Deutschland	1	1920-39	
V.P. 1^b	- Italien	1-2	1922-39	
	Vatikan-Post	1	1929-39	
V.P. 3	Weltpostverein	1	1921-39	
V.P. 4	Deutsch-italienischer Postverkehr	1	1920-39	

Akten-zeichen	Inhalt	Band	Datum	Serial Nr.
V.P. 5	Drahtlose Telegrafie und Radio-wesen	1-2	1920-36	
V.P. 6	Kabel	1	1920-36	
V.P. 7	Post und Telegrafen-Kongresse	1	1920-33	
V.S. 1^a	Schiffahrtswesen, allgemein Deutschland	1-3	1920-39	
V.S.1$^{a\ 1}$	Motorschiff Barbara	1	1926-37	
V.S. 1^b	Schiffahrtswesen, allgemein Italien	1-3	1920-39	
V.S. 1^c	Verschiedenes in Schiffahrtsan-gelegenheiten	1	1920-39	
V.S. 2	Deutsch-italienische Schiffahrts-fragen	1-6	1920-39	
V.S. 2^b	Deutsch-italienische Schiffahrts-angelegenheiten	1	1920-27	
V.S. 3^a	Deutsche Seeschiffahrt	1	1924-39	
V.S. 3^b	Italienische Seeschiffahrt	1	1922-39	
V.S. 4^a	Binnenschiffahrt, Allgemeines und Verschiedenes	1	1922-37	
V.S. 4^b	Donau	1-2 3 4	1922-39	7356/E534534-82 7356/E534583-85
V.S. 4^c	Binnenschiffahrt Elbe	1	1923-36	
	– Oder	1	1936-39	
V.S. 4^d	Schiffahrtswesen Rhein	1-4	1926-39	
V.S. 5^a	Häfen und Freihafenzonen Deutschland-Italien, allgemein	1	1924-39	
V.S. 5^b	Italienische Häfen: Fiume	1	1921-39	
	– Genua	1	1921-39	
	– Neapel	1	1923-39	
	– Triest	1-3	1920-39	
	– Venedig	1	1925-32	
	– verschiedene	1	1920-39	
V.S. 6	Kanäle	1 2	1920-39	5216/E308266-68
V.S. 7	Schiffbau Subventionen	1-2	1920-39	
V.S. 8	Schiffahrtsgesellschaften	1-3	1920-39	
V.S. 9	Internationale Schiffahrtsfragen und Konferenzen	1-2	1920-39	
V.S.10	Deutsche Schiffe in Italien	1	1920	
V.W.	Wege, Strassen, Wasser u.Brücken	1-2	1925-39	

Akten-zeichen	Inhalt	Band	Datum	Serial Nr.
Fi. 1^a	Aufwertung von Wertpapieren, Generelles	1-2	1925-38	
Fi.1^a 1	Deutsche Finanzen (Haushalt, Währung)	1-2	1920-31	
		3	1931-39	L815/L237031-33
		4-6		
	– Devisenüberweisungen	1-2	1934-39	
Fi. 1^b	Aufwertung von Wertpapieren, Einzelfälle und Verschiedenes	1	1926-35	
Fi.1^b 1	Italienische Finanzen	1-11	1921-39	
	Sonderband zu Band 3 Aufwertung italienischer Wertpapiere		1928-33	
	Italienische Anleihen	1	1926-32	
Fi.1^b 2	Laufende Berichte über den Haushalt, Italien	1-2	1920-27	
Fi.1^b 3	Sanierung der italienischen Währung	1	1925-29	
Fi. 2	Deutsch-italienische Finanz-fragen	1	1939	
Fi. 3^a	Finanz- und Steuergesetzgebung, Deutschland	1	1920-39	
	Reichsnotopfer	1	1920-21	
Fi. 3^b	Finanz- und Steuergesetzgebung, Italien	1-5	1920-39	
	Steuer auf das Kapital auslän-discher Gesellschaften, Sdbd.	1-2	1935-37	
Fi. 4	Monopole	1	1920-38	
Fi. 5	Gold-, Münz- und Notenwesen	1	1920-26	
	Devisenhandel	1	1920	
Fi. 8^a	Banken, Börsen, Sparkassen	1-4	1920-39	
Fi. 8^b	Italienische Banken u. Sparkassen	1-3	1920-39	
Fi. 9	Kursgarantie des Istituto per i Cambi con l'Estero für den deutsch-italienischen Verrech-nungsverkehr	1	1939	
	Verschiedenes Material über Finanz- und Bankfragen		1920-21	
Z. 1^a	Deutsches Zollwesen	1-3	1920-39	
Z. 2	Italien, Zollwesen, Zolltarif, allgemein	1	1921-25	
	– –	1-4	1920-38	
	15%iger Wertzoll, Sonderband zu Band 3		1936-37	
Z. 2^b	Italienisches Zollwesen	1	1920-26	
Z. 3	Zollfragen verschiedener Länder	1	1937	

Akten-zeichen	Inhalt	Band	Datum	Serial Nr.
Z. 5	Gegenseitigkeitsvereinbarungen über Zollfreiheit	1	1939	
Z.10	Zollreklamationen, Zollvergünstigungen	1	1921-26	
	Rechtswesen, allgemein,Beiband		1924-39	
	Fortbildung deutscher Akademiker in Italien		1925-29	
	Italienische Justizgesetzgebung	1	1921-29	
		2	1931-39	
	– Beamten und Staatsarbeiterrecht		1922-34	
	– Wappen- und Flaggenrecht		1925-34	
	– Vereinsgesetze		1925	
	– Haushaltswesen		1924-25	
	– einzelne Gesetze auf wirtschaftspolitischem Gebiet, Handels-, Verkehrs-, Finanzfragen		1926-34	
	– Aktiengesellschaften und Handelsgesellschaften		1926-35	
	Gewerblicher Rechtsschutz		1930-36	
	Italienische Gesetzgebung auf Kunst- und wissenschaftlichem und kulturellem Gebiet		1920-38	
	Ital.verschiedene einzelne Gesetze		1920-39	
	Alimentationspflichten italienischer Väter		1934	
	Italienische Adelslisten		1934	
	– Jugendgerichtsbarkeit		1935	
	Deutsch-italienische Rechtsverträge und Abkommen		1920-24	
	Deutsch-italienischer Rechtsverkehr, Zeugenvernehmungen, Zustellungen		1922-36	
	Haft und Auslieferungen		1922-32	
	Allgemeine Strafregisterauszüge		1927-38	
	Rechtspflege und Gerichtswesen, gen.		1921-26	
	Polizeisachen, allgemein		1921-38	
R. 1	Reformen	1	1925-26	
R. 2	Italien – Gesetzgebung	1	1925-26	
R. 2ᵃ 1	Staats- und Verfassungsrecht, allgemein	1-3	1924-39	

Akten-zeichen	Inhalt	Band	Datum	Serial Nr.
R. 2^{a} 1	Sonderband - Faschistische Reform des italienischen Staats- und Verfassungsrechts	1	1928-33	
R.4^{a} 2-5	Deutsch-italienischer Rechtsver-kehr	1	1921-27	
R.2^{a} 2	Justizgesetzgebung, Italien	1	1929-30	
R.4^{b} 1	Deutsch-italienischer Rechtsver-kehr - Vollstreckbarkeit deut-scher Urteile in Italien	1	1920-36	
	Internationales Recht, Druck- sachen	1-2	1921-39	
	-	1	1928-33	
R.10	Vermittlungen in Rechts-, Gerichts-und Strafsachen	1-4	1920-27	
	Giovanni Marchetti	1	1926-32	
	Vermittlungen in Rechtssachen	5-7	1927-39	
		1	1926-27	
R.10^{a}	Rechtshilfsverkehr	1	1932-34	
R.10	Vermittlungen in Rechtssachen Einzelfälle	1	1934-36	
R.10^{a}	Auskünfte über Vermittlungen in Rechtssachen, Einzelfälle	1-2	1930-32	
R.11	Ersuchungsschreiben deutscher Gerichtsbehörden um Vernehmung von Zeugen	1-2	1921-27	
	Zeugenvernehmungen	1-8	1927-38	
R.12	Gerichtliche Zustellungen	1-4	1923-38	
R.13^{a}	Auslieferungen A - L	1	1920-27	
R.13	Auslieferungsersuchen	1-2	1927-33	
	Haft und Auslieferungsersuchen Einzelfälle	1	1934-39	
R.13^{a}	Haftsachen - Einzelfälle	1-2	1920-27	
R.31	Rechtssachen - Verschiedenes	1	1921-23	
R.22	Rechtsauskünfte	1	1923-27	
R.18 III	Nachlassangelegenheiten, Ein-zelfälle	1	1920-24	
R.17	Rechtskongresse	1	1925-27	
R.16	Austausch von Strafnachrichten	1	1920-25	
	Anklageschrift in dem Verfahren gegen Dr.Neumann, v.Sass	1		
R.22	Interventionen	1	1921-25	
R.14	- verschiedener Art	1	1923-27	
R.12	Rechtssachen - Interzessionen	1	1924-26	
R.13	Interzessionen	1-2	1921-27	

Akten-zeichen	Inhalt	Band	Datum	Serial Nr.
R.3 Nr.6^d	Strafrecht, Rechtshilfe in Straf-sachen, Auslieferungen, Straf-vollzug, Gefangenenaustausch, Allgemeines	1-3	1940-41	
	Unterstützungs- und Heimschaf-fungssachen, Einzelfälle		1922-25	
	Heimschaffungssachen		1920-21	
	Unterstützungen und Heimschaf-fungen	1-5	1922-32	
	Heimschaffungen, Geschwister Dall'Armi	1	1920-22	
	Abgelegte Sachen, Heimschaffun-gen A - Z	1-3	1932	
	Heimschaffungen A - Z	1-2	1930-34	
	- und Unterstützungen, Einzelfälle A - Z	1-2	1936-39	
	- von Deutschland nach Ita-lien	1	1919-20	
	Unterstützungs- und Heimschaf-fungssachen Reichsdeutscher	1	1921-26	
	Heimschaffung von Italienern aus Deutschland	1	1920-25	
	Unterstützungen, Einzelfälle	1-3	1922-29	
E.7^c	Rentensachen, Armenhilfe, Unterstützungen, Einzelfälle	1	1920-26	
	Unterstützungs- und Unterhalts-angelegenheiten von Italienern in Deutschland	1	1922-25	
E.7^a	Unterstützungs- und Rentensachen Pensionsangelegenheiten, Armen-hilfe (Generelles)	1	1921-28	
	Briefumschlag mit Quittungen der notleidenden Deutschen, die aus der Unterstützungskasse Beträge erhalten haben(mit anliegendem Verzeichnis)		1930	
	Ein Band mit gleichem Inhalt (Blatt 1-130)		1936-38	
	Ein Band (Bl.1-8) Verfügungen und Erlasse betr.: Unterstützun-gen, Darlehn, Heimschaffungen		1924	
	Ein Paket enthaltend Heimschaf-fungsakten	1-6	1932-39	
	Verpflegungskosten, allgemein	1	1940	
	Unterstützungen im Ausland, allg.	1-2	1940	
	Heimschaffungen, allgemein	1	1939-41	
E.5	Bescheinigungen seitens der Bot-schaft	1-6	1927-33	
	Bescheinigungen	1-4	1934-39	

Akten-zeichen	Inhalt	Band	Datum	Serial Nr.
M.18^a	Beglaubigung der Unterschriften von Privatpersonen	1	1920-24	
M.12^b	Sterbefälle, Leichentransporte	1	1922-26	
M.12^a	- allgemein	1	1920-24	
M.12^c	- verschiedene	1	1924-26	
M.18^c	Atteste, Bescheinigungen	1	1921-26	
M.18^b	Legalisationen	1	1921-26	
E.3	Empfehlungen	1	1920-23	
	- und Einführungsschreiben	1	1920-24	
	Empfehlungsschreiben	1	1924-25	
	Empfehlungen u. Einführungs-schreiben	1-6	1925-39	
E.3 Sbd	Reise Dr.Otto Wohlberedt		1934	
	Expedition Frobenius	4	1932-37	
E.6^a	Stellengesuche	1-3	1920-35	
	Vermittlungen (Varia)	1	1920-24	
E.10	Darbietung und Übermittlung von Geschenken	1	1920-26	
	Grenzempfehlungen	1-7	1921-35	
	Schwarze Liste	1-5	1921-37	
E.8	Verschiedenes	1-4	1920-27	
	Auskünfte privat	1	1922-23	
	Behändigung und Weiterleitung von Briefen	1	1920-23	
E.1^a	Behändigung von Briefen	1	1922-24	
	- und Weiterleitungen	1	1925-27	
E.1	Weiterleitung von Briefen	1	1927-30	
E.1^a	Behändigung u. Weiterleitung	3-5	1930-37	
	- Verschiedenes	1	1925-27	
E.1		6-8	1937-39	
E.2^a	Beschaffung von Gesetzen, Statistiken für das Auswärtige Amt	1	1920-27	
E.2^c	- Material für amtliche deutsche Stellen	1	1920-25	
	Drucksachenaustausch zwischen deutschen und italienischen Behörden	1	1921-26	
E.1^b	Übermittlung deutscher Bücher und Drucksachen an italienische Behörden	1	1921-27	

Akten-zeichen	Inhalt	Band	Datum	Serial Nr.
E.1^c	Übermittlung italienischer Bücher und Drucksachen an deutsche Behörden	1	1923-27	
	Verzeichnis der Austauschdrucksachen	1	1929-30	
E.2	Beschaffung von Drucksachen, Statistiken, allgemein	1	1920-26	
E.2^d	Beschaffung von Gesetzen, Statistiken, Material für italienische Stellen und privat	1	1919-26	
		1	1920-26	
E.2^c	Austausch amtlicher Drucksachen für Bayern	1	1923-27	
E.2^b	Beschaffung von Gesetzen, Statistiken für das Auswärtige Amt	1	1920-26	
Ma.1^b 1-3	Deutsche Staatsangehörigkeit, Gesetzgebung, italienische Staatsangehörigkeit, Gesetzgebung	1	1921-35	
	Matrikel-, Legalisationen,- Staatsangehörigkeits-, Personenstands- und Notariatssachen, Gen.	1-2	1925-39	
	Frage der doppelten Staatsangehörigkeit	2	1936-39	
	Staatsangehörigkeitsfragen anderer Länder		1927-29	
M.1^a	Beibehalt oder Wiedererwerb der deutschen Staatsangehörigkeit	1	1920-23	
M.3	Ausstellung von Heimatscheinen	1	1920-26	
M.2	Staatsangehörigkeitsbescheinigungen	1	1920-26	
M.4	Bestätigungen der deutschen Staatszugehörigkeit	1	1921-24	
M.6	Entlassung aus der deutschen und Erwerb der italienischen Staatsangehörigkeit	1	1921-26	
M. 7	Entlassung aus der deutschen Staatsangehörigkeit	1	1920-25	
M.5^a	Aufnahme und Wiederaufnahme in den deutschen Staatsverband	1	1921-27	
M.1^b	Erwerb der italienischen Staatsangehörigkeit	1	1921	
Ma.3	Sonstige Vermittlung in Staatsangehörigkeits-, Personenstands-, Notariatssachen und Verschiedenes sofern nicht Konsulatssache	1	1921-26	
	Austausch von standesamtlichen Urkunden, Ehegesetzgebung und Bestimmungen über Eheschliessungen (Haager Abkommen, Geburt, Todesfälle, Leichenpässe)	1	1921-29	

Akten-zeichen	Inhalt	Band	Datum	Serial Nr.
Ma.2	Austausch von Zivilstandsre-gisterauszügen, standesamtlichen Urkunden	1-3	1921-35	
	Austausch von standesamtlichen Urkunden	4-6	1935-39	
M.13	Beschaffung von standesamtlichen Urkunden	1	1921-26	
M.11^c	Beschaffung von Heiratspapieren	1	1921-26	
Sdbd.	Uneheliche Geburten	1	1938	
Ma.	Eheschliessungsakten	1-5	1920-31	
B.1	Bevölkerungsfragen, allgemein Volkszählungen, Bevölkerungs-politik	2-3	1931-39	
	Bevölkerung - Statstisches	1	1926	
B.2	Ein- und Auswanderungsfragen	1-3	1920-39	
B.2^b	Ein- und Auswanderung Deutsch-land-Italien	1	1921-26	
B.2^c 1	Italienisches Wanderungswesen	1-2	1921-39	
B.2^c 2	Aus- und Rückwanderung zwischen Italien und anderen Ländern		1921-39	
B.2^c 3	- Deutschland - Italien	1-2	1921-39	
Sdbd.	Austausch von Hotel- und Gast-wirtschafts-Angestellten		1925-30	
	Beschäftigung ausländischer Musiker in Italien		1929-35	
B.2^c	Wanderungswesen, Einzelfälle	1	1932-34	
B.2^c 3	Deutsch-italienischer Arbeits- und Auswanderungsvertrag, Ange-stellten-Austausch Einzelfälle A - Z	1-2	1936-39	
	Sloman-Angestellte		1927-32	
B.3	Siedlungs- und Wohnungswesen		1920-25	
		2-3	1929-39	
	Einreise- und Niederlassungsver-hältnisse (allg.)	1	1925-26	
D.E.1^a	Grosses deutsches Eigentum	1-13	1922-39	
D.E.1 Sdbd.	Villa Thode	1	1922-24	
		1	1937-38	
D.E.6^a	Deutsches Eigentum - Südtirol und sonstige neue Provinzen	1-7	1920-27	
E.1	Beschlagnahmte Versicherungen		1924-26	
	Freigabe beschlagnahmter Waren	1	1919-24	
	Freigabe beschlagnahmten deut-schen Eigentums	1	1920-27	

Akten-zeichen	Inhalt	Band	Datum	Serial Nr.
E.1	Akte betr. Freigabe beschlag-nahmten deutschen Eigentums	1	1920-24	
D.E.gen.5	Deutsches Eigentum - Entschädi-gungsangelegenheiten, Freigabe und Rückbeförderung	1	1920-21	
	Akte betr.Rückkauf beschlagnahmt gewesenen deutschen Eigentums	1	1920-26	
	Akte betr.Freigabe von Klein-eigentum	1	1921-23	
	Entschädigungen, Freigabe von Kleineigentum	1-2	1920-27	
	Handakten betr.deutsches Eigen-tum in Italien	1-3	1920-22	
	Behandlung des im Weltkrieg beschlagnahmten Eigentums (Anfra-gen)	1	1922-23	
D.E.7 Sdbd.	James v.Pourtales-Stiftung	1	1928-34	
	Lenz	1	1935	
	Sautter	1	1932-36	
D.E.gen.	Deutsches Eigentum	1-2	1919-25	
D.E.gen.2	- (Allgemein)	1-2	1919-21	
D.E.1[a]	- Niederschrift über die Besprechung mit Vertre-tern der italienischen Regierung betr.Ablösung des deutschen Eigentums in Italien	1	1922	
	Ratifikation des deutsch-italie-nischen Eigentumabkommens	1	1927	
	Anfragen aus dem Publikum betr. Aufwertung des Altbesitzes	1	1927-28	
D.E.spez.	Palazzo Vidoni	1	1923-35	
	- Caffarelli	1	1922-25	
	Verletzung deutscher Interessen bei den Eigentumsverkäufen in Genua	1	1919-20	
	Deutsche Institute in Italien	1	1922	
	Archäologisches Institut	1	1920	
D.E.	Italienische Verzeichnisse des deutschen Eigentums	1		
	Akte betr. Rückgabe beschlagnahm-ten deutschen Eigentums der Amalia Böhm	1	1932-34	
	Akte betr.Freigabe einer Hypo-thek des Ernst Göbel in Feuer-bach	1	1929-32	
D.E.1[a]	Doppel von Noten und Berichten	1	1922-23	
D.E.1	Verschiedenes deutsches Eigentum	1	1920-23	

Akten-zeichen	Inhalt	Band	Datum	Serial Nr.
D.E.7	Deutsches Eigentum, Einzelfälle	1-12	1920-33	
S.1 Fasz.1 -S.8 Fasz. 9	Alt-italienische Freigabefälle		1928-31	
S.9 Fasz. 10	Südtirol, Tiroler Einzelfälle (81-136)	1-3	1927-31	
S.10 Fa.13				
S.11 Fasz 14	Anleihe-Altbesitz, Einzelakten	1	1927-29	
S.12 Fasz 15	Erl.dtsch.Eigentum,Einzelakten	1	1920-23	
S.13 Fasz 16		1	1920-23	
S.14 Fasz 17	Bescheide u.a.Akten	1	1926-30	
S.15 Fasz 18	Journal 1925-28 und Verschiedenes	1	1926-30	
S.24 Fasz 1	Verschiedene Hilfsakten	1	1928-30	
2	Arbitro-Sachen	1	1929	
S.25	Verzichterklärungen	1	1927-29	
S.26	Geschäftsakten des Reichsvertre-ters beim gem.Schiedsgericht in Rom	1	1923-29	
S.27	Geschäftsakten des deutsch-italienischen Sondergerichts-hofes in Rom	1	1923-29	
S.28	Graf Henckel-Donnersmarck Eigentum - Nationalisierung	1	1927-30	
S.29	Südtiroler Einzelfälle Fasz. 1 Nr. 1-40 2 Nr.41-60		1927-31	
S.30	Urteil des italienisch-bulgari-schen Schiedsgerichts		1924-30	
S.31	Entschädigungen und Auszahlungen Einzelfälle und Freigabe von Hypothekenbriefen		1924-30	
Soz.1^a	Allgemeines über Sozial- und Arbeiterrecht deutsch und italienisch	1-4	1922-39	
Soz.1^b 1	Italienisches Arbeitsrecht, Gesetzgebung	1-4	1925-39	
Soz.1^b 2	Arbeitszeit	1	1922-39	
Soz.1^b 3	Arbeitsgerichtsbarkeit	1	1923-39	
Soz.2	Internationale sozialpolitische Angelegenheiten, Internationales Arbeitsamt Genf	1-3	1921-39	
Soz.3	Genossenschaftswesen, Gewerk-schaftswesen, Berufsorganisa-tionen	1	1920-39	
	Opera Nazionale Del Dopolavoro	1	1926-39	

Akten-zeichen	Inhalt	Band	Datum	Serial Nr.
Soz.3[b]	Kraft durch Freude	1	1934-39	
Soz.4	Internationales Institut für Soziologie	1	1924-39	
Soz.5	Sozialisierung	1	1920-39	
Soz.6	Betriebsräte	1	1920-39	
Soz.7	Tarifverträge, Arbeitslöhne	1	1921-39	
Soz.9	Arbeiterbewegungen (Streiks)	1	1920-39	
Soz.10	Arbeits- und Erwerbslosenfürsorge	1-2	1920-39	
Soz.10[a]	Freiwilliger Arbeitsdienst.	1	1933-39	
Soz.11	Sozialversicherung	1-3	1927-39	
Soz.11[a]	- allgemein	1	1920-27	
Soz.11[b]	Invaliditäts- und Altersversicherung	1	1920-24	
R.3 Nr.5 f	Sozialversicherung für Südtiroler Rückwanderer	1	9.40-10.41	
	Rentenempfänger, Pensionsempfänger, Hinterbliebenenfürsorge	2	9.40- 9.41	
		3	3.41-12.41	
R.6 Nr.2	Stellung und Bestrebungen Italiens in der internationalen Sozialpolitik	1	4.39-10.40	
R.4 Nr.8[b]	Internationale Handwerkszentrale	1	6.40-11.41	
R.6 Nr.9	Auslandspropaganda durch Verbreitung der Ziele, Maßnahmen und Erfolge der deutschen Sozialpolitik	1	10.39-11.40	
		2	10.40-11.41	
	Vorlage des "Nachrichtenblattes über die Faschistischen Korporationen"		12.39-12.41	
R.4 Nr.4[b]	Arcari		9.40-12.40	
R.4 B	Berichte und Nachrichten italienischer Dienststellen über sozialpolitische Vorgänge in anderen Ländern	1	10.39- 5.40	
R.6 A III 1a	Verbindungsstelle Italien, Aufgaben und Geschäftsbereich, Allgemeines	1	12.39- 1.42	
1[f]	- Verfügungen des Dienststellenleiters	1	3.42-12.42	
1[h]	- Dienstwagen	1	1.42- 5.43	
1[k]	- Briefweiterleitungen	1	1.42- 9.42	
R.6 B I 2	Besuchsreisen führender Persönlichkeiten, Italiener nach Deutschland	1	7.41- 1.43	
R.6 B II 2	Studienkommissionen, Italiener nach Deutschland	1	4.40-12.41	

Akten-zeichen	Inhalt	Band	Datum	Serial Nr.
R.4 A VIII	Sozialversicherung	2	1.40-11.41	
R.6 B III 3	Berufserziehung und Frauenarbeit Politische und fachliche Zusammenarbeit. Beschaffung deutschen sozial-politischen Materials für Italiener	1	3.39- 4.42	
R.6 B III 6	Siedlungswesen-Städtebau; politische und fachliche Zusammenarbeit. Beschaffung deutschen sozialpolitischen Materials für Italiener		3.39- 6.39	
		1	7.39- 5.40	
R.6 B IV 1	Schrifttum und Propaganda Zeitschriftenaustausch	1	11.40- 5.42	
R.6 B IV 4[b]	– Broschüren und Buchpropaganda, sozialpoltische Propaganda in Italien	1	3.40- 8.42	
R.6 C II 3	Einzelgesuche italienischer Staatsangehöriger.Gewerbliche Arbeitskräfte. Weiterleitungen A-K und L-Z	1a	12.40- 2.42	
R.6CIII 1	Landwirtschaftliche Arbeitskräfte, Verträge, Vereinbarungen	1	3.39- 2.42	
R.6 C V	Einzelgesuche italienischer Staatsangehöriger, Angestellte, Ingenieure, Techniker	1	8.39- 6.42	
K.W.1	Deutsch-italienische Kunstbeziehungen	1	1925-26	
K.W.1[a]	Kunst und Wissenschaft allgemein, Deutschland	1	1921-37	
K.W.1[b]	– Italien	1	1921-38	
K.W.1[c]	– deutsch-italienische Beziehungen,(Allgemeines)	1-3 4	1921-39	7440/E540194-96
K.W.1[c] 1	– deutsche Lektorate in Italien und italienische Lektorate in Deutschland	1-5	1921-39	
K.W.1[c] 1 Sonderbd.	– Lektorate in Deutschland und Italien, Einzelfälle	2	1934	
K.W.1[c] 1	– Lektoren, Einzelfälle	Sbd	1939	
K.W.1[c] 2	– Deutscher akademischer Austauschdienst	1-3	1934-39	
K.W.1[c] 3	– deutsch-italienischer Kulturvertrag	1-4	1937-39	
K.W.1[d]	Internationale Kunst und wissenschaftliche Beziehungen Italien - andere Länder	1	1925-39	
K.W.1[e] 4	Italienische Kulturpropaganda Fahrpreisermässigung	1	1939˙	
K.W.4	Übermittlung und Beschaffung von wissenschaftlichem Material für deutsche und italienische Stellen	1	1920-26	

Akten-zeichen	Inhalt	Band	Datum	Serial Nr.
K.W.4^a	Handschriftenentleihung	1-7	1920-39	
K.W.5	Literatur und wissenschaftliche Zeitschriften	1-3	1920-40	
K.W.5^a	Das deutsche Buch in Italien	1-3	1920-39	
K.W.5^b	Das italienische Buch	1	1926-39	
K.W.5^c	Deutsche Bücher im Ausland, ausser Italien	1	1927-39	
K.W.6	Deutsche Institute in Italien (allgemeines)	1	1920-39	
K.W.6^a 1	Archäologisches Institut	1-3	1920-39	
K.W.6^a 2	- Kassen-u.Personalangelegenheiten	1	1921-38	
K.W.6^a 3	Villa Amelung	1-2	1923-39	
K.W.6^b	Vulkan-Institut	1-2	1920-39	
K.W.6^c	Zoologisches Institut Neapel	1-2	1920-39	
K.W.6^d	Kunsthistorisches Institut Florenz	1-2	1920-39	
K.W.6^e	Biblioteca Hertziana	1-2	1920-39	
K.W.6^f	Zoologische Station Rovigno	1-4	1913-39	
K.W.6^g	Preussisch-historisches Institut Rom	1	1921-39	
K.W.6^g 2	Grundstück Valle Giulia	1-2	1927-36	
K.W.6^h	Collegio Germania-Ungaria	1	1920-39	
K.W.6^i	Villa Böcklin	1	1936	
K.W.6^L	Stockung in der Überweisung von Geldmitteln für die Kulturinstitute	1	1939	
K.W.6^n	Deutsche Akademie, München	1	1939-40	
K.W.7	Reale Academia d'Italia	1	1939	
K.W.7^a	Deutsch-italienische Institute in Rom und Köln	1-3	1928-39	
K.W.7^d	Villa Sciarra	1	1939	
K.W.7^b 1	Italienisches Institut in Berlin	1	1920-39	
K.W.7^b 2	Italienisches Archäologisches und Kunsthistorisches Institut	1	1921-26	
K.W.7^c	Verschiedene italienische Kunst- und wissenschaftliche Institute und Vereinigungen	1-2	1921-39	
K.W.8	Wissenschaftliche Institute und Kunststätten in Deutschland	1	1921-37	
K.W.8^a	Deutsch-italienische Studienstiftung	1	1939	

Akten-zeichen	Inhalt	Band	Datum	Serial Nr.
K.W.9^a	Kunst- und wissenschaftliche Institute und Vereinigungen anderer Länder	1-2	1921-34	
K.W.9$^{b\ 1}$	Internationales Laboratorium auf dem Gold'Olen	1	1921-31	
K.W.9$^{b\ 3}$	Erdbebenforschung	1	1923	
K.W.9$^{b\ 4}$	Internationales Malaria-Institut Rom	1	1920-39	
K.W.10	Künstler und Gelehrte aller Nationen	1	1929-39	
	Goethe	1-6	1921-39	
	Platen	2	1937	
	Dante	2	1935-39	
K.W.10^a	Gruppo Letterario dei Dieci	1	1928-39	
K.W.10^b	Preis San Remo für einen auslän- dischen Schriftsteller	1	1939	
K.W.11	Kunstausstellungen	1	1925-26	
K.W.11^a	- Verschiedenes	1-2	1921-39	
K.W.11$^{b\ 1}$	Verschiedene Kunst- und wissen- schaftliche Ausstellungen	1	1923-39	
	Internationale Kunstausstellung (Biennale)	Sbd.	1923-25	
	Internationale Lehrmittelausstel- lung	1	1923	
	Internationale Kunstausstellung für religiöse Kunst	1	1933-34	
K.W.11$^{b\ 2}$	Kunstausstellung in Venedig	1-3	1922-39	
K.W.11$^{b\ 3}$	- Florenz	1-3	1922-39	
	Florentiner Freunde der Deut- schen Akademie	Sbd	1927-31	
K.W.11$^{b\ 4}$	Verschiedene Kunstausstellungen in anderen Ländern	1-2	1929-39	
K.W.12	Wissenschaftliche Kongresse	1	1921-27	
K.W.13	Hochschul- und Studentenangele- genheiten	1-4	1921-39	
K.W.14^a	Erlaubnis zum Besuch italieni- scher Kunststätten, Generell	1	1921-39	
K.W.14^b	- Einzelfälle	1-7	1920-39	
K.W.15 Sdbd.	Wohltätigkeitskonzerte	1-2	1935-39	
K.W.15	Vorträge, Referate	1-2	1937-40	
	Kunst und Wissenschaft: Theaterwesen	1-2	1937-39	
	- italienisch	1	1940	
	- Vorträge, Theater, Musik	1-17	1920-39	

Akten-zeichen	Inhalt	Band	Datum	Serial Nr.
K.W.15 Sdbd.	Konzertreise Reichs-Symphonie-Orchester durch Italien, Herbst 1933	1	1933	
	Deutsche Pressestimmen zum Gastspiel der Mailänder Scala unter Toscanini	1	1929	
K.W.17	Verschiedenes in Kunst- und wissenschaftlichen Angelegenheiten	1-28	1921-39	
	Kunst und Wissenschaft: Sonderband: Palombini	1	1938-39	
	– Observatorium	1	1939	
	– Codex Aesinas	1	1938-39	
	– Deutsch-italienische Kulturgesellschaft	1	1938-39	
	– Besuch Reichsminister Dr.Frank	1	1936	
	– Ankauf der Statue des Diskuswerfers	1	1938	
K.W.20^a	Sport: allgemein	1-3	1926-39	
K.W.20^b 1	– Lawn-Tennis	1-2	1921-39	
K.W.20^b 2	– Pferde-Sport	1-6	1922-39	
	– – Internationales Turnier in Aachen	1	1929-35	
K.W.20^b 3	– Auto-Sport	1-3	1924-39	
K.W.20^b 5	– Jugenderziehung	1-2	1927-39	
K.W.20^c	– Verschiedenes	1-4	1920-33	
K.W.20^c 1	– XI.Olympiade Berlin 1936	1	1934-38	
	– – Olympiaorden	1	1936-37	
K.W.20^c 2	Studentenspiele Wien	1	1939	
K.W.21	Jugendaustausch	1	1933-34	
K.W.22	V.Olympische Winterspiele 1940 in Garmisch-Partenkirchen	1	1939	
Schu.1^{a1}	Unterrichtswesen Deutschland	1	1920-39	
Schu.1^{a2}	Deutsches Schulwesen im Ausland	1-3	1920-39	
Schu.1^{a3}	Deutsches Gewerbe- und Fachschulwesen in Italien (auch Privatschulen)	1-2	1922-39	
Schu.1^b 1	Italienisches Unterrichtswesen	1-4	1920-39	
	Opera Nationale Balilla	1	1926	
Schu.1^b 2	Italienisches Schulwesen im Ausland	1	1920-39	
Schu.1^b 3	– Fachschulwesen	1-2	1922-39	
Schu.1^b 4	– Hochschulwesen	1-2	1922-39	

Akten-zeichen	Inhalt	Band	Datum	Serial Nr.
Schu.1^b 5	Schulwesen in Südtirol	1-2	1922-39	
Schu.1^b 6	Französische Schulbücher in italienischen Schulen	1	1925-32	
Schu.1^c	Schulwesen anderer Länder (ausser Italien und Deutschland)	1	1923-36	
Schu.2^b	Deutsche Schule Rom	1-12	1910-39	
Schu.2^b Sdbd.	Satzungen der Deutschen Schule Rom	1	1939	
Schu.2^b	Deutsche Schule bei den Schwestern der christlichen Liebe,Rom	1	1926-33	
	Deutsche Schule in Bari	1	1938-39	
	— Bozen	1	1938-39	
	— Florenz	1-3	1920-39	
	— Genua	1	1920-39	
	— Livorno	1	1938-39	
	— Mailand	1-2	1920-39	
	— Meran	1	1921-39	
	— Neapel	1	1933-39	
	— Palermo	1	1927-39	
	— San Remo	1	1931-35	
	— Venedig	1-2	1925-39	
	— Triest	1	1924-39	
	— Turin	1-2	1931-39	
Schu.2^c	Lehrkräfte deutscher Schulen in Italien	1	1920-22	
Schu.2^d	Schulbücher und sonstiges Unterrichtsmaterial für deutsche Schulen	1	1921-36	
Schu.2^e	Beihilfen für die deutschen Schulen in Italien	1-6	1920-37	
Schu.3^a	Zulassung von Ausländern auf deutschen Hochschulen (allgemein)	1-3	1920-39	
Schu.3^b	Ausländer an italienischen Schulen, Hochschulen, Kunstschulen Studentenaustausch	1-3	1920-36	
Schu.3^b Sdbd.	Italienische Universität für Ausländer in Perugia	1	1926-39	
Schu.3^c	Einzelbewerbungen: von Deutschen zum Besuch italienischer, von Italienern zum Besuch deutscher Schulen	1	1920-39	
Schu.3^d	Deutsch-italienischer Schüleraustausch	1	1932-39	
Schu.4	Verschiedener Schriftwechsel in Schulangelegenheiten	1	1920-27	

Akten-zeichen	Inhalt	Band	Datum	Serial Nr.
Schu.4	Bücher und Zeitschriften für die deutschen Schulen in Italien, Buchprämien	2-4	1928-39	
Schu.4 Sdbd.	Bücherstiftung für Reichsdeutsche Vereinigung Rom	1	1938-39	
Schu.4[a]	Deutsch-Unterricht an italienischen Schulen, Buchprämien	1	1939	
Schu.5	Alexander v.Humboldt-Stiftung	1-3	1925-39	
	- 1 Sonderband	1	1931-35	
Schu.5[a]	Denisfonds	1	1939	
Wo.1[a]	Wohlfahrt und Vereinswesen Allgemeines	1	1921-39	
Wo.1[b]	- Weisungen des Auswärtigen Amtes	1	1920-39	
Wo.2	Italienische Kinderferienheime	1	1939	
Wo.3[a]	Deutsche Vereine und Wohlfahrtseinrichtungen in Italien und sonstigem Ausland (Allgemeines)	1	1922-36	
Wo.3[b]	Deutsche Vereinigung Rom	1-3	1920-39	
	Reichsdeutsche Vereinigung, Italien	1	1939	
	Deutscher Hilfsverein Rom	1	1920-33	
	- Bozen	1	1922-39	
	- Florenz	1	1925-39	
	Frauenverein und Marienheim in Florenz	1	1922-39	
	Deutsche Heime Fiume und Abbazia	1	1939	
	Deutsche Wohltätigkeitsanstalten und Vereine Genua	1	1920-39	
	- Livorno	1	1937-39	
	- Mailand	1	1920-36	
	- Meran	1	1938-39	
	- Neapel	1	1925-39	
	- Palermo	1-2	1925-39	
	- Turin	1	1923-39	
	- Triest	1-2	1922-39	
	- Venedig	1	1923-39	
	- Messina	1	1933-39	
	Evangelisches Diakonissenhaus Rom	1-2	1920-39	
	Ortsgruppe Rom der NSDAP	1	1933-34	
	Deutscher Arbeitsausschuss	1-2	1934-36	
Wo.3[c]	Deutsche Seemannsheime	1	1921-39	
Wo.3[b]	Kaiser Friedrich Krankenhaus San Remo	1-5	1920-39	
Wo.4	Stiftungen, Verschiedenes	1	1929-39	

Akten-zeichen	Inhalt	Band	Datum	Serial Nr.
Wo.4[a]	Schwanenfeld-Stiftung	1	1920-39	
Wo.4[b]	Gerhardt-Stiftung	1	1920-37	
Wo.4[c]	Müller - Stiftung	1	1921-31	
Wo.4[e]	Golla'sche Stiftung	1	1921-31	
Wo.5	Wohlfahrt und Vereine Villa Massimo	1-4	1920-39	
	- Villa Falconieri	3	1928-39	
Wo.7	- Romana, Florenz	1-2	1921-39	
Wo.10	Sammlungen von italienischen Wohltätigkeitsanstalten, Bettel-briefe	1	1921-27	
Wo.11	Rotes Kreuz	1	1921-39	
Wo.20	Bund der Auslandsdeutschen	1-2	1922-35	
Wo.21	Winterhilfe	1-3	1931-39	
	Sammlungen	1-4	1927-39	
Wo.22	Wohlfahrt und Vereine,Verschie-denes	1	1924-37	
	Verschiedene Korrespondenzen	1	1921-34	
	Notlage in Deutschland	1	1921-24	
G.1	Gesundheitswesen Allgemeines	1	1922-39	
G.2	- Italien	1	1928-39	
G.3	Sanitätskongresse und Konferen-zen	1-2	1929-39	
G.3[a]	Internationales Gesundheitsamt in Paris	1	1920-34	
G.3[b]	Internationale Hygiene - Ausstel-lung Dresden	1	1928-32	
G.4[a]	Krankheiten und Seuchen	1	1923-39	
G.4[b]	Meldungen über das Auftreten ansteckender Krankheiten	1	1920-39	
G.5	Austausch von amtlichen Drucksa-chen über Gesundheitswesen	1	1921-39	
G.11[a]	Deutsche Ärzte und Apotheker in Italien	1-2	1920-39	
G.11[b]	Zulassung deutscher Ärzte und Apotheker in Italien(Einzelfälle)	1-2	1920-39	
G.12	Krankenhauswesen	1	1925-39	
G.13	Krankenfürsorge, Generelles	1	1935	
G.14	Schriftwechsel mit dem Istituto Italiano d'Igiene Providenza ed Assistenza Sociale (Prof.Dr.Levi)	1	1921-39	
Ki.1	Kirchenpolitisches, allgemein	1-2	1920-39	
	Palästina-Gesellschaft in Bari	1	1937	

Akten-zeichen	Inhalt	Band	Datum	Serial Nr.
Ki.11	Deutsch-evangelische Gemeinden in Italien, allgemein	1	1920-39	
Ki.12	Deutsche evangelische Gemeinde in Rom	1-2	1920-39	
Ki.13	– Abbazia	1	1927-39	
	– Florenz	1	1921-30	
	– Gardone	1	1921-34	
	– Genua	1	1920-39	
	– Neapel und Palermo	1	1921-36	
	– Triest	1	1935-39	
	Sonstige deutsche Gemeinden und Kapellen in Italien	1	1921-39	
Ki.17	Bestattungswesen	1	1921-37	
Ki.18	Deutsche Nationalkirche der "Anima" Rom	1	1939	
Kult 1	Allgemeine Kulturpolitik des Gastlandes – Kulturelle Organisationen und Vereinigungen	1	1940-42	
Kult 1 Nr.1	Verschiedene italienische Kunst- und wissenschaftliche Institute und Vereinigungen	1	1940	
Kult 1 Nr.1a	Deutsche Kulturpolitik in Italien	1	1938-41	
Kult 1 Nr.1b	– Zweigstelle Mailand	1	1941	
Kult 1 Nr.1c	Fonds für Kulturarbeit	1	1941	
Kult 1 Nr.4	Istituto di Studi Romani	1	1940	
Kult 1 Nr.5	Istituto Italiano di Studi Germanici	1	1939-41	
Kult 1 Nr.6	Italienisches Institut für Malaria-Forschung	1	1939-41	
Kult 2	Kulturpolitische Beziehungen Italiens zu Deutschland, allgem.	1	1941	
Kult 2 Nr.1		1-2	1940-41	
Kult 2 Nr.1a	Deutscher akademischer Austausch-dienst	1	1940-41	
	Deutsche Kultur- und wissenschaftliche Institute in Italien, allgemein	1	1940-41	
Kult 2 Nr.1b	Deutsches Archäologisches Institut in Rom	1	1939-41	
Kult 2 Nr.1c+1d	Kaiser-Wilhelm-Institut in Rom	1-2	1939-41	
Kult 2 Nr.1e	Deutsches Historisches Institut in Rom	1	1939-41	
Kult 1 Nr.1e	Ehemals Tschechisches Historisches Institut in Rom	1	1939-41	

Akten-zeichen	Inhalt	Band	Datum	Serial Nr.
Kult 2 Nr.1e	Polnisches Historisches Institut in Rom	1	1940	
Kult 2 Nr.1f	Deutsche Akademie (Villa Massimo in Rom)	1	1939-41	
Kult 2 Nr.1g	Collegium Germanicus	1	1939-40	
Kult 2 Nr.1h	Kunsthistorisches Institut, Florenz	1	1940-41	
	Sonderband: Florentiner Freunde der deutschen Akademie	1	1940-41	
Kult 2 Nr.1 i	Villa Romana, Florenz	1	1939-41	
Kult 2 Nr.1p	Deutsch-italienische Studien-stiftung	1	1940-41	
Kult 2 Nr.1 u	Deutsch-italienisches Kultur-institut, Mailand	1	1941	
Kult 2 Nr.2a	Englische Kulturinstitute in Italien	1	1940-41	
Kult 2 Nr.2c	Deutsche wissenschaftliche Insti-tute und Kunststätten in Deutsch-land[sic]	1	1940-41	
Kult 2 Nr.3	Fremde Kulturpolitik (ausländi-sche)	1	1940	
Kult 3	Reichs- und Volksdeutsche im Gastland	1	1940	
Kult 3 Nr.1	Reichsdeutsche Kolonie in Italien	1	1939-41	
Kult 3 Nr.2	Deutsche Vereine in Italien	1	1940-42	
Kult 3 Nr.4	Kultur: Deutsche Heime	1	1940-41	
Kult 6	Nachforschungen und Verwendungen für ehemalige polnische Staatsan-gehörige	1-2	1940	
Kult 7	Jugendbewegung - Jugendtreffen und Jugendkongresse	1	1940-42	
Kult 7 Nr.1	Reisen HJ und BdM nach Italien	1	1940-41	
D.Kult 8	Schulwesen in Deutschland	1	1940-41	
Kult 8	Reichsbeihilfen, Schulfonds	1-2	1939-41	
	- Kulturfonds	1-2	1939-41	
	Bücherspenden für Schulbibliothek	1	1941	
	- allgemein	1	1940-41	
	Reichsbeihilfen, Buchprämien für Sprachkurse	1	1940	
	Deutsches Schulwesen im Gastland	1-2	1940-41	
	Deutsche Schule in Rom	1-2	1939-41	

Akten-zeichen	Inhalt	Band	Datum	Serial Nr.
Kult 8 Nr.1	Kauf des neuen Schulgebäudes in der Via Savoia 13-15, Sonderband	1	1936-39	
Kult 8 Nr.1c	Sprachkurse der Deutschen Schule in Rom	1	1941	
Kult 8 Nr.1d	Lehrer an der Deutschen Schule in Rom A - Z	1-3	1940-41	
Kult 8 Nr.1g	Deutsche Lehrkräfte	1	1939-41	
Kult 8 Nr.1h	Reifeprüfungen	1	1940-41	
Kult 8 Nr.1 i	Kindergärten	1	1940-41	
Kult 8 Nr.1k	Schülerheime	1	1941	
D.Kult 8 Nr.2	Auswahl, Vermittlung und Betreuung der Lehrkräfte	1	1939-41	
D.Kult 8 Nr.3	Deutscher Lehrer- und Schüler- austausch	1	1939-41	
Kult 8 Nr.2	Deutsche Schule, Mailand	1	1940-41	
Kult 8 Nr.4	- Triest	1	1940-41	
Kult 8 Nr.6	- Genua	1	1940-41	
Kult 8 Nr.7	- Venedig	1	1940-41	
Kult 8 Nr.10	- Bozen	1	1940-41	
Kult 8 Nr.12	Bücher und Zeitschriften für Schulen	1	1940-41	
Kult 8 Nr.14	Schule, Livorno	1	1940	
Kult 8 Nr.15	- Fiume	1	1940-41	
Kult 9	Sprachwerbung, allgemein	1	1940-41	
Kult 9 Nr.1 b	Deutsche Sprachwerbung Lektoren A - Z	1-5	1940-41	
Kult 9 Nr.1c	- Sprachkurse	1	1940-41	
Kult 9 Nr.1 f	Tschechische Lektoren	1	1940-41	
Kult 10	Hochschulwesen in Deutschland	1	1939-40	
	- im Gastland	1	1939-41	
Kult 10 Nr.1	- Auskünfte, Ver- schiedenes	1	1940-41	
Kult 11	Wissenschaft	1	1941	
Kult 11 Nr.1	Wissenschaftliche Institute und Vereinigungen	1	1940-41	

Akten-zeichen	Inhalt	Band	Datum	Serial Nr.
Kult 11 Nr.1	Wissenschaftliche Kongresse und Ausstellungen	1	1940-41	
Kult 11 Nr.1a	Vortragsreisen nach Italien	1-9	1940-41	
Kult 11 Nr.2	Studien und Forschungsreisen A - Z	1-2	1940-41	
Kult 11 Nr.4a	Wissenschaft, Verschiedenes A - Z	1-3	1940-41	
Kult 11 Nr.4b	Bücheraustausch und Drucksachen-austausch	1	1939-41	
Kult 11 Nr.8	Buchwerbung und Buchausstellun-gen	1	1940-42	
Kult 11 Nr.8a	Bücher und Zeitschriften allgem. Bibliotheken	1-4	1940-41	
	- A - Z	2-4	1940-42	
Kult 11 Nr.8b	Übersetzungen deutscher und italienischer Literatur	1-3	1940-41	
Kult 11 Nr.8c	Deutsche Buchinteressen in Italien und italienische Buch-handlungen in Deutschland	1	1941	
Kult 11 Nr.9	Archäologie	1	1940-41	
Kult 11 Nr.10	Erdbebenforschung	1	1940-41	
Kult 12 Nr.1	Kunst in Deutschland	1	1940-41	
	- Italien	1-2	1940-41	
	- - A - Z	1-2	1940-41	
Kult 12 Nr.1a	- Truppenbetreuung, Sonderbd.	1	1941	
Kult 12 Nr.2	Theaterwesen in Deutschland	1	1940-41	
	- Italien	1-2	1940-41	
Kult 12 Nr.3	Musikwesen, Konzerte allgemein, Sonderbände	1-20	1940-42	
Kult 12 Nr.5	Sportwesen, Verschiedenes	1-4	1940-41	
Kult 12 Nr.6	Theaterwesen in Italien	1	1940-41	
Kult 12 Nr.7	Zirkus Busch	1	1940-41	
Kult 13 Nr.1	Deutsche Propaganda,allgemein	1	1940-41	
Kult 13 Nr.2a	Beiträge zu italienischen Zei-tungen und Zeitschriften	1	1941	
Kult 13 Nr.2c	Deutsche Zeitungen und Zeit-schriften	1-2	1940-41	
Kult 13 Nr.2c	Italienische Zeitungen und Zeit-schriften	1	1940-41	

Akten-zeichen	Inhalt	Band	Datum	Serial Nr.
Kult 13 Nr.2d	Deutsche politische Druckwerke, Bücher, Broschüren	1-5	1940-41	
Kult 13 Nr.2f	Informationsmaterial	1	1941	
Kult 13 Nr.2g	Propagandamaterial versch. Quellen	1	1940-41	
Kult 13 Nr.2h	Begleitschreiben, Weiterleitung von Briefen, Propagandamaterial	1	1940-41	
Kult 13 Nr.2k	Versand verschiedenen Propagandamaterials	1	1941	
Kult 13 Nr.2m	Giornale Parlato	1	1940-41	
Kult 13 Nr.2n	Zuschriften und Anregungen zur Propaganda	1	1941	
Kult 13 Nr.2p	Kartenmaterial	1	1941	
Kult 13 Nr.2qu	Gegenpropaganda	1	1941	
Pr.1[a]	Pressewesen, Deutschland allgem.	1-3	1921-39	
Pr.1[b]	Presse, Deutschland	1+3	1922-39	
	- einzelne deutsche Zeitungen	1	1920-39	
	- Italien - Zeitung	1	1928-34	
Pr.1[c]	Deutschsprachige Zeitungen im Ausland	1	1921-39	
Pr.2[a]	Italien, Presse, allgemeine Lage, Veränderungen	1-3	1921-37	
	Sonderband: Presseübersichten	1	1928-33	
Pr.2[b]	Presse Italien, einzelne Zeitungen, Verschiedenes	1-2	1922-34	
	Italienische Presse, einzelne Zeitungen	1	1920-34	
Pr.2[c]	Italien, Sonstiges die italienische Presse betreffend	1	1923-28	
Pr.2[d]	- Presseübersichten	1	1922-25	
Pr.2 Nr.1	Koordination (dtsch-ital.)	1-5	1940-41	
Pr.2 Nr.1d	Zeitschrift Berlin-Rom-Tokio	1-2	1940-41	
	- - Anhang Kritiken	1	1939-40	
	Sonderband: Presse und Propaganda (England)	1	1939-40	
Pr.3	Pressewesen und Presseangelegenheiten anderer Länder	1	1921-37	
Pr.4	Deutsch-italienisches Pressewesen	1-5	1920-39	
Pr.4 Nr.1	Reise italienischer Pressevertreter nach Deutschland	1	1940	

Akten-zeichen	Inhalt	Band	Datum	Serial Nr.
Pr.4 Nr.2	Reise deutscher Pressevertreter nach Italien	1	1940	
Pr.5^a	Deutsch-italienisches Nachrich-tenwesen, allgemein	1	1920-35	
Pr.5^b	Einzelnachrichten und Telegra-fenagenturen	1-2	1920-39	
Pr.6^a	Presseverbände, Journalismus	1-2	1921-36	
Pr.6^b 1	Italienische Pressevertreter Sammelband	1	1932-39	
	Italienischer Journalist Smare-glia	1	1940-41	
	Italienische Pressevertreter Sammelband	1	1920-39	
Pr.6^b 2	Deutsche Pressevertreter, Sammel-band	1	1920-39	
	- Einzelfälle,Sammelbd.	1	1920-35	
Pr.6^b 3	Fremde Pressevertreter, -	1	1920-37	
Pr.6^b 4	Einzelne Journalisten	1	1920-37	
Pr.6^c	Gegenseitige Abberufung von Pressevertretern	1	1939	
Pr.7	Interviews	1	1920-34	
Pr.8	Pressewesen,Verschiedenes	1-6	1920-39	
Pr.9	Ausländische Pressemeldungen, Erlass des Auswärtigen Amtes "Presse"	1	1939	
Pr.9^a	Die Presse über Deutschland	1	1920-23	
Pr.9^b	Artikel italienischer Journa-listen aus Deutschland	1	1922-25	
Pr.9^c	Artikel und Aufsätze zur Ver-wertung in der Presse	1	1922-24	
Pr.10	Pressekongresse	1	1920-32	
Pr.11	Übersendung von Broschüren und Büchern	1	1939	
Pr.12	Rassenfragen	1	1938-39	
Pr.13 Nr. 2a	Propaganda in italienischer Presse	1	1936-37	
	Deutsche Beiträge zur italieni-schen Presse (Artikel)	2	1940-41	
Pr.13 Nr.2b	Bild-Propaganda	1	1939-41	
Pr.13 Nr.2d	Deutsche politische Druckwerke, Bücher	1	1939-40	
Pr.13 Nr.2g	Reichsministerium für Volksauf-klärung und Propaganda	1	1936-39	
	Propagandamaterial, verschiedene Quellen	1	1939-40	8336/E589866-75

Akten-zeichen	Inhalt	Band	Datum	Serial Nr.
P.13 Nr.2f	Informationsmaterial, speziell	1-2	1939-41	
	Berichte an das Propaganda-Ministerium Berlin	1	1939	
P.18 Nr.1	Filmwesen	1-4	1940-41	
	– Verschiedenes	1-4	1940-41	
	– Einzelne Filme A-Z	1-2	1941	
P.18 Nr.2	– Hetzfilme	1	1940-41	
	Presse-Referat, Weltpolitik	1	1930	
	– – Konferenzen	1	1929-30	
	– Räumung, Entwaff-nung,Reparationen	1	1928	
	– Flottenpakt, Eng-land-Frankreich-Amerika, Kellogpakt Südamerika	1	1928-29	
	– Balkan-Österreich, Kleine Entente Rumänien,Bulgarien, Tschechoslowakei	1-3	1928-30	
	– Vatikan	1-4	1928-30	
	– Schweiz	1	1928-29	
	– Südtirol	1	1928-29	
	– Italien	1-2	1928-30	
	– – Frankreich	1	1929-30	
	– Italienische Arbei-ter in Frankreich	1	1929-30	
	Bank für internationale Zahlungen	1	1930	
	Presse-Referat Spezialberichte berichte, italieni-sche Aussenpolitik	1	1929	
	– Fucruscitti	1	1928-30	
	Zeitungsausschnitte zum Dawes-plan, Youngplan	1	1929	
	– Deutschland	1-2	1928-29	
	– und Berichte, ver-schiedenes	1-19	1920-39	
	Presseberichte, Verschiedenes	1-4	1926-38	
	Berichtverzeichnis Mailand	1	1927-32	
	Berichtverzeichnisse an das Aus-wärtige Amt	1-5	1927-33	
	Verzeichnis der nat.Güter	1	1923-27	
	Firmenverzeichnis Einladungen, Abrechnung über Frühstück, Abendessen,Tees, Theater	1-3		

Akten-zeichen	Inhalt	Band	Datum	Serial Nr.
	Oesterreichische ungebrauchte Reisepässe, eingezogene reichs-deutsche Pässe, Stimmzettel, Verzeichnis zu den Abstimmungen			
R.3 Nr.5[b]	Zustellungen	1-5	1940-42	
	Vernehmungen	1-4	1940-42	
Ks.2	Eheschliessungen	1-2	1940-42	
Ks.3	Nachlassangelegenheiten Todesfälle	1	1940-42	
Ks.4	Dokumentenbeschaffung	1-3	1940-43	
Ks.5	Vaterschaftserklärungen - Unterhalt für Minderjährige	1-4	1941-42	
Ks.6	Arbeitsbewilligungen	1	1941-42	
Ks.7	Matrikelaustausch - Personen-standsurkunden	1-2	1941-43	
Ks.8	Ein- und Ausbürgerungen - Optantenfrage	1-4	1940-42	
Ks.9	Darlehen	1	1940-42	
Ks.10[c]	Aufenthaltsermittlungen	1	1941-42	
Ks.12	Verschiedenes	1-3	1941-42	
Ks.14	Prozesse - Forderungen	1-2	1941-42	
Ks.15	Rentenangelegenheiten	1	1941-42	
Ks.16	Verhaftungen - Verfehlungen, Konzentrationslager	1-2	1941-42	
Ks.17	Verbalnoten für fremde Sichtver-merke		1940-41	
	- für jüdische Auswan-derer	1	1940	
	Passangelegenheiten	1-6	1941-42	
R.5 Nr.1	Pass-Sachen Gen.Kons.Genua		1942	
Ks.18	Ausstellungen von Zeugnissen	1-3	1940-42	
Ks.24	Weiterleitungen	1	1941-42	
Ks.26	Nachforschungen	1	1941-42	
Ks.28	Krankenhausbehandlungen, Verpflegung	1	1941-43	
Ks.31	Zollwesen	1	1941	
Ks.33	Übersetzungen von Urkunden und Beglaubigungen	1	1942	
	Einbürgerung - Südtiroler	1	1940	
B	Belgien - Nachforschungen und Auskünfte	1	1940	
F	Frankreich - Nachforschungen und Auskünfte A - Z	1-2	1940	

Akten-zeichen	Inhalt	Band	Datum	Serial Nr.
N	Nachforschungen in anderen Ländern	1	1940–41	
	Abwanderungsanträge von Optanten	1	1940–41	
Mil.10	Streichungen aus den italienischen Stellungslisten	1	1941–42	
	Schmuck – Generalakten	1–2	1940–42	
	Ehrenkreuze	1	1939–43	
	Journal 1001–10514		1920	
	Journal, Abt.I 1 – 8399		1921	
	– 1 – 5881		1922	
	– 1 – 6734		1923	
	– 1 – 6039		1924	
	– 1 – 5563		1925	
	– 1 – 5479		1926	
	– 1 – 5267		1927	
	– 1 – 5491		1928	
	– 1 – 4291		1929	
	– 1 – 1950		1930	
	– 1 – 1779		1931	
	– 1 – 1819		1932	
	– 1 – 1876		1933	
	– 1 – 1388		1934	
	– 1 – 999		1935	
	– 350 – 1699		1936	
	– 1 – 1673		1937	
	– 1 – 1680		1938	
	– Abt.II 1 – 1536		1921	
	– 1 – 964		1922	
	– 1 – 679		1924	
	– 730 – 968		1926	
	– 1 – 1064		1927	
	– 1 – 1056		1928	
	– 1 – 1154		1929	
	– 1 – 752		1930	
	– 1 – 492		1931	
	– 1 – 450		1932	
	– 1 – 386		1934	
	– 1 – 346		1935	

Akten- zeichen	Inhalt	Band	Datum	Serial Nr.
	Journal,Abt.III 1 - 1670		1921	
	– 1 - 1751		1922	
	– 1 - 1595		1923	
	– 1 - 1125		1924	
	– 1 - 1316		1925	
	– 1 - 1548		1926	
	– 1 - 1809		1927	
	– Abt.III H 2000 - 2729		1920	
	– 1 - 2766		1921	
	– 1 - 1176		1922	
	– 1 - 456		1923	
	– 1 - 368		1924	
	– 1 - 452		1925	
	– 1 - 525		1926	
	– 1 - 424		1927	
	– 1 - 493		1928	
	– 1 - 516		1929	
	– 1 - 481		1930	
	– 1 - 587		1931	
	– 1 - 514		1932	
	– 1 - 442		1933	
	– 1 - 484		1934	
	– 1 - 1006		1935	
	– 1 - 349		1936	
	Eingänge der Konsulate		1925-35	
	Namensverzeichnis I Index II		1921-23	
	– – III		1923-34	
	Reg.		1934	
	Sachregister		1934	
	Ausgabenbuch Rechnungsjahre		1923-33	
	Nebenkassenbuch –		1920-32	
	Kontokorrent u. Bankkonten		1927-32	
	Kassenbuch		1920	
	– Sachbuch u.Ein-u.Auszah- lungen		1933	
	Hauptbuch – Einzahlungen		1934-35	
	– Auszahlungen		1934	

Akten-zeichen	Inhalt	Band	Datum	Serial Nr.
	Gebührenbuch		1934-35	
	Sachbuch		1934	
	Einnahmen		1919-33	
	Kontobuch		1922-27	
	Auslagenbuch		1928-29	
	Portoauslagen		1929-30	
	Kurier- und Frachtenbuch		1926-28	
	Eingangsbuch,Erlasse des A.A.		1920-21	
	- - Noten d'Esteri		1926-30	
	- - - Privatbriefe		1931-35	
	Passjournal		1921-24	
	Reisepassverzeichnis		1929-32	
	-		1935-37	
	Namensverzeichnisse zu den Pass-registern		1927-37	
	Passregister		1925-29	
	-		1936-37	
	Sichtvermerk-Verzeichnis		1921-22	
	-		1925-30	
	Schwarze Liste, Heimschaffung, Schwindler		1926-37	
	Aktenverzeichnis			

Akten-zeichen	Inhalt	Band	Datum	Serial Nr.
G Pol 1a	Politische Beziehungen Deutschland – Oesterreich		1925–34	5266/E322381–51
Pol 1	– Polen		1925–33	5266/E322518–64
	– Russland		1924–34	5266/E322646–860
G Pol 1a	– Belgien		1927–30	5266/E322861–929
Pol 3	Spanien		1931–34	
	Politische Beziehungen England – Frankreich		1928–29	5266/E322930–44
Pol 8c	Südtirol		1920–33	8038/E578080–89 K653/K171280–418
Wo	Papstspenden		1920–22	
Mil	Militärwesen		1925–34	M36/M001036–41
Pol 6g	Internationale politische Verträge		1921–22	5267/E322946–85
Pol 9	Völkerbund		1924–28	5267/E322986–3098
Fr. 5	Militärkontrolle und Abrüstungsfrage		1924–29	5267/E323099–336
Fr. 1 b g	Revision der Friedensverträge		1933	
Fr. 8	Reparationen, Allgemeines	1	1922–23	5268/E323338–626
		2	1924–31	5268/E323627–938
Pol 3	Russland		1920–34	5268/E323939–4098
	Oesterreich		1931–34	5269/E324100–212
Pol 17	Vatikan		1925–29	5269/E324213–31
W.1 b	Deutsch-österreichische Zollunion	1	3.1931	5269/E324232–510
		2	4.1931	5269/E324511–777
		3	5.1931	5269/E324778–5143
		4	5.31– 6.31	5270/E325145–296
Pol 3	Amerika		1928	5270/E325297–308
	Litauen		1927	5270/E325309–49
	Ungarn		5.28– 6.28	5270/E325350–70
	Frankreich		1922–33	5270/E325371–460
V. Pl.	Flugwesen		1921–32	5270/E325461–686
Pol 2	Politische Beziehungen Italien – England		1925–29	5270/E325687–725
Pol 2 a	– Ungarn		1923–29	5271/E325727–48
	Deutschland– Italien	1	1922–27	5271/E325749–6056
		2	1928–34	8038/E578090–99 K1043/K268798–826
	Innen-und Aussenpolitik Italiens		1923–30	5271/E326057–171

Akten-zeichen	Inhalt	Band	Datum	Serial Nr.
Pol 2	Politische Beziehungen Italien - Polen		1926-29	5271/E326172-220
Pol 2b geh.	Italien, innere Lage		1930-31	5271/E326221-33
Pol 2a	Politische Beziehungen Italien - Russland		1933	
Pol 2	- Frankreich		1922-33	K1044/K868827-59 K1733/K426292-97
	- Oesterreich		1922-31	5271/E326234-327
	Hitler und Südtirol		1929-30	5272/E326329-63
G.Pol.lb	Allgemeines über Aussen- und inn. politische Angelegenheiten		1920,23-25	5272/E326364-562
	Beschwerde über G.K.Graf Luxburg, Palermo		1930	
Pol 9 b 2	Marchese Paulucie		1929	5272/E326563-71
	Abkommen zwischen Deutschland und Italien		1922	
	Pressefonds		1926-32	
	Botschaftseinbruch		1923	5257/E315421-84
	Hitlers Besuch in Rom		1931	5257/E315485-95
	Aufzeichnung Botsch.v.Hassell über Dreierpakt		1934	5257/E315496-502
	Aufzeichnung Begegnung Hitler-Mussolini		1934	5257/E315503-15
	Hauptmann Freiherr von Richthofen		1929-32	L758/L224654-752
	Emil Ludwig		1929-30	5257/E315516-654
	Veränderungen in der ungari- schen Obersten Heereleitung und sonstigen Generalität		1935	4680/E224545-47
	Ausl.Organ der NSDAP schlägt vor, H.Madl zum Vertrauensmann des G.K.Mailand zu bestellen			
	Deutsche Stellungnahme zu den schwebenden politischen Fragen			4680/E224548-61
	- Telegramm des Botschafters v.Hoesch			4680/E224562-67
	Italienische Kriegsmaterialver- schiffungen nach Ethiopien			4680/E224568-72
				4680/E224573-80
	Verhalten der italienischen Be- hörden gegenüber Angehörigen der NSDAP			4680/E224581-88
	Lehrer Erich Thiede, Neapel			
	Wahlkonsulat Venedig			
	Exposé d.RM. über römische Abmachungen und Ostpaktfrage			4680/E224589-99

Akten-zeichen	Inhalt	Band	Datum	Serial Nr.
	Angebliche Agenten der Geheimen Staatspolizei sind abzuweisen		1935	4680/E224600-01
	Broschüre betr. Vergiftung des Vernältnisses zwischen Waffen-träger der Nation und Träger von Weltanschauung in Staat und Partei			
	Überwachung von Mitgliedern der NSDAP			4680/E224602-05
	G.V.Erteilung an den türkischen Staatsangehörigen Novitz Carp			
	Angebliche italienische Truppen-zusammenziehungen an der öster-reichischen Grenze			4680/E224606-10
	Übernahme eines Betrages von 500.000 Liren (Lire Depot)			4680/E224611-12
	Aufnahme von Österreichern in die NSDAP			
	Grenzstelle frei			4680/E224613-14
	Pressepolitische Fonds			
	Chiffre-Material			
	Dienstkraftwagen des Militär- und Marine-Attachés			
	Lire Depot			
	Herstellung amerikanischer Zün-der			4680/E224615-17
	Dispositionsfonds für 1935			
	Litauenfrage			
	Verstärkung der Luftschutzanla-gen in Palermo, Boothafen Syrakus			4680/E224618-19
	Truppenverschiebungen			4680/E224620-21
	Verhältnisse in Süd-Tirol			
	Stützung der Zeitung "Schlem"			4680/E224622-81
	Vertretung der Reichsinteressen in Südtirol			4680/E224682-711
	Abrüstungsfrage			
	Amerikanische Freiwillige für Abessinien - Fliegerkorps			
	Politische Lage in Österreich			4680/E224712-25
	Fernsprechleitung			
	Lire-Depot			
	Abrechnung Pressefonds			
	Tel. für Gestapo			
	Dispositionsfonds (Abh.Juli-Sept)			

Akten-zeichen	Inhalt	Band	Datum	Serial Nr.
	Entwurf eines Donaupaktes		1935	4680/E224726-39
	Briefwechsel Gen.Kons.Lindner, Genua Botschaftsrat v.Plessen			
	Bestätigung des Empfanges des Chiffre-Schlüssels			
	Italienische Agenten in Abessinien			4680/E224740-44
	Englische Regierung zur Memelfrage			4680/E224745-47
	Internationale Behandlung des abessinischen Konflikts			4680/E224748-50
	Warnung an Gen.Kons.Immelen			4680/E224751-56
	Pressepolitische Fonds			
	Reichskanzler a.D. Wirth			4680/E224757-75
	Engl.Botschaft an Mussolini: Englands Einstellung zum Sanktionsproblem			4680/E224776-84
	Stellung Deutschlands zum Abessinien-Konflikt			4680/E224785-87
	Besprechung Canaris-Roatta			4680/E224788-94
	Erhöhung des Weizenpreises			4680/E224795-97
	Zahlungsbedingungen bei Kriegsbedarflieferungen nach Italien			4680/E224798-801
	Militärische Lage in Ostafrika			4680/E224802-07
	Notwendigkeit, die Gehälter den gestiegenen Preisen anzupassen			
	Verhältnisse in Kairo			4680/E224808-58
	Sanktionskonferenz			4680/E224859-64
	Oberinspektor Kahlenberg			
	Angebliche Zusammenziehung italienischer Truppen in Bari und Brindisi			4680/E224865-68
	Führerbild an Dr.med.Galler			4680/E224869-70
	Aufdeckung einer umstürzlerischen Bewegung			4680/E224871-75
	Empfang des Universitätsprofessors durch den Führer			4680/E224876-90
	Emigranten			
	Zusammenarbeit der deutschen und italienischen politischen Polizei			4680/E224891-948
	Verteilung der italienischen und englischen Streitkräfte im Mittelmeer			4680/E224949-58
	Neubesetzung der Dienststelle der Deutschen Schule			4680/E224959-60

Akten-zeichen	Inhalt	Band	Datum	Serial Nr.
	Italienisch-abessinischer Krieg, auch Berichte aus Neapel		1935	4680/E224961-70
	Berichte des Luftattachés			
	Unterredung Führer - Englischer Botschafter			4680/E224971-77
	Stellung Bischof Hudal in Rom zu Deutschland und US.			4680/E224978-95
	Italienische Propaganda			4680/E224996-99
	Unterredung Botschafter mit Vertretern der Partei in Italien			4680/E225000-03
	Englische Kriegsvorbereitungen		1936	3175/D682371-73
	Chiffriersachen			
	Kassettenschlüssel für Marine-attaché			
	Umgruppierung in Österreich Aussprache Papen-Starhemberg			3175/D682374-82
	Reise Schuschnigg nach Prag			3175/D682383-86
	Berichterstattung des Luftatta-chés			
	Jude Ziffer			K1686/K405701-03
	Aufzeichnung über Unterredung Botschafter - Führer			3175/D682387-94
	Briefwechsel Renthe-Fink/Lot-scher über Verhältnis Russland-Italien, Deutschland-Österreich			3175/D682395-99
	Bericht des Militärattachés			3175/D682400-09
	Freimaurerei			3175/D682410-14
	Berichterstattung W.Wingund und Lady Haz in Abessinien Knickerbocker			
	Politische Lage - Äusserungen Balbos			3175/D682415-24
	Rückberufung Badoglios			3175/D682425-27
	Unterredung Botschafter - Chamhun			3175/D682428-32
	Besuch Unterstaatssekr.Ricci			3175/D682433-35
	Telegramm Badoglios über Lazar in Abessinien			3175/D682436-38
	Einstellung Ciano gegenüber Aussenministerium			3175/D682439-43
	Unterredung Chamhun - Luvich			3175/D682444-47
	- mit Mussolini über allge-meine Lage			3175/D682448-59
	Spionageabwehr Fischer Rinecker in Oberitalien			

Akten-zeichen	Inhalt	Band	Datum	Serial Nr.
	Türkische Luftrüstungen		1936	3175/D682460-62
	Bericht des hiesigen Luftattachés			
	Einstellungen beim Heer			
	Emigranten in Italien			
	Politische Polizei			
	Italien zum Locarno- und Russen-pakt			3175/D682463-90
	Italienische Niederschrift über Unterhaltung Botschafter - Mussolini			
	Engl.-soz.Militärabmachungen			3175/D682491-93
	Deutschfeindliche Haltung Ceruttis			3175/D682494-96
	Kurierpost für evangelische Kirche Rom			
	Österreichfrage			3175/D682497-514
	Unterredung Botschafter - Japan Botschafter			3175/D682515-18
	Vorgänge über Lumbrosa			
	Flieger Hansen in Abessinien			
	Memorandum betr.Locarnokündigung			3175/D682519-50 7880/E570580-92
	Wirtschaftliche Mobilmachung in Italien			
	Warnung vor Gindler			
	Spionagepolizeiliche Ermittlun-gen			
	Betätigung deutscher Facharbei-ter im Ausland			
	Besprechung über tchechisch-russisches Militärbündnis			3175/D682551-55
	VI.Internationaler Gemeinde-kongress			3175/D682556-60
	Mitwirkung der politischen Lei-ter der NSDAP bei Heranziehung der deutschen Staatsangehörigen im Ausland zum Wehr- und Arbeits-dienst			
	Postchiffre, österr.Wehrpflicht-meldung Mil.Akt. aus Prag			3175/D682561-63
	Bildstreifen "Standschütze Bruggler"			3175/D682564-67
	Dienstpflicht in Österreich			3175/D682568-70
	Schulunterricht in Südtirol			3175/D682571-76
	Zahlenmässige Erfassung der Reichsdeutschen			

Akten-zeichen	Inhalt	Band	Datum	Serial Nr.
	Anton Heyer		1936	
	Angebliche italienische Bereit-willigkeit zu Generalstabs- Be-sprechungen mit Frankreich			3175/D682577-82
	Chilenischer Antrag zur Aufhe-bung der Sanktionen			3175/D682583-85
	Abessinische Eingeborene für Kolonial-Armee			3175/D682586-88
	Verzifferungsbräuche			
	Auslands-Pressebüro G.m.b.H.			3175/D682589-90
	Namen von Kurieren			
	Beziehungen zwischen Italien und Sowjet-Rußland			3175/D682591-96
	Vorschläge der Vertreter der Rest-Locarno-Mächte			3175/D682597-601
	Truppenansammlungen in Südtirol			3175/D682602-03
	Geheim-Material für Konsulat Neapel			
	Besuch einer italienischen Wehr-machts-Abteilung in Berlin			3175/D682604-05
	Unterredung Surich – Sowjetbot-schafter Stein			3175/D682606-08
	Zusammenziehung italienischer Truppen			3175/D682609-11
	Argentinischer Antrag auf Ein-berufung Völkerbundsversammlung			3175/D682612-14
	Unterredung Krofta – österrei-chischer Gesandte Marek			3175/D682615-17
	Abordnung eines Beamten der Geheimen Staatspolizei nach Rom			
	Bericht über Lage in Frankreich			3175/D682618-24
	Gegenbesuch der deutschen Mili-tärabordnung in Italien			3175/D682625-26
	Wechsel des Marineattachés			
	Urteil Dr.Mollers über Dr.Keller			
	Aufzeichnung über Besprechung Botschafter – Mussolini v.7.3.36			3175/D682627-30
	Aufzeichnung betr.v.Herrn Dr. Bruhn empfohlenen Südtiroler			
	Bericht über den Pressevertreter Kramer wegen "Deutsche Zukunft"			
	Geheime Abmachungen der Türkei und Sowjetrußland betr.Sicherung der Dardanellen			3175/D682631-33
	Hochverratsprozess gegen Edgar André			

Akten-zeichen	Inhalt	Band	Datum	Serial Nr.
	Deutsch-österreichische Verstän-digung		1936	3175/D682634-43
	Zusammenstellung über Auslands-verschuldung Deutschlands			3175/D682644-50
	Entwicklung des Rundfunks im Ausland			3175/D682651-56
	Militärische Lage in Abessinien			3175/D682657-63
	Berichte an das Auslandspresse-büro			
	Anlaufen von fremden Häfen deutscher Kriegsschiffe Anlaufen deutscher Kriegsschiffe von italienischen Häfen in span. Gewässern			3175/D682664-68
	Aufzeichnung betr.Teilnahme von Maltzahns an italienischen Manövern 1936			
	Admiral Canaris kommt auf die Botschaft			7675/E547605-07
	Übernahme der Parteiakten in die Botschaft			3175/D682669-71
	Informationsreise Oberstlt. Frapper-Picco			
	Beurteilung des "Deutschen See-hilfsvereins" Genua und seiner leitenden Persönlichkeiten			
	Vorlage der Wehrmachtsattaché-Berichterstattung			
	Vertreter für Firmen, die Kriegs-geräte ausführen			
	Geldbeträge für Prälat Steinmann			
	Auslandsreise Kreuzer "Emden"			
	Brief RM.Dr.Goebbels an Alfieri			3175/D682672-77
	Waffenlieferungen nach Spanien			3175/D682678-82
	"Paula" (Chiffriersache)			
	Vernichtung des Verzifferungs-blattes 3461			
	Richtlinien für Kriegsgerätege-schäfte			3175/D682683-87
	Erteilung von Heimatscheinen an Emigranten			
	Sekretär des Konsulats Pg.Hezinger			
	Gesetz über den Widerruf und Aberkennung deutscher Staatsange-hörigkeit			
	Französische und türkische Be-sprechungen laut Mitteilung ungarischen Geschäftsträgers in Berlin			3175/D682688-94

Akten-zeichen	Inhalt	Band	Datum	Serial Nr.
	Lage in Danzig		1936	3175/D682695-98
	Leitung der kommun. Zentrale gegen Italien in Wien (Seymann-Scheinin M.Gregor)			
	Einstellung des Ortsgruppenleiters Gerhard Otto beim Deutschen Konsulat in Neapel			
	Lage in Südtirol und Wünsche der Südtiroler			3175/D682700-25
	Italien unterstützt Wünsche Polens und Griechenlands um Aufnahme in Donaukommission			3175/D682726-27
	Ausbau des Wirtschaftsdienstes der deutschen Auslandsvertretungen			3175/D682728-60
	Verbot von Rassemischehen			
	Angaben über Aufrüstung der wichtigsten Mächte			3175/D682761-69
	Protokoll über Besuch Ciano in Berlin			3175/D682770-91
	Vorträge in der Wehrmachtsakademie			
	Auskunft über Walter Opitz			
	Aufzeichnung des Herrn Reichsministers über Besuch Ciano			3175/D682792-802
	Danziger Frage			3175/D682803-05
	Handelsvertragsverhandlungen in Rom			
	Rudolf von Gerlach			
	Weiterleitung von Erlassen an Generalkonsulat Genua und Konsulat Turin			
	Lage in Spanien und deutsche Hilfe			701/261138-43
	Deutsch-italienischer Kulturvertrag			
	Anerkennung Manschukuos durch Italien			3175/D682806-08
	Schreiben Windels an Botschafter betr.deutschen Unterricht in Bozen und Meran			
	Revision der Donau-Akte. England und Frankreich will Klage bei ständigem internationalen Gerichtshof betreiben			3175/D682809-10

Akten-zeichen	Inhalt	Band	Datum	Serial Nr.
	Stellung der autoritären Regierung Metaxas		1936	3175/D682811-16
	Eintritt deutscher Kinder in Südtirol in die Balilla			
	Emigranten und Juden			
	Auskunft über Bösch, Markus			
	Englische Öffentlichkeit über Vorgänge in Südtirol			
	Verbal-Noten der tschechoslowakischen und jugoslawischen Gesandten in Paris, betr.Ergebnis der Pressburger Tagung der Kleinen Entente			3175/D682817-26
	Deutsch-japanisches Abkommen			967/302375-77
	Ausfallen der Verzifferungsblätter Nr. 3700 und 3708			
	Entlassung Konsul Hellwig, Florenz			
	Italienisch-spanisches Abkommen			701/261144-288
	Sitzung am 6.12.36 über spanische Aktion			701/261289-93
	Berliner Besprechungen mit dem österreichischen Staatssekretär für Auswärtige Angelegenheiten Dr.Guido Schmidt; deutsch-österreichisches Verhältnis			3175/D682827-37
	Erfindung eines neuartig angetriebenen Motors durch Hidrnelli			
	Italienisch-spanische Beziehungen			701/261294-96
	Gespräch Eden-Grandi betr.Aktion in Spanien			701/261297-98
	"Spanien" Geheim-Telegramm über Spanien			
	Italienisch-englisches Abkommen			3175/D682838-40
	Chiffriermaterial "Perle"			
	Besuch des Herzogs von Aosta beim deutschen Botschafter			3175/D682841-43
	Waffenlieferung Italiens an Portugal			3175/D682844-48
	Chiffriermaterial für Neapel			
	Englands Politik gegen Deutschland			701/261299-303
	Angeblicher Nachrichtenaustausch über Italien und Deutschland durch Sowjets			
	Weitergabe-Nachrichten (W.-Nachrichten) für Handelsschiffe			
	- im Kriegsfall über Berufsvertretungen			

Akten-zeichen	Inhalt	Band	Datum	Serial Nr.
	Unterstützung der Kriegsmarine im Frieden und im Kriegsfall durch Reichsvertreter im Ausland		1936	701/261304-13
	Kornicker, Kurt, Journalist			
	Mantelberichte des Mil.Att.			
	Sammlung von Telegrammen im Berichtsdoppel aus den Handakten des Herrn Botschafters Juli-Dez.			701/261314-39
	Sammlung von Aufzeichnungen und Telegrammen aus den Handakten des Herrn Botschafters Februar 36			701/261340-99
	Ausführungen von Staraces über italienische Politik vor Partei-funktionären in Turin		1937	
	Italienisch-jugoslawische Be-sprechungen			2127/462726-37
	Kriegsschuldforschung Lumbroso			2127/462738-96
	Aufzeichnung über Mitteilung des österreichischen Gesandten über seine Unterhaltung mit Herrn Generaloberst Göring und Aufzeichnung über Göring-Besuch			2127/462797-834
	Übersendung von Lirenoten			2127/462835-37
	Äusserungen des französischen Generalstabschefs Gamelin			2127/462838-49
	Durchfahrt von Kriegsschiffen und Kriegsfahrzeugen fremder Mächte durch den Kaiser-Wilhelm-Kanal			
	Funkpersonal für Empfänger und Sender auf der Botschaft			
	Italienische Luftschutzübung und Graf Ciano			2127/462850-52
	Deutsch-italienische Gesell-schaft			2127/462853-950
	Übersicht über den Stand der fremden Heere			2127/462951-57
	Englische Einstellung zu franzö-sischem Plan einer militärischen Annäherung zwischen Frankreich, Tschechoslowakei, Rumänien und Jugoslawien			2127/462958-61
	Auskunft über Dr.Lorenzo Biseo			2127/462962-3002
	Übermittlung von Weisungen an die Auslandsdienststellen durch Rund-funk			
	Der Deutsche Wahlkonsul in Vene-dig soll bei jedem Aufenthalt in Berlin bei dem Leiter des Refe-rats Pol IM vorsprechen			

Akten-zeichen	Inhalt	Band	Datum	Serial Nr.
	Stellungnahme des deutschen Militärattachés in Moskau betr. Trotzkisten-Prozess		1937	2127/463003-13
	Angebliche Äusserungen Cianos gegenüber dem jugoslawischen Gesandten Drutchitch			2127/463014-31
	Habsburger Frage			2127/463032-35
	Deutscher Bodenbesitz in Südtirol			2127/463036-55
	Reise Schüllers nach Rom zur Verbesserung der italienisch-österreichischen Wirtschaftsbeziehungen			2127/463056-71
	Maßnahmen bei Kriegsgefahr (Spannungszeit)			
	Dr.Richard Koderle: Mitglied des Vergleichsrats auf Grund des deutsch-italienischen Vergleichsvertrags			2127/463072-76
	Italienreise einer portugiesischen Offizierskommission			
	Englisch-französische Verhandlungen betr.Belgien			2127/463077-81
	Aufzeichnung betr.Reise von Brumer nach Italien			2127/463082-91
	Unterausschuss für Autarkiefragen der deutsch-italienischen Regierungsausschüsse für Wirtschaftsfragen			2127/463092-215
	Felix Kraus - Geldaushändigung an F.Kraus			2127/463216-21
				2127/463222-26
	Südtirol			2127/463227-49
	Korrespondent für "Neuentstehender Welt-Presse-Konzern" Bewerbungen an Dr.Hugon-Budapest Poste Restante			2127/463250-52
	Wirtschaftsberichte			
	Romreise von Catroux			2127/463253-56
	Anschrift Reichskanzler a.D. Dr.Wirth			2127/463257-61
	Karte der illegalen SA.- und SS.-Formationen in Steiermark			2127/463262-66
	Grundsätzliche Richtlinien für Vorschläge über die Aberkennung der Reichsangehörigkeit			
	Deutsch-japanisches Antikomintern-Abkommen			967/302378-81
	Einsetzung einer Sonderkommission zur Unterstützung der Gesetzesveten des litauischen Gouverneurs			2127/463267-73

Akten-zeichen	Inhalt	Band	Datum	Serial Nr.
	Weiterleitung eines Briefes an die Deutsche Gesandtschaft in Tirana		1937	
	Geplanter Besuch Mussolinis in Deutschland			2127/463274-75
	Geheime Blattsammlung des Protokolls			2127/463276-94
	Deutsch-italienische Wirtschaftsverhandlungen in München (3 Protokolle)			
	Lieferung von Aluminium an Italien			2127/463295-99
	Aufzeichnung des Herrn Reichsministers Frhr.v.Neurath über seinen Besuch in Rom und seine Besprechungen mit Mussolini			2127/463300-11
	Reise des Herrn Reichsministers Frhr.v.Neurath nach London. Mitteilung an italienische Regierung			
	Zahlungen des VDA an Dr.Wilhelm Witter			2127/463312-18
	Entwicklung der italienischen Handelsbilanz			2127/463319-23
	Errichtung eines Seminars für deutsche Sprache und Literatur an Universität Mailand			
	Abwehr von Lügenmeldungen			
	Sonderkuriere für Spanien			
	Italienische Mitteilung über angeblich durch Franzosen abgefangene deutsche Telegramme nach Algier			
	Abtretung des Judalandes durch Engländer			2128/463328-32
	Errichtung eines Flugzeugwerkes in Ostia			2128/463333-50
	Italienisch-jugoslawisches Wirtschaftsprotokoll, ital.-jugosl. Wirtschaftsabkommen, Gewährung von indirekten Präferenzen für Südosten			2128/463351-71
	Beförderung von 2 Briefen nach Gesandtschaft Tirana			
	Angebliche kommunistische Betätigung des amerikanischen Staatsbürgers Schmacke in Deutschland			2128/463372-80
	AO.-Akademischer Austauschdienst Angelegenheit Lektor Leifhelm, Palermo			
	Spanienkurier			
	Prüfung der Fahrzeuge bei Staatsbesuchen			

Akten-zeichen	Inhalt	Band	Datum	Serial Nr.
	Italien und der chinesisch-japanische Konflikt und chine-sisch-japanischer Konflikt allg.		1937	2128/463381-401
	Zahlungen an Kriminalkommissar Dr.Helmerking			2128/463402-05
	Beitrag von RM 500,- für "Italien-Beobachter"			2128/463406-08
	Meerengenabkommen von Montreux			2128/463409-21
	Verhinderung der Durchfahrt russischer Transportschiffe			2128/463422-23
	Flottenstützpunkte			2128/463424-41
	Maßnahmen für die Erzeugung synthetischer Gummis in Italien			2128/463442-45
	Unterredung Ciano-Plessen über Spanien-Ostasien-England			2128/463446-47
	Waffenausfuhrverbot			2128/463448-53
	Journalist von Langen			
	Aufenthalt der Spanienverbände in Cagliari			
	Unterhaltung mit italienischem Geschäftsträger über Wirt-schaftspolitik im Donauraum			2128/463454-56
	Wettbewerb zwischen der deut-schen und italienischen Luft-fahrtindustrie			2128/463457-59
	Italienische Konkurrenz beim Absatz deutscher Flugzeuge in Portugal			2128/463460-65
	Deutscher Militärattaché in Rom auch für Tirana			2128/463466-70
	Eventuelle Heimbeförderung des Friedrich Konnig			
	U-Boote im Mittelmeer			
	Reise und Besuch des Kreuzers "Emden" 1937 und 1938			8267/E588076-121
	- des Kadettenschul-schiffes "Schleswig-Holstein"			8267/E588122-36
	Stand der deutsch-belgischen Unterhaltungen betr.die künftige internationale Stellung Belgiens			2128/463471-83
	Angelegenheit Hyran - Vingh			
	Unterredung Greiser-Burckhardt (Danzig)			2128/463484-91
	Zusammenarbeit mit dem italie-nischen Tropen-Ministerium z. Störung der kommunistischen Schwarzsender			2128/463492-502

Akten-zeichen	Inhalt	Band	Datum	Serial Nr.
	Bericht des Kommandanten des Kreuzers "Köln" über seinen Aufenthalt in Livorno		1937	
	Oktawja Maria Wielopolska in Verdacht für den polnischen und französischen Nachrichtendienst tätig zu sein			
	"Spanien" Geheimtelegramme über Spanien			2128/463503-15
	Deutsch-italienischer Kulturvertrag			2128/463516-640
	Ernst Beduarek angeblich im polnischen und französischen Spionagedienst			
	Wehrwirtschaftliche Mobilmachung in Italien und entsprechende Berichterstattung			2128/463641-51
	Besuch Ribbentrop bei Mussolini			2128/463652-63
	Vertrag der Reederei Sloman über spanische Schiffe			2128/463664-68
	Angeblicher Brief von General Ludendorff			
	Beabsichtigtes Abkommen anlässlich Besuch Mussolinis			2128/463669-708
	Wirtschaftliche Vorbereitungen für einen Krieg - Finanzielle Lage			2128/463709-14
	Italienische Goldsendungen nach Deutschland			2128/463715-18
	Italienisch-englisches Verhältnis 2 Briefe an Eden betr.Ausgleich			2128/463719-21
	Auskunft Dr.M.Salpke			
	Panzerschiff "Deutschland" und 4. Torpedobootflottille in Neapel (21.12.-2.1.1938)			8267/E588137-38
	Auskunft über Richard Kühl			
	Ergebnis der ungarisch-italienischen Wirtschaftsverhandlungen			2128/463722-40
	Bewaffnung rotspanischer Handelsschiffe. Schritte des italienischen Botschafters in Ankara			2128/463741-46
	Unterredung Hitler-Halifax			2128/463747-59
	Austritt Italiens aus dem Völkerbund			2128/463760-62
	Anfliegen deutscher Kriegsschiffe in spanischen Gewässern durch fremde Flugzeuge			
	Deutsch-italienische Wirtschaftsverhandlungen (Telegramm vom 14.12. Nr.355)			2128/463764-66

Akten-zeichen	Inhalt	Band	Datum	Serial Nr.
	Besuch von Zeelands in Italien		1937	2128/463767-74
	Sammlung der Vorträge in der Wehrmachts-Akademie			
	Tätigkeit des Herzogs von Alba in England			2128/463775-77
	Festnahme der Frau Katharina Hoffmann			
	Auskunft über Grete Assmann			
	Beteiligung Italiens am spanischen Bürgerkrieg und Spanien allgemein		1938	2129/463783-4028
	Fühlungnahme französischer und russischer Elemente mit Bot-schaftsangehörigen			
	Chinesisch-japanischer Konflikt			967/302382-83
	Auskunft, welche italienische Persönlichkeiten befugt sind, über Autarkiefragen zu verhan-deln			2129/464029-36
	Konferenz von Gewerkschaftsgrup-pen in London am 19.12.37 und in Plymouth am 21.12.37 betreff Spanien			2129/464037-53
	Vortrag des Botschafters Graf v.Schulenburg über Russland			2129/464054-95
	Französische Waffenlieferungen nach Russland			2129/464096-98
	Chiffriermaterial			
	Aufgabengebiet des Wehrmachts-attachés			2129/464099-101
	Zusammenarbeit der englisch-französischen Marine			2129/464102-10
	Deutsch-italienisches Clearing-Abkommen			2129/464111-16
	Konferenz der internationalen Werkschaftsverbände vom 23.12. 1937 in Manchester			2129/464117-24
	Beziehungen zwischen USA und Deutschland. Das deutsch-ameri-kanische Element			2129/464125-45
	Italien und die Stellung der Schweiz zum Völkerbund			2129/464146-50
	Ansichten gewisser Kreise des Quai d'Orsay zur politischen Lage			2129/464151-57
	Zentralstelle für kommunistische Hilfe Rot-Spanien			2129/464158-60
	Behandlung von Geheimsachen, Panzerschrank			
	Lage in Weiss- und Rotspanien			2129/464161-67

Akten-zeichen	Inhalt	Band	Datum	Serial Nr.
	Heirat des Albanischen Königs		1938	
	Aussen-und innerpolitische Lage Japans			2129/464168-89
	Bemühungen der italienischen .Rüstungsindustrie um türkische Aufträge			2129/464190-92
	Tee-Empfang bei Graf Coudenhove-Kalergi zu Ehren Pater Mücker-mann			2129/464193-98
	Besprechungen auf dem Obersalz-berg			2129/464199-205
	Jugoslawien und Gleichschaltung Österreichs			2129/464206-08
	Auskunft über Hedwig Voigt			
	Einwanderung Volksdeutscher			2129/464209-37
	Attentatsverdächtig Sowjet-Agen-ten			
	Berichterstattung über diploma-tische und konsularische Vertre-ter Österreichs			2129/464238-54
	Unterredung Führer und Briti-scher Botschafter			2129/464255-61
	Russlands Stellung zum polnisch-litauischen Konflikt			2129/464262-68
	Anlaufen italienischer Häfen durch deutsche Kriegsschiffe			
	Beitritt zum Meerengenpakt (Konferenz von Montreux)			2129/464269-305
	Konferenz der internationalen Gewerksschaftsverbände bezüglich Einmischung in Spanienkonflikt			2129/464306-09
	Soellner, Auskunft über Ingenieur Guido, Emil			
	Kett, Auskunft über Maria			
	Zahlung von Lire 300.000 an H.Carrara			
	Verhandlungen der britischen und portugiesischen Militärkom-mission über die Verteidigung Portugals und seiner Kolonien			2129/464310-12
	Überblick über die wehrwirt-schaftlichen Organisationen des Auslandes			2129/464313-15
	Zwischenfall zwischen General-konsul Fricke und Vize-General-gouverneur Cerulli			
	Angaben über Möglichkeit zum Eintritt in die Nationalspani-sche Armee			2129/464316-17
	Mobilmachungsvorbereitung im Inland			

Akten-zeichen	Inhalt	Band	Datum	Serial Nr.
	Führerbesuch		1938	2129/464318-28
	Angebliche grosse Bestellungen Italiens in England für Fabriken und zukünftige Unternehmungen in Abessinien			2129/464329-35
	Aufdeckung einer Zivil- und Militärverschwörung in Lissabon			2129/464336-42
	Englisch-französische Minister-besprechungen			2129/464343-46
	Durchmarschrecht für sowjetrussische Truppen durch rumänisches Gebiet			2129/464347-51
	Sowjetrussische Flugzeuge für die Tschechei			2129/464352-54
	Besprechungen über Südtirol			2129/464355-75
	Aufzeichnungen D.R.M. betr. Südtirol			2129/464376-79
	Pressepolitische Abrechnung Januar bis März 1938			
	Ankauf des Betyna'schen Führer-bildes			
	Verhandlungsergebnis der Wirtschaftsbesprechungen betr. Italien-Österreich			2129/464380-96
	Bekanntgabe beziehungsweise Zugänglichmachung von amtlichen Akten an Angestellte			
	Uniformtragen fremdländischer Wehrmachtsangehöriger in Deutschland			
	Weisung betr. Abwehr von Lügen- und Hetzmeldungen			2129/464397-403
	Auskunft über Helene Haussmann geb. Boetticher			
	Vorsicht bei Telefongesprächen			
	Erscheinen von Nachrichten in hiesiger Presse, ohne dass die deutsche Herkunft erkennbar			2129/464404-06
	Italienisch-englische Besprechungen			2129/464407-20
	Gewinnung militärischer Nachrichten durch D. Auslandsvertretungen			2129/464421-32
	Wehrwirtschaftliche Vorbereitung für einen Krieg			
	Empfang von Südtirolern durch den Führer			2129/464433-37
	Auskunft über Ing. Hubert Gasteiner			
	Behandlung des deutsch-tschechoslowakischen Schiedsvertrages v. 1925			2129/464438-43

Akten-zeichen	Inhalt	Band	Datum	Serial Nr.
	Haltung des deutschen Gesandten in Tirana		1938	2129/464444-57
	Tschechoslowakei und Ukrainische Frage			2129/464458-61
	Sudetendeutsche und Tschechoslowakei			2129/464462-632
	Italien und die Reduzierung der Truppen in Lybien			2129/464633-39
	Bericht des Direktors Eltze von der Ausfuhrgemeinschaft für Kriegsgerät über Aufenthalt in Portugal			2129/464640-46
	Ungarischer Besuch in Rom			2129/464647-55
	Bewilligung für die kirchliche kulturelle Deutschtumsarbeit im Ausland			2129/464656-66
	Versetzung Eden's als Botschafter nach Washington			2129/464667-69
	Französisch-türkisches Sandschak-abkommen			2129/464670-76
	Auskunft über Frl.Anneliese Boecker, geb.29.10.1912			
	Deutschlandreise Infant Don Juan da Borbón			
	Die wirtschaftliche Bedeutung der Schweiz für Deutschland im Kriegsfalle			2129/464677-713
	Verhalten und Dienstpflicht der Auslandsdeutschen im Kriegsfalle			2129/464714-21
	Paul Schulz, Verhaftung in Italien			
	Deutsch-türkisches Verhältnis			2129/464722-25
	Berichtigung eines Hetzartikels in der estnischen Zeitung "Rahvakeht"			2129/464726-36
	Vorschrift für Verschlußsachen			
	Rundtelegramm unter Kennwort "lural"			
	Vorschriften für Geheim-Sende-dienst			
	Anleitung für Verschleierungs-verfahren			
	Chiffrierwesen für Notfall			
	Vorschriften für Verschlußsachen			
	Erdöl für italienische Kriegs-marine aus Albanien			2129/464737-51
	Alarmtelegramm London-Danzig			2129/464752-53
	China-Japan Konflikt Angriff auf Hankow			967/302384-87

Akten-zeichen	Inhalt	Band	Datum	Serial Mr.
	Munitions-Bestellung für Mexiko		1938	2129/464754-59
	Post-Chiffré über Geheimerlasse			
	Mob.Maßnahmen			
	Ausfuhr von Kriegsgerät nach Italien			2129/464760-62
	Bestätigung über Empfang von Verschlußsachen			
	Durchmarsch russischer Truppen durch Rumänien			2129/464763-64
	Bericht Kairo: Militärische Maß-nahmen der Engländer und Ägypter			2129/464765-69
	Aufsatz Korvettenkapitän E.A.Brenning: "Die neuen Neutra-litätsregeln der nordischen Staaten"			
	Innere Entwicklung und Lage Frankreichs			2129/464770-73
	Einstellung der Propaganda an italienischen Sendern bezüglich deutscher Legion Condor			2129/464774-76
	Weiterleitung von Verschlußsa-chen			
	Beurteilung einer etwaigen Ver-letzung der belgischen Neutra-lität durch englische Flugzeuge			
	Auslands-Ausbildungsreise des Kreuzers "Emden"			
	Lage in Südtirol			2129/464777-83
	Wirtschaftliche Maßnahmen anderer Länder beim deutsch-tschechi-schen Konflikt			2129/464784-89
	Sicherung des Geldbedarfs der Auslandsbehörden im Kriegsfall			
	Bericht über Persönlichkeiten (Wirtschaftler), die als jüdisch gelten			
	Spannung zwischen Deutschland-Italien-Brasilien, Botschafter-frage			2129/464790-824
	Kommission A der deutsch-italie-nischen Regierungsausschüsse			2129/464825-30
	Betätigung deutscher Facharbei-ter im Ausland			
	Herstellung von Geschossführungs-ringen			2129/464831-34
	Deutsch-italienische General-stabsbesprechungen			2129/464835-41
	Deutsch-französischer Erklärungs-austausch			2129/464842-58

Akten-zeichen	Inhalt	Band	Datum	Serial Nr.
	Inkraftsetzen des italienisch-englischen Paktes		1938	2129/464859-60
	Absichten der englischen Regierung hinsichtlich der Aufnahme von Besprechungen mit Deutschland			2129/464861-67
	Anwendung des § 71 DBG auf die Beamten			
	Auskunft über Andreas Kofol			
	Zahlung an Legationssekretär von Reichert von RM 1.000,-			
	Eindruck im Palazzo Chigi des Besuches des R.M. von Ribbentrop			2129/464868-72
	Rücktritt Ungarischen Aussen-ministers Komya [sic]			2129/464873-75
	Ungarn und die Besetzung der Karpatho-Ukraine			2129/464876-78
	Verschiebung der Reise Reichs-ministers Rust			2129/464879-83
	Deutsch-französische Erklärung und Empfang des französischen Botschafters Francois Poncet durch Italiener			2129/464884-88
	Äusserungen Ciano's über süd-afrikanischen Minister Pirow			2129/464889-91
	Warnung vor Paul Radzki			
	Sicherung deutscher Handels-schiffe			2129/464892-94
	Ausbau der deutschen Flotte gemäß deutsch-englischer Flot-tenvereinbarungen			2129/464895-932
	Ungarn und die Achsenmächte (auch Beitritt Ungarns und Mand-schukuos zum Antikominternpakt)			2129/464933-48
	Auskunft über Viktor Boitin			
	Luftschutzkeller			
	Zerreissmaschinen			
	Umschläge "Castor" und "Pollux"			
	Umschlag "Regenschirm""Erdriss"			
	Briefwechsel des Herrn Botschaf-ters mit Kurt Kircheis, Florenz, betr.Deutsche Schule in Florenz			2129/464949-69
	Spanien		1939	2130/464975/2-5095
	Tschechoslowakei			2130/465096-141
	Deutsche Antarktische Expedition 1938-1939			
	Besuch Chamberlain in Rom			2130/465142-211

Akten-zeichen	Inhalt	Band	Datum	Serial Nr.
	Schreiben Ettel an den Herrn Botschafter betr. Konsul Thisson		1939	2130/465212-19
	Aufnahmebereitschaft telegrafischer Nachrichten			
	Gasmasken für Angehörige der Botschaft			
	Rückbeorderung der Auslands-Italiener			
	Telegramm Nr.38			2130/465220-22
	Umsiedlung von Deutschen aus Südtirol			2130/465223-74
	Angebliche Äusserung von Frau Hiltebrand			
	Angebliche Absichten Deutschlands auf Erdöl aus Albanien			2130/465275-82
	Einschreiten Ungarns gegen Karpaten-Ukraine			2130/465283-84
	Auszahlung von RM 130,- an Fürst Urach			
	Stellung Italiens zum deutsch-spanischen Freundschaftsabkommen			2130/465285-87
	Mitteilung über wehrwirtschaftliche Organisation Italiens			
	Vorschrift für Verschlußsachen und eine Anleitung			
	Schreiben für Leg.Sekr.z.D. Schmid-Krutina			
	Vorschrift für Verschlußsachen			
	Betr.Dr.Graeff			
	Auskunft über drei Detektiv-Institute			
	Militärische Nachrichten			2130/465288-93
	Verfahren bei Ausbürgerung			
	Vorschrift für Verschlußsachen (Entsendung Funkangest.Köhler)			
	Unabkömmlichkeit des Schriftleiters Rich.Gerlach			
	Runderlass betr.Mob.Vorbereitungen			
	Mobilmachung			2130/465294-98
	Sicherung der Geheimakten			
	Telegramm: Unterredung Botschafter Ciano betr.kroatische Frage			2130/465299-316
	Aufforderung Mandschukuos an Spanien zum Beitritt Antinkominternpakt			2130/465317-19

Akten-zeichen	Inhalt	Band	Datum	Serial Nr.
	Beschaffung von Witzblättern des Auslandes		1939	
	Für pressepolitische Ausgaben werden RM 13.000,- zur Verfügung gestellt			
	Schreiben Prinz Valery G.de Santamaura betr.kroatische Frage			2130/465320-23
	Brief von Chamberlain an Duce und dessen Antwort			2130/465324-28
	Papst hat Protest der Demokratien gegen Besetzung Böhmens und Mährens abgelehnt			2130/465329-30
	Kredit auf Finanzierung jugoslawischer Staatsaufträge			2130/465331-39
	Tel.Nr.117 betr.Maßnahmen Italiens gegen Albanien, evtl. Protektorat			2130/465340-44
	Deutsch-polnische Politik			2130/465345-52
	Gespräch Staatspräsident Greiser mit Staatssekretär über Danziger Fragen			2130/465353-55
	Zahlungen an Ges.Rat Ettel			
	Zurückbeförderung schwarzer Chiffrierbände			
	Telegramm für Herrn Botschafter persönlich betr.Albanien			
	Englische Einkreisungsaktion Deutschland insbesondere Demarche in Ankara			2130/465356-58
	Einladung des Generaloberst v.Brauchitsch durch General Pariani			2130/465359-60
	Chiffrierangelegenheit			
	Haltung der Türkei zu Achse			
	Bericht Cianos über neue Situation in Stellung d.Militäratt. in Albanien			2130/465361-85
	Begrenzung des Schlachtschiffbaus			2130/465386-88
	Informierung Cianos über Gespräch von Papens mit türkischem Aussenminister			2130/465389-411
	Gespräch von Papens mit türkischem Aussenminister			
	Austausch der in Spanien gefangenen Besatzung des sowjetrussischen Dampfers "Komsomol"			2130/465412-33
	Südtiroler Angelegenheiten			
	Nachrichtenaustausch über Flottenbau			2130/465434-37

Akten-zeichen	Inhalt	Band	Datum	Serial Nr.
	G.F.M.Göring in San Remo		1939	2130/465438-40
	Probemunition für die Schweiz			2130/465441-48
	Postchiffré wegen Hetzpropaganda			2130/465449-52
	Erfahrungsbericht eines Kapitäns Lampe über Luftschutzmaßnahmen in Gibraltar			
	Beitritt Portugals zum Antiko-minternpakt			2130/465453-58
	Kartenwerk über Posen und West-preussen			2130/465459-60
	Aufzeichnung über Reise Rust			2130/465461-62
	Einstellung von Angehörigen nichtdeutscher Volksgruppen in den Reichsarbeitsdienst und Wehrdienst			2130/465463-64
	Ehrung des Bürgermeisters La Guardia durch italienischen Botschafter Fürst Colonna			2130/465465-67
	Aktion des Papstes Pius XII			2130/465468-71
	Angelegenheit Willy Schön, Waldhof			
	Presseabkommen			
	Gespräch mit Graf Ciano über Empfang des englischen Botschaf-ters beim Duce und über Entsen-dung General Cavallero			2130/465472-81
	Telegramm und Antwort betr.die Zusammenkunft Alfieri/Goebbels in Wien			2130/465482-500
	Aufzeichnung über Gespräch von Mackensen mit englischem Bot-schafter			2130/465501-06
	Gespräch Botschafter/Duce mit dem Spanier Sunner. Reise Sunner nach Portugal			721/264497-501
	Bericht über den Besuch der Zer-störer "Friedrich Ihn" und "Erich Steinbrink" Bericht des Kreuzers"Leipzig"			
	Bezug spanischer Schwefelkiese			2130/465507-10
	Amerikanischer Legationssekretär Geist			
	Aufzeichnungen, Berichte, Tele-gramme über den Fall des Orts-gruppenführers Kauffmann in Bozen			2130/465511-80
	Mobilmachung			
	Politisches Gespräch Botschafter -Duce anlässlich Überreichung der Manesse-Handschrift			2130/465581-93

Akten-zeichen	Inhalt	Band	Datum	Serial Nr.
	Politische Übersicht Nr.4+5+6+7		1939	2130/465594-754
	Teilnahme des Generals Halder an italienischen Manövern			8392/E591814-16
	Verhalten Jugoslawiens zum Völkerbund			2130/465755-57
	Schiffsmeldedienst Behandlung der Handelsschiffskapitäne durch Wahlkonsuln			
	Wirtschaftspolitische Beziehungen Deutschlands zum Ausland im Jahre 1938			2130/465758-869
	Mobilmachungsvorbereitungen, Entbindung von Rückkehrverpflichtung für kulturell tätige Personen			
	Diplomatische Behandlung der Danziger Frage			2130/465870-98
	Paktverhandlung mit der Sowjet-Union			2130/465899-901
	Zusammenstellung von Pressestimmen			2130/465902-43
	Unterredung Botschafter/Duce			2130/465944-50
	Luftverteidigung neutraler Staaten			2130/465951-59
	Umsiedlung Südtirol			
	Goldreserve Jugoslawiens			2130/465960-61
	Fragen der spanischen Neutralität			2130/465962-67
	Nachforschung nach Gräfin Vitzthum			
	Munitionslieferung an Rotspanien			
	Stellung der deutschen Wehrmachtsbeamten			
	General Aranda über seinen Aufenthalt in Deutschland			
	Betrifft Ungarn. Csacky-Besuch in Rom			2130/465968-6007
	Material gegen Polen aus der Zeit des Friedensvertrages von Versailles			
	Devisenzahlungen durch G.K.Addis Abeba			2130/466008-11
	Persönliche und sachliche Verluste des Deutschtums in Polen			2130/466012-39
	Arbeiten an der griechisch-jugoslawischen Grenze			2130/466040-42
	Englisch-japanischer Konflikt			2130/466043-46
	Anordnung über Verzifferungen			

Akten-zeichen	Inhalt	Band	Datum	Serial Nr.
	Wirtschaftspolitische Beziehungen Deutschlands		1939	2131/466052-155
	Stand der deutsch-russischen Gespräche (Weizsäcker); Gespräch Botschafter Ciano über die Haltung Japans			2131/466156-60
	Aufzeichnungen über Besuch des Grafen Ciano in Fuschl. Gedanken des Duce und Ciano bei einem Konflikt mit Polen (England, Frankreich)			2131/466161-89
	Abfindungssummen der Diener der ehemal. österreichischen Gesandtschaft Armando Desidera und Ernesto Fantozzi			
	Spaniens Haltung gegenüber Polen			2131/466190-93
	Militär- und Marine-Missionen			2131/466194-97
	Fliegerkdrg. nach Italien			2131/466198-200
	Heimschaffung von Wehrpflichtigen			
	Konflikt mit Polen, Reise von Ribbentrop nach Moskau			
	Wehrwirtschaftsorganisation Italiens			
	Wehrwirtschaftliche Planung über Rohstoffversorgung Italiens			
	Wehrpflicht für die deutscher Volkswirtschaft wichtigen Auslandsdeutscher			
	Tätigkeit der Fa "Miag", Braunschweig			
	Kassenangelegenheit			
	Telegramme und Aufzeichnungen über Unterredung mit japanischem Botschafter Shiratori			967/302388-415
	Vierzig Exemplare der Schrift "Anschlag gegen den Frieden" von Diewerge (Grünspan-Prozess)			2131/466201-02
	Politischer Bericht aus Pressburg			2131/466203-10
	Ferngespräch mit den Dienststellen des Auswärtigen Amtes im Ausland			
	Unabkömmlichkeitsstellung von Gefolgschaftsmitgliedern der Deutschen Luft-Hansa			
	Amanullah von Afghanistan			2131/466211- 21
	"Depot M"			
	Ferngespräche mit Auswärtigem Amt im Kriege			
	Französische Angehörige Yvonne Delidaise			

Akten-zeichen	Inhalt	Band	Datum	Serial Nr.
	Frankreichs Kriegsabsichten		1939	
	Geldhinterlegung Deutscher in Italien			2131/466222-38
	Unterhaltung mit einflussreichen Türken			2131/466239-41
	Waffengeschäft Spanien-Jugosla-wien			2131/466242-43
	Befestigungsbauten an den unga-risch-russischen Grenzen			2131/466244-46
	Vertretung von Firmen des feind-lichen Auslands seitens deut-scher Firmen			2131/466247-50
	Deutsch-spanischer Warenverkehr über Italien			2131/466251-53
	Telegramme nach Rom			2131/466254-57
	Mobilmachungsmaßnahmen			
	Erschliessung albanischer Boden-schätze durch Italien			
	Reg.Ausschußverhandlungen Telegramme Clodius/Auswärtiges Amt			2131/466258-66
	Verbindung mit der Reichsbahn-zentrale			
	Wehrwirtschaftliche Organisation Italiens			
	Reg.Rat Dr.Spakler, Antrag auf Entlassung aus dem Heeresdienst			
	Russisches Vorgehen gegen Bess-arabien			2131/466267-68
	Mitgliederlisten der Alliance Francaise			
	Chiffriermaterial für Konsulat Tripolis			
	Rohstoffbezug über Italien			2131/466269-80
	Neuorientierung der englisch-französischen Propaganda			2131/466281-87
	Türkisch-sowjetrussische Ver-handlungen			2131/466288-97
	Sprachregelung betr.Umsiedlung der Nationalitäten im Auslande			2131/466298-301
	Span. Aussenminister und Unter-staatssekr. zur Rede des Herrn Reichsaussenministers in Danzig und Folgerung hieraus für Krieg gegen England			2131/466302-04
	Geschäftsreisen nach Italien			
	Einreise Kaltbrenner nach Italien und Spanien zu Einfuhr-verhandlungen			

Akten-zeichen	Inhalt	Band	Datum	Serial Nr.
	Tätigkeit von Dr.Franz Reichert, Rom		1939	
	Bezug Drahterlass Nr.30 vom 13.11. an Neapel: Dampfer Marburg Duisburg, Leverkusen			
	Dampfer Coburg und Askari			
	Bereitstellung Blech			
	Telegramm 746 vom 1.11.39 an Auswärtiges Amt Anbietung von Kupfer			
	Weiterleitung von Filmen der Ufa nach New York auf Veranlassung eines Holländers Vaut			
	Charterung griechischer Schiffe durch Feindmächte			2131/466305-29
	Anforderung einer Karte betr. Kraftwerke Italiens			
	Eintritt Englands in den Krieg			2131/466330-33
	Deckadressen für südamerikani-sche Vertretungen			
	Kriegswichtige Lieferungen an die Westmächte			
	Artikel "Deutschland", "Italien" und "Sowjet"			2131/466334-36
	Deutsch-spanische Zusammenarbeit in Argentinien			721/264502-04
	Beförderung diplomatischer Post durch Luft-Hansa			
	Vorbereitung Schwarzer Listen			
	Begegnung Ley - Cianetti			8332/E589818-35
	Bildung eines Balkanblocks			2131/466337-68
	Reichsangehöriger Bruno Kögl Verbindung zu Lock(Loch)			
	Beobachtung der Behandlung Reichsdeutscher durch Behörden und Zivilbevölkerung im neutralen Ausland			
	Rede des Reichsstatthalters von Sachsen anlässlich eines Jagd-essens in Riesa, an dem auch der italienische Generalkonsul Luppis teilnahm			
	Spanischer Plan, Handelsschiffe unter Convoy nach neutralen Ländern fahren zu lassen			2131/466369-75
	Internationale Donaukommission			2131/466376-82
	Agent des Intelligence Service in Genua: Mr.Smith			
	Kohlentransporte nach Italien			2131/466383-443

Akten-zeichen	Inhalt	Band	Datum	Serial Nr.
	Dr.Ing.Otto May, Einkauf von Artillerie-Munitionslehren		1939	
	Flugzeugtorpedos			
	Spanien und der Krieg			2131/466444-67
	Wortlaut des amerikanischen Neutrlitätsgesetzes			
	Auskünfte über Bettina Bomhard geb.Klippenberg			
	Tätigkeit des Dr.Reichert in Rom			
	Italienische Kriegsmaterial-lieferungen an Frenkreich			2131/466468-78
	Chiffriermaterial			
	Unabkömmlichkeitsstellung der deutschen Angestellten des Internationalen landwirtschaftlichen Instituts			
	Reichsinstitut für ausländische und koloniale Forstwirtschaft			
	Zustrom polnischer Wehrpflichtiger nach Frankreich			2131/466479-96
	Äusserung des bulgarischen Oberkomm. der Luftwaffe zu dem Verhältnis Bulgarien-Russland			2131/466497-99
	Telegramm von Papen über Russlands Stellung zur Türkei; auch finnisch-russische Auseinandersetzung			2131/466500-02
	Lage in der Dobrutscha			
	Informationsdienst			2131/466503-11
	Austausch der Ratifikationsurkunden des geh.Deutsch-Spanischen Freundschf.V.; Mitteilung an Italienische Regierung			2131/466512-16
	- erneute Auflage der strengen Geheimhaltung für italienische Regierung			
	Berichtigung betr.Aufzeichnung Nickelerze aus Griechenland			2131/466517-43
	Darstellung des Aufbaus des sogenannten Lassen-Konzerns Verdacht der Handelsspionage, Beobachtung			
	Chiffrierverfahren			
	Neue italienische Bestimmungen über die Ein- und Ausfuhr von Banknoten			2131/466544-59
	Lieferung von Seide durch Firma Pietro Ruffini, Mailand, an Firma Bordoni, Chemnitz			

Akten-zeichen	Inhalt	Band	Datum	Serial Nr.
	"Amt für Handel mit England"in Budapest		1939	
	Vorwürfe Molotow's betr.Lieferung von Flugzeugen der Italienischen Regierung an Finnland über Deutschland			2131/466560-82
	Sicherheitsmaßnahmen der Kurier-beförderung nach Spanien			
	Flugzeuglieferung der Isotta-Fraschini an Frankreich. Telegramm Nr.1084 an Auswärtiges Amt über Rücksprache mit Ciano. Weiterverfolgung und Bericht in der Angelegenheit erbeten			2131/466583-99
	Auskunft über Hubert Mohr - Erinnerung			
Pers.	Personalangelegenheiten		1920-34	
	Handakten Botschafters v.Neurath Personalangelegenheiten von Botschaftsangehörigen		1923-29	
	Reise des Generalkonsuls v.Herff		1919-20	
	Gesandtschaftsrat Dr.Thomas		1920	
	Vertretung des Reichsausgleichs-amtes und des Deutsch-Italieni-schen Schiedsgerichts in Rom		1923-24	
	von Richthofen		1932	
	Beschwerde der SA in Rom gegen Leg.Sekr.Marsch.v.Bieberstein		1933	
	Ortsgruppenführer der NSDAP,Rom, nimmt Beleidigung des Botschaf-ters zurück		1934	
	Sache Francis Hartmann-Venedig		1934	
	Planiglob ./. Comites		1922-23	
	Klagesache Offredi		1921-28	
	Neuordnung der konsularischen Vertretungen in Italien		3.1920	
	Konsulatswesen		1933	
	Dienstbetrieb		1925-34	K1045/K268860-65
	Chiffreangelegenheiten		1921-35	
	Radioausstattung der Botschaft		1934	
	Diverses politisches Material		1920-34	K655/K171422-51
	"Englischer Kollektenfonds"		1921-35	
	Kassenbuch und Belege betr. geheime-politische Fonds		4.31 - 3.33	
	Briefwechsel betr.geheime Zahlungen		1922	
	"Monte"-Zahlungen		1920	

Akten-zeichen	Inhalt	Band	Datum	Serial Nr.
	Abfindung Garcia und Nicolosi		1920-21	
Pol.3 Tschecho-slowakei Sdbd.	Grundstückakten Villa Rava (Anlage z.Dt.Botschaft Rom 3874/39)		6.1939	
	Deutschland			
Pol.2 a	Innere Lage		1921	2158/469642-50
Pol.1	Sammelsachen		1924-32	2158/469640-41 2158/469651-714
Pol.1 a	Politische Beziehungen Deutschland-England		1924	
	- Frankreich		1923-27	2158/469750-71
	- Italien		1922-34	2158/469715-49
	- Österreich		1934	2158/469772
	- Ungarn		1934	2158/469773-829
	- Polen		1934	2158/469830-98
	- Russland		1921-34	2158/469899-909
	- Tschechoslowakei		1928-39	2158/469910-35 3114/D633017-24
	Italiens Beziehungen		1919-35	K656/K171452-77
Pol.2 a	Italien - Frankreich		1920-29	2194/473244-46
	- England		1922	2194/473211-22
	- Österreich		1922-34	2194/473223-43
	- Jugoslawien		1924-28	2194/473154-67
Pol.2	- Russland		1924-30	2194/473168-210
Pol.2 a	- Albanien		1927	2194/473247-51
Pol.2	- Tschechoslowakei		1923-24	2194/473262-86
	- Vereinigte Staaten		1926	2194/473252-56
	- Schweiz		1924	
Pol.2 a	- Spanien		1923	2194/473257-61
Pol.2 c Pol.4 b	- Türkei		1921-29	2194/473287-97
Pol.3	- Kleine Entente		1924-33	2243/477010-47
	- Tschechoslowakei		1931-34	2158/469936- 2243/477104-21
	- Jugoslawien		1929-34	2243/477064-87
	- Rumänien		1933-34	2243/477094-103
	Politische Beziehungen Frankreich -Russland, besonders Ostpaktfrage		1932-34	2218/475095-158
	England		1925-33	2218/475052-94

Akten-zeichen	Inhalt	Band	Datum	Serial Nr.
Pol.1 c	Politische Beziehungen England - Russland		1922-27	
W.3	Russland		1921-33	
	Finnland		1931	2265/479305-10
	Alandfrage		1920	2265/479295-304
	Randstaaten		1934	2265/479311-21
Pol.3	Memel und Litauen		1921-34	2265/479344-423
	Polen		1920-28	2265/479192-294
	Danzig		1927-33	2265/479322-43
	Politische Beziehungen Schweiz- Frankreich		1920	2243/477088-93
	Tanger-Algeciras-Akte		1934	2266/479438-43
	Unabhängigkeit Österreichs		1934	2243/477122-37
	Österreich		1922-34	
	Donau-Problem		1934	2243/477058-63
	Ungarn		1933-34	2243/477048-57
	Türkei-Bulgarien-Balkan		1920-33	2157/469607-36 K657/K171478-87
	Ägypten		1920	2266/479426-30
	Abessinien		1934	2266/479431-37
	China, Ostasien		1927	2266/479444-55
Pol.7	Dritter Jüdischer Weltkongress: Boykott deutscher Waren		1934	K1687/K405704-18
	Liste deutscher Nichtarier Studenten in Bologna		1935	
Pol.8	Minderheiten		1929	
Pol.10	Faschismus, Kommunismus, Freimaurer			
Pol.10 a	Terracini			
Pol.11	Politische und sonstige Persön-lichkeiten		1920-29	K658/K171488-543
	Gräfin Treuberg		1923-27	
Pol.12	Diplomatische Vertretungen und Persönlichkeiten		1921-30	K659/K171544-78
Pol.12 b 2	Chiffre-Diebstahl bei italieni-scher Botschaft in Berlin		1929	
	Dr.Sonnenschein in Mailand		1921	K660/K171579-91
Pol.19	Politische Propaganda, Spionage		1920-34	
	Botschafters von Hassells Be-richt: Wege zur Information der italienischen Regierung und öffentlichen Meinung		1920	K661/171592-99

Akten-zeichen	Inhalt	Band	Datum	Serial Nr.
Pol.19	Gewinnung von Zeitungen zur Propaganda		1921	K662/K171600-04
	Lumbroso,Kriegsschuldforscher		1921-35	
	Fürst Georg Abchasi		1920	
	Felix Heinemann-Paulucci		1921	
	Fall von Kothen, stellvertreten-der Gauleiter von Kärnten		1933-34	
	Schriftwechsel von Simson und Bergmann über die deutschen Reparationsverpflichtungen		2.20- 3.20	K663/K171605-17
	Bitte an Nitti um Intervention zwecks Zurückziehung der franzö-sischen Truppen aus dem Einfall-gebiet		4.20	K664/K171618-22
Pol.7	Konferenz in Stresa		1920	K665/K171623-29
	Internationale Donaukonferenz		1920	
	Instruktionen für Spa		5.20	K666/K171630-38
	Konferenz in Genf		1920	
	Finanzkonferenz Brüssel		12.20	
	Streit um die Insel Yap und die deutschen Kabel		12.20	
	Genua-Konferenz		4.22	K667/K171639-78
	Vorbereitungs-Ausschuss für Ab-rüstungskonferenz in Genf		1.26	
	Besprechung mit Henderson über Abrüstungsfrage		6.33	
	Parallel-Aktion von deutschen und italienischen Sozialisten und Gewerkschaften zur Genua-Konfe-renz		1922	
Fr.1 a	Schuldfrage		1921	K668/K171679-96
Fr.3	Besetzte Gebiete, Rheinland, Ruhr und Sicherheitsfrage		1920-25	
	Friedensvertrag: Abstimmungs-gebiete		1927-32	
	- Eupen-Malmedy		1920-26	
Fr.3 a	- Oberschlesien		1920-21	
	Saargebiet		1934	8723/E609779-90 M166 /M005376-78
Fr.3	Entwaffnung		12.20- 1.21	
	Abrüstung: Brief Forster's an französischen Militärattaché Durand		8.29	
Fr.5 a		2	1930-34	K1046/K268866-72
Fr.3 Sich.	Sitzungs-Niederschriften der Kon-ferenz von Locarno 5.-16.10.25		1925	

Akten-zeichen	Inhalt	Band	Datum	Serial Nr.
Fr.13 c	Schlussprotokoll von Locarno und Anlagen		10.25	
Fr.4	Kohlenlieferungen, Wirkung des Kohlenabkommens von Spa		7.20	
Fr.4 a	Verteilung der oberschlesischen Kohlen: Verhandlungen in Paris 27.-28.12.1920		1.21	
Fr.8	Friedensvertrag: Reparationen und damit zusammenhängende Fragen		1920-21	K669/K171697-736
	Deutsche Friedens-Delegation, Mutius-Lord Hardinge über deutsche Zahlungsfähigkeit für Reparationen		12.20	
	Lloyd George will Giolitti zu den Verhandlungen nach London bitten		2.21	
Fr.8 a	Besprechung in London		2.21	
	Giolitti zur Reparationsfrage		4.21	
	Französischer Plan der Beschlagnahme deutscher Bankguthaben im neutralen Ausland für Reparationszwecke		12.21	
	Übersetzung einer italienischen Denkschrift über Art der deutschen Waren als Reparationslieferungen an Italien		9.21	
	Denkschrift an italienischen Minister Belotti über Reparationslieferungen		10.21	
	Unterredungen von Simson in London mit italienischen Minister Schanzer und englischen Ministern		7.22	
Fr.8 a Rep.	Telegramme vom 31.7.1922 über Reparationen und Rheinland		1922	
Fr.8 a 1	Telegramme über englische Note an Schuldner-Staaten wegen Schuldenregulierung		8.22	
	Deutsche als Führer des an Italien abgelieferten Zeppelin-Luftschiffes		1.21	
W.	Geheimakte in wirtschaftspolitischen Angelegenheiten		1920-33	K670/K171737-860
	Wirtschaftliche und finanzielle Lage Deutschlands, Italiens und anderer Länder in den Nachkriegsjahren 1919		1919-22	K671/K171861-92
	Verhandlungen über Ablösung deutschen Eigentums in Italien		1919-22	K672/K171893-947
W.	Schriftwechsel Bonnemann und Transatlantica		1920-21	K673/K171948-99
	Schriftwechsel Gebr.Perrone im Zusammenhang mit Berichtsfälschung Idea Nazionale (Affaire Straheker)		1920-21	

Akten-zeichen	Inhalt	Band	Datum	Serial Nr.
W.	Messaggerie Italiane		1920-25	
DE 7	Frage der Abtretung des Schnee-berggipfels		1926-33	
W.	Deutsch-italienische Wirtschafts-beziehungen		8.31	K674/K172000-55
	Protokoll zur Regelung kaufmän-nischer Verbindlichkeiten Italien - Deutschland		10.32	
	Wirtschaftspolitik Italien - Österreich-Ungarn		12.32-34	8038/E578100-33
	Französisch-russisches Protokoll über die Prinzipien zu einem künftigen Wirtschaftsabkommen		8.33	
	Runderlass des Auswärtigen Amtes Die gegenwärtige Lage und die Ziele der deutschen Aussenhan-delspolitik		6.34	8756/E610816-32
	Deutsche Devisenlage erschwert Entschädigung von Auslands-Deutschen		11.34	
W.2 b	Wirtschaftsbeziehungen Italien-Albanien		1.33	
V.s	Hanseatischer Abwehrverband Hamburg-Bremen gegen Bevorzu-gung des Hafens Triest wegen Frachtrückvergütungen		1934	
	Neue Zahlungsabkommen Deutsch-land - Italien		6.34	
W.1	Deutsch-jugoslawischer Handels-vertrag, geheime Vereinbarung zur Förderung deutsch-jugosla-wischen Warenverkehrs, Reiseve-kehrsabkommen von Belgrad		5.34	
	Vergleichs- und Schiedsgerichts-vertrag, Rom		12.26	
	Vertrag der Verständigung und Zusammenarbeit Deutschland, Gr.Britannien, Frankreich, Ita-lien Doppel des Vertrages		1933	8910/E621745-53
	Vertrag der Verständigung und Zusammenarbeit Viererpakt,Rom		6.33	8903/E621666-77
	Politischer Bericht: Unterredung über den Viererpakt		5.33	8904/E621680-84
Pr.2	Italienische Presse, einzelne Zeitungen		1922-29	
Pr.2 b	- "Il Paese"		1921-22	
	Verschiedene Presseangelegen-heiten		1920-23	K675/K172056-58
Pr.5	Presse, Nachrichtenwesen		1921-30	
	Transocean(Telegrammgesellschaft)		1920-23	

Akten-zeichen	Inhalt	Band	Datum	Serial Nr.
Pr.6	Presse, einzelne Journalisten und Pressevertreter		1920-33	
	Journalist Dr.Ulrich Schmid		1920-34	
	– Todaldi		1920	
Pr.5 b	Frage der Entsendung des Österei-chers Graf Thun als DNB-Mitar-beiter nach Rom		11.34	
	Streichungen von Journalisten aus der deutschen Berufsliste		11.34	
	Abberufungen deutscher Auslands-berichterstatter wegen Devisen-not		1934	
	Kassenakten		1919-35	
K.W.10	Gerhart Hauptmann		1929-33	
K.W.	Kunst und Wissenschaft		1920-34	K676/K172059-64
	Verzeichnis der deutschen evan-gelischen Gemeinden in Italien		1920	
Ki.	Pfarrer Lessing, Florenz		1921-23	
Schu.1 c	Bericht Studiendirektors Gaster, Berlin über Schulbesichtigungs-reise nach Florenz und Rom		5.22- 6.22	
	NSDAP-"Gleichschaltung" des Vorstandes der deutschen Schule in Venedig		1934	
	Prälat Baumgarten Verein für das Deutschtum im Ausland		1920	
	Politische Übersicht Nr. 11 vom 27.3.1920			
	Politische Übersichten		1933-34	
	– Nr. 1 – 4		1935	
	– 1 – 9		1936	
	Sonstige A-Berichte		12.19- 4.20	K677/K172065-207
	B-Berichte, erstes Halbjahr		1920	
	Doppel der Berichte		11.19- 1.20	
	Bericht vom Silvesterbesuch des deutschen Gesandten Adolf Müller in Bern bei französischem Bot-schafter Allisé und Päpstlichem Nuntius Maglione		1.22	
	Kreuzerhandbusch: Band A Europa Band B Asien, Australien Band C Amerika, Afrika		1933 1934 1935	
110/39	Deutsch-polnischer Konflikt	1	8.39-10.39	2290/483305-29 7987/E575387-91
	Informations-Telegramme		10.39	
	Telegramme	1	8.39-12.39	2290/483373-403 7987/E575392-424 8395/E591847-50

Akten-zeichen	Inhalt	Band	Datum	Serial Nr.
110/39	Deutsch-polnischer Konflikt, Schriftwechsel,Aufzeichnungen	1	8.39-11.39	2290/483341-72 7987/E575425-27
		2	12.39	
	- Handelsangelegenheiten	1	8.39- 9.39	2290/483404-40
	Englisch-französischer Krieg gegen Deutschland, Informations-telegramme und Schriftwechsel betreffend Presse	2	11.39-12.39	2290/483330-40
	Schliessung der Missionen in Algier, Bagdad, Beirut, Bombay, Jerusalem, Kairo, Kenya,Nairobi, Tanganjika, Sidney, Tunis		1939-41	K1688/K405719-24
	Englisch-französischer Krieg gegen Deutschland, Handelsange-legenheit	1	10.39-11.39	
		2	11.39-12.39	
	Informationsdienst betr.neutrale Schiffahrt	1	9.39-12.39	
	Englische Blockade-Maßnahmen Handelsangelegenheit (englische und französische Schwarze Listen)	1	9.39-12.39	
	Prisenrecht; Nichtanwendung auf italienische, spanische und japanische Schiffe	1	10.39-12.39	
	Warnungen an die neutrale Schiff-fahrt	1	11.39- 2.40	
	Englische und französische Schiffskäufe in neutralen Ländern und Ankäufe ausländischer Schif-fe durch italienische Reedereien	1	11.39-12.39	
	Italienische und andere Schiffe (neutrale Schiffe in englischen Geleitzügen)	1	9.39-12.39	
	Deutsche Schiffe in italieni-schen Häfen (auch Tankdampfer)	1-2	8.39-12.39	
	Deutsche Schiffe in Häfen von AOJ (Italien-Ostafrika)	Sbd	9.39-12.39	
	Eisenbahn-Schiffs- und Flugver-bindungen	1	9.39-12.39	
	Deutsche auf italienischen Schif-fen, Grundsätzliches (französische und englische Hal-tung) Reisemöglichkeit für deut-sche Passagiere	1	10.39-12.39	
	Anfragen deutscher Reichsangehö-riger, die auf italienischen Schiffen nach Übersee reisen wollen	1	11.39-12.39	
	Flüchtlinge, Betreuung durch die Auslandsorganisation	1	9.39-12.39	
	Herunterholen Deutscher von italienischen Schiffen	1	9.39-12.39	

Akten-zeichen	Inhalt	Band	Datum	Serial Nr.
110/39	Deutsche Post auf italienischen Schiffen, Beschlagnahme deutscher Post auch auf anderen neutralen Schiffen	1	10.39- 1.40	
	Verwendung italienischer Transportmittel zu Transporten nach den Feindländern	1	11.39-12.39	
	Italienische Bestellungen in Deutschland für England		1940	
	Befürchtungen des Königs von Bulgarien			1044/311149-51 2281/480306-12
	Italienische Stellen bei Vornahme britischer Kontrollmaßnahmen			
	Freistellung des Ob.St.Direktors Dr.Döhner			
	Berichte der Gesandtschaft Budapest über den Fortgang der Unterhaltung mit dem rumänischen Aussenminister			2281/480313-21
	Weiterbeförderung diplomatischer Post mit italienischem Kurier nach Übersee für deutsche Vertretungen Es können bis zu 5000 Lit dem dem Esteri zur Verfügung gestellt werden			
	Kurierverbindung mit Rom (Marine)			
	Neue Vordrucke der Reisevisen und Pässe			
	Polizei-Attachés bei den Auslandsbehörden			
	Innerpolitische Unruhen in Spanien			
	Auslandsdienstreisen von Mitarbeitern der Dienststelle Ribbentrop			4459/E086871-72
	Herzog von Windsor (Eduard VIII)			
	Äusserungen des französischen Marineministers Campinchi			
	Lieferung von Tankanlagen (Host Venturi)			
	Verschiffung spanischer Waren über Italien			
	Stellungnahme des Reichsverkehrsministeriums zu Blockadebrechereinsatz			
	Reise des Gesandten Grobba nach Djidda (Schumacher)			
	Passhefte für New York und Addis Abeba			
	Bauxit aus Jugoslawien nach Triest			

Akten-zeichen	Inhalt	Band	Datum	Serial Nr.
	Militärangelegenheiten, Berichte der Konsulate		Jan.1940	
	Unterredung v.Reichert mit Hermanin v.Reichenfeld (Brief Botschafter an Staatssekretär)			2281/480328-40
	Unterredung Gesandter v.Blessen mit General Roatta			1044/311152-54
	Entlassung des Dr.Walter Steiner aus dem Heeresdienst			
	Russischer Einmarsch in Bess-arabien			1044/311155-62 2281/480341-53
	Getarnte Ausfuhr über Italien			
	Belieferung Englands mit Lebens-mitteln durch Italien. Dampfer TEBRE und Dampfer AMSTERDAM			
	Antideutsche Einstellung des tschechischen Staatsangehörigen Sieber, Handesreferent beim tschechisch-slowakischen General-konsulat in Triest			
	Schriftwechsel v.Bergen/v.Macken-sen über die Verwendung des Gesandten v.Hindenburg			
	Beobachtungen über Verbindungen von Speditionsfirmen zum feind-lichen Ausland			
	Aufzeichnung über die Prinzessin von Battenberg			1044/311163-66
	Deutsch-italienische Farbstoff-Sondergeschäfte			
	Spanische Quecksilberlieferun-gen an Italien			
	Geldüberweisungen eines Musikver-lages New York		Febr.1940	
	Chiffrematerial			
	Erkundigungen über Gunhild Papendieck			
	Faschistische Partei als Organ der italienischen Wehrwirtschaft			
	Angebliche Lieferungen italieni-scher Firmen von Kriegsmaterial an die Feindstaaten			
	Tankanlagen in Triest, Lager der Shell Floridsdorf			
	Geheimhaltungsvermerk auf Tele-grammen			
	Die Türkei und der Krieg			1044/311167-68
	Italienische Freiwillige für Finnland			1044/311169-84
	Deutsche Transportflugzeuge zum Transport von Wolframerz aus Spanien			1044/311185-224

Akten-zeichen	Inhalt	Band	Datum	Serial Nr.
	Warenbezüge aus Spanien über Italien		Febr.1940	
	III.Ergänzung des Rahmenerlasses "Getarnte Ausfuhr" v.9.11.39			
	Filmapparat für Dr.Bergmann (Bozen) oder Peter Hofer			
	Mündliche Übereinkommen zwischen Gen.Sekret. des Türkischen Aussenministeriums und bulgari-schem Ministerpräsident in Sofia			
	Vorgänge über deutschen Reichs-angehörigen Victor Boitin, Mai-land			
	Propaganda durch Informations-abteilung			
	Einfuhr von Wolle aus Peru			
	Kostenlose Heimbeförderung deut-scher Wehrpflichtiger Gegenseitige Vereinbarung Deutschland - Italien			
	Bericht erwünscht über Gesetze des Gastlandes strafrechtlichen, sowie staats- und verwaltungs-rechtlichen Inhalts			
	Nachrichten über Aufstellung eines alliierten Expeditions-korps im östlichen Mittelmeer			1044/311225-66
	Anfrage von Herrn Joachim Herts-let für OKM			
	Entwicklung der politischen Lage im Südosten (Balkan)			2281/480354-65
	Telegramm des deutschen Gesan-dten in Oslo v.24.1.40 über Gespräch mit norwegischem Aus-senminister über Rede Winston Churchill			2281/480366-68
	Telegramm des deutschen Bot-schafters Madrid v.23.I.40 über Kriegsplan der französischen Regierung für den Osten			1044/311267-73
	Dienstreise Stabsingenieur Beine und Stabsingenieur Thiene nach Italien. Prüfung der Her-stellungsmöglichkeiten von Luft-waffengeräten			
	Beschäftigung des Angestellten Kübber bei der Botschaft auf Grund der Mobilmachungsmaßnahmen			
	Betr. den der Botschaft zugeteil-ten Kriminalkommissar			
	Auskunft über Magda Tscherner			
	Aufstellung deutscher "Schwarze Listen"			

Akten-zeichen	Inhalt	Band	Datum	Serial Nr.
	Kriegswichtige Einfuhren Frankreichs aus Italien, Spanien und Portugal		Febr.1940	
	Lieferung von Materialien und technischen Anlagen aus Deutschland an Italien			
	Kontrolle der Feindmächte über italienischen Transithandel für Deutschland			
	Weiterleitung eines Briefes des ehem.irischen Gesandten in Berlin, Ch.Bewley, an eine Berliner Adresse			1044/311274-79
	Aktivierung der Pressearbeit			
	Verhaftung der Elisabet Bruner			
	Aufzeichnung über Lage des internationalen Handels			
	Vermittlung der amtlichen Post für Lourenzo-Marquez, Batavia, Bangkok durch die italienischen Vertretungen			
	Dampferkauf Litauens in Italien			
	Von England gewünschte Kriegslieferungen Italiens			
	Abwehr: Verhalten gegenüber sich anbietenden Agenten			
	Bericht Generalkonsulat Mailand v.20.12.1939 Geh.Nr.103 betr. Dipl.Schriftstücke mit Nachgang (3 versiegelte Umschläge)			1044/311280-308
	Verfrachtungen über Genua Verschiffungszertifikate			
	Lieferungen von Kriegsmaterial Italiens an Frankreich			
	Italienische Aufträge auf Lieferung von Eisen und Maschinen			
	Unterstützung englischer Kontrolle durch Hafenpersonal gegen Bezahlung			
	Brief, den eine Firma im Protektorat von einem italienischen Lieferanten erhielt			
	Lieferung von Benzol			
	Transitgeschäfte Italien			
	Ruhr-Chemie A.G. und ital. Best. Benzinsynthese			
	Hinterlegung von 500 Liren durch Oberst Busch			
	Telegramm aus Madrid:Unterredung des Herzogs von Alba mit Lord Halifax betr.Russland			1044/311309-17

Akten-zeichen	Inhalt	Band	Datum	Serial Nr.
	Angebliche Unzuverlässigkeit des slowakischen Gesandten		Febr.1940	
	Spanische Kriegsschuld an Italien			
	Wehrwirtschaftliche Beurteilung Englands und Frankreichs			
	Aufzeichnungen betr.L'origine della guerra und betr.Propaganda			
	Nachrichtenanlagen der Botschaft			
	Kriegsmaterial für die Türkei			2281/480369-72
	Heimbeförderung deutscher Marineoffiziersanwärter aus Massaua			
	Balkanbund-Konferenz im Februar 1940			2281/481284-303
	Zusammenkunft Czaky-Ciano in Venedig im Januar 1940			
	Weiterleitung von Schlüsseln nach Caracas			
	Verurteilung des Hans Arnheim zum Tode			
	Lebensmittelpakete nach Deutschland			
	Dobrudschfrage			4459/E086873-82
	Sonderaudienz italienischer Gesandter beim König von Dänemark			1044/311318-20
	Kassenschrank für die Registratur Schlüssel für Kassenschrank der Registratur (Mar.Att.) (Bode-Bank-Marke C)			
	Lage in Brasilien, Einstellung zu Deutschland			2281/480373-78
	Äusserungen eines französischen Generals zu Marschall Balbo		März 1940	
	Blei und sonstige Rohstoffe aus Spanien über Italien nach Deutschland			
	Bitte der Königin von Italien um Ausreisegenehmigung für Prinzessin Rupprecht von Bayern			
	Intervention des Marineattachés bei Admiral Somigli(in Vertretung des Admirals Cavagnari)			4459/E086883-87
	Sumner Welles, Europareise			2281/480380-87
	Hanflieferungen Italien an Deutschland			
	Grenzbahnhof Brenner			
	Anlagen von unterirdischen Tanks für Rohöl und Heizöl			

Akten-zeichen	Inhalt	Band	Datum	Serial Nr.
	Einsatz von Schnellbooten zwischen Italien und Spanien. Eintreffen des Beauftragten Einhart		März 1940	
	Geschenk des Königs von Yemen			
	Sowjetisches Wirtschaftsabkommen vom 11.2.1940			
	Kronprinz Rupprecht von Bayern Pass und andere Angelegenheiten des deutschen Hochadels und bayrischer Prinzen			
	Versendung von Verschlußsachen			
	Personen die für Aufklärung des Münchener Attentats von Bedeutung			
	Molybdänerz und Wolframerz für Deutschland			
	Deutsch-italienisches Clearing Grundsätzliche Vereinbarungen und Verhandlungen im Regierungsausschuss vom 21.10.1939			
	Deutsch-italienischer geheimer Briefwechsel			
	Italienische Fischereifahrzeuge für Frankreich			
	Bitte italienischer Regierung zwei Caproni-Flugzeuge über Deutschland fliegen zu lassen			
	Aufzeichnung Dr.Spakler über Unterredung mit Prof.Visco betr. Errichtung einer deutsch-italienischen Rassen-Akademie			2281/480388-90
	Protestnote der italienischen Regierung an England wegen Unterbindung der Kohlenzufuhr auf dem Seewege			
	Verkauf deutscher Schiffe in italienischen Häfen an Italien Verwendung in der Adria und Sardinienschiffahrt (Reg.Aussch. Verh.)			
	Deutsche Maßnahmen gegen englisch-französische Ausfuhrblockade			2281/480391-94
	Besuch des Herrn Reichsaussenministers von Ribbentrop			4459/E086888-97
	Flugzeuge der Firma Walter A.G., Prag, über Italien nach Frankreich			
	Eindrücke des rumänischen Gesandten, Berlin, von seiner Reise nach Bukarest			
	Aus- und Einreise-Sichtvermerk für Nelly Catelli			

Akten-zeichen	Inhalt	Band	Datum	Serial Nr.
	Charterung italienischer Schiffe zum Fleischtransport für Frankreich von La Plata nach Marseille		März 1940	
	Maßnahmen gegen die englische und französische Warenausfuhr, Anordnungen des Führers			
	Belgischer Journalist R.H.Wéry			
	Unterhaltung des Konsuls in Palermo mit Italienern über die allgemeine Stimmung und Lage			
	Heimschaffung der Prometheus-Besatzung von den Kap-Verdischen Inseln			
	Auskunft über italienischen Staatsangehörigen Buda, Vertreter in kosmetischen Artikeln			
	Rangordnung der Waffenattachés, hinter Botschaftern und Botschaftsräten			
	Sendungen nach Dublin			
	Früherer Präsident Svinhufvud zur Lage			
	Einreisesichtvermerk für Lilia d'Albore			
	Wehrpolitischer Atlas von Frankreich und von England (2 Anlagen)			
	Empfehlungen fremder Regierungsstellen für Sichtvermerke			
	Ismet Zeki arbeitet für England		März/April 1940	
	Schiffsbewegungen nach den Feindstaaten			
	Zugänglichkeit des Handelsattaché beim französischen Generalkonsulat in Genua			
	Getarnte Ausfuhr von Kalziumchlorat aus Deutschland			
	Bericht des Vertreters der Deutsch-Südamerikanischen Bank			
	Britische Truppenbewegungen im Nahen Osten			
	Notiz über zollfreie Bestellungen			
	Schmieröleinfuhr über Italien			
	Unterredung der Berner Gesandten Italiens und Spaniens			
	Schlüssel für Panzerschrank Tripolis			
	Bildung und Anerkennung der Regierung Wang Ching Wei			8783/E612077-89
	Englisch-französische Kriegsauffassung			

Akten-zeichen	Inhalt	Band	Datum	Serial Nr.
	Anweisungen für geheimzuhaltende Schriftstücke		März/April 1940	
	Chiffrierangelegenheit (Kennzeichnung der Chiffrierbände)			
	Buna-Verfahren			
	Schiffbauaufträge Englands an Italien			
	Ermittlungen über Therese Centola			
	Finnisch-russischer Konflikt Durchbruch auf der Karelischen Enge. Beendigung des Konflikts			2281/480395-405
	Mittel für besondere Zwecke für die Konsularbehörden in Italien			
	Übersendung von Propagandamaterial		April 1940	
	Vorschriften für Verschlußsachen (Kons.Bozen)			
	Telegramm der Deutschen Botschaft Buenos Aires über die Kriegsaussichten der Alliierten			
	Lieferung von Naphtalin, Rohbenzol, Aceton			
	Unterstellung der Parteidienststellen unter die Missions-Chefs			
	Artikel des Generalkonsuls Wüster in der "Deutschen Zeitung in der Schweiz"			
	Vorschrift für Verschlußsachen (Konsulat Florenz)			
	Zahlungen an Gesandtschaftsrat Ehrich und an Hermann Kahrs			
	Sichtvermerk für den finnischen Generalkonsul Karl Hjelt			
	Chiffresache			
	Anfrage bei Werken auf Lieferung von Zünderteilen			
	Amerikanischer Journalist Wiegang über die amerikanischen Botschafter in Paris und London			2281/480406-08
	Äusserungen des Ex-Königs Alfonso XIII			2281/480409-15
	Umfang der Überseepost			
	Reise Dr.Bohn, Ölreferent im RWiMi.			
	Stimmung in den Wirtschaftskreisen Mailands			
	Sendung für Generalkonsul Druffel Triest			

Akten-zeichen	Inhalt	Band	Datum	Serial Nr.
	Unabkömmlichstellung		April 1940	
	Erteilen von Sichtvermerken für Aufenthaltsorte in der Grenzzone			
	Charterung italienischer Schiffe im Schwarzen Meer			
	Kurier Tafel			
	Tätigkeit des Krämer, Gerken und Schumann			
	Äuserungen des Präsidenten der Agenzia Stefani			
	Besuch des Grafen Teleki in Rom			2281/480416-33
	Haltung der jugoslawischen Kommunisten zum europäischen Konflikt			2281/480434-35
	Information des ungarischen Gesandten in Madrid über die Alliierten			
	Erteilen von Dringlichkeitsbescheinigungen für Geschäftsreisen nach Italien			
	Vorschriften für Verschlußsachen			
	Hafensperre in Triest			
	Weiterbeförderung eines Päckchens nach Dublin			
	Direkter Funkverkehr mit Barcelona			
	Funkverkehr mit dem jeweiligen Aufenthaltsort des Herrn RAM			
	Transitgeschäfte über italienische Monopolverwaltung			
	Sowjet-Iranischer Handelsvertrag			2281/480436-38
	Abschleppen eines italienischen Schiffes von Yarmouth nach Rotterdam			
	Dienstanweisungen für Major Helffrich			
	Gespräch mit belgischem Botschafter Graf van Kerkhove			2281/480439-43
	Bezahlung von Rechnungen des GFM.Göring			
	Jüdischer Journalist Augur Poljakow			2281/480444-48
	Italienisch-russische Beziehungen			2281/480449-53
	Gerüchte über Besetzung Korfus durch Italien			
	Möglichkeit deutsche beschlagnahmte Waren freizubekommen			

Akten-zeichen	Inhalt	Band	Datum	Serial Nr.
	Bemühungen Turi, Dresdner Bank, um Mineralöl-Einfuhr nach Deutschland		April 1940	
	Rücktritt des spanischen Aussen-ministers Beigbeder			
	Moskaus Haltung gegenüber der Türkei			
	Export von Erdöl aus Rumänien			
	Vorgang über "Aktion" Artikel			
	Dokumente zur Begegnung des Führers mit dem Duce für St.S. Frh.v.Weizsäcker			2281/480455-532
	Doppel der Anlagen zu einem Führerbrief an den Duce			
	Aushändigung des Führerbriefes betr. militärische Aktionen in Holland, Belgien, Dänemark			
	Beschäftigung von Schiffahrts-sachverständigen			
	Antideutsche Propagandatätigkeit des polnischen Kapitäns Klon-kowsky			
	Auskunft über Prinz Windischgrätz			
	- Ing.Tilo Bavastro			
	Wetterfunkbetrieb			
	Orden für den Hafenkommandanten von Neapel Colonello di Porto Amedeo Lauro			
	Pressepolitischer Friedensfonds			
	Material über IRCE			
	Zinnmenge aus Russland für Italien		April/Mai 1940	
	Waffenangebot an türkische Re-gierung durch Giacomo Recupito			
	Kriegsvorbereitungen Italiens			
	Stimmungsberichte der Konsulate			
	Japanisch-russisches Verhältnis			967/302416-20
	Mercedes-Benz Flugmotore für Italien			
	Geburtstag von Rom Nichtveröffentlichte Rede des Duce			2281/481304-19
	Gespräch Sikorski's mit Reynaud			
	Verhältnis Ciano's zum Duce			4459/E086898-903
	Türkei hält an Montroux-Bestim-mungen fest			
	Politische Lage in Ostasien			2281/480533-49

Akten-zeichen	Inhalt	Band	Datum	Serial Nr.
	Vertrauliche Ausführungen Cianetti's zur Lage		April/Mai 1940	2281/480550-57
	Kupferlieferungen nach Deutsch-land			
	Artikel des Dr.Theodor Blahut			
	Aktivität des ehem. japanischen Botschafters Shiratori in Rom hinsichtlich Zusammenschluss Rom-Tokio-Berlin			8782/E612069-75
	Spanischer Flottenbesuch in Portugal			
	Aufgabenstellung der Nachrichten- und Presseabteilung des Auswärti-gen Amtes			
	Präsident der Agenzia Stefani, Senatore Morgagni zur deutsch-italienischen Achsenpolitik, ins-besondere über Verhältnis Duce – Führer			4459/E086904-10
	Italienische Haltung in Prag, Generalkonsul Caruso, Giovanni Riccoboni			
	Haltung des italienischen Kon-suls in Prag			
	Versuch der Firma Roditi & Sons, S.A., Florenz, Maschinen für englische und französische Rech-nung zu kaufen			
	Heimschaffung deutscher Seeleute aus Spanien mit Ala Littoria			
	Italienreise des Organisations-leiters des Fichtebundes e.V., Herrn Theo Kessemeier			
	Spanien im Falle des Eintritts Italiens in den Krieg			2281/480558-59
	Postverpackung aus Amerika			
	Frachtverkehr zwischen dem Kongo			
	Zahlungen an Herrn Clemm von Hohenberg			
	Personalien des Konsulats Palermo			
	Unterredung mit dem slowakischen Gesandten Cermak, Slowakischer Gesandter Zorskovec in Rom			
	Besuch des jugoslawischen Ge-sandten			
	Empfang des Fürsten Bismarck bei Conte Ciano			2281/480560-65

Akten-zeichen	Inhalt	Band	Datum	Serial Nr.
	Militärische Operationen in Norwegen, Memorandum an skandinawische Regierungen sowie Mitteilungen des Führers und RAM an den Duce und Ciano, Brief des Herrn RAM an den Herrn Botschafter v.Mackensen		April/Mai 1940	2281/481320-30
	Spanien beim Eintritt Italiens in den Krieg			4459/E086911-16
	Wetternachrichten für ausserheimische Gewässer			
	Zahlungen an Gesandten Fürst v.Bismarck			
	Haltung der Türkei bei Eintritt Italiens in den Krieg			2281/481331-41
	Deutsch-italienische Regierungsausschussverhandlungen vom 21.1.bis 24.2.40			
	Annunziatenorden für G.F.M. Göring, Grosskreuz Deutscher Adler für Kronprinz und Jahrestag des Stahlpaktes		Mai 1940	4459/E086917-28
	Besprechungen britischer Diplomaten auf dem Balkan, Türkei, Sowjet-Union Anfang April 1940 in London			
	Gesandter Bene und Korpsführer Hühnlein, Brief des VLR Luther in dieser Angelegenheit			
	Brief des Gesandten v.Dörnberg an Viconte Travaglini betr. Verwaltung der Güter des Malteser-Ordens			
	Rede des Oberbürgermeisters Pfitzner, Prag			2281/480566-69
	Stellung des stellvertretenden Landesgruppenleiters L. Dr.Butting			
	Beschäftigung des Gen.Kons.Toepke			
	Angelegenheit des Dr.Rust (DAF)			
	Rückbeförderung deutscher Seeleute aus AOJ			
	Passverlust im Ausland			
	Post und Handelsspionage der Engländer in Genua			
	Französischer Botschafter in Ankara über die Lage			
	Telegramm des Papstes an Holland und Belgien			
	Cessiertes Telegramm über Aushändigung des Führerbriefes an den Duce			

Akten-zeichen	Inhalt	Band	Datum	Serial Nr.
	Französische Reaktion auf Besetzung im Norden		Mai 1940	
	Weiterleitung eines Erlasses nach Genua (betr.Fürst Adolf Schwarzenberg)			
	Einfuhr von Zinkerzen aus Italien			
	Unterrichts-Telegramm für Luftattachés			
	Eisenbahnlinie Rom-Istanbul			
	Lieferung italienischer Lastkraftwagen an Frankreich			
	Fürst Adolf Schwarzenberg			
	Wirtschaftliche Lage der besetzten nordischen Staaten			
	Unterredung Prinz von Hessen mit Ciano			
	Überfliegen italienischen Hoheitsgebietes			
	Reise Ministerialrat Fetzer, Okdo K.M. nach Rom			
	Wirtschaftsspionage v.Miller,Rom			
	Übersendung von Chiffrematerial			
	Telegramm Sofia über Besuch des englischen Botschafters in Ankara			
	Unterhaltung des H.Botschafters mit Graf Ciano Mai 1940 betr. Botschaften Churchills und Roosevelts an den Duce			4459/E086929-54
	Bericht über den Schweizer Staatsangehörigen Guy Blanc			
	Einfuhr von Rohseide aus Italien			
	Lieferung von Kriegsgerät an fremde Staaten			
	Heimschaffung deutscher Reichsangehöriger			
	Speditionsfirma Francesco Parisi			
	Bericht der Gesandtschaft für Mittelamerika			
	Englischer Botschafter Sir Hugh Knatchbull			
	Kabinettswechsel in Rumänien			
	Bericht von Ucello			
	Bewachung deutscher Handelsschiffe in Triest			
	Kapltn.a.D.Erich G.Gerth			

Akten-zeichen	Inhalt	Band	Datum	Serial Nr.
	Chiffrematerial des Generalkon-sulats Batavia		Mai 1940	
	Kommandierung Generalmajor v.Pohl Luftattaché			
	Englische Blockade gegenüber Italien			
	Hinterlegungsgelder für Verwal-tungszwecke			
	Antwortbrief des Führers an Graf Teleki			2281/481342-64
	Grundsätzlicher Befehl des Führers und Reichskanzlers			4459/E086955-56
	Rotspanische Flüchtlingsorgane in Frankreich und Mexiko			
	Angelegenheit Emir Schekib Arslan			
	Besuch des japanischen Aussen-ministers a.D.Sato			152/82016/2-42
	Telegramm aus Budapest über Ver-hältnis Ungarn-Russland			
	Spanische Antwort auf französi-schen Fühler			
	Totalfälschung eines Reisepasses			
	Bericht eines V-Mannes über Besprechung mit Reynaud			
	Bestochener Tel.-Beamter in Triest			
	Frachtsonderdienst nach Barcelona			
	Lieferungen aus dem Südosten Europas an die Feindmächte im Transit durch Italien			
	Lieferung mexikanischen Benzins für Italien			
	Italienische Sprengstofflliefe-rungen an Rumänien		Mai/Juni 1940	
	Entmilitarisierung der Stadt Rom im Falle des Kriegseintritts Italiens			4459/E086957-63
	Angebliches Ersuchen Ungarn an Italien um Übernahme Protektorats			
	Einkauf von Flugzeugtorpedos in Italien			
	Italienische Tankschiffe im Schwarzen Meer			
	Tarnungsgeschäfte (Teak-Holz)			
	Devisenbedarf für Propaganda-zwecke und Frage des Privat-transfers.Aktivierung der Presse-arbeit			

Akten-zeichen	Inhalt	Band	Datum	Serial Nr.
	Brennstoff und Schmieröl für Transportflugzeuge		Mai/Juni 1940	
	Geschützladung auf Dampfer "Liebenfels"			
	Gerüchte über ungarisch-italienische Schiffahrtsunternehmen			
	Eintritt Italiens in den Krieg			2281/481365-81 9863/E692871-73
	Quecksilberlieferungen spanischer Herkunft			
	Fernschreibschlüssel Rom-Berlin Juni 1940, 2.Ausgabe			
	Frontreise des Luftattachés			
	Verhältnis Russlands zur Türkei			2281/480571-87
	Tankflottenverhältnis auf der Donau			
	Broschürenübersendung			
	Verhältnis des belgischen Botschafters Graf Kerkhove zum König von Belgien bezw. zur belgischen Regierung			
	Polnische Scheinregierung		Juni 1940	
	Indizierung der Werke Orianis			
	Sogenannte "Schwarze Gelder" (Helffrich)			
	Aufkündigungen von U.K.-Stellungen			
	Kommandierung Flaggoffizier zum italienischen Marineministerium Stellung des Gen.v. Pohl und Admiral Weichhold zum Botschafter			
	Botschafterfrage in Rom und Moskau			2281/480588-90 4459/E086964-82
	Löschen deutscher Schiffe in A.O.J.			
	Italienischer Luftangriff auf Haifa			
	Erbeutete Flakgeschütze für Italien			
	Telegramm aus Washington über Lieferungssperre Russland			2281/480591-94
	Verhältnis Italiens zu Jugoslawien			
	Dritter Transport via Suez (Wehrmacht)			
	Visum für Pg.Hans-Joachim Böttcher			
	Geflüchtete Deutsche aus fremder Kriegsgefangenschaft			

Akten-zeichen	Inhalt	Band	Datum	Serial Nr.
	Tee-Einladung der Prinzessin Radziwill bei Frau v.Mackensen		Juni 1940	
	Waffenstillstand mit Frankreich			2281/481382-404
	Verhältnis Russlands zu Italien, Balkan sowie Bessarabienfrage			2281/481405-27 9863/E692874-75 9866/E692888-91
	Schreiben Habersberg in Sachen Merrum			
	Deutsch-italienische technische Zusammenarbeit			
	Drahtmeldung des Major Heggenreiner			
	Abschuss deutscher Flugzeuge durch die Schweiz			2281/480595-601
	Einreisesichtvermerke für fremde Wehrmachtsangehörige		Juli 1940	
	Vorschlag des G.Arena an den Führer			
	Japan und der europäische Krieg			967/302421-25
	Patronenlieferung an Italien			
	Nickel aus Norwegen für Italien und Kupfertransitgeschäfte, italienische Kupferlieferungen			
	Kapazität italienischer Munitionsfabriken			
	Besoldungsgrundsätze für Schreibdamen			
	Exportlieferungen von Luftfahrtgerät			
	Amerikaner Friedrich Arntz (Textilfachmann)			
	Zahlungen für Weissbuch Nr.3			
	Verhältnis der Sowjet-Union zu Iran			2281/480602-03
	Fernschreibverbindung Berlin-Rom			
	Seestreitkräfte im Mittelmeer Vercharterung jugoslawischer Schiffe an England			
	Skodawerke in Pilsen			
	Beschlagnahmen durch italienische Regierung			
	Lage an der französisch-spanischen Zonengrenze			2281/480604-07
	Ausweisung Zankl und andere			
	Zahlungen Istituto Cambi (Wife)			
	Versenkung französischer Kriegsschiffe in Oran			

Akten-zeichen	Inhalt	Band	Datum	Serial Nr.
	Angelegenheit des Gesandtschaft-rates Deiters		Juli 1940	
	Lloyds Register of Shipping 1940			
	Knallkapsel unter einer Kohlen-lieferung			
	Verhältnis Deutschlands zu Russ-land			2281/481428-48
	Innerpolitische Lage in Spanien und Verhältnis Spaniens zur Achse			2281/481449-66 4241/E074560-61/3
	Verhältnis Griechenlands zur Achse			2281/481467-68
	Lage und Stimmung in England			2281/480609-12 3090/D625962-81
	Auseinandersetzung mit Promi und Besuch Ministerialrat Fritzsche in Rom			
	Geschenk Flakbatterie des Führers an den Duce			2281/480613-14
	Reise des Grafen Ciano am 19.7. nach Berlin			2281/480615-18
	Spionageabwehr Fr.Dr.med.M.Roth			
	Bombenangriffe auf Palermo und Tripolis			
	Bestellung Dr.Gräff zum Referen-ten für wehrwirtschaftliche Fra-gen			
	Versteifung der Haltung Frank-reichs und italienische Truppen-verschiebungen an der französi-schen Grenze			2281/480619-23 4459/E086983-7000
	Verkehrskonferenz Rom 26.6. bis 8.7.40 Verhandlungen des Ge-sandten Martius			
	Verhandlungen über deutsch-italienische Zusammenarbeit auf dem Gebiet der Kriegswirtschaft vom 15. bis 18.6.40			
	Deutsche Propaganda gegen Frankreich			2281/480624-29
	Besuch der Rumänen und Bulgaren in Berlin, Besprechungen und Aufzeichnungen über Csaky-Besuch in Rom, Alexander Gregorian			2281/481469-96
	Telefonischer Presseberichts-dienst		Juli/August 1940	
	Deutsch-italienische Maßnahmen des Handels- und Wirtschafts-krieges			
	Einreisesichtvermerk Frederikson und v.Horn			

Akten-zeichen	Inhalt	Band	Datum	Serial Nr.
	Reise Bernhardt nach Madrid		Juli/August 1940	
	Land- und Seekontrolle der französischen Grenzen			
	Sichtvermerksantrag Arved Grebert			
	Haltung der Vereinigten Staaten von Amerika zum Krieg			2281/480630-45 4421/E084030-44
	Angelegenheit Bentz/Hlobil			
	Koordination des Wirtschafts-krieges mit Italien			
	Ein- und Ausreisevisen für Kyhoegen, Harmsen, Hans Daufeld, Horst Issel, Dr.Heinz Tornet, Helmut Knochen, Alfred Söhlmann, Karl Mercier, Karl Janssen, Albert Heilmann, Hans Daufeld, Greifelt, Harry Peters			
	Verhältnis der Schweiz zum Krieg			2281/481497-508 4459/E087001-07
	- Jugoslawiens zum Krieg und - - zu den Achsenmächten			
	Rüstungsausgaben der kriegfüh-renden Mächte			
	Abessinische Stammesfürsten (Ras Makonnen)			
	Spionagesache Alfons Hammer-schmidt			
	Überführung deutscher Schiffe von Sardinien			
	Stellung Irlands zum europäi-schen Krieg			
	Italiens Absichten im Balkan und Mittelmeer			2281/481509-13
	Stellung Spaniens und Portugals zum Krieg.Spanische Kriegsziele			2281/481514-19 4104/E070568-74
	Lage in französisch Marokko			2281/480646-50
	Totale Blockade über England			
	Visumsanträge Major Helffrich			
	Spionagetätigkeit der Herzogin Sermonette			
	Bulgarien-Rumänien-Balkan			2281/481520-31
	Arabische Länder			K1690/K405728-41
	Deutsche Aussenhandelsbilanz			
	Sechstes geheimes Protokoll über deutsch-italienische Wirt-schaftsbeziehungen			
	Wirtschaftsverhandlungen			

Akten-zeichen	Inhalt	Band	Datum	Serial Nr.
	Eisen- und Stahllieferungen und Erze		August 1940	
	Koffer und 600 Zloty des Herrn Alex Bauermeister			
	Italien und das deutsch-türkische Handelsabkommen.			
	Maffia-Narodua-Ochrana, Rechtsanwalt Rasin			
	Einrichtungsgegenstände Hauptmann Dr.Scholz			
	Ausweisung Parkers			
	Zahlungen an Clemm v.Hohenberg			
	Wirtschaftsverhandlungen in Berlin vom 12.-17.August 1940			
	Veröffentlichung italienischer Bilder in deutscher Presse und umgekehrt			
	Telegramm aus Tarabya über Deutschland-Russland-Türkei		September 1940	
	Briefwechsel des deutsch-italienischen Regierungsausschusses v.17.8.40 (Finanzierungsgeschäfte v. 21.10.39)			
	Synthetische Auto- und Möbelstoffe			
	Feindhetze betr.Polen			
	Verhältnis Russland-Iran			
	Handels- und Wirtschaftskriegführung			
	Bewaffneter türkischer Dampfer UGUR und andere türkische Handelsschiffe			
	Deutsche Schiffsverbindungen			
	Briefe für Herrn Prof.Petriconi			
	Türkisch-britisch-französischer Beistandspakt vom 19.10.39			2281/481533-50
	Deutsche Blockadeerklärung gegen England und Verhalten Griechenlands und Jugoslawiens hierzu			
	Ausbürgerung Zita von Habsburg			2281/480652-57
	Autoreifen für Italien und Frankreich			
	Vorschläge des Grossmuftis betr. Syrien, Palestina, Transjordanien			2281/481551-628
	Chiffresachen (Verschlußsachen) für Florenz in Genua zu verwahren			
	Wirtschaftsverhandlungen Italien-Frankreich			

Akten-zeichen	Inhalt	Band	Datum	Serial Nr.
	Bericht des spanischen Botschaf-ters in London über General de Gaulle, Churchill und de Gaulle		September 1940	
	Spanischer Geheimbericht über Französisch Marokko			
	Griechischer Gesandter am 26.8.40 beim Herrn RAM in Fuschl			2281/480658-61
	Zusatzprotokoll zum portugisisch-spanischen Freundschafts- und Nichtangriffspakt			4459/E087008-13
	Lage in Aequatorial-Afrika, Kontrolle in Nordafrika, Propa-ganda-Auswertung der Lage in französisch-Afrika			2281/480662-99
	Druckschriften-Propaganda in Italien G.Kreides Vorschläge, G.Zeigner			
	Rumänisch-ungarische Verhandlun-gen mit neuer Grenzkarte			
	Wirkungen englischer Bombenan-griffe in Deutschland und umge-kehrt			
	Missglückter Putsch der Eisernen Garde in Rumänien			
	Überweisungen für deutsche Marineangehörige, die zurück-kehrten			
	Kommunistische Propaganda im Balkan			
	Schiffsverkehr im Mittelmeer, Kontrolle durch England und Italien			
	Wiener Schiedsspruch Exposé Graf Csaky, Aufnahme bei der ungarischen Bevölkerung, in Bulgarien, in Rumänien			2281/481629-59
	Politische Lage im Irak, Iraks Ministerpräsident über die Achsenmächte			2281/481660-63
	Innenpolitische Lage in England Deutsche Luftangriffe auf England Gespräch des türkischen Botschaf-ters mit Churchill, Lageberichte über England			2281/480700-14 3090/D625982-92
	RM.2200,-- für Südostdienst			
	Haltung und Lage der Schweiz			4459/E087014-22
	Russland-Türkei-Syrien Verhältnis der Türkei zur Achse			
	Fräulein Duday			
	JAPAN TIMES über französisch Indochina			

Akten-zeichen	Inhalt	Band	Datum	Serial Nr.
	Entlassung des S.Hübernig aus italienischem Rüstungsbetrieb		September 1940	
	Aussenpolitische Rundfunkarbeit			
	Nichtangriffspakt Frankreich – Tailand			152/82048-51
	100 to. Glyzerin für Italien monatlich			
	Gewinnung von Kalisalzen am Toten Meer			
	Einreiseangelegenheit Laraque, Plesch und Janucelli			
	Schweizer Transitverkehr über Genua			
	Liniendienst Genua-Barcelona			
	Warnung vor Einstellung des Karl Wiel			
	Fernsprechverkehr mit Spanien und Portugal			
	Deutsche Währungspolitik in den Balkanländern			
	Vorfall mit SS-Obersturmführer Lorenz			
	Bunkerkohle für den D.NORDERNEY			
	Reise des Franz Winkler		Oktober 1940	
	Rückständige Lieferungen von deutschen Textilmaschinen nach Italien			
	Schrift über Staatssystem Sowjet-Russlands			
	Ägypt.Staatsangeh.Dr.Riskala			
	Arbeitsschutz für deutsche Wehrpflichtige in Italien			
	Tätigkeit des Funkbeauftragten (Jäger)			
	Beitritt Ungarns zum Dreimächtepakt Beitritt anderer europäischer Länder			2281/480716-47 2366/489192-293
	Deutsche Militärmission nach Rumänien			2281/481664-82
	Ehemaliger Presseattaché Alex.Gregorian, Rom			2281/480748-63
	Ausrüstung des Konsulats Tripolis mit Chiffrematerial			
	Generalkonsul von Pannwitz und interimistische Entsendung des Ges. Rat Pfeiffer			2281/480764-82

Akten-zeichen	Inhalt	Band	Datum	Serial Nr.
	Verhältnis Italiens zu Griechen-land		Oktober 1940	2281/481683-719
	Italienische Staatsangehörige jüdischer Rasse Liquidation des Judenvermögens			K1691/K405742-81
	Italienisch-deutsche Kommission wegen der Greueltaten Ungarn-Rumänien			4459/E087023-41
	Getreideversorgung Deutschland - Italien im Jahre 1940			
	Direktor Mieth der Osram-Ges., Mailand			
	Anfrage wegen Berichts des Mar. Att.3184 Kdos			
	Chiffreangelegenheiten, Ver-schlußsachen-Vorschrift			
	Spanische Eisenerze für Italien und Warnliste			
	Schriftwechsel über Reise der Kronprinzessin von Italien zu ihrem Bruder König von Belgien und Reise der Königinmutter von Belgien			
	Auslagen des Marineattachés Rom			
	Abgabe von 20 Torpedos an die italienische Luftwaffe			
	Vatikan			
	Annahme des Stephanordens durch den Duce			
	Besuch Antonescus in Rom			2281/481720-24
	Aktivität Englands in Griechen-land			
	Begegnung des Führers mit Laval, Franco, Pétain und Treffen des Führers mit dem Duce in Florenz			2281/481725-33
	Überwachung der Ausfuhr kriegs-wichtiger Schweizer Waren, Geleitscheinverfahren			
	Entsendung italienischer Flug-zeuge nach Flandern			2281/480783-90
	Verhältnis Bulgariens zur Achse			
	Japanische Benzinlieferungen nach Äthiopien			
	Wechsel des Parteisekretärs Muti-Serena			
	Besuch des Caudillo in Rom Rücksprache Fürst Bismarck mit Pansa			
	In Florenz Herrn Botschafter durch Herrn RAM angekündigte Reise nach Berlin			

Akten-zeichen	Inhalt	Band	Datum	Serial Nr.
	Äusserungen des Generals Weygand		Oktober 1940	
	Nachforschung nach dem Brief des irischen Gesandten Bewley (800 Dollar)			
	Versorgung der englischen Mittelmeerflotte mit rumänischem Öl			
	Entlassung und Erpressungsversuch Luger			
	Stimmung Duce-Ciano über die italienischen Heerführer			2281/481734-37
	Beschaffung eines Vatikan-Code			
	Freigeleit für amerikanisches Schiff durch italienische Regierung			
	Bombardierung der Stadt Bitolj und Susak			
	Havarierte italienische U-Boote in Tanger			
	Gespräche mit dem König von Ägypten			K1689/K405725-27
	Halbjude Tischler			
	Dampfer Aegina, Einsatz für Fruchtfahrt		November 1940	
	Nachrichtendienst des italienischen Ministeriums für Volkskultur			
	Grenzpolitischer Bericht der Gauleitung Tirol			
	Italienische Kriegführung			2281/481738-80
	Reise des Vizepräsidenten der Fiatwerke nach Paris und Berlin			
	Unterredung des Herrn RAM mit thailändischem Staatsminister Montri			2281/480791-811
	Entsendung des Arztes Kersten zur Behandlung des Grafen Ciano			
	Gräfin Klara Wurmbrand Stuppach			
	Tass-Vertreter Belloussov in Rom			
	Prinzessin von Piemonte - Staatsminister Dr.Meissner		Dezember 1940	
	Klärung einer Einzelfrage aus dem Brief des Duce an den Führer vom November 1940			
	Erzbezüge der Vereinigten Stahlwerke aus Spanien über Italien			
	Nachfrage nach dem Beamten Mascia im italienischen Aussenministerium			
	Legionärbewegung in Rumänien			

Akten-zeichen	Inhalt	Band	Datum	Serial Nr.
	Firmen in Spanien, die mit England arbeiten		Dezember 1940	
	Italienische Luftangriffe auf Bahrein			2281/480812-28
	Generalfeldmarschall Milch in Rom 6.12.40			
	Aufenthaltsrecht für ehemalige rumänische Minister			4459/E087042-46
	Aldo Chiesi, faschistischer Gauleiter in Köln			
	Freundschaftspakt Ungarn - Jugo-slawien			
	Zahlungen an Prinz von Hessen Sonderfonds zum Erwerb von Kunstgegenständen durch den Führer und Beschaffung anderer Kunstgegenstände			2281/481781-854
	Angelegenheit K.S.Malhamé/Joh. Bondy			
	Exkönig CAROL von Rumänien in Spanien			
	Dr.ing. Max Hähnle, Rom			
	Brief an Gen.Dir.Masi, Rom			
	Beihilfe für Bürohilfsarbeiter Sieber			
	Versendung belgischen Goldes durch Frankreich			
	Abgabe von Kautschuk nach Italien			
	Hereinnahme von Lirebeträgen			
	Slowakischer Gesandter beim Vatikan Sidor			
	Staatenlose Semen Mecaj und Schulgin			
	Wehrwirtschaftliche Angaben über Italien			
	Zusammenstellung von Ereignissen und Vorgängen aus der Rundfunk-arbeit			
	Einsatz deutscher Truppen in Italien			
	Wirtschaftswunschlisten der Italiener - der Deutschen			
	Wirtschaftsverhandlungen Rom Januar 1940			
	Schulden Spaniens an Deutschland und Italien			
	Sendungen dür den Auslandspres-seclub Berlin			

Akten-zeichen	Inhalt	Band	Datum	Serial Nr.
	Wirtschaftsverhandlungen am 3.12.in Berlin		Dezember 1940	
	Aufzeichnung des Herrn Botschafters Gespräche mit Italienern			
	Aufzeichnung des Fürsten Bismarck Deutsch-italienische militärische Zusammenarbeit			2281/481855-72
	Italienische Kriegführung		Januar 1941	2281/481874-931 4865/E248660-63
	(ebenfalls Bericht über Albanien)			2281/481932-70 4865/E248664-67
	Beiband: Stimmungsberichte der Konsulate			2281/480830-919
	Ausländische Handelsschiffe in Amerika			5129/E295938-44
	Italienischer Schiffsbau Tanker für mexikanische Regierung			
	Verhältnis Italiens zu Russland Italienisch-russische Gespräche			2281/481971-84
	Bulgarien, Rumänien, Jugoslawien, Ungarn Beitritt Bulgariens zum Dreimächtepakt			2281/481985-88 4865/E248668-99
	Wirtschaftliche Besprechungen Favagossas in Berlin vom 29.12.40 bis 5.1.41 Käufe durch Prof.Canci von der AMMI			
	Arabische Länder, Syrien Grossmufti Lage in Ägypten und Türkei			2281/481989-2058 4865/E248700-36 K1693/K405823-57
	Beiband: Irak			2281/482059-69 4865/E248737-67
	Mineralölversorgung Italiens			
	Französische Kolonien de Gaulle Unterredung Ciano-Darlan in Turin Dezember 41			2281/480920-1020 4640/E209236-50
	Audienz beim Duce, Auftrag des Führers und Vorbereitung der Begegnung Führer-Duce			2281/481022-24
	Fürst Colonna			
	Kurierdienst innerhalb Italiens			
	Gesandter von Twardowsky			
	Drahtlose Verbindung Dublin-Berlin und Angelegenheiten Irland (allgemein)			
	Übergabe des Konsulats Tripolis bei einer englischen Besetzung			
	Weiterleitung eines Schreibens der Deutschen Werke an jugoslawischen Militärattaché			

Akten-zeichen	Inhalt	Band	Datum	Serial Nr.
	Spanien: Lebensmittel aus Amerika für Spanien		Dezember 1940	
	Deutsche Schiffe in Italien, Ostafrika Rückführung der UCKERMARK			
	Angebot Abschriften jugoslawischer Zifferntelegramme			
	Verhaftung Volksdeutscher in Südtirol			2281/481025-33
	Geplanter Besuch Ricci und militärische Verwendung			2281/481034-39
	Besuch Franco's in Rom Ende Januar 1941			4865/E248768-84
	Graf Ciano begibt sich an die Front, Angelegenheiten des Grafen Ciano			2281/481040-71
	Erklärung eines Luftsperrgebietes			
	Lage in den italienischen Kolonien (Abessinien)			
	Lage in Ostasien. Japan und China, Siam. Verhältnis Japans zu Deutschland			4865/E248785-90
	Beiband: Japan-Amerika			2281/482071-89 4865/E248791-844
	Verhalten der Vereinigten Staaten von Amerika und der südamerikanischen Staaten zum europäischen Krieg			4865/E248845-86
	Beiband: Schliessung der Konsulate			
	Ex-König Amman Ullah von Afghanistan			
	Innerpolitische Lage in England (Besuch Willkie)			2281/481072-84
	Ein- und Ausreise-Sichtvermerke für Clary-Aldringen, Fast Stock, Leicht, Prof.F.Clauss, Pergendorfer, Kopkow, Posse, Max Müller Daufeldt, Claus Daufeldt, Schalva, Maglakelidse, Ratynski, Mayjjas, Acsay, Fehrmann, Massow, Martens, van Veen, Friedrich Anton, Jamil Raouf, Rosetti, Arntz, Ludevici, Aliquo, Roth, Martens		Februar 1941	
	Lieferung von Kriegsmaterial an Italien			
	Italienische Schiffe im Iran (Bender Abbas)			
	Rumänische Gesandten Grigorcea und Bossi			
	Brief Pétains und Nachrichten aus Frankreich			2281/481085-93 4640/E209251-56

Akten-zeichen	Inhalt	Band	Datum	Serial Nr.
	Behandlung des Diplomatischen Korps		Februar 1941	
	Reise des Grossadmirals Raeder nach Italien			2281/481094-101
	Sendungen des Wehrbezirkskommandos Ausland Uk.-Stellungen: Friedrich			
	Entsendung des Oberleutnant Otzen als Vertreter des Militär-attachés			
	Deutsch-italienische Offiziers-kommission in Siebenbürgen und Kronstadt und Klausenburg			2281/482090-116
	Französische Schiffahrt			
	Kein Verkauf schwedischer Schiffe an Italien			
	Jugoslawische Staatsmänner in Fuschl, Stand der deutsch-jugo-slawischen Gespräche Dreimächte-pakt, Entwicklung der Lage Dreimächtepakt mit Kroatien			2281/482117-49
	Deutsche Schiffe in italieni-schen Häfen, Erz- und Bauxit-verschiffungen			
	Lage in den italienischen Kolonien, Lybien			
	Gräfin Rosi de Waldeck geb. Ullstein		März 1941	
	Südamerik.diplom.Vertreter (Mercado)			
	Bericht des Dr.Reichert, DNB			
	Lage in Tanger Spanien und der Krieg Gibraltar, Portugal, Marokko			4865/E248887-958
	Türkei/Dodekanes			2281/482151-86
	Personal des Konsulats Palermo			
	Abwehrdienst Betätigung für den S.D. durch Angehörige des Auswärtigen Amtes (Angelegenheit SS Scharführer Vincent) (auch Skalak) (Vorgänge K.K.Kappler verg.185/41 geh.) Vorgänge: Podessar, Rainer, Vlasek			
	Reise des Gauleiterstellvertr. Fr.Schmidt			
	Japanische Staatsangehörige Frau v.Wrede-Pai			
	Sonderanweisung für Handels-schiff "Marburg"			
	Reise Alfieri nach Fuschl und Berlin und Botschafterwechsel Attolico/Alfieri			

Akten-zeichen	Inhalt	Band	Datum	Serial Nr.
	Wirtschaftswerbung durch Verband der Deutschen Wirtschaft		März 1941	
	Reise Georg Wild über Rom nach Brasilien			
	Besuch des japanischen Aussen-ministers Matsuoka			2281/482187-93 4865/E248959-65
	Feindhetze betr. besetzte und angegliederte Gebiete			K1692/K405782-822
	Indische Freiheitsbewegung - Bose - Politische Lage in Indien Shedai Himalaja Sender			41/28467/1-658
	Schliessung der amerikanischen Konsulate			
	Deutsche Operationen gegen Griechenland und Waffenniederlegung			2281/482194-210 4865/E248966-79
	Deutsche Operationen gegen Jugoslawien, neue Grenzen nach der Niederwerfung			2281/482211-27 4865/E248980-9184
	Staatsoper Berlin - Vatikan und Kgl.Oper Rom in Berlin		März/April 1941	
	Auskünfte über Marchesa Ferrante - Johanna Ams			
	Strafverfahren gegen den Journalisten Heinz Leschke			
	Annahme einer englischen Anleihe durch Spanien			4865/E248640-41
	Stellung Grandis zu Deutschland			
	Rundfunkangelegenheiten Errichtung eines Senders in Agram (Rundfunk über Flug Rud.Hess nach Schottland)			2281/481103-16
	Abhörverbot der englischen Sender und anderer ausländischer Sender (auch Italien)			
	Angebliche Reden des Grafen Viola während seines Aufenthaltes in Spanien			
	Zahlungen an den OGL in Venedig Kahrs			
	Innenpolitik Ungarns Reise Bardossys nach Rom			4865/E248642-47
	Zusammenarbeit Südamerikanischer Staaten mit Nordamerika			
	Ex-Königin von Spanien Prinz Juan von Spanien			4865/E249184/1-/
	Unabhängigkeit Kroatiens Reise Graf Cianos nach Wien Neue Grenzen			2281/482229-60 4849/E247259-547
	Dreimächtepakt			4865/E249185-225

Akten-zeichen	Inhalt	Band	Datum	Serial Nr.
	Anonyme Schmähbriefe		März/April 1941	
	Auftrag für Konsul Freiherr v.Neurath			
	Handstreich auf Nizza			2281/482261-83
	Verhältnis Deutschlands zu Norwegen, Skandinavien im allgem.			2281/481117/2-40
	Fernsprechverbindungen Rom - Auswärtiges Amt			
	Lage in Japan		Mai 1941	
	Verhältnis Japans zur Sowjet-Union			4865/E249226-29
	Direkter telefonischer Verkehr innerer Ressorts			
	Äusserungen Matsuokas über Eden			152/82043-47
	Ablieferung holländischer Gulden und Depot "M"			
	Vorführung Chiffriermaschine Enigma			
	Besuch des Königs von Italien in Albanien			
	Errichtung Standortoffiziere Rom und Neapel			
	Besprechung ung.Herr Szilassy - Oberstltn.Helfferich			
	Ausweisung Reichsangehöriger Jos.Haubner			
	Reise des Gesandten Grobba nach Bagdad			2281/481141-42
	Britische Kriegsmaßnahmen auf dem Gebiet des Urheberschutz-rechtes und des Urheberrechts			
	Zahlungen an Landesgruppenleiter Dr.Butting bezw. Dr.Ehrich			
	Reichsmarkzahlungsmittel, Befehl Oberkommando des Heeres			
	Begleitung des Herrn RAM			
	Zahlung durch den Militärattaché			
	Erkrankung des Herrn Botschafters			
	Entsendung Vizekonsul Dr.Pausch nach Laibach			
	Amtsenthebung Starace Reise nach Deutschland			
	Gnadengesuch v.Salvini-Plawen			
	Bewirtschaftung der Mittel für Aufgaben der Aufklärung			
	Frau Bertha Honig geb.Finkel		Juni 1941	

Akten-zeichen	Inhalt	Band	Datum	Serial Nr.
	Auskunft über Herrn Schultze		Juni 1941	
	Rücktritt Sebastianis			
	Fräulein Thyxa Voges			
	Lage im Mittelmeer			
	Postverkehr mit Griechenland			
	Prinz Michael von Montenegro			
	Kabinettsumbildung			
	Amerikan.Vizekonsul Getzinger			
	Armenische Unabhängigkeitspartei			
	Organisation der faschistischen Miliz Galbiati			2281/482284-302
	Sozialgestaltung in Italien nach dem Krieg			
	Bilder von Rudolf Hess in Diensträumen			
	Zeitungsaustausch an Kriegsgefangene			
	Versenkung spanischer Dampfer CRESPI und ANTONIO			
	Deutsch-sowjetrussischer Krieg Freiwilligenmeldungen im Ausland (Prinz von Dorsprung,Messoyedoff) Informationsberichte des OKW			2281/482303-416
	– Sonderband			2281/482417-24
	Verschluß-Sachen-Anweisung für sämtliche Verwaltungsbehörden			
	Freies Geleit für ein niederländisches Lazarettschiff			
	Versetzung General von Bülow, Ernennung General von Pohl zum Luftattaché Komm.Oberstleutnant v.Veltheim als Gehilfe			
	Spanische Devisengenehmigung zur Übertragung von 20 Mill.Peseten an Deutsche Botschaft in Madrid			
	Deutsches Propagandazentrum in Libyen		Juli 1941	
	Reden und Schriften Mussolinis			2281/482426-33
	Stellung deutscher Heeresdienststellen zu den Militärattachés			2281/482434-36
	Höhe der italienischen Diplomatenbezüge und Besoldung des Auswärtigen Dienstes			
	Tschechische Legion in Frankreich			2281/481143-46

Akten-zeichen	Inhalt	Band	Datum	Serial Nr.
	Ein- und Ausreise-Sichtvermerke: Adalbert Bieleck, Lorenz Karbus, Johann Christ (Hr.Hofmann), Canzani Lamonato		Juli 1941	
	Unruhen in Montenegro und Serbien Unruhen in Kroatien, Dalmatien			2281/482437-48 4865/E249230-60
	Aufdeckung einer Verschwörung gegen die faschistische Regierung			
	Besuch Tuka in Rom und Angelegenheit Galvanek			4865/E249261-319
	Zuteilung Dr.Kirschbaum			
	Irakische Offiziere als Gäste der italienischen Regierung			K1694/K405858-78
	Tagung der Kulturreferenten und Dienstantritt Oberbannführer Wilke bei der Kultur-Abteilung			
	Besetzung der bulgarischen Grube Jessarina durch Italien		August 1941	
	Diapositive zur Weitersendung nach Buenos Aires			
	Afghanistan			4865/E249320-27
	Zuständigkeitsgrundsätze für das Auswärtige Amt und Promi (anläßlich des Besuches Pavolinis bei Reichsminister Dr.Goebbels) (auch Besuch Farinacci in Berlin) Fotokopie Arbeitsabkommen Auswärtiges Amt/Promi			2281/482449-79
	Sonderkurier, Reisen des Herrn Botschafters			2281/481147-49
	Lage und Stimmung in den italienisch gewordenen Teilen Dalmatiens			
	Bericht Dr.Lodygensky über den russischen Krieg			
	Lit 15.000,-- für Verbreitung von Propagandamaterial			
	Duce Reise, Liste der Begleitung			
	Vernichtung von Geheimmaterial			
	Generalkonsul Dr.Mayr, Genua			
	Anti-Nationalsozialisten und rechtsfeindliche Strömungen in Italien			
	Schwierigkeiten mit italienischen Arbeitern in Deutschland			2281/482480-553 4865/E249328-48
	Beschlagnahme deutschen Kuriergepäcks durch Argentinien, Abtransport des Funkgerätes durch die Lati			

Akten-zeichen	Inhalt	Band	Datum	Serial Nr.
	Umsiedlung Südtirol (auch frühere Vorgänge)		August 1941	2281/482555-95 4865/E249349-699
	Italienische Rotekreuzschwester M.Bogner			
	Angelegenheiten des Funkbeauftragten Bawart		September 1941	
	Weiterleitung von Briefen			
	Zuteilung des Gesandtschaftsrat Hofmann an die Botschaft und Personalbesetzung der Kulturabteilung der Botschaft			
	Verhaftung des japanischen Honorarkonsuls Schnabel			
	Deutsche Einkäufe in Italien und Verhalten Deutscher in Italien			
	Unterredung des amerikanischen Botschafters beim Papst und Äusserungen Serena über den Vatikan			2281/481151-93
	Untergang der deutschen Dampfer FREIENFELS und GEIERFELS			
	Beurteilung der Handelsattachés			4865/E249700-34
	Antrag der Fürstin Radziwill zur Reise ihrer Tochter Fürstin Th. Lubomirska Warschau-Rom			
	Einsatz deutscher und italienischer Schiffe als Blockadebrecher			
	Angelegenheiten des Generalkonsuls v.Druffel			
	Zahlungen für Minister Schröder an v.Reichert			
	Reise einer italienischen Abordnung in die Steiermark Deutschfeindliches Verhalten in der Provinz Laibach, Bandenunwesen			
	Zahlungen an Angehörige von Seeleuten der von uns besetzten Länder			
	Austausch italienischer und amerikanischer Stattsangehöriger			
	Italien und der Vatikan			
	Verlängerung des Antikominternpaktes			2281/482596-646
	Freigabe eines von Oberst Busch hinterlegten Betrages		Oktober/ November 1941	
	Besuch des Gauleiters Bohle in Rom Oktober 1941			
	Besatzung des versenkten Dampfers ASKARI			

Akten-zeichen	Inhalt	Band	Datum	Serial Nr.
	Neuregelung des europäischen Luftverkehrs		Oktober/ November 1941	2281/481194-211
	Erkundigungen über Elsa Küchenmeister			
	Italienischer Schiffskode			4865/E248648-49
	Wachewechsel in den italienisch-fasc.Berufsverbänden			
	Aufzeichnung Capomazza über seine Deutschlandreise			2281/481212-36
	Angelegenheiten Grossmufti			2281/482647-701
	Herstellung und Versand DAF Feldpostdienst			
	Verhaftung des tschechischen Diplomaten Masaryk, Prag			2281/481237-45
	Eindrücke des Grafen Ciano über Deutschlandbesuch			4865/E249735-47
	Einrichtung eines Wehrwirtschaftsoffiziers in Rom und Zusammenarbeit mit den Dienststellen der Wehrmacht			
	Sachbearbeiter für koloniale Angelegenheiten in Rom			2281/482702-42
	Anmusterung griechischer Seeleute, die im feindlichen Nachrichtendienst stehen			
	Kautionsliste für Grundstück Via San Giovanni			
	Ernennung Polizeikommissars Kappler zum Polizeiattaché			
	Ernennung Anfusos zum italienischen Gesandten in Budapest			4865/E248650-59
	Reichsangehöriger Fr.Czerwenka			
	Lage im Mitrowizagebiet			4865/E249748-809
	Zahlungen an Herrn Laube			
	Rumänisch-ungarische Spannungen			
	Ersetzung des Generals Pricolo durch General Fougier			
	Dolmetscher für das Afrikakorps			
	Zuständigkeit der A.O. der NSDAP		November/ Dezember 1941	2281/482743-49
	Beauftragung deutscher innerer Stellen in Italien			
	Krieg Japan-England-USA-Südamerika			2281/482750-99 4865/E249810-24
	Schrift des Vittorio Calestani			
	Kriegsverdienstkreuz(Dr.Mollier)			

Akten-zeichen	Inhalt	Band	Datum	Serial Nr.
	Behandlung amerikanischer Gefan-gener in Libyen, Überführung des amerikanischen Journalisten Harold Denny nach Deutschland		November/Dezember 1941	2281/481246-66
	Leutnant a.D.Joachim v.Reichl Gen.v.Kürenberg			
	Geheime Pressetelegramme			2281/481267-77
	Stenotypistin Charlotte Thurian			
	Zahlung Aufwandsentschädigung an Gesandtschaftsrat Hofmann			
	Ehemaliger Fremdenlegionär Hans Wieg			
	Britischer Jude Morpurgo und Fa.Stock			
	Enthebung Serenas, Vidussoni:Par-teisekretär. Auseinandersetzung G.K.Müller und Ortsgruppenleiter in Meran			4865/E249825-31
	Reise des Dipl.Ing.Morgenstern im Auftrag des OKM			
	Italienischer Handelsrat in Berlin			
	Pflicht der Behördenmitglieder am Leben der Partei teilzunehmen			
	Urschrift des Abkommens über die gütliche Erledigung vor dem Deutsch-Italienischen Gemischten Schiedsgericht schwebender Ent-schädigungsklagen vom 20.Aug.24			
	Lose Vorgänge zum Botschafts-einbruch in Rom aus dem Jahre 1923 und 1926			
	Sammlung des Herrn Botschafters v.Hassell von Berichten über die Lage in Italien (Ende 1932 und später)			8038/E578134-63 K1047/K268873-951
	Privater Briefwechsel des Herrn Botschafters v.Hassell (Sekreta) 1932-1933			8038/E578164-215 K678/K172208-36
	Mobilmachungsangelegenheiten Allgemeine Anweisungen		1938-39	
	- UK.Stellungen		1939-40	
Mil.Nr.2	- Wehrpflicht	1	6.35- 9.38	
D.Pol 7	Wehrmachts- und Arbeitsdienst-angelegenheiten, Generelles	1	9.38-12.40	
	- Beihefte		9.38-12.40	
Spi.1-2	Spionage, Agenten	1	12.39- 6.40	2281/481278-82 3090/D625993-6003
	-	2	6.40-12.41	

Akten-zeichen	Inhalt	Band	Datum	Serial Nr.
Pol 1	Italien - Aussenpolitik	1	1.42-12.42	4924/E257257-79 5590/E401167-69
Pol 1 Nr. 1	Italienische Kriegführung (auch deutscher Einsatz)	1	1.42- 5.43	4924/E257280-524 5589/E401163-65
Pol 3	Italien - Innenpolitik (auch faschistische Parteiorgani- sation, auch Judenfragen)	1	1.42-12.42	4924/E257525-786
		2	1.43- 5.43	4924/E257787- 8013
Pol 3 Nr.8a	Italienisch-Ostafrika	1	1.42- 3.42	4925/E258016
Pol 3 Nr.8b	Libyen	1	1.42- 2.43	4925/E258017
Pol 3 Nr.8c	Südtirol	1	1.42-12.42	4925/E258018-97
Pol 3 Nr.8d	Albanien	1	1.42-12.42	4925/E258098 5255/E314837-52
		2	1.43- 5.43	4925/E258099 6181/E464392-455
Pol 3 Nr.8e,8f	Provinz Laibach, Dalmatien und Grenzgebiete	1	1.42- 5.43	4925/E258100 5670/E411427-34
Pol 3 Nr.10	Stimmungsberichte über die Lage in Italien, Berichte der Konsu- late und anderer Stellen	1	1.42-12.42	4925/E258101-27
	-	2	1.43- 5.43	4925/E258128
D Pol 1 Nr. 2	Deutsche Wehrmacht in Italien	1	1.42- 5.43	
D Pol 1 Nr. 2a	Abkommen zwischen dem Deutschen Reich und dem Königreich Italien auf dem Gebiet der Strafgerichts- barkeit bei einem Einsatz von Teilen der Wehrmacht	1	1.42-12.42	
D Pol 1 Nr. 3	Abwehrdienst	1	1.42-12.42	
D.Pol 1 Nr. 3 Sdbd. 1	- Schwendt und Blaschke	1	1.42-12.42	
D Pol 2 IIa	Krieg Englands (Alliierten) gegen die Achsenmächte(auch "Zweite Front")	1	1.42- 5.43	5439/E364430-44 6091/E451717-39
D Pol 2 IIb	Frankreich und französische Ko- lonien (auch italienisch-franzö- sische Beziehungen)	1	1.42-10.42	4639/E209047-233 5701/E413800-15
	-	2	11.42- 4.43	6444/E481888-912
D Pol 2 IIc	Tunis (auch arabische Bewegung)	1	11.42-12.42	5580/E400795-1010
		2	1.43- 5.43	6445/E481914-74 7230/E530538-40
D Pol 2 III	Spanien - Portugal	1	1.42-12.42	688/259276-630
		2	1.43- 5.43	719/263972-4194
D Pol 2 IIIa	Vatikan	1	1.42- 5.43	824/279868- 80046

Akten-zeichen	Inhalt	Band	Datum	Serial Nr.
D Pol 2 IV a	Ungarn	1	1.42- 5.43	4926/E258131-277
D Pol 2 IV b	Rumänien	1	1.42- 5.43	4926/E258278-362
D Pol 2 IV c	Deutsch-italienische Offiziers-kommission in Siebenbürgen und ungarisch-rumänische Beziehungen	1	1.42-12.42	4926/E258363 5258/E315656-702
		2	1.43- 5.43	4926/E258364 6961/E518952-9065
D Pol 2 IV d	Kroatien(und restliche ehemalige jugoslawische Gebiete) Bulgarien Slowakei	1	1.42- 6.42	4927/E258367-711
		2	7.42- 9.42	4927/E258712-9250
		3	10.42- 2.43	4927/E259251-634
D Pol 2 IV e	Griechenland	1	1.42- 5.43	4927/E259635-912
D Pol 2 IV f	Grenzfragen auf dem Balkan	1	8.42-12.42	4927/E259913-60096
D Pol 2 V a	Kriegführung Sowjetrusslands gegen die Achsenmächte	1	1.42- 5.43	4928/E260099-286
D Pol 2 V c	Russische Emigranten	1	1.42- 4.43	4928/E260287-398
D Pol 2 V d	Kriegsführung Sowjetrusslands gegen die Achsenmächte (Infor-mationsmaterial)	1	1.42-12.42	4928/E260399
D Pol 2 VI	Skandinavische Länder Dänemark, Schweden, Norwegen, Island, Finnland	1	1.42- 5.43	4928/E260400-56
D Pol 2 VII a	Arabische Länder, Arabien, Ceylon Cypern, Palestina, Syrien	1	1.42- 1.43	4929/E260459-557
D Pol 2 VII b	Arabien Unabhängigkeitsbewegung (Grossmufti-Gailani)	1	1.42- 4.42	4929/E260558-973
		2	4.42-12.42	4929/E260974-1356
D Pol 2 VII c	Türkei	1	1.42- 5.43	4929/E261357-597
D Pol 2 VII d	Ägypten	1	1.42-12.42	4929/E261598-793
D Pol 2 VII e	Indien	1	1.42- 6.42	4930/E261796-2038
		2	7.42-12.42	4930/E262039-311
		3	1.43- 5.43	4930/E262312-95
D Pol 2 VII e Sdbd. 1	Indische Legion in Deutschland und arabische Legion in Italien	1	1.42-12.42	86/62799-897 4930/E262395/1
Sdbd. 2	Indien, Berichte vom "Sonder-referat Indien"	1	1.42-12.42	4930/E262396
D Pol 2 VII f	Japanische Indienpropaganda (bezw.Indienpropaganda der Dreierpaktmächte)	1	1.42-12.42	978/303467-523 4930/E262397

Akten-zeichen	Inhalt	Band	Datum	Serial Nr.
D Pol 2 VII g	Afghanistan	1	1.42- 5.43	86/62899-975 4930/E262398
D Pol 2 VIII a	Japan, China, Mandschukuo	1	1.42- 5.43	166/131935/1-48 4931/E262401 5521/E383933-61 6552/E489441-44
D Pol 2 IX	Amerika: Vereinigte Staaten, Kanada, Mittel- und Südamerika	1	1.42- 7.42	4931/E262402-653
		2	8.42- 1.43	4931/E262654-854
D Pol 2 IX a	Kriegführung Amerikas gegen die Dreierpaktmächte	1	1.42-12.42	4931/E262855-923
Prot 1	Zeremonielles	1	1.42- 5.43	4932/E262926- 3009
Prot 2a	Italienisches diplomatisches Korps	1	1.42- 6.43	4932/E263010-117
Prot 2b	Ausländisches diplomatisches Korps	1	1.42- 6.43	4932/E263118
Prot 3	Orden	1	1.42- 5.43	4932/E263119-63
Prot 5	Besuche hoher Persönlichkeiten	1	1.42-12.42	4932/E263164-320
		2	1.43- 7.43	4932/E263321-449
R 4	Italienische Arbeiter in Deutschland	1	1.42-12.42	4933/E263452-88
D R 5	Passangelegenheiten	1	1.42-12.42	4933/E263489
D R 5 Nr. 1	Sichtvermerke an Angehörige deutscher Fürstenhäuser und des Hochadels	1	1.42- 5.43	4933/E263490-628
D R 7 Nr. 1	Warngebiete für die Seekrieg-führung	1	1.42- 6.42	4933/E263629-757
D R 7 Nr. 2	Lazarettschiff für Malta	1	5.42- 7.42	4933/E263758-830
Kult 2	Ankauf von Kunstwerken in Italien	1	1.42-12.42	4934/E263833
	Presse-Angelegenheiten (auch Propaganda)	1	1.42-12.42	4934/E263834
W	Wirtschaftsangelegenheiten	1	1.42- 5.43	4934/E263835-74
W Sch.	Heimschaffung deutscher See-leute des Dampfers "Prometheus" Sonderband 1	1	1.42-10.42	4934/E263875
R 3 Nr.3	Inag-Streitfall Direktor Kapferer Sonderband 1	1	1.42- 5.42	4934/E263876
R 3 Nr.6	Strafrecht, Auslieferungen, Verhaftungen	1	1.42-12.42	4934/E263877
	Fall Harbeck Sonderband 1	1	2.42- 3.42	4934/E263878
	Fall Obmann-Urbanek Sonderband 2	1	4.42- 6.42	4934/E263879
	Fall Dr.V.von Somogyi Sonderband 3	1	10.41- 5.42	4934/E263880

Akten-zeichen	Inhalt	Band	Datum	Serial Nr.
R 3.Nr.6	Fall Lt.Pederiva Sonderband 4	1	4.42- 1.43	4934/E263881
	Geheim-Tagebuch (Journal) der Deutschen Botschaft, Rom (Quir.)			
	Nr.I		1.20-12.36	
	Nr.II		1.37- 5.40	
	Nr.III		5.40-12.41	

Akten-zeichen	Inhalt	Band	Datum	Serial Nr.
8	Preussen. Berichterstattungs-pflicht	1	1920-29	
8 Nuntius	Preussen und der Apostlische Gesandte (Nuntius) in Berlin und der deutsche Botschafter in Rom (Beglaubigung des deutschen Bot-schafters zum Preussischen Gesandten)	1	1924-29	
8 Becker	Schriftwechsel mit Minister Becker	1	1927-30	
8	Schriftwechsel mit Ministerial-dirigenten von Bülow, Vortrag Legationsrat Meyer-Rodehüser und Gesandtschaftsrat Klee	1	1928-31	
	Briefwechsel mit Ministerial-direktor Tendelenburg und Staats-sekretär Weismann	1	1928-32	
8 Pr.Ges.	Aufhebung des Preussischen Gesandtenpostens	1	1934	
8 Kano	Besetzung von Kanonikaten	1	11.30-12.31	
	- Switalski, Frauenburg	2	12.32- 2.33	
	-	3	1.33-10.33	
8 a	Preussische Kirchenangelegen-heiten	1	4.22- 7.39	
8 b	Militärseelsorge	1-5	1920-42	
9 Schuld am Kriege	Schuldfrage	1-5	1920-37	
9	Parlamentarischer Untersuchungs-ausschuss	1	1919-23	4057/E066326_405
	Sicherheitspakt, Konferenz Locarno	1	1925-26	
	Schiedsgerichte, Gem.Schiedshöfe	1	1922	
	Deutschland und Völkerbund	1-4	1922-32	
	Völkerbund, internationales Komitee für Hygiene, Sterilisa-tion	1	1932-33	
	Ständisches Büro in Genf (Union Catholique d'Etudes Interna-tionale)	1	1927	
9 All.	Deutschland, Allgemeines	1-5	1920-33	
9 All.Nat	- Nationalistische Strömun-gen, Ludendorff, Hitlerprozess und Ähnliches	1	1923-31	
9 Kr.Verb	Kriegsverbrecher	1-2	1920-22	
9 Schw. Trup.	Schwarze Truppen	1-2	1920-25	
9 Rotes Kr.	Rotes Kreuz, Sammelakten		1922-31	
9 Kr.Gef.	Kriegsgefangene		1920-22	

Akten-zeichen	Inhalt	Band	Datum	Serial Nr.
9 Bes.Ko.	Besatzungskosten		1920-24	
9	Kinderelend, Papstspenden, Ernährung, Gesundheitszustand, Notstand in Deutschland	1	1919-23	
	Notleidende Wissenschaft. Kinder-elend, Papstspenden, Ernährung, Gesundheitszustand, Notstand in Deutschland	2	1923-27	
	Ablieferung von Milchkühen	1	1920	
	Deutsches Eigentum, Bund der Auslandsdeutschen, Auslands-deutsche im allgemeinen, Verband reichsdeutscher Vereine im Ausland	1	1921-28	
		2	1932-37	
	Deutsch-österreichische Wirt-schaftsvereinbarung	1	1931-32	
	Nachrichten (Meyer-Rodehüser, Zech, v.Bülow)	1	1927-28	
9 Rep.	Reparationsproblem, London Ultimatum	1-2 3 4-7	1921-23	L1594/L486691-98
	- Ruhrepisode	8-13	1923	
	Reparationen ab 4.VI.1923	14	1923	
	- (26.Juni 1923 Papstbrief)	15	1923	
	-	16	1923	
	- Krupp. Vermittlung der Kurie	17a	1923-24	
	Vermittlung der Kurie in Straf-verfahren	17b	1923-24	
	Reparationen. Rechtsgutachten	18a	1923	
	Reparationen	18b	1923	
9 Rep. Spez.	Vermittlung der Kurie in Straf-sachen - Deportationsfrage	19a	1923	
	Freilassung deutscher Gefangener (Rapport Rintelen) Belgien	19b	1923-24	
	Reparationen, Ruhr	20 -25	1923-32	
9 S.G.	Saargebiet	1-7 8 9-17	1919-37	M165/005365-75
	- Rémond und Schulen	18	1921-24	
9 EM.	Eupen-Malmedy	1-7	1919-32	
	- Hirtenbriefe belgischer Bischöfe			
	Haltung des Bischofs von Lüttich. Kaplan Gilles	8	1932-40	
9 O.P.	Abstimmungsgebiet Ost- und West-preussen	1-2	1919-30	

Akten-zeichen	Inhalt	Band	Datum	Serial Nr.
9 Memel	Memel	1	1922-40	
9 O.S.	Gleiwitz	1	1926	
	Oberschlesien	1	1921-25	
9	Minderheiten, Oberschlesien	1	1931-32	
Versch.	Verschiedene Akten über Ober-schlesien	1	1921-23	

9 NSDAP	NSDAP
	I. Ortsgruppe Rom
	II. S.A. Rom
	III. Besuchsweise Anwesenheit
	   von Parteigenossen, Künst-
	   lern
		1	1931-42	

9 NSDAP Beamte	Zugehörigkeit und Verhalten des Botschaftspersonals zur NSDAP und zur Ortsgruppe Rom	1	1933-39	
9 Prop. Material	Propagandamaterial auch des Reichsministeriums für Volks-aufklärung	1	1933-41	
9 RK	Besuche April 1933	1	1933-43	
9 Führer	Adolf Hitler	1	1934-43	
9	Viererpakt	1	1933	
	30. Juni 1934 und damit Zusam-menhängendes	1	6.34- 7.35	8754/E610803-08
	Neuaufbau des Reiches	1	1934-37	
	Reichsparteitag Nürnberg 1935	1	1935-39	
	Allgemeine Wehrpflicht (Wehrmacht), Arbeitsdienst	3	1938-43	
	Deutschland Drittes Reich	9-10	1936-43	
	Deutschen Jugend im Dritten Reich	1-3	1933-42	
	Rassengesetzgebung und Ähnliches, Neuheidentum, Christentum	1-3	1933-43	
	Sterilisation	1	1933-41	
9 B.B.	Berufsbeamtentum	1	1933-42	
9	Finanz- und Wirtschaftsangelegen-heiten	1	1936-43	
	Universitätsangelegenheiten	1	1934-42	
	Rosenberg, Bergmann, Schmidtke	1	1934-42	
	Hitler-Jugend Rom (Villa Bona-parte) und Hitler-Jugend zu Besuch in Rom	1	1934-41	
	Hetze gegen Deutschland durch Schrift, Film	1-5	1924-43	
	Deutschland, Drittes Reich, Krieg	1-5	1939-43	
	Neuordnung Europas	1-2	1940-43	

Akten-zeichen	Inhalt	Band	Datum	Serial Nr.
9	Bolschewismus und Kommunismus	1-2	1936-43	
	Festlegung des Osterfestes, gemeinsamer Kalender	1-2	1900-28	
	Acta Apostolicae Sedis. Inhaltsangabe	1	1927-36	
9 Ifa	Religionsverspottung - Ifa- Ausstellung und Aähnliches	1	1930-36	
9 Um-wandl.	Umwandlung der Preussischen Gesandtschaft beim Päpstlichen Stuhl in eine Deutsche Botschaft. Pacelli Apostolische Nuntiatur in Berlin	1	1919-42	
9	Spannung zwischen der deutschen Regierung und der Kurie wegen der Rede des Kardinals Mundelein - Chicago	1	1937	
	Absetzung von Geistlichen	1-2	1920-32	
9 Uk.	Uditore der S.R.R. Konsultor	1	1920-33	
9	Schulwesen in Deutschland und deutsche Schulen im Ausland	1	1917-34	
	Professor Kehr	1	1922-36	
	Deutsche Geistliche in Rom. Schwaighofer	1	1919-23	
	Katholikentage	1	1920-25	
	Thoiry	1	1926	
	Posen und Posen-Gnesen	1-2	1919-23	
	Kanonisationen	1-2	1921-43	
	Prozesse und Verurteilungen von Ordensleuten wegen Devisen-schiebungen	1-3	1935-37	
	Minderheiten	1	1931-35	
	Katholische Belange im Dritten Reich	1-4	1933-43	
	Überwachungen im Inland, Verurteilungen von Geistlichen und Ähnliches, Verfahren gegen H.J.Führer, Demonstrationen	1-8	1933-43	
	Beiheft zu Band 8	1	1937	
	Hirtenbrief des Deutschen Episkopats vom 7.Juni 1934	1	1934-43	
	Anfragen des Pax-Vereins katholischer Priester Deutsch-lands	1	1931-35	
	Eidesleistung deutscher Bischöfe und Bischofswahlen im Dritten Reich	1	1933-36	
9 a	Kirchliche Angelegenheiten des Dritten Reiches und des Kirchen-ministeriums	1	1934-40	

Akten-zeichen	Inhalt	Band	Datum	Serial Nr.
9	Pilgerzüge und katholische Studienfahrten	1-2	1920-39	
	Missionen	1-2	1919-43	
	Frontkämpfer - Pilgerfahrt nach Rom	1	1935	
	Diözese Oppeln	1	1930-32	
	Gumprecht, Klinke, Steuer, Paech, Sedak (Stankowski, Krug), Kunze	1-3	1921-41	
	Russische Emigranten und deren Seelsorge	1	1923-39	
	Pastorisierung. Polen-Deutschland, Deutschland-Polen	1	1927-30	
	Katholikentage und Tagung ähnlicher katholischer Verbände	2	1926-34	
	Katholische Aktion in Deutschland und anderen Ländern	1	1927-40	
	Protestanten in Italien	1	1926-35	
	Preussen, Konkordat	1-3	1920-42	
	Konkordat	1-5	1920-28	
	Reichskonkordat	1		8125/E581642-91
		2		8125/E581692-719
		3		8125/E581720-45
		4	1933-34	8125/E581746-60
		5		8125/E581761-95
		6		8125/E581796-857
		7		8125/E581858-914
		8		8125/E581915-51 M132/M004893-963
		9		8125/E581952-55
		10	1934-36	8125/E581956-87
		11		8125/E581988-93
		12		7048/E523145-239
		13		8125/E581994-2003
		14		7048/E523240-75
		15	1936-43	7048/E523276-92
		16		
	Frühere Reichskonkordatentwürfe	1	1921-25	
	Zeitungsartikel Konkordat ab Januar 1927	1	1927-29	
	Deutsche und schweizer Zeitungsartikel (Juni-Juli 1933/34)	1	1933-34	
	Italienische Zeitungsausschnitte zum Reichskonkordat 1933/34	1	1933-34	
	Französische und spanische Zeitungsausschnitte 1933-34	1	1933-34	
	Erlass des Auswärtigen Amtes über Berlin an die Missionen (?)	1	1933	
	Fürstbistum Breslau	1-4	1919-27	

Akten-zeichen	Inhalt	Band	Datum	Serial Nr.
14	Bistum Fulda	1	1932-36	
	– Hildesheim	1	1929-34	
	– Limburg	1	1925-38	
	– Mainz	1	1920-35	
	– Meissen	1	1921-38	
	– Osnabrück	1	1921-35	
	Danzig	1-4	1920-35	
	Konkordat	1	1933-35	
	Kalthof	1	1931-34	
17	Franziskanerkirche in Posen	1	1921-29	
	Jesuitenkirche in Bromberg	1	1930-36	
	Bischof von Kattowitz, Schlesischer Bischof, Bistum Schlesien	1	1930-37	
	Breslau Güter, Kattowitz	1	1932-37	
	Polen	1-15	1920-40	
	Korridor	1	1927-39	
	Minoritätenschutz, Minderheiten aller Länder	1-5	1922-36	
	– , Einzelfälle	1	1922-31	
	Sauermann	1	1924-27	
	Minoritätenschutz, Einzelfälle:			
	– Betsche	1	1923-29	
	– Bielitz	1	1926-30	
	– Buschmann in Bielschowitz	1	1928-30	
	P.Kempf und Nachfolger (Breitinger)	1	1934	
	Polnische Terrorakte bei Wahlen	1	1930	
	Angriffe, Ausfälle und Ähnliches polnischer Geistlicher gegen Deutschland	1	1929-39	
	– Dr.Bromboscz	1	1935-37	
	Polnisches Konkordat, Bistum Schlesien, Schriftwechsel	1-4	1926-39	
	Doppel zum Polnischen Konkordat	Bdl.	1925	
18	Bischofswahlen und Weihbischöfe in Preussen und sonst in Deutschland	1	1919-33	
19	Bayern	1	1919-36	
	Konkordat Bayern	1	1920-39	
	Separatisten	1	1920-24	
	Traunstein (Ersatz)	1	1934	
	Aufhebung 1)der Bayerischen Gesandtschaft Rom 2)der Apostolischen Nuntiatur München	1	1934-38	

Akten-zeichen	Inhalt	Band	Datum	Serial Nr.

19	Aufhebung
	3) Kardinal Faulhaber, Legat,
	                   Delegat,
	4) Französische Gesandtschaft,
	    München
		1	1934-38	

20	Württemberg	1	1922-38	
21	Baden Konkordat	1	1931-38	
22	Zentrum	1	1927-34	
25	Sandwich-Inseln	1	1921-23	
28	Eidesformel der Päpste	1	1926	
28^1	Conclave 1922, + Benedikt XV.	5	1922	
28^3	Gratulationen für Benedikt XV.	2	1915-21	
	Erkrankung und Tod Benedikts XV.	3	1922-29	
	Benedikt XV.		1920-21	
28^3 Spez.	Audienzen bei S.Heiligkeit Benedikt XV.	Sbd.	1920-21	
28^4	Pius XI.	1-4	1922-42	
	Weihnachtsansprache Pius XI. an die Kardinäle	1-2	1930-39	
	Goldenes Priesterjubiläum	1-2	1927-31	
	Ausfahrten aus dem Stato della Città del Vaticano	1	1931-35	
	Verhältnis Pius XI. und Kirchen- fürsten zu Künstlern	1	1932-35	
28^4 Spez.	Pius XI. Audienzen, Äusserungen, Ansprachen, Briefe	1-4	1922-40	
	Pius XI. Krankheit und Tod	1	1936-39	
	- Gratulationen	1	1922-41	
	-	1	1936	
28^5	Pius X. Beatifikation	1	1921-39	
29	+ Benedikt XV.1922. Kardinals- kolleg bis Konklave	2	1922	
	Kardinal Gasparri und Tod	1	1922-35	
	Kardinalskolleg, Konsistorien, Kardinals-Charakteristik	1-4	1919-35	
	Ehrle	1	1924-35	
	Konsistorium, Frage der Birett- Aufsetzung	1	1929-33	
	Römischer Nationalismus, Inter- nationalisierung der Kurie	1	1928-35	
	Konklavebestimmungen, Kondulationen bei Ableben der Päpste	1	1922-37	
	Kardinal Pacelli	1-2	1929-38	

Akten-zeichen	Inhalt	Band	Datum	Serial Nr.
29	Polnisches Informationsbüro im Vatikan (Staatssekretariat)	1	1940	
30 Allg.	Verschiedene Angelegenheiten der Kurie	1-5	1921-32	
	Encyclica	1-2	1924-36	
	Casti connubii vom 31.12.30	1	1931-35	
	Littera Encyclica, "Morialium animos"	1	1928	
	Encyclica "Summi Pontificatus"	1	1939-42	
30 c	Encyclica: "Caritate Christi" vom 3.5.1932. "Dilectissima nobis" vom 3.6.1933	1	1932-33	
30	Encyclica "Rerum Novarum" und Encyclica "Quadragesimo anno"	1	1919-41	
	- "Ubi arcano Dei"	1	1922-23	
	Azione Cattolica	1-6	1925-43	
	Jubeljahr 1925	1-3	1924-28	
	Anno Santo extra ordinem 1929	1	1929-30	
	Anno Santo	1	1933-35	
	Centenario Aloisiano, Centenario des Hl.Stanislaus Kostka	1	1926-27	
	Tod des Pilgers Leonhard Werden	1	1925	
	Material für Bericht über das erste Halbjahr des Anno Santo 1933-1934	1	1933	
	700 Jahrfeier des Todestages des Hl.Antonius von Padua	1	1930-32	
	Hl.Franziskus von Assisi	1	1925-28	
	Jubelfeier des Konzils von Ephesus	1	1931	
	Missionswerk zur Verbreitung des Glaubens und Propaganda Fide	1-3	1920-42	
	Missionsausstellung Rom 1925	1-2	1923-27	
	Präparate (Missionsausstellung)	1	1926-27	
	Geldangelegenheiten der Missions-ausstellung	1	1924-25	
	Vulgata	1	1926-34	
	Zentralausschuss für Pilgerfahr-ten nach Rom. Peregrinatio romano ad Petri Sedem	1	1935-38	
	Opera Cardinal Ferrari. Opera Bonomelli	1	1925-31	
	- Pontificia S.Pietro Aposto-lo. Einheim.Klerus	1	1926-35	
	- Pia Tedesca. Deutsche fromme Stiftung in Loreto	1	1938-40	

Akten-zeichen	Inhalt	Band	Datum	Serial Nr.
30	Ritenkongregation. Kongregation der Orientalischen Kirche. Kongregation der Propaganda Fide	1	1929-40	
	Stellungnahme des Vatikans zur katholischen Gesellschaftslehre und damit zusammenhängende Fragen	1	1925-33	
	Päpstliche Institute, Kommission und katholische, wissenschaftliche Verbände	1-3	1921-43	
30 c	Katholische und internationale Vereine, Kongresse und Ähnliches	1-2	1920-26	
	Religiöse, kirchliche und Missionskongresse, Konferenzen und Vereinigungen	1	1926-43	
	Eucharistische Kongresse	2	1931-43	
	Nationalsozialistische Kongresse	1	1935-39	
	Politische Kongresse und Verbände	1	1926-37	
30	Rota	1	1929-43	
	Konzile	1	1923-42	
	Pax Romana	1	1921-43	
	Ordenskongregationen in Rom, in Italien und Ähnliches	1	1922-43	
	Kirchenmusik, Kirchengesang und damit Zusammenhängendes	1	1933-42	
30 P.Do.	Veröffentlichung päpstlicher Dokumente in Friedensvermittlungsfragen	1 2	1917-28	4057/E066407-605 4057/E066607-749
30	Amerika Vermittlung - Pressestimmen	1	1921	
	Vermittlung Amerika	1	1921	K2185/K603165-82
	- Kongress Washington	2	1921-23	
	Papst und Völkerbund	1	1929-36	
30 Vat.	Schiedsrichteramt des Papstes. Eintreten für Abrüstung und Frieden	1	1930-38	
	Stato della Città del Vaticano. (innerpolitisches und politisches, Allgemeines)	1-3	1929-36	
30 b	Parteien in Italien, katholische und internationale Vereine	1-6	1919-28	
30 C.N.	Centro Nazionale	1	1924-30	
	Politische Übersichten über die Tätigkeit des Hl.Stuhles	1	1928-43	
	Verträge: Vatikan, Italien	1	1929-41	
	Besuch fremder Staatsoberhäupter beim Papst; und Staatsmänner	1-2	1919-40	

Akten-zeichen	Inhalt	Band	Datum	Serial Nr.
30	Protokolle für die Fürsten-besuche bei S.Heiligkeit	1	1928-30	
	Erzberger			
	Papst und Hospitalisierung			
30 Vat.E.	Kunst und Wissenschaft in der Vatikanstadt. Pontificia Accademia delle Scienze	4-5	1933-43	
30	Wissenschaftliche und verwandte Verbände, Kongresse, Tagungen (auch Freimaurerkongresse)	1	1926-42	
	Päpstliches archäologisches Institut	1	1926-41	
	Italienische Weltausstellung 1942	1	1938-40	
	Rundfunk. Katholischer Radio-Pressedienst	1	1929-40	
	Vatikansender und sonstige Radiomeldungen	2	1940-43	
	Film	2	1937-43	
	Artikel des "Osservatore Romano"	10-12	1937-43	
	- des"Avvenire d'Italia"	3	1935-42	
	- " Regime Fascista"	1	1939-42	
	- aus italienischen katholi-lischen Blättern	1	1933-43	
	Katholische Presse und Bücher	1	1929-42	
30 c	Pressekongresse	1	1929-42	
30	Vatikanische Zeitungen und Verkehr mit den fremden Journa-listen	1	1929-42	
	Flugwesen auch für Missions-zwecke	1	1929-38	
	Vatikan und Arbeiter, Arbeitszeit	1	1932-33	
	Eisenbahn	1	1929-35	
	Wünsche und Beschwerden des Vatikans	1	1934-36	
	Geldverhältnisse des Vatikans (Gehälter, Zahlungen, Münzen, Medaillen)	1	1925-42	
	Ein- und Ausfuhr von Kunstgegen-ständen bei Umzug der Diplomaten	1	1930-38	
	Kaufmännische Angebote und Anfragen aller Art wegen Lie-ferungen an die Vatikanstadt oder Kirchen in Italien und Rom	1	1931-42	
	Verordnungen der Vatikanstadt	1	1929-30	
	Kirchliche Gesetzgebung und Verordnungen	1	1925-41	

Akten-zeichen	Inhalt	Band	Datum	Serial Nr.
30	Allgemeine, nichtpolitische Angelegenheiten	1	1929-43	
	Ehe, Eheschliessungen	1	1929-34	
	Ehe, Ehescheidungen, Reichs-gesetz über Ehescheidungen	2	1935-42	
	Attentate, Straftaten, Prozesse	1	1929-42	
	Vatikan und Jugenderziehung	1	1926-43	
	Jüdische Fragen, Judenmission	1	1926-40	K1685/K405625-700
31	Päpstlicher Hofstaat und Diplomatie, Marchetti, Maglione, Cerretti	1-4	1916-29	
	Vatikanisches, diplomatisches Corps, Delegaten, Beamte	1	1929-35	
	Päpstliche Beamte und Würden-träger, diplomatisches Corps, Reden, Empfänge	1	1928-32	
	Personalverhältnisse (Zeitdauer) Geldaufwendungen der Missionen beim Heiligen Stuhl und Aufwen-dungen des Heiligen Stuhles für seine diplomatischen Vertretun-gen	1	1928-38	
	Diplomatisches Corps beim Heiligen Stuhl	1	1929-37	
	Ordo Costantiniano di San Giorgio. Ordine Sacro Militare di Nostra Signora di Betlemme	1	1934-39	
	Orden des Hl.Lazarus. Tiberi-nische Akademie in Rom. Institut Héraldique et Historique de France. Arcadia	1	1932-35	
	Orden vom Heiligen Grabe	1	1932-40	
	Malteser-Orden	1	1929-43	
33	Jesuiten und Jesuitenniederlas-sungen	1	1920-43	
	Unionsbestrebungen und Weltkir-chenkonferenzen	1	1920-32	
34	Ehen, Ehedispense, Ehescheidun-gen	1	1921-29	
35	Ordens- und päpstliche Titelver-leihungen, Goldene Rose	1-2	1922-42	
35 a	Verkehr des schwarzen diploma-tischen Corps mit dem weissen und Repräsentationen	1	1920-29	
35	Päpstliche Doktortitel, Reife-zeugnisse geistlicher Schulen und Ähnliches	1	1928-35	
	Reform der kirchlichen Fakultäten "Deus scientiarum Dominus"	1	1930-36	

Akten-zeichen	Inhalt	Band	Datum	Serial Nr.
36	Index, Kirchenstrafen und Ähnliches, Widerrufe	1	1924-43	
37	Santa Maria dell'Anima	1	1885-1930	
	Katholischer, deutscher Gesellenverein in Rom und die anderen Gesellenvereine	1	1922-40	
	Collegium Cultorum Martyrum	1	1929-35	
	Karmelitinnen in Rocca di Papa	1	1929-35	
	Italienisch-deutsche Studentenvereinigung	1	1933-35	
	Collegium Germanicum-Hungaricum	1-2	1927-40	
	Katholischer, deutscher Leseverein	1	1920-35	
	Instituto Femminile Villa			
	Paolino. Suore dell'Immacolata Concezione Malinckrodt	1	1922-33	
	Katholischer Marienverein, katholisches Altersheim, katholische Mädchenheime	1	1926-36	
	Deutscher katholischer Leseverein, Lichtbildvorträge, Film, Veranstaltungen	1	1927-38	
	St.Vinzenz-Verein St.Elisabethen-Verein	1	1926-34	
	Deutsche katholische Gemeinde in Genua	1	1928-41	
	Deutsches Schwesternheim in Gardone	1	1939-41	
	Deutsche katholische Gemeinde in Venedig	1	1928-40	
	Deutsche Schule in Turin	1	1936-41	
	- katholische Gemeinde in Rom	1	1923-41	
	- in Palermo	1	1929-41	
	- Florenz	1	1925-41	
	- Mailand	1	1924-41	
	- Neapel	1	1928-41	
	- Triest	1	1930-40	
	- Bologna u.Gardone	1	1930-35	
	- Palermo	1	1931-32	
	Deutsche katholische Gemeinden in Italien, gen.	1	1923-39	
	Schwestern Unserer Lieben Frau	1	1926-40	
	Genossenschaft der Salvatorianerinnen, Mutterhaus in Rom	1	1939	
	Anstalten der Grauen Schwestern in Italien	1	1924-42	

Akten-zeichen	Inhalt	Band	Datum	Serial Nr.
37	Istituto Femminile Villa Paolina (Malinckrodt-Schwestern)	1	1934–43	
	Deutsche Schule in Rom	1	1924–43	
	Deutsche Akademie Villa Massimo	1	1930–42	
	Römisches Institut	1	1922–42	
	Archäologisches Institut in Rom	1	1927–40	
	Deutsches Haus, deutsche Verei-nigung	1	1925–43	
	Laienkongregation der Christli-chen Schulbrüder	1	1939–40	
	Biblioteca Hertziana (Kaiser Wilhelm-Institut für Kunst und Kulturwissenschaft in Rom)	1	1926–39	
	Notarius Sander, Bücherstube	1	1925–27	
	Klub deutscher Pressevertreter	1	1929–30	
	Katholischer kaufmännischer Verein	1		
	Benediktusstiftung	1	1922–23	
	Generalrat der Katholischen Gesellenvereine Köln	1	1934	
	Evangelische Gemeinde in Rom und Neapel und Italien	1	1925–35	
	Fremdenhaus der deutschen Kapu-zinerinnen in Assisi	1	1921–35	
	S.M. dell'Anima Neapel	1	1915–36	
	Verhandlungen	1	1925–30	
	Pilger-Komitee, Pilgerbewegung und Zusammenhängendes	1-2	1926–34	
37 A	Campo Santo	1	1917–33	
37	Besetzung des Rektorpostens des Campo Santo Teutonico 1930/1931 Rektoren-Personalia	1	1930–31	
	Allgemeine Anträge für kulturelle Zwecke und Versendung der Gelder	1-2	1926–35	
38	Feier des XX.September Freimaurerei und auf ähnlicher Grundlage aufgebaute Logen. Rotary	1	1923–38	
39	Italien	1-6	1920–38	
	Dante	1	1920–21	
	Monaco	1	1933	
	Minderheiten Venezia Giulia, Fürsterzbischof Sedej von Görz, Triest, Gorizia, Fiume	1	1931–36	
	San Marino	1	1926–42	

Akten-zeichen	Inhalt	Band	Datum	Serial Nr.
39	Religionsunterricht in den italienischen Schulen und Ähnliches	1	1930-41	
	II Nostra Internazionale d'Arte Sacra 1933/34 Roma	1	1932-34	
40	Römische Frage	1-6	1919-29	
41	Frankreich, Allgemeines	1-4	1920-36	
	Frankreich ohne Kultusassozia-tionen, Elsass-Lothringen, Action francaise	5-6	1936-43	
	Frankreich und Vatikan	1-2	1920-23	
	Pastorisierung von Ausländern in Frankreich	1	1931-34	
	Action francaise	1-2	1926-41	
	Elsass-Lothringen	1-3	1922-41	
	Kultus-Assoziationen (Frankreich)	1-2	1906-28	
42	Österreich, Vorarlberg, Liechtenstein	1 2-3	1920-39	K1182/K303706-949
	Österreich, Wiedervereinigung mit dem Deutschen Reich	1	1938-39	
42 Spez.	Österreich 25.Juli 1934	1	1934	
42	Ungarn	1	1921-43	
	Südtirol	1-4	1921-36	
	Hirtenbrief des österreichischen Episkopats vom 21.12.33	1	1933-37	
43	Russland, Regierung und inner-kirchliche Angelegenheiten	1-3	1921-30	
	Russland, Regierung und innen- und aussenpolitische Angelegen-heiten	4-6	1930-39	
	Russland, Litauen	1	1917-21	
	– Allgemeines, Unter-stützung	1	1919-26	
	Missionierung Russlands	1	1921-29	
	Konkordat mit Russland	1	1933	
	Georgien	1	1922-28	
43 a	Tschechoslowakei	1-6	1919-39	
	Breslauer Güterfrage und Tschechoslowakei	4	1935-38	
43 b	Estland (Reval)	1	1919-43	
	Litauen (Kowno)	1-2 3	1921-43	5146/E303507-17
	Lettland (Riga)	1	1920-42	
44	Rumänien	2	1929-43	

Akten-zeichen	Inhalt	Band	Datum	Serial Nr.
44	Msgr.Steinmanns Korrespondenz über Minderheiten, Schule	1	1925-34	
	Rumänien Szatmar-Grosswardein	1	1928-35	
	Griechenland	1	1921-43	
	Albanien	1	1923-40	
45	Bulgarien	1	1922-42	
45 a	Gemischte Ehe des bulgarischen Königspaares. Taufe der Kinder	1	1929-37	
46	Spanien	1-2 2a 3	1922-39	5157/E303712-21
47	Portugal	1 2	1920-43	4426/E084160-203 4426/E084204-05
48	Belgien	1 2 3	1919-43	4425/E084148-57 5312/E337848-53
49	England	1 2 3	1920-40	3099/D626326-54 3099/D626313-25
	- Dominien, Ceylon, Britisch-Indien, Canada	1	1927-42	
	Irland	1	1920-43	3095/D626222-29
	Schweiz	1	1924-42	4419/E083934-43
	Schweden	1	1921-43	
	Malta	1-2	1928-38	
50 a	Süd- und Ostafrika	1	1922-37	
50 b	Nordafrika und Ägypten	1	1925-38	
50 c	Liberia	1	1928-32	
51	Türkei	1	1921-41	
	Arabien	1	1926-33	
	Iran, Irak	1	1921-38	
	Palästina, Zionismus	1-3	1919-43	
	Französisches Protektorat im Orient	1-2	1903-42	
	Abessinien, auch italienisch-abessinischer Konflikt und Sanktionen	1-2	1929-42	
51	Syrien - Libanon	1	1928-42	
52 a	China, Delegatur in Peking	1 2 3	1918-43	5416/E362581-601
52	Indo-China	1	1928-42	
	Mandschukuo	1	1933-38	
53	Japan	1	1919-43	

Akten-zeichen	Inhalt	Band	Datum	Serial Nr.
54	Vereinigte Staaten von Nord-amerika	2-3	1927-41	
	Philippinen	1	1930-43	
	Australien	1	1932-42	
55	Columbien	1	1924-42	
	Peru	1	1921-43	
	Venezuela	1	1923-42	
	Haiti, Cuba und Dominikanische Republik	1	1924-42	
	Brasilien	1	1922-42	
	Argentinien	1	1923-43	
	Chile	1	1923-43	4794/E236443-46 5678/E412369-73
	Bolivien, Paraguay	1	1925-43	
	Mexiko	3	1929-42	
	Honduras, San Salvador	1	1921-42	
	Ecuador	1	1925-42	
	Uruguay	1	1921-42	
	Nicaragua	1	1937-42	
	Guatemala, Panama, Costa-Rica	1	1921-42	
57 spez.	Informierung von Pressevertre-tern durch Botschaft	1	1927-43	
57	Westdeutscher Beobachter	1	1935-38	
	Presse, Bücher politischen In-halts, Drucksachen (nicht spe-ziell NSDAP-Inhalts)	1	1936-43	
	Agenzia Urbs, Agenzia Fides, KIPA, Ecclesia-Korrespondenz	1	1925-41	
	Nationale Presse und Bücher, deutsches Zeitungswesen, Maß-nahmen gegen die katholischen Diözesen und ähnliche Presse, auch ausländisches Schrifttum über Nationalsozialismus	1	1935-42	
	Académie Diplomatique Inter-nationale	1	1927-40	
	Lettres de Rome sur l'athéisme, mod.Arbeitskreis Dr.Ehrt, Bolschewismus	1	1935-39	
	Italia	1	1932-39	
	Baumgarten	1	1916-23	
26	Politische Berichte der öster-reichischen Quirinal-Gesandt-schaft	1	1920-27	
27	Informationsberichte des Bundes-pressedienstes	1	1920-27	

Akten-zeichen	Inhalt	Band	Datum	Serial Nr.
28	Ein Bündel Diverses: Anima, Gesellenverein, katholische Aktion, Benediktinerklöster, Bischof Hudal, versiegelter Aktenband	1	1920-37	
29	Diverses, Geheimberichte 1928, Msgr.Pablikowski, Konklave 1922	1	1920-27	
30	Konkordatsakten	1	1920-37	
31	Österreichische und vatikanische Ordensverleihungen	1	1933-37	
32	Politische Weisungen 1921 - 1928. Apostolischer Nuntius in Wien. Bistum Brixen	1	1921-28	
33	Politische Berichte	1	1920-24	
34		1	1925-29	
35		1	1930-33	
	Berichtskopien aus Wien 32, 33, 34	1		
36	Politische Berichte	1-4	1934-37	
		1	1938	
	Berichtskopien der Quirinal-Gesandtschaft		1937-38	8892/E621569-72
	Einsichtsakten		1937-38	
	Konkordatsvergleichstabelle			
38	Personalakten: Frhr.von Pastor, Legationsrat Blaas, Gesandter Dr. Kohlruss	1		
	Personalien Zimmermann M.9. Botschaftsarchiv	1	1920-35	
	Akten der ehemaligen Österreichi-schen Gesandtschaft beim Heiligen Stuhl	1	1929-37	K1177/K303272-96 K1178/K303297-357 K1179/K303358-426

Akten-zeichen	Inhalt	Band	Datum	Serial Nr.
74	Allgemeines	1	8.23- 3.37	74/53395-733
		2	3.22- 9.32	74/53735-976
		3	1.33- 6.36	8112/E579741-59
		4	7.36- 9.38	74/54110-391
		5	10.38- 4.40	74/54393-720
Geh.C-Akt Spez.V	VAA-Material (Geheime Lagebe-richte von der Front)	1	7.42-11.42	74/53978-4107
	Politica	1	2.19- 9.20	74/54722-5091
		2	10.20- 1.21	74/55093-392
	Diverses		6.25-11.35	74/55394-506
9 Emigr. Allg.	Emigranten, Überwachung im Aus-land· (auch Nicht-Emigranten) Gestapo	1	5.33- 4.38	74/55508-869
	Gestapo	2	5.38- 5.40	74/55871-6451
Beiheft zu 9 Emigr.	Emigranten - Einzelfälle		1933-39	74/56453-652
	Geh. Personalien		8.19- 6.35	
	Personalien der Botschaft, Diplomaten		6.25- 3.37	
	Personalien (ausser Presse)		5.19- 5.23	
	57, Presse		1.20- 5.23	
	"Corriere d'Italia" und "P.P.J."		7.20- 5.24	
	"Sonnenschein"		6.21- 9.23	
	Geldsachen		1.21- 4.22	
37	Rector Anima (Besetzung des Rektorpostens)		6.26- 6.33	
	Anima, Generelles		7.30- 4.34	
9	Deutsche in Kongregationen und päpstlichen Behörden		3.28- 1.38	
	Seelsorge in Italien		4.31- 5.37	
8	Wirth, ehemaliger Reichskanzler		7.32- 5.41	5128/E295870-935
	von Olpinski (Osten)		11.34- 2.40	
	Gerlach		1.17- 7.20	

Akten-zeichen	Inhalt	Band	Datum	Serial Nr.
Po 1	Allgemeine politische Lage auf dem Balkan	1	1927-35	
Po 2	Politische und wirtschaftliche Beziehungen der Balkanstaaten zueinander, Balkankonferenzen	1-2	1921-38	
Po 3	− Kleine Entente	1	1921-38	
Po 4	− Balkanpakt	1	1925-38	
Po 5	− Donaufragen, Donaukonferenzen	1-5	1920-38	
Po 6	− Donaublock, Agrar-konferenzen, Römi-scher Dreierpakt	1-4	1930-37	
Po 7	Bulgarische Aussenpolitik, Allgemeines	1-2	1921-38	
Po 8	Politische Beziehungen Bulga-riens zu Deutschland	1 2	1921-38	3775/E041097-132
Po 8 a	Deutsch-bulgarische Auseinander-setzungen über gegenseitige Forderungen aus dem Weltkriege	1	1920-25	
Po 8 b	Bulgarische Staatsangehörige in Abessinien	1	1936-38	
Po 9	Deutsch-bulgarische Verträge und Verhandlungen	1-3	1925-38	
Po 10	Politische Beziehungen Bulgariens zu Frankreich	1	1921-38	
	Griechenland	1-2	1924-38	
Po 12	Thrazische Fragen	1	1922-36	
Po 13	Politische Beziehungen Bulgariens zu Italien	1	1923-38	
Po 14	Jugoslawien	1-3	1921-38	
Po 15	Mazedonische Frage	1	1922-37	
Po 16	Politische Beziehungen Bulgariens zu Rumänien	1	1921-38	
Po 17	Dobrudscha-Frage	1	1927-34	
Po 18	Politische Beziehungen Bulgariens zu Russland	1	1921-36	
Po 19	− Tschechoslowakei	1	1922-38	
Po 20	− Türkei	1-2	1921-38	
Po 21	− Ungarn	1	1929-36	
Po 22	− anderen Staaten	1	1921-38	
Po 23	Allgemeine innerpolitische Lage und Entwicklung Bulgariens	1-3	1922-38	
Po 24	Kabinettfragen,Regierungswechsel Ministerkrisen, Personalien von bulgarischen Staatsmännern	1-4	1921-38	
Po 24 a	Wahlen in Bulgarien	1	1926-34	

Akten-zeichen	Inhalt	Band	Datum	Serial Nr.
Po 25	Parteiwesen, Parteikämpfe, politische Organisationen, Personalien bulgarischer Partei-politiker, Freimaurer, Juden-frage	1-3	1921-38	
Po 25 a	Einreise von Emigranten und Ostjuden nach Deutschland, geheim	1	1933-39	
Po 25^1	Innenpolitisches: Kommunismus, nationale Bewegungen	1	1942-43	
Po 26	Umsturzbewegungen, Kommunisti-sche Bewegung, Gesetz zum Schut-ze des Staates, politische Pro-zesse, Amnestien, Bandenwesen	1-3	1922-38	
Po 26 a	Prozess gegen Kabinett Rados-lawow	1	1921-23	
Po 27	Mazedonische Bewegung	1-2	1921-38	
Po 28	Königsfrage, Angelegenheiten des königliches Hauses	1	1924-38	
Po 29	Politische Unterredungen mit dem König, Reisen des Königs	1	1926-38	
Po 30	Ausländische diplomatische und konsularische Vertretungen in Bulgarien	1-3	1923-38	
Po 31	Bulgarische diplomatische und konsularische Vertretungen im Auslande, bulgarische Militär-attachés	1-2	1921-38	
Po 34	Bulgarische Arbeitsdienstpflicht	1	1921-35	
Po 32	Etikette, Ceremonialien, Ordensverleihungen	1	1923-36	
Po 33	Deutscher Militär- und Luft-attaché für Bulgarien, auslän-dische Militärattachés in Bulgarien	1-2	1929-39	
Po 34	Bulgarische Armee und Flotte, Flugwaffe, Polizei und Gendarmerie	1	1921-38	
Po 34 a	Ein- und Ausfuhr von Kriegsgerät, Aufrüstung Bulgariens, Waffen-lieferungen, Geheimakten	1	1935-38	3767/E040714-50 M243/M008097-10?
Po 36	Staat und Kirche	1	1922-38	
Po 37	Minderheiten und Flüchtlings-wesen	1-4	1925-38	
	- Sonderheft	1	1931-34	
Po 38	Wirtschaftspolitische Fragen Bulgariens	1	1921-37	
Po 39	Bulgarische Staatsfinanzen, Finanzpolitik, Anleihen, Berich-te des Völkerbundkommissars	1-7	1921-38	
Po 39 a	Pernik-Minen	1	1923-25	

Akten-zeichen	Inhalt	Band	Datum	Serial Nr.
Po 40	Reparationen	1-2	1928-33	
Po 41	Vertrag von Versailles	1-3	1924-33	
Po 42	– von Neuilly	1-2	1921-33	
Po 43	Völkerbundfragen	1-4	1923-38	
Po 43 a	Deutschland und der Völkerbund	1	1926-37	
Po 43 b	Ratstagungen des Völkerbundes	1-2	1927-38	
Po 43 c	Abrüstungsfragen im Völkerbund	1-4	1927-37	
	Drucksachenmaterial zur Abrüstungsfrage	1	1933-34	
Po 43 e	Weltwirtschaftskonferenz in Genf, Zollfriedenskonferenz	1	1927-31	
Po 43 f	Paneuropa	1	1929-31	
Po 44	Garantiepakt (Locarnopakt)	1	1925-29	
Po 45	Deutsch-österreichische Zoll-union, Anschlussfragen	1	1931-38	
Po 46	Internationale Konferenzen und Kongresse, Teilnahme bezw. Aus-schliessung Deutschlands, Internationales Arbeitsamt	1-2	1922-38	
Po 47	Presseangelegenheiten, Propa-ganda	1-7	1923-39	
Po 47 a	Reichsjugendführung	1	1938-39	
Po 47 b	Bulgarische Pressedirektion, Redaktionen und Behörden	1	1938-39	
Po 47 c	Fahrterleichterungen für bul-garische Journalisten in Deutschland	1	1938-39	
Po 47 d	Deutsche Zeitungen und Zeit-schriften	1	1938-39	
Po 47 e	Betreuung durchreisender Journa-listen und Presseleute	1	1937-39	
Po 47 f	Auskünfte in Presseangelegen-heiten	1	1936-39	
Po 47 g	Deutsch-bulgarisches Presseab-kommen, Pressebesuche	1	1939	
Po 47 h	Deutsches Nachrichtenbüro Berlin	1	1939	
Po 47 i	Reichsverband der deutschen Presse	1	1939	
Po 47 k	Flugschriften	1	1939	
Po 47 l	Lanciertes Material	1	1939	
Po 47 m	Sammelmappe für unverlangte Manuskripte und Berichte	1	1938	
Po 47 Instr.	Promi Instruktionen	1	1938	
Po 47 n	Pressetätigkeit der Frau Müller-Neudorf	1	1933-36	

Akten-zeichen	Inhalt	Band	Datum	Serial Nr.
Po 48	Deutsche Pressevertreter in Bulgarien, DNB-Vertreter, WTB-Vorgänge, Pressebeirat Dr.Laufer	1-2	1924-38	
Po 49	Verschiedene Geheimangelegen-heiten	1-3	1921-38	
Po 49 II	Deutscher Arbeitsdienst	1	1935-39	
Po 49 III	Besuch des Ministerpräsidenten Hermann Göring in Sofia	1	1935-36	
Po 49 IV	Hilfsaktion für die bulgarischen Kriegsbeschädigten	1	1935-36	
Po 49 V	Hebung des deutschen U-Bootes 45	1	1935-38	
Po 49 VIII	Aufrüstung fremder Staaten (ausschliesslich Bulgarien)	1	1936	
Po 49 IX	Besuch des Kreuzers "Emden" in Varna	1	1934-38	
Po 50	Allgemeine inner- und aussen-politische Lage Deutschlands	1-10	1921-38	
Po 50 a	Danzig, Polnischer Korridor, die deutsch-polnischen Streit-fälle, deutsch-polnische Be-ziehungen	1	1930-38	
Po 50 a	Lage des Deutschtums in Polen (Sammlung)	1	1939	
Po 50 b	Saargebiet	1-2	1933-35	
Po 50 c	Beteiligung der Auslandsdeut-schen an den deutschen Wahlen und Volksabstimmungen	1	1936-38	
Po 51	Allgemeine inner- und aussen-politische Lage Albaniens	1	1921-36	
Po 52	- Nord-u.Südamerika	1	1921-38	
Po 53	- Belgien	1	1923-37	
Po 54	- England und seine Überseebesitzungen, Irland	1	1922-38	7632/E545358-6(
Po 55	- Frankreich	1	1923-38	
Po 56	- Griechenland	1-4	1921-38	
Po 57	- Italien, Romverein-barungen, römischer Pakt	1-2	1922-38	
Po 58	- Jugoslawien (Marseiller Königs-mord)	1-4	1921-38	
Po 58 a	Freihafenzone von Saloniki	1	1922-29	
Po 59	Allgemeine innen- und aussenpo-litische Lage Polens	1-2	1922-38	
Po 60	- Österreich	1	1923-37	
Po 61	- Russland und Randstaaten	1-3	1921-36	

Akten-zeichen	Inhalt	Band	Datum	Serial Nr.
61 a	Wrangelarmee und zaristische-russische Organisationen	1	1922-33	
62	Allgemeine innen- und aussenpolitische Lage Rumäniens	1-2	1921-38	
63	- Spanien	1-2	1930-38	
64	- Tschechoslowakei	1-2	1921-38	
65	- Türkei	1-3	1921-38	
65 a	Dardanellenfrage, Meerengenkonferenz in Montreux, Mittelmeerkonferenzen	1	1936	
66	Allgemeine innen- und aussenpolitische Lage Ungarns	1-2	1923-38	
67	- Aiatische Staaten	1	1926-33	
68	Vatikan, Interventionen in politischen und kirchlichen Fragen sowie kirchliche Vertreter	1	1923-38	
69	Allgemeine innen- und aussenpolitische Lage anderer Länder, Informationserlasse vom Auswärtigen Amt	1-7	1935-38	
70	Persönlicher Briefwechsel Gesandter Beckerle	1	1941-43	
	Persönliche Aufzeichnungen Gesandter Beckerle	1 2	1941-44	5548/E387601-33 6960/E518775-820 6960/E518821-950
	Erwerb eines Grundstückes: Gesandtschaftsgebäude und Bau einer Dienstwohnung	1-3	1920-39	
	Gemeindeschwester	1	1935-36	
	Personalien Spezielles v.Heutik, KS.Walter, LS.Stefani	1	1921-23	
	Personalangelegenheiten Gesandter Rümelin	1-3	1921-38	
	Persönliche Angelegenheiten des Gesandten Rümelin	1	1923-39	
	Personalien: LS.Dr.Altenburg	1	1925-31	
	Stenotyp.Becker, Liselotte	1	1935-38	
	Attaché Berger, Karl	1	1935-36	
	Attaché de Chapeaurouge, Alfred	1	1936-38	
	LS. Dr.Clodius	1	1932-34	
	KS.Damerau	1	1925-27	
	KS. Galle	1	1924-26	
	KS.Geiger	1	1929-34	
	Havrilow	1	1923-24	
	KS.Hörner	1	1934-39	
	Stenotyp. Hübener, Ursula	1	1934-35	
	KS. Konitzer	1	1925-29	
	Amtsgeh. Leibowitsch	1	1923-25	

Akten-zeichen	Inhalt	Band	Datum	Serial Nr.
	Personalien:			
	LS.D.Lütkens	1	1923-25	
	KS. Michel	1	1928-34	
	Stenotyp. Milewski	1	1926-30	
	GS. Dr. Noebel	1	1924-27	
	Attaché Dr. Northe	1	1934-35	
	KS. Paulus, Dietas	1	1924-25	
	Attaché Graf zu Pappenheim	1	1937-38	
	Stenotyp.Poschmann	1	1926-34	
	LS.v.Saucken	1	1931-32	
	LS. Prinz zu Schaumburg-Lippe	1	1933-35	
	Theodoroff, Annemarie, Frau	1	1924-35	
	Theodoroff, Peter	1	1922-37	
	v. Ungelter	1	1935	
	v. Wühlisch	1	1927-33	
	Gehaltsfragen - Kassenfragen	1	1924-26	
	Verwaltung des Konsulats Rustschuk	1	1914-24	
	Verwaltung des Konsulats Varna	1	1922-32	
H 1	Aussenhandel Bulgariens. Deutsch-bulgarischer Aussenhandel	1-4	1936-39	
H 2	Handelsvertrag zwischen Deutschland und Bulgarien	1	1931-38	
H 2 a	Zusatzabkommen zum Deutsch-bulgarischen Handelsvertrag	1	1933-35	
H 2 b	Deutsch-bulgarische Vereinbarungen über die Überleitung des österreichisch-bulgarischen Wirtschaftsverkehrs in das deutsch-bulgarische Vertrags-system vom 19.V.1938	1	1938-39	
H 2 c 1.	Austro-Bulg. Handelskammer	1	1937-38	
2.	Austro-Bulg. Tabak A.-G., Sofia			
3.	Bulg.-österr. Wirtschaftsvereinbarungen			
H 3 a	Bulgarische Handelsvertragspolitik	2	1930-36	
H 4	Kompensationsgeschäfte	2+4	1932-34 1936-39	
H 5	Wirtschaftslage Bulgariens	1-2	1928-39	
H 7	Devisenbewirtschaftung in Bulgarien	1	1936-39	
H 8	Zahlungsverkehr mit Bulgarien	2	1936-39	
H 10	Verletzung des Urheberrechts	1	1928-39	
H 10 a	Marken- und Warenzeichenschutz	1	1934-39	
H 11	Zinsendienst bulgarischer Vor-kriegsanleihen	1-2	1924-28	
H 11 a	Bulgarisches Budget und Bank-(verein) wesen	1+3	1924-31 1936-39	

Akten-zeichen	Inhalt	Band	Datum	Serial Nr.
H 11 b	Bankwesen	1	1926-37	
H 12	Entschuldung der bulgarischen Landwirtschaft	1	1931-37	
H 15	Ausgestaltung der wirtschaftlichen Berichterstattung und wirtschaftlichen Aussenhandels-förderung	1	1926-36	
H 16	Deutsche Handelskammer in Sofia	1	1934-38	
H 18	Abkommen zur Vermeidung der Doppelbesteuerung	1	1926-37	
H 19	Bulgarische Staatsmonopole	1	1934-36	
H 20 a	Zolltarif und Zolltarifgesetz	1-2	1924-39	
H 21	Zolltarifentscheidungen und Gesetzgebung	1	1928-35	
H 22	Zollauskünfte und Reklamationen	4-6	1936-39	
H 23	Statistische Gebühren	1	1928-39	
H 24	Bulgarische Verfügungen über den Verkehr mit pharmazeutischen Erzeugnissen	1	1929-37	
H 25	Rosenblätter- und Rosenölernten	1	1925-37	
	Viehzucht	1	1936-39	
	Eierausfuhr	1	1931-39	
	Bulgarischer Tabakmarkt	1	1930-36	
H 26	Arbeitsmarkt	1	1926-39	
	Arbeitsbewilligungen für Reichs-deutsche	1	1931-39	
H 27	Jüdische Vertreter in Bulgarien	1	1935-39	K1696 /K406200-397
H 28	Bulgarische Konzessionen an Aus-länder	1	1924-31	
H 29	Schiffahrt	1	1926-39	
H 29 a	Neue Geschäftsordnung für Schiffsagenten	1	1936-37	
H 29 b	Schiffsgebührentarif	1	1932-34	
H 30	Eisenbahnwesen	1	1929-39	
H 30 a	Ausländische Anleihen für Bulgarien, Eisenbahn-Kredit-Geschäft	1-2	1937-39	
H 31	Industrie und Bergbau	1	1929-39	
H 31 a	Bodenschätze	1	1936-39	
H 32	Reichsstelle für den Aussenhandel	1	1935-39	
H 34	Lieferungsverzug deutscher Firmen	1	1935-39	
	Forderungen der Hansa-G.m.b.H., Bremen	1	1927-34	

Akten-zeichen	Inhalt	Band	Datum	Serial Nr.
	Forderungen der Firma Hermann Köbe, Luckenwalde	1	1936	
	Reklamationen der Firma Pittel & Brausewetter	1	1934-36	
	Angelegenheit Neuhausen	1	1936-38	
Allg.9	Südost-Ausstellung Breslau-Landmaschinenmarkt	1	1935-39	
Allg.10	Mustermesse Plovdiv	1	1934-39	
	Ausstellungen, Kongresse in Bulgarien	1	1936-39	
	Standesamtsangelegenheiten, Geburten, Eheschliessungen, Sterbefälle	1-3	1911-24	
	- Standesamtsregister	1-2	1911-30	
	Gerichtsangelegenheiten, Vormundschaftssachen	1-7	1890-1922	
	- Alimentenforderungen	1-3	1915-23	
	Rechtshilfeersuchen, Zustellungen, Zeugenvernehmungen	4-5	1938-39	
	Goldbrunner/Tunteff Ehescheidungen	1	1925-39	
	Unterhalt der geschiedenen Frau Rosengart, Plovdiv	1	1932-37	
	Gerichtsangelegenheiten, Nachlasssachen, Einzelfälle	1-6	1916-24	
	Staatsangehörigkeitsangelegenheiten	1-2	1921-24	
	-	2-3	1935-38	
	Optionsanträge	1	1939	
	Heimschaffungen, Heimreisedarlehen	1	1935-39	
	Mitteilungen bulgarischer Behörden über: Geburten, Eheschliessungen, Sterbefälle von deutschen Staatsangehörigen in Bulgarien	1	1935-39	
	Soziale und berufsorganisatorische Entwicklung in Bulgarien, ausländische und internationale Sozialpolitik	1	1935-39	
	Erdbeben (Unterstützungen)	1	1928	
Ku 1	Deutsches Lektorat in Bulgarien	1-2	1921-39	
Ku 2	Sprachkurse, Hebung des deutschen Unterrichts in bulgarischen Schulen	1-2	1930-39	
Ku 3	Deutsche Buchhandlung und das Deutsche Buch	1	1924-34	
	Bücherspenden, Bücherwesen	1-8	1933-39	

Akten-zeichen	Inhalt	Band	Datum	Serial Nr.
Ku 3	Deutsche Buchausstellung in Sofia	1	1937	
Ku 6	Stipendien aus der Alexander v.Humboldt-Stiftung	1-5	1925-39	
Ku 7	Deutsch-bulgarischer Kultur-verein in Sofia	1	1926-38	
	Deutsch-bulgarische Kultur-vereine in Bulgarien	1	1932-37	
	Deutsche Kulturwerbung in Bulgarien	1	1936	
Ku 7 b	Deutsche Vorträge und Konzerte	1-4	1932-39	
Ku 7 c	Verband Deutsch-bulgarischer Kulturvereine	1	1932-38	
Ku 8	Zahlungen, Zuschüsse an die Deutsch-bulgarischen Kultur-vereine	1	1931-38	
Ku 9	Kulturpolitische Bestrebungen	1-2	1932-39	
Ku 10	Kulturpropaganda fremder Staaten in Bulgarien	1	1931-39	
Ku 11	Rundfunkwesen (Allgemeines)	1	1932-39	
Ku 12	Reichsmusikkammer, Auskünfte über bulgarische Künstler und Musiker	1	1938-39	
16 a	Bulgarische Studenten an deut-schen Hochschulen, Allgemeines	1-2	1921-24	
16 b	- Anträge auf Zulassung zum Studium	1-4	1921-24	
Sch 1	Unterstützungsversuche der deutschen Schulen in Bulgarien, Auszahlung der Beihilfen an die Schulen	1-5	1929-39	
Sch 2	Schulfragen allgemeiner Art	1-3	1934-39	
	Befreiung der Deutschen Schulen von der Stageantensteuer	1	1936-37	
Sch 3	Beihilfe für die Hinterbliebenen des verstorbenen Lehrers Schnorr in Russe	1	1933-38	
Sch 4	Schulgesetze	1	1932-33	
Sch 5	Lehrkräfte der Deutschen Schule Sofia	1-5	1925-39	
Sch 5 a	- in Plovdiv	1	1925-30	
Sch 5 b	Lehrmittelausstellung	1	1926	
Sch 6	Neubau der Deutschen Schule Sofia	1-2	1927-37	
Sch 6 a	Deutsche Schulen in Sofia	1-4	1917-23	
	- in Sofia und Plovdiv	1-8	1925-39	
Sch 7	Deutsche Schule in Burgas	1-2	1925-39	

Akten-zeichen	Inhalt	Band	Datum	Serial Nr.
Sch 8	Neubau Schule Burgas	1	1934-37	
Sch 9	Deutsche Schule in (Philippopel) Plovdiv	1-7	1917-39	
Sch 10	– in Rustschuk	1-5	1907-39	
Sch 11	– in Varna	1-4	1916-39	
Sch 12	Neubau der Deutschen Schule in Varna	1	1935	
Sch 13	Deutsche Schule in Bardarski-Geran	1	1925-37	
Sch 14	– in Endje(Zarevbrod)	1-2	1910-39	
Sch 15	Deutschlandfahrt einer Schüler-gruppe der Deutschen Schule, Sofia	1	1934-38	
	Kirchen- und Unterrichtswesen, Vereine	1-2	1920-24	
	Deutsche Vereine und Gesellschaf-ten in Bulgarien, Bund der Auslandsdeutschen	1	1921-22	
	Geheimakten.			
	Akten	1	1.35- 6.38	3774/E041028-76
		2	7.38-12.38	3774/E041077-92
	Lose A-Akten		1926-37	3744/E040348-402 9338/E661676-77 K2149/K599618-33
	Spionageverdächtige: Journalist Hans Wagner Hauptmann a.D.Walter E.Brell		1931-34	K2150/K599634-73
	Liste des schädlichen und uner-wünschten Schrifttums der Reichs-schrifttumskammer mit Nachtrag und Benutzungsakte, 1 Umschlag		1935-38	

Akten-zeichen	Inhalt	Band	Datum	Serial Nr.
130 I	Personalien im Ministerium des Äusseren in Stockholm	1 2	1911-39	6219/H047538-42 6219/H047543-66
130 II	Personalien des Auswärtigen Amtes in Berlin	1	1918-39	
130 III	Personalien bei anderen Behörden in Berlin und Stockholm	1	1912-39	6220/H047568-84
G V Nr.1	Generalkonsul von Herff		1915-22	
G V Nr.3	Konsul Maenes		1917-21	
P II	Personalien der Passabteilung Dienstbetrieb		1920-22	
	Gesandter von Rosenberg	2	1932-34	
86	Gesuche und Bewerbungen verschiedener Art	5	1932-39	
18 VII	Urlaub	1	1921-39	
18 V	Organisation der Gesandtschaft	2	1923-39	6221/H047586-616
17 II	Gesandtschaftsgebäude	5-10	1922-36	
17 I	Inventar, Bücher	10	1938-39	
17 III	Abonnements von Zeitschriften	1-2	1919-39	
8 I	Geschäftsgang	3	1924-39	3506/E020300-302
8 IV	Hoheitszeichen des Deutschen Reiches (Flagge)	1	1920-38	
20	Steuern der Beamten und Angestellten	9	1892-1939	
14 II	Angestellten- und Invalidenversicherung	2	1925-38	
94	Kassenangelegenheiten, Pensionen	4-5	1916-37	
94 II	Zahlung von Pensionen	1	1920-38	
94 III	Devisenanmeldungen und Überweisungen	1-2	1934-39	
161	Lebensmittelkarten für Beamte der Gesandtschaft	1-3	1916-22	
	Überweisungslisten	1-7	1929-36	
	Pressepropagandistischer Fond	1	1934-40	6223/H047628-49 3510/E020419-24
8 II	Chiffres geheim	1-2	1867-1924	
10 I	Gen. Kuriere, Depeschenkasten	1	1875-1938	
10 II	Telegramm-Depeschenkasten und Kurierdienst	1-4	1914-39	
161	Verzeichnisse der Kuriersendungen	1-2	1917-23	
	- der Berichte an das Auswärtige Amt	10 -12	1922-25	
	Weiterleitungen, Brief- und Nachrichtenvermittlung	1-5	1916-24	

Akten-zeichen	Inhalt	Band	Datum	Serial Nr.
161 Pers G.12	Weiterleitungen und Vermittlung von Briefen, Paketen, Telegrammen	1 2 3 4	1937–42	4298/E077808–09 6224/H047651–54
227	Sammlungen, Generelles	1	1920–38	
		1–4	1920–23	
		5 7–11	1923–26	
		2,6, 12,13 16	1923–39	
Pers. G.13	Spenden, Darbietungen	1 2	1915–41	6225/H047656–71
161	Liebesgaben und Spenden	1–3	1914–28	
52	Anfragen verschiedener Art	5 6 7	1928–38	6227/H047673–83
58 Sonderakt	Audienzen	1	1908–35	
92	Hof- und Zeremonialangelegenheiten, Generelles	1	1912–38	
92 II		2–5	1920–37	
92 II Abt.3	Geburtstag der Königin von Schweden (Tod und Beisetzung)	1	1917–31	
92 Abt.2	Ableben des Reichspräsidenten von Hindenburg	5a	1934	
92 II	Glückwünsche an den Führer	6	1937–39	
92 III	Glückwunsch- und Beileidskundgebungen	4–5	1934–39	
71 III	Deutsche Reichsfeiern, Feier des Verfassungstages (11.August)	1	1922–33	
71 VII	Vorbereitung zur Reichsgründungsfeier (18.Januar)	1–2	1921–33	
71	Deutscher Nationalfeiertag, Tag der Nationalen Arbeit	1	1933–40	
125	Verleihung von Titeln, Orden (Rückgabe von Orden)	5–10	1918–38	
	– (Rote Kreuz-Medaille)	5–8	1918–24	
	Ordenssachen, Verleihung von Titeln (Abteilungen)	6	1918–27	
	– Johanniterorden	1	1912–32	
126	– schwedische an Ausländer	1	1913–22	
125	Ehrenzeichen des Deutschen Roten Kreuzes	2–6	1924–39	
	Ehrenkreuz des Weltkrieges	1–2	1934–40	
	Gedenksteine in Trelleborg	1–2	1921–38	
136	Reisen fürstlicher Personen	1	1906–34	

Akten-zeichen	Inhalt	Band	Datum	Serial Nr.
136	Reisen fürstlicher Personen (Staatsoberhäupter)	1	1906-34	
136 III	- des Königs und der Königin von Schweden	1	1909-39	6228/H047685-98
217	Innen- und Aussenpolitik Schweden	1		6239/H048430-55
		2		6239/H048456-93
		3	1918-26	6239/H048494-501
		4		6239/H048502-44
		5		6239/H048545-95
		6		6239/H048596-625
		7		6239/H048626-77
		8		6239/H048678-747
		9	1926-33	6239/H048748-81
		10		6239/H048782-808
		11		6239/H048809-56/12
		12		5912/E433834-57
		13		5912/E433858-66
		14	1933-36	5912/E433867-83
		15		3504/E020291-93
				5912/E433884-957
		16		3513/E020521-53
				5912/E433958-95
				5913/E434164-88
		17		3513/E020554-91
				5912/E433996-4008
				5913/E434189-233
				7556/E541888-92
		18		3513/E020592-684
				5912/E434009-53
				5913/E434234-90/1
		19	1938-39	3513/E020685-731
				5912/E434054-105
				5913/E434291-306
				7556/E541893-903
		20		3514/E020735-63
				5912/E434106-20
		21		3514/E020764-75
				5912/E434121-41
		22		3514/E020776-91
				5912/E434142-62
199	Innen-und Aussenpolitik Deutschland	1-5	1920-24	
		6-15	1924-33	
		17		6241/H048858-64
		18		
		19	1933-34	
		20		
		21		6241/H048865-80
		22		6241/H048881-85
		23		
		24	1934-39	
		25		5929/E435777-826
		26		6241/H048885-90
	- Belgien	1	1919-39	
	- Bulgarien, Ukraine, Persien	1	1917-38	
	- China	1	1920-38	
	- Danzig	1	1925-38	

Akten-zeichen	Inhalt	Band	Datum	Serial Nr.
199	Innen- und Aussenpolitik Dänemark	1 2 3	1919-39	6242/H048892-96 6242/H048897-903
	- England	1 2	1918-39	6243/H048905-25 2913/D566540-42
S III/18	- Finnland	1 2 3 4	1918-22	L284/L086904-7315 L284/L087316-43 L284/L087344-51 L284/L087352-455
173 I	-	1 2 3 4	1915-22	L289/L087679-8031 L289/L088032-41 L289/L088042-86
199	-	1 2 3 4 5	1922-33	L290/L088087-413 L290/L088414-705 L290/L088706-996 L290/L088997-9336 L290/L089337-495
	-	6 7 8 9	1933-39	6244/H048927-68 L290/L089496-788 6244/H048969-85 L290/L089789-985 6244/H048986-9002 L290/L089986- 90068 6244/H049003-50 L290/L090069-176
	- Frankreich	1-4	1918-39	
	- Holland	1	1916-39	
	- Italien	1-2	1917-39	
	- Japan	1-2	1915-37	
	- Memel	1-2	1923-39	
	- Norwegen	1-5	1914-39	
	- Österreich und Schweiz	1	1918-39	
	- Österreich	2-4	1932-39	
	- Polen	1-4	1916-26	
		5-8	1926-39	
204	- Randstaaten (Baltikum)	1-4	1918-32	
		6-8	1934-39	
199	- Rumänien	1	1915-38	
204 I - IV	- Russland	1 2 3 4 5	1916-21	L889/L251404- 2058 L889/L252059- 783 L889/L252784- 3057 L889/L253058-238
204 VI		1 2 3	1919-21	L889/L253312-24

Akten-zeichen	Inhalt	Band	Datum	Serial Nr.
204 VI	Innen- und Aussenpolitik Russland	4-8	1921-27	
		9 10 11 12	1927-39	6245/H049052-59 7557/E541905-08
199	— Skandinavien	1		3517/E020930-41 5914/E434308-26
		2	1921-39	3517/E020942-1016 5914/E434327-36 5915/E434338-53
		3		3517/E021017-029
	— Spanien	1-4	1919-39	
	— Tschechoslowakei	1 2	1921-39	3122/D641976-84
	— Türkei und Armenien	1	1917-38	
	— Vereinigte Staaten von Amerika	1-2	1918-39	
	— verschiedene Länder	1-3	1919-38	
135	Schwedische Reichstagsprotokolle, Reichstagseröffnung, Thronrede	1-2	1894-1939	
231	Ostsee- und Nordseeabkommen	1-2	1907-32	
47	Spitzbergenfrage	1	1920-35	
S II 14	Alandinseln, geh.	1		L292/L090177-281 6248/H049107-171
		2 3 4 5	1917-30	6248/H049172-256 6248/H049257-95 6248/H049296-336 6248/H049337-49
101 I	Inder-National-Komitee: Chattopadhyaya-Acharya	1-2	1917-21	
235	Die deutsche Reichsflagge	1 2	1921-39	6250/H049351-62
Pol 3 Nr. 7	Parteiwesen, politische Verbände in Schweden	1	1939-40	3512/E020444-516
161	Sympathiekundgebungen für Deutschland und Schmähungen	1-2	1914-21	
240	Behelligung von Ausländern (Schweden) in Deutschland	1-2	1933-38	
242	Spionage, geheim	1	1934-38	6251/H049364-74
96	Kolonialfrage	2-3	1938-39	
96 adh.	Kolonialpolitik in der Welt-publizistik	1	1938	
230	Völkerbund	1-6	1918-26	
		13	1937-38	
237	Abrüstung	8 9	1936-38	7455/E540391-95

Akten-zeichen	Inhalt	Band	Datum	Serial Nr.
236	Kommunismus	1 2 3 4 5	1925–39	6252/H049376–78 6252/H049379–85 6252/H049386–95
243	Judenfrage	1–2	1936–39	
222	Verschiedenes (politisch)	1	1918–22	
		3 4	1934–39	6253/H049397–418
S II 5	Geheime Akten (nicht geheftet) Sammlung II und III (Verzeichnis inliegend)		1917–24	
233	Abwicklung der Geschäfte des Militärbevollmächtigten	1	1920–22	
239	Militärattaché (Generalia)	1	1933–39	
112	Berichterstattung über das Heer- wesen	1–2 3 4	1907–38	5930/E435828–43
214	Gendarmerie-Offiziere in Persien	1–2	1918–32	
115	Militaria, Verschiedenes	1	1907–34	
	Kommandierung deutscher Offi- ziere nach Schweden und schwedi- scher nach Deutschland	1	1910–37	
	Beurlaubungen von deutschen Offizieren nach Schweden	1	1913–38	
167	Militärangelegenheiten	1	1915–23	
197	Marineangelegenheiten, Verschiedenes	1–3	1915–21	
206	Der Ubootkrieg. Versenkte Dampfer	1–3	1917–21	
232	Abwicklung der Geschäfte des Marineattachés	1	1919–21	
238	Marineattaché, Verschiedenes	1	1933–39	
	– Berichte	1–5	1933–38	
107	Kriegsmarine, Verschiedenes	1–2	1908–38	
	– deutsche, Generalia	1	1921–38	
	– Kassensachen	1	1926–38	
	Berichterstattung über die schwedische Marine	1	1923–38	
28	Besuch schwedischer Häfen durch deutsche und deutscher Häfen durch fremde Kriegsschiffe	1	1896–1922	
107	Deutsche Schiffsbesuche in Schweden	1–4	1914–32	
		1–5	1933–39	
	Fremde Kriegsmarine	1	1929–38	
	Besuch schwedischer Kriegsfahr- zeuge in Deutschland und anderen Ländern	1	1929–38	

Akten-zeichen	Inhalt	Band	Datum	Serial Nr.
) Pol 2 c	Telegrafischer Informations-dienst betr. Behinderung der neutralen Schiffahrt durch englische und französische Ein-griffe	1	1939	3505/E020296-97
108	Geschenke, Remunerationen, Orden, Medaillen an Kapitäne und See-leute für Rettungen	1-2	1910-33	
218 VI	Frieden und Wiederaufbau (Reparationen)	1-40	1920-30	
	- Ruhrbesetzung	1-9	1923-26	
	Sicherheitsfragen, Verträge	1	1925	
218 VII	Konferenz in Spa: Reparations-kohlen	1-3	1920-24	
218 VIII	Auslegung und Milderung des Friedensvertrages, Übergriffe farbiger französischer Truppen in den besetzten Gebieten und Bekämpfung der schwarzen Schmach durch das neutrale Ausland	1	1921-25	
218 IX	Saargebiet	1-9	1921-35	
218 X	Schuldfrage	1-4	1921-38	
186	Aktenpublikationen des Auswärti-gen Amtes	1	1922-29	
218 XI	Leistungen aus dem Friedensver-trag	1-2	1922-23	
218 XII	Schieds- und Vergleichsverträge, Schiedsgerichtshöfe	3-4	1931-39	
224 Abt.1	Abstimmungsgebiet Schleswig	1-5	1919-38	
Abt. 2-3	- Eupen und Malmedy, Ober-schlesien	1-6	1920-21	
II A 1	Wirtschaftslage Deutschlands	6-11	1923-33	
II A 2	- Schwedens	3-4	1922-27	
II A 2a	Weltwirtschaftskonferenz	1-3	1926-30	
II A 4	Wirtschaftslage anderer Länder	1-7	1920-36	
II A 4a	- Randstaaten	1	1926-30	
II A 5	Deutsch-schwedischer Handels- und Schiffahrtsvertrag	1-11	1918-36	
II A 6	Deutsche Ein- und Ausfuhrbestim-mungen	1-3	1921-30	
II A 7	Schwedische Ein-, Aus- und Durch-fuhrbestimmungen	1-4	1920-27	
II A 8	Durchfuhr durch Deutschland	3	1921-26	
	Gesetz über den Waffenhandel von Deutschland nach China	1	1928-29	
II A 9	Differenzen im deutsch-schwedi-schen Handelsverkehr	4-7	1921-33	

Akten- zeichen	Inhalt	Band	Datum	Serial Nr.
II B 1	Deutschlands Handel mit Schweden, Ein- und Ausfuhr	6-7	1922-31	
	Deutsch-schwedischer Spezial-handel	10	1935-36	
II B 2	Handel Schwedens mit Russland und Nachrichten über Russland	3-4	1920-25	
II B 3	Handel Schwedens mit anderen Ländern	1	1919-28	
II A 10	Deutsche Handelskammer in Schwe-den	1	1920-26	
		3-5	1927-36	
II A 11	Deutsch-skandinavische Wirt-schaftsverbände	1	1919-29	
II A 15	Warenpreise und Einzelmarkt-berichte	1-2	1919-27	
90	Handel, Gewerbe und Industrie, Verschiedenes	1-2	1919-23	
II A 7a	Allgemeine Handelserlaubnis, Bestimmungen für Ausländer	1-2	1921-36	
	Besteuerung von Handelsreisenden (Handelsreisendenpatent)	1-2	1906-27	
II A 21	Vertretungen des deutschen Han-dels und der deutschen Industrie in Schweden	1	1920-23	
II F 1	Fachzeitschriften	1-2	1919-26	
II F 2	Zeitungen und Bücher	1	1919-27	
169	Wirtschaftliche Spionage der Entente	1	1920	
118	Masse und Gewichte, Normung	1	1900-24	
I 1	Besondere Bestimmungen für den Handel	1-2	1919-26	
I 6	Handelsmerkblatt und Winke für den Aussenhandel	1	1923-27	
I 8	Warennachfragen	1	1925-27	
188	Handelsauskunftsstelle Vizekonsul Grumme	1-2	1914-26	
169	Erteilung von Handelsauskünften	1	1919-20	
84	Geschäftsempfehlungen	1	1910-23	
II A 19	Verschiedenes, Empfehlungen, Adressen, Auskünfte über Firmen	2-3	1921-30	
226	Messen	1	1919-21	
II A 12	Deutsche Ausstellungen und Messen	1-4	1921-30	
II A 13	Schwedische und andere ausser-deutsche Ausstellungen und Messen	4-5	1923-28	

Akten-zeichen	Inhalt	Band	Datum	Serial Nr.
II A 22	Schwedische Wirtschaftspropaganda	1	1920-31	
I 5	Exportkartothek Firma Kasch & Co.	1	1922-24	
II C 1	Schwedische Industrie und Verhältnisse	2-5	1921-30	
II C 2	Erze	1-2	1920-36	
II C 6	Tabakmonopol, Tabakeinfuhr, Tabakbesteuerung, Tabakzölle und Tabakanbau	1	1911-32	
II C 7	Alkohol in Schweden	1-2	1920-36	
II C 7a	Alkoholeinfuhr und Schmuggel (Konferenzen)	1	1925-31	
II C 8	Schwedische Zündholzindustrie	1-3	1924-36	
II C 9	Eisen und Stahl	1	1926-29	
II C 10	Schwedische Filmindustrie	1	1927-36	
II C 11	- Holz-und Holzveredlungsindustrie	1	1930-36	
II A 18	Erfindungen und Patentwesen, Markenschutz	1-2	1920-27	
II C 4	Landwirtschaft, Gartenbau, Forstwirtschaft	1-3	1923-31	
II C 5	Viehzucht (einschliesslich Ein- und Ausfuhr)	1	1924-29	
221	Versorgung Deutschlands mit Lebensmitteln	1-2	1918-21	
80	Fischereiabkommen, Jagd und Vogelschutz	1-4	1900-28	
33	Marineangelegenheiten, Verschiedenes	2-5	1914-21	
110	Handelsmarine, Verschiedenes	1-2	1912-21	
111	Übersendungsschreiben zu Marinedrucksachen	1-2	1907-27	
II G 1	Marineangelegenheiten	1-2	1920-22	
II D 1	Schiffahrt (allgemein)	5-10	1921-27	
II D 1a	Schiffahrtsabgeben in Schweden	1	1921-27	
30	Schiffsvermessungen und Messbriefe	1-3	1888-1927	
II D 3	Eisenbahnen und Güterverkehr	1-2	1921-27	
105	Luftschiffahrt (Flugwesen)	1-3	1908-21	
II D 2		1-6	1919-30	
II D 2a	- und Expeditionspläne	1-2	1924-27	
D 30	Flugwesen	1	1929-40	
D II 5	Grenzverkehr und sonstiger Reiseverkehr	1	1922-27	

Akten-zeichen	Inhalt	Band	Datum	Serial Nr.
131	Postangelegenheiten, Verordnungen, Reklamationen, Verträge	1	1906-22	
144	Telegrafen- und Telefonangelegenheiten, Verträge, Kabel, Verordnungen	1	1910-21	
169 XX	Berichte des Finanzbeirates der Gesandtschaft	1-4	1920-21	
81	Geld-,Bank- und Börsenwesen, finanzielle Angelegenheiten, Staatsanleihen, Verschiedenes	1-2	1908-21	
81 Abt.1-12		1	1901-21	
81 Abt.13	Internationale Valutakonferenz	1-2	1919-21	
81 Abt.14-16	Deutsch-schwedisches Kreditabkommen, deutsch-holländisches Kreditabkommen. Das Loch im Westen	1	1920	
II A 1	Deutsch-schwedisches Verrechnungsabkommen, Clearing	16	1934-36	
II E 1	Finanzangelegenheiten	1-4	1923-29	
II E 2	Währungsfragen	1	1921-24	
II E 3	Anleihen und Kreditgewährungen	1	1919-23	
225	Rubel	1	1917-22	
177	Reklamationen gegen Steuer, - Zoll und dergleichen. Behörden	1-3	1908-21	
156	Zollsachen, Verschiedenes	1	1909-21	
II A 16	Zölle	4-10	1924-33	
23	Doppelbesteuerung	1	1901-20	
II E 4	Steuern	1	1921-27	
C I/7	Unzuverlässige Firmen	Ord.	1.37- 6.38	
C I/7,8		Ord.	7.38- 5.39	
	Dienstreisen des Handelsattachés			
C II/1-9	Wirtschaftliche Verhältnisse in Deutschland Allgemeines (auch Jahresbericht) Wirtschaftsorganisationen Merkblatt für den deutschen Aussenhandel, Industrie, Handel (Aussenhandel), Preisunterbietungen, Staatsfinanzen, Währungsfragen, Bankwesen, Land- und Forstwirtschaft	Ord.	1.37- 5.39	
C II/ 1-18	Fischerei, Jagd, Pelztierzucht Handwerk und Genossenschaftswesen, Versicherungswesen, Energiewirtschaft, Rechtsfragen, Kulturfragen, Verkehrswesen (auch Posten) Vierjahresplan und Rohstoffversorgung, soziale Fragen	Ord.	1.37- 5.39	

Akten-zeichen	Inhalt	Band	Datum	Serial Nr.
C II/ 19-21	Ausstellungen, Messen, Kongresse Pressestimmen über Deutschland, Zeitungen, Kataloge, Druck-schriften, Vorträge und Reden über Deutschland	Ord.	1.37- 5.39	
C II/24	Deutsche Devisenbestimmungen	Ord.	1.37- 5.39	
C II/ 25/26	Verschiedenes	Ord.	1.37- 5.39	
	Folgen des österreichischen Anschlusses	Ord.	3.38- 5.39	
C II/28	Folgen der Angliederung Sude-tendeutschlands, Protektorat Böhmen und Mähren	Ord.	10.38- 5.39	
	Wirtschaftl.Verhandlungen in Schweden			
C III/ 6-9a	Staatsmonopole, Verstaatlichun-gen, Standardisierung und Normung, Handel (auch Handels-bilanz) Ein- und Ausfuhrbestim-mungen, Kohlen	Bdl.	1.37- 5.39	
C III/ 13-24	Staatsfinanzen, Währungsfragen, Anleihen, Bankwesen, Sparkassen, Clearing, Landwirtschaft, Forst-wirtschaft, Fischerei, Jagd, Pelztierzucht, Handwerk, Genos-senschaftswesen, Versicherungs-wesen, Energiewirtschaft, Ver-kehrswesen	Ord.	1.37- 5.39	
C III/30	Pressewesen, Zeitungen, Kataloge, Druckschriften	Bdl.	1.37- 5.39	
C III/32	Marktberichte und Absatzmöglich-keiten, Einfuhrmöglichkeiten	Bdl.	1.37- 5.39	
/33	Verschiedenes			
C IV/1-7	Wirtschaftliche Verhältnisse in anderen Ländern als Deutschland und Schweden Dänemark, Norwegen, Finnland, England, USA, UdSSR, sonstige Staaten	Ord.	1.37- 5.39	
C V/1-5	Wirtschaftliche Beziehungen zwischen Deutschland und Schweden Allgemeines, Spezielles, Beanstandungen und Beschwerden Studienreisen (Vortragsreisen) Empfehlungen und Einführungen	Bdl.	1.37- 5.39	7073/E526779-90
C V/7-8	Austausch (Studenten, Handwerker, Kaufleute)	Ord.	1.37- 5.39	
	Förderung der Ausfuhr			
C VIII 5-7	Mehrseitige internationale Wirt-schaftsbeziehungen und Abkommen Wirtschaftliche Zusammenarbeit der nordischen Länder in Kriegs-fällen. Sonstige nicht genannte Nordische Vorbehaltsklausel	Ord.	7.37- 5.39	
C IX/1	Anfragen aus Deutschland die urschriftlich mit Notizen zur Erledigung an die RfA abge-geben werden	Ord.	1.37- 5.39	

Akten-zeichen	Inhalt	Band	Datum	Serial Nr.
C IX/2a,b	Anfragen aus Deutschland betr. Vertreter, die urschrift-lich an die DHK abgegeben werden – die hier bearbeitet werden	Bd1.	1.37- 5.39	
C IX/3	betr. Forderungsangelegenheiten, die urschriftlich an die DHK abgegeben werden	Bd1.	10.36- 5.39	
C IX/4	sonstige Forderungsangelegen-heiten	Bd1.	1.37- 5.39	
C IX/5	Einholung von Auskünften über Firmen (Begleitschreiben)	Ord. Bd1.	1.37- 5.39	
C IX/8,9	Erwirkung von Jagdscheinen Bescheinigung für Umzugsgut, Heiratsgut	Bd1.	1.37- 5.39	
C X	Anfragen aus Schweden Bewerber um Vertretungen	Bd1.	1.37- 5.39	
	Firmenauskünfte A - O	Bd1.	1.30-12.37	
	– Arier	Bd1.	11.37- 1.38	
	– A - Å	Bd1.	1.38- 5.39	
Einzel-akte Ia,b b	Handelsauskünfte über schwedi-sche Verhältnisse bearbeitet bei der Gesandtschaft zur Bearbeitung abgegeben an RfA, DHK, Konsulate		6.39-12.39	
Einzel-akte I a,b,c	Einfuhrverbote		1.40-12.40	
Sonder-akte I	Schiffsmeldungen und damit in Zusammenhang stehende Angelegen-heiten		8.39- 1.42	
	Schiffsmeldungen		1939-42	
Sonder-akten III	Protektorat Böhmen und Mähren		2.40- 6.42	
C Pers G 5	Bezug von Zeitungen, Zeitschrif-ten, Büchern, Weiterleitung und Austausch von Druckschriften		6.39- 5.41	
	Alte österreichische Akten Internationale Holzwirtschafts-konferenz Holz 87		1934-38	
20	Deutsche Gesetzgebung	1-2	1934-39	
	Schwedische Gesetzgebung	1	1934-39	
19	Schutz im Ausland lebender Deutscher	1	1912-31	
37	Rechtshilfe in Zivilsachen	1	1874-1921	
D 14	Zustellungen	Bd1.	1938-42	
154	Auskünfte, Rechtsgutachten in Zivil- und Strafsachen	1-2	1912-21	
D 12	Warnungen, Straffällige	Bd1.	1925-34	

Akten-zeichen	Inhalt	Band	Datum	Serial Nr.
A 23	Nachforschungen nach dem Verbleib vermisster Personen	1	1902-22	
D 20	Ermittlungen	Bd1.	1935-37	
59	Auslieferungen von Verbrechern, Verträge	1-3	1893-1934	
228	Kriegsbeschuldigte und Auslieferungsfrage	1	1919-22	
64	Prozess- und Handelsrecht, Forderungen gegen Privatpersonen und Firmen	1-2	1907-22	
D 10	Forderungen und Differenzen	Bd1.	1935-38	
121	Nachlass- und Erbschaftsangelegenheiten	1	1907-21	
215	Forderungsangelegenheit Tufvesson in Teneriffa	3	1922-27	
Sonder-akten	Nachlass und Unterhalt: Max Roth More, Gesch. Rausch, Victor Bocks, Else Fils-Mazukuly	1	1936-41	
D 5	Verschiedenes, Auskünfte, Ermittlungen	Bd1.	1934-38	
73	Empfehlungen	3	1933-38	
	Alimentensachen	Bd1.	1928-34	
D 11	Heiratssachen	Bd1.	1924-38	
	Vermittlung in Familienrechtsangelegenheiten	Bd1.	1920-34	
22	Erwerb und Verlust der Staatsangehörigkeit	1	1894-1922	
128	Paßsachen	8-9	1923-25	
	Visa, Pässe, Grenzempfehlungen, Aufenthaltsgenehmigungen, Bescheinigungen	30 -33	1924-28	
		36	1933-38	
44	Grenzempfehlungen	1	1920-36	
53	Arbeitergesetzgebung	1-2	1900-23	
56	Ausstände und Aussperrungen	1	1909-23	
II C 1a	Soziale Verhältnisse	1-2	1924-29	
54	Versicherungswesen (allgemein)	1-2	1903-27	
D 23	Unfallrenten, Versicherungen, Pensionen	1	1925-32	
134	Übernahmen, Unterstützungen	1-4	1911-35	
146	Unterstützungswesen	1	1903-22	
D 19	Unterstützungen und Heimschaffungen	Bd1.	1934-36	
48	Rotes Kreuz	1-2	1923-39	

Akten-zeichen	Inhalt	Band	Datum	Serial Nr.
190 3	Deutsche Interessenvertretung durch Schweden in Russland, schwedische Delegierte und Verschiedenes	1-3	1918-21	
Beiheft	Rückblick auf die Fürsorgetätigkeit für deutsche Kriegs- und Zivilgefangene (Hall.)		1921	
190 4 Nr. 1	Rubelüberweisungen vom Schwedischen Generalkonsulat Moskau	10	1919-21	
	Briefvermittlung zwischen deutschen Zivilgefangenen und ihren Angehörigen			
	Rubelüberweisungen vom Schwedischen Generalkonsulat Moskau	11 -12	1918-21	
	Beschaffung von Urkunden über Zivilgefangene in Russland, Todesfälle, Vollmachten, Nachlässe	1-6	1917-26	
190 4 Nr. 2	Berichte der schwedischen Delegierten über den Besuch der Gefangenenlager in Russland	1-3	1917-21	
	Beschwerde über deutsche Zivilgefangene oder wegen Vergehen gegen deutsche Zivilgefangene	11	1917-21	
190 4 Nr. 3	Deutsche Kriegsgefangene in Russland, Heimschaffung der Gefangenen in Sibirien	1-3	1917-23	
	Nachrichtenvermittlung	1-3	1917-21	
	Ermittlungen nach deutschen Kriegsgefangenen in Russland, Forderungen, Entschädigungen laut Inhaltsverzeichnis	13	1917-24	
190 5	Nachforschungen nach Kriegs- und Zivilgefangenen, Geld- und Paketsendungen	4 6-7	1918-31	
190 6	Gewährung von Darlehn an Zivilinternierte	1-2	1917-21	
	Abrechnungen	4	1914-22	
	Darlehn an Kriegsgefangene	1-3	1916-22	
	Amtliche Geldüberweisungen nach Russland	8-9	1918-22	
190 18		4-6	1917-23	
190 19	Schadens- und Vermögensersatzansprüche aus Anlass von Verlusten in Russland	1-2	1917-22	
26	Angestellte der Mühlgrabener (Schichau)-Werft, Unterstützungen, Auskünfte	1-2	1914-21	
190	Vertretung der deutschen Interessen in Russland durch Schweden, Verschiedenes	1-5	1920-32	
207	Eigentum deutscher Beamter	11-13	1920-21	

Akten-zeichen	Inhalt	Band	Datum	Serial Nr.
215	Vertretung deutscher Interessen:			
223	Triest desgleichen Fiume	1	1919-21	
220	Attaché Mannberg, Legationsrat Lind av Hageby, Konsulatssekretär Pallat (Verschiedenes) Frage der Durchfahrt deutscher Schiffe durch die Meerengen nach dem Schwarzen Meer (Verschiedenes)	6-10	1920-22	
	Abrechnungen der B-Abt.des Ministeriums des Äussern in Stockholm (Verschiedenes) Legationsrat Wisén (Versch.)	11 -15	1922-25	
147	Vereine und Stiftungen	1-3	1910-30	
	Deutscher Hilfsverein	1	1877-1921	
	Verschiedenes, Vereine und Stiftungen	1 2 3	1909-39	6260/H049953-72 6260/H049973-76
	Deutsch-schwedische Vereinigung	4	1920-37	6261/H049978_89
	Vereine	5	1925-37	
147 Abt.3	Nordische Gesellschaft	1 2	1924-38	6262/H049991-50003 3516/E020817-73 6262/H050004-05 3516/E020874-926
147 Abt.4	Svensk-Tyska-Föreningen, Stockholm	1-2 4	1920-39	3511/E020427-42
147 Abt.6	Deutsche Vereinigung	1	1913-36	
71	Deutschtum im Auslande	3	1932-38	3503/E020283-88
124	Nobel-Stiftung	1-3	1897-1937	
3	Auswanderungswesen	1	1898-1926	
62	Auswanderung und Einwanderung	1	1908-23	
128	Jugendbewegung: Reisen deutscher Wandervögel und Pfadfinder, Schülerreisen, Hitlerjugend	1-3	1924-39	
95	Evangelische Kirchengemeinde in Malmö	1-3	1908-36	
	Katholische Kirche in Schweden	1 2	1911-39	3509/E020390-416
	Deutsche Kirche in Göteborg	1	1933-38	
	Kirchenangelegenheiten, Verschiedenes	2 3	1934-39	3515/E020794-801 3515/E020802-12
	Kirchen, Schulen, wissenschaftliche Anstalten, Hochschulen	1	1928-37	
95 B Sonder-akte KII		1	1908-23	

Akten-zeichen	Inhalt	Band	Datum	Serial Nr.
95	Schulen, Hochschulen, wissen-schaftliche Anstalten, Versch.	8 9	1933-39	6263/H050007-25 6263/H050026-40
	Deutsche Schule in Stockholm	1	1935-38	
	Deutsch-schwedischer Schüler-austausch	1-2	1933-39	
	Deutsche Sprache an schwedi-schen Lehranstalten, Lektoren, Sprachkurse	1-2	1932-39	
	Buchprämien für gute Leistungen in der deutschen Sprache	1	1928-39	
	Studienreisen	6 7 8 9	1935-39	6264/H050042-58 6264/H050059-61
	Deutsch-akademischer Austausch-dienst (Dr.Kappner)	1 2	1934-38	6265/H050063-85 6265/H050086-89
	Ausländer an deutschen Hoch-, Fach- und anderen Schulen, Ferienkurse	7-8	1931-39	
	Germanistische Professur an der Hochschule in Stockholm	1	1927-31	
	Alexander von Humboldt-Stiftung	1	1925-39	
67	Wissenschaftliche Kongresse und Konferenzen	7 8 9	1934-39	6266/H050091-103
S III 22	Sven Hedin und die Firma Junkers (Expedition)	1 2	1926-32	6267/H050105-107 6267/H050108-110
60	Kunstausstellungen	3	1917-21	
61	–　　　München	1	1909-22	
99	Ausstellungen, Kunst und Wissen-schaft	7	1938	
	Kunst, Verschiedenes	1	1931-39	
	Wissenschaft, Verschiedenes	2+4	1935-39	
116	Kulturelles, Verschiedenes	1-3	1918-25	
		8	1934-39	
162	Deutsche Kinder in Schweden	1-2	1919-27	
20	Königlich-Gymnastisches Zentral-institut	10	1926-38	
161	Drucksachen, Veröffentlichungen und Vorträge	1-3	1917-21	
186	Vortragspropaganda	1-4	1918-27	
		5+9	1927-30 1937-39	
	Vortragsreise des Grafen Luckner	1	1921-22	
	Professor Dr.Walter Lund	1 2	1917-39	6268/H050112-34

Akten-zeichen	Inhalt	Band	Datum	Serial Nr.
186	Buchpropaganda, Absatz deutscher Bücher und Zeitschriften	1-4	1919-39	
	Französische Propaganda	1-2	1920-39	
	Künstlerische Propaganda, Musik, Theater	1-6	1915-33	
		12-13	1937-39	
	Filmpropaganda	1-4	1916-24	
	Filme	7	1937-39	6269/H050136-45
	Propaganda, Verschiedenes	3	1935-39	6270/H050147-52 3507/E020305-35
	Deutsche Kulturarbeit im Auslande	4	1936-39	3508/E020338-87
159	Sport aller Art, Olympische Spiele	1-5	1911-38	
	Olympiaden	1-2	1919-38	
	Sport, Verschiedenes	1	1922-39	
	Leichtathletik	1	1920-39	
178 I	Presse, Sonderfonds geheim	1	1915-32	L892/L253407-54 6276/H050339-72
		2		6276/H050373-415
		3		6276/H050416-74
178 V/VII	Die Presse, Verschiedenes	1	1916-24	6280/H050589-617
		2		6281/H050619-48
		3		6282/H050650-73
		4		6282/H050674-93
178 XIV		1-9	1919-31	
		16	1936-39	6283/H050752-69
		17		6283/H050770-76
		18		6283/H050777-82
		19		
178 XV	Deutsche Zeitungen	1	1921-39	
178 XVI	Ausländische Zeitungen	1	1914-39	6284/H050784-824
	Svenska Dagblatt	1	1921-39	6284/H050825-58
	Sozialdemokraten	1	1920-39	
	Dagens Nyheter	1	1927-39	
	Nya Dagligt Allehanda	1	1929-39	6284/H050859-88
	Stockholms Tidningen	1	1930-39	6284/H050889-905
	Göteborgs Handels-Och Sjöfart-stidning	1	1934-39	
S III	Göteborgs Morgonpost	1	1917-33	6284/H050906-50
		2		6284/H050951-78
S III 8	Svenska Telegrammbyrå	1	1918-21	6285/H050980-1033
178 XVII	Korrespondenten	1	1914-26	6286/H051035-78
		2		6286/H051079-111
		3		6286/H051112-32
		4		6286/H051133-47
		5		
		1-2	1927-39	

Akten-zeichen	Inhalt	Band	Datum	Serial Nr.
178 XVII	Korrespondenten, Dr.Konrad Flex	1-3	1925-29	
	– Uddgren	1	1926-35	6287/H051149-58
178 XVIII	Jüdische politische Nachrichten	1	1923	
178 XXI	Veröffentlichung der politischen West-Ost-Nachrichten-Agentur Polwona	1	1920-21	
178 XIX	Presseberichte des Auswärtigen Amtes	1-5	1919-22	
178 IV Abt.13	Pressetelefonate nach Berlin	1	1923-28	
178 IV Abt.10	Presse-Wochenberichte	1-5	1918-31	
178 IV Abt.11	Politische Wochenübersicht	1-2	1923-30	
Abt.12	Politische Wochenberichte des Auswärtigen Amtes	1	1928-32	
186	Verteilung von Drucksachen	1-10	1918-28	
241	– von Propagandamaterial	2	1934-39	
D P 1	Deutschland, Presse- und Propagandawesen, Allgemeines	1	1939-41	6288/H051160-97
P 2 Nr.1	Schweden, Presse- und Propagandawesen, Beziehungen zu Deutschland	1 2 3 4 5	1939-41	6289/H051199-259 6289/H051260-302 6289/H051303-36 6289/H051337-72 6289/H051373-426
P 2 Nr.2	Beziehungen zu anderen Staaten und zwischen anderen Staaten	1 2	1939-41	6290/H051428-35
P 2 Nr.3	Greuel- und Lügenmeldungen der ausländischen Presse und deren Bekämpfung	1	1939	6291/H051437-39
P 3	Schweden, Presse-Verlagsanstalten, Zeitungen	1	1939-40	6292/H051441-86
P 3 Nr.3	Südschwedische Presse	1	1939-41	6293/H051488-500
P 6	Schweden, Presse, Beanstandungen in Presse, Rundfunk, Film und Propaganda	1 2 3 4	1939-41	6294/H051502-38 6294/H051539-51 6294/H051552-65
98	Jahresberichte der Konsulate	1-4	1923-35	
	Konsulate in Schweden	1	1921-29	
	– Gothenburg	1-4	1915-29	
	– Karlskrona	1	1907-30	
	Vizekonsulat in Karlshamm	1	1902-33	
	– Luleå	1	1902-22	
	Konsulat Malmö	1 2 3	1902-36	6295/H051567-86

Akten-zeichen	Inhalt	Band	Datum	Serial Nr.
98	Konsulat Norrköping Akten	Ord. 1 2 3	1939-41	6296/H051588-93 6296/H051594-97 6296/H051598-603
Pers.G.1	Akten	1	1940-43	6297/H051605-98
Pers.7 b		1	1940-43	
D.W.H.7 c		1	1940-43	
W.2 Nr.4		1	1940-43	
R.3 Nr.4		1	1940-43	
Kult 3		1	1940-43	
	Konsulat Östersund	Heft		
Pers.G.4	Grundstücksverwaltung, Mietvertrag	1	1940-41	
Pers.R.14	Heimschaffung	1	1940	
D.Pol.3 Nr.7	Betr. Spielen des Badenweiler Marsches	1	1940	
	Parteiangelegenheiten	1	1940-41	6298/H051700-03
D.Pol.3 Nr.9	Militär, Marine, Luftfahrt	1	1940-41	
Pol.3 Nr.3	Militär	1	1940	
R.3.Nr.3	Gerichtswesen	1	1940-41	
R.3.Nr.6	Strafrecht	1	1940	
R.4	Arbeits- und Gewerberecht	1	1940-41	
D.R.3	Staatsrecht, Zivil- und Strafrecht	1	1940-41	
D.R.3 Nr.4	Familienrecht, Ehe und Personenstand	1	1940	
D.R.6	Sozial- und Fürsorgewesen	1	1941	
D.R.5	Paßerlasse	1	1940-41	
D.R.6 Nr.2	Winterhilfswerk	1	1940	
	Österreichische Gesandtschaft Stockholm	1-3	1924-28	
16	A-Journale		1914-39	
26	B-Journale		1914-39	
Index	2 Bücher		1931-39	
Index	2 Bücher		1931-39	
	Tagebuch des Finanzbeirats der deutschen Gesandtschaft			

Akten-zeichen	Inhalt	Band	Datum	Serial Nr.
A	Botschaftsakten	1	1939	
A I 1 a	Allgemeine Angelegenheiten der deutschen Auslandsvertretungen	1	1933-39	4006/E058691-98
A I 1 c	NSDAP. Anordnungen ihrer Organisationen und Gliederungen, Mitgliedschaft	1	1935-39	
A I 1 e	Auswärtiges Amt	1	1936-39	4094/E069529-49
A I 2 f	Devisenzuteilung an Beamte des Auswärtigen Dienstes	1	1934-39	
A I 2 g	Dienstreisen und Reisekosten	1	1924-38	
A I 2 k	Allgemeine Wehrpflicht und Beamte des Auswärtigen Dienstes	1	1935-39	
A II 2 a	Personalangelegenheiten der Botschaft Beamte	1	1936-38	
A II 2 c	– Angestellte	1	1934-39	
A II 2 d	Dienstakten Militärattaché	1 2	1928-39	4073/E068777-80
	Persönliches, Militärattaché und sein Personal	1	1934-39	
A II 2 e	Besteuerung der Angestellten	1	1934-36	
A II 2 f	Reichsangestellten- und Invalidenversicherung	1	1924-39	
A II 2 g	Polnische Sozialversicherung für Büroangestellte	1	1932-38	
A II 2 i	Autoangelegenheiten der Botschaftsmitglieder	1	1936-38	
A II 2 m	Aufbau des Wirtschaftsdienstes der Deutschen Botschaft in Warschau	1	1937-38	
A II 2 n	Übernahme von Beamten und Angestellten der ehem.österreichischen Vertretungen	1	1937-39	
Pers.Botschafter	Persönliche Angelegenheiten des Herrn Botschafters und Personal	1-2	1931-39	
	Personalien:			
	Achtnig, Friedrich	1	1927-38	
	Grf.Attems	1	1938-39	
	Bachian, Martha	1	1934-38	
	Baum, Wilhelm	1	1937-38	
	Birnbaum, Imanuel	1	1937	
	Blissmer, Georg	1	1925-39	
	Boldt, Gerhard	1	1935-39	
	Brandtner, Gustav	1	1934-39	
	Bürgam, Karl	1	1933-38	
	Danek, Johann	1	1938-39	
	Daniel, Alfred	1	1939-40	
	Duchow, Willy	1	1939-40	
	Dziemba, Lothar	1	1939	

Akten-zeichen	Inhalt	Band	Datum	Serial Nr.
Pers. Botsch.	Personalien:			
	Engel, Elisabeth	1	1937-39	
	Espe, Wilhelm	1	1938-39	
	Fibich, Alfred	1	1920-39	
	George, Erika	1	1936-39	
	Geuther, Fritz	1	1937-38	
	Grytz, Paul	1	1938-39	
	Habermann, Kurt	1	1935-39	
	Hannighofer, Heinrich	1	1932-39	
	Henschke, Willi	1	1921-40	
	Hoffmann, Hedwig	1	1930-39	
	Holitzner, Wilhelm	1	1937-38	
	Dr.Jalowietzki, Gerhard	1	1926-39	
	John, Herbert	1	1938-39	
	Jüttemann, Hermann	1	1920-39	
	Kegel, Gerhard	1-2	1934-39	
	Knaepper, Paula	1	1931-39	
	Koischwitz, Karl	1	1929-39	
	Kruhöffer, Ilse	1	1932-39	
	Dr.Krümmer, Ewald	1	1932-39	
	Küchel, Martha	1	1938	
	Kulschewski, Ewald	1	1936-38	
	Losereit, Herbert	1	1939-40	
	Marganski, Henryk	1	1936-38	
	Matz, Elfriede	1	1933-39	
	Maudanz, Karl	1	1939	
	Metge, Ilse	1	1938-39	
	Mottl, Alexander	1	1936-39	
	Müller, Hermann	1	1937-39	
	v.Nostitz-Wallwitz	1	1938-39	
	Otto, Käte	1	1937-39	
	Potrykus, Anna	1	1938-39	
	Romuald Rebczynski	1	1935-38	
	Rominski, Sophie	1	1937-39	
	Ross, Erwin	1	1934-39	
	Sadowski, Alexander	1	1929-32	
	Schambeck, Jacob	1	1935-39	
	Schatten, Willi	1	1938-40	
	von Scheliha	1	1932-39	4084/E069212-15
	Schroeder, Christel	1	1936-40	
	Schulz, Heinrich	1	1928-40	
	Dr.Seelos, Gebhard	1	1935-38	
	v.Sperber, Ilse	1	1937-39	
	Spickermann, Willi	1	1938-39	
	Sprink, Georg	1	1936-39	
	Dr.Struve, Gustav	1	1937-39	
	Thurnhofer, Alice	1	1938-39	
	Tornow, Hedwig	1	1934-39	

Akten-zeichen	Inhalt	Band	Datum	Serial Nr.
Pers. Botsch.	Personalien:			
	v.Trotha, Ingeborg	1	1938-39	
	v.Trütschler	1	1939	
	Werner, Ilse-Dorothea	1	1937-39	
	v.Wühlisch	1	1936-39	
	Zinsser, Christian	1	1937-38	
	Hilfspersonal, allgemein	1	1929-39	
	Einstellung einer Hilfskraft	1	1928-35	
A 3	Dienstgebäude (Hauskauf)	1-5	1921-33	
	Wohnungsangelegenheiten	1	1921-22	
A 3 b	Materialienbeschaffung für das Dienstgebäude	1	1921-35	
A II 3 a	Dienstgebäude der Botschaft	1	1933-35	
A II 3 b	Neues Dienstgebäude bezw.Grund-stück (Kaufangebot)	1-3	1934-39	
	Neubau Botschaft, Lieferungs-angebote	1	1935-38	
A II 3 d	Deutsch-polnisches Abkommen über gegenseitige Freistellung der beiderseitigen Botschafts- und Konsulatsgrundstücke	1	1927-39	
A II 3 e	Heizungsanlage, Lieferung von Koks und Brennmaterial	1	1935-38	
A II 3 f	Fernsprecher (Hausanlage)	1-2	1935-39	
A II 3 g	Dienstkraftwagen	1	1935-39	
A II 3 h	- Versicherung	1	1934-39	
A II 3 k	Dienstwohnungen	2	1934-39	
A II 5 b	Ausstattung des Dienstgebäudes und der Diensträume	1	1923-36	
A II 3 m	Übernahme der ehemaligen öster-reichischen Gesandtschaft in Warschau	1	1933-38	
A II 3 n	Übernahme der ehemaligen tsche-choslowakischen Gesandtschaft und des Personals	1	1939	
B I	Angelegenheiten der Beamten und Angestellten der ehemaligen deutschen Botschaft Warschau	1-2	1939-40	
B IX	Urkundenbeschaffung	1	1938-40	
B X	Gebäude der ehemaligen Tsche-chischen Gesandtschaft in Warschau	1	1939-40	
B XII	Inventar der ehemaligen Tsche-chischen Gesandtschaft in Warschau	1	1940	
A II 4 a	Haushaltswesen, Voranschläge	1	1937	
A II 4 k	Kulturfonds (geheim)	1-4	1934-38	

Akten-zeichen	Inhalt	Band	Datum	Serial Nr.
A II 4 i	Pressefonds (geheim)	1-2	1926-39	
A II 4 m	Fonds zur Ausgestaltung der wirtschaftlichen Berichterstattung und zur Aussenhandelsförderung	1	1935-39	
A II 8 a	Chiffrierwesen I (geheim)	1	1935-39	
A II 8 b	Telegrammwesen	1	1924-38	
A II 8 c	Chiffrierwesen II (Rundfunk) geheim	1	1934-39	7983/E575229-32
A III 1 a	Allgemeine Angelegenheiten der deutschen Konsularbehörden in Polen	1	1936-38	
A III 1 b	Personalveränderungslisten der bei den deutschen Vertretungen in Polen beschäftigten Beamten und Angestellten	1	1935-39	4095/E069552-600
A III 1 c	Vereinbarung mit Polen über die steuerliche Behandlung der beiderseitigen Konsulatsbeamten und Angestellten	1	1933-36	
A III 1 d	Wohnungssteuer von deutschen Konsulatsbeamten und Angestellten in Polen	1	1932-36	
A III 2 a	Generalkonsulat Posen	1	1935-39	
A III 2 b	- Kattowitz	1	1935-39	
A III 2 c	Neubau des deutschen Generalkonsulats in Kattowitz	1	1934-37	
A III 2 d	Deutsches Konsulat Thorn	1	1935-39	
A III 2 e	Erhebung des Konsulats in Thorn zum Generalkonsulat	1	1934-39	
A III 2 f	Konsulat Krakau	1	1935-39	
A III 2 g	- Lodz	1	1935-39	
A III 2 h	Paßstelle Bromberg	1	1935-39	
A III 2 i	Generalkonsulat Danzig	1	1935-38	
A III 2 k	Errichtung eines deutschen Konsulats in Wilna	1	1935	
A III 2 L	Konsularische Vertretung in Gdingen	1	1928-39	
A III 2 m	Konsulat Lemberg	1	1938-39	
A III 2 n	- Bielitz	1	1938-39	
A III p	Auflösung der ehemaligen österreichischen Konsulate in Polen	1	1938	
A III r	Konsulat Teschen	1	1938-39	
A IV 1 a	Diplomatisches Korps in Warschau	1	1932-39	
A IV 1 b	Minister für auswärtige Angelegenheiten	1	1935-39	

Akten-zeichen	Inhalt	Band	Datum	Serial Nr.
A IV 1 c	Polnische diplomatische und konsularische Vertretungen im Ausland	1	1935-39	
A IV 1 d	Deutsche diplomatische und kon-sularische Vertretungen im Ausland	1	1936-39	
A IV 1 e	Fremde diplomatische und konsu-larische Vertretungen in Polen	1	1935-39	
A IV 1 f	- im Ausland	1	1935-39	
A IV 1 g	Polnische diplomatische und konsularische Vertretungen in Deutschland	1	1935-39	
A IV 1 h	Fremde diplomatische Vertretun-gen in Deutschland	1	1936-38	
A V 1 a	Etikette, Protokollangelegen-heiten	1-2	1935-39	
A V 2 a	Verleihung von Ehrenzeichen, Orden	1	1933-39	
A V 2 b	Ehrenzeichen des Deutschen Roten Kreuzes	1-2	1921-39	
A V 2 d	Ehrenkreuz für polnische Staats-angehörige	1	1934-35	
A V 2 e	Verleihung des Verwundetenabzei-chens	1	1936	
A V 2 f	Verleihung des Treudienstehren-abzeichens	1	1938-39	
A V 3 a	Spenden, Sammlungen	1	1933-39	
A VI 1 a	Deutscher Klub Warschau	1	1935-39	
A VI 1 b	- Hilfsverein Warschau	1-2	1920-37	
A VI 1 c	Verein Deutscher Hochschüler	1	1936-37	
	Verschiedene Briefe von und an Herrn Botschafter v.Moltke, sowie gehaltene Reden	1	1934-35	
	Briefe Dr.Krümmer	1	1935-39	
	- von Scheliha	1	1935-39	
	- Schliep	1	1936-39	7260/E532758-62 4010/E058726-37
	- Struve	1	1938-39	
	- v.Wühlisch	1	1938-39	4011/E058740-41
P 2 a	Deutsch-polnische Vereinbarung vom 26.I.1934		1934	9984/E697408-17
P 2 i	Polens Beziehungen zu Danzig	1-6	1929-35	
P 2 k	Polnischer Westmarkenverein	1	1929-35	
P 2 L	Französisch-russischer und polnisch-russischer Vertrags-abschluss-Verhandlungen (Nichtangriffspakt)	1-2	1931-34	

Akten-zeichen	Inhalt	Band	Datum	Serial Nr.
3 sp.	Verfassungsreform		1929-35	
3	Polens innere Politik	1-8a	1920-36	
3 a	Polnische Presse und Propaganda-fonds	1-3	1930-35	
3 b	Personalien prominenter Persön-lichkeiten		1931-35	
4	Polens Sozialpolitik	1-4	1922-34	
4 a	Streiks		1921-26	
5	Unterrichts-, Kirchen-, Schul- und Vereinswesen	6-8	1929-33	
	Welt· Goethe-Ehrung	8a	1931-32	
	Vereins-, Kirchen- und Schulwesen Künstler	9-11	1933-35	
5 a	Kirchenwesen	4-7	1929-34	
5 b	Schulgelderhebung für die Kinder deutscher Diplomaten in Polen		1924-31	
	Schulfrage der Minderheiten in Oberschlesien	1-2	1927-33	
	Schulangelegenheiten	4-6	1931-34	
5 c	Deutsche Kunstausstellung in Warschau		1928-30	
5 d	Studienreisen nach Polen	1-3	1929-35	
5 e	Polnische Vereine in Deutschland		1927-33	
5 f	Klagen über Unterdrückung pol-nischer Minderheiten in Deutsch-land	1	1928-32	
	Polnisches Schulwesen in Deutsch-land		1930-35	
5 g	Internationale Reiterturniere in Warschau, Sportangelegen-heiten	1-4	1927-35	
5 h	Theater, Musikwesen, Deutsche Kunstgesellschaft	1-3 4	1929-33	6249/E470338-43
6	Nationalitäten, Minderheiten, Judenfragen	1		K1698/K406502-23
		2	1920-27	K1698/K406524-74
		3		K1698/K406575-608
		4		K1698/K406609-27
		5		K1698/K406628-29
		6	1928-33	K1698/K406630-43
		7		K1698/K406644-53
		8		
		9	1934-35	K1698/K406654-71
		10		9396/E665514-19
	Verhaftung des Abgeordneten Ulitz		1929	

Akten-zeichen	Inhalt	Band	Datum	Serial Nr.
P 6 b	Deutscher Kultur- und Wirt-schaftsbund		1929-32	
P 8	Militär- und Marineangelegen-heiten	4	1927-29	
	Manöver, Truppentransporte aus Ostpreussen ins übrige Deutsch-land	4a	1926-34	
	Militärangelegenheiten	5	1934-35	
	Technische Truppenteile	3	1927-33	
P 8 a	Marineangelegenheiten		1922-34	
P 8 b	Polizei, Gendarmerie, Feuerwehr		1929-33	
P 9 a	Spionage-Übergriffe		1921-25	
	Nachrichtendienst, Sonderakten		1920-28	
P 10	Bolschewismus - Kommunismus	1-2	1920-34	
P 11	Sowjetrussland	5-8	1926-34	
P 11 a	Deutsch-russischer Vertrag von Rapallo		1922-34	
P 12	Ukraine	1-5	1920-34	
P 13	Randstaaten	14 -22	1927-35	
P 13 a	Deutsch-litauische Beziehungen		1923-34	
P 14	Galizien		1922-34	
P 15	Danzig	1-14	1920-35	
	Deutscher Flottenbesuch in Danzig		1925-32	
P 16	Pomerellen		1920-35	
P 17	Oberschlesien	12 -17	1922-35	
P 17 a	- Grenzfestsetzungen		1922-27	
P 23	Ostsee		1921-33	
P 24	Oder	1-2	1921-34	
P 25	Weichsel, Hela,Gdingen, Wester-platte	1-1a	1921-29	
P 25	Weichsel und Weichselniederung	2	1934	
	- Sonderakte	2a	1924-34	
P 25 a	Warthe, Netze,Küddow, Proma		1929-33	
P 25 b	Danzigs Klage gegen Polen, Sonderakten		1930-35	
	Gdingen, Hela, Westerplatte		1927-33	
P 25 c	Danzig-polnische Vereinbarungen über den Port d'attaché		1925-34	

Akten-zeichen	Inhalt	Band	Datum	Serial Nr.
I 1 a	Polnische Politik im allgemeinen	1-2	1936-39	
I 1 b	Polnische Aussenpolitik	1	1935-39	4089/E069257-79
		2		3929/E051708-22
I 2 a	Polnische Innenpolitik, allg.	1-3	1935-38	
I 2 c	Polnisches Parteiwesen	1-2	1935-39	
I 2 d	Sejm und Gemeindewahlen (Wahlordnungsgesetz)	1-2	1935-39	
I 2 e	Tod Pilsudskis	1-2	1935-39	
I 2 f	Polnisches Gesetz über Abzeichen und Uniformen	1-2	1933-38	
I 2 g	Minderheiten in Polen (ausser deutscher Minderheit), Ukrainer	1	1937-39	
I 2 h	Weissrussische Minderheit in Polen	1	1938	
I 3 a	Poln. Verbände	1-2	1935-39	
I 3 b	- Westverband	1-2	1935-39	
I 3 c	- Gedenktage	1-2	1935-39	
I 3 d	- Arbeitsdienst	1	1936-39	
I 3 e	Polen, Freimaurertum, geheim	1	1936-39	
I 3 f	Poln. Polizeiwesen	1	1936-38	
I 3 g	- Winterhilfe	1	1936-37	
I 3 h	Attentate in Polen	1	1937	
I 4 a	Polnische Presse und Propaganda-wesen	1-2	1935-39	
I 4 b	Polnische Tageszeitungen	1-2	1935-39	
I 4 c	Verzeichnis der englischen und amerikanischen Journalisten in Warschau	1	1931-38	
I 4 d	Warschauer Club der Auslands-presse	1	1934-36	
I 5 a	Polnisches Schul- und Unterrichts-wesen	1-2	1936-38	
I 5 b	Polen, Schulreform und Ehe-gesetzgebung	1	1931-35	
I 6 a	- Kirchenwesen	1-2	1936-39	
I 6 b	Orthodoxe und griechisch-katholische Kirche in Polen	1	1937-38	
I 7 a	Judenangelegenheiten in Polen	1-2	1935-39	
I 8 a	Polen, Militärwesen	1 -2	1936-39	8154/E582584-86
I 8 b	- Marineangelegenheiten	1	1937-38	
I 8 c	Militärfliegerei	1-2	1936-39	

Akten-zeichen	Inhalt	Band	Datum	Serial Nr.
P I 8 d	Befestigung der Halbinsel Hela	1-2	1937-39	
P I 9 a	Posen und Pomerellen	1-2	1935-39	
P I 9 c	Oberschlesien	1	1938	
P I 9 e	Kongresspolen, Lodz	1	1938	
P I 9 f	Kleinpolen, Galizien	1	1936	
P I 9 g	Wilna	1	1935-37	
P I 9 h	Wilnaer "Slowo"	1	1935-36	
P I 10 a	Auslandspolen	1-2	1929-39	
P I 10 b	Polnische Fürsorge für die Lands-leute in der Fremde	1	1930-32	
P I 10 c	- Auswanderung	1-3	1925-38	
P I 11 a	- See- und Kolonialliga	1 2	1933-39	7589/E543281-90 4024/E059437-47
P I 12 a	Volksgruppen in Polen	1-2	1935-39	
P	Neueingänge, Politik, Verschied.	1	1939	
P I 1-12		1	1939	7983/E575233-35 8278/E588246-49
P II 1 a	Deutsche Politik, allgemein	1	1935-38	
P II 1 b	- Aussenpolitik	1 2	1935-39	4008/E058707-11
P II 1 c	Reichsparteitage und Stuttgarter Tagungen	1-2	1936-39	
P II 2 a	Deutsche Innenpolitik im allgem.	1-2	1935-39	
P II 2 b	Deutschland, Arbeitsdienst	1-2	1935-39	
P II 2 c	Gedenktage in Deutschland	1-2	1935-39	
P II 2 d	Minderheiten in Deutschland (ausser Polen)	1	1936-38	
P II 3 a	Deutschland, Rassegesetzgebung, Bevölkerungspolitik	1	1935-37	
	Rassenlehre gegen Slawentum	1	1934-37	
P II 3 b	Deutschland, Auswanderung	1	1934-37	
P II 3 c	Reichstagswahlen, Deutschland	1	1936-38	
P II 4 a	Deutschland, Pressewesen,Gen.	1	1935-38	
P II 4 b	Deutsche Tageszeitungen und Pressevertreter	1	1935-38	
P II 4 c	Deutsche Propaganda für das Ausland	1-2	1935-39	
P II 4 d	Lügenhetze und Angriffe der aus-ländischen Presse gegen Deutsch-land	1	1935-37	
P II 4 e	Greuelhetze in Polen, antideut-sche Hetze	1-2	1933-34	

Akten-zeichen	Inhalt	Band	Datum	Serial Nr.
P II 5 a	Deutschland, Schul-und Unter-richtswesen	1	1935-37	
P II 6 a	- Kirchenwesen	1-2	1935-39	
P II 7 a	Lösung der Judenfrage in Deutschland	1-2	1935-39	
P II 8 a	Deutschland, Heer, Militärange-legenheiten	1-2	1935-39	
P II 8 b	- Marineangelegen-heiten	1	1935-37	
P II 8 c	- Luftwaffe	1	1930	
P II 8 d	Allgemeine Wehr- und Arbeits-dienstpflicht	1-2	1935-39	
P II 10 a	Auslandsdeutschtum V.D.A.	1-2	1935-39	
P II 10 b	Beteiligung der Auslandsdeut-schen an Wahlen	1-2	1936-38	
P II 10 c	Deutsche Minderheiten im Ausland	1	1936-37	
P II 11 a	Kolonialfragen	1-2	1936-38	
P II	Neueingänge Politik, Verschied.	1	1939	
P III 1 a	Allgemeine politische Beziehun-gen zwischen Deutschland und Polen	1 2	1935-39	5815/E423857-62 3925/E051623-49 3924/E051607-21
P III 1 b	Deutsche Staatsbesuche in Polen	1 2	1936-39	4009/E058714-23 4005/E058679-88
P III 1 b - s	Besuchsreisen von Reichsdeut-schen und deutschen Organisa-tionen in Polen	1	1937-39	
P III 1 c	Polnische Staatsbesuche in Deutschland	1	1935-37	4074/E068783-810
P III 1 c - s	Besuchsreisen von polnischen Organisationen in Deutschland	1	1938-39	
P III 1 d	Stimmung und Hetze gegen Deutschland (nicht Presse)	1-5	1935-39	
P III 1 e	Deutsche Emigranten in Polen	1	1933-36	
P III 1 f	NSDAP in Polen	1-2	1936-39	
P III 1	Neueingänge, Verschiedenes	1	1939	3927/E051661-62
P III 2 a	Deutsche Minderheiten in Polen, Generalia	1 2-4	1935-39	9395/E665507-11
P III 2 a - s	Minderheiten - Erklärungen	1 2	1937-38	6214/E470030-33 7589/E543291-316
P III 2 b	Deutsche Minderheiten in Pommerellen	1-3	1935-39	
P III 2 b - J	- (J)	1-2	1935-37	

Akten-zeichen	Inhalt	Band	Datum	Serial Nr.
P III 2 c	Deutsche Minderheiten in Oberschlesien	1	1935-39	
P III 2 c - J	- (J)	1-2	1935-38	
P III 2 c - s	Prozess gegen die NSDAP in Kattowitz, geheim	1	1936	
P III 2 d	Entlassungen von Deutschen in Ost-Oberschlesien	1-2	1935-39	
P III 2 e	Deutsche Minderheiten in Polen, Genfer Abkommen	1 2-6	1935-38	7598/E543749-52
P III 2 f	Organisierung von Reichsdeut-schen in Polen	1	1935-38	
P III 2 g	Deutsch-polnischer Volksgruppen-vertrag	1	1936	7589/E543370-412
P III 2 h	Ehemalige österreichische Staats-angehörige in Polen	1	1938	
P III 2 i	Bisherige Deutschtumsarbeit Österreichs in Polen	1	1938	
P III 2 k	Organisationen (Vereine,Verbände) der deutschen Minderheiten in Polen	1	1938-39	
P III 2	Neueingänge, Verschiedenes	1	1939	8155/E582588-99
P III 3 a	Polnische Minderheiten in Deutschland, Generalia	1-3	1935-39	
P III 3 a - J	- (J)	1	1935-37	
P III 3	Neueingänge, Verschiedenes	1	1939	
P IV		1	1939	
P III 4 a	Pressetelegramme über polnische Presse	1	1936-37	
P III 4 b	Wochenberichte über polnische Presse	1-6	1935-39	
P III 4 c	Deutschsprachige Zeitungen und Zeitschriften in Polen	1	1933-39	
P III 4 d	Deutsche Pressevertreter in Polen	1-2	1934-39	
P III 4 e	Deutschfeindliches Schrifttum in Polen	1	1935-39	
P III 4 f	Deutsche Beanstandungen über die polnische Presse	1-5	1934-39	
P III 4 g	Polnische Beanstandungen über die deutsche Presse	1-3	1934-39	
P III 4 h	Polnische Pressevertreter in Deutschland	1-2	1935-39	
P III 4 k	Deutsch-polnische Presseabkommen	1-2	1934-39	
P III 4 m	Schrifttum über den National-sozialismus in Polen	1	1938	

Akten-zeichen	Inhalt	Band	Datum	Serial Nr.
P III 4	Neueingänge, Pressewesen, Verschiedenes	1	1939	
P III 4 b	Neueingänge, Wochenberichte, Verschiedenes	1	1939	7983/E575236-40
P III 5 a	Deutsches Schulwesen in Polen	1-4	1934-39	
P III 5 a J	- (J)	1-3	1935-39	
P III 5 b	Polnisches Schulwesen in Deutschland	1-2	1935-38	
P III 5 b J	- (J)	1	1935-38	
P III 5	Neueingänge,Schulwesen,Verschiedenes	1	1939	
P III 6 a	Evangelische Kirche in Polen	1-3	1933-39	
P III 6 b	Lage der Deutschen Evangelischen Kirche in Polen	1-3	1935-39	
P III 6 c	Deutsche katholische Kirchenangelegenheiten in Polen	1 2	1935-37	3926/E051652-59 4007/E058700-04
P III 7 a	Polnische Juden in Deutschland	1 2	1935-39	3928/E051665-705
P III 8 a	Deutsche Flottenbesuche in Gdingen	1	1935	
P III 8 b	Polnische Flottenbesuche in Deutschland	1	1934-35	
P III 8 c	Militärdienst von deutschen Minderheitsangehörigen in Polen	1	1935-39	
P III 8 d	Überfliegen des Korridors durch deutsche Militärflugzeuge	1	1935-39	
P III 8 e	Überfliegen von deutschem Gebiet durch polnische Militärflugzeuge	1	1936-39	
P III 9 a	Posen und Pommerellen	1-2	1935-39	
P III 9 c	Oberschlesien	1-2	1935-38	
P III 9 d	Begutachtender Ausschuss für Arbeitsfragen in Oberschlesien	1	1927-37	
P III 9 e	Gemischte Kommission für Oberschlesien	1	1936-38	
P III 9 f	Interessengemeinschaft Kattowitz geheim	1 2 3	1932-38	9093/E639580-645 9093/E639646-55
P III 9 g	Pless-Besitz in Oberschlesien	1 2	1935-39	4025/E059450-84
P III 9 h	St.Julius-Hospital in Rybnik	1	1936-39	
P III 9 i	Olsa-Gebiet	1-2	1938-39	
P III 10a	Spionagefälle gegen Deutschland	1-2	1934-39	
P III 10c	Deutsch-polnischer Austausch von politischen Gefangenen	1-2	1935-38	

Akten-zeichen	Inhalt	Band	Datum	Serial Nr.
P III 10d	Persönlichkeit Stefan Olpinski	1	1933-38	
P III 11a	Ansprüche polnischer Staatsange-höriger gegen den deutschen Fiskus, Generalia	1	1935-39	
P III 11b	- Einzelfälle	1	1935-37	
P	Neueingänge, Verschiedenes	1	1939	7983/E575241-44
P III 6 - 10		1	1939	
P IV 10	Beziehungen Deutschlands - Balkanstaaten	1	1938	
P IV 11	- Belgien	1	1935-38	
P IV 12	- Brasilien	1	1938	
P IV 17	- Danzig	1	1936-39	
P IV 18	- England	1	1935-39	
P IV 19	- Estland	1	1935-39	
P IV 20	- Finnland	1	1935-38	
P IV 21	- Frankreich	1	1935-38	
P IV 23	- Holland	1	1936	
P IV 27	- Italien	1	1935-38	
P IV 28	- Japan	1	1936-38	
P IV 29	- Jugoslawien	1	1935-36	
P IV 32	- Lettland	1	1935-38	
P IV 34	- Litauen	1	1935-39	
P IV 39	- Österreich	1	1934-36	
P IV 41	- Randstaaten	1	1936	
P IV 42	- Rumänien	1	1937-39	
P IV 44	- Schweiz	1	1936-38	
P IV 46	- Spanien	1	1936-38	
P IV 47	- Tschechoslowakei	1	1935-39	
P IV 49	- UdSSR	1	1935-39	4083/E069208-09
P IV 50	- Ukraine	1	1936-38	
P IV 51	- Ungarn	1	1935-39	
P IV 52	- Vereinigte Staa-ten von Amerika	1-2	1935-39	
P IV	Neueingänge, Verschiedenes	1	1939	
P V 2	Beziehungen Polen - Afghanistan	1	1936	
P V 4	- Ägypten	1	1937	
P V 6	- Amerika	1	1935-37	
P V 11	- Belgien	1	1936-38	
P V 13	- Bulgarien	1	1935-36	
P V 16	- Dänemark	1	1936-38	
P V 17	- Danzig	1-2	1935-39	
P V 17 J	- - Information	1-4	1935-38	

Akten-zeichen	Inhalt	Band	Datum	Serial Nr.
P V 17 a	Danzig - polnische Verhandlungen zur Beilegung des Zollkonfliktes Devisen	1-3	1935-36	
P V 17 b	Benutzung des Danziger Hafens durch polnische Kriegsschiffe	1	1932-38	
P V 18	Beziehungen Polen - England	1	1936-39	
P V 19	– Estland	1	1936-39	
P V 20	– Finnland	1-2	1935-38	
P V 21	– Frankreich	1	1935-39	7589/E543317-49
		2		2884/D565335-45
P V 22	– Griechenland	1	1938	
P V 24	– Indien·	1	1937	
P V 27	– Italien	1-2	1936-39	
P V 21-27	Französische und italienische Kulturpropaganda in Polen	1	1936-37	
P V 28	Beziehungen Polen - Japan	1	1936-39	
P V 29	– Jugoslawien	1-2	1936-39	
P V 32	– Lettland	1	1935-38	
P V 34	– Litauen	1-2	1935-38	
P V 37	– Norwegen	1	1935-38	
P V 39	– Österreich	1	1937	
P V 40	– Portugal	1	1937-38	
P V 42	– Rumänien	1-2	1935-38	
P V 43	– Schweden	1-2	1935-38	
P V 44	– Schweiz	1	1935	
P V 46	– Spanien	1-2	1935-39	
P V 47	– Tschechoslowakei	1-2	1935-38	
P V 48	– Türkei	1	1937	
P V 49	– UdSSR	1-2	1935-38	
P V 50	– Ukraine	1	1935-38	
P V 51	– Ungarn	1-2	1935-38	
P V 52	– USA	1	1936-39	
P V	– zu mehreren Staaten	1	1936	
	Neueingänge, Verschiedenes	1	1939	
P VI 2	Politik Afghanistan	1	1935	
P VI 3	– Afrika	1	1939	
P VI 4	– Ägypten	1	1935-36	
P VI 8	– Argentinien	1	1938-39	
P VI 10	– Balkanstaaten	1-2	1936-39	
P VI 11	– Belgien	1-2	1936-39	
P VI 12	– Brasilien	1	1938	
P VI 13	– Bulgarien	1	1935-39	
P VI 14	– Chile	1	1938-39	
P VI 15	– China	1	1938	
P VI 16	– Dänemark	1	1936-39	
P VI 17	– Danzig	1		
		2	1935-39	5816/E423864-949
		3		5816/E423950-61
		4-5		

Akten-zeichen	Inhalt	Band	Datum	Serial Nr.
P VI 17 J	Politik Danzig (Inf.)	1-5 6 7-8	1935-39	7589/E543350-55
P VI 18	– England	1	1935-39	7626/E545160-72
P VI 18 a	– Irland (Eire)	1	1937-39	
P VI 19	– Estland	1-2	1935-39	
P VI 20	– Finnland	1-2	1935-39	
P VI 21	– Frankreich	1 2	1935-39	2888/D565522-28
P VI 22	– Griechenland	1-3	1935-39	
P VI 23	– Holland	1 2	1936-39	2889/D565531-35
P VI 24	– Indien	1	1935	
P VI 25	– Iran	1	1935	
P VI 27	– Italien	1-2	1935-39	
P VI 28	– Japan	1	1938-39	
P VI 29	– Jugoslawien	1	1935-39	
P VI 31	– Kleine Entente	1	1935-39	
P VI 32	– Lettland	1	1935-39	
P VI 33	– Liberia (Afrika)	1	1935	
P VI 34	– Litauen	1-2	1935-39	
P VI 34 a	– Memelgebiet	1-2	1935-39	
P VI 35	– Luxemburg	1	1937-38	
P VI 37	– Norwegen	1	1936-39	
P VI 38	– Ostasien	1	1935-36	
P VI 39	– Österreich	1	1935-38	9788/E687334-36
P VI 41	– Randstaaten	1-4	1935-38	
P VI 42	– Rumänien	1-2	1935-39	
P VI 43	– Schweden	1-2	1935-39	
P VI 44	– Schweiz	1	1936-39	2890/D565538-44
P VI 46	– Spanien	1-3	1936-39	
P VI 47	– Tschechoslowakei	1-2	1935-39	
P VI 48	– Türkei	1-2	1936-39	
P VI 49	– UdSSR	1-3	1933-39	
P VI 50	– Ukraine	1-2	1935-39	
P VI 51	– Ungarn	1-2	1935-39	
P VI 52	– Vereinigte Staaten von Amerika	1-2	1936-39	
P VI 53	– Palästina	1	1936-37	
P VI 1-20	Neueingänge, Verschiedenes	1	1939	8368/E590641-44
P VI 21-52		1-2	1939	
P VII	Politische Beziehungen zwischen mehreren Staaten:	1	1936	
P VII 13-29	Bulgarien-Jugoslawien	1	1935-37	
P VII 18-20	England – Finnland	1	1937	
P VII 18-27	– Italien	1	1936-38	

Akten-zeichen	Inhalt	Band	Datum	Serial Nr.
P VII 18-28	Politische Beziehungen zwischen England – Japan	1	1935–37	7628/E545199–214
P VII 18-32	– Lettland	1	1936–37	
P VII 18-48	– Türkei	1	1936	
P VII 18-51	– Ungarn	1	1936	
P VII 19-20	Finnland – Estland	1	1935–38	
P VII 19-32	Estland – Lettland	1	1937–38	
P VII 19-34	– – Litauen	1	1937	
P VII 20-32	Finnland – Lettland	1	1935–38	
P VII 21-11	Frankreich – Belgien	1	1936–37	
P VII 21-18	– England	1	1935–38	
P VII 21-27	– Italien	1	1935–38	
P VII 21-29	– Jugoslawien	1	1937	
P VII 21-34	– Litauen	1	1936–38	
P VII 21-42	– Rumänien	1	1935–37	
P VII 21-43	– Schweden	1	1937	
P VII 21-48	– Türkei	1	1937	
P VII 21-49	– Russland	1	1935–38	
P VII 27-6	Italien – Amerika	1	1936	
P VII 27-17	– Danzig	1	1936	
P VII 27-29	– Jugoslawien	1	1936–37	
P VII 27-39	– Österreich	1	1936–37	
P VII 27-49	– Russland	1	1935–36	
P VII 27-51	– Ungarn	1	1936–38	
P VII 28-15	China – Japan	1	1937–38	
P VII 29-42	Jugoslawien – Rumänien	1	1936	
P VII 39-51	Österreich – Ungarn	1	1935–37	
P VII 42-48	Rumänien – Türkei	1	1936–38	
P VII 42-49	– Russland	1	1935–38	
P VII 43-19	Schweden – Estland	1	1937	

Akten-zeichen	Inhalt	Band	Datum	Serial Nr.
P VII 43-20	Politische Beziehungen Schweden - Finnland	1	1936-37	
P VII 47-19	Tschechoslowakei - Estland	1	1935	
P VII 47-34	- Litauen	1	1935	
P VII 47-39	- Österreich	1	1936	
P VII 47-42	- Rumänien	1	1936-38	
P VII 47-49	- Russland	1	1935-38	
P VII 48-22	Türkei - Griechenland	1	1937	
P VII 49-2	Russland - Afghanistan	1	1936	
P VII 49-11	- Belgien	1	1935-36	
P VII 49-18	- England	1	1935-38	
P VII 49-19	- Estland	1	1937-38	
P VII 49-20	- Finnland	1	1936-38	
P VII 49-28	- Japan	1	1936-38	
P VII 49-29	- Jugoslawien	1	1935-36	
P VII 49-32	- Lettland	1	1935-38	
P VII 49-34	- Litauen	1	1935-38	
P VII 49-37	- Norwegen	1	1936	
P VII 49-41	- Randstaaten	1	1935-37	
P VII 49-43	- Schweden	1	1937	
P VII 49-44	- Schweiz	1	1935-36	
P VII 49-46	- Spanien	1	1936-37	
P VII 49-48	- Türkei	1	1935-37	
P VII 51-19	Ungarn - Estland	1	1936	
P VIII 1 a	Völkerbund	1-2	1936-38	
P VIII 1 b	Internationale politische Arbeitsgemeinschaften, Kongresse	1	1936-38	
P VIII 1 c	Internationaler Frauen-, Mädchen- und Kinderhandel	1	1938	
P VIII 2 a	Minderheiten in Europa	1	1935	
P VIII 6 a	Internationalismus, Kirchenwesen	1	1935-36	
P VIII 7 a	- Juden	1	1935-38	
P VIII 8 a	Internationales Militärwesen	1	1936-37	

Akten-zeichen	Inhalt	Band	Datum	Serial Nr.
P VIII 8b	Internationale Marineangelegen-heiten (Flottenvertrag)	1	1936-38	
P VIII 9a	Ostsee	1	1935	
P VIII 10a	Kommunismus	1-2	1934-39	
P VIII	Neueingänge, Verschiedenes	1	1939	
P 1/35	Ostpakt	1	1935-36	
P 2/35	Mitteleuropäischer Pakt (Donaupakt)	1	1935-36	
P 3/35	Londoner Kommunique vom 3.II.35 Besuch Simons in Berlin am 25. und 26.III.1935	1	1935	7624/E545062-121
P 4/35	Allgemeine Wehrpflicht in Deutschland, Gesetz vom 16.3.35, Konferenz in Stresa, Völkerbunds-beschluss gegen Deutschland 16.4.1935, Protest gegen Be-schluss 20.4.35	1	1935	
P 5/35	Besuch Edens in Moskau 28.3.35, Warschau 1.4.35	1	1935	7624/E545122-33
P 6/35	Besuch Lavals in Warschau vom 10.- 12.5.1935 und Moskau vom 13.- 15.5.35	1	1935	
P 7/35	Reichstagsrede des Führers und Reichskanzlers am 21.5.35	1	1935-38	
P 8/35	Französisch-sowjetischer Bei-standspakt vom 2.5.35	1	1935-36	
P 9/35	Beistandspakt zwischen der Tschechoslowakei und der Sowjet-Union vom 16.5.35	1	1935-36	
P 10/35	Entwurf eines westeuropäischen Luftpaktes	1	1935-36	
P 11/35	Deutsch-englisches Flottenabkom-men vom 18.6.35	1	1935-37	
P 12/35	Rumänien und der französisch-tschechoslowakisch-russische Beistandspakt, Durchmarsch rus-sischer Truppen durch Rumänien			
	Polens Stellung hierzu, Polnisch-rumänisches Bündnis	1	1935-36	
P 13	Italienisch-abessinischer Kon-flikt, Sanktionen	1-7	1935-36	
P 14	Wiederherstellung der vollen Souveränität im Rheinland; deut-scher und französischer Friedens-plan. Rede des Führers vom 7.III.36	1-2	1936	
P 15	Dreierkonferenz in Rom am 23. März 36 (Römische Protokolle vom 17.III.34)	1	1934-36	
P 16	Fünfmächtebesprechung, Westpakt	1	1936-37	

Akten-zeichen	Inhalt	Band	Datum	Serial Nr.
P 17	Wiederherstellung der Souveräni-tät auf den deutschen Strömen (Note vom 14.11.36)	1	1936-37	7307/E554506-13
P 18	Allgemeine europäische Politik	1	1936-38	
P 19	Wiedervereinigung Deutschland-Österreich	1	1938	
P 21	Ungarisch-polnisch-tchechische Grenzfragen	1	1938	
P 22	Auflösung der Tschechoslowakei	1	1939	7983/E575245-46 2892/D565559-72
P 23	Anschluss des Memelgebietes an das Reich	1	1939	
P 24	Politische Berichte	1	1939	7804/E566356-60 7983/E575247-49 8277/E588235-44 2908/D566058-114
H I 1 a	Polen: Handel-Wirtschaft-Industrie, Allgemeines	1	1935-39	
H I 1 b	Jahresberichte über die allge-meine Wirtschaftslage in Polen	1	1935-39	
H I 2 a	Aussenhandel, Handelsvertrags-politik	1	1935-39	
H I 2 b	Holzabkommen vom 19.I.1929	1-2	1927-31	
H I 2 c	Einfuhr und Registrierung von Sonderheilmitteln, Gen.	1	1934-39	
H I 2 d	Einfuhrverbote für Waren nach Polen	1	1935-38	
H I 2 e	Polnische Ursprungszeugnisse	1	1935-39	
H I 2 f	- Ausfuhr, Gen.	1	1935-39	
H I 3 b	Polen, Waffenhandel	1	1935	
H I 3 c	Handel, Wirtschaft, Industrie, Preisstatistik	1	1936	
H I 3 d	Baumwollhandel in Polen	1	1930-34	
H I 4 a	Polen, Industrie	1	1936-39	
H I 4 b	Industriegebiet von Sandomierz	1	1937-39	
H I 4 c	Polnische Kraftwagen-Industrie	1	1935-39	
H I 4 d	- Fahrrad-Industrie	1	1936-39	
H I 4 e	- Textilindustrie	1	1936-39	
I 1	Bergwerk- und Hüttenindustrie	1-2	1923-33	
I 3	Farbenindustrie	1	1927-34	
I 4	Polnische Kohlenindustrie	1	1928-34	
I 7	Elektrotechnische Industrie Polens	1	1929-34	
I 8	Papierindustrie in Polen		1927-34	

Akten-zeichen	Inhalt	Band	Datum	Serial Nr.
I 9	Elektrizität, Gas- und Wasser-versorgung in Polen		1932-35	
I 10	Zuckerindustrie		1929-34	
I 11	Chemische Industrie		1929-34	
I 12	Leder-Industrie		1928-34	
I 13	Erdöl-Industrie		1926-34	
H I 5	Löhne, Arbeitszeit und soziale Fürsorge des Arbeiters	1-2	1928-35	
H I 5 a	Polnisches Genossenschaftswesen	1	1936-37	
H I 6 a	Gewerkschaftswesen in Polen	1	1935	
H I 6 b	Lohnverhältnisse, Arbeitslosig-keit	1	1936-38	
H I 7 a	Messe- und Ausstellungswesen, Generalia	1	1936-39	
H I 8 a	Polnische Bauwirtschaft	1-2	1926-36	
H I 9 a	- Industrie-u.Handelskammer	1	1935-39	
H I 9 b	Auslandshandelskammern	1	1937-39	
W	Wehrwirtschaft in Polen	1	1936-39	
H II 1 a	Deutschland, Handel,Wirtschaft, Industrie	1	1935-39	
H II 2 a	- Aussenhandel	1	1935-39	
H II 2 b	- Einfuhr	1	1935-39	
H II 2 c	- Ausfuhr	1	1934-39	
H II 2 d	Einfuhr von Milcherzeugnissen nach Deutschland	1	1935-39	
H II 2 e	- von Hühnereiern nach Deutschland	1	1935-36	
H II 2 f	Deutschland, Ein-und Ausfuhr-verbote	1	1935-39	
H II 2 g	- - von Kriegsgerät	1	1935-38	7589/E543366-69
H II 4 a	- Industrie	1	1935-39	
H II 8 a	Bauwirtschaft in Deutschland	1	1938	
H II 9 a	Deutsche Industrie-und Handels-kammern, Auslandshandelskammern, Aussenhandelsstellen	1	1935-38	
	Sammelberichte Kegel	1	1935-39	
	Wirtschaftsberichte, Reichs-stelle für den Aussenhandel und Verschiedenes	1-2	1935-39	
H III 1 a	Wirtschaftsbeziehungen Deutschland - Polen	1	1935-39	
H III 1 b	Deutsch-polnische Vereinbarung über gegenseitige Anerkennung von Lufttüchtigkeitszeugnissen	1	1935-37	

Akten-zeichen	Inhalt	Band	Datum	Serial Nr.
H III 1 c	In Deutschland eingefrorene polnische Warenforderungen	1	1934-36	
H III 1 d	Artikel 218 des Genfer Abkommens	1	1934-36	9390/E665322-24
H III 1 e	Deutsch-polnisches Roggenabkommen	1	1935-38	
H III 1 g	Deutschland - Polen, Ein- und Ausreise	1	1939	
H III 1 i	Vertreterprovisionen aus dem Eisenbahn-Transitabkommen	1	1937-38	
H III 2	Deutsch-polnischer Handelsver-trag vom 17.III.30	1	1930	
	Verhandlungen über ein deutsch-polnisches Niederlassungsabkom-men	1	1926-33	
H III 2 a	Deutsch-polnisches Kompensa-tionsgeschäft	1 2	1934-39	9389/E665292-315 9389/E665316-19
H III 2 b	Monatsberichte der deutschen Handelskammer für Polen über das deutsch-polnische Kompensations-abkommen vom 11.X.34	1	1934-36	
H III 2 c	Polnische Gesellschaft für den Kompensationshandel (Zahan)	1	1935-38	
H III 3 a	Wortlaut des deutsch-polnischen Wirtschaftsabkommens vom 17.3.30	1	1930	
	Deutsch-polnisches Wirtschafts-abkommen und Verhandlungen	1 2 3	1934-36	9391/E665327-77 9392/E665380-426
		4-6	1937	
H III 3a S	Deutsch-polnische Wirtschafts-verhandlungen über den Anschluß Osterreichs	1	1938-39	
H III 3 b	Wünsche der Wirtschaft zu den deutsch-polnischen Wirtschafts-verhandlungen 1935	1	1934-37	
H III 3 d	Wertgrenzen für Devisenbeschei-nigungen	1-2	1935-38	
H III 4 a	Vertrieb deutscher Kraftwagen und Motorräder in Polen	1-2	1935-39	
H III 4 b	Kreditaktion für polnische In-vestitionszwecke	1	1938-39	
H III 5 a	Deutsches Genossenschaftswesen in Polen	1	1934-39	
H III 5 b	Polnisches Genossenschaftswesen in Deutschland	1	1935-39	
H IV 27	Wirtschaftliche Beziehungen: Deutschland - Italien	1	1935-36	
H IV 32	- Lettland	1	1938	
H IV 34	- Litauen	1	1936-39	
H IV 38	- Ostasien	1	1935	
H IV 42	- Rumänien	1	1935	

Akten-zeichen	Inhalt	Band	Datum	Serial Nr.
IV 43	Wirtschaftliche Beziehungen: Deutschland - Russland	1	1935-39	
IV 47	– Tschechoslowakei	1	1935-38	
IV 48	– Türkei	1	1938	
IV 52	– Amerika	1	1938	
V 6 a	Wirtschaftliche Beziehungen: Polen - Amerika	1	1935-36	
V 13	– Bulgarien	1	1936-38	
V 17	– Danzig	1	1935-39	
V 18	– England	1	1935-39	
V 21	– Frankreich	1	1935-39	
V 39	– Österreich	1	1935-39	
V 47	– Tschechoslowakei	1-2	1925-35	
V 48	– Türkei	1	1923-35	
VI 6	Wirtschaft in Amerika	1	1937	
VI 16	– Dänemark	1	1937	
VI 17	– Danzig	1	1935-39	
VI 19	– Estland	1	1936-39	
VI 20	– Finnland	1	1936	
VI 23	– Holland	1	1936	
VI 27	– Italien	1	1935-36	
VI 30	– Kanada	1	1937	
VI 32	– Lettland	1	1936-38	
VI 34	– Litauen	1	1937	
VI 39	– Österreich	1	1935	
VI 41	– Randstaaten	1	1936	
VI 43	– Schweden	1	1936-37	
VI 46	– Spanien	1	1938	
VI 47	– Tschechoslowakei	1	1935-36	
VI 49	– UdSSR	1	1936-39	
VI 51	– Ungarn	1	1936	
VII 18/20	Wirtschaftsbeziehungen: England - Finnland	1	1939	
VII 18/29	– Jugoslawien	1	1935-36	
VII 18/49	– UdSSR	1	1939	
VII 18/20	Estland - Finnland	1	1937	
VII 19/49	– UdSSR	1	1935	
VII 19/32	– Lettland	1	1937-38	
VII 20/49	Finnland - UdSSR	1	1939	
VII 27/39	Italien - Österreich	1	1935	
VII 27/48	– Türkei	1	1935	
VII 34/49	Litauen - UdSSR	1	1939	

Akten-zeichen	Inhalt	Band	Datum	Serial Nr.
H VII 39/ 47	Wirtschaftsbeziehungen Österreich – Tschechoslowakei	1	1936-37	
H VIII 1a	Internationales Wirtschaftswesen	1	1935-37	
H VIII 2a	Internationale Währungsfragen	1	1936	
W.-Abt.	Wirtschaft, Neueingänge, Verschiedenes	1 2	1939	7983/E575254-56 8157/E582674-78
L.allg.	Berichte des landwirtschaftlichen Sachverständigen	1	1925-27	
L I 1 a	Polnische Landwirtschaft, Ackerbau	1	1935-39	
L I 1 b	Entschuldung der polnischen Landwirtschaft	1	1934-38	
L I 1 d	Poln.Hypothekenmoratorium	1	1932-38	
L I 1 f	– Agrarreform, Parzellierungsplan	1	1935-39	
L I 1 f-S	– – Parzellierung	1-2	1938-39	
L I 2 a	Forstwirtschaft in Polen	1	1936-37	
L I 3 a	Fischereiwesen in Polen	1	1935-38	
L II 1 a	Deutschland, Landwirtschaft	1	1935-38	
L II 2 a	– Forstwirtschaft	1	1939	
L III 1 a	Landwirtschaft zwischen Polen und Deutschland	1	1939	
L III 6 a	Gemeinsame Schädlingsbekämpfung	1	1936-37	
L VIII 1a	Internationale Landwirtschaft	1	1936-39	
F I 1 a	Polen: Allgemeines Finanzwesen	1	1933-36	
F I 1 b	Finanzen der polnischen Selbstverwaltungskörperschaften	1	1934-35	
F I 1 c	Polnischer Staatshaushalt	1	1935-39	
F I 1 d	Polen: Arbeits-und Arbeitslosenfonds	1	1935-37	
F I 1 e	– Anleihen	1	1936-38	
F I 1 f	– Bank-und Börsenwesen	1	1936-39	
F I 1 g	– Geldverkehr, Währungswesen	1	1936-37	
F I 1 h	– Monopolwesen	1	1939	
F I 1 k	– Devisenbestimmungen	1-2	1936-39	
F I 1 k S	–	1	1936-39	
F I 2 a	– Steuerwesen	1	1933-37	
F I 2 b	– Einkommensteuer	1	1935-36	
F I 2 c	– Umsatzsteuer,Gewerbesteuer	1	1935-39	

Akten-zeichen	Inhalt	Band	Datum	Serial Nr.
I 2 e	Polen: Stempelsteuer	1	1935-38	
I 2 f	– Verbrauchssteuern	1	1935-37	
I 2 g	– sonstige Steuern	1	1935-37	
I 2 h	– Kraftfahrzeugsteuer	1	1936-39	
I 3 a	– Zollwesen	1	1935-39	
I 3 b	– Zolltarif	1	1935-38	
I 3 c	Zollbefreiungen und Ermässigung in Polen	1	1935-39	
I 3 d	Polen: Zertifikate für Passagierschiffe	1	1935	
I 3 e	– Exportprämien	1	1935-39	
I 3 f	– Ausfuhrzölle	1	1937-39	
I 3 g	– – für Erlenrundholz	1	1935-36	
I 4 a	– Lotteriewesen	1	1936	
II 1 a	Deutschland: Allgem.Finanzwesen	1	1935-39	
II 1 b	– Devisenbestimmungen	1	1934-39	
II 1 c	– Registermark	1	1934-36	
II 1 d	– Geldverkehr und Währung	1	1936-38	
II 1 e	– Bedienung der Zinsscheine für die Dawes-u.Younganleihe	1	1934-38	
II 2 a	Steuerwesen in Deutschland	1	1936-38	
II 2 b	Zollwesen in Deutschland	1	1937-39	
III 1 a	Allgemeine finanzielle Beziehungen zwischen Deutschland und Polen	1	1937-39	
III 1a S	Deutsch-polnische Finanzverhandlungen	1	1939	
III 1 a R	Finanzwesen Deutschland - Polen	1	1939	
III 2 a	Deutsch-polnische Vereinbarung zur Vermeidung der Doppelbesteuerung	1	1938	
III 2 c	Doppelbesteuerung der in Deutsch-O.S. wohnenden und in Polen-O.S. beschäftigten Arbeitnehmer	1	1931-39	
III 2 d	Deutsch-polnisches Abkommen über die Behandlung der Emigrantenkautionen vom 29.3.35	1-2	1933-38	
III 2 e	Steuererleichterungen für den Kraftfahrzeugverkehr zwischen Deutschland und Polen	1	1933-38	
VIII 1a	Internationales Finanzwesen	1	1935	

Akten-zeichen	Inhalt	Band	Datum	Serial Nr.
V I 1 a	Flugwesen in Polen	1	1935-39	
V I 2	Schiffahrtswesen	1-6	1922-35	
	Schiffahrtskonzessionen	1-2	1924-34	
	Binnenschiffahrtsverkehr polnische Wasserstrassen	1-2	1922-35	
V I 2 a	Binnenschiffahrt in Polen	1	1935-39	
V I 2 b	Ausbau des Hafens von Gdingen	1	1935-39	
V I 2 c	Nachrichtenblatt des Hafens von Gdingen	1	1935-39	
V I 2 d	Polnischer Überseehandel - Handelsflotte	1	1934-39	
V I 2 e	Polen: Hafenangelegenheiten	1	1933-39	
V I 2 f	Weichselschiffahrt	1	1927-37	
V I 2 g	Transitverkehr über die Häfen des polnischen Zollgebietes	1	1939	
V I 3	Eisenbahnverkehr	1-2	1924-27	
V I 3	Bahnbau Oberschlesien-Gdingen	1	1930-31	
V I 3 a	Poln. Eisenbahnwesen	1	1935-39	
V I 3 b	- Eisenbahntarife	1	1935-38	
V I 3 c	Bau neuer Eisenbahnstrecken in Polen	1	1935-39	
V I 4 a	Pass- und Sichtvermerksangelegen-heiten in Polen	1-2	1935-39	
V I 4 b	Poln. Staatsgrenzen	1-2	1936-39	
V I 5 a	- Reiseverkehr - Verkehrs-werbung	1	1936-39	
V I 6 a	Wasserbauarbeiten in Polen	1	1935-39	
V I 6 b	Wasserwesen und Wasserorganisa-tion in Polen	1	1935	
V I 7 a	Strassenwesen in Polen	1	1934-38	
V I 7 b	Kraftfahrzeugverkehr auf öffent-lichen Strassen	1	1936-39	
V I 9 a	Post-und Telegrafenwesen in Polen	1	1935-39	
V II 1 a	Flugwesen in Deutschland	1	1935-39	
V II 1 b	Deutschlandflug	1	1933-35	
V II 2 a	Schiffahrtswesen in Deutschland	1	1936-39	
V II 3 a	Fahrpreisermässigung auf deut-schen Eisenbahnen	1	1935-37	
V II 4 a	Pass-und Sichtvermerksangelegen-heiten, Generalia	1	1935-39	
V II 4 b	- Sperre, Einzelfälle	1-2	1934-39	

Akten-zeichen	Inhalt	Band	Datum	Serial Nr.
V II 4 e	Autopassierscheine, Generalia	1	1935-37	
V II 4 g	Behandlung der Kraftfahrzeuge beim Grenzübertritt	1	1928-39	
V II 4 h	Deutsche Grenzzonenverordnung	1	1937-39	
V II 5 a	Deutschland, Reiseverkehr	1	1936-39	
V II 7 a	– Strassenwesen	1	1935-38	
V II 9 a	– Post-und Telegrafenwesen	1	1935-39	
V III 1 a	Deutsch-polnisches Luftverkehrsabkommen vom 28.8.29	1	1931-38	
V III 1 b	Warschauer Luftbeförderungsabkommen vom 12.10.29	1	1929-35	
V III 1 c	Vereinbarung über den deutsch-polnischen Luftverkehr	1-2	1933-39	
V III 1 d	Flugverkehr und -linien Deutschland-Polen	1	1934-36	
V III 1 e	Überfluggenehmigungen deutscher Flugzeuge über polnisches Gebiet	1	1935-39	
V III 1 f	Grenzverletzungen durch deutsche und polnische Flugzeuge	1	1934-39	
V III 2 a	Deutsch-polnischer Binnenschiffahrtsverkehr	1	1926-39	
V III 2 b	Amtliche Liste der deutschen und polnischen Seeschiffe	1	1929-38	
V III 2 c	Deutsche Hafenkonsulate in Polen	1	1935-39	
V III 2 d	Beteiligung deutscher Schiffahrtslinien am polnischen Auswandererverkehr	1	1934-36	
V III 3 a	Eisenbahnzahlungen an Polen aus dem Durchgangsverkehr durch den Korridor	1 2 3	1933-39	9172/E645119-284 9172/E645285-408 9172/E645409-532
	Handakten zu den Transitverhandlungen in Berlin vom 11.November bis 21.12.36	1	1936	9172/E645533-35
V III 3 a D	Eisenbahndurchgangsverkehr durch polnisches Gebiet	1	1936-39	
V III 3 b	Deutsch-polnischer Triebwagenverkehr durch den Korridor	1	1934-35	
V III 3 c	Remontetransporte durch den Korridor	1	1934-37	
V III 3 d	Transitverkehr durch Ostpreussen	1	1935	
V III 3 e	Deutsch-poln.Eisenbahnwesen	1	1936-38	
	– Eisenbahnverhandlungen, Abkommen, Konferenzen	1-2	1930-39	
V III 3 g	Vertretung der Reichsbahnzentrale für den deutschen Reiseverkehr	1	1938-39	

Akten-zeichen	Inhalt	Band	Datum	Serial Nr.
V III 3 h	Transitverkehr durch Polen	1	1939	
V III 4 a	Deutsch-polnischer Vertrag zur Regelung der Grenzverhältnisse vom 27.1.26	1	1927-39	
V III 4 b	Vereinbarung wegen Zulassung von Zollstrafen Übergang über die deutsch-polnische Grenze	1	1925-39	
V III 4 c	Deutsch-polnisches Abkommen	1	1926-39	
V III 4 d	- über die Unterhaltung des Wasserlaufs des Drewenz-Flusses	1	1927-39	
V III 4 e	- über Erleichterung im kleinen Grenzverkehr	1-2	1934-39	
V III 4 e S	Mißstände bei der Ausstellung von Grenzausweisen	1	1936-39	
V III 4 f	Vorflutregelung im Tal der oberen Liszwarte	1	1934-38	
V III 4 g	- der Prosna	1	1933-34	
V III 4 h	Wiedereröffnung von deutsch-polnischen Eisenbahnübergängen	1	1935-38	
V III 4 i	Deutsch-polnische Vereinbarung über Ermässigung der Sichtver-merksgebühren für den Binnen-schiffahrtsverkehr	1	1930-38	
V III 4 k	Illegale Grenzüberschreitung an der deutsch-polnischen Grenze	1	1926-38	
V III 4 m	Grenzzwischenfälle, Generalia	1-2	1933-39	
V III 4 n	- Inf.	1	1935-39	
V III 4 p	Schmuggel von Betäubungsmitteln	1	1933-38	
V III 5 a	Touristenverkehr Deutschland - Polen	1	1934-39	
V III 5 b	Transitverkehr durch den Korridor (nicht Eisenbahn)	1	1935-39	
V III 7 a	Reise polnischer Ingenieure durch Deutschland	1	1938	
V IV	Verkehrsbeziehungen zwischen Deutschland und mehreren anderen Staaten	1	1938-39	
V IV 34	Verkehrsbeziehungen: Deutschland - Litauen	1	1936	
V IV 39	- Österreich	1	1936	
V IV 47	- Tschechoslowakei	1	1938	
V IV 49	- UdSSR	1	1936	
V V 10	Polen -Balkanstaaten	1	1938	
V V 16	- Dänemark	1	1939	
V V 17	- Danzig	1	1936-38	
V V 18	- England	1	1935-39	

Akten-zeichen	Inhalt	Band	Datum	Serial Nr.
V V 20	Verkehrsbeziehungen: Polen - Finnland	1	1936-39	
V V 21	– Frankreich	1	1937	
V V 23	– Holland	1	1935	
V V 27	– Italien	1	1937	
V V 33	– Liberia	1	1938	
V V 34	– Litauen	1	1937-39	
V V 42	– Rumänien	1	1936-38	
V V 43	– Schweden	1	1934-39	
V V 47	– Tschechoslowakei	1	1935-39	
V V 51	– Ungarn	1	1936-39	
V V 53	– Palästina	1	1934-37	
V VI 17	Verkehrswesen in Danzig	1	1936-39	
V VI 19	– Estland	1	1936	
V VI 20	– Finnland	1	1936	
V VI 27	– Italien	1	1935	
V VI 49	– UdSSR	1	1938-39	
V VII 43/ 4	Verkehrsbeziehungen Schweden - Ungarn	1	1938	
V VIII	Internationalismus, Verkehrs- wesen, Generalia	1	1935-39	
V VIII 1 a	Internationales Flugwesen	1	1936-39	
V VIII 2 a	Internationalismus, Donaukommis- sion	1	1935-36	
V VIII 2 b	Internat. Schiffahrtswesen	1	1938-39	
V VIII 4 a	– Konvention zur Bekämpfung des Alkoholschmuggels	1	1936-37	
V VIII 5 a	– Reiseverkehr	1	1936	
V VIII 9 a	– Post-und Telegrafenwesen	1	1936	
V	Neueingänge, Verkehrswesen	1	1939	
R 1 dtsch	Deutsch-polnisches Abkommen über Pfandbriefanstalt in Posen	1	1930-31	
	– Aufwertungsabkommen	1-2	1928-33	
	– – Artikel 37 u.47	1	1929-31	
	– Sparkassenabkommen	1	1930-31	
	Aufwertung in Deutschland	1-2 2a-4	1923-35	
R 1 a	Agrar-Reform in Polen	1-5	1925-35	
	Beschwerden der deutschen Minder- heit Posens und Pommerellen	1	1929-33	

Akten-zeichen	Inhalt	Band	Datum	Serial Nr.
R 1 a	Handelsrecht, Pfandrecht	1	1920-33	
R 1 c	Rückzahlung von Steuer- und Emigrantenkaution	1	1922-34	
	Verhandlungen über Rückzahlung von Steuer- und Emigrantenkaution	2	1930-33	
R 1 d	Aufwertung von Sparkassenguthaben	1	1930-35	
R 1 e	- Hypotheken	1	1930-35	
R 1 f	Verzeichnis der Hypotheken der preussischen Landschaften. Tilgung von Hypothekenschulden	1	1929-35	
R 1 g	Aufwertung der 4% Lodzer Fabrik-Eisenbahn-Obligationen	1	1930-34	
R 1 h	Aufwertungsansprüche gegen deutsche Versicherungsgesellschaften	1	1932-33	
R 1 russ.	Aufwertung von Forderungen gegen russische Versicherungsgesellschaften	1	1929-33	
R 3	Sabotageprozess Kingsland	1-2	1931-33	
R 3 a	Kriegergräber und Denkmäler, Fürsorge	1	1924-31	
R 3 b	Deutsch-polnische Frühjahrsverhandlungen	1	1920	
R 3 c	- allgemeine Verhandlungen	1-3	1922-25	
R 3 d	Konferenz Genua und Haag		1922	
R 3 e	Ruhrgebiet		1923-29	
R 3 f	Versailler Vertrag Ausführung durch Polen		1921-34	
R 3 g	Völkerbundsentscheidungen in Minderheitssachen	1-7	1925-35	
R 3 k	Kriegsächtungspakt Kellogpakt	1	1928-30	
R 3 L	Haager Konferenz	1-2	1929-31	
R 4	Liquidationssache Prinz Pless	1-3	1930-35	
	- allgemein	10-11	1925-29	
	- Karl Sachs	13	1927-31	
	Strittige Staatsangehörigkeitsfälle	15	1927-29	
	Entschädigungszahlungen des polnischen Staates für Liquidationsverhöre	16	1930-31	
R Liqui 87	Liquidation Fürst Thurn und Taxis	1-2	1925-39	
R 4 a	Reklamationen	16-18	1932-34	
R 4 b	Ansiedler	1	1921-22	

Akten-zeichen	Inhalt	Band	Datum	Serial Nr.
R 4 b	Ansiedler Sonderakten v.Tiedemann	2	1921-34	
		2-3	1922-33	
R 4 c	Domänenpächter		1921-28	
R 4 d	Liquidation von Gütern	2-6	1922-34	
R 4 e	Steuersicherheiten von Auswan-derern	1	1923-33	
	Emigrantenkaution	2	1934	
R 4 f	Chorzow-Werke	1-2	1926-30	
R 4 g	Schlichtungsabkommensverhand-lungen	1	1926-33	
R 4 h	Liquidationsverzichtverhand-lungen	1	1929	
R 4 i	Rentengutsvertrag, Vorkaufsrecht, Wiederkaufsrecht	1-2	1926-34	
R 4 L	Deutsch-polnische Staatsangehö-rigkeitsverhandlungen in Genf		1929	
	Verhandlungen der technischen Delegierten über Staatsangehö-rigkeit und Liquidationsfragen	2	1930-33	
	Einzelne Liquidationsfälle und Aufhebung der deutsch-polnisch gemischten Schiedsgerichte	4	1931-33	
R 4 m	Deutsch-polnisches Arrangement	1	1929-30	
	Gegenwirkung gegen deutsch-pol-nisches Ausgleichsabkommen	3	1929	
	Deutsch-polnisches Liquidations-abkommen und Haager Verträge	4	1930	
	Liquidationsabkommen	5	1929-32	
R 5	Abwanderungsaufforderungen		1925-30	
sp R 5	Aide-Mémoire		1925-26	
	Zusammenstellung der Aide-Mémoires betr.Richtigkeit der polnischen Optantenlisten		1925-27	
	Aide-Memoire Fall Goga	1	1925-26	
	- 22 Fälle	1	1925-26	
	Zusammenstellung der Aide-Mémoires betr.Berichtigung der deutschen Optantenliste	1	1925-27	
	Polnische Optanten in Deutsch-land		1924-25	
	Staatsangehörigkeits- und Optan-tenfragen, Wiener Vertrag	1-2	1924-29	
	- Einleitung von Verhand-lungen	1	1920-29	

Akten-zeichen	Inhalt	Band	Datum	Serial Nr.
sp R 5	Option (Staatsangehörigkeit) Registrierung von Optanten allg.	2	1932-34	
	Registrierung von Optanten, Optanten-Ausweisungen	3	1925-32	
	Optionserklärungen	1	1922-24	
sp R 5 a	Einzelfälle, Aide-Mémoires (Auswanderungs-Sichtvermerks-fälle)	1-4	1922-30	
	Registrierung der Ausländer-Aufenthaltsbewilligung für Optanten	5	1929-33	
	Staatsangehörigkeit Einzelfälle	6-7	1931-33	
sp R 6	Rechts- und Paßsachen, Gen.	1	1938	
sp R 6 a	Korridorprovisorium	1	1920-22	
	Korridorabkommen	1	1933	
sp R 6 b	Deutsch-polnisches Schiedsgericht in Korridorfragen	1	1922-33	
sp R 6 c	Durchgangs-Schiffsverkehr, Zollsachen	1-2	1922-29	
	Abbruch der Opalenier Brücke	3	1928-31	
	Zollsachen im Durchgangsverkehr	1	1929-34	
sp R 6 d	Kreuzburger Abkommen (Schnellzugsverkehr)	1	1922-29	
sp R 7	Abstimmung Ost- und Westpreussen	1-2	1920	
sp R 10	Aide-Mémoires-Verwendung Einzelfälle	2	1920-23	
	- Mittellose,Ferienkin-der	3	1926-33	
	Unterstützung, Mittellose, Ferienkinder		1934-35	
sp R 10 a	Deutsch-polnischer Austausch der Schuljugend während der Sommer-ferien		1924-35	
sp R 11	Übergriffe polnischer Behörden, Misshandlungen	3-5	1920-34	
sp R 12	Occupationsangelegenheiten		1920	
R 13	Gefangenenaustausch deutsch-polnisch	1-2	1920-34	
R 13 a	- - russisch		1920-25	
R 14	Ausweisungen Deutscher	16-33	1928-35	
R 14 a	Ausweisung von Polen und umge-kehrt, Liste 1-4	1-2	1923-24	
R 14 b	Ausweisungen aus Bayern		1923-24	
R 14 c	- Mecklenburg		1923-24	
R 15	Übernahmesachen	1-7	1922-34	

Akten-zeichen	Inhalt	Band	Datum	Serial Nr.
R 16	Grenzverletzungen	1-11	1921-34	
R 16 a	'- durch fremde Flugzeuge	1-2	1925-33	
R 18	Rückwanderer, Auswanderer	1	1920-29	
R 22	Entziehung von Schankkonzessio-nen in Polen	1-2	1927-33	
	Regelung des weiteren Schicksals reichsdeutscher Gastwirte in Polen und polnischer Gastwirte in Deutschland	3	1927-32	
	Schankkonzessionen. Liste uner-ledigter Fälle Schankkonzessions-verlängerungen	4	1932-35	
R 23	Gewerbeausübung in Polen		1931-33	
R	Eigentümer Walter Friese, Schadensersatzklage gegen polnischen Fiskus		1922-35	
	Enteignung des Gutes Hohenbirken, Magistrat Ratibor		1930-31	
R I 1 a	Rechtswesen allgemein, Staats-recht in Polen	1	1936-38	
R I 1 b	Juristische Organisationen, Vereinigungen	1	1936	
R I 2 a	Polnische Gesetze und Verordnun-gen	1	1935-39	
R I 2 b	Urheberrecht in Polen	1	1935	
R I 2 d	Deutsch-polnische Vereinbarung über die Frage der Ortsnamen-bezeichnung	1	1937-39	
R I 2 e	Statistik (Rechtslage)	1	1935-38	
R I 2 f	Polnisches Konsulatsgebühren-gesetz	1	1937	
R I 3 a	Gerichtswesen, Strafrecht in Polen	1	1935-39	
R I 4 a	Neues polnisches Handelsgesetz-buch	1	1933-35	
R I 4 b	Handels- und Gewerberecht	1	1936-39	
R I 5 a	Ausländerverordnung	1	1938-39	
R I 6 a	Staatsangehörigkeitsfragen	1	1936-39	
R I 8 b	Versicherungswesen in Polen	1	1935	
R I 8 c	Arbeitsgesetzgebung	1	1937	
R I 9 a	Fürsorgewesen in Polen	1	1936	
R II 1 a	Deutsches Rechtswesen im allge-meinen	1	1936-39	
R II 2 a	Bürgerlich - rechtliche-und verwaltungsrechtliche Angelegen-heiten	1	1935-38	

Akten-zeichen	Inhalt	Band	Datum	Serial Nr.
R II 3 a	Gerichtswesen in Deutschland	1	1935-37	
R II 3 b	Kriminal- und Justizstatistik in Deutschland	1	1932-38	
R II 4 a	Handels-und Gewerberecht in Deutschland	1	1936	
R II 5 a	Nachweisung über Ausweisung von Ausländern	1	1937-39	
R II 6 a	Reichs- und Staatsbürgerrecht	1	1935-39	
R II 6 b	Aberkennung der deutschen Staatsangehörigkeit, Ausbürgerungen (Gen.)	1	1936-39	
R II 8 a	Sozialwesen in Deutschland	1	1935-39	
R II 9 a	Fürsorgewesen in Deutschland	1	1938-39	
R III 1 a	Deutsch-polnische Zusammenarbeit auf juristischem Gebiet	1	1937-39	
R III 1 b	Verträge, Abkommen	1	1939	
R III 2 a	Deutsch-polnischer Konsular-vertrag	1	1926-33	
R III 2 b	Beischreibung von Randvermerken zu polnischen Personenstandsre-gistern	1	1922-37	
R III 2 c	Austausch von Urkunden auf Grund des Haager Eheschliessungsabkom-men vom 12.6.1902	1	1934-37	
R III 3 a	Deutsch-polnischer Auslieferungs-vertrag	1	1930-35	
R III 3 b	Verhaftungen und Verurteilungen von Volksdeutschen	1	1938-39	
R III 3 c	Behandlung von in Strafhaft be-findlichen Personen	1	1935-39	
R III 3 d	Rechtshilfeersuchen	1	1935-39	
R III 5 b	Abwanderungen von Volksdeutschen ins Reich	1	1936-39	
R III 5 c	Polnische Wanderarbeiter in Deutschland	1	1937-39	
R III 5 c W.	Anwerbung polnischer Arbeiter	1	1938-39	
R III 6 a	Polnische Liste gem.Art.7 § 3 Abs.2 des Wiener Abkommens vom 30.8.1924	1	1930-36	
R III 6 b	Deutsch-polnische Schlichtungs-kommission für strittige Staats-angehörigkeitssachen	1	1936-38	
R III 6 c	Deutsch-polnischer Austausch von Einbürgerungsnachrichten	1	1937-38	
R III 7 b	Deutsch-polnisches Abkommen über die Einlösung der westpreussi-schen Anleihescheine	1	1929-37	

Akten-zeichen	Inhalt	Band	Datum	Serial Nr.
III 8 a	Deutsch-poln.Sozialversicherungs-vertrag	1	1931-38	
III 8 b	– Abkommen über Er-werbslosenfürsorge und Arbeitslosen-unterstützung	1	1927-39	
III 8 c	Deutsche private Versicherungs-gesellschaften in Polnisch-Ober-schlesien	1	1936-37	
III 9 a	Öffentliche Fürsorge Deutschland-Polen	1-2	1932-38	
III 9 b	Deutsch-polnischer Kinderaus-tausch	1	1937-39	
III 10 a	Übertragung von Rentengrund-stücken	1	1935-38	
III 10 b	Polnischer Grundbesitz in Deutschland	1	1936	
III 10 c	Überleitung der an Polen abge-tretenen Gebiete in Bromberg und Posen	1	1936	
IV 6	Rechtsbeziehungen:			
	Deutschland – Amerika	1	1935	
IV 42	– Rumänien	1	1936-37	
V 6	Polen – Amerika	1	1936	
V 13	– Bulgarien	1	1935	
V 17	– Danzig	1	1935-38	
V 27	– Italien	1	1935-36	
V 32	– Lettland	1	1935	
V 35	– Luxemburg	1	1936	
V 51	– Ungarn	1	1936	
V	– mehrere andere Staaten	1	1935-37	
VI 17	Rechtswesen Danzig	1	1936-37	
VIII 2 a	Internationales Handels-, Wechsel-und Scheckrecht	1	1937	
VIII 3 a	Ständiger internationaler Gerichtshof im Haag	1	1935-36	
	Neueingänge Rechtswesen, Versch.	1	1939	
I 1 a	Kulturelle Angelegenheiten in Polen	1	1939	
I 1 b	Kulturelle Organisationen, Vereinigungen	1	1935-39	
I 2 a	Filmwesen in Polen	1	1934-39	
I 3 a	Theater und Bühne, Gen.	1	1936-37	
I 4 a	Musik-, Konzert- und Vortrags-wesen in Polen	1	1936-39	
I 5 a	Kunst, Wissenschaft und Fort-bildung in Polen	1	1936-38	

Akten-zeichen	Inhalt	Band	Datum	Serial Nr.
K I 6 a	Universitäts- und Hochschulange-legenheiten	1	1935-38	
K I 8 a	Rundfunkwesen in Polen	1	1935-39	
K I 9 a	Sport und Erziehung, körperliche Ertüchtigung	1	1935-39	
K I 10 a	Statistik über Menschenkrankhei-ten und Tierseuchen in Polen	1	1927-37	
K II 1 a	Kulturelle Angelegenheiten in Deutschland	1	1936	
K II 1 b	Deutsche Kulturwerbung im Ausland	1	1935-39	
K II 1 c	Deutsche Kongresszentrale	1	1935-39	
K II 1 d	Kulturelle Organisation	1	1935-39	
K II 2 a	Filmwesen in Deutschland	1	1939	
K II 3 a	Theater und Bühne in Deutschland	1	1937-38	
K II 4 a	Musik-, Konzert und Vortragswesen	1	1937-39	
K II 6 a	Universitäts- und Hochschulange-legenheiten	1	1929-38	
K II 8 a	Rundfunkwesen in Deutschland	1	1935-39	
K II 9 a	Sport und körperliche Erziehung in Deutschland	1	1936-38	
K II 10 a	Veterinär- und Gesundheitswesen in Deutschland	1	1938-39	
K III 1 a	Deutsche Kulturpropaganda in Polen	1	1935-39	
K III 1 c	Deutsch-poln.Kulturpropaganda	1	1935-39	
K III 2 a	- Filmverhandlungen, Filmaustausch	1-4	1932-38	
	Filme und Kino	1-3	1925-35	
K III 2 b	Deutsche Filme in Polen und polnische in Deutschland	1	1934-37	
K III 2 c	Hetzfilme	1	1934-39	
K III 2 d	Filmboykott	1	1935-39	
K III 2 e	Deutsch-polnischer Gemeinschafts-film	1	1935-38	
K III 2 f	Vertretung der Ufa in Polen	1	1935-37	
K III 3 a	Deutsch-polnischer Theateraus-tausch	1	1935-39	
K III 4 a	Gastspielreisen deutscher Künst-ler in Polen	1	1934-39	
K III 4 b	Polnischer Musikboykott	1	1936	
K III 4 c	Deutsche Musik- und Konzert-veranstaltungen in Polen	1	1936-37	

Akten-zeichen	Inhalt	Band	Datum	Serial Nr.
K III 5 a	Lehrtätigkeit deutscher Professoren und Wissenschaftler in Polen	1	1929-39	
K III 5 b	Berufung abgebauter Professoren, Ärzte (Emigranten) nach Polen	1	1934-36	
K III 5 c	Einsichtnahme in polnische Staatsarchive	1	1935-39	
K III 5 d	Preussisches Geheimes Staatsarchiv, Publikationsstelle	1	1934-38	
K III 5 e	Einsicht in deutsche Staatsarchive	1	1935-39	
K III 5 f	Austausch von Arbeitnehmern zur beruflichen und sprachlichen Fortbildung	1	1934-39	
K III 5 g	Deutsch-polnischer Buchaustausch	1	1938-39	
K III 5 h	Deutsche Sprachkurse	1-2	1934-38	
K III 6 a	Deutsch-polnische Hochschulangelegenheiten	1	1935-39	
K III 6 b	Vorlesungsaustausch zwischen deutschen und polnischen Universitäten	1	1935-38	
K III 6 c	Verleihung von Ehrendoktorwürden an polnische Wissenschaftler durch deutsche Universitäten	1	1936-39	
K III 7 a	Deutsch-polnischer Studentenaustausch, Alexander von Humboldt-Stiftung	1-3	1931-39	
K III 7 b	Stipendiaten des Gustav Adolf Vereins	1	1934-39	
K III 7 c	Zusammenarbeit zwischen der deutschen Studentenschaft und der polnischen Liga	1	1935-39	
K III 8 a	Rundfunk Deutschland - Polen	1	1935-38	
K III 9 a	Deutsch-polnische Sportveranstaltungen	1	1936-39	
K III 9 b	Deutsche Sportveranstaltungen in Polen	1	1935-39	
K III 9 b J	- Information	1	1936-39	
K III 9 c	Deutsche Turn-und Sportvereine in Polen	1	1936-38	
K III 10 a	Nachrichtenaustausch über Auftreten übertragbarer Krankheiten auf Grund des deutsch-polnischen Abkommens vom 18.12.22	1	1923-37	
K VIII 2a	Internationales Filmwesen	1	1935-37	
K VIII 5a	Internationalismus, Wissenschaft	1	1930-36	
K VIII 9a	Internationales Sport-und Ertüchtigungswesen	1	1937	
K	Neueingänge, Kult,Verschiedenes	1	1939	

Akten-zeichen	Inhalt	Band	Datum	Serial Nr.
	2 A.Journale		1933-35	
	3 Passjournale		1920-39	
	1 Aktenplan		1936	
	Geheimakten:			
	Geheimsachen	1	1923-24	
Geh.Akten	Verhältnis zwischen der ukraini-schen Minderheit und der polni-schen Regierung (Untersuchungs-verfahren gegen den Undoführer Lewicki)	1	1931-32	
Geh.Akten Sonderakte	Deutsches St.Johannis-Kranken-haus in Lodz	1	1929-33	
	Telegramme, geheim	1	1938-39	
	U.K.-Stellung, geheim	1	1938-39	
	Geheime Reichssachen	1	1938-39	2927/D566821-74
		1	1937-39	7250/E532096-98 2927/D566876-81
	-(Wirtschaft)	1	1938-39	7983/E575250-53
H	H.-Geheim, Wirtschaft	1	1937-39	2918/D566659-81
	R.-Geheim - Runderlasse	1	1935-38	3922/E051581-96
	K.-Geheim - Kult	1	1936-39	2917/D566646-56
	V.-Geheim- Verkehr	1	1935-39	
	Karteisachen - Geheim	1	1935-39	
		2		2906/D566033-41

Akten-zeichen	Inhalt	Band	Datum	Serial Nr.
	Reparationen (Dawes-Plan)	1-19	1922-30	
	– (Young-Plan)	20 -28	1930-32	
Nebenakte	– Gegenaktion zum Wigginbericht	1	1931-32	
V 6 a	Völkerbund, allgemein	1-8	1921-33	
V 6 c	Haager Schiedsgerichtshof	1-4	1923-34	
V 6 d	Locarno	1-4	1924-27	
V 7 a	Konferenzen	1	1921-29	
V 7 b I	III.Haager Konferenz	1	1922-27	
V 7 b	Genua-Konferenz	1	1922	
V 7 c	Wirtschafts- und Finanzkonferenz	1-2	1922-30	
V 7 l	Donaukonferenzen	1	1932	
V 7 d	Telegrafen- und Radiokonferenz	1-2	1924-33	
V 7 f	Abrüstung (Genfer Abrüstungskon-ferenz)	1-9	1928-34	
V 7 g	See-Abrüstung	1-3	1928-34	
1	Wirtschaftliche Lage in Deutsch-land	1+4 5-7	1920-32	
2	– allgemein und in Ameri-ka	1-3	1921-34	
	Wirtschaft: Runderlasse	1	1920-22	
2 a	Berichte des Handelsattachés Becker	1	1934-35	
	Deutsche Wirtschaftszahlen	1-4	1925-28	
a	Statistik	1	1922-33	
	– Volkszählung	1	1924-33	
6 a	Aussenhandel Deutschlands,allg.	1	1922-33	
6 b	– der Vereinigten Staaten	1-2	1923-30	
	Ausstellungen Philadelphia	1-2	1922-27	
8	Deutsche Bestimmungen über Aus- und Einfuhr	1	1921-33	
	Handel - Verschiedenes	1-3	1921-34	
	– (Ostsyndikat Breslau)	1	1922-23	
20	Internationale Handelskammern	1	1923-31	
24	Handelsauskünfte	1-7	1922-34	
24 a	Auskünfte über Patentanmeldungen	1	1927-32	
	Beschlagnahmte Patente	1	1924-26	
	Auskünfte über beschlagnahmte Patente	1	1924-28	

Akten-zeichen	Inhalt	Band	Datum	Serial Nr.
	Patentwesen, Einzelfälle		1928	
	Handel-u.Industrieberichte			
	New York	1	1925-31	
	- Chicago	1	1925-29	
	- Seattle	1	1927-36	
	- Atlanta	1	1928-30	
J 1	Industrie, allgemein	1-2	1922-35	
J 1 a	Chemische Industrie, Amerika	1	1928-33	
	I.G.Farbenindustrie	1	1928-30	
J 3 a	Bestrebungen auf ausschliess-liche Verwendung heimischen Materials	1	1926-33	
J	Verschiedene Normungsbestrebun-gen	1	1922-27	
L 1	Landwirtschaft, Acker- und Gartenbau	1-2	1922-32	
L 1 a	Landwirtschaftliche Hilfsgesetz-gebung	1-3	1926-35	
L 1 b	Landwirtschaft, Verschiedenes	1	1922-36	
L 36	Forstwirtschaft	1	1925-31	
E	Eisenbahnwesen	1-2	1922-31	
Kr	Kraftfahrwesen	1-3	1924-34	
Lu 1	Luftschiffahrt, allgemein	1-6	1922-34	
Lu 1 a	Zivil-Luftfahrtkonferenz	1	1927-34	
Lu 1 b	Meteorologische Karte des Atlantischen Ozeans	1	1927-36	
Lu 1 c	Amerikanische Veröffentlichungen über Luftfahrtwesen	1	1927-36	
Lu 1 d	Panamerikanischer Flugverkehr "Scadtka"	1	1924-33	
Lu 1 g	Luftverkehr - Kanalzone	1	1931-34	
Lu 3	Transozeanflug - Bremen	1-2	1928	
Lu 4	Graf Zeppelin	1-4	1928-36	
V 1	Verkehrswesen - Wasserstrassen	1-2	1923-34	
V 6	Fremdenverkehr	1-3	1922-31	
V 6 c	Bäderführer	1	1924-27	
V 6 d	Verkehrswerbung (Information - Office)	1	1925-29	
Post 3	Postalische Beziehungen Amerika - Deutschland	1	1922-31	
Post	Verschiedenes - Markensammlung	1	1924-32	
Post 3 d	Rundfunk	1-2	1928-33	

Akten-zeichen	Inhalt	Band	Datum	Serial Nr.
ch 6	Amerikanische Schiffahrtsunter-nehmungen	1-3	1922-35	
ch 6 a	Deutsche Schiffahrtsunternehmun-gen	1-2	1923-33	
ch 1 b	Seeleute - Ausbildung, Legiti-mationen	1-2	1922-32	
ch 1 c	Schmuggel auf Schiffen	1	1922-31	
ch 12	Schiffsunfälle, Rettungswesen	1	1922-30	
ch	Desertionen von deutschen Schiffen	1-2	1923-31	
	Verschiedenes - Schiffahrt	1-2	1922-33	
i 1	Deutsche Staatsfinanzen	1-6	1922-32	
i 1 a	- Finanzen und Kredite	1	1923-26	
i 1 c	Goldverschiffungen der Reichs-bank	1	1923-30	
i 1 b	Silberkauf	1	1924-31	
i 1 d	Amerikanische Staatsfinanzen	1-2	1924-33	
i 3	Deutsche Anleihen	1-3	1922-33	
i 3 a	Kriegsanleihe-Aufwertung	1-8	1924-31	
i 3 b	Anleihen und Kreditgesuche	1-4	1924-33	
	Kredite für Lebensmittel, Fishbill	1-2	1923-25	
i 4	Treasury Bonds, Rückzahlung der Anleihen	1-3	1922-25	
i 4 a	Valorisierung der Markschulden	1	1922-25	
i 20	Bankwesen, Sparkassen, Kredit-institute	1-3	1922-33	
i 19	Bankenkrise	1	1933-36	
i 15	Reichsbankvertreter	1	1930-32	
	Schatzanweisungen	1	1929-30	
	Zahlungsverfahren	1	1928-31	
	Bendix-Berichte	1-4	1921-25	
	- Situationsberichte	1	1922-23	
	- Wochenberichte	1	1924-25	
	- Aufklärungsarbeit	1	1923-25	
	- Presseberichte	1	1922-23	
i 8	Kriegsschulden der Alliierten	1-9	1922-33	
i 5	Rückgabe des deutschen Eigentums	1-6	1922-23	
i 5 a	M.C.C.	1 2	1922-28	K2034/K527687-745

Akten-zeichen	Inhalt	Band	Datum	Serial Nr.
Fi 5 a	M.C.C.	3	1929-31	K2034/K527746-8
		4		K2034/K527849-5
		5	1931-32	K2034/K527860-9
Fi 5 b	Rückgabe des deutschen Eigentums, Ausführungen	1-2	1922-23	
Fi 5 c	Durchführung des Gesetzes betr. Freigabe deutschen Eigentums	1	1922-23	
Fi 5 d	Beschlagnahmte deutsche Schiffe	1-2	1923-35	
Fi 5 e	Bestrebungen auf Gesamtfreigabe	1	1923-25	
Fi 5 f	Lacques-Plan	1	1932-33	K2034/K527977-8150
Fi 5 E I	Donovan-Plan	1	1931-32	K2034/K528151-35
Fi 7	Deutsche Auslandsguthaben	1	1923	
	In England, Frankreich, Deutschland befindliche Zertifikate über shares deutscher Reichsangehöriger in amerikanischen Gesellschaften	1-2	1925-29	
Fi 5 I	Deutsches Eigentum, Freigabe	1-16	1924-28	
	- Zeitungsausschnitte	1-3	1925-26	
Fi 5 I a	- Vorschläge zum Freigabegesetz	1	1926	
Fi 5 I b	- Verschiedenes	1-3	1925-27	
St 1	Steuerwesen - Steuergesetzgebung	1	1921-32	
St 1 a	Amerikanische Bundessteuergesetzgebung - Steueraufkommen	1-4	1922-33	
St 1 b	Sondersteuer für im Auslande erbaute Wasserfahrzeuge	1	1926-33	
St 1 c	Amerikanische Einfuhrsteuer, Diverses	1	1932	
St 1 d	- auf Kohle	1	1932-33	
St	Runderlasse - Steuerfragen	1	1920-22	
	Steuern - Verschiedenes	1	1922-31	
Z 4	USA-Zollpolitik	1-3	1922-29	
Z 4 b	Zollzuschlag für deutsche Eisen- und Stahlprodukte	1-2	1926-27	
Z 4 c	Zoll-Schatzamtsagenten	1	1922-26	
Z 4 d	USA-Tarif-Commission	1-3	1926-29	
Z 4 e	Europäische Zoll-Union	1	1926-30	
Z 4 f	Anti-Dumpingzölle	1-2	1926-28	
Z 7 e	Amerikanisches Zollwesen (Sträflingsarbeiten)	1	1930-34	
Z 4 h	- (Untersuchungen)	1	1926-31	

Akten-zeichen	Inhalt	Band	Datum	Serial Nr.
Z 4 i	Amerikanische Zolltarifrevision (allgemein)	1-2	1928-30	
	Amerikanisches Zollwesen Schedule 8-15	1	1929-30	
	- Flußspat	1	1927-30	
R	Verschiedenes betr. Rechtsange-legenheiten	1-2	1922-32	
	- Akte: Witzke und Ackermann	1-2	1921-25	
R 1	Rechtswesen - Gesetzgebung	1-3	1922-31	
R 15	Strafverfolgungen, Begnadigungen von Deutschen in Amerika, allg.	1	1929-33	
	Maehler 1 u. 2 nebst Anlage Strafverfolgungen und Begnadi-gungen	1-3	1922-30	
	Bischoff, Strafverfolgungen und Begnadigungen	1	1920-24	
	Dehne, Strafverfolgungen und Begnadigungen	1	1921-23	
	Palow, Strafverfolgungen und Begnadigungen	1	1922-26	
	Strafprozess gegen den früheren A.P.C. Miller	1	1925-28	
	A - Z	1-2	1922-31	
R 20	Beschlagnahme fremden Eigentums in Deutschland	1	1922-28	
R 27	Forderungen, Beschwerden und Entschädigungsansprüche aus USA gegen Deutschland A - Z	1-2	1921-28	
	Runderlasse	1	1920	
	Haak, Meiss, Pocahontas	1	1922-23	
R 27 u. 27 a	Forderungen, Beschwerden, Ent-schädigungsansprüche gegen Deutschland und Forderungen der amerikanischen Regierung für Beförderungen von Kriegsgefange-nen	1	1922-30	
R 27 b .R 27 c	Kriegsschädengesetz und Ortszu-lage und Beihilfe für Kriegs-teilnehmer	1	1925-33	
R 28	Forderung gegen die amerikani-sche Regierung aus Deutschland A - Z	1-6	1922-30	
	Forderungen aus Deutschland gegen die Vereinigten Staaten Sonderakte Wiegel, Otto	1	1923	
	- Dolores Liebisch	1	1918-23	
	- F.Petersen	1	1923-24	
	- Allgemeines	1	1925-32	

Akten-zeichen	Inhalt	Band	Datum	Serial Nr.
R 31	Verwendungen, Vermittlung, Nachforschungen A – Z	1–3	1922–30	
	– A – W	1–7	1925–34	
R 32	Legalisationen und Bescheinigungen American Red Cross	1	1931–33	
R 35	Rechtshilfe	1	1921–32	
R 36	Rechtspflege – Handelssachen	1	1923–32	
R 40	– und Justizverwaltung	1	1921–32	
R 42	Internierte	1	1922–33	
R 42 a	– Sanitäter	1	1922–32	
R 45	Reichsverfassung	1	1921–34	
R 47	Vormundschaft	1	1922–30	
R 48	Zustellungen	1	1922–32	
V 1 b	Polizei	1	1924–31	
R	Staatsangehörigkeit, allgemein	1	1922–27	
	– A – Z	1	1922–30	
	– Einzelfälle A – Z	1–26	1929–38	
R 43	Nachlaßsachen	1	1922–28	
R	– Einzelfälle A – Z	1–2	1922–30	
	Nachlässe-Freigabe, Einzelfälle	1–3	1921–28	
	Passangelegenheiten, allgemein	1–3	1922–38	
	– Einzelfälle	1–7	1922–35	
Vw 14	Übernahme, Heimschaffung von Reichsangehörigen, Deportationen A – Z	1–2	1922–30	
V 10	Grenzempfehlungen A – Z	1–2	1922–30	
S 1	Soziale Verhältnisse Sozialpolitik, allgemein	1–2	1922–35	
S 2	Arbeiterfragen	1–4	1919–32	
S 2 b	Lage des deutschen Arbeitsmarktes	1	1924–33	
S 2 c	Amerikanisches Beamtenwesen	1	1925–31	
S 3	Streiks, Aussperrungen	1	1922–32	
R 46	Versicherungen	1	1926–37	
	Pensionen, Einzelfälle A – Z	1–4	1922–33	
S 6	Runderlasse, Auslandssammlungen	1	1920–21	
	Wohltätigkeit, Liebesgaben	1–9	1921–32	
S 6 a	Auslandssammlungen	1	1922–29	

Akten-zeichen	Inhalt	Band	Datum	Serial Nr.
S 6 b	Besteuerung von Schenkungen, Liebesgaben und Unterstützungen in Deutschland	1	1922-32	
S 10	Siedlungs- und Wohnungswesen	1-2	1921-33	
S	Frauenbewegung	2	1922-34	
	- N.A.: Kriegsverhütung	1	1929-32	
S 12 e	Mädchen- und Kinderhandel	1	1930-33	
S 12 d	Bekämpfung der Sklaverei	1	1928-32	
S 12	Alkoholbewirtschaftung	1	1929-33	
S 12 a	Alkohol auf Schiffen	1-3	1922-33	
S 12 b	Prohibitionsfragen	1-5	1922-32	
S 12 c	Bekämpfung des Missbrauchs narkotischer Mittel	1-3	1923-32	
A 2 a	Hilfswerk, Privates	1-3	1922-24	
A 2 b	- Politisches	1-2	1922-24	
A 2 c	Rotes Kreuz	1-2	1924-28	
A 2 d	Katholisches Hilfswerk	1	1923-26	
A 2 e	Selbsthilfe	1	1924-27	
A.D.E. Gen.	Abwicklungsstelle für Deutsches Eigentum: Verkehr mit dem Auswärtigen Amt	2	1923-25	
	Konsulaten	3	1923-26	
	Banken	4	1923-26	
	Interessenvertre-tungen	5	1923	
	Beglaubigungen auf Antrag von Behörden und Privaten	7	1923	
	Verkehr mit amerikanischen An-wälten	8	1923-27	
	Aufzeichnungen und Besprechungen	10	1923	
	Shares	11	1923	
	Hearings über Winslow Bill vor dem House Commitee	12	1923	
	Gesetzentwurf sowie endgültige Fassung des Winslow-Gesetzes	13	1923	
	Verschiedenes	14	1923-26	
	Zeitungsausschnitte	15	1923-31	
A.D.E.	Claims, Einzelfälle	1-2	1922-26	
R 19	Freigabe des beschlagnahmten Eigentums, Einzelfälle	1-2	1922-28	
A.D.E.	Berichterstattung und Aufzeich-nungen über die mit der Freigabe des deutschen Eigentums auf Grund der Winslow Bill zusammenhängen-den Fragen	1	1923-27	

Akten-zeichen	Inhalt	Band	Datum	Serial Nr.
A.D.E.	Beglaubigungen von Urkunden, die dem A.P.C. zur Unterstützung von Freigabeanträgen eingereicht werden	1	1927	
	Veröffentlichungen und Aufsätze betr.Behandlung des beschlagnahmten deutschen Privateigentums	2	1925-28	
	Schrift- und Telegrammwechsel mit dem Auswärtigen Amt	1	1929	
Claims	Norddeutscher Lloyd, Ship Claims	1	1928-29	
	Hapag, Ship Claims	1	1928-29	
	Ships Einzel-Claims	1	1928	
	SS. Wiegand Claims	1	1928-29	
	Friedr.Krupp	1	1928	
	Radio-Station Sayville	1	1928	
	Karl W.Sonntag	1	1928	
	Claims, Einzelfälle Nr. 1-8473 - Nr.10562 - 12348	1-13 14-16	1922-26 1922-29	
	Lose Akten betr.Freigabe deutschen Eigentums	1	1922-29	
	- betr.Claims, Einzelfälle	1-5	1922-29	
D.A.F.	Studienreisen, Vorträge (wissenschaftliche) Reisen A - Z	1-5	1925-29	
	Gesellschaftsreisen, allgemein	1-2	1934-37	
V 6 e	Kulturwerbung (Terramare Office)	1	1926-33	
G 1	Gesundheitswesen allgemein	1-3	1921-37	
G 2	Seuchenmeldungen	1-2	1924-36	
Aw 1	Aus- und Einwanderungswesen allgemein	1-5	1921-28	
	Nebenakte: Statistische Mitteilungen	1-4	1925-30	
Aw 2 a	Arbeits- und Landangebote, Angebote für deutsche Einwanderer	1-2	1924-32	
Aw 2 b	Auskünfte betr.Ein- und Auswanderung, allgemein	1	1925-33	
	Auskünfte betr.Ein- und Auswanderung Einzelfälle A - Z	1-9	1925-36	
Aw 2 c	Geheimrat Schmidt, Southern Alluvial Land Association	1	1922-26	
Aw 2 d	Ansiedlung deutsch-russischer Mennoniten	1	1929-32	
A 5	Sammlung Jüdisch-Politischer Berichte, jüdische Angelegenheiten	1-8	1922-33	
	Liberty-Artikel	1	1931	

Akten-zeichen	Inhalt	Band	Datum	Serial Nr.
	Sonderakten:			
	Allen, General	1	1923-33	
	Bendix, Ludwig	1	1927-33	
	Bernsdorff, Graf	1	1923-36	
	Böhmer, Walter	1	1924-26	
	Boess, Oberbürgermeister	1	1929-	
	Boy-Ed, Karl	1	1922-32	
	Charles, Heinrich	1	1922-26	
	de Haas, Ministerialdirektor	1	1925-31	
	de Kalb, Johann	1	1930	
	Dietrich, Bruno	1	1925-28	
	Edel, Fritz	1	1929-30	
	Fischer, S.H.	1	1923-24	
	Frobenius, Leo	1	1922-26	
	Gould, W.D.	1	1923	
	Hanson, Harry W.	1	1923-27	
	Harden, Max	1	1923-27	
	Hoetsch, Professor	1	1924-29	
	Iswolski	1	1924-26	
	Jaeckh, Professor, Ernst	1	1924-33	
	Jordan, Max	1	1925-30	
	Joyner, Sterling	1	1923-24	
	Klein, Julius	1	1925-33	
	Kurze, Walter	1	1924-32	
	Ludendorff, General	1	1925-30	
	Lima, Oliveria	1	1924-26	
	Lerchenfeld, Graf	1	1923-24	
	Luckner, Felix	1	1925-27	
	Ludwig, Emil	1	1925-35	
	Mücke, Kapitänleutnant	1	1922-23	
	Merck, Walter	1	1929-32	
	Newcomb, Robinson	1	1925-27	
	Oberfohren, J.	1	1927-31	
	Peltzer, Otto	1	1926-32	
	Parker, Judge	1	1925-29	
	Rohrbach, Paul	1	1922-31	
	Schmidt, Carl, E.	1	1922-34	
	Simonds, Frank	1	1925-36	
	Stein, Professor	1	1923-30	
	Sumner, Malcom	1	1922	
	Steuben, General, von	1-2	1923-31	
	Thompson, William Hale	1	1927-28	
	Treut, Robert	1	1925-33	
	Viereck, George Sylvester	1	1922-32	
	Vollbehr, Otto	1-2	1926-36	

Akten-zeichen	Inhalt	Band	Datum	Serial Nr.
	Academy of Pol.Science	1	1928-33	
	Amerik.Academy of Pol.& Social Science	1	1923-29	
	American Committee	1	1923-26	
	– Legion	1-3	1922-37	
	– Peace Society	1	1927-33	
	Bureau of Efficiency	1	1922-24	
	Brocks Bright Foundation	1	1929-30	
	Briarcliff Conference	1	1926	
	Buchhandel	1-2	1926-35	
	Carnegie Endowment	1-2	1925-36	
	Chemikalientrust, europäisch	1	1927	
	Chautauqua Konferenz	1	1921-22	
	Department of Commerce	1	1924-28	
	Freiburg Passionsspiele	1	1928-34	
	Frauenkunstgewerbe	1	1928-29	
	German Commerce Yearbook	1	1928-32	
	Int.Trust Co.of N.Y.	1	1927-30	
	Internationaler Frauenbund	1	1925	
	Institute of Economics	1	1922-31	
	– Politics	1-3	1922-31	
	Jahresberichte	1	1926-36	
	Loewen-Universität	1	1925-33	
	Pollak Foundation	1	1925	
	Panamerikanische Handelskonferenz	1	1927-36	
	Przemysl-Motorschiff	1	1927-29	
	Panamerikanische Konferenz	1-3	1924-34	
	Quarter-Collection	1	1924-31	
	Reichszentrale für Heimatdienst	1	1927-31	
	Rotary Bewegung	1	1926-32	
	Shenandoah Luftschiff	1	1925-26	
	Stahltrust, europäisch	1	1926-33	
	Southern Commercial Congress	1	1922-23	
	Tacna Arica	1-2	1922-29	
	Waffenstillstandsfeier	1-3	1924-33	
	War Finance Corporation	1	1921-29	
	Weltreise amerikanischer Studenten	1	1925-30	

Akten-zeichen	Inhalt	Band	Datum	Serial Nr.
	Yorktown Feier	1	1931-33	
	Handakten Dr.W.Kiesselbach 58 Hefte		1922-28	
Priv.	Private Anfragen verschiedener Art, allgemein	1-3	1921-22	
	Anfragen und Auskünfte verschiedener Art, Privat	1-65	1922-38	
	Verschiedene Broschüren betr. Claims-Kommission, Bauzeichnungen			
	2 Journale			

Akten-zeichen	Inhalt	Band	Datum	Serial Nr.
A	Chiffre		1910-22	
	Albanien	2-3	1920-38	
Af	Afrika	1-2	1912-38	
Afg	Afghanistan		1911-30	
Am	Amerika	1-2	1911-38	
As	Asien, ohne türkische Besitzungen und Sibirien	1-2	1911-38	
Bu	Bulgarien	1-2	1916-37	
A D I	Deutschland	2		
		3	1920-36	K1859/K464359-6059
		4-5		
A D	- politische Emigranten	1-8	1933-38	
A E	Großbritannien und Kolonien	1	1911-38	7621/E544971-91
		2		7621/E544992-5031
	Ägypten	1-2	1911-38	
A F	Frankreich und Kolonien	1-3	1911-38	
A Gr.(S)	Griechenland	2-3	1915-37	
A It.	Italien	3	1916-27	
		4	1928-35	8026/E577760-67
		5-6	1935-38	
A It. I	Südtirol	1-2	1928-38	
A Js	Jugoslawien	1-2	1917-38	
A M	Mitteleuropäische Kleinstaaten: Belgien, Holland, Luxemburg, Schweiz, Liechtenstein	1-2	1911-38	
A N	Nordische Kleinstaaten: Schweden, Finnland, Norwegen, Dänemark	1-2	1911-38	
A Oe	Österreichische innere Angelegenheiten	6-11	1920-30	
		12	1931-32	K1196/K306695-7267
		13		K1860/K466060-7379
		14 -34	1933-38	
A Oe f	Anschlußfrage	1-2	1918-34	
A Oe V	- Vorarlberg		1919-23	
A Oe W	Der Wiederaufbau Österreichs, Bericht des Generalkommissars Zimmermann		1922-26	
A Oe I	Österreich: Beziehungen zu anderen Ländern, Betrachtungen	1-2	1920-31	
A Oe 2	Deutsch-österreichisches Abkommen	1	1935-36	8678/E607201-83
		2	1936-37	
		3	1937-38	7821/E567296-301
A Oe 3	Neue Regierung Schuschnigg		1938	

Akten-zeichen	Inhalt	Band	Datum	Serial Nr.
A Oe 4	Proklamation des Führers		1938	
A Oe 5	Habsburger Frage	1	1932-37	K1066/K274719-5129
		2	1937-38	K1066/K275130-207
A Oe 6	Vaterländische Front	1-2	1934-38	
A Oe 7	Schutzkorps der Vaterländischen Front		1937-38	
A Oe 8	Runderlasse der österreichischen Behörden	1-2	1936-38	
A Oe 9	Befriedigungsaktion		1936-38	
A Oe 10	Briefzensur, Grußform "Heil, Hitler", Postkarten mit Haken-kreuz		1934-38	
A Oe 11	Verzeichnis der ausgebürgerten Österreicher		1934-38	
A Oe 12	Auswirkung des deutsch-österrei-chischen Abkommens	1-2	1936-37	
A Oe 13	Amnestie		1937	
A Oe 14	Freiheits- und Todesstrafen	1-2	1934-37	
A Oe 15	Flugschriften, Hetzplakette	1	1934-35	
A Oe 16	Belästigungen wegen Tragens des Hakenkreuzes		1937-38	
A Oe 17	Zur Lage nach der Proklamation		1938	
A Oe 18	Abwicklung des ehemaligen österreichischen Aussendienstes		1938-39	K1183/K303950-4335
A Oe 21	Österreichische Kreditanstalt	1	1931-32	K1861/K467380-576
		2	1931-37	K1862/K467577-897
A Oe 22	- Völkerbundsanleihe	1	1931-32	K1195/K306039-269
		2	1932	K1195/K306270-445
		3	1933-35	K1195/K306446-694
A Oe	Protestnoten		1933-39	
A	Politische Haftfälle		1934-38	
A P (F III 3)	Polen, Danzig	3-7	1918-38	
A P I	- Oberschlesien		1920-31	
A R	Russland und Sibirien	3-4	1920-38	
A Re	Rumänien	3-4	1916-38	
A Q			1914-23	
A Sp	Spanien und Portugal	1-3	1911-38	
A T (O)	Türkei	5	1913-34	
A (3) 1	Die orientalischen Eisenbahnen	6	1935-38	
A T	Tschechoslowakei	1-2	1920-38	

Akten-zeichen	Inhalt	Band	Datum	Serial Nr.
A Ts I	Tschechoslowakei, Fremdvölker		1920-26	
A U	Ungarn	2-4	1920-38	
A U I	– Fremdvölker		1914-23	
A Uk	Ukraine			
A Vat.	Vatikan	1-2	1911-38	
A (5) 1	Zionismus		1917-32	
A 1	Zeremonielles, Audienzen, Staatsfesttage, Notifikationen, Nationalversammlung		1924-38	
	Nationaler Feiertag des deutschen Volkes		1935-37	
	Erntedankfest		1935-37	
	Heldengedenktag		1936-38	
	Tag der Machtergreifung		1938	
	Feier des Geburtstages des Führers		1937-38	
	Freiherr von Neurath in Wien		1937	
	Dr.Hjalmar Schacht in Wien		1937	
A 2	Westliche russische Randvölker, Memelland		1918-30	
	Orden, Aufzeichnungen, Rang-und Titelwesen, Adel, Privilegien		1937-38	
A 4 (9)	Georgier, Kaukasier, Tartaren		1915-25	
	Ukraine	3	1918-35	
	Heer, Marine, Polizei, Gendarmerie, Kriegergräber, Flaggenfrage, Hoheitszeichen		1937-38	
A 5 (10)	Friedensverhandlungen		1919	K1184/K304336-572
	Versailler Vertrag	1-2	1930-38	
A 5 a	Völkerbund		1920-24	
	– österreichische Völkerbundsliga		1934-38	
A 5 b	Minderheiten		1929-38	
A 6	Kirchenangelegenheiten, Kurie Katholizismus, Protestantismus		1919-35	K1185/K304573-784
A 6	Literatur, Kunst, Wissenschaft, Studien- und Konzertreisen		1936-38	
A 7	Die kleine Entente, Donaukonföderation, Balkanbund		1923-37	
A 9	Verwendungssuche, Forderungssachen		1938	
b	Bolschewismus, Kommunismus, Anarchismus, Sozialismus, Gewerkschaftssachen	2-5	1920-38	

Akten-zeichen	Inhalt	Band	Datum	Serial Nr.
A c	Presse, insbesondere Österreichs		1920-30	
A d	Vertretungen, österreichischer Aussendienst, fremde Diplomatie Zollvergünstigungen	1 2	1920-32 1932-36	K1188/K305158-286
	Diplomatisches Korps, amtliche Persönlichkeiten, Politiker		1937-38	K1189/K305287-371
	Berichte über das Diplomatische Korps, die Mitglieder der Regierung		1937	
A e	Verschiedenes	1-3	1911-38	
A f	Nationalismus, Faschismus, Heimwehr, Stahlhelm, Monarchismus	1 2-8	1923-34 1934-38	K1863/K467898-9662
	Heimatschutz		1936-37	
	Aufenthaltsbewilligung	1-2	1936-38	
	Rückeinbürgerung ausgebürgerter politischer Flüchtlinge		1937-38	
	Emigrantenrückkehr, Gen.u.Spez.		1937-38	
	Rückkehr von Emigranten nach Österreich	1-2	1936-38	
	Emigrantenrückkehr, Listen	1 2	1937-38	K1192/K305598-708
	Namenlisten österreichischer Emigranten, die die Heimkehr nach Österreich anstreben		1936-37	
	Dr. Richard Koderle		1934-38	
	H.H.Sadila - Mantau		1936-38	
A g	Militärangelegenheiten	1 2	1930-35 1936-38	K1190/K305372-547
A I c Generalia	Geschäftsverteilung, Büroverfügungen, Auslandsgebührengesetz		1919-38	
	Dienststelle des Auswärtigen Amtes, Abwicklung		1938-39	
A II	Lebenshaltungskosten in Österreich, Besoldung		1934-39	
A III	Dienstkraftwagen		1917-38	
	Abgabe von Akten an das Auswärtige Amt		1920-39	
A IV	Gesandtschaftsgebäude		1922-38	
	Haushaltssachen		1934-38	
A VII	Wahrnehmung österreichischer Interessen durch das Deutsche Reich, österreichische Diplomaten-liste		1921-38	
A IX	Deutschtum in Österreich (Verschiedene Vereine)		1929-38	
IX a	Bund der Reichsdeutschen		1935-38	

Akten-zeichen	Inhalt	Band	Datum	Serial Nr.
IX b	Reichsdeutschenhilfe in Wien	1-2	1926-38	
Pa	Presseangelegenheiten allgemein	1-5	1919-24	
		6	1925-27	K1864/K469663-965
		7-14	1928-38	
	Tschechischer Einfluss auf die österreichische Presse		1927-38	
	Deutschsprachige Zeitungen und Zeitschriften in Österreich		1933-38	
	Handbuch der deutschsprachigen Zeitungen im Ausland		1934-37	
	Schönere Zukunft		1934-37	
	Wiener Neueste Nachrichten		1934-38	
	Verbot deutscher Zeitungen	2	1936-37	
	- österreichischer Zeitungen	2	1933-38	
	Hetzschriften und Bücher gegen den Führer und das Reich		1935-38	
Pa gen.	Abbau der Zeitungsverbote		1936-37	
Pa	Deutsch-österreichische Presse-vereinbarung vom 10.Juli 1937		1937-38	
	VLR.Braun von Stumm (Nachrichten- und Presseabteilung des Auswärti-gen Amtes)		1938	
Pb	Presseberichte, Pressekonferenzen Pressevertreter	1-5	1920-37	
	Presseberichte des Pressebeirats an Promi	1-2	1933-38	
Pc	Presse, Neugründungen, Subven-tionen	1-3	1920-36	
Pc V	Deutsches Volksblatt		1919-22	
Pc	Mitteleuropäische Korrespondenz (Miko)		1935-38	
	Monatsschrift "Wehr und Waffen"		1936-38	
	Verschiedene Zeitungen	1-2	1937-38	
Pf	Filme		1919-34	
B I b	Personalangelegenheiten der mittleren und Unterbeamten: Wivenot, Todt, Adler, Brücklmaier, Dr.Euler, Hollmann, v.Mutius, Weidel, Eßlang, Kolasius, Siegert, Jesuiter, Reinhard, Platzer, Schmidt, Werner, Jack, Marschall		1912-33	
	Arlt, Eckel, Einderle, Fack-ler, Hartmeyer, Haupt, Heller, Hofmann Joh.,Hofmann Max, Jesgarz, Kern, Kroß, Lauterböck, Wegner, Porath, Puppel, Reisgen, Witrisch, Reinmachefrauen		1922-39	

Akten-zeichen	Inhalt	Band	Datum	Serial Nr.

B I b	Personalangelegenheiten der mittleren und Unterbeamten:
	    v.Stotzingen, Rore, Märkl, Ethofer, Kleiner, Lamerdin, Zugmayr, Piest, Dentzer, Klein, Bethke, Schmidt
	
	    Bruckhaus, Ewald, Gramms, Steuermann, Krüger, Wagner, Piesczek, Hinz, Troika, Mansfeld
	
	    de la Trobe, Kundt, Best-mann, v.Haeften, Schwaynoch Schellhorn, Junker, Berner, Below, Hoffmann, Hesse, Clodius, Engelberg, Bles-sing, Dornbusch
	
	    Stenotypistinnen, Telefo-nistinnen, Hilfsarbeiter, Lektoren, untere Beamte
			1922-39	

B I c	Geschäftsgang der Gesandtschaft, allgemein. Dienstangelegenheiten und -vorschriften, Sparerlasse, Auslandsgebührengesetz	2-4	1918-38	
	Urlaub		1921-38	
	Dienstreisenbestimmungen		1924-37	
	Umzugskostenbestimmungen		1924-38	
	Gewährung von Beihilfen		1928-38	
	Kinder- und Verheiratetenzu-schlag		1935-38	
B II	Kassen- und Etatssachen Lebensmittelversorgung		1874-1927	
	Invaliden- und Angestelltenver-sicherung		1919-37	
	Angestelltenversicherung		1919-38	
	Steuern		1922-38	
B III	Amtslokal, Archiv, Inventar, Auto, Bibliothek	2-3	1918-38	
B III/IV	Gesandtschaftsgebäude, Inventar, Etatsvoranschläge		1918-32	
B IV	Bau. Einrichtung und Unterhaltung des Gesandtschaftsgebäudes, Gesandtschaftsgarten, Dienstwoh-nungen, Telefon, Bewirtschaftung von Haushaltungsmitteln	1 4-6	1866-1923 1922-36	
B VII	Fremde Diplomatie, Vertretungen		1919-33	
B VIII	Konsulate, Generelles (Karten)		1888-1938	
	Konsulat Graz	1-2	1919-38	
	- Innsbruck		1921-38	
	- Klagenfurth		1935-38	
	- Linz	1-2	1921-38	
	- Salzburg, Klagenfurth		1923-38	

Akten-zeichen	Inhalt	Band	Datum	Serial Nr.
B VIII	Konsulat Wien		1910-37	
	Paßstelle Bregenz		1916-35	
	– Wien		1916-35	
B IX	Vereine u.Gesellschaften		1899-35	
B IX	Verschiedene Vereine, Unterstützungen		1919-35	
B 1	Kurierangelegenheiten v.Rosenberg, Pfeifer		1905-23	K643/K168100-22
B 5	Kirchen- und Unterrichtswesen, Kulturfragen, Humanitäres		1933-38	
	Konsulatsakademie Wien		1921-36	
B 8	Verträge, Abkommen		1910-20	
B 13	Studienreisen, Kunst und Wissenschaft		1923	
B 24	Wohlfahrtsangelegenheiten, Kriegsunterstützungen, Kleinrentner Generalia		1920-38	
D h II	Anwerbung und Vermittlung österreichischer landwirtschaftlicher Arbeiter nach dem Deutschen Reich		1928-38	
	Arbeitsgesuche deutscher Rück- und Zuwanderer, Arbeitsvermittlung für Österreicher		1935-38	
W d II	Devisenschmuggel, devisenfahndungsstelle		1934-38	
W h II	Handelsverträge: Allgemeines, Abessinien, Albanien, Ägypten, Amerika, Argentinien, Belgien, Brasilien, Bulgarien, Kolumbien,China, Dänemark, England		1924-38	
	– Deutschland,(Schriftwechsel über Einzelsachen)		1933-38	
	– Frankreich, England, Griechenland, Holland, Italien		1923-38	
	– Japan, Jugoslawien, Kanada, Kuba, Lettland, Litauen, Norwegen, Persien, Portugal Polen		1924-38	
	– Rumänien mit Präferenzverträgen, Rußland, Schweden, Schweiz		1926-38	
	– Spanien, Tschechoslowakei, Türkei, Ungarn		1924-38	7858/E569875-82
	Deutsch-österreichische Obst-Kohlekompensationen Broochiverträge, Römischer Dreierpakt		1932-35	
Wp VII	Erdölkonzession K.G. Schmidt, Wien (Denkschrift)			
Wt 10	Deutsche Revisions- und Treuhandgesellschaft		1935-38	

Akten-zeichen	Inhalt	Band	Datum	Serial Nr.
v VII	Versicherungen (Allgemeines, Viktoria, Phönix)		1935-38	
	Geheime Sachen O - X und L		1882-1921	
	Geheim III Ganz geheime Sachen		1913-21	9852/H316824-7280 L413/L118741-50
	Presse, Allgemeines		1919-25	4938/E264189-399
	Geheimakten 1925			
218/25	Sicherheitsfrage: deutsche Anregungen hierzu			4938/E265184-341
225/25	Anschlußfrage: Bericht der Gesandten von Rosenberg und Dr. Pfeiffer			
379/25	Tschechoslowakische Wirtschaftsspionage			
530/25	Einreiseerlaubnis für die jugoslawischen Staatsangehörigen Golubitsch Mustafa, Paul und Memed Baschitsch			
	Dr. Bam, Journalist			
948/25	Amerikanisches Chiffrierverfahren (Verhandlungen des Generals Kundt)			
	Richter, Samuel; Spionageangebot			
	Geheimakten 1926			
46/26	Stellung der Reichsregierung zu den Investigationsbeschlüssen des Völkerbundsrats			4938/E265342-520
	Spende für den Bund der Reichsdeutschen			
125/26	Ratssitzfrage beim Eintritt Deutschlands in den Völkerbund			
169/26	Die Locarno-Verträge und das Verhältnis Deutschlands zu Rußland			
200/26	Balkan Lage: Deutsches und österreichisches Memorandum			
224/26	Politische Aussprache beim Berliner Besuch des Bundeskanzlers Ramek am 27./28.3.1926			
289/26	Italiens Wunsch auf freie Hand an der Donau			
401/26	Pasitsch's angebliche Verhandlungen mit Deutschland, einen Thronwechsel in Serbien betreffend			

Akten-zeichen	Inhalt	Band	Datum	Serial Nr.
	Geheimakten 1926			
A 401/26	Dr.Preindlsperger von Preindl-spergs Vorschlag eines Deutsch-jugoslawischen Wirtschaftsbünd-nisses			
A 492/26	Vorgänge in polnischen Regierungs-kreisen			
	Geheimakten 1927			
	Deutsch-russische Zusammenarbeit (Aufzeichnung General Kundt)			
	Aufzeichnung über die Besprechun-gen am 30.5.1927 gelegentlich der Anwesenheit des Staatssekre-tärs von Schubert			
A 425/27	Graf Lerchenfeld über das Ver-hältnis Österreichs zum Reich (Bericht nach einjähriger Tätig-keit des Gesandten in Wien)			
A 547/27	Italienisch-albanischer Vertrag			
A 583/27	Abrüstungskonferenz (Tagung 30.11.- 3.12.1927)			
A 584/27	Aufzeichnungen über die Be-sprechungen am 14.11.1927 gelegentlich des Wiener Besuches des Reichskanzlers Dr.Marx und Reichsaussenministers Dr.Strese-mann			4938/E265521-77
A 590/27	Petrucci, Legationsrat; Vertrau-ensmann Mussolinis			
	Geheimakten 1928			
A 53/28 A 133/28	Sicherheitskomitee: Bemerkungen der deutschen Regierung zum Arbeitsprogramm			4938/E265780-6092
A 59/28 A 77/28	Angebliche Bemühungen des Ge-sandten Graf Lerchenfeld und Reichsaussenministers Dr.Strese-mann um Herstellung einer christlichsozial-sozialdemokra-tischen Regierungskoalition			
A 123/28	Verlegung des Völkerbundsitzes nach Wien			
A 149/28	Wirth, Reichskanzler a.D.: Unterredung mit Bundeskanzler Dr. Seipel			
A 205/28	Polens Absichten zur Errichtung von Botschaften			
A 422/28	Dr.Benesch, tschechischer Aussen-minister: Besuch Berlin			
A 296/28 A 320/28 A 423/28	Dr.Klein: Intervention in Süd-tiroler Frage			

Akten- zeichen	Inhalt	Band	Datum	Serial Nr.
	Geheimakten 1928			
A 456/28	Minister Painlevé in Wien			
A 1862/28	Minderheitenregelung			
	Schreiben des Ministerialdirektors Köpke an den Gesandten Graf Lerchenfeld vom 29.Mai und 25.Juni 1928 betr.Verhandlungen wegen eines ungarisch-rumänischen Ausgleichs			
	Geheimakten 1929			
A 76	Österreichische Staatsanleihe in Amerika (Vermittlungsversuche)			4938/E266093-367
B 292 B 494 B 580	Minderheitenfrage			
	Privatbrief des Gesandten Graf Lerchenfeld an Ministerialdirektor Köpke den neuen Bundeskanzler Streruwitz betreffend			
	– vom 1.6.1929 betr.die Vergrößerung des tschechischen Nachrichtendienstes (Ankauf des Europa-Press)			
A 103 A 185	Kundschafterangebot des Tschechoslowaken Navratil			
	Schreiben des Generals Kundt betr. die Rede Bauers vor dem antifaschistischen Komitee (Afkao)			
	Privatbrief des Dir.Zechlin an den Gesandten Graf Lerchenfeld betr. Ufa-Angelegenheit, Elbemühlblätter, Nachrichtenagentur der Kleinen Entente			
	Korrespondenz des Gesandten Graf Lerchenfeld über Anschlußfrage und Einwirkung auf Katholizismus Gutachten Hollnsteiner und Abt Reetz. Brief an Msgr.Arata, Lissabon			
B 1275	Korrespondenz mit Botschafter von Prittwitz in Sachen des Vertriebes eines Werkes zu Gunsten der Reichsdeutschenhilfe			
	Schreiben des Botschaftsrats Hoffmann an Ministerialdirektor Köpke vom 10.9.1929 betr.Unterredung mit dem Landtagsabgeordneten Dr.Hölscher über die österreichische Heimwehr			
	Korrespondenz zwischen Botschaftsrat Hoffmann und Herrn von Bülow – AA – betr.die österreichische Heimwehrfrage und Pater Innerkofler			

Akten-zeichen	Inhalt	Band	Datum	Serial Nr.
	Geheimakten 1929			
A 269	Bericht betr. Zusammenkunft Steruwitz mit Benesch			
A 392	Gespräch des Gesandten Graf Lerchenfeld mit Reichsminister Dr.Hilferding über innerpolitische Lage in Österreich			
	Schreiben des Herrn von Bülow an den Gesandten Graf Lerchenfeld vom 20.9.1929 betr.Möglichkeit eines österreich-italienischen Ausgleichs durch Verzicht auf den Anschluss			
	Bericht des Deutschen Konsulats Innsbruck vom 11.11.1929 betr. Heimatwehr und Alpenländische Rundschau			
	Korrespondenz mit Herrn v.Bülow betr.Professor Otte und den Wiener Heimatbund			
	- betr.Oskar Bam und den Landbund			
A 497	Schreiben des Herrn von Bülow den Vertreter der Agenzia Steffani, Herrn Villa, betreffend			
	Geheimakten 1930			4938/E266368-839
	Papst Waldemar, Major a.D.			
	Auslandsreisen des Bundeskanzlers Schober			
A 15	Angebliche Abmachungen der Generalstäbe der Kleinen Entente und Frankreichs			
	Schreiben des Staatssekretärs von Schubert			
	Beabsichtigte Ernennung des Gesandten Post zum Leiter der Politischen Abteilung im Bundeskanzleramt			
	Abberufung des Generals Kundt, Vertretung der Reichswehr in Wien			
	Hofrat Siechart und sein Verhältnis zur Bodenkreditanstalt und zu den Steyermühlblättern			
A 195	Bericht der Deutschen Botschaft Rom betr.Ausführungen Mussolinis zur aussenpolitischen Lage			
	Schreiben des Botschaftsrats Hoffmann an Geh.Rat von Bülow vom 25.4.1930 betr.Wiener Neueste Nachrichten,Reisen des Bundeskanzlers Schober nach Paris und London, geplante Annäherungsversuche Italiens an Deutschland, Austausch politischer Berichte zwischen Deutschland u.Österreich			

Akten-zeichen	Inhalt	Band	Datum	Serial Nr.
	Geheimakten 1930			
A 303	Militärischer Nachrichtendienst Suppantschitsch			
	Schreiben des Gesandten Graf Lerchenfeld an den Pressechef Dr.Zechlin, den Herausgeber der "Uta", Herrn Otto betreffend			
A 334	Niederschrift über die politi-schen Besprechungen in Berlin mit Bundeskanzler Schober			
A 335	Tschechische Blättermeldungen wonach Bundeskanzler Schober sich während seiner Londoner und Pariser Reise zur Wiederher-stellung der Donauföderation bereit erklärt habe			
	Österreichs Aussenpolitik			
	Erlasse des Auswärtigen Amtes vom 1.7. und 3.12.1930 die unga-rische Königsfrage betreffend			
A 399	Erlass vom 28.7.1930 - II Alb.98 betr.früheres Parlamentsmitglied Alexander Freundlich in Wien und hier lebenden Albaner Hassan Bey Prischtina, Mittelperson des König Zogu			
A 382	Österreichischer Gesandter Hein (Bericht der Deutschen Botschaft Moskau, Erlaß vom 18.7.1930 - II Oe 1183 -)			
A 445	Österreichische Politik betr. Südtirol (Erlaß vom 2.9.1930 - II Jt 1264 -)			
A 469 A 677	Österreichischer Bundesverlag			
A 507	Polnischer Nachrichtendienst (Dr.Krantz)			
	Schreiben an Reichsminister Wirth betr.Unterstützung des Österreichischen Volksbundes			
	Schreiben an Reichsminister Curtius,vom 15.11.1930 betr.: persönliche Fühlungnahme durch Sonderbeauftragten des deutschen und Österreichischen Aussenamtes			
	Aufzeichnung über die Besprechun-gen mit dem Grafen Bethlen an-läßlich seines Besuches in Berlin			
	Preikoschat, Erich und Wolter, Klara; Spionageverdacht			
	Geheimakten 1931			4938/D266840-7179
	Beihilfen für die Österreichisch-Deutsche Arbeitergemeinschaft			
	Wiener Neueste Nachrichten			

Akten-zeichen	Inhalt	Band	Datum	Serial Nr.
	Geheimakten 1931			
	Serbisches Beutearchiv			
	Kandidatur Benesch für Vorsitz Abrüstungskonferenz			
	Aufzeichnung anläßlich Besuchs Reichsministers Dr.Curtius in Wien			
A 132	Überlassung der Gesandtschafts-festräume an den Deutschen Schul-verein Südmark			
A 817/32	Österreichischer Bundesverlag (Gooß)			
A 304/31	Bestellung von Militärgewehren bei den Steyrwerken durch Grie-chenland			
A 543/31	Erfindung von Guttenberg; Tor-pedo, Schiffsantriebskonstruk-tion, Fernlenksteuerung			
A 596/31	Schreiben gegen Bundeskanzler Schober			
A 743/31	Schreiben von Bülow an Gesandten Dr.Rieth betr.Zusammenkunft Dr.Schober-Benesch			
A 758/31	Aufzeichnungen des Reichsmini-sters Dr.Curtius über Besprechun-gen in Rom 1931			
A 896/31	Erlaß des Auswärtigen Amtes vom 9.10.1931 betr. Urlaubsreisen der Missionschefs			
	Verschlossene Briefe			
A 1048/31	Zusammenkunft Dr.Brüning - Dr. Buresch			
A 799/32	Angelegenheit Langenhan - Ossa Brief an Bürgermeister Winkler			
A 1073/32	Organisation des Österreichisch-Deutschen Volksbundes			
	Geheimakten 1932			4938/E267180-767
A 363/32	Kölnische Zeitung; Wiener Ver-tretung			
A 299/32	Landbund			
A 300/32	Bildungs- und Erholungsheim der christlichen Gewerkschaften Österreichs (Staud)			
A 394/32	Angriffe auf Gesandtschaftsrat Dr.Clodius			
A 379	Deutsche Allgemeine Zeitung (Frau Klausberger)			
A 423	Zahlungen an Alfred Stein			

Akten-zeichen	Inhalt	Band	Datum	Serial Nr.
	Geheimakten 1932			
B 2443/32	Erzbischöflicher Stuhl in Wien, Nachfolge für Kardinal Dr.Piffl betreffend			
A 357	Zusammenstellung für die Besprechungen des Gesandten Dr.Rieth in Berlin			
A 513	Militärabkommen der Kleinen Entente in Bukarest			
A 839/32	Neue Freie Presse			
A 700/32	Gerda Luise von Einem, Spionageverdacht			
	Aufzeichnung über Unterredung Bundeskanzler Dr.Streruwitz mit Gesandtschaftsrat Dr.Clodius			
	Schreiben des Geheimrats von Friedberg an Gesandten Dr.Rieth vom 20.10.1932			
A 1075/31	Briefaustausch zwischen dem Reichswehrministerium und dem Bundesministerium für Landesverteidigung			
	Geheimakten 1933			
A 777/31	Österreichisch-Deutsche Arbeitsgemeinschaft			4938/E267768-8594
A 346/33	Grossdeutschgesinnte katholische Studentenschaft in Österreich			
A 332/32	Freiheit, Zeitung; Konflikt mit der Gesandtschaft			
A 36/33	Österreichischer Gesandtenposten in Berlin, Tauschitz Nachfolger von Dr.Frank			
A 1792/34	Hirtenberger Patronenfabrik, Waffenlieferungen			
A 59/33	Aufrüstung Österreichs			
A 1083/33	Bestrebungen zur Neutralisierung Österreichs			
A 151/33	Ernennung von Pflügls zum österreichischen Gesandten in Paris (Hohenlohe/Liechtenstein)			
	Une formidable affaire d'espionage			
A 238/33	Niederösterreichische Eskomptebank			
A 368/33	Schreiben des Gesandten Dr.Rieth an Herrn von Bülow betr.österreichische Wünsche bei eventuellen Revisionsverhandlungen der Friedensverträge			
A 444/33	Englischer Gesandter Sir Erik Phipps			

Akten-zeichen	Inhalt	Band	Datum	Serial Nr.
	Geheimakten 1933			
A 667/33	Habicht, Theo und Cohrs, Heinz; Ernennung zu Gesandtschafts-beamten			
A 374/33	Aussenpolitische Lage Deutsch-lands im März 1933			
A 1033/32	Colloredo, Graf Ferdinand; poli-tische Mission in Rom			
B 2623/33	Sudetendeutscher Heimatbund in Wien			
	Berichte des Militärattachés Generalleutnant Muff			
	Geheimakten 1934			
346/33	Berichte des NS-Nachrichtendien-stes Gau Wien			4938/E268595-9218
	Österreichischer Volkswirt			
	Aufzeichnung über eine Unterre-dung des Gesandten Dr.Rieth in Berlin am 10.2.1934			
A 2220	Politische Lage in Österreich			
A 791/35	Amerikanische Sabotage Claims (Willy Kissling)			
A 3391/34	Wiener Neueste Nachrichten			
A 1842/33	Neue Zeitung (Baron Wallerstein-Marnegg)			
A 1226/34	Hilfsaktion für verhaftete öster-reichische Nationalsozialisten			
A 1874/34	Hitler - Mussolini; Zusammen-kunft in Venedig			
	Quittungen (Dr.Junker 1933)			
A 631/33	Dr.Schreiber; Anbietung für Nachrichtendienst			
A 639/33	Neubachers Stellung zur NSDAP			
A 760/33	Schreiben des Gesandten Dr.Rieth an Herrn von Bülow betr.Unter-redung mit Bundeskanzler Dr.Dollfuß (Annäherung)			4938/E269219-478
A 2096/33	Kommunistische Kurierverbindung nach Berlin			
A 874/33	Meindl'sche Aktion			
	Madarasz,Josef, Oberregierungs-rat			
B 1331/34	Dr.Hans Neuwirth			
A 1603/33	Italienisch-französisch-engli-sches Demarche in deutsch-öster-reichischem Konflikt			

Akten-zeichen	Inhalt	Band	Datum	Serial Nr.
	Geheimakten 1934			
A 1998/33	Hans Sachs (Jellinek)			4938/E269479-70060
A 1166/33	Republikanischer Schutzbund in Österreich			
A 1290/33	Tschechoslowakische Einflüsse auf Innenpolitik in Österreich			
A 455/34	Alpine Montan in Österreich, Streik bei derselben			
	Karwinski			
	Schreiben des Gesandtschaftsrats Dr.Clodius an den Gesandten Dr.Rieth über die Wirtschaftsverhältnisse in Österreich			
A 47/34	Schwarze Front (Otto Strasser)			
	Großdeutsche in Österreich			
	Arco			
A 1690/33	Pekny, Jaroslaus, Österreichischer Kriminalbeamter			
	Berichte des Militärattachés Generalleutnant Muff			
A 1840/33	Patzner, Jugendsekretär der christlichsozialen Partei			
A 1793/33	Schönburg-Hartenstein, Fürst, Generaloberst			
A 1965/33	Wolf, Reichsbahndirektor über die Regelung des internationalen europäischen Eisenbahnverkehrs			
B 3139/33	WTB-Vertreter Baron Hahn			
A 1648/33	Österreichische Druck- und Verlagsgesellschaft			
A 151/34	Erbprinz zu Waldeck, Angelegenheit Habicht			
	Kaltenböck, Bodo, Major a.D.			
	Schreiben des Gesandten Dr.Rieth vom 17.März an Herrn von Grünau			
	Aufzeichnung über Dr.Viktor Kienböck			
	Schreiben des Gesandten Dr.Rieth vom 23.7.1934 an Herrn von Bülow über die innerpolitische Lage Österreichs			
	Geheimakten 1935-38			
A 2013/37	Deutsch-österreichisches Polizeiabkommen			4938/E270061-80
A 1434/38	Legales Hilfswerk			4938/E270081-260
A 1125/38	Angelegenheit von Tschirschki			
	UTA,Korresondenz (Wilhelm Otto)			

Akten-zeichen	Inhalt	Band	Datum	Serial Nr.
	Geheimakten 1935-38			
A 3819/36	Defektenangelegenheit des Hofrats Paul Ewald			4938/E270261-700
A 4501/35	Wehrmachtattaché betr.Erlasse			
B 4501/35	Russek, Ida, Stenotypistin			
A 66/35	Donauraumfrage			
A 78/38	Amerikanische Sabotageprozesse			4938/E270701-927
	Luppe, Kapitän a.D., Klagenfurt			4938/E270928-1084
	Wirth, Dr.Josef, Reichskanzler a.D.			
A 899/35	Nachrichtenbeschaffung			
B 4260/35	Konsul von Druffel, Preßburg			
B 4278/35	H.R. Wiese			
	Dr.Kohl, Klagenfurt			
B 3112/34	Megerle, Dr.Karl; Entsendung als Attaché			
A 1087/35	Wiener Neueste Nachrichten			
A 5944/37	Beihilfen für politische Häftlinge, Honorierung der Rechtsbeistände			4938/E271085-271
A 2067/36	Meldungen über Österreich			4938/E271272-401
A 1349/35	Zahlung an Kraus, Felix			
A 721/36	Major Finkl-Karl Hartl			
A 4649/36	Kanzler Gaerte, Linz			
A 2877/37	Kriegsmaßnahmen			
A 5505/37	Liste des schädlichen und unerwünschten Schrifttums			
A 5012/37 A 7412/37	Geheime Verschlußsachen			
	Quittungen			
	Engelberg, Dr. Konsulatssekretär			
	Berichte des Militärattachés Generalleutnant Muff			4938/E271402-759
	NSDAP in Österreich			4939/E271762-835 8675/E606961-64
	In der Maur			4939/E271836
	Dr.Vogel			4939/E271837
	Dr.Herbert Schneider, Dr.Gustav von Wächter			4939/E271838 8676/E606966-75
	Berichte des Botschafters von Papen an den Führer und Reichskanzler	1		4939/E271839-2191
		2	10.34- 2.38	4939/E272192-404
		3		4939/E272405-704

Akten-zeichen	Inhalt	Band	Datum	Serial Nr.
	Geheimakten 1935-1938			
	Angriffe österreichischer und reichsdeutscher Presse		1938	4939/E272705
	Privatakten von Papen		1935-36	4939/E272706-906
A 218/27	Briefumschlag an Graf Lerchenfeld			4939/E272907
	− an Gerrison (Frhr.von Romberg) versiegelt			4939/E272908
	Privatbriefe des Botschafters, Informatorische Aufzeichnungen		1914-19	5002/E283355-4248
D Oe 20 Geh.11	Deutsch-österreichische Zoll-union		1931-32	
	Nr. 143 - 233	1		5002/E284249-505
	Nr. 235 - 299	2		5002/E284506-667
	Nr. 302 - 384	3		5002/E284668-941
	Nr. 385 - 498	4		5002/E284942-5105
	Nr. 506 - 718	5		5002/E285106-311
	Nr. 734 - 789	6		5002/E285312-569
A.Oe.19 Geh.26	Donauföderation		1931-32	
	Nr. 846/31 - 25/32	1		5101/E294026-217
	Nr. 30 -222/32	2		5101/E294218-493
	Nr. 221 -365/32	3		5101/E294494-871
	Nr. 373 -654/32	4		5101/E294872-5228
A II Geh.	Personalbestand		1936-38	
D a I	Alimentensachen	1-2	1935-38	
D e II	Ehesachen	1	1934-38	
D n II	Nachlaßsachen	1-8	1928-38	
	Ein Aktenband Nachlass	1	1928-37	
	Wien Generalia	1	1938	
	Diverses	1	1938	
	Staatsangehörigkeit Einzelfälle 1 - 5472		1931-38	
	Akten des Generalmajors a.D. Kundt	1-5	1920-29	
	9 Journale		1885-1927	
	Fragebogen		1927	
	Landkarten			

Akten-zeichen	Inhalt	Band	Datum	Serial Nr.
Pers.A.	Das Auswärtige Amt, Organisation, Geschäftsübersichten (Geschäftsgang des A.D.)	1	1921-39	
Pers.A 1, 2	Auswärtiges Amt und Auslandsver-tretungen, Organisation, Geschäftsübersichten	1-5	1940-44	
Pers.A gen.	Allgemeines	1	1942	
Pers.P	Personalakten, allgemein	1-3	1924-39	
Pers.P 1, 2	Personalien der Beamten und Angestellten der Behörde, Allgemeines, Urlaub	1-5	1940-44	
Pers.P gen.	Allgemeines	1	1943	
Pers.P	Namen-Einzelakten, Beamte A - Z	3	1940-44	
	- Angestellte A - Z	20	1940-44	
	- - R.A.D.	1	1940-44	
P.-Anst.	Bewerbungen	1-7	1933-44	
Pers.G 1	Aktenplan der Behörde	1	1935-42	
Pers.G 2	Dienstbetrieb, Anordnungen, Organisationen	1-2	1921-39	
Pers.G 2 a	Einteilung des Amtsbezirks	1	1925-39	
Pers.G 1-5	Dienstbetrieb, Anordnungen	1	1940	
Pers.G 1-4	Dienstbetrieb, Anordnungen, Organisation, Grundstücksverwal-tung, Dienstwohnungen, Dienst-kraftwagen	1-4	1941-44	
Pers.G 2	Dienstbetrieb, allgemein	1	1943-44	
Pers.G 4	Grundstücksverwaltung, Mietsver-trag, Dienstwohnung, Dienst-kraftwagen	1-7	1921-44	
Pers.G 5	Ausstattungsgegenstände und Geräte in Diensträumen und Dienstwohnungen, Inventar	1-18	1940-44	
Pers.G 6	Beflaggung der Behörde, Feier-tage			
Pers.G 7	Drucksachenaustausch, Zeitungsbezug			
Pers.G 8	Deutsche Vertretungen des Auswärtigen Amtes im Ausland (Amtsbezirk)			
Pers.G 9	Deutsche Kommissionen und Delagationen			
Pers.G 10	Verkehr mit Behörden Kroatiens, Anschriften			
Pers.G 11	Verkehr mit innerdeutschen Behörden, mit deutschen Dienst-stellen in Kroatien			

Akten-zeichen	Inhalt	Band	Datum	Serial Nr.
Pers.G 12	Zustellungen	1-5	1941-44	
Pers.G gen.	Generalien	1	1939-44	
Pers.G 15	Weiterleitungen von Briefen	1-2	1936-39	
Pers.R 1	Haushaltswesen, Voranschläge, Bedarfsnachweisungen	1	1924-39	
Pers.R 2	Kassenordnung, Kassenprüfung	1	1922-32	
Pers.R 1	Haushaltswesen, Voranschläge, Bedarfsanweisungen			
Pers.R 2	Kassenordnung-, führung und - prüfung			
Pers.R 3	Beschaffung von Betriebsmitteln, Kassenbestandsverstärkung	1-3	1941-43	
Pers.R 4	Fonds: Pers R 4 Kult I (Lektoren) Pers R 4 Kult, Pr Ru Spr K	1-3	1942-44	
Pers.R 5	Abrechnungen	24	1921-44	
	Auftragszahlungen	1-2	1942	
	Einzahlungen Dritter	1-2	1942-43	
	Abrechnungen, Vorschüsse, Frachten			
Pers.R 6	Prüfungsbemerkungen			
Pers.R 7	Gebühren			
Pers.R 8	Besoldungen, Löhne, Unterstützungen an Beamte und Angestellte, Zahlungslisten			
Pers.R 9	Umzugs- und Reisekosten			
Pers.R 10	Steuern, Angestellten- und Krankenversicherung			
Pers.R 11	Devisenangelegenheiten	1-5	1940-44	
Pers.R 8	Gehaltsfragen, Gehälter	1-2	1922-39	
	Gehalts- und Zahlungslisten	1-3	1941-43	
	Besoldungen, Löhne, Unterstützungen an Beamte und Angestellte, Zahlungslisten	1-3	1940-44	
Pers.R 7	Gebühren	1	1921-40	
Pers.R 10	Steuern, Angestellten- und Invalidenversicherung	1-2	1921-39	
Pers.R 13	Unterstützungen im Ausland, Heft	1-5	1940-43	
	Heimschaffungen Heft	1-5	1940-43	

Akten-zeichen	Inhalt	Band	Datum	Serial Nr.
Pers.R gen.	Allgemeines	1	1941-44	
Pers.Si 1	Sicherung der Gebäude und Geheimakten gegen Anschläge, Einbruch, Feuer; Luftschutz			
Pers.Si 2	Maßnahmen bei Kriegsgefahr und inneren Unruhen (Ausweichstellen)			
Pers.Si 3	Telegramm-, Erlass- und Berichtskontrolle			
Pers.Si 4	Aktenvernichtung und -versendung			
Pers.Si 5	Chiffrierdienst			
Pers.Si 6	Kurierangelegenheiten	1-9	1923-44	
Pers.Si gen.	Allgemein	1	1921-42	
Pers. Bibl.	Bibliothek	1-4	1941-44	
Pers.Var.	Verschiedenes	1-3	1941-43	
Em.Be.	Empfehlungen und Bescheinigungen	1-4	1941-44	
Pers.	Einkaufsangebote	1	1935-39	
	Berichtsverzeichnisse für Auswärtiges Amt	1-2	1941-43	
Prot 1	Protokoll, Allgemeines	1	1933-39	
Prot 2	Diplomatisches und konsularisches Korps (hiesige Konsulate)	1	1933-36	
	Nationale Feiertage und Festlichkeiten, Verfassung	1	1926-37	
Prot 3	Glückwünsche und Beileidsschreiben	1	1937-38	
	Etikette	1-3	1937-41	
Prot 1 Nr. 1	Einführung beim Staatsoberhaupt des Gastlandes, Zeremoniell, Staatswappen	1	1941-43	
Prot 1 Nr. 2 a	Glückwunschliste, Glückwunschnoten	1-2	1941-44	
Prot 1 Nr. 2 b	Geschenke	1	1941-44	
Prot 1 Nr.2c,d,e	Strassen- und Platzbenennungen, Beflaggung, Schreiben des kroatischen Volkes an den Führer	1	1941-44	
Prot 1 Nr. 3a	Empfänge, Einladungen, Feiern und Ansprachen hierbei (eigene)	1	1941-44	
Prot 1 Nr.3b	Kroatische und volksdeutsche Feiern	1	1941-44	
Prot 1 Nr.3c	Zwischenstaatliche Feiern	1	1941-44	
Prot 1 Nr. 4	Doyennat	1	1941-44	

Akten-zeichen	Inhalt	Band	Datum	Serial Nr.
Prot 1 Nr. 5	Besuchslisten, Rangfolge	1	1941-43	
Prot 1 Nr. 6	Telegrafischer, telefonischer und Schriftverkehr der fremden Missionen und Konsulate im Reich	1	1942-44	
Prot 2 Nr. 1a	Diplomatisches Korps (personell) (Deutschland)	1	1941-44	
	(Kroatien) Geheimakten Minister Dr.Toth, Drahterlass Nr. 1443 vom 7.9.1944 (Reise-Peric-Slowakei) Kroatische Wirtschaftsdelegation - Lyon Gesandter Benzon, Gesandter Kosak	1-2	1941-44	
	Bulgarien Geheimakten: Umsturz Bulgarien		1941-44	
	China		1942	
	Finnland Geheimakten: Umsturz Finnland		1941-44	
	Italien Geheimakten: Umsturz Italien		1941-44	
	Indien		1943	
	Japan Geheimakten: Äusserung des japanischen diplomatischen Vertreters gegenüber Kroaten		1943-44	
	Rumänien		1941-44	
	Slowakei		1941-44	
	Spanien		1941-44	
	Thailand		1943	
	Ungarn		1941-44	
Prot 2 Nr. 1b	Diplomatisches Korps (Besondere Rechte)	1-2	1941-44	
Prot 2 Nr. 1c	Allgemeiner Schriftverkehr	1	1941-44	
Prot 2 Nr. 1d	Grenzempfehlungen (alphabetisch)	1	1941-44	
Prot 2 Nr. 2a	Konsularisches Korps Personell Kroatien		1941-44	
	Argentinien		1941-44	
	Finnland		1941	
	Frankreich		1941-44	
	Italien		1941-43	
	Schweden		1940	
	Schweiz	1	1941	
Prot 2 Nr. 2b	Konsularisches Korps Deutschland	1	1941-44	
Prot 2 Nr. 2c	Allgemeiner Schriftverkehr		1941-43	
	Nicht mehr bestehende Konsularvertretungen in Kroatien (ehemals Jugoslawien)	1		

Akten-zeichen	Inhalt	Band	Datum	Serial Nr.
Prot 3	Orden und Ehrenzeichen, verschiedene	1	1936-39	
Prot 3 a	– deutsche	1	1941-43	
Prot 3 b	Fremde Ordenszeichen	1	1941-44	
Prot 4	Staatsbesuche zwischen Deutsch-land und dem Gastlande	1	1941-44	9820/H310106-85
	Besuch führender deutscher Persönlichkeiten im Gastlande, angebliche Reise Führer-Keitel-Himmler nach Kroatien			
	Besuch führender Persönlichkei-ten des Gastlandes im Reich Geheimakten: Reise Poglavnik-Führerhauptquartier. Reise Susić-Deutschland Reise Mandio-Peric ins Führer-hauptquartier			
Prot 5	Staatsbesuche zwischen dem Gast-lande und anderen Staaten und zwischen anderen Staaten	1	1941-44	9820/H310186-368
	Vizekonsulat Susak	1	1931-37	9820/H310369
	Personal- und Inventarsache des ehemalig tschechoslowakischen Konsulats	1	1939	
	Übernahme des ehemalig österrei-chischen Konsulats	1	1938	
	Konsulat Ljubljana	1	1938	
	Sammelpost für Konsulate Laibach, Sarajewo, Marburg	1	1941	
Adj.4	Allgemeiner Schriftverkehr A – Z	1	1941-44	9820/H310186-368
Adj.5	Anschriftenverzeichnisse a) Gesandtschaften, Konsulate b) Ministerien, Behörden, Ämter c) Persönlichkeiten privat d) deutsche Dienststellen	1	1941-43	
Adj.6	a) Verbindung zur Ustascha Geheimakten:Tgb.Nr.5/43 Waffeneinkäufe durch Ustascha im Reich	1	1942-43	
	b) Aufstandsbekämpfung	1	1942-43	
Adj.7	Kroatische Wehrmacht, kroatische Landwehr, Vor- und Nachschulung	1	1941-44	
Adj.8	a) Kroatischer Arbeitsdienst b) Volksdeutscher Arbeitsdienst c) Sonstige kroatische Organisa-tionen	1	1941-42 1942 1942-43	
	d) Sozialpolitik	1	1941-43	
Adj.10	Personaleinstellung (Gesandt-schaftswache)	1	1941-44	
Pol 1	Aussenpolitik Kroatiens	1	1941	
Pol 2 Nr. 1	Politische Beziehungen Kroatiens zu Deutschland	1-5	1941-44	
Pol 2 Nr. 1a	Minderheitenfragen, Beschwerden			

Akten-zeichen	Inhalt	Band	Datum	Serial Nr.
Pol 2 Nr. 1b	Grenzzwischenfälle	1-5	1941-44	
Pol 2 Nr. 1c	Grundenteignung von Kroaten in Untersteiermark			
Pol 2 Nr. 1d	Umsiedlung von Aufständischen. Wikingaktion			9820/H310369-74
Pol 2 Nr. 1e	Deutsch-kroatische Interventionen, beiderseitige Beschwerden	1-5	1941-44	
Pol 2 Nr. 1 Ums.	Umsiedlungen von Slovenen, Ungarn, Kroaten, Serben und Ukrainern	1-2 3 4-7	1939-44	4828/E241287-387
	A - Z	1-2	1942	
Pol 2 Nr. 2	Deutscher Militärattaché, Luftattaché, Marineattaché, Polizeiattaché	1-2 3	1941-43	9820/H310375-87
Pol 2 Nr. 3	Politische Beziehungen Kroatiens zu anderen Staaten, Grenzfragen, Verträge	1-3		
Pol 2 Nr. 3a	Kroatisch-serbischer Aktenaustausch	4		4827/E241075-284 9820/H310388-97
Pol 2 Nr. 3b	Politische Interventionen für Serben (siehe auch Akte Pol Int)			
Pol 2 Nr. 3c	Politische Interventionen für Kroaten			
Pol 2 Nr. 3d	Grenzzwischenfälle	5	1941-44	4832/E243134-353
Pol 2 Nr. 3e	Rüstungsarbeiter	6		
Pol 2 Nr. 3 Ums.	Serbenumsiedlung aus Kroatien	7		
Pol 2 Nr. 3 Sem.	Semliner Gebietsfragen	8		
Pol 3	Innenpolitik Kroatiens	1 2 3 4	1941-44	9820/H310398-517 9820/H310518-620 9820/H310621-67 9820/H310668-81
Pol 3 Nr. 1	Kroatische Ministerien			
Pol 3 Nr. 2	Personalien des Staatsoberhauptes, politischer Führer	1-4	1941-44	9820/H310682-98
Pol 3 Nr. 2a	Gegensätze in der Staatsführung			
Pol 3 Nr. 2b	Gesetzgebung, innerpolitische Anordnungen			
Pol 3 Nr. 2 Mus	Muselmanenfrage			

Akten-zeichen	Inhalt	Band	Datum	Serial Nr.
Pol 3 Nr. 3	Kroatisches Militär, Marine, Luftfahrt, Gendarmerie	1-4	1941-44	
Pol 3 Nr. 3b	Kroatischer Arbeitsdienst in Verbindung mit deutschen RAD-Sachbearbeitern			
Pol 3 Nr. 3a	Einberufung fremder Staatsange-höriger zum kroatischen Militär-dienst A - Z	1-9	1940-44	
Pol 3 Nr. 4	Aufstandsbewegung, Spionagewesen	1 2 3 4	1941-44	9820/H310699-83 9820/H310834-151 9820/H311512-99 6186/E464558-62 9820/H311997-215
Pol 3 Nr. 4 It	Zusammenarbeit Cetniks und Italiener	1		9820/H312160-212
Cet.	Cetnikfragen	2	1941-44	9820/H312213-39
Mus	Aufständische gegen Muselmanen	3		
Kom	Kommunistenangelegenheiten	4		9820/H312240-58
Pol 3 Nr. 4a	Emigrantenwesen (ausser deut-schen Emigranten)	1-4	1941-44	
Pol 3 Nr. 4b	Flugblätter, Hetzschriften			
Pol 3 Nr. 4c	Übergriffe durch Ustascha			
Pol 3 Nr. 5	Hoheitszeichen, Flaggen, Feiertage	1 2		9820/H312259-583 9820/H312584-99
Pol 3 Nr. 6	Wahlen in Kroatien, Sabor	3	1940-44	9820/H312600-07
Pol 3 Nr. 7	Parteiwesen	4-5		
Pol 3 Nr. 7a	Cetnik in Kroatien Handakten über Cetnikaufstand			
Pol 3 Nr. 8	Kolonialfragen			
Pol 3 Nr. 9	Propaganda der Feindstaaten			
Pol 3 Nr. 10	Werbung von Legionen gegen Achsenmächte			
Pol 3 Nr. 11	Denunzierungen			
Pol 3 Nr. 11a	Attentate, Sabotage			
Pol 3 Nr. 12	Politische Auskunft, Nachfor-schungen			
Pol 3 Nr.13	Luftschutzmaßnahmen Kroatiens			
Pol 3 Nr. 14	Lage der kroatischen Arbeiter-schaft			

Akten-zeichen	Inhalt	Band	Datum	Serial Nr.
Pol 4 Nr. 1	Völkerbund	1 2		K1700/K406672-704 K1701/K406705-43
Pol 4 Nr. 2	Kommunismus, Sozialismus	3-4	1933-44	
Pol 4 Nr. 3	Freimaurer	5 6		9820/H312608-23
Pol 4 Nr. 5	Judenfrage			
Pol 4 Nr. 6	Kirchenfragen, Religionen			
Mus	Muselmanen und muselmanische Fragen			
Pol 5	Politisch verdächtige Personen und Völkerschaften			
Pol 6	Kriegsfreiwillige für Achsen-mächte			
Pol 7	Feindtätigkeit im jetzigen Kriege			
Pol 7 Nr. 1	Feindtätigkeit in Kroatien			
Nr. 2	— in Serbien			
Pol 8	Verhältnis deutscher Militär-stellen in Kroatien			
Pol 8 Nr. 1	Militärische Operationen bezw. Vorbereitungen			
Pol 8 Nr. 2	Kroatisches Militär in Kampf-gebieten			
Pol 8 Nr. 3	Übergriffe deutscher Wehrmacht			
Pol 9	Deutsch-kroatische Interventionen und Beschwerden			
Pol R	Politische Rechtsangelegenheiten	1 2 3	1941-44	9820/H312624-50 9820/H312651-60 9820/H312661-67
Pol R 2 Nr. 1	Rechtliche Beziehungen Kroatiens zu Deutschland	4		
Nr. 2	— zu anderen Staaten			
Pol R 3 Nr. 1	Ausserordentliche Gerichte Kroatiens			
Pol R 3 Nr. 3	Zivilrecht, Gerichtswesen, Justizverwaltung, Grundeigentum			
Pol R 3 Nr. 4	Ehescheidungen			
Pol R 3 Nr. 5	Handelsrecht, Rechtshilfe in Zivilsachen			
Pol R 6	Strafrecht, Auslieferung, Gefangenenaustausch			
Pol R 5 Nr. 1	Polizei, Kriminalitätsbekämpfung Aufenthaltsangelegenheiten			

Akten-zeichen	Inhalt	Band	Datum	Serial Nr.
Pol R 6 Nr. 2	Sozialversicherung			
Pol R 7 Nr. 6	Rotes Kreuz Genfer Konvention			
Pol R 7 Nr. 10	Briefrecht, Neutralität, Schutzrecht			
Pol R 7 Nr. 13	Beschlagnahme von Waffen			
Pol R 7 Nr. 18	Kriegsgefangenenangelegenheiten			
Pol R 7 Nr. 19	Kriegs- und Aufstandsschaden, Beschlagnahme			
Pol R 7 Nr. 20	Beleidigung des Staatsoberhauptes und des Staates			
Pol Arch	Politisches Material	1 2 3 4	1941-44	9820/H312668-706 9820/H312707-14
Pol Inf	Berichte über Politik Dritter Staaten	1 2 3 4	1941-44	9820/H312715-28 9820/H312729-62 9820/H312763-82
Pol Pr	Politische Pressenotizen	1-2	1941-42	
Pol Var	Verschiedene politische Angelegenheiten	1-3	1942-44	
Pol Int	Politische Interventionen, Verschiedenes	1 2-5	1941-42	9820/H312783-92
Pol Ausk	Politische Auskunft	1-3	1941-44	
D Pol	Deutscher Aufbau	1	1933-38	
D Pol 1	Deutsche Aussenpolitik und Propaganda	2 3	1941-44	4841/E245132-48
D Pol 2	Politische Beziehungen Deutschlands zu anderen Staaten	4		
D Pol 3	Innenpolitik	5		
D Pol 3 Nr. 1a	Parteisachen	1	1941-44	
D Pol 3 Nr. 1b	Wollsammlung für Soldaten an der Ostfront	1	1941-42	
D Pol 3 Nr. 1c	WHW	1-2	1934-44	
D Pol 3 Nr. 1d	Verbrauchergenossenschaft	1	1942-43	
D Pol 3 Nr. 1e	Truppen- und Verwundetenbetreuung	1	1941-44	
D Pol 3 Nr. 2a	Freimaurerfragen	1	1941-42	
D Pol 3 Nr. 2b	Judenfragen	1	1941-42	K1702/K406744-75

Akten-zeichen	Inhalt	Band	Datum	Serial Nr.
D Pol 3 Nr. 9	U.K.Stellung von Gefolgschafts-mitgliedern der Deutschen Luft-hansa A.-G., Kroatische Staatsangehörigkeit	1	1943	
D Pol 3 Nr. 5	NSDAP	1	1933-38	9820/H312793-98
	Wahl und Wahlliste 1938	1-2 3 4	1938	9820/H312799-800
	Versailler Vertrag	1	1933-35	
	Abrüstung	1	1935-37	
	Kriegsschuldfrage	1	1933-38	
	Krieg	1	1939	
Mil Ref	Militär, Generalia,	1	1935-39	
	- , allgemein	1-2	1938-42	
	- Wehrpflicht A - J	2	1937-40	
	- K - O	3	1937-40	9820/H312801-12
	- P - Z	4-5	1937-40	
	- A - G	6	1941-42	9820/H312813-23
	- H - Z	7-9	1941-42	
	- A - Z	10 -15	1942-43	
	- A - E	16	1943-44	9820/H312824-26
	- F - Z	17 -20	1943-44	
	- Einberufung	21	1941-44	
	- gen., Erlasse	22	1940-44	
	R. A. D.	23	1941-44	
	Organisation Todt, O.T.	24	1943-44	
W 1	Wirtschaftspolitik und Berichte	1-5	1941-43	
W 1 Nr.2	Wirtschaftsberichte der kroati-schen Regierung	1	1941-43	
W 1 Dal	Dalmatien	1	1944	
W 1 Nr.3	Wirtschaftsverflechtung	1-5	1941-44	
	Gruppe Malzacher	1	1941	
	Werk Vistad	1	1941-43	
	Waggonfabrik Brod	1	1941-42	
W 1 P	Persönlichkeiten des Wirtschafts-lebens	1	1943	
W 1 Nr.4	Lebenshaltungskosten in Kroatien	1-2	1941-43	
W 1 Nr.8	Berater bei kroatischer Regierung	1	1941-42	

Akten-zeichen	Inhalt	Band	Datum	Serial Nr.
W 2 Nr. 1	Wirtschaftliche Beziehungen Kroatien - Deutschland	1-2	1941-44	
W 2 Nr. 2	– Serbien	1-3	1941-44	
	– Frankreich	1	1941-43	
	– Schweiz	1	1943	
	– Slowakei	1	1943	
	– Bulgarien	1	1943	
	– Spanien	1	1942	
	– Belgien	1	1942	
	– Rumänien	1	1941-43	
	– Holland	1	1942-43	
	– Dänemark	1	1942	
	– Griechenland	1	1941-43	
	– Ungarn	1	1941-43	
	– Italien	1	1941-43	
	– andere Länder	1		
W 2 Nr. 3	Deutsch-kroatische Wirtschafts-besprechungen	1-3	1941-44	
	Fünfte Regierungsausschuss-tagung Juni 1943	1-2	1943	
	Sechste Regierungsausschuss-tagung Oktober 43 - März 44	1-2	1943-44	
	Kroatische Wunschlisten und Bezugswünsche deutscher Volks-gruppe	1	1943-44	
W 2 Nr. 4	Wirtschaftsstatistik	1	1941-44	
W 2 Nr. 5	Handelspropaganda	1	1941-42	
W 2 Nr. 6	Beziehungen der deutschen Volks-gruppe zu Kroatien	1-5	1941-44	
W 3	Boykottbewegung	1	1933-36	
W 4	Wirtschaftliche Kriegsmaßnahmen, Beutefragen, Beschlagnahme durch Wehrmacht	1 2 3-4	1941-44	9820/H312827-33
W 4 Nr. 1	Maßnahmen gegen deutschen Besitz, Enteignung, Einsatz von Kommissaren	1-4	1941-44	
	L.u.C.Hardtmuth in Zagreb	1	1941-42	
W 4 Nr. 2	Einfuhrgenehmigungen	1	1941-42	
W 4 b	Deutsche Wehrmacht in Kroatien	1	1943-44	
W 4 It.	Kriegsmaßnahmen Italiens in	1	1942-43	
W 4 Sch.	Schadenersatz - Kriegsschäden	1	1941-44	
W 5	Ausschreibungen, Kautionen	1-2	1941-44	
W 6	Grosse öffentliche Arbeiten, Saveregulierung	1-3	1941-44	

Akten-zeichen	Inhalt	Band	Datum	Serial Nr.
W 10	Film und Kino	1	1942-44	
W 12	Bescheinigungen	1-4	1941-44	
W 14	Abwicklung ehemaliger jugo-slawischer wirtschaftlicher Beziehungen	1-5	1941-43	
	Sonderauftrag Fabricius	1	1942	
W 17	Arbeiteranwerbung, Arbeitsein-satz	1-4	1941-44	
W 18	Kongresse und Veranstaltungen (wirtschaftspolitische)	1	1941-43	
W 19	Bestellung von Kriegsgerät durch Kroatien	1	1942-44	
W 21	Alkohol	1	1943	
D W 1	Deutsch-jugoslawisches Wirt-schaftsabkommen	1-2	1933-39	
	Deutsche Wirtschaft	1	1942-44	
D W 2	Beziehungen Deutschlands zu anderen Ländern	2	1941-43	
D W 2 It	Deutsch-italienische Beziehungen			
D W 3 Rus	Russland, Einsatz im Osten	1	1942-43	
W A O	Wirtschaft, Auslandsorganisation	1	1942-44	
	Wirtschaftliche Berichte	1-3	1922-39	
	Runderlasse wirtschaftlichen Inhalts	1-5	1933-39	
	Wirtschaftliche Berichtsdurch-schläge	1	1943	
	Täglicher Wirtschaftsbericht (Ordner)	2	1942-44	
W R 1	Rohstoffe und Waren, allgemein	1-5	1941-44	
W R 2	Hanf	1-2	1943-44	
W R 3 B	Bauxit, allgemein	1	1942-44	
	Vereinigte Aluminiumwerke	1-2	1941-44	
	Hansa-Leichtmetall	1	1941-44	
	Bauxitfirmen	1-3	1941-44	
	Bauxittransporte	1-2 3 4 5	1941-44	9820/H312834-43 9820/H312844-61
	Montan-Transport, Bauxit	1	1942-44	9820/H312862-64
	Bauxit-Vermerke O.T.	1-2	1943-44	
	Bauprogramm O.T.	1	1942-43	
	Bauxit-Approvisation	1-2	1943-44	
	Deutsche Bauxitinteressen	1	1941-42	9820/H312865-3067

Akten-zeichen	Inhalt	Band	Datum	Serial Nr.
W R 3 B	Bauxitförderung	1	1943	
	Bauxitkarten	1	1942	
W R 3 E	Erze, Bergbau	1-3	1941-44	
	Schwerspatwerke Alberti & Co.	1	1942-43	
W R 3 K	Kohle, allgemein	1-4	1941-44	
	Kohlenvorkommen in Kroatien	1	1941-42	
	Kohlenlieferungen	1-2	1941-43	
	Kohle, Verflechtung	1	1941-44	
W R 4	Holz	1-5	1941-44	
	Holz Einzelfirmen	1-2	1941-43	
	Hobag	1	1942-43	
	Mitrovacka	1	1941-42	
	Naschitzer A.-G.	1-2	1942-44	
	Gutmann-Aktien	1	1942-43	
	Edelmann	1	1941-43	
W R 5 Nr. 1	Fleisch und Konserven	1	1941	
Nr. 2	Fische	1	1942-43	
Nr. 3	Obst	1-2	1942-44	
Nr. 4	Milch, Eier, Geflügel	1-2	1943-44	
W R 5 La	Getreide und Futtermittel	1	1941-43	
W R 6	Mineralöl, technische Öle und Fette	1-3	1942-44	
	Tierische Fette	1	1942	9820/H313068-84
	Ölschiefer	1	1943	
	Erdgas	1	1942-43	
	Standard Vacuum	1	1942-44	
	Petrolej A.-G.	1	1942-43	
	Shell A.-G.	1	1942-43	
	Mineralöl, Verschiedenes	1	1942	
W R 7	Pferde	1	1941-44	
W R 8	Därme, Schlachthausabfälle	1	1941-44	
W R 10	Tannin, Leder	1-2	1941-44	
W R 11	Tabak	1	1941-44	
W R 12	Salz	1	1941	
W R 13	Baumwolle	1	1941	
W R 14	Wolle	1	1941-44	
W R 15	Bettfedern	1	1941-42	
W R 16	Heilkräuter	1	1941-44	
W R 17	Magnesit	1	1941-44	
W R 18	Ätherische Öle	1	1941-42	
W R 19	Sojabohnen	1	1942-44	
W R 20	Eisen und Stahl	1	1941-44	
W R 21	Likör, Alkohol	1	1942-44	

Akten-zeichen	Inhalt	Band	Datum	Serial Nr.
W J 2 Nr. 1	Wirtschaft, Industrie, allgemein	1	1942-44	
W J 2 Nr. 4	Hütten und Bergbau	1	1941-44	
W J 2 Nr. 6	Textilindustrie	1	1941-44	
W J 2 Nr. 7	Chemische Industrie	1-2	1942-44	
W J 2 Nr. 8	Elektrifizierung Uridat	1	1942-43	
	Gaswerk Zagreb	1	1942-43	
	Noris - Elin	1	1942-43	
	Munja - Kontakt	1	1942-43	
	Elektrizität und Gas	1	1942-43	
W J 2 Nr. 10	Stärkeindustrie	1	1943	
W J 2 Nr. 12	Glasindustrie und Keramik	1	1941-42	
W J 2 Nr. 13	Nahrungsmittelindustrie	1-2	1942-44	
W J 2 Nr. 15	Kraftfahrzeugindustrie	1	1941	
W J 2 Nr. 16	Verschiedenes	1	1942	
W J 2 Nr. 18	Lederindustrie	1	1942-43	
W J 2 Nr. 19	Farbenindustrie	1	1941	
W J 2 Nr. 20	Industrieverschleppung	1	1941-42	
W J 2 Nr. 21	Papierindustrie	1	1942-44	
W J 2 Nr. 22	Zementindustrie	1	1942-44	
W J 2 Nr. 24	Sprengstoff	1	1942-43	
W J 2 Nr. 25	Erdgas	1	1941-42	
W J 2 Nr. 26	Monopolindustrie	1	1942-44	
W J 2 Nr. 23	Graphische Industrie	1	1941-42	
W J 2 Nr. 27	Aluminiumindustrie	1	1942-43	
W J 2 Nr. 28	Bleistiftindustrie	1	1942	
W J 3 Nr. 1	Auftragsverlagerung	1	1942-44	
D W H	Deutsche wirtschaftliche Nachrichten - Handel	1	1941-43	
W H 2 Nr. 1	Allgemeine Handelsbeziehungen Kroatien zu Deutschland	1	1944	
W H 2 Nr. 2	- Ausfuhr	1	1944	

Akten-zeichen	Inhalt	Band	Datum	Serial Nr.
W H 2 Nr. 4	Einfuhr aus Deutschland, allgemein	1	1942-43	
W H 7	Handelskammer	1	1941-44	
	- , Berichte	1	1942-44	
	- , Wirtschaftlicher Wochenbericht	1	1942-44	
W H 26	Wirtschaftsbücher	1	1942-44	
W H 30	Rechtsanwälte in Kroatien	1	1943-44	
W L 1	Landwirtschaft	1-3	1941-44	
W L 2		1	1941	
W L 2 Nr. 2	Kunstdüngungsversuche	1	1941-42	
W L 2 Nr. 8	Obst- und Gartenbau	1	1941-44	
W L 2 Nr. 9	Viehzucht	1	1944	
W L 2 Nr.10	Saatgut	1-3	1942-44	
W L 2 Nr.12	Landwirtschaftliche Geräte	1-2	1942-44	
W L 2 Nr.13	Weinbau	1	1942	
W L 2 Nr.14	Seidenraupenzucht	1	1942-44	
D L W	Deutsche Landwirtschaft	1	1941-44	
W Fs	Seefischerei, Fischerei im allgemeinen	1	1942-43	
W 1 E	Ernährungslage in Kroatien	1-5	1941-44	
W F	Devisen- und Finanzangelegen-heiten, Aufwertung, allgemein	1-6	1925-44	
W F 1	Finanzielle Fragen	1-2	1941-44	
W F 1 Nr. 4	Wertpapiere, Aktien	1	1941-43	
W F 2 Nr. 1	Finanzielle Beziehungen Kroatien - Deutschland	1	1941-44	
W F 2 Nr. 2	- zu anderen Ländern	1	1942-44	
W F 2 Nr. 3	Geldwesen und Zahlungsverkehr	1-2	1942-44	
W F 2 Nr. 6	Clearing	1	1943-44	
W F 2 Nr. 7a	Devisen- und Zollstrafsachen	1	1942-44	
W F 2 Nr.12	Börse	1	1942	

Akten-zeichen	Inhalt	Band	Datum	Serial Nr.
W F 2 Nr.15	Versicherungswesen	1-3	1941-44	
W St	Steuersachen	1	1941-44	
W Z	Zollsachen	1-6	1940-44	
D W Z	Deutsches Zollwesen	1	1942	
W V 2 Nr. 1	Verkehrsfragen, allgemein	1-2 3	1941-44	9820/H313085-87
W V 2 Nr. 2	Verkehrsbeziehungen Kroatiens zu anderen Ländern	1	1941	
W V 2 Nr. 3	Reiseverkehr	1	1941-44	
W V 2 Nr. 5	Reisebüro	1	1941-42	
W V 2 Nr.10	Strassenbau O.T.	1	1941-44	
W V 10	-	1	1941	
W V 2 Nr.13	Spediteure	1	1941-44	
W V 2 Nr.16	Hotels	1	1941-43	
W V 2 Nr.17	Kraftwagenverkehr	1	1941-43	
W V 3 Nr. 1	Grenzverkehrsfragen Deutschland - Kroatien	1-3	1941-44	
W V 3 Nr. 2	Kroatien - Serbien	1	1941	
W V 3 Nr. 3	- Italien	1	1941	
W V 3 Nr. 4	- Ungarn	1	1941	
W V 3 Nr. 2	Semliner Grenzverkehr	1	1943	
D W V 2	Deutscher Reiseverkehr ins italienische Gebiet	1	1942	
W P 2 Nr. 1	Postwesen	1	1941-44	
W P 2 Nr. 2	- Beziehungen Kroatiens zu anderen Ländern	1	1941-43	
D W P	Deutsches Postwesen	1	1942-44	
W E 2	Eisenbahnverkehr	1 2 3	1942-44	9820/H313088-102 9820/H313103-115 9820/H313116-18
W E 2 Nr. 2	Eisenbahnbeziehungen Kroatiens zu anderen Ländern	1	1941-42	
W E 2 Nr.11	Eisenbahnbrücken	1	1941-43	9820/H313119-21
W Kr	Kraftfahrwesen	1-2	1941-43	

Akten-zeichen	Inhalt	Band	Datum	Serial Nr.
W Kr 1	Anschaffungen von Kraftwagen	1	1944	
W Kr 2	Holzgasgeneratoren	1	1942-43	
W Kr 3	Kraftwagen, Fahrbewilligungen, Kontrolle	1-2	1942-44	
	P.K.W. Kontrolle und Beschlagnahme	1	1942-43	
W Kr 4	Reifen	1	1943-44	
W Lu	Luftfahrt	1	1942-44	
W Sch 1	Seeschiffahrt, allgemein	1	1941-44	
W Sch 2 Nr. 2	Binnenschiffahrt, allgemein	1-4	1941-44	
	Kroatische Flußschiffahrt "Hribrod"	1	1942-43	
	Vukovar- und Zigeuner- Werft	1	1942-44	
W Sch 3 Nr. 1	Seeschiffahrt, allgemein	1	1941-44	
W Sch 3 Nr. 2	Binnenschiffahrt, Kroatien - andere Länder	1	1941	
W Sch 4 Nr. 1	Schiffswerften	1-2	1941-42	
D W Sch	Deutsche Seeschiffahrt	1	1942-44	
W A 1	Ausstellungen, allgemein	1	1941-42	
W A 2	Mustermessen und Ausstellungen	1	1941-43	
	Prager Mustermesse	1	1940	
W A 4	Zagreber Messe	1	1939-43	
D W A	Deutsche Ausstellungen	1	1942-44	
W Verm	Vermittlungen, Einzelsachen	1-5	1942-44	
W Ausk	Auskünfte über Firmen und Personen	1-2	1941-44	
W Int	Interventionen gegen hiesige Firmen	1	1941-42	
W Ford	Forderungen	1	1940-43	
W Vertra	Wirtschaftliche Vertrauensleute	1	1940-42	
W H Kred	Kreditauskünfte	1	1940-41	
	- (Ordner)	1-3	1942-44	
W H C	Anfragen d. R.f.A., Einzelsachen	1-2	1936-44	
	(Ordner)	1-12	1941-44	
W H Frag	Vertreter-Fragebogen A - Z	1-3	1939-42	
W.H.Sicht verm.	Sichtvermerke	1-2	1942-43	
	- A - Z	1-2	1943-44	
W H Hiver	Vertreter, hiesige A - Z	11	1941-44	

Akten-zeichen	Inhalt	Band	Datum	Serial Nr.
	Deutsche Vertretungen	1	1923-35	
	Vertreterliste	1		
W H Unverl	Kartei der unsicheren Firmen des Auslandes	1-5	1921-44	
W H - A R	Arisierung	1	1941-44	
W H - J	Juden	1-4	1938-40	
W H U	Mitteilungen über jüdische Firmen und deren Beziehungen zu deutschen Firmen	1	1940	
	Deutsch-jugoslawische Unternehmungen	1	1933-40	
W Wi Wo	Wehrwirtschaftsoffizier	1	1941-44	
W Mil	Militärsachen, Einzelsachen	1	1942	
W Zu	Wirtschaft - Zustellungen	1	1943-44	
W Anst	Wirtschaft - Anstellungen	1	1942	
W Pat	Patentangelegenheiten	1-2	1937-43	
W Re	Wirtschaft - Rechtssachen	1	1942	
W D R	– Rotes Kreuz	1	1942-43	
W Übers	– Übersiedlungen	1	1942-44	
W Ums	– Umsiedlungen	1	1942-44	
W Prot	Ragusaer Bäder und Hotel A.-G.	1	1940-42	
W Pers	Vorträge Dr.Kühn	1	1941-44	
W Prop	Wirtschaft - Propaganda	1	1941-44	
W Va	– Varia	1	1941-43	
	Wirtschafts - Archiv Regierung, Behörden, Einrichtungen		1941-44	
Mappen	Sabor, Regierung, Ministerien, Abteilungen, Institutionen	1		
	Gespanschaften, staatliche Einrichtungen, Ämter, Behörden			
	Staatliche Wirtschaftskommission, Inspektorate, Fachausschüsse, Räte, Anstalten			
	Staatliche Unternehmungen			
	Erneuerung - Nationalisierung			
	Verstaatlichungen - Enteignungen			
	Korporationen, Organisationen, Ustascha-Verbände			
	Judengesetze - Juden in der Wirtschaft			
	Pers - Nachrichten			

Akten-zeichen	Inhalt	Band	Datum	Serial Nr.
Mappen 10	Statistik			
11	Allgemeine Gesetze und Verord-nungen			
12	Magistrate	2		
13	Deutsche Volksgruppe	2		
	Volkswirtschaft 1941-1944			
1	Wirtschaftsaufbau, Planung, Leitung	2		
2	Wirtschaftspolitik			
3	Wirtschaftsgesetze, Verordnungen, Verfügungen			
4	Wirtschaftsbeaufsichtigung			
5	Berichte (Wirtschaftsberichte)	2		
6	Kroatische amtliche Wirtschafts-berichte			
7	Artikel über Wirtschaftspatente			
8	Wirtschaftliches aus Gespan-schaften und Gebieten	2		
9	Wirtschaftliches und Statisti-sches aus Städten			
10	Normierung, Normen			
11	Fachgemeinschaften und Zentral-stellen	2		
12	Abfallsammlung			
13	Genossenschaftswesen	2		
14	Kommissare			
15	Veräusserungsverbote			
	Landwirtschaft 1941-1944			
1	Landwirtschaftliche Berichte	2		
2	- Maßnahmen	2		
3	Artikel über Landwirtschaft			
4	Bauernwirtschaftsgemeinschaft			
5	Agrarpolitik			
6	Meliorationen			
7	Getreideerzeugungsmaßnahmen			
8	Industriepflanzen	2		
9	Hackfrucht, Hülsenfrüchte, Gemüse			
10	Futtermittel			
11	Obstbau			
12	Weinbau			

Akten-zeichen	Inhalt	Band	Datum	Serial Nr.
Mappen 13	Zuckerindustrie			
14	Lebensmittelindustrie			
15	Spiritus, Hefe			
16	Obst- und Gemüsekonservierung			
17	Düngemittel			
	Viehzucht - Fischerei		1941-44	
1	Allgemeines über Viehzucht			
2	Förderung der Viehzucht			
3	Zuchtvieh			
4	Schlachtvieh			
5	Pferde, Zugtiere			
6	Viehhandel			
7	Geflügel, Eier, Federn			
8	Bienenzucht			
9	Felle, Häute, Därme, Hörner, Haare, Unschlitt			
10	Wolle			
11	Fleischverarbeitende Industrie			
12	Milchwirtschaft			
13	Leder			
14	Fischerei			
	Forstwirtschaft		1941-44	
1	Allgemeines, Maßnahmen, Berichte	2		
2	Forsterzeugung, Brennholz, Holz-kohle			
3	Jagdwesen, Tierzucht			
4	Holzindustrie			
5	Zellulose, Holzstoff, Holz-destillation			
6	Gerbstoffe, Tannin			
	Bergbau		1941-44	
1	Allgemeines			
2	Bauxit			
3	Eisenerzförderung, Eisenerzeu-gung			
4	Kohle			
5	Sonstige Erze und Metalle			
6	Minerale und Mineralölindustrie			
7	Erdöl, Erdgas, Ölschiefer			

Akten- zeichen	Inhalt	Band	Datum	Serial Nr.
Mappen	Bergbau		1941-44	
8	Mineralquellen			
1	Allgemeines		1941-44	
2	Kartelle, Truste, Konzerne			
3	Elektrizitätswirtschaft, Gaswerke, Wasserkräfte			
4	Schwerindustrie			
5	Metallindustrie			
6	Papierindustrie			
7	Textilindustrie			
8	Chemisch-pharmazeutische Industrie			
9	Tonindustrie - Keramik			
10	Glas- und Porzellanindustrie			
11	Elektrotechnische Industrie			
12	Horn - Kunstharz			
13	Bekleidungsindustrie			
14	Gummi- und Gummiwarenindustrie			
15	Sonstige verarbeitende Industrien			
	Handel		1941-44	
1	Allgemeines			
2	Marktberichte, Marktordnung			
3	Innenhandel, Wirtschaftspolizei	2		
4	Preis- und Lohngestaltung	2		
5	Lebensmittelpreise	2		
6	Sonstige Preise			
7	Aussenhandel - Allgemeines			
8	Aussenhandelsstatistik			
9	Ausfuhr			
10	Einfuhr			
11	Kompensation - Kontingente			
12	Vertreterwesen, Handelsreisende, Auskunfteien			
13	Neue Firmen			
14	Hauptversammlungen, Angaben über Wirtschaftsunternehmen	2		
15	Anzeigen			
16	Staatliche Beteiligung an Wirtschaftsunternehmen			

Akten-zeichen	Inhalt	Band	Datum	Serial Nr.
Mappen	Zwischenstaatliche Wirtschafts-beziehungen Kroatiens zu		1941-44	
1, 2, 3	Deutschland			
4	– Güteraustausch			
5	– Wehrwirtschaftliches			
6	Untersteiermark, Kärnten, Krain			
7, 8	Italien			
9	– Güteraustausch			
10	Ungarn			
11	Rumänien			
12	Slowakei			
13	Bulgarien			
14	Schweiz			
15	Protektorat, Generalgouvernement, besetzte Gebiete			
16	sonstige Staaten (Finnland, Frankreich, Spanien, Portugal)			
17	Verflechtung			
18	Internationale Tagungen			
	Soziale Fragen		1941-44	
1	Volksernährung	2		
2	Versorgungsmaßnahmen	2		
2a	Dopos			
3	Rationierung	2		
4	Lebenshaltungskosten			
5	Lohnfragen, Kollektivverträge			
6	Arbeitsmarkt			
7	Kroatische Arbeiter in Deutsch-land			
8	Organisation der Arbeit, Arbeitsdienst	2		
9	Versicherungswesen			
10	Soziale Maßnahmen			
	Wirtschaftsförderung und Werbung		1941-44	
1	Kroatische Wirtschaftskammern			
2	Deutsche, ausländische, inter-nationale und gemischte Wirt-schaftskammern			
3	Wirtschaftswerbung, Vorträge			
4	Wirtschaftsverlag			

Akten-zeichen	Inhalt	Band	Datum	Serial Nr.
Mappen	Wirtschaftsförderung und Werbung		1941-44	
5	Zagreber Messe, kroatische Aus-stellungen	2		
6	Beteiligung Kroatiens an aus-ländischen Messen			
7	Fachbildungswesen			
8	Reklamewesen, Kino - Filme			
9	Nachrichtenbüros			
	Verkehr		1941-44	
1	Verkehrsfragen - Allgemeines			
2	Eisenbahnverkehr, Allgemeines	2		
3	- Statistik, Verordnungen, Tarife			
4	Durchfuhr			
5	Bahnstrecken und Brückenbau			
6	Verkehrsnachrichten			
7	Seeschiffahrt			
8	Binnenschiffahrt			
9	Wasserwege			
10	Landverkehr - Kraftfahrwesen			
11	Strassenbau - Instandhaltung			
12	Flugverkehr			
13	Speditionswesen			
14	Post, Telegraf - Telefon			
15	Rundfunk			
16	Reiseverkehr			
17	Öffentliche Arbeiten			
	Finanzwesen		1941-44	
1	Staatsfinanzen			
2	Anleihen			
3	Währungsfragen			
4	Steuern, Abgaben, Gebühren	2		
5	Zollwesen, Zollfreilager			
6	Monopole			
7	Zahlungsverkehr, Devisenvor-schriften			
8	Verordnungen über Finanzfragen			
9	Staatliche und öffentliche Geldanstalten			

Akten-zeichen	Inhalt	Band	Datum	Serial Nr.
Mappen	Finanzwesen		1941-44	
10	Schadenersatz			
11	Börsenwesen			
12	**Finanzmarkt, Banken**			
13	Versicherungswesen			
14	Deutsche Kapitalbeteiligungen			
15	Ausländische Kapitalbeteiligungen			
Gruppe XIV	Gewerbe und Handwerk		1941-44	
Gruppe V:	1 Warnungen			
	4 Reichsstellen			
	5 Wirtschaftliches aus dem Reich			
Kult 1 a	Kulturelle Organisationen und Vereinigungen des Gastlandes (Gesellschaft der Freunde Deutschlands)	1	1932-39	
		1	1943	
	Verschiedene fremde Vereinigungen im Gastland	1	1943-44	
Kult 1 b	Deutsch-kroatische Gesellschaft	1	1943-44	
Kult 2 Nr. 1	Kulturpolitische Beziehungen zu Deutschland, Rundfunk	1	1943-44	
Kult 2 Nr. 2	Kulturpolitische Beziehungen zu anderen Ländern	1	1943-44	
Kult 3	Wehrmachtsangelegenheiten und Betreuung	1	1943-44	
Kult 3 Nr. 2	Reichsdeutscher Hilfsverein	1-2	1930-44	
Kult 3 Nr. 4	Vaterländische Front (Liquid.)	1	1938-39	
Kult 3 Nr. 3	Zustellungen an die Volksgruppe	1	1943-44	
	Schwäbisch-deutscher Kulturbund	1	1934-39	
Kult 3 Nr. 4	Slowenen und Wenden	1	1933-39	
Kult 4	Kirchenwesen	2	1935-44	
Kult 4 Nr. 5	Deutsche Kirche im Gastland	1	1943-44	
Kult 5	Ein-, Aus- und Rückwanderung	1-5	1939-44	
Kult 6	Kroatische Schulen, Lehrpläne und Bücher		1943-44	
Kult 7	Kroatische Jugendbewegung, Treffen, Wanderungen		1943-44	
Kult 8 Nr. 1	Reichsdeutscher Schulbetrieb, laufende Angelegenheiten		1943-44	
Kult 8 Nr. 3	Beihilfe für die Schule		1943-44	

Akten-zeichen	Inhalt	Band	Datum	Serial Nr.
Kult 8 Nr. 4	Neubau der deutschen Oberschule		1943-44	
Kult 8 Nr. 5	Lehrer der deutschen Oberschule		1943-44	
Kult 8	Allgemeines Schulwesen	1	1935-39	
	Deutsche evangelische Schule	1	1935-39	
	Deutsche Erziehungsanstalten	1	1935-39	
Kult 9 Nr. 1	Deutsche Sprachwerbung		1944	
Kult 9 Nr. 2	Kroatische Verlagsanstalten und Druckereien		1943-44	
Kult 9 Nr. 3	Kroatische Bücher, Zeitungen und Zeitschriften	1	1943-44	
Kult 9 Nr. 2	Press-Import		1943-44	
	Rad-Verlag		1943-44	
	Europa-Verlag		1943-44	
Kult 9 Nr. 4	Kroatische Wörterbücher	2	1942	
Kult 10	Hiesige Hochschulen	1	1936-39	
Kult 10 Nr. 4	Stipendien	1	1938-39	
Kult 10 Nr. 7	Studienreisen und Wanderfahrten	1-3	1933-39	
Kult 10 Nr. 8	Studentenaustausch	1	1939	
Kult 10	Kroatische Hochschulangelegen-heiten		1943-44	
Kult 10 Nr. 2	Kroatische Stipendien für Deutsche		1943-44	
Kult 10 Nr. 4	Studentenwesen		1944	
Kult 10 Nr. 3	Lektorate und Lektoren	1	1943-44	
Kult 11 Nr. 1	Vorträge in Kroatien		1943-44	
Kult 11 Nr. 2	Ehrung von kroatischen Wissen-schaftlern		1943	
Kult 11 Nr. 4	Drucksachenaustausch		1943-44	
Kult 11 Nr. 5	Reisen von Professoren		1943-44	
Kult 11 Nr. 6	Ausgrabungen und Forschungen		1943-44	
Kult 11 Nr. 7	Tagungen im Gastland		1943	
Kult 11 Nr. 8	Buchwerbung und Buchausstellung		1943	

Akten-zeichen	Inhalt	Band	Datum	Serial Nr.
ult 11 r. 8 b	Büchereien im Ausland		1943-44	
ult 11 r. 8 a	Buchspenden	1	1943-44	
ult 11 r. 1	Kongresse	1	1937-39	
ult 11 r. 6	Erdbeben	1	1923-38	
ult 11 r. 7	Medizin	1	1935-39	
ult 11 r. 8	Deutsche Bücher	1-3	1928-39	
	Hiesige Bücher	1-2	1921-39	
	Bücherangebot	1	1938-39	
	Deutsche Zeitschriften	1	1936-39	
ult 12	Theater, Kunst und Literatur	1-2	1933-39	
ult 12 r. 4	Film	1	1937-39	
ult 12 r. 5	Sport	1	1939	
ult 12 r. 6	Olympia	1	1933-36	
ult 12 r. 8	Ausstellungspavillon des Protek-torates Böhmen und Mähren	1	1939-42	
ult 12 r. 1	Kunstschaffen in Kroatien	1	1943-44	
ult 12 r. 2	Theaterwesen in Kroatien	2	1943-44	
ult 12 r. 3	Musikwesen und Konzerte	3	1943-44	
ult 12 r. 4	Filmwesen in Kroatien	4	1943-44	
ult 12 r. 5	Sportwesen in Kroatien	5	1943-44	
ult 12 r. 6	Sportpropaganda		1943	
ult 12 r. 8	Ausstellungen in Kroatien	6	1943-44	
ult La	Landwirtschaftliche Angelegen-heiten	1	1943-44	
ult La 6	Landwirtschaftliche Propaganda	1	1943-44	
ult La nst.	Anstellungen an landwirtschaft-lichen Betrieben	1	1943	
ult Techn.	Technischer Apparat	1	1942-44	
m Be Zoll	Zollabfertigungen	1	1943-44	
ult Zu u. P Zu	Zustellungen	1	1943-44	

Akten-zeichen	Inhalt	Band	Datum	Serial Nr.
Kult Em Be	Empfehlungen und Bestätigungen	1	1943-44	
Kult Int	Interventionen	1	1943-44	
Kult Ausk	Auskünfte und Nachforschungen	1	1943-44	
Kult Anst	Anstellungsanträge	1	1943-44	
Kult Var	Verschiedene Angelegenheiten	1	1943-44	
Kult Inf	Informationen zur Propagandistischen Auswertung	2	1943-44	
D Kult 1a	Deutsche kulturelle Organisationen und Vereinigungen	1	1943-44	
D Kult 1b	Deutscher Auslandsrundfunk	1	1943-44	
D Kult 1 Nr. 1	Kroatisch-italienischer Kulturvertrag	1	1943	
D Kult 1 Nr. 2	Veranstaltungsplan	1	1943-44	
D Kult 1 Nr. 3	Deutsche Kriegspropaganda	1-12	1944	
D Kult 2	Kulturpolitische Beziehungen Deutschlands zu anderen Staaten	1	1943	
D Kult 2 Nr. 1	Kulturelle und soziale Maßnahmen	1	1943	
D Kult 2 Nr. 2	Kulturpolitische Arbeit			
D Kult 3	Deutsche Propaganda, Verschied.	1-5	1943	
	Hinter den Kulissen des "Weissen Hauses"	1	1943	
	Albion zieht in den Krieg	1	1943	
	Bildaushangdienst, Schaufensterpropaganda	1	1943	
D Kult 5	Ein-, Rück- und Auswanderung	1-5	1940-44	
D Kult 7	Deutsche Jugendbewegung	1	1943-44	
D Kult 8	Schulen in Deutschland	1	1943	
D Kult 8 Nr. 5	Besuch von Volks-, Bürger- und Mittelschulen in Deutschland	1	1943	
D Kult 8 Nr. 6	Deutsche Bücher	1	1943-44	
D Kult 8 Nr. 6a	Deutsche Zeitungen und Zeitschriften	1	1943-44	
D Kult 8 Nr. 7	Übersetzung deutscher Bücher	1	1943-44	
D Kult 10	Deutsche Hochschulen	1-2	1930-39	
D Kult 10 Nr. 2	Stipendien	1	1936-37	

Akten-zeichen	Inhalt	Band	Datum	Serial Nr.
D Kult 10 Nr. 2a	Humboldtstiftung	1-2	1925-39	
D Kult 10 Nr. 3	Studienreisen	1-2	1921-39	
D Kult 10 Nr. 2	Stipendien für Studien in Deutschland (Ausländer)	1	1943-44	
D Kult 10 Nr. 2a	Studium an deutschen Hochschulen		1943-44	
D Kult 10 Nr. 3	Kroatische Lektorate in Deutschland		1944	
D Kult 10 Nr. 4	Ferienkurse an deutschen Hochschulen	1	1943	
D Kult 11 Nr. 4	Reisen deutscher Wissenschaftler ins Ausland	1	1943	
D Kult 11 Nr. 6	Vorträge in Deutschland	1	1943-44	
D Kult 11 Nr. 7	Tagungen in Deutschland	1	1943-44	
D Kult 12 Nr. 1	Kunstschaffen in Deutschland	1	1943	
D Kult 12 Nr. 2	Theaterwesen	1	1943-44	
D Kult 12 Nr. 3	Musikwesen	1-2	1943-44	
D Kult 12 Nr. 4	Filmwesen	1	1943-44	
D Kult 12 Nr. 5	Sport	1	1943-44	
D Kult 12 Nr. 8	Messen und Ausstellungen	1	1943-44	
	Volkstumsreferat		1941-44	
Kult 3 I a	Politik		1941-44	
	Geheimakten: Verschlechterung der Lage der Volksgruppe			
	Vereinbarung über die Zuständigkeit in Volkstumsfragen			
	Teilumsiedlung Westslavonien			
	Tendenziöse und unwahre Anschuldigungen gegen die Volksgruppe			
	Verleumderische Berichte von Ustascha-Amtswaltern über die Volksgruppe und volksgruppenangehörende Beamte			
	Sicherung des Anteils der Volksgruppe an beschlagnahmten Judenvermögen			
	Besprechung mit Volksgruppenführung und Volksgruppenführer			

Akten-zeichen	Inhalt	Band	Datum	Serial Nr.
Kult 3 I b	Organisation der Deutschen Volks-gruppe Geheimakten: Deckabkürzungen (einzelne Dienststellen) Bezeichnung der Volksgruppe als Minderheit Einrücken Volksgruppenführer Altgayers zur Waffen-SS		1941-44	
Kult 3 I c	Beschwerden Geheimakten: Herabsetzende Behandlung Volks-deutscher Wühlarbeit gegen Grossgespan Dr.Elicker		1943-44	
Kult 3 I d	Tagungen Geheimakten: Deutsch-kroatische Konferenz in Syrmien		1943-44	
Kult 3 I e	Reisen	1-3	1941-44	
Kult 3 II	a) Schulen, Schulung		1941-44	
	b) Propaganda		1941-44	
	c) Zeitung Geheimakten: Veröffentlichen von amtlichen Verlautbarungen der Deutschen Volksgruppe in Kroatien durch die "Deutsche Zeitung in Kroa-tien"			
Kult 3 II	d) Bücherwesen, Bücherspenden, Büchersendungen		1941-44	
	e) Reisen von Lehrkräften nach Kroatien		1941-44	
	f) Landkarten	1-3		
Kult 3 III	a) Kulturangelegenheit, Kunst		1941-44	
	b) Rundfunk, Kino, Theater		1941-44	
	d) Schrifttum		1941-44	
	e) Glaubensangelegenheit		1941-44	
	Geheimakten: Verfassung der deutschen evan-gelischen Kirche in Kroatien			
	f) Sozialangelegenheiten	1	1941-44	
Kult 3 IV	a) Handel Geheimakten: Bau einer volksdeutschen Zucker-fabrik in Kroatien	1-3	1941-44	
	b) Industrie und Gewerbe		1941-44	
	c) Landwirtschaft, Feldzuweisung			
	d) Arbeitskräftevermittlung		1941-44	
	e) Bankwesen, Rechnungen		1941-44	

Akten-zeichen	Inhalt	Band	Datum	Serial Nr.
Kult 3 Va	a) Werbung zur Waffen-SS		1941-44	6182/E464457-512 9820/H313122-226
	Geheimakten: Einziehung von 6000 Volksgruppenangehörigen zur Waffen-SS			
	Verstärkung der vorhandenen militärischen Kräfte durch volksdeutsche Regimenter			
	Aufzeichnung des Volksgruppenführers, Sicherung der deutschen Siedlung gegen Partisanen			
	Vermerk von Oberstubaf.Hruschka, Werbung der Volksdeutschen zur Waffen-SS			
	Besprechung mit SS-Obergruppenführer Lorenz und SS-Brigadeführer Behrens			
	Aussiedlung der Bosniendeutschen ins Reich			
	Bisher zur Waffen-SS Gemusterte			
	Zeittafel wegen Werbung zur Waffen-SS			
	Abgehende Transporte zur Waffen-SS Gemusterter			
	Rekrutierung zur Waffen-SS			
	Rechtliche Lage bei weiterer Werbung durch die Waffen-SS			
Kult 3 V	Deutsche Einsatzstaffel			
	Neuaufstellung von SS-Verbänden (Kroatische Legion)			
	Wehrüberwachung Freiwilliger der bosnischen Division			
	Abmachung, nach welcher alle Volksdeutschen in Kroatien dem Reichsführer-SS zur Ableistung ihrer Wehrdienstpflicht zur Verfügung zu stellen sind, nicht getroffen			
	b) Weiterleitungen		1943-44	
	c) Vermerke, Aufzeichnungen		1942-44	
	Geheimakten: betr. Syrmien Vermerk des Herrn Gesandten: Besprechung mit dem Poglavnik 12. 8. 1942 - Besprechung mit Aussenminister Dr.Lorkovio betr. Obersturmbannführer Keller			
	d) Zahlenmaterial über Transporte der zur Waffen-SS Eingerückten			
	e) Annahmeuntersuchungspläne		1942-43	
	f) Dienstreisen von Angehörigen der Wehrmachtsformationen		1941-43	

Akten-zeichen	Inhalt	Band	Datum	Serial Nr.
Kult 3 V	Eisenbahnschutzbataillon Geheimakten: Zur Verstärkung des Eisenbahn-schutzes legt die Wehrmacht zwei Landesschützenbataillone nach Kroatien		1942-43	
	Verwendung von Einheiten des Eisenbahnschutzbataillons XI, XII, und XIII			
	h) Arbeitsdienst		1941-44	
	Geheimakten: Überfall auf volksdeutsche Arbeitsdienstlager bei Ober-josefsdorf			
	i) Verschiedene Verzeichnisse	1	1943	
	j) Fliegerhorst Semlin		1942-43	
	Geheimakten: Wehrpflichtentziehung der Ar-beitnahme beim Fliegerhorst Semlin Lage der Volksdeutschen in Semlin			
	k) Fürsorgeoffizier		1941-43	
	Geheimakten: Sitz des Fürsorgeoffiziers			
	Verlegung des Dienstsitzes des Fürsorgeoffiziers der Waffen-SS			
	Errichtung von drei Nebenstellen des Ersatzkommandos			
	Nebenstelle des Ersatzkommandos Südost der Waffen-SS in Kroatien			
	Besprechung beim deutschen Gesandten wegen Überstellung volksdeutscher Truppen in Waffen-SS und Schutz der zurück-bleibenden Familien			
	l) Angelegenheit Kammerhofer Polizei, Gendarmerie Geheimakten: UK-Stellungsverfahren für die Volksdeutschen		1942-43	
	m) Musterung der Batschka-Deutschen		1942-43	
	n) Vereinbarungen		1941-43	
	Geheimakten: Dienst der Angehörigen der Deutschen Volksgruppe in Kroatien in der Kroatischen Wehrmacht			
	o) Staatsangehörigkeit der zur Waffen-SS Eingerückten		1941-43	
	Geheimakten: Staatsangehörigkeit der Angehöri-gen der zur Waffen-SS Einberu-fenen			
	p) Feldpostangelegenheit		1942-43	
	Geheimakten: Errichtung eines SS-Zweigfeld-postamtes in Essegg/Kroatien Auswertung der Feldpostprüfstelle			

Akten-zeichen	Inhalt	Band	Datum	Serial Nr.
Kult 3 V	r) Aufruf des Volksgruppen-führers	2	1942	
	Geheimakten: Dolmetscher für den Ausbau kroatischer Truppenteile an der Ostfront			
	s) Wehrangelegenheit einzelner Personen (alphab.geordnet)		1941-43	
	t) Kroatische Einheiten, Landwehr		1941-44	
	Geheimakten: Vereinbarungswidrige Behandlung volksgruppenangehöriger Rekruten		7.42	9820/H313227-34
	Einziehung volksgruppenangehöri-ger Rekruten zu kroatischen Spezialformationen			
	Einberufung Volksgruppenangehö-riger zu kroatischen Einheiten			
	u) Wehrangelegenheit der Deutschen Volksgruppe im allgemeinen		1941-44	
	Geheimakten: Briefwechsel mit kroatischem Generalstab wegen Verhältnisse in Bijeljina			
	Vorschriften über die Zugehörig-keit Volksdeutscher in volks-deutschen Organisationen	3	1941-44	
	Zur Verfügungstellung volks-deutscher Dolmetscher für die in die Heimatflak einzustellenden Kroaten durch das SS-Hauptamt nicht möglich			
	v) Einsatzstaffel	4		9820/H313235-69
	Geheimakten: Einsatzstaffel der deutschen Mannschaft			
	Stellung der volksdeutschen Einheiten unter deutsche Kriegs-gerichtsbarkeit			
	Führer der Heimschutzeinheiten der Einsatzstaffel			
	Aufnahme von ES-Deserteuren bei reichsdeutschen Dienststellen und Organisationen in Serbien			
	Gerichtsbarkeit der Einsatz-staffel, Anschluss an die Wehr-machtsleitung			
	Mannschaft des Eisenbahnsiche-rungsbataillons, Bearbeitung eigener landwirtschaftlicher Betriebe.			

Akten-zeichen	Inhalt	Band	Datum	Serial Nr.
Kult 3 V	v) Rechts-und materielle Stellung der volksgruppenangehörigen Offiziere der kroatischen Landwehr und der Einsatzstaffel bei der SS-Gebirgsjäger Division "Prinz Eugen" und der 13.SS-Freiwilligen Division.			
	z) Stärkemeldung der ES		1942-43	
	Geheimakten: Stärkemeldung der deutschen Truppen in der kroatischen Wehrmacht.			
	x) Stabsbefehle der Einsatzstaffel			
	Geheimakten: Befehl 3 "Aufstellung des 3.Ber.Btl.der ES der deutschen Mannschaft"			
	Befehl vom 26.3.1943 Umbau der Einsatzstaffel - Befehlsverhältnisse			
	Befehl 5 (3/4.1943) Einsatzstaffel - Heimatschutzregiment - Aufstellung			
	y) Kosakendivision			
	Geheimakten: Kosakeneinheiten in deutschen Siedlungen			
Kult 3 VI	Partisanentätigkeit	1	1941-44	9820/H313270-944
	Geheimakten: Vertraulicher Bericht der Deutschen Volksgruppenführung			
	Vertraulicher Bericht der Deutschen Volksgruppe über Lage in der Fruska Gora			
	Verschleppung Volksdeutscher			
	Partisanenüberfall auf das Dorf Bingula			
	Lagebericht über Varazdin			
Kult 3 VII	a) Weiterleitung von Schriftstücken b) Weiterleitung des Verordnungsblattes der deutschen Volksgruppe c) Weiterleitung von Wandzeitungen der deutschen Volksgruppe d) Weiterleitung der Zeitung der deutschen Volksgruppe "Volk am Pflug"	1	1941-44	
Kult 3 VIII	a) Umsiedlung Bosnien	1	1942-44	9820/H313945-68
	Geheimakten: Vermerk des Herrn Gesandten betr. Maßnahmen zur Sicherung der deutschen Siedlungen zwischen Banja Luka und Gradiska			
	Runderlass betr.Umsiedlung Bosnien Feststellung des hier verbleibenden Vermögens			
	Umsiedlung aller Volksdeutschen aus Kroatien erscheint bejahenswert			

Akten-zeichen	Inhalt	Band	Datum	Serial Nr.
Kult 3 VIII	Erteilung der deutschen Staats-angehörigkeit für von der Um-siedlung Zurückgestellten			
	Aussiedlung der Volksdeutschen aus Velika Pisanica im Winter			
	Aussiedlung der Volksdeutschen aus Grgurevci			
	Niederschrift über Aussagen deutscher Flüchtlinge aus Litzmannstadt Lager Tuschinwald in der Volksgruppenführung in Zagreb			
	Interne Umsiedlung Syrmien			
	b) Umsiedlung Untersteiermark	2	1942-44	
	Geheimakten: Abschluss Umsiedlungsvereinba-rung in Zagreb erwünscht			
	d) Umsiedlungsangelegenheit einzelner Personen	3	1942-44	
	Geheimakten: Einsatz eines Volksdeutschen			
	c) Schätzrahmen			
	e) Rückwanderung	4-5	1942-44	
Kult 3 IX	Staatsangehörigkeit	1	1941-44	
Kult 3 X	Auskunft, Nachforschungen	1	1941-44	
	Geheimakten: Post aus dem Reich an die DUT in Agram unterliegt der Prüfung durch die Auslandsbriefprüf-stelle			
Kult 3 XI	Interventionen	1	1941-44	
Kult 3 XII	Vermerke, Berichte, Aufzeich-nungen			
	Geheimakten: Veranstaltete volkspolitische Tagungen			9820/H313969-4094
	Streng vertraulicher Bericht aus dem Konzentrationslager "Ustaski-izzeljenicki logor" Slav.Pozega			
	Lage der Volksdeutschen in Slavonien und Syrmien und andere Beobachtungen			
	Eingabe an das Innenministerium. Antrag zur Überbrückung von Spannungen			
	Bericht über die durchgeführten Maßnahmen zur Sicherung deutscher Siedlungen zwischen Banja Luka und Bos.Gradiska			9820/H314095-102
	Aufzeichnung vom 6.10.1943 betr. Unterhaltung mit Volksgruppen-führer Altgayer und Stabsleiter Kutschera über verschiedene Fra-gen zwischen der Volksgruppe und der Gesandtschaft			

Akten-zeichen	Inhalt	Band	Datum	Serial Nr.
Kult 3 XII	Vermerk des Herrn Gesandten vom 15.11.1943. Text über die Vereidigung der Kroaten in der in Kroatien eingesetzten deutschen Gendarmerie			9820/H314103-04
	Niederschrift über Besprechung mit Volksgruppenführer Altgayer und Hauptamtsleiter Gasteiger am 3.September 1944			
	Vermerke, Berichte, Aufzeichnungen			
	Geheimakten: Lage in Ruma	1-3	1941-44	
	Lage in Syrmien			
Kult 3 XIII	Verschiedenes, Programme, Adressenmaterial	1	1942-44	
Kult 3 XIV	Gesetzesverfügungen	1-2	1941-44	
Kult 3 Name	Dienstreisen einzelner Personen aus dem Reich nach Kroatien	1	1941-44	
Kult 3 Nr. 3	A 85/42 und A 342/44			
D Kult 3 3 a	Verbindung zur Deutschen Volksgruppe	1	1941-43	
D Kult 3 3 b	Verbindung zur Volksdeutschen Mittelstelle		1941	
D Kult 11 1 a	Kartenstelle	1	1941-43	
D Kult 11 1 b	Bücherei	1	1941-42	
	Einbürgerungsanträge von der Deutschen Volksgruppe	1	1942	
	Mitteilungen der Ortsgruppe Zagreb der Deutschen Volksgruppe in Kroatien	1	1942	
	Verordnungsblätter	1	1941-44	
	Presse des Gastlandes			
P Inf	Sämtliche für die Presse bestimmten Angelegenheiten, wie Bilder, Informationen	1	1943-44	
P 1	Presse und Propagandawesen	1	1943-44	
P 3	Zeitungen des Gastlandes	1	1943-44	
P 3 Nr. 2	Deutsche Zeitungen und Zeitschriften im Gastland	1	1943-44	
P 3 Nr. 2a	Kroatische Zeitungen und Zeitschriften	1	1943-44	
P 4 Nr. 1	Pressevertreter, Redakteure, Berichterstatter	1	1943-44	
P 6 Nr. 1	Hetzpresse gegen Deutschland	1	1943	
	An hiesige Presse weitergeleitete Veröffentlichungen	1	1943	

Akten-zeichen	Inhalt	Band	Datum	Serial Nr.
D P Inf	Presse Deutschland			
	Sämtliche für die Presse bestimm-te Angelegenheiten	1	1943-44	
D P 1	Presse- und Propagandawesen in Deutschland		1943-44	
D P 1 b	Presseempfang		1943	
D P 3	Verlagsanstalten, Zeitungswesen, Nachrichtenbüros		1943-44	
D P 4	Zeitschriften		1943-44	
D P 4 Nr. 1	Pressevertreter, Berichterstatter	1	1943-44	
	Allgemeine Presse, Erlasse	1	1935-39	
	Presse- und Propagandawesen in Deutschland	1	1932-39	
	Dr.Kurt Johannsen, Hamburg (Aufklärungsausschuss)	1	1932-37	
R	Rechtsfragen, Rechtswesen, Allgemeines	1-2	1936-41	
R 2 Nr.1	Kriegsgräberfürsorge	1-6	1929-44	
R 3 Nr. 1-4	Staatsrecht, Zivil- und Straf-recht,Familienrecht,Staatsange-hörigkeit	1-13	1940-44	
R 3 Nr.4a	Beschaffung von Urkunden A - Z	1-35	1940-43	
R 3 Nr.4b	Eherecht und Ehescheidung Einzelfälle	1-7	1940-44	
R 3 Nr.5	Handels- und Prozessrecht, Rechtshilfe in Zivilsachen	1-5	1940-44	
R 3 Nr.6	Strafrecht, Rechtshilfe in Strafsachen, Auslieferung, Haft	1-6	1934-44	
R 4 Nr. 1-3	Arbeitsrecht, Lohnfragen, Streiks, Arbeitsbewilligungen	1-5	1940-44	
R 5 Nr.1	Paßrecht, Aufenthaltsbestimmun-gen	1-2	1940-43	
	- A - Z	1-28	1940-44	
R 5 Nr.2	Reisepässe, Sichtvermerke	1-7	1940-44	
R 6 Nr.1	Sozial- und Fürsorgewesen, allg.	1-5	1940-41	
R 6 Nr. 1-4		1-5	1940-44	
R 6 Nr.6	Familienunterhalt	1-3	1942-44	
R 7	Internationales Rechtswesen, allgemein	14 Heft	1941-44	
R 7 Nr.17	- Einzelfälle	1-8	1941-44	
R 7 Nr.19	Schadenersatzforderung Partisanenüberfall	1-3	1942-44	
D R 1 Nr. 1-3	Rechtswesen in Deutschland, allgemein Mappen	5	1940-44	
D R 3	Staatsrecht, Zivil- und Straf-recht Mappen	3	1940-44	

Akten-zeichen	Inhalt	Band	Datum	Serial Nr.
D R 3 Nr. 1	Staatsangehörigkeitsfragen, Einbürgerungen	1-6	1939-44	
	Staatsangehörigkeitsfragen A - Z	1-17	1942-43	
D R 3 Nr. 1a	Ausbürgerungen, Einzelfälle	1-4	1934-44	
D R 3 Nr. 2	Beglaubigungen, Notariatssachen	1-3	1941-43	
D R 3 Nr. 3a	Ferntrauung deutscher Staatsan-gehöriger, die sich im Ausland aufhalten	1	1941	
D R 4	Arbeitsrecht und Arbeitsvermitt-lung, allgemein	1-2	1940-41	
	- A - Z	1-13	1940-44	
D R 5	Passrecht, Sichtvermerke Allgemeines	1-8	1938-42	
D R 5 Nr. 2	Sichtvermerke, Passangelegenhei-ten, Einzelsachen	1-38	1940-44	
D R 6 Nr. 1-7	Sozial- und Fürsorgewesen, allg. Mappen	15	1940-44	
D R 6 Nr. 6	Unterstützungen, Versorgungen A - Z Mappen		1940-44	
	Unterstützungen, Renten und Versorgungen A - Z	1-9	1941-44	
D R 6 Nr. 6 W	Wehrmachtsfürsorge, Hinterblie-benenrente A - Z	1-10	1942-43	
	Familienunterhalt A - Z Mappen		1942-44	
D R 8	Referat Hauschild Arbeitsamt	1	1942	
	Arbeitseinsatz, Anwerbungen, Betreuungen	1-4	1941-44	
Not.	Notariatssachen, Beglaubigungen	1-7	1924-43	
Na	Nachlasssachen	1-7	1935-44	
Zeu	Zeugenvernehmung	1-6	1922-44	
Zu	Zustellungen	1-17	1938-44	
R a	Rechtsanwälte	1-2	1940-41	
Uns	Unsichere, Hochstapler, Verbre-cher	1	1936-42	
Sta	Personen- und Ehestandsangele-genheiten, generell	1	1935-39	
	- Einzelfälle	1-25	1934-39	
Al	Alimentensachen und Vormund-schaft	1-3	1922-39	
	- Einzelfälle	4-17	1940-44	
Vorm	Vormundschaft	1-4	1940-44	
Ado	Adoptionssache	1	1939-40	

Akten-zeichen	Inhalt	Band	Datum	Serial Nr.
Auspez	Arbeitsmarkt, Arbeitsbewilligun-gen, Einzelfälle	1-5	1925-39	
	- generell	1-2	1937-39	
	Hausierer	1	1928-37	
Ausw	Aufenthaltsbewilligungen, Ausweisungen	1-4	1928-39	
Pa	Paßangelegenheiten und Reise-bestätigungen	1-4	1921-42	
Me	Meldewesen	1-7	1938-44	
Em-Be	Empfehlungen und Bescheinigungen	1-9	1935-44	
Fl	Flüchtlingswesen und Flüchlings-kartei	1-5	1934-39	
Rei	Reichsdeutsche, allgemein	1-5	1933-39	
Hei	Heimschaffungen	1-2	1924-39	
U	Unterstützungen	1-2	1921-39	
Ford	Forderungen, Einzelfälle	1-8	1932-44	
	- Deutsch (Max), Mappen Angeli (Stefan) und Pavlovie	3	1938-41	
Voll	Zwangsvollstreckungen	1-2	1931-39	
	Liquidationen	1	1938-40	
	Akten Muthesius	1	1921-29	
Ausk	Auskünfte und Nachforschungen	1-22	1933-44	
Verl	Verluste und Funde	1-7	1929-44	
Int	Interventionen	1-16	1933-44	
Var	Varia, allgemein	1-9	1922-44	
	Verschiedenes Mappen	10	1932-43	
	Sichtvermerke, Passierscheine und Paßangelegenheiten A - Z	335	1936-44	
	Deutsches wissenschaftliches Institut, Zagreb			
Pers P	Personalakten des D.W.J.	1	1942-44	
	Personalien, weibliche	1	1942-44	
	- männliche	1	1942-44	
	Verzeichnis der Stellen, Assistenten	1	1942-44	
	Inventar-Verzeichnis	1	1942-44	
Pers R 4	Haushaltspläne und Verwaltung	1	1941-43	
Pers R 5	Abrechnungen	1	1942-43	
	Hauptbuch (Auszahlungen)	1	1944	

Akten-zeichen	Inhalt	Band	Datum	Serial Nr.
Kult	Wissenschaftliche Vorträge in Zagreb (Inhaltsverzeichnis auf Paket)	1-3	1942-44	
	Vorträge und Reisen (Inhaltsverzeichnis auf Paket)	1	1942-44	
	Zeitungsartikel und Veröffentlichungen, Professor Stadler Mappen	2	1942-44	
	Tagungen, Kongresse und Bücher-spende (Inhaltsverzeichnis auf Paket)	1	1942-44	
	Wissenschaftliche Zeitschriften, Jahrbücher, Literatur und Ver-öffentlichungen (Inhaltsverzeich-nis auf Paket)	1	1942-44	
	Universitäten, Neuernennungen, Veränderungen, Hochschule (Inhaltsverzeichnis auf Paket)	1	1942-44	
D Kult	D.W.J.- Eröffnung	1	1942-44	
Kult	Veranstaltungen, Filme, Aus-künfte, Manuskripte (Inhaltsverzeichnis auf Paket)	1	1942-44	
	Kulturelle Angelegenheiten, Verschiedenes (Inhaltsverzeichnis auf Paket)	1	1942-44	
	Zeitungsausschnitte bezw. Über-setzungen (Inhaltsverzeichnis auf Paket)	2	1942-44	
	- Tagung der DWJ-Leiter in Berlin, Auswärtiges Amt und Reichswissenschafts-ministerium	1	1942-44	
1	Ein Ordner mit Lebensläufen kroatischer Professoren		1942-44	
2	Ein Päckchen Umschläge mit Anschriften kroatischer Profes-soren			
3	Ein Hefter mit Mitgliederlisten der Kroatischen Akademie			
4	Zwei Karteikästen: kroatische Professoren, nach Fakultäten geordnet			
5	Ein Karteikasten: Stipendiaten		1942-44	
6	Zwei Karteikästen: Geschäftsvorgänge			
7	Zwei Karteikästen: Allgemeine Anschriften			
8	Ein Ordner: Berichte, Listen, Durchdrucke			
9	Ein Ordner: Assistentenbewerbun-gen			
10	Ein Ordner: Schulwesen und Heimschulen			

Akten-zeichen	Inhalt	Band	Datum	Serial Nr.
11	Ein Ordner: Auskünfte über Studium			
12	– Studium in Deutsch-land			
13	– Verteilerlisten			
14	– Studentenführung		1942–44	
15	– Abgelehnte Anträge			
16	– –			
17	– Schriftwechsel mit Studienwerk			
18	– Schriftwechsel mit Mitteleurop.Wirt-schaftstag			
19	– Schriftwechsel mit Südoststiftung			
20	– Prinz Eugen Stipen-dium, Praktikanten, Ingenieurkurs			
21	– Sonstige Stipendien			
22	– Humboldtstiftung A – J			
23	– K – Z			
24	– Sichtvermerke			
25	– Presseausschnitte			
26	– –			
27	– Schriftwechsel A – N			
28	– – O – Z			
29	Ein Paket mit 24 Mappen: Stipendienanträge			
32	Praktikanten, Sommerkurse, Studienwerk	6	1942–44	
	Akten der Landwirtschaftsabtei-lung			
	Aufstellungen, Tabellen, Acker-bau (Inhaltsverzeichnis a/Paket)	1	1942–44	
	Vermögensaufnahme, statistisches Material, Bodenuntersuchungen, Tierzucht (Inhaltsverzeichnis auf Paket)	1	1942–44	
	Landwirtschaftliche Arbeiten und wissenschaftliche Unterlagen der Landwirtschaftsabteilung (Inhalt-verzeichnis auf Paket)	1	1942–44	
	Wissenschaftliche Unterlagen der Landwirtschaftsabteilung	1	1942–44	
	Zeitungsausschnitte, verschiedene (Inhaltsverzeichnis auf Paket)	1	1942–44	

Akten-zeichen	Inhalt	Band	Datum	Serial Nr.
	Zeitungsausschnitte, verschiedene (Inhaltsverzeichnis auf Paket)	4	1942-44	
	Verschiedene Zeitungsausschnitte über Landwirtschaft	2	1942-44	
	Ausgefüllte Formulare über Land-besitz, nach Bezirken und Zeit-schriften bearbeitet im Statis-tischen Reichsamt (vertraulich zu behandeln)	1	1942-44	
La 1, 1a	Briefe A - Z	2 Ordn.	1942-44	
La 2	Aufsätz und Artikel Dr.Parsche	1 Ordn.	1942-44	
La 4	Ackerbau, Diverses	1 Ordn.	1942-44	
La 6	Listen - Anschriften	1 Ordn.	1942-44	
	Verschiedenes, A - Z	1 Ordn.	1942-44	
	Wirtschaftsnachrichten, Südosteuropa-Gesellschaft Mappe	1	1943-44	
	Akten der Wirtschaftsabteilung, Verschiedenes (s.Inhalt a/Paket)	1 Bdl.	1942-44	
	Interner Wirtschaftsdienst der Deutschen Volksgruppe	1	1942-44	
	Wirtschaftsabteilung, Vermerke, Kult, Wi., Gesandte	1 Ordn	1942-44	
	Landkarten und Fotos			
	drei Tagebücher und Portobuch		1942-44	
	11 Tagebücher		1923-43	
	3 Journale		1941-44	
	3 Sachregister		1941-43	
	5 W.-Tagebücher		1921-44	
	4 W.H.-Namensverzeichnisse		1921-41	
	1 W.-Sachregister		1941-43	
	1 Tagebuch des Sozialreferenten		1941	
	1 Passregister		1930-34	
	2 Namensverzeichnis-Pass		1939-42	
	3 Sichtvermerke		1940-43	
	2 Visa		1939-42	
	6 H.und V.L.		1939-43	
	2 Nebenkassenbücher		1921-33	
	14 Einnahmebücher		1921-42	
	13 Ausgabebücher		1921-42	
	9 Gebührenbücher		1934-43	
	2 Fragebogenregister		1942-43	
	4 Telegrammbücher			

Akten-zeichen	Inhalt	Band	Datum	Serial Nr.
	Baupläne für die deutsche Schule und das deutsche Heim in Agram			
	Amtsblatt "Narodne novine"	3 Bd1.	1941-43	
1.	Satzungen des Verbandes der Genossenschaften des "Napredak" in Sarajewo			
2.	Rundschreiben der Deutschen Handelskammer in Kroatien vom 30.6.1942 - Einfuhrbestimmungen in Kroatien			
3.	Stand der landesplanerischen Studienarbeiten zum Ausbau der Sawe		1943	
4.	Zbornik, Sammlung der Gesetze und Verfügungen des U.St.Kroatien			
	1 Karteikasten des D.W.J.			
	Karteikarten über Personen A - Z.			
	Geheimakten			
Pol 2 Nr. 3	Politische Beziehungen Kroatiens zu anderen Staaten		1944	9787/H302166-71
Pol 3 Nr. 1	Innenpolitik Kroatiens		1942-44	3894/E049041-53 9787/H302172-412
Pol 3 Nr. 3	Militär-, Marine- und Luftange-legenheiten		1943-44	6136/E458375-401 9787/H302413-570
Pol 3 Nr. 4	Bekämpfung der Aufständischen-Partisanen		1943-44	9787/H302471-504
D Pol Nr. 1	Deutsche Aussenpolitik		1944	3894/E049005-22 9787/H302505-15
D Pol Nr. 2	Politische Beziehungen Deutsch-lands zu anderen Staaten als dem Gastland		1942+44	6356/E473993-95
D Pol Nr. 3	Deutsche Innenpolitik		1942+44	3894/E049023-40 9787/H302516-25
Pol 3 Nr. 4 Ko	Bekämpfung der Kommunisten-Agitation		1943	9787/H302526-40
Pol 4 Nr. 6	Zwischenstaatliche aussenpoliti-sche Probleme, Kirchenfragen, Religion		1942-44	9787/H302541-71
Pol 4 Nr. 2	Bolschewismus		1943	6136/E458402-28 9787/H302572-99
Pol 3 Nr 7,9,10	Werbung von Legionen gegen Achsenmächte		1942-43	6136/E458429-40
Pol 3 Nr. 13	Ustasche		1942-44	9787/H302600-26
Pol 7 Nr. 1,2	Feindtätigkeit		1943-44	9787/H302627-34

Akten-zeichen	Inhalt	Band	Datum	Serial Nr.
Pol 8 Nr. 1,2,3	Verhältnis deutscher Dienststellen in Kroatien		1944	9787/H302635-67
Kult 2	Kulturpolitische Beziehungen Kroatiens zu Deutschland		1941+43	6136/E458441-49
Kult 3	Reichs- und Volksdeutsche in Kroatien		1942-44	9787/H302668-713
Pol 2 Nr. 2	Deutscher Polizeiattaché in Kroatien		1941-44	9787/H302714-839
D R 5	Passrecht und Fremdenpolizei		1940-41 1944	9787/H302840-43
Pol Inf	Politisches Informationsmaterial dritter Staaten		1943-44	6136/E458450-59 9787/H302844-97
Pers P	Personalien der Beamten, Angestellten, Arbeiter und Sachverständigen der Behörde		1941-44	9787/H302898-903
K II/1	Deutsche in Kroatischer Wehrmacht Verträge, Abkommen, Vereinigtes kroatisches Wehrgesetz	1	1942-44	9787/H302904-3043
		2	1944	9787/H303044-131
K II/2/B		1	1944	9787/H303132-200
		2	1944	9787/H303201-330
		3	1944	9787/H303331-40
		4	1944	9787/H303341-59
K III/1		1	1944	9787/H303360-430
		2	1944	9787/H303431-51
K III/2		1	1944	9787/H303452-55
		2	1944	9787/H303456-57
K IV/1		1	1943-44	9787/H303458-78
K IV/2		1	1944	9787/H303479-96
K III/2 Kr. L.	Kroatische Lageberichte 4 Mappen		1943-44	9787/H303497-862
				9787/H303863-4167
				9787/H304168-450
				9787/H304451-67
K III/1	Deutsche Tagesrapporte			9787/H304468-536
	Mitteilungen des Polizeiattachés		1943-44	9787/H304537-820
	Dienstanweisungen		1943-44	9787/H304821-35
	Schreiben des kroatischen Innenministeriums		1944	9787/H304836-87 9787/H310027-102
	Mitteilungen der Abwehrstellen		1943	9787/H304888-988
	Arbeitsausschuss für den Kriegseinsatz		1943-44	9787/H304989-5236

Akten-zeichen	Inhalt	Band	Datum	Serial Nr.
	Geheime Reichssachen		1942–44	3014/D588976-9165
				3903/E049705-11
				3903/E049712-26
				6137/E458461-74
				9787/H305237-934
				3014/D589166-291
				9787/H305935-6168
				3014/D589292-364
				6137/E458475-553
				9787/H306169-602
				3014/D589365-443
				9787/H306603-744
				3903/E049727-914
				6137/E458554-726
				9787/H306745-7232
	Bauxit Mappe I-IV		1941–42	5554/E395034-41
				9787/H307233-385
			1943	9787/H307386-553
			1943	9787/H307554-675
			1943–44	9787/H307676-91
	Bauxit - Hafen Ploce		1941–43	9787/H307692-8121
			1943	9787/H308122-38
	Einsatzgruppe Bergbau, bis		3.44	9787/H308139-251
	Bauxitprogramm Führerbefehl		1943–44	9787/H308252-72
	Mineralöl - G WR 6		1941–44	9787/H308273-77
	Holz - G WR 4		1942–44	9787/H308278-321
	Eisenerze - G WR 3 E		1942–44	9787/H308322-72
	Finanzangelegenheiten		1943–44	9787/H308373-532
	Eisenbahn und Strassenbau		1943–44	9787/H308533-64
	Ernährungsfragen		1943–44	9787/H308565-703
	Preise		1942–44	9787/H308704-32
	Deutsch-kroatische Handelsbe-ziehungen		1943–44	9787/H308733-67
	Kroatisch-italienische Beziehun-gen		1942–44	9787/H308768-75
	Kroatische Beziehungen zu anderen Ländern		1943–44	9787/H308776-77

Akten-zeichen	Inhalt	Band	Datum	Serial Nr.
	Mappe I bis IV aus Mesnicks		1942	9787/H308778-80
			1942-43	9787/H308781-887
	Lageberichte des WO VII		1941-44	9787/H308888-9235
	Protokolle		1941-44	9787/H309236-806
	Dienstreise GR Dr.Kühn Holzgebiet		1944	9787/H309807-23
Kult Var	Verschiedenes		1944	9787/H309824-36
Kult Inf	Informationen zur propagandistischen Auswertung		1944	9787/H309837-39
P 4 Nr.1	Pressevertreter, Berichterstatter in Kroatien		1944	9787/H309840-43
Propaganda-Archiv Kult E	Gegner, Flugzettel, Cetnini-Greuel, Juden		1942-44	9787/H309844-76
	Bolschewismus		1942-43	9787/H309877-83
	Geheime Aufzeichnungen und Korrespondenz des Gesandten und seines Adjutanten		1941-44	9787/H309884-10026

Akten-zeichen	Inhalt	Band	Datum	Serial Nr.
W.F.	Fahndungen, Devisen, Schmuggel		5.37- 6.39	
Pol 4	Kommunismus, Kommunisten	II	3.25-12.38	K2151/K599674-884
Pol g.8	Sabotage-Akte auf deutschen Schiffen	1	7.38-12.39	
	Professor Eggen van Terlan		1.34- 8.34	
V	Verschiedenes, Geheim	II	1.34-11.36	K2152/K599885-99
A 15	Politische Angelegenheiten, Verschiedenes	VII	4.31-12.35	
		VIII	1.36- 5.39	
D.1.i	Personalien, Verschiedenes	IX	10.32- 6.38	

KONSULAT APENRADE

Akten-zeichen	Inhalt	Band	Datum	Serial Nr.
Pers.R. 5	Belege zum H.u.V. Buch Einzahlung	1	1939-41	4862/E248185-86
Po 1	Politik, Verschiedenes	1	7.20- 4.22	4861/E247980-82
	Nordschleswig	2	5.22- 9.26	4861/E247983-8025
		3	9.26-11.30	4861/E248026-59
		4	12.30-12.38	4861/E248060-182
Po 2	Dänische Politik im abgetretenen Gebiet	1	7.20- 7.23	4860/E247835-61
		2	7.23-11.37	4860/E247862-946
		3	11.37- 2.39	4860/E247947-77
Po 3	Dänische Politik und Propaganda südlich der Grenze	1	8.20-12.38	4778/E234698-722
Po 4	Militär-und Marineangelegenheiten	1	8.20- 9.35	4791/E235804-46
Po 5	Schulwesen im abgetretenen Gebiet	1	8.20- 9.23	4822/E239365-453
		2	10.23-11.28	4822/E239454-502
		3	11.28- 4.33	4822/E239503-61
		4	4.33- 5.39	4822/E239562-612
Po 9	Kirche	1	8.20- 6.39	4816/E239155-89
Po 11 a	Deutsche kulturelle Bestrebungen in Nordschleswig	1	2.21-12.38	4817/E239192-309
Po 12	Verschiedenes Pol.	2	2.37- 9.39	4818/E239312-23
Po 13	Dänische Presse	1	2.29- 2.37	4819/E239326-30
Po 14	Auslandsdeutschtum	1	2.24- 3.39	4820/E239341-50
Po Kult	Kulturelles	1	12.27- 1.39	4821/E239353-62
Kult 3 Nr. 2	Deutsche Volksgruppen und ihre Organisation	1	1939-42	4813/E238398-653
		2	1939-42	4813/E238654-895

Akten-zeichen	Inhalt	Band	Datum	Serial Nr.
S./N.Schl.	Angelegenheiten Nordschleswigs	1	1927–42	4846/E245621–826
		2	1927–42	4846/E245827–6033
		3	1927–42	4846/E246034–215
		4	1927–42	4846/E246216–444
		5	1942–43	4846/E246445–672
		6	1942–43	4846/E246673–983
		7	1942–43	4846/E246984–7204
Wi 2 spez.	Kreditanstalt Vogelsang	1	1933–41	4812/E238313–95
S/Zw.Verst	Zwangsversteigerungen	1	1939–40	4811/E238197–311
	GENERALKONSULAT DANZIG			
I 2	Danzig-polnische Beziehungen (auch Entscheidungen des Völkerbundkommissars und des Völkerbundes)	27	1932–34	9170/E644891–914 9747/E685233–35
		29	1932–34	9170/E644915–17
		31	1934–36	9815/E691128–45
		33	1934–36	9170/E644918–20
		35	1936–37	7596/E543672–76
		36	1936–37	7596/E543677–87
		37	1937–38	7596/E543688–89
II 2	Volkstag und Parteiwesen	6	1935–38	7596/E543690–94
IX 3	Reichswehr. Militärische Angelegenheiten	1	1929–38	9163/E644513–42 L1509/L447095–250
	Hoher Kommissar des Völkerbundes in der Freien Stadt Danzig: c) Kostin	3	1932–34	9059/E634258–74
	– d) Burckhardt	4	1937–38	7596/E543695–705
	– e) Lester	5	1933–36	9168/E644822–42
	Professor Dr.Noé	1	1927–38	9051/E633965–79
	Danziger Werft	1	1930–38	7596/E543706–08
	Überbrückungskredite und Maßnahmen zur Sanierung der Danziger Staatsfinanzen	1	1925–36	9058/E634237–55 M122/M004666–67
	Besprechungen mit dem Hohen Kommissar	1	1933–39	9060/E634277–367
		2	1933–39	9087/E638722–870
		3	1933–39	9166/E644735–812
		4	1933–39	7249/E532046–94
	Verschiedene G.–Sachen	1	1933–39	9057/E634202–34

Akten-zeichen	Inhalt	Band	Datum	Serial Nr.
	Verschiedene G.-Sachen	2	1933-39	7596/E543709-25 9086/E638685-720
		3	1933-39	7596/E543726-29
		4	1933-39	7248/E532005-44
	Handakten, Berichtsdurchschläge an das Auswärtige Amt	1	1933	9620/E678915-17
		1	1935	9215/E647996-97
		1	1935	9215/E647998-8004
Prot.5 a	Kriegsschiffbesuche: Schleswig-Holstein	1	1939	8287/E588325-38
Pol 3 Nr.8	Das Polentum in Danzig	1	1939	8471/E596096-101
Pol 4 Nr.1	Völkerbund und Hoher Kommissar	1	1939	7261/E532764-72
D Pol 2 Nr. 2	Deutschlands Beziehungen zu Polen	1	1939	8265/E586067-79
	KONSULAT FLORENZ			
	Geheimakten	1	1940-43	5605/E401622-30
	KONSULAT GALATZ			
Geheim	Geheimakten verschiedenen Inhalts 2 Ordner		1938-43	
	Berichterstattung Bessarabien	1	1939-42	
	Entwürfe für antikommunistische Broschüren betr. Tschechen, Bulgaren	1		
	Direktor Dr.Ing.Gerhard Erlemann	1	1940-44	
Geh.K.W. 1	Konsulatswesen	1	1925	
Geh.K.W. 2	− Konstantza	1	1925-36	
Geh.K.W. 3	− Braila	1	1927-37	
Geh.Sch.III	Schiffahrt, Hafenfreizonen	1	1926-38	
Kult 3/2	Schriftwechsel mit Ges.Bukarest und Auswärtigem Amt	1	1939	
	− mit dem Gaurat für Bessarabien	1	1939	
	Deutsche Volksgruppen und ihre Organisationen	1	1938-40	
Kult 8	Schulwesen: Beihilfe	1	1938-40	
Pol 3	Innenpolitik Rumäniens	1	1938-40	
Pol 3/1	NSDAP-Gliederungen und Verbände	1	1939	
Pol 4/1	Zwischenstaatliche aussenpolitische Probleme	1	1938-40	
Pol 7	Angelegenheiten der NSDAP 2 Deckel mit losen Sachen	1	1937-38	

Akten-zeichen	Inhalt	Band	Datum	Serial Nr.
Pol 7	Angelegenheiten der NSDAP			
	Ein Umschlag mit Sachen zu Pers R 7725/44 Guido Henkel, Galatz			
C D D	Internationale Donau-Kommission			
	Ein Paket mit Urkunden der R.f.G. und Briefumschlag Spiess-winkel			
	Ein Paket und ein Brief des Generalkonsuls Dr.Loerner			
	1 Journal		1943	
	1 Sichtvermerkbuch		1941	
	2 Passjournale		1939-43	
	1 Geh.Tagebuch		1939-43	
	1 Verzeichnis der an das Aus-wärtige Amt abgegebenen Berichte			

KONSULAT GENF

| Po 1, 1 | Deutschland und der Völkerbund und Internationales Arbeitsamt | 1 | 1933-39 | 4019/E059068-106 |
| | Minderheiten   Generalia | 3 | 1929-39 | M41/M001095-106 |

GENERALKONSULAT GÖTEBORG

| Pol 3 | Schwedische innerpolitische Verhältnisse   Beiakte | | 1941-42 | 5406/E362487-89 |

Akten-zeichen	Inhalt	Band	Datum	Serial Nr.
P.K.	Personalien des Konsuls	1	1921-27	
	- des Hilfsamtsgehilfen Krüger	1	1925-26	
	- der Beamten	1	1928-31	
P.A.	- der Angestellten	1	1920-31	
Gg 3 b	Inventar Schriftwechsel	3	1933-38	
Gg 15 b	Hausangelegenheiten Schriftwechsel	1	1932-40	
	Wertsendungen	1	1925-31	
Pers A	Geheim-Erlasse	1	1938	
Prot 3	Orden- und Ehrenzeichen Schriftwechsel	1	1934-36	
Pol 1	Politisches	1-4	1921-36	
	Aussenpolitik des Gastlandes	5	1936-39	
Pers Polen	Personalien polnischer Staats-männer und Diplomaten sowie fremder Diplomaten und Konsuln	1	1932-38	
Pol	Optionsliste Deutsches Konsulat Lodz	1	1921-22	
Pol 3	Militärakten	1	1934-39	
D P 2	Beziehungen Deutschlands zu anderen Staaten als dem Gast-lande, allgemeine Bestimmun-gen	1	1934-39	
	- Schriftwechsel	1	1933-38	
Po 6 g	Jungdeutsche Partei in Polen	1	1934-37	
Po 7 a	Rassenfrage, Nationalitätenfrage, Fremdvölker, allgemeine Bestim-mungen	1	1935-38	
Po 12 a	NSDAP Auslandsorganisation, allg.Bestimmungen	1	1937-39	
Po 12 b	- Schriftwechsel	1	1937-39	
Po 13 a	Agenten-und Spionagewesen allg.Bestimmungen	1	1935	
Po 13 b	- Schriftwechsel	1	1933-38	
W 1	Wirtschaft	8-14	1926-33	
H 2	Handelsbeziehungen Deutschlands zu Polen	1	1933-38	
Wi 4 b I	Deutsches Genossenschaftswesen in Polen	1	1919-35	
Wi 7 a	Deutsch-polnisches Wirtschafts-abkommen vom 4.11.35 allgemeine Bestimmungen	1	1935-36	
R 1 a	Rechtswesen, allgemeine Bestim-mungen	1	1930-39	

Akten-zeichen	Inhalt	Band	Datum	Serial Nr.
R 1 b	Rechtswesen, Schriftwechsel	1	1931-38	
R 1 c	— Auskünfte	1	1937-39	
R 3 b	Beglaubigungen und Legalisa-tionen, Schriftwechsel	1	1924-35	
S 2 a	Wohltätigkeit und Liebesgaben (Spenden und Unterstützungen)	1	1923-39	
S 2 c	Nationalsozialistische Volks-wohlfahrt	1	1935-39	
F V 1	Versailler Vertrag	1	1921-33	
F V 2		2	1934-37	
Deutschtum Po 6 a	Deutschtum	1-7	1922-35	
	— enthaltend wichtige Erlasse aus den bereits an das Auswärtige Amt abgeliefer-ten Aktenbänden vom Jahre 1927-1930	1	1927-30	
P 3 Nr.2 f	Der Deutsche Wegweiser	1	1931-39	
Po 6 d	Deutscher Kultur- und Wirt-schaftsbund	1	1931-38	
Kirche	Kirche, geheim	1-2	1924-29	
Po 10 b	Kirchenwesen in Polen	1	1928-35	
Kult 4 Nr. 1	— Protestantismus	1	1935-39	
Kult 4 Nr. 2	— Katholizismus	1	1930-38	
Schulwesen	Schulwesen	1	1925-27	
	— geheim	2	1927-28	
	— —	3	1928-29	
	—	4-6	1929-35	
Po 5 a	— enthaltend wichtige Erlas-se aus den bereits an das Auswärtige Amt abgeliefer-ten Aktenbänden v.1925-30	1	1925-30	
Po 5 d	Schulbeschwerden der deutschen Minderheit in Polen beim Völker-bund	1	1931-36	
G 2	Deutsche Krankenhäuser in Polen, Johanniskrankenhaus	1-3	1926-30	
Kult 11		4	1931-39	
K W 2	Schenkungen, Stiftungen und Stipendien	1	1938	
K W 4	Filmwesen	2	1938-39	
	Presse	1-2	1922-31	

Akten-zeichen	Inhalt	Band	Datum	Serial Nr.
	Geheimerlasse aus den Akten:			
	I. Kult 3 a	1	1938-39	
	III. Po 4 a	1	1936-38	
	IV. Pol 12 a	1	1939	
	V. Kult 3	1	1937-38	
	VI. R 7 a	1	1937	
	VII. Kult 2 Nr. 1	1	1939	
	VIII. Vw 3 a	1	1939	
	IX. Kult 8	1	1938-39	
	X. D Kult 4	1	1935-39	
	XI. D Kult 1 g	1	1939	
	XII. Vw 8	1	1936	
	XIII. Po 6 b	1		
Journale	Ausgabenbuch	1	1931	
	Urkunden - Kassenbuch	1	1937-39	
	Weiterleitung von Briefen	1	1939	
	Einzahlungen	1	1933	
	Nebenkassenbuch	1	1932-33	
	Überweisungslisten	1-2	1926-27	
	Notariatsregister	1	1933-39	
	Matrikel-Eintragungen	1	1930	
	Legalisationen I, II, III	1-3	1921-39	
	Liste der Einreisesichtvermerke	1	1933-34	
	Sichtvermerke I, II, III, IV, V, VI, VII, VIII	1-8	1929-39	
Material	Material des Schul- und Bildungs-vereins (Fotografische Aufnahmen)			
	GENERALKONSULAT MEMEL			
P 2 g M	Deutsch-litauische Wirtschafts-verhandlungen spez. Gerichtsver-fassungsgesetz	2	1933	9797/E687565-75
P 2 i M	Entziehung der Arbeitsgenehmi-gung und Ausweisung von Beamten und Angestellten	1	1933-34	9795/E687378-498
		2	2.34- 3.34	9795/E687499-510
P 6 M		1	2.34- 8.34	9795/E687511-38
P 23 M	Deutsch-litauischer Handelsver-trag und das Memelgebiet	1	1935-39	9799/E687633-67
P 25 M	Memelländisches Parteiwesen	1	1934	9796/E687540-63

Akten-zeichen	Inhalt	Band	Datum	Serial Nr.
II 9 d	Die deutschen Minderheiten Minderheitsfragen		1928–39	3228/D700063-75
XI 8 g 1	Seemannsamt, Explosion auf der Vancouver		1938–39	3229/D700077-85
	KONSULAT TRIEST			
	Akten	1	1921–24	1017/308541-952
		2	1925–27	1024/309353-670
		3	1928–29	1025/309672-870
		4	1930–39	1026/309872-10067
	GENERALKONSULAT ZÜRICH			
	Auswärtiges Amt Ref.D. III	1	1940–42	5325/E337999-8004
H 7 a	Geheimakten Handel, Finanz und Wirtschaft	1	9.31–12.37	6110/E452431-73
Pers.Si 2 a	Krieg 1939/40	1	9.39– 8.40	2402/D500527-85
Pers.Si 7 a	Informationen A – Bo	1	1939–43	1897/426973-7105
	— Br– E	1	1939–43	1897/427106-56
	— F – G	1	1939–43	1897/427157-214
	— H – Ki	1	1939–43	1897/427215-81
	— Kl– L	1	1939–43	1897/427282-350
	— M – Po	1	1939–43	1913/430338-58
	— R – Schn	1	1939–43	1913/430359-424
	— Scho – Tyer	1	1939–43	1913/430425-463
	— U – Z	1	1939–43	1913/430464-578
Pers.Si 7	Geheimakten allgemein	1	9.39– 3.41	2402/D500586-99
		2	4.41– 5.42	2402/D500600-19
		3	5.42–11.42	2402/D500620-37 5326/E338006-15
		4	11.42– 4.44	1865/423342-76 3942/E053942-4000
Pers.Si 7 a	— speziell	1	10.43– 5.44	3942/E053919-38
adh 1,2	— Alfred Reutschi	1	10.43–44	1865/423377-453 3942/E053939-41

Akten-zeichen	Inhalt	Band	Datum	Serial Nr.
Po III	Fremde Missionen in Albanien	1	1924-39	
	Albanische Missionen im Ausland	1	1925-39	
	Politische Berichte und Tele-gramme bis 31.12.1925	1	1923-25	
	Politik: Staaten ausser Albanien Politische Berichte	1	1932-39	
	Erlasse, aussenpolitisch ab 1938	1	1936-38	
	Eingänge, I.Balkankonferenz in Athen Oktober 1930 Istanbul 1931 Bukarest 1932 II.Balkanpakt vom 9.II. 1934	1	1931-36	
	Aufzeichnungen: Albanien 1926-1929 politisch und wirtschaftlich	1	1926-29	
	Politik Albanien (bis einschließ-lich Fjeri-Revolte, August 1935)	1	1924-35	
Pol 1(u. Pol 2 Nr.2)	Aussenpolitik Albaniens ab 1940	1	1940-42	656/256490-522
Pol 2 Nr. 1	Deutschland und Albanien	1	1934-39	
	Deutsch-Österreicher Wiedervereinigung Österreichs mit dem Reich	1	1938	
	Tschechoslowakei - Protektorat Böhmen-Mähren	1	1939	3114/D633025-30
Pol 2 Nr. 2	Beziehungen Albaniens zu anderen Staaten	1	1926-37	
	Albanien und der Völkerbund	1	1926-39	
	Italiener in Albanien Albanisch-italienische Beziehun-gen (bis Ende 1938)	1	1927-40	
	Pressezwischenfall Italien-Albanien vom Mai 1930	1	1930	
	Albanisch-jugoslawischer Konflikt Gjureschkowitsch, Ausgänge und Eingänge		1927	
	Italienisch-jugoslawische Aus-gänge und Eingänge		1926-27	
Pol 3 Nr. 4	Innenpolitik. Parlamentarisches und albanisches Innerpolitisches (Faschistischer Ständerat)	1	1925-40	
Pol 3 Nr. 1	Albanische Personalien, auch fremde, prominente Persönlich-keiten mit Beziehungen auf Albanien	1	1925-38	
Pol 3 Nr. 2	Militär- und Luftfahrtangelegen-heiten (Albanisches Heer)	1	1925-42	
	Monarchie Albanien 1.September 28	1	8.28- 4.31	

Akten-zeichen	Inhalt	Band	Datum	Serial Nr.
Pol 3 Nr. 2	Attentat auf König Ahmed Zogu am 20.II.1931	1	1931	
Pol 3 Nr. 3 K	Agenten- und Spionagewesen, Bekämpfung kommunistischer Agitation (Kommunismus in Albanien)	1	1925-42	661/257067-81 K2148/K599552-617
Pol 3 Bd. 1	Innenpolitik Albaniens	1	1938-43	652/255873-907
Pol 3	- Albanien - Italien Nach italienischer Besetzung	1	1939-40	531/238685-831
	Verlobung und Heirat des Königs, Geburt des Thronerben	1	1938-39	
Pol 4	Italo/albanisch-griechischer Krieg sowie Krieg Italiens gegen England	1	1940-41	
Pol 6	Besuch des Königs von Italien und sonstiger Fürstlichkeiten und Staatsmänner in Albanien	1	1941	
	Kulturpolitisches, Eingänge	1	1925-34	
	Schulwesen in Albanien, Deutsche Sprachlehrer für Albanien	1	1925-36	
	Franziskaner	1	1925-32	
	Kultur- und Schulfonds 1937	1	1928-38	
	Kulturpolitik 1936	1	1936-38	
	Deutsche Kulturpolitik 1938 auch Anmeldung zum Kultur-und Schulfonds	1	1937-38	
	Albanische Studenten in Deutschland	1	1924-38	
W 3	Zementfabriken	1	1927-37	
W F 1	V/2 Anleihe	1	1927-32	
W F 2 Nr. 1	Banken, Albanische Nationalbank	1	1925-39	

APPENDIX I

List of Serials

The following pages list in numerical order all serials which
appear in this volume, together with their title. In some cases the
title differs from the corresponding title of the file listed in the
main section of the volume. As distinguished from the practice in the
volumes of Documents on German Foreign Policy, serials which are supple-
mentary to earlier serials are not so identified. (Serials 2129, 2130,
2131, 2281, differ from the rest, inasmuch as not complete files but
single documents were filmed under those numbers. Thus only a general
description of their contents has been given and researchers should con-
sult the pertinent pages in this volume). The National Archives Supplement should be consulted about details of how to order copies of all
microfilms in this volume.

28	Gesandtschaft Prag, Geheim:	Telegramme an und vom Auswärtigen Amt und anderen Behörden
37	Gesandtschaft Prag, Geheim:	Telegrammabschriften, Aufzeich-nungen
41	Botschaft Rom (Quirinal), Geheim:	Indische Freiheitsbewegung; Poli-tische Lage in Indien. Bose. Shedai Himalaja Sender
74	Botschaft Rom Vatikan, Geheim:	Allgemeines. VAA-Material (Geheime Lageberichte von der Front). Emi-granten (auch nicht-Emigranten) Überwachung im Ausland. Gestapo. Einzelfälle. Politika. Diverses
86	Botschaft Rom (Quirinal), Geheim:	Indische Legion in Deutschland; arabische Legion in Italien
127	Botschaft Moskau, Geheim:	Politische Beziehungen: Sowjet Union - Deutschland
152	Botschaft Rom (Quirinal), Geheim:	Äusserungen Matsuokas über Eden, Besuch des japanischen Aussenmini-sters a.D.Sato, Nichtangriffspakt Frankreich-Tailand
165	Botschaft Moskau, Geheim:	Politische Akten
166	Botschaft Rom (Quirinal), Geheim:	Japan, China, Mandschukuo
166	Botschaft Moskau, Geheim:	Politische Beziehungen: Sowjet Union - Japan (Mandschkuo, chinesisch-japa-nischer Krieg; Zwischenfälle an der mongolisch-mandschurischen Grenze)
167	Botschaft Moskau, Geheim:	Politische Beziehungen: Sowjet Union - andere Staaten
171	Botschaft Moskau, Geheim:	Politische Beziehungen: Sowjet Union - Nordische Staaten (Finnland, Schweden, Norwegen, Dänemark) Aaland-frage, Finnische Inseln
215	Botschaft Moskau, Geheim:	Zwischenstaatliche, aussenpolitische Probleme.Bolschewismus, Sozialismus.

215	Botschaft Moskau, Geheim:	Russische Emigranten. Innenpolitik der Sowjet Union. Militär, Marine, Luftfahrt. Politische Beziehungen: Deutschland-Baltische Staaten (auch Memel). Deutschland-Balkanstaaten. Deutschland-England (Einkreisungspolitik)
258	Botschaft Moskau, Geheim:	Politische Beziehungen: Sowjet Union - England (englische Einkreisungspolitik) Garantien, Paktverhandlungen mit der Sowjet Union und der Türkei
270	Botschaft Moskau, Geheim:	Politische Akten
273	Botschaft Moskau, Geheim:	Schulenburg, Personalia
276	Botschaft Moskau, Geheim:	Politisches, Schulenburg
277	Botschaft Moskau, Geheim:	Politisches, Schulenburg
279	Botschaft Paris, Geheim:	Verhaftungen, Interventionen, Auslieferungen A - Z
282	Botschaft Paris, Geheim:	Italien, italienische diplomatische und konsularische Vertretungen in Frankreich
285	Botschaft Moskau, Geheim:	Politische Akten
292	Botschaft Moskau, Geheim:	Politik, geheim
315	Botschaft Moskau, Geheim:	Lose G-Vorgänge
349	Botschaft Moskau, Geheim:	Personalia
352	Botschaft Moskau, Geheim:	Politische Beziehungen: Deutschland-andere Staaten. Krieg mit Polen
354	Botschaft Moskau, Geheim:	Politische Beziehungen:Deutschland - andere Staaten. Krieg mit Polen
357	Botschaft Moskau, Geheim:	Politische Beziehungen: Deutschland-andere Staaten. Krieg mit Polen
359	Botschaft Moskau, Geheim:	Litauischer Gebietsstreifen. Politische Beziehungen: Deutschland-andere Staaten. Krieg mit Polen
361	Botschaft Moskau, Geheim:	Politische Beziehungen: Sowjet Union-England (englische Einkreisungspolitik, Garantien, Paktverhandlungen mit der Sowjet Union und der Türkei)
363	Botschaft Moskau, Geheim:	Politische Beziehungen: Deutschland-Italien
366	Botschaft Moskau, Geheim:	Politische Beziehungen: Sowjet Union-Italien
370	Botschaft Moskau, Geheim:	Politische Beziehungen: Sowjet Union-Balkan Pakt Staaten (Bulgarien, Griechenland, Jugoslawien, Rumänien, Türkei) Balkan Pakt, Mittelmeerfragen, Schwarzes Meer Pakt, Bessarabien
372	Botschaft Moskau, Geheim:	Politische Beziehungen: Sowjet Union-Balkan-Staaten (Bulgarien,Griechenland, Jugoslawien, Rumänien, Türkei) Balkan Pakt,Mittelmeerfragen, Schwarzes Meer Pakt, Bessarabien

380	Botschaft Moskau, Geheim:	Politische Beziehungen Sowjet Union-Balkan Pakt Staaten (Bulgarien, Griechenland, Jugoslawien, Rumänien, Türkei) Balkan Pakt, Mittelmeerfragen, Schwarzes Meer Pakt, Bessarabien
397	Botschaft Moskau, Geheim:	Tschechoslowakei
410	Botschaft Moskau, Geheim:	Pressevertreter, Redakteure, Berichterstatter und ihre Organisationen. Vertreter des DNB und deutscher Zeitungen
414	Botschaft Moskau, Geheim:	Deutsche Innenpolitik: Protektorat Böhmen und Mähren
418	Botschaft Moskau, Geheim:	Deutsche Innenpolitik, Staatsschutzbestimmungen, Antikommitern
425	Botschaft Moskau, Geheim:	G-Sachen, Verschiedenes
426	Botschaft Moskau, Geheim:	Militärische Angelegenheiten
429	Botschaft Moskau, Geheim:	Politische Beziehungen:Sowjet Union-Nordische Staaten (Finnland, Schweden, Norwegen, Dänemark) Aalandfrage, Finnische Inseln
432	Botschaft Moskau, Geheim:	Politische Beziehungen:Sowjet Union-Baltische Staaten
433	Botschaft Moskau, Geheim:	Politische Verhältnisse in anderen Ländern (innerpolitische Informationserlasse)
441	Botschaft Moskau, Geheim:	Politische Beziehungen: Deutschland-Nordische Staaten
445	Botschaft Madrid, Geheim:	Periodische Meldungen des Polizeiattachés über die Besucher in der Englischen Botschaft
446	Botschaft Madrid, Geheim:	Diplomatische und konsularische Vertretungen der Scheinregierungen in Spanien
448	Botschaft Madrid, Geheim:	Diplomatische und konsularische Vertretungen der Scheinregierungen in Spanien
450	Botschaft Paris, Geheim:	Kriegsgefangenenwesen. Friedensvorbereitungen, - fühler, - angebote.
454	Botschaft Madrid, Geheim:	Fremde Vertretungen in Spanien, ausser England, Frankreich, Italien, USA, Scheinregierungen. Italien und italienische Beziehungen zu Spanien. Frankreich, Beziehungen zu Spanien.
455	Botschaft Paris, Geheim:	Berichterstattung Botschafter Abetz; Schriftwechsel Schleier-Abetz
457	Botschaft Madrid, Geheim:	Berlin, Verschiedenes
461	Botschaft Moskau, Geheim:	Politische Beziehungen: Deutschland-Polen und Danzig
462	Botschaft Madrid, Geheim:	Antikominternpakt Verlängerung; Reise Serrano Suner nach Berlin
466	Botschaft Moskau, Geheim:	Politische Beziehungen: Sowjet Union-Baltische Staaten

477	Botschaft Moskau, Geheim:	Politische Beziehungen: Deutschland-Polen und Danzig
478	Botschaft Paris, Geheim:	Abwehrsachen
479	Botschaft Madrid, Geheim:	Kurierverkehr, Depeschenbeförderung
480	Botschaft Madrid, Geheim:	Fernsprech- und Fernschreibebetrieb der Botschaft
481	Botschaft Madrid, Geheim:	Deutsch-spanische Beziehungen betr. Arbeitsrecht; Einsatz spanischer Arbeiter in Deutschland
487	Botschaft Moskau, Geheim:	Politische Beziehungen: Deutschland-Spanien
488	Botschaft Moskau, Geheim:	Politische Beziehungen: Deutschland-Polen (Scheinregierung)
492	Botschaft Madrid, Geheim:	Innere Lage in Spanien
493	Botschaft Moskau, Geheim:	Innenpolitik der Sowjet Union
494	Botschaft Moskau, Geheim:	Innenpolitik der Sowjet Union
497	Botschaft Madrid, Geheim:	Restaurationsfrage in Spanien: Wiedereinführung der Monarchie
498	Botschaft Madrid, Geheim:	Innere Lage in Spanien
499	Botschaft Madrid, Geheim:	Berichterstattung der spanischen Auslandsvertretung über Zustände im neutralen und feindlichen Ausland
500	Botschaft Moskau, Geheim:	Politische Beziehungen: Sowjet Union – Polen (Ukraine Frage, Russisch-Polen)
502	Botschaft Madrid, Geheim:	Spanische Freiwillige in Russland "Blaue Division"
515	Gesandtschaft Lissabon, Geheim:	Vertrauliche Akten: Pol., Kult., Pers., Presse, Recht
516	Gesandtschaft Lissabon, Geheim:	Wolfram-Abkommen
531	Generalkonsulat Tirana	Albanien: Innenpolitik; Italien. Nach italienischer Besetzung
597	Botschaft Moskau, Geheim:	Politische Akten
644	Botschaft Moskau, Geheim:	Litauischer Gebietsstreifen. Politische Beziehungen: Sowjet Union – Deutschland
652	Generalkonsulat Tirana:	Albanien: Innenpolitik
656	Generalkonsulat Tirana:	Albanien: Aussenpolitik ab 1940
659	Gesandtschaft Bern:	Geheimakten
661	Generalkonsulat Tirana,	Agenten, Spionagewesen; Bekämpfung kommunistischer Agitation (Kommunismus in Albanien)
672	Gesandtschaft Bern:	Geheimakten
688	Botschaft Rom (Quirinal), Geheim:	Spanien-Portugal

695	Botschaft Moskau, Geheim:	Politische Beziehungen: Sowjet Union – Deutschland
701	Botschaft Rom (Quirinal), Geheim:	Italienisch-spanisches Abkommen Sitzung am 6.12.1936 über spanische Aktion. Italienisch-spanische Beziehungen. Gespräch Eden-Grandi betr. Aktion in Spanien. Englands Politik gegen Deutschland. Unterstützung der Kriegsmarine im Frieden und im Kriegsfall durch Reichsvertreter im Ausland. Sammlung von Telegrammen im Berichtsdoppel aus den Handakten des Herrn Botschafters Juli-Dezember. Sammlung von Aufzeichnungen und Telegrammen aus den Handakten des Herrn Botschafters Februar 1936. Lage in Spanien und deutsche Hilfe.
719	Botschaft Rom (Quirinal), Geheim:	Spanien – Portugal
721	Botschaft Rom (Quirinal) Geheim:	Gespräch Botschafter-Duce mit Sunner. Reise Sunner nach Portugal. Deutsch-spanische Zusammenarbeit in Argentinien.
731	Botschaft Paris :	Entwaffnung Deutschlands
732	Botschaft Paris :	Entwaffnung Deutschlands
824	Botschaft Rom (Quirinal), Geheim:	Vatikan
889	Gesnadtschaft Bukarest, Geheim:	Verschiedenes
895	Gesandtschaft Bukarest, Geheim:	Politisches
902	Gesandtschaft Bukarest, Geheim:	Personalien
903	Gesandtschaft Bukarest, Geheim:	Wirtschaftliches
967	Botschaft Rom (Quirinal), Geheim:	Deutsch-japanisches Abkommen. Chinesisch-japanischer Konflikt. Deutsch-japanisches Antikomintern Abkommen. China – Japan – Konflikt. Angriff auf Hankow. Telegramme und Aufzeichnungen über Unterredung mit japanischem Botschafter Shiratori. Japan und der europäische Krieg. Japanisch-russisches Verhältnis.
978	Botschaft Rom (Quirinal), Geheim:	Japanische Indienpropaganda
1017	Konsulat Triest	Akten
1024	Konsulat Triest	Akten
1025	Konsulat Triest	Akten
1026	Konsulat Triest	Akten

1044	Botschaft Rom (Quirinal), Geheim:	Befürchtungen des Königs von Bulgarien. Unterredung Gesandter v.Plessen mit Gen. Roatta. Russischer Einmarsch in Bessarabien. Aufzeichnung über die Prinzessin von Battenberg. Die Türkei und der Krieg. Italienische Freiwillige für Finnland. Deutsche Transportflugzeuge zum Transport von Wolframerz aus Spanien. Aufstellung eines alliierten Expeditionskorps im östlichen Mittelmeer. Kriegsplan der französischen Regierung für den Osten. Weiterleitung eines Briefes des ehemaligen irischen Gesandten in Berlin Bewley an eine Berliner Adresse. Gen.Kons. Mailand: Schriftstücke. Unterredung Herzog von Alba mit Lord Halifax, betr. Russland. Sonderaudienz des italienischen Gesandten beim König von Dänemark.
1089	Botschaft Brüssel:	Oslo Konvention
1090	Botschaft Brüssel:	Presseabteilung. Beschwerden
1091	Botschaft Brüssel:	Presseabteilung
1094	Gesandtschaft Lissabon:	Konsulat Luanda
1095	Gesandtschaft Lissabon:	Portugiesische Kolonialpolitik
1096	Gesandtschaft Lissabon:	Konsulat Lourenco Marques und Mozambique
1115	Gesandtschaft Lissabon:	Fremde diplomatische und konsularische Vertretungen in Portugal
1116	Gesandtschaft Lissabon:	Deutsch-polnischer Krieg 1939 und dessen Auswirkung auf England und Frankreich
1156	Gesandtschaft Bern:	Geheimakten
1157	Gesandtschaft Bern:	Geheimakten
1175	Gesandtschaft Bern:	Geheimakten
1177	Gesandtschaft Bern:	Geheimakten
1186	Gesandtschaft Bern:	Geheimakten
1192	Gesandtschaft Bern:	Geheimakten
1290	Botschaft Brüssel:	Secreta. Informationsdienst
1307	Botschaft Brüssel:	Secreta.
1308	Botschaft Madrid, Geheim:	Verschiedenes. Quecksilber. Sofindus. Störungskäufe. Projekt Lieferungen für Luftfahrtindustrie. Luftfrachtsonderdienst Wolfram. Handelsvertragsverhandlungen Deutschland-Spanien und andere Länder. Wehrwirtschaftliche Beurteilung Englands und Frankreichs.Getreidelieferungen. Transitverkehr. Deutsche Beteiligung in Spanien. P.P.P./Campsa.Verrechnungspartner mit Spanien.Eigentumsübertragungen und "Orconera". Ausländische Kapitalbeteiligung in Spanien.

1308	Botschaft Madrid, Geheim:	Störungskäufe der Feindmächte, feindliche Firmen. Verschiedenes. Besprechungen mit dem spanischen Handelsminister Carceller. Bernhardt (Sofindus) Zollpolitik Wolfram
1315	Gesandtschaft Bern:	Geheimakten
1330	Gesandtschaft Bern:	Geheimakten
1331	Botschaft Madrid:	Madrid
1333	Botschaft Brüssel:	Secreta
1338	Gesandtschaft Bern:	Geheimakten
1345	Gesandtschaft Bern:	Geheimakten
1348	Gesandtschaft Bern:	Geheimakten
1349	Gesandtschaft Bern:	Geheimakten
1379	Botschaft Moskau, Geheim:	Politische Beziehungen: Sowjet Union-Deutschland
1425	Botschaft Brüssel:	Secreta
1444	Botschaft Brüssel:	Secreta
1447	Botschaft Moskau, Geheim:	Politische Akten
1448	Botschaft Moskau, Geheim:	Politische Akten
1456	Botschaft Brüssel:	Secreta
1496	Botschaft Brüssel:	Secreta
1524	Botschaft Brüssel:	Secreta
1536	Botschaft Moskau:	Allgemeine auswärtige Politik Russlands
1537	Botschaft Moskau:	Allgemeine auswärtige Politik Russlands
1538	Botschaft Moskau:	Allgemeine auswärtige Politik Russlands
1539	Botschaft Moskau:	Allgemeine auswärtige Politik Russlands
1544	Botschaft Brüssel:	Secreta
1559	Botschaft Brüssel:	Deutsche Aussenpolitik, allgemein
1563	Botschaft Moskau:	Politische Beziehungen: Russland - Deutschland
1564	Botschaft Moskau:	Politische Beziehungen: Russland - Deutschland
1565	Botschaft Moskau:	Politische Beziehungen: Russland - Deutschland
1566	Botschaft Moskau:	Politische Beziehungen: Russland - Deutschland
1567	Botschaft Moskau:	Politische Beziehungen: Russland - Deutschland, geheim
1572	Botschaft London, Geheim:	Gespräch zwischen Führer und Sir John Simon 25.März 1935 Presse. Personalia

1587	Botschaft Brüssel:	Propaganda
1589	Botschaft Moskau:	Politische Beziehungen: Sowjet Union - Türkei
1590	Botschaft Moskau:	Politische Beziehungen: Sowjet Union - Türkei
1600	Botschaft Brüssel:	Propaganda
1601	Botschaft Brüssel:	Aussenpolitik Belgiens
1602	Botschaft Brüssel:	Politische Beziehungen: Belgien - Deutschland. Verträge, allgemeines
1630	Botschaft Madrid,Geheim:	Meldungen über Landungsabsichten der Alliierten (Schaffung einer zweiten Front) Landung der Alliierten in West- und Nordafrika
1631	Botschaft Madrid, Geheim:	Entwicklung der allgemeinen Kriegslage
1636	Botschaft Brüssel:	Politische Beziehungen: Deutschland - Frankreich. Berichte Dr. Sieburg
1653	Botschaft Madrid, Geheim:	Illegaler Grenzverkehr (Durchschleusung Wehrfähiger der Feindmächte)
1654	Botschaft Madrid, Geheim:	Illegaler Grenzverkehr (Durchschleusung Wehrfähiger der Feindmächte)
1672	Botschaft Madrid, Geheim:	Seekrieg und seine Auswirkungen auf Spanien
1673	Botschaft Madrid, Geheim:	Seekrieg und seine Auswirkungen auf Spanien
1674	Botschaft Madrid, Geheim:	"Bandalona"
1679	Botschaft Brüssel:	Politische Beziehungen: Deutschland - Frankreich. Berichte Dr. Sieburg
1694	Botschaft Brüssel:	Deutsche Innenpolitik. Militär-, Marine-, Luftfahrtangelegenheiten. Arbeitsdienstpflicht.
1716	Botschaft Paris:	Österreich-Wiedervereinigung
1734	Botschaft Brüssel:	Innenpolitik Belgiens. Ministerien
1740	Botschaft Brüssel:	Militär-, Marine-, und Luftfahrtangelegenheiten
1747	Botschaft Brüssel:	Politische Beziehungen: Belgien - Niederlande
1748	Botschaft Brüssel:	Staatsschutzbestimmungen. Agenten, Spionage, Kommunismus
1791	Botschaft Paris:	Russland
1810	Botschaft Moskau:	Politische Beziehungen: Sowjet Union - Spanien
1811	Botschaft Moskau:	Politische Beziehungen: Sowjet Union - Spanien
1812	Botschaft Moskau:	Politische Beziehungen: Sowjet Union - Tschechoslowakei

1813	Botschaft Moskau:	Politische Beziehungen: Sowjet Union-Tschechoslowakei
1814	Botschaft Moskau:	Politische Beziehungen: Sowjet Union-Südamerika
1819	Botschaft Paris:	Spanien
1841	Botschaft Moskau:	Politische Beziehungen: Deutschland - UdSSR
1842	Botschaft Moskau:	Politische Beziehungen: Deutschland - UdSSR
1843	Botschaft Moskau:	Politische Beziehungen: Deutschland - UdSSR
1844	Botschaft Moskau:	Politische Beziehungen: Deutschland - UdSSR
1865	Generalkonsulat Zürich, Geheim:	Allgemein. Alfred Reutschi
1882	Botschaft Moskau:	Politische Beziehungen: Deutschland - UdSSR
1883	Botschaft Moskau:	Politische Beziehungen: Deutschland - UdSSR
1884	Botschaft Moskau:	Politische Beziehungen: Deutschland - UdSSR
1885	Botschaft Moskau:	Politische Beziehungen: Deutschland - UdSSR
1897	Generalkonsulat Zürich:	Informationen: A - L
1899	Botschaft Madrid:	Falange Espanola. Auswärtige Angelegenheiten
1904	Botschaft Moskau:	Politische Beziehungen: Deutschland - UdSSR
1905	Botschaft Moskau:	Politische Beziehungen: Deutschland - UdSSR
1906	Botschaft Moskau:	Politische Beziehungen: Deutschland - UdSSR
1907	Botschaft Moskau:	Politische Beziehungen: Deutschland - UdSSR
1908	Botschaft Moskau:	Politische Beziehungen: Deutschland - UdSSR
1909	Botschaft Moskau:	Politische Beziehungen: Deutschland - UdSSR
1912	Botschaft Madrid:	Spanisch-französische Beziehungen. Spanisch-russische Beziehungen. Spanischer Volkssturm im Ausland
1913	Generalkonsulat Zürich:	Informationen: M - Z
1931	Botschaft Moskau:	Politische Jahresberichte der Botschaft an das Auswärtige Amt (geheim)

1937	Botschaft Madrid:	Argentinien. Bolivien. Brasilien. Chile. Columbien. Cuba (Dominikanische Republik) Ecuador. Guatemala. Mexiko. Panama. Paraguay. Peru.
1948	Botschaft Paris:	Polen
1961	Botschaft Madrid:	Preispolitik. Olivenöl. Emilio Kiechle. Roubaud. Kriegsgewinnsteuer
1965	Gesandtschaft Bern:	Politische Beziehungen: Deutschland – Türkei
1976	Gesandtschaft Prag:	Politische Beziehungen zu Deutschland
2004	Gesandtschaft Budapest:	Tschechoslowakei; Kleine Entente. Tschechoslowakischer Konflikt; eingehende Telegramme, Erlasse, Berichte, Karpathorussland
2010	Botschaft Madrid:	Geleitscheinwesen, Verbleibskontrolle. Carbonell y Cia de Cordoba, SA. Cordoba; H.Bade & Co., Hamburg. Spanische und deutsche Bezugswünsche innerhalb des normalen Warenverkehrs. Wirtschaftskrieg, Deutsch-italienische Zusammenarbeit
2039	Botschaft Paris:	Italien
2045	Botschaft Madrid:	Kirchen, allgemeines. Deutsch-evangelische Gemeinden in Spanien. Deutsch-evangelische Gemeinde in Madrid
2046	Botschaft Madrid:	Deutsch-evangelische Gemeinde in Madrid
2119	Botschaft Moskau,Geheim:	Handakten Schulenburg (aus verschiedenen Sachgebieten, überwiegend Mai – Juni 1941
2127	Botschaft Rom (Quirinal), Geheim:	Italienisch-jugoslawische Besprechungen. Kriegsschuldforschung Lumbroso. Göring Besuch und Gespräch Österreichischer Gesandter-Göring. Übersendung von Lirenoten. Äusserungen des französischen Generalstabschef Gamelin. Italienische Luftschutzübung. Graf Ciano. Deutsch-italienische Gesellschaft. Übersicht über den Stand der fremden Heere. Englische Einstellung zu französischem Plan einer militärischen Annäherung zwischen Frankreich , Tschechoslowakei, Rumänien und Jugoslawien. Auskunft über Dr.Lorenzo Biseo. Stellungnahme des deutschen Militärattachés in Moskau betr.Trotzkisten-Prozess. Angebliche Äusserung Cianos gegenüber dem jugoslawischen Gesandten Drutchitch. Habsburger Frage. Deutscher Bodenbesitz in Südtirol. Reise Schüllers nach Rom zur Verbesserung der italienisch-österreichischen Wirtschaftsbeziehungen. Dr.Richard Koderle. Englisch-französische Verhandlungen, betr. Belgien. Reise Brumer nach Italien. Unterausschuss für Autarkiefragen der deutsch-italienischen Regierungsausschüsse für Wirtschaftsfragen. Geldaushändigung an Felix Kraus. Südtirol. Korrespondent für "Neuentstehender Welt-Presse-Konzern". Romreise Catroux. Anschrift Reichskanzler a.D. Dr.Wirth.

2127   Botschaft Rom (Quirinal),   Karte der illegalen SA und SS For-
                 Geheim: mationen in Steiermark. Einsetzung
                                         einer Sonderkommission zur Unter-
                                         stützung der Gesetzesveten des li-
                                         tauischen Gouverneurs. Geplanter
                                         Besuch Mussolinis in Deutschland.
                                         Geheime Blattsammlung des Proto-
                                         kolls. Lieferung von Aluminium an
                                         Italien. Aufzeichnung RM von Neurath
                                         über seinen Besuch in Rom und Be-
                                         sprechung mit Mussolini. Zahlung des
                                         VDA an Dr. Wilhelm Witter. Entwick-
                                         lung der italienischen Handelsbilanz.

2128   Botschaft Rom (Quirinal),   Abtretung des Judalandes durch
                 Geheim: Engländer. Errichtung eines Flug-
                                           zeugwerkes in Ostia.Italienisch-
                                         Jugoslawisches Wirtschaftsprotokoll
                                         und Wirtschaftsabkommen. Angebliche
                                         kommunistische Betätigung des ameri-
                                         kanischen Staatsbürgers Schmacke in
                                         Deutschland. Italien und der Chine-
                                         sisch-japanische Konflikt. Zahlung
                                         an Kriminalkommissar Dr.Helmerking.
                                         Beitrag von RM 500.00 für "Italien
                                         Beobachter". Meerengenabkommen von
                                         Montreux. Verhinderung der Durch-
                                         fahrt russischer Transportschiffe.
                                         Flottenstützpunkte. Massnahmen für
                                         die Erzeugung synthetischer Gummis
                                         in Italien. Unterredung Ciano - Ples-
                                         sen über Spanien-Ostasien-England.
                                         Waffenausfuhrverbot. Unterhaltung mit
                                         italienischem Geschäftsträger über
                                         Wirtschaftspolitik im Donauraum.Wett-
                                         bewerb zwischen der deutschen und
                                         italienischen Luftfahrtindustrie.
                                         Italienische Konkurrenz beim Absatz
                                         deutscher Flugzeuge in Portugal.
                                         Deutscher Militärattaché in Rom, auch
                                         für Tirana. Stand der deutsch-belgi-
                                         schen Unterhaltungen betr.die künf-
                                         tige internationale Stellung Belgiens.
                                         Unterredung Greiser-Burckhardt
                                         (Danzig) Zusammenarbeit mit dem ita-
                                         lienischen Tropen Ministerium zur
                                         Störung der kommunistischen Schwarz-
                                         sender. Geheimtelegramme über Spanien.
                                         Deutsch-italienischer Kulturvertrag.
                                         Wehrwirtschaftliche Mobilmachung in
                                         Italien. Besuch Ribbentrop bei Musso-
                                         lini. Vertrag der Reederei Sloman
                                         über spanische Schiffe. Beabsichtigtes
                                         Abkommen anlässlich Besuch Mussolinis.
                                         Wirtschaftliche Vorbereitungen für
                                         einen Krieg, finanzielle Lage. Italie-
                                         nische Goldsendungen nach Deutschland.
                                         Italienisch-englisches Verhältnis:
                                         2 Briefe an Eden betr.Ausgleich.
                                         Ergebnis der ungarisch-italienischen
                                         Wirtschaftsverhandlungen. Bewaffnung
                                         rotspanischer Handelsschiffe.Schritte
                                         des italienischen Botschafters in
                                         Ankara. Unterredung Hitler-Halifax.
                                         Austritt Italiens aus dem Völkerbund.
                                         Deutsch-italienische Wirtschaftsver-
                                         handlungen. Besuch von Zeelands in
                                         Italien. Tätigkeit des Herzogs von
                                         Alba in England.

2129	Botschaft Rom (Quirinal), Geheim:	Für 1938: Spanischer Bürgerkrieg. Anschluss Österreichs. Südtirol. Kriegsvorbereitungen. Englisch-französische Militär- und Ministerbesprechungen. Wehrwirtschaftliche Vorbereitungen. Polnisch-litauischer Konflikt. Sudetendeutschland. Tschechoslowakei. China-Japan Konflikt. Deutsch-italienische Generalstabsbesprechungen. Antikominternpakt. (pp.639-44)
2130	Botschaft Rom (Quirinal), Geheim:	Für 1939: Spanien. Tschechoslowakei. Chamberlain in Rom. Südtirol. Mobilmachung.Aufforderung Spaniens und Mandschukuos zum Beitritt in Antikominternpakt. Besetzung Böhmens und Mährens. Albanien. Göring in San Remo. Pius XII. Danzig. Paktverhandlungen mit der Sowjet Union. Ungarn. (pp.644-48)
2131	Botschaft Rom (Quirinal), Geheim:	Für 1939: Deutsch-russische Verhandlungen.Ciano in Fuschl. Militär-, Luft- und Marineangelegenheiten. Spaniens Haltung gegenüber Polen.Grünspan Prozess. Amanullah von Afghanistan. Russisches Vorgehen gegen Bessarabien. Englisch-französische Propaganda. Rohstoffe für Deutschland über Italien. Griechische Schiffe für Feindmächte. Eintritt Englands in den Krieg. Balkanblock. Kohle für Italien. Spanische Handelsschiffe nach neutralen Ländern. Italienisches Kriegsmaterial für Frankreich. Russlands Stellung zur Türkei. Finnisch-russische Auseinandersetzung. Italienische Flugzeuglieferungen an Frankreich und Finnland. (pp.649-53)
2144	Botschaft Brüssel:	Deutsche Aussenpolitik, allgemein
2157	Botschaft Rom (Quirinal), Geheim:	Türkei-Bulgarien-Balkan
2158	Botschaft Rom (Quirinal), Geheim:	Innere Lage. Sammelsachen. Politische Beziehungen: Deutschland zu Frankreich, Italien, Österreich, Ungarn, Polen, Russland, Tschechoslowakei
2194	Botschaft Rom (Quirinal), Geheim:	Italiens Beziehungen zu Frankreich, England, Österreich, Jugoslawien, Russland, Albanien, Tschechoslowakei, Vereinigte Staaten, Spanien, Türkei
2218	Botschaft Rom (Quirinal), Geheim:	Politische Beziehungen: Frankreich - Russland, besonders Ostpaktfrage. England
2243	Botschaft Rom (Quirinal), Geheim:	Italiens Beziehungen zu: Kleine Entente Tschechoslowakei, Jugoslawien, Rumänien.Politische Beziehungen: Schweiz - Frankreich.Unabhängigkeit Österreichs. Donau Problem. Ungarn
2265	Botschaft Rom (Quirinal), Geheim:	Finnland. Alandfrage. Randstaaten. Memel und Litauen. Polen. Danzig.

2266	Botschaft Rom (Quirinal), Geheim:	Tanger-Algeciras Akte. Ägypten. Abessinien. China, Ostasien.
2273	Botschaft Paris, Geheim:	Ereignisse August 1939

2281   Botschaft Rom (Quirinal), Geheim:

Für 1940: Ungarn. Rumänien. Bulgarien. Russland. Balkan. Norwegen. Türkei. Brasilien. Sumner Welles Europareise. Italien. Englisch-französische Ausfuhrblockade. Finnisch-russischer Konflikt. Amerikanischer Journalist Wiegand. Ex-König Alfonso XIII. Graf Teleki in Rom. Jugoslawien. Belgien. Iran. Augur Poliakow. Italienisch-russische Beziehungen. Begegnung Führer-Duce. Ostasien. Militärische Operationen in Norwegen. Pfitzner, Prag. Eintritt Italiens in den Krieg. USA Lieferungssperre Russland.
Für 1941: Begegnung Führer-Duce. Südtirol. Ciano. Innerpolitische Lage in England. Raeder in Italien. Deutsch-italienische Offizierskommission in Siebenbürgen. Jugoslawische Staatsmänner in Fuschl. Türkei-Dodekanes. Rundfunkangelegenheiten. Handstreich auf Nizza. Deutschland-Norwegen, Skandinavien. Reise Grobba nach Bagdad. Organisation der faschistischen Miliz. Deutsch-russischer Krieg. Mussolini. Tschechische Legion in Frankreich. Zuständigkeitsgrundsätze für AA und Promi. Sonderkurier. Unterredung des amerikanischen Botschafters mit dem Papst. Verlängerung des Antikominternpaktes. Grossmufti. NSDAP/AO. Behandlung amerikanischer Kriegsgefangener in Libyen. Pressetelegramme. Deutsch-russisches Verhältnis. Griechenland und die Achse. Ciano in Berlin. Waffenstillstand mit Frankreich. Iran-Sowjet Union. Französisch-spanische Zonengrenze. Italiens Absichten im Mittelmeer und Balkan. Lage in französisch Marokko. Balkan. Türkisch-britisch-französischer Beistandspakt. Zita von Habsburg. Vorschläge des Grossmufti. Äquatorial und Nordafrika. Wiener Schiedsspruch. Lage in Irak. Deutsche Militärkommission Rumänien. Pannwitz, Pfeiffer. Italien-Griechenland. Antonescu in Rom. Treffen Führer-Laval, Pétain, Franco, Duce. Italienische Flugzeuge in Flandern, Italienische Kriegführung. RAM-Montri. Prinz von Hessen. Deutsch-italienische militärische Zusammenarbeit. Italien - Russland (pp.661-94; auch ser.nrs.: 3039, 4865, 2366, 3090, 4104, 4459, 4421, 4241, 9863)

2290   Botschaft Rom (Quirinal), Geheim:

Deutsch-polnischer Konflikt. Telegramme. Englisch-französischer Krieg gegen Deutschland; Informationstelegramme und Schriftwechsel, betr.Presse. Handelsangelegenheiten

2318   Botschaft Paris:

Politische Beziehungen: Deutschland - Frankreich, Verhältnis Pétain-Laval, internierte Minister: Reynaud, Mandel, Blum. Innenpolitik Frankreich, allgemein

2335	Botschaft Paris:	Militär-, Marine- und Luftfahrtan-gelegenheiten. Groupe Collaboration
2342	Botschaft Madrid, Geheim:	Illegaler Grenzverkehr (Durch-schleusung Wehrfähiger der Feind-mächte)
2343	Botschaft Madrid, Geheim:	Illegaler Grenzverkehr (Durch-schleusung Wehrfähiger der Feind-mächte)
2346	Botschaft Paris:	Parteiwesen. Politische Verbände. Comité Ouvrier de Secoure Immediat.
2361	Botschaft Ankara:	Geheime Erlasse, Berichte, Tele-gramme. Rüstungsindustrie.
2366	Botschaft Rom (Quirinal), Geheim:	Beitritt Ungarns zum Dreimächte-pakt
2371	Botschaft Paris:	Danzig
2402	Generalkonsulat Zürich:	Krieg 1939/40. Geheimakten,allgemein
2455	Botschaft Paris:	Kassensachen, allgemein; Voran-schläge. Kassenordnung, Kassenfüh-rung. Beschaffung von Betriebsmit-teln (Fonds). Abrechnung Kult-R, Rundfunk und Presse. Löhne, Gehäl-ter, Zahlungslisten
2456	Botschaft Paris:	Aufenthaltsbestimmungen, Sichtver-merke. Berichtsammlung, Auswärtiges Amt. Sammlung Schwendemann
2469	Botschaft Paris:	Auswärtige Angelegenheiten
2484	Botschaft Paris:	Kolonien
2485	Botschaft Paris:	Deutsch-französische Wirtschafts-politik, Handelsvertragsverhand-lungen
2492	Botschaft Moskau, Geheim:	Politische Beziehungen: Sowjet Union-Nordische Staaten (Finnland, Schwe-den, Norwegen, Dänemark) Aalandfrage, Finnische Inseln
2493	Botschaft Paris:	Französische Presse
2494	Botschaft Moskau, Geheim:	Politische Beziehungen: Sowjet Union-Polen (Ukraine Frage, Russisch Polen)
2504	Gesandtschaft Kopenhagen:	Besatzungskosten
2505	Gesandtschaft Kopenhagen:	Winterschule für Nordschleswig
2533	Botschaft Moskau, Geheim:	Politische Beziehungen: Deutschland-Ungarn und Slowakei
2536	Botschaft Paris:	Innere Angelegenheiten
2537	Botschaft Paris:	Beziehungen zu Italien
2543	Botschaft Paris:	Monatsberichte
2594	Botschaft Paris:	Innere Angelegenheiten
2623	Botschaft Paris:	Rahn. Cinepress

2624	Botschaft Paris, Geheim:	Beziehungen: Frankreich-Deutschland
2654	Botschaft Paris:	Spanien
2655	Botschaft Paris:	Spanien
2667	Botschaft Madrid:	Frankreich
2670	Botschaft Paris, Geheim:	Beziehungen: Frankreich-Deutschland
2685	Botschaft Madrid, Geheim:	Sudetendeutsche Frage und mittel-europäische Krise
2695	Gesandtschaft Kopenhagen:	Konterbande (Prisenordnung)
2697	Gesandtschaft Kopenhagen:	Kreditinstitut Vogelsang
2698	Gesandtschaft Kopenhagen:	Pastor Schmidt-Wodder und Cornelius Petersens Bendestyre Bergung
2699	Gesandtschaft Kopenhagen:	Minderheiten und Schulfragen
2700	Gesandtschaft Kopenhagen:	Minderheiten und Schulfragen
2701	Gesandtschaft Kopenhagen:	Politische Agenten; vertrauliche Auskünfte über Personen
2702	Gesandtschaft Kopenhagen:	Nordschleswig
2703	Gesandtschaft Kopenhagen:	Nordschleswig
2704	Gesandtschaft Kopenhagen:	Deutsch-dänische Verhandlungen
2724	Botschaft Paris, Geheim:	Beziehungen: Frankreich-Deutschland
2748	Gesandtschaft Kopenhagen:	Deutsche Zeitungen in Nordschleswig; deutsche Einheitszeitung
2763	Botschaft Moskau, Geheim:	Politische Beziehungen: Deutschland-andere Staaten. Krieg mit Polen
2772	Botschaft Madrid:	England (auch Dominien)
2789	Botschaft Ankara:	Politische Beziehungen zu Deutschland; deutsche Militär-, Luft- und Marine-attachés (persönliches), Chiffretele-gramme in geheimen Kommandosachen. Militär- und Marineangelegenheiten
2801	Botschaft Moskau, Geheim:	Politische Beziehungen: Sowjet Union-Spanien (Gefangenenaustausch). Sonderakten Abteilung D.
2806	Botschaft Madrid:	Frankreich
2807	Botschaft Paris:	Politische Beziehungen: Deutschland-Frankreich
2808	Botschaft Paris:	Innere Angelegenheiten
2819	Botschaft Paris:	Protektorat Böhmen und Mähren
2830	Botschaft Moskau, Geheim:	Presse und Propagandawesen in Deutschland, allgemeines
2841	Botschaft Brüssel:	Presseabteilung
2845	Botschaft Brüssel:	Secreta
2847	Botschaft Brüssel:	Parteiwesen. Politische Verbände
2852	Gesandtschaft Haag	Aussenpolitik

2854	Gesandtschaft Haag:	Nationalsozialistische Bewegung in den Niederlanden
2856	Botschaft Brüssel:	Aussenpolitik Belgiens
2863	Gesandtschaft Luxemburg:	Luxemburgs Eintritt in den Völkerbund, Neutralitätsfragen
2864	Gesandtschaft Luxemburg:	Luxemburgs Eintritt in den Völkerbund, Neutralitätsfragen
2865	Gesandtschaft Luxemburg:	Luftschutz in Luxemburg
2866	Gesandtschaft Luxemburg:	Französisch-sowjetrussischer Beistandspakt und Militärisierung der Rheinlandzone
2867	Gesandtschaft Luxemburg:	Konferenz der Neutralen
2868	Gesandtschaft Luxemburg:	Luxemburgische Regierung: Personalien, Innenpolitik
2869	Gesandtschaft Luxemburg:	Internierte, Deserteure
2870	Gesandtschaft Luxemburg:	Luxemburg, "Moderne Garantien"
2872	Gesandtschaft Luxemburg:	Erzlieferungen
2876	Gesandtschaft Luxemburg:	Dienstanweisungen für Auslandsvertretungen, Telegramme
2878	Gesandtschaft Luxemburg:	NSDAP Landesgruppe Luxemburg, allgemein
2879	Gesandtschaft Luxemburg:	Politische Beziehungen: Luxemburg-Belgien-Frankreich
2884	Botschaft Warschau:	Beziehungen: Polen-Frankreich
2885	Gesandtschaft Haag:	Deutschland: Kolonialpolitik
2888	Botschaft Warschau:	Politik: Frankreich
2889	Botschaft Warschau:	Politik: Holland
2890	Botschaft Warschau:	Politik: Schweiz
2892	Botschaft Warschau:	Auflösung der Tschechoslowakei
2906	Botschaft Warschau, Geheim:	Karteisachen - Geheim
2908	Botschaft Warschau:	Politische Berichte
2913	Gesandtschaft Stockholm:	England: Innen- und Aussenpolitik
2917	Botschaft Warschau, Geheim:	K.-Geheim, Kult
2918	Botschaft Warschau, Geheim:	H.-Geheim, Wirtschaft
2922	Botschaft Moskau, Geheim:	Deutsche Innenpolitik: Protektorat Böhmen und Mähren
2927	Botschaft Warschau, Geheim:	Geheime Reichssachen
2932	Botschaft Paris, Geheim	Beziehungen: Frankreich-Deutschland, Gesuche
2936	Gesandtschaft Lissabon:	Politik fremder Staaten
2937	Gesandtschaft Lissabon:	Spanien, spanischer Bürgerkrieg, Nichteinmischung, Aufbau

2939	Botschaft Paris, Geheim:	Beziehungen: Frankreich-Deutschland, Gesuche
2940	Botschaft Paris, Geheim:	Beziehungen: Frankreich-Deutschland, Gesuche
2941	Gesandtschaft Kopenhagen:	Völkerbund
2941	Botschaft Paris:	Spanien
2942	Gesandtschaft Lissabon:	Politische Beziehungen: Deutschland-Portugal
2946	Botschaft Madrid, Geheim:	Montana
2947	Botschaft Madrid, Geheim:	Handakten Kanzler; Pressepolitik und Propaganda
2948	Botschaft Madrid, Geheim:	Legion Condor
2949	Gesandtschaft Lissabon:	Portugiesische Aussenpolitik, allgemein
2953	Gesandtschaft Oslo:	Besetzung Norwegens, geheim
2960	Botschaft Madrid:	Frankreich
2969	Gesandtschaft Oslo:	Besetzung Norwegens, Okkupationspolitik
2970	Gesandtschaft Oslo:	Geheimer Pressefonds
2972	Gesandtschaft Oslo:	Geheime Reichssachen, Einzelfälle
2973	Gesandtschaft Oslo:	Dr. U.Noack
2974	Gesandtschaft Oslo:	Verschiedenes
2975	Gesandtschaft Oslo:	Geheimakten
2976	Gesandtschaft Oslo:	Filmwesen und -vermittlung
2977	Gesandtschaft Oslo:	Attachés
2982	Gesandtschaft Oslo:	Wochenberichte
2983	Gesandtschaft Oslo:	Propaganda
2985	Botschaft Paris, Geheim:	Häftlinge
3007	Gesandtschaft Oslo:	"City of Flint"
3014	Gesandtschaft Zagreb, Geheim:	Geheime Reichssachen
3025	Botschaft Madrid, Geheim:	Entwicklung der allgemeinen Kriegslage
3027	Botschaft Madrid:	Ursachen des Krieges, Vorgeschichte, Schuldfrage. Weissbücher. Kriegserklärung. Kriegseintritt. Stand des Kampfes, Aussichten 1939. Wirtschaft, Kriegswirtschaft. England und Frankreich, Beistandspflicht gegen Polen. Kriegsakten, ausgezeichnet. Ziele, Massnahmen, Methoden der feindlichen Kriegsführung (Blockade). Kriegshandlungen der Feindstaaten, Neutralitätsbrüche. Feindliche Kriegspropaganda, Pressehetze. Haltung der Neutralen (ausser Spanien,USA,Russland, Italien). Konferenz der Oslo Staaten

3038	Botschaft Paris, Geheim:	Politische Beziehungen: Frankreich - andere Staaten
3050	Botschaft Madrid:	England (auch Dominien)
3066	Botschaft Moskau, Geheim:	Politische Beziehungen: Deutschland - andere Staaten. Krieg mit Polen
3073	Gesandtschaft Oslo:	Friedensbestrebungen
3074	Gesandtschaft Oslo:	Vercharterung norwegischen Schiffsraums
3075	Gesandtschaft Oslo:	Norwegische Neutralitätspolitik
3076	Gesandtschaft Oslo:	Überfall des M/S " Altmark "
3077	Gesandtschaft Oslo:	Respektierung norwegischer Hoheitsgewässer
3078	Gesandtschaft Oslo:	Englische Neutralitätsverletzungen in den norwegischen Hoheitsgewässern
3079	Gesandtschaft Oslo:	U 21
3080	Gesandtschaft Oslo:	Besetzung Norwegens, Okkupationsverwaltung
3081	Gesandtschaft Oslo:	Besetzung Norwegens, Okkupation, Militär
3084	Gesandtschaft Lissabon:	Geheimakten: Lage in England
3089	Botschaft Paris, Geheim:	Irland. England
3090	Botschaft Rom (Quirinal), Geheim:	Lage und Stimmung in England. Innenpolitische Lage in England. Spionage, Agenten.
3091	Gesandtschaft Oslo:	England, Frankreich, Italien, Irland, Portugal, Schweiz, Spanien
3095	Botschaft Rom Vatikan:	Irland
3099	Botschaft Rom Vatikan:	England
3102	Gesandtschaft Athen:	Englisch-griechische Wirtschaftsverhandlungen 1940
3103	Botschaft Ankara	England
3104	Botschaft Rom (Quirinal):	England
3105	Botschaft Paris:	Rundfunkreferat. Verhandlungen mit der französischen Regierung. Radio-Diffusion National. Radio-Paris. Funkspiegel. Ru-Mitarbeiter
3106	Botschaft Paris, Geheim:	Diplomatische und konsularische Vertretungen Frankreichs und anderer Staaten
3108	Gesandtschaft Prag:	Konsulat Reichenberg. Konsulat Eger. Sonstiges. Geheime Zahlungen. Schutz deutscher Reichsangehöriger. Aussenpolitik. Politische Beziehungen zu Deutschland
3109	Gesandtschaft Prag:	Innenpolitik.Abtretung des sudetendeutschen Gebietes. Präsident der Republik. Kabinett. Präsident Masaryk.

3109	Gesandtschaft Prag:	Innenpolitik, Verwaltung, Gesetzgebung. Sudetendeutsche Heimatfront (Henlein). Auseinandersetzung in der SDP. Nationalitätsfragen, allgemein. Lage des Sudetendeutschtums in der CSR. Deutsches Landestheater. Armeespionage.
3110	Gesandtschaft Prag:	Armee, Militärvorbereitungen. Presse, Rundfunk. Kunst, Film, Sport. Auskünfte über Personen. Fälschungen von Bezugsscheinen über Margarine (geheim). Agenten. Kommunisten. Tschechische Schulen in Deutschland, allgemein. Protektorat Böhmen, Mähren (Militärische Besatzungs- und Flüchtlingsfragen, Verhaftungen) Deutschland - Tschechoslowakei. Reichsregierung. Kulturelle Einrichtungen in Deutschland, Alexander von Humboldt-Stiftung. Kongresse, Tagungen.
3112	Botschaft Paris:	Geheime Akten
3114	Generalkonsulat Tirana:	Tschechoslowakei; Protektorat Böhmen-Mähren
3114	Botschaft Rom (Quirinal), Geheim:	Politische Beziehungen: Deutschland - Tschechoslowakei
3114	Botschaft Paris:	Protektorat Böhmen und Mähren. Slowakei. Kleine Entente
3115	Gesandtschaft Pressburg:	Kirchenwesen. Waffen SS. Slowakei: Aussenpolitik. Dr.Tuka. Kleine Entente. Balkankonferenz. Kroatien. Rumänien. Vatikan. Deutschland. Politische Beziehungen: Slowakei-Ungarn. Slowakei: Innenpolitik. Sidor. Dr.Klinovsky. Staatspräsidentenwahl. Marine, Luftfahrt, Militär, Arbeitsdienst. Hoheitszeichen. Wahlen. Parteien. Tschechische Restaurationsbestrebungen, Benesch, Masaryk. Liquidierung tschechischen Vermögens. Deutsche Aussenpolitik. Umsiedlung deutscher Volksgruppen.
3117	Botschaft Rom (Quirinal):	Zusammenkunft Mussolini-Hitler in Venedig, Sonderband
3120	Botschaft Paris, Geheim:	Französische Regierung, Zusammensetzung der Kabinette, Übersiedlung nach Versailles
3121	Botschaft Paris, Geheim:	Französische Persönlichkeiten
3122	Gesandtschaft Belgrad:	Politische Beziehungen und Verträge Jugoslawiens und Deutschland zu Polen, Slowakei, Protektorat. Übernahme der ehemaligen tschechoslowakischen Gesandtschaft.
3122	Gesandtschaft Bern:	Übernahme des Protektorats über die Tschechei. Tschechische Mappe, Einzelfälle.
3122	Gesandtschaft Stockholm:	Tschechoslowakei: Innen- und Aussenpolitik
3122	Gesandtschaft Riga:	Protektorat Böhmen-Mähren
3122	Gesandtschaft Haag:	Protektorat Böhmen und Mähren; Slowakei.

3175   Botschaft Rom (Quirinal),
                   Geheim:

Englische Kriegsvorbereitungen. Umgruppierung in Österreich: Aussprache Papen-Starhemberg. Reise Schuschnigg nach Prag. Aufzeichnung Unterredung Führer-Botschafter. Briefwechsel Renthe-Fink/Lotscher über Verhältnis Russland-Italien, Deutschland-Österreich. Bericht des Militärattachés. Freimaurerei. Politische Lage, Äusserungen Balbos. Rückberufung Badoglios. Unterredung Botschafter - Chamhun. Besuch Unterstaatssekretär Ricci. Telegramm Badoglios über Lazar in Abessinien. Unterredung Chamhun - Luvich. Unterredung mit Mussolini über allgemeine Lage. Türkische Luftrüstung. Italien zum Locarno- und Russenpakt. Engl.-soz.Militärabmachungen. Deutschfeindliche Haltung Ceruttis. Österreichfrage. Unterredung Botschafter-japan. Botschafter. Memorandum betr. Locarnokündigung. Besprechung über tschechisch-russisches Militärbündnis. VI.Internationaler Gemeindekongress. Postchiffre, österreichische Wehrpflichtmeldung, mil.Aktion aus Prag. Bildstreifen "Standschütze Bruggler". Dienstpflicht in Österreich. Schulunterricht in Südtirol. Angebliche italienische Bereitschaft zu Generalstabsbesprechungen mit Frankreich. Chilenischer Antrag zur Aufhebung der Sanktionen. Abessinische Eingeborene für Kolonial-Armee. Auslands-Pressebüro. Beziehungen zwischen Italien und Sowjet-Russland. Vorschläge der Vertreter der Rest-Locarno-Mächte. Truppensammlungen in Südtirol. Besuch einer italienischen Wehrmachtsabteilung in Berlin. Unterredung Surich - Sowjetbotschafter Stein. Zusammenziehung italienischer Truppen. Argentinischer Antrag auf Einberufung Völkerbundsversammlung. Unterredung Krofta - österreichischem Gesandten Marek. Bericht über Lage in Frankreich. Gegenbesuch der deutschen Militärabordnung in Italien. Aufzeichnung über Besprechung Botschafter - Mussolini. Geheime Abmachung Türkei - Sowjetrussland betr.Sicherung der Dardanellen. Deutsch-österreichische Verständigung. Zusammenstellung über Auslandsverschuldung Deutschlands. Entwicklung des Rundfunks im Ausland. Militärische Lage in Abessinien. Anlaufen von fremden Häfen deutscher Kriegsschiffe. Übernahme der Parteiakten in die Botschaft. Brief RM Goebbels an Alfieri. Waffenlieferungen nach Spanien. Richtlinien für Kriegsgerätegeschäfte. Französische und türkische Besprechungen laut Mitteilung des ungarischen Geschäftsträgers in Berlin. Lage in Danzig. Lage in Südtirol und Wünsche der Südtiroler. Italien unterstützt Wünsche Polens und Griechenlands um Aufnahme in Donaukommission. Ausbau des Wirtschaftsdienstes der deutschen Auslandsvertretungen. Angaben über Aufrüstung der wichtigsten Mächte.

3175	Botschaft Rom (Quirinal), Geheim:	Protokoll über Besuch Ciano in Berlin. Aufzeichnung des RAM über Besuch Ciano. Danziger Frage. Anerkennung Mandschukuos durch Italien. Revision der Donau Akte. Stellung der autoritären Regierung Metaxas. Verbal Noten der tschechoslowakischen und jugoslawischen Gesandten in Paris, betr.Ergebnis der Pressburger Tagung der Kleinen Entente. Berliner Besprechung mit dem österreichischen Staatssekretär Dr.G. Schmidt; deutsch-österreichisches Verhältnis. Italienisch-englisches Abkommen. Besuch Herzog von Aosta beim deutschen Botschafter. Waffenlieferung Italiens an Portugal.
3202	Botschaft Madrid, Geheim:	Lieferungen deutschen Kriegsgerätes
3203	Botschaft Madrid, Geheim:	Antikominternpakt, Verlängerung, Reise Serrano Suner nach Berlin
3206	Botschaft Paris:	Spanien
3207	Botschaft Madrid:	Nationale Erhebung
3228	Generalkonsulat San Franzisko:	Deutsche Minderheiten; Minderheitenfragen
3229	Generalkonsulat San Franzisko:	Seemannsamt; Explosion auf der "Vancouver"
3248	Botschaft Paris, Geheim:	Fanzösische Vereine, Versammlungen, Veranstaltungen, Genehmigungen
3369	Gesandtschaft Lissabon:	Spanien: Nichteinmischungspakt, Waffenembargo, Freiwilligenfrage
3371	Gesandtschaft Lissabon:	Waffenlieferung an Spanien 1936
3372	Botschaft Madrid:	Nichtinterventionspolitik
3376	Botschaft Madrid:	Marokko
3426	Botschaft Moskau, Geheim:	Politische Beziehungen: Sowjet Union-Nordische Staaten (Finnland, Schweden, Norwegen, Dänemark) Aalandfrage, Finnische Inseln.
3467	Gesandtschaft Lissabon:	Spanien: Nichteinmischungspakt, Waffenembargo, Freiwilligenfrage
3468	Botschaft Madrid:	Nichtinterventionspolitik
3485	Botschaft Paris, Geheim:	Beziehungen: Frankreich-Deutschland
3503	Gesandtschaft Stockholm:	Deutschtum im Ausland
3504	Gesandtschaft Stockholm:	Schweden: Innen- und Aussenpolitik
3505	Gesandtschaft Stockholm:	Behinderung neutraler Schiffe durch Engländer und Franzosen
3506	Gesandtschaft Stockholm:	Geschäftsgang
3507	Gesandtschaft Stockholm:	Propaganda, verschiedenes
3508	Gesandtschaft Stockholm:	Deutsche Kulturarbeit im Ausland
3509	Gesandtschaft Stockholm:	Katholische Kirche in Schweden

3510	Gesandtschaft Stockholm:	Pressepropagandistischer Fonds
3511	Gesandtschaft Stockholm:	Svensk-Tyska-Foreningen, Sockholm
3512	Gesandtschaft Stockholm:	Schweden: Parteiwesen, politische Verbände
3513	Gesandtschaft Stockholm:	Schweden: Innen- und Aussenpolitik
3514	Gesandtschaft Stockholm:	Schweden: Innen- und Aussenpolitik
3515	Gesandtschaft Stockholm:	Kirchenangelegenheiten, verschiedenes
3516	Gesandtschaft Stockholm:	Nordische Gesellschaft
3517	Gesandtschaft Stockholm:	Skandinavien: Innen- und Aussenpolitik
3521	Botschaft Paris:	Politische Beziehungen zu Deutschland
3522	Botschaft Paris:	Politische Beziehungen: Frankreich - England
3523	Botschaft Paris:	Verhältnis Pétain-Laval
3545	Botschaft Paris:	Besuch Dr. Schacht
3546	Botschaft Paris:	Politische Beziehungen: Deutschland - Frankreich
3547	Botschaft Paris:	Presse, geheim
3548	Botschaft Paris, Geheim:	Beziehungen: Deutschland - USA
3550	Botschaft Paris:	Donauproblem
3551	Botschaft Paris:	Innenpolitik Frankreich, allgemein
3562	Botschaft Ankara:	Geheime Erlasse, Berichte, Telegramme
3578	Botschaft Ankara:	Geheime und streng geheime Erlasse, Berichte, Telegramme
3590	Botschaft Moskau, Geheim:	Politische Beziehungen: Sowjet Union - Deutschland
3597	Botschaft Paris, Geheim:	Lageberichte über Nordafrika und Besetzung Frankreichs durch Achsentruppen
3599	Botschaft Paris, Geheim:	Algerien und Marokko
3613	Botschaft Ankara:	Geheime und streng geheime Erlasse, Berichte, Telegramme
3614	Botschaft Ankara:	Geheime und streng geheime Erlasse, Berichte, Telegramme
3616	Botschaft Paris, Geheim:	Antillen
3624	Botschaft Paris, Geheim:	Französisch Nordafrika
3626	Gesandtschaft Budapest:	Geheimsachen
3633	Botschaft Paris, Geheim:	Politische Beziehungen: Frankreich - Italien
3636	Botschaft Ankara:	Geheime und streng geheime Erlasse, Berichte, Telegramme

3637	Botschaft Ankara:	Geheime una streng geheime Erlasse, Berichte, Telegramme
3645	Gesandtschaft Kowno:	Politische Beziehungen: Litauen - Deutschland
3647	Gesandtschaft Belgrad:	Politisches, geheim
3649	Botschaft Paris, Geheim:	Beziehungen: Frankreich-Deutschland, Gesuche
3652	Botschaft Paris, Geheim:	Besetzung Frankreichs
3660	Gesandtschaft Oslo:	Luftverkehr, Sperrballons, deutsche Flugzeuge
3661	Gesandtschaft Oslo:	Schiffahrtssachverständige in Norwegen
3662	Gesandtschaft Oslo:	Verletzung norwegischer Neutralität durch Flugzeuge
3663	Gesandtschaft Oslo:	Vercharterung norwegischen Schiffs- raums
3664	Gesandtschaft Oslo:	Besetzung Norwegens, Okkupations- politik
3668	Gesandtschaft Oslo:	Englische Neutralitätsverletzungen in den norwegischen Hoheitsgewässern
3676	Gesandtschaft Oslo:	Seekriegsführung
3677	Gesandtschaft Oslo:	Friedensbestrebungen
3681	Botschaft Paris, Geheim:	Persönlichkeiten
3686	Gesandtschaft Oslo:	Respektierung norwegischer Hoheits- gewässer
3687	Gesandtschaft Oslo:	Überfall des M/S "Altmark"
3697	Botschaft Paris, Geheim:	Waffenstillstandskommission (Wako)
3698	Botschaft Paris, Geheim:	Politische Beziehungen: Frankreich - andere Staaten
3699	Botschaft Paris, Geheim:	Französische Regierung, Zusammenset- zung der Kabinette, Übersiedlung nach Versailles
3701	Gesandtschaft Prag:	Beziehungen zu Russland
3702	Botschaft Paris, Geheim:	Beziehungen: Deutschland - UdSSR
3704	Gesandtschaft Oslo:	Geheime Pressefonds
3705	Gesandtschaft Oslo:	Propagandafonds
3706	Gesandtschaft Oslo:	Norwegische Neutralitätspolitik
3709	Gesandtschaft Bukarest:	Deutschlands Aussenpolitik: Ost- und Westpakt
3710	Gesandtschaft Bukarest:	Geheimakten: Militärisches
3711	Gesandtschaft Bukarest:	Geheimakten: Minderheiten
3712	Gesandtschaft Bukarest:	Geheimakten: Verwaltungsorganisation

3713	Botschaft Paris:	Reisen ausländischer Journalisten: Europa
3714	Botschaft Paris:	Reisen ausländischer Journalisten: Europa
3715	Gesandtschaft Bukarest:	Politische Beziehungen: Deutschland – Rumänien
3717	Gesandtschaft Belgrad:	Wirtschaftliches, geheim
3735	Gesandtschaft Oslo:	Vertreter des Auswärtigen Amtes beim Reichskommissar
3740	Gesandtschaft Oslo:	Gehaltszahlungen an Landeskreisleiter der NSDAP, Pg. Spanaus
3741	Gesandtschaft Oslo:	Geheime Verschlussachen
3742	Gesandtschaft Oslo:	Besprechungen mit den Konsuln
3743	Gesandtschaft Oslo:	Abwicklung der Geschäfte
3745	Gesandtschaft Oslo:	Filmwesen und -vermittlung
3746	Gesandtschaft Oslo:	Besetzung Norwegens, Okkupations- verwaltung
3747	Gesandtschaft Oslo:	Nordische Gesellschaft
3748	Botschaft Paris, Geheim:	Juden und Freimaurer in Frankreich
3758	Botschaft Paris, Geheim:	Der Militärbefehlshaber in Frankreich
3760	Botschaft Paris, Geheim:	Der höhere SS und Polizeiführer in Frankreich
3761	Botschaft Paris, Geheim:	Der Befehlshaber der Sicherheits- polizei und des SD in Frankreich
3764	Gesandtschaft Bukarest:	Deutschlands Aussenpolitik: Ost- und Westpakt
3766	Gesandtschaft Oslo:	Besetzung Norwegens, Okkupation, militär.
3767	Gesandtschaft Sofia:	Ein- und Ausfuhr von Kriegsgerät, Aufrüstung Bulgariens, Waffenlie- ferungen; Geheimakten
3774	Gesandtschaft Sofia, Geheim:	Akten. Lose A-Akten
3775	Gesandtschaft Sofia:	Politische Beziehungen:Bulgarien – Deutschland
3779	Gesandtschaft Oslo:	Gesandter
3780	Botschaft Paris, Geheim:	Kampf gegen Kommunisten
3789	Botschaft Paris:	Arbeiterfragen, allgemein. Sammlung von ein- und ausgehenden Telegrammen. Sammlung Schwendemann
3790	Botschaft Paris, Geheim:	Frankreich: Innere Verhältnisse
3793	Botschaft Rom (Quirinal):	Deutsch-italienische Beziehungen, allgemein
3796	Botschaft Paris:	Judenfrage

3797	Botschaft Paris:	Militär-, Marine-und Luftfahrtangelegenheiten
3799	Gesandtschaft Oslo:	Gesandter
3813	Botschaft Paris:	Anwerbung französischer Arbeitskräfte für Deutschland
3814	Botschaft Paris:	Groupe Collaboration
3821	Botschaft Paris, Geheim:	Französisches Gewerksschaftswesen, Sozialpolitik, französische Arbeiter in Deutschland
3833	Botschaft Paris, Geheim:	Frankreich: Aussenpolitik
3835	Gesandtschaft Bern:	Schweiz, allgemeines
3837	Gesandtschaft Bern:	Politische Beziehungen: Deutschland - Frankreich
3839	Botschaft Paris, Geheim:	Deutsche Waffenstillstandskommission in Wiesbaden, deutsche Waffenstillstandskommission für Wirtschaft
3841	Gesandtschaft Bern:	Völkerbund. Deutschland und der Völkerbund
3842	Gesandtschaft Bern:	Beziehungen zu Deutschland
3843	Botschaft Paris, Geheim:	Demarkationslinie, Rhonelinie
3844	Botschaft Paris:	Geheime Akten
3847	Botschaft Madrid, Geheim:	Ladung des französischen Dampfers San Diego, Bilbao
3848	Botschaft Madrid, Geheim:	Übergabe Mercedes Wagens an Franco als Geburtstagsgeschenk des Führers
3849	Botschaft Madrid, Geheim:	Illegaler Grenzverkehr (Durchschleusung Wehrfähiger der Feindmächte)
3850	Botschaft Madrid, Geheim:	Verschiedenes
3851	Botschaft Madrid, Geheim:	Wehrwirtschaftliche Beurteilung Englands und Frankreichs
3852	Botschaft Madrid, Geheim:	Handakten Kanzler; Schiffsmeldungen Einzelfälle
3853	Botschaft Madrid, Geheim:	U-Boot 167 Las Palmas, Besatzung des deutschen versenkten U-Bootes
3855	Botschaft Madrid, Geheim:	U-Boot 573 in Cartagena beschädigt eingelaufen
3856	Gesandtschaft Bern:	Massnahme gegen den Kommunismus in der Schweiz
3857	Gesandtschaft Bern:	Ermordung Gustloffs
3862	Botschaft Ankara:	Geheime und streng geheime Erlasse, Berichte, Telegramme
3864	Botschaft Ankara:	Syrien, geheim
3865	Botschaft Ankara:	Geheime und streng geheime Erlasse, Berichte, Telegramme

3867	Botschaft Ankara:	Geheime Erlasse
3869	Botschaft Madrid, Geheim:	Deutschlandreise des spanischen Parteiministers Arrese, Januar 1943
3871	Botschaft Madrid, Geheim:	Getarnte Warensendung aus Übersee "Get.Sdgn."
3874	Gesandtschaft Bern:	Deutsche Aussenpolitik
3879	Gesandtschaft Bern:	Stimmungsberichte
3880	Gesandtschaft Athen:	Geheimakten 1937/38
3883	Botschaft Ankara:	Geheime und streng geheime Erlasse, Berichte, Telegramme
3890	Botschaft Ankara:	Deutsche Innenpolitik, Auslands-organisation
3891	Botschaft Madrid, Geheim:	Entwicklung der allgemeinen Kriegs-lage
3893	Botschaft Madrid, Geheim:	Seekrieg und seine Auswirkungen auf Spanien
3894	Gesandtschaft Zagreb, Geheim:	Kroatien: Innenpolitik. Deutsche Aussenpolitik
3895	Botschaft Madrid, Geheim:	Meldungen über Landungsabsichten der Alliierten (Schaffung einer zweiten Front) Landung der Alliierten in West- und Nordafrika
3898	Gesandtschaft Bern:	Flucht des französischen Generals Giraud aus deutscher Kriegsgefangen-schaft
3899	Gesandtschaft Bern:	Der Führer und Reichskanzler
3900	Gesandtschaft Bern:	Carol von Rumänien
3901	Gesandtschaft Bern:	Krieg mit Frankreich, allgemeines 1939/42. Berichtesammlung des Kon-sulats in Genf über Frankreich 1940
3902	Botschaft Madrid, Geheim:	Deutsches Konsulat San Sebastian
3903	Gesandtschaft Zagreb, Geheim:	Geheime Reichssachen
3904	Gesandtschaft Bern:	NSDAP und ihre Gliederungen
3905	Gesandtschaft Bern:	Politische Beziehungen: Deutschland – Portugal
3907	Gesandtschaft Bern:	Elsass-Lothringen, politisches
3908	Botschaft Madrid, Geheim:	Carol Geheim: Exkönig Carol von Rumänien
3911	Gesandtschaft Bern:	Militärische Angelegenheiten in der Schweiz
3918	Gesandtschaft Bern:	Politische Beziehungen: Schweiz – Deutschland
3919	Gesandtschaft Bern:	Abwehr, Spionage
3920	Gesandtschaft Bern:	Kommunistische Partei der Schweiz Bekämpfung kommunistischer Agitation

3921	Gesandtschaft Bern:	Berichte über Verhältnisse in den Feindstaaten. Kriegsziele, Friedensfühler
3922	Botschaft Warschau, Geheim:	H.-Geheim, Wirtschaft
3923	Gesandtschaft Riga:	Politische Beziehungen: Lettland - Russland
3924	Botschaft Warschau:	Politische Beziehungen: Deutschland - Polen
3925	Botschaft Warschau:	Politische Beziehungen: Deutschland - Polen
3926	Botschaft Warschau:	Deutsche katholische Kirchenangelegenheiten in Polen
3927	Botschaft Warschau:	Neueingänge, verschiedenes
3928	Botschaft Warschau:	Polnische Juden in Deutschland
3929	Botschaft Warschau:	Polnische Aussenpolitik
3938	Gesandtschaft Bern:	Die nationale Erneuerungsbewegung in der Schweiz
3942	Generalkonsulat Zürich:	Geheimakten, allgemein; speziell. Alfred Reutschi
3944	Botschaft Brüssel:	Secreta
3947	Botschaft Brüssel:	Eupen-Malmedy
3948	Botschaft Brüssel:	Parteiwesen. Politische Verbände
3949	Botschaft Brüssel:	Innenpolitik Belgiens, allgemeines
3950	Botschaft Brüssel:	Presseabteilung
3997	Gesandtschaft Bern:	Berichte der Verbindungsoffiziere des Auswärtigen Amtes bei den Armee-Oberkommandos
4001	Botschaft Brüssel:	Deutsche Aussenpolitik, allgemein
4005	Botschaft Warschau:	Deutsche Staatsbesuche in Polen
4006	Botschaft Warschau:	Allgemeine Angelegenheiten der deutschen Auslandsvertretungen
4007	Botschaft Warschau:	Deutsche katholische Kirchenangelegenheiten in Polen
4008	Botschaft Warschau:	Deutsche Aussenpolitik
4009	Botschaft Warschau:	Deutsche Staatsbesuche in Polen
4010	Botschaft Warschau:	Briefe, Schliep
4011	Botschaft Warschau:	Briefe, v.Wuehlisch
4019	Konsulat Genf:	Deutschland, Völkerbund, Internationales Arbeitsamt
4020	Botschaft Brüssel:	Politische Beziehungen: Deutschland - Frankreich, Berichte Dr.Sieburg
4021	Botschaft Brüssel:	Aussenpolitik Belgiens
4024	Botschaft Warschau:	Polen: See- und Kolonialliga

4025	Botschaft Warschau:	Pless-Besitz in Oberschlesien
4027	Gesandtschaft Bern:	Attentat auf den Führer in München
4052	Botschaft Brüssel:	Propaganda
4057	Botschaft Rom (Vatikan):	Veröffentlichung päpstlicher Dokumente in Friedensvermittlungsfragen. Parlamentarischer Untersuchungsausschuss.
4073	Botschaft Warschau:	Dienstakten Militärattaché
4074	Botschaft Warschau:	Polnische Staatsbesuche in Deutschland
4082	Botschaft Moskau, Geheim:	Geheime Sachen der Abteilung C
4083	Botschaft Warschau:	Beziehungen: Deutschland - UdSSR
4084	Botschaft Warschau:	v.Scheliha
4085	Botschaft Moskau, Geheim:	Geheime Sachen der Passabteilung
4086	Botschaft Moskau, Geheim:	Geheime Sachen der Abteilung B
4087	Botschaft Moskau, Geheim:	Sicherheitsfragen: MOB und Nachrichtenwesen
4089	Botschaft Warschau;	Polnische Aussenpolitik
4090	Botschaft Madrid:	Die Tangerzone
4091	Botschaft Madrid:	Auswärtige Angelegenheiten
4094	Botschaft Warschau:	Auswärtiges Amt
4095	Botschaft Warschau:	Personalveränderungslisten der bei den deutschen Vertretungen in Polen beschäftigten Beamten und Angestellten
4096	Botschaft Madrid:	Marokko, allgemeines
4100	Botschaft Moskau, Geheim:	Litauischer Gebietsstreifen
4103	Botschaft Madrid:	Haltung Spaniens 1939
4104	Botschaft Rom (Quirinal), Geheim:	Stellung Spaniens und Portugals zum Krieg, spanische Kriegsziele
4137	Botschaft Moskau, Geheim:	Geheime Sache der Abteilung P A
4138	Botschaft Moskau, Geheim:	Politische Beziehungen: Sowjet Union - Deutschland
4139	Botschaft Moskau, Geheim:	Politische Beziehungen: Sowjet Union - Deutschland
4183	Botschaft Moskau, Geheim:	Politische Beziehungen: Sowjet Union - Balkan Pakt Staaten (Bulgarien, Griechenland, Jugoslawien, Rumänien, Türkei) Balkan Pakt, Mittelmeerfragen, Schwarzes Meer Pakt, Bessarabien
4184	Botschaft Moskau, Geheim:	Politische Beziehungen: Sowjet Union - Balkan Pakt Staaten (Bulgarien, Griechenland, Jugoslawien, Rumänien, Türkei) Balkan Pakt, Mittelmeerfragen, Schwarzes Meer Pakt, Bessarabien

4185	Botschaft Moskau, Geheim:	Politische Beziehungen: Deutschland - Italien
4189	Botschaft Moskau, Geheim:	Politische Beziehungen: Deutschland - andere Staaten. Krieg mit Polen
4190	Botschaft Moskau, Geheim:	Politische Beziehungen: Deutschland - andere Staaten. Krieg mit Polen
4191	Botschaft Moskau, Geheim:	Deutsche Innenpolitik: Militär-, Marine-, Luftfahrtangelegenheiten; Wehr- und Arbeitsdienstpflicht
4218	Botschaft Madrid:	Haltung der Neutralen (ausser Spanien, USA, Russland, Italien)
4219	Botschaft Rom (Quirinal):	Spanien
4241	Botschaft Rom (Quirinal), Geheim:	Innerpolitische Lage in Spanien und Verhältnis Spaniens zur Achse
4243	Botschaft Brüssel:	Secreta
4244	Botschaft Madrid:	Spanische und deutsche Bezugswünsche innerhalb des normalen Warenverkehrs
4245	Botschaft Madrid:	Prisenwesen-Konterbande, Banngut, Schwarze Liste
4246	Botschaft Paris, Geheim:	Spanien
4247	Botschaft Madrid:	Schwefelkies- und Eisenerzverschiffungen nach England
4250	Gesandtschaft Oslo:	Belgien, Holland, Luxemburg
4298	Gesandtschaft Stockholm:	Weiterleitung und Vermittlung von Briefen, Paketen, Telegrammen
4299	Gesandtschaft Oslo:	Skandinavien, Dänemark, Finnland, Schweden
4305	Botschaft Madrid:	Spanischer Krieg
4306	Botschaft Madrid:	Regierungspolitik allgemein
4360	Gesandtschaft Lissabon:	Geheimakten: Wolfram Angelegenheiten, Grube Borralha
4362	Gesandtschaft Lissabon:	Geheimakten: Lage in England
4363	Botschaft Rom (Quirinal):	Portugal
4365	Botschaft Madrid, Geheim:	Material für Handelsvertrag
4366	Botschaft Madrid, Geheim:	Handels- und Wirtschaftsangelegenheiten
4367	Botschaft Madrid, Geheim:	Deutschlands Zahlungen an Spanien; Finanzplan Ein- und Ausfuhrstation Spanien
4368	Botschaft Madrid, Geheim:	Telegrammwechsel Wirtschaftsverhandlungen
4369	Botschaft Madrid, Geheim:	Oliven für Amerika
4370	Botschaft Madrid, Geheim:	Wolfram
4371	Botschaft Madrid, Geheim:	Chinin und Lebertran

4372	Botschaft Madrid, Geheim:	Angaben über spanische Kolonien
4373	Botschaft Madrid, Geheim:	Kohle
4374	Botschaft Madrid, Geheim:	Handels- und Wirtschaftsangelegenheiten
4375	Gesandtschaft Lissabon:	Geheimakten: Lage in Amerika
4376	Gesandtschaft Lissabon:	Geheimakten: W-Bezüge Feindmächte (auch Verträge)
4377	Gesandtschaft Lissabon:	Geheimakten: Kohlen
4391	Botschaft Madrid:	Auswärtige Angelegenheiten
4392	Botschaft Madrid:	Spanisches dipolmatisches und konsularisches Korps
4393	Botschaft Madrid:	Spanische Militär-, Marine- und Luftattachés
4394	Botschaft Madrid:	Manifestationen gegen deutsche Vertretungen in Spanien
4395	Botschaft Madrid:	Spanisch-russische Beziehungen
4399	Botschaft Madrid:	Deutschfeindliche Propaganda in Marokko
4400	Botschaft Madrid:	Presse, allgemeines (Deutscher Einfluss auf spanische Presse)
4401	Botschaft Madrid:	Deutscher Fichtebund
4403	Botschaft Madrid:	Spanische Kundgebungen gegen deutsche Regierung Hitler
4405	Botschaft Paris:	Spanien
4406	Botschaft Madrid:	Ministerien, Minister und Staatsmänner
4409	Botschaft Madrid:	Diplomatisches und konsularisches Korps in Spanien
4410	Botschaft Madrid:	Abgegangene Verbalnoten
4411	Botschaft Madrid:	Falange Espanola
4412	Botschaft Ankara:	England
4413	Botschaft Rom (Quirinal):	England - Frankreich
4414	Botschaft Rom (Quirinal):	Schweiz
4419	Botschaft Rom (Vatikan):	Schweiz
4421	Botschaft Rom (Quirinal), Geheim:	Haltung der Vereinigten Staaten von Amerika zum Krieg
4423	Gesandtschaft Luxemburg:	Brüssel
4424	Gesandtschaft Luxemburg:	Geheime Eingänge und Ausgaben seit 10.Mai 1940
4425	Botschaft Rom (Vatikan):	Belgien
4426	Botschaft Rom (Vatikan):	Portugal
4427	Gesandtschaft Luxemburg:	Luxemburg: Faschistische Bewegung

4428	Gesandtschaft Luxemburg:	Telegramme
4430	Botschaft Paris, Geheim:	Französische Regierung, Zusammensetzung der Kabinette, Übersiedlung nach Versailles
4431	Gesandtschaft Pressburg:	Dr.Klinovsky
4433	Gesandtschaft Pressburg:	Slowakei: Wirtschaftspolitik, allgemein
4434	Gesandtschaft Pressburg:	Slowakei: Wirtschaftspolitik, allgemein
4435	Botschaft Moskau, Geheim:	Politische Beziehungen: Deutschland – Ungarn und Slowakei
4444	Botschaft Paris:	Spanien
4445	Botschaft Madrid, Geheim:	Montana
4447	Botschaft Moskau, Geheim:	Politische Beziehungen: Sowjet Union – Nordische Staaten (Finnland, Schweden, Norwegen, Dänemark) Aalandfrage, Finnische Inseln
4448	Botschaft Moskau, Geheim:	Politische Beziehungen: Sowjet Union – Nordische Staaten (Finnland, Schweden, Norwegen, Dänemark) Aalandfrage, Finnische Inseln
4452	Gesandtschaft Oslo:	Besetzung Norwegens, Okkupationsverwaltung
4459	Botschaft Rom (Quirinal), Geheim:	Auslandsdienstreisen von Mitarbeitern der Dienststelle Ribbentrop. Dobrudschafrage. Intervention des Marineattachés bei Admiral Somigli Besuch RAM Ribbentrop. Verhältnis Ciano's zum Duce. Deutsch-italienische Achsenpolitik, Verhältnis Duce – Führer. Spanien beim Eintritt Italiens in den Krieg. Orden für Göring und Kronprinz. Churchill und Roosevelts Botschaft an Duce. Grundsätzliche Befehle des Führers. Entmilitärisierung Roms. Botschafterfrage in Rom und Moskau. Versteifung der Haltung Frankreichs und italienische Truppenverschiebungen an der französischen Grenze. Verhältnis der Schweiz zum Krieg. Zusatzprotokoll zum portugiesisch-spanischen Freundschafts- und Nichtangriffspakt. Haltung und Lage der Schweiz. Italienisch-deutsche Kommission wegen der Greueltaten Ungarn – Rumänien. Aufenthaltsrecht für ehemalige rumänische Minister
4511	Botschaft Ankara:	Geheime Erlasse, Berichte, Telegramme
4544	Gesandtschaft Riga:	Lettland: Innere Politik
4554	Botschaft Ankara:	Geheime und streng geheime Erlasse, Berichte, Telegramme
4635	Botschaft Paris, Geheim:	Waffenstillstandskommission (Wako)
4636	Botschaft Paris, Geheim:	Juden und Freimaurer in Frankreich

4637	Botschaft Paris, Geheim:	Frankreich: Innere Verhältnisse
4638	Botschaft Paris, Geheim:	Fremde Volksgruppen in Frankreich
4639	Botschaft Rom (Quirinal), Geheim:	Frankreich, französische Kolonien; italienisch-französische Beziehungen
4640	Botschaft Rom (Quirinal), Geheim:	Französische Kolonien; de Gaulle, Unterredung Ciano-Darlan. Brief Pétain
4642	Botschaft Paris, Geheim:	Privater Schriftwechsel Botschafter von Hoesch-Staatssekretär von Schubert
4644	Botschaft Paris, Geheim:	Der höhere SS und Polizeiführer in Frankreich
4645	Botschaft Paris, Geheim:	Arbeitseinsatz, Unterstützungen
4646	Botschaft Paris, Geheim:	Friedensvorbereitungen
4647	Botschaft Paris, Geheim:	Kampf gegen Kommunisten
4648	Botschaft Paris:	Afrika
4649	Botschaft Paris, Geheim:	Französische Kolonien, Mandate, Protektorate; Kolonialministerium
4650	Botschaft Paris, Geheim:	Deutsch-französisches Liquidationsabkommen
4651	Botschaft Paris, Geheim:	Französische Regierung, Zusammensetzung der Kabinette, Übersiedlung nach Versailles
4652	Botschaft Paris, Geheim:	Französische Persönlichkeiten
4653	Botschaft Paris, Geheim:	Kampf gegen Kommunisten
4654	Botschaft Paris, Geheim:	Französische Kolonien, Mandate, Protektorate; Kolonialministerium
4655	Botschaft Paris, Geheim:	Französisches Gewerkschaftswesen, Sozialpolitik, französische Arbeiter in Deutschland
4659	Botschaft Paris, Geheim:	Vertreter des Auswärtigen Amtes beim AOK (VAA)
4660	Botschaft Paris, Geheim:	Französisches Gewerksschaftswesen, Sozialpolitik, französische Arbeiter in Deutschland
4661	Botschaft Paris, Geheim:	Gardes Territoriaux
4673	Gesandtschaft Belgrad:	Politische Beziehungen: Jugoslawien - Deutschland
4680	Botschaft Rom (Quirinal), Geheim:	Veränderungen in der ungarischen obersten Heeresleitung und sonstigen Generalität. Deutsche Stellungnahme zu den schwebenden politischen Fragen. Telegramm des Botschafters v.Hoesch. Italienische Kriegsmaterialverschiffungen nach Ethiopien. Verhalten der italienischen Behörden gegenüber Angehörigen der NSDAP.Expose des Reichsministers über römische Abmachungen und Ostpaktfrage.

4680	Botschaft Rom (Quirinal), Geheim:	Angebliche Agenten der Geheimen Staatspolizei sind abzuweisen. Überwachung von Mitgliedern der NSDAP. Angebliche italienische Truppenzusammenziehung an der österreichischen Grenze. Übernahme von 500.000 Liren. Grenzstelle frei. Herstellung amerikanischer Zünder. Verstärkung der Luftschutzanlagen in Palermo, Boothafen Syrakus. Truppenverschiebungen. Stützung der Zeitung "Schlem". Politische Lage in Österreich. Entwurf eines Donaupaktes. Italienische Agenten in Abessinien. Englische Regierung zur Memelfrage. Internationale Behandlung des abessinischen Konflikts. Warnung an Gen.Kon.Immelen. Reichskanzler a.D. Wirth. Englische Botschaft an Mussolini: Englands Einstellung zum Sanktionsproblem. Stellung Deutschlands zum Abessinien-Konflikt. Besprechung Canaris-Roatta. Erhöhung des Weizenpreises. Zahlungsbedingungen bei Kriegsbedarfslieferungen nach Italien. Militärische Lage in Ostafrika. Verhältnis in Kairo. Sanktionskonferenz. Angebliche Zusammenziehung italienischer Truppen in Bari und Brindisi. Führerbild an Dr.Galler. Aufdeckung umstürzlerischer Bewegung. Empfang des Universitätsprofessors durch den Führer. Zusammenarbeit der deutschen und italienischen Polizei. Verteilung der italienischen und englischen Streitkräfte im Mittelmeer. Neubesetzung der Dienststelle der deutschen Schule. Italienisch-abessinischer Krieg, auch Berichte aus Neapel. Unterredung Führer-engl. Botschafter. Stellung Bischof Hudal in Rom zu Deutschland und USA. Italienische Propaganda. Unterredung Botschafter mit Vertretern der Partei in Italien.
4682	Botschaft Paris, Geheim:	Thailand
4683	Botschaft Paris, Geheim:	China
4685	Gesandtschaft Bukarest:	Geheimakten: Telegramme aus Berlin
4687	Botschaft Madrid:	Nationale Erhebung
4692	Gesandtschaft Bern:	Geheimakten
4704	Botschaft Ankara:	Deutsche Innenpolitik. Auslandsorganisation.
4713	Botschaft Paris, Geheim:	Protektorat Böhmen und Mähren
4737	Gesandtschaft Pressburg:	Slowakei: Wirtschaftspolitik, allgemein
4743	Botschaft Paris, Geheim:	Irak
4745	Gesandtschaft Kopenhagen:	Kulturelle Angelegenheiten, Sport
4749	Gesandtschaft Kopenhagen:	Schiffahrt und Fischerei
4750	Gesandtschaft Kopenhagen:	Generalia
4751	Gesandtschaft Kopenhagen:	Diplomaten

4752	Gesandtschaft Kopenhagen:	Dienstbetrieb
4753	Gesandtschaft Kopenhagen:	Dienstbetrieb
4754	Gesandtschaft Kopenhagen:	Zusammenlegung des Generalkonsulates und der Gesandtschaft
4755	Gesandtschaft Kopenhagen:	Vorträge, Musik, Theater
4759	Botschaft Ankara:	Syrien, geheim
4760	Botschaft Paris, Geheim:	Syrien
4761	Gesandtschaft Kopenhagen:	Eisenbahn, Post, Telegrafie, Zollwesen
4762	Gesandtschaft Kopenhagen:	Luftverkehr, Kraftfahrzeuge
4763	Gesandtschaft Kopenhagen:	Internationale Abkommen und Institute, Ausstellungen, Konferenzen
4764	Gesandtschaft Kopenhagen:	Rechtssachen
4765	Gesandtschaft Kopenhagen:	Handel, Industrie, Landwirtschaft
4766	Gesandtschaft Kopenhagen:	Journalist Ernst Harthern
4767	Gesandtschaft Kopenhagen:	Presse, Telegramme, Presseberichterstattung
4768	Gesandtschaft Kopenhagen:	Presse
4769	Gesandtschaft Kopenhagen:	Reichsparteitag
4770	Gesandtschaft Kopenhagen:	Berufskonsulat Apenrade
4771	Gesandtschaft Kopenhagen:	Pressebeirat Dietrich
4772	Gesandtschaft Kopenhagen:	Wahlkonsulate, Konsularagenturen; Allgemeines, Verschiedenes
4773	Gesandtschaft Kopenhagen:	Rechtshilfe, Auslieferungen, Heimschaffungen, Fürsorge, Auslandsdeutschtum, Kirchen, Schulen, Religion
4774	Gesandtschaft Kopenhagen:	Drucklegung des deutschen Weissbuches in dänischer Sprache
4775	Gesandtschaft Kopenhagen:	Der Ausbruch des Krieges und Haltung der dänischen Regierung gegenüber Polen
4776	Gesandtschaft Kopenhagen:	Wirtschaftspolitische Front der Neutralen gegen England
4777	Gesandtschaft Kopenhagen:	Deutsche Flaggen, allgemein
4778	Konsulat Apenrade:	Dänische Politik und Propaganda südlich der Grenze
4779	Gesandtschaft Kopenhagen:	Schleswig-Holsteinischer Universitätstag, Dr. Schifferer, Professor Scheel
4780	Gesandtschaft Kopenhagen:	Deutsch-nordische Woche in Kiel
4781	Gesandtschaft Kopenhagen:	Deutsch-dänischer Schiedsvertrag

4782	Gesandtschaft Kopenhagen:	Deutsch-dänische Passfrage
4783	Gesandtschaft Kopenhagen:	Die dänische Grenzwehr; militärische Mittelungen betr.Nordschleswig
4784	Gesandtschaft Kopenhagen:	Gestellung und Einziehung Deutscher zur dänischen Wehrpflicht
4785	Gesandtschaft Kopenhagen:	Anlaufen von Bornholm und Christiana; Durchfahrt bei Samso durch deutsche Kriegsfahrzeuge; jährliche Anmeldung der Dienstsegelboote
4786	Gesandtschaft Kopenhagen:	Fischerei in der Flensburger Föhrde
4788	Gesandtschaft Kopenhagen:	Dänischer Kapitän Lembourn
4791	Konsulat Apenrade:	Militär- und Marineangelegenheiten
4792	Gesandtschaft Kopenhagen:	Wichtige Akten allgemein politischen Inhalts 1917/20
4794	Botschaft Rom (Vatikan):	Chile
4798	Botschaft Paris:	Spanien
4799	Gesandtschaft Bern:	Politische Beziehungen: Deutschland - Ägypten
4803	Botschaft Paris, Geheim:	Holland
4807	Botschaft Paris, Geheim:	Belgien
4810	Botschaft Paris, Geheim:	Südamerika
4811	Konsulat Apenrade:	Zwangsversteigerungen
4812	Konsulat Apenrade:	Kreditanstalt Vogelsang
4813	Konsulat Apenrade:	Deutsche Volksgruppen und ihre Organisationen
4814	Gesandtschaft Kopenhagen:	Das Ostseeproblem
4815	Gesandtschaft Kopenhagen:	Dänische Lotsenordnung
4816	Konsulat Apenrade:	Kirche
4817	Konsulat Apenrade:	Deutsche kulturelle Bestrebungen in Nordschleswig
4818	Konsulat Apenrade:	Verschiedenes Pol.
4819	Konsulat Apenrade:	Dänische Presse
4820	Konsulat Apenrade:	Auslandsdeutschtum
4821	Konsulat Apenrade:	Kulturelles
4822	Konsulat Apenrade:	Schulwesen im abgetretenen Gebiet
4823	Gesandtschaft Kopenhagen:	Deutsch-dänische Verhandlungen
4825	Gesandtschaft Bern:	Allgemeine Aussenpolitik der Schweiz
4826	Botschaft Paris, Geheim:	Schweiz
4827	Gesandtschaft Zagreb:	Kroatisch-serbischer Aktenaustausch

4828	Gesandtschaft Zagreb:	Umsiedlung von Slovenen, Ungarn, Kroaten, Serben und Ukrainern
4830	Gesandtschaft Bern	Einstellung und Annahme von Schweizern zum Kampf gegen die Bolschewisten
4832	Gesandtschaft Zagreb:	Grenzzwischenfälle
4833	Gesandtschaft Kopenhagen:	Nordschleswig
4835	Gesandtschaft Bern:	Alt Bundesrat Musy
4838	Gesandtschaft Kopenhagen:	Nordschleswig
4840	Botschaft Paris, Geheim:	Portugal
4841	Gesandtschaft Zagreb:	Deutsche Aussenpolitik und Propaganda
4842	Gesandtschaft Kopenhagen:	Tischler Verhandlungsprotokolle
4843	Gesandtschaft Kopenhagen:	Pastor Schmidt-Wodder und Cornelius Bendestyre Bergung
4844	Gesandtschaft Kopenhagen:	Ausstückung in Nordschleswig
4845	Gesandtschaft Kopenhagen:	Minderheiten und Schulfragen
4846	Konsulat Apenrade:	Angelegenheiten Nordschleswigs
4849	Botschaft Rom (Quirinal), Geheim:	Unabhängigkeit Kroatiens; Neue Grenzen; Reise Cianos nach Wien
4850	Gesandtschaft Bern:	Geheimakten
4852	Gesandtschaft Lissabon:	Deutsch-polnischer Krieg 1939 und dessen Auswirkung auf England und Frankreich
4860	Konsulat Apenrade:	Dänische Politik im abgetretenen Gebiet
4861	Konsulat Apenrade:	Politik, verschiedenes. Nordschleswig
4862	Konsulat Apenrade:	Belege zum H.u.V.Buch, Einzahlungen
4864	Botschaft Paris:	Russland
4865	Botschaft Rom (Quirinal), Geheim:	Italienische Kriegsführung. Bulgarien, Rumänien, Jugoslawien, Ungarn; Beitritt Bulgariens zum Dreimächtepakt. Lage in Ägypten und Türkei. Irak. Besuch Francos in Rom. Lage in Ostasien. Verhalten Nord- und Südamerikas zum Krieg. Lage in Tanger. Spanien und der Krieg. Besuch Matsuoka. Deutsche Operationen in Griechenland, Jugoslawien. Englische Anleihe an Spanien. Innenpolitik Ungarns; Bardossy in Rom. Ex-Königin und Prinz Juan von Spanien. Dreimächtepakt. Verhältnis Japan - Sowjet Union. Unruhen in Montenegro, Serbien, Kroatien, Dalmatien. Tuka in Rom; Angelegenheit Galvanek. Afghanistan. Italienische Arbeiter in Deutschland. Umsiedlung Südtirol. Beurteilung der Handelsattachés.Italienische Schiffskode.

4865	Botschaft Rom (Quirinal), Geheim:	Eindrücke Ciano über Deutschland-besuch. Ernennung Anfuso zum ita-lienischen Gesandten in Budapest. Lage im Mitrowizagebiet. Krieg Japan-USA-England-Südamerika. Ent-hebung Serenas, Vidussoni: Partei-sekretär
4867	Gesandtschaft Kopenhagen:	Nordschleswig
4868	Gesandtschaft Kopenhagen:	Nordschleswig
4869	Gesandtschaft Kopenhagen:	Nordschleswig
4870	Gesandtschaft Kopenhagen:	Nordschleswig
4871	Gesandtschaft Kopenhagen:	Nordschleswig
4889	Gesandtschaft Kopenhagen:	Die dänische Abrüstungsfrage; dänisches Heer und Flotte
4891	Gesandtschaft Kopenhagen:	Professor Aage Fries
4892	Gesandtschaft Kopenhagen:	Kranken-, Invaliden-, Angestellten- und Altersversicherung Nordschles-wig; Kriegsverletzte, Hinterbliebene
4893	Botschaft Madrid:	Militär und Polizei
4894	Botschaft Madrid:	Regierungs Politik Allgemein
4895	Botschaft Madrid:	Regierungs Politik Allgemein
4897	Botschaft Madrid:	Regierungs Politik Allgemein
4898	Gesandtschaft Kopenhagen:	Presse
4901	Gesandtschaft Kopenhagen:	Presse
4902	Gesandtschaft Kopenhagen:	Presse
4903	Gesandtschaft Kopenhagen:	Presse
4915	Cesandtschaft Kopenhagen:	Minderheiten und Schulfragen, Spezialakten
4916	Gesandtschaft Kopenhagen:	Arbeiterbewegung, Sozialpolitik
4917	Gesandtschaft Kopenhagen:	Presse, Propaganda
4918	Gesandtschaft Kopenhagen:	Arbeiterbewegung, Sozialpolitik; Kommunisten, Emigranten
4924	Botschaft Rom (Quirinal), Geheim:	Italien: Aussenpolitik, Kriegführung, Innenpolitik
4925	Botschaft Rom (Quirinal), Geheim:	Italienisch-Ostafrika. Libyen. Süd-tirol. Albanien. Laibach, Dalmatien, Grenzgebiete. Lage in Italien
4926	Botschaft Rom (Quirinal), Geheim:	Ungarn. Rumänien. Deutsch-italie-nische Offizierskommission in Sieben-bürgen; ungarisch-rumänische Be-ziehungen. Afghanistan
4927	Botschaft Rom (Quirinal), Geheim:	Kroatien; Bulgarien; Slowakei. Grie-chenland. Grenzfragen auf dem Balkan
4928	Botschaft Rom (Quirinal), Geheim:	Kriegsführung Sowjetrusslands gegen die Achsenmächte.Russische Emigran-ten.

4928	Botschaft Rom (Quirinal), Geheim:	Skandinavische Länder: Dänemark, Schweden, Norwegen, Island, Finnland.
4929	Botschaft Rom (Quirinal), Geheim:	Arabische Länder: Arabien, Ceylon, Cypern, Palästina, Syrien. Arabien: Unabhängigkeitsbewegung; Grossmufti Gailani. Türkei. Ägypten.
4930	Botschaft Rom (Quirinal), Geheim:	Indien. Indische Legion in Deutschland; arabische Legion in Italien. "Sonderreferat Indien", Japanische Indienpropaganda. Afghanistan.
4931	Botschaft Rom (Quirinal), Geheim:	Japan, China, Mandschukuo. Amerika: Vereinigte Staaten, Kanada, Mittel- und Südamerika. Kriegführung Amerikas gegen die Dreierpaktmächte.
4932	Botschaft Rom (Quirinal), Geheim:	Zeremonielles. Italienisches diplomatisches Korps. Ausländisches diplomatisches Korps. Orden. Besuch hoher Persönlichkeiten.
4933	Botschaft Rom (Quirinal), Geheim:	Italienische Arbeiter in Deutschland. Passangelegenheiten. Sichtvermerke an Angehörige deutscher Fürstenhäuser und des Hochadels. Warngebiete für die Seekriegsführung. Lazarettschiff für Malta
4934	Botschaft Rom (Quirinal), Geheim:	Ankauf von Kunstwerken in Italien. Presse- und Propagandaangelegenheiten. Wirtschaftsangelegenheiten. Heimschaffung deutscher Seeleute des Dampfers "Prometheus". Inag-Streitfall: Direktor Kapferer. Strafrecht, Auslieferungen, Verhaftungen. Fall Harbeck, Fall Obmann-Urbanek. Fall Dr.V.v.Somogyi. Fall Lt.Pederiva.
4937	Botschaft Madrid:	Marokko, allgemeines
4938	Botschaft Wien, Geheim:	Sicherheitsfrage: deutsche Anregungen. Stellung der Reichsregierung zu den Investigationsbeschlüssen des Völkerbundrates. Besuch RK Marx und RM Stresemann. Sicherheitskomitée: Bemerkungen der deutschen Regierung zum Arbeitsprogramm. Österreichische Staatsanleihe in Amerika (Vermittlungsversuche). Geheimakten: 1930, 1931, 1932, 1933, 1934. Gesandter Rieths Unterredung mit Bundeskanzler Dollfuss.(Annäherung). Deutsch-österreichisches Polizeiabkommen. Legales Hilfswerk. Defektenangelegenheit Paul Ewald. Amerikanische Sabotageprozesse. Luppe, Klagenfurt. Beihilfen für politische Häftlinge. Meldungen über Österreich. Berichte des Militärattachés Gen. Lt. Muff. W.Papst. Presse, allgemeines
4939	Botschaft Wien, Geheim:	NSDAP in Österreich. In der Maur. Dr.Vogel. Dr. Herbert Schneider. Berichte Papens an Führer. Angriff österreichischer und reichsdeutscher Presse. Privatakten: v.Papen. Briefumschlag an Graf Lerchenfeld. Briefumschlag an Gerrison (v.Romberg).

4941	Gesandtschaft Kopenhagen:	Völkerbund
4942	Gesandtschaft Kopenhagen:	Militär- und Marineangelegenheiten
4943	Gesandtschaft Kopenhagen:	Heer und Marine
4944	Gesandtschaft Kopenhagen:	Pontoppidan Affaire
4953	Gesandtschaft Kopenhagen:	Musiklehrer Modis der St.Petri Schule. Studienrat Heidrich, deutsche Petri Schule
4963	Gesandtschaft Helsinki:	Berichte, Drahtberichte
4964	Gesandtschaft Helsinki:	Petsamo Telegramme
4969	Gesandtschaft Bern:	Politische Beziehungen: Deutschland – Baltische Staaten
4980	Botschaft Madrid:	Sammlung der Berichte
4991	Gesandtschaft Kopenhagen:	Skandinavien
4996	Gesandtschaft Kopenhagen:	Deutsch-dänische Beziehungen
4997	Gesandtschaft Kopenhagen:	England. Frankreich, Belgien, Niederlande, Spanien, Portugal, Italien, Schweiz, Luxemburg
4999	Gesandtschaft Kopenhagen:	Deutsche Politik
5000	Gesandtschaft Kopenhagen:	Dänische Politik. Vertrag zwischen Deutschland und Dänemark 1922
5002	Botschaft Wien, Geheim:	Privatbriefe des Botschafters; Informatorische Aufzeichnungen. Deutsch-österreichische Zollunion.
5007	Gesandtschaft Kopenhagen:	Dänische Politik: Deutsch-dänische Beziehungen
5008	Gesandtschaft Kopenhagen:	Dänische Nebenländer: Grönland, Island, Färöer
5009	Gesandtschaft Kopenhagen:	Randstaaten
5010	Gesandtschaft Kopenhagen:	Dänisches Filmwesen, allgemein
5011	Gesandtschaft Kopenhagen:	Verschiedenes
5012	Gesandtschaft Kopenhagen:	Verdienstorden vom deutschen Adler
5014	Gesandtschaft Kopenhagen:	Verschiedenes. Legate, Dienstreisen
5015	Gesandtschaft Kopenhagen:	Verschiedenes.
5016	Gesandtschaft Kopenhagen:	Afrika, Amerika, Asien
5017	Gesandtschaft Kopenhagen:	Verschiedenes
5018	Gesandtschaft Kopenhagen:	Protokollangelegenheiten
5019	Gesandtschaft Kopenhagen:	Politische Angelegenheiten. Presseangelegenheiten
5020	Gesandtschaft Kopenhagen:	Deutsche Politik
5072	Botschaft Paris:	Spanien
5076	Botschaft Madrid:	Nationale Erhebung

5085	Gesandtschaft Helsinki:	Erlasse
5101	Botschaft Wien, Geheim:	Donauföderation
5112	Gesandtschaft Helsinki:	Schriftwechsel, geheim
5128	Botschaft Rom (Vatikan), Geheim:	Wirth, ehemaliger Reichskanzler
5129	Botschaft Rom (Quirinal), Geheim:	Ausländische Handelsschiffe in Amerika
5130	Gesandtschaft Lissabon:	Politische Beziehungen zu anderen Staaten, ausser Portugal; Verträge und Abkommen
5139	Botschaft Ankara:	Geheime und streng geheime Erlasse, Berichte, Telegramme
5145	Botschaft Madrid:	Innere Angelegenheiten
5146	Botschaft Rom (Vatikan) :	Litauen (Kowno)
5148	Botschaft Rom:	Spanien
5149	Botschaft Madrid, Geheim:	Montana
5154	Botschaft Paris:	Spanien
5156	Botschaft Madrid, Geheim:	Montana
5157	Botschaft Rom (Vatikan):	Spanien
5160	Gesandtschaft Helsinki:	Multex Telegramme
5165	Botschaft Ankara:	Geheime und streng geheime Erlasse, Berichte, Telegramme
5166	Botschaft Ankara:	Geheime und streng geheime Erlasse, Berichte, Telegramme
5167	Botschaft Ankara:	Presse und Propaganda, geheim
5169	Botschaft Ankara:	Geheime Erlasse
5171	Gesandtschaft Helsinki:	Multex Telegramme
5174	Botschaft Madrid:	Diplomatische Vertretungen in Rotspanien, Asylfrage
5177	Botschaft Rom (Quirinal):	Spanien
5178	Botschaft Madrid, Geheim:	Handels- und Wirtschaftsangelegenheiten
5184	Botschaft Paris, Geheim:	Spanien
5185	Botschaft Madrid, Geheim:	"Gr.Plan" Grosser Plan 1942
5187	Botschaft Madrid, Geheim:	Übergabe Mercedes Wagen an Franco als Geburtstagsgeschenk des Führers
5188	Botschaft Madrid, Geheim:	Deutschlandreise des spanischen Parteiministers Arrese, Januar 1943
5189	Gesandtschaft Bern:	Deutsche Aussenpolitik
5190	Botschaft Madrid, Geheim:	Deutsches Konsulat San Sebastian
5194	Botschaft Madrid, Geheim:	Sudetendeutsche Frage und mitteleuropäische Krise

5200	Gesandtschaft Prag:	Minderheiten
5201	Gesandtschaft Prag:	Aussenpolitik
5206	Botschaft Madrid, Geheim:	Handels- und Wirtschaftsangelegenheiten
5207	Botschaft Paris:	Innere Angelegenheiten
5210	Botschaft Rom (Quirinal):	Deutsch-italienische Wirtschaftsverhandlungen und Vertrag
5211	Botschaft Rom (Quirinal):	Politische Beziehungen: Italien - Jugoslawien
5216	Botschaft Rom (Quirinal):	Kanäle
5217	Botschaft Rom (Quirinal):	Politische Beziehungen: Italien - Frankreich
5218	Botschaft Paris:	Marokko
5222	Botschaft Rom (Quirinal):	Politik, Vatikan
5223	Gesandtschaft Helsinki:	Schriftwechsel, geheim. Drahtberichte
5255	Botschaft Rom (Quirinal), Geheim:	Albanien
5257	Botschaft Rom (Quirinal), Geheim:	Botschaftseinbruch. Hitlers Besuch in Rom 1931. Aufzeichnung Botschafter v.Hassell über Dreierpakt. Aufzeichnung Begegnung Hitler-Mussolini. Emil Ludwig
5258	Botschaft Rom (Quirinal), Geheim:	Deutsch-italienische Offizierskommission in Siebenbürgen; ungarisch-rumänische Beziehungen. Afghanistan.
5266	Botschaft Rom (Quirinal), Geheim:	Politische Beziehungen: Deutschland - Österreich. Deutschland - Polen. Deutschland - Russland. Deutschland - Belgien. England - Frankreich
5267	Botschaft Rom (Quirinal), Geheim:	Internationale politische Verträge. Völkerbund. Militärkontrolle und Abrüstungsfrage
5268	Botschaft Rom (Quirinal), Geheim:	Reparationen, allgemeines. Russland
5269	Botschaft Rom (Quirinal), Geheim:	Österreich, Vatikan. Deutsch-österreichische Zollunion
5270	Botschaft Rom (Quirinal), Geheim:	Deutsch-österreichische Zollunion. Amerika. Litauen. Ungarn. Frankreich. Politische Beziehungen: Italien - England, Flugwesen
5271	Botschaft Rom (Quirinal), Geheim:	Politische Beziehungen: Italien - Ungarn. Deutschland - Italien. Innen- und Aussenpolitik Italiens. Politische Beziehungen: Italien - Polen. Italien, innere Lage. Politische Beziehungen: Italien - Österreich
5272	Botschaft Rom (Quirinal), Geheim:	Hitler und Südtirol. Aussen- und innere Politik, allgemeines. Marchese Pauluci.
5312	Botschaft Rom (Vatikan):	Belgien

5319	Gesandtschaft Bern:	Kriegsmassnahmen der Schweiz
5320	Gesandtschaft Bern:	Politische Beziehungen: Schweiz – Deutschland
5321	Gesandtschaft Bern:	Politische Reden und Vorträge
5322	Gesandtschaft Bern:	Freimaurer Logen
5323	Gesandtschaft Bern:	Kommunistische Partei der Schweiz. Bekämpfung kommunistischer Agitation
5324	Gesandtschaft Bern:	Schweizer Ärztemissionen für die Ostfront
5325	Generalkonsulat Zürich:	Auswärtiges Amt, Ref.D.III
5326	Generalkonsulat Zürich:	Geheimakten, allgemein
5391	Botschaft Madrid, Geheim:	Seekrieg und seine Auswirkungen auf Spanien
5392	Gesandtschaft Lissabon:	Deutsch-polnischer Krieg 1939 und dessen Auswirkung auf England und Frankreich
5406	Generalkonsulat Göteborg	Schweden: Innerpolitische Verhältnisse, Beiakte
5416	Botschaft Rom (Vatikan):	China, Delegatur in Peking
5429	Gesandtschaft Bern:	Rumänisch-ungarische Gegensätze, Friedensfühler beider Länder
5430	Gesandtschaft Bukarest:	Geheimakten: Telegramme aus Berlin
5434	Gesandtschaft Lissabon:	Geheimakten: Lage in England
5435	Gesandtschaft Lissabon:	Geheimakten: Lage in England
5436	Gesandtschaft Bern:	Berichte über Verhältnisse in den Feindstaaten, Kriegsziele, Friedensfühler
5437	Gesandtschaft Bern:	Berichte über Verhältnisse in den Feindstaaten, Kriegsziele, Friedensfühler
5439	Botschaft Rom (Quirinal), Geheim:	Krieg Englands gegen die Achsenmächte (auch "Zweite Front")
5446	Botschaft Ankara:	Geheime und streng geheime Erlasse, Berichte, Telegramme
5469	Botschaft Ankara:	Presse und Propaganda, geheim
5500	Botschaft Paris:	Beziehungen zu Deutschland
5501	Botschaft Paris:	Marokko
5521	Botschaft Rom (Quirinal), Geheim:	Japan, China, Mandschukuo
5522	Botschaft Paris:	Beziehungen zu Deutschland
5548	Gesandtschaft Sofia:	Gesandter Beckerle: Persönliche Aufzeichnungen
5554	Gesandtschaft Zagreb,Geheim:	Bauxit, Mappe I-IV
5580	Botschaft Rom (Quirinal), Geheim:	Tunis; arabische Bewegung

5589	Botschaft Rom (Quirinal), Geheim:	Deutsche Kriegsführung
5590	Botschaft Rom (Quirinal), Geheim:	Italienische Aussenpolitik
5605	Konsulat Florenz:	Geheimakten
5616	Botschaft Paris:	Westafrika
5633	Botschaft Paris, Geheim:	Französische Kolonien, Mandate, Protektorate; Kolonialministerium
5634	Botschaft Paris:	Rion Prozesse
5635	Botschaft Paris, Geheim:	Französisches Gewerkschaftswesen, Sozialpolitik, französische Arbeiter in Deutschland
5636	Botschaft Paris, Geheim:	Französisches Gewerkschaftswesen, Sozialpolitik, französische Arbeiter in Deutschland
5637	Botschaft Paris, Geheim:	Französisches Gewerkschafswesen, Sozialpolitik, französische Arbeiter in Deutschland
5638	Botschaft Paris:	Marokko
5639	Botschaft Paris:	Deutsche Kulturpolitik
5670	Botschaft Rom (Quirinal), Geheim:	Laibach, Dalmatien, Grenzgebiete
5678	Botschaft Rom (Vatikan):	Chile
5683	Gesandtschaft Helsinki:	Drahtberichte und Erlasse, auch geheim. Schriftwechsel, geheim.
5701	Botschaft Rom (Quirinal), Geheim:	Frankreich, französische Kolonien; italienisch-französische Beziehungen
5758	Botschaft London, Geheim:	Grossbritanniens Armee
5759	Botschaft London, Geheim:	Deutschland, Armee und Kriegsflugwesen
5798	Gesandtschaft Lissabon:	Lösung der Judenfrage
5799	Gesandtschaft Belgrad:	Judenangelegenheiten
5800	Botschaft Paris, Geheim:	Frankreich: Innere Verhältnisse
5808	Gesandtschaft Oslo:	Finnland
5815	Botschaft Warschau:	Politische Beziehungen: Deutschland – Polen
5816	Botschaft Warschau:	Politik: Danzig
5827	Gesandtschaft Bern:	Russischer Massenmord polnischer Offiziere in Katyn. Massenmorde in Winniza
5835	Botschaft Ankara:	England
5836	Botschaft Paris:	England
5837	Botschaft Rom (Quirinal):	Politische Beziehungen: Italien – England
5840	Gesandtschaft Kopenhagen:	England

5844	Gesandtschaft Belgrad:	Berichte der Botschaft London 1923/36
5852	Botschaft Rom (Quirinal):	Deutsch-italienische Beziehungen: Besuch Reichsaussenminister von Ribbentrop
5857	Botschaft Paris, Geheim:	Frankreich
5896	Botschaft Paris, Geheim:	Belgien
5898	Gesandtschaft Bern:	Politische Beziehungen: Deutschland - Italien
5911	Gesandtschaft Oslo:	Schweden
5912	Gesandtschaft Stockholm:	Schweden: Innen- und Aussenpolitik
5913	Gesandtschaft Stockholm:	Schweden: Innen- und Aussenpolitik
5914	Gesandtschaft Stockholm:	Skandinavien: Innen- und Aussenpolitik
5915	Gesandtschaft Stockholm:	Skandinavien: Innen- und Aussenpolitik
5921	Gesandtschaft Kowno:	Politik, Allgemeine Angelegenheiten: Jahresübersichten der Gesandtschaft und anderer deutschen Auslandsbehörden
5922	Gesandtschaft Reval:	Estlands Beziehungen zu Deutschland. Innere Politik. Militärattaché
5923	Botschaft Paris:	Estland
5929	Gesandtschaft Stockholm:	Deutschland: Innen- und Aussenpolitik
5930	Gesandtschaft Stockholm:	Heerwesen
5944	Botschaft Moskau:	Trotzkistenprozess, Pjatzkow-Radek
5951	Gesandtschaft Kopenhagen:	Heer und Marine
5952	Gesandtschaft Oslo:	Dänemark, Island, Färöer
5954	Gesandtschaft Bern:	Dänemark, allgemein
6003	Gesandtschaft Bern:	Politische Reden und Vorträge
6020	Gesandtschaft Kopenhagen:	Skandinavien
6021	Gesandtschaft Oslo:	Politische Beziehungen: Norwegen - andere Staaten. Ministerien, Minister, prominente Persönlichkeiten, Armee
6027	Botschaft Paris, Geheim:	Der Militärbefehlshaber in Frankreich
6028	Botschaft Paris, Geheim:	Lageberichte über Nordafrika und Besetzung Frankreichs durch Achsentruppen
6091	Botschaft Rom (Quirinal), Geheim:	Krieg Englands gegen die Achsenmächte (auch "Zweite Front")
6093	Gesandtschaft Lissabon:	Geheimakten: Lage in England
6099	Gesandtschaft Bern:	Schweiz, Innere Verwaltung
6100	Gesandtschaft Bern:	Deutscher Nationalsozialismus in der Schweiz
6101	Gesandtschaft Bern:	Neutralität der Schweiz
6102	Gesandtschaft Bern:	Schweizer Nationalsozialismus und Frontenbewegung

6108	Gesandtschaft Bern:	Ermordung Gustloffs. Prozess Frankfurter
6109	Gesandtschaft Bern:	Handelsbeziehungen: Schweiz - Deutschland
6110	Generalkonsulat Zürich:	Geheimakten: Handel, Finanz, Wirtschaft
6136	Gesandtschaft Zagreb,Geheim:	Militär-, Marine- und Luftangelegenheiten. Bolschewismus. Werbung von Legionen gegen Achsenmächte. Kulturpolitische Beziehungen: Kroatien - Deutschland. Politisches Informationsmaterial dritter Staaten
6137	Gesandtschaft Zagreb,Geheim:	Geheime Reichssachen
6181	Botschaft Rom (Quirinal), Geheim:	Albanien
6182	Gesandtschaft Zagreb,Geheim:	Werbung zur Waffen-SS
6183	Gesandtschaft Belgrad:	Kommunismus und seine Bekämpfung
6184	Gesandtschaft Belgrad:	Spione, Agenten, Tito-Partisanen
6185	Gesandtschaft Belgrad:	Politische Beziehungen und Verträge Jugoslawiens und Deutschlands zu Serbien, 1944
6186	Gesandtschaft Zagreb:	Aufstandsbewegung, Spionagewesen
6214	Botschaft Warschau:	Minderheiten: Erklärungen
6219	Gesandtschaft Stockholm:	Personalien im Ministerium des Äusseren in Stockholm
6220	Gesandtschaft Stockholm:	Personalien bei anderen Behörden in Berlin und Stockholm
6221	Gesandtschaft Stockholm:	Organisation der Gesandtschaft
6223	Gesandtschaft Stockholm:	Pressepropagandistischer Fonds
6224	Gesandtschaft Stockholm:	Weiterleitung und Vermittlung von Briefen, Paketen und Telegrammen
6225	Gesandtschaft Stockholm:	Spenden, Darbietungen
6227	Gesandtschaft Stockholm:	Anfragen verschiedener Art
6228	Gesandtschaft Stockholm:	Reisen des Königs und der Königin von Schweden
6239	Gesandtschaft Stockholm:	Schweden: Innen- und Aussenpolitik
6241	Gesandtschaft Stockholm:	Deutschland: Innen- und Aussenpolitik
6242	Gesandtschaft Stockholm:	Dänemark: Innen- und Aussenpolitik
6243	Gesandtschaft Stockholm:	England: Innen- und Aussenpolitik
6244	Gesandtschaft Stockholm:	Finnland: Innen- und Aussenpolitik
6245	Gesandtschaft Stockholm:	Russland: Innen- und Aussenpolitik
6248	Gesandtschaft Stockholm:	Aalandinseln, geheim
6249	Botschaft Warschau:	Theater, Musikwesen, Deutsche Kunstgesellschaft

6250	Gesandtschaft Stockholm:	Die deutsche Reichsflagge
6251	Gesandtschaft Stockholm:	Spionage, geheim
6252	Gesandtschaft Stockholm:	Kommunismus
6253	Gesandtschaft Stockholm:	Verschiedenes (politisch)
6260	Gesandtschaft Stockholm:	Verschiedenes; Vereine und Stiftungen
6261	Gesandtschaft Stockholm:	Deutsch-schwedische Vereinigung
6262	Gesandtschaft Stockholm:	Nordische Gesellschaft
6263	Gesandtschaft Stockholm:	Schulen, Hochschulen, wissenschaftliche Anstalten
6264	Gesandtschaft Stockholm:	Studienreisen
6265	Gesandtschaft Stockholm:	Deutsch-akademischer Austauschdienst (Dr.Kappner)
6266	Gesandtschaft Stockholm:	Wissenschaftliche Kongresse und Konferenzen
6267	Gesandtschaft Stockholm:	Sven Hedin und die Firma Junkers (Expedition)
6268	Gesandtschaft Stockholm:	Professor Dr. Walter Lund
6269	Gesandtschaft Stockholm:	Filme
6270	Gesandtschaft Stockholm:	Propaganda, verschiedenes
6276	Gesandtschaft Stockholm:	Presse, Sonderfonds, geheim
6280	Gesandtschaft Stockholm:	Presse, verschiedenes
6281	Gesandtschaft Stockholm:	Presse, verschiedenes
6282	Gesandtschaft Stockholm:	Presse, verschiedenes
6283	Gesandtschaft Stockholm:	Presse, verschiedenes
6284	Gesandtschaft Stockholm:	Ausländische Zeitungen. Svenska Dagblatt. Göteborgs Morgonpost
6285	Gesandtschaft Stockholm:	Svenska Telegrammbyrå
6286	Gesandtschaft Stockholm:	Korrespondenten
6287	Gesandtschaft Stockholm:	Korrespondenten: Uddgren
6288	Gesandtschaft Stockholm:	Deutschland: Presse- und Propagandawesen, allgemeines
6289	Gesandtschaft Stockholm:	Schweden: Presse- und Propagandawesen; Beziehungen zu Deutschland
6290	Gesandtschaft Stockholm:	Beziehungen zu und zwischen anderen Staaten
6291	Gesandtschaft Stockholm:	Greuel- und Lügenmeldungen der ausländischen Presse und deren Bekämpfung
6292	Gesandtschaft Stockholm:	Schweden: Presse, Verlagsanstalten, Zeitungen
6293	Gesandtschaft Stockholm:	Südschwedische Presse

6294	Gesandtschaft Stockholm:	Schweden: Presse, Beanstandungen in Presse, Rundfunk, Film, Propaganda
6295	Gesandtschaft Stockholm:	Konsulat Malmö
6296	Gesandtschaft Stockholm:	Konsulat Norrköping, Akten
6297	Gesandtschaft Stockholm:	Akten
6298	Gesandtschaft Stockholm:	Parteiangelegenheiten
6339	Botschaft Paris:	Wirtschaftliche Beziehungen: Frankreich-USA, Kanada
6356	Gesandtschaft Zagreb,Geheim:	Politische Beziehungen: Deutschland - andere Staaten
6381	Botschaft Rom (Quirinal):	Politische Beziehungen: Italien - Polen
6396	Gesandtschaft Bern:	Reparationen. Sicherheitsfrage, Investigationen, Lokarnopakt
6397	Gesandtschaft Bern:	Völkerbund, allgemein
6398	Gesandtschaft Bukarest:	Völkerbund, allgemein
6399	Gesandtschaft Kowno:	Völkerbund
6399	Botschaft Paris:	Völkerbund
6400	Botschaft Paris:	Allgemeine Abrüstung und Rüstung
6403	Botschaft Paris:	Deutsches Garantieangebot; Sicherheitspakt Locarno
6428	Gesandtschaft Lissabon:	Völkerbundsfragen
6434	Gesandtschaft Helsinki:	Erlasse
6435	Gesandtschaft Helsinki:	Erlasse
6436	Gesandtschaft Helsinki:	Drahterlasse und Berichte, auch geheim
6437	Gesandtschaft Helsinki:	Drahterlasse
6438	Gesandtschaft Helsinki:	Drahterlasse
6440	Gesandtschaft Helsinki:	Berichte
6441	Gesandtschaft Helsinki:	Drahtberichte
6442	Botschaft Paris, Geheim:	Juden und Freimaurer in Frankreich. Arbeitseinsatz, Unterstützungen. Französische Kolonien, Mandate, Protektorate; Kolonialministerium. Berichte über innere Verhältnisse in Frankreich
6443	Botschaft Paris, Geheim:	Französisches Gewerkschaftswesen, Sozialpolitik, französische Arbeiter in Deutschland. Besetzung Frankreichs. Französisch-Nordafrika. Frankreich: Aussenpolitik. Demarkations- und Rhonelinie. Illegaler Grenzverkehr. Tunis. Katholische Kirche. Deutschland: Innenpolitik
6444	Botschaft Rom (Quirinal), Geheim:	Frankreich, französische Kolonien; italienisch-französische Beziehungen

6445	Botschaft Rom (Quirinal), Geheim:	Tunis; arabische Bewegung
6453	Botschaft Paris:	Freimaurer
6462	Botschaft Madrid, Geheim:	Meldungen über Landungsabsichten der Alliierten (Schaffung einer zweiten Front) Landung der Alliierten in West- und Nordafrika
6506	Gesandtschaft Helsinki:	Multex Telegramme
6507	Gesandtschaft Helsinki:	Multex Telegramme
6508	Gesandtschaft Helsinki:	Persönliche Reklamationen
6509	Gesandtschaft Helsinki:	Wehrpflichtigenliste. Buch X für Schiffs- und Seemannsangelegenheiten. Telegramme. Freiwilligenfrage. Schriftwechsel des Schiffahrtssachverständigen beim deutschen Konsulat Petsamo. Petsamo Telegramme
6510	Gesandtschaft Helsinki:	Schiffe. Freigabe deutscher Schiffe "Irma" "Ravensberg" "Worms". Freigabe finnischer Schiffe "Aallotar" "Helmi". Nachforschungen. Nachlass Becker
6511	Gesandtschaft Helsinki:	Pass Sachen
6512	Gesandtschaft Helsinki:	Nachlass. Notenwechsel über Waffenhilfe, Prisenschiffe, Schiffsabgaben. Nordische Woche. Deutsche Schule in Helsingfors. Deutsche Vereine. Juden
6513	Gesandtschaft Helsinki:	Oberschlesien. Transoceanic o/a Schichau. Notariatsakte. Hauptgräberlisten
6514	Gesandtschaft Helsinki:	Politik
6515	Gesandtschaft Helsinki:	Politik
6516	Gesandtschaft Helsinki:	Politik
6517	Gesandtschaft Helsinki:	Hilfsamtsdiener Hartig. Attaché Karl Kuno Overbeck. Kanzler Schaller. Pache. Fräulein Schreiber, Frau Haaser. Legationsrat Hoffmann Crull. H.Toivonen Siilinjärvi. Dr.Friedmann. Militärattaché und Marinevertreter. Graf du Moulin. Brueck. Meynen. Hintze
6518	Gesandtschaft Helsinki:	Fogelholm. Kanzler Wucherpfennig. Hahn. Lampe. v.Küchler. Gesandtschaftsrat Dr.v.Grundherr. Preusker. Marta Teiskonen. Personalien S.Milewski. Hollberg. Handelsabteilung Personalien H.l. Personalien ausgeschiedener Personen, höhere und mittlere Beamte.
6520	Gesandtschaft Bukarest:	Rumäniens Aussenpolitik
6521	Gesandtschaft Athen:	Einkreisungspolitik
6528	Gesandtschaft Lissabon:	Geheimakten: Kohlen
6551	Botschaft Paris, Geheim:	Französische Wirtschaft, Handel, Industrie, Verkehr

6552	Botschaft Rom (Quirinal), Geheim:	Japan, China, Mandschukuo
6559	Botschaft Paris, Geheim:	Französisch Nordafrika
6597	Gesandtschaft Bern:	Berichte über Verhältnisse in den Feindstaaten, Kriegsziele, Friedensfühler
6641	Gesandtschaft Athen:	Sudetendeutschtum
6642	Gesandtschaft Budapest:	Geheimsachen
6643	Gesandtschaft Bukarest:	Politische Beziehungen: Deutschland - Rumänien
6644	Gesandtschaft Bukarest:	Deutsche Pressevertreter in Rumänien
6645	Botschaft Rom (Quirinal):	Rumänien
6671	Gesandtschaft Helsinki:	Deutsche Bestimmungen betr. Entschädigung von Kriegsschäden. Deutsche Zivilschäden in Finnland. Material für deutsche Zivilschaden Anmeldungen. Schriftwechsel mit Geschädigten, A-O.
6672	Gesandtschaft Helsinki:	Aufruhrschäden, Schriftwechsel mit Geschädigten, A-Z. Protokolle des deutschen Ausschusses, Abrechnungen des Kulturbeitrages. Walther. Frau Irene Schmidt
6673	Gesandtschaft Helsinki:	Berichtverzeichnisse
6674	Gesandtschaft Helsinki:	Schriftwechsel, geheim
6675	Gesandtschaft Helsinki:	Schriftwechsel, geheim
6676	Gesandtschaft Helsinki:	Schriftwechsel, geheim. Depots. Verfügungen des Auswärtigen Amtes, Tagebücher
6677	Gesandtschaft Helsinki:	Privata: Schnetzer, Schnapp, Goldbeck. Berichte vom VAA beim AHQ über sowjetrussisches Heer. Varia.
6791	Gesandtschaft Pressburg:	Zwischenstaatliche aussenpolitische Probleme
6792	Gesandtschaft Pressburg:	Zwischenstaatliche aussenpolitische Probleme
6809	Gesandtschaft Luxemburg:	Berichtsammlung
6810	Gesandtschaft Haag:	Jahres- und Lageberichte über Holland
6811	Botschaft Rom (Quirinal):	Belgien
6855	Botschaft Ankara:	Deutsche Innenpolitik. Auslandsorganisation
6859	Gesandtschaft Bern:	Schweizer Nationalsozialismus und Frontenbewegung
6860	Gesandtschaft Bern:	Schweizer Presse
6861	Gesandtschaft Bern:	Deutschenhetze, Greuelpropaganda
6862	Gesandtschaft Bern:	Deutschenhetze, Greuelpropaganda
6863	Botschaft Ankara:	Geheime und streng geheime Erlasse, Berichte, Telegramme

6906	Botschaft Rom (Quirinal):	Chile
6960	Gesandtschaft Sofia:	Gesandter Beckerle: Persönliche Aufzeichnungen
6961	Botschaft Rom (Quirinal), Geheim:	Deutsch-italienische Offizierskommission in Siebenbürgen; ungarisch-rumänische Beziehungen
6984	Gesandtschaft Lissabon:	Vertrauliche Erlasse des Auswärtigen Amtes
7028	Gesandtschaft Kopenhagen:	Skandinavien
7048	Botschaft Rom (Vatikan):	Reichskonkordat
7063	Gesandtschaft Bukarest:	Politische Beziehungen: Ungarn - Rumänien
7073	Gesandtschaft Stockholm:	Wirtschaftliche Beziehungen: Deutschland - Schweden
7207	Botschaft Paris:	Italien
7208	Botschaft Rom (Quirinal):	Italien: Aussenpolitik, allgemein
7209	Botschaft Rom (Quirinal):	Politische Beziehungen: Italien - Japan
7210	Botschaft Rom (Quirinal):	Politische Beziehungen: Italien - Österreich
7211	Botschaft Rom (Quirinal):	Politische Beziehungen: Italien - Russland
7212	Botschaft Rom (Quirinal):	Deutsch-italienische Beziehungen, Besuch Mussolini in Deutschland
7213	Botschaft Rom (Quirinal):	Deutsch-italienische Beziehungen: Besuch Ciano
7214	Botschaft Rom (Quirinal):	Deutsch-italienische Beziehungen: Besuch Reichsaussenminister v.Neurath
7215	Botschaft Rom (Quirinal):	Abessinien
7216	Botschaft Rom (Quirinal):	Abessinien: Sonderband; Sanktionen
7217	Gesandtschaft Bern:	Italien, allgemein
7218	Botschaft Rom (Quirinal):	Deutsch-italienischer Handelsvertrag
7219	Botschaft Rom (Quirinal):	Deutsch italienische Wirtschaftsverhandlungen und Vertrag
7220	Botschaft Moskau:	November Verhaftungen 1936
7221	Botschaft Moskau:	Politische Beziehungen: Sowjet Union - Italien
7222	Botschaft Moskau:	Neue Verfassung in der UdSSR
7223	Botschaft Moskau:	Innerpolitische Verhältnisse in der UdSSR
7225	Gesandtschaft Bern:	Russischer Massenmord polnischer Offiziere in Katyn. Massenmorde in Winniza
7230	Botschaft Rom (Quirinal), Geheim:	Tunis; arabische Bewegung

7231	Gesandtschaft Lissabon:	Deutsche Propaganda und Aufklärung. Pressebeziehungen: Deutschland - Portugal
7238	Botschaft Rom (Quirinal):	Türkei
7239	Botschaft Ankara:	Türkische Wirtschafts- und Handelspolitik
7240	Botschaft Ankara:	Politische Übersichten
7241	Botschaft Rom (Quirinal):	Politische Beziehungen: Italien-Türkei
7242	Botschaft Ankara:	Deutsch-türkische Wirtschaftsverhandlungen
7243	Botschaft Ankara:	Deutsch-türkische Wirtschaftsabkommen
7248	Generalkonsulat Danzig:	Verschiedene G.-Sachen
7249	Generalkonsulat Danzig:	Besprechungen mit dem Hohen Kommissar
7250	Botschaft Warschau, Geheim:	Geheime Reichssache
7251	Gesandtschaft Riga:	Randstaatenpolitik; Warschau-Rigaer Konferenz; östliche Garantieverträge
7260	Botschaft Warschau:	Briefe Schliep
7261	Generalkonsulat Danzig:	Völkerbund und Hoher Kommissar
7307	Botschaft Warschau:	Wiederherstellung der Souveränität auf den deutschen Strömen
7308	Gesandtschaft Bukarest:	Europäische und Internationale Donaukommission
7356	Botschaft Rom (Quirinal):	Donau
7358	Botschaft Moskau:	Deutsche Presse. DNB, Pressebeirat Baum, Stein, Dr.Schüle; Hellschreiberanlage
7364	Botschaft London, Geheim:	Marine
7368	Gesandtschaft Budapest:	Deutsch-ungarische Besprechungen zur Minderheitenfrage
7437	Botschaft London, Geheim:	Schweden
7440	Botschaft Rom (Quirinal):	Kunst und Wissenschaft: Deutsch-italienische Beziehungen, allgemein
7450	Botschaft Rom (Quirinal):	Politische Beziehungen: Italien - England
7453	Botschaft Paris:	Türkei
7455	Gesandtschaft Stockholm:	Abrüstung
7486	Gesandtschaft Bukarest:	Politische Beziehungen: Deutschland - Rumänien
7498	Botschaft Moskau:	Abt.D.geh. Akten aller Art; Inhaltsverzeichnis
7508	Botschaft Rom (Quirinal):	Deutsche Kolonialpolitik
7538	Botschaft Moskau:	Presse, speziell deutsche.
7549	Botschaft Ankara:	Deutsche Aussenhandelspolitik (Runderlasse)

7550	Gesandtschaft Kopenhagen:	Skandinavien
7551	Gesandtschaft Kopenhagen:	Dänische Politik
7552	Botschaft Moskau:	Politische Beziehungen: Sowjet Union - Finnland
7553	Gesandtschaft Oslo:	Thronreden und Stortingwahlen
7554	Gesandtschaft Oslo:	Nobelpreis
7555	Gesandtschaft Prag:	Deutsche Handelspolitik, Verträge, Gesamtübersicht
7556	Gesandtschaft Stockholm:	Schweden: Innen- und Aussenpolitik
7557	Gesandtschaft Stockholm:	Russland: Innen- und Aussenpolitik
7568	Botschaft London, Geheim:	Auswärtige Angelegenheiten
7589	Botschaft Warschau:	Minderheiten: Erklärungen. Deutsch-polnischer Volksgruppenvertrag. Beziehungen: Polen-Frankreich. Politik: Danzig. Deutschland: Ein- und Ausfuhrverbot von Kriegsgerät. Polen: See- und Kolonialliga.
7596	Generalkonsulat Danzig:	Beziehungen: Danzig-Polen (auch Entscheidungen des Völkerbundkommissars und des Völkerbundes). Volkstag und Parteiwesen. Hoher Kommissar Burckhart. Danziger Werft. Verschiedene G.-Sachen.
7597	Botschaft Brüssel:	Secreta
7598	Botschaft Warschau:	Deutsche Minderheiten in Polen: Genfer Abkommen
7599	Gesandtschaft Haag:	Belgien
7600	Gesandtschaft Riga:	Politische Beziehungen: Lettland - Russland
7601	Botschaft Moskau:	Politische Beziehungen: Sowjet Union - Randstaaten: Estland, Lettland, Litauen, Finnland
7603	Botschaft Paris:	Beziehungen zu Deutschland
7604	Botschaft Paris:	Deutsch-französische Wirtschaftspolitik, Handelsvertragsverhandlungen
7621	Botschaft Wien:	Grossbritannien und Kolonien
7622	Botschaft Ankara:	England
7623	Botschaft Rom (Quirinal):	Politische Beziehungen: Deutschland - Afghanistan
7624	Botschaft Warschau:	Londoner Kommuniqué vom 3.II.35; Besuch Simons in Berlin 25./26.III.35 Besuch Edens in Moskau 28.III.35 und Warschau 1.IV.35
7625	Botschaft Rom (Quirinal):	England-Frankreich. England-Japan. England-Russland
7626	Botschaft Warschau:	Politik: England

7628	Botschaft Warschau:	Politische Beziehungen: England - Japan
7629	Botschaft Rom (Quirinal):	England
7630	Botschaft Moskau:	Beziehungen Deutschlands zu England
7631	Botschaft London, Geheim:	Marine
7632	Gesandtschaft Sofia:	Allgemeine innen- und aussenpolitische Lage Englands und seine Überseebesitzungen. Irland
7633	Botschaft Paris:	England
7636	Gesandtschaft Riga:	Politische Beziehungen: Deutschland - Lettland
7640	Botschaft Paris:	Deutsch-französische Wirtschaftspolitik, Handelsvertragsverhandlungen
7664	Botschaft Rom (Quirinal):	Spanien
7675	Botschaft Rom (Quirinal), Geheim:	Admiral Canaris kommt auf die Botschaft
7680	Botschaft Rom (Quirinal):	Wirtschaftsbeziehungen: Italien - Ungarn. Politische Beziehungen: Italien-Japan. Donaustaaten
7681	Gesandtschaft Budapest:	Deutschlands auswärtige politische Beziehungen
7689	Botschaft Rom (Quirinal):	Wirtschaftsbeziehungen: Italien - Tschechoslowakei
7700	Botschaft Paris:	Deutschland; Präsident und Minister
7701	Botschaft Paris:	Internationale Ausstellung, Paris 1937
7728	Botschaft Paris:	Beziehungen zu Deutschland
7775	Botschaft Moskau, Geheim:	Politische Beziehungen: Deutschland - andere Staaten. Krieg mit Polen
7777	Gesandtschaft Haag:	Vertreter des Auswärtigen Amtes, Pressereferent
7778	Gesandtschaft Haag:	Der Vertreter des Auswärtigen Amtes im Stabe des Reichskommissars für das besetzte niederländische Gebiet, allgemeines
7779	Gesandtschaft Haag:	Urlaubsbestimmungen
7780	Gesandtschaft Haag:	UK-Stellung
7781	Gesandtschaft Haag:	General v.Unruh Aktion
7782	Gesandtschaft Haag:	W.Janke
7783	Gesandtschaft Haag:	Gesandter Bene
7784	Gesandtschaft Haag:	Personalia. Pressereferat
7785	Gesandtschaft Haag:	Legationssekretär Betz
7786	Gesandtschaft Haag:	Abteilung Rundfunk
7795	Gesandtschaft Reval:	Estlands Beziehungen zu Deutschland

7802	Gesandtschaft Reval:	Politische Fragen
7804	Botschaft Warschau:	Politische Berichte
7805	Botschaft Paris:	Auswärtige Angelegenheiten
7814	Botschaft Rom (Quirinal):	Deutsche Wirtschaftspolitik, allgemein
7821	Botschaft Wien:	Deutsch-österreichisches Abkommen
7829	Botschaft Paris:	Deutsch-französische Wirtschafts-politik, Handelsvertragsverhandlungen
7831	Botschaft Paris:	Elsass-Lothringen
7834	Botschaft Paris:	Comité des Forges
7845	Botschaft Paris:	Luftpakt, Handakten Köster
7851	Gesandtschaft Prag:	Deutsche Devisenordnung
7852	Botschaft Rom (Quirinal):	Politische Beziehungen: Italien - Jugoslawien
7853	Botschaft Ankara:	Besuche führender Staatsmänner
7854	Gesandtschaft Athen:	Griechenland und andere Staaten. Kommunismus, Freimaurertum, Soziali-stische Bewegungen
7858	Botschaft Wien:	Handelsverträge: Spanien, Tschecho-slowakei, Türkei, Ungarn
7859	Botschaft Moskau:	Politische Beziehungen: Sowjet Union - Bulgarien
7860	Gesandtschaft Bukarest:	Rumäniens Aussenpolitik. Rumäniens Innenpolitik: Jahresberichte
7861	Gesandtschaft Belgrad:	Politisches, geheim
7864	Gesandtschaft Budapest:	Deutsch-ungarische Beziehungen. Ungarns innere politische Lage. Nationalitäten in Ungarn; deutsche Minderheiten. Ungarns auswärtige politische Beziehun-gen. Geheimsachen
7875	Botschaft Ankara	Deutsche Aussenhandelspolitik (Rund-erlasse)
7880	Botschaft Rom (Quirinal), Geheim:	Memorandum betr.Locarnokündigung
7885	Botschaft Rom (Quirinal):	Minderheitenfragen, Südtirol
7887	Gesandtschaft Bukarest:	Rumäniens Innenpolitik: Prozess Codreanus
7889	Gesandtschaft Belgrad:	Jugoslawien: Innere Politik, Parlament, Parteiwesen
7965	Botschaft Paris:	Deutsches Garantieangebot; Sicherheits-pakt Locarno
7983	Botschaft Warschau:	Neueingänge, Wochenberichte, verschie-denes. Wirtschaft. Auflösung der Tschechoslowakei. Politische Berichte. Chiffrierwesen II (Rundfunk) geheim Geheime Reichssache (Wirtschaft)

7987	Botschaft Rom (Quirinal), Geheim:	Deutsch-polnischer Konflikt: Schrift-wechsel, Aufzeichnungen, Handelsange-legenheiten. Telegramme. Englisch-französischer Krieg gegen Deutschland, Informationstelegramme und Schrift-wechsel, betr.Presse
7990	Botschaft Rom (Quirinal):	Deutsch-italienische Beziehungen: Besuch Benni. Polen
7991	Botschaft Paris:	Informationstelegramme. Danzig
7992	Botschaft Moskau, Geheim:	Politische Beziehungen: Deutschland – Polen und Danzig. Deutsche Innenpolitik: Militär-, Marine-, Luftfahrtangelegen-heiten; Wehr- und Arbeitsdienstpflicht. Innenpolitik der Sowjet Union. Presse- und Propagandawesen: Beziehungen zu Deutschland, Presseattachés. Presse- und Propagandawesen in Deutschland, allgemeines. Sicherheitsfragen. Politische Beziehungen: Sowjet Union – Spanien (Gefangenenaustausch) Poli-tische Beziehungen: Sowjet-Union –Japan (Mandschukuo, chinesisch-japanischer Krieg; Zwischenfälle an der mongolisch-mandschurischen Grenze)
7995	Botschaft Moskau, Geheim:	Politische Beziehungen: Sowjet Union – Japan (Mandschukuo, chinesich-japani-scher Krieg; Zwischenfälle an der mon-golisch-mandschurischen Grenze)
7997	Gesandtschaft Bukarest:	Rumänische Aufrüstung
7998	Gesandtschaft Bukarest:	Räterussland, politisch
7999	Gesandtschaft Bukarest:	Rumäniens Aussenpolitik
8002	Botschaft Rom (Quirinal):	Deutsch-italienische Beziehungen, all-gemein
8026	Botschaft Wien:	Italien
8036	Botschaft Rom (Quirinal):	Donaustaaten
8038	Botschaft Rom (Quirinal), Geheim:	Berichtesammlung Hassels über Lage in Italien; Privater Briefwechsel. Wirtschaftspolitik: Italien-Österreich-Ungarn. Deutschland-Italien. Südtirol.
8054	Botschaft Rom (Quirinal):	Deutsch-italienische Beziehungen, all-gemein
8055	Botschaft Rom (Quirinal):	Abessinien
8057	Botschaft Rom (Quirinal):	Abessinien, Sonderband: Sanktionen
8058	Botschaft Rom (Quirinal):	Minderheitenfragen, Südtirol
8059	Botschaft Rom (Quirinal):	Italienische Ministerien
8065	Botschaft Rom (Quirinal):	Botschafter v.Hassell, privater Schriftwechsel
8066	Botschaft Rom (Quirinal):	Deutschland: Innen- und Aussenpolitik, allgemein
8067	Botschaft Rom (Quirinal):	Deutschland: Nationalsozialismus

8073	Botschaft Rom (Quirinal):	Italien: Aussenpolitik, allgemein
8075	Botschaft Rom (Quirinal):	Wirtschaftsbeziehungen: Italien - Österreich
8076	Botschaft Rom (Quirinal):	Wirtschaftsbeziehungen: Italien - Ungarn
8077	Botschaft Rom (Quirinal):	Deutsch-italienische Wirtschaftsbeziehungen, allgemein
8078	Botschaft Rom (Quirinal):	Deutsch-italienische Wirtschaftsverhandlungen und Vertrag
8079	Botschaft Rom (Quirinal):	Internationale Wirtschaftsfragen
8112	Botschaft Rom (Vatikan), Geheim:	Allgemeines
8125	Botschaft Rom (Vatikan):	Reichskonkordat
8132	Botschaft Paris:	Informationstelegramme
8153	Gesandtschaft Oslo:	Auflösung der Tschechoslowakei, Rückkehr Memel
8154	Botschaft Warschau:	Polen, Militärwesen
8155	Botschaft Warschau:	Neueingänge, verschiedenes
8157	Botschaft Warschau:	Wirtschaft, Neueingänge, verschiedenes
8203	Botschaft Paris:	Innere Angelegenheiten
8211	Botschaft Paris:	Francois Poncet, Handakten Köster
8212	Gesandtschaft Kowno:	Diplomatisch- und konsularisches Korps. Auswärtiger Dienst
8213	Botschaft Paris:	Französische Missionen und Konsularvertretungen in Deutschland
8265	Generalkonsulat Danzig:	Beziehungen: Deutschland - Polen
8267	Botschaft Rom (Quirinal), Geheim:	Reise und Besuch des Kreuzers "Emden" 1937, 1938 und des Kadettenschulschiffes "Schleswig-Holstein". Panzerschiff "Deutschland" und 4.Torpedobootflotille in Neapel
8275	Botschaft Rom (Quirinal):	Bulgarien
8276	Gesandtschaft Kopenhagen:	Minderheiten und Schulfragen
8277	Botschaft Warschau:	Politische Berichte
8278	Botschaft Warschau:	Neueingänge, Politik, verschiedenes
8279	Botschaft Rom (Quirinal):	Deutschland: Reichsparteitag, Sonderband
8283	Gesandtschaft Belgrad:	Jugoslawiens Haltung zu Deutschland nach September 1939 gegenseitige Lieferungen
8284	Gesandtschaft Kopenhagen:	Politische Angelegenheiten
8285	Gesandtschaft Luxemburg:	Berichtsammlung

8286	Gesandtschaft Bern:	Neutralität der Schweiz
8287	Generalkonsulat Danzig:	Kriegsschiffsbesuche: Schleswig - Holstein
8302	Gesandtschaft Luxemburg:	Geheim-Tagebuch des Gesandten
8332	Botschaft Rom (Quirinal), Geheim:	Begegnung Ley-Cianetti
8336	Botschaft Rom (Quirinal):	Propagandamaterial; verschiedene Quellen
8341	Botschaft Rom (Quirinal):	Deutsch-italienische Beziehungen, Sammelband
8342	Botschaft Ankara:	Deutsch-Türkische Wirtschaftsbeziehungen und Verhandlungen
8343	Botschaft Ankara:	Rüstungsindustrie
8346	Botschaft Brüssel:	Aussenpolitik Belgiens
8356	Botschaft Rom (Quirinal):	Deutsch-italienische Beziehungen, Sammelband
8357	Gesandtschaft Bukarest:	Rumäniens Aussenpolitik
8367	Gesandtschaft Bern:	Geheimakten
8368	Botschaft Warschau:	Neueingänge, verschiedenes
8369	Gesandtschaft Bern:	Geheimakten
8371	Botschaft Paris:	Parteitag, Tagungen, Zusammenkünfte
8372	Botschaft Paris:	Ansprüche und Beschwerden gegen den deutschen Staat
8376	Gesandtschaft Budapest:	Ausgehende Telegramme
8377	Gesandtschaft Bukarest:	Rumänische Aussenpolitik
8378	Gesandtschaft Bukarest:	Politische Beziehungen: Ungarn - Rumänien
8389	Gesandtschaft Oslo:	Überfall des M/S "Altmark"
8392	Botschaft Rom (Quirinal), Geheim:	Teilnahme des Generals Halder an italienischen Manövern.
8395	Botschaft Rom (Quirinal), Geheim:	Telegramme
8402	Botschaft Madrid:	Spanische Militär-, Marine- und Luftattachés
8417	Botschaft Rom (Quirinal):	Adolf Hitler
8419	Gesandtschaft Belgrad:	Politische Beziehungen: Jugoslawien - Deutschland
8420	Botschaft Rom (Quirinal):	Deutsch-italienische Beziehungen: Besuch Göring
8422	Botschaft Moskau, Geheim:	Politische Beziehungen: Sowjet Union - Spanien (Gefangenenaustausch)
8433	Botschaft Moskau:	Akten und Karten der Umsiedlungskommission

8439	Gesandtschaft Kowno:	Politische Beziehungen: Litauen-Polen
8471	Generalkonsulat Danzig:	Das Polentum in Danzig
8490	Botschaft Ankara:	Änderung der deutschen Prisenordnung in Europakonflikt
8491	Botschaft Ankara:	Rüstungsindustrie
8493	Botschaft Ankara:	Deutsch-Türkische Wirtschaftsbeziehungen und Verhandlungen
8501	Botschaft Rom (Quirinal):	Deutsch-italienische Beziehungen, Sammelband
8505	Gesandtschaft Luxemburg:	Luxemburgische Sicherheitsfragen
8511	Gesandtschaft Reval:	Politische Beziehungen: Estland - Räterussland
8515	Botschaft Moskau, Geheim:	Politische Beziehungen: Sowjet Union - Deutschland
8544	Gesandtschaft Bern:	Deutscher Nationalsozialismus in der Schweiz
8568	Gesandtschaft Oslo:	Neutralität Norwegens
8583	Botschaft Rom (Quirinal):	Deutschland: Reichsparteitag, Sonderband
8624	Botschaft Rom (Quirinal):	Türkei
8675	Botschaft Wien, Geheim:	NSDAP in Österreich
8676	Botschaft Wien, Geheim:	Dr.Gustav v.Wächter
8678	Botschaft Wien:	Deutsch-österreichisches Abkommen
8680	Botschaft Rom (Quirinal):	Italien: Aussenpolitik, allgemein
8681	Botschaft Paris:	Abrüstung, Handakten Köster
8684	Botschaft Rom (Quirinal):	Allgemeine Abrüstungsfragen
8723	Botschaft Rom (Quirinal), Geheim:	Saargebiet
8747	Botschaft Paris:	Beziehungen zu Russland
8748	Botschaft Paris:	Frankreich-Russland (Handakten Köster)
8754	Botschaft Rom (Vatikan):	30. Juni 1934 und damit Zusammenhängendes
8756	Botschaft Rom (Quirinal), Geheim:	Runderlass des Auswärtigen Amtes: Die gegenwärtige Lage und die Ziele der deutschen Aussenhandelspolitik
8758	Botschaft Moskau:	Litwinow-Barthou Ostpakt
8759	Botschaft Paris:	Ostpakt
8760	Botschaft Paris:	Ostpakt
8762	Botschaft Rom (Quirinal):	Deutschland: Innen- und Aussenpolitik, allgemein
8782	Botschaft Rom (Quirinal), Geheim:	Aktivität des ehemaligen japanischen Botschafters in Rom betr.Zusammenschluss Rom-Tokio-Berlin

8783	Botschaft Rom (Quirinal), Geheim:	Bildung und Anerkennung der Regierund Wang Ching Wei
8812	Botschaft Moskau:	Litwinow-Barthou Ostpakt
8836	Botschaft Moskau, Geheim:	Politische Beziehungen: Deutschland - andere Staaten. Krieg mit Polen
8840	Botschaft Rom (Quirinal):	Sonderband: Mussolini Paktvorschlag
8892	Botschaft Rom (Vatikan)	Berichtskopien der Quirinal-Gesandtschaft
8903	Botschaft Rom (Quirinal), Geheim:	Vertrag der Verständigung und Zusammenarbeit: Viererpakt, Rom
8904	Botschaft Rom (Quirinal), Geheim:	Politischer Bericht: Unterredung über den Viererpakt
8906	Botschaft Paris:	Viermächtepakt, Handakten Köster
8910	Botschaft Rom (Quirinal), Geheim:	Vertrag der Verständigung und Zusammenarbeit Deutschland, Grossbritannien, Frankreich, Italien
8916	Botschaft Rom (Quirinal):	Politische Beziehungen: Italien - Frankreich
8920	Gesandtschaft Bukarest:	Ordensangelegenheiten, besonderes
8932	Botschaft Rom (Quirinal):	Donaustaaten
8949	Botschaft Rom (Quirinal):	Deutschland: Nationalsozialismus, Sonderband
8951	Botschaft Rom (Quirinal):	Wirtschaftspolitik: Deutschland - Frankreich
8970	Botschaft Rom (Quirinal):	Abstimmungsgebiete: Saargebiet
8973	Botschaft Rom (Quirinal):	Wirtschaftsbeziehungen: Italien-Österreich
8983	Botschaft Rom (Quirinal):	Österreich
8984	Botschaft Moskau:	Politische Beziehungen: Sowjet Union - Japan
9007	Gesandtschaft Kowno:	Deutsch-litauische Wirtschaftsverhandlungen
9043	Botschaft Rom (Quirinal):	Italien: Aussenpolitik, allgemein
9045	Botschaft Rom (Quirinal):	Minderheitenfragen, Südtirol
9051	Generalkonsulat Danzig:	Professor Dr. Noe
9053	Botschaft Rom (Quirinal):	Deutsch-italienische Wirtschaftsverhandlungen und Vertrag
9057	Generalkonsulat Danzig:	Verschiedene G.-Sachen
9058	Generalkonsulat Danzig:	Überbrückungskredite und Massnahmen zur Sanierung der Danziger Staatsfinanzen
9059	Generalkonsulat Danzig:	Hoher Kommissar Kostin
9060	Generalkonsulat Danzig:	Besprechungen mit dem Hohen Kommissar

9086	Generalkonsulat Danzig:	Verschiedene G.-Sachen
9087	Generalkonsulat Danzig:	Besprechungen mit dem Hohen Kommissar
9093	Botschaft Warschau:	Interessengemeinschaft in Kattowitz, geheim
9113	Botschaft Moskau:	Politische Beziehungen: Sowjet Union - China
9148	Botschaft Moskau:	Lage im fernen Osten
9163	Generalkonsulat Danzig:	Reichswehr; Militärische Angelegenheiten
9166	Generalkonsulat Danzig:	Besprechungen mit dem Hohen Kommissar
9168	Generalkonsulat Danzig:	Hoher Kommissar Lester
9170	Generalkonsulat Danzig:	Beziehungen: Danzig-Polen (auch Entscheidungen des Völkerbundkommissars und des Völkerbundes)
9172	Botschaft Warschau:	Eisenbahnzahlungen an Polen aus dem Durchgangsverkehr durch den Korridor. Handakten zu den Transitverhandlungen in Berlin vom 11. bis 21.XII.1936
9214	Botschaft Paris:	Danzig und Ostfrage; Handakten Köster
9215	Generalkonsulat Danzig:	Handakten, Berichtsdurchschläge
9222	Botschaft Moskau:	Beziehungen Deutschlands zu Polen
9257	Botschaft Ankara:	Deutsch-Türkische Wirtschaftsbeziehungen und Verhandlungen
9258	Botschaft Ankara:	Wirtschaftsbeziehungen und Bestrebungen Frankreichs auf dem Balkan
9338	Gesandtschaft Sofia, Geheim:	Lose A-Akten
9340	Gesandtschaft Belgrad:	Wirtschaftliches, geheim
9349	Botschaft Rom (Quirinal):	Politische Beziehungen: Italien - Jugoslawien
9389	Botschaft Warschau:	Deutsch-polnisches Kompensationsgeschäft
9390	Botschaft Warschau:	Artikel 218 des Genfer Abkommens
9391	Botschaft Warschau:	Deutsch-polnisches Wirtschaftsabkommen und Verhandlungen
9392	Botschaft Warschau:	Deutsch-polnisches Wirtschaftsabkommen und Verhandlungen
9395	Botschaft Warschau:	Deutsche Minderheiten in Polen, generalia
9396	Botschaft Warschau:	Nationalitäten, Minderheiten, Judenfrage
9399	Botschaft Paris:	Wirtschaftsangelegenheiten
9400	Botschaft Rom (Quirinal):	Deutsche Wirtschaftspolitik, allgemein
9411	Botschaft Rom (Quirinal):	Internationale Wirtschaftsfragen
9443	Gesandtschaft Prag:	Deutsche Devisenordnung

9444	Botschaft Moskau:	Namen A-R. Verhaftungen in Tiflis und Batum. Abteilung D.H.6 Junkerswerke
9446	Botschaft Moskau:	Politische Beziehungen: Sowjet Union - Frankreich (Nichtangriffspakt)
9456	Botschaft Moskau:	Konsulntreffen und -besprechungen
9459	Botschaft Moskau:	Politische Beziehungen, geheim: Vergehen gegen "Derop"
9462	Botschaft Moskau:	Politische Beziehungen: Sowjet Union - Italien
9472	Botschaft Moskau:	Entwicklung der Beziehungen zu Junkers und dem Reich, bezgl. Zusammenarbeit in Russland
9506	Gesandtschaft Budapest:	Ausgehende Telegramme
9525	Botschaft Moskau:	Russische Beschwerden über Verhaftungen, Haussuchungen bei Sowjet Staatsangehörigen in Deutschland
9535	Botschaft Moskau:	Deutschfeindliche und Gegenpropaganda
9538	Gesandtschaft Belgrad:	Politische Beziehungen: Jugoslawien - Deutschland
9542	Gesandtschaft Prag:	NSDAP
9586	Gesandtschaft Budapest:	Geheimsachen
9600	Gesandtschaft Budapest:	Donaupaktfragen
9620	Generalkonsulat Danzig:	Handakten; Berichtsdurchschläge
9623	Gesandtschaft Reval:	Estlands Beziehungen zu Deutschland
9653	Botschaft Rom (Quirinal):	Allgemeine Abrüstungsfragen
9685	Botschaft Rom (Quirinal):	Donaustaaten
9706	Gesandtschaft Prag:	Schwarze Front
9708	Gesandtschaft Belgrad:	Politik, Kleine Entente
9722	Gesandtschaft Budapest:	Nationalitäten in Ungarn; deutsche Minderheiten
9747	Generalkonsulat Danzig:	Beziehungen: Danzig-Polen (auch Entscheidungen des Völkerbundkommissars und des Völkerbundes)
9784	Gesandtschaft Budapest:	Entwicklung des deutsch-ungarischen Warenverkehrs
9787	Gesandtschaft Zagreb, Geheim:	Politische Beziehungen: Kroatien - andere Staaten. Kroatien: Innenpolitik. Militär-, Marine- und Luftangelegenheiten. Bekämpfung der aufständischen Partisanen. Deutsche Aussen- und Innenpolitik. Bekämpfung der Kommunisten. Zwischenstaatliche aussenpolitische Probleme, Kirchenfragen, Religion. Bolschwismus. Ustasche. Feindtätigkeit. Deutsche Dienststellen. Reichs- und Volksdeutsche. Deutsche Polizeiattachés. Passrecht. Personalien. Informationsmaterial. Vorträge, Abkommen, Kroatisches Wehrgesetz. Lageberichte.

928

9787 Gesandtschaft Zagreb, Geheim: Dienstanweisungen. Kriegseinsatz. Geheime Reichssachen. Bauxit. Mineralöl. Holz. Eisenerze. Finanzangelegenheiten. Eisenbahn. Ernährungsfragen. Handelsbeziehungen. Beziehungen mit Italien und anderen Ländern. Protokolle. Verschiedenes. Pressevertreter. Cetnini-Greuel, Juden. Korrespondenz des Gesandten (auch ser.no. 3894, 6136, 3014, 3903, 6137, 5554, pp.853-56)

9788 Botschaft Warschau: Politik: Österreich

9792 Botschaft Ankara: Deutsch-Türkische Wirtschaftsbeziehungen und Verhandlungen

9795 Generalkonsulat Memel: Entziehung der Arbeitsgenehmigung und Ausweisung von Beamten und Angestellten

9796 Generalkonsulat Memel: Memelländisches Parteiwesen

9797 Generalkonsulat Memel: Deutsch-litauische Wirtschaftsverhandlungen

9798 Gesandtschaft Kowno: Memel, Politik, Sonderband: Entlassung reichsdeutscher Beamte und Verweigerung von Arbeitsgenehmigungen für reichsdeutsche Arbeitnehmer im Memelgebiet

9799 Generalkonsulat Memel: Deutsch-litauischer Handelsvertrag; Memelgebiet

9800 Gesandtschaft Kowno: Deutsch-litauische Wirtschaftsverhandlungen

9801 Gesandtschaft Kowno: Deutsch-litauischer Handelsvertrag

9807 Botschaft Rom (Quirinal): Deutsch-italienische Beziehungen, allgemein

9812 Gesandtschaft Kowno: Deutsch-litauische Beziehungen

9814 Gesandtschaft Kowno: Politik, allgemeine Angelegenheiten: Jahresübersichten der Gesandtschaft und anderer deutschen Auslandsbehörden

9815 Generalkonsulat Danzig: Beziehungen: Danzig-Polen (auch Entscheidungen des Völkerbundkommissars und des Völkerbundes)

9820 Gesandtschaft Zagreb: Staatsbesuche. Vizekonsulat Susak. Allgemeiner Schriftverkehr. Umsiedlung von Aufständischen. Militär-, Luft-, Marine-, Polizeiattaché. Kroatien: Innenpolitik. Staatsoberhaupt. Aufstandsbewegung, Spionagewesen. Cetnikfrage. Kommunisten. Wahlen. Hoheitszeichen. Freimaurer. Politische Rechtsangelegenheiten. Politisches Material. NSDAP. Militär, Wehrpflicht. Wirtschaftliche Kriegsmassnahmen. Bauxittransporte. Fette. Verkehrsfragen. Eisenbahnverkehr. Geheimakte: Rekruten. Einsatzstaffel. Partisanentätigkeit. Umsiedlung Bosnien. Volkspolitische Tagungen. Sicherung deutscher Siedlungen.

9820	Gesandtschaft Zagreb:	Vereidigung von Kroaten in der deutschen Gendarmerie. Kroatisch-serbischer Aktenaustausch. Werbung zur Waffen SS
9827	Gesandtschaft Bukarest:	Kleine Entente, politisch
9848	Gesandtschaft Bukarest:	Donauföderation
9852	Botschaft Wien:	Geheim III; Ganz geheime Sachen
9863	Botschaft Rom (Quirinal), Geheim:	Eintritt Italiens in den Krieg. Verhältnis Russlands zu Italien, Balkan, Bessarabienfrage
9866	Botschaft Rom (Quirinal), Geheim):	Verhältnis Russland zu Italien, Balkan, Bessarabienfrage
9868	Gesandtschaft Oslo:	Vercharterung norwegischen Schiffraums
9877	Gesandtschaft Bern:	Kriegsmassnahmen der Schweiz
9885	Botschaft Ankara:	Deutsch-Türkische Wirtschaftsbeziehungen und Verhandlungen
9886	Botschaft Ankara:	Deutsch-Türkische Wirtschaftsbeziehungen und Verhandlungen
9887	Botschaft Paris:	Informationstelegramme
9902	Botschaft Ankara:	Geheime und streng geheime Erlasse, Berichte, Telegramme
9905	Botschaft Ankara:	Geheime Erlasse
9906	Botschaft Ankara:	Deutsch-Türkische Wirtschaftsbeziehungen und Verhandlungen
9910	Botschaft Rom (Quirinal):	Italien: Aussenpolitik, allgemein
9911	Botschaft Paris:	Abessinien
9912	Gesandtschaft Bern:	Schweizer Nationalsozialismus und Frontenbewegung
9913	Gesandtschaft Bern:	Belästigung und Angriffe auf Deutsche
9914	Gesandtschaft Bern:	Neutralitätswidriges Verhalten der Schweizer Presse
9919	Gesandtschaft Budapest:	Eingehende Multex Telegramme
9920	Gesandtschaft Lissabon:	Deutsch-polnischer Krieg 1939 und dessen Auswirkung auf England und Frankreich
9925	Gesandtschaft Lissabon:	Geheimakten
9931	Botschaft Rom (Quirinal):	Sonderband: Mussolini Paktvorschlag
9932	Botschaft Rom (Quirinal):	Diplomatische Privilegien
9958	Botschaft Rom (Quirinal):	Politische Beziehungen: Italien - Österreich
9968	Botschaft Paris:	Informationstelegramme
9971	Botschaft Rom (Quirinal):	Politische Beziehungen: Italien - Österreich

9973	Gesandtschaft Kowno:	Grenzverkehr, allgemeines
9974	Gesandtschaft Kowno:	Militärangelegenheiten, geheim
9984	Botschaft Warschau:	Deutsch-polnische Vereinbarungen vom 26.I.1934
K 553	Botschaft Rom (Quirinal):	Missionschef
K 554	Botschaft Rom (Quirinal):	Botschafter von Neurath, verschiedener Schriftwechsel
K 555	Botschaft Rom (Quirinal):	Botschaftsrat v.Prittwitz, Handakten
K 556	Botschaft Rom (Quirinal):	Botschaftsrat v.Prittwitz, Schriftwechsel
K 557	Botschaft Rom (Quirinal):	Generalkonsul v.Herff
K 579	Botschaft Rom (Quirinal):	Stadtrat Sassenbach
K 580	Botschaft Rom (Quirinal):	Legationssekretär Dr.Ulrich
K 643	Botschaft Wien:	Kurierangelegenheiten: v.Rosenberg, Pfeifer
K 653	Botschaft Rom (Quirinal), Geheim:	Südtirol
K 655	Botschaft Rom (Quirinal), Geheim:	Diverses politisches Material
K 656	Botschaft Rom (Quirinal), Geheim:	Italiens Beziehungen
K 657	Botschaft Rom (Quirinal), Geheim:	Türkei-Bulgarien-Balkan
K 658	Botschaft Rom (Quirinal), Geheim:	Politische und sonstige Persönlichkeiten
K 659	Botschaft Rom (Quirinal), Geheim:	Diplomatische Vertretungen und Persönlichkeiten
K 660	Botschaft Rom (Quirinal), Geheim:	Dr.Sonnenschein in Mailand
K 661	Botschaft Rom (Quirinal), Geheim:	Botschafter v.Hassels Bericht: Wege zur Information der italienischen Regierung und öffentlichen Meinung
K 662	Botschaft Rom (Quirinal), Geheim:	Gewinnung von Zeitungen zur Propaganda
K 663	Botschaft Rom (Quirinal), Geheim:	Schriftwechsel von Simson und Bergmann über die deutschen Reparationsverpflichtungen
K 664	Botschaft Rom (Quirinal), Geheim:	Bitte an Nitti um Intervention zwecks Zurückziehung der französischen Truppen aus dem Einfallsgebiet
K 665	Botschaft Rom (Quirinal), Geheim:	Konferenz in Stresa
K 666	Botschaft Rom (Quirinal), Geheim:	Instruktionen für Spa
K 667	Botschaft Rom (Quirinal), Geheim:	Genua Konferenz

K 668	Botschaft Rom (Quirinal), Geheim:	Schuldfrage
K 669	Botschaft Rom (Quirinal), Geheim:	Friedensvertrag: Reparationen und damit zusammenhängende Fragen
K 670	Botschaft Rom (Quirinal), Geheim:	Geheimakte in wirtschaftlichen Angelegenheiten
K 671	Botschaft Rom (Quirinal), Geheim:	Wirtschaftliche und finanzielle Lage Deutschlands, Italiens und anderer Länder in den Nachkriegsjahren
K 672	Botschaft Rom (Quirinal), Geheim:	Verhandlungen über Ablösung deutschen Eigentums in Italien
K 673	Botschaft Rom (Quirinal), Geheim:	Schriftwechsel Bonnemann und Transatlantica
K 674	Botschaft Rom (Quirinal), Geheim:	Deutsch-italienische Wirtschaftsbeziehungen
K 675	Botschaft Rom (Quirinal), Geheim:	Verschiedene Presseangelegenheiten
K 676	Botschaft Rom (Quirinal), Geheim:	Kunst und Wissenschaft
K 677	Botschaft Rom (Quirinal), Geheim:	Sonstige A Berichte
K 678	Botschaft Rom (Quirinal), Geheim:	Hassel: Privater Briefwechsel
K 706	Botschaft Rom (Quirinal):	Verhandlungen über einen deutsch-italienischen Schiedsvertrag
K 1006	Botschaft Paris:	Ägypten
K 1043	Botschaft Rom (Quirinal), Geheim:	Deutschland-Italien
K 1044	Botschaft Rom (Quirinal), Geheim:	Politische Beziehungen: Italien - Frankreich
K 1045	Botschaft Rom (Quirinal), Geheim:	Dienstbetrieb
K 1046	Botschaft Rom (Quirinal), Geheim:	Abrüstung: Brief Forster's an französischen Militärattaché Durand
K 1047	Botschaft Rom (Quirinal), Geheim:	Berichtesammlung Hassel über Lage in Italien
K 1048	Botschaft Rom (Quirinal):	Militärattaché, allgemein
K 1049	Botschaft Rom (Quirinal):	Balkanstaaten
K 1050	Botschaft Rom (Quirinal):	Junkers-Siemens
K 1051	Botschaft Rom (Quirinal):	Wirtschaftsbeziehungen: Italien - Österreich
K 1066	Botschaft Wien:	Habsburger Frage
K 1167	Botschaft Paris:	Österreich
K 1168	Botschaft Paris:	Deutsch-österreichisches Zollabkommen
K 1170	Gesandtschaft Budapest:	Deutsch-Österreich

K 1171	Gesandtschaft Bern:	Donaukonföderation
K 1172	Gesandtschaft Belgrad:	Frage Anschluss Österreich an Deutschland
K 1173	Gesandtschaft Prag:	Beziehungen zu Österreich
K 1177	Botschaft Rom (Vatikan):	Akten der ehemaligen österreichischen Gesandtschaft beim Heiligen Stuhl
K 1178	Botschaft Rom (Vatikan):	Akten der ehemaligen österreichischen Gesandtschaft beim Heiligen Stuhl
K 1179	Botschaft Rom (Vatikan):	Akten der ehemaligen österreichischen Gesandtschaft beim Heiligen Stuhl
K 1180	Botschaft London, Geheim:	Österreich
K 1181	Botschaft London, Geheim:	Österreich
K 1182	Botschaft Rom (Vatikan):	Österreich, Vorarlberg, Liechtenstein
K 1183	Botschaft Wien:	Abwicklung des ehemaligen österreichischen Aussendienstes
K 1184	Botschaft Wien:	Friedensverhandlungen
K 1185	Botschaft Wien:	Kirchenangelegenheiten, Kurie, Katholizismus, Protestantismus
K 1188	Botschaft Wien:	Vertretungen, österreichischer Aussendienst, fremde Diplomatie, Zollvergünstigungen
K 1189	Botschaft Wien:	Diplomatisches Korps, amtliche Persönlichkeiten, Politiker
K 1190	Botschaft Wien:	Militärangelegenheiten
K 1191	Botschaft Rom (Quirinal):	Österreich
K 1192	Botschaft Wien:	Emigrantenrückkehr, Listen
K 1195	Botschaft Wien:	Österreichische Völkerbundsanleihe
K 1196	Botschaft Wien:	Österreich: Innere Angelegenheiten
K 1554	Botschaft Ankara:	Botschaftsrat Fabricius, dienstlicher Schriftwechsel
K 1555	Botschaft Ankara:	Vertrauensarzt der Botschaft
K 1556	Botschaft Ankara:	Deutsche Konsularbehörden in der Türkei, Konsulatsbezirke
K 1557	Botschaft Ankara:	Deutsch-türkische Beziehungen
K 1558	Botschaft Ankara:	Politische Beziehungen zu Deutschland, zu und zwischen anderen Staaten. Verträge
K 1559	Botschaft Ankara:	Weltpolitik
K 1560	Botschaft Ankara:	Politische Stimmungsberichte der Konsulate
K 1561	Botschaft Ankara:	Sandjak Alexandrette
K 1562	Botschaft Ankara:	Europakonflikt 1939/40
K 1563	Botschaft Ankara:	Europakonflikt 1940/42

K 1564	Botschaft Ankara:	Syrien geheim
K 1565	Botschaft Ankara:	Arabien, Ägypten, Irak, Palästina, Persien, Syrien
K 1566	Botschaft Ankara:	Innenpolitik der Türkei
K 1567	Botschaft Ankara:	Judentum
K 1568	Botschaft Ankara:	Berichte, Telegramme, geheime und streng geheime Erlasse
K 1569	Botschaft Ankara:	Deutsche Innenpolitik. Auslandsorganisation
K 1570	Botschaft Ankara:	Politische Attentate
K 1571	Botschaft Ankara:	Presse, allgemeines
K 1572	Botschaft Ankara:	Türkische Presse, allgemein
K 1573	Botschaft Ankara:	Pressepropaganda in der Türkei
K 1574	Botschaft Ankara:	Verwertung und Verbreitung pressepropagandistischer Nachrichten; Türkische Presseartikel
K 1575	Botschaft Ankara:	Wochenfunkspiegel
K 1576	Botschaft Ankara:	Presse- und Propagandawesen. Berichte des Pressereferenten
K 1577	Botschaft Ankara:	Pressedienst Berlin
K 1578	Botschaft Ankara:	Erlasse von, und Berichte an, die Informationsabteilung in Propagandaangelegenheiten
K 1579	Botschaft Ankara:	Druckschriften der Propagandaabteilung
K 1580	Botschaft Ankara:	Bücher, Zeitschriften, Drucksachen, Propagandamaterial; Beanstandung durch die Türkei
K 1581	Botschaft Ankara:	Pressevertreter, allgemein
K 1582	Botschaft Ankara:	Deutsches Nachrichten Büro
K 1583	Botschaft Ankara:	Syrien. Pressepropaganda
K 1584	Botschaft Ankara:	Geheimerlasse der Informationsabteilung und D IV. Presse und Propaganda, geheim
K 1585	Gesandtschaft Bern:	Massnahmen gegen schweizerische Staatsangehörige in Deutschland
K 1586	Gesandtschaft Bern:	Verfahren gegen Schweizer
K 1587	Gesandtschaft Bern:	Palästina
K 1588	Gesandtschaft Bern:	Polen, allgemein
K 1589	Gesandtschaft Bern:	Jüdische Angelegenheiten
K 1590	Gesandtschaft Bern:	Prozess "Protokolle der Weisen von Zion"
K 1591	Gesandtschaft Bern:	Belästigung und Angriffe auf Deutsche
K 1592	Gesandtschaft Bern:	Judenfrage in der Schweiz

K 1593	Gesandtschaft Bern:	Polnische Greuelpropaganda und deren Bekämpfung
K 1594	Gesandtschaft Belgrad:	Deutschlands innere Politik
K 1595	Gesandtschaft Belgrad:	Politisches, geheim
K 1596	Gesandtschaft Belgrad:	Verhaftungen, Internierte. Serbien-Kroatien, 1942
K 1597	Gesandtschaft Belgrad:	Judenangelegenheiten
K 1598	Gesandtschaft Belgrad:	Reichs- und Protektoratsangehörige in Jugoslawien
K 1599	Gesandtschaft Budapest:	Geheimsachen
K 1600	Gesandtschaft Budapest:	Freimaurertum und Judenfragen
K 1601	Gesandtschaft Budapest:	Kolonialfragen
K 1602	Gesandtschaft Budapest:	Ungarische Wirtschaftspolitik
K 1603	Gesandtschaft Budapest:	Nichtarische Professoren
K 1604	Gesandtschaft Bukarest:	Judenfrage
K 1605	Gesandtschaft Lissabon:	Lösung der Judenfrage
K 1607	Botschaft Paris:	Indien
K 1608	Botschaft Paris:	Mesopotamien
K 1609	Botschaft Paris:	Mittelmeer
K 1610	Botschaft Paris:	Palästina
K 1611	Botschaft Paris:	Syrien
K 1612	Botschaft Paris:	Türkei
K 1613	Botschaft Paris:	Ukraine
K 1614	Botschaft Paris:	Antinationalsozialistische Ausstellung in Paris
K 1615	Botschaft Paris:	Innere Angelegenheiten
K 1616	Botschaft Paris:	Juden und Freimaurer
K 1617	Botschaft Paris:	Wirtschaftliche Beziehungen: Frankreich - Ägypten, Abessinien
K 1618	Botschaft Paris:	Personal, allgemein
K 1619	Botschaft Paris:	Schriftverkehr mit Parteistellen und anderen deutschen Stellen (nicht Militär)
K 1620	Botschaft Paris:	Arbeiterfragen, allgemein
K 1621	Botschaft Paris:	Presse- und Propagandawesen in Frankreich
K 1622	Botschaft Paris:	Presse- und Propagandawesen in Frankreich
K 1623	Botschaft Paris:	Jüdische Zeitungen; Judentum im Kampf gegen Hitler-Deutschland

K 1624	Botschaft Paris:	Danzig
K 1625	Botschaft Paris:	Deutsche Kontrollkommission im unbesetzten Frankreich und in den französischen Kolonien
K 1626	Botschaft Paris:	Innenpolitik Frankreich, allgemein
K 1627	Botschaft Paris:	Judenfrage
K 1628	Botschaft Paris:	Rahn
K 1629	Botschaft Paris:	Algerien
K 1630	Botschaft Paris:	Syrien
K 1631	Botschaft Paris:	Neukaledonien
K 1632	Botschaft Paris, Geheim:	Gesuche, Schadenersatzansprüche, Erlaubnisscheine
K 1633	Botschaft Paris, Geheim:	Juden und Freimaurer in Frankreich
K 1634	Botschaft Paris, Geheim:	Frankreich: Innere Verhältnisse
K 1635	Botschaft Paris, Geheim:	Protektorat Böhmen und Mähren
K 1636	Botschaft Paris, Geheim:	Juden und Freimaurer in Frankreich. Ägypten und Palästina
K 1637	Botschaft Paris, Geheim:	Arabien
K 1638	Botschaft Paris, Geheim:	Belgien
K 1639	Botschaft Paris, Geheim:	Irak
K 1640	Botschaft Paris, Geheim:	Jugoslawien
K 1641	Botschaft Paris, Geheim:	Türkei
K 1642	Botschaft Paris, Geheim:	UdSSR
K 1643	Gesandtschaft Pressburg:	Juden, Emigranten, Pass-Sachen, allgemein; Einzelfälle
K 1644	Gesandtschaft Pressburg:	Judentum, Freimaurertum, Gesetze, Vorträge, Reden
K 1645	Gesandtschaft Pressburg:	Staatsschutzbestimmungen, Kommunismus, Freimaurertum, Judenfrage in Deutschland
K 1646	Gesandtschaft Pressburg:	Judenfrage, generell, Einzelfälle
K 1649	Gesandtschaft Riga:	Kulturpropaganda, Studentenaustausch, Sportvereine
K 1650	Gesandtschaft Riga:	Kulturpropaganda, Geschenkwerte, Propagandamaterial
K 1651	Gesandtschaft Riga:	Kirchenwesen
K 1652	Gesandtschaft Riga:	Studien- und Gesellschaftsreisen
K 1653	Gesandtschaft Riga:	Politische Beziehungen: Deutschland - Österreich
K 1654	Gesandtschaft Riga:	Politische Beziehungen: Deutschland - Litauen. Deutschland - Polen

K 1655	Gesandtschaft Riga:	Politische Beziehungen: Deutschland - Russland
K 1656	Gesandtschaft Riga:	Politische Beziehungen: Deutschland - Skandinavien
K 1657	Gesandtschaft Riga:	Innere und äussere Politik der Staaten Asiens
K 1658	Gesandtschaft Riga:	Innere und äussere Politik: England. Estland.
K 1659	Gesandtschaft Riga:	Innere und äussere Politik: Balkan, Skandinavien, Danzig und Osteuropa. Finnland
K 1660	Gesandtschaft Riga:	Innere und äussere Politik: Litauen
K 1661	Gesandtschaft Riga:	Innere und äussere Politik: Polen. Russland
K 1662	Gesandtschaft Riga:	Innere und äussere Politik: Skandinavien (Schweden, Norwegen, Dänemark).
K 1663	Gesandtschaft Riga:	Innere und äussere Politik: Spanien
K 1664	Gesandtschaft Riga:	Deutschland: Innere Politik, Parlaments- und Parteiwesen; Kabinette
K 1665	Gesandtschaft Riga:	Wahlberechtigung Auslandsdeutscher
K 1666	Gesandtschaft Riga:	Nationalsozialistische Emigranten in Deutschland
K 1667	Gesandtschaft Riga:	Lettland: Innere Politik
K 1668	Gesandtschaft Riga:	Nationalsozialismus in Lettland
K 1669	Gesandtschaft Riga:	NSDAP Stützpunkt in Lettland und Auslandsorganisation der NSDAP
K 1670	Gesandtschaft Riga:	Nationalitätenfrage, Minoritäten, Fremdvölker, Judenfragen
K 1671	Gesandtschaft Riga:	Minderheiten in Lettland
K 1672	Gesandtschaft Riga:	Bolschewismus, Kommunismus, Faschismus
K 1673	Gesandtschaft Riga:	Krieg, Kriegsmaterial
K 1674	Gesandtschaft Riga:	Unterstützung der lettischen Presse
K 1675	Gesandtschaft Riga:	Lettische Presse
K 1676	Gesandtschaft Riga:	Jüdische Presse (Hajnt)
K 1677	Gesandtschaft Riga:	Politische Propaganda; Übersendung von Bild- und Zeitungsmaterial
K 1678	Gesandtschaft Riga:	Politische Emigranten; Matteotti Komitee
K 1680	Gesandtschaft Riga:	Lettlands Wirtschafts- und Handelspolitik, allgemein
K 1681	Gesandtschaft Riga:	Sonderakte: Schenker & Co; Deutsche Wirtschaftsinteressen in Sowjet - Lettland
K 1682	Gesandtschaft Riga:	Sonderakte: Wertpapiere

K 1683	Gesandtschaft Riga:	Antideutsche Wirtschaftspropaganda
K 1684	Gesandtschaft Riga:	Förderung deutschen Handels in Lettland
K 1685	Botschaft Rom (Vatikan):	Jüdische Fragen, Judenmission
K 1686	Botschaft Rom (Quirinal), Geheim:	Jude Ziffer
K 1687	Botschaft Rom (Quirinal), Geheim:	Dritter Jüdischer Weltkongress: Boykott deutscher Waren
K 1688	Botschaft Rom (Quirinal), Geheim:	Schliessung der Missionen in Algier, Bagdad, Beirut, Bombay, Jerusalem, Kairo, Kenya, Nairobi, Tanganjika, Sidney, Tunis.
K 1689	Botschaft Rom (Quirinal), Geheim:	Gespräch mit dem König von Ägypten
K 1690	Botschaft Rom (Quirinal), Geheim:	Arabische Länder
K 1691	Botschaft Rom (Quirinal), Geheim:	Italienische Staatsangehörige jüdischer Rasse; Liquidation des Judenvermögens
K 1692	Botschaft Rom (Quirinal), Geheim:	Feindhetze betr.besetzte und angegliederte Gebiete
K 1693	Botschaft Rom (Quirinal), Geheim:	Lage in Ägypten und Türkei
K 1694	Botschaft Rom (Quirinal), Geheim:	Irakische Offiziere als Gäste der italienischen Regierung
K 1695	Botschaft Rom (Quirinal):	Deutschland: Juden; Aufnahme der deutschen Judenpolitik in Italien. Fall Ziffer
K 1696	Gesandtschaft Sofia:	Jüdische Vertreter in Bulgarien
K 1698	Botschaft Warschau:	Nationalitäten, Minderheiten, Judenfrage
K 1700	Gesandtschaft Zagreb:	Völkerbund
K 1701	Gesandtschaft Zagreb:	Völkerbund
K 1702	Gesandtschaft Zagreb:	Judenfragen
K 1733	Botschaft Rom (Quirinal), Geheim:	Politische Beziehungen: Italien - Frankreich
K 1785	Botschaft Paris:	Allgemeine Abrüstung und Rüstung
K 1859	Botschaft Wien:	Deutschland
K 1860	Botschaft Wien:	Österreich: Innere Angelegenheiten
K 1861	Botschaft Wien:	Österreichische Kreditanstalt
K 1862	Botschaft Wien:	Österreichische Kreditanstalt
K 1863	Botschaft Wien:	Nationalismus, Faschismus, Heimwehr, Stahlhelm, Monarchismus
K 1864	Botschaft Wien:	Presseangelegenheiten, allgemein

K 1904	Botschaft Moskau:	Sowjetisch-polnische Nichtangriffs-paktverhandlungen
K 1905	Botschaft Moskau:	Politische Berichte
K 1906	Botschaft Moskau:	Zwischenfall Berliner Handelsvertre-tung
K 2034	Botschaft Washington:	M.C.C. Lacques-Plan. Donovan-Plan
K 2090	Botschaft London, Geheim:	Gespräch zwischen Führer und Sir John Simon 25.März 1935
K 2091	Botschaft London, Geheim:	Friedensvertrag
K 2092	Botschaft London, Geheim:	Rostin über Unterredung mit Russen, Bogolomov, Lindenberg und Rosengolz
K 2093	Botschaft London, Geheim:	Flottenverhandlungen 1937
K 2094	Botschaft London, Geheim:	Handelsbeziehungen zu Deutschland
K 2095	Botschaft London, Geheim:	Deutsch-englische Zusammenarbeit zur Erschliessung Russlands
K 2096	Botschaft London, Geheim:	Sicherheitsfrage
K 2097	Botschaft Paris:	Deutsch-französisches Studienkommitee (Mayrisch-Komité). Plan de Vignaud.
K 2098	Botschaft Paris, Geheim:	Beziehungen: Frankreich-Deutschland, Gesuche
K 2099	Botschaft Paris, Geheim:	Häftlinge
K 2100	Botschaft Paris, Geheim:	Kampf gegen Kommunisten
K 2101	Botschaft Paris:	Berichterstattung Militärattachés
K 2102	Botschaft Paris:	Vereinigte Staaten von Europa
K 2148	Generalkonsulat Tirana:	Agenten, Spionagewesen; Bekämpfung kommunistischer Agitation (Kommunis-mus in Albanien)
K 2149	Gesandtschaft Sofia,Geheim:	Lose A-Akten
K 2150	Gesandtschaft Sofia,Geheim:	Spionageverdächtige: Hans Wagner, Walter E.Brell
K 2151	Generalkonsulat Antwerpen:	Kommunismus, Kommunisten
K 2152	Generalkonsulat Antwerpen:	Verschiedenes, geheim
K 2185	Botschaft Rom (Vatikan):	Vermittlung Amerika
L 284	Gesandtschaft Stockholm:	Finnland: Innen- und Aussenpolitik
L 286	Botschaft Moskau, Geheim:	Politische Beziehungen: Sowjet Union-Nordische Staaten (Finnland, Schweden, Norwegen, Dänemark) Aalandfrage, Finnische Inseln
L 287	Botschaft Moskau, Geheim:	Politische Beziehungen: Deutschland – Nordische Staaten
L 288	Botschaft Moskau:	Politische Beziehungen: Sowjet Union – Finnland
L 289	Gesandtschaft Stockholm:	Finnland: Innen-und Aussenpolitik

L 290	Gesandtschaft Stockholm:	Finnland: Innen- und Aussenpolitik
L 292	Gesandtschaft Stockholm:	Aalandinseln, geheim
L 336	Botschaft Moskau:	Schriftwechsel mit Reichsminister des Auswärtigen, von Rosenberg
L 337	Botschaft Moskau:	"Kupferberg-Gold" Aufzeichnungen. Briefwechsel mit Reichskanzler und Minister des Auswärtigen
L 338	Botschaft Moskau:	v.Körner, dienstliche Korrespondenz
L 339	Botschaft Moskau:	Völkerbund, Locarno
L 340	Botschaft Moskau:	Mission Heller-Morsbach, Aufzeichnungen für Berlin
L 354	Botschaft Moskau:	Wirtschaftliche Beziehungen: Russland - Deutschland
L 355	Botschaft Moskau:	Wirtschaftliche Beziehungen: Russland-Deutschland. Handelsvertrag
L 356	Botschaft Moskau:	Wirtschaftliche Beziehungen: Russland-Deutschland. Deutsch-französische wirtschaftliche Zusammenarbeit in der UdSSR
L 361	Botschaft Rom (Quirinal):	Kohlenlieferungen, allgemeines
L 363	Botschaft Rom (Quirinal):	Sonderband: Besuch des Reichskanzlers Brüning und des Reichsaussenministers Curtius in Rom, August 1931
L 364	Botschaft Rom (Quirinal):	Reparationsfragen, Kriegsschulden, internationale Verhandlungen, Ministerbesuche
L 388	Gesandtschaft Riga:	Utag
L 413	Botschaft Wien:	Geheim III; Ganz geheime Sachen
L 731	Botschaft Rom (Quirinal):	Deutsch-italienische Wirtschaftsverhandlungen und Vertrag
L 758	Botschaft Rom (Quirinal), Geheim:	Hauptmann Freiherr v.Richthofen
L 759	Botschaft Rom (Quirinal):	Italienische Wirtschaftspolitik, allgemein
L 760	Botschaft Rom (Quirinal):	Deutsche Wirtschaftspolitik, allgemein
L 761	Botschaft Rom (Quirinal):	Vorbereitungen für deutsch-italienischen Handelsvertrag, allgemein
L 809	Botschaft Rom (Quirinal):	Alte Handelsverträge und Verhandlungen
L 810	Botschaft Rom (Quirinal):	Vorbereitungen für deutsch-italienischen Handelsvertrag, allgemein
L 811	Botschaft Rom (Quirinal):	Alte Handelsverträge und Verhandlungen
L 812	Botschaft Rom (Quirinal):	Deutsch-italienische Wirtschaftsverhandlungen und Vertrag
L 813	Botschaft Rom (Quirinal):	Battaglia economica Italia. Einfuhrverbote und Beschränkungen

L 814	Botschaft Rom (Quirinal):	Verhandlungen mit Italien; Kohlenlieferungen
L 815	Botschaft Rom (Quirinal):	Deutsche Finanzen (Haushalt,Währung)
L 816	Botschaft Rom (Quirinal):	Gross- und Schwerindustrie
L 817	Botschaft Rom (Quirinal):	Gross- und Schwerindustrie
L 818	Botschaft Rom (Quirinal):	Deutsche und italienische Industrie: Bergbau
L 889	Gesandtschaft Stockholm:	Russland: Innen- und Aussenpolitik
L 892	Gesandtschaft Stockholm:	Presse, Sonderfonds, geheim
L 944	Botschaft London, Geheim:	Australien
L 945	Botschaft Paris:	Australien
L 947	Botschaft Rom (Quirinal):	Wirtschaftsbeziehungen: Italien - Australien. Politische Beziehungen: Italien - Australien. Australien.
L 981	Botschaft London, Geheim:	Kolonialangelegenheiten. Beziehungen zu den Besitzungen. Koloniale Konferenzen
L 982	Botschaft Paris:	Kolonien
L 1509	Generalkonsulat Danzig:	Reichswehr; Militärische Angelegenheiten
L 1514	Botschaft Rom (Quirinal):	Minderheitenfragen, Südtirol
L 1594	Botschaft Rom (Vatikan):	Reparationsproblem: London Ultimatum
L 1701	Botschaft Rom (Quirinal):	Deutschland: Innen- und Aussenpolitik, allgemein
L 1702	Botschaft Rom (Quirinal):	Deutschland: Innen- und Aussenpolitik, allgemein
L 1703	Botschaft Rom (Quirinal):	Deutschland: Nationalsozialismus
L 1704	Botschaft Rom (Quirinal):	Deutsch-italienische Beziehungen: Besuch Dr.Goebbels
L 1705	Botschaft Rom (Quirinal):	Deutsch-italienische Beziehungen: Besuch R.Hess
L 1706	Botschaft Rom (Quirinal):	Deutsch-italienische Beziehungen: Besuch Dr.Ley
L 1803	Botschaft Rom (Quirinal):	Minoritätenfragen, allgemein
L 1804	Botschaft Rom (Quirinal):	Minderheitenfrage, Südtirol
L 1805	Botschaft Rom (Quirinal):	Donaustaaten
L 1806	Botschaft Rom (Quirinal):	Deutsch-italienische Beziehungen: Besuch v.Blomberg
L 1807	Botschaft Rom (Quirinal):	Deutsch-italienische Beziehungen: Besuch Himmler
M 11	Botschaft Paris:	Londoner Communiqué, Handakten Köster

M 31	Botschaft Paris:	Handakten Botschafter Köster
M 32	Botschaft Rom (Quirinal):	Abstimmungsgebiete: Saargebiet
M 36	Botschaft Rom (Quirinal), Geheim:	Militärwesen
M 37	Botschaft Paris:	Ostpakt
M 38	Botschaft Paris:	Abrüstung, Handakten Köster
M 41	Konsulat Genf:	Minderheiten, Generalia
M 48	Botschaft Paris:	Francois Poncet, Handakten Köster
M 49	Botschaft Paris:	Kriegsteilnehmer und Kriegsbeschädigte
M 62	Gesandtschaft Bern:	Neutralität der Schweiz
M 74	Botschaft Paris, Geheim:	Lageberichte über Nordafrika und Besetzung Frankreichs durch Achsentruppen
M 75	Gesandtschaft Prag:	Politische Beziehungen zu Deutschland
M 76	Gesandtschaft Budapest:	Nationalitäten in Ungarn; deutsche Minderheiten
M 87	Botschaft Rom (Quirinal):	Deutsche Wirtschaftspolitik, allgemein
M 95	Botschaft Rom (Quirinal):	Italien: Aussenpolitik, allgemein
M 117	Gesandtschaft Kowno:	Litauen: Innere Politik
M 122	Generalkonsulat Danzig:	Überbrückungskredite und Massnahmen zur Sanierung der Danziger Staatsfinanzen
M 126	Botschaft Rom (Quirinal):	v.Hassell
M 127	Botschaft Paris:	Deutschland; Präsident und Minister
M 132	Botschaft Rom (Vatikan):	Reichskonkordat
M 144	Botschaft Moskau:	Politische Beziehungen: Sowjet Union - Japan
M 149	Botschaft Rom (Quirinal):	Allgemeine Abrüstungsfragen
M 150	Botschaft Moskau:	Französisch-sowjetischer Beistandspakt
M 165	Botschaft Rom (Vatikan):	Saargebiet
M 166	Botschaft Rom (Quirinal), Geheim:	Saargebiet
M 167	Botschaft Rom (Quirinal):	Abstimmungsgebiete: Saargebiet
M 173	Botschaft Paris:	Südafrika
M 181	Botschaft Paris:	Angeblich deutsches Propagandadokument
M 189	Botschaft Paris:	Deutsch-österreichisches Zollabkommen
M 197	Botschaft Paris:	Beziehungen zu Russland
M 198	Botschaft Paris:	Frankreich-Russland (Handakten Köster)
M 208	Botschaft Paris:	Deutsches Garantieangebot; Sicherheitspakt Locarno. Reparationsfrage.

M 240	Gesandtschaft Budapest:	Nationalitäten in Ungarn; Deutsche Minderheiten
M 241	Gesandtschaft Budapest:	Donaupaktfragen
M 242	Botschaft Rom (Quirinal):	Donaustaaten
M 243	Gesandtschaft Sofia:	Ein- und Ausfuhr von Kriegsgerät, Aufrüstung Bulgariens, Waffenlieferungen; Geheimakten
M 254	Botschaft Rom (Quirinal):	Abessinien
M 268	Botschaft Moskau:	Litwinow Vorschlag über Unabhängigkeit der Baltischen Staaten
M 272	Botschaft Rom (Quirinal):	Abessinien
M 276	Gesandtschaft Lissabon:	Portugiesische Presse; neue Kolonien für Deutschland
M 281	Botschaft Rom (Quirinal):	Locarnopakt, französisch-russischer Pakt, Westpakt
M 285	Botschaft Rom (Quirinal):	Abessinien, Sonderband: Sanktionen
M 286	Botschaft Rom (Quirinal):	Locarnopakt, französisch-russischer Pakt, Westpakt
M 287	Botschaft Paris:	Deutsches Garantieangebot; Sicherheitspakt Locarno. Reparationsfrage.
M 297	Botschaft Rom (Quirinal):	Deutsch-italienische Beziehungen: Besuch Ciano
M 298	Botschaft Rom (Quirinal):	Donaustaaten
M 299	Botschaft Rom (Quirinal):	Italien: Aussenpolitik, allgemein
M 318	Botschaft Moskau:	Anti-Sowjet Campagne
M 335	Botschaft London, Geheim:	Flottenkonferenz 1934/35
M 336	Botschaft London, Geheim:	Privatbriefe
M 355	Botschaft Rom (Quirinal):	Sonderband: Sonderabkommen mit Italien über Reparationen
P 6 a	Botschaft Brüssel:	Legationsrat Werkmeister

N A T I O N A L   A R C H I V E S   S U P P L E M E N T

Serial-Roll Conversion List for
National Archives Microfilm of
German Foreign Ministry and other
Records Described in this Volume

This list gives the number of the microfilm roll (reel or container) on which each of the serials described in this volume is reproduced. An asterisk in the roll column indicates that the roll or rolls had not yet been received by the National Archives.

Some serials extend over more than one roll. Anyone interested in buying only part of such a serial can cite inclusive frame numbers to the National Archives, which will furnish the corresponding roll numbers and their cost.

Where rolls include more than one serial, some of these serial numbers may be either widely separated in this volume or not listed at all. It follows that such rolls may contain serials in addition to those selected.

In any case, the National Archives does not sell parts of rolls, only complete rolls, but 8- by 10-inch paper prints made from the microfilm may be purchased.

Positive copies of the microfilm rolls described in this volume or prints of single frames may be purchased at prices quoted by our Publications Sales Branch. Single rolls may be purchased separately. Prices are subject to change without advance public notice. The price includes postage or shipping on orders for the United States, Mexico, or Canada and on small orders sent to other countries. Orders of more than 40 rolls from foreign countries other than Canada and Mexico are subject to an added 5-percent shipping charge. There are no discounts for quantity orders.

Orders should be submitted on GSA Form 6784, Microfilm Order, or on institutional or commercial purchase order forms. Orders can be handled more quickly when they include the correct microfilm publication number(s), roll number(s), and price(s). Titles and dates of publications are not needed. Order forms will be sent on request.

Payment must accompany each order and should be in the form of a check or money order; cash payments are discouraged. Payments from outside the United States should be made by international money order or check drawn on a U.S. bank. Make checks or money orders payable to GSA (NATS) and mail to Cashier, National Archives (GSA), Washington, DC 20408.

Serial	Roll	Serial	Roll	Serial	Roll
28	12-13	425	289	659	296-347
37	22	426	279	661	296
41	28	429	285	672	348
74	67-71	432	288	688	349
86	83	433	291	695	353
127	133	441,445	285	701	352
152,165	163	446,448	284	719	355
166	170	450	285	721	352
167	169	454	294	731	354
171	173	455	*	732	769
215	201,203	457	292	824	368
258	222	461	298	889	379
270	240	462,466	308	895	386
273	241	477	302	902-903	381
276	249	478	308	967	379
277	241	479	297	978	391
279	245	480	304	1017	399
282	248	481,487	305	1024	401
285	219	488	303	1025	694
292	248	492	309	1026	401
315	126	493	301	1044	691
349	256	494	297	1089	694
352	263-264	497	309	1090-1091	690
354	680	498	310	1094-1095	692
357	256	499	301	1096	708
359,361	277	500	299	1115-1116	719
363	266	502	295	1156	726
366	276	515	306	1157	712
370	280	516	311	1175,1177	705
372	276	531	313	1186	713
380	282	597	337	1192	710
397	281	644	344	1290	754
410,414, 418	265	652,656	324	1307	757

Serial	Roll	Serial	Roll	Serial	Roll
1308	758-761	1672	1017	2010	1141
1315	755	1673-1674, 1679	1005	2039,2045	1144
1330-1331, 1333,1338	741	1694	1013	2046	1146
1345	735,747	1716	1014	2119	1130
1348	747	1734	1015	2127-2128	1128
1349	750	1740	1008	2129	1157
1379	740	1747-1748	1028	2130	1158
1425	737	1791	1029	2131	1159
1444,1447-1448	766	1810	1042	2144	1174
1456	753	1811-1814	1038	2157	1174
1496	776	1819	1044	2158	1161
1524, 1536-1537	782	1841-1842	1052	2194	1172
1538	783	1843-1844	1053	2218	1173
1539	777	1865	1056	2243	1175
1544	783	1882	1058	2265	1206
1559	778	1883	1059	2266	1205
1563	785	1884	1057	2273	1206
1564	778	1885	1059	2281	1298-1300, 1302
1565	911	1897	1069	2290	1297
1566	909	1899	1070	2318	1280
1567	785	1904-1905	1068	2335,2342-2343,2346	1304
1572	908	1906	1071	2361	1303
1587	912	1907	1057	2366	1306
1589	911	1908	1071	2371	1315
1590	912	1909	1070	2402	1319
1600	913	1912	1069	2455-2456	1326
1601	915	1913	1068	2469,2484-2485,2492-2494	1327
1602	914	1931	1071	2504-2505	1345
1630-1631, 1636	919	1937,1948	1076	2533	1364
1653	1002	1961,1965	1078	2536-2537 2543	1365
1654	1005	1976	1082		
		2004	1142		

Serial	Roll	Serial	Roll	Serial	Roll
2594	1370	2973-2977 2982-2983, 2985	1442	3578	1721
2623	1371			3590,3597	1722
2624	1372	3007	1449	3599,3613	1721
2654-2655	1373	3014	1450	3614,3616, 3624,3626, 3633	1766
2667,2670	1374	3025,3027	1452		
2885	1418	3038,3050	1453	3636-3637, 3645,3647	1768
2695, 2697-2698	1376	3066	1495	3649	1773
2699-2701	1377	3073-3081	1481	3652,3660- 3660-3664	1786
2702	1379	3084	1482		
2703-2704	1377	3089-3091, 3095,3099, 3102-3106	1496	3668, 3676-3677, 3681	1801
2724	1379	3108	1497	3686-3687	1802
2748,2763	1382	3109	1501	3697-3699	1811
2772	1383	3110,3112, 3114-	1502	3701-3702, 3704-3706	1802
2789,2801, 2806-2808, 2819	1399	3115	1506-1508	3709-3715, 3717	1814
2830,2841	1400	3117, 3120-3122	1531	3735, 3740-3741	1847
2845,2847	1402	3175	1594	3742-3743, 3745-3747, 3748,3758, 3760	1854
2852,2854 2856	1403	3202-3203, 3206-3207	1615		
2863-2870, 2872,2876, 2878-2879, 2884-2885, 2888-2890, 2892	1418	3228-3229, 3248	1624	3761,3764, 3766-3767	1856
		3369,3371	1641	3774-3775	1856A
2906,2908, 2913	1421	3372	1728	3779-	1857
		3376	1641	3780	3967
2917-2918, 2922	1422	3426	1663	3789	1856
2927	1423	3467	1725	3790	1856A
2932	1422	3468	1724	3793	3967
2936-2937, 2939-2942	1423	3485	1830	3796,3797, 3799, 3813-3814	3966
		3503-3517	1831		
2946-2949, 2953	1432	3521-3523	1637	3821,3833, 3835	3968
2960	1433	3545-3548, 3550-3551	1639	3837,3839, 3841-3843	3967
2969-2970, 2972	1434	3562	1587		

Serial	Roll	Serial	Roll	Serial	Roll
3844	3970	4137-4139	2129	4647-4655	2399
3847-3853	3967	4183-4185, 4189-4191	2130	4659-4661	2401
3855	3970	4218-4219	2132	4673	2415
3856-3857	3967	4241, 4243-4244	2133	4680	2420
3862	3970	4245-4247, 4250	2135-2136	4682-4683, 4685,4687	2421
3864-3865, 3867	3969	4298-4299, 4305	2157	4692	2423
3869,3871, 3874,3879	3972	4306	2158-2159	4704	2424
3880,3883, 3890-3891	3973	4360	*	4713	2425
3893	3974	4362	2186	4737	2432
3894-3895	3973	4363	2187	4743,4745, 4749-4752	2433
3898-3903	3980	4365	2189-2190	4753-4755, 2759-4765	2434
3904-3905, 3907-3908	3981	4366	2189	4766-4781	2435
3911, 3918-3919	3982	4367-4370	2191	4782-4786, 4788,4791	2436
3920-3929	1888	4371	2191-2192	4792	2437
3938	1906	4372-4377	2192	4794, 4798-4799	2438
3942	1934	4391-4395, 4399-4401, 4403	2193	4803,4807	2439
3944	1913	4405-4406, 4409-4414	2194	4810-4812	2440
3947-3950	1903	4419,4421, 4423-4426	2195	4813-4816	2441
3997,4001	1917	4427-4428, 4430-4431, 4433-4435	2199	4817-4823	2442
4005-4011, 4019-4021	1936	4444-4445	2198	4825-4827	2445
4024-4025 4027	1956	4447-4448	2207	4829	2457-2458
4052	1999	4452	2208	4830,4832	2459
4057	1998-1999	4459	2292	4833	2460
4073-4074	2042	4511	2275	4835,4838	2461
4082-4085	1960	4544	2296	4840-4845	2462
4086	2130	4554	2297	4846	2463-2465
4087, 4089-4091, 4094	2042	4635-4636	2397	4849-4850, 4852,4860	2466
4095-4096, 4100, 4103-4104	2064	4637-4640, 4642, 4644-4646	2398	4861-4862, 4864	2467
				4865	2468-2469
				4867	2471-2472

Serial	Roll	Serial	Roll	Serial	Roll
4868	2450	5112, 5128-5130	2541	5605	2675
4869	2451-2452			5616	2677
4870-4871	2453	5139, 5145-5146	2552	5633-5639	2655
4889, 4891-4895	2454	5148-5149, 5154, 5156-5157, 5160,5165	2553	5670	2679
				5678,5683	2683
4897-4898, 4901-4903	2456			5701	2694
4915-4916	2474	5166-5167, 5169	2554	5758-5759	2717
4917-4918	2475	5171	2557	5798-5800	2723
4924	2477	5174, 5177-5178, 5184-5185, 5187-5190, 5194,5200-5201	2559	5808, 5815-5816	2732
4925-4926	2478			5827	2733
4927	2479-2481			5835-5836	2734
4928	2482	5206-5207, 5210-5211, 5216-5218, 5222-5223	2560	5837	2734,2761
4929	2483-2484			5840	2734
4930	2485			5844	2735
4931	2486	5255	2567	5852,5857	2740
4932	2487	5257-5258	2568	5896,5898, 5911	2761
4933-4934, 4937	2488	5266-5267	2577-2578		
		5268	2578-2579	5912-5915	2795
4938	2489-2498	5269	2579-2581	5921-5923, 5929-5930	2797
4939	2499-2500	5270	2581		
4941-4944	2501	5271	2581-2582	5944,5951	2801
4953	2503	5272	2582	5952,5954	2802
4963-4964, 4969	2504	5312, 5319-5326	2600	6003	2812
4980	2507	5391-5392, 5406,5416	2614	6020-6021	2825
4991	2512			6027-6028	2826
4996-4997	2514	5429-5430, 5434-5437, 5439,5446	2618	6091,6093, 6099-6102	2834
4999-5000	2515			6108-6110	2835
5002	2519-2521	5469	2620	6136-6137	2898
5007-5012, 5014-5015	2523	5500-5501, 5521-5522	2666	6181-6186	2908
				6214	2955
5016-5020	2524	5548	2651	6219-6221, 6223-6225, 6227-6228	2813
5072,5076	2532	5554	2680		
5085	2533	5580, 5589-5590	2674	6239, 6241-6244	2816
5101	2535-2536				

Serial	Roll	Serial	Roll	Serial	Roll
6245,6248	2793	6516	2883-2885	7364	3208
6249	2815	6517	2886	7368	3209
6250-6253	2793	6518	2887-2888	7437,7440, 7450,7453, 7455	3210
6260-6270, 6276	2817	6520-6521	3011		
6280-6286	2818	6528	3012	7486	3107
6287-6298	2819	6551-6552	3014	7498,7508	3211
6339	2959	6559	3015	7538, 7549-7557	3212
6356,6381, 6396	2961	6597	3024	7568	3213
		6641-6645	3142	7589	3214
6397-6400, 6403	2962	6671	2976,2979, 2995	7596-7601, 7603-7604	3215
6428	2969	6672	2977,2980- 2981	7621-7626, 7628-7633	3217
6434	2849-2850	6673	2996		
6435	2860	6674	2978,2982	7636	3151
6436	2851-2852	6675	2983,3001	7640	3218
6437	2853-2854	6676	2984-2985, 2997	7664,7675, 7680-7682	3220
6438	2855,2861			7700-7701	3237
6440	2856,2862- 2863	6677	2986	7728	3260
6441	2864-2865	6791-6792	3137	7775	3278
6442	2994	6809-6811, 6855, 6859-6863	3154	7777-7782	3279
6443	2799	6906	3155	7783-7786	3282
6444-6445, 6453	2971	6960-6961	3156	7795,7802, 7804-7805	3222
6462	2972	6984,7028	3181	7814	3283
6506	2866	7048	3182	7821	3284
6507	2867	7063	3179	7829,7831, 7834,7845	3287
6508	2868	7073	3185		
6509	2869-2870	7207,7208	3197	7851-7854, 7858-7861, 7864	3286
6510	2871-2872	7209-7223, 7225, 7230-7231	3193	7875,7880	3288
6511	2873-2875			7885	
6512	2876-2877	7238-7243	3199	7887,7889	3245
6513	2878	7248-7251	3194	7965	3296
6514	2879-2880	7260-7261	3195	7983,7987, 7990-7992	3262
6515	2881-2882	7307-7308 7356,7358	3202		

Serial	Roll	Serial	Roll	Serial	Roll
7995, 7997-7999, 8002	3263	8568	3356	9214-9215, 9222	3530
		8583	3357	9257-9258	3442
8026	3299	8624	3390	9338	3561
8036,8038	3300	8675-8676, 8678, 8680-8681, 8684	3395	9340,9349	3562
8054-8055, 8057-8059, 8065-8067, 8073, 8075-8079	3301			9389-9392, 9395-9396, 9399-9400, 9411	3565
		8723	3400		
8112	3309	8747-8748, 8754,8756, 8758-8760, 8762	3401	9443	3552
8125	3313			9444	3662
8132	3302	8782-8783	3377	9446	3552
8153-8155, 8157,8203	3303	8812	3404	9456,9459, 9462	3553
		8836	3379	9472	3663
8211-8213	3313	8840	3405	9506	3505
8265	3324	8892	3469	9525	3569
8267, 8275-8279, 8283-8287	3307	8903-8904, 8906,8910	3407	9535	3555
8302	3351	8916	3469	9538	3540
8332,8336, 8341-8343, 8346	3329	8920,8932	3416	9542	3555
		8949	3498	9586	3581
8356-8357, 8367-8369	3330	8951	3417	9600	3582
8371-8372	3353	8970,8973, 8983	3418	9620	3591
				9623	3541
8376-8378	3332	8984	3502	9653	3589
8389,8392, 8395	3334	9007	3506	9685	3584
8402	3354	9043,9045, 9051,9053, 9057-9058	3510	9706,9708	3610
8417, 8419-8420	3333	9059-9060	3511	9722	3592
8422	3345	9086-9087	3517	9747	3605
8433,8439	3346	9093	3518	9784	3607
8471	3335	9113	3519	9787	5788-5797
8490-8491, 8493,8501, 8505	3347	9148	3523	9788	3607
		9163,9166	3525	9792	3572
8511,8515	3355	9168,9170, 9172	3526	9795-9801	3611
8544	3365			9807	3780

Serial	Roll	Serial	Roll	Serial	Roll
9812, 9814-9815	3781	K 1188-1192	5441	K 2090	5539-5540
9820	5798-5803	K 1195,	5443	K 2091-2093	5541
9827	3782	K 1196	5444	K 2094-2095	5542
9848	3843	K 1554-1564	4718	K 2096	5543-5544
9852	3785	K 1565	4719	K 2097-2100	5545
9863	3665	K 1566-1568	4720	K 2101-2102	5546
9866,9868, 9877, 9885-9887	3595	K 1569-1582	4721	K 2148-2152	5580
		K 1583	4722-4724	K 2185	5585
9902	3658	K 1584-1590	4725	L 284	4239
9905-9906	3671	K 1591-1601	4726	L 286-288	4240
9910-9914	3672	K 1602-1605	4727	L 289	4241
9919-9920	3690	K 1607	4729	L 290	4242-4244
9925	3777	K 1608	4730	L 292	4245
9931-9932	3891	K 1609-1610	4731	L 336	4261
9958	3935	K 1611	4732-4734	L 337-340	4262
9968	3994	K 1612	4735-4739	L 354-356	4378
9971, 9973-9974	3995	K 1613-1631	4740	L 361,363	4379
9984	3989	K 1632	4741	L 364	4380-4381
K 553-557	4159	K 1633	4742-4743	L 388	4263
K 579-580	4162	K 1634-1646	4744	L 413	4411
K 643	4178	K 1649-1669	4745	L 731	5061
K 653, K 655-678	4183	K 1670-1678	4746	L 758-761	5063
K 706	4343-4344	K 1680-1695	4747	L 809-812	5109
K 1006	4607	K 1696,1698, K 1700-1702	4748	L 813-818	5110
K 1043-1051	4613	K 1733	5156	L 889	4828-4829
K 1066	4621	K 1785	5166	L 892	4830
K 1167	5433-5434	K 1859	5191-5192	L 944-945, L 947	4847
K 1168	5435	K 1860	5193-5194	L 981	4856
K 1170-1171	5436	K 1861-1862	5195	L 982	4857
K 1172-1173	5437	K 1863	5196-5197	L 1509	5367
K 1177-1182	5439	K 1864	5198	L 1514	5368
K 1183-1185	5440	K 1904-1906	5215	L 1594	5678
		K 2034	5474-5475	L 1701-1706	5697

Serial	Roll	Serial	Roll	Serial	Roll
L 1803–1807	5673	M 122	4554	M 240–243	5040
M 11	4267	M 126–127, M 132	4555	M 254	5045
M 31–32, M 36–38, M 41	4272	M 144	4593	M 268,272	5047
M 48–49	4275	M 149	5017	M 276,281	5049
M 62	4283	M 150	5018	M 285–287	5120
M 74	4322	M 165–167	5021	M 297–299	5122
M 75–76	4323	M 173	5023	M 318	5484
M 87	4324	M 181	5024	M 335–336	5486
M 95	4433	M 189	5026	M 355	5125
M 117	4551	M 197–198	5029	P 6 a	5780
		M 208	5033		

INDEX

The following index lists, in alphabetical order: countries; topics; and names of persons. As far as practicable, the wording of the file title has been maintained. Files dealing with political or economic relationship between two countries have been listed under each country and the same has been done for files dealing with treaties and agreements between different countries.

In order not to make the Index too long and complicated, references to the lesser files (e.g. Rechtswesen, Sozialpolitik, etc.) and to some of the subject headings of the country files, have been omitted. Appendix II in volume I should be consulted as a guide to the subject headings of the classification system used in the Archives of the German Foreign Ministry for the country files.

ADDENDA and ERRATA

Volume I, p.xiv: the reference to Curtius should have been omitted

        p.670: to serial number 3086 add Tschechoslowakei

        p.758: Appendix II (not Appendix IV) should be consulted

Volume II, p.vii: "... volumes III and IV those from 1936 to 1945"
            should be changed to: volume III the files from
            1936 to 1945, volume IV files from 1920 to 1945.

        p.777: Brasilien. Presse, Propaganda und Allgemeines
            the serial number should be 6493 NOT 6439

        p.1162: serial number 6439 should be changed to 6493

        p.1277: 6439 2994 7 should be deleted; 6493   3008 8
            should be substituted

        p.1307: HAIMHAUSEN, E.H.v., should have been listed as
            HANIEL, Haimhausen E.H.v.

        p.1318: to Südafrika, add p.31

Volume III, p.4: under Deutsch-Französische Beziehungen serial 396
            should be changed to 386

        p. 455: under Nachtrag 1939, (7) it should be Pannwitz,
            NOT Pannwik

        p. 536: insert 386 Staatssekretär: Deutsch-Französische Be-
            ziehungen

        p. 537: under serial 396 Staatssekretär: Deutsch-Französi-
            sche Beziehungen should be taken out.

        p. 775: 386 should be added to 387, both are on roll 680